Transnational Management

■ ■ ■ ■ ■ ■ ■ ■ ■ ■ ■ ■ ■ ■ ■ ■ ■

Transnational Management

TEXT, CASES, AND READINGS IN CROSS-BORDER MANAGEMENT

SEVENTH EDITION

Christopher A. Bartlett
Harvard Business School

Paul W. Beamish
Ivey Business School
The University of Western Ontario

10 9 8 7 6 5 4 3 2 1
CTP MPM
20 16 15 14

When ordering this title, use **ISBN 978-1-259-25376-8** or **MHID 1-259-25376-7**

Printed in Singapore

COVENTRY UNIVERSITY LONDON CAMPUS

About the Authors

Christopher Bartlett is the Thomas D. Casserly Professor Emeritus of Business Administration at the Harvard Graduate School of Business Administration. He received an economics degree from the University of Queensland, Australia, and both masters and doctorate degrees in business administration from Harvard University. Prior to his academic career, he was a marketing manager with Alcoa in Australia, a management consultant in McKinsey and Company's London office, and the country general manager of a subsidiary company of Baxter Laboratories in France.

He joined the faculty of Harvard Business School (HBS) in 1979, and over the following 30 years, his research, teaching, and consulting interests have focused on strategic and organizational challenges confronting managers in multinational corporations and on the process of managing transformational change. While at HBS, he served as chair of the International Senior Management Program, area head of the General Management Unit, faculty chairman of the Program for Global Leadership, and chair of the Humanitarian Leadership Program.

He is the author or co-author of nine books, including *Managing Across Borders: The Transnational Solution* (co-authored with Sumantra Ghoshal), which was named by *Financial Times* as one of the 50 most influential business books of the century. *The Individualized Corporation,* another subsequent major research book that he co-wrote with Ghoshal, was the winner of the Igor Ansoff Award for the best new work in strategic management and was named one of the Best Business Books for the Millennium by *Strategy+Business* magazine. Both books have been translated into over 10 foreign languages.

His articles have appeared in journals such as the *Harvard Business Review, Sloan Management Review, Strategic Management Journal, Academy of Management Review,* and *Journal of International Business Studies.* He has also researched and written over 100 case studies and teaching notes, and their sales of over 4 million copies make him Harvard's best-selling case author ever. He has been elected by his colleagues as a Fellow of the Academy of Management, the Academy of International Business, the Strategic Management Society, and the World Economic Forum.

Paul Beamish is the Donald Triggs Canada Research Chair in International Business at the Ivey Business School, Western University. He is the author or co-author of numerous books, articles, contributed chapters, and teaching cases. His articles have appeared in the *Academy of Management Review, Academy of Management Journal, Strategic Management Journal, Journal of International Business Studies* (JIBS), *Organization Science,* and elsewhere. He has received best research awards from the Academy of Management and the Academy of International Business (AIB). In 2008, he was recognized in *International Business Review* as the second most productive international business scholar worldwide in the previous decade. He served as editor-in-chief of *JIBS* from 1993–1997 and worked for Procter & Gamble Canada and Wilfrid Laurier University before joining Ivey's faculty in 1987.

He has supervised 27 doctoral dissertations, many involving international joint ventures and alliances. His consulting, management training, and joint venture facilitation activities have been in both the public and private sector.

At Ivey, he has taught in a variety of school programs, including the Executive MBA offered at its campus in Hong Kong and in the MSc in International Business program. In 2012, he was the recipient of the International Management Outstanding Educator Award from the Academy of Management. From 1999–2004, he served as associate dean of research. He currently serves as director of Ivey Publishing, the distributor of Ivey's collection of over 4,600 current cases; Ivey's Asian Management Institute (AMI); and the cross-enterprise center, Engaging Emerging Markets.

He is a Fellow of the Academy of International Business, Royal Society of Canada, and Asia Pacific Foundation of Canada.

Preface

This book grew out of the authors' strongly held belief that the best research in the academic fields of international business and cross-border management did more than capture the challenges, activities, perceptions, and best practices from the field. It also translated those findings into practical and relevant lessons for managers and students of management. That philosophy and commitment has remained at the core of the seven editions of this volume.

So in preparing this new edition, we have done all we can to ensure that the frameworks, concepts, and practical examples we have included are topical, relevant, and significant to practitioners working in today's global business environment. We believe that those are the issues that are described in the case studies, illuminated by the articles, and embedded in the conceptual chapters that provide the framework for this course-long voyage in transnational management.

In the 22 years since the first edition of *Transnational Management* appeared, much has changed in the field of cross-border business management—new external demands have emerged, new strategic responses have been developed, new organizational capabilities have evolved, and new managerial competencies have become necessary. But old international hands will insist that these differences are largely superficial. They make a fairly convincing case that beyond inevitable and never-ending adjustments, the basic challenges of managing a worldwide operation remain much as they have always been: understanding one's host-country environment, being sensitive to cross-cultural differences, seeing the world as an integrated strategic reality, and being able to deal with the complexities of managing operations separated by the barriers of distance, language, time, and culture.

In many ways, both views are correct, and we are reminded of that fact with each revision of this volume. On the one hand, we receive passionate input from teaching faculty anxious for fresh new material that reflects the vibrancy of the field and keeps up with the latest developments. But we also hear from those who recognize the importance of teaching the timeless international management issues that they believe are often best captured in their favorite classic cases and readings.

Based on input that we constantly receive from the users of this text, we have sought to maintain this balance: undertaking a major updating of the chapters while maintaining their intellectual integrity; adding new articles that reflect current thinking while maintaining the classics; and adding new case material that captures emerging issues to keep courses fresh, while retaining timeless cases that have proven ability to keep students challenged. The result is that, as in all the previous editions, all the chapters have been updated, and around half the cases and readings have been retained, and about half are new to the seventh edition.

▥ Chapter Changes from the Sixth Edition

INTRODUCTION: So What Is Transnational Management?

- A new introductory chapter outlining the overall agenda and objectives of the book.

CHAPTER 1: Expanding Abroad

- Chapter text:
  - Chapter text significantly revised and updated
  - Table 1 updated
  - Two new tables regarding indicators of foreign direct investment (FDI) and internationalization statistics
  - New examples from companies including Dunkin' Donuts, Facebook, Google, GE Healthcare, and Sinopec
- Case studies:
  - Two new cases: "Sherwood-Hockey Sticks: Global Sourcing"; and "Mahindra & Mahindra in South Africa"
- Supplemental readings:
  - A new reading: "The Global Entrepreneur: A New Breed of Entrepreneur Is Thinking Across Borders—From Day One"

CHAPTER 2: Understanding the International Context

- Chapter text:
  - Chapter text significantly revised and updated
  - New discussion of nationally owned corporations investing in other countries
  - New discussion about localization at the city level
  - New examples from companies including Procter & Gamble, GLOBE study, Unilever, the auto industry, the airline industry, Anheuser-Busch In-Bev, the U.N. Global Compact, and Hyundai
- Case studies:
  - A new case: "A Speed Race: Benelli and QJ Compete in the International Motorbike Arena"
- Supplemental readings:
  - A new reading: "Managing Risk in an Unstable World"

CHAPTER 3: Developing Transnational Strategies

- Chapter text:
  - Chapter text significantly revised and updated
  - New figure and discussion regarding strategies to serve emerging market consumers
  - New examples from companies including Toyota, Irdeto, Kraft, Unilever, Canon, Apple, Electrolux, Dell, and Tata Motors

- Case studies:
  - A new case: "United Cereal: Lora Brill's Eurobrand Challenge"
- Supplemental readings:
  - Two new readings: "Capturing the World's Emerging Middle Class" and "New Business Models in Emerging Markets"

CHAPTER 4: Developing a Transnational Organization

- Chapter text:
  - Chapter text significantly revised and edited
  - Added reference to developing countries and high-tech industries
  - New examples from companies including Haier, General Electric, Google, Cisco, Procter & Gamble, and IBM
- Case studies:
  - Two new cases: "Lundbeck Korea: Managing an International Growth Engine" and "Kent Chemical: Organizing for International Growth"
- Supplemental readings:
  - Two new readings: "Have You Restructured for Global Success?" and "Organizing for an Emerging World"

CHAPTER 5: Creating Worldwide Innovation and Learning

- Chapter text:
  - Chapter text significantly revised and edited
  - Added reference to developing countries and knowledge-based industries such as telecom, biotech, and pharmaceuticals
  - A new section on the worldwide generation and distribution of patent and trademark data
  - New examples from companies including QUALCOMM, Sharp, Nokia, John Deere, and Mahindra & Mahindra
- Case studies:
  - A new case: "Applied Research Technologies, Inc.: Global Innovation's Challenges"
- Supplemental readings:
  - Two new readings: "How GE is Disrupting Itself" and "How to Build Collaborative Advantage"

CHAPTER 6: Engaging in Cross-Border Collaboration

- Chapter text:
  - Chapter text significantly revised and updated
  - New discussion of governance in JVs

- New examples from companies including Unisys, energy technology JV, airline alliances, Lenovo-NEC, Dow Chemical, BMW and PSA-Peugeot-Citroen, Virgin Mobile and Tata Teleservices, Carlsberg and Scottish & Newcastle, Fiat and Nanjing Automotive, and John Hopkins Medicine International
- Case studies:
  - A new case: "Sharp Corporation: Beyond Japan"
  - The Nora-Sakari case was slightly condensed
- Supplemental readings:
  - A new reading: "How to Manage Alliances Better Than One at a Time"
  - Updated reading: "The Design and Management of International Joint Ventures"

CHAPTER 7: Implementing the Strategy

- Chapter text:
  - Chapter text significantly revised and edited
  - Added references to developing countries and the alternative energy industry (solar, wind, etc.)
  - New examples from companies including Procter & Gamble, KFC, General Electric, BRL Hardy, Tsingtao Brewery, Apple Computer, and Nokia
- Case studies:
  - Three new cases: "Levendary Café: The China Challenge"; "Clayton Industries, Inc.: Peter Arnell, Country Manager for Italy"; "Managing a Global Team: Greg James at Sun Microsystems, Inc."
- Supplemental readings:
  - Two new readings: "Managing Executive Attention in the Global Company" and "The Collaboration Imperative"

CHAPTER 8: The Future of the Transnational

- Chapter text:
  - Chapter text significantly revised and edited.
  - Update information and data on the World Bank, the Foreign Corrupt Practices Act, and the Global Compact
  - New examples from companies including Wal-Mart, BP, British American Tobacco, Apple, Starbucks, Heineken, and Unilever
- Case studies:
  - A new case: "Barrick Gold Corporation—Tanzania"
- Supplemental readings:
  - A new reading: "A Global Leader's Guide to Managing Business Conduct"

Acknowledgments

Transnational Management has greatly benefited from comments, suggestions, and insights generously offered by colleagues at the hundreds of institutions around the world that have adopted this book. In particular, we would like to acknowledge the role played by our Editorial Advisory Board, whose members are listed on page xii. These faculty adopters have committed significant effort to providing a detailed critique of the sixth edition that helped us decide what to include and what to change in this edition.

We are also extraordinarily grateful to the researchers and colleagues who have contributed new materials to this edition. In addition to our own classroom materials, new case studies have been provided by Megan (Min) Zhang, Jean-Louis Schaan, Chandrasekhar Ramasastry, Francesca Spigarelli, Ilan Alon, William Wei, Carole Carlson, Michael Roberts, Laura Winig, Heather Beckham, Derek Lehmberg, Arar Han, Benjamin H. Barlow, Tsedal Neeley, Thomas J. DeLong, and Aloysius Newenham-Kahindi. Articles that bring important recent research to this edition for the first time have been contributed by Daniel J. Isenberg, Ian Bremmer, David Court, Laxman Narasimhan, Matthew J. Eyring, Mark W. Johnson, Hari Nair, Nirmalya Kumar, Phanish Puranam, Toby Gibbs, Suzanne Heywood, Leigh Weiss, Jeffrey R. Immelt, Vijay Govindarajan, Chris Trimble, Morten T. Hansen, Nitin Nohria, Ulrich Wassmer, Pierre Dussauge, Marcel Planellas, Rick Lash, Lynn S. Paine, Rohit Deshpandé, and Joshua D. Margolis.

We would also like to acknowledge the coordination undertaken by support staff at our respective institutions, who worked over many months to coordinate the flow of e-mails, phone calls, manuscripts, and other documents between the United States, Canada, and Australia. At Ivey, this includes PhD candidates Bassam Farah, Majid Eghbali-Zarch, Michael Sartor, Vanessa Hasse, and Megan Zhang. In particular, we would like to offer a special thanks to Mary Roberts for helping us through the long and arduous revision process.

To Anke Weekes, our sponsoring editor, and Heather Darr, our editorial coordinator, at McGraw-Hill, we thank you for your patience and tolerance through this long process and look forward to continuing our productive working relationship for many years to come.

Finally, we would like to acknowledge the lasting contribution of our good friend and colleague, the late Sumantra Ghoshal, who was a founding co-author of this book. Sumantra left an enduring imprint on the field of international management and beyond, and his wisdom and insights still glow brightly in this volume. But more than his brilliance, we miss his convivial, energetic company.

Despite the best efforts of all the contributors, however, we must accept responsibility for the shortcomings of the book that remain. Our only hope is that they are outweighed by the value that you'll find in these pages and the exciting challenges that they represent in the constantly changing field of transnational management.

Christopher A. Bartlett
Paul W. Beamish

Editorial Advisory Board

Our sincere thanks to the following faculty, who provided detailed feedback and suggestions on the materials for this edition:

Stephen E. Courter	University of Texas McCombs School of Business, USA
Yang Fan	Rotterdam School of Management, Erasmus University, Netherlands
P. Roberto Garcia	Indiana University, Kelley School of Business, USA
Axele Giroud	Manchester Business School, UK
Sumit K. Kundu	Florida International University, USA
Gary Schwarz	Nottingham University Business School, China
Sivakumar Venkataramany	Dauch College of Business and Economics, Ashland University, USA
Chris Williams	Richard Ivey School of Business, University of Western Ontario, Canada

Contents

PART 3 THE MANAGERIAL IMPLICATION   541

Chapter 7

Implementing the Strategy: Building Multidimensional Capabilities   *541*

Cases

Readings

Chapter 8

The Future of the Transnational: An Evolving Global Role   *625*

Cases

Readings

Index   697

Introduction:
So What Is Transnational Management?

Few managers operating in today's international business environment would dispute that this is an extremely exciting time to be engaged in almost any aspect of cross-border management. Fast-changing global developments have created big challenges that appear exceptionally complex, but at the same time they have opened up new opportunities that seem almost limitless.

Around the world, managers are asking questions like the following: What can we do to limit our exposure to the ongoing economic crisis in the Eurozone? How can we take advantage of the remarkable rise in Asian markets? How should we deal with the threat of new competitors emerging from developing countries? Can we exploit the coming boom in big data to track and exploit new global trends? Should we harness the fast growing social networks to leverage our cross-border management connections and organizational processes?

These are all issues that we will confront in the pages of this book. But before launching into those rich and engaging discussions, perhaps we should step back for a moment to review the broad territory we will be exploring on our voyage of discovery. A good place to start might be with the title of this book. What exactly does Transnational Management mean?

Transnational: What Does That Imply?

The first word on the cover of this book may not be familiar to some. While the terms "multinational", "international", and "global" are in widespread general use, it may not be entirely clear to you why we chose to use the less familiar description "transnational" in the title of this book.

Good question. And we promise to respond to it by the end of Chapter 1. By the end of that opening chapter it should be clear to you that we use those four terms quite specifically. Furthermore, you will find that our distinction between "multinational", "international", "global", and "transnational" will become a strong theme that runs through this book in our discussion of strategy, organization, and management.

But more of that later. For the purpose of this introduction, let's just recognize that the "transnational" qualifier indicates that our focus will be on the management challenges that face companies whose operations extend across national boundaries. Indeed, the concepts we will be presenting in the text are grounded in extensive research published in a book titled *Managing Across Borders: The Transnational Solution*. The challenging cross-border management issues identified in that five year long, multi-company, worldwide research project supplemented with a large body of subsequent research frames our agenda.

So what is different about cross-border management? In what ways do the challenges facing a manager of a multinational enterprise (MNE) differ from those facing his or her counterpart in a purely domestic organization? There are many such differences, but let's begin by identifying half a dozen of the most important that will be reflected in the issues we explore throughout this book:

- The most obvious contrast derives from the fact that by definition, MNEs have operations in multiple nation states, a difference that has huge strategic, organizational, and management implications. Although domestic companies must take account of local and state governments, what distinguishes inter-country differences from the intra-country ones is the powerful force of national sovereignty. Unlike the local or regional bodies, the nation-state generally represents the ultimate rule-making authority against whom no appeal is feasible. Consequently, the MNE faces an additional and unique element of risk: the political risk of operating in countries with different legislative requirements, legal systems, and political philosophies regarding a host of issues including private property, free enterprise, human rights, and corporate responsibility that a domestic company can simply take for granted.
- Cross-border management also must deal with a greater range of social and cultural differences. Again, domestic companies experience some regional cultural differences, but in cross-border operations the stakes are much higher. An MNE will quickly flounder unless management is not only embedded in the community and able to speak the local language, but also is both sensitive and responsive to local cultural norms, practices, preferences and values.
- By having operations in foreign countries, an MNE is exposed to a wide range of economic systems and conditions which they must understand and to which they must adapt. The differences may be built into political systems ranging from unfettered free enterprise to highly regulated socialist economies; they may be reflected in various stages of economic development from advanced OECD countries to extremely poor less developed countries; and they may be facilitated or constrained by differences in national infrastructure ranging from subtle differences in technical standards to the quality of basic communications services. Each variation in the underlying standards or support systems demands significant modifications to an MNE's strategy and operations.
- Another major way in which cross-border management diverges from domestic management relates to differences in competitive strategy. The purely domestic company can respond to competitive challenges within the context of its single market; the MNE can, and often must, play a much more complex competitive game. Global-scale efficiencies or cross-border sourcing may be necessary to achieve a competitive position, implying the need for complex international logistical coordination. Furthermore, on the global chessboard, effective competitive strategy might require that a competitive challenge in one country might call for a response in a different country—perhaps the competitor's home market. These are options and complexities a purely domestic company does not face.

- In terms of metrics, a purely domestic company can measure its performance in a single comparable unit—the local currency. But because currency values fluctuate against each other, the MNE is required to measure results with a flexible and sometimes distorted measuring stick. In addition, its results are exposed to the economic risks associated with shifts in both nominal and real exchange rates.
- Finally, the purely domestic company manages its activities through organizational structures and management systems that reflect its product and functional variety; the MNE organization is intrinsically more complex because it must provide for management control over its product, functional, *and* geographic diversity. And the resolution of this three-way tension must be accomplished in an organization whose managers are divided by barriers of distance and time and impeded by differences in language and culture.

Management: Why This Focus?

The "Transnational" in the title is simply a qualifier for "Management", and in the final analysis, that is what this book is really about. In many ways, it is a focus that distinguishes this volume from many others in the field. For that reason, let's take a moment to understand why.

The serious study of cross-border management is a relatively recent phenomenon. For many decades, international business research focused mainly on global environmental forces, international systems and structures, and powerful institutions like home- and host-country governments, all of which framed the context within which the MNE had to operate. In these studies, countries and industries rather than companies were the primary units of analysis, and most international policy attention (as well as academic research) focused on macro analysis of key indicators such as trade flows and foreign direct investment patterns.

During the 1960s and 1970s, this interest in global economic forces and international institutions began to be matched by an equal focus on the MNE as the primary driver of the rapidly expanding international economy. A decade later, as the task of running such companies became more complex, attention again expanded to encompass an understanding the roles, responsibilities, and relationships of those running the MNEs.

And so there opened a field of management that had been largely neglected by both practitioners and researchers up to that point. Indeed, until the 1970s, many companies had staffed their international operations with aging or less competent managers, instructing them to simply take the most successful domestic products, strategies, and practices, and transfer them abroad. But in the closing decades of the 20th century, as new offshore markets opened up, global competition intensified, and worldwide operations became more complex, it was clear that such an approach was doomed to failure. Only the most capable managers would be able to run the modern MNE.

This book builds on the lessons that came out of that burst of innovation in cross-border management that has continued into the first decades of the 21st century. So while we will reflect on the changes taking place in the macro global environment, and specifically on the way in which these forces affect MNEs, we will do so by adopting a management interpretation, viewing these fast-changing global forces through the eyes of the executives who operate in the thick of it.

It is this management perspective that has framed the design of this book and the pedagogy that supports it. But unlike many other courses in international management that have been constructed around the traditional functions of the company—R&D, manufacturing, marketing, etc.—we have rejected this conceptual approach. Our experience is that the most important issues facing today's business leaders rarely come packaged in such neatly defined and hermetically sealed bundles. Almost all real-world problems cut across functional boundaries and require executives to understand the issue in a broader and more systemic sense. Furthermore, they demand integrative solutions that bring together, rather than divide, the people working in their traditional functional silos. For that reason, our dominant perspective throughout this book will be that of a general manager—whether that is the CEO of the corporation, the global business vice president, the national subsidiary manager, or the frontline country product manager.

By adopting the perspective of the transnational general manager, however, we do not ignore the important and legitimate perspectives, interests, and influences of other key actors both inside and outside the company. We view the effects of these other key players from the perspective of a MNE general manager however, and focus on understanding how they shape or influence the strategic, organizational, and operational decisions that the general manager must take.

Text, Cases, and Readings: How Will We Learn?

If the title *Transnational Management* describes the field of study and the content of the book, the subtitle *Text, Cases, and Readings in Cross-Border Management* provides clues to the teaching philosophy and materials that will be employed. Because this book may be different in structure and format from some others you have used, it's probably worth spending a little time describing the classroom materials you will find between these covers and the pedagogic philosophy we followed in assembling them.

As the previous paragraphs have suggested, taking on the responsibility of the general manager in a 21st-century MNE may well represent the most complex task to which a manager could be assigned. So creating a course that prepares one for such a role requires some creativity. It's clear that the challenges cannot be reduced for example to a few global strategy recipes, a standardized international organization chart, or a simple check list of the six most important things a country manager must do to succeed.

But neither is it helpful to suggest that everything is too complex to reduce to specifics. In the chapters that follow, we will seek a middle way that presents some broad concepts, frameworks, and principles that allow some generalization and conceptualization of the issues. But we will also provide material that allows students to take these generalized models for a "test drive" to apply, adapt, enhance and embed the ideas in a practice-based, decision-oriented approach that is both grounded and flexible.

The Structure

The book is structured around into three parts which are divided into eight integrated text chapters, each representing a topic that builds on the chapters that precede it. The basic outline is shown in this figure.

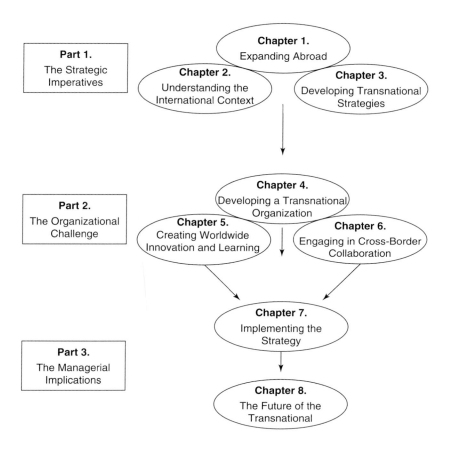

Part I of the book consists of three chapters that focus on the *strategic imperatives* facing the emerging MNE.

- In Chapter 1, we will examine the internal strategic motivations that drive, attract, or compel MNEs to expand offshore.
- Chapter 2 helps us understand the complex and often conflicting external environmental forces that shape the strategy of the MNE as it expands abroad.
- Chapter 3 explores how MNEs resolve the tension between their internal motivations and the external forces and to develop a strategy based on building layers of competitive advantage.

Part II has three chapters that examine the *organizational challenges* flowing from the strategic imperatives.

- Chapter 4 examines the task of building an organization able to deliver the multi-layered strategic capabilities required by a multidimensional transnational strategy.
- Chapter 5 focuses on the critical strategic task of developing the capability to develop and diffuse innovations on a worldwide platform.

- In Chapter 6, we explore the growing organizational challenge of managing collaborations across corporate boundaries.

Part III has two chapters focusing on the *managerial implications* of both the strategic imperatives and the organizational challenges we have identified.

- Chapter 7 allows us to explore the managerial roles and responsibilities required in implementing MNEs strategy.
- Chapter 8 considers the evolving roles and responsibilities of transnational organizations and managers in today's global political economy.

The Learning Materials

To help us through this big agenda, the book is constructed around three major learning resources: the eight text chapters described above, 27 case studies relevant to the chapter topics, and 21 supplemental readings. Let's briefly explain how each of these components to contribute to the overall learning.

The supplemental readings, drawn primarily from practitioner-oriented journals such as *Harvard Business Review* and the *McKinsey Quarterly,* have been carefully selected to provide supplemental perspectives to those presented in the text chapters. Some are classic articles whose wisdom has endured over time, while others are contemporary and reflect the latest thinking on the topic being addressed. In all instances, their objective is to expand and enrich the mental maps being created as we progress on this voyage of discovery.

But as we have emphasized, because the challenges facing the modern MNE represent perhaps the most complex environment in which a manager can operate, no amount of concepts, models, theories, or frameworks can capture the task. We believe that the most powerful way to allow students to enter this complexity is to employ real-life cases that require the complexity to be unravelled and decisions to be made. Most of those in this book provide the reader not only with data on the macro business and company context, but also with detailed information about the key actors and what they bring to the situation: their personal motivations, their strengths and weaknesses, their roles and responsibilities. In many instances, videos and follow-up cases lead to further insight.

Although a few of the cases have been disguised, all of them are real, and almost all have been prepared on the basis of detailed field research. While the vast majority of them document current best practice or illustrate managers facing contemporary challenges, we have also included a handful of classic cases, enduring favorites that have been shown to be effective in illustrating persistent issues in cross-border management.

For those who are less familiar with the use of cases in a classroom setting, it is worthwhile emphasizing that the purpose of this classroom material is to present you with the kinds of important challenges a manager might encounter only once a year, once in a decade, or even once in a career. They present you with an opportunity to go through the same process as the case protagonist—sorting through the information, analyzing the situation, evaluating the options, deciding on action, thinking through the implementation steps required to bring about the necessary change, and then convincing your colleagues of the wisdom of your approach. Repeating this process a couple of dozen times through the course can significantly increase one's ability to translate abstract concepts and general theories into real on-the-ground practice.

Getting Started

But enough overview, background, and analysis; it's time to launch headlong into this fascinating and exciting new world of transnational management. So let's begin our voyage to explore the challenges and opportunities of those who have the responsibility for the strategy and operations of organizations that stretch across the barriers of distance, language, and culture. It should be quite a trip.

Expanding Abroad:
Motivations, Means, and Mentalities

In this chapter, we look at a number of important questions that companies must resolve before taking the leap to operate outside their home environment. What market opportunities, sourcing advantages, or strategic imperatives provide the *motivation* for their international expansion? By what *means* will they expand their overseas presence—through modes such as exports, licensing, joint ventures, wholly owned subsidiaries, or some other means? And how will the management *mentalities*—their embedded attitudes, assumptions, and beliefs—that they bring to their international ventures affect their chances of success? Before exploring these important questions, however, we need to develop a definition of this entity—the multinational enterprise (MNE)—that we plan to study, and develop a sense of its size and importance in the global economy.

This book focuses on the management challenges associated with developing the strategies, building the organizations, and managing the operations of companies whose activities stretch across national boundaries. Clearly, operating in an international rather than a domestic arena presents managers with many new opportunities. Having worldwide operations not only gives a company access to new markets and low-cost resources, it also opens up new sources of information and knowledge and broadens the options for strategic moves that the company might make to compete with its domestic and international rivals. However, with all these new opportunities come the challenges of managing strategy, organization, and operations that are innately more complex, diverse, and uncertain.

Our starting point is to focus on the dominant vehicle of internationalization, the multinational enterprise (MNE), and briefly review its role and influence in the global economy.[1] Only after understanding the origins, interests, and objectives of this key factor will we be in a position to explore the strategies it pursues and the organization it develops to achieve them.

In this chapter, we introduce the MNE by defining its key characteristics, discussing its origins, interests, and objectives, and reviewing its major role and influence in the global economy. We then describe the motivations that drive these companies abroad, the means they adopt to expand internationally, and the mentalities of management that shape the strategies MNEs pursue and the organizations they develop to achieve them.

[1]Such entities are referred to variously—and often interchangeably—as *multinational, international,* and *global enterprises.* (Note that we use the term *enterprise* rather than *corporation* because some of the cross-border entities that we will examine are nonprofit organizations whose strategies and operations are every bit as complex as that of their corporate brethren.) At the end of this chapter, we assign each of those terms—*multinational, international,* and *global*—specific meanings, but throughout the book, we adopt the widely used *MNE* abbreviation in a broader, more general sense to refer to all enterprises whose operations extend across national borders.

The MNE: Definition, Scope, and Influence

An economic historian could trace the origins of international business back thousands of years to the seafaring traders of Greece and Egypt,[2] through the merchant traders of medieval Venice and the great British and Dutch trading companies of the 17th and 18th centuries. By the 19th century, the newly emerged capitalists in industrialized Europe began investing in the less-developed areas of the world (including the United States), but particularly within the vast empires held by Britain, France, Holland, and Germany.

Definition

In terms of the working definition that we use, few if any of these entities throughout history could be called true MNEs. Most early traders would be excluded by our first qualification, which requires that an MNE have *substantial direct investment* in foreign countries, not just the trading relationships of an import-export business. And even most of the companies that had established international operations in the 19th century would be excluded by our second criterion, which requires that they be engaged in the *active management* of these offshore assets rather than simply holding them in a passive investment portfolio.

Thus, though companies that source their raw materials offshore, license their technologies abroad, export their products into foreign markets, or even hold minor equity positions in overseas ventures without any management involvement may regard themselves as "international," by our definition, they are not true MNEs unless they have substantial, direct investment in foreign countries *and* actively manage and regard those operations as integral parts of the company, both strategically and organizationally.

Scope

According to our definition, then, the MNE is a very recent phenomenon, with the vast majority developing only in the post–World War II years. However, the motivations for international expansion and the nature of MNEs' offshore activities have evolved significantly over this relatively short period, and we will explore some of these changes later in this chapter.

It is interesting to observe how the United Nations (U.N.) has changed its definition of the MNE as these companies have grown in size and importance.[3] In 1973, it defined such an enterprise as one "which controls assets, factories, mines, sales offices, and the like in two or more countries." By 1984, it had changed the definition to an enterprise (a) which comprises entities in two or more countries, regardless of the legal form and fields of activity of those entities; (b) which operates under a system of decision making that permits coherent policies and a common strategy through one or more decision-making centers; and (c) in which the entities are so linked, by ownership or otherwise, that one or more of them may be able to exercise a significant influence over the activities of the others, in particular to share knowledge, resources, and responsibilities.

[2]See Karl Moore and David Lewis, *The Origins of Globalization* (New York: Routledge, 2009).

[3]The generic term for companies operating across national borders in most U.N. studies is *transnational corporation* (TNC). Because we use that term very specifically, we continue to define the general form of organizations with international operations as MNEs.

Table 1-1   Selected Indicators of FDI and International Production, 2001–2010

Item	Value at Current Prices (billions of dollars)			Annual Growth Rate or Change on Return (percent)		
	2005–2007 average	2009	2010	2001–2005	2009	2010
FDI inflows	1,472	1,185	1,244	5.3	−32.1	4.9
FDI outflows	1,487	1,171	1,323	9.1	−38.7	13.1
FDI inward stock	14,407	17,950	19,141	13.4	17.4	6.6
FDI outward stock	15,705	19,197	20,408	14.7	20.1	6.3
Income on inward FDI	990	945	1,137	32.0	−11.3	20.3
Rate of return on inward FDI[a]	*5.9*	*7.0*	*7.3*	*0.1*	*−0.3*	*0.3*
Income on outward FDI[a]	1,083	1,037	1,251	31.3	−6.8	20.6
Rate of return on outward FDI[a]	*6.2*	*6.9*	*7.2*	*—*	*−0.2*	*0.3*
Cross-border M&As	703	250	339	0.6	−64.7	35.7
Sales of foreign affiliates	21,293	30,213[b]	32,960[b]	14.9	−9.3	9.1
Value-added (product) of foreign affiliates	3,570	6,129[b]	6,636[b]	10.9	−1.4	8.3
Total assets of foreign affiliates	43,324	53,601[b]	56,998[b]	15.5	−16.8	6.3
Exports of foreign affiliates	5,003	5,262[c]	6,239[c]	14.7	−20.3	18.6
Employment by foreign affiliates (thousands)	55,001	66,688[b]	68,218[b]	4.1	3.4	2.3

Source: UNCTAD.
[a]Calculated with FDI income for the countries that have the data for both this and FDI stock.
[b]Data for 2009 and 2010 are estimated based on a fixed effects panel regression of each variable against outward stock and a lagged dependent variable for the period 1980–2008.
[c]For 1998–2010, the share of exports of foreign affiliates in world export in 1998 (33.3 percent) was applied to obtain values.
Note: Not included in this table is the value of worldwide sales by foreign affiliates associated with their parent firms through nonequity relationships and of the sales of the parent firms themselves. Worldwide sales, gross product, total assets, exports, and employment of foreign affiliates are sometimes estimated.

In essence, the changing definition highlights the importance of both strategic and organizational integration, and thereby, the *active, coordinated management* of operations located in different countries, as the key differentiating characteristic of an MNE. The resources committed to those units can take the form of skilled people or research equipment just as easily as plants and machinery or computer hardware. What really differentiates the MNE is that it creates an internal organization to carry out key cross-border tasks and transactions internally, rather than depending on trade through the external markets, just as the companies in Table 1-1 do. This more recent U.N. definition also expands earlier assumptions of traditional ownership patterns to encompass a more varied set of financial, legal, and contractual relationships with different foreign affiliates. With this understanding, our definition of MNEs includes Apple, BP, and Honda Motors, but also Intercontinental Hotels, Deloitte Consulting, and McDonald's.

MNE Influence in the Global Economy

Most frequent international business travelers have had an experience like this: A woman arrives on her Singapore Airlines flight, rents a Toyota at Hertz, and drives to the downtown Marriott Hotel. In her room, she flips on the LG television and absentmindedly gazes out at neon signs flashing "Pepsi," "Samsung," and "Lexus." The latest episode of *Modern Family* is flickering on the screen when room service delivers dinner, along with a bottle of Perrier. All of a sudden, a feeling of disorientation engulfs her. Is she in Sydney, Shanghai, Sao Paulo, or San Francisco? Her surroundings and points of reference over the past few hours have provided few clues.

Such experiences, more than any data, provide the best indication of the enormous influence of MNEs in the global economy. As the cases and articles in this book show, few sectors of the economy and few firms—not even those that are purely domestic in their operations—are free of this pervasive influence. According to U.N. estimates, even in the midst of the 2010 recession, the total number of MNEs exceeded 65,000. Their collective operations, both abroad and at home, generated value added of approximately $16 trillion, about a quarter of total global gross domestic product (GDP). MNEs' foreign affiliates generated value added of approximately $7 trillion, more than one-tenth of global GDP and one-third of world exports.

Not all MNEs are large, but most large companies in the world are MNEs. Indeed, the largest 100 MNEs, excluding those in banking and finance, accounted for $12.1 trillion of total worldwide assets in 2010, of which $7.5 trillion was located outside their respective home countries.

Moreover, as Table 1-1 shows, despite the 2008–2009 economic crisis international production is expanding, with sales, employment, and assets of foreign affiliates all increasing. This is due to the consistent high rates of return earned by MNEs on foreign direct investment (FDI). MNEs' rate of return on outward FDI has gone back up to 7.3 percent in 2010 after a one-year dip during the crisis.

However, the importance of developing and transition economies is rising. As Table 1-2 shows, while the total worldwide assets of the 100 largest MNEs (or Transnational Corporations, as the United Nations refers to them) increased by 7 percent to $11,543 billion between 2008 and 2009, in the same period, the total assets of the 100 largest TNCs from developing and transition economies increased by 17.9 percent from $2,673 billion to $3,152 billion. In addition, the total employment of the 100 largest TNCs worldwide decreased by 3.7 percent to 15,144,000 between 2008 and 2009, in the same period, the total employment of the 100 largest TNCs from developing and transition economies increased by 21.9 percent to 8,259,000.

A different perspective on the size and potential impact of MNEs is provided in Table 1-3, which compares the overall revenues of several MNEs with the GDPs of selected countries. By comparing company revenues and country GDPs, it is clear that some of the world's largest MNEs are equivalent in their economic importance to medium-sized economies such as Venezuela, Denmark, or Malaysia, and considerably more economically important than smaller or less developed economies such as Cameroon, Paraguay, or Barbados. They have considerable influence on the global economy, employ a high percentage of business graduates, and pose the most complex

Table 1-2   Internationalization Statistics of the 100 Largest Non-Financial MNEs
Worldwide and from Developing and Transition Economies
(Billions of dollars, thousands of employees, and percent)

Variable	100 Largest MNEs Worldwide			100 Largest MNEs from Developing and Transition Economies	
	2008	2009	2010	2008	2009
Assets					
Foreign	6,161	7,147	7,512	899	997
Total	10,790	11,543	12,075	2,673	3,152
Foreign as % of total	57	62	62	34	32
Sales					
Foreign	5,168	4,602	5,005	989	911
Total	8,406	6,979	7,847	2,234	1,914
Foreign as % of total	61	66	64	44	48
Employment					
Foreign	9,008	8,568	8,726	2,651	3,399
Total	15,729	15,144	15,489	6,778	8,259
Foreign as % of total	57	57	56	39	41

Source: UNCTAD.
Note: From 2009 onward, data refer to fiscal year results reported between April 1 of the base year to March 31 of the following year. 2010 data are unavailable for the 100 largest MNEs from developing and transition economies due to lengthier reporting deadlines in these economies.

strategic and organizational challenges for their managers. For the same reasons, they provide the focus for much of our attention in this book.

The Motivations: Pushes and Pulls to Internationalize

What motivates companies to expand their operations internationally? Although occasionally the motives may be entirely idiosyncratic, such as the desire of the CEO to spend time in Mexico or link to old family ties in Europe, an extensive body of research suggests some more systematic patterns.

Traditional Motivations

Among the earliest motivations that drove companies to invest abroad was the need to *secure key supplies*. Aluminum producers needed to ensure their supply of bauxite, tire companies went abroad to develop rubber plantations, and oil companies wanted to open new fields in Canada, the Middle East, and Venezuela. By the early part of the last

Table 1-3   Comparison of Top MNEs and Selected Countries: 2010

Company*	Revenues (Millions USD)	Company Rank	Country**	GDP (Current Millions, USD)	Country GDP Rank
Wal-Mart Stores	408,214	1	United States	14,586,736	1
Royal Dutch Shell	285,129	2	China	5,926,612	2
Exxon Mobil	284,650	3	Japan	5,458,836	3
BP	246,138	4	Germany	3,280,529	4
Toyota Motor	204,106	5	Venezuela	391,848	25
Sinopec	187,518	7	Denmark	311,989	30
AXA	175,257	9	Malaysia	237,797	35
China National Petroleum	165,496	10	Hungary	128,632	52
Chevron	163,527	11	Cameroon	22,480	90
General Electric (GE)	156, 779	13	Barbados	4,109	143

Note: The purpose of this table is merely illustrative of the economic importance of some of the world's largest MNEs. One has to be cautious when comparing the above company and country numbers. That is because country GDPs and company revenues are not perfectly comparable, while country value-added and company value-added are. A country's GDP represents its value-added, whereas a company's revenue is typically higher than its value-added. Thus, from a comparison point of view, the above company numbers may be somewhat inflated relative to the country numbers.
*Data are from Fortune Global 500 and CNN Money's Ranking of world's largest corporations in 2010 by revenue http://money.cnn.com/magazines/fortune/global500/2010/full_list/
**Data are from World Development Indicators published by the World Bank: http://data.worldbank.org/indicator/NY.GDP.MKTP.CD

century, Standard Oil, Alcoa, Goodyear, Anaconda Copper, and International Nickel were among the largest of the emerging MNEs.

Another strong trigger for internationalization could be described as *market-seeking* behavior. This motivation was particularly strong for companies that had some intrinsic advantage, typically related to their technology or brand recognition, which gave them a competitive advantage in offshore markets. Their initial moves were often opportunistic, frequently originating with an unsolicited export order. However, many companies eventually realized that additional sales enabled them to exploit economies of scale and scope, thereby providing a source of competitive advantage over their domestic rivals. This market seeking was a particularly strong motive for some European multinationals, whose small home markets were insufficient to support the volume-intensive manufacturing processes that were sweeping through industries ranging from food and tobacco to chemicals and automobiles. Companies like Philips, Volkswagen, and Unilever expanded internationally primarily in search of new markets.

Another traditional and important trigger of internationalization was the desire to *access low-cost factors* of production. Particularly as tariff barriers declined in the 1960s, the United States and many European countries, for which labor represented a major cost, found that their products faced a competitive disadvantage compared with imports. In response, a number of companies in clothing, electronics, household appliances, watch-making, and other such industries established offshore sourcing locations to produce components or even complete product lines. For example, General Electric (GE) moved production from its lamp plant in Virginia to China and GE Healthcare, one of

GE's most strategic businesses, invested in three world-class plants in India and more recently started manufacturing high-end CT imaging systems there for India and the world.

Labor was not the only productive factor that could be sourced more economically overseas. For example, the availability of lower-cost capital (often through a government investment subsidy) also became a strong force for internationalization. It was the provision of such government financial incentives that induced General Motors (GM) to expand its basic assembly operation in Brazil into a fully integrated operation that is now the company's fourth most important R&D facility worldwide.

These three motives traditionally were the main driving forces behind the overseas expansion of MNEs. The ways in which these motives interacted to push companies— particularly those from the United States—to become MNEs are captured in the well-known product cycle theory espoused by long time Harvard Professor Ray Vernon.[4]

This theory suggests that the starting point for an internationalization process is typically an innovation that a company creates in its home country. In the first phase of exploiting the development, the company—let's assume that it is in the United States— builds production facilities in its home market not only because this is where its main customer base is located, but also because of the need to maintain close linkages between research and production in this phase of its development cycle. In this early stage, some demand also may be created in other developed countries—in European countries, for example—where consumer needs and market developments are similar to those of the United States. These requirements normally would be met with home production, thereby generating exports for the United States.

During this pre-MNE stage, firms would typically establish an export unit within the home office, to oversee the growing export levels. Committing to this sort of organizational structure would in turn typically lead to stronger performance than would treating exports simply as part of the domestic business.[5]

As the product matures and production processes become standardized, the company enters a new stage. By this time, demand in the European countries has become quite sizable, and export sales, originally a marginal side benefit, have become an important part of the revenues from the new business. Furthermore, competitors probably have begun to see the growing demand for the new product as a potential opportunity to establish themselves in the markets served by exports. To prevent or counteract such competition and to meet the foreign demand more effectively, the innovating company typically sets up production facilities in the importing countries, thereby making the transition from being an exporter to becoming a true MNE.

Finally, in the third stage, the product becomes highly standardized, and many competitors enter the business. Competition focuses on price and, therefore, on cost. This trend activates the resource-seeking motive, and the company moves production to low-wage, developing countries to meet the demands of its customers in the developed markets at a lower cost. In this final phase, the developing countries may become net exporters of the product, while the developed countries become net importers.

[4]Raymond Vernon, "International Investment and International Trade in the Product Cycle," *Quarterly Journal of Economics,* May 1966, pp. 190–207.
[5]Paul W. Beamish, Lambros Karavis, Anthony Goerzen, and Christopher Lane, "The Relationship Between Organizational Structure and Export Performance," *Management International Review* 39 (1999), pp. 37–54.

Although the product cycle theory provided a useful way to describe much of the internationalization of the postwar decades,[6] by the 1980s, its explanatory power was beginning to wane, as Professor Vernon himself was quick to point out. As the international business environment became increasingly complex and sophisticated, companies developed a much richer rationale for their worldwide operations.

Emerging Motivations

Once MNEs had established international sales and production operations, their perceptions and strategic motivations gradually changed. Initially, the typical attitude was that the foreign operations were mere strategic and organizational appendages to the domestic business and should be managed opportunistically. Gradually, however, managers began to think about their strategy in a more integrated, worldwide sense. In this process, the forces that originally triggered their expansion overseas often became secondary to a new set of motivations that underlay their emerging global strategies.

The first such set of forces was the increasing *scale economies, ballooning R&D investments,* and *shortening product life cycles* that transformed many industries into global rather than national structures and made a worldwide scope of activities not a matter of choice, but an essential prerequisite for companies to survive in those businesses. These forces are described in detail in the next chapter.

A second factor that often became critical to a company's international strategy—though it was rarely the original motivating trigger—was its global *scanning and learning* capability.[7] A company drawn offshore to secure supplies of raw materials was more likely to become aware of alternative, low-cost production sources around the globe; a company tempted to go abroad by market opportunities was often exposed to new technologies or market needs that stimulated innovative product development. The very nature of an MNE's worldwide presence gave it a huge informational advantage that could result in it locating more efficient sources or more advanced product and process technologies. Thus, a company whose international strategy was triggered by a technological or marketing advantage could enhance that advantage through the scanning and learning potential inherent in its worldwide network of operations. (This has become an increasingly important strategic advantage, which we will explore in detail in Chapter 5.)

A third benefit that soon became evident was that being a multinational rather than a national company brought important advantages of *competitive positioning.* Certainly, the most controversial of the many global competitive strategic actions taken by MNEs in recent years have been those based on cross-subsidization of markets. For example, a Chinese energy company, such as China Petroleum and Chemical Group (Sinopec), could challenge a competitor in the United States by subsidizing its U.S. losses with funds from its profitable operations in the Middle East or South America.

---

[6]The record of international expansion of countries in the post–World War II era is quite consistent with the pattern suggested by the product cycle theory. For example, between 1950 and 1980, U.S. firms' foreign direct investment (FDI) increased from $11.8 billion to $200 billion. In the 1950s, much of this investment focused on neighboring countries in Latin America and Canada. By the early 1960s, attention had shifted to Europe, and the European Economic Community's share of U.S. firms' FDI increased from 16 percent in 1957 to 32 percent by 1966. Finally, in the 1970s, attention shifted to developing countries, whose share of U.S. firms' FDI grew from 18 percent in 1974 to 25 percent in 1980.

[7]This motivation is highlighted by Raymond Vernon in "Gone Are the Cash Cows of Yesteryear," *Harvard Business Review,* November–December 1980, pp. 150–55.

If the U.S. company did not have strong positions in the Chinese company's key markets, its competitive response could only be to defend its home market positions—typically by seeking government intervention or matching or offsetting the Chinese challenger's competitive price reductions. Recognition of these competitive implications of multicountry operations led some companies to change the criteria for their international investment decisions to reflect not only market attractiveness or cost-efficiency choices, but also the leverage that such investments provided over competitors.[8]

Although for the purposes of analysis—and to reflect some sense of historical development—the motives behind the expansion of MNEs have been reduced to a few distinct categories, it should be clear that companies were rarely driven by a single motivating force. More adaptable companies soon learned how to capitalize on the potential advantages available from their international operations—ensuring critical supplies, entering new markets, tapping low-cost factors of production, leveraging their global information access, and capitalizing on the competitive advantage of their multiple market positions—and began to use these strengths to play a new strategic game that we will describe in later chapters as *global chess*.

The Means of Internationalization: Prerequisites and Processes

Having explored *why* an aspiring MNE wants to expand abroad (i.e., its motivation), we must now understand *how* it does so by exploring the means of internationalization. Beyond the desire to expand offshore, a company must possess certain competencies—attributes that we describe as *prerequisites*—if it is to succeed in overseas markets. Then it must be able to implement its plan to expand abroad through a series of decisions and commitments that define the internationalization process.

Prerequisites for Internationalization

In each national market, a foreign company suffers from some disadvantages in comparison with local competitors, at least initially. Because of their greater familiarity with the national culture, industry structure, government requirements, and other aspects of doing business in that country, domestic companies have a huge natural advantage over foreign companies. Their existing relationships with relevant customers, suppliers, regulators, and so on provide additional advantages that the foreign company must either match or counteract with some unique strategic capability. Most often, this countervailing strategic advantage comes from the MNE's superior knowledge or skills, which typically take the form of advanced technological expertise or specific marketing competencies. At other times, scale economies in R&D, production, or some other part of the value chain become the main source of the MNE's advantage over domestic firms. It is important to note, however, that the MNE cannot expect to succeed in the international environment unless it has some distinctive competency to overcome the liability of its foreignness.[9]

---

[8]These competitive aspects of global operations are discussed in detail in Chapter 3.

[9]The need for such strategic advantages for a company to become an MNE is highlighted by the *market imperfections theory of MNEs*. For a comprehensive review of this theory, see Richard E. Caves, *Multinational Enterprise and Economic Analysis*, 2d ed. (Cambridge: Cambridge University Press, 1996).

Such knowledge or scale-based strategic advantages are, by themselves, insufficient to justify the internationalization of operations. Often with much less effort, a company could sell or license its technology to foreign producers, franchise its brand name internationally, or sell its products abroad through general trading companies or local distributors, without having to set up its own offshore operations. This approach was explicitly adopted by Dunkin' Donuts, which decided to proactively and aggressively franchise its brand domestically (in the United States) as well as internationally, rather than solely set up its own domestic and international restaurants. Dunkin's founder, Bill Rosenberg, was so enamored by the franchising concept that he founded the International Franchise Association (IFA) in 1960. He believed that franchising is a wonderful way to expand further and faster. By 2011, Dunkin' had around 10,000 restaurants worldwide in 31 countries, around 7,000 of which were in the United States and 3,000 abroad. Approximately 70 percent of these restaurants were franchised operations. Dunkin' claimed to serve more than 2.7 million customers a day! One may argue that Dunkin' could not have grown as fast domestically and internationally were it not for the franchising strategy that it followed.

The other precondition for a company to become an MNE, therefore, is that it must have the organizational capability to leverage its strategic assets more effectively through its own subsidiaries than through contractual relations with outside parties. If superior knowledge is the main source of an MNE's competitive advantage, for example, it must have an organizational system that provides better returns from extending and exploiting its knowledge through direct foreign operations than the return it could get by selling or licensing that knowledge.[10]

To summarize, three conditions must be met for the existence of an MNE. First, there must be foreign countries that offer certain location-specific advantages to provide the requisite *motivation* for the company to invest there. Second, the company must have some *strategic competencies* or ownership-specific advantages to counteract the disadvantages of its relative unfamiliarity with foreign markets. Third, it must possess some *organizational capabilities* to achieve better returns from leveraging its strategic strengths internally, rather than through external market mechanisms such as contracts or licenses.[11] Understanding these prerequisites is important not only because they explain why MNEs exist, but also, as we show in Chapter 3, because they help define the strategic options for competing in worldwide businesses.

The Process of Internationalization

The process of developing these strategic and organizational attributes lies at the heart of the internationalization process through which a company builds its position in world markets. This process is rarely well thought out in advance, and it typically builds on

---

[10]The issue of organizational capability is the focus of what has come to be known as the *internalization theory of MNEs*. See Alan M. Rugman, "A New Theory of the Multinational Enterprise: Internationalization versus Internalization," *Columbia Journal of World Business*, Spring 1982, pp. 54–61. For a more detailed exposition, see Peter J. Buckley and Mark Casson, *The Future of Multinational Enterprise* (London: MacMillan, 1976).

[11]These three conditions are highlighted in John Dunning's eclectic theory. See John H. Dunning and Sarianna M. Lundan, *Multinational Enterprises and the Global Economy*, 2d ed. (Cheltenham, UK: Edward Elgar, 2008).

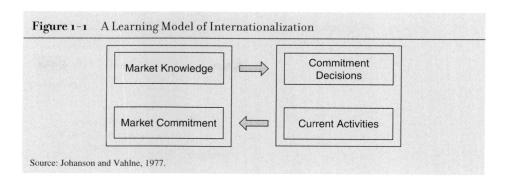

Figure 1-1   A Learning Model of Internationalization

Market Knowledge ⟹ Commitment Decisions

Market Commitment ⟸ Current Activities

Source: Johanson and Vahlne, 1977.

a combination of rational analysis, opportunism, and pure luck. Nonetheless, it is still possible to discern some general patterns of behavior that firms typically follow.

The best-known model for internationalization was developed by two Swedish academics based in Uppsala, who described foreign-market entry as a learning process.[12] The company makes an initial commitment of resources to the foreign market, and through this investment, it gains local market knowledge about customers, competitors, and regulatory conditions. On the basis of this market knowledge, the company is able to evaluate its current activities, the extent of its commitment to the market, and thus its opportunities for additional investment. It then makes a subsequent resource commitment, perhaps buying out its local distributor or investing in a local manufacturing plant, which allows it to develop additional market knowledge. Gradually, and through several cycles of investment, the company develops the necessary levels of local capability and market knowledge to become an effective competitor in the foreign country (see Figure 1-1).

Whereas many companies internationalize in the incremental approach depicted by the so-called Uppsala model, a great many do not.[13] Some companies invest in or acquire local partners to shortcut the process of building up local market knowledge. For example, Wal-Mart entered the United Kingdom by buying the supermarket chain ASDA rather than developing its own stores. Others speed up this process even more by starting up as "born globals" (see page 12 for a definition of a "born global" company). For example, Facebook, the social networking firm founded in 2004, became global at a surprising speed because it was started as an internet company. By 2012, Facebook had around 850 million monthly active users (MAUs) and around 500 million daily active users (DAUs) in more than 200 countries, and it managed its millions of users and thousands of advertisers and developers from just four regional centers, namely from California, Texas, Ireland, and India. Cases such as these highlight the complexity of the decisions that MNEs face in entering a foreign market.

[12]Jan Johanson and Jan-Erik Vahlne, "The Internationalization Process of the Firm—A Model of Knowledge Development and Increasing Foreign Market Commitments," *Journal of International Business Studies* 88 (1977), pp. 23–32.
Jan Johanson and Jan-Erik Vahlne, "The Uppsala Internationalization Process Model Revisited: From Liability of Foreignness to Liability of Outsidership," *Journal of International Business Studies* 40 (2009), pp. 1411–1431.
[13]Jonathan Calof and Paul W. Beamish, "Adapting to Foreign Markets: Explaining Internationalization," *International Business Review* 4 (1995), pp. 115–131.

Figure 1-2   Approaches to Foreign Market Entry

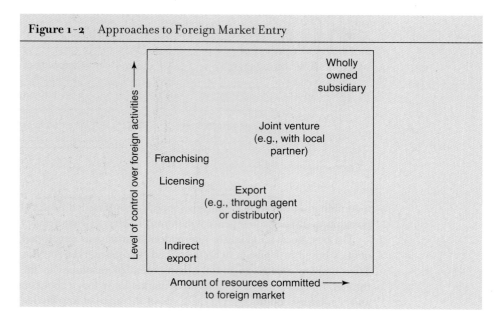

One important set of factors is the assimilation of local market knowledge by the subsidiary unit, as suggested by the Uppsala model. But other, equally important factors to the MNE include its overall level of commitment to the foreign market in question, the required level of control of foreign operations, and the timing of its entry. To help make sense of these different factors, it is useful to think of the different modes of operating overseas in terms of two factors: the level of market commitment made and the level of control needed (see Figure 1-2).

Some companies internationalize by gradually moving up the scale, from exporting through joint venturing to direct foreign investment. Others, like Wal-Mart, prefer to move straight to the high-commitment, high-control mode of operating, in part because they are entering mature markets in which it would be very difficult to build a business from nothing. Still others choose to adopt a low-commitment, low-control mode, such as some "born global" companies. "Born globals" establish significant international operations at or near their founding. Whether this is due to their internal orientation,[14] or the need to move quickly due to the nature of their product or services, such firms do not take such an incremental approach.

One of the most well-known "born globals" of our time is Google. Google was able to make this approach work because it started as an online search company whose users could access its web-based search engine from any country in the world without Google's brick-and-mortar investment in that country. To be clear, none of these approaches is necessarily right or wrong, but they should be consistent with the overall strategic intentions and motivations of the MNE.

[14]Jane Lu and Paul W. Beamish, "Internationalization and Performance of SMEs," *Strategic Management Journal* 22 (2001), pp. 565–586.

Coventry University
London Campus
Tel 024 7765 1016

Borrowed Items 04/02/2016 10:54
XXXXX0139

Item Title	Due Date
48001000036956	11/02/2016

* Transnational management : text, cases, and readings in cross-border management

---

* Indicates items borrowed today
Thankyou for using this unit

www.coventry.ac.uk

Similarly, not all MNEs are large firms. By definition, most large MNEs started out small. Yet many small and medium-sized enterprises (SMEs) retain such a size, while still being MNEs in their own right. Other SMEs, observing a positive impact on performance as a consequence of their FDI activity,[14] will grow.[15]

The Evolving Mentality: International to Transnational

Even from this brief description of the changing motivations for and means of internationalization, it should be clear that a gradual evolution has occurred in the strategic role that foreign operations play in emerging MNEs. We can categorize this evolutionary pattern into four stages that reflect the way in which management thinking has developed over time as changes have occurred in both the international business environment and the MNE as a unique corporate form.

Although such a classification is necessarily generalized and somewhat arbitrary, it enables us to achieve two objectives. First, it highlights that for most MNEs, the objectives that initially induced management to go overseas evolve into a very different set of motivations over time, thereby progressively changing management attitudes and actions. Second, such a classification provides a specific language system that we use throughout this book to describe the very different strategic approaches adopted by various MNEs.[16]

International Mentality

In the earliest stages of internationalization, many MNE managers tend to think of the company's overseas operations as distant outposts whose main role is to support the domestic parent company in different ways, such as contributing incremental sales to the domestic manufacturing operations. We label this approach the *international* strategic mentality.

The *international* terminology derives directly from the international product cycle theory, which reflects many of the assumptions implicit in this approach. Products are developed for the domestic market and only subsequently sold abroad; technology and other sources of knowledge are transferred from the parent company to the overseas operators; and offshore manufacturing represents a means to protect the company's home market. Companies with this mentality regard themselves fundamentally as domestic with some foreign appendages. Managers assigned to overseas operations may be selected because they happen to know a foreign language or have previously lived abroad. Decisions related to the foreign operations tend to be made in an opportunistic or ad hoc manner. Many firms at this stage will prefer to enter only countries where there is low "psychic distance" between it and the home market.

[15]In his Ivey Business Journal article entitled "Growing Big by Targeting Small," Wunker (2012) argues that leaders of internationalizing firms are typically trained to focus on growing their companies in established, large, attractive markets. However, some of the greatest sources of firm growth arise from new markets that start out as small footholds. To support his argument, he provides a table showing that 8 of the 10 most valuable U.S. companies started serving very small new markets that they developed over time. And that following this strategy, they grew along with their markets to become giants.

[16]The terms *international, multinational, global,* and *transnational* have been used very differently—and sometimes interchangeably—by various writers. We want to give each term a specific and different meaning and ask that readers put aside their previous usage of the terms—at least for the duration of this book.

Multinational Mentality

The exposure of the organization to foreign environments and the growing importance of sales and profits from these sources gradually convince managers that international activities can provide opportunities of more than marginal significance. Increasingly, they also realize that to leverage those opportunities, they must do more than ship out old equipment, technology, or product lines that had been developed for the home market. The success of local competitors in the foreign markets and the demands of host governments often accelerate the learning of companies that otherwise would retain an unresponsive, international mentality for too long.

A *multinational* strategic mentality develops as managers begin to recognize and emphasize the differences among national markets and operating environments. Companies with this mentality adopt a more flexible approach to their international operations by modifying their products, strategies, and even management practices country by country. As they develop national companies that are increasingly sensitive and responsive to their local environments, these companies undertake a strategic approach that is literally multinational: Their strategy is built on the foundation of the multiple, nationally responsive strategies of the company's worldwide subsidiaries.

In companies operating with such a multinational mentality, managers of foreign operations tend to be highly independent entrepreneurs, often nationals of the host country. Using their local market knowledge and the parent company's willingness to invest in these growing opportunities, these entrepreneurial managers often can build significant local growth and establish a considerable independence from headquarters.

Global Mentality

Although the multinational mentality typically results in very responsive marketing approaches in the different national markets, it also gives rise to an inefficient manufacturing infrastructure within the company. Plants are built more to provide local marketing advantages or improve political relations than to maximize production efficiency. Similarly, the proliferation of products designed to meet local needs contributes to a general loss of efficiency in design, production, logistics, distribution, and other functional tasks.

In an operating environment of improving transportation and communication facilities and falling trade barriers, some companies adopt a very different strategic approach in their international operations. These companies think in terms of creating products for a world market and manufacturing them on a global scale in a few highly efficient plants, often at the corporate center.

We define this approach as a classic *global* strategy mentality because it views the world, not individual national markets, as its basic unit of analysis. The underlying assumption is that national tastes and preferences are more similar than different, or that they can be made similar by providing customers with standardized products at adequate cost and with quality advantages over those national varieties that they know. Managers with this global strategic approach subscribe to Harvard marketing Professor Theodore Levitt's provocative argument in the mid-1980s that the future belongs to companies that make and sell "the same thing, the same way, everywhere."[17]

This strategic approach requires considerably more central coordination and control than the others and is typically associated with an organizational structure in which various product or business managers have worldwide responsibility. In such companies, R&D and manufacturing activities are typically managed from the headquarters, and most strategic decisions also take place at the center.

Transnational Mentality

In the closing decades of the twentieth century, many of these global companies seemed invincible, chalking up overwhelming victories over not only local competitors but international and multinational ones as well. Their success, however, created and strengthened a set of countervailing forces of localization.

To many host governments, for example, these global companies appeared to be a more powerful and thus more threatening version of earlier unresponsive companies with their unsophisticated international strategic mentality. Many host governments increased both the restrictions and the demands that they placed on global companies, requiring them to invest in, transfer technology to, and meet local content requirements of the host countries.

Customers also contributed to this strengthening of localizing forces by rejecting homogenized global products and reasserting their national preferences—albeit without relaxing their expectations of high quality and low costs that global products offered. Finally, the increasing volatility in the international economic and political environments, especially rapid changes in currency exchange rates, undermined the efficiency of such a centralized global approach.

As a result of these developments, many worldwide companies recognized that demands to be responsive to local market and political needs *and* pressures to develop global-scale competitive efficiency were simultaneous, if sometimes conflicting, imperatives.

In these conditions, the either/or attitude reflected in both the multinational and the global strategic mentalities became increasingly inappropriate. The emerging requirement was for companies to become more responsive to local needs while capturing the benefits of global efficiency—an approach to worldwide management that we call the *transnational* strategic mentality.

In such companies, key activities and resources are neither centralized in the parent company nor so decentralized that each subsidiary can carry out its own tasks on a local-for-local basis. Instead, the resources and activities are dispersed but specialized, to achieve efficiency and flexibility at the same time. Furthermore, these dispersed resources are integrated into an interdependent network of worldwide operations.

In contrast to the global model, the transnational mentality recognizes the importance of flexible and responsive country-level operations—hence the return of the word *national* into the terminology. And compared with the multinational approach, it provides for means to link and coordinate those operations to retain competitive effectiveness and economic efficiency, as is indicated by the prefix *trans*. The resulting need for

---

[17]See Theodore Levitt, "The Globalization of Markets," *Harvard Business Review,* May–June 1983, pp. 92–102.

intensive, organizationwide coordination and shared decision making implies that this is a much more sophisticated and subtle approach to MNE management. In subsequent chapters, we will explore its strategic, organizational, and managerial implications.

It should be clear, however, that there is no inevitability in either the direction or the endpoint of this evolving strategic mentality in worldwide companies. Depending on the industry, the company's strategic position, the host countries' diverse needs, and a variety of other factors, a company might reasonably operate with any one of these strategic mentalities. More likely, bearing in mind that ours is an arbitrary classification, most companies probably exhibit some attributes of each of these different strategic approaches.[18]

■ Concluding Comments

This chapter has provided the historical context of the nature of the MNE and introduced a number of important concepts on which subsequent chapters will build. In particular, we have described the evolving set of *motivations* that led companies to expand abroad in the first place; the *means* of expansion, as shaped by the processes of internationalization they followed; and the typical *mentalities* that they developed. Collectively, these motivations, means, and mentalities are the prime drivers of what we call a company's *administrative heritage,* the unique and deeply embedded structural, process, and cultural biases that play an important part in shaping every company's strategic and organizational capabilities. We will explore this concept in more detail in later chapters.

Chapter 1 Readings

- In Reading 1-1, "The Global Entrepreneur: A New Breed of Entrepreneur Is Thinking Across Borders—From Day One," Isenberg describes the unconventional business thinking and behavior of the global entrepreneur; how he or she sees the opportunity in the *distance* challenge; and the challenges he or she faces and the skills he or she needs to succeed.
- In Reading 1-2, "Distance Still Matters: The Hard Reality of Global Expansion," Ghemawat introduces the cultural, administrative, geographic, economic (CAGE) distance framework. The intent of this framework is to help managers understand which attributes create distance, and the impact that this has on various industries.
- In Reading 1-3, the now classic "The Tortuous Evolution of the Multinational Corporation," Perlmutter introduces the primary types of headquarters orientation toward subsidiaries: ethnocentric, polycentric, and geocentric, and the forces that move an organization toward—or away from—a geocentric mindset.

All three readings are intended to underscore the motivations, means, and mentalities required to expand abroad.

---

[18]Professor Howard Perlmutter was perhaps the first to highlight the different strategic mentalities. See his article, "The Tortuous Evolution of the Multinational Corporation," *Columbia Journal of World Business,* January–February 1969, pp. 9–18, reproduced in the Readings section of this chapter.

Case 1-1   Sher-Wood Hockey Sticks: Global Sourcing

In early 2011, the senior executives of Sher-Wood Hockey (Sher-Wood), the venerable Canadian hockey stick manufacturer, were pondering whether to move the remaining high-end composite hockey and goalie stick production to its suppliers in China. Sher-Wood had been losing market share for its high-priced, high-end, one-piece composite sticks as retail prices continued to fall. Would outsourcing the production of the iconic Canadian-made hockey sticks to China help Sher-Wood to boost demand significantly? Was there any other choice?

The History of Ice Hockey[1]

From the time of early civilization in places as diverse as Rome, Scotland, Egypt and South America, the "ball and stick" game has been played. The game has had different names, but its basic idea has been the same; the Irish, for instance, used the word "hockie" to refer to the sport. Some reports trace the origins of the game to 4,000 years ago, but it has survived to the present.

IVEY

Richard Ivey School of Business
The University of Western Ontario

Megan (Min) Zhang wrote this case under the supervision of Professor Paul W. Beamish solely to provide material for class discussion. The authors do not intend to illustrate either effective or ineffective handling of a managerial situation. The authors may have disguised certain names and other identifying information to protect confidentiality.

[1]Summarized from Jacqueline L. Longe, *How Products Are Made (Volume 4)* (Farmington Hills: Gale Research,1998); http://www.historyhockey.net, accessed on July 18, 2011; http://www.mcgilltribune.com, accessed on July 18, 2011; and http://www.madehow.com, accessed on July 18, 2011.

The modern version of ice hockey emerged from the rules laid down by two Canadians, James Creighton and Henry Joseph, when they studied at McGill University in the late nineteenth century. Their rules were used in the first modern game, which was played in Montreal, Quebec in 1875. In 1892, Canada's governor general, Lord Stanley, introduced the game's first national title, the "Lord Stanley's Dominion Challenge Trophy," later simply referred to as the Stanley Cup. In 1917, the National Hockey League (NHL) was founded in Montreal.

Ice hockey found its way to the United States in 1893. By the early 1900s, it had also become prevalent in Europe. Ice hockey was played as a part of the Olympic Summer Games for the first time in April 1920 in Antwerp, Belgium.

By the late twentieth century, ice hockey represented an important source of national pride to Canadians, and it had become popular in other countries in the northern hemisphere, especially the United States, Czech Republic, Finland, Russia and Sweden.

Ice Hockey Stick[2]

In ice hockey, players use specialized equipment both to facilitate their participation in the game and for protection from injuries. The equipment can be classified into five categories: goalie, head/face (helmet, neck guard), protective (shoulder pads, shin pads, elbow pads, hockey pants and gloves), sticks and skates. "Head-to-toe equipment suppliers" typically offered all equipment except for goalie equipment. Among the five categories of equipment, sticks and skates drove the industry, accounting for almost two-thirds of global equipment sales.[3]

A hockey stick is a piece of equipment used in ice hockey to shoot, pass and carry the puck. It is composed of a long, slender shaft with a flat extension

[2]Summarized from J. L. Longe, *How Products Are Made*, 1999, http://www.prohockeystuff.com, accessed on July 18, 2011; and http://www.nhlhockeyice.com, accessed on July 18, 2011.

[3]http://www.thehockeysource.tv, accessed on July 18, 2011.

at one end called the blade. The goaltender (goalie) has a slightly modified shaft with a wider paddle. Hockey stick dimensions can vary to suit a player's comfort, size, usage and stickhandling skills.

Hockey sticks are manufactured either as one-piece sticks with the blade permanently fused to the shaft or as two-piece sticks, where the blade and shaft are made as separate pieces that are joined later in the manufacturing process. One-piece hockey sticks emerged more recently with the advent of new component materials.

The three qualities that players seek in a hockey stick are lightness, responsiveness and "the feel." There were three characteristics which professional players looked for: lie, flex and blade pattern. The lie of a stick refers to the angle between the shaft and the blade. Players usually seek a lie that will put the blade flat on the ice when they are in their skating stance. Hockey stick shafts are highly flexible, and this flexibility is a key component in their performance. Flex, bend, stiffness and whip are all terms used to describe the amount of force required to bend a given length of stick shaft.

Until the late 1950s, hockey stick blades were rarely curved. However, in the 1960s, players began asking their stick manufacturers to create sticks with pre-curved blades for better performance. Soon after, many NHL players became proponents of the "banana blade." In 2011, the legal limit for hockey blade curves in the NHL was 19 mm, or ¾ of an inch. In addition, players generally expected a hockey stick to be light enough to use easily and flexibly.

To satisfy these qualities, the greatest change came in the materials used to make a hockey stick. One consequence of employing more advanced (composite) materials was that the manufacturing process became more complicated and required more innovations. Custom designs were prevalent among professional players who wanted their sticks to fit their own physical features (i.e., height and strength) and skills.

The three primary materials for manufacturing hockey sticks were wood, aluminum and composite. The earliest hockey sticks were made with solid wood. These sticks were not very durable and were inconsistent in length and shape. In the 1940s, laminated sticks were created with layers of wood glued together to create a more flexible and durable design. In the 1960s, manufacturers began adding additional fibreglass lamination or other synthetic coatings, which further enhanced the durability of the sticks.

In the early 1980s, Easton Hockey introduced single piece, all-aluminum sticks that were much lighter than wooden sticks. Because the stiff aluminum did not have the proper "feel" to players, manufacturers then developed a light aluminum shaft with a replaceable wooden blade. The design became popular in the late 1980s and early 1990s.

In the mid-1990s, advanced composite sticks were developed. Composites were comprised of reinforcing fibres, such as graphite (carbon) and Kevlar, and binders such as polyester, epoxy or other polymeric resins that held the fibres together. In the following decade, graphite had become by far the most popular material for sticks used in the NHL, and it was growing rapidly in popularity for amateur and recreational players. Although graphite sticks were originally sold as shafts alone while a separate blade was purchased by the hockey player, one-piece sticks that included both the shaft and the blade eventually predominated. Some manufacturers also used titanium to produce composite sticks. Moreover, Sher-Wood used foam materials, such as polyurethane, to fill blades and paddles of goalie sticks for shock absorption and stiffness.

New, lighter and more durable composites were always being developed. Ice hockey sticks, roller hockey sticks, lacrosse sticks, baseball bats, softball bats and hockey skates required similar technologies to manufacture because almost all of these athletic products incorporated composite materials. R&D, manufacturing and quality control processes continued to advance in the industry. Increasingly, precise technologies were employed throughout the production process.

For most composite and aluminum sticks, the stick's flex characteristic was expressed numerically. This number, which ranged from 50 through 120, was printed on the stick and corresponded to the amount of force (in pounds-force) that it took to deflect or bend the shaft one inch. By contrast, the flex characteristic of their wooden counterparts could not be derived precisely, because the sticks were produced using a high-volume production process that yielded sticks with variable flex properties.

Basics of Hockey Equipment Industry[4]

According to most industry analysts, the global hockey equipment market was showing signs of maturity, growing at just 1 to 2 per cent per annum.[5] The global hockey equipment market in 2010 was $555 million, with skates and sticks accounting for an estimated 62 per cent of industry sales.

Ice hockey equipment sales were driven primarily by global ice hockey participation rates (registered and unregistered). There were about 600,000 hockey players in Canada in 2010. The number of registered hockey players in Canada between the ages of 5 and 25 was expected to shrink by 30,000 players, or 5 per cent, over the next five years. Nevertheless, some industry analysts believed that growth rates of casual and unregistered hockey participation, especially in the United States, as well as growth rates in Eastern Europe (particularly Russia) and women's hockey had exceeded that of the registered segment as a whole. Other drivers of equipment sales included demand creation efforts, the introduction of innovative products, a shorter product replacement cycle, general macroeconomic conditions and the level of consumer discretionary spending.

Relative to European football (soccer) or American baseball, all of the equipment required to participate in organized hockey was more expensive to purchase. Outfitting a teenager or an adult to play recreational hockey cost approximately $600. The equipment for younger players was less expensive. However, nearly 40 per cent of all ice hockey players lived in homes where the annual household income was more than $100,000 per year.

The hockey sticks endorsed by professional hockey players enjoyed a strong position in the hockey stick market. Children and amateur players liked to have sticks embossed with specific players' names. Hockey stick manufacturers typically paid NHL players to use their sticks and provided the players with custom designed sticks.

Competitor Brands and Strategies[6]

Before a Montreal company began manufacturing ice hockey sticks in the late 1880s, most players made their own. By the early twenty-first century, more than 20 brands of ice hockey sticks existed in North America and Europe, and many of the smaller equipment manufacturers had failed or been purchased by larger competitors. The main brands were Easton (Easton-Bell Sports), Bauer (Bauer Performance Sports), CCM (Reebok-CCM Hockey), Warrior (Warrior Sports), Sher-Wood (Sher-Wood Hockey), Mission ITECH (acquired by Bauer) and Louisville/TPS (acquired by Sher-Wood). Bauer, CCM and Sher-Wood originated in Canada, and Easton and Warrior originated in the United States.

Over 80 per cent of the ice hockey equipment market was shared by three major competitors: Bauer, Reebok (which owned both the Reebok and CCM brands) and Easton, each of which was a head-to-toe supplier offering players a full range of products (skates, sticks and full protective equipment). Moreover, Bauer and Reebok also provided goalie equipment. The balance of the equipment market was highly fragmented with many smaller equipment manufacturers, such as Warrior and Sher-Wood, offering specific products and

[4]Summarized from Preliminary Prospectus of Bauer Performance Sports Ltd. (January 27, 2011), http://www.secure.globeadvisor.com/servlet/ArticleNews/story/gam/20110614/GIVOXBAUERMILSTEADATL, accessed on July 18, 2011; http://www.sgma.com/press/93_Sanctioned-Team-Sports-Play-In-the-US-Remains-Strong-But, accessed on July 18, 2011; and http://www.ehow.com/way_5191903_ice-hockey-equipment-guide.html, accessed on July 18, 2011.
[5]Source: https://secure.globeadvisor.com/servlet/ArticleNews/story/gam/20110614/GIVOXBAUERMILSTEADATL, accessed on July 18, 2011.

[6]Summarized from Preliminary Prospectus of Bauer Performance Sports Ltd., http://www.fundinguniverse.com, accessed on July 18, 2011; http://www.eastonbellsports.com, accessed on July 18, 2011; http://www.bauer.com, accessed on July 18, 2011; http://www.sher-wood.com, accessed on July 18, 2011; http://www.adidas-group.corporate-publication.com, accessed on July 18, 2011; http://www.warrior.com, accessed on July 18, 2011; http://www.stickshack.com, accessed on July 18, 2011; and http://www.hockeystickexpert.com, accessed on July 18, 2011.

Exhibit 1   NHL Share of Hockey Stick Brands and Their Manufacturing Sites

Company	NHL Share	Manufacturing Sites
Easton	45.1%	Tijuana, Mexico, and China
Bauer	15.7%	Composite sticks made in China and Thailand
RBK/CCM	13.7%	Composites sticks in China, wooden sticks in Canada and Finland
Warrior	11.8%	Tijuana, Mexico (insourcing), China (outsourcing)
Sher-Wood	2.3%	Composite, high-end wood goalie sticks in Canada and China, most wood stick production in Eastern Europe
Louisville TPS, Mission, and others	11.4%	N/A

Source: http://www.usatoday.com/, January 2008, accessed on May 29, 2011.

catering to niche segments within the broader market. **Exhibit 1** lists the proportion of NHL players using sticks made by the five major suppliers. Each of the five major companies sought new growth in diverse categories.

Easton-Bell Sports   operated divisions dedicated to hockey, baseball, lacrosse and softball. Easton established itself as a worldwide leader in designing, developing and marketing performance sports equipment, as well as a broad spectrum of accessories for athletic and recreational activities. Easton Hockey's technical prowess made its stick the number one choice among NHL players and amateurs alike and kept its gloves, skates and helmets at the forefront of technological advance. For years, Easton Hockey had signed head-to-toe contract extensions with NHL players. Easton's innovation processes followed a unique routine—developing new technologies for composite ice hockey sticks first and then applying the advances in materials to skates, baseball bats and softball bats. In 2011, Easton-Bell offered 48 types of player and goalie sticks in its Synergy and Stealth lines. Easton-Bell's net sales for 2006 were $639 million compared to $379.9 million in 2005, an increase of 68 per cent. Gross profit for 2006 was $212.9 million or 33.3 per cent of net sales, as compared to $134.9 million or 35.5 per cent of net sales for 2005.

Bauer Performance Sports   manufactured ice hockey, roller hockey and lacrosse equipment

as well as related apparel. Bauer was focused on building a leadership position and growing its market share in all ice hockey and roller hockey equipment products through continued innovation at all performance levels. It produced products at competitive prices using alternative materials, sourcing arrangements and supply-chain efficiencies. It also targeted emerging and underdeveloped consumer segments, including Russian players and female players. In 2008, Bauer Performance implemented several strategic acquisitions to enter new industries and to enhance its market leadership in its chosen categories. In 2011, Bauer offered 20 types of player and goalie sticks in its Supreme and Vapor lines. Bauer was the number one manufacturer of skates, helmets, protective gear and goalie equipment, and a close number two to Easton of sticks in 2010. It enjoyed a 45 per cent share of the global hockey equipment market. Bauer's profit margin as a percentage of net revenues was 37 per cent.

Reebok-CCM Hockey   concentrated on providing hockey equipment and apparel. The company leveraged its multi-brand approach to target different consumer segments. In particular, it developed innovative technologies that appealed to image-conscious consumers. Its products were best suited to the physical side of the game and were frequently purchased by consumers seeking performance and quality. In 2011, they offered 32 types of player and goalie sticks. Reebok-CCM's net sales in

Exhibit 2   Types of Global Sourcing

	Insourcing	Outsourcing
Offshoring	Keeping work in a wholly owned subsidiary in a distant country.	Contracting work with a service provider in a distant country.
Near-shoring	Keeping work in a wholly owned subsidiary in a neighbouring country.	Contracting work with a service provider in a neighbouring country
On-shoring	Keeping work in a wholly owned subsidiary in the home country.	Contracting work with a service provider in the home country.

Source: Derived from Oshri, Korlarksy, and Willcocks, *The Handbook of Global Outsourcing and Offshoring,* 2009; Macmillan Publishers.

2010 were $280 million, and its key markets were Canada, the United States, Scandinavia and Russia.

Warrior Sports concentrated on providing lacrosse and ice hockey equipment, apparel and footwear. The company was dedicated to a core set of philosophies and strengths: technical superiority, grassroots marketing, original and creative youthful expression, and strong partnerships with retailers and suppliers. In 2011, Warrior offered 15 types of player and goalie sticks.

Generally, hockey companies provided one type of hockey sticks at three different price points—junior, intermediate and senior. The reference retail prices of the five competitors' best senior composite sticks varied. The Bauer Supreme TotalOne Composite, Easton Stealth S19 Composite and Warrior Widow Composite Senior were all priced at $229.99. The CCM U+ Crazy Light Composite and Reebok 11K Sickkick III Composite came in at $209.99, while the Sher-Wood T90 Pro Composite was priced at $139.99.[7]

Global Sourcing in the Hockey Equipment Industry

Similar to other industries, the hockey industry eventually entered the global sourcing era. Global sourcing is the process by which the work is

contracted or delegated to a company that may be situated anywhere in the world.[8] Sourcing activities can be categorized along both organizational and locational dimensions (**Exhibit 2** lists several types of global sourcing). From an organizational perspective, the choice between insourcing and outsourcing involves deciding whether to keep the work within the firm or contract it out to an independent service provider. From a locational perspective, three choices are available—onshoring (within the nation), nearshoring (to a neighbouring country) and offshoring (to a geographically distant country). To optimize the overall benefits and hedge risks, companies often seek to balance their global outsourcing and insourcing activities. **Exhibit 3** lists several of the factors typically considered by manufacturers faced with the decision of whether to onshore insource or offshore outsource.

As early as the 1980s, western sports equipment manufacturers, such as Nike and Reebok, started to outsource the manufacture of sporting goods, such as running shoes, to Asia. Nevertheless, before the year 2000, hockey companies preferred insourcing over outsourcing and executed this strategic focus through organic growth, strategic acquisitions and establishing company-owned factories in other countries; for example, Easton and Warrior had factories in Tijuana, Mexico. During the past decade, the hockey industry began to outsource. In 2004, Bauer Nike Hockey shut down or downsized three plants in Ontario and Quebec, eliminating 321 manufacturing jobs. The company outsourced about 90 per cent of its production to other makers

[7]Source for all, http://www.amazon.com, accessed on May 29, 2011.
[8]This paragraph is summarized from Ilan Oshri, Julia Kotlarsky, and Leslie P. Willcocks, *The Handbook of Global Outsourcing and Offshoring* (Hampshire: Macmillan, 2009); and Marc J. Schniederjans, Ashlyn M. Schniederjans, and Dara G. Schniederjans, *Outsourcing and Insourcing in an International Context* (New York: M.E. Sharpe, 2005).

Exhibit 3   Evalution of Global Sourcing

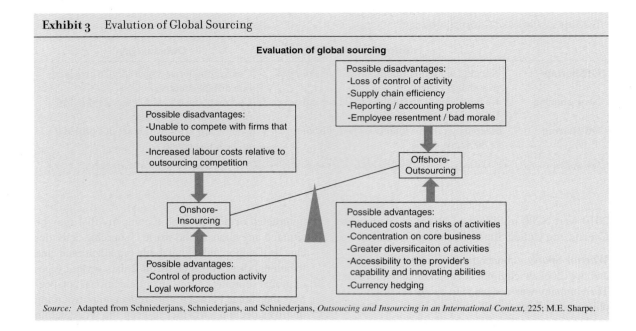

Source: Adapted from Schniederjans, Schniederjans, and Schniederjans, *Outsoucing and Insourcing in an International Context,* 225; M.E. Sharpe.

in Canada and the rest to international suppliers. From 2002 to 2008, Reebok-CCM closed five plants in Ontario and Quebec and outsourced manufacturing to other countries, eliminating about 600 manufacturing jobs. Easton and Warrior also outsourced part of their manufacturing to Asia but still kept their factories in Mexico. The capacity of Warrior's Mexican factory was estimated to be 4,000 composite sticks per week produced by 250 employees in 2008. (Exhibit 1 lists the manufacturing sites associated with several of the leading hockey stick brands.)

Global manufacturing outsourcing was characterized by some drawbacks. It separated manufacturing activities from R&D and marketing activities and challenged a company's ability to coordinate initiatives between these functions, such as product innovation, designing for manufacturability, supply chain efficiency and quality control. Especially in offshore outsourcing, cultural differences caused miscommunication, technology

distance necessitated extra training, and geographic distance resulted in extra lead time or cycle time.[9] In March 2010, Bauer Hockey recalled 13 models of junior hockey sticks, manufactured outside of Canada, due to excessive lead levels in the sticks' paint that was detected by public health officials in random testing.

Offshore outsourcing also threatened to negatively impact a company's public image if it reduced domestic employment. In November 2008, UNITE HERE[10] launched a national campaign to persuade Reebok to repatriate the production of its hockey equipment and jerseys.[11]

Additionally, global economic dynamics, such as changing labour costs, raw material costs and exchange rates, introduced new uncertainties into global sourcing. **Exhibit 4** lists a sample of comparative labour rates prevailing in Canada, the United States, Mexico and China. In 2011, the Boston Consulting Group (BCG) concluded that with Chinese wages rising and the value of the Yuan

[9]This paragraph is summarized from Masaaki Kotabe, *Global Sourcing Strategy: R&D, Manufacturing, and Marketing Interfaces* (New York: Quorum Books, 1992.)

[10]UNITE HERE: a union representing 50,000 food service, apparel, textile, hotel and distribution workers across Canada.
[11]http://www.cbc.ca/news/story/2010/03/18/nike-hockeystick-recall .html, accessed on July 18, 2011.

Exhibit 4   Hourly Compensation Costs in Manufacturing (US$)

Year	China (urban)	China[1]	Canada	USA	Mexico	Estonia	Finland
2002	0.95	0.41	18.39	27.01	5.33	3.09	22.65
2003	1.07	0.44	21.49	28.18	5.06	4.07	28.15
2004	1.19	0.45	24.14	28.94	5.02	4.81	32.50
2005	1.30	0.49	26.81	29.74	5.36	5.44	33.72
2006	1.47	0.53	29.21	29.98	5.59	6.43	35.27
2007	1.83	0.64	31.92	31.51	5.87	8.49	39.45
2008	2.38	0.82	32.70	32.23	6.12	10.34	44.68
2009	N/A	N/A	29.60	33.53	5.38	9.83	43.77

[1]The data is for town or village.
Source: http://www.bls.gov, accessed on July 18, 2011.

continuing to increase, the gap between U.S. and Chinese wages was narrowing rapidly.

Industries other than sporting goods had already begun to practice repatriating manufacturing, also known as reshoring or backshoring. In fact, reshoring had been an alternative in global sourcing planning from the beginning. For German manufacturing companies in the period 1999 to 2006, every fourth to sixth offshoring activity was followed by a reshoring activity within the following four years, mainly due to lack of flexibility and quality problems at the foreign location. This served as a short-term correction of the prior location misjudgement rather than a long-term reaction to slowly emerging economic trends.[12]

Sher-Wood Hockey Inc.: Company Timeline[13]

Sher-Wood Hockey Inc. manufactured and distributed hockey sticks and equipment in Canada. Based in Sherbrooke, Quebec, it was founded in 1949 and was formerly known as Sherwood-Drolet, Ltd. For more than 60 years, it had been one of Canada's best-known hockey equipment manufacturers.

In 1976, Sherwood-Drolet introduced its flagship wooden stick, the PMP 5030, which was described as "the best stick in the world" by NHL legend Guy Lafleur. By 2007, the company had made more than 6 million PMP 5030s.

In 2006, Sherwood-Drolet sold about one million wooden and 350,000 composite sticks. The company anticipated that the composite stick business would continue to grow in terms of volume and profitability. Earlier, Sherwood-Drolet had started contracting out the production of its lower end wooden models to producers in Estonia and China. In 2007, it outsourced the production of PMP 5030 (mid to high end wooden) sticks to a local provider in Victoriaville, Quebec. Meanwhile, the company concentrated on making composite sticks fashioned from graphite, Kevlar and other synthetics. Notwithstanding the company's efforts to move its wooden stick production offshore, it claimed that it would continue to make custom wooden models for professional hockey players, such as Jason Spezza of the Ottawa Senators.

However, when Spezza learned that Sherwood-Drolet would no longer be manufacturing his favourite wooden sticks in Canada, he decided to move to another company. "They [local manufacturers] can get sticks to me in a week now. If it's over there [China], the process will probably be just too much," said Spezza.[14] Ultimately, Montreal-based

[12]Source: S. Kinkel and S. Maloca. "Drivers and Antecedents of Manufacturing Offshoring and Backshoring: A German Perspective," *Journal of Purchasing and Supply Management* 15.3 (2009): 154–65.
[13]Summarized from http://www.sher-wood.com, accessed on July 18, 2011; http://hockeystickexpert.com, accessed on July 18, 2011; http:// www.canada.com/topics/sports/story.html?id=87c5d6b3-8872-496a-8d4f-01f5f4e36342, accessed on July 18, 2011; and http://www.thestar .com/News/Canada/article/273561, accessed on July 18, 2011.

[14]http://www.canada.com/topics/sports/story.html?id=87c5d6b3-8872-496a-8d4f-01f5f4e36342, accessed on July 18, 2011

Reebok designed and produced a stick for him that had a graphite shaft and wooden blade, but the look of a one-piece. In November 2008, Reebok issued a press release announcing that Spezza would start using their sticks, ". . . we are excited to work with Jason, not only on marketing initiatives, but also on the research, design and development of future Reebok Hockey equipment."[15]

By May 2008, Sherwood-Drolet had filed a proposal to its creditors under the Bankruptcy and Insolvency Act. CBC News reported, "It has been hurt in recent years by shift from wooden hockey sticks to composite sticks."[16] Richmond Hill, Ontario-based Carpe Diem Growth Capital bought the company and changed its name to Sher-Wood Hockey Inc.

In September 2008, Sher-Wood purchased the hockey novelty and licensed assets of Inglasco. In December that same year, it purchased TPS Sports Group, a leading manufacturer and distributor of hockey sticks and protective equipment. Sher-Wood transported TPS's assets from Wallaceburg and Strathroy, Ontario to Quebec, consolidated three companies and invested an additional $1.5 million to set up the new factory.

Production

As of March 2011,[17] Sher-Wood produced sticks (sticks, shafts, blades), protective equipment (gloves, pants, shoulder pads, elbow pads, shin pads), goalie gear (goalie pads, catcher, blocker, knee protector, arm and body protector, pants) and other accessories (pucks, bags, puck holders, mini sticks, bottles, carry cases) for ice hockey. The company also sold some equipment and accessories for street hockey (goalie kit, sticks, pucks, balls), as well as sports novelties for hockey fans.

The company introduced new sticks twice a year—in May/June and at the end of October. The life cycle of a product line in the market was about 18 to 24 months. By the end of 2010, Sher-Wood provided 27 types of player and goalie sticks. Thirteen of them were wooden.

Although Sher-Wood had targeted various NHL players in order to support the credibility of the brand, the company mostly targeted junior teams, AAA teams and a couple of senior leagues. Sher-Wood only conducted a low volume of custom design for high-end players and mainly provided custom products from a cosmetic standpoint. For example, personalizing the graphic or colour of the sticks. Sher-Wood used to need two to three weeks to produce customized sticks for an NHL player.

In 2010, Sher-Wood sales volume for sticks produced in Sherbrooke dropped almost 50 per cent compared to 2009. Its Chinese partners manufactured most of their composite hockey sticks. Sher-Wood's plant manufactured the remaining high-end, one-piece composite sticks and goalie foam sticks, about 100,000 units annually, with 33 workers in the factory and seven staff in the office. The return on investment of the fixed cost in Canada was low.

Executives believed that they needed to provide a competitive retail price to boost the demand. To do so, they also needed to afford retailers a higher margin than their competitors did, so that retailers would help with product presentations in stores and marketing efforts. These approaches called for low cost production as well as decent quality. To reduce the cost and fully utilize the facilities, they could outsource the remaining production to the partner based in Victoriaville and move facilities there. However, according to regulations in Quebec, Sher-Wood did not have enough latitude to move or sell the equipment to their subcontractor in Quebec. They also considered backshoring the manufacturing out of China. They concluded that it would be more advantageous to stay in China from both cost reduction and R&D standpoints.

Chinese Partners' Condition and Collaboration

Sher-Wood's suppliers were located in Shanghai, Shenzhen and Zhongshan City near Hong Kong. They were producing tennis and badminton rackets,

---

[15]http://www.reebokhockey.com/labs/labs-blog/entries/2008/Nov/25/entry/jason-spezza-reebok-hockey-family/, accessed on July 18, 2011.
[16]http://www.cbc.ca/news/business/story/2008/05/05/sherwood-filing.html?ref=rss, accessed on July 18, 2011.
[17]Summarized from http://www.sher-wood.com, accessed on May 29, 2011.

developing the expertise in composite technology and relevant sporting goods production. Sher-Wood began to cooperate with them about 10 years ago when it started selling composite sticks. For years, these suppliers manufactured one-piece and two-piece composite hockey sticks for hockey companies around the world. Gradually, they accumulated manufacturing capacity and R&D capability. Sher-Wood's main supplier in Zhongshan City operated two shifts for 10 hours a day, six days a week. Their annual capacity was more than 1 million units. Moreover, they possessed an R&D team with 10 to 15 engineers, which was able to produce a prototype within one day with full information. On the contrary, it would cost Sher-Wood four to five months with a team of two to three engineers to produce a similar prototype. More importantly, as a consequence of their long-term cooperation, the main supplier had developed a certain feeling about hockey so that language and cultural barriers were not problems any more. "They were becoming a partner rather than one section within the supply chain," said Eric Rodrigue, Sher-Wood's marketing vice president.

Sher-Wood and its Chinese supplier partner needed to collaborate closely. On one hand, Sher-Wood had to send their experts to China to coach the partner about how to produce sticks according to their specifications. On the other hand, although Sher-Wood and the partner had similar on-site labs to conduct product tests, Sher-Wood mainly focused on the feeling of the stick, that is, the reproduction of how the slap shot, passes, reception, etc., would feel when a player placed his or her hands a certain way on the stick. Sher-Wood also conducted tests on ice with professional players, something their supplier could not do.

Moreover, with young, passionate and knowledgeable new managers in management and marketing, company executives thought they were ready to meet the extra cost and effort in market collaboration between Sher-Wood, the partner in China and retailers.

Company executives were concerned with rising labour costs, material costs and the currency exchange rate in China. Nevertheless, the overall cost of manufacturing in China was still lower than the cost in Quebec. They estimated that cost reduction was 0 to 15 per cent per unit depending on the model, with good quality and fast turnaround time. Moreover, some industries such as textiles had started to relocate their manufacturing to new emerging countries, such as Vietnam and Cambodia, for low labour and equipment costs; however, there was no R&D advantage in composite materials in these alternative locales.

Executives were also concerned with other issues. First, although the main supplier was able to produce customized sticks for an NHL player within 24 hours, the shipping was quite expensive from China to Quebec. Second, the main supplier used to produce huge volumes fast but without product personalization. Third, the game of hockey was perceived as a Western cultural heritage sport, so anything relevant to hockey which was made in China had the potential to negatively influence the market perception. However, all their competitors had outsourced manufacturing to China for years.

The Challenge

In early 2011, the question for Sher-Wood senior executives was how to boost their hockey stick sales. They believed that they should cope with this challenge by providing sticks with better quality, better retail price and better margin for retailers. They wondered whether they should move the manufacturing of the remaining high-end composite sticks to their suppliers in China or whether there was any alternative.

If they decided to shift their remaining manufacturing outside of the company, they needed to deal with a variety of issues. To fully utilize the facilities in Sherbrooke, they needed to move equipment to China, which was difficult and time-consuming because of export regulations. To set up the manufacturing machines and guide the manufacturing team, they would need to send experts there. To complete the coming hockey season between September and April but still implement the decision, they needed to plan every phase precisely. They also needed to figure out what to say and do about the 40 affected employees. Many had worked for Sher-Wood for more than 30 years, and their average age was 56. How could this be communicated to the public? They needed to make a final decision soon.

Case 1-2   Jollibee Foods Corporation (A): International Expansion

Christopher A. Bartlett

Protected by his office air conditioner from Manila's humid August air, in mid-1997, Manolo P. ("Noli") Tingzon pondered an analysis of demographic trends in California. As the new head of Jollibee's International Division, he wondered if a Philippine hamburger chain could appeal to mainstream American consumers or whether the chain's proposed U.S. operations could succeed by focusing on recent immigrants and Philippine expatriates. On the other side of the Pacific, a possible store opening in the Kowloon district of Hong Kong raised other issues for Tingzon. While Jollibee was established in the region, local managers were urging the company to adjust its menu, change its operations, and refocus its marketing on ethnic Chinese customers. Finally, he wondered whether entering the nearly virgin fast food territory of Papua New Guinea would position Jollibee to dominate an emerging market—or simply stretch his recently-slimmed division's resources too far.

With only a few weeks of experience in his new company, Noli Tingzon knew that he would have to weigh these decisions carefully. Not only would they shape the direction of Jollibee's future internalization strategy, they would also help him establish his own authority and credibility within the organization.

▌ Professor Christopher A. Bartlett and Research Associate Jamie O'Connell prepared this case. HBS cases are developed solely as the basis for class discussion. Cases are not intended to serve as endorsements, sources of primary data, or illustrations of effective or ineffective management.

▌ Company History

Started in 1975 as an ice cream parlor owned and run by the Chinese-Filipino Tan family, Jollibee had diversified into sandwiches after company President Tony Tan Caktiong (better known as TTC) realized that events triggered by the 1977 oil crisis would double the price of ice cream. The Tans' hamburger, made to a home-style Philippine recipe developed by Tony's chef father, quickly became a customer favorite. A year later, with five stores in metropolitan Manila, the family incorporated as Jollibee Foods Corporation.

The company's name came from TTC's vision of employees working happily and efficiently, like bees in a hive. Reflecting a pervasive courtesy in the company, everyone addressed each other by first names prefaced by the honorific "Sir" or "Ma'am," whether addressing a superior or subordinate. Friendliness pervaded the organization and become one of the "Five Fs" that summed up Jollibee's philosophy. The others were flavorful food, a fun atmosphere, flexibility in catering to customer needs, and a focus on families (children flocked to the company's bee mascot whenever it appeared in public). Key to Jollibee's ability to offer all of these to customers at an affordable price was a well developed operations management capability. A senior manager explained:

> It is not easy to deliver quality food and service consistently and efficiently. Behind all that fun and friendly environment that the customer experiences is a well oiled machine that keeps close tabs on our day-to-day operations. It's one of our key success factors.

Jollibee expanded quickly throughout the Philippines, financing all growth internally until 1993. (**Exhibit 1** shows growth in sales and outlets.)

Exhibit 1   Jollibee Philippines Growth, 1975–1997

Year	Total Sales (millions of pesos)	Total Stores at End of Year	Company-Owned Stores	Franchises
1975	NA	2	2	0
1980	NA	7	4	3
1985	174	28	10	18
1990	1,229	65	12	54
1991	1,744	99	21	80
1992	2,644	112	25	89
1993	3,386	124	30	96
1994	4,044	148	44	106
1995	5,118	166	55	113
1996	6,588	205	84	124
1997 (projected)	7,778	223	96	134

NA = Not available

Tan family members occupied several key positions particularly in the vital operations functions, but brought in professional managers to supplement their expertise. "The heads of marketing and finance have always been outsiders," TTC noted. (**Exhibit 2** shows a 1997 organization chart.) Many franchisees were also members or friends of the Tan family.

In 1993, Jollibee went public and in an initial public offering raised 216 million pesos (approximately US $8 million). The Tan family, however, retained the majority ownership and clearly controlled Jollibee. Although the acquisition of Greenwich Pizza Corporation in 1994 and the formation of a joint venture with Deli France in 1995 diversified the company's fast food offerings, in 1996 the chain of Jollibee stores still generated about 85% of the parent company's revenues. (**Exhibit 3** and **4** present Jollibee's consolidated financial statements from 1992 through 1996.)

McDonald's: Going Burger to Burger   The company's first serious challenge arose in 1981, when McDonald's entered the Philippines. Although Jollibee already had 11 stores, many saw McDonald's as a juggernaut and urged TTC to concentrate on building a strong second-place position in the market. A special meeting of senior management concluded that although McDonald's had more money and highly developed operating systems, Jollibee had one major asset: Philippine consumers preferred the taste of Jollibee's hamburger by a wide margin. The group decided to go head to head with McDonald's. "Maybe we were very young, but we felt we could do anything," TTC recalled. "We felt no fear."

McDonald's moved briskly at first, opening six restaurants within two years and spending large sums on advertising. Per store sales quickly surpassed Jollibee's and, by 1983, McDonald's had grabbed a 27% share of the fast food market, within striking range of Jollibee's 32%. The impressive performance of the Big Mac, McDonald's largest and best-known sandwich, led Jollibee to respond with a large hamburger of its own, called the Champ. Jollibee executives bet that the Champ's one wide hamburger patty, rather than the Big Mac's smaller two, would appeal more to Filipinos' large appetites. Market research indicated that Filipinos still preferred Jollibee burgers' spicy taste to McDonald's plain beef patty, so the Champ's promotions focused on its taste, as well as its size.

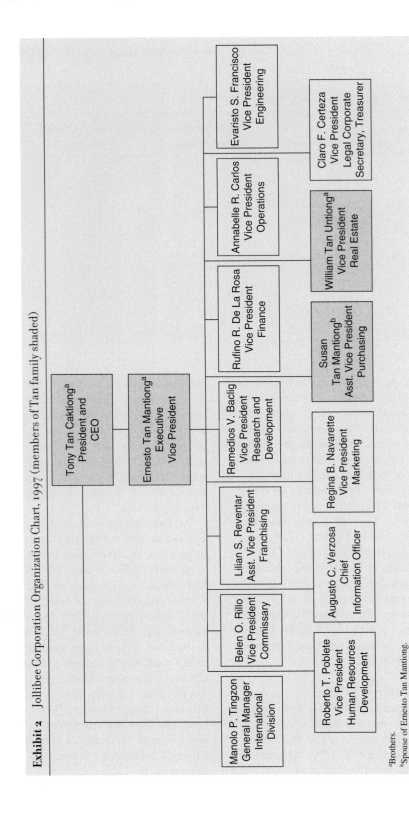

Exhibit 2 Jollibee Corporation Organization Chart, 1997 (members of Tan family shaded)

Tony Tan Caktiong[a]
President and CEO

Ernesto Tan Mantiong[a]
Executive Vice President

Manolo P. Tingzon
General Manager
International Division

Roberto T. Poblete
Vice President
Human Resources Development

Belen O. Rillo
Vice President
Commissary

Augusto C. Verzosa
Chief Information Officer

Lilian S. Reventar
Asst. Vice President
Franchising

Regina B. Navarette
Vice President
Marketing

Remedios V. Baclig
Vice President
Research and Development

Susan Tan Mantiong[b]
Asst. Vice President
Purchasing

Rufino R. De La Rosa
Vice President
Finance

Annabelle R. Carlos
Vice President
Operations

William Tan Untiong[a]
Vice President
Real Estate

Evaristo S. Francisco
Vice President
Engineering

Claro F. Certeza
Vice President
Legal Corporate
Secretary, Treasurer

[a]Brothers.
[b]Spouse of Ernesto Tan Mantiong.

28

Exhibit 3 Jollibee Foods Corporation Consolidated Balance Sheets (in Philippine pesos)

Years Ended December 31,

	1996	1995	1994	1993	1992
Assets					
Current assets					
Cash and cash equivalents	480,822,919	355,577,847	474,480,298	327,298,749	116,716,643
Accounts receivable:					
Trade	579,089,680	206,045,303	135,663,597	107,680,327	86,885,668
Advances and others	105,836,646	70,731,546	66,224,534	35,838,295	15,091,648
Inventories	323,019,198	201,239,667	183,154,582	135,263,988	116,828,086
Prepaid expenses and other current assets	223,680,221	132,077,935	88,995,824	41,462,780	66,028,987
Total current assets	1,712,448,664	965,672,298	948,518,835	647,544,139	401,551,032
Investments and advances	283,758,590	274,878,713	132,277,028	67,000,362	60,780,936
Property and equipment	2,177,944,193	1,181,184,783	753,876,765	568,904,831	478,857,474
Refundable deposits and other assets—net	363,648,234	224,052,247	91,575,543	92,035,464	72,310,079
Total assets	4,537,799,681	2,645,788,041	1,926,248,171	1,375,484,796	1,013,499,521
Liabilities and Stockholders' Equity					
Current liabilities:					
Bank loans	771,690,724	—	—	—	—
Accounts payable and accrued expenses	1,274,801,219	715,474,384	497,238,433	323,029,967	297,029,436
Income tax payable	58,803,916	28,103,867	17,205,603	23,206,109	19,851,315
Notes payable	—	—	—	—	133,000,000
Current portion of long-term debt	6,707,027	7,524,098	—	—	22,034,635
Dividends payable	16,810,812	—	—	—	—
Total current liabilities	2,128,813,698	751,102,349	514,444,036	346,236,076	471,915,386
Long-term debt	28,936,769	33,725,902	—	—	21,127,827
Minority interest	45,204,131	1,479,723	1,331,529	—	—
Stockholders' equity					
Capital stock—par value	880,781,250	704,625,000	563,315,000	372,000,000	66,000,000
Additional paid-in capital	190,503,244	190,503,244	190,503,244	190,503,244	—
Retained earnings	1,263,560,589	964,351,823	656,654,362	466,745,476	454,456,308
Total stockholders' equity	2,334,845,083	1,859,480,067	1,410,472,606	1,029,248,720	520,456,308
Total liabilities	4,537,799,681	2,645,788,041	1,926,248,171	1,375,484,796	1,013,499,521
Average exchange rate during year: pesos per US$	26.22	25.71	26.42	27.12	25.51

29

Exhibit 4 Jollibee Foods Corporation Consolidated Statements of Income and Retained Earnings (in Philippine pesos)

	Years Ended December 31				
	1996	**1995**	**1994**	**1993**	**1992**
Systemwide Sales (incl. franchisees)	8,577,067,000	6,894,670,000	5,277,640,000	4,102,270,000	NA
Company sales	6,393,092,135	4,403,272,755	3,277,383,084	2,446,866,690	2,074,153,386
Royalties and franchise fees	511,510,191	448,200,271	328,824,566	255,325,825	221,884,104
	6,904,602,326	4,851,473,026	3,606,207,650	2,702,192,515	2,296,037,490
Cost and Expenses					
Cost of sales	4,180,809,230	2,858,056,701	2,133,240,206	1,663,600,632	1,469,449,458
Operating expenses	1,943,536,384	1,403,151,840	1,013,999,640	674,288,268	545,749,275
Operating income	780,256,712	590,264,485	458,967,804	364,303,615	280,838,757
Interest and other income—net	44,670,811	102,134,296	83,342,805	32,716,223	(13,599,219)
Minority share in net earnings of a subsidiary	—	—	499,770		
Provision for income tax	219,900,353	168,589,520	138,001,953	104,230,670	66,172,056
Income before minority interest and cumulative effect of accounting change	605,027,170	523,809,261	403,808,886	292,789,168	201,067,482
Minority interest	2,829,654	137,694	—		
Cumulative effect of accounting change		13,733,644	—	—	—
Net income	602,197,516	537,405,211	403,808,886	292,789,168	201,067,482
Earnings per share	0.68	0.61	0.81	0.59	0.58
Average exchange rate (pesos per $US)	26.22	25.71	26.42	27.12	25.51

But the Champ's intended knockout punch was eclipsed by larger events. In August 1983, political opposition leader Benigno Aquino was assassinated as he returned from exile. The economic and political crisis that followed led most foreign investors, including McDonald's, to slow their investment in the Philippines. Riding a wave of national pride, Jollibee pressed ahead, broadening its core menu with taste-tested offerings of chicken, spaghetti and a unique peach-mango dessert pie, all developed to local consumer tastes. By 1984, McDonald's foreign brand appeal was fading.

In 1986, dictator Ferdinand Marcos fled the Philippines in the face of mass demonstrations of "people power" led by Aquino's widow, Corazon. After she took office as president, optimism returned to the country, encouraging foreign companies to reinvest. As the local McDonald's franchisee once again moved to expand, however, its management found that Jollibee now had 31 stores and was clearly the dominant presence in the market.

Industry Background

In the 1960s, fast food industry pioneers, such as Ray Kroc of McDonald's and Colonel Sanders of Kentucky Fried Chicken, had developed a value proposition that became the standard for the industry in the United States and abroad. Major fast food outlets in the United States, which provided a model for the rest of the world, aimed to serve time-constrained customers by providing good-quality food in a clean dining environment and at a low price.

Managing a Store   At the store level, profitability in the fast food business depended on high customer traffic and tight operations management. Opening an outlet required large investments in equipment and store fittings, and keeping it open imposed high fixed costs for rent, utilities, and labor. This meant attracting large numbers of customers ("traffic") and, when possible, increasing the size of the average order (or "ticket"). The need for high volume put a premium on convenience and made store location critical. In choosing a site, attention had to

be paid not only to the potential of a city or neighborhood but also to the traffic patterns and competition on particular streets or even blocks.

Yet even an excellent location could not make a store viable in the absence of good operations management, the critical ingredient in reducing waste, ensuring quality service and increasing staff productivity. Store managers were the key to motivating and controlling crew members responsible for taking orders, preparing food, and keeping the restaurant clean. Efficient use of their time-preparing raw materials and ingredients in advance, for example—not only enabled faster service, but could also reduce the number of crew members needed.

Managing a Chain   The high capital investment required to open new stores led to the growth of franchising which enabled chains to stake out new territory by rapidly acquiring market share and building brand recognition in an area. Such expansion created the critical mass needed to achieve economies of scale in both advertising and purchasing.

Fast food executives generally believed that chain-wide consistency and reliability was a key driver of success. Customers patronized chains because they knew, after eating at one restaurant in a chain, what they could expect at any other restaurant. This not only required standardization of the menu, raw material quality, and food preparation, but also the assurance of uniform standards of cleanliness and service. Particularly among the U.S. chains that dominated the industry, there also was agreement that uniformity of image also differentiated the chain from competitors: beyond selling hamburger or chicken, they believed they were selling an image of American pop culture. Consequently, most major fast food chains pushed their international subsidiaries to maintain or impose standardized menus, recipes, advertising themes, and store designs.

Moving Offshore: 1986–1997

Jollibee's success in the Philippines brought opportunities in other Asian countries. Foreign businesspeople, some of them friends of the Tan family, heard about the chain's success against McDonald's and began approaching TTC for franchise rights in their countries. While most of his family and other executives were caught up in the thriving Philippine business, TTC was curious to see how Jollibee would fare abroad.

Early Forays: Early Lessons

Singapore   Jollibee's first venture abroad began in 1985, when a friend of a Philippine franchisee persuaded TTC to let him open and manage Jollibee stores in Singapore. The franchise was owned by a partnership consisting of Jollibee, the local manager, and five Philippine-Chinese investors, each with a one-seventh stake. Soon after the first store opened, however, relations between Jollibee and the local manager began to deteriorate. When corporate inspectors visited to check quality, cleanliness, and efficiency in operations, the franchisee would not let them into his offices to verify the local records. In 1986, Jollibee revoked the franchise agreement and shut down the Singapore store. "When we were closing down the store, we found that all the local company funds were gone, but some suppliers had not been paid," said TTC. "We had no hard evidence that something was wrong, but we had lost each other's trust."

Taiwan   Soon after the closure in Singapore, Jollibee formed a 50/50 joint venture with a Tan family friend in Taiwan. Although sales boomed immediately after opening, low pedestrian traffic by the site eventually led to disappointing revenues. Over time, conflict arose over day-to-day management issues between the Jollibee operations staff assigned to maintain local oversight and the Taiwanese partner. "Because the business demands excellent operations, we felt we had to back our experienced Jollibee operations guy, but the partner was saying, 'I'm your partner, I've put in equity. Who do you trust?'" When the property market in Taiwan took off and store rent increased dramatically, Jollibee decided to dissolve the joint venture and pulled out of Taiwan in 1988.

Brunei   Meanwhile, another joint venture opened in August 1987 in the small sultanate of Brunei, located on the northern side of the island of Borneo. (**Exhibit 5** shows the locations of Jollibee International stores as of mid-1997.) The CEO of Shoemart, one of the Philippines' largest department stores, proposed that Jollibee form a joint-venture with a Shoemart partner in Brunei. By the end of 1993, with four successful stores in Brunei, TTC identified a key difference in the Brunei entry strategy: "In Singapore and Taiwan, the local partners ran the operation, and resented our operating control. In Brunei, the local investor was a silent partner. We sent managers from the Philippines to run the operations and the local partner supported us."

Indonesia   An opportunity to enter southeast Asia's largest market came through a family friend. In 1989, Jollibee opened its first store, in Jakarta. Initially, the operation struggled, facing competition from street vendors and cheap local fast food chains. When conflict between the local partners and the manager they had hired paralyzed the operation, in late 1994, Jollibee dissolved the partnership and sold the operation to a new franchisee. Nevertheless, the company viewed the market as promising.

TTC summed up the lessons Jollibee had learned from its first international ventures:

> McDonald's succeeded everywhere because they were very good at selecting the right partners. They can get 100 candidates and choose the best—we don't have the name to generate that choice yet.
>
> Another key factor in this business is location. If you're an unknown brand entering a new country or city, you have trouble getting access to prime locations. McDonald's name gets it the best sites. People were telling us not to go international until we had solved these two issues: location and partner.

Building an Organization   In 1993, TTC decided that Jollibee's international operations required greater structure and more resources. Because most of his management team was more interested in the fast-growing domestic side of the business, in January 1994, he decided to hire an experienced outsider as Vice President for International Operations.

Exhibit 5   Locations of Jollibee International Division stores, mid-1997
(Locations with Jollibee outlets are underlined.)

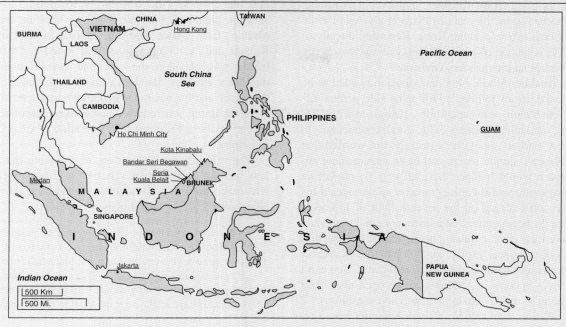

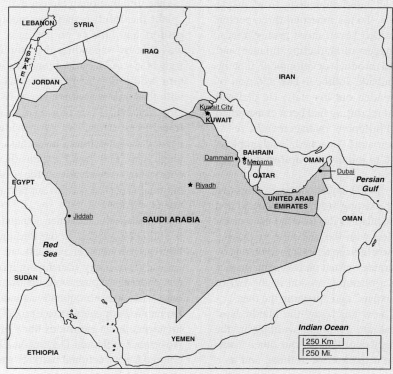

He selected Tony Kitchner, a native of Australia, who had spent 14 years in Pizza Hut's Asia-Pacific regional office in Hong Kong. Reporting directly to TTC, Kitchner asked for the resources and autonomy to create an International Division.

Kitchner felt that his new division needed to be separate from Jollibee's Philippine side, with a different identity and capabilities. He agreed with TTC that attracting partners with good connections in their markets should be a priority, but worried that Jollibee's simple image and basic management approach would hamper these efforts. To project an image of a world-class company, he remodeled his division's offices on the seventh floor of Jollibee's Manila headquarters and instituted the company's first dress code, requiring his managers to wear ties. As one manager explained, "We had to look and act like a multinational, not like a local chain. You can't have someone in a short-sleeved open-neck shirt asking a wealthy businessman to invest millions."

Within weeks of his arrival, Kitchner began recruiting experienced internationalists from inside and outside Jollibee. To his inherited three-person staff, he quickly added seven more professionals, including new managers of marketing, finance, and quality control and product development that he brought in from outside Jollibee. The addition of two secretaries rounded out his staff. He claimed that greater internal recruiting had been constrained by two factors—Philippine management's resistance to having their staff "poached," and employees' lack of interest in joining this upstart division.

Strategic Thrust   While endeavoring to improve the performance of existing stores in Indonesia and Brunei, Kitchner decided to increase the pace of international expansion with the objective of making Jollibee one of the world's top ten fast food brands by 2000. Kitchner's strategy rested on two main themes formulated during a planning session in the fall of 1994—"targeting expats" and "planting the flag."

The Division's new chief saw the hundreds of thousands of expatriate Filipinos working in the Middle East, Hong Kong, Guam, and other Asian territories as a latent market for Jollibee and as a good initial base to support entry. Looking for a new market to test this concept, he focused on the concentrations of Filipino guest-workers in the Middle East. After opening stores in Dubai, Kuwait, and Dammam, however, he found that this market was limited on the lower end by restrictions on poorer workers' freedom of movement, and on the upper end by wealthier expatriates' preference for hotel dining, where they could consume alcohol. Not all overseas Filipinos were potential customers, it seemed.

The other strategic criterion for choosing markets rested on Kitchner's belief in first-mover advantages in the fast food industry. Jay Visco, International's Marketing manager, explained:

> We saw that in Brunei, where we were the pioneers in fast food, we were able to set the pace and standards. Now, we have six stores there, while McDonald's has only one and KFC has three. . . . That was a key learning: even if your foreign counterparts come in later, you already have set the pace and are at top of the heap.

The International Division therefore began to "plant the Jollibee flag" in countries where competitors had little or no presence. The expectation was that by expanding the number of stores, the franchise could build brand awareness which in turn would positively impact sales. One problem with this approach proved to be its circularity: only after achieving a certain level of sales could most franchisees afford the advertising and promotion needed to build brand awareness. The other challenge was that rapid expansion led to resource constraints—especially in the availability of International Division staff to support multiple simultaneous startups.

Nonetheless, Kitchner expanded rapidly. Due to Jollibee's success in the Philippines and the Tan family's network of contacts, he found he could choose from many franchising inquiries from various countries. Some were far from Jollibee's home base—like the subsequently abandoned plan to enter Romania ("our gateway to Europe" according to one manager). In an enormous burst of energy, between November 1994 and December 1996, the company entered 8 new national markets and opened 18 new stores. The flag was being planted. (See **Exhibit 6.**)

Exhibit 6   Jollibee International Store Openings

Location	Date Opened	
Bandar Seri Begawan, *Brunei*	August 1987	
Bandar Seri Begawan, Brunei (second store)	June 1989	
Seria, Brunei	August 1992	
Jakarta, *Indonesia*	August 1992	
Jakarta, Indonesia (second store)	March 1993	
Bandar Seri Begawan, Brunei (third store)	November 1993	International Division created
Kuala Belait, Brunei	November 1994	
Dubai, *United Arab Emirates*	April 1995	
Kuwait City, *Kuwait*	December 1995	
Dammam, *Saudi Arabia*	December 1995	
Guam	December 1995	
Jiddah, Saudi Arabia	January 1996	
Bahrain	January 1996	
Kota Kinabalu, *Malaysia*	February 1996	
Dubai (second store)	June 1996	
Riyadh, Saudi Arabia	July 1996	
Kuwait City, Kuwait (second store)	August 1996	
Kuwait City, Kuwait (third store)	August 1996	
Jiddah, Saudi Arabia (second store)	August 1996	
Hong Kong	September 1996	
Bandar Seri Begawan, Brunei (fourth store)	October 1996	
Ho Chi Minh City, *Vietnam*	October 1996	
Medan, Indonesia	December 1996	
Hong Kong (second store)	December 1996	
Dammam, Saudi Arabia	April 1997	
Hong Kong (third store)	June 1997	
Jakarta, Indonesia (third store)	July 1997	
Jakarta, Indonesia (fourth store)	September 1997	

Italics represent new market entry.

Operational Management

Market entry   Once Jollibee had decided to enter a new market, Tony Kitchner negotiated the franchise agreement, often with an investment by the parent company, to create a partnership with the franchisee. At that point he handed responsibility for the opening to one of the division's Franchise Services Managers (FSM). These were the key contacts between the company and its franchisees, and Kitchner was rapidly building a substantial support group in Manila to provide them with the resources and expertise they needed to start up and manage an offshore franchise. (See **Exhibit 7.**)

About a month before the opening, the FSM hired a project manager, typically a native of the new market who normally would go on to manage the first store. The FSM and project manager made most of the important decisions during the startup process, with the franchisees' level of involvement varying from country to country. However, one responsibility in which franchisee was deeply involved was the key first step of selecting and securing the site of the first store, often with advice from International Division staff, who visited the country several times to direct market research. (Sometimes the franchisee had been chosen partly for access to

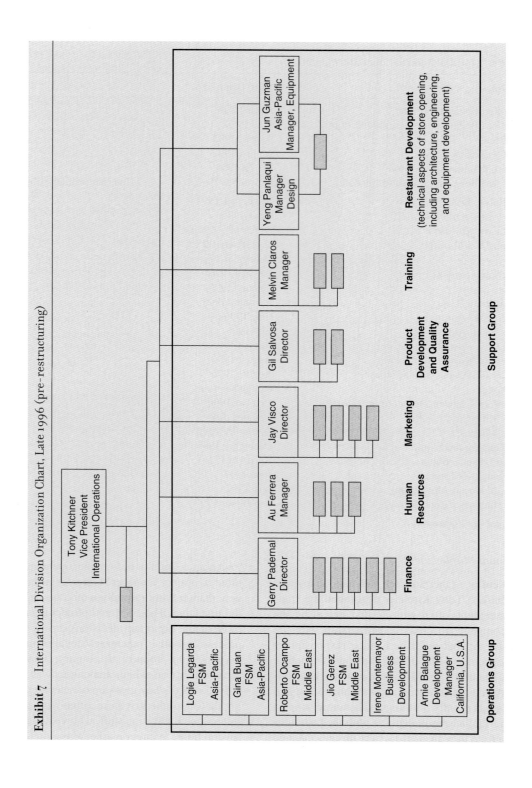

Exhibit 7 International Division Organization Chart, Late 1996 (pre–restructuring)

Tony Kitchner
Vice President
International Operations

Operations Group

Logie Legarda
FSM
Asia-Pacific

Gina Buan
FSM
Asia-Pacific

Roberto Ocampo
FSM
Middle East

Jio Gerez
FSM
Middle East

Irene Montemayor
Business
Development

Arnie Balague
Development
Manager
California, U.S.A.

Support Group

Gerry Padernal
Director

Finance

Au Ferrera
Manager

**Human
Resources**

Jay Visco
Director

Marketing

Gil Salvosa
Director

**Product
Development
and Quality
Assurance**

Melvin Claros
Manager

Training

Yeng Panlaqui
Manager
Design

Jun Guzman
Asia-Pacific
Manager, Equipment

Restaurant Development
(technical aspects of store opening,
including architecture, engineering,
and equipment development)

particularly good sites.) Once the franchisee had negotiated the lease or purchase, the project manager
began recruiting local store managers.

The FSM was responsible for engaging local
architects to plan the store. The kitchen followed
a standard Jollibee design that ensured proper production flow, but Kitchner encouraged FSMs to
adapt the counter and dining areas to the demands
of the space and the preferences of the franchisee.
A design manager in the International Division provided support

During the planning phase, the project manager
worked with International Division finance staff to
develop a budget for raw materials, labor, and other
major items in the operation's cost structure. He or
she also identified local suppliers, and—once International Division quality assurance staff had accred-
ited their standards—negotiated prices. (Some raw
materials and paper goods were sourced centrally
and distributed to franchisees throughout Asia.)

Once architectural and engineering plans were
approved, construction began. As it often did in
other offshore activities, the International Division staff had to develop skills very different from
those of their Jollibee colleagues working in the
Philippines. For example, high rents in Hong Kong
forced them to learn how to manage highly com-
pacted construction schedules: construction there
could take one-third to one-half the time required
for similar work in the Philippines.

Under FSM leadership, the International Division staff prepared marketing plans for the opening
and first year's operation. They included positioning and communications strategies and were based
on their advance consumer surveys, aggregate market data, and analysis of major competitors. Division staff also trained the local marketing manager
and the local store manager and assistant managers who typically spent three months in Philippine
stores. (Where appropriate local managers had not
been found, the store managers were sometimes
drawn from Jollibee's Philippine operations.) Just
before opening, the project manager hired crew
members, and International Division trainers from
Manila instructed them for two weeks on cooking,

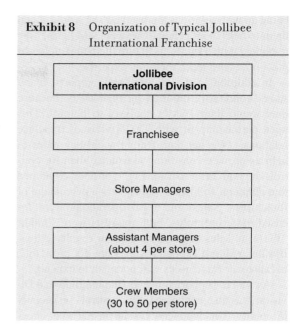

Exhibit 8   Organization of Typical Jollibee
International Franchise

```
┌─────────────────────────────┐
│         Jollibee            │
│  International Division     │
└─────────────────────────────┘
              │
┌─────────────────────────────┐
│         Franchisee          │
└─────────────────────────────┘
              │
┌─────────────────────────────┐
│       Store Managers        │
└─────────────────────────────┘
              │
┌─────────────────────────────┐
│     Assistant Managers      │
│    (about 4 per store)      │
└─────────────────────────────┘
              │
┌─────────────────────────────┐
│       Crew Members          │
│    (30 to 50 per store)     │
└─────────────────────────────┘
```

serving customers, and maintaining the store. (See
Exhibit 8 for a typical franchise's organization.)

Oversight and Continuing Support   After a
store opened, the FSM remained its key contact
with Jollibee, monitoring financial and operational
performance and working to support and develop
the store manager. For approximately two months
after opening, FSMs required stores in their jurisdictions to fax them every day their figures for sales
by product, customer traffic, and average ticket. As
operations stabilized and the store manager started
to see patterns in sales and operational needs, FSMs
allowed stores to report the same data weekly and
provide a monthly summary.

FSMs used this information not only to project
and track royalty income for corporate purposes, but
also to identify ways they could support the local
franchisee. When the data suggested problems, the
FSM would contact the store manager, highlight the
issue, and ask for an appropriate plan of action. For
example, if FSM Gina Buan saw a decline in sales for
two consecutive weeks, she demanded specific plans
within 24 hours of her call. If managers could not

come up with solutions themselves, she would coach them to help them generate answers. "My aim," she remarked with a smile, "is to turn them into clones of me—or at least teach them my expertise."

In addition to the required sales reports, many stores voluntarily reported on their costs, because they found their FSM's analysis so helpful. This open partnership fit with TTC's view of franchise relations. "We get data from franchisees more to help us provide consulting assistance than for control," he said. Ernesto Tan, TTC's brother, explained that although Jollibee's royalty was a percentage of franchisees' sales, and local operations were focused more on profits, both interests were similar: "We want sales to grow, so that our royalty grows. But this will not happen if stores are not profitable, because our franchisees will not push to expand."

As well as support, however, the International Division was also concerned with control—especially in quality. Unannounced on-site inspections every quarter were Jollibee's primary tool. Over two days, the FSM evaluated every aspect of operations in detail, including product quality and preparation (taste, temperature, freshness, availability, and appearance), cleanliness, restaurant appearance, service speed, and friendliness. The manual for intensive checks was several inches thick. All international staff had been trained in Jollibee's quality standards and conducted less detailed "quick checks" whenever they traveled. Based on a 15-page questionnaire, a quick check took roughly two hours to complete and covered all of the areas that intensive ones did, although with less rigor and detail. Each store received an average of two quick checks per quarter.

In addition to FSMs' own rich industry experiences—Gina Buan, for example, had managed stores, districts, and countries for Jollibee and another chain—these field managers engaged the expertise of International Division functional staff. While they tried to shift responsibility gradually to the franchisee, division support staff often bore much of the responsibility long after startup. For example, the marketing staff tried to limit their franchise support role to creating initial marketing plans for new openings and reviewing new store plans. However, often they were drawn into the planning of more routine campaigns for particular stores, work they felt should be handled by the franchisee and store managers.

International vs. Domestic Practice   As operations grew, Kitchner and his staff discovered that international expansion was not quite as simple as the metaphor of "planting flags" might suggest. It sometimes felt more like struggling up an unconquered, hostile mountain. After numerous market entry battles, the international team decided that a number of elements of Jollibee's Philippine business model needed to be modified overseas. For example, the company's experience in Indonesia led Visco to criticize the transplantation of Jollibee's "mass-based positioning":

> When Jollibee arrived in Indonesia, they assumed that the market would be similar to the Philippines. But the Indonesian masses are not willing to spend as much on fast food as the Philippine working and lower-middle class consumers, and there were lots of cheap alternatives available. We decided that we needed to reposition ourselves to target a more up-market clientele.

Kitchner and Visco also felt that Jollibee needed to present itself as "world class," not "local" or "regional." In particular, they disliked the Philippine store design—a "trellis" theme with a garden motif—which had been transferred unchanged as Jollibee exported internationally. Working with an outside architect, a five-person panel from the International Division developed three new store decors, with better lighting and higher quality furniture. After Kitchner got TTC's approval, the Division remodeled the Indonesian stores and used the designs for all subsequent openings.

International also redesigned the Jollibee logo. While retaining the bee mascot, it changed the red background to orange and added the slogan, "great burgers, great chicken." Visco pointed out that the orange background differentiated the chain's logo from those of other major brands, such as KFC, Coca-Cola, and Marlboro, which all had red-and-white logos. The slogan was added to link the Jollibee name and logo with its products in people's minds. Visco also noted that, unlike Wendy's Old

Fashioned Hamburgers, Kentucky Fried Chicken, and Pizza Hut, Jollibee did not incorporate its product in its name and market tests had found that consumers outside the Philippines guessed the logo signified a toy chain or candy store.

Kitchner and his staff made numerous other changes to Jollibee's Philippine business operating model. For example, rather than preparing new advertising materials for each new promotion as they did in the Philippines, the international marketing group created a library of promotional photographs of each food product that could be assembled, in-house, into collages illustrating new promotions (e.g., a discounted price for buying a burger, fries, and soda). And purchasing changed from styrofoam to paper packaging to appeal to foreign consumers' greater environmental consciousness.

Customizing for Local Tastes   While such changes provoked grumbling from many in the large domestic business who saw the upstart international group as newcomers fiddling with proven concepts, nothing triggered more controversy than the experiments with menu items. Arguing that the "flexibility" aspect of Jollibee's "Five Fs" corporate creed stood for a willingness to accommodate differences in customer tastes, managers in the International Division believed that menus should be adjusted to local preferences.

The practice had started in 1992 when a manager was dispatched from the Philippines to respond to the Indonesian franchisee's request to create a fast food version of the local favorite *nasi lema,* a mixture of rice and coconut milk. Building on this precedent, Kitchner's team created an international menu item they called the Jollimeal. This was typically a rice-based meal with a topping that could vary by country–in Hong Kong, for example, the rice was covered with hot and sour chicken, while in Vietnam it was chicken curry. Although it accounted for only 5% of international sales, Kitchner saw Jollimeals as an important way to "localize" the Jollibee image.

But the International Division expanded beyond the Jollimeal concept. On a trip to Dubai, in response to the local franchisee's request to create a salad for the menu, product development manager Gil Salvosa spent a night chopping vegetables in his hotel room to create a standard recipe. That same trip, he acquired a recipe for chicken masala from the franchisee's cook, later adapting it to fast food production methods for the Dubai store. The International Division also added idiosyncratic items to menus, such as dried fish, a Malaysian favorite. Since other menu items were seldom removed, these additions generally increased the size of menus abroad.

Although increased menu diversity almost always came at the cost of some operating efficiency (and, by implication, complicated the task of store level operating control), Kitchner was convinced that such concessions to local tastes were necessary. In Guam, for example, to accommodate extra-large local appetites, division staff added a fried egg and two strips of bacon to the Champ's standard large beef patty. And franchisees in the Middle East asked the Division's R&D staff to come up with a spicier version of Jollibee's fried chicken. Although Kentucky Fried Chicken (KFC) was captivating customers with their spicy recipe, R&D staff on the Philippine side objected strenuously. As a compromise, International developed a spicy sauce that customers could add to the standard Jollibee chicken.

Overall, the International Division's modification of menus and products caused considerable tension with the Philippine side of Jollibee. While there was no controversy about reformulating hamburgers for Muslim countries to eliminate traces of pork, for example, adding new products or changing existing ones led to major arguments. As a result, International received little cooperation from the larger Philippine research and development staff and customization remained a source of disagreement and friction.

Strained International-Domestic Relations   As the International Division expanded, its relations with the Philippine-based operations seemed to deteriorate. Tensions over menu modifications reflected more serious issues that had surfaced soon after Kitchner began building his international group. Philippine staff saw International as newcomers who, despite their lack of experience in Jollibee, "discarded practices built over 16 years." On the other side, International Division staff reported that they found the Philippine organization bureaucratic and slow-moving. They felt stymied by requirements to follow certain procedures and go through proper channels to obtain assistance.

The two parts of Jollibee continued to operate largely independently, but strained relations gradually eroded any sense of cooperation and reduced already limited exchanges to a minimum. Some International Division staff felt that the Philippine side, which controlled most of Jollibee's resources, should do more to help their efforts to improve and adapt existing products and practices. Visco recalled that when he wanted assistance designing new packaging, the Philippine marketing manager took the attitude that international could fend for itself. Similarly, Salvosa wanted more cooperation on product development from Philippine R&D, but was frustrated by the lengthy discussions and approvals that seemed to be required.

However, the domestic side viewed things differently. Executive Vice President Ernesto Tan, who was in charge of Jollibee in the Philippines, recalled:

> The strains came from several things. It started when International tried to recruit people directly from the Philippine side, without consulting with their superiors. There also was some jealousy on a personal level because the people recruited were immediately promoted to the next level, with better pay and benefits.
> The international people also seemed to develop a superiority complex. They wanted to do everything differently, so that if their stores did well, they could take all the credit. At one point, they proposed running a store in the Philippines as a training facility, but we thought they also wanted to show us that they could do it better than us. We saw them as lavish spenders while we paid very close attention to costs. Our people were saying, "We are earning the money, and they are spending it!" There was essentially no communication to work out these problems. So we spoke to TTC, because Kitchner reported to him.

Matters grew worse throughout 1996. One of the first signs of serious trouble came during a project to redesign the Jollibee logo, which TTC initiated in mid-1995. Triggered by International's modification of the old logo, the redesign project committee had representatives from across the company. Having overseen International's redesign, Kitchner was included. During the committee's deliberations, some domestic managers felt that the International vice-president's strong opinions were obstructive, and early in 1996 Kitchner stopped attending the meetings.

During this time, TTC was growing increasingly concerned about the International Division's continuing struggles. Around November 1996, he decided that he could no longer support Kitchner's strategy of rapid expansion due to the financial problems it was creating. Many of the International stores were losing money, but the cost of supporting these widespread unprofitable activities was increasing. Despite the fact that even unprofitable stores generated franchise fees calculated as a percentage of sales, TTC was uncomfortable:

> Kitchner wanted to put up lots of stores, maximizing revenue for Jollibee. Initially, I had supported this approach, thinking we could learn from an experienced outsider, but I came to believe that was not viable in the long term. We preferred to go slower, making sure that each store was profitable so that it would generate money for the franchisee, as well as for us. In general, we believe that whoever we do business with—suppliers and especially franchisees—should make money. This creates a good, long-term relationship.

In February 1997, Kitchner left Jollibee to return to Australia. A restructuring supervised directly by TTC shrank the International Division's staff from 32 to 14, merging the finance, MIS and human resources functions with their bigger Philippine counterparts. (See **Exhibit 9.**) Jay Visco became interim head of International while TTC searched for a new Division leader.

A New International Era: 1997

In the wake of Kitchner's departure, TTC consulted intensively with Jollibee's suppliers and other contacts in fast food in the Philippines regarding a replacement. The name that kept recurring was

Exhibit 9 International Division Organization Chart, March 1997 (post-restructuring)

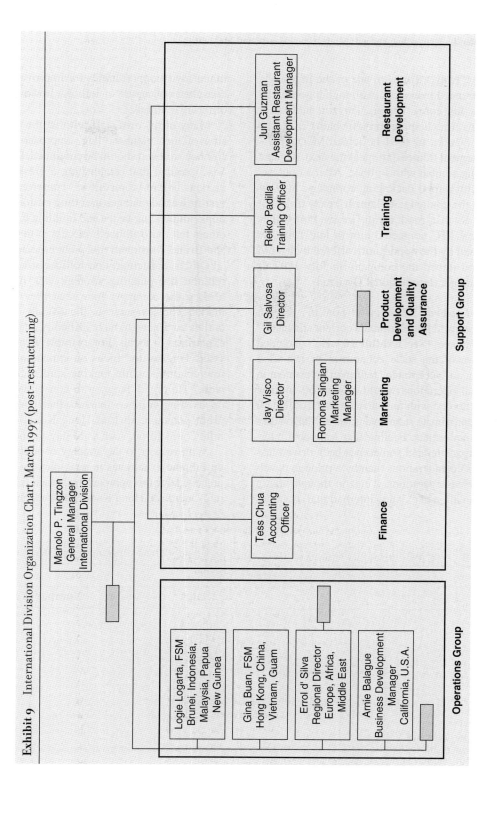

Manolo P. ("Noli") Tingzon, one of the industry's most experienced managers. Although based in the Philippines his entire career, Tingzon had spent much of this time helping foreign chains crack the Philippine market. In 1981 he joined McDonald's as a management trainee and spent the next 10 years in frustrating combat with Jollibee. After a brief experience with a food packaging company, in 1994 he took on the challenge to launch Texas Chicken, another U.S. fast food chain, in its Philippines entry. When TTC contacted him in late 1996, he was intrigued by the opportunity offered by his old nemesis and joined the company in July 1997 as general manager, International Division.

A Fresh Look at Strategy Upon his arrival, Tingzon reviewed International's current and historical performance. (See **Exhibit 10.**) He concluded that because of the scale economies of fast food franchising, an "acceptable" return on investment in international operations would require 60 Jollibee restaurants abroad with annual sales of US$800,000 each, the approximate store level sales at McDonald's smaller Asian outlets. Feeling that Jollibee's international expansion had sometimes been driven less by business considerations than by a pride in developing overseas operations, Tingzon thought that a fresh examination of existing international strategies might reveal opportunities for improvement. As he consulted colleagues at Jollibee, however, he heard differing opinions.

Many of his own staff felt that the rapid expansion of the "plant-the-flag" approach had served Jollibee well and should be continued. For example, Visco argued that establishing a presence in each market before competitors conferred important first-mover advantages in setting customer expectations, influencing tastes and building brand. He and others felt that Jollibee's success in the Philippines and Brunei illustrated this point especially well.

Others, particularly on Jollibee's domestic side, felt the flag-planting strategy was ill-conceived, leading the company into what they saw as rash market choices such as the Middle East, where outlets continued to have difficulty attracting either expatriates or locals. For example, Ernesto Tan advised Tingzon to "focus on expanding share in a few countries while making sure each store does well." He urged Tingzon to consolidate and build on existing Jollibee markets that had either high profit potential, such as Hong Kong, or relatively mild competition, such as Malaysia and Indonesia.

With respect to the strategy of initially focusing on Filipino expatriates in new markets, Tingzon appreciated that this approach had eased Jollibee's entry into Guam and Hong Kong, but wondered whether it

Exhibit 10   International Store Sales by Country: 1996 (in U.S. dollars at contemporary exchange rates)

		1996	
		Sales	**Number of Stores**
Bahrain		262,361	1
Brunei		2,439,538	6
Guam		1,771,202	1
Hong Kong		1,142,240	2
Indonesia		854,259	3
Kuwait		864,531	3
Malaysia		391,328	1
Saudi Arabia		976,748	4
United Arab Emirates		487,438	2
Vietnam		112,578	1
Total	US$	9,302,223	24

might trap the chain. "Might we risk boxing ourselves into a Filipino niche that prevents us from growing enough to support operations in each country?" he asked. Again opinion was divided between those favoring the expatriate-led strategy and those who felt it was time for Jollibee to shake its Philippine identity and target the mainstream market wherever it went.

Strategy in Action: Three Decisions   Although he eventually wanted to resolve these issues at the level of policy, Tingzon faced three immediate growth opportunities that he knew would shape the emergence of the future strategy.

Papua New Guinea: Raising the Standard   In early 1996, at the recommendation of Quality Assurance Manager Gil Salvosa, a local New Guinea entrepreneur in the poultry business approached Tony Kitchner about a Jollibee franchise. He described a country of five million people served by only one poorly managed, 3-store fast-food chain, that had recently broken ties with its Australian chicken restaurant franchise. "Port Moresby does not have a single decent place to eat," he told Kitchner. He believed Jollibee could raise the quality of service and food enough to take much of the Australian chain's market share while discouraging further entrants.

Although the original plan had been to open just one store in the foreseeable future—in the capital, Port Moresby—Tingzon was certain that the franchisee could only cover the costs of developing the market if he put in at least three or four stores soon after. But he was uncertain whether Papua New Guinea could support the 20 stores that he saw as the target critical mass for new markets. (For comparison, in the Philippines, approximately 1,200 fast food outlets competed for the business of 75 million people. GNP per capita in both countries was almost at US$2,500.)

When Tingzon explained his concerns, the would-be franchisee's response was that he would negotiate with a major petroleum retailer and try to open stores in five of their service stations around the country. Furthermore, he emphasized that he was willing to build more stores if necessary and would put up all the capital so that Jollibee would risk no equity in the venture.

Hong Kong: Expanding the Base   Also on Tingzon's plate was a proposal to expand to a fourth store in Hong Kong. The franchise, owned by Jollibee in partnership with local businessmen and managed by Tommy King, TTC's brother-in-law, opened its first store in September 1996 to instant, overwhelming success. Located near a major transit hub in the Central district, it became a gathering place for Filipino expatriates, primarily domestic workers. However, appealing to the locals had proven more difficult. While volume was high on weekends, when the Filipinos came to Central to socialize, it fell off during the week, when business was primarily from local office workers.

Although two more stores in Central had attracted many Filipinos, they both relied extensively on Chinese customers and generated sales of only about one-third of the first outlet. One problem was that, despite strenuous efforts, Jollibee had been unable to hire many local Chinese as crew members. According to one manager, Chinese customers who did not speak English well were worried that they would be embarrassed if they were not understood by the predominantly Philippine and Nepalese counter staff. Another problem was that in a city dominated by McDonald's, Jollibee's brand recognition among locals was weak. Working with Henry Shih, the sub-franchisee who owned the second store, Jollibee staff were trying to help launch a thematic advertising campaign, but due to the Hong Kong operation's small size, the franchise could not inject sufficient funds.

Shih also blamed rigidity over menu offerings for Jollibee's difficulties appealing to Chinese customers. In early 1997, his Chinese managers had suggested serving tea the Hong Kong way—using tea dust (powdered tea leaves) rather than tea bags and adding evaporated milk. More than six months later, he had still not received a go-ahead. His proposal to develop a less-fatty recipe for Chicken Joy, one of Jollibee's core menu items, had met more direct resistance. "The Chinese say that if you eat lots of deep-fried food you become hot inside and will develop health problems," said Shih who believed that the domestic side had pressured the International Division to reject any experimentation with this "core" menu item.

Meanwhile, staffing problems were worsening. The four locally-recruited Chinese managers clashed with the five Filipinos imported from Tommy King's Philippine franchise, with the Chinese calling the Filipinos' discipline lax and their style arrogant, while the Filipinos saw the Chinese managers as uncommitted. By August 1997, all of the Chinese managers had resigned, leaving Jollibee with only Filipinos in store-level management positions. Shih was afraid this would further undermine Jollibee's ability to hire local crews, as Chinese preferred to work for Chinese.

Partly due to staff turnover, store managers were focused on dealing with day-to-day operations issues such as uneven product quality and had little time to design even short-term marketing strategies. King's focus on his Philippine stores slowed decision-making. And while Gina Buan, the FSM, had visited Hong Kong more often than any other markets she supervised (including for an extraordinary month-long stay), she had been unable to resolve the management problems. In June, King appointed Shih General Manager to oversee the entire Hong Kong venture.

In this context, Shih and King proposed to open a fourth store. The site in the Kowloon district was one of the busiest in Hong Kong, located at one of just two intersections of the subway and the rail line that was the only public transport from the New Territories, where much of the city's workforce resided. However, the area saw far fewer Filipinos than Central and the store would have to depend on locals. Acknowledging that the fourth store would test Jollibee's ability to appeal to Hong Kong people, Shih argued that the menu would have to be customized more radically. However, Tingzon wondered whether expansion was even viable at this time, given the Hong Kong venture's managerial problems. Even if he were to approve the store, he wondered if he should support the menu variations that might complicate quality control. On the other hand, expansion into such a busy site might enhance Jollibee's visibility and brand recognition among locals, helping increase business even without changing the menu. It was another tough call.

California: Supporting the Settlers   Soon after signing his contract, Tingzon had learned of a year-old plan to open one Jollibee store per quarter in California starting in the first quarter of 1998. Supporting TTC's long-held belief that Jollibee could win enormous prestige and publicity by gaining a foothold in the birthplace of fast food, Kitchner had drawn up plans with a group of Manila-based businessmen as 40% partners in the venture. Once the company stores were established, they hoped to franchise in California and beyond in 1999.

Much of the confidence for this bold expansion plan came from Jollibee's success in Guam, a territory of the U.S. Although they initially targeted the 25% of the population of Filipino extraction, management discovered that their menu appealed to other groups of Americans based there. They also found they could adapt the labor-intensive Philippine operating methods by developing different equipment and cooking processes more in keeping with a high labor cost environment. In the words of one International Division veteran, "In Guam, we learned how to do business in the United States. After succeeding there, we felt we were ready for the mainland."

The plan called for the first store to be located in Daly City, a community with a large Filipino population but relatively low concentration of fast-food competitors in the San Francisco area. (With more than a million immigrants from the Philippines living in California, most relatively affluent, this state had one of the highest concentrations of Filipino expatriates in the world.) The menu would be transplanted from the Philippines without changes. After initially targeting Filipinos, the plan was to branch out geographically to the San Francisco and San Diego regions, and demographically to appeal to other Asian-American and, eventually, Hispanic-American consumers. The hope was that Jollibee would then expand to all consumers throughout the U.S.

Like the expansion strategies in PNG and Hong Kong, this project had momentum behind it, including visible support from Filipino-Americans, strong interest of local investors, and, not least, TTC's great interest in succeeding in McDonald's back-yard. Yet Tingzon realized that he would be the one held accountable for its final success and wanted to bring an objective outsider's perspective to this plan before it became accepted wisdom. Could Jollibee hope to succeed in the world's most competitive fast-food market? Could they provide the necessary support and control to operations located 12 hours by plane and eight time zones away? And was the Filipino-to-Asian-to-Hispanic-to-mainstream entry strategy viable or did it risk boxing them into an economically unviable niche?

Looking Forward   Noli Tingzon had only been in his job a few weeks, but already it was clear that his predecessor's plan to open 1000 Jollibee stores abroad before the turn of the century was a pipe dream. "It took McDonald's 20 years for its international operations to count for more than 50% of total sales," he said. "I'll be happy if I can do it in 10." But even this was an ambitious goal. And the decisions he made on the three entry options would have a significant impact on the strategic direction his international division took and on the organizational capabilities it needed to get there.

Case 1-3   Mahindra & Mahindra in South Africa

In May 2011, Pravin Shah, chief executive, International Operations (Automotive and Farm Equipment Sectors) at Mahindra & Mahindra Ltd. (M&M), a leading multinational automotive manufacturer headquartered in Mumbai, India, was weighing his options on the company's growth strategy in the South African market. Shah's dilemma was four-fold. Since 2005, Mahindra & Mahindra South Africa (Proprietary) Ltd. (M&M (SA)), the company's fully owned subsidiary based in Pretoria, South Africa, had grown the market by

▮ R Chandrasekhar wrote this case under the supervision of Professor Jean-Louis Schaan solely to provide material for class discussion. The authors do not intend to illustrate either effective or ineffective handling of a managerial situation. The authors may have disguised certain names and other identifying information to protect confidentiality.

importing completely built units (CBUs) from its Indian operations. Shah needed to decide whether M&M (SA) should move to the next logical step of an agreement with a local vendor to use the latter's surplus facility for contract assembly of M&M vehicles. Or, M&M (SA) could skip that step altogether and invest in its own manufacturing facility. Alternatively, Shah could wait and watch until the subsidiary logged a critical mass of vehicle sales volumes that would be sustainable in the long term. The fourth option would be to grow the current business model of importing CBUs from India by using South Africa as the hub from which to sell them to other countries in the African continent and, thereby, expand the export market. Said Shah:

> Each option involves tradeoffs. They have to be evaluated in light of M&M (SA)'s long-term view of the South African automotive market, which, in some ways, is unlike other international markets where we are present. South Africa is clearly a growth market. It is also competitive and fragmented. The basic question is: what is the fit that we want in it? There are issues about how we can build on the competencies we have developed during the last six years and the skills we need to develop, going forward, locally. The larger consideration for whatever call we take in South Africa is the globalization strategy of M&M, which defines the boundary.

Shah needed to present his recommendation to the four-member board of M&M (SA). The board, of which he was himself a member, was chaired by Dr. Pawan Goenka, president (Automotive and Farm Equipment Sectors), M&M. The decision of the board of the South African subsidiary would need to be, in turn, formally approved by the board of M&M, which, as the parent company, had 12 directors, more than half of whom were independent directors. The M&M board was meeting an average of six times in a year to discuss and decide on matters of strategic importance.

Context

M&M, the parent company, had six assembly plants worldwide. One was located in Egypt as part of a non-exclusive arrangement between M&M in India and a contract-manufacturing vendor in Egypt. M&M exported components from India for assembly in Egypt of vehicles intended either for local sales or for export. The Egyptian vendor assembled an average of 200 vehicles per month for M&M when the plant capacity was partially dedicated to M&M, thus proving the basic viability of local assembly as a strategic option for M&M (SA).

South Africa was one of M&M's biggest and most important export markets and was crucial to M&M's strategic growth. M&M had long-term plans to launch a global sport-utility vehicle (SUV) brand from South Africa. It was also planning to launch a new SUV for the South African market built on an altogether new platform. Both plans supported M&M launching its own manufacturing facility.

The wait-and-watch policy was a result of the South African automotive industry having just recovered from a sharp decline in new-vehicle sales in three consecutive years—2007, 2008 and 2009. In 2010, sales growth had turned positive and was expected to gather momentum. However, the global automotive market had not yet fully recovered from the recession, which had led to the downturn in the South African automotive market. An annual survey of auto executives worldwide, had pointed to over-capacity as the major concern globally during

2011.[1] Over-capacity prevailed in both mature automotive markets (e.g., in the United States, Germany and Japan) and in emerging automotive markets (e.g., China and India). In the automobile industry, which was cyclical in nature, over-capacity was not a unique problem but it always made everyone cautious.

Finally, with the exceptions of Egypt and South Africa, none of the 54 countries in the African continent had a sizeable middle class that could warrant M&M having a presence along the lines of the inroads M&M had made in South Africa or Egypt. Each individual market needed to be developed over time. In the interim, M&M could cater to the African markets from its South African base, which could be used as a re-export hub. Said Shah:

> Contract assembly is the way to go for companies with low volumes [of less than a few thousand vehicles per annum]. Of late, a growing number of multi-brand assemblers are coming up in Eastern Cape Province. It is also noteworthy that contract manufacturing is common in the industry even between established players who are otherwise competing for market share. Fiat, for example, assembles vehicles for Nissan, which assembles vehicles for Renault. The major factor for consideration is the availability of surplus capacity. On the other hand, it is possible for a company to set up its own manufacturing facility in South Africa once it has reached annual sales of 6,000 units in which a single brand in its portfolio sells approximately 1,500 units annually. It places you firmly on the path of both localization of content and scaling up, which are major issues in auto manufacturing globally. A volume of that order also helps build brand equity in the local market.

South African Automotive Industry

South Africa fared better than its neighbors (both in and out of African continent) in the business environment rankings from 2006 to 2010. The country was expected to retain the lead for the period 2010 to 2015 in several of the 55 parameters used as the basis for rankings (see **Exhibit 1**).

The South African automotive industry accounted for about 10 per cent of the country's manufacturing

---

[1] Dieter Becker et al, *"Global Automotive Executive Survey 2011: Creating a Future Roadmap for the Automotive Industry,"* pp. 24–26, www .kpmg.com/Global/en/IssuesAndInsights/ArticlesPublications/Documents/ Global-Auto-Executive-Survey-2011.pdf, accessed August 25, 2011.

Exhibit 1   South Africa—Business Environment Rankings

#	Indicators	2006–2010		2010–2015	
		South Africa	Regional average	South Africa	Regional average
	Political environment				
1	Risk of armed conflict	4	3.2	5	3.4
2	Risk of social unrest	3	2.8	2	2.1
3	Constitutional mechanisms for the orderly transfer of power	3	2.4	3	2.4
4	Government and opposition	4	3.2	3	3.1
5	Threat of politically motivated violence	3	2.6	3	2.7
6	International disputes or tensions	3	2.8	4	2.9
7	Government policy towards business	3	3.1	3	3.1
8	Effectiveness of system in policy formulation and execution	3	2.6	3	2.7
9	Quality of the bureaucracy	3	2.2	2	2.2
10	Transparency and fairness of legal system	2	1.8	4	2.2
11	Efficiency of legal system	4	2.4	4	2.4
12	Corruption	3	2.4	3	2.4
13	Impact of crime	1	3.3	1	3.2
	Taxes				
1	Corporate tax burden	4	3.4	4	3.9
2	Top marginal personal income tax	3	3.9	3	4.0
3	Value-added tax	4	4.2	4	4.1
4	Employers' social security contributions	5	3.7	4	3.9
5	Degree of encouragement for new investment	2	2.5	3	3.0
6	Consistency and fairness of the tax system	2	2.5	3	2.6
7	Tax complexity	4	3.2	4	3.4
	Financing				
1	Openness of the banking sector	3	2.9	3	2.9
2	Stockmarket capitalization	4	2.9	3	3.2
3	Distortions in financial markets	3	3.2	3	3.3
4	Quality of the financial regulatory system	3	2.4	3	2.9
5	Access of foreigners to local capital market	4	2.6	4	2.8
6	Access to medium-term finance for investment	3	2.8	3	2.8

(Continued)

Exhibit 1   South Africa—Business Environment Rankings (*Continued*)

		2006–2010		2010–2015	
#	Indicators	South Africa	Regional average	South Africa	Regional average
	Labour market				
1	Labour costs adjusted for productivity	3	3.9	3	3.9
2	Availability of skilled labour	2	2.3	3	2.6
3	Quality of workforce	3	2.5	3	2.8
4	Quality of local managers	3	2.5	3	2.6
5	Language skills	4	3.0	4	3.2
6	Health of the workforce	1	2.9	1	2.9
7	Level of technical skills	3	2.9	3	2.9
8	Cost of living	4	2.8	4	2.2
9	Incidence of strikes	3	3.5	3	3.3

Source: Pratibha Thaker, ed., *Economist Intelligence Unit—Country Forecast—South Africa,* May 2011, www.eiu.com/countries, accessed November 10, 2011.

Notes: 1. Rankings are on a scale from 1 (very bad for business) to 10 (very good for business); 2. Regional average is the total for 17 countries: Algeria, Bahrain, Egypt, Iran, Israel, Jordan, Kuwait, Libya, Morocco, Qatar, Saudi Arabia, Tunisia, UAE, Angola, Kenya, Nigeria and South Africa.

exports. Although its annual vehicle production was less than one per cent of global vehicle production, the industry contributed about 7.5 per cent to the gross domestic product (GDP) of South Africa.

The industry was picking up momentum after three consecutive years of negative growth, which had been preceded by three consecutive years of record-breaking growth. According to the National Association of Automobile Manufacturers of South Africa (NAAMSA), new vehicle sales fell by 5.1 per cent in 2007, 21.1 per cent in 2008 and 25.9 per cent in 2009. The decline was largely due to the global recession, which had reduced the flow of credit in the financial system. Locally, the South African government had passed the National Credit Act[2] in July 2007, which regulated the flow of credit and further limited its availability. In 2010, however, a turnaround began. The industry had grown at 24 per cent over the previous year, exceeding initial projections of a 7 per cent increase. The momentum was expected to be sustainable. The government had targeted a production of 1.2 million vehicles in 2020 from about 0.5 million in 2010 (see **Exhibit 2**).

[2]Republic of South Africa, *National Credit Act, 2005,* www.ncr.org.za/pdfs/NATIONAL_CREDIT_ACT.pdf, accessed August 28, 2011.

South Africa exported vehicles to more than 70 countries, mainly Japan, Australia, the United Kingdom and the United States. African export destinations included Algeria, Botswana, Zambia, Zimbabwe, Lesotho, Mozambique, Namibia and Nigeria.

South Africans drove 1,390 variants of cars, recreational vehicles and light commercial vehicles. Domestic consumption was limited to well-known brands, such as Toyota, Volkswagen, Ford, Mazda and BMW. These brands together accounted for more than 80 per cent of new-vehicle sales in the country (see **Exhibit 3**). Present in South Africa were eight of the top 10 global vehicle makers, which sourced components and assembled vehicles for both local and overseas markets. South Africa also had three of the world's largest tire manufacturers. More than 200 automotive component manufacturers were located in South Africa, including several multinationals.

Growth Catalyst

The catalyst for the growth of the South African auto industry had been the government's Motor Industry Development Programme (MIDP).

Exhibit 2   South Africa: Total Vehicle Sales, Production, Exports and Imports, 2006–2010

	2010	2009	2008	2007	2006
Cars					
a) Local sales	113,740	94,379	125,454	169,558	215,311
b) Exports (CBUs)	181,654	128,602	195,670	106,460	119,171
c) Total domestic production	295,394	222,981	321,124	276,018	334,482
d) CBU imports	223,390	163,750	203,808	265,095	266,247
e) Total car market (a+d)	337,130	258,129	329,262	434,653	481,558
Light Commercial Vehicles					
a) Local sales	96,823	85,663	118,641	156,626	159,469
b) Exports (CBU)	56,950	45,514	87,314	64,127	60,149
c) Total domestic production	163,773	131,777	205,955	220,763	219,618
d) CBU imports	36,911	32,496	50,825	47,760	40,208
e) Total LCV market (a+d)	133,734	118,159	169,466	204,386	199,677
Medium & Heavy Vehicles					
Sales including imports	22,021	18,934	34,659	37,069	33,080
Exports	861	831	1,227	650	539
Total MCV/HCV market	22,021	18,934	34,659	37,069	33,080
Total Aggregate Market	492,907	395,222	533,387	676,108	714,315
Total Aggregate Exports	239,465	174,947	284,211	171,237	179,859
Total Domestic Production	472,049	373,923	562,965	534,490	587,719
GDP Growth Rate (%)	2.8	(1.7)	3.7	5.5	5.6

Source: National Association of Automobile Manufacturers of South Africa, "New Vehicle Sales Statistics," www.naamsa.co.za/flash/total.asp?/ total_market_at_a_glance, accessed August 22, 2011.
Note: CBUs = completely built units; LCV = light commercial vehicle; MCV = medium commercial vehicle; HCV = heavy commercial vehicle; GDP = gross domestic product

Exhibit 3   Mahindra & Mahindra South Africa—Leader Brands' Production

#	Market Segment	Leader Brands	2010	2009	2008	2007	2006
1	Light Commercial Vehicles	Toyota	34,709	29,444	32,273	38,816	28,009
		Isuzu	10,886	10,550	17,191	18,754	22,135
		Nissan	13,082	10,217	12,406	21,102	23,554
		Ford	7,433	7,184	9,938	10,813	12,107
		Mazda	3,835	3,585	4,992	5,097	5,748
2	Sport-Utility Vehicles	Toyota	16,083	10,349	10,362	11,570	10,315
		Land Rover	4,349	3,630	4,363	5,363	4,380
		BMW	4,713	2,831	3,223	3,692	3,050
		Mercedes	3,713	3,070	3,445	5,207	3,970
		Chrysler	2,735	2,299	2,523	3,745	3,583
		M&M	1,555	1,148	1,662	3,160	3,315

Source: Company files

Introduced in 1995, MIDP had been legislated to last until 2009 and was to be phased out by 2012. It would be replaced in 2013 by the Automotive Production and Development Programme (APDP).

Pre-MIDP, the import duty rates for CBUs and completely knocked-down (CKD) components were 115 per cent and 80 per cent, respectively. The high duty rates were aimed at protecting the local industry from global competition. In 1995, under the MIDP, the tariffs were reduced to 65 per cent and 49 per cent, respectively. They had continued to decline at a steady rate, reducing year-on-year to 25 per cent for CBUs and 20 per cent for CKDs in 2012.

Several MIDP provisions had helped boost automotive exports from South Africa. For example, the MIDP enabled local vehicle manufacturers to import goods duty-free to the extent of the value of their exports, thus allowing them to concentrate on manufacturing for export. The MIDP also granted vehicle manufacturers a production-asset allowance to invest in new plant and equipment, reimbursing 20 per cent of their capital expenditure in the form of import-duty rebates over a period of five years.

The APDP was meant to create long-term sustainability by concentrating on localization of vehicle content. Meant to last until 2020, the APDP was built around four key elements: tariffs, local assembly allowance, production incentives and automotive investment allowance. The program aimed to create a stable and moderate import tariffs regime from 2013, set at 25 per cent for CBUs and 20 per cent for components. It would also offer a local assembly allowance (LAA), which would enable vehicle manufacturers with a plant volume of at least 50,000 units per annum to import a percentage of their components duty-free. The investment allowance of 20 per cent would also be carried forward from the MIDP regime.

All rebates of import duty were given in the form of certificates that were tradable in the open market and could, therefore, be converted into cash. However, many automotive manufacturers used the certificates themselves to offset the cost of their imports. For example, to reduce the cost of their imports trading companies such as M&M (SA) purchased these certificates, when they were available at low prices in the open market. Said Nico M. Vermeulen, director, NAAMSA:

> A trading company, which imports CBUs at 25 per cent duty and sells them either in the domestic or export markets, will not get any certificate because it is neither manufacturing nor adding value locally. An assembly plant, which imports CKDs at 20 per cent import duty, must meet with three conditions in order to be eligible for a certificate: be registered with the Department of Trade and Industry; assemble a minimum of 50,000 vehicles per annum; and export. The value of the certificate for an assembly plant is linked to the value of export income it generates. A manufacturing company must produce 50,000 vehicles per annum to be eligible for a certificate which is linked, not to exports as in an assembly plant, but to the value added in the form of local content. A manufacturer gets the certificate, irrespective of whether the products are sold locally or exported, as long as it provides evidence of content localization.[3]

MIDP differed from APDP because it incentivized exports of vehicles and components, whereas APDP incentivized value added through local production. Both incentives were in tune with the outcomes the government was seeking at different points of time. The gradual decline in tariff protection was aimed at helping the domestic auto manufacturing companies become efficient in several ways. They could secure economies of scale, rationalize product platforms, focus on exports, compete globally and benchmark their operations against the best in the world. NAAMSA had estimated that the average annual volumes of production per platform would need to increase to a minimum of 80,000 units for a local company to become globally competitive. Similarly, employee productivity would need to improve from 15 vehicles to 30 vehicles per employee per annum.

Consumer Classification

South Africa had a population of 50.6 million, of which the black Africans comprised 40.2 million, white Africans 4.6 million, coloured Africans 4.5 million and Indian/Asian Africans 1.27 million.[4]

[3]Interview with case author, September 02, 2011.

[4]South Africa.info, "South Africa's Population," www.southafrica .info/about/people/population.htm, accessed August 18, 2011.

The South African Advertising Research Foundation (SAARF), an independent trade body, had segmented South African adult consumers (ranging in age from 15 to 50-plus) into 10 categories known as Living Standards Measures (LSMs). The measures graded people from 1 to 10 in an ascending order of their standard of living. Instead of using traditional metrics such as race and income, the SAARF LSM, which had won an award as the "media innovator of the year," grouped people by using such criteria as degree of urbanization and ownership of cars and major appliances. The grading was meant to help marketers and advertisers

of goods and services to identify, as accurately as possible, their target markets (see **Exhibit 4**).

The data for the year ending December 2010 had reiterated a major trend that had long been evident in South African marketing. The buying power of black African consumers, comprising the largest group in the middle-income (LSM 5–8) market, was rising. Said Ashok Thakur, CEO of M&M (SA):

> The mindset of white African consumers, who have been the bedrock of the vehicles market in South Africa, is similar to the mindset of consumers in the countries of West Europe. They buy well-known brands because they trust them. That explains why there has been

Exhibit 4   South Africa—Customer Segmentation, December 2010

	LSM1	LSM2	LSM3	LSM4	LSM5	LSM6	LSM7	LSM8	LSM9	LSM10
Population ('000s)	808	1,944	2,394	4,744	5,636	6,891	3,621	2,830	3,038	2,114
Population Group (%)										
• Black African	98.4	98.0	98.8	96.8	94.9	82.3	58.7	48.6	34.0	18.9
• Coloured African	1.6	1.9	1.2	3.2	4.3	11.3	18.8	16.1	13.9	6.4
• White African	—	—	—	—	0.2	1.5	4.6	6.7	8.1	9.9
• Indian/Asian African	—	—	—	0.1	0.7	4.9	17.9	28.6	44.0	64.7
Household income (%)										
• >R799	23.1	13.9	12.7	6.8	4.5	1.1	0.3	0.2	0.1	—
• R800–R1,399	38.0	33.8	28.2	22.1	16.1	6.9	2.2	0.9	0.2	—
• R1,400–R2,499	28.0	32.9	30.8	23.3	17.2	9.8	3.6	1.8	0.7	0.2
• R2,500–R4,999	9.7	17.5	23.4	33.4	34.7	25.2	13.3	6.2	2.3	0.6
• R5,000–R7,999	1.1	1.0	4.4	11.5	18.6	28.0	24.3	16.1	8.9	2.5
• R8,000–R10,999	0.1	0.6	0.1	2.1	6.0	16.3	25.2	22.0	17.6	7.2
• R11,000–R19,999	—	0.4	0.5	0.9	2.6	10.6	23.2	31.3	32.2	18.4
• >R20,000	—	—	—	—	0.4	2.1	7.9	21.4	38.1	71.0
Age (% of population)										
• 15–24	30.6	29.5	31.4	32.0	33.9	29.3	25.5	25.9	26.3	26.9
• 25–34	21.2	18.9	20.3	23.1	23.6	26.1	25.7	21.3	19.7	17.2
• 35–49	17.3	22.8	24.7	22.8	23.4	25.1	27.3	28.0	28.8	29.0
• 50 plus	30.8	28.8	23.6	22.1	19.1	19.5	21.5	24.7	25.2	26.9
Community (%)										
• Metro (250,000 plus)	—	29.5	31.4	32.0	33.9	29.3	25.5	25.9	26.3	26.9
• Urban (<250,000)	—	18.9	20.3	23.1	23.6	26.1	25.7	21.3	19.7	17.2
• Villages (<40,000)	—	22.8	24.7	22.8	23.4	25.1	27.3	28.0	28.8	29.0
• Rural	100	28.8	23.6	22.1	19.1	19.5	21.5	24.7	25.2	26.9

Source: www.saarf.co.za/SAARF_LSM/SAARF_Demographics/Table 40, accessed August 26. 2011.

a strong influence, for decades, of German brands in the South African automotive market. However, as the percentage of black African consumers entering higher income bands goes up, one would think that black Africans will acquire the buying habits and preferences of white Africans who are already in those bands. But, our experience in South Africa proves the opposite.

The black African consumers were buying Western European brands, and more recently Japanese and Korean brands, not because they trusted them but because they did not trust the local brands. This element of rebound had strategic implications for companies such as M&M (SA). The brand savviness of black Africans provided room for automotive brands other than those from Europe, Japan and Korea to strengthen their brand equity so that they could lock in sales from the growing black African consumers. M&M (SA) saw this situation as an entry-level opportunity.

A June 2010 *McKinsey Quarterly* research article into South African consumer goods had led to similar conclusions. It showed that 49 per cent of middle-income black consumers but only 26 per cent of middle-income white consumers agreed with the statement: "I purchase branded food products because they make me feel good." Among upper-income black Africans, those agreeing with the statement jumped to 65 per cent, while only 22 per cent of upper-income white Africans agreed. Of all black African consumers surveyed, 71 per cent agreed with the statement: "I have to pay careful attention so stores do not cheat me." In electronic goods, more than 60 per cent of black African consumers agreed that "products with no brands or less-known brands might be unsafe to use." In both cases, far fewer white consumers concurred.[5]

According to Thakur, the South African automotive market was also witness to three other trends that contrasted white African and black African consumers. White Africans earned more and also spent more, leaving them with less disposable income to

invest in discretionary purchases, such as automobiles. Black Africans earned less but also spent less and seemed to have higher disposable incomes. Second, white Africans were buying used vehicles rather than new vehicles although their brand preferences remained. Black Africans, on the other hand, were buying new vehicles. Third, white Africans preferred functional attributes (such as good mileage), whereas black Africans preferred features, based on aesthetics, design and comfort, in their automobiles.

M&M Company Background

M&M was founded as a steel trading company in Mumbai, India, in 1945, by two brothers, J. C. Mahindra and K. C. Mahindra. Two years later, M&M entered into automotive manufacturing by launching Willys, the iconic World War II jeep, on a franchise from Willys-Overland Motors, the American maker of general purpose utility vehicles (UVs). Willys was the country's first UV. The company began manufacturing farm equipment in 1960. The UV and tractor platform gradually became the company's core competence.

The company had extended its core competence, over time, into the full spectrum of the automotive value chain. By 2011, it was producing two-wheelers at one end, small turbo prop aircraft at the other, and trucks, buses, pickups and cars in between. Positioning itself on the platform of "motorized mobility," the company had also started making powerboats, securing a presence in the transportation media across "land, sea and sky."

The mobility platform had generated opportunities for synergies across the company's auto categories. Broadly, they prevailed in sourcing, product development and quality control. Common for all products was the use of raw materials such as steel and aluminum, which were used in castings and forgings. The automotive and tractor divisions had a common engine development team. The processes for quality improvements at the supplier end were uniform across categories. Synergies also prevailed at the level of operations. For example, transmissions and other aggregates were shared between different vehicles.

[5]Bronwen Chase et al., "A Seismic Shift in South Africa's Consumer Landscape," *McKinsey Quarterly,* June 2010, www.mckinseyquarterly.com/search.aspx?q=south Africa, accessed August 16, 2011.

Exhibit 5   Mahindra and Mahindra—Business Segments

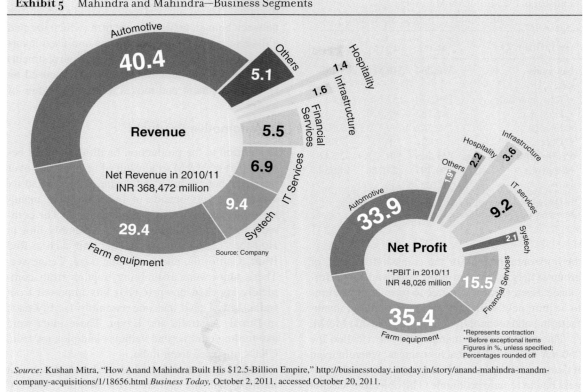

Source: Kushan Mitra, "How Anand Mahindra Built His $12.5-Billion Empire," http://businesstoday.intoday.in/story/anand-mahindra-mandm-company-acquisitions/1/18656.html *Business Today,* October 2, 2011, accessed October 20, 2011.

M&M had also diversified into unrelated areas branching into financial services, information technology (IT), hospitality, infrastructure and other areas. The group was in a total of eight businesses (see **Exhibit 5**). Each business operated autonomously under its own CEO. Some of the CEOs were members of the Group Executive Board of the parent company. Each was a growing business in an emerging market like India. The group had 45 operating companies, some of which were listed on local stock exchanges.

M&M was one of India's leading multinationals and had 113,000-plus employees, of whom 12 per cent were foreigners and Indian expatriates, located across 79 countries. It had consolidated revenues of ₹370 billion for the year ending

⁶Indian rupee (₹44.9908 = 1US$), www.exchange-rates.org/Rate/USD/INR/5-20-2011, accessed November 16, 2011.

March 2011 and profit before tax of ₹45 billion (see **Exhibit 6**). The group was cash flow positive. It had $650 million surplus and internal accruals were growing every year.

Business Model

The business model followed by M&M was rooted in what the company called "engine theory." The parent company was viewed as an engine with multiple pistons. Each business vertical was in the nature of a piston. For example, the automotive sector was one piston, IT was another and so on. Each piston was a driver in its own right, focused not only on what it did best but also on improving the performance of the engine. The more verticals the company added, the longer and stronger the crankshaft grew. Each vertical was also receiving

Exhibit 6   Mahindra & Mahindra—
Consolidated Income Statement

(in million ₹)	2011	2010	2009
Net sales	370,264	316,880	269,198
Less			
• Raw materials	199,970	152,679	130,637
• Personnel	42,183	45,825	42,749
• Interest	9,742	9,798	7,501
• Depreciation	9,724	8,735	7,493
Profit before taxation	**45,149**	40,328	**22,541**
Net profit	**30,797**	**24,786**	**14,054**

Source: Mahindra & Mahindra Annual Report, 2010–11, page 129
and Mahindra & Mahindra Annual Report, 2009–10, page 138.
Note: Net sales includes other income.

the horizontal benefit, or the crankshaft benefit, of group synergies that, in turn, improved its performance. Each vertical was free to form joint ventures to acquire new skills and leverage sourcing, manufacturing and technology of partners outside M&M.

The company had mandated what it called the "50 per cent rule" for each business, wherein even if demand fell by as much as 50 per cent, each business had to remain profitable. The objective was not only to provide enough room for business cycles, global shocks and other external factors but also to create a multiplier effect when volumes grew in times of more consistent activity.

The analyst community was treating M&M as a conglomerate on the ground that it had ventured, over the years, into newer businesses, which they considered to be non-core areas. While valuing the company, analysts were, therefore, giving it a conglomerate discount of 10 to 15 per cent. But the management of M&M saw the group as a federation of independent companies, benefiting from both business focus and group synergies. It was of the view that unlike a conglomerate, M&M provided an opportunity for investors in the parent company to participate in the equity of distinctive businesses that were creating shareholder value. Thus, according to the management, M&M should have received a federation premium, instead of a conglomerate discount.

The parent company saw its role as an allocator of capital. The group was trying to find a sweet spot between being a private equity firm (which juggled a diverse portfolio of investments and used leverage to create short-term value for each investment) and a family-run conglomerate (which focused on skill development and took a longer-term view of business).

Automotive Products

In addition to the production facilities that had become part of M&M as a result of acquisitions over the years, both in India and overseas, M&M had six assembly plants outside of India and nine manufacturing plants of its own within India. The company had an 88,000 square foot assembly unit in Houston, Texas, and one smaller unit each in Red Bluff, California, and in Chattanooga, Tennessee. These units were assembling tractors from completely knocked down (CKD) kits imported from India. M&M also had one assembly facility each in Brazil, Australia and Egypt. These units were assembling commercial vehicles and pickups from CKDs imported from India.

M&M had entered the India urban UV segment in 2002 with the launch of the Scorpio. The UV segment was small in India and growing at about 14 per cent per annum. Although the Scorpio was a UV, it was billed as "more than a car" (or "car plus")—a new segment M&M had created on a price-value proposition (of between ₹500,000 and ₹700,000) aimed at both the B segment (cars selling up to ₹500,000) and the C segment (cars selling at ₹700,000). By positioning the Scorpio as a mid-size car competing with car makers in B and C segments rather than with UV makers, M&M was able to grow the Scorpio sales in India at 30 per cent.

M&M had a 60 per cent share of the domestic UV market by value and 52 per cent by volume (see **Exhibit 7**). Its UV products consisted of multipurpose vehicles, sport-utility vehicles (SUV) and pickup trucks characterized by ruggedness and reliability. The company's long-term goal was to build a global brand in the SUV and pickups segment.

Exhibit 7   Mahindra & Mahindra—Indian Domestic Market Shares by Volume

	2011			2010		
Category	Total Domestic sales	M&M sales	M&M share (%)	Total Domestic sales	M&M sales	M&M share (%)
Utility Vehicles	323,896	169,205	52.2	272,741	150,726	55.2
Light Commercial Vehicles	353,621	114,856	32.4	287,777	86,217	—
Three-wheelers	526,022	62,142	11.8	440,392	44,438	3.0
Two-wheelers	11,790,305	163,914	1.4	9,371,231	70,008	0.7
Cars	1,982,990	10,009	0.5	1,528,337	5,332	0.3
Medium/Heavy Commercial Vehicles	322,749	843	0.4	244,944	—	—
Multi-Purpose Vehicles	213,507	966	0.4	150,256	—	—
Total Auto Products	15,513,090	521,935		12,295,678	356,721	
Tractors	480,377	—	—	400,203	—	—

Source: Mahindra & Mahindra Annual Report, 2010–11 pages 28 and 29 of 172.
Note: Industry sales attributed in the report to the Society of Indian Automotive Manufacturers (SIAM).

M&M was also the largest producer of tractors in the world by volume.

Globalization

A global perspective was a hallmark at M&M from the beginning. The company had entered into a series of joint ventures with overseas companies. The launch of economic reforms by the federal government of India in July 1991 had given the ongoing perspective a new push. M&M was of the view that it each of its businesses would be facing new competition from international companies entering India; consequently, it had to prepare to defend its turf on the home ground. Said Shah:

> The anchor of our globalization strategy is that competing with multinational companies in overseas markets helps us compete with them better in India. Globalization gives us access to new technologies, new markets and new skill sets. It makes us competitive in emerging markets like Brazil, Russia, India and China and, of late, South Africa, which will be the growth markets of the future. M&M believes in

the Africa story. South Africa, in particular, is of interest to us not just because it is one of the most important export markets for M&M but because it is a springboard for the larger African market. South Africa is also where there is a good fit between what the customers need and what we can provide and between the price we offer and the value perceived by the customer

The long-term aspiration of M&M was to be recognized as a global SUV brand. In line with that aspiration, M&M had acquired a majority stake in SsangYong Motor Company (SsangYong) of Korea in February 2011. SsangYong was a major SUV manufacturer and a natural fit for M&M. The product range, the markets and the price range created a continuum for M&M, opening up new markets for M&M's SUV brands in Russia, China and Korea.[7]

[7]Mahindra & Mahindra, "Inside an International Acquisition," video clip, http://rise.mahindra.com/rise_topics/inside-an-international-acquisition, between 3:11 and 4:35 of 7:45-minute video, accessed September 1, 2011.

M&M in South Africa

M&M formally entered the South African market in February 2005, by setting up a 51 per cent subsidiary, Mahindra & Mahindra SA (M&M (SA)). The balance of 49 per cent was held by a local partner whose investment wing of the business had helped finance the venture. M&M had been exporting its automobiles to South Africa since October 2004 and had appointed dealers in all nine provinces of South Africa. M&M (SA) had also created a network of customer service outlets and collaborated with a local logistics company to ensure distribution of spare parts to service outlets countrywide within 24 hours.

By October 2004, M&M (SA) started importing two of its leading Indian brands—Bolero and Scorpio—both SUVs, in five models, fully assembled. Subsequently, it was importing two other SUV brands, Xylo and Thar, from M&M's plants in India. Before being launched in South Africa, all models had been tested in the hazardous terrains of Australia and Europe, in high altitudes, low levels, deserts and cold conditions, in addition to being tested in the local terrain by local testing agencies. Said Thakur:

> Our entry strategy into South Africa was two-fold. First, we wanted a niche in the SUV segment straddling both cargo and passenger traffic. We did not want to play in the mass market. We identified four-wheeler passenger vehicles and pickups and delivery vehicles carrying cargo as our market segments. Second, we offered a value proposition by pricing Bolero, our launch vehicle, at between 20 per cent and 30 per cent lower than the prevailing competition. Bolero caught up with farming and small business segments and did very well with customers in semi-urban and rural areas and in villages where it was identified with "toughness"—an attribute which is valued in an African terrain. Scorpio reinforced it. We now need to build on it in the urban markets.

The global launch of the Scorpio pickup range of vehicles was held in South Africa in 2006, highlighting the strategic importance of South Africa as a market in the company's global growth plans. The company was making new brands available in South Africa, around the same time it launched the brands in India. For example, Xylo, a multi-purpose vehicle, was launched in India in January 2009 and in South Africa in March 2009.

M&M (SA) bought out its local partner's stake in August 2009, with a view to fully control and manage the business. It had the mission of "providing world-class products and services, at an unbeatable all round value to the customer, by unleashing the power of our people to benefit both partner countries and the communities we serve."[8] In five years of doing business in South Africa, M&M (SA) had sold a total of 11,000 vehicles. By 2011, it had a turnover of $40.3 million for the year ending March 2010 (see **Exhibit 8**). It had secured a market share of about 1.2 per cent in the pickup market and in the low to medium range SUV markets, and the goal was to increase these markets to 5 per cent (see **Exhibit 9**).

The Mahindra brand in South Africa used different SUVs to target different segments—individuals, families, mining companies and farmers. It competed with Kia, Hyundai and Nissan for SUVs and with Toyota for pickups. Soon, M&M (SA) was a player of choice in the used-car market. Many local customers were becoming second-time buyers, indicating a strong loyalty for the Mahindra brand.

The medium to long-term plan was to make M&M (SA) the entry point into Africa. A major constraint M&M (SA) faced in this regard was the vehicle ordering cycle from India, which took more than two months. This long cycle was a limitation when bidding for contracts from the African governments, particularly those in the sub-Sahara region, which were the single largest buyers of new vehicles. A short lead time was often a competitive advantage in winning those contracts.

Issues Before Shah

Contract Assembly   M&M (SA) had been in talks with a few vendors in South Africa regarding the assembly of pickup vehicles, which were being shipped out of India to countries in West Africa. Local

---

[8]www.mahindra.com/spotlight, accessed September 10, 2011.

Exhibit 8   Mahindra & Mahindra South Africa—Income Statement

Year ending March	2011	2010	2009
in South African Rand (ZAR)			
Sale of Vehicles	235,876,218	161,563,355	157,855,190
Sales of Spares	34,448,679	29,318,826	30,217,514
Sale of Tractors	273,000	1,511,999	9,483,660
Sale of Accessories	169,051	69,583	176,020
Sale of Services	—	—	952,766
Total Revenue	**270,766,948**	**192,463,763**	**198,685,150**
Less Cost of sales	221,703,228	166,470,257	199,642,431
Gross Profit	49,063,720	25,993,506	(957,281)
Add Other Income	138,082	1,653,520	369,597
Add Investment Revenue	3,145,901	2,970,225	1,138,512
Less Finance Cost	2,409,208	4,518,481	11,985,817
Less Operating Expenses	23,900,437	22,425,423	41,954,297
Profit Before Tax	**26,038,058**	**3,673,347**	**(53,389,286)**
Tax	7,293,834	1,044,461	14,664,466
Profit After Tax	**18,744,224**	**2,628,886**	**(38,724,820)**

Source: www.mahindra.com/investors/mahindra&mahindra/resources/2010-11/subsidiary_annual_report_part_2 and www.mahindra.com?investors/mahindra &mahindra/resources/2009-10/subsidiary_annual_report, p. 6 and p. 13 of the Subsidiary Annual Report, 2010–11 Part 2 and p. 746 of the Subsidiary Annual Report, 2009–10, accessed October 01, 2011.
Note: 1 ZAR = US$ 0.148954.

assembly would improve margins by reducing, by about 25 per cent, the cost of shipping CBUs from India to African destinations. The vehicles could be assembled in South Africa for export to African destinations. Costs could be further reduced by launching variants that were in demand and by locally sourcing some of the components and extra fitments. Once M&M (SA) made the decision to assemble the vehicles locally, only three-months lead time would be needed to commence operations. Local assembly also meant that M&M (SA) would not need to make any major upfront investment in the vendor's facilities.

Brand equity was a major driver in the South African automobile market, where consumers bought cars and trucks on the basis of brand recall. Consumers preferred global brands because South Africa had no home-grown automobile brands. In spite of more than five years of presence in South Africa, M&M (SA)'s volume of sales was not comparable to global players operating in South Africa. Its brand equity was also not comparable with such global competitors as Toyota, Nissan and others.

M&M was accustomed to occupying the driver's seat. The mindset of being in charge prevailed throughout the organization, from the way it structured joint ventures (in which it invariably held the majority shareholding), to its staffing of key positions at the top with its own people. As a result, a contract assembly, in which the vendor ruled, particularly in mobilizing and deploying resources, would be a difficult proposition for M&M managers.

For the past two years, the company had contracted an assembly plant in Egypt for the Scorpio vehicle and another in Brazil for a pickup vehicle. When using local assembly, the vehicle ordering cycle would be about 10 days. The choice of contract assembly depended upon the availability of surplus capacity, the ability of the vendor to ramp up capacity consistent with changing needs and the vendor's knowledge and technical know-how, financial capability and management bandwidth.

Certification of the locally assembled vehicles local agencies was an area in which M&M (SA) did not have competence since it was only importing

Exhibit 9 Mahindra & Mahindra South Africa — Sales Volume

#	M&M Models	Models	Year of launch	Main attributes	Target customer segments	2010	2009	2008	2007	2006	2005
1	Bolero	S/Cab D/Cab	2004	Tough Durable Work and play	Contractors Farmers Service providers	387	342	725	1,429	1,442	579
2	Scorpio	Manual Auto Petrol Diesel	2004	7–8 seater Off-road use Safety features	Urban consumers	211	267	355	810	1,128	366
3	Scorpio Pickup	S/Cab D/Cab 2-Wheel 4-Wheel	2006	Multi-Utility Vehicle	Contractors Farmers Small businesses	612	375	582	921	745	—
4	Mahindra Thar	4 by 4	2010	Sports Utility Vehicle	Outdoor customers Off-roaders Retro-look seekers	107	—	—	—	—	—
5	Mahindra Xylo	E8 E2	2009 2009	Luxury People mover	Taxi operators Ferry owners Shuttle providers	238	164	—	—	—	—
	Total					1,555	1,148	1,662	3,160	3,315	945

Source: Company files.

CBUs from its Indian operations. The certification could be outsourced in South Africa; however, doing so would be a departure from the norm at M&M, which typically retained all critical business processes under its control.

Own Manufacturing

Setting up a manufacturing plant in South Africa would be consistent with M&M's mission of being a long-term player. It would also demonstrate to customers its commitment to the local market, which would be a major factor in an industry where after-sales service, such as a warranty, was a crucial factor in attracting sales. Setting up its own manufacturing plant would also present an opportunity to lock in customers at the beginning of the growth curve in the South African market, which was the biggest export market for the parent company M&M. Raising funds in this option was not an area of concern because M&M had always operated as a cash surplus company.

Manufacturing was the easier part in automobiles. The real challenge, particularly in South-Africa, was localization of content. Gross margins in the automobile industry fluctuated with production volume because many of the costs related to vehicle production were fixed. Once M&M (SA) got into manufacturing, it would be under pressure to sustain high production levels just to break even. Beyond the break-even point, fixed costs could be spread over more units, opening the doors for profitability.

Wait and Watch

M&M (SA) sales had suffered during the downturn but the confidence levels of the subsidiary had been high. The subsidiary had used the recessionary period to reduce fixed costs (through outsourcing, among other solutions), streamline operations (particularly for shipping and port-related work), improve its business processes and enlarge the reach and quality of its dealer network so that when the recession ended, M&M (SA) could become stronger and would be better prepared to face competition.

M&M (SA) could continue its prevailing business model of importing automotive products from India and exporting them from South Africa. This approach would help the company tide over the recession from which it was only mid-way to recovery. However, it would need to bear the higher rate of import duty of 25 per cent compared with local assemblers and manufacturers.

Use South Africa as a Hub

M&M (SA) had an opportunity to develop markets in the 54 countries on the African continent, which were just opening up. Africa and Asia (with the exception of Japan) were the only continents that grew during the recession years of 2007 to 2009. Africa's GDP growth slowed to 2 per cent in 2009 but recovered to 4.7 per cent in 2010 and was expected to move upward. Companies entering the African continent at the beginning of the new growth period could take the lead in shaping industry structures, segmenting markets and establishing brands.

The boom in commodity prices in early 2007 had led global companies to show interest in the African region, which, in addition to having rich deposits of minerals and metals, had 10 per cent of the world's oil reserves. But many companies were guarded in developing entry strategies for the region because of the ongoing recession. The political turmoil in countries such as Algeria, Egypt, Libya, Morocco and Tunisia added to the uncertainty. The paradox for a multinational was that the fastest growing economies in the region also carried the highest macro-economic risks.

In a study entitled "Lions on the Move" published in June 2010, McKinsey Global Institute had categorized the African economies into four buckets: oil exporters, diversified economies, transition economies and pre-transition economies. It had further categorized the African economies on the basis of GDP per capita. Algeria, Botswana, Equatorial Guinea, Gabon, Libya and Mauritius ranked first with South Africa, with per capita GDP in excess of $5,000 per annum. Congo Republic, Morocco, Namibia and Tunisia ranked second with GDP per capita ranging between $2,000 and $5,000. Cameroon, Côte d'Ivoire, Egypt, Nigeria, Sudan,

Senegal and Zambia ranked third with GDP per capita ranging between $1,000 and $2,000.[9] These 17 countries together comprised the first line of target for re-exports from South Africa. Said Shah:

[9]McKinsey Global Institute, *Lions on the Move: The Progress and Potential of African Economies,* www.mckinsey.com/mgi/publications/progress_and_potential_of_african_economies/index.asp, p. 5, accessed September 12, 2011.

The board would be interested in understanding the trade-offs involved in each of the four options. The members would, of course, want to know the level of investment and the expected return. These are quantitative and it would not take long to reach a consensus on them. The litmus test would be qualitative; it will be about the growth potential of the South African market. Their question would be something like, "Where will our decision now take M&M (SA) by 2015?"

Case 1-4   Acer, Inc: Taiwan's Rampaging Dragon

With a sense of real excitement, Stan Shih, CEO of Acer, Inc., boarded a plane for San Francisco in early February 1995. The founder of the Taiwanese personal computer (PC) company was on his way to see the Aspire, a new home PC being developed by Acer America Corporation (AAC) Acer's North American subsidiary. Although Shih had heard that a young American team was working on a truly innovative product, featuring a unique design, voice

▌ Professor Christopher A. Bartlett and Research Associate Anthony St. George prepared this case as the basis for class discussion rather than to illustrate either effective or ineffective handling of an administrative situation. Some historical information was drawn from Robert H. Chen, "Made in Taiwan: The Story of Acer Computers," Linking Publishing Co., Taiwan, 1996, and Stan Shih, "Me-too is Not My Style," Acer Foundation, Taiwan, 1996. We would like to thank Eugene Hwang and Professor Robert H. Hayes for their help and advice.

recognition, ease-of-use, and cutting-edge multimedia capabilities, he knew little of the project until Ronald Chwang, President of AAC had invited him to the upcoming product presentation. From Chwang's description, Shih thought that Aspire could have the potential to become a blockbuster product worldwide. But he was equally excited that this was the first Acer product conceived, designed, and championed by a sales-and-marketing oriented regional business unit (RBU) rather than one of Acer's production-and-engineering focused strategic business units (SBUs) in Taiwan.

Somewhere in mid-flight, however, Shih's characteristic enthusiasm was tempered by his equally well-known pragmatism. Recently, AAC had been one of the company's more problematic overseas units, and had been losing money for five years. Was this the group on whom he should pin his hopes for Acer's next important growth initiative? Could such a radical new product succeed in the highly competitive American PC market? And if so, did this unit—one of the company's sales-and-marketing-oriented

Exhibit 1   Selected Financials: Sales, Net Income, and Headcount, 1976–1994

	1976	1977	1978	1979	1980	1981	1982	1983	1984
Sales ($M)	0.003	0.311	0.80	0.77	3.83	7.08	18.1	28.3	51.6
Net Income ($M)	N/A	N/A	N/A	N/A	N/A	N/A	N/A	1.4	0.4
Employees	11	12	18	46	104	175	306	592	1,130

RBUs—have the resources and capabilities to lead the development of this important new product, and, perhaps, even its global rollout?

Birth of the Company

Originally known as Multitech, the company was founded in Taiwan in 1976 by Shih, his wife, and three friends. From the beginning, Shih served as CEO and Chairman, his wife as company accountant. With $25,000 of capital and 11 employees, Multitech's grand mission was "to promote the application of the emerging microprocessor technology." It grew by grasping every opportunity available—providing engineering and product design advice to local companies, importing electronic components, offering technological training courses, and publishing trade journals. "We will sell anything except our wives," joked Shih. Little did the founders realize that they were laying the foundations for one of Taiwan's great entrepreneurial success stories. (See **Exhibit 1.**)

Laying the Foundations   Because Multitech was capital constrained, the new CEO instituted a strong norm of frugality. Acting on what he described as "a poor man's philosophy," he leased just enough space for current needs (leading to 28 office relocations over the next 20 years) and, in the early years, encouraged employees to supplement their income by "moonlighting" at second jobs. Yet while Multitech paid modest salaries, it offered key employees equity, often giving them substantial ownership positions in subsidiary companies.

Frugality was one of many business principles Shih had learned while growing up in his mother's tiny store. He told employees that high-tech products, like his mother's duck eggs, had to be priced with a low margin to ensure turnover. He preached the importance of receiving cash payment quickly and avoiding the use of debt. But above all, he told them that customers came first, employees second, and shareholders third, a principle later referred to as "Acer 1-2-3."

Shih's early experience biased him against the patriarch-dominated, family-run company model that was common in Taiwan. "It tends to generate opinions which are neither balanced nor objective," he said. He delegated substantial decision-making responsibility to his employees to harness "the natural entrepreneurial spirit of the Taiwanese." With his informal manner, bias for delegation, and "hands-off" style, Shih trusted employees to act in the best interests of the firm. "We don't believe in control in the normal sense. . . . We rely on people and build our business around them," he said. It was an approach many saw as the polar opposite of the classic Chinese entrepreneur's tight personal control. As a result, the young company soon developed a reputation as a very attractive place for bright young engineers.

Shih's philosophy was reflected in his commitment to employee education and his belief that he could create a company where employees would constantly be challenged to "think and learn." In the early years, superiors were referred to as "shifu," a title usually reserved for teachers and masters of the martial arts. The development of strong teaching relationships between manager and subordinate was encouraged by making the cultivation and grooming of one's staff a primary criterion for promotion. The slogan, "Tutors conceal nothing from their pupils" emphasized the open nature

1985	1986	1987	1988	1989	1990	1991	1992	1993	1994
94.8	165.3	331.2	530.9	688.9	949.5	985.2	1,259.8	1,883	3,220
5.1	3.9	15.3	26.5	5.8	(0.7)	(26.0)	(2.8)	85.6	205
1,632	2,188	3,639	5,072	5,540	5.711	5,216	5,352	7,200	5,825

of the relationship and reminded managers of their responsibility.

This created a close-knit culture, where coworkers treated each other like family, and the norm was to do whatever was necessary for the greater good of the company. But is was a very demanding "family," and as the patriarch, Stan Shih worked hard to combat complacency—what he called "the big rice bowl" sense of entitlement—by creating a constant sense of crisis and showering subordinates with ideas and challenges for their examination and follow-up. As long as the managers took responsibility for their actions—acted as responsible older sons or daughters—they had the freedom to make decisions in the intense, chaotic, yet laissez-faire organization. Besides his constant flow of new ideas, Shih's guidance came mainly in the form of the slogans, stories, and concepts he constantly communicated.

This philosophy of delegation extended to organizational units, which, to the extent possible, Shih forced to operate as independent entities and to compete with outside companies. Extending the model externally, Shih began experimenting with joint ventures as a way of expanding sales. The first such arrangement was struck with a couple of entrepreneurs in central and southern Taiwan. While capturing the partners' knowledge of those regional markets, this approach allowed Multitech to expand its sales without the risk of hiring more people or raising more capital.

Early successes through employee ownership, delegated accountability, management frugality, and joint ventures led to what Shih called a "commoner's culture." This reflected his belief that the way to succeed against wealthy multinationals—"the nobility"—was to join forces with other "commoners"—mass-market customers, local distributors, owner-employees, small investors and supplier-partners, for example. The "poor man's" values supported this culture and guided early expansion. As early as 1978, Shih targeted smaller neighboring markets that were of lesser interest to the global giants. At first, response to Multitech's promotional letters was poor since few foreign distributors believed that a Taiwanese company could supply quality hi-tech products. Through persistence, however, Multitech established partnerships with dealers and distributors in Indonesia, Malaysia, Singapore, and Thailand. Shih described this early expansion strategy:

> It is like the strategy in the Japanese game *Go*—one plays from the corner, because you need fewer resources to occupy the corner. Without the kind of resources that Japanese and American companies had, we started in smaller markets. That gives us the advantage because these smaller markets are becoming bigger and bigger and the combination of many small markets is not small.

Expansion abroad—primarily through Asia, Middle East and Latin America—was greatly helped by a growing number of new products. In 1981, Multitech introduced its first mainstream commercial product, the "Microprofessor" computer. Following the success of this inexpensive, simple computer (little more than an elaborate scientific calculator), Shih and his colleagues began to recognize the enormous potential of the developing PC market. In 1983, Multitech began to manufacture IBM-compatible PCs—primarily as an original equipment manufacturer (OEM) for major brands but also under its own Multitech brand. In 1984 sales reached $51 million, representing a sevenfold increase on revenues three years earlier.

By 1986, the company felt it was ready to stake a claim in Europe, establishing a marketing office in Dusseldorf and a warehouse in Amsterdam. Multitech also supplemented the commission-based purchasing unit it had previously opened in the United States with a fully-fledged sales office.

Birth of the Dragon Dream   By the mid-1980s, Multitech's sales were doubling each year and confidence was high. As the company approached its tenth anniversary, Shih announced a plan for the next ten years that he described as "Dragon Dreams." With expected 1986 revenues of $150 million, employees and outsiders alike gasped at his projected sales of $5 billion by 1996. Critics soon began quoting the old Chinese aphorism, "To allay your hunger, draw a picture of a big cake."

But Shih saw huge potential in overseas expansion. After only a few years of international experience, the company's overseas sales already accounted for half the total. In several Asian countries Multitech was already a major player: in Singapore, for example, it had a 25% market share by 1986. To build on this Asian base and the new offices in Europe and the United States, Shih created the slogan, "The Rampaging Dragon Goes International." To implement the initiative, he emphasized the need to identify potential overseas acquisitions, set up offshore companies, and seek foreign partners and distributors.

When the number of Acer employees exceeded 2000 during the tenth year anniversary, Shih held a "Renewal of Company Culture Seminar" at which he invited his board and vice presidents to identify and evaluate the philosophies that had guided Multitech in its first ten years. Middle-level managers were then asked to participate in the process, reviewing, debating, and eventually voting on the key principles that would carry the company forward. The outcome was a statement of four values that captured the essence of their shared beliefs: an assumption that human nature is essentially good; a commitment to maintaining a fundamental pragmatism and accountability in all business affairs; a belief in placing the customer first; and a norm of pooling effort and sharing knowledge. (A decade later, these principles could still be found on office walls worldwide.)

Finally, the anniversary year was capped by another major achievement: Acer became the second company in the world to develop and launch a 32-bit PC, even beating IBM to market. Not only did the product win Taiwan's Outstanding Product Design Award—Acer's fifth such award in seven years—it also attracted the attention of such major overseas high-tech companies as Unisys, ICL and ITT, who began negotiations for OEM supply, and even technology licensing agreements.

Rebirth as Acer: Going Public   Unfortunately, Multitech's growing visibility also led to a major problem. A U.S. company with the registered name "Multitech" informed its Taiwanese namesake that they were infringing its trademark. After ten years of building a corporate reputation and brand identity, Shih conceded he had to start over. He chose the name "Acer" because its Latin root meant "sharp" or "clever", because "Ace" implied first or highest value in cards—but mostly because it would be first in alphabetical listings. Despite advice to focus on the profitable OEM business and avoid the huge costs of creating a new global brand, Shih was determined to make Acer a globally recognized name.

Beyond branding, the success of the 32-bit PC convinced Shih that Acer would also have to maintain its rapid design, development and manufacturing capability as a continuing source of competitive advantage. Together with the planned aggressive international expansion, these new strategic imperatives—to build a brand and maintain its technological edge—created investment needs that exceeded Acer's internal financing capability. When officials from Taiwan's Securities and Exchange Commission approached Shih about a public offering, he agreed to study the possibility although he knew that many Taiwanese were suspicious of private companies that went public.

A program that allowed any employee with one year of company service to purchase shares had already diluted the Shihs' original 50% equity to about 35%, but in 1987 they felt it may be time to go further. (Shih had long preached that it was "better to lose control but make money" and that "real control came through ensuring common interest.") An internal committee asked to study the issue of going public concluded that the company would not only raise needed funds for expansion but also would provide a market for employee-owned shares. In 1988, Acer negotiated a complex multi-tiered financing involving investments by companies (such as Prudential, Chase Manhattan, China Development Corporation, and Sumitomo), additional sales to employees and, finally, a public offering. In total, Acer raised NT $2.2 billion (US $88 million). Issued at NT $27.5, the stock opened trading at NT $47 and soon rose to well over NT $100. After the IPO, Acer employees held about 65% of the equity including the Shihs' share, which had fallen to less than 25%.

The Professionalization of Acer

While the public offering had taken care of Acer's capital shortage, Shih worried about the company's acute shortage of management caused by its rapid growth. In early 1985, when the number of employees first exceeded 1,000, he began to look outside for new recruits "to take charge and stir things up with new ideas." Over the next few years, he brought in about a dozen top-level executives and 100 middle managers. To many of the self-styled "ground troops" (the old-timers), these "paratroopers" were intruders who didn't understand Acer's culture or values but were attracted by the soaring stock. For the first time, Acer experienced significant turnover.

Paratroopers and Price Pressures Because internally-grown managers lacked international experience, one of the key tasks assigned to the "paratroopers" was to implement the company's ambitious offshore expansion plans. In late 1987, Acer acquired Counterpoint, the U.S.-based manufacturer of low-end minicomputers—a business with significantly higher margins than PCs. To support this new business entry, Acer then acquired and expanded the operations of Service Intelligence, a computer service and support organization. Subsequently, a dramatic decline in the market for minicomputers led to Acer's first new product for this segment, the Concer, being a dismal disappointment. Worse still, the substantial infrastructure installed to support it began generating huge losses.

Meanwhile, the competitive dynamics in the PC market were changing. In the closing years of the 1980s, Packard Bell made department and discount stores into major computer retailers, while Dell established its direct sales model. Both moves led to dramatic PC price reductions, and Acer's historic gross margin of about 35% began eroding rapidly, eventually dropping ten percentage points. Yet despite these problems, spirits were high in Acer,

and in mid-1989 the company shipped its one millionth PC. Flush with new capital, the company purchased properties and companies within Taiwan worth $150 million. However, Acer's drift from its "commoner's culture" worried Shih, who felt he needed help to restore discipline to the "rampaging dragon." The ambition to grow had to be reconciled with the reality of Acer's financial situation.

Enter Leonard Liu Projected 1989 results indicated that the overextended company was in a tailspin. Earnings per share were expected to fall from NT $5 to NT $1.42. The share price, which had been as high as NT $150, fell to under NT $20. (See **Exhibit 2.**) Concerned by the growing problems, Shih decided to bring in an experienced top-level executive. After more than a year of courting, in late 1989, he signed Leonard Liu, Taiwan-born, U.S.-based, senior IBM executive with a reputation for a no-nonsense professional management style. In an announcement that caught many by surprise, Shih stepped down as president of the Acer Group, handing over that day-to-day management role to Liu. In addition, Liu was named CEO and Chairman of AAC, the company's North American subsidiary.

Given Shih's desire to generate $5 billion in sales by 1996, Liu began to focus on opportunities in the networking market in the United States. Despite the continuing problems at Counterpoint and Service Intelligence, he agreed with those who argued that Acer could exploit this market by building on its position in high-end products, particularly in the advanced markets of the United States and Europe. In particular, Liu became interested in the highly regarded multi-user minicomputer specialist, Altos. Founded in 1977, this Silicon Valley networking company had 700 employees, worldwide distribution in 60 countries, and projected sales of $170 million for 1990. Although it had generated losses of $3 million and $5 million in the previous two years, Liu felt that Altos's $30 million in cash reserves and $20 million in real estate made it an attractive acquisition. In August 1990, Acer paid $94 million to acquire the respected Altos brand,

Exhibit 2 Acer Share Price History, November 1988–January 1995

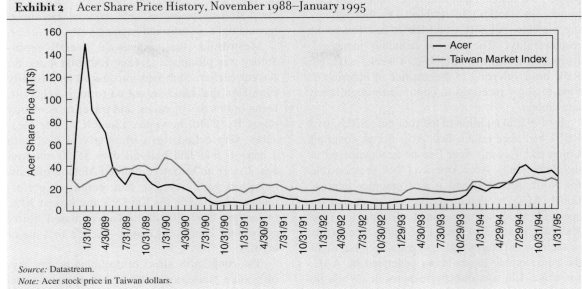

Source: Datastream.
Note: Acer stock price in Taiwan dollars.

its technology and its distribution network.[1] Almost immediately, however, powerful new PCs began to offer an alternative means of multi-user networking, and, as if to remind management of the eclipse of Counterpoint's minicomputers, within a year of its purchase, Altos was losing $20 million. Through the 1990s, AAC's losses increased.

In addition to this strategic thrust, Liu also began working on Acer's established organization and management approaches. For example, under Shih's leadership, while managers had been given considerable independence to oversee their business units, they had not been given profit and loss responsibility. Furthermore, because of the family-style relationship that existed among long-time company members, inter-company transfers were often priced to do friends a favor and ensure that a buyer did not "lose face" on a transaction. Even

outsourced products were often bought at prices negotiated to make long-term suppliers look good. With no accountability for the profits of their business units, managers had little incentive to ensure quality or price, and would let the group absorb the loss. As one Acer observer noted, the company was "frugal and hard-working, but with little organizational structure or procedure-based administration."

As Shih had hoped, Liu brought to Acer some of IBM's professional management structures, practices and systems. To increase accountability at Acer, the new president reduced management layers, established standards for intra-company communications, and introduced productivity and performance evaluations. Most significantly, he introduced the Regional Business Unit/Strategic Business Unit (RBU/SBU) organization. Acer's long-established product divisions became SBUs responsible for the design, development, and production of PC components and system products, including OEM product sales. Simultaneously, the company's major overseas subsidiaries and marketing companies became RBUs responsible for developing distribution channels, providing

---

[1]Because this was a much larger deal than either Counterpoint (acquired for $1 million plus a stock swap) or Service Intelligence (a $500,000 transaction), Shih suggested the deal be structured as a joint venture to maintain the Altos managers' stake in the business. However, Liu insisted on an outright acquisition to ensure control, and Shih deferred to his new president's judgment.

support for dealers, distributor networks, and customers, and working to establish JVs in neighboring markets. All SBUs and RBUs had full profit responsibility. "The pressure definitely increased. I was eating fourteen rice boxes a week," said one RBU head, referring to the practice of ordering in food to allow meetings to continue through lunch and dinner.

By 1992, in addition to the four core SBUs, five RBUs had been established: Acer Sertek covering China and Taiwan; Acer Europe headquartered in the Netherlands; Acer America (AAC) responsible for North America; and Acer Computer International (ACI), headquartered in Singapore and responsible for Asia, Africa, and Latin America. (See **Exhibits 3a** and **3b.**) One of the immediate effects of the new structures and systems was to highlight the considerable losses being generated by AAC, for which Liu was directly responsible. While no longer formally engaged in operations, Shih was urging the free-spending Altos management to adopt the more frugal Acer norms, and even began preaching his "duck egg" pricing theory. But

demand was dropping precipitously and Liu decided stronger measures were required. He implemented tight controls and began layoffs.

Meanwhile, the company's overall profitability was plummeting. (See **Exhibits 4** and **5.**) A year earlier, Shih had introduced an austerity campaign that had focused on turning lights off, using both sides of paper, and traveling economy class. By 1990, however, Liu felt sterner measures were called for, particularly to deal with a payroll that had ballooned to 5,700 employees. Under an initiative dubbed Metamorphosis, managers were asked to rank employee performance, identifying the top 15% and lowest 30%. In January 1991, 300 of the Taiwan-based "thirty percenters" were terminated—Acer's first major layoffs.

The cumulative effect of declining profits, layoffs, more "paratroopers," and particularly the new iron-fisted management style challenged Acer's traditional culture. In contrast to Shih's supportive, family-oriented approach, Liu's "by-the-numbers" management model proved grating. There was

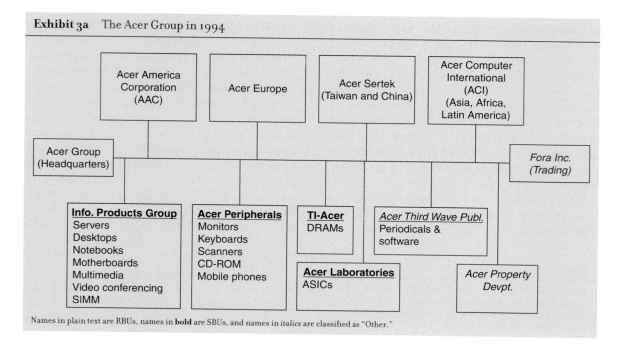

Exhibit 3a   The Acer Group in 1994

Names in plain text are RBUs, names in **bold** are SBUs, and names in *italics* are classified as "Other."

Exhibit 3b   Acer's Geographical Distribution in 1994

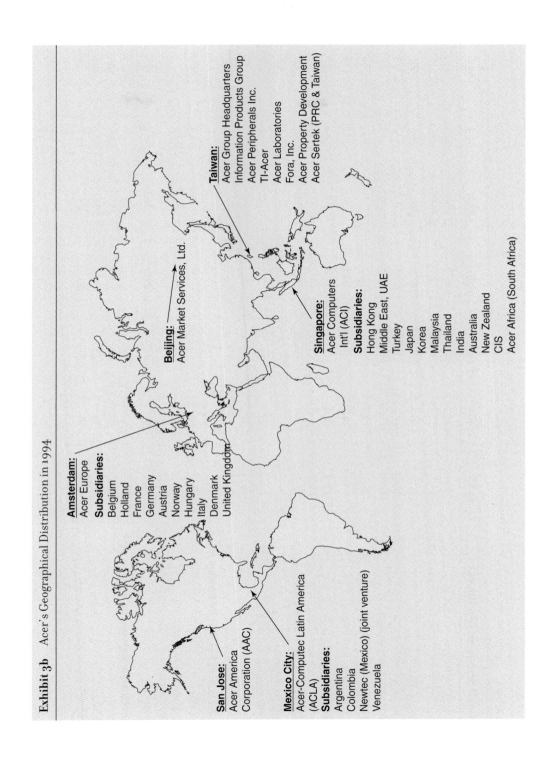

Amsterdam:
Acer Europe
Subsidiaries:
Belgium
Holland
France
Germany
Austria
Norway
Hungary
Italy
Denmark
United Kingdom

Beijing:
Acer Market Services, Ltd.

Taiwan:
Acer Group Headquarters
Information Products Group
Acer Peripherals Inc.
TI-Acer
Acer Laboratories
Fora, Inc.
Acer Property Development
Acer Sertek (PRC & Taiwan)

Singapore:
Acer Computers
Int'l (ACI)
Subsidiaries:
Hong Kong
Middle East, UAE
Turkey
Japan
Korea
Malaysia
Thailand
India
Australia
New Zealand
CIS
Acer Africa (South Africa)

San Jose:
Acer America
Corporation (AAC)

Mexico City:
Acer-Computec Latin America
(ACLA)
Subsidiaries:
Argentina
Colombia
Newtec (Mexico) (joint venture)
Venezuela

67

Exhibit 4 Acer Combination Income Statement, 1988–1994

Income Statement ($ millions)	1988	1989	1990	1991	1992	1993	1994
TURNOVER	530.9	688.9	949.5	985.2	1,260	1,883	3,220
Cost of sales	(389.4)	(532.7)	(716.7)	(737.7)	(1,000)	(1,498)	(2,615)
GROSS PROFIT	141.6	156.3	232.8	247.5	260	385	605
SG&A expenses	(88.2)	(118.2)	(192.2)	(217.2)	(217)	(237)	(316)
R&D and other expenses	(17.9)	(25.4)	(47.7)	(42.3)	(38)	(48)	(59)
OPERATING PROFIT/(LOSS)	35.6	12.7	(7.1)	(12.0)	5	100	230
Non-operating profit/(loss)	(8)	(6.3)	(1.5)	(15)	(4)	(11)	(19)
PROFIT BEFORE TAX	27.6	6.4	(8.6)	(27.0)	1	89	212
Tax	(1.2)	(1)	(1.2)	1	(3)	(3)	(7)
PROFIT (LOSS) AFTER TAX	26.4	5.4	(9.8)	(26.0)	(3)	86	205
Sales by Region (%)							
North America	na	31	31	31	38	44	39
Europe	na	32	28	28	22	23	17
Rest of World	na	37	41	41	40	33	44
Combination Revenue by Product (%)							
Portables	na	na	3.2	2.9	7.9	18 ⎫	60%
Desktops and Motherboards	na	na	60.9	56.3	54.9	47 ⎬	
Minicomputers	na	na	13.9	11.3	6.6		
Peripherals and Other	na	na	22	29.5	30.6	35	40%
Combination Revenue by Business (%)							
Brand	na	53	47	na	58	68	56%
OEM	na	34	22	na	18	32	36%
Trading	na	13	31	na	24	na	7%

Source: Company Annual Reports Year ending December 31.

Exhibit 5   Consolidated Balance Sheet, 1988–1994

Acer Group Balance Sheet ($ millions)	1988	1989	1990	1991	1992	1993	1994
Current Assets	277.30	448.80	579.50	600.90	700.20	925.00	1355.00
Fixed Assets							
Land, Plant, and Equipment (after depreciation)	53.10	126.90	191.10	161.50	179.60	590.00	645.00
Deferred charges and other assets	11.50	22.90	60.90	239.50	212.30	69.00	82.00
Total Assets	341.90	598.60	831.50	1001.90	1092.10	1584.00	2082.00
Total Current Liabilities	189.40	248.60	464.60	505.80	504.20	752.00	1067.00
Long-Term Liabilities	11.20	16.60	43.70	168.50	214.30	342.00	312.00
Total Liabilities	200.6	265.20	508.40	674.30	718.50	1094.00	1379.00
Stockholders Equity and Minority Interest (including new capital infusions)	141.30	333.40	323.10	327.60	373.60	490.00	703.00

Source: Company documents.

also growing resentment of his tendency to spend lavishly on top accounting and law firms and hire people who stayed at first-class hotels, all of which seemed out of step with Acer's "commoner's culture." Soon, his credibility as a highly respected world-class executive was eroding and Acer managers began questioning his judgement and implementing his directives half-heartedly.

In January 1992, when Shih realized that Acer's 1991 results would be disastrous, he offered his resignation. The board unanimously rejected the offer, suggesting instead that he resume his old role as CEO. In May 1992, Leonard Liu resigned.

Rebuilding the Base

Shih had long regarded mistakes and their resulting losses as "tuition" for Acer employees' growth— the price paid for a system based on delegation. He saw the losses generated in the early 1990s as part of his personal learning, considering it an investment rather than a waste. ("To make Acer an organization that can think and learn," he said, "we must continue to pay tuition as long as mistakes are unintentional and long-term profits exceed the cost of the education.") As he reclaimed the CEO role, Shih saw the need to fundamentally rethink Acer's management philosophy, the organizational model that reflected it, and even the underlying basic business concept.

"Global Brand, Local Touch" Philosophy   At Acer's 1992 International Distributors Meeting in Cancun, Mexico, Shih articulated a commitment to linking the company more closely to its national markets, describing his vision as "Global Brand, Local Touch." Under this vision, he wanted Acer to evolve from a Taiwanese company with offshore sales to a truly global organization with deeply-planted local roots.

Building on the company's long tradition of taking minority positions in expansionary ventures, Shih began to offer established Acer distributors equity partnerships in the RBU they served. Four months after the Cancun meeting, Acer acquired a 19% interest in Computec, its Mexican distributor. Because of its role in building Acer into Mexico's leading PC brand, Shih invited Computec to form a joint venture company responsible for all Latin America. The result was Acer Computec Latin America (ACLA), a company subsequently floated on the Mexican stock exchange. Similarly, Acer Computers International (ACI), the company responsible for sales in Southeast Asia planned an initial public offering in Singapore in mid-1995. And in Taiwan, Shih was even considering taking some of Acer's core SBUs public.

As these events unfolded, Shih began to articulate an objective of "21 in 21," a vision of the Acer Group as a federation of 21 public companies, each with significant local ownership, by the 21st century. It was what he described as "the fourth way," a strategy of globalization radically different from the control-based European, American or Japanese models, relying instead on mutual interest and voluntary cooperation of a network of interdependent companies.

Client Server Organization Model   To reinforce the more networked approach of this new management philosophy, in 1993, Shih unveiled his client-server organization model. Using the metaphor of the network computer, he described the role of the Taiwan headquarters as a "server" that used its resources (finance, people, intellectual property) to support "client" business units, which controlled key operating activities. Under this concept of a company as a network, business units could leverage their own ideas or initiatives directly through other RBUs or SBUs without having to go through the corporate center which was there to help and mediate, not dictate or control. Shih believed that this model would allow Acer to develop speed and flexibility as competitive weapons.

While the concept was intriguing, it was a long way from Acer's operating reality. Despite the long-established philosophy of decentralization and the introduction of independent profit-responsible business units in 1992, even the largest RBUs were still viewed as little more than the sales and distribution arms of the Taiwan-based SBUs. To operationalize the client server concept, Shih began to emphasize several key principles. "Every man is lord of his

castle," became his battle cry to confirm the independence of SBU and RBU heads. Thus, when two SBUs—Acer Peripherals (API) and Information Products (IPG)—both decided to produce CD-ROM drives, Shih did not intervene to provide a top-down decision, opting instead to let the market decide. The result was that both units succeeded, eventually supplying CD-ROMs to almost 70% of PCs made in Taiwan, by far the world's leading source of OEM and branded PCs.

In another initiative, Shih began urging that at least half of all Acer products and components be sold outside the Group, hoping to ensure internal sources were competitive. Then, introducing the principle, "If it doesn't hurt, help," he spread a doctrine that favored internal suppliers. However, under the "lord of the castle" principle, if an RBU decided to improve its bottom line by sourcing externally, it could do so. But it was equally clear that the affected SBU could then find an alternative distributor for its output in that RBU's region. In practice, this mutual deterrence—referred to as the "nuclear option"—was recognized as a strategy of last resort that was rarely exercised. Despite Shih's communication of these new operating principles, the roles and relationships between SBU and RBUs remained in flux over several years as managers worked to understand the full implications of the client server model on their day-to-day responsibilities.

The Fast Food Business Concept   But the biggest challenges Shih faced on his return were strategic. Even during the two and a half years he had stepped back to allow Liu to lead Acer, competition in the PC business had escalated significantly, with the product cycle shortening to 6 to 9 months and prices dropping. As if to highlight this new reality, in May 1992, the month Liu left, Compaq announced a 30% across-the-board price reduction on its PCs. Industry expectations were for a major shakeout of marginal players. Given Acer's financial plight, some insiders urged the chairman to focus on OEM sales only, while others suggested a retreat from the difficult U.S. market. But Shih believed that crisis was a normal condition in business and that persistence usually paid off. His immediate priority was to halve Acer's five months of inventory—two months being inventory "in transit."

Under Shih's stimulus, various parts of the organization began to create new back-to-basics initiatives. For example, the System PC unit developed the "ChipUp" concept. This patented technology allowed a motherboard to accept different types of CPU chips—various versions of Intel's 386 and 486 chips, for example—drastically reducing inventory of both chips and motherboards. Another unit, Home Office Automation, developed the "2-3-1 System" to reduce the new product introduction process to two months for development, three months for selling and one month for phaseout. And about the same time, a cross-unit initiative to support the launch of Acer's home PC, Acros, developed a screwless assembly process, allowing an entire computer to be assembled by snapping together components, motherboard, power source, etc.[2] Integrating all these initiatives and several others, a team of engineers developed Uniload, a production concept that configured components in a standard parts palette for easy unpacking, assembly, and testing, facilitating the transfer of final assembly to RBU operations abroad. The underlying objective was to increase flexibility and responsiveness by moving more assembly offshore.

Uniload's ability to assemble products close to the customer led the CEO to articulate what he termed his "fast-food" business model. Under this approach, small, expensive components with fast-changing technology that represented 50%–80% of total cost (e.g., motherboards, CPUs, hard disc drives) were airshipped "hot and fresh" from SBU sources in Taiwan to RBUs in key markets, while less-volatile items (e.g., casings, monitors, power supplies) were shipped by sea. Savings in logistics, inventories and import duties on assembled products easily offset higher local labor assembly cost, which typically represented less than 1% of product cost.

[2]To promote the innovative idea, Shih sponsored internal contests to see who could assemble a computer the fastest. Although his personal best time was more than a minute, experts accomplished the task in 30 seconds.

As Shih began promoting his fast-food business concept, he met with some internal opposition, particularly from SBUs concerned that giving up systems assembly would mean losing power and control. To convince them that they could increase competitiveness more by focusing on component development, he created a presentation on the value added elements in the PC industry. "Assembly means you are making money from manual labor," he said. "In components and marketing you add value with your brains." To illustrate the point, Shih developed a disintegrated value added chart that was soon dubbed "Stan's Smiling Curve." (See **Exhibit 6.**)

The Turnaround   Describing his role as "to provide innovative stimulus, to recognize the new strategy which first emerges in vague ideas, then to communicate it, form consensus, and agree on action," Shih traveled constantly for two years, taking his message to the organization. Through 1993, the impact of the changes began to appear. Most dramatically, the fast-food business concept (supported by Liu's systems) caused inventory turnover to double by late 1993, reducing carrying costs, while lowering the obsolescence risk. In early 1994, the Group reported a return to profit after three years of losses.

Acer America and the Aspire

After Liu's resignation in April 1992, Shih named Ronald Chwang to head AAC. With a Ph.D. in Electrical Engineering, Chwang joined Acer in 1986 in technical development. After overseeing the start-up of Acer's peripherals business, in 1991 he was given the responsibility for integrating the newly acquired Altos into AAC as president of the Acer/Altos Business Unit.

Because AAC had been losing money since 1987, Chwang's first actions as CEO focused on stemming further losses. As part of that effort, he embraced the dramatic changes being initiated in Taiwan, making AAC's Palo Alto plant the first test assembly site of the Uniload system. Under the new system, manufacture and delivery time was cut

Exhibit 6   Stan Shih's PC Industry Conceptualization

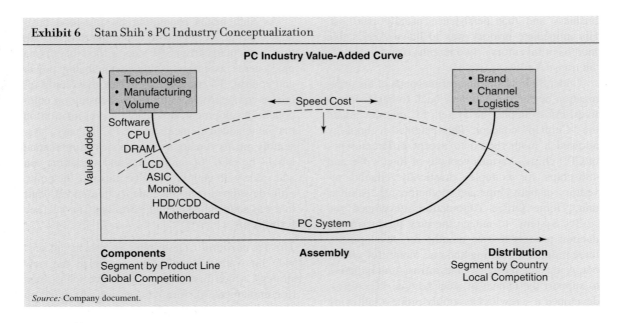

PC Industry Value-Added Curve

Source: Company document.

from 80 days to 45 days, reducing inventory levels by almost 45%. To support its Uniload site, AAC established a department of approximately 20 engineers, primarily to manage component testing, but also to adapt software design to local market needs. By 1994, AAC was breaking even. (See **Exhibit 7.**)

Birth of Aspire Despite these improvements, AAC and other RBUs still felt that Acer's Taiwan-based SBUs were too distant to develop product configurations that would appeal to diverse consumer and competitive situations around the globe. What might sell well in Southeast Asia could be a year out of date in the United States, for example. However, the emerging "global brand, local touch" philosophy and the client server organization model supporting it gave them hope that they could change the situation.

In January 1994, Mike Culver was promoted to become AAC's Director of Product Management, a role that gave him responsibility for the product development mandate he felt RBUs could assume under the new client-server model. The 29-year-old engineer and recent MBA graduate had joined Acer America just 2½; years earlier as AAC's product

manager for notebook computers. Recently, however, he had become aware of new opportunities in home computing.

Several factors caught Culver's attention. First, data showed an increasing trend to working at home—from 26 million people in 1993 to a projected 29 million in 1994. In addition, there was a rapidly growing interest in the Internet. And finally, developments in audio, telecom, video, and computing technologies were leading to industry rumblings of a new kind of multimedia home PC. Indeed, rumor had it that competitors like Hewlett Packard were already racing to develop new multimedia systems. Sharing this vision, Culver believed the time was right to create "the first Wintel-based PC that could compete with Apple in design, ease-of-use, and multimedia capabilities."

In October of 1994, Culver commissioned a series of focus groups to explore the emerging opportunity. In one of the groups, a consumer made a comment that had a profound impact on him. She said she wanted a computer that wouldn't remind her of work. At that moment, Culver decided that Acer's new home PC would incorporate radically new design aesthetics to differentiate it from the

Exhibit 7   AAC Selected Financials (1990–1994)

AAC Results ($ millions)	1990	1991	1992	1993	1994
Revenue	161	235	304	434	858
Cost of Sales	133	190	283	399	764
Selling and Marketing	27	61	25	23	55
General Administration	20	16	17	19	20
Research and Development	5	8	6	4	4
Operating Profit/(Loss)	(24)	(40)	(26)	(11)	15
Non-operating Profit/(Loss)	(1)	(7)	(3)	(5)	(3)
Profit/(Loss) Before Tax	(25)	(47)	(29)	(16)	12
Tax	1	(2)	0	0	1
Net Income/(Loss)	(26)	(45)	(29)	(16)	11
Current Assets	155	153	123	144	242
Fixed Assets (net)	39	43	28	25	25
Other Assets (net)	37	37	31	19	11
TOTAL Assets	231	233	182	188	278
Current Liabilities	155	169	154	136	218
Long-term debt	17	15	18	58	47
Stockholder Equity (including additional capita)	58	50	10	(6)	12
Total Liabilities	231	233	182	188	278

Source: Company documents.
(*Note*: Totals may not add due to rounding.)

standard putty-colored, boxy PCs that sat in offices throughout the world.

By November, Culver was convinced of the potential for an innovative multimedia consumer PC, and began assembling a project team to develop the concept. While the team believed the Acer Group probably had the engineering capability to develop the product's new technical features, they were equally sure they would have to go outside to get the kind of innovative design they envisioned. After an exhaustive review, the team selected Frog Design, a leading Silicon Valley design firm that had a reputation for "thinking outside of the box." Up to this point, Culver had been using internal resources and operating within his normal budget. The selection of Frog Design, however, meant that he had to go to Chwang for additional support. "The approval was incredibly informal," related Culver, "it literally took place in one 20 minute discussion in the hallway in late November. I told Ronald we

would need $200,000 for outside consulting to create the cosmetic prototype." Chwang agreed on the spot, and the design process began.

In 1994, Acer was in ninth place in the U.S. market, with 2.4% market share, largely from sales of the Acros, Acer's initial PC product, which was an adaptation of its commercial product, the Acer Power. (See **Exhibit 8** for 1994 market shares.) Culver and Chwang were convinced they could not only substantially improve Acer's U.S. share, but also create a product with potential to take a larger share of the global multimedia desktop market estimated at 10.4 million units and growing at more than 20% annually, primarily in Europe and Asia.

Working jointly with designers from Frog Design, the project team talked to consumers, visited computer retail stores and held discussions to brainstorm the new product's form. After almost two months, Frog Design developed six foam models of possible designs. In January 1995, the Acer team

Exhibit 8   Top Ten PC Manufacturers in the
U.S. and Worldwide in 1994

Company	U.S. Market Share	Worldwide Market Share
Compaq	12.6%	9.8%
Apple	11.5%	8.1%
Packard Bell	11.4%	5.1%
IBM	9.0%	8.5%
Gateway 2000	5.2%	2.3%
Dell	4.2%	2.6%
AST	3.9%	2.7%
Toshiba	3.6%	2.4%
Acer	2.4%	2.6%
Hewlett Packard	2.4%	2.5%

Source: Los Angeles Times, January 31, 1996.

Exhibit 9   First Generation Aspire
Prototype Design

chose a striking and sleek profile that bore little resemblance to the traditional PC. Market research
also indicated that customers wanted a choice of
colors, so the team decided that the newly named
Aspire PC would be offered in charcoal grey and
emerald green. (See **Exhibit 9.**)

Meanwhile, the team had been working with
AAC software engineers and a development group in
Taiwan to incorporate the new multimedia capabilities into the computer. One significant introduction
was voice-recognition software that enabled users
to open, close, and save documents by voice commands. However, such enhancements also required
new hardware design: to accommodate the voice-
recognition feature, for example, a microphone had
to be built in, and to properly exploit the machine's
enhanced audio capabilities, speakers had to be integrated into the monitor. The multimedia concept also
required the integration of CD-ROM capabilities,
and a built-in modem and answering machine incorporating fax and telephone capabilities. This type of
configuration was a radical innovation for Acer, requiring significant design and tooling changes.

In early 1995 the price differential between upper-
tier PCs (IBM, for example) and lower-end products
(represented by Packard Bell) was about 20%.
Culver's team felt the Aspire could be positioned

between these two segments offering a high quality innovative product at a less-than-premium
price. They felt they could gain a strong foothold
by offering a product range priced from $1,199
for the basic product to $2,999 for the highest-
end system with monitor. With a September launch,
they budgeted U.S. sales of $570 million and prof-
its of $17 million for 1995. A global rollout would
be even more attractive with an expectation of
breakeven within the first few months.

Stan Shih's Decisions

On his way to San Jose in February 1995, Stan Shih
pondered the significance of the Aspire project.
Clearly, it represented the client-server system at
work: this could become the first product designed
and developed by an RBU, in response to a locally
sensed market opportunity. Beyond that, he had
the feeling it might have the potential to become
Acer's first global blockbuster product.

Despite its promise, however, Shih wanted to
listen to the views of the project's critics. Some
pointed out that AAC had just begun to generate
profits in the first quarter of 1994, largely on the

basis of its solid OEM sales, which accounted for almost 50% of revenues. Given its delicate profit position, they argued that AAC should not be staking its future on the extremely expensive and highly competitive branded consumer products business. Established competitors were likely to launch their own multimedia home PCs—perhaps even before Acer. Building a new brand in this crowded, competitive market was extremely difficult as proven by many failed attempts, including the costly failure of Taiwan-based Mitac, launched as a branded PC in the early 1990s.

Even among those who saw potential in the product, there were several who expressed concern about the project's implementation. With all the company's engineering and production expertise located in Taiwan, these critics argued that the task of coordinating the development and delivery of such an innovative new product was just too risky

to leave to an inexperienced group in an RBU with limited development resources. If the project were to be approved, they suggested it be transferred back to the SBUs in Taiwan for implementation.

Finally, some wondered whether Acer's client-server organization model and "local touch" management would support Aspire becoming a viable global product. With the growing independence of the RBUs worldwide, they were concerned that each one would want to redesign the product and marketing strategy for its local market, thereby negating any potential scale economies.

As his plane touched down in San Francisco, Shih tried to resolve his feelings of excitement and concern. Should he support the Aspire project, change it, or put it on hold? And what implications would his decisions have for the new corporate model he had been building?

Reading 1-1   The Global Entrepreneur

by Daniel J. Isenberg

For a century and more, companies have ventured abroad only after establishing themselves at home. Moreover, when they have looked overseas, they haven't ventured too far afield, initially. Consumer health care company Johnson & Johnson set up its first foreign subsidiary in Montreal in 1919—33 years after its founding in 1886. Sony, established in 1946, took 11 years to export its first product to the United States, the TR-63 transistor radio. The Gap, founded in 1969—the year Neil Armstrong walked on the moon—opened its first overseas store in London in 1987, a year after the *Challenger* **space shuttle disaster.**

Companies are being born global today, by contrast. Entrepreneurs don't automatically buy raw

materials from nearby suppliers or set up factories close to their headquarters. They hunt for the planet's best manufacturing locations because political and economic barriers have fallen and vast quantities of information are at their fingertips. They also scout for talent across the globe, tap investors wherever they may be located, and learn to manage operations from a distance—the moment they go into business.

Take Bento Koike, who set up Tecsis to manufacture wind turbine blades in 1995. The company imports raw materials from North America and Europe, and its customers are located on those two continents. Yet Koike created his globe-girding start-up near São Paulo in his native Brazil because a sophisticated aerospace industry had emerged there, which enabled him to develop innovative blade designs and manufacturing know-how. Tecsis has become one of the world's market leaders, having installed 12,000 blades in 10 countries

Daniel J. Isenberg (disenberg@hbs.edu) is a senior lecturer at Harvard Business School in Boston.

Reprinted by permission of Harvard Business Review From "The Global Entrepreneur" by Daniel J. Isenberg, issue December /2008 Copyright © 2008, 2012 by the Harvard Business School Publishing Corporation; all rights reserved.

in the past decade and racked up revenues of $350 million in 2007.

Standing conventional theory on its head, start-ups now do business in many countries before dominating their home markets. In late 2001, Ron Zwanziger, David Scott, and Jerry McAleer teamed up to launch their third medical diagnostics business, even though Zwanziger lives in the United States and Scott and McAleer live in England. They started Inverness Medical Innovations by retaining the pieces of their company that Johnson & Johnson didn't acquire and immediately gained a presence in Belgium, Germany, Ireland, Israel, the United Kingdom, and the United States. The troika didn't skip a beat. In seven years, they wanted to grow the new venture into an enterprise valued at $7 billion and believed that being born global was the way to do it. They're getting there: Inverness Medical's assets were valued at $5 billion as of August 2008.

Today's entrepreneurs cross borders for two reasons. One is defensive: To be competitive, many ventures, like Tecsis and Inverness Medical, have to globalize some aspects of their business—manufacturing, service delivery, capital sourcing, or talent acquisition, for instance—the moment they start up. That may sound obvious today, but until a few years ago, it was standard practice for U.S. venture capitalists, in particular, to require that the companies they invested in focus on domestic markets.

The other reason is to take the offense. Many new ventures are discovering that a new business opportunity spans more than one country or that they can use distance to create new products or services. Take Racing ThePlanet, which Mary Gadams founded in 2002 to stage marathons, each 250 kilometers long and lasting seven days, in the world's most hostile environments. Her team works out of a small Hong Kong office, but the company operates in the Gobi Desert in Mongolia, the Atacama Desert in Chile, the Sahara Desert in Egypt, and Antarctica. Distance has generated the opportunity: If the deserts were accessible, participants and audiences would find the races less attractive, and the brand would be diluted. Racing

ThePlanet isn't just about running; it's also about creating a global lifestyle brand, which Gadams uses to sell backpacks, emergency supplies, clothing, and other merchandise, as well as to generate content for the multimedia division, which sells video for websites and GPS mapping systems. The company may be just six years old, but brand awareness is high, and RacingThePlanet is already profitable.

In this article, I'll describe the challenges start-ups face when they are born global and the skills entrepreneurs need to tackle them.

Key Challenges   Global entrepreneurs, my research shows, face three distinct challenges.

Distance.   New ventures usually lack the infrastructure to cope with dispersed operations and faraway markets. Moreover, physical distances create time differences, which can be remarkably tough to navigate. Even dealing with various countries' workweeks takes a toll on a start-up's limited staff: In North America, Europe, China, and India, corporate offices generally operate Monday through Friday. In Israel, they're open Sunday through Thursday. In Saudi Arabia and the UAE, the workweek runs Saturday through Wednesday, but in other predominantly Muslim countries like Lebanon, Morocco, and Turkey, people work from Monday through Friday or Saturday.

A greater challenge for global entrepreneurs is bridging what the British economist Wilfred Beckerman called in 1956 "psychic distance." This arises from such factors as culture, language, education systems, political systems, religion, and economic development levels. It can heighten—or reduce—psychological barriers between regions and often prompt entrepreneurs to make counterintuitive choices. Take the case of Encantos de Puerto Rico, set up in 1998 to manufacture and market premium Puerto Rican coffee. When founder-CEO Angel Santiago sought new markets in 2002, he didn't enter the nearby U.S. market but chose Spain instead. That's because, he felt, Puerto Ricans and Spaniards have similar tastes in coffee and because of the ease of doing business in Spanish, which reduced the psychic distance between the two countries. When two years later, Encantos de Puerto Rico did enter the United States, it focused initially on Miami, which has a large Hispanic population.

Context. Nations' political, regulatory, judicial, tax, environmental, and labor systems vary. The choices entrepreneurs make about, say, where to locate their companies' headquarters will affect shareholder returns and also their ability to raise capital. When the husband-and-wife team of Andrew Prihodko, a Ukrainian studying at MIT, and Sharon Peyer, a Swiss-American citizen studying at Harvard, set up an online photo management company, they thought hard about where to domicile Pixamo. Should they incorporate it in Ukraine, which has a simple and low tax structure but a problematic legal history? Or Switzerland, where taxes are higher but the legal system is well established? Or Delaware, where taxes are higher still but most U.S. start-ups are domiciled? Prihodko and Peyer eventually chose to base the company in the relatively tax-friendly Swiss canton of Zug, a decision that helped shareholders when they sold Pixamo to NameMedia in 2007.

Some global entrepreneurs must deal with several countries simultaneously, which is complex. In 1994, Gary Mueller launched Internet Securities to provide investors with data on emerging markets. Three years later, the start-up had offices in 18 countries and had to cope with the jurisdictions of Brazil, China, and Russia on any given day. By learning to do so, Internet Securities became a market leader, and in 1999, Euromoney acquired 80% of the company's equity for the tidy sum of $43 million.

Resources. Customers expect start-ups to possess the skills and deliver the levels of quality that larger companies do. That's a tall order for resource-stretched new ventures. Still, they have no option but to do whatever it takes to retain customers. In 1987, Jim Sharpe acquired a small business, XTech, now a manufacturer of faceplates for telecommunications equipment. Initially, the company made its products in the United States and sold them overseas through sales representatives and distributors. However, by 2006, Cisco, Lucent, Intel, IBM, and other XTech customers had shifted most of their manufacturing to China. They became reluctant to do business with suppliers that didn't make products or have customer service operations in China. So Sharpe had no choice but to set up a subsidiary in China at that stage.

Competencies Global Entrepreneurs Need   All entrepreneurs must be able to identify opportunities, gather resources, and strike deals. They all must also possess soft skills like vision, leadership, and passion. To win globally, though, they must hone four additional competencies.

Articulating a global purpose. Developing a crystal clear rationale for being global is critical. In 1999, for example, Robert Wessman took control of a small pharmaceuticals maker in his native Iceland. Within weeks, he concluded that the generics player had to globalize its core functions—manufacturing, R&D, and marketing—to gain economies of scale, develop a large product portfolio, and be first to market with drugs as they came off patent. Since then, Actavis has entered 40 countries, often by taking over local companies. Wessman faced numerous hurdles, but he stuck to the strategy. Actavis now makes 650 products and has 350 more in the pipeline. In 2007, it generated revenues of $2 billion and had become one of the world's top five generics manufacturers.

Alliance building. Start-ups can quickly attain global reach by striking partnerships with large companies headquartered in other countries. However, most entrepreneurs have to enter into such deals from positions of weakness. An established company has managers who can conduct due diligence, the money to fly teams over for meetings, and the power to extract favorable terms from would-be partners. It has a reasonable period within which to negotiate a deal, and it has options in case talks with one company fail. A start-up has few of those resources or bargaining chips.

Start-ups also have problems communicating with global partners because their alliances have to span geographic and psychic distances. Take the case of Trolltech, an open-source software company founded in 1994 in Oslo by Eirik Chambe-Eng and Haavard Nord. In 2001, the start-up landed a contract to supply a Japanese manufacturer with a Linux-based software platform for personal digital assistants (PDAs). The dream order quickly turned into a nightmare. There were differences between what the Japanese company thought it would get and what the Norwegian supplier felt it should provide, and the start-up struggled to deliver the modifications its partner began to demand. Suspecting that Trolltech wouldn't deliver the software on time, the Japanese company offered to send over a team of software engineers. However, when it suggested that both companies work through the Christmas break to meet a deadline—a common practice in Japan—Trolltech refused, citing the importance of the Christmas vacation in Norway. The relationship almost collapsed, but Chambe-Eng and Nord managed to negotiate a new deadline that they could meet without having to work during the holiday season.

Supply-chain creation   Entrepreneurs must often choose suppliers on the other side of the world and monitor them without having managers nearby. Besides, the best manufacturing locations change as labor and fuel costs rise and as quality problems show up, as they did in China.

Start-ups find it daunting to manage complex supply networks, but they gain competitive advantage by doing so. Sometimes the global supply chain lies at the heart of the business opportunity. Take the case of Winery Exchange, cofounded by Peter Byck in 1999. The California-based venture manages a 22-country network of wineries and breweries. Winery Exchange works closely with retail chains, such as Kroger, Tesco, and Costco, to develop premium private label products, and it gets its suppliers to produce and package the wines as inexpensively as possible. The venture has succeeded because it links relatively small market-needy suppliers with mammoth product-hungry retailers and provides both with its product development expertise. In 2006, Winery Exchange sold 2 million cases of 330 different brands of wine, beer, and spirits to retailers on four continents.

In addition to raw materials and components, start-ups are increasingly buying intellectual property from across the world. Hands-On Mobile, started by David Kranzler, is a Silicon Valley-based developer of the mobile versions of Guitar Hero III, Iron Man, and other games. When the company started in 2001, the markets for mobile multimedia content were developing faster in Asia and Europe than in the United States, and gamers were creating attractive products in China, South Korea, and Japan. Kranzler realized that his company had to acquire intellectual property and design capacity overseas in order to offer customers a comprehensive catalog of games and the latest delivery technologies. Hands-On Mobile therefore picked up MobileGame Korea, as well as two Chinese content development companies, which has helped it become a market leader.

Multinational organization   In 2006, I conducted a simulation exercise called the **Virtual Entrepreneurial Team Exercise** (VETE) for 450 MBA students in 10 business schools in Argentina, Austria, Brazil, England, Hong Kong, Liechtenstein, the Netherlands, Japan, and the United States. The teams, each composed of students from different schools and different countries, developed hypothetical pitches for Asia Renal Care, a Hong Kong-based medical services start-up, that had raised its first round of capital in 1999. They experienced a slice of global entrepreneurial life in real time, using technologies like Skype, wikis, virtual chat rooms, and, of course, e-mail to communicate with one another. The students learned how to build trust, compensate for the lack of visual cues, respect cultural differences, and deal with different institutional frameworks and incentives—the competencies entrepreneurs need for coordination, control, and communication in global enterprises. The would-be entrepreneurs' emotions ranged from elation to frustration, and their output varied from good to excellent.

Start-ups cope with the challenges of managing a global organization in different ways. Internet Securities used a knowledge database to share information among its offices around the world, increasing managers' ability to recognize and solve problems. RacingThePlanet used intensive training to ensure that volunteers perform at a consistently high level during the events it holds. Trolltech worked round the clock to meet deadlines, passing off development tasks from teams in Norway to those in Australia as the day ends in one place and begins in the other. Inverness Medical hired key executives wherever it could and organized the company around them rather than move people all over the world.

Still, there are no easy answers to the challenges of managing a start-up in the topsy-turvy world of global entrepreneurship. Take the case of Mei Zhang, who founded WildChina, a high-end adventure-tourism company in China, in 2000. Three years later, Zhang hired an American expatriate, Jim Stent, who had a deep interest in Chinese history and culture, as her COO. Zhang moved to Los Angeles in 2004, anointing Stent as CEO in Beijing and appointing herself chairperson. Thus, a Chinese expatriate living in the United States had to supervise an American expatriate living in Beijing. And when the two amicably parted ways in 2006, Zhang started managing the Chinese company from Los Angeles. These are contingencies no textbook provides for.

How Diaspora Networks Help Start-Ups Go Global

Many entrepreneurs have taken advantage of ethnic networks to formulate and execute a global strategy. The culture, values, and social norms members hold in common forge understanding and trust, making it easier to establish and enforce contracts.

Through diaspora networks, global entrepreneurs can quickly gain access to information, funding, talent, technology—and, of course, contacts. In the late 1990s, for instance, Boston-based Desh Deshpande, who had set up several high-tech ventures in the United States, was keen to start something in his native India. In April 2000, he met an optical communications expert, Kumar Sivarajan, who had worked at IBM's Watson Research Center before returning to India to take up a teaching position at the Indian Institute of Science in Bangalore. Deshpande introduced Sivarajan to two other Indians, Sanjay Nayak and Arnob Roy, who had both worked in the Indian subsidiaries of American high-tech companies. The trust among the four enabled the creation of the start-up Tejas Networks in two months' time. Deshpande and Sycamore Networks, the major investors, wired the initial capital of $5 million, attaching few of the usual conditions to the investment. Tejas Networks has become a leading telecommunications equipment manufacturer, generating revenues of around $100 million over the past year.

The research that my HBS colleague William Kerr and I have done suggests that entrepreneurs who most successfully exploit diaspora networks take these four steps:

Map networks.   The members of a diaspora often cluster in residential areas, public organizations, or industries. For instance, in Tokyo, Americans tend to work for professional service firms such as Morgan Stanley and McKinsey, live in Azabu, shop in Omotesandō, and hang out at the American Club.

Identify organizations that can help.   Many countries have offices overseas that facilitate trade and investment, and they open their doors to people visiting from home. These organizations can provide the names of influential individuals, companies, and informal organizations, clubs, or groups.

Tap informal groups.   Informal organizations of ethnic entrepreneurs and executives are usually located in communities where immigrant professionals are concentrated. In the United States, for instance, they thrive in high-tech industry neighborhoods such as Silicon Valley or universities like MIT.

Identify the influentials.   It can be tough to identify people who have standing with local businesses and also within the diaspora network. A board member or coach that both respect is an invaluable resource for a would-be entrepreneur.

How Social Entrepreneurs Think Global

Atsumasa Tochisako is an unlikely entrepreneur. When he was in his mid-fifties, he left a senior position at the Bank of Tokyo-Mitsubishi to set up Microfinance International, a global for-profit social enterprise (FOPSE, for short), based in Washington, D.C. Having also been stationed in Latin America for many years, Tochisako had observed the large cash remittances coming from immigrants in the United States, as well as the exorbitant charges they paid commercial banks and the poor service they received. Sensing a business opportunity and the chance to do some good, he decided to provide immigrant workers with inexpensive remittance, check-cashing, insurance, and microlending services.

MFI was international from its birth in June 2003, with operations in the United States and El Salvador. Since then, it has expanded into a dozen Latin American countries and further extended its reach by allowing multinational financial institutions, such as the UAE Exchange, to use its proprietary Internet-based settlement platform.

Like Tochisako, many entrepreneurs today combine social values, profit motive, and a global focus. Social entrepreneurs are global from birth for three reasons. First, disease, malnutrition, poverty, illiteracy, and other social problems exist on a large scale in many developing countries. Second, the resources—funds, institutions, and governance systems—to tackle those issues are mainly in the developed world. Third, FOPSEs that tackle specific conditions can often be adapted to other countries. For instance, in 2002, Shane Immelman founded The Lapdesk Company to provide portable desks to South African schoolchildren, a third of whom are taught in schoolrooms that don't have adequate surfaces on which to write. The company asks large corporations in South Africa to donate desks—with some advertising on them—for entire school districts. By doing so, these companies are able to meet the South African government's requirement that they invest part of their profits in black empowerment programs. Since then, Immelman has adapted the business model to Kenya, Nigeria, and the Democratic Republic of Congo and has launched programs in India and Latin America.

• • •

Entrepreneurs shouldn't fear the fact that the world isn't flat. Being global may not be a pursuit for the fainthearted, but even start-ups can thrive by using distance to gain competitive advantage.

Reading 1-2   Distance Still Matters: The Hard Reality of Global Expansion

by Pankaj Ghemawat

When it was launched in 1991, Star TV looked like a surefire winner. The plan was straightforward: The company would deliver television

▌*Pankaj Ghemawat is the Jaime and Josefina Chua Tiampo Professor of Business Administration at Harvard Business School in Boston. His article "The Dubious Logic of Global Megamergers," coauthored by Fariborz Ghadar, was published in the JulyAugust 2000 issue of HBR.*

programming to a media-starved Asian audience. It would target the top 5% of Asia's socioeconomic pyramid, a newly rich elite who could not only afford the services but who also represented an attractive advertising market. Since English was the second language for most of the target consumers, Star would be able to use readily available and fairly cheap English-language programming rather than having to invest heavily in creating new local programs. And by using satellites to beam programs into people's homes, it would sidestep the constraints of geographic distance that had hitherto kept traditional broadcasters out of Asia. Media mogul Rupert Murdoch was so taken with this plan—especially with the appeal of leveraging his Twentieth Century Fox film library across the Asian market—that his company, News Corporation, bought out Star's founders for $825 million between 1993 and 1995.

The results have not been quite what Murdoch expected. In its fiscal year ending June 30, 1999, Star reportedly lost $141 million, pretax, on revenues of $111 million. Losses in fiscal years 1996 through 1999 came to about $500 million all told, not including losses on joint ventures such as Phoenix TV in China. Star is not expected to turn in a positive operating profit until 2002.

Star has been a high-profile disaster, but similar stories are played out all the time as companies pursue global expansion. Why? Because, like Star, they routinely overestimate the attractiveness of foreign markets. They become so dazzled by the sheer size of untapped markets that they lose sight of the vast difficulties of pioneering new, often very different territories. The problem is rooted in the very analytic tools that managers rely on in making judgments about international investments, tools that consistently underestimate the costs of doing business internationally. The most prominent of these is country portfolio analysis (CPA), the hoary but still widely used technique for deciding where a company should compete. By focusing on national GDP, levels of consumer wealth, and people's propensity to consume, CPA places all the emphasis on potential sales. It ignores the costs and risks of doing business in a new market.

Most of those costs and risks result from barriers created by distance. By distance, I don't mean only geographic separation, though that is important. Distance also has cultural, administrative or political, and economic dimensions that can make foreign markets considerably more or less attractive. Just how much difference does distance make? A recent study by economists Jeffrey Frankel and Andrew Rose estimates the impact of various

factors on a country's trade flows. Traditional economic factors, such as the country's wealth and size (GDP), still matter; a 1% increase in either of those measures creates, on average, a .7% to .8% increase in trade. But other factors related to distance, it turns out, matter even more. The amount of trade that takes place between countries 5,000 miles apart is only 20% of the amount that would be predicted to take place if the same countries were 1,000 miles apart. Cultural and administrative distance produces even larger effects. A company is likely to trade ten times as much with a country that is a former colony, for instance, than with a country to which it has no such ties. A common currency increases trade by 340%. Common membership in a regional trading bloc increases trade by 330%. And so on. (For a summary of Frankel and Rose's findings, see the exhibit "Measuring the Impact of Distance.")

Much has been made of the death of distance in recent years. It's been argued that information technologies and, in particular, global communications are shrinking the world, turning it into a small and relatively homogeneous place. But when it comes to business, that's not only an incorrect assumption, it's a dangerous one. Distance still matters, and companies must explicitly and thoroughly account for it when they make decisions about global expansion. Traditional country portfolio analysis needs to be tempered by a clear-eyed evaluation of the many dimensions of distance and their probable impact on opportunities in foreign markets.

The Four Dimensions of Distance

Distance between two countries can manifest itself along four basic dimensions: cultural, administrative, geographic, and economic. The types of distance influence different businesses in different ways. Geographic distance, for instance, affects the costs of transportation and communications, so it is of particular importance to companies that deal with heavy or bulky products, or whose operations require a high degree of coordination among highly dispersed people or activities. Cultural distance, by contrast, affects consumers' product preferences. It is a crucial consideration for any consumer goods or media company, but it is much less important for a cement or steel business.

Each of these dimensions of distance encompasses many different factors, some of which are readily apparent; others are quite subtle. (See the exhibit "The CAGE Distance Framework" for an overview of the factors and the ways in which they affect particular industries.) In this article, I will review the four principal dimensions of distance, starting with the two overlooked the most—cultural distance and administrative distance.

Cultural Distance.   A country's cultural attributes determine how people interact with one another and with companies and institutions. Differences in religious beliefs, race, social norms, and language are all capable of creating distance between two countries. Indeed, they can have a huge impact on trade: All other things being equal, trade between countries that share a language, for example, will be three times greater than between countries without a common language.

Some cultural attributes, like language, are easily perceived and understood. Others are much more subtle. Social norms, the deeply rooted system of unspoken principles that guide individuals in their everyday choices and interactions, are often nearly invisible, even to the people who abide by them. Take, for instance, the long-standing tolerance of the Chinese for copyright infringement. As William Alford points out in his book *To Steal a Book Is an Elegant Offense* (Stanford University Press, 1995), many people ascribe this social norm to China's recent communist past. More likely, Alford argues, it flows from a precept of Confucius that encourages replication of the results of past intellectual endeavors: "I transmit rather than create; I believe in and love the Ancients." Indeed, copyright infringement was a problem for Western publishers well before communism. Back in the 1920s, for example, Merriam Webster, about to introduce a bilingual dictionary in China, found

that the Commercial Press in Shanghai had already begun to distribute its own version of the new dictionary. The U.S. publisher took the press to a Chinese court, which imposed a small fine for using the Merriam Webster seal but did nothing to halt publication. As the film and music industries well know, little has changed. Yet this social norm still confounds many Westerners.

Most often, cultural attributes create distance by influencing the choices that consumers make between substitute products because of their preferences for specific features. Color tastes, for example, are closely linked to cultural prejudices. The word "red" in Russian also means beautiful. Consumer durable industries are particularly sensitive to differences in consumer taste at this level. The Japanese, for example, prefer automobiles and household appliances to be small, reflecting a social norm common in countries where space is highly valued.

Sometimes products can touch a deeper nerve, triggering associations related to the consumer's identity as a member of a particular community. In these cases, cultural distance affects entire categories of products. The food industry is particularly sensitive to religious attributes. Hindus, for example, do not eat beef because it is expressly forbidden by their religion. Products that elicit a strong response of this kind are usually quite easy to identify, though some countries will provide a few surprises. In Japan, rice, which Americans treat as a commodity, carries an enormous amount of cultural baggage.

Ignoring cultural distance was one of Star TV's biggest mistakes. By supposing that Asian viewers would be happy with English-language programming, the company assumed that the TV business was insensitive to culture. Managers either dismissed or were unaware of evidence from Europe that mass audiences in countries large enough to support the development of local content generally prefer local TV programming. If they had taken cultural distance into account, China and India could have been predicted to

Measuring the Impact of Distance

Economists often rely on the so-called gravity theory of trade flows, which says there is a positive relationship between economic size and trade and a negative relationship between distance and

trade. Models based on this theory explain up to two-thirds of the observed variations in trade flows between pairs of countries. Using such a model, economists Jeffrey Frankel and Andrew Rose[1] have predicted how much certain distance variables will affect trade.

Distance Attribute	Change in International Trade (%)
Income level: GDP per capita (1% increase)	+0.7
Economic size: GDP (1% increase)	+0.8
Physical distance (1% increase)	−1.1
Physical size (1% increase)*	−0.2
Access to ocean*	+50
Common border	+80
Common language	+200
Common regional trading bloc	+330
Colony-colonizer relationship	+900
Common colonizer	+190
Common polity	+300
Common currency	+340

[1]Jeffrey Frankel and Andrew Rose, "An Estimate of the Effects of Currency Unions on Growth," unpublished working paper, May 2000.
*Estimated effects exclude the last four variables in the table.

require significant investments in localization. TV is hardly cement.

Administrative or Political Distance.   Historical and political associations shared by countries greatly affect trade between them. Colony-colonizer links between countries, for example, boost trade by 900%, which is perhaps not too surprising given Britain's continuing ties with its former colonies in the commonwealth, France's with the franc zone of West Africa, and Spain's with Latin America. Preferential trading arrangements, common currency, and political union can also increase trade by more than 300% each. The integration of the European Union is probably the leading example of deliberate efforts to diminish administrative and political distance among trading partners. (Needless to say, ties must be friendly to have a positive influence on trade. Although India

and Pakistan share a colonial history—not to mention a border and linguistic ties—their mutual hostility means that trade between them is virtually nil.)

Countries can also create administrative and political distance through unilateral measures. Indeed, policies of individual governments pose the most common barriers to cross-border competition. In some cases, the difficulties arise in a company's home country. For companies from the United States, for instance, domestic prohibitions on bribery and the prescription of health, safety, and environmental policies have a dampening effect on their international businesses.

More commonly, though, it is the target country's government that raises barriers to foreign competition: tariffs, trade quotas, restrictions on foreign direct investment, and preferences for domestic competitors in the form of subsidies and favoritism in regulation and procurement. Such measures are expressly intended to protect domestic industries, and they are most likely to be implemented if a domestic industry meets one or more of the following criteria:

- *It is a large employer.* Industries that represent large voting blocs often receive state support in the form of subsidies and import protection. Europe's farmers are a case in point.
- *It is seen as a national champion.* Reflecting a kind of patriotism, some industries or companies serve as symbols of a country's modernity and competitiveness. Thus the showdown between Boeing and Airbus in capturing the large passenger-jet market has caused feelings on both sides of the Atlantic to run high and could even spark a broader trade war. Also, the more that a government has invested in the industry, the more protective it is likely to be, and the harder it will be for an outsider to gain a beachhead.
- *It is vital to national security.* Governments will intervene to protect industries that are deemed vital to national security—especially in high tech sectors such as telecommunications and aerospace. The FBI, for instance, delayed Deutsche Telekom's acquisition of Voicestream for reasons of national security.
- *It produces staples.* Governments will also take measures to prevent foreign companies from dominating markets for goods essential to their citizens' everyday lives. Food staples, fuel, and electricity are obvious examples.
- *It produces an "entitlement" good or service.* Some industries, notably the health care sector, produce goods or services that people believe they are entitled to as a basic human right. In these industries, governments are prone to intervene to set quality standards and control pricing.
- *It exploits natural resources.* A country's physical assets are often seen as part of a national heritage. Foreign companies can easily be considered robbers. Nationalization, therefore, is a constant threat to international oil and mining multinationals.

- *It involves high sunk-cost commitments.* Industries that require large, geography-specific sunk investments—in the shape, say, of oil refineries or aluminum smelting plants or railway lines—are highly vulnerable to interference from local governments. Irreversibility expands the scope for holdups once the investment has been made.

Finally, a target country's weak institutional infrastructure can serve to dampen cross-border economic activity. Companies typically shy away from doing business in countries known for corruption or social conflict. Indeed, some research suggests that these conditions depress trade and investment far more than any explicit administrative policy or restriction. But when a country's institutional infrastructure is strong—for instance, if it has a well-functioning legal system—it is much more attractive to outsiders.

Ignoring administrative and political sensitivities was Star TV's other big mistake. Foreign ownership of broadcasting businesses—even in an open society like the United States—is always politically loaded because of television's power to influence people. Yet shortly after acquiring the company, Rupert Murdoch declared on record that satellite television was "an unambiguous threat to totalitarian regimes everywhere" because it permitted people to bypass government-controlled news sources. Not surprisingly, the Chinese government enacted a ban on the reception of foreign satellite TV services soon thereafter. News Corporation has begun to mend fences with the Chinese authorities, but it has yet to score any major breakthroughs in a country that accounts for nearly 60% of Star TV's potential customers. Murdoch of all people should have foreseen this outcome, given his experience in the United States, where he was required to become a citizen in order buy the television companies that now form the core of the Fox network.

Geographic Distance.   In general, the farther you are from a country, the harder it will be to conduct business in that country. But geographic distance is not simply a matter of how far away the country is in miles or kilometers. Other attributes that must be considered include the physical size of the country, average within-country distances to borders, access

The CAGE Distance Framework

The cultural, administrative, geographic, and economic (CAGE) distance framework helps managers identify and assess the impact of distance on various industries. The upper portion of the table lists the key attributes underlying the four dimensions of distance. The lower portion shows how they affect different products and industries.

Cultural Distance	Administrative Distance	Geographic Distance	Economic Distance
Attributes Creating Distance			
Different languages Different ethnicities; lack of connective ethnic or social networks Different religions Different social norms	Absence of colonial ties Absence of shared monetary or political association Political hostility Government policies Institutional weakness	Physical remoteness Lack of a common border Lack of sea or river access Size of country Weak transportation or communication links Differences in climates	Differences in consumer incomes Differences in costs and quality of: • natural resources • financial resources • human resources • infrastructure • intermediate inputs • information or knowledge
Industries or Products Affected by Distance			
Products have high linguistic content (TV) Products affect cultural or national identity of consumers (foods) Product features vary in terms of: • size (cars) • standards (electrical appliances) • packaging Products carry country-specific quality associations (wines)	Government involvement is high in industries that are: • producers of staple goods (electricity) • producers of other "entitlements" (drugs) • large employers (farming) • large suppliers to government (mass transportation) • national champions (aerospace) • vital to national security (telecommunications) • exploiters of natural resources (oil, mining) • subject to high sunk costs (infrastructure)	Products have a low value-to-weight or bulk ratio (cement) Products are fragile or perishable (glass, fruit) Communications and connectivity are important (financial services) Local supervision and operational requirements are high (many services)	Nature of demand varies with income level (cars) Economies of standardization or scale are important (mobile phones) Labor and other factor cost differences are salient (garments) Distribution or business systems are different (insurance) Companies need to be responsive and agile (home appliances)

How Far Away Is China, Really?

As Star TV discovered, China is a particularly tough nut to crack. In a recent survey of nearly 100 multinationals, 54% admitted that their total business performance in China had been "worse than planned," compared with just 25% reporting "better than planned." Why was the failure rate so high? The survey provides the predictable answer: 62% of respondents reported that they had overestimated market potential for their products or services.

A quick analysis of the country along the dimensions of distance might have spared those companies much disappointment. Culturally, China is a long way away from nearly everywhere. First, the many dialects of the Chinese language are notoriously difficult for foreigners to learn, and the local population's foreign-language skills are limited. Second, the well-developed Chinese business culture based on personal connections, often summarized in the term *guanxi*, creates barriers to economic interchange with Westerners who focus on transactions rather than relationships. It can even be argued that Chinese consumers are "home-biased";

market research indicates much less preference for foreign brands over domestic ones than seems to be true in India, for example. In fact, greater China plays a disproportionate role in China's economic relations with the rest of the world.

Administrative barriers are probably even more important. A survey of members of the American Chamber of Commerce in China flagged market-access restrictions, high taxes, and customs duties as the biggest barriers to profitability in China. The level of state involvement in the economy continues to be high, with severe economic strains imposed by loss-making state-owned enterprises and technically insolvent state-owned banks. Corruption, too, is a fairly significant problem. In 2000, Transparency International ranked the country 63rd out of 90, with a rating of one indicating the least perceived corruption. Considerations such as these led Standard & Poor's to assign China a political-risk ranking of five in 2000, with six being the worst possible score.

So, yes, China is a big market, but that is far from the whole story. Distance matters, too, and along many dimensions.

to waterways and the ocean, and topography. Manmade geographic attributes also must be taken into account—most notably, a country's transportation and communications infrastructures.

Obviously, geographic attributes influence the costs of transportation. Products with low value-to-weight or bulk ratios, such as steel and cement, incur particularly high costs as geographic distance increases. Likewise, costs for transporting fragile or perishable products become significant across large distances.

Beyond physical products, intangible goods and services are affected by geographic distance as well. One recent study indicates that cross-border equity flows between two countries fall off significantly as the geographic distance between them rises. This phenomenon clearly cannot be explained by transportation costs—capital, after all, is not a physical good. Instead, the level of information infrastructure (crudely measured by telephone

traffic and the number of branches of multinational banks) accounts for much of the effect of physical distance on cross-border equity flows.

Interestingly, companies that find geography a barrier to trade are often expected to switch to direct investment in local plant and equipment as an alternative way to access target markets. But current research suggests that this approach may be flawed: Geographic distance has a dampening effect, overall, on investment flows as well as on trade flows. In short, it is important to keep both information networks and transportation infrastructures in mind when assessing the geographic influences on cross-border economic activity.

Economic Distance   The wealth or income of consumers is the most important economic attribute that creates distance between countries, and it has a marked effect on the levels of trade and the types of partners a country trades with. Rich countries, research suggests, engage in relatively more cross-border economic activity relative to their economic size than do their poorer cousins. Most of this activity is with other rich countries, as the positive correlation between per capita GDP and trade flows implies. But poor countries also trade more with rich countries than with other poor ones.

Of course, these patterns mask variations in the effects of economic disparities—in the cost and quality of financial, human, and other resources. Companies that rely on economies of experience, scale, and standardization should focus more on countries that have similar economic profiles. That's because they have to replicate their existing business model to exploit their competitive advantage, which is hard to pull off in a country where customer incomes—not to mention the cost and quality of resources—are very different. Wal-Mart in India, for instance, would be a very different business from Wal-Mart in the United States. But Wal-Mart in Canada is virtually a carbon copy.

In other industries, however, competitive advantage comes from economic arbitrage—the exploitation of cost and price differentials between markets. Companies in industries whose major cost components vary widely across countries—like the garment and footwear industries, where labor costs are important—are particularly likely to target countries with different economic profiles for investment or trade.

Whether they expand abroad for purposes of replication or arbitrage, all companies find that major disparities in supply chains and distribution channels are a significant barrier to business. A recent study concluded that margins on distribution within the United States—the costs of domestic transportation, wholesaling, and retailing—play a bigger role, on average, in erecting barriers to imports into the United States than do international transportation costs and tariffs combined.

More broadly, cross-country complexity and change place a premium on responsiveness and agility, making it hard for cross-border competitors, particularly replicators, to match the performance of locally focused ones because of the added operational complexity. In the home appliance business, for instance, companies like Maytag that concentrate on a limited number of geographies produce far better returns for investors than companies like Electrolux and Whirlpool, whose geographic spread has come at the expense of simplicity and profitability.

A Case Study in Distance

Taking the four dimensions of distance into account can dramatically change a company's assessment of the relative attractiveness of foreign markets. One company that has wrestled with global expansion is Tricon Restaurants International (TRI), the international operating arm of Tricon, which manages the Pizza Hut, Taco Bell, and KFC fast-food chains, and which was spun off from Pepsico in 1997.

When Tricon became an independent company, TRI's operations were far-flung, with restaurants in 27 countries. But the profitability of its markets varied greatly: Two-thirds of revenues and an even higher proportion of profits came from just seven markets. Furthermore, TRI's limited operating cash flow and Tricon's debt service obligations left TRI with less than one-tenth as much money as archrival McDonald's International to invest outside the United States. As a result, in 1998, TRI's president, Pete Bassi, decided to rationalize its global operations by focusing its equity investments in a limited number of markets.

But which markets? The exhibit "Country Portfolio Analysis: A Flawed Approach" provides a portfolio analysis of international markets for the fast-food restaurant business, based on data used by TRI for its strategy discussions. The analysis suggests that the company's top markets in terms of size of opportunity would be the larger bubbles to the center and right of the chart.

Applying the effects of distance, however, changes the map dramatically. Consider the Mexican market. Using the CPA method, Mexico, with a total fast-food consumption of $700 million, is a relatively small market, ranking 16th of 20. When combined with estimates of individual consumer wealth

Industry Sensitivity to Distance

The various types of distance affect different industries in different ways. To estimate industry sensitivity to distance, Rajiv Mallick, a research associate at Harvard Business School, and I regressed trade between every possible pair of countries in the world in each of 70 industries (according to their SIC designations) on each dimension of distance.

The results confirm the importance of distinguishing between the various components of distance in assessing foreign market opportunities. Electricity, for instance, is highly sensitive to administrative and geographic factors but not at all to cultural factors. The following table lists some of the industries that are more and less sensitive to distance.

CULTURAL DISTANCE Linguistic Ties	ADMINISTRATIVE DISTANCE Preferential Trading Agreements	GEOGRAPHIC DISTANCE Physical Remoteness	ECONOMIC DISTANCE Wealth Differences
More Sensitive			
Meat and meat preparations	Gold, nonmonetary	Electricity current	*(Economic distance decreases trade)*
Cereals and cereal preparations	Electricity current	Gas, natural and manufactured	Nonferrous metals
Miscellaneous edible products and preparations	Coffee, tea, cocoa, spices	Paper, paperboard	Manufactured fertilizers
Tobacco and tobacco products	Textile fibers	Live animals	Meat and meat preparations
Office machines and automatic data-processing equipment	Sugar, sugar preparations, and honey	Sugar, sugar preparations, and honey	Iron and steel Pulp and waste paper
Less Sensitive			
Photographic apparatuses, optical goods, watches	Gas, natural and manufactured	Pulp and waste paper	*(Economic distance increases trade)*
Road vehicles	Travel goods, handbags	Photographic apparatuses, optical goods, watches	Coffee, tea, cocoa, spices
Cork and wood	Footwear	Telecommunications and sound-recording apparatuses	Animal oils and fats
Metalworking machinery	Sanitary, plumbing, heating, and lighting fixtures	Coffee, tea, cocoa, spices	Office machines and automatic data-processing equipment
Electricity current	Furniture and furniture parts	Gold, nonmonetary	Power-generating machinery and equipment
			Photographic apparatuses, optical goods, watches

MORE SENSITIVE ◄───────────────────────────► LESS SENSITIVE

Exhibit 1a Country Portfolio Analysis (a flawed approach)

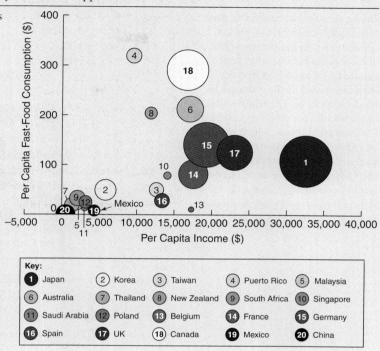

Here's how country portfolio analysis (CPA) works. A company's actual and potential markets are plotted on a simple grid, with a measure of per capita income on one axis and some measure of product performance, often penetration rates, on the other. The location of the market on the grid reflects the attractiveness of the market in terms of individual consumer wealth and propensity to consume. The size of the bubble represents the total size of the market in terms of GDP or the absolute consumption of the product or service in question. The bubbles provide a rough estimate of how large the relative revenue opportunities are. This CPA map compares a number of non–U.S. markets for fast-food restaurants.

Key:

1 Japan   2 Korea   3 Taiwan   4 Puerto Rico   5 Malaysia
6 Australia   7 Thailand   8 New Zealand   9 South Africa   10 Singapore
11 Saudi Arabia   12 Poland   13 Belgium   14 France   15 Germany
16 Spain   17 UK   18 Canada   19 Mexico   20 China

and per capita consumption, this ranking would imply that TRI should dispose of its investments there. But the exhibit "Country Portfolio Analysis: Adjusted for Distance" tells a different story. When the fast-food consumption numbers for each country are adjusted for their geographic distance from Dallas, TRI's home base, Mexico's consumption decreases less than any other country's, as you might expect, given Mexico's proximity to Dallas. Based on just this readjustment, Mexico leaps to sixth place in terms of market opportunity.

Further adjusting the numbers for a common land border and for membership in a trade agreement with the United States pushes Mexico's ranking all the way up to second, after Canada. Not all the adjustments are positive: adjusting for a common language—not a characteristic of Mexico—pushes Mexico into a tie for second place with the United Kingdom. Additional adjustments could also be made, but the overall message is plain. Once distance is taken into account, the size of the market opportunity in Mexico looks very different. If TRI had used the CPA approach and neglected distance, the company's planners might well have ended up abandoning a core market. Instead, they concluded, in Bassi's words, that "Mexico is one of TRI's top two or three priorities."

Factoring in the industry effects of distance is only a first step. A full analysis should consider how a company's own characteristics operate to increase or reduce distance from foreign markets. Companies with a large cadre of cosmopolitan managers, for instance, will be less affected by cultural differences than companies whose managers are all from the home country. In TRI's case, consideration of company-specific features made

Exhibit 1b   Country Portfolio Analysis (adjusted for distance)

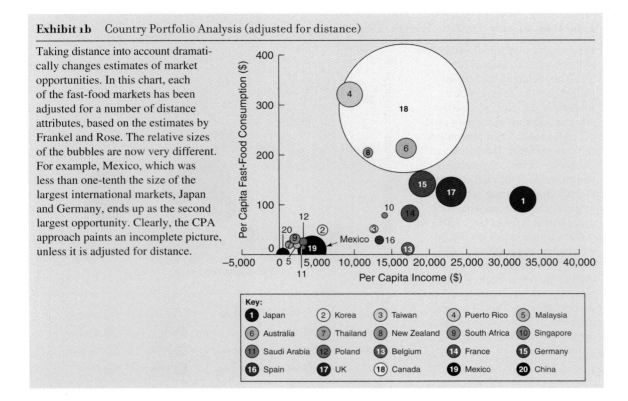

Taking distance into account dramatically changes estimates of market opportunities. In this chart, each of the fast-food markets has been adjusted for a number of distance attributes, based on the estimates by Frankel and Rose. The relative sizes of the bubbles are now very different. For example, Mexico, which was less than one-tenth the size of the largest international markets, Japan and Germany, ends up as the second largest opportunity. Clearly, the CPA approach paints an incomplete picture, unless it is adjusted for distance.

Key:
1	Japan	2	Korea	3	Taiwan	4	Puerto Rico	5	Malaysia
6	Australia	7	Thailand	8	New Zealand	9	South Africa	10	Singapore
11	Saudi Arabia	12	Poland	13	Belgium	14	France	15	Germany
16	Spain	17	UK	18	Canada	19	Mexico	20	China

Mexico even more attractive. The company already owned more than four-fifths of its Mexican outlets and had a 38% share of the local market, well ahead of McDonald's.

Consideration of the interaction of company-specific features and distance is beyond the scope of this article. But whether the analysis is at the industry or company level, the message is the same: Managers must always be conscious of distance—in all its dimensions. The CAGE distance framework is intended to help managers meet that challenge. While it is necessarily subjective, it represents an important complement to the tools used by most companies seeking to build or rationalize their country market portfolios. Technology may indeed be making the world a smaller place, but it is not eliminating the very real—and often very high—costs of distance.

Reading 1-3   The Tortuous Evolution of the Multinational Corporation

Howard V. Perlmutter

Four senior executives of the world's largest firms with extensive holdings outside the home country speak:

Company A: "We are a multinational firm. We distribute our products in about 100 countries. We manufacture in over 17 countries and do research and development in three countries. We look at all new investment projects—both domestic and overseas—using exactly the same criteria."

Company B: "We are a multinational firm. Only 1% of the personnel in our affiliate companies are non-nationals. Most of these are U.S. executives on temporary assignments. In all major markets, the affiliate's managing director is of the local nationality."

Company C: "We are a multinational firm. Our product division executives have worldwide profit responsibility. As our organizational chart shows, the United States is just one region on a par with Europe, Latin America, Africa, etc., in each product division."

Company D (non-American): "We are a multinational firm. We have at least 18 nationalities represented at our headquarters. Most senior executives speak at least two languages. About 30% of our staff at headquarters are foreigners."

While a claim to multinationality based on their years of experience and the significant proportion of sales generated overseas is justified in each of these four companies, a more penetrating analysis changes the image.

The executive from Company A tells us that most of the key posts in Company A's subsidiaries are held by home-country nationals. Whenever replacements for these men are sought, it is the practice, if not the policy, to "look next to you at the head office" and "pick someone (usually a home-country national) you know and trust."

The executive from Company B does not hide the fact that there are very few non-Americans in the key posts at headquarters. The few who are there are "so Americanized" that their foreign nationality literally has no meaning. His explanation for this paucity of non-Americans seems reasonable enough: "You can't find good foreigners who are willing to live in the United States, where our headquarters is located. American executives are more mobile. In addition, Americans have the drive and initiative we like. In fact, the European nationals would prefer to report to an American rather than to some other European."

The executive from Company C goes on to explain that the worldwide product division concept is rather difficult to implement. The senior executives in charge of these divisions have little overseas experience. They have been promoted from domestic posts and tend to view foreign consumer needs "as really basically the same as ours." Also, product division executives tend to focus on the domestic market because the domestic market is larger and generates more revenue than the fragmented European markets. The rewards are for global performance, but the strategy is to focus on domestic. His colleagues say "one pays attention to what one understands—and our senior executives simply do not understand what happens overseas

Trained as an engineer and a psychologist, Howard V. Perlmutter spent eight years at M.I.T.'s Center for International Studies and five years at the Institut pour l'Etude des Methodes de Direction de l'Enterprise (IMEDE) in Lausanne, Switzerland. His main interests are in the theory and practice of institution building, particularly the international corporation. He has recently been appointed Director for Research and Development of Worldwide Institutions in association with the Management Science Center at the University of Pennsylvania, as well as a member of the faculty at the Wharton School.
Used with permission of Howard V. Perlmutter.

and really do not trust foreign executives in key positions here or overseas."

The executive from the European Company D begins by explaining that since the voting shareholders must by law come from the home country, the home country's interest must be given careful consideration. In the final analysis he insists: "We are proud of our nationality; we shouldn't be ashamed of it." He cites examples of the previous reluctance of headquarters to use home-country ideas overseas, to their detriment, especially in their U.S. subsidiary. "Our country produces good executives, who tend to stay with us a long time. It is harder to keep executives from the United States."

A Rose by Any Other Name . . .

Why quibble about how multinational a firm is? To these executives, apparently being multinational is prestigious. They know that multinational firms tend to be regarded as more progressive, dynamic, geared to the future than provincial companies which avoid foreign frontiers and their attendant risks and opportunities.

It is natural that these senior executives would want to justify the multinationality of their enterprise, even if they use different yardsticks: ownership criteria, organizational structure, nationality of senior executives, percent of investment overseas, etc.

Two hypotheses seem to be forming in the minds of executives from international firms that make the extent of their firm's multinationality of real interest. The first hypothesis is that the degree of multinationality of an enterprise is positively related to the firm's long-term viability. The "multinational" category makes sense for executives if it means a quality of decision making which leads to survival, growth and profitability in our evolving world economy.

The second hypothesis stems from the proposition that the multinational corporation is a new kind of institution—a new type of industrial social architecture particularly suitable for the latter third of the twentieth century. This type of institution could make a valuable contribution to world order and conceivably exercise a constructive impact on the nation-state. Some executives want to understand how to create an institution whose presence is considered legitimate and valuable in each nation-state. They want to prove that the greater the degree of multinationality of a firm, the greater its total constructive impact will be on host and home nation-states as well as other institutions. Since multinational firms may produce a significant proportion of the world's GNP, both hypotheses justify a more precise analysis of the varieties and degrees of multinationality.[1] However, the confirming evidence is limited.

State of Mind

Part of the difficulty in defining the degree of multinationality comes from the variety of parameters along which a firm doing business overseas can be described. The examples from the four companies argue that (1) no single criterion of multinationality such as ownership or the number of nationals overseas is sufficient, and that (2) external and quantifiable measures such as the percentage of investment overseas or the distribution of equity by nationality are useful but not enough. The more one penetrates into the living reality of an international firm, the more one finds it is necessary to give serious weight to the way executives think about doing business around the world. The orientation toward "foreign people, ideas, resources," in headquarters and subsidiaries, and in host and home environments, becomes crucial in estimating the multinationality of a firm. To be sure, such external indices as the proportion of nationals in different countries holding equity and the number of foreign nationals who have reached top positions, including president, are good indices of multinationality. But one can still behave with a home-country orientation despite foreign shareholders, and one can have a few home-country nationals overseas but still pick

---

[1]H. V. Perlmutter, "Super-Giant Firms in the Future," *Wharton Quarterly,* Winter 1968.

those local executives who are home-country oriented or who are provincial and chauvinistic. The attitudes men hold are clearly more relevant than their passports.

Three primary attitudes among international executives toward building a multinational enterprise are identifiable. These attitudes can be inferred from the assumptions upon which key product, functional and geographical decisions were made.

These states of mind or attitudes may be described as ethnocentric (or home-country oriented), polycentric (or host-country oriented) and geocentric (or world-oriented).[2] While they never appear in pure form, they are clearly distinguishable. There is some degree of ethnocentricity, polycentricity or geocentricity in all firms, but management's analysis does not usually correlate with public pronouncements about the firm's multinationality.

Home-Country Attitudes

The ethnocentric attitude can be found in companies of any nationality with extensive overseas holdings. The attitude, revealed in executive actions and experienced by foreign subsidiary managers, is: "We, the home nationals of X company, are superior to, more trustworthy and more reliable than any foreigners in headquarters or subsidiaries. We will be willing to build facilities in your country if you acknowledge our inherent superiority and accept our methods and conditions for doing the job."

Of course, such attitudes are never so crudely expressed, but they often determine how a certain type of "multinational" firm is designed. Table 1 illustrates how ethnocentric attitudes are expressed in determining the managerial process at home and overseas. For example, the ethnocentric executive is more apt to say: "Let us manufacture the simple products overseas. Those foreign nationals are not yet ready or reliable. We should

manufacture the complex products in our country and keep the secrets among our trusted home-country nationals."

In a firm where ethnocentric attitudes prevailed, the performance criteria for men and products are "home-made." "We have found that a salesman should make 12 calls per day in Hoboken, New Jersey (the headquarters location), and therefore we apply these criteria everywhere in the world. The salesman in Brazzaville is naturally lazy, unmotivated. He shows little drive because he makes only two calls per day (despite the Congolese salesman's explanation that it takes time to reach customers by boat)."

Ethnocentric attitudes are revealed in the communication process where "advice," "counsel," and directives flow from headquarters to the subsidiary in a steady stream, bearing this message: "This works at home; therefore, it must work in your country."

Executives in both headquarters and affiliates express the national identity of the firm by associating the company with the nationality of the headquarters: this is "a Swedish company," "a Swiss company," "an American company," depending on the location of headquarters. "You have to accept the fact that the only way to reach a senior post in our firm," an English executive in a U.S. firm said, "is to take out an American passport."

Crucial to the ethnocentric concept is the current policy that men of the home nationality are recruited and trained for key positions everywhere in the world. Foreigners feel like "second-class" citizens.

There is no international firm today whose executives will say that ethnocentrism is absent in their company. In the firms whose multinational investment began a decade ago, one is more likely to hear, "We are still in a transitional stage from our ethnocentric era. The traces are still around! But we are making progress."

Host-Country Orientation

Polycentric firms are those which, by experience or by the inclination of a top executive (usually one of the founders), begin with the assumption

[2]H. V. Perlmutter, "Three Conceptions of a World Enterprise," *Revue Economique et Sociale*, May 1965.

Table 1   Three Types of Headquarters Orientation toward Subsidiaries in an International Enterprise

Organization Design	Ethnocentric	Polycentric	Geocentric
Complexity of organization	Complex in home country, simple in subsidiaries	Varied and independent	Increasingly complex and interdependent
Authority; decision making	High in headquarters	Relatively low in headquarters	Aim for a collaborative approach between headquarters and subsidiaries
Evaluation and control	Home standards applied for persons and performance	Determined locally	Find standards which are universal and local
Rewards and punishments; incentives	High in headquarters, low in subsidiaries	Wide variation; can be high or low rewards for subsidiary performance	International and local executives rewarded for reaching local and worldwide objectives
Communication; information flow	High volume to subsidiaries; orders, commands, advice	Little to and from headquarters; little between subsidiaries	Both ways and between subsidiaries; heads of subsidiaries part of management team
Identification	Nationality of owner	Nationality of host country	Truly international company but identifying with national interests
Perpetuation (recruiting, staffing, development)	Recruit and develop people of home country for key positions everywhere in the world	Develop people of local nationality for key positions in their own country	Develop best men everywhere in the world for key positions everywhere in the world

that host-country cultures are different and that foreigners are difficult to understand. Local people know what is best for them, and the part of the firm which is located in the host country should be as "local in identity" as possible. The senior executives at headquarters believe that their multinational enterprise can be held together by good financial controls. A polycentric firm, literally, is a loosely connected group with quasi-independent subsidiaries as centers—more akin to a confederation.

European multinational firms tend to follow this pattern, using a top local executive who is strong and trustworthy, of the "right" family and who has an intimate understanding of the workings of the host government. This policy seems to have worked until the advent of the Common Market.

Executives in the headquarters of such a company are apt to say: "Let the Romans do it their way. We really don't understand what is going on there, but we have to have confidence in them. As long as they earn a profit, we want to remain in the background." They assume that since people are different in each country, standards for performance, incentives and training methods must be different. Local environmental factors are given greater weight (see Table 1).

Many executives mistakenly equate polycentrism with multinationalism. This is evidenced in the legalistic definition of a multinational enterprise as a cluster of corporations of diverse nationality joined together by ties of common ownership. It is no accident that many senior executives in headquarters take pride in the absence of non-nationals in their subsidiaries, especially people from the head office. The implication is clearly that each subsidiary is a distinct national entity, since it is incorporated in a different sovereign state. Lonely senior executives in the subsidiaries of polycentric companies complain that: "The home office never tells us anything."

Polycentrism is not the ultimate form of multinationalism. It is a landmark on a highway. Polycentrism is encouraged by local marketing managers who contend that: "Headquarters will never understand us, our people, our consumer needs, our laws, our distribution, etc. . . . ."

Headquarters takes pride in the fact that few outsiders know that the firm is foreign-owned. "We want to be a good local company. How many Americans know that Shell and Lever Brothers are foreign-owned?"

But the polycentric personnel policy is also revealed in the fact that no local manager can seriously aspire to a senior position at headquarters. "You know the French are so provincial; it is better to keep them in France. Uproot them and you are in trouble," a senior executive says to justify the paucity of non-Americans at headquarters.

One consequence (and perhaps cause) of polycentrism is a virulent ethnocentrism among the country managers.

A World-Oriented Concept

The third attitude which is beginning to emerge at an accelerating rate is geocentrism. Senior executives with this orientation do not equate superiority with nationality. Within legal and political limits, they seek the best men, regardless of nationality, to solve the company's problems anywhere in the world. The senior executives attempt to build an organization in which the subsidiary is not only a good citizen of the host nation but is a leading exporter from this nation in the international community and contributes such benefits as (1) an increasing

supply of hard currency, (2) new skills and (3) a knowledge of advanced technology. Geocentrism is summed up in a Unilever board chairman's statement of objectives: "We want to Unileverize our Indians and Indianize our Unileverans."

The ultimate goal of geocentrism is a world-wide approach in both headquarters and subsidiaries. The firm's subsidiaries are thus neither satellites nor independent city states, but parts of a whole whose focus is on worldwide objectives as well as local objectives, each part making its unique contribution with its unique competence. Geocentrism is expressed by function, product and geography. The question asked in headquarters and the subsidiaries is: "Where in the world shall we raise money, build our plant, conduct R&D, get and launch new ideas to serve our present and future customers?"

This conception of geocentrism involves a collaborative effort between subsidiaries and headquarters to establish universal standards and permissible local variations, to make key allocational decisions on new products, new plants, new laboratories. The international management team includes the affiliate heads.

Subsidiary managers must ask: "Where in the world can I get the help to serve my customers best in this country?" "Where in the world can I export products developed in this country—products which meet worldwide standards as opposed to purely local standards?"

Geocentrism, furthermore, requires a reward system for subsidiary managers which motivates them to work for worldwide objectives, not just to defend country objectives. In firms where geocentrism prevails, it is not uncommon to hear a subsidiary manager say, "While I am paid to defend our interests in this country and to get the best resources for this affiliate, I must still ask myself the question 'Where in the world (instead of where in my country) should we build this plant?'" This approach is still rare today.

In contrast to the ethnocentric and polycentric patterns, communication is encouraged among subsidiaries in geocentric-oriented firms. "It is your duty to help us solve problems anywhere in the world," one chief executive continually reminds the heads of his company's affiliates. (See Table 1.)

The geocentric firm identifies with local company needs. "We aim not to be just a good local company but the best local company in terms of the quality of management and the worldwide (not local) standards we establish in domestic and export production." "If we were only as good as local companies, we would deserve to be nationalized."

The geocentric personnel policy is based on the belief that we should bring in the best man in the world regardless of his nationality. His passport should not be the criterion for promotion.

The EPG Profile

Executives can draw their firm's profile in ethnocentric (E), polycentric (P) and geocentric (G) dimensions. They are called EPG profiles. The degree of ethnocentrism, polycentrism and geocentrism by product, function and geography can be established. Typically R&D often turns out to be more geocentric (truth is universal, perhaps) and less ethnocentric than finance. Financial managers are likely to see their decisions as ethnocentric. The marketing function is more polycentric, particularly in the advanced economies and in the larger affiliate markets.

The tendency toward ethnocentrism in relations with subsidiaries in the developing countries is marked. Polycentric attitudes develop in consumer goods divisions, and ethnocentrism appears to be greater in industrial product divisions. The agreement is almost unanimous in both U.S.- and European-based international firms that their companies are at various stages on a route toward geocentrism but none has reached this state of affairs. Their executives would agree, however, that:

1. A description of their firms as multinational obscures more than it illuminates the state of affairs;
2. The EPG mix, once defined, is a more precise way to describe the point they have reached;

3. The present profile is not static but a landmark along a difficult road to genuine geocentrism;
4. There are forces both to change and to maintain the present attitudinal "mix," some of which are under their control.

Forces Toward and Against

What are the forces that determine the EPG mix of a firm? "You must think of the struggle toward functioning as a worldwide firm as just a beginning—a few steps forward and a step backward," a chief executive puts it. "It is a painful process, and every firm is different."

Executives of some of the world's largest multinational firms have been able to identify a series of external and internal factors that contribute to or hinder the growth of geocentric attitudes and decisions. Table 2 summarizes the factors most frequently mentioned by over 500 executives from at least 17 countries and 20 firms.

From the external environmental side, the growing world markets, the increase in availability of managerial and technological know-how in different countries, global competition and international customers' advances in telecommunications, regional political and economic communities are positive factors, as is the host country's desire to increase its balance-of-payments surplus through the location of export-oriented subsidiaries of international firms within its borders.

In different firms, senior executives see in various degrees these positive factors toward geocentrism: top management's increasing desire to use human and material resources optimally, the observed lowering of morale after decades of ethnocentric practices, the evidence of waste and duplication under polycentric thinking, the increased awareness and respect for good men of other than the home nationality, and, most importantly, top management's own commitment to building a geocentric firm as evidenced in policies, practices and procedures.

The obstacles toward geocentrism from the environment stem largely from the rising political and economic nationalism in the world today, the suspicions of political leaders of the aims and increasing

Table 2   International Executives' View of Forces and Obstacles towards Geocentrism in Their Firms

Forces towards Geocentrism		Obstacles towards Geocentrism	
Environmental	**Intra-Organizational**	**Environmental**	**Intra-Organizational**
1. Technological and managerial know-how increasing in availability in different countries	1. Desire to use human versus material resources optimally	1. Economic nationalism in host and home countries	1. Management inexperience in overseas markets
2. International customers	2. Observed lowering of morale in affiliates of an ethnocentric company	2. Political nationalism in host and home countries	2. Nation-centered reward and punishment structure
3. Local customers' demand for best product at fair price	3. Evidence of waste and duplication in polycentrism	3. Military secrecy associated with research in home country	3. Mutual distrust between home-country people and foreign executives
4. Host country's desire to increase balance of payments	4. Increasing awareness and respect for good people of other than home nationality	4. Distrust of big international firms by host-country political leaders	4. Resistance to letting foreigners into the power structure
5. Growing world markets	5. Risk diversification in having a worldwide production and distribution system	5. Lack of international monetary system	5. Anticipated costs and risks of geocentrism
6. Global competition among international firms for scarce human and material resources	6. Need for recruitment of good people on a worldwide basis	6. Growing differences between the rich and poor countries	6. Nationalistic tendencies in staff
7. Major advances in integration of international transport and telecommunications	7. Need for worldwide information system	7. Host-country belief that home countries get disproportionate benefits of international firms' profits	7. Increasing immobility of staff
8. Regional supranational economic and political communities	8. Worldwide appeal products	8. Home-country political leaders' attempts to control firm's policy	8. Linguistic problems and different cultural backgrounds
	9. Senior management's long-term commitment to geocentrism as related to survival and growth		9. Centralization tendencies in headquarters

power of the multinational firm. On the internal side, the obstacles cited most frequently in U.S.-based multinational firms were management's inexperience in overseas markets, mutual distrust between home-country people and foreign executives, the resistance to participation by foreigners in the power structure at headquarters, the increasing difficulty of getting good men overseas to move, nationalistic tendencies in staff, and linguistic and other communication difficulties of a cultural nature.

Any given firm is seen as moving toward geocentrism at a rate determined by its capacities to build on the positive internal factors over which it has control and to change the negative internal factors which are controllable. In some firms the geocentric goal is openly discussed among executives of different nationalities and from different subsidiaries as well as headquarters. There is a consequent improvement in the climate of trust and acceptance of each other's views.

Programs are instituted to assure greater experience in foreign markets, task forces of executives are upgraded, and international careers for executives of all nationalities are being designed.

But the seriousness of the obstacles cannot be underestimated. A world of rising nationalism is hardly a precondition for geocentrism; and overcoming distrust of foreigners even within one's own firm is not accomplished in a short span of time. The route to pervasive geocentric thinking is long and tortuous.

Costs, Risks, Payoffs

What conclusions will executives from multinational firms draw from the balance sheet of advantages and disadvantages of maintaining one's present state of ethnocentrism, polycentrism or geocentrism? Not too surprisingly, the costs and risks of ethnocentrism are seen to out-balance the payoffs in the long run. The costs of ethnocentrism are ineffective planning because of a lack of good feedback, the departure of the best men in the subsidiaries, fewer innovations, and an inability to build a high calibre local organization. The risks are political and

social repercussions and a less flexible response to local changes.

The payoffs of ethnocentrism are real enough in the short term, they say. Organization is simpler. There is a higher rate of communication of knowhow from headquarters to new markets. There is more control over appointments to senior posts in subsidiaries.

Polycentrism's costs are waste due to duplication, to decisions to make products for local use but which could be universal, and to inefficient use of home-country experience. The risks include an excessive regard for local traditions and local growth at the expense of global growth. The main advantages are an intense exploitation of local markets, better sales since local management is often better informed, more local initiative for new products, more host-government support, and good local managers with high morale.

Geocentrism's costs are largely related to communication and travel expenses, educational costs at all levels, time spent in decision making because consensus seeking among more people is required, and an international headquarters bureaucracy. Risks include those due to too wide a distribution of power, personnel problems and those of reentry of international executives. The payoffs are a more powerful total company throughout, a better quality of products and service, worldwide utilization of best resources, improvement of local company management, a greater sense of commitment to worldwide objectives, and last, but not least, more profit.

Jacques Maisonrouge, the French-born president of IBM World Trade, understands the geocentric concept and its benefits. He wrote recently:

> "The first step to a geocentric organization is when a corporation, faced with the choice of whether to grow and expand or decline, realizes the need to mobilize its resources on a world scale. It will sooner or later have to face the issue that the home country does not have a monopoly of either men or ideas. . . .
>
> "I strongly believe that the future belongs to geocentric companies. . . . What is of fundamental importance is the attitude of the company's top management. If it is dedicated to 'geocentrism,' good international management will be possible. If not, the

best men of different nations will soon understand that they do not belong to the 'race des seigneurs' and will leave the business."[3]

Geocentrism is not inevitable in any given firm. Some companies have experienced a "regression" to ethnocentrism after trying a long period of polycentrism, of letting subsidiaries do it "their way." The local directors built little empires and did not train successors from their own country. Headquarters had to send home-country nationals to take over. A period of home-country thinking took over.

There appears to be evidence of a need for evolutionary movement from ethnocentrism to polycentrism to geocentrism. The polycentric stage is likened to an adolescent protest period during which subsidiary managers gain their confidence as equals by fighting headquarters and proving "their manhood," after a long period of being under headquarters' ethnocentric thumb.

"It is hard to move from a period of headquarters domination to a worldwide management team quickly. A period of letting affiliates make mistakes may be necessary," said one executive.

Window Dressing

In the rush toward appearing geocentric, many U.S. firms have found it necessary to emphasize progress by appointing one or two non-nationals to senior posts—even on occasion to headquarters. The foreigner is often effectively counteracted by the number of nationals around him, and his influence is really small. Tokenism does have some positive effects, but it does not mean geocentrism has arrived.

Window dressing is also a temptation. Here an attempt is made to demonstrate influence by appointing a number of incompetent "foreigners" to key positions. The results are not impressive for either the individuals or the company.

Too often what is called "the multinational view" is really a screen for ethnocentrism. Foreign affiliate managers must, in order to succeed, take

[3]Jacques Maisonrouge, "The Education of International Managers," *Quarterly Journal of AIESEC International*, February 1967.

on the traits and behavior of the ruling nationality. In short, in a U.S.-owned firm the foreigner must "Americanize"—not only in attitude but in dress and speech—in order to be accepted.

Tokenism and window dressing are transitional episodes where aspirations toward multinationalism outstrip present attitudes and resources. The fault does not lie only with the enterprise. The human demands of ethnocentrism are great.

A Geocentric Man—?

The geocentric enterprise depends on having an adequate supply of men who are geocentrically oriented. It would be a mistake to underestimate the human stresses which a geocentric career creates. Moving where the company needs an executive involves major adjustments for families, wives and children. The sacrifices are often great and, for some families, outweigh the rewards forthcoming—at least in personal terms. Many executives find it difficult to learn new languages and overcome their cultural superiority complexes, national pride and discomfort with foreigners. Furthermore, international careers can be hazardous when ethnocentrism prevails at headquarters. "It is easy to get lost in the world of the subsidiaries and to be 'out of sight, out of mind' when promotions come up at headquarters," as one executive expressed it following a visit to headquarters after five years overseas. To his disappointment, he knew few senior executives. And fewer knew him!

The economic rewards, the challenge of new countries, the personal and professional development that comes from working in a variety of countries and cultures are surely incentives, but companies have not solved by any means the human costs of international mobility to executives and their families.

A firm's multinationality may be judged by the pervasiveness with which executives think geocentrically—by function, marketing, finance, production, R&D, etc., by product division and by country. The takeoff to geocentrism may begin with executives in one function, say marketing, seeking to find a truly worldwide product line. Only when this worldwide attitude extends throughout the firm, in headquarters and subsidiaries, can executives feel that it is becoming genuinely geocentric.

But no single yardstick, such as the number of foreign nationals in key positions, is sufficient to establish a firm's multinationality. The multinational firm's route to geocentrism is still long because political and economic nationalism is on the rise, and, more importantly, since within the firm ethnocentrism and polycentrism are not easy to overcome. Building trust between persons of different nationality is a central obstacle. Indeed, if we are to judge men, as Paul Weiss put it, "by the kind of world they are trying to build," the senior executives engaged in building the geocentric enterprise could well be the most important social architects of the last third of the twentieth century. For the institution they are trying to erect promises a greater universal sharing of wealth and a consequent control of the explosive centrifugal tendencies of our evolving world community.

The geocentric enterprise offers an institutional and supranational framework which could conceivably make war less likely, on the assumption that bombing customers, suppliers and employees is in nobody's interest. The difficulty of the task is thus matched by its worthwhileness. A clearer image of the features of genuine geocentricity is thus indispensable both as a guideline and as an inviting prospect.

Understanding the International Context:
Responding to Conflicting Environmental Forces

This chapter shifts our focus from the internal forces that drive companies to expand to the larger, external, international environment in which they must operate. In particular, we consider three sets of macro forces that drive, constrain, and shape the industries in which entities compete globally. First, we examine the pressures—mostly economic—that drive companies in many industries to integrate and coordinate their activities across national boundaries to capture scale economies or other sources of competitive advantage. Second, we explore the forces—often social and political—that shape other industries and examine how they can drive multinational enterprises (MNEs) to disaggregate their operations and activities to respond to national, regional, and local needs and demands. And third, we examine how, in an information-based, knowledge-intensive economy, players in a growing number of industries must adapt to opportunities or threats wherever they occur in the world by developing innovative responses and initiatives that they diffuse rapidly and globally to capture a knowledge-based competitive advantage.

Continual change in the international business environment has always characterized the task facing MNE managers, and the situation in the second decade of the 21st century is no different. Important shifts in political, social, economic, and technological forces have combined to create management challenges for today's MNEs that differ fundamentally from those facing companies just a couple of decades ago. Yet despite intense study by academics, consultants, and practicing managers, both the nature of the various external forces and their strategic and organizational implications are still widely disputed.

When Professor Theodore Levitt's classic *Harvard Business Review* article, "The Globalization of Markets," was first published, his ideas provoked widespread debate. In Levitt's view, technological, social, and economic trends were combining to create a unified world marketplace that was driving companies to develop globally standardized products that would enable them to capture global economies. Critics, however, claimed that Levitt presented only one side of the story. They suggested that, like many managers, he had become so focused on the forces for globalization that he was blind to their limitations and equally powerful countervailing forces.

The ensuing debate helped better define the diverse, changeable, and often contradictory forces that reshaped so many industries. In this chapter, we summarize a few of the most powerful of these environmental forces, trace their historical evolution, and suggest how they have led collectively to a new and complex set of challenges that require managers of MNEs to respond to three simultaneous yet often conflicting sets of external demands: the need for cross-market integration, national responsiveness, and worldwide innovation and learning.

Forces for Global Integration and Coordination

The phenomenon of globalization in certain industries, as described by Levitt, was not a sudden or discontinuous development. It was simply the latest round of change brought about by economic, technological, and competitive factors that, 100 years earlier, had transformed the structures of many industries from regional to national in scope. Economies of scale, economies of scope, and differences in the availability and cost of productive resources were the three principal economic forces that drove this process of structural transformation of businesses. Globalization was simply the latest stage of this long transformation.[1] The impact of these forces on MNE strategy had been facilitated by the increasingly liberal trading environment of the 1980s, 1990s, and 2000s. We will now examine these forces of change in more detail.

Forces of Change: Scale, Scope, Factor Costs, and Free Trade

The Industrial Revolution created pressures for much larger plants that could capture the benefits of the *economies of scale* offered by the new technologies that it spawned. These pressures led to the combining of cheap and abundant energy, good transportation networks, and new production technologies to restructure capital-intensive industries. For the first time, companies combined intermediate processes into single plants and developed large-batch or continuous-process technologies to achieve low-cost volume production.

As those pressures continued into the twentieth century, the level of scale intensity often increased further. In industries such as fine chemicals, automobiles, airframes, electronics, and oil refining, production at scale-economy volumes often exceeded the sales levels that individual companies could achieve in all but the largest nations, pushing them to seek markets abroad. Even in industries in which the leading companies could retain a large enough share of their domestic markets to achieve scale economies without exports, those on the next rung were forced to seek markets outside their home countries if they were to remain competitive.

In less capital-intensive industries, companies that were largely unaffected by scale economies often were transformed by the opportunities for *economies of scope* that were opened by more efficient, worldwide communication and transportation networks.

One classic example of how such economies could be exploited internationally was provided by trading companies that handled consumer goods. By exporting the products of many companies, they achieved a greater volume and lower per-unit cost than any narrow-line manufacturer could in marketing and distributing its own products abroad.

In many industries, MNEs discovered that there were opportunities to exploit both scale and scope economies. For example, consumer electronics companies such as Panasonic (at the time known as Matsushita) derived scale advantages from their highly

---

[1]For a more detailed analysis of these environmental forces, see Alfred D. Chandler Jr., "The Evolution of the Modern Global Corporation," in *Competition in Global Industries,* ed. Michael Porter (Boston: Harvard Business School Press, 1986), pp. 405–48. For those interested in an even more detailed exposition, Chandler's book, *Scale and Scope* (Cambridge, MA: Harvard University Press, 1990) will prove compelling reading.

specialized plants producing TVs, video recorders, and DVD players, and scope advantages through their marketing and sales networks that offered service, repair, and credit for a broad range of consumer electronics.

With changes in technology and markets came the requirement for access to new resources at the best possible prices, making differences in *factor costs* a powerful driver of globalization. Often no home-country key inputs were available to companies wishing to expand into new industry segments. European petroleum companies, for example, explored the Middle East because of Europe's limited domestic crude oil sources. Other companies went overseas in search of bauxite from which to produce aluminum, rubber to produce tires for a growing automobile industry, or tea to be consumed by an expanding middle class.

Labor-intensive industries such as textiles, apparel, and shoes turned to international markets as a source of cheap labor. The increased costs of transportation and logistics management were more than offset by the much-lower production costs. However, companies usually found that once people in these other countries became educated, the cheap labor rapidly got more expensive. Indeed, the typical life cycle of a country as a source of cheap labor for an industry today is only about five years. Therefore, companies seeking this source of competitive advantage often chased cheap labor from southern Europe to Central America to the Far East to Eastern Europe.

Whereas the economics of scale and scope and the differences in factor costs between countries provided the initial motivation for global coordination, the *liberalization of world trade* agreements became an equally powerful source of change in the past half-century. Beginning with the formation of the General Agreement on Tariffs and Trade (GATT) in 1945 and moving through various rounds of trade talks, the creation of regional free trade agreements such as the European Union (E.U.) and North American Free Trade Agreement (NAFTA), and the formation of the World Trade Organization (WTO), the dominant trend has been toward the reduction of barriers to international trade. While few new multicountry trading agreements have been reached during the 2000s, there has been a dramatic rise in the number of bilateral agreements involving the emerging markets in Asia and South America. The result is that the international trading environment of the 21st century is less restricted than in recent decades, which has enabled MNEs to realize most of the potential economic benefits that arise from global coordination.

This opening of world markets has coincided with the growing opportunities presented by the high economic growth rates of emerging markets, which are attracting a new round of MNE investment. Once attracted to countries like China and India as sources of low-cost labor, MNEs now recognize them as key sources of growth in coming decades. Today, the strategic role of developing countries has radically changed for many MNEs. Not only have they played a key role in the reconfiguration of their worldwide assets as companies continue to seek access to low-cost factors of production, they are now becoming important sources of revenue growth and drivers of global scale efficiency.

Driving an Expanding Spiral of Globalization

During the 1970s and 1980s, these forces began to globalize the structure and competitive characteristics of a variety of industries. In some, the change was driven by a major technological innovation that forced a fundamental realignment of industry economics.

For example, in the 1960s, transistors and integrated circuits revolutionized the design and production of radios, televisions, and other consumer electronics and drove the minimum efficient scale of production beyond the demand of most single markets.

Later, advances in semiconductor technology led to the boom in the PC industry, and innovations in wireless technology resulted in the creation of the mobile phone industry. Advances in both of these latter technologies, triggered by convergence of the telecommunications and consumer electronics industry, resulted in the smart phone. Today, the growing dominance of digital media for music and books and the rapid growth of social media are combining to transform the publishing and music industries, as well as creating an online retail distribution industry that is capable of low-cost, seamless global distribution.

In market terms, the spread of global forces expanded from businesses in which the global standardization of products was relatively easy (e.g., watches, cameras) to others in which consumers' preferences and habits converged only slowly (e.g., automobiles, appliances). Again, major external discontinuities often facilitated the change process, as in the case of global oil price increases in 2005, which triggered a worldwide demand for smaller, more fuel-efficient, and/or alternative-energy cars. An entirely different event initiated another major restructuring of the worldwide auto industry when the 2008 financial crisis saw the bankruptcy of General Motors (GM). Leaner and more efficient automakers, such as Hyundai Motors, took advantage of the ensuing industry shakeup to increase the U.S. market share of its Hyundai and Kia product lines from 5.2% in 2008 to 9% in 2011.

Global Competitors as Change Agents

As the previous section highlighted, many industries were driven to become more globally integrated primarily through external forces of change. But other industries less affected by such external imperatives were transformed mainly through the internal restructuring efforts of competitors who recognized that by so doing, they could gain significant competitive advantage. This led to a further wave of globalization as companies in industries as diverse as automobiles, office equipment, industrial bearings, construction equipment, and machine tools rolled out initiatives that involved rationalizing their product lines, standardizing parts design, and specializing manufacturing operations. By capturing scale economies beyond national markets, these company-initiated actions led to the global transformation of their industries.

Competitors have even been successful in changing the structure of industries in which national tastes or behaviors traditionally varied widely around the world and were not susceptible to global convergence. Food tastes and eating habits were long thought to be the most culture-bound of all consumer behaviors. Yet, companies like McDonald's, Coca-Cola, and Starbucks have shown that, in Eastern and Western countries alike, even these culturally linked preferences can be changed, with the result that the restaurant industry around the world has been transformed.

Other companies in traditionally local businesses have also begun to exploit the opportunities for capturing economies beyond their national borders. Rather than responding to the enduring differences in consumer practices and market structures across

European countries, many large branded packaged goods companies such as Procter and Gamble (P&G) and Unilever have recognized that there were potential economies that could transform traditionally national businesses like soap and detergent manufacturing. By standardizing product formulations, rationalizing package sizes, and printing multilingual labels, they have been able to restructure and specialize their nationally dominated plant configurations and achieve substantial scale economies, giving them significant advantages over purely local competitors.

Even labor-intensive local industries such as office cleaning and catering are not immune to the forces of globalization. For example, the Danish cleaning services company ISS has built a successful international business by transferring practices and know-how across countries, thereby offering consistent, high-quality service to its international customers.

But beyond these initiatives to capture global scale advantages, there has been another competitor-driven force that has accelerated the global integration of many industries. In the closing decades of the 20th century, there emerged a new competitive strategy, which could be used only by companies that implemented a coordinated global strategy by managing their worldwide operations as interdependent units. Unlike the traditional multinational strategic approach based on the assumption that each national market was unique and independent of the others, these global competitive games assumed that a company's competitive position in all markets was linked, and that funds generated in one market could be used to subsidize its position in another. While strategists termed this approach *global chess* and economists referred to it as *cross-subsidization of markets,* politicians simply labeled it "dumping."

Whereas the classic exponents of this strategy were several Japanese companies that used the profit sanctuary of a protected home market to subsidize their unprofitable expansions abroad in the 1980s, many others soon learned to play global chess. For example, British Airways grew in part because its dominant position at Heathrow Airport enabled it to make large profits on its long-haul routes (particularly the trans-Atlantic route) and essentially subsidize its lower-margin or unprofitable U.K. and European business. In turn, it could fend off new entrants in Europe by pushing its prices down there, while not putting its most profitable routes at risk. As a result, existing competitors such as British Midland suffered because they lacked access to the lucrative Heathrow-U.S. routes.

Although few challenged the existence or growing influence of these diverse globalizing forces that were transforming the nature of competition worldwide, some questioned the unidimensionality of their influence and the universality of their strategic implications. They took issue, for example, with Levitt's suggestions that "the world's needs and desires have been irrevocably homogenized," that "no one is exempt and nothing can stop the process," and that "the commonality of preference leads inescapably to the standardization of products, manufacturing, and the institution of trade and commerce." Critics argued that although these might indeed be long-term trends in many industries, there were important short- and medium-term impediments and countertrends that had to be taken into account if companies were to operate successfully in an international economy that jolts along—*perhaps* eventually toward Levitt's "global village," but perhaps not.

▨ Forces for Local Differentiation and Responsiveness

There are many different stories of multinational companies making major blunders in transferring their successful products or ideas from their home countries to foreign markets. GM is reported to have faced difficulties in selling the popular Chevrolet Nova in Mexico, where the product name sounded like "no va," meaning "does not go" in Spanish.[2] Similarly, when managers began investigating why the advertising campaign built around the highly successful "Come alive with Pepsi" theme was not having the expected impact in Thailand, they discovered that the Thai copy translation read more like "Come out of the grave with Pepsi." Although these and other such cases have been widely cited, they represent extreme examples of an important strategic task facing managers of all MNEs: how to sense, respond to, and even exploit the differences in the environments of the many different countries in which their company operates.

National environments differ on many dimensions. For example, there are clear differences in the per-capita gross national product (GNP) or the industry-specific technological capabilities of Japan, Australia, Brazil, and Poland. They also differ in terms of political systems, government regulations, social norms, and the cultural values of their people. It is these differences that require managers to be sensitive and responsive to national, social, economic, and political characteristics of the host countries in which they operate.

Far from being overshadowed by the pressures of globalization, the impact of these localizing forces have been felt with increasing intensity and urgency throughout recent decades. Even companies that had been most committed to global integration began to change. In the early 1990s, many Japanese companies that had ridden the wave of globalization so successfully began to feel the strong need to become much more sensitive to host-country economic and political forces. This shift led to a wave of investment abroad, as Japanese companies sought to become closer to their export markets and more responsive to host governments.

By the millennium, many North American and European companies also realized that they had pushed the logic of globalization too far and that a reconnection with the local environments in which they were doing business was necessary. For example, Coca-Cola's incoming CEO, Douglas Daft, explained his company's shift in policy in the *Financial Times*: "As the 1990s were drawing to a close, the world had changed course, and Coca-Cola had not. We were operating as a big, slow, insulated, sometimes even insensitive 'global' company; and we were doing it in an era when nimbleness, speed, transparency, and local sensitivity had become absolutely essential."

In an effort to catch up with Unilever's leading market share in developing countries, P&G has begun a major effort to emulate its old competitor's ability to adapt its products to local markets. For example, in India, it has introduced Guard, a very inexpensive razor that comes with a small comb in front of the blade to make the local practice of weekly shaving more comfortable.

▨ [2] For this and many other such examples of international marketing problems, see David A. Ricks, *Blunders in International Business*, 4th ed. (Cornwall: Blackwell Publishing, 2006).

Cultural Differences

A large body of academic research provides strong evidence that nationality plays an important and enduring role in shaping the assumptions, beliefs, and values of individuals. The most celebrated work describing and categorizing these differences in the orientations and values of people in different countries is Geert Hofstede's classic research. Hofstede describes national cultural differences along four key dimensions: power distance, uncertainty avoidance, individualism, and "masculinity."[3] The study demonstrates how distinct cultural differences across countries result in wide variations in social norms and individual behavior (e.g., the Japanese respect for elders, the American responsiveness to time pressure) and is reflected in the effectiveness of different organizational forms (e.g., the widespread French difficulty with the dual-reporting relationships of a matrix organization) and management systems (e.g., the Swedes' egalitarian culture, which leads them to prefer flatter organizations and smaller wage differentials). More recently, the GLOBE Study[4] has refined Hofstede's landmark work and developed new measures of organizational culture and leadership, and the division of societies into cultural clusters.

However, cultural differences are also reflected in nationally differentiated consumption patterns, including the way people dress or the foods they prefer. Take the example of tea as a beverage consumed around the globe. The British typically drink their tea hot and diluted with milk, whereas Americans often consume it as a summer drink served over ice, and Saudi Arabians drink theirs as a thick, hot, heavily sweetened brew. To succeed in a world of such diversity, companies often must modify their quest for global efficiency through standardization and find ways to respond to the needs and opportunities created by cultural differences. So Unilever produces 20 separate brands of black tea, each blended to meet the specific tastes of local consumers around the world. It adapted its Lipton brand to offer a canned iced tea in the United States, and sells Lipton Cold Brew tea bags in markets around the world. Even more ambitious is the Starbucks strategy of serving green tea lattes in its Chinese outlets in a bid to get that traditionally tea-drinking nation hooked on coffee eventually.

Government Demands

Inasmuch as cultural differences among countries have been an important localizing force, the diverse demands and expectations of home and host governments have perhaps been the most severe constraint to the global strategies of many MNEs. Traditionally, the interactions between companies and host governments have had many attributes of classic love-hate relationships.

The "love" of this equation was built on the benefits that each could bring to the other. To the host government, the MNE represented an important source of funds,

[3]For a more detailed exposition, see Hofstede's book *Culture's Consequences,* 2d ed. (Beverly Hills, CA: Sage Publications, 2001). For managerial implications of such differences in national culture, see also Nancy J. Adler and A. Gundersen, *International Dimensions of Organizational Behavior,* 5th ed. (Mason, Ohio: Thomson South-Western, 2008), and Fons Trompenaars and Charles Hampden-Turner, *Riding the Waves of Culture* (London: Nicholas Brealey Publishing, 1997).
[4]*Culture, Leadership, and Organizations: The Globe Study of 62 Societies*, eds. R. J. House, P. J. Hanges, M. Javiden, P. W. Dorfman, and V. Gupta (Thousand Oaks, California: Sage, 2004).

technology, and expertise that could help further national priorities, such as regional development, employment, import substitution, and export promotion. To the MNE, the host government represented the key to local market or resource access, which provided new opportunities for profit, growth, and improvement of its competitive position.

The "hate" side of the relationship—more often emerging as frustration rather than outright antagonism—arose from the differences in the motivations and objectives of the two partners. To be effective global competitors, MNEs sought three important operating objectives: unrestricted access to resources and markets throughout the world; the freedom to integrate manufacturing and other operations across national boundaries; and the unimpeded right to coordinate and control all aspects of the company on a worldwide basis. The host government, in contrast, sought to develop an economy that could survive and prosper in a competitive international environment. At times, this objective led to the designation of another company—perhaps a "national champion"—as its standard bearer in the specific industry, bringing it into direct conflict with the MNE.

This conflict is particularly visible in the international airline business, in which flag-carrying companies—from struggling developing country airlines such as Air Malawi or Pakistan International Airlines to Gulf State powerhouses like Emirates Airlines, Etihad Airways, Qatar Airways, or Gulf Air—compete only after receiving substantial government subsidies. But it also has been a thorny issue among their biggest suppliers, with Boeing complaining to the WTO that Airbus is violating free trade agreements through the support it receives from various European governments.

Even when the host government does not have such a national champion and is willing to permit and even support an MNE's operations within its boundaries, it usually does so only at a price. Although both parties might be partners in the search for global competitiveness, the MNE typically tried to achieve that objective within its global system, whereas the host government strove to capture it within its national boundaries, thereby leading to conflict and mutual resentment.

The potential for conflict between the host government and the MNE arose not only from economic but also from social, political, and cultural issues. MNE operations often cause social disruption in the host country through rural exodus, rising consumerism, rejection of indigenous values, or a breakdown of traditional community structures.

Similarly, even without the maliciousness of MNEs that, in previous decades, blatantly tried to manipulate host government structures or policies (e.g., ITT's attempt to overthrow the Salvador Allende government in Chile), MNEs can still represent a political threat because of their size, power, and influence, particularly in developing economies.

Because of these differences in objectives and motivations, MNE–host government relationships are often seen as a zero-sum game, in which the outcome depends on the balance between the government's power (arising from its control over local market access and competition among different MNEs for that access) and the MNE's power (arising from its financial, technological, and managerial resources and the competition among national governments for those resources).

If, in the 1960s, the multinational companies had been able to hold "sovereignty at bay,"[5] by the 1980s, the balance had tipped in the other direction. In an effort to stem the

---

[5]Raymond Vernon, *Sovereignty at Bay* (New York: Basic Books, 1971).

flood of imports, many countries began bending or sidestepping trade agreements signed in previous years. By the early 1980s, even the U.S. government, traditionally one of the strongest advocates of free trade, began to negotiate a series of orderly marketing agreements and voluntary restraints on Japanese exports, while threats of sanctions were debated with increasing emotion in legislative chambers around the globe. And countries became more sophisticated in the demands that they placed on inward-investing MNEs. Rather than allowing superficial investment in so-called screwdriver plants that provided only limited, low-skill employment, governments began to specify the levels of local content, technology transfer, and a variety of other conditions, from re-export commitment to plant location requirements.

In the 1990s, however, the power of national governments was once again on the wane. The success of countries such as Ireland and Singapore in driving their economic development through foreign investment led many other countries—both developed and developing—to launch aggressive inward investment policies of their own.

This increased demand for investment allowed MNEs to play countries off one another and, in many cases, to extract a high price from the host country. For example, according to *The Economist,* the incentives paid by Alabama to Mercedes to establish its 1993 auto plant there cost the state $167,000 per direct employee.

In the first years of the new millennium, the once-troublesome issue of MNE-country bargaining power evolved into a relatively efficient market system for inward investment, at least in the developed world. However, the developing world was a rather different story, with MNEs continuing to be embroiled in political disputes, such as the 1995 hanging of environmental activist Ken Saro-Wiwa by the Nigerian government because of his opposition to what he saw as Shell's exploitation of his people's land. In addition, MNEs have regularly attracted the brunt of criticism from so-called antiglobalization protestors during WTO meetings. The antiglobalization movement included a diverse mix of groups with different agendas, but united in their belief that the increasing liberalization of trade through the WTO was being pursued for the benefit of MNEs and at the expense of people and companies in less developed parts of the world.

Although this movement did not have a coherent set of policy proposals of its own, it provided a salutary reminder to policymakers and the executives managing MNEs that the globalization of business remains a contentious issue. The rewards are not spread evenly, and for many people in many parts of the world, the process of globalization often makes things worse before it makes them better. This forced MNEs to rethink their more contentious policies and encouraged them to articulate the benefits that they bring to less developed countries. By 2012, more than 8,500 companies from 130 countries had signed the U.N. Global Compact, committing themselves to aligning their operations and strategies with 10 aspirational principles in the areas of human rights, labor, environment, and anti-corruption.

A new trend is emerging that is set to alter the MNE-government relationship during the 2010s. Cash-rich governments and their nationally owned corporations in emerging markets, particularly China, are looking to invest in foreign resources, with such investments often packaged as part of a government-to-government diplomatic relationship. Not only are the government investors looking to earn returns on investment, but perhaps more importantly, they are securing the natural resources to ensure the future economic security of their own countries, and particularly the need to continue to grow and prosper. This policy-based partnership of governments and national corporations engaging in the global business arena via such mechanisms as sovereign wealth funds is significantly different from the "national champion" strategy of an earlier era, and it is certain to have important global competitive implications over the next decades.

Growing Pressures for Localization

Although there is no doubt that the increasing frequency of world travel and the ease with which communication linkages occur across the globe have done a great deal to reduce the effects of national consumer differences, it would be naïve to believe that worldwide tastes, habits, and preferences have become anywhere near homogenous. One need only look at the breakfast buffet items on display at any major hotel in Beijing. These hotels need to appeal to large groups of consumers from within China, from North America, from Europe, from Japan, and elsewhere. So separate breakfast stations will provide steamed breads and noodles, bacon and eggs, cold cuts and cheese, and miso soup.

Although many companies have succeeded in appealing to—and accelerating—convergence worldwide, even the trend toward standardized products that are designed to appeal to a lowest common denominator of consumer demand has a flip side. In industry after industry, a large group of consumers has emerged to reject the homogenized product design and performance of standardized global products.

By reasserting traditional preferences for more differentiated products, they have created openings—often very profitable ones—for companies willing to respond to, and even expand, the need for products and services that are more responsive to those needs.

When the U.S.-based office supply retail chain Office Depot issued a request of its vendors for refrigerators that could be locked for improved security in U.S. offices and dormitories, Haier, a Chinese appliance company, was the one willing to create such a customized product.[6] The fact that such an innovation originated in a firm from China underscores how localization solutions may appear from previously unlikely locales. Increasingly, it is MNEs from emerging markets that seem best equipped to compete in other emerging markets.

Other consumer and market trends are emerging to counterbalance the forces of global standardization of products. In an increasing number of markets, from telecommunications to office equipment to consumer electronics, consumers are not so much buying individual products as selecting systems. For example, with advances in wireless, 3G, and other Internet technologies, the television is becoming part of a home entertainment and information network, connected through a home computer, smart phone, or gaming system, to an online databank of music, video, text, and social media. This transformation is forcing companies to adapt their standard hardware-oriented products to more flexible and locally differentiated systems that consist of hardware plus software plus services. In such an environment, the competitive edge lies less with the company that has the most scale-efficient global production capability and more with the one that is sensitive and

---

[6]For more detail, see Peter J. Williamson and Ming Zeng, *Dragons at Your Door: How Chinese Cost Innovation Is Disrupting Global Competition* (Boston: Harvard Business School Press, 2007).

responsive to local requirements and able to develop the software and services. Unsurprisingly, most of the profit lies in the downstream parts of the value chain.

In addition to such barriers to global standardization, other important impediments exist. Although the benefits of scale economies obviously must outweigh the additional costs of supplying markets from a central point, companies often ignore that those costs consist of more than just freight charges. In particular, the administrative costs of coordination and scheduling worldwide demand through global-scale plants usually is quite significant and must be taken into account. For some products, lead times are so short or market service requirements so high that these scale economies may well be offset by other such costs.

More significantly, developments in computer-aided design and manufacturing, robotics, and other advanced production technologies have made the concept of flexible manufacturing a viable reality. Companies that previously had to produce tens or hundreds of thousands of standardized printed circuit boards (PCBs) in a central, global-scale plant now can achieve the minimum efficient scale in smaller, distributed, national plants closer to their customers. Flexible manufacturing technologies mean that there is little difference in unit cost between making 1,000 or 100,000 PCBs. When linked to the consumer's growing disenchantment with homogenized global products, this technology appears to offer multinational companies an important tool that will enable them to respond to localized consumer preferences and national political constraints without compromising their economic efficiency.

The pressure for localization can extend down to the regional or city level in some countries. The growth opportunities in many national markets are not evenly distributed throughout each country. As a result, there is considerable intra-country variance in infrastructure development, industry structure, demographics, and consumer characteristics among cities or clusters of cities. For example, McKinsey segmented China into "22 city clusters, each homogenous enough to be considered one market for strategic decision making. Prioritizing several clusters or sequencing the order in which they are targeted can help a company boost the effectiveness of its distribution networks, supply chains, sales forces, and media and marketing strategies."[7] Similarly, when Interbrew (now part of Anheuser-Busch In-Bev) was establishing Stella Artois beer as a global brand, their efforts were concentrated on 20 major cities around the world.

Forces for Worldwide Innovation and Learning

The trends that we have described in this chapter have created an extremely difficult competitive environment in many industries, and only those firms that have been able to adapt to the often-conflicting forces for global coordination and national differentiation have been able to survive and prosper. But on top of these forces, another set of competitive demands has been growing rapidly around the need for fast, globally coordinated innovation. Indeed, in the emerging competitive game, and particularly in technology intensive industries, victory most often goes to the company that can harness its access to information and expertise around the globe most effectively to develop and diffuse innovative products and processes on a worldwide basis.

[7]Yuval Atsmon, Ari Kertesz, and Ireena Vittal, "Is Your Emerging-Market Strategy Local Enough?" *McKinsey Quarterly* 2 (2011) pp. 50–61.

This ability to develop worldwide innovation and learning is such a vital strategic capability for MNEs today that we will simply outline the issue here, and return to examine it in greater detail in Chapter 5.

The trends driving this shift in the competitive game in many ways derive from the globalizing and localizing forces that we described previously. The increasing cost of R&D, coupled with shortening life cycles of new technologies and the products they spawn, have combined to reinforce the need for companies to seek global volume to amortize their heavy research investments as quickly as possible. At the same time, even the most advanced technology has often diffused rapidly around the globe, particularly during the past few decades. In part, this trend has been a response to the demands, pressures, and coaxing of host governments as they bargain for increasing levels of national production and high levels of local content in the leading-edge products being sold in their markets. But the high cost of product and process development has also encouraged companies to transfer new technologies voluntarily, with licensing becoming an important source of funding, cross-licensing a means to fill technology gaps, and joint development programs and strategic alliances a strategy for rapidly building global competitive advantage.

When coupled with converging consumer preferences worldwide, this diffusion of technology has had an important effect on both the pace and locus of innovation. No longer can U.S.-based companies assume that their domestic environment provides them with the most sophisticated consumer needs and the most advanced technological capabilities, and thus the most innovative environment in the world. Today, the newest consumer trend or market need might emerge in Australia or Italy, and the latest technologies to respond to those needs may be located in South Korea or Sweden. Innovations are springing up worldwide, and companies are recognizing that they can gain competitive advantage by sensing needs in one country, responding with capabilities located in a second, and diffusing the resulting innovation to markets around the globe.

A related trend is the increasing importance of global standards in such industries as computer software, telecommunications, consumer electronics, and even consumer goods. The winners in the battle for a new standard—from software platforms to razor blade cartridges—can build and defend dominant competitive positions that can endure worldwide for decades. First-mover advantages have increased substantially and provided strong incentives for companies to focus attention not only on the internal task of rapidly creating and diffusing innovations within their own worldwide operations, but also on the external task of establishing the new product as an industry standard. Chapter 5 will examine this vital strategic issue in greater detail.

◼ Responding to the Diverse Forces Simultaneously

Trying to distill key environmental demands in large and complex industries is a hazardous venture but, at the risk of oversimplification, we can make the case that until the late 1980s, most worldwide industries presented relatively unidimensional environmental requirements. This led to the development of industries with very different characteristics—those we distinguish as global, multinational, and international industries. More recently, however, this differentiation has been eroding with important consequences for companies' strategies.

Global, Multinational, and International Industries

In some businesses, the economic forces of globalization were historically strong enough to dominate other environmental demands. For example, in the consumer electronics industry, the invention of the transistor led to decades of inexorable expansion in the benefits of scale economics: successive rounds of technological change, such as the introduction of integrated circuits and microprocessors, led to a huge increase in the minimum efficient scale of operations for television sets. In an environment of falling transportation costs, low tariffs, and increasing homogenization of national market demand, these huge-scale economies dominated the strategic tasks for managers of consumer electronics companies in the closing decades of the last century.

Such industries, in which the economic forces of globalization are dominant, we designate as *global industries*. In these businesses, success typically belongs to companies that adopt the classic *global strategies* of capitalizing on highly centralized, scale-intensive manufacturing and R&D operations and leveraging them through worldwide exports of standardized global products.

In other businesses, the localizing forces of national, cultural, social, and political differences dominate the development of industry characteristics. In laundry detergents, for example, R&D and manufacturing costs were relatively small parts of a company's total expenses, and all but the smallest markets could justify an investment in a detergent manufacturing tower and benefit from its scale economies. At the same time, sharp differences in laundry practices, perfume preferences, phosphate legislation, distribution channels, labeling requirements, and other such attributes of different national markets led to significant benefits from differentiating products and strategies on a country-by-country basis.

This differentiation is typical of what we call *multinational industries*—worldwide businesses in which the dominance of national differences in cultural, social, and political environments allow multiple national industry structures to flourish. Success in such businesses typically belongs to companies that follow *multinational strategies* of building strong and resourceful national subsidiaries that are sensitive to local market needs and opportunities and allow them to manage their local businesses by developing or adapting products and strategies to respond to the powerful localizing forces.

Finally, in some other industries, technological forces are central, and the need for companies to develop and diffuse innovations is the dominant source of competitive advantage. For example, the most critical task for manufacturers of telecommunications switching equipment has been the ability to develop and harness new technologies and exploit them worldwide. In these *international industries,* it is the ability to innovate and appropriate the benefits of those innovations in multiple national markets that differentiates the winners from the losers.

In such industries, the key to success lies in a company's ability to exploit technological forces by creating new products and to leverage the international life cycles of the product by effectively transferring technologies to overseas units. We describe this as an *international strategy*—the ability to manage the creation of new products and processes in one's home market effectively and diffuse those innovations to foreign affiliates sequentially.

Transition to Transnationality

Our portrayal of the traditional demands in some major worldwide industries is clearly oversimplified. Different tasks in the value-added chains of different businesses are subject to different levels of economic, political, cultural, and technological forces. We have described what can be called the *center of gravity* of these activities—the environmental forces that have the most significant impact on industry's strategic task demands.

By the closing years of the 20th century, however, these external demands were undergoing some important changes. In many industries, the earlier dominance of a single set of environmental forces was replaced by much more complex environmental demands, in which each of the different sets of forces was becoming strong simultaneously. For example, new economies of scale and scope and intensifying competition among a few competitors were enhancing the economic forces toward increased global integration in many multinational and international industries. In the detergent business, product standardization has become more feasible because the growing penetration and standardization of washing machines has narrowed the differences in washing practices across countries. Particularly in regional markets such as Europe or South America, companies have leveraged this potential for product standardization by developing regional brands, uniform product formulation, multilingual packaging, and common advertising themes, all of which have led to additional economies.

Similarly, localizing forces are growing in strength in global industries such as consumer electronics. Although the strengths of the economic forces of scale and scope have continued to increase, host government pressures and renewed customer demand for differentiated products are forcing companies with global strategies to reverse their earlier strategies, which were based on exporting standard products. To protect their competitive positions, they have begun to emphasize the local design and production of differentiated product ranges in different countries and for different international segments. And the growing need to supplement standard hardware-oriented products with more locally differentiated systems, software and services is increasing the need for more flexibility and responsiveness in local markets.

Finally, in the emerging competitive battle among a few large firms with comparable capabilities in global-scale efficiency and nationally responsive strategies, the ability to innovate and exploit the resulting developments globally is becoming more and more important for building durable comparative advantage, even in industries in which global economic forces or local political and cultural influences had previously been dominant. In the highly competitive mobile phone business, for example, all surviving major competitors must have captured the minimum scale efficiency to play on the global field, as well as the requisite government relationships and consumer understanding to respond to market differences. Today, competition in this industry consists primarily of a company's ability to develop innovative new products—perhaps in response to a consumer trend in Japan, a government requirement in Germany, or a technological development in the United States—and then diffuse it rapidly around the world.

In the emerging international environment, therefore, there are fewer and fewer examples of pure global, textbook multinational, or classic international industries. Instead, more and more businesses are driven to a greater or lesser extent by *simultaneous* demands for global efficiency, national responsiveness, and worldwide innovation. These are the characteristics of what we call a *transnational industry*. In such industries, companies find it increasingly difficult to defend a competitive position on the basis of only one dominant capability. They need to develop their ability to respond effectively to all forces at the same time to manage the often-conflicting demands for efficiency, responsiveness, and innovation without sacrificing any one for the other.

The emergence of the transnational industry has not only made the needs for efficiency, responsiveness, and innovation simultaneous, it has also made the tasks required to achieve each of these capabilities more demanding and complex. Rather than achieve world-scale economies through centralized and standardized production, companies must instead build global efficiency through a worldwide infrastructure of distributed but specialized assets and capabilities that exploit comparative advantages, scale economies, and scope economies simultaneously. (In Chapter 4, we will return to elaborate on this challenging organization requirement in more detail.)

Consequently, in most industries, a few global competitors now compete head to head in almost all major markets.

To succeed in such an environment, companies must develop new strategic capabilities, including a mastery of the logic of global chess: the ability to build and defend profit sanctuaries that are impenetrable to competitors; to leverage existing strengths in order to cross-subsidize weaker products and market positions; to make high-risk, pre-emptive investments that raise the stakes and force out rivals with weaker stomachs and purse strings; and to form alliances and coalitions to isolate and outflank competitors. These and other similar maneuvers must now be combined with world-scale economies to develop and maintain global competitive efficiency.

Similarly, responsiveness through differentiated and tailor-made local-for-local products and strategies in each host environment is rarely necessary or feasible anymore. National customers no longer demand differentiation; they demand sensitivity to their needs, along with the level of cost and quality standards for global products to which they have become accustomed. At the same time, host governments' desire to build their national competitiveness dominates economic policy in many countries, and MNEs are frequently viewed as key instruments in the implementation of national competitive strategies. Changes in regulations, tastes, exchange rates, and related factors have become less predictable and more frequent. In such an environment, simple market-by-market responsiveness is usually inadequate. The flexibility to change product designs, sourcing patterns, and pricing policies to remain responsive to continually changing national environments has become essential for survival.

And finally, exploiting centrally developed products and technologies is no longer enough. MNEs must build the capability to learn from the many environments to which they are exposed and to appropriate the benefits of such learning throughout their global operations. Although some products and processes still must be developed centrally for worldwide use, and others must be created locally in each environment to meet purely local demands, MNEs must increasingly use their access to multiple centers of technologies and familiarity with diverse customer preferences in different countries to create truly transnational innovations. Similarly, environmental and competitive information acquired in different parts of the world must be collated and interpreted to become a part of the company's shared knowledge base and provide input to future strategies.

(In Chapter 3, we will develop this discussion of the required strategic capabilities and highlight the need for MNEs to build layers of competitive advantage.)

Concluding Comments

The increasing complexity of forces in the global environment and the need to respond simultaneously to their diverse and often conflicting demands have created some major challenges for many MNEs. The classic global companies, such as many highly successful Japanese and Korean companies whose competitive advantage was historically rooted in a highly efficient and centralized system, have been forced to respond more effectively to the demands for national responsiveness and worldwide innovation. The traditional multinational companies—many of them European—long had the advantage of being the masters of national responsiveness, but today they face the challenge of exploiting global-scale economic and technological forces more effectively. And U.S. companies, with their more international approach to leveraging home country innovations abroad, have had to struggle to build a better understanding of cultural and political forces and respond to national differences more effectively while simultaneously enhancing global-scale efficiency through improved scale economies.

For most MNEs, the challenge of the 2000s is both strategic and organizational. On the one hand, they are forced to develop a more complex array of strategic capabilities which enable them to capture the competitive advantages that accrue to efficiency, responsiveness, and learning. On the other hand, the traditional organizational approaches of these companies, developed to support their earlier global, multinational, or international approaches, have become inadequate for the more complex strategic tasks that they now must accomplish. In Chapters 3 and 4, we will discuss some of the ways in which companies can respond to these new strategic and organizational challenges.

Chapter 2 Readings

- In Reading 2-1, "Clusters and the New Economics of Competition," Porter details how clusters—critical masses in one place of unusual success in a particular field—influence competitiveness. By co-locating in near proximity, companies, customers, and suppliers are better able to innovate, thereby creating a competitive advantage within a particular country.
- In Reading 2-2, "Managing Risk in an Unstable World," Bremmer provides insights on the political risk analysis needed by MNEs to guide their worldwide investment activities. Emphasis is placed on the types of information required, and the more nuanced ways that are needed to interpret it.

These readings all elaborate on the environmental forces facing MNEs and reinforce how they need to respond to their often-conflicting demands.

Case 2-1   Global Wine War 2009: New World versus Old

Christopher A. Bartlett

"We have the people, expertise, technology and commitment to gain global preeminence for Australian wine by 2025. It will come by anticipating the market, influencing consumer demand, and building on our strategy of sustainable growth."

—Sam Toley, CEO of Australian Wine and Brandy Corporation.

"By phasing out the buyback of excess wine and increasing incentives for farmers to uproot their vines, the EC reforms will only bring in the New World's agro-industry model. We need to protect the age-old European model built on traditional vineyards."

—Jean-Louis Piton, Copa-Cogeca Farmers Association.

In 2009, these two views reflected some of the very different sentiments unleashed by the fierce competitive battle raging between traditional wine makers and some new industry players as they fought for a share of the $230 billion global wine market. Many Old World wine producers—France, Italy, and Spain, for example—found themselves constrained by embedded wine-making traditions, restrictive industry regulations, and complex national and European Community legislation. This provided an opportunity for New World wine companies—from Australia, the United States, and Chile, for instance—to challenge the more established Old World producers by introducing innovations at every stage of the value chain.

In the Beginning[1]

Grape growing and wine making have been human preoccupations at least since the times when ancient Egyptians and Greeks offered wine as tributes to dead pharaohs and tempestuous gods. It was under the Roman Empire that viticulture spread throughout the Mediterranean region, and almost every town had its local vineyards and wine was a peasant's beverage to accompany everyday meals. By the Christian era, wine became part of liturgical services, and monasteries planted vines and built wineries. By the Middle Ages, the European nobility began planting vineyards as a mark of prestige, competing with one another in the quality of wine served at their tables—the first niche market for premium wine.

Wine Production   Tending and harvesting grapes has always been labor intensive, and one worker could typically look after only a three hectare lot. (1 hectare = 2.47 acres) The introduction of vineyard horses in the early 19th century led to vines being planted in rows and to more efficient tending and allowed one person to work a plot of 7 hectares.

Yet despite these efficiencies, vineyards became smaller, not larger. Over many centuries, small agricultural holdings were continually fragmented as land was parceled out by kings, taken in wars,

[1]Historical discussions are indebted to Harry W. Paul, *Science, Vine and Wine in Modern France* (Cambridge University Press, 1996), pp. 2–15; to Jancis Robinson, ed., *The Oxford Companion to Wine, 2nd Ed.* (Oxford University Press, 1999); and to James Wilson, *Terroir* (Berkeley: University of California Press, 1998), pp. 10–45.

or broken up through inheritance. During the French Revolution, many large estates were seized, divided, and sold at auction. And after 1815, the Napoleonic inheritance code prescribed how land had to be passed on to all rightful heirs. By the mid-19th century, the average holding in France was 5.5 ha. and was still being subdivided. (In Italy, similar events left the average vineyard at 0.8 ha.)

While the largest estates made their own wine, most small farmers sold their grapes to the local wine maker or *vintner*. With payment based on weight, there was little incentive to pursue quality by reducing yield. Some small growers formed cooperatives, hoping to participate in wine making's downstream profit, but grape growing and wine making remained highly fragmented.

Distribution and Marketing   Traditionally, wine was sold in bulk to merchant traders—*négociants* in France—who often blended and bottled the product before distributing it. But poor roads and complex toll and tax systems made cross-border shipping extremely expensive. In the early 19th century, for example, a shipment of wine from Strasbourg to the Dutch border had to pass through 31 toll stations.[2] And since wine did not travel well, much of it spoiled on the long journeys. As a result, only the most sophisticated *négociants* could handle exports, and only the rich could afford the imported luxury.

Late 18th century innovations such as mass production of glass bottles, the use of cork stoppers, and the development of pasteurization revolutionized the industry. With greater wine stability and longevity, distribution to distant markets and bottle aging of good vintages became the norm. Increased vine plantings and expanded production followed, and a global market for wine was born.

Regulation and Classification   As the industry developed, it became increasingly important to the cultural and economic life of the producing countries. By the mid-18th century in France, grape growing supported 1.5 million families and an equal number in wine-related businesses. Eventually, it accounted

for one-sixth of France's total trading revenue, and was the country's second-largest export.

The industry's growing cultural and economic importance attracted political attention, and with it, laws and regulations to control almost every aspect of wine making. For example, Germany's 1644 wine classification scheme prescribed 65 classes of quality, with rules for everything from ripeness required for harvesting to minimum sugar content. (Even in 1971, a law was passed in Germany requiring a government panel to taste each vineyard's annual vintage and assign it a quality level.[3]) Similar regulations prescribing wine-making practices also existed in France and Italy.

Rather than resisting such government classifications and controls, producers often supported and even augmented them as a way of differentiating their products and raising entry barriers. For example, the current French classification system was created by a Bordeaux committee prior to the 1855 Exposition in Paris. To help consumers identify their finest wines, they classified about 500 vineyards into five levels of quality, from *premier cru* (first growth) to *cinquième cru* (fifth growth).

Because it helped consumers sort through the complexity of a highly fragmented market, this marketing tool soon gained wide recognition, leading the government to codify and expand it in the *Appellation d'Origin Controllée* (AOC) laws of 1935. These laws also defined regional boundaries and set detailed and quite rigid standards for vineyards and wine makers.[4] Eventually, more than 300 AOC designations were authorized, from the well known (Saint Emilion or Beaujolais) to the obscure (Fitou or St. Péray). (A similar classification scheme was later introduced in Italy defining 213 *Denominazione di Origne Controllate* (or DOC) regions, each with regulations prescribing area, allowed grape varieties, yields, required growing practices, acceptable alcohol content, label design etc.[5])

---

[3]Ibid., p. 312.
[4]Dewey Markham, *1855: A History of the Bordeaux Classification* (New York: Wiley, 1998), p. 177.
[5]Robinson, p. 235.

[2]Robinson, p. 308.

Later, other wine regions of France were given official recognition with the classification of *Vins Delimités de Qualité Superieure* (VDQS), but these were usually regarded as of lower rank than AOC wines. Below VDQS were *Vins de Pays,* or country wine—inexpensive but very drinkable wines for French tables, and increasingly, for export. These categories were quite rigid with almost no movement across them. This was due to a belief that quality was linked to *terroir*, the almost mystical combination of soil, aspect, microclimate, rainfall, and cultivation that the French passionately believed gave the wine from each region—and indeed, each vineyard—its unique character.

But *terroir* could not guarantee consistent quality. As an agricultural product, wine was always subject to the vagaries of weather and disease. In the last quarter of the 19th century, a deadly New World insect, phylloxera, devastated the French vine stock. From a production level of 500 million liters in 1876, output dropped to just 2 million liters in 1885. But a solution was found in an unexpected quarter: French vines were grafted onto phylloxera-resistant vine roots native to the United States and imported from the upstart Californian wine industry. It was the first time many in the Old World acknowledged the existence of a New World wine industry. It would not be the last.

Stirrings in the New World

Although insignificant in both size and reputation compared with the well-established industry in traditional wine-producing countries, vineyards and wine makers had been set up in many New World countries since the 18th century. In the United States, for example, Thomas Jefferson, an enthusiastic oenologist, became a leading voice for establishing vineyards in Virginia. And in Australia, vines were brought over along with the first fleet carrying convicts and settlers in 1788. Nascent wine industries were also developing at this time in Argentina, Chile, and South Africa, usually under the influence of immigrants from the Old World wine countries.

Opening New Markets While climate and soil allowed grape growing to flourish in the New World, the consumption of wine in these countries varied widely. It became part of the national cultures in Argentina and Chile, where per capita annual consumption reached about 80 liters in Argentina and 50 liters in Chile in the 1960s. While such rates were well behind France and Italy, both of which boasted per capita consumption of 110–120 liters in this era, they were comparable with those of Spain.

Other New World cultures did not embrace the new industry as quickly. In Australia, the hot climate and a dominant British heritage made beer the alcoholic beverage of preference, with wine being consumed mostly by Old World immigrants. The U.S. market was more complex. In keeping with the country's central role in the rum trade, one segment of the population followed a tradition of drinking hard liquor. But another group reflected the country's Puritan heritage and espoused temperance or abstinence. (As recently as 1994, a Gallup survey found that 45% of U.S. respondents did not drink at all, and 21% favored a renewal of prohibition.) As a result, in the pre-World War II era, wine was largely made by and sold to European immigrant communities.

In the postwar era, however, demand for wine increased rapidly in the United States, Australia, and other New World producers. In the United States, for example, consumption grew from a postprohibition per capita level of 1 liter per annum to 9 liters by 2006. In Australia the rate of increase was even more rapid, from less than 2 liters in 1960 to 24 liters by 2006. This growth in consumption was coupled with a growing demand for higher quality wines, resulting in a boom in domestic demand that proved a boost for the young New World wine industry.

Challenging Production Norms On the back of the postwar economic boom, New World wine producers developed in an industry environment different from their European counterparts. First, suitable land was widely available and less expensive, allowing the growth of much more extensive vineyards. As a result, in 2006, the average vineyard holding in the United States was 213 hectares and in Australia 167 hectares, compared to an

Italian average of 1.3 hectares, and 7.4 hectares in France.[6]

Unconstrained by tradition, New World producers also began to experiment with grape growing and winemaking technology. In Australia, controlled drip irrigation allowed expansion into marginal land and reduced vintage variability. (In contrast, irrigation was strictly forbidden in France under AOC regulations.) The larger vineyards also allowed the use of specialized equipment such as mechanical harvesters and mechanical pruners which greatly reduced labor costs.

Innovation also extended into viniculture where New World producers pursued techniques such as night harvesting to maximize grape sugars, while innovative trellis systems permitted vines to be planted at twice the traditional density. Other experiments with fertilizers and pruning methods increased yield and improved grape flavor. These innovations, when coupled with typically sunny climates, freed New World farmers from many of the stresses of their counterparts in regions like Bordeaux where the rainy maritime climate made late autumn harvests risky, and held wine producers hostage to wide year-to-year vintage variations.

New World wine companies also broke many wine making traditions. Large estates usually had on-site labs to provide analysis helpful in making growing and harvest decisions. In the 1990s, some experimented with a reverse osmosis technology to concentrate the juice (or *must*), ensuring a deeper-colored, richer-tasting wine. (Ironically, the technique was developed in France, but most French producers deplored it as "removing the poetry of wine." Needless to say, it was a forbidden practice under AOC regulations.) New World wine makers also developed processes that allowed fermentation and aging to occur in huge, computer-controlled, stainless steel tanks rather than in traditional oak barrels. To provide oak flavor, some added oak chips while aging their popular priced wines—another practice strictly forbidden in most traditional-producing countries.

Exhibit 1   Consumer Price Breakdown: French Popular Wines

Cost Structure	EUR/ litre	EUR/ bottle
Juice	0.50	
Wine making	0.06	
Bulk wine (total)	0.56[a] =	0.42
Bottling packaging		0.35
Local taxes		0.08
Logistics storage		0.10
Margins/overhead		0.10
Wholesale price		1.05
Excise duties[a]		0.45
Retail and wholesale margins		1.14
If VAT		0.05
Consumer price in EUR		3.14

[a]Example from the Netherlands.

Source: Changing Competitiveness in the Wine Industry, Rabobank Market Study, 2006, p. 16.

The economic impact of these and other innovations became clear in a comparison of the costs of production in the Langedoc region of France with the Riverina district in Australia, both big producers of popular priced wines. The French cost per tonne of €238 was 74% higher than the Australian cost of €137.[7] And South American grape costs were even lower, driving down the price of popular premium wine in Europe to €2 a bottle, while the French vins de pays was priced above €3. (**Exhibit 1** shows the cost composition of a bottle of French wine.)

Reinventing the Marketing Model   Beyond their experiments in growing and winemaking, New World producers also innovated in packaging and marketing. While the European targeted the huge basic wine market by selling the popular liter bottle of *vin de table,* the Australians developed the innovative "wine-in-a-box" package. Employing a collapsible plastic bag in a compact cardboard box with a dispensing spigot, the box's shape and weight not only saved shipping costs, it also made

[6]Heijbrock, Arend "Changing Competitiveness in the Wine Industry," Rabobank Research Publication, 2007, p. 5.

[7]Heijbrock, p. 16.

storage in the consumer's refrigerator more convenient. More recently, Australian producers began replacing cork stoppers with screw caps, even on premium wines. The logic was based not just on economics, but also on the fact that many wines, particularly the delicate whites, were susceptible to spoiling if corks were deficient.

From their earliest experiences in the marketplace, New World producers learned the value of differentiating their products and making them more appealing to palates unaccustomed to wine. Several early products developed for unsophisticated palates were wildly successful—Ripple in the United States and Barossa Pearl in Australia, for example—but were dismissed by connoisseurs as evidence of the New World's inferior winemaking skills. Yet these experiments provided valuable lessons in branding and marketing—skills that were rare in this industry prior to the 1970s.

With wine showing the potential for mass appeal, in 1977 Coca-Cola acquired Taylor California Cellars. Other experienced consumer marketers such as Nestlé, Pillsbury, and Seagram followed, and conventional wisdom was that their sophisticated marketing techniques would finally crack the last major largely unbranded consumer product. But the challenge proved more difficult than expected, and within a decade the outsiders had sold out. Yet their influence endured in the consumer focused attitudes and the sophisticated marketing skills they left behind.

The other major change driven by New World companies occurred in distribution. Historically, fragmented producers and tight government regulations had created a long, multilevel value chain, with service providers in many of the links lacking either the scale or the expertise to operate efficiently. (See **Exhibit 2** for a representation.) In contrast, the large New World wine companies typically controlled the full value chain, extracting margins at every level and retaining bargaining power with increasingly concentrated retailers. And because their name was on the final product, they controlled quality at every step.

Exhibit 2   Wine Industry Value Chain

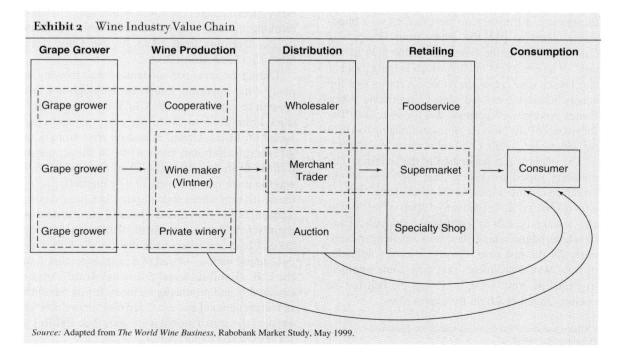

Source: Adapted from *The World Wine Business*, Rabobank Market Study, May 1999.

To traditionalists, the New World's breaks with established grape-growing and wine-making ways were sacrilege. They argued that in the drive for efficiency and consistency, and in the desire to cater to less sophisticated palates, New World producers had lost the character that came with more variable vintages made in traditional ways. And they were shocked that many of these "engineered products" were sold using appellation names—Chablis, Burgundy, Champagne, and so on. In response, the European Community (EC) passed regulations making such practices illegal. New World wine makers gradually adjusted by identifying their wines by the grape variety used, and eventually consumers recognized and developed preferences defined by the varietal name—cabernet sauvignon versus merlot, or chardonnay versus sauvignon blanc, for example. Indeed, many seemed to find this easier to understand than trying to penetrate the many complex regional designations that each of the traditional wine-producing countries had promoted.

The Judgment of Paris   On May 24, 1976, in a publicity-seeking activity linked to America's Bicentenary, a British wine merchant set up a blind-tasting panel to rate top wines from France and California. Despite the enormous "home field advantage" of an event held in Paris with a judging panel of nine French wine critics, the American entries took top honors in both the red and white competitions. When French producers complained that the so called "The Judgment of Paris" was rigged, a new judging was held two years later. Again, Californian wines triumphed.[8]

The event was a watershed in the industry. The publicity raised awareness that the New World produced quality wines, to the great shock of those who dismissed their innovative approaches. It was also a wake-up call to traditional producers, many of whom began taking their new challengers seriously for the first time. Finally, it gave confidence to New World producers that they could compete in global markets. In short, it was the bell for the opening round in a fight for export sales.

[8]Gideon Rachman, "The Globe in a Glass," *The Economist*, December 18, 1999, p. 91.

Maturing Markets, Changing Demand

"The Judgment of Paris" signaled the start of many disruptive changes in wine industry during the last quarter of the 20th century. More immediately alarming for most traditional producers was a pattern of declining demand that saw a 20% drop in worldwide consumption from 1970 to 1990, and a subsequent flattening of demand. When combined with radical changes in consumer tastes, consolidation in the distribution channels, and shifts in government support, these trends presented industry participants with an important new set of opportunities and threats.

Changing Global Demand Patterns   The most dramatic decline in demand occurred in the highest-consumption countries, France and Italy. In the mid-1960s, per capita annual consumption in both countries was around 110 to 120 liters; by 2005 it was about 50 litres. Key causes of the decline were a younger generation's different drinking preferences, an older generation's concern about health issues, and stricter drunk-driving penalties. Simultaneously, steep declines occurred in other major of wine drinking cultures—Spain dropped from 60 liters to 35, Argentina from 80 to 30, and Chile from 50 to 15. (See **Exhibit 3.**)

During the same period, demand was growing in many wine-importing countries, although not fast enough to offset losses in Old World wine countries. From 1966 to 2005, per capita annual consumption in the United Kingdom rose from 3 to 20 liters, in Belgium from 10 to 26 liters, and in Canada from 3 to 10 liters. Even more promising was the more recent growth of new markets, particularly in Asia where consumption in China, Japan, Taiwan, South Korea, and Thailand grew at double digit annual rates through the 1990s. In fact, by 2005, China had emerged as the world's fifth wine consuming nation—ahead of Spain, Argentina, and the U.K. (**Exhibits 4** and **5** lists the world's major consuming and producing nations). It was this shift in market demand that escalated the competition for export sales into a global wine war. (See **Exhibit 6** for import and export data.)

Exhibit 3   Wine Consumption Per Capita, Selected Countries, 1966–2006

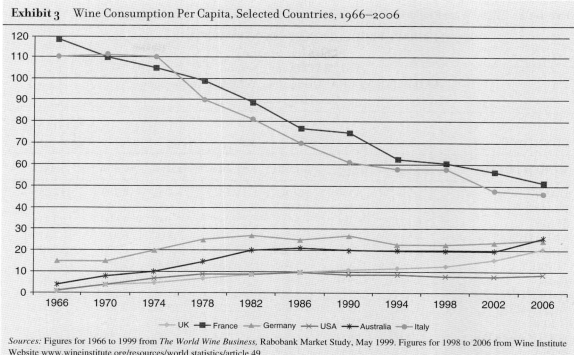

Sources: Figures for 1966 to 1999 from *The World Wine Business,* Rabobank Market Study, May 1999. Figures for 1998 to 2006 from Wine Institute Website www.wineinstitute.org/resources/world statistics/article 49.

Shift to Quality, Rise of Fashion   Partially off-setting the overall volume decline was a growing demand for higher-quality wines. While the basic segment (less than $5 a bottle) still accounted for half the world market in volume, the premium ($5 to $7) and the super-premium ($7 to $14) now represented 40% of the total—and more than 50% of the market in younger markets such as the United States and Australia. (**Exhibit 7** shows one version of price segmentation as defined by a leading industry analyst.)

The trend was worldwide. Even in Old World wine countries where total demand was in decline, consumption of premium wine kept rising. Despite government subsidies, per capita consumption of basic wine in the EU fell from 31 liters in 1985 to 18 liters in 2005, while demand for quality wine increased from 10 liters to 15 liters. In that same 20 year period, jug wine sales in the United States declined from 800 million to 600 million liters,

while consumption of premium wines increased from 150 million to 600 million liters.

With the shift to quality, a greater fashion element began to influence demand. The decline in importance of working families' daily consumption of locally produced table wine was offset by upscale urban consumers who chose bottles on the basis of grape variety, vintage, source—and increasingly fashion. The 1980s' emphasis on lighter foods led to an increase in demand for white wines, making white wine spritzers (wine with soda water) a fashionable drink in the United States market. By the late 1980s, white wine represented over 75% of U.S. sales.

This all changed following the 1991 publication of a medical report identifying red-wine as a partial explanation of the "French paradox"—low rates of heart disease in a population well known for its love of rich food. Featured on the U.S. television show *60 Minutes,* the report soon led to an increase

Exhibit 4   World Wine Production: By Country

			WORLD GRAPE PRODUCTION BY COUNTRY AVERAGE 1996–2000 ACTUAL 2002–2004 ESTIMATED 2005 & 2006 AND PERCENT CHANGE 2006 vs AVERAGE 1996–2000 U.S. TONS (000)[1]				
COUNTRY[2]	96–00	2002	2003	2004	2005	2006	% CHANGE 2006/96–00
WORLD TOTAL	65,648	67,755	69,081	73,490	72,271	71,089	8.29%
ITALY	9,914	8,150	8,249	9,581	8,700	8,700	(12.25%)
FRANCE	8,295	7,544	6,952	8,314	7,600	7,700	(7.17%)
SPAIN	6,127	6,481	7,998	8,037	7,500	7,500	22.41%
UNITED STATES[3]	6,513	7,339	6,573	6,240	7,814	6,417	(1.47%)
CHINA	2,704	4,938	5,705	6,099	6,100	6,100	125.61%
TURKEY	3,968	3,858	3,968	3,858	3,900	3,900	(1.72%)
IRAN	2,484	2,981	3,086	3,086	3,100	3,100	24.82%
ARGENTINA	2,456	2,474	2,537	2,922	2,700	2,700	9.94%
AUSTRALIA	1,261	1,933	1,650	2,221	2,300	2,400	90.37%
CHILE	1,827	2,064	2,386	2,149	2,200	2,200	20.42%
SOUTH AFRICA	1,597	1,654	1,809	1,916	1,790	1,790	12.07%
INDIA	1,057	1,334	1,268	1,323	1,300	1,300	23.03%
GERMANY	1,515	1,453	1,233	1,235	1,300	1,300	(14.21%)
GREECE	1,353	1,213	1,268	1,323	1,300	1,300	(3.92%)
EGYPT	1,070	1,217	1,217	1,406	1,280	1,280	19.61%
BRAZIL	939	1,235	1,163	1,414	1,200	1,200	27.77%
ROMANIA	1,299	1,179	1,162	1,169	1,170	1,170	(9.93%)
PORTUGAL	1,000	1,211	1,042	1,134	1,130	1,130	13.03%
MOLDOVA	576	707	732	661	700	700	21.63%
HUNGARY	757	633	665	698	670	670	(11.45%)

Source: Trade Data and Analysis, The World Wine Institute, 2006.

in demand, with red wine's market share growing from 27% in 1991 to 43% five years later.

Even within this broad trend of red versus white preference, the demand for different grape varieties also moved with fashion. During the white wine boom, chardonnay was the grape of choice, but by the late 1990s, Pinot Gris and Sauvignon Blanc were emerging white wine fashion favorites. In red wine, a love affair with Cabernet Sauvignon was followed by a mini-boom for Merlot, which in turn was succeeded by a demand spike for Pinot Noir.

Such swings in fashion posed a problem for growers. Although vines had a productive life of 60 to 70 years, they typically took 3 to 4 years to produce their first harvest, 5 to 7 years to reach full productive capacity, and 35 years to produce top quality grapes. But New World wine regions had the capacity and the regulatory freedom to plant new varieties in new vineyards and could respond. For example, in the 1990s, the California acreage planted with chardonnay increased 36%, and merlot plantings increased 31%.

Exhibit 5   World Wine Consumption: By Country

COUNTRY [2]	2002	2003	2004	2005	2006	% Change 2006/2002
WORLD WINE CONSUMPTION CATEGORY A[1] 2002–2006 AND % CHANGE 2006/2002 HECTOLITERS (000)						
CATEGORY A TOTAL	**226,179**	**231,547**	**234,064**	**236,991**	**241,553**	**6.80%**
FRANCE	34,820.00	33,340.00	33,141.00	33,000.00	32,800.00	(5.80%)
ITALY	27,709.00	29,343.00	28,300.00	27,600.00	27,300.00	(1.48%)
UNITED STATES[3]	23,650.00	24,363.00	25,114.00	26,180.00	26,883.00	13.67%
GERMANY	20,272.00	20,150.00	19,593.00	19,437.00	19,850.00	(2.08%)
CHINA	11,469.88	11,586.02	13,286.00	15,000.00	16,000 00	39.50%
SPAIN	13,960.00	13,798.00	13,898.00	13,735.00	13,735.00	(1.61%)
UNITED KINGDOM	9,916.00	10,622.00	10,729.00	12,000.00	11,700.00	17.99%
RUSSIA	6,404.00	8,682.00	10,159.00	11,200.00	11,200.00	74.89%
ARGENTINA	11,988.00	12,338.00	11,113.00	11,113.00	10,972.00	(8.48%)
ROMANIA	4,964.00	5,049.70	5,800.00	2,379.00	5,600.00	12.81%
PORTUGAL	4,650.00	5,290.00	4,828.00	4,820.00	4,700.00	1.08%
AUSTRALIA	4,007.00	4,196.00	4,361.00	4,523.00	4,600.00	14.80%
CANADA	2,883.58	3,440.00	3,607.00	4,000.00	4,200.00	45.65%
BRAZIL	3,178.00	3,077.00	3,177.00	3,710.00	3,553.00	11.80%
SOUTH AFRICA	3,884.00	3,487.00	3,509.00	3,450.00	3,519.00	(9.40%)
NETHERLANDS	3,330.00	3,563.00	3,340.00	3,474.00	3,350.00	0.60%
GREECE	2,420.10	2,450.00	3,275.00	3,480.00	3,350.00	38.42%
HUNGARY	3,454.00	3,120.00	3,080.00	3,200.00	3,200.00	(7.35%)
CHILE	2,297.00	2,552.00	2,547.00	2,740.00	2,850.00	24.07%
BELGIUM	2,724.00	2,614.00	2,741.00	2,813.00	2,775.00	1.87%

Source: Trade and Data Analysis, The World Wine Institute, 2006.

As these various demand trends continued, the rankings of the world's top wine companies underwent radical change. Despite their relative newness and the comparative smallness of their home markets, New World companies took nine slots in a list of the world's top 15 wine companies, a list previously dominated by Old World companies. (See **Exhibit 8** for the listing).

Increasing Distribution Power   Because marketing had typically been handled by their *négociants,* most Old World producers were still isolated from such fast-changing consumer tastes and market trends—particularly when they occurred in distant export markets. Equally problematic was their lack of understanding of the rapidly concentrating retail channels. In contrast, because most large New World wine companies controlled their distribution chain from the vineyard to the retailer, they were able to sense changes in consumer preferences and respond to shifts in distribution channels.

Furthermore, the New World companies were able to capture even more economic advantage by him and reducing handling stages, holding less inventory, and capturing the intermediaries' markup. Even the transportation economics that once favored European suppliers' proximity to the huge United Kingdom market changed. As trucking costs rose, container-ship rates fell, making the cost of shipping wine from Australia to the

Exhibit 6   Consumption, Production, Export, and Import Figures for Selected Old World and New World Wine Producing and Consuming Countries, 2001

	Consumption		Production	Exports		Imports		
	Liters Per Capita	Total hls 000s	Total hls (000s)	Total hls (000s)	Total hls (000s)	Value ($Millions)	$/Litre
France	52	34,200	45,400	15,180	5,370	789	1.40
Italy	46	28,150	45,900	18,480	1,750	474	2.70
Argentina	31	12,200	15,050	3,260	140	NA	1.30
Spain	27	14,260	34,700	15,280	200	NA	3.20
Germany	26	20,380	10,500	3,450	14,240	2,710	1.90
Australia	28	5,960	14,304	7,980	340	NA	4.70
United Kingdom	22	12,760	—	—	12,910	5,090	3.90
United States	9	25,125	20,000	4,240	8,450	4,624	5.40

Source: Rabobank *World Wine Map,* 2008.
Note: In several European countries, production does not equal consumption (plus exports minus imports) due to excess production being subject to government purchase.

Exhibit 7   Quality Segments in the Wine Industry (Rabobank's Categories)

	Icon	Ultra Premium	Super Premium	Premium	Basic
Price range (approx)	More than $50	$20–$50	$10–$20	$5–$10	Less than $5
Consumer profile	Connaisseur	Wine lover	Experimenting consumer	Experimenting consumer	Price-focused consumer
Purchase driver	Image, style	Quality, image	Brand, quality	Price, brand	Price
Retail outlets	Winery, boutique, food service	Specialty shop, food service	Better supermarket, specialty shop	Supermarket	Supermarket, discounter
Market trend	Little growth	Little growth	Growing	Growing	Decreasing
Competition	Limited, "closed" segment	Gradually increasing	Increasing, based on brand and quality/price ratio	Fierce, based on brand, price	Based on price
Volume market share	1%	5%	10%	34%	50%
Availability	Scarce	Scarce	Sufficient, year round	Large quantities, year round	Surplus

Source: Adapted by casewriters from *The World Wine Business,* Market Study, May 1999.

Exhibit 8   Top 15 World Wine Companies: 2007/08

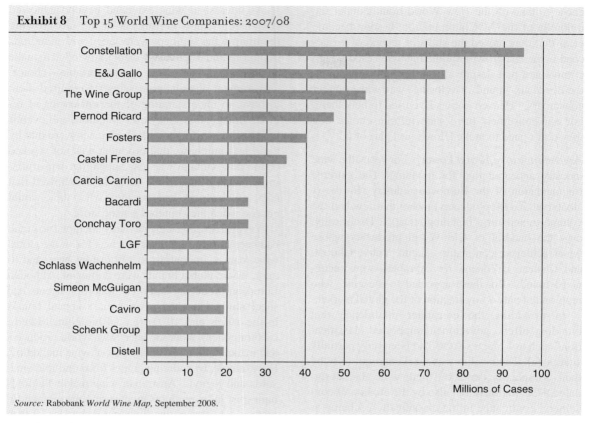

Source: Rabobank *World Wine Map*, September 2008.

UK about the same as trucking it from the south of France.

Size also gave New World companies bargaining power in the sophisticated negotiations that a concentrated retail sector now demanded. For example, following the huge wine surpluses flooding the market in the early 2000s, Australian producers used their cost advantage to drive prices lower. But equally important in the battle for volume sales was their ability to respond to retailers' need for a consistent supply of strong brands at a good price/quality ratio.[9] In the face of this head-on competitive challenge, the French tried to defend their position through frequent promotions.[10] But they were

hampered by their lack of consumer knowledge and marketing skills.

The Old World suppliers' problems became clear from their dealings with Tesco, the world's largest wine retailer with wine sales of £1.5 billion in 2007. To maximize sales, Tesco emphasized that it wanted to work with creative suppliers. "Don't just bring the deals, bring me innovation," said Dan Jago, Tesco's Wine, Beer, and Spirits division head. "If you want your prices to rise, you have to persuade customers why they should pay more."[11]

While a handful of icon brands prospered at the top of the market based on image and quality, the fragmentation of Old World vineyards forced most to compete at the low end on price. When some

[9]Rachman, p. 99.

[10]Annemiek Geene, Arend Heijbroek, Anne Lagerwerf, and Rafi Wazir, "The World Wine Business," Market Study, May 1999, available from Rabobank International.

[11]Anonymous, "The World's Largest Wine Retailer," *Meininger's Wine Business International*, June 2007, pp. 42–45.

chose to take on the New World brands under the umbrella of the AOC's reputation, it soon became clear that they lacked the skills or resources to succeed in the last growth middle market. Tesco's Jago complained that despite its once strong reputation, the Bordeaux "brand" was losing sway with younger consumers. "Heaven knows I've tried to help them, but our consumers have such infinite choice that they don't need to make [Bordeaux] part of it."[12]

Ascendancy in of Brand Power   For years, the wine industry appeared ripe for branding. The extreme fragmentation of the European industry (Bordeaux alone had 20,000 producers) meant that few had the volume to support a branding strategy. Historically, only the handful of Old World producers whose wines achieved icon status—Lafite, Veuve Cliquot, and Chateau d'Yquem, for example—were recognized brands. But these appealed to the elite, who represented only a tiny fraction of the global market.

In providing the consumer confidence that branding offers, government-supported classifications such as France's AOC had been only partially successful. Their value was weakened not only by their complexity (in 2009 there were 327 designated AOC regions), but also by the erosion of consumers' confidence in the classification scheme as an assurance of quality.[13] For example, Burgundy's most famous vineyard, Chambertin, had its 32 acres divided among 23 proprietors. While most produced the high-quality wine that had earned its *grand cru* status, others rode on that reputation to sell—at $150 a bottle—legitimately labeled Chambertin that wine critic Robert Parker described as "thin, watery, and a complete rip-off."[14]

As interest in wine extended beyond educated connoisseurs, new consumers in the fast-growing premium wine segment were faced with hundreds of options and often insufficient knowledge to make an informed—or even a comfortable—choice. Government classification schemes required them to have an understanding of the intricacies of region, vintage, and vineyard reputation, and even if they found a wine they liked, chances were that by their next purchase, that producer was not stocked or the new vintage was less appealing. Unsurprisingly, survey data in the early 1990s showed that 65% of shoppers had no idea what they would choose when they entered a wine store.

Yet even in 2009, despite many attempts, no brand had been able to capture as much as 1% of the global wine market, in contrast to soft drinks, beer, and liquor, where global brands were dominant. Although European producers and their importing agents had successfully launched several mass appeal brands in the 1960s and 1970s (e.g., Blue Nun, Mateus, Liebfraumilch), a decade later New World producers had made branding a routine part of wine marketing. For example, by sourcing grapes from multiple vineyards and regions, Australian wine maker Penfolds built trust in its products by ensuring the vintage-to-vintage consistency that branding demanded. It then leveraged its trusted brand name by creating a hierarchy of Penfolds wines that allowed consumers to move up each step from $9 to $185 wines as their tastes—and their budgets–developed. (See **Exhibit 9.**)

New World producers who built their marketing expertise in their home markets during the 1960s and 1970s, learned how to respond to consumer preferences for the simpler, more fruit-driven wines that were easy to appreciate. They then took those wines and the marketing and branding skills they had developed at home into the export markets. By 2007, New World companies claimed 14 of the world's top 20 wine brands. (See **Exhibit 10**).

The Government Solution   The radical shifts in demand proved extremely challenging to Old World producers. First, there was often no new land available to plant, particularly in controlled AOC regions.

---

[12]Ibid.

[13]The same problem plagued wines from Italy, where DOC regulations were so often violated that the government eventually introduced a DOCG classification in 1980 (the G stood for *guarantita*) to restore consumer confidence in notable wine regions. And in Germany, government standards were so diluted that, even in mediocre years, over 75% of wine produced was labeled *Qualitatswein* (quality wine), while less than 5% earned the more modest *Tatelwein* (table wine) designation.

[14]Robert M. Parker, Jr., *Parker Wine Buyer's Guide*, 5th Edition (New York: Fireside Press, 1999), p. 276.

Exhibit 9   Penfolds Red Wine U.S. Brand Structure, 2009

Label	Varietal Type	Years Before Release	Price Segment	Suggested U.S. Retail Price per Bottle ($US)
Rawson's Retreat	Varietal range[a]	1	Premium	$8.99
Koonunga Hill	Varietal range[a]	1–2	Premium	$10.99
Thomas Hyland	Varietal range[a]	1–2	Premium	$14.99
Bin 138	Shiraz Mourvedre Grenache	2	Super Premium	$19.00
Bin 128	Shiraz	3	Super Premium	$24.00
Bin 28	Shiraz	3	Super Premium	$24.00
Bin 389	Cabernet Shiraz	3	Super Premium	$26.00
Bin 407	Cabernet Sauvignon	3	Super Premium	$26.00
St. Henri	Shiraz	5	Ultra Premium	$39.00
Magill Estate	Shiraz	4	Ultra Premium	$50.00
RWT	Shiraz	4	Ultra Premium	$69.00
Bin 707	Cabernet Sauvignon	4	Ultra Premium	$80.00
Grange	Shiraz	6	Icon	$185.00

[a]Typical red varietal range included of these brands Merlot, Shiraz Cabernet, and Cabernet Sauvignon. (These brands also offer a range of white wines.)

Source: Southcorp Wines, the Americas.

Equally restrictive were the regulations prescribing permitted grape varieties and winemaking techniques that greatly limited their flexibility. So, for example, when fashion switched away from sweeter white wines, the German wine industry which was constrained by tight regulations on sugar content, watched its exports drop from over 3 million hectoliters in 1992 to under 2 million just five years later.

But the biggest problem was that declining demand at home and a loss of share in export markets had caused a structural wine surplus—popularly called the European wine lake. The EU's initial response was to pay farmers to uproot their vineyards, leading to 500,000 hectares (13% of production) being uprooted between 1988 and 1996. A parallel "crisis distillation program" provided for the EU to purchase surplus wine for distillation into industrial alcohol. An average of 26 million hectoliters (15% of total production) was distilled annually in the decade since 1999. In a 2006 reform proposal, the EU aimed to uproot a further 200,000 hectares—equal to the size of the U.S. wine industry—and gradually phase out crisis distillation.

Critics contended that despite their intent to move towards more market-driven policies, the EU regulators were still dealing with challenges from the supply-side perspective of the grape growers. Little was being done to address marketing support, wine style, the freedom and willingness to innovate, or the business models Old World wine companies were pursuing so successfully.

But New World wine companies were also facing challenges. Problems of global oversupply were made worse by emerging signs of saturation in several major export markets. For example, after 2003, Australia's wine export value to its major UK market was growing at less than half the rate of volume sales. And by 2005, its UK export volume increase slowed to only 1.6% while its average price in that market declined by 4.4%. There was also some evidence that New World wines were developing image problems born of their willingness to lower prices aggressively in an era of excess supply. The challenge now was to remake their image and move out of the highly competitive low price segment.

Exhibit 10   Top 20 Wine Brands 2004–2008

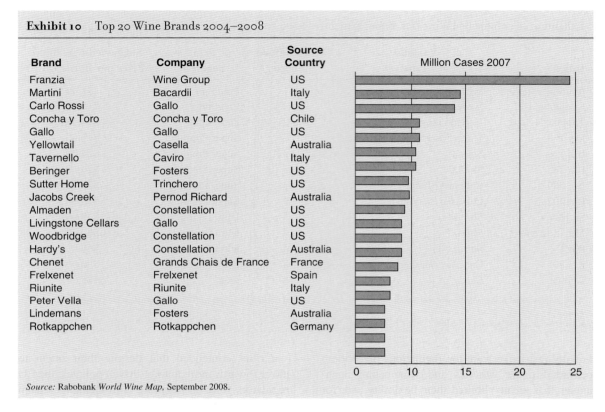

Brand	Company	Source Country
Franzia	Wine Group	US
Martini	Bacardii	Italy
Carlo Rossi	Gallo	US
Concha y Toro	Concha y Toro	Chile
Gallo	Gallo	US
Yellowtail	Casella	Australia
Tavernello	Caviro	Italy
Beringer	Fosters	US
Sutter Home	Trinchero	US
Jacobs Creek	Pernod Richard	Australia
Almaden	Constellation	US
Livingstone Cellars	Gallo	US
Woodbridge	Constellation	US
Hardy's	Constellation	Australia
Chenet	Grands Chais de France	France
Frelxenet	Frelxenet	Spain
Riunite	Riunite	Italy
Peter Vella	Gallo	US
Lindemans	Fosters	Australia
Rotkappchen	Rotkappchen	Germany

Source: Rabobank *World Wine Map*, September 2008.

The Battle for the U.S. Market

Squeezed by chronic oversupply in producer countries and declining demand in mature markets, the Old and New World were again locked in a competitive battle for export markets which in 2008 accounted for 33% of global demand. Nowhere was the battle more intense than in the United States, which one industry analyst called "perhaps the most attractive market in the world."[15]

The U.S. Market   It was easy to see why the U.S. was so attractive. In Germany, the world's largest wine importer, 65% of the market was accounted for by basic wine that sold for less than €2 a bottle. As the second largest importer, the U.K. offered a more attractive market (the €3–5 segment accounted for

57% of sales), but it was showing signs of saturation. But as third-place importer, the United States market had grown faster than any other major wine market— from $11 billion in 1993 to $30 billion in 2007. Better yet, the rate of increase in value was four times the volume growth. This reflected the fact that wine that sold for more than €5 ($7) accounted for 48% of the market, and this segment was growing at 15% p.a.— three times the rate of lower price segments.

Still, the U.S. wine market had long been one of the most difficult for imports to crack due to its distance from most producing countries, its state-by-state regulatory strictures, and particularly its complex three-tier distribution system that forced all sales to pass through state-licensed wholesalers. Not only did these wholesalers add cost, they also exercised great power. (The largest of them, Southern Wine and Spirits, had twice the sales of Consolation Brands, the world's largest wine company.) But all

[15]Stephen Rannekiev, "The Future of the California Wine Industry," F&A Research Advisory, Rabobank Industry Note, August 2007, p. 1.

this changed when a 2005 Supreme Court ruling allowed interstate wine shipments, triggering a series of state and federal regulation challenges that began to open up the U.S. distribution system. Finally, the largest entry barrier for imports began to erode.

One of the key drivers of U.S. market growth was due to Generation Y (born after 1997) embracing wine much more than Generation X, and almost as much as the Baby Boomers. These new consumers were not only price-sensitive, but also very Internet savvy, and consequently were well educated about their purchases. As they came of drinking age, research showed that they chose imported wines more than earlier generations, a cause for concern for in the U.S. industry.

Not surprisingly, in the first decade of the millennium, the U.S. became a major battleground in the fight for exports. Despite the fact that it had a successful domestic industry, wine imports into the U.S. increased by 185% between 1995 and 2006, by which time they claimed a record 31% market share. Soon, the champions of the Old World and New World were battling head-to-head—the Americans defending their home market against the three countries that accounted for 77% of imports by value: Italy, France, and Australia. It had become a microcosm of the global wine wars.

The American Defense   Some industry critics suggested that because American producers had long focused on their large, high priced domestic market, they had fallen behind the prevailing global price/quality ratio, not only at the low end, but even at the higher price points. One wake-up call was an analysis comparing the prices of all 2004 vintage Cabernet Sauvignon wines that achieved a Robert Parker Wine Enthusiast rating of 90. The average price for the Californian wines was $55, while the price for similarly rated wines from Australia was $20.[16]

Having become a high cost producer, the U.S. industry recognized that it needed to respond to the new competitive challenges. One of the greatest problems was that its land costs were extremely high. In 2008, an average acre of land in Napa cost

$150,000, more than 10 times the price of an average Australian vineyard, and 20 times the cost in Chile. Furthermore, there was virtually no land available for expansion in Napa or other premium wine areas. And labor costs were being squeezed as control over illegal immigration increased. The cost of pruning an acre in Napa in 2008 was $350, similar to the cost in France, but much higher than in highly mechanized Australia ($120 an acre), or in low labor cost Chile ($75 an acre).

Because of their high cost, vineyards in North Coast locations such as Napa and Sonoma targeted the super-premium and ultra-premium segments at $12 a bottle and above. Meanwhile, the Central Valley which produced 70% of California's wine volume was focused on the basic segment typified by Gallo's Carlo Rossi brand. And as market oversupply grew in 2002 and beyond, surplus wine purchased on the spot market created the Charles Shaw brand, nicknamed "Two Buck Chuck" for its $1.99 price. Soon it was selling 5 million cases a year.

This bifurcated focus led to the middle segment of the market ($5–$8 a bottle) being underserved. Into that gap stepped Yellow-Tail, an Australian import with a trendy label, and the full-bodied fruity wine the U.S. market preferred. Soon it was selling 10 million cases a year worldwide. With little ability to respond quickly from domestic sources, U.S. wineries began looking to an unexpected source— imported wine from low-cost producing countries, a development we will describe below.

Europe's Renewed Advance   As EU agricultural policy changes shifted the focus from reducing oversupply to subsidizing marketing and promotion, European wines began growing their market share in the U.S. Finally, after years of beating a retreat to New World competitors, the major EU wine exporting countries could boast that they captured 99% of the 2006 dollar volume increase in imported wine sales into the U.S.

With the Australians charging into the popular premium segment, French wines extended their penetration into the super premium segment. While ranked number three in imports by volume, France

[16]Ibid, p. 5.

beat all other countries in terms of import value. Its price per bottle, at 77% above the average of all imports, reflected its strong position in the luxury segment including champagne. In contrast, the growth in Italian imports was occurring mostly in the popular priced range that was their historic strength. Promoting well-known brands such as Riunite, Cavit and Bolla, they increased their 2006 volume by 2 billion cases, thereby retaining their position as the number one importer by volume.

But ironically, the success of the European imports was also helped by U.S. domestic producers. As they became more global in scope, many U.S. wine companies began divesting vineyards and expanding their marketing role. Foreign wine suppliers benefited from this shift in two ways. First, when domestic companies took advantage of a law that permitted up to 25% foreign wine in products that could still be labeled as American, the imports became the source of the less expensive bulk wine required for blending. Foreign suppliers also benefited when domestic companies broadened their line by importing and marketing country specific wines. Gallo became particularly adept at this strategy, and successfully launched brands such as Bella Sera and Ecco Domani with wines sourced in Italy, and Red Bicyclette, its brand of imported French wine. In essence, the American companies filled the gap in marketing capability and distribution expertise that had previously been a barrier to entry for many European imports.

Australia's New Challenge   For more than a decade, Australia's wine producers had become accustomed to success. In 1996, the industry's "Strategy 2025" plan had detailed a "total commitment to innovation and style" as its means of becoming "the world's most influential and profitable supplier of branded wines by 2025." Ten years later, grape production had more than doubled and exports of had grown by 530% to 782 million liters in 2006, making Australia the world's number four wine exporter. In fact, most of Strategy 2025's goals had been achieved by 2006, almost 20 years ahead of schedule.

But celebrations were dampened by the recognition that in the mid-2000s, exports to the U.K., its largest market, were stagnating and average price was eroding. Fortunately, the U.S. market was growing rapidly, and by 2007 represented 31% of Australia's wine export market value, compared to 33% for the U.K. But with an average price per liter of $4.46 for Australian imports into the US, it represented a much more attractive market than the U.K. where the average had slipped to $3.35.

But Australian wine was also facing price and image problems in the U.S. market. Challenged by overproduction since 2000, its bumper crops of 2004, 2005, and 2006 had led Australian producers to aggressively reduce prices in all export markets. While this led to a boom in export sales, it also established an image of Australian wines as "cheap and cheerful." The image was typified by Yellow Tail, the phenomenally successful brand that sold 8.1 million cases into the U.S. in 2007, accounting for 36% of all Australian imports to the country.

Being trapped by this image was particularly problematic as costs started to rise. Serious droughts in Australia led to major cost increases for water at the same time as global energy prices were soaring. Together, these factors caused an increase in production cost of almost $200 at tonne, and forced Australian producers to recognize that regardless of their greater efficiency, Argentina and Chile were lower cost producers. For example, while Australia could land its bulk table wine in the U.S. at $0.80 a liter, Argentina's price was $0.36 a liter.

Like other countries, the Argentineans and Chileans had learned from Australia's success, and had copied its successful strategy to develop their own accessible wines marketed under consistent brands. For example, Concha y Toro was the world's fourth largest wine brand, ahead of Gallo and Yellow Tail, for example. And even where emerging New World producers had not developed the necessary marketing skills, a growing number of global wine companies could offset that shortcoming. For example, in 2007, the top selling new wine in the U.S. was the popular premium South African brand Sebeka—sourced, bottled, branded, and marketed by Gallo. In short, Australia's competitive position in the U.S. was being seriously challenged.

Behind the Battle Lines: Strategy in France and Australia

Buoyed by a decade of success, yet also concerned by the recent weakening of the average price recorded by Australian export wines, the Australian Wine and Brandy Corporation, the government's wine export body, linked up with the industry-led Winemakers Federation of Australia to develop a new strategy supporting the continued growth of the industry. Under the title "Directions to 2025," the document detailed how the industry would implement the second stage of the landmark "Strategy 2025" which had emphasized volume growth to 2002, value growth to 2015, and achieving global preeminence for Australian wine by 2025.

On a broad platform of Wine Australia, "Directions to 2025" planned to support four sub-brands, each targeting a separate consumer group. "Brand Champions" would cover accessible premium brand wines and promote ease of enjoyment; "Generation Next" would emphasize innovation which was important to younger consumers who associated wine with social occasions not grape attributes; "Regional Heroes" would develop an association between Australian regions and wine varieties or styles; and "Landmark Australia" would support Australia's high profile aspirational wines and provide an umbrella of world-class reputation. (**Exhibit 11** shows a map off brand attributes.)

But a 2008 crush of 32% more than the previous year led many to believe that the recent drought-related production declines were over. Within the industry, there were concerns that as supply increased, producers would abandon the long-term strategy and return to their earlier discounting practices, particularly for popular brands that could generate the volume to remove excess supply. Australian wine making icon Wolf Blass despaired at what he called "a wrongheaded approach." He felt that Australian wine could not compete long-term in a low-cost battle, and argued that the export business should focus on full-bodied, quality wines that would raise its image. That would be a real challenge in an industry that was forecasting a 7% oversupply of fruit by 2013.

Meanwhile, in France, the industry and the government were responding differently to the global surplus. In 2005, the grower-led Comite d'Action Viticole (CAV) launched its campaign of violence against imports, blocking highways and the overturning trucks of foreign wine. In a subsequent meeting with the prime minister, a delegation of winemakers extracted his commitment to support a national strategy "to help French wine recover lost markets." The plan, funded to €90 million, offered direct support to wineries in financial difficulty, and promised funds to relaunch French wines into the world market. Furthermore, a new national wine committee would work on simplifying the complex classification systems, perhaps moving towards larger, simpler regional appellations such as Bordeaux or Burgundy. Finally, the prime minister directed his agriculture minister to go to Brussels and argue for more funds to distill surplus wine into industrial alcohol.

But the EU was moving in a different direction. In 2007, it announced plans to use its annual €1.3 billion wine budget more effectively. It would be ending the €500 million annual buyback of unsold wine, redirecting those funds to new incentives encouraging farmers to uproot vines on 200,000 hectares of vineyards, and providing €120 million a year for a marketing campaign. The plans were extremely unpopular with farmers, and when the EU plan passed in spite of their objections, the protests escalated. In France, the CAV claimed responsibility for explosions at supermarkets selling imported wines, particularly in the high productivity Languedoc-Roussillon wine region in the south of France. Then, five balaclava-clad men appeared on French television threatening more violence unless wine prices increased.

Most in the industry felt such actions were unhelpful, and undermined their marketing efforts. They urged winemakers to get behind the new promotion campaign for "South of France" wines that was supported with €20 million from government and industry coffers. In an unusual display of unity, producers from various AOC, VDQS, and

Exhibit 11   Wine Australia's Market Segment

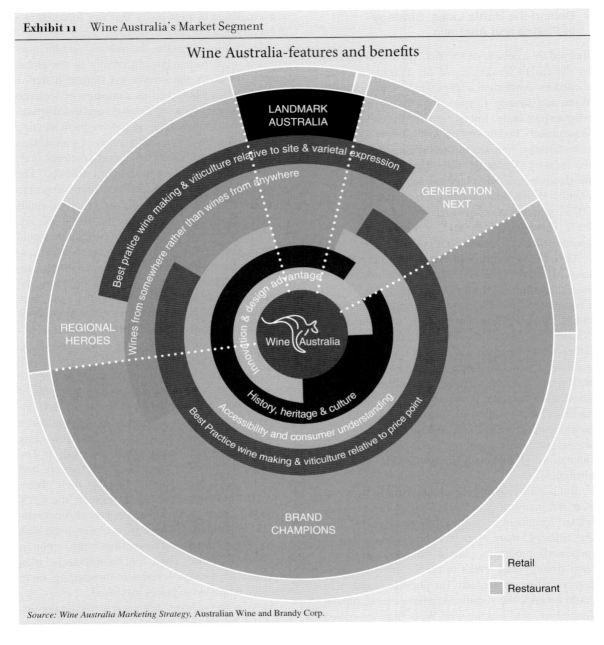

Wine Australia-features and benefits

Source: Wine Australia Marketing Strategy, Australian Wine and Brandy Corp.

Vin de Pays regions had agreed to launch products under this common banner. While some felt it was the only chance they had to compete against strongly branded New World wines, others worried that the "South of France" brand was too generic, and hid the richness of the area's diverse sources of wine. But in the battle for export markets, everyone agreed that something had to be done.

Case 2-2   The Globalization of CEMEX

Pankaj Ghemawat

Geographic diversification enables us to operate in multiple regions with different business cycles. For the long term, we are trying to ensure that no one market accounts for more than one third of our business. Yet we do not diversify simply to balance cyclic downturns and upswings. We do not see volatility as an occasional, random element added to the cost of doing business in an interconnected global marketplace. We plan for volatility. We prepare for it. We have learned how to profit from it.

—Lorenzo Zambrano, CEO of CEMEX[1]

In 1990, Cementos Mexicanos was a Mexican cement company that faced trade sanctions in its major export market, the United States. By the end of 1999, CEMEX operated cement plants in 15 countries, owned production or distribution facilities in a total of 30, and traded cement in more than 60. Non-Mexican operations accounted for nearly 60% of assets, slightly over 50% of revenues and 40% of EBITDA (earnings before interest, taxes, depreciation, and amortization) that year. CEMEX's sales revenues had increased from less than $1 billion in 1989 to nearly $5 billion in 1999, and it had become the third largest cement company in the world in terms of capacity, as well as the largest international trader. Growth had been achieved without compromising profitability: in the late 1990s, its ratio of EBITDA to sales ranged between 30% and 40%—ten to fifteen percentage points higher than its leading global competitors. In addition, the company was celebrated as one of the few multinationals from Latin America, and as a model user of information technology in an otherwise low-tech setting.

CEMEX executives sometimes characterized the company's international operations as a "ring of grey gold," comprising commitments to high-growth markets, mostly developing and mostly falling in a band that circled the globe north of the Equator. By the end of 1990s, the addition of countries such as Indonesia and Egypt to the ring had prompted discussions about the scope and speed of CEMEX's international expansion. So had the hostile bid, in early 2000, by Lafarge, the second-largest cement competitor worldwide in cement for Blue Circle, the sixth largest. Hector Medina, CEMEX's Executive Vice President of Planning and Finance, likened the takeover struggle to "ripples in an agitated environment" that could have significant implications for the other cement majors.

This case begins with a brief overview of the cement industry and international competition within it. It then describes the globalization of CEMEX and how it was managed.

The Cement Industry

Cement had been used since antiquity as a binding agent that hardened when mixed with water. It was first made in its modern form in England during the early part of the 19th century. The production process, which remained broadly unchanged, involved burning a blend of limestone (or other calcareous rocks) and smaller quantities of materials containing aluminum, silicon, and iron in a kiln at high temperatures to yield marble-sized pellets of "clinker." Clinker was then ground with gypsum and other minerals to yield cement, a fine gray powder. The mixture of

‖ Professor Pankaj Ghemawat and Research Associate Jamie L. Matthews prepared this case drawing, in part, on a course paper by Pau Cortes, Heriberto Diarte and Enrique A. Garcia. HBS cases are developed solely as the basis for class discussion. Cases are not intended to serve as endorsements, sources of primary data, or illustrations of effective or ineffective management.

‖ [1]CEMEX 1998 annual report, p. 4.

Exhibit 1   How CEMEX Makes Cement

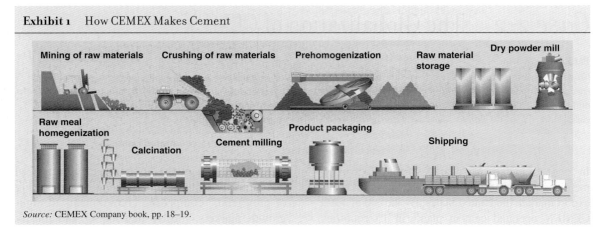

Source: CEMEX Company book, pp. 18–19.

cement, aggregates, and water that hardened into a rocklike mass after hydration was known as concrete. Concrete could be mixed "on site" where it was to be used, or it could be obtained in "ready-mix" form from a central drum at the plant or a ready-mix truck.

Supply   Since limestone, clay and the other raw materials required were abundant in many regions of the world, cement could usually be produced locally. Cement companies often owned raw material quarries and located their production facilities close by to minimize materials handling. The production technology was continuous process, consisted of a number of stages (see **Exhibit 1**) and was marked by high capital- and energy-intensity. It was also considered relatively mature: no major innovations had been recorded in the last 20 years. The minimum efficient scale (MES) for a cement plant approximated 1 million tons of capacity per year. New capacity cost about $120–$180 per ton, depending on local factors such as the cost of land, environmental legislation, and the need for ancillary equipment and infrastructure, including investment in quarries and kilns. A cement plant's assets were largely dedicated to the production of cement and might last for decades. Operating costs typically ranged from $20–$50 per ton, with labor accounting for well under $10 per ton.[2] Transportation costs, in contrast, could account for as much as one-third of total delivered costs.

High transportation costs in relation to production costs meant that there was only a limited distance within which a plant could deliver cement at competitive prices. Road transportation was the most expensive, and limited the effective distribution radius to 150–300 miles.[3] Waterborne transportation was the most economical and, as a result of innovations since the mid-1950s, had led to a substantial expansion of MES.[4] New systems of loading and unloading barges were introduced and specialized ships for carrying cement were developed. As a result, cement producers began to establish much larger plants that shipped cement to distribution terminals in distant markets as well as serving local ones. Still, a host of other costs had to be layered on top of the costs of ocean freight for long-distance trade to take place (see **Exhibit 2**). In the late 1990s, international seaborne traffic in cement and clinker averaged about 50 million tons per year. It was believed that about 10 million tons of this traffic was carried by small vessels on short coastal or estuarial voyages, and about 40 million tons by oceangoing vessels.[5]

Demand   Cross-country comparisons indicated that the long-run demand for cement was directly related to GDP, with per capita consumption

[2]Merrill Lynch, Ownership Changes in Asian Cement, December 3, 1999, p. 117.

[3]ING Barings, *European Cement Review,* February 2000, p. 24.
[4]Hervé Dumez and Alain Jeunemaître, *Understanding and Regulating the Market at a Time of Globalization: The Case of the Cement Industry,* p. 113.
[5]Drewry Shipping Consultants, *Cement Shipping: Opportunities in a Complex and Volatile Market,* January 1998.

Exhibit 2   Cost Structure of Asian Exports to the United States

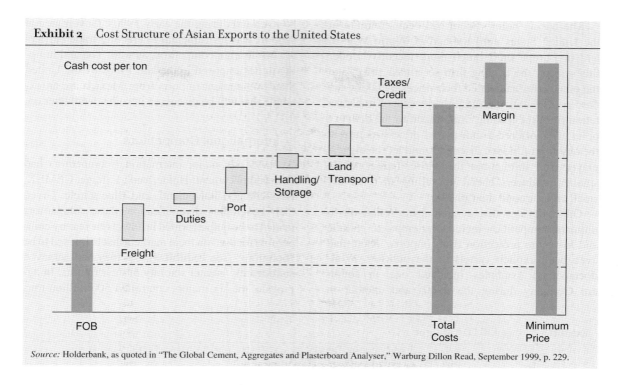

Source: Holderbank, as quoted in "The Global Cement, Aggregates and Plasterboard Analyser," Warburg Dillon Read, September 1999, p. 229.

increasing up to the $20,000-plus per capita income mark and then declining very gradually. Numerous other local attributes affected cement demand as well. Rainfall had a negative effect since it made cement-based construction more difficult and increased the likelihood of using substitutes such as wood or steel instead. Population density had a positive effect, as higher density led to taller buildings and more complex infrastructure. Demand also tended to be higher in areas with a warm climate and lower under extremes of heat or cold. Demand generally decreased with a long coastline, since more sea transport meant fewer roads, and increased with the share of governmental expenditures in GDP. CEMEX forecast total world demand to grow at slightly under 4% per annum through 2010. Demand growth was expected to be highest in the developing Asian economies, Central America, the Caribbean, and Sub-Saharan Africa, where it would approach or exceed 5%, and lowest in Western Europe and North America, where it would be closer to 1%.

In the short run, cement demand varied directly with GDP and, even more reliably, with construction expenditure/investment. As a result, construction plans could be used to develop short-run forecasts for cement demand. However, the cyclicality of the construction sector made medium-run forecasts somewhat dicey. Bulk sales were very sensitive to GDP growth, interest rates, and other macroeconomic factors that affected the formal construction market. Retail sales to individual consumers for home construction and the like, which were important in developing countries, were discovered to be less cyclical and also offered opportunities for some branding, as described below.

Competition   Cyclicality on the demand side combined with capital-intensity, durability, and specialization on the supply side to mean that overcapacity in the cement industry could be ruinous in its effects. Cement firms tried to cushion their interactions under conditions of overcapacity by relying on "basing point" pricing systems, other leadership strategies, and even direct restraints on competition.

The basing point system had been common in the United States until the end of World War II, and in Europe until much more recently. Under this system, the leading firm set a base price, and the other firms calculated their prices by taking the base price and increasing it by the cost of transportation from the leading firm's plant to the delivery point. This offered a transparent price structure in the absence of hidden discounts, and let the biggest players sell throughout the entire market, while smaller producers ended up selling in relatively small areas around their plants.

Other devices that cement firms relied on to mitigate competition included attempts to collude and to secure protection from imports. There had even been explicit cartels in the industry. Well-documented examples included one in southern Germany during the 1980s and another in

Switzerland during the early 1990s. Governmental support was instrumental in erecting trade barriers to curb foreign competitors as well. The antidumping duties imposed in the late 1980s by the United States on cement imports from Mexico are an example that will be discussed in some detail later on.

International Competitors

By 1999, six major international competitors had emerged in cement: Holderbank, Lafarge, CEMEX, Heidelberger, Italcementi, and Blue Circle. Given their geographic diversification, these competitors tended to be outperformed in any given year by competitors focused on local markets that happened to be "booming" (see **Exhibit 3**), but they had achieved significantly greater stability in their returns. In aggregate, the six majors controlled 500 million tons

Exhibit 3   1999 EBITDA Margin

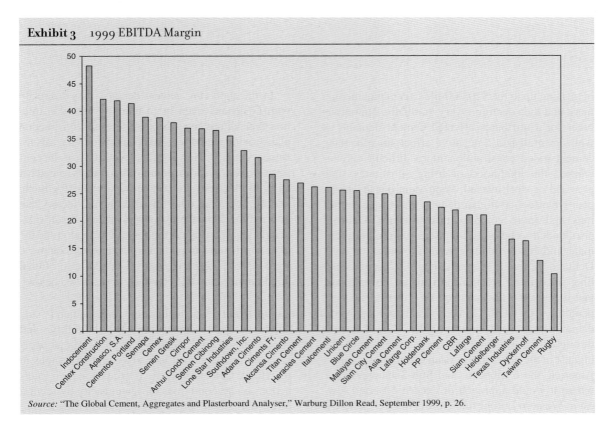

Source: "The Global Cement, Aggregates and Plasterboard Analyser," Warburg Dillon Read, September 1999, p. 26.

Exhibit 4   Selected Data on Global Competitors (December 1999)

Company	Holder-bank	Lafarge	CEMEX	Heidel-berger	Ital-cementi	Blue Circle
Accounting Data						
Sales (US$ m)	7,618	10,552	4,828	6,404	3,414	3,604
Cement volume (m tons)	74.6	64.3	39.1	46.0	37.8	NA
EBIT (US$ m)	1,066	1,766	1,436	645	511	466
EBITDA (US$ m)	1,785	2,446	1,791	1,195	838	684
CAPEX (US$ m)	784	1,144	262	540	310	295
Free Cash Flow (US$ m)	144	511	862	487	200	(294)
Net debt (US$ m)	4,767	5,422	4,794	2,957	1,731	538
Net debt/EBITDA	.7	2.2	2.7	2.5	2.1	0.8
Total debt to capitalization	54.1%	46.5%	44.1%	51.3%	43.0%	31.0%
Interest coverage	4.6	6.6	3.6	4.8	6.8	5.7
Stock Market Data[a] (to Dec. '99)						
Market value (US$ m)	11,122	12,132	7,203	4,209	2,488	4,707
Profitability of stock US$[b] (12 mth)	16%	22%	114%	3%	9%	12%
TEV[c] (US$ m)	17,015	19,157	12,500	7,373	5,050	5,593
TEV adjusted/ton (US$)[d]	160	130	172	86	90	93
Capacity Data						
Footprint[e] (m tons)	140	107	85	71	55	45
Degree of control of footprint	72%	79%	77%	75%	98%	97%
Controlled capacity (m tons)	101	85	65	53	54	44
Number of Countries	53	38	15	33	14	14

Sources: Annual Reports; Datastream; JP Morgan; CEMEX
[a]End-of-period exchange rate used for calculations.
[b]For Holderbank, class B stock; for CEMEX, New CPO.
[c]TEV defined as total enterprise value (debt plus equity).
[d]Excluding non-cement assets for Lafarge (35%), Heidelberger (10%) and Blue Circle (25%).
[e]Footprint defined as total capacity in which a given company has a significant stake.

of capacity, representing slightly over one-quarter of capacity, representing slightly over one-quarter of the world total, or over one-third of the total excluding China. The six-firm concentration ratio had been only 12% in 1988, with Votorantim of Brazil edging out CEMEX for the sixth spot.[6]

In 1999, each of the six major international competitors still had clearly identifiable national origins and controlled a significant share of its home market. But each had also come to operate production facilities

[6]Podolny, Joel, John Roberts, Joon Han, and Andrea Hodge, 1999, "CEMEX, S.A. de C.V.: Global Competition in a Local Business," Stanford, CA: Stanford University. ECCH #IB17.

in anywhere between a dozen and several dozen countries around the world. **Exhibit 4** supplies financial data on the six majors, and **Exhibit 5** summarizes their capacity shares in a number of major markets.

Although some of the majors, such as Holderbank, had operated in several countries for decades, internationalization, particularly in an interregional sense, did not begin until the 1970s. This was when European players began to penetrate the United States. During the 1960s and 1970s, the U.S. cement industry had fallen into a crisis as profitability dropped with the collapse in prices, and domestic firms responded by

Exhibit 5   Capacity Shares of the Big 6 in Selected Markets

Country	Holderbank	Lafarge	CEMEX	Heidelberger	Italcementi	Blue Circle
Japan	0.0%	0.0%	0.0%	0.0%	0.0%	0.0%
Korea	0.0%	12.0%	0.0%	0.0%	0.0%	0.0%
Taiwan	0.0%	0.0%	0.0%	0.0%	0.0%	0.0%
Indonesia	0.0%	2.6%	43.7%	0.0%	0.0%	0.0%
Malaysia	0.0%	6.6%	0.0%	3.9%	0.0%	46.4%
Philippines	37.5%	20.5%	22.0%	0.0%	0.0%	16.7%
Thailand	25.3%	0.0%	0.0%	0.0%	13.2%	0.0%
India	1.4%	0.3%	0.0%	0.0%	0.0%	0.0%
South Africa	36.3%	25.8%	0.0%	0.0%	0.0%	0.0%
Egypt	5.4%	5.0%	16.9%	0.0%	0.0%	3.3%
Greece	0.0%	0.0%	0.0%	0.0%	5.5%	58.9%
Poland	0.0%	21.2%	0.0%	22.4%	0.0%	0.0%
Turkey	0.0%	8.3%	0.0%	17.3%	9.2%	0.0%
France	12.6%	33.9%	0.0%	26.8%	26.4%	0.0%
Germany	6.6%	7.0%	0.0%	25.3%	0.0%	0.0%
Italy	6.2%	5.0%	0.0%	0.0%	36.9%	0.0%
Portugal	0.0%	0.0%	0.0%	0.0%	0.0%	0.0%
Spain	9.9%	19.3%	26.5%	0.0%	6.6%	0.0%
UK	0.0%	0.0%	0.0%	23.8%	0.0%	50.3%
Canada	19.1%	32.9%	0.0%	20.4%	11.2%	13.8%
U.S.	13.5%	8.3%	1.8%	11.2%	4.6%	6.2%
Argentina	37.6%	11.2%	0.0%	0.0%	0.0%	0.0%
Brazil	10.0%	13.4%	0.0%	0.0%	0.0%	0.0%
Mexico	19.2%	4.3%	64.6%	0.0%	0.0%	0.0%
Venezuela	24.5%	23.6%	40.6%	0.0%	0.0%	0.0%

Source: CEMEX

lowering investment in cement and diversifying into other lines of business. This resulted in shortages in some regional markets and provided an opening for European cement firms that had remained strong and were looking to expand. By 2000, European groups controlled 65% of the U.S. market.

Cross-border investment in the United States had been concentrated in certain periods—most recently, 1985–1988 and 1991–1993—instead of trickling in more continuously. Such waves were characteristic of cross-border investment in other regions as well, given the cement majors' emphasis on buying existing capacity rather than adding new capacity to enter new markets (see **Exhibit 6**). Obviously,

Exhibit 6   Waves of Acquisitions

Period	Region	Period	Region
1985–1988	U.S./ Canada	1995–1997	Latin America
1987–1990	Latin America	1996–1998	E. Europe
1989–1991	Mediterranean	1998 onwards	SE. Asia
1991–1993	U.S.	1999 onwards	W. Europe
1990–1994	E. Europe		

Source: Adapted by casewriters from ING Barings, European Cement Review, February 2000.

acquisitions were most attractive to them when the market values of target companies were less than their underlying values—a condition more likely to be fulfilled at the bottom of the local economic cycle rather than the top. The underlying values of acquired franchises could be assessed by estimating their average profitability, capacity utilization, weighted average cost of capital and, probably most problematically, expected long-run growth rates. See **Exhibit 7** for an attempt by an investment bank to perform such calculations at the country level. In practice, of course, such country-level analyses had to be supplemented with target-specific considerations such as the target's cost position and market share, and the kind of base it afforded for further cost-reduction and expansion.

Starting in 1997 and particularly after the summer of 1998, the largest and most concentrated wave of cross-border investment ever began in South East Asia. The international players had their eye on the market for many years, but had been unable to justify the entry premium—some companies in the region had been valued at up to $300 per ton of capacity on an enterprise value basis! The Asian crisis that began in 1997 changed the situation dramatically and gave the majors the opportunity they were waiting for. The six majors' Asian cement deals through fall 1999 are summarized in **Exhibit 8.** They quickly increased their share of capacity in Asia, excluding China, from less than 20% to about 60%.

Of the leading international competitors in cement, two, Holderbank and Lafarge, were larger than CEMEX. Holderbank had cement operations on five continents and in more than 50 countries, making it the most global as well as the largest international competitor. Its globalization strategy could be traced back to the early 1920s when the company (formed in 1912) first moved out of Switzerland and into neighboring France, Belgium, and the Netherlands. The company's 1999 sales were $7,618 million and its EBIT was $1,066 million. Cement accounted for 68% of 1999 sales and concrete and aggregates for 24%.

Lafarge was ranked second in the global cement market and also had strong positions in other

building such as plaster, aggregates, concrete, and gypsum. Its 1999 sales were $10,552 million and EBIT was $1,766 million. Cement accounted for 35% of 1999 sales and concrete and aggregates for another 30%. Lafarge was not as focused on emerging markets as some of the other global players. In February 2000, it mounted a hostile bid, valued at nearly $5.5 billion, for Britain's Blue Circle, the sixth-largest cement competitor. Motives for the deal included achieving a certain size in order to remain visible and attractive to investors, expanding cashflow and, relatedly, geographic presence and, probably, dislodging Holderbank from the top spot in the global cement industry. However, by May, Lafarge had managed to attract only 44% of Blue Circle's shares with its aggressively priced offer.

CEMEX

By the year 2000, CEMEX had become the third largest cement company in the world with approximately 65 million tons of capacity (see **Exhibit 9** for historical financial data). CEMEX traced its origins back to 1906 when the Cementos Hidalgo cement plant was opened, with a capacity of less than 5,000 tons per year, in northern Mexico, near Monterrey. In 1931, it was merged with Cementos Portland Monterrey, founded by Lorenzo Zambrano, to form Cementos Mexicanos, later renamed CEMEX. Over the next half-century, the company expanded its capacity to about 15 million tons, and was well on its way to becoming Mexico's market leader by the early 1980s.

In 1985, Lorenzo Zambrano, scion of the Zambrano family that still controlled CEMEX and a grandson as well as namesake of the company's founder, took over as CEO. In his first few years at the helm, CEMEX continued to grow by constructing additional cement capacity. It also began to diversify horizontally into areas such as petrochemicals, mining, and tourism in order to reduce the risks related to its dependence on a highly cyclical core business. However, it wasn't long before Zambrano decided to refocus the company on cement and cement-related businesses. Based partly on the work of the Boston Consulting Group, he had

Exhibit 7 Market Statistics and Valuations for Selected Countries[a]

Country	Ex-plant Price per Ton (US$)	Cash Cost per Ton (US$)	EBITDA per Ton (US$)	Risk Free Rate (%)	Equity Risk Premium (%)	Market Gearing (%)	WACC (%)	Value/ Ton of Demand (US$)	Domestic Demand (m tons)	Domestic Capacity (m tons)	Value/Ton of Capacity (no growth) (US$)	Trend Growth (%)	Value/ Ton of Capacity (trended) (US$)
Japan	48	38	10	1.8	5.0	50.0	4.8	208	72.8	97.0	156	0.1	160
Korea	50	33	17	8.5	8.0	20.0	15.1	113	47.6	62.1	86	5.0	129
Taiwan	58	37	21	5.7	8.0	25.0	12.0	176	20.5	24.5	147	3.0	196
Indonesia	41	23	18	12.0	8.0	50.0	16.5	109	18.1	45.3	44	7.5	80
Malaysia	41	28	13	8.0	8.0	25.0	14.3	90	8.2	17.5	42	7.8	93
Philippines	49	34	15	14.0	8.0	50.0	18.5	81	12.5	20.4	50	8.0	88
Thailand	48	26	22	10.0	8.0	40.0	15.2	145	25.6	58.0	64	8.0	135
India	52	38	14	9.5	8.0	40.0	19.0	74	80.8	85.0	70	7.5	116
S. Africa	55	37	18	15.0	6.0	15.0	20.3	89	8.8	12.0	65	0.9	68
Egypt	53	33	20	10.0	8.0	0.0	18.0	111	24.7	23.0	119	5.9	178
Greece	58	30	28	6.4	6.0	20.0	11.4	246	8.5	15.0	139	1.5	161
Poland	38	28	10	9.5	6.0	20.0	14.5	69	13.8	16.3	58	5.0	89
Turkey	40	26	14	10.3	8.0	0.0	18.3	77	36.4	61.0	46	6.5	71
France	78	49	29	4.7	4.0	30.0	7.8	372	19.1	28.1	253	-1.5	211
Germany	72	51	21	4.6	4.0	25.0	7.9	268	37.0	51.0	194	1.0	221
Italy	55	38	17	4.8	4.0	25.0	8.1	211	35.0	52.5	141	-0.3	136
Portugal	66	40	26	4.8	5.0	10.0	9.4	277	10.0	9.6	289	0.0	289
Spain	64	40	24	4.8	5.0	10.0	9.4	255	31.0	39.3	201	2.7	283
UK	74	51	23	5.4	4.0	10.0	9.1	253	12.8	14.4	225	-0.2	219
Argentina	62	40	22	12.0	8.0	40.0	17.2	128	8.2	9.5	110	3.0	134
Brazil	59	39	20	13.0	8.0	40.0	18.2	110	40.1	45.8	96	5.0	133
Mexico	96	40	56	12.0	8.0	50.0	16.5	339	25.7	44.0	198	2.5	233
Venezuela	95	35	60	15.0	8.0	20.0	21.6	278	4.5	8.6	145	-0.5	142
Canada	67	42	25	5.5	4.0	0.0	9.5	263	8.6	15.2	148	0.5	157
U.S.	69	48	21	5.7	4.0	0.0	9.7	216	107.1	97.3	238	1.0	266

Source: Adapted by casewriters from ING Barings, European Cement Review, February 2000, p. 29.

[a]Franchise value represents the theoretical value of one ton of capacity (assuming all sales are made domestically). The first step in its derivation is to obtain the capital value of cash flow generated in perpetuity by one ton of production. This is calculated by taking EBITDA per ton ($) and dividing by the weighted average cost of capital. The second step is to find the ratio of domestic demand to domestic supply. Dividing the value of one ton of production by the ratio calculated in the second step gives the value of one ton of capacity. (The idea is that if domestic demand exceeds available supply then the value of owning capacity is greater than the value suggested by current EBITDA alone). The final step is to adjust franchise value for growth in domestic demand, trend growth, which is defined as the average of rolling averages for the previous 5, 10 and 20 years and is therefore less vulnerable to short-run fluctuations in growth rates.

Exhibit 8   Cement Majors' Asian Deals after the Asian Crisis

	Country	Date	Stake %	Price (US$ m)	Capacity (m tons)	Value/Ton (US$)	Source
Holderbank							
Union Cement	Philippines	Jul-98	40%	210	5.8	146	A
Alsons Cement	Philippines	Jan-99	25%	22	2.5	130	B
Tengara Cement	Malaysia	Jun-98	70%	28	1.1	42	A
Siam City Cement	Thailand	Aug-98	25%	153	12.3	95	A
Huaxin Cement	China	Jan-99	23%	20	1.4	61	A
Total				**433**	**23.1**	**107**	
Lafarge							
Republic Cement	Philippines	Feb-98	14%	25	1.6	119	A
Continental Cement and South East Asia Cement	Philippines	Oct-98	100% 64%	460	4.6	132	C
Haifa Cement	Korea	Jul-99	33%	100	7.4	68	A
Andalas	Indonesia	n/a	16%	10	1.2		D
Tisco	India	1999	100%	127	0.3	107	A
Total[a]				**712**	**13.9**	**109**	
CEMEX							
Rizal and Solid Cement	Philippines	Dec 97, Nov 98	70%	219	2.8	166	C
Apo Cement	Philippines	Jan-99	100%	400	3.0	164	A
Semen Gresik	Indonesia	mid-98	14%	115	20.1	55	A
Semen Gresik	Indonesia	Nov-98	8%	49	20.1	56	A
Semen Gresik	Indonesia	1999	4%	28	20.1	58	A
Total				**811**	**25.9**	**109**	
Italcementi							
Jalaprathan Cement	Thailand	Oct-98	55%	26	1.6	58	A
Asia Cement	Thailand	Jul-99	53%	180	4.8	131	A
Total				**206**	**6.4**	**112**	
Blue Circle							
Iligan Cement Corp	Philippines	Jul-99	95%	53	0.5	109	C
Kedah Cement	Malaysia	Oct-98	65%	185	3.5	164	A
APMC	Malaysia	Dec-98	50%	309	4.7	157	A
Inflow from Minorities in Malaysian rights	Malaysia	Dec-98	65%	−118			D
Republic Cement	Philippines	1998	54%	90	1.6	138	C
Fortune Cement	Philippines	Jul-98	20%	35	1.9	114	A
Fortune Cement	Philippines	Jan-99	31%	86	1.9	147	A
Zeus Holdings	Philippines	Jul-98	73%	31	0.4	204	A
Total[b]				**671**	**12.6**	**153**	

Sources: Adapted by casewriters from: A) CEMEX; B) SDC database, Cembureau, *World Cement Directory 1996*, p. 322; C) Warburg Dillon Read, Global Equity Research, *The Global Cement, Aggregates and Plasterboard Analyser,* September 1999, p. 230; D) Merrill Lynch, *Asian Cement,* December 1999, p. 5.
[a]Excludes Andalas. Also, value/ton includes a weighting of 94% for Continental/SEACem to reflect breakdown of capacity between the companies.
[b]Includes inflow from minorities in Malaysian rights in total price.

Exhibit 9 CEMEX Financials (Millions of US dollars, except share and per share amounts)

Income Statement	1988	1989	1990	1991	1992	1993	1994	1995	1996	1997	1998	1999
Net Sales	612	988	1,305	1,706	2,194	2,897	2,101	2,564	3,365	3,788	4,315	4,828
Cost of Sales	428	772	928	1,064	1,371	1,747	1,212	1,564	2,041	2,322	2,495	2,690
Gross Profit	184	215	377	642	823	1,150	889	1,000	1,325	1,467	1,820	2,138
Operating Expenses	61	120	178	221	286	444	325	388	522	572	642	702
Operating Income	123	95	199	420	537	706	564	612	802	895	1,178	1,436
Comprehensive Financing (Cost)	2	52	(5)	124	179	25	(16)	567	529	159	(132)	(29)
Other Income (Expenses) Net	70	4	(42)	(47)	(89)	(101)	(133)	(162)	(171)	(138)	(152)	(296)
Income Before Taxes & Others	195	151	152	498	628	630	415	1,017	1,160	916	893	1,111
Minority Interest	26	25	30	60	70	97	45	109	119	107	39	56
Majority Net Income	167	121	148	442	545	522	376	759	977	761	803	973
Earnings per Share	0.15	0.11	0.13	0.40	0.52	0.49	0.35	0.59	0.75	0.59	0.64	0.77
Dividends per Share	0.01	0.01	0.02	0.06	0.07	0.09	0.06	0.07	0.0	0.12	0.14	0.17
Shares Outstanding (millions)	1,114	1,114	1,114	1,114	1,056	1,056	1,077	1,286	1,303	1,268	1,258	1,366
ROE	14.2	9.5	10.6	24.1	18.7	16.2	13.3	26.4	29.3	21.7	20.7	18.8
Balance Sheet												
Cash and Temporary Investments	189	186	145	202	384	326	484	355	409	380	407	326
Net Working Capital	140	226	236	286	562	595	528	567	611	588	638	699
Property, Plant, & Equipment, Net	1,117	2,037	2,357	2,614	4,124	4,407	4,093	4,939	5,743	6,006	6,142	6,922
Total Assets	1,710	2,940	3,438	3,848	7,457	8,018	7,894	8,370	9,942	10,231	10,460	11,864
Short-Term Debt	69	360	261	144	884	684	648	870	815	657	1,106	1,030
Long-Term Debt	142	792	1,043	1,267	2,436	2,866	3,116	3,034	3,954	3,961	3,136	3,341
Total Liabilities	355	1,354	1,566	1,607	3,897	4,022	4,291	4,603	5,605	5,535	5,321	5,430
Minority Interest	182	306	474	408	649	771	771	889	1,000	1,181	1,251	1,253
Stockholders' Equity, excluding Minority Interest	1,173	1,280	1,398	1,833	2,911	3,225	2,832	2878	3,337	3,515	3,887	5,182
Total Stockholders' Equity	1,355	1,586	1,872	2,242	3,560	3,996	3,603	3767	4,337	4,696	5,138	6,435
Book Value per Share	1.05	1.15	1.25	1.65	2.76	3.05	2.63	2.24	2.57	2.74	3.08	3.79
Other Financial Data												
Operating Margin (%)	20.2	9.6	15.3	24.6	24.5	24.4	26.9	23.9	23.8	23.6	27.3	29.8
EBITDA Margin (%)	28.6	17.9	24.8	33.2	31.9	31.6	34.2	31.8	32.3	31.5	34.4	37.1
EBITDA	175	177	324	567	700	914	719	815	1,087	1,193	1,485	1,791

Source: CEMEX

concluded that geographic diversification within the cement business was preferable to horizontal diversification outside it. All the non-core assets were eventually divested and CEMEX switched to a strategy of growth through acquisitions.

This strategy focused, in the first instance, on Mexico. As Mexico began to open up in the late 1980s, large firms such as Holderbank and Lafarge viewed it as a possible market to expand their operations. Faced with this threat, CEMEX decided to unify its Mexican operations. In 1987, CEMEX acquired Cementos Anahuac, giving the company access to Mexico's central market and bolstering its export capabilities with the addition of two plants and four million tons of capacity. Two years later, the acquisition of Cementos Tolteca, Mexico's second-largest cement producer with seven new plants and 6.6 million tons of capacity, made CE-MEX Mexico's largest producer. These mergers, which cost CEMEX nearly $1 billion, secured its position in Mexico and gave it the size and financial resources to begin the process of geographic expansion.

When the 1994/1995 peso crisis struck, CEMEX had just finished a plan for revamping its Mexican operations. In December 1994, after a year of political instability that included the assassination of a presidential candidate, Mexico's foreign reserves dropped to about $5 billion, down from nearly $30 billion in March. Incoming President Zedillo warned his citizens to prepare for tough times. CEMEX quickly reworked its planned Mexican revamp and compressed it from 18 months to 3 months. Despite the recession that followed, it managed to maintain margins at reasonable levels. One reason was that many Mexicans did not have credit, so the self-construction part of the market was affected to only a limited extent, even though demand from the formal sector went down by 50%.[7] Another was that the company had already begun to expand into foreign markets. At the start of the year 2000, CEMEX was the leader in the Mexican market, with an installed capacity of 28 million tons, or about 60% of the country's total. Apasco, which Holderbank had acquired and invested heavily in expanding in the early 1990s, was the second largest player, with another 9 million tons of capacity. Analysts did not expect further increases in CEMEX's share of the Mexican market.

International Expansion   After having secured its leadership in Mexico, CEMEX began to look for opportunities beyond Mexico's borders. Internationalization began with exports, principally to the United States. By 2000, CEMEX was the largest international cement trader in the world, with projected trading volumes of 13 million tons of cement and clinker that year, 60% of which was expected to be third-party product.[8] International trade offered opportunities to arbitrage price differentials across national boundaries and to divert low-priced imports away from one's own markets. It also expanded the range of options available to deal with threats from particular competitors and let CEMEX study local markets and their structure at minimal cost before deciding whether to make more of a commitment to them by acquiring capacity locally.

After the imposition of trade sanctions by the United States, foreign direct investment had become a much more important component of CE-MEX's internationalization strategy than pure trade. CEMEX's foreign investments focused on acquiring existing capacity rather than building "greenfield" plants. Its major international moves are summarized in **Exhibit 10** and described in more detail in the rest of this section.

The United States   CEMEX had begun to export to the U.S. market in the early 1970s. In the late 1980s, it established distribution facilities in the southern United States in order to expand this effort. However, the U.S. economy and the construction industry in particular were experiencing a downturn. As a result, eight U.S. producers banded together to file an antidumping petition claiming that they were

---

[7]Interview with Hector Medina, Executive Vice President—Planning and Finance.

[8]Interview with Jose L. Saenz de Miera, President of Europe-Asia Region.

Exhibit 10   Timeline of CEMEX's International Expansion

Year	Event
1985	GATT signed; CEMEX began to concentrate on cement and divests other business lines
1987	Acquired Cementos Anáhuac in Mexico
1989	Acquired Cementos Tolteca; became Mexico's largest producer and one of ten largest worldwide
1992	Acquired Valenciana and Sanson in Spain; became world's fifth largest cement producer
1993–1994	Acquired 0.7 mt of capacity in Jamaica, 0.4 mt in Barbados, and 0.7 mt in Trinidad & Tobago
1994	Acquired Vencemos in Venezuela, Cemento Bayano in Panama, and the Balcones plant in Texas
1995	Acquired Cementos Nacionales in the Dominican Republic
1996	Acquired a majority stake in Colombia's Cementos Diamante and Industrias e Inversiones Samper; became world's third largest cement company
1997	Acquired 30% stake in Rizal Cement Company in the Philippines
1998–1999	Acquired a 20% interest in PT Semen Gresik in Indonesia; acquired an additional 40% of Rizal, and 99.9% of APO Cement Corp, also in the Philippines
1999	Acquired Assiut in Egypt, a 12% stake in Bio Bio in Chile, and Cemento del Pacifico in Costa Rica
2000	Announced availability of $1.175 billion for global acquisitions during the course of the year (36% more than 1999 spending)

Source: CEMEX

being harmed by low-cost Mexican imports and demanding protection. After finding that cement prices were higher in Mexico than in the southern United States and inferring that Mexican producers were dumping cement in the U.S. market at artificially low prices, the U.S. International Trade Commission (ITC) imposed a 58% countervailing duty on CEMEX's exports from Mexico to the United States. The duty was reduced to 31% after CEMEX started limiting exports to U.S. states where prices were relatively high.[9] The company tried to fight these actions before the relevant U.S. bodies, but this proved very difficult. Medina recalled that at one point, CEMEX was simultaneously being investigated by the ITC for artificially lowering prices and by the U.S. Federal Trade Commission for purchasing a distribution terminal with the intent of artificially raising them! A ruling by the General Agreement on Tariffs and Trade (GATT) in 1992 sided with Mexico in this dispute, but the

United States refused to give way. As of early 2000, the countervailing duty was still in place, although there were also reports that the United States was finally moving closer to repealing it.

After the countervailing duty was imposed, CEMEX had acquired a 1 million ton cement plant in Texas to reinforce its ready-mix and distribution facilities in the southern United States. Zambrano sometimes referred to this constellation of facilities as a firewall protecting the Mexican market from incursions from the United States. In addition, CEMEX's coastal terminals in the United States continued to import cement into the United States, from third parties as well as from the company's other plants. Thus, CEMEX credited imports of Chinese cement to the west coast of the United States for doubling the profits of its activities in the United States during 1999, to the point where they accounted for 12% of CEMEX's total sales and 7% of its EBITDA.

Spain   In 1991, CEMEX built distribution terminals in Spain to trade cement that was produced in Mexico, and also to study the European market.

[9]David P. Baron, "Integrated Strategy: Market and Nonmarket Components," *California Management Review,* vol. 37, no. 2 (Winter 1995), pp. 51–52.

In July 1992, it spent about $1.8 billion to acquire what ended up being 68% of the stock and 94% of the voting rights in two large Spanish cement companies, Valenciana and Sanson, with a total of nearly 12 million tons of capacity. These acquisitions yielded a market-leading 28% share in one of Europe's largest cement markets, which then happened to be in the throes of a major boom. The acquisitions also lowered dependence on the Mexican market, gave CEMEX significant capacity in a major market for Holderbank and Lafarge, and raised its international profile. But shareholders generally took a dim view of the deals: CEMEX's American Depositary Receipts, issued just a year earlier (another first for a Latin American company), tumbled by about one-third around the dates at which the acquisitions were announced. And immediately afterwards, the Spanish economy plunged into its deepest recession in 30 years, with the Spanish peseta having to be devalued three times during late 1992 and 1993. These developments added to the urgency of orchestrating major turnarounds at the two Spanish companies.

It was in this context that CEMEX began to develop and codify its post-merger integration process. Every aspect of the Spanish acquisitions was reviewed, from procurement policies to the location of the mines to the use of automation. Processes were streamlined, as was the workforce (by 25%) and investments in information technology were stepped up. Simultaneously, CEMEX moved quickly to harmonize and integrate the systems for its Spanish operations with its Mexican ones. The post-merger integration process reportedly took a little more than a year, or less than one-half the amount of time originally budgeted, and was followed by major improvements in operating margins, from 7% at the time of the acquisitions to about 20% by 1994 and an average of 25% for the second half of the 1990s. The Spanish operations turned out to be critical in helping CEMEX weather the Mexican peso crisis of 1994/1995.

In 1998, CEMEX sold its cement plant in Sevilla for $260 million. The Sevilla plant, which had accounted for about 10% of CEMEX's capacity in Spain, was relatively old, and had high production costs. CEMEX remained the largest competitor in the Spanish market after the sale. It used the proceeds to invest in capacity in South East Asia, particularly Indonesia. According to its annual report for 1998, "We effectively exchanged one million metric tons of production capacity in Spain for the equivalent of approximately 4 million metric tons in Southeast Asia, a higher long-term growth market." In 1999, Spain accounted for 16% of CEMEX's revenues and 15% of EBITDA.

Latin America   CEMEX's next major international move was entry into Venezuela, which initiated a broader series of engagements in Latin America, mostly around the Caribbean Basin. Venezuela had been wracked by macroeconomic instability since the late 1980s, depressing demand for cement and forcing large losses on the industry. In April 1994, CEMEX paid $360 million for a 61% stake in industry leader Vencemos, which operated about 4 million tons of capacity, or about 40% of the Venezuelan total. Virtually all remaining Venezuelan capacity ended up in the hands of Holderbank and Lafarge. As in Spain, CEMEX moved quickly to integrate and improve the efficiency of its Venezuelan operations. Vencemos' operating margin improved from 9% in the third quarter of 1994 to 41% a year later,[10] and stood at 34% in 1998.[11] Although the Venezuelan economy had continued to disappoint, Vencemos was able to keep capacity utilization high even when domestic demand was low because it was located near a major port facility. This permitted it to export surplus production to places such as the Caribbean islands and the southern United States. In 1998, Venezuela accounted for 12% of CEMEX's revenues and 13% of EBITDA. Earnings were down in 1999, however.

In mid-1996, CEMEX acquired a 54% interest—subsequently increased—in Cementos Diamante, Colombia's second-largest cement producer, for $400 million, and a 94% interest in Inversiones Samper, the third-largest producer, for $300 million. The

[10]"Global Invasion," *International Cement Review,* Jan. 2000, p. 35.
[11]Company fact book.

acquisitions gave CEMEX 3.5 million tons of capacity, or a bit less than one-third of the Colombian total, behind industry leader Sindicato Antioqueño—a loose confederation of small cement producers—with a share of about 50%. Weak demand topped off by a price war caused CEMEX's operating margins in Colombia to decline from more than 20% at the beginning of 1998 to 3% by late in the year. Margins began to recover, however, during 1999.[12] That year, Colombia accounted for 3–4% of CEMEX's revenues and EBITDA.

Next, CEMEX entered Chile, paying $34 million for an 12% stake in Cementos Bio-Bio, Chile's third-largest competitor. The largest producer in Chile was Cement Polpaico, a subsidiary of Holderbank, and the second-largest was one of Blue Circle's subsidiaries. Compared to them, Bio-Bio was relatively focused on the northern and southern parts of Chile rather than on its populous middle. Elsewhere in Latin America, CEMEX acquired controlling stakes in the largest producers in Panama, the Dominican Republic, and Costa Rica.[13]

Other regions Between late 1997 and early 1999, CEMEX invested in Filipino cement producers Rizal (a 70% interest in 2.3 million tons of capacity for $218 million) and APO (a 100% interest in 2.0 million tons of capacity for $400 million). Both Rizal and APO were close to ports and therefore had export as well as domestic potential. The Philippines itself had been a Spanish colony in the 19th century, and was one of the first East Asian economies to experience macroeconomic pressures in the second half of the 1990s. Less than 20% of Filipino cement capacity had been controlled by foreign firms in early 1997, when there had been nearly 20 producers and a supply shortage as the result of a decade in which demand had grown at about 10% per year.[14] But the Filipino market just as large capacity additions by domestic competitors were coming on line. This gave international competitors their opening. CEMEX ended up controlling about 22% of Filipino cement capacity, well behind Holderbank but slightly ahead of Lafarge and Blue Circle. In 1999, the Philippines accounted for 2.5% of CEMEX's revenues and approximately one-half that percentage of its EBITDA.

Indonesia was the other Southeast Asian market in which CEMEX had established a presence: in September 1998, it paid $115 million for a 14% stake in Semen Gresik, Indonesia's largest cement company with 17 million tons of capacity, and considered by many to be its most efficient. Originally, 35% of the company was supposed to have been sold (out of a total of 65% held by the Indonesian government), but public protests reduced the number of shares offered. By 2000, CEMEX had increased its stake to 25% by spending another $77 million, but continued to have the Indonesian state as a major partner. The political and economic environment in Indonesia remained fluid, and further negotiations to buy out more of the government's stake were complicated by weakened institutions and the turnover of officials as well as by continued public opposition. In addition, excess capacity of almost 20 million tons—the largest such amount in the region—needed to be restructured. Still, the Indonesian market had significant long-run potential, not least because its population numbered 220 million (three times that of the Philippines). As the dollar value of the Indonesian rupiah collapsed, the dollar price of cement in the local market had decreased from about $65 per ton in early 1997 to less than $20 per ton in 1998, before starting to recover in 1999. As part of its investment in Semen Gresik, CEMEX had also entered into export commitments, which it intended to fulfill in part by setting up a grinding mill in Bangladesh to receive and process shipments of clinker from Indonesia.

In November 1999, CEMEX acquired a 77% stake in Assiut Cement Company, the largest cement producer in Egypt with about 4 million tons in capacity, for a total of about $370 million. In May 2000, CEMEX announced plans to invest in expanding Assiut's capacity to 5 million tons, and to add 1.5 million tons of capacity in a new Egyptian facility. These plans catered to the Egyptian

---

[12]*International Cement Review,* January 2000, pp. 35–36.
[13]Ibid, p. 36.
[14]*International Cement Review*, January 2000, p. 37.

Exhibit 11   Capacity Consolidation Potential (millions of tons)

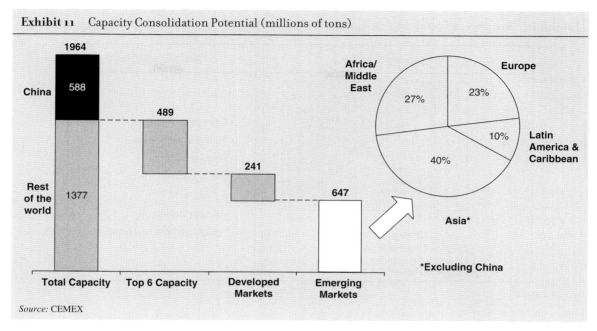

Source: CEMEX

government's interest in increasing domestic production of cement to help meet demand that had been growing at an average annual rate of 11% since 1995. But the Egyptian market remained fragmented—Assiut accounted for only 17% of it—and the Egyptian regulatory context cumbersome.

The future   In May 2000, CEMEX announced that it had accumulated $1.175 billion to spend on global acquisitions. China was an obvious target because of the size of its market, variously pegged at about half a billion tons by official estimates and closer to half that according to independent analysts.[15] However, approximately 75% of Chinese production took place in small, technologically obsolete kilns owned by local authorities and not run on a commercial basis. Even after discounting opportunities in China, the bulk of the capacity that might be consolidated by the six major international competitors was located in emerging markets, particularly in Asia and Africa/the Middle East (see **Exhibit 11**). CEMEX was thought likely to enter India, where it thought the restructuring process was farther advanced,

before China. Indian demand amounted to about 100 million tons, or more than three times Mexico's, and was served by 28 competitors, the eight largest of which combined to account for two-thirds of total demand. Holderbank and Lafarge already had a degree of presence there. In Latin America, CEMEX had its eye on Brazil, although it was unwilling to pay prices for acquisitions that, at $250 or more per ton, exceeded its capacity valuations. In May 2000, the company announced that it was negotiating with the Portuguese government over a 10% stake in Cimentos de Portugal (Cimpor), that country's largest cement maker. Such a deal might permit consolidation of operations around the Mediterranean as well as giving CEMEX access to Brazil and some African markets. Holderbank and Lafarge were reportedly also interested.

The Expansion Process   As CEMEX moved to more distant markets, the various stages in the expansion process—opportunity identification, due diligence, and post-merger integration—became more formalized and greater attempts were made to standardize them, reflecting past experiences.

[15]ING Barings, *European Cement Review,* February 2000, p. 40.

Exhibit 12   Framework for Acquisition Analyses

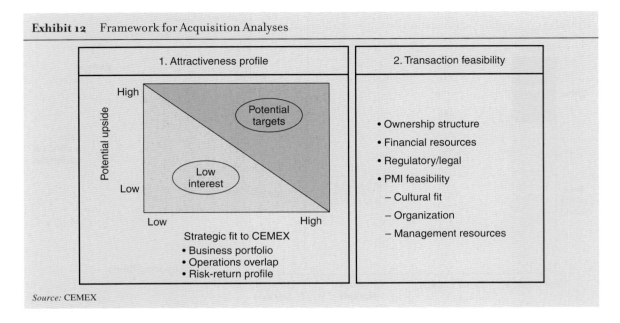

Source: CEMEX

Opportunity identification   While the logic of expanding to the U.S., Spain, and, in particular, Latin America, had been relatively obvious, CEMEX had had to develop better tools for screening opportunities as it ventured farther afield. CEMEX looked at several factors in deciding whether to invest in other countries. A country had to have a large population and high population growth as well as a relatively low level of current consumption. In addition, CEMEX wanted to lead the market or at least control 25% of it. These considerations tended to favor opportunities in emerging countries. Quantitative factors were assigned a 65% weight in country analysis, and qualitative factors, such as political risk, a weight of 35%. The analysis was complicated by the fact that CEMEX looked at countries in a regional context rather than as independent markets and was particularly interested in the Caribbean Basin, South East Asia, and the Mediterranean. According to CFO Rodrigo Treviño, "We now have a very balanced and well-diversified portfolio and we can afford to be more selective."[16]

[16]Tim Duffy, "CEMEX's CFO: Still Eying International Markets for Diversification," *Dow Jones International News*, March 7, 2000.

If detailed market analysis was the top-down component of the process for identifying opportunities, the process of identifying target companies constituted its bottom-up component. CEMEX's conceptual framework for looking at targets is summarized in **Exhibit 12.** CEMEX pursued controlling stakes—often as close to 100% as possible—in the companies that it bought into, in order to maximize flexibility. When identifying a possible acquisition target, CEMEX also examined the potential for restructuring both the target company and the market as a whole. Restructuring the target company meant increasing its efficiency and optimizing capacity utilization. Restructuring the market might involve reductions in the number of players or volume of imports, moves toward rational pricing, fragmentation of distribution channels, product differentiation and other attempts to get closer to the customer. Speed in both respects was very important to improving target valuations.

Due diligence   After a target was identified, a process of due diligence was performed whereby it was assessed in depth by a team of people. In 1999, about 20 processes of due diligence were undertaken, resulting in three acquisitions. The due diligence process typically lasted one to two weeks and involved about ten people per team, half of whom usually had prior experience with the process. Once a team was formed, it was briefed on the target company and given a standardized methodology to follow in assessing it. Negotiations with the government usually continued through the due diligence process, and meetings with local competitors and industry associations were often held as well to allay any concerns about the acquisition. The final output from the due diligence process was a standardized report, to be presented to the Executive Vice President of Planning and Finance, Hector Medina, that was critical in pricing deals. Only rarely, however, would CEMEX bid prices that exceeded top-down estimates of the value of capacity in particular markets (as illustrated in **Exhibit 7**).

Especially in Southeast Asia, CEMEX had recently found itself looking at the same targets as other international cement companies. CEMEX believed that its due diligence process was more specific and systematic. To cite just one example, the human resources component of its process looked at the age, education, and average years of service of the target's employees, and at labor union affiliations, government involvement, and relationship to the community in order to estimate the optimal number of employees and recommend strategies for moving towards those targets. Other issues related to human resources, such as training programs and organizational restructuring, were also covered. Such thoroughness was thought to reduce the possibility of unpleasant surprises down the road, and to speed up the post-merger integration process if an acquisition was, in fact, undertaken. The process methodology was revised every six months to reflect recent experiences.

Post-Merger integration (PMI) process Once the decision to proceed with an acquisition was made, CEMEX formed a PMI team. The purpose was to improve the efficiency of the newly obtained operation and adapt it to CEMEX's standards and culture. PMI teams had become more diverse and multinational over time. The PMI process took anywhere from six months to a year, during which team members kept their original positions and salaries, returning home one week in every six. At the beginning of the process, the team was briefed on the country and methodology, and attended cultural awareness and teambuilding workshops. The process itself had a monthly cadence: the regional director visited every month, the country president of the new operation reported to headquarters in Monterrey every month in the same format as the other CEMEX country presidents, and CEO Zambrano, the regional directors and all the country presidents met every month in Monterrey or, occasionally, New York or Madrid.

The PMI process involved integration at three levels: the improvement of the situation at the plant acquired, the sharing or replication of basic management principles, and the harmonization of cultural beliefs. CEMEX tried to send in a PMI team as soon after an acquisition as possible and, while there were differences in terms of how quickly and to what extent the team tried to take charge, regarded itself as moving much more quickly in this respect than its leading international competitors. Integration almost always involved substantial manpower reductions, most of which were concentrated within the first six months. But the PMI team also tried to discover whom to retain or promote to managerial positions. It was possible for as many as half the members of a PMI team to stay on as expatriates after the process was over. CEMEX also viewed the PMI process as a vehicle for continuous improvement in existing operations. Thus, every two or three years, a PMI process was performed on CEMEX's Mexican operations, which were looked at as if they had just been acquired.

Management As CEMEX expanded internationally, other broad aspects of its management changed as well. Geographic diversification had reduced earnings volatility: thus, over 1994–1997, the standard deviation of quarterly cash flow margins averaged 7.1% for CEMEX as a whole, compared to 9.5% for Mexico, 12% for Spain, 22% for the U.S., and

30% for Venezuela. Financing, nevertheless loomed large as an issue because of the asset-intensity of the international acquisition strategy, which included not only paying for equity but also the assumption of significant debt and incurral of large investments in modernization—up to 50% of purchase prices in some cases. While high costs of capital had always been a major issue for Mexican companies, the situation was exacerbated by the peso crisis, which simultaneously raised domestic interest rates and restricted the extent to which Mexican cashflows could be used to finance foreign direct investment (because of the 70% devaluation of the peso against the U.S. dollar). CEMEX responded by folding the ownership of its non-Mexican assets into its Spanish operations and financing new acquisitions through the latter. This was several hundred basis points cheaper for CEMEX, partly because Spain had an investment-grade sovereign rating, and partly because all interest expenses were tax-deductible in Spain (compared to just real interest expenses in Mexico). Consolidating its bank debt through the Spanish operations in 1996 was estimated to have saved CEMEX about $100 million per year in interest costs, and to have better matched dollar-linked assets and its principally dollar-denominated debt.[17]

CEMEX's net debt amounted to $4.8 billion at the end of 1999, leaving it relatively close to the 55% limit on debt-to-total-capital that was specified in bank covenants. The company had managed, however, to satisfy the cap on leverage and the floor on interest coverage that it had set for itself more than one year ahead of schedule, and further strengthening of capital structure had been promised. CEMEX had also tried to broaden its sources of capital. In 1998, it sold its plant in Sevilla, as described above. In early 1999, it partnered with AIG, the insurance company, and the private equity arm of the Government of Singapore Investment Corporation, among others, to set up a fund of up to $1.2 billion to invest in some of the cement assets it was acquiring in Asia. In September 1999, CEMEX listed and started to trade on the New York Stock Exchange. And while no new shares were offered in conjunction with that listing, the company issued $500 million of warrants later on in the year.

CEMEX also continued to distinguish itself by the intent of its emphasis on emerging markets, even though some of its competitors had moved in the same direction. The company calculated that the weighted average growth rate in cement demand in thecountries in which it was present was close to 4%, compared to 3% for Holderbank and Lafarge and 2% for the three other international majors. CEMEXalso thought that its emerging market business should command higher price-earnings ratios in cement than business in advanced markets—the reverse of the situation that prevailed. According to CEO Lorenzo Zambrano, "They assign us the ratios of developing-country companies, even though we have very little volatility and our risk is limited due to our geographical diversification."[18]

Despite the increasing number of countries in which CEMEX participated, Mexico continued to play a critical role in its strategy as a lab for developing, testing, and refining new ideas about how to compete in emerging markets. Thus, in addition to reinforcing CEMEX's skills at handling macroeconomic fluctuations, the peso crisis had led to the discovery of a distinct customer segment involving informal construction that demanded bagged cement through retail channels, exhibited less cyclicality than the formal construction sector, and was apparently ubiquitous in emerging markets. Such demand lent itself to branding and promotion, which CEMEX first worked out in Mexico, before rolling out marketing campaigns to other countries. Another example was provided by the idea of using global positioning satellites to link dispatchers, truckers, and customers in a system that could track deliveries and guarantee them to within 20 minutes, rather than the usual three-hours-plus. This idea originated with visits to Federal Express in Memphis and an emergency call center in Houston and required the assistance of consultants from the U.S. in using complexity theory to model cement delivery logistics. The innovation

[17]CEMEX 1997 Annual Report, and *International Cement Review*, December 1999, p. 40.

[18]James F. Smith, "Making Cement a Household Word," *Los Angeles Times*, January 16, 2000, p. C1.

was, once again, first implemented in Mexico, aided by imaginative advertising comparing the speeds of cement and pizza delivery. Customer willingness-to-pay went up while fuel, maintenance, and payroll costs came down.

CEMEX's organizational arrangements also differed in important ways from its competitors'. One key difference was that country-level managers at CEMEX reported directly to regional directors whereas competitors often had an extra layer of area managers between regional and country managers. CEMEX plants were organized into 7–9 departments, each with its own vice president. Every month, the vice presidents reported to the country president and the regional manager during the latter's visit. The reports covered all aspects of the plants and used a standardized format. In addition, the country presidents, regional directors, CEO Zambrano, and his executive committee all met every month as well. Other global competitors might hold such meetings as infrequently as once a quarter and tended to be more decentralized in their decision-making. CEMEX had recently reorganized from a structure with a Mexican division and an international one to a structure with three regional divisions: North America, South America and the Caribbean, and Europe and Asia. Also, while it resisted setting up full-fledged regional offices, it had made some recent attempts to coordinate more formally across different countries within a region. For example, it had consolidated the administrative and financial functions for six countries in the South American and Caribbean region in Venezuela.

At the apex of this structure sat CEMEX's CEO, Lorenzo Zambrano. Zambrano had begun working at CEMEX during the summers in the early 1960s while he was a teenager attending nearby ITESM (Monterrey Tech), and had returned to the company after earning his MBA from Stanford University in 1968. Lorenzo Zambrano favored a very hands-on approach to running CEMEX, often checking kiln statistics and sales data on a daily basis. He was a bachelor who devoted the vast majority of his time to the company, and encouraged his subordinates to do the same. He also got personally involved in sending and receiving e-mail and using Lotus Notes, which was still unusual among local CEOs.

Zambrano's personal commitment to information technology mirrored CEMEX's early and consistent use of IT. When Zambrano took over as CEO in the mid-1980s, heavy investments in IT in Mexico seemed to be overruled by the country's weak telecom infrastructure. Zambrano was convinced, however, that the importance of using IT to increase productivity would become more apparent as the Mexican economy opened up, and that the optimal private response to the disabilities of Mexico's public infrastructure was to invest more rather than less in this area. In 1987, CEMEX created a satellite system to link the Mexican plants it had begun to acquire. In 1988, the company transferred internal voice and data communications to its own private network. The Spanish acquisitions were also connected immediately to each other as well as to the Mexican operations. In 1992, the company founded Cemtec, which was supposed to complement the company's IT department by performing the functions of software development and hardware installation, and which was eventually spun off. In 1987, CEMEX spent about 0.25% of its sales on IT; by 1999, this figure had increased to about 1%. CEMEX's competitors were considered slower at capitalizing on the possibilities afforded by IT, although they were moving in the same direction.

CEMEX's use of IT had transformed the way the company worked in numerous ways. The 20-minute site delivery guarantee, already described, was a very visible example that led to the company's being canonized as a master of "digital business design."[19] The company was also connected via the Internet to distributors and suppliers. More recently, it had announced plans to launch a Latin American e-business development accelerator and, in alliance with B2B specialist Ariba and three large Latin American companies (Alfa of Mexico, and Bradespar and Votorantim of Brazil), a neutral business-to-business

---

[19]Adrian J. Slywotzky and David J. Morrison, with Ted Moser, Kevin A. Mundt, and James A. Quella, *Profit Patterns: 30 Ways to Anticipate and Profit from Strategic Forces Reshaping Your Business*, New York: Times Business/Random House, April 1999.

integrated supplier exchange, Latinexus, that was supposed to become the leading e-procurement marketplace in Latin America. Within CEMEX, IT made an enormous amount of information became available to Zambrano and his top management. Sales figures were reported daily, broken out by product and geography. On the production side, various operating metrics were available kiln by kiln. Even emissions data were included. And information flowed sideways as well as upwards: country managers could view data from other countries, and kiln managers were able to look at other kilns.

CEMEX provided its employees with a number of IT training programs and had also been aggressive in using new technology to overhaul its training function. A private satellite TV channel was acquired for this purpose, and CEMEX developed a virtual MBA program in collaboration with Monterrey Tech that combined satellite TV, the Internet, and the university's network of campuses to deliver courses to executive (part-time) MBA students. Recruitment was greatly aided by the company's public profile and included not only the graduates of Mexico's top educational institutions, but also Mexican graduates of top foreign business schools and alumni of other leading firms. Thus, while the Boston Consulting Group

had long been CEMEX's principal strategy consultant, more than one of the professionals in the company's strategic planning function was a McKinsey alumnus. Overall, many regarded CEMEX as having shifted over time from an engineering-driven approach to one more dependent on economics.

Outlook

While CEMEX faced a number of issues in 2000, perhaps the most important one concerned how far its competitive advantage could travel. CEMEX's entry into Indonesia and Egypt, in particular, stirred some concerns about the difficulties of working across language barriers and the challenges of adapting to different cultures—such as incorporating prayer-breaks into continuous process operations in Muslim countries. Others, however, were more optimistic, pointing out that the CEMEX already used English as its semiofficial language, arguing that cement itself was a language of sorts, and noting that the company had its own strong culture that could serve as a binder. And everybody recognized that while Lafarge's hostile bid for Blue Circle appeared to have failed, consolidation at a new level—of international competitors rather than by them—might be the next big dynamic in the cement industry.

Case 2-3   A Speed Race: Benelli and QJ Compete in the International Motorbike Arena

Marta Zhang, the young Chinese managing director of Italian motorcycle manufacturer Benelli, was sitting in her office in Pesaro, Italy, reflecting on the purchase of the company by Qianjiang Group (QJ)

IVEY

Richard Ivey School of Business
The University of Western Ontario

Francesca Spigarelli, Ilan Alon and William Wei wrote this case solely to provide material for class discussion. The authors do not intend to illustrate either effective or ineffective handling of a managerial situation. The authors may have disguised certain names and other identifying information to protect confidentiality. The authors would like to thank

four years earlier in 2005. After the Chinese won a bid to acquire the company, QJ had gotten off to a very good start: the local authorities had helped to

Gianluca Galasso, Susanna Carloni, Pierluigi Marconi and Yan Haimei for all the information and support they gave us during the writing of the case.

Ivey Management Services prohibits any form of reproduction, storage or transmittal without its written permission. Reproduction of this material is not covered under authorization by any reproduction rights organization. To order copies or request permission to reproduce materials, contact Ivey Publishing, Ivey Management Services, c/o Richard Ivey School of Business, The University of Western Ontario, London, Ontario, Canada, N6A 3K7; phone (519) 661-3208; fax (519) 661-3882; e-mail cases@ivey.uwo.ca.

Copyright © 2009, Ivey Management Services

create a welcoming environment, the two production lines were operational, new motorbikes were being projected by skilled engineers and the new scooters were very attractive.

While this new relationship began well, many differences were emerging between China and Italy: cultural attitude, work methods, civil and fiscal rules and access to credit were some areas of dispute. Despite industrial investments in order to gain efficiency and reduce prices, penetration of Western markets was difficult due to a high level of competition, especially from Japanese brands.

The European and U.S. press had welcomed the new motorbike models very enthusiastically, but sales results were not consistent with such technical success and with QJ's plans; moreover, the technical departments in Pesaro and in China had not agreed on the industrial plan to produce a new motorbike, which was projected two years before, and already presented—with great success—to a specialist public.

Mario Tonis, the press office director, interrupted Zhang's thoughts with some good news: the motorbike tests last month had produced brilliant results with the press. *Ultimate Motorcycling* reported:

> Retaining the original Benelli staff and leaving all design and manufacturing still in Pesaro, the combination of Asian work ethic and Italian design flair has proven a potent combination, indeed. The result has produced several new Benelli models, and the Tornado, although identical in appearance to previous iterations, has evolved into a superbike that retains the design brilliance of the original but without its quirky nature.[1]

The products were available and potentially successful, but how could Zhang integrate the new company, create a common corporate culture, help transfer the know-how, expand the business and win out over the strong Japanese competition?

The Acquired Company

Benelli was established as a family firm in Pesaro, Italy (in the Marche Region on the Adriatic coast), in 1911. Initially specializing in automobile and motorcycle repairs as well as the manufacturing of spare parts, over the years the firm also began manufacturing motorcycles that were successful in various sports competitions, winning numerous national and international titles.

To offer a stable work for her six sons, Teresa Benelli, a young widow, opened the "Benelli Garage" to repair cars and motorcycles. The business was successful and the sons begun first to produce spare parts and then engines too. In 1920, the first engine was ready: a single-cylinder two-stroke 75 cc model. In the following year, the first Benelli motorcycle was built with a complete in-house engine of 98 cc.

In 1923, a special model of motorcycle was projected and produced to enter race competitions. One of Teresa's sons, Antonio—nicknamed "Tonino the Terrible"—had a natural talent as a rider. Running a Benelli 175, he started a brilliant career winning four Italian championship titles in 1927, 1928 and 1930 with the single overhead camshaft model, and in 1931 with the double overhead camshaft model. The success in races contributed to affirm the brand and capacity of the company in projecting and producing competitive bikes at an international level. In 1932, during a race, Tonino had a terrible accident and had to stop his career. He died in 1937 in a road accident.

In 1949, one of Teresa's sons, Giuseppe, founded his own motorbike company—Motobi—due to disagreements with his brothers. Some years later, as problems with the family were solved, he attached to the parent company.

In 1962, Benelli and Motobi were able to produce about 300 motorcycles per day, with a workforce of 550 employees.[2] Toward the end of the 1960s, growing competition with the Japanese led to the sale of Benelli to De Tomaso Industries Inc. Despite various attempts to differentiate itself from its Japanese competitors, as well as a merger with Moto Guzzi in 1988, the company's manufacturing operations eventually ceased.[3]

---

[1] Arthur Coldwells, "Stormbringer: Benelli Tornado Tre 1130, A Brilliant Return," *Ultimate Motorcycling,* April/May 2009, p. 27.

[2] www.benelli.com/eng/storia.asp.

[3] Francesca Spigarelli and Paola Bellabona, "The transnational dimension of the Chinese Economy," in M. Abbiati, *Economic and cultural characteristics of the Chinese Market,* Ca' Foscarina, Venice, 2006, p. 157.

Exhibit 1   Company Activities Before the Acquisition

2001

- Launch of a new strategic plan. The main decisions concerned the following: focusing on high displacement motorcycles, partnerships with other producers in the scooter sector and reducing costs to be more competitive in terms of sales prices.
- Cooperative agreement with Renault Sport in the scooter sector. The commercial purpose was to sell Benelli's products in both France and Italy through the Renault network.
- Participation in the Superbike championship with the new Tornado 900 cc. Good results helped the company win a consensus in the market (relaunching the company image).

2002

- Cooperation with Renault Sport did not bring the expected results because of negative market conditions and trends.
- Management focused on motorbike production. A new motorbike was launched: the Tornado 900 Tre, with 101 units sold within several months (85 per cent abroad).
- In the scooter sector, the company looked for more flexibility by reducing stocks and outsourcing production. The most knowledge-intensive activities remained inside. The new Velvet 400 cc was projected.

2003

- Benelli stopped production of scooters to focus exclusively on motorbike production.
- The new Tornado RS model was launched, with production of 1,600 units. A new motorbike in the naked sector, the Tornado Naked Tre (TNT), was projected, which was due to be launched in 2004. Many orders from both Italy and abroad were placed by customers due to the success in the press.

2004

- The new TNT was launched in the naked sector. Within seven months 930 units were sold. Good results in race competition supported sales activities. New versions of the TNT were projected and due to be launched in 2005 (many orders were already placed).
- A new line of accessories and spare parts was projected to enter the market: high margins on those products should have brought higher profits to the company.

Source: Benelli financial statements and balance sheet.

In 1989, an entrepreneur also from the Pesaro area attempted to relaunch the company, but his efforts were unsuccessful. Operations only resumed in 1995 when the Indesit Group[4] purchased the brand and again relaunched the company. Although the group focused immediately on the scooter sector (trying to gain profits from the high volume of production despite low margins), in 2001, the group decided to enter the motorcycle sector in a niche market; however, the need for sizable investments, coupled with enormous financial difficulties, eventually brought a halt to production in

2005 and sent the company into liquidation (see **Exhibit 1**). Following an intense period of negotiations for the acquisition of Benelli by the John Galt Investment Ltd company owned by Russian Nikolai Smolenski, son of Alexander Smolenski,[5] the company was eventually purchased by QJ.[6]

[4]The Indesit Group, the largest company in the Marche Region, Italy (€3,438 million in turnover in 2007 and 17,418 employees), was producing electric home appliances. The company belonged to the Merloni family. See www.indesitcompany.com.

[5]Giorgio Leonardi, "A 24 year old Russian billionaire running Benelli's bikes," La Repubblica, July 30, 2005, p. 41, http://ricerca .repubblica.it/repubblica/archivio/repubblica/2005/07/30/un-miliardario-russo-di-24-anni-monta.html; accessed July 1, 2009; Federico De Rosa, "Benelli. A rush between Russians and Chinese. Qianjiang Motor Group is arriving," Corriere della Sera, September 6, 2005, http://archiviostorico.corriere.it/2005/settembre/06/Benelli_testa_testa_russo_cinese_co_9_050906051.shtml, accessed July 1, 2009.
[6]Jeff Israey, "China in Italy: Kick Start," Time, August 9, 2007, www.time.com/time/magazine/article/0,9171,1651236,00.html, accessed June 30, 2009.

An acquisition by the Russian group would have probably resulted in the company being dismantled, with its machinery transferred to the United Kingdom and the loss not only of the brand but also of local jobs. Instead, QJ intended to relaunch the company by adopting an interesting industrial plan.

▓ The Acquirer Company[7]

QJ was situated in Wenling, China, 480 kilometres from Shanghai. QJ was a large-scale state-owned group, and one of the 520 key state enterprises certified by the Chinese State Council. QJ was the largest Chinese company producing and selling motorcycles, with an annual output of more than one million units. It was chosen by the Motor Cycle Industry Association as one of the 10 best enterprises with strong competitive power in China. At the beginning of 2002, the "Qianjiang" trademark was given the award of "Famous Chinese Trademark."

QJ had formerly been the Wenling Chemical Engineering Machinery Factory, established in 1971. The factory changed its line of production to motorcycles in May 1985, and then moved to Wenling. In January 1993, its name was changed to the Zhejiang Motorcycle Factory. After restructuring in 1996, the enterprise became Zhejiang Qianjiang Motorcycle Group. With government support, QJ successively merged with and acquired the Wenling Saccharification Factory, the Wenling Locomotive Factory, the Wenling Vehicle Repair Factory and the Wenling Electric Tools Factory, among others. These mergers allowed the group to achieve low-cost expansion and to double its economic indicators within a short time. The Zhejiang Qianjiang Motorcycle Company, Ltd. was established in 1999 with the approval of the People's Government of Zhejiang Province. The group was the primary founder of the subsidiary Zhejiang Wenling Motorcycle Company, and owned 75 per cent equity of Zhejiang Meikeda Motorcycle Company, Ltd., which was co-founded with Bright Steel Pte. Ltd.[8] Zhejiang Qianjiang Motorcycle Company, Ltd. had been a public company listed on the Shenzhen Stock Exchange since May 14, 1999.

Strengths of the Company   The primary business of QJ was research and development (R&D), as well as the manufacturing and marketing of motorcycles and engine parts. The company's motorcycle products constituted approximately seven per cent of market share in China.

The QJ Group designed, developed and produced Qianjiang machinery and electrical products. It produced motorcycles ranging from 50 cc to 250 cc, and also manufactured motorcycle-related products such as engines and parts, as well as race cars, miniature motorcycles, all-terrain vehicles (ATVs), gas scooters, generators, high pressure water cleaners, garden tools, power pumps, vacuum pumps and lawn mowers, among other products. Forty per cent of the group's products were exported to Europe, America, the Middle East, Northeast Asia and Africa—to a total of more than 110 countries throughout the world.

Eight years after the company went public, it had produced and sold more than seven million motorcycles (among which 0.93 million were exported). Total sales reached RMB21.2 billion, and RMB4.5 billion was paid in taxes. Among the total sales, 9,377,000 finished motorcycles were sold on the domestic market and 2,654,000 were exported, earning US$140.4 million in foreign exchange. The assets of QJ totaled RMB3.6 billion, with a total investment of RMB260 million.

The company covered an area of more than seven million square feet in the Wenling Economic Development Zone and was the largest motorcycle

▓ [7]The information about the acquirer company and strengths of the company is from Qianjiang Motor. Company Profile (Gong si jie jie), www.qjmotor.com/qjmotor/JieShao/aboutus.jsp, accessed December 11, 2009; Qianjiang Motor. Financial Report (Cai wu bao gao), First Quarter 2009 accessed December 11, 2009; www.qjmotor.com/qjmotor/newsAction.do?method=view&id=4028882f20f0be6901 2108d4445e0019, accessed December 11, 2009; Qianjiang Motor. Interim Report (Zhong qi bao gao), 2006, http://disclosure.szse.cn/m/finalpage/2006-08-17/18034278.PDF, accessed December 11, 2009.

▓ [8]Zhejiang Meikeda Motorcycle Co., Ltd. was a joint venture of the Qianjiang Group and Singapore Kedeng Investment Co., Ltd., with registered capital of US$2.8 million; 75 per cent of equity was held by the Qianjiang Group and 25 per cent held by Singapore Kedeng Investment Co., Ltd.

production base in Asia and the most advanced in China, with an annual production capacity of 1.5 million finished motorcycles. It had one joint-stock company and five joint-venture companies: these included many sub-departments such as a graduate school, an R&D centre, a testing centre, a machine-processing factory and an assembly factory. The company possessed both high and new technology and first-class equipment, and utilized advanced three-dimensional Pro/ENGINEER and CAD Design Software manufacturing technology. At the same time, it also imported advanced equipment (e.g. a processing-centre machine as well as a line-cutting machine, etc.) from the United States, Germany, Switzerland and Japan to develop its products and to process mouldings and machines.

The enterprise had a complete quality management system, and was issued an International Organization for Standardization certificate (ISO9001) in 1997 by the authorized international attestation organization, TUV Product Service, Ltd. The company's series of products passed CE, GS, CSA and UL standards and received quality licences from the National Import and Export Commodity Inspection Bureau. QJ also received "Well-Known Brand of China," "Chinese Famous Trademark," "Inspection-free Product," "State-level Technical Centre" and "State-level Laboratory" awards.

International Expansion   To upgrade its products, Qianjiang Motor cooperated with AVL—one of the two most important European automobile and motorcycle research institutes—and with a French engine design corporation that was a cooperative partner of Renault to develop motorcycle engines. Working with design company Bluesky Design (www.blueskydsn.com), Qianjiang Motor developed fashionable vehicles such as dune buggies, scooters, beam sport-utility vehicles and off-road vehicles for overseas markets.[9]

In 1999, Jiang Zuyun joined forces with QJ to sell motorcycles in the Indonesian market. Within

two years, QJ held almost half of the Indonesian motorcycle market share. On August 20, 2001, the largest joint venture between China and Indonesia, Sanex Qianjiang Motor International (Sanex Qianjiang), inaugurated a US$12 million motorcycle assembly plant in Indonesia. Established as a joint venture in March 2000, Sanex Qianjiang was owned by Qianjiang Motor International, Malaysia's Lion Group and Taiwan's CPI, who together held 35 per cent of the shares, and Indonesia's PT Sanex. Beginning in April 2000, Sanex Qianjiang imported fully-assembled motorcycles from its Chinese headquarter and sold them in Indonesia; however, about two months before the inauguration of the plant, the company gradually began to reduce its imports when the local plant started producing 400 to 500 units per day. The plant eventually had a total production capacity of 30,000 units per month. Sanex Qianjiang thus created many employment opportunities for Indonesians. The company had 43 main dealerships and 273 sub-dealerships across Indonesia, and it also planned to establish a subsidiary called PT Sanex Agung Motor Indonesia to produce spare parts for the company.

To target the European market, QJ established a joint venture with an Austrian company to create the Generic brand that would produce European-style motorcycle products; in the meantime, QJ also acquired Hungarian company Keeway Motor, establishing Qianjiang-Keeway Europe. In 2005, QJ acquired Benelli. With these three leading brands—Benelli, Generic and Keeway—QJ was planning to build and expand its markets in Europe and North America, to accelerate technical innovations and to establish itself in a more competitive position in the international market.

In terms of its strategic development, QJ also targeted the Taiwanese market. Taiwan had the highest density of motorcycles in the world, with more than 300 motorcycles per square kilometre. Approximately 50 per cent of the population owned a motorcycle, and due to the high labour costs for repairs and maintenance, Taiwanese people preferred to buy new motorcycles rather than repairing

[9]X. Xia, "Qianjiang Motor: Exporting to European and American Markets," April 30, 2007, www.atvchina.com.cn/viewnews-7354.html, accessed December 11, 2009.

them.[10] Due to the new leadership in Taiwan, the relationship with mainland China had become closer and therefore opened up shipping, postal communications and trading connections with the mainland. At the same time, the production costs of local Taiwanese companies were increasing and the investment environment had deteriorated, thus providing a great opportunity for the development of the mainland motorcycle industry. Qianjiang Motor, located in Wenling, China, was situated to the northeast of the Taiwan Strait. In addition to its geographical advantages, several senior QJ executives who were dispatched by the foreign shareholders were Taiwanese, giving them the advantage of familiarity with the Taiwanese motorcycle market. QJ opened up the Taiwan market by relying on its geographical location, advanced techniques and competitive pricing. Its gross profits almost doubled due to the rise in exports to Taiwan.

Industry Analysis

The Industry   Benelli was part of the motorcycle industry, which included companies involved in manufacturing motorcycles and related equipment, parts and accessories. Motorcycles were classified by their engine size and vehicle use. Engines were measured according to their displacement by cubic centimetre (cc): scooters were less than 50 cc, standard were from 50 cc to 650 cc and heavy were more than 650 cc. Motorcycles were usually classified for commercial purposes into one of the following three categories: street, off-road or dual-purpose, depending on the surface on which they were intended to be used.

Street motorcycles were designed for riding on paved roads. Their engines were generally in the 125 cc and greater range. They included the following categories: cruiser, sport bike, touring, sport touring, naked, feet-forward motorcycles, scooters and mopeds. Off-road motorcycles, also known as dirt bikes, included motocross, rally raids, trials and track racing. Dual-purpose motorcycles were street legal motorbikes that were also designed for off-road situations. This class included adventure-touring, enduro and supermotard.

Benelli had products in both the scooter sector and in the heavy segment of the motorcycle industry: in the naked, sport and touring segments. With a wide range of scooters and standard products in a variety of models, QJ focused on the low-price segment of the market. Its slogan was, "Dedicated to a combination of European design, Japanese quality, and Chinese cost." It also had several typical Chinese-style low-power motorcycles.

Global Trends   Several key competitors in the motorcycle industry shared the majority of worldwide sales. The industry could be described as global and highly competitive. Price, design and engine performance were the key elements in customer choice. Japanese manufacturers such as Yamaha, Suzuki, Kawasaki and Honda had large market shares in many countries by combining innovative designs with low prices; however, in certain geographic markets, a single producer may have had a dominant position due to its specific core competencies or due to customer loyalty. For example, this was the case for Harley Davidson in North America, where the company held almost one-third of the market (**Exhibit 2**),[11] or of Ducati, in the sports or race segments, where the company offered high technical performance, which was supported by good sports/race results.[12]

In the period 2003–2007, the motorcycle market in USA, Canada, Germany, France, United Kingdom, Italy, Russia and Japan grew by 4.7 per cent. The total value of the so-called G8 market was, at the end of 2007, US$24.3 billion (41 per cent related

---

[10]Q. Li, "Qianjiang Motor: Penetrating market in Taiwan," April 4, 2008, http://www.tzgb.com/Motorcycle/Qiyezhichuang/200804/3766 .html, accessed December 11, 2009.

[11]Don J. Brown, "What's Next for the Motor Co.?," *Dealernews*, February 1, 2009, www.dealernews.com/dealernews/Research/Whats-Next-for-the-Motor-Co/ArticleStandard/Article/detail/579349 accessed June 30, 2009. As for Ducati, see "Ducati Grows United States Market Share," Motorcycleusa.com, 2009, www.motorcycle-usa.com/577/3542/ Motorcycle-Article/Ducati-Grows-United-States-Market-Share.aspx, accessed December 10, 2009.

[12]As for Ducati competitive position, see "Ducati Grows United States Market Share," Motorcycleusa.com, 2009, www.motorcycle-usa .com/577/3542/Motorcycle-Article/Ducati-Grows-United-States-Market-Share.aspx, accessed December 10, 2009.

Exhibit 2   Market Share of Top 10 Motorbike Producers in the United States (Sales Estimates for 2008)

Producer	Market Share (%)
Harley Davidson	27.3
Honda	20.9
Yamaha	17.0
Kawasaki	13.8
Suzuki	12.5
KTM	2.0
BMW	1.4
Triumph	1.3
Victory	1.3
Ducati	1.0

Source: Don J. Brown (2009), "What's Next for the Motor Co.?" Dealernews, February 1, 2009, www.dealernews.com/dealernews/Research/Whats-Next-for-the-Motor-Co/ArticleStandard/Article/detail/579349, accessed June 30, 2009.

Exhibit 3   Market Share of Top 10 Motorbike Producers in Italy (% on Number of Registrations, February 28, 2009)

Producer	Market Share (%)
Honda	19.4
Piaggio	16.3
Yamaha	14.9
Kymco	7.8
Suzuki	6.8
Altre	6.7
Aprilia	5.5
Kawasaki	4.2
BMW	3.6
Ducati	2.6

Source: authors calculation on data from www.ancma.it/it/publishing.asp, acquired through Benelli QJ srl.

to the U.S.), with a projection of a further growth of 5.1 per cent by 2012.

An interesting trend in the global arena was due to the appearance of small companies, from emerging markets, Brazil, Russia, India and China in particular (BRIC area). Those markets were becoming more and more interesting both for supply and demand of motorcycles. In the period 2003–2007, the BRIC motorcycle market grew by 14.5 per cent and its total value was US$27.2 billion at the end of 2007.[13] Brazil was the fastest growing area with a compound annual growth rate of 28.3 per cent. Following the projections available, by 2012 the BRIC market should reach a value of US$67.4 billion, with an increase of 19.9 per cent from 2007.[14]

Local Trends: Italy   In Italy, the motorcycle industry was very competitive: Japanese manufacturers had the biggest market share, especially in the motorcycle sector. In 2008, Honda and

Yamaha held more than 30 per cent of new vehicle registrations and gained a dominant position despite negative market trends (see **Exhibit 3**). In the same year, Kawasaki sold the most of a single motorcycle model (see **Exhibit 4**). In the scooter segment, the Italian Piaggio Group had a good market share.[15]

Benelli had a small market share in the Italian industry, operating in a niche segment. The company tried to compete with Aprilia, Ducati and Honda, but its real direct competitors both on the Italian market and abroad were three Italian producers: Moto Morini (Morini), MV Augusta (MV) and Triumph Motorcycles (Triumph). Morini was its direct competitor in terms of both proposed models and annual sales. Although it was in the same market segment, MV produced more exclusive/luxury motorcycles, with higher prices and better performance. Benelli was Triumph's competitor because these two companies were the only manufacturers of three-cylinder Italian motorcycles; however, in comparison to Benelli, Triumph's market share was much larger (**Exhibit 5**).

[13]"Motorcycles—Global Group of Eight (G8) Industry Guide," Research and Markets, www.researchandmarkets.com/reportinfo.asp?report_id=706788, accessed June 30, 2009.

[14]"Motorcycles—BRIC (Brazil, Russia, India, China) Industry Guide," Research and Markets, www.researchandmarkets.com/reportinfo.asp?report_id=706787, accessed June 30, 2009.

[15]www.ancma.it/common/file/articolo_220sezione_7.pdf and www.ancma.it/common/file/articolo_224sezione_8.pdf, accessed December 10, 2009.

Exhibit 4   Top 10 Motorbikes Sold in Italy in 2008 (Number of Registrations)

	Producer	Product	Class	Number
1	Kawasaki	Z 750	Naked	6,745
2	Honda Italia	Hornet 600	Naked	5,207
3	BMW	R 1200 GS	Enduro	5,087
4	Honda	XL 700 V Transalp	Enduro	4,198
5	Yamaha	FZ6 Fazer	Naked	4,025
6	Suzuki	GSR 600	Naked	3,172
7	Ducati	M 696	Naked	3,113
8	Suzuki	DL650 U V-Strom	Enduro	2,655
9	Kawasaki	ER-6n	Naked	2,560
10	BMW	R 1200 R	Naked	2,258

Source: authors calculation on data from www.ancma.it/it/publishing.asp, acquired through Benelli QJ srl.

Exhibit 5   Motorbike and Scooter (More Than 50 cc) Registrations per Year

Producers	2006	2007	2008
Benelli	262	401	484
Moto Morini	340	356	351
MV Augusta	1,987	1,891	1,274
Triumph Motorcycles	3,781	5,233	5,978

Source: authors calculation on data from www.ancma.it/it/publishing.asp, acquired through Benelli QJ srl.

Local Trends: China   The Chinese motorcycle market was the largest in the world and accounted for 59.1 per cent of market volume in the Asia-Pacific region (see **Exhibit 6**). In 2006, the domestic market grew by 7.9 per cent to reach a value of US$5.8 billion and a volume of 14.9 million units. It was projected to have a value of US$9.9 billion in 2011, an increase of 69.4 per cent since 2006; the forecast volume would reach 24.6 million units, an increase of 65.7 per cent since 2006.

Based on volume, Jiangmen Grand River Group Company, Ltd. was the leading player in the Chinese motorcycle market, accounting for 16.2 per cent of market share in 2006. In the same year, Chongqing Loncin Industry (Group) Company, Ltd. and China Jialing Industrial Company, Ltd. held 8.3 per cent and 7.4 per cent of market share respectively. Due to the lack of a dominant leading player in the market, there was an increasing number of manufacturers, including Qianjiang Motors and other emerging firms that competed for the remaining 68 per cent of market share.

To understand actual trends in the Chinese market and QJ's position, some background information on the Chinese legal and regulatory environment is required. Focusing on the exhaustion of traditional natural resources, the deterioration of the environment and the excessive carbon dioxide emissions, the Chinese Ministry of Finance, Ministry of Science and Technology, Ministry of Industry and Technology Information and the National Development and Reform Commission issued a financial compensation plan for pure electric and fuel cell-powered vehicles. Energy-saving and environment-protecting vehicles were leading the R&D trend. QJ put the development of new-energy motorcycles onto its agenda: the company took the lead in releasing motorcycles with an engine management system, catering to national policies. Strengthening its technical input, QJ also introduced an electronic control injection system, reducing noise and gas emissions; at the same time, QJ was devoted to developing electric and liquid gas-powered motorcycles, as well as to participating in the formulation of national electric motorcycle standards.

According to a Chinese State Council resolution, motorcycles would officially be included in the "to the countryside" plan. From March 1, 2009 to December 31, 2009, the state was to allocate RMB5 billion for farmers in the countryside to trade old motorcycles and automobiles for new ones. This would mean considerable growth in the domestic motorcycle market. In the countryside, motorcycles were indispensible vehicles for feed, poultry and product transport, as well as for commuting. Compared to computers and other home appliances, farmers relied the most on motorcycles. The plan would be implemented over the course of

Exhibit 6   Country Backgrounds

China   China was the world's second largest economy in terms of gross domestic product (GDP) at purchasing power parity (PPP), and the world's most populous nation. Huge trade surpluses (China was the third largest world trader) and a large capacity to attract foreign direct investment (FDI)—China was the world's number 1 recipient of FDI—provided China with a huge amount of foreign reserves to be invested.[1] Real GDP grew at 11 per cent from 2003 to 2007 (Table A) and even after the economic crisis the economy was projected to expand at very high rates (Table B). Government stimulus packages, formally launched at the end of 2008 with an initial investment of about US$600 billion (equivalent to 13 per cent of GDP), provided a great boost to the country's economic growth. China would have remained the fastest-growing major economy in the world in the period 2009–10.[2]

While China's outlook appeared promising, extraordinary economic growth was unbalanced and, according to some, even unsustainable. Problems included the growing pollution in urban and industrial areas, the unbalanced growth of the cities compared to the countryside, social pressures, human rights violations and lack of democracy.[3] In the business sector, many Chinese companies that had entered international markets were not profitable, and they faced huge problems in terms of being competitive and adopting international management standards. Chinese companies had difficulties getting their products accepted in Western countries; moreover, some foreign

Table A   Outlook for China

Annual data	2007	Historical averages from 2003–2007	%
Population (millions)	1,321.3	Population growth	0.6
GDP (billions of US$; market exchange rate)	3,46	Real GDP growth	11.0
GDP (billions of US$; PPP)	7,316	Real domestic demand growth	9.9
GDP per head (US$; market exchange rate)	2,620	Inflation	2.6
GDP per head (US$; PPP)	5,540	Current account balance (% of GDP)	5.6
Average exchange rate RMB:US$	7.61	FDI inflows (% of GDP)	3.0

Source: Factsheet, May 6, 2009, Economist Intelligence Unit (Country ViewsWire).

Table B   China's Main Macroeconomic Data: Projections

Key indicators	2008	2009	2010	2011	2012	2013
Real GDP growth (%)	9.0	6.0	7.0	8.4	8.7	8.9
Consumer price inflation (%)	5.9	−0.2	2.5	3.5	4.1	4.1
Budget balance (% of GDP)	−0.1	−3.6	−2.1	−1.6	−1.1	−1.0
Current account balance (% of GDP)	10.2	6.1	4.5	3.6	2.9	2.0
Commercial bank prime rate (%)	5.6	5.4	6.6	7.0	7.1	7.4

Source: Factsheet, May 6, 2009, Economist Intelligence Unit (Country ViewsWire).

[1] For a deep analysis on aspects related to Chinese outward and inward foreign direct investments see "OECD Investment Policy Reviews China: Encouraging Responsible Business Conduct," OECD Publishing, 2008.
[2] Economist Intelligence Unit, "China economy: Stimulus report card," http:// viewswire.eiu.com/index.asp?layout=VWArticleVW3& article_id=715063456&country_id=1800000180&page_title=Latest+analysis, accessed December 10, 2009.
[3] Economist Intelligence Unit, Country Profile 2009—China, The EIU Limited, London, 2009 (printed and distributed by Patersons Dartford, Questor Trade Park, 151 Avery Way, Dartford, Kent DA1 1JS, UK); EIU, Country Profile, China, www.eiu.com.

Exhibit 6   Country Backgrounds (*Continued*)

companies were redirecting their investments to other emerging nations or to developing countries where they could find lower labor costs.

Italy   Italy was part of the Group of Seven (G7) industrialized nations. Its economic strength was in the processing and manufacturing of goods. Exports of luxury goods, consumer durables and investment goods led its competitiveness abroad. The industrial system was based mainly on small and medium-sized family-owned firms.

Economic growth in Italy ranged from one per cent in 1996 to a 3.7 per cent peak in 2000 and gradually slowed down thereafter in the two periods of recession in 2003 and 2008. Recent growth rates were among the lowest of the industrialized countries, due mainly to several years of low productivity growth and loss

of competitiveness. Like many Western countries, Italy was facing the consequences of the global financial turmoil, with a strong decrease in output and a rise in public spending after a period of substantial reductions in the budget deficit (Table C and Table D). The economy weakened during 2008: exports fell sharply due to the export structure. Investment demand also fell sharply, as did consumer expenditures, especially for cars and durables.

The government faced challenges related to long-term budget consolidation. The key issues included the extension of the pension reform process and reforms to improve the efficiency of public administration. At the same time, measures to relaunch firm competitiveness were needed to sustain an industrial system that was based mainly on small and medium enterprises (SMEs).

Table C   Outlook for Italy

Annual data	2008	Historical averages from 2004–2008	%
Population (millions)	58.1	Population growth	0.1
GDP (billions of US$; market exchange rate)	2,311	Real GDP growth	0.9
GDP (billions of US$; PPP)	1,797	Real domestic demand growth	0.9
GDP per head (US$; market exchange rate)	39,744	Inflation	2.3
GDP per head (US$; PPP)	30,910	Current account balance (% of GDP)	−2.2
Average exchange rate €:US$	0.680	FDI inflows (% of GDP)	1.3

Source: Factsheet, May 6, 2009, *Economist Intelligence Unit* (Country ViewsWire).

Table D   Italy's Main Macroeconomic Data: Projections

Key indicators	2008	2009	2010	2011	2012	2013
Real GDP growth (%)	−1.0	−4.5	−0.5	0.6	0.9	0.9
Consumer price inflation (av; %)	3.4	0.5	0.8	1.7	1.9	1.6
Consumer price inflation (av, %; EU harmonized measure)	3.5	0.6	0.9	1.8	2.0	1.7
Budget balance (% of GDP)	−2.7	−5.3	−5.2	−3.6	−3.7	−3.6
Current account balance (% of GDP)	−3.2	−2.2	−2.0	−3.0	−2.8	−2.7
Short-term interest rate (av; %)	4.6	1.7	1.8	2.6	3.5	4.1

Source: Factsheet, May 6, 2009, *Economist Intelligence Unit* (Country ViewsWire).

four years, until 2013. As the leading company in the domestic motorcycle industry, QJ would greatly benefit from this compensation policy.[16]

The Acquisition

Benelli and QJ made contact for the first time in June 2005: they were looking for an agreement that matched their relative strengths. Benelli had a recognizable brand name, knowledge of Western markets and projection skills, while QJ had high-efficiency plants and low production costs. In September 2005, a deal was reached concerning the founding of Benelli QJ. Industrial activities began in October 2005.

The main reasons for QJ to purchase Benelli was to utilize a well-known and recognized brand in terms of quality and sporting tradition, as well as to capitalize on Benelli's professionalism and knowledge in order to offer a high-quality product in segments that had not yet been penetrated by the QJ Group; therefore, the strategic objective of the initiative was to relaunch the Benelli brand by leveraging its history and tradition in order to achieve high-quality production. Benelli's products and spare parts were also to be used in China in order to increase the quality of domestically-manufactured products and to further diversify production to new categories of clients. Increased efficiency and a wide range of quality products were expected to help QJ to compete with the leading Japanese companies in the motorbike market.

At the time of the acquisition, there were no particular expectations with respect to Benelli's geographic location in central Italy, but QJ actually found some competitive benefits in the Marche Region. There was a lot of support from local public organizations, which facilitated negotiations and helped QJ win in the 'competition' with the Russian entrepreneur to purchase the company. The directors of QJ—which was in part a publicly-controlled company—welcomed the involvement of the local organizations, as well as the relationships forged

[16]L. Qu, "Great Prospects for Motorcycle Industry in China," March 2009, http://money.zjol.com.cn/05money/system/ 2009/03/31/ 015391068.shtml, accessed December 11, 2009.

between the Chinese local government and that of town, provincial and regional organizations in Italy.

There was much unexpected common ground in terms of culture and society between Pesaro, the Marche Region and the location in China. In addition to being located in a coastal town, QJ appreciated that the people in Pesaro had a strong work ethic and an approach to work that was similar to that in China.

The Post-Acquisition Phase

Main Organizational and Operating Changes Introduced After the Acquisition   Operations relating to administration, production and R&D were maintained in Pesaro. The main changes related to production operations, which were restructured to increase capacity at the Pesaro site: innovations included an expansion of in-house operations, such as the three-cylinder engine assembly that had previously been outsourced. As a result, the original workforce of 45 at the time of purchase was increased to 100 employees.

As for human resources, the sales director, parts quality manager and managing director were Chinese. The sales director was working on restructuring the sales network and expanding it to the West. The quality manager was handling the production relationship with the parent company especially to coordinate the production of Benelli parts that were made in China and then imported for assembly. All of the engineers, workers and technicians were Italian. The previous technical director became vice managing director. Generally, Chinese employees from the QJ Group came to Pesaro and vice versa for short periods of time, on a rotating basis, to learn from mutual experience (especially for designing and testing of motors).

For Benelli, the greatest positive changes after the acquisition included the following:

- efficiency-building efforts to reduce some avoidable costs that had been increasing with the previous owners and leading to significant losses;
- a new way of managing human resources: QJ gave increased decision-making power and

Exhibit 7 Two 2009 Benelli Products

Source: Courtesy of Benelli QJ srl.

responsibility to the staff, including young employees and women. QJ was attempting to let
all of the staff become involved in the future of
the company, by spreading a teamwork approach
through periodical meetings and encouraging
suggestions and ideas from the bottom to the top.

Industrial Activities: Present and Future In
2009, two production lines were operating at the
original industrial plant: one for engine production and assembly and one for motorcycle production and assembly. Before the acquisition, engines
were produced and tested through outsourcing, so
only one line of production was in use. The decision to outsource the engines had been a mistake:
it resulted in high production costs and problems in
quality and performance control. The Chinese thus
decided to bring production in-house, following
the suggestions of the Italian technical director. In
order to realize the new plan, the agreements with
local professional and technical schools were reinforced, to create apprenticeships and subsequent
placements for students. No changes were made in
the relationships with the local suppliers.

The QJ Group devised a challenging industrial
plan for the development of the company, with a resulting increase in the workforce: the industrial plan
involved manufacturing new products within four
years. Motorcycle production increased from only
three models prior to the company's acquisition to
nine in 2007 and 10 in 2008 (**Exhibit 7** shows two
2009 Benelli products). Each motorcycle model was
different, and three new engines were used; they
were designed in the technical department in Pesaro.
Designs and prototypes were then transferred to the
QJ technical department, where both the Chinese
and Italian technical departments worked cooperatively to oversee the industrial development of the
project. Once the industrial plan for the product was
completed, production began in Italy.

Prior to the acquisition, Benelli produced only
one model of scooter. Since 2008, two new models
were added to their product range. As of August
2009, there were four models: they were all designed and projected in Italy, completely produced
in China by QJ, and then imported with Benelli's
brand for distribution in Italy.

A key factor in the relaunching of Benelli's activities was to reduce production costs and sales
prices. It was estimated that it would take 10 years
to achieve a truly competitive price in relation to
the Japanese manufacturers. More parts would be
produced in China to reach this strategic goal, while
all high-value—knowledge-based—activities were

maintained in Italy. While trying to win competitiveness in terms of price and build on QJ's strengths, Benelli was working on QJ products to improve their technical performance as well as their style and design.

Benelli's products were expected to enter the Chinese market in 2009–2010. In 2009, import restrictions on motorbikes with a displacement of more than 250 cc were abolished, so sales activities could now be organized; several dealers were ready to sell Benelli's motorbikes in China. Scooters would not be distributed in China because they were not competitive in terms of price. After the industrial plan was completed, the relaunching of Benelli would also focus on racing activity: QJ was planning to have new competitive bikes ready for the MotoGP (in the next five years) and for the World Superbike races.[17]

Sales Activities Abroad and the Commercial Network

Another key element for improving Benelli's competitive position and strengthening QJ's competitiveness on international markets was the commercial network. Benelli's business relationships abroad were being restructured, starting with the development of new branches in Europe and the United States. A great part of Benelli's sales came from the European Union, particularly in Italy. Germany was the most important foreign market. The second most important foreign market for Benelli should have been the United States; however, there was a big differential between *sell in* and *sell out* (i.e. the number of imported motorbikes and the number of motorbikes sold). The key problems related to sales in the United States were customer-assistance services and distribution channels. The United Kingdom was another important market.

The Italian commercial network was based on 179 official sellers: 30 per cent located in the north, 33 per cent in the centre and 37 per cent in the south. Benelli also set up 21 "authorized workshops," eight in the north, three in the centre and 48 in the south.

The distribution network abroad consisted primarily of joint subsidiaries with Benelli and KW brand products. KW was a new brand intended to sell scooters: it was launched by the group after the acquisition of the Hungarian company Keeway (later Qianjiang-Keeway Europe). These brands were differentiated by their price and quality, but they were sold through the same network. Aside from the KW subsidiaries, the commercial network was based on official importers—usually one for each country—that sold to different dealers. The dealers did not usually operate as mono-brand sellers. Benelli had importers in 37 countries across Europe, Asia and America.

QJ's commercial strategy was differentiated on the basis of the geographic area: while there was a strong sales network in Indonesia through dealers and subdealers, Qianjiang Motor kept its sales away from the Southeast Asian market where national brands grouped together to compete and force down prices. Companies in countries such as Vietnam mainly relied on low prices to compete, and Qianjiang's prices were entirely uncompetitive.

QJ was now turning to the North American and European markets. Europe had a very strict technical standard to pass as a threshold, so it was difficult to enter the market. In Europe, motorcycle repairs had a high cost per hour that could erode the margins made through sales. Therefore, first-rate products with good quality were needed to enter the European market.

What Is Next?

After the acquisition, some problems arose due to the cultural differences between the Chinese and the Italians in terms of behaviour, specifically concerning business approach. Human relationships were difficult due to different mentalities, habits and background. Problems stemmed not only from differing organizational cultures, but also from the differing working environments in China and Italy.

There were many examples of such communication problems in the technical area. The Chinese

---

[17]Aaron Frank, "Benelli, BMW, and MV Agusta—Onward and Upward," *Motorcyclist*, www.motorcyclistonline.com/ newsandupdates/122_0804_benelli_bmw_mv_agusta/index.html, accessed December 10, 2009.

and the Italian technical departments should have worked together in harmony to combine and optimize their complementary skills; however, working together was difficult due to language and cultural differences. These problems were delaying the development of important projects.

Another critical field was that relating to rules and laws. In some cases, administrative actions were perceived as nonsense by both Italians and Chinese. Behaviours relating to specific Italian fiscal or civil rules were sometimes judged as "wrong" by the Chinese; likewise, Chinese rules seemed "strange" or unacceptable to Italian employees. In this sense, the problem facing Benelli and its new Chinese owners concerned how to improve cross-cultural understanding. Problems in communications and cultural differences created a rift between management and employees, impeding the implementation of strategy and harming the company's potential.

Other difficulties in managing the "new" Benelli were due to the great focus on efficiency, which also had negative consequences. Domestic consumers in China were price-oriented: in general, this resulted in Chinese companies paying more attention to reducing costs and cutting investments that had long-term or intangible returns. QJ's international expansion required it to give up this traditional way of doing business and to reconsider the low-cost approach. This focus on cost-savings led the company to give less importance to sales promotion.

A key problem for Benelli and its new Chinese owners was to improve the worldwide strength of the brand as well as the effectiveness of the sales network to increase market share. Benelli's products, especially its motorcycles, had a huge potential to compete with the most important players in the market, but their market share in both Europe and in the United States was low. QJ had expected fewer problems in penetrating the western market through the Benelli brand; however, delays were caused as a result of having to rebuild and relaunch the brand image internationally, as well as having to re-establish international supplier relationships. Marketing investments, especially for sales promotion, post-sales assistance and customer care were needed.

Reading 2-1   Clusters and the New Economics of Competition

by Michael E. Porter

Now that companies can source capital, goods, information, and technology from around the world, often with the click of a mouse, much of the conventional wisdom about how companies and nations compete needs to be overhauled. In theory, more open global markets and faster transportation and communication should diminish the role of location in competition. After all, anything that can be efficiently sourced from a distance through global markets and corporate networks is available to any company and therefore is essentially nullified as a source of competitive advantage.

But if location matters less, why, then, is it true that the odds of finding a world-class mutual-fund company in Boston are much higher than in most any other place? Why could the same be said of textile-related companies in North Carolina and South Carolina, of high-performance auto companies in southern Germany, or of fashion shoe companies in northern Italy?

Today's economic map of the world is dominated by what I call clusters: critical masses—in one place—of unusual competitive success in particular fields. Clusters are a striking feature of virtually every national, regional, state, and even metropolitan economy, especially in more economically advanced nations. Silicon Valley and Hollywood may be the world's best-known clusters. Clusters are not unique, however; they are highly typical—and therein lies a paradox: the enduring competitive advantages in a global economy lie increasingly in local things—knowledge, relationships, motivation—that distant rivals cannot match.

Although location remains fundamental to competition, its role today differs vastly from a generation ago. In an era when competition was driven heavily by input costs, locations with some important endowment—a natural harbor, for example, or a supply of cheap labor—often enjoyed a comparative advantage that was both competitively decisive and persistent over time.

Competition in today's economy is far more dynamic. Companies can mitigate many input-cost disadvantages through global sourcing, rendering the old notion of comparative advantage less relevant. Instead, competitive advantage rests on making more productive use of inputs, which requires continual innovation.

Untangling the paradox of location in a global economy reveals a number of key insights about how companies continually create competitive advantage. What happens inside companies is important, but clusters reveal that the immediate business environment outside companies plays a vital role as well. This role of locations has been long overlooked, despite striking evidence that innovation and competitive success in so many fields are geographically concentrated—whether it's entertainment in Hollywood, finance on Wall Street, or consumer electronics in Japan.

Clusters affect competitiveness within countries as well as across national borders. Therefore, they lead to new agendas for all business executives—not just those who compete globally. More broadly, clusters represent a new way of thinking about location, challenging much of the conventional wisdom about how companies should be configured, how institutions such as universities can contribute to competitive success, and how governments can promote economic development and prosperity.

▌ Michael E. Porter is the C. Roland Christensen Professor of Business Administration at the Harvard Business School in Boston, Massachusetts. Further discussion of clusters can be found in two new essays—"Clusters and Competition" and "Competing Across Locations"—in his new collection titled On Competition (Harvard Business School Press, 1998).

What Is a Cluster?

Clusters are geographic concentrations of interconnected companies and institutions in a particular field. Clusters encompass an array of linked industries and other entities important to competition. They include, for example, suppliers of specialized inputs such as components, machinery, and services, and providers of specialized infrastructure. Clusters also often extend downstream to channels and customers and laterally to manufacturers of complementary products and to companies in industries related by skills, technologies, or common inputs. Finally, many clusters include governmental and other institutions—such as universities, standards-setting agencies, think tanks, vocational training providers, and trade associations—that provide specialized training, education, information, research, and technical support.

The California wine cluster is a good example. It includes 680 commercial wineries as well as several thousand independent wine grape growers. (See the exhibit "Anatomy of the California Wine Cluster.") An extensive complement of industries supporting both wine making and grape growing exists, including suppliers of grape stock, irrigation and harvesting equipment, barrels, and labels; specialized public relations and advertising firms; and numerous wine publications aimed at consumer and trade audiences. A host of local institutions is involved with wine, such as the world-renowned viticulture and enology program at the University of California at Davis, the Wine Institute, and special committees of the California senate and assembly. The cluster also enjoys weaker linkages to other California clusters in agriculture, food and restaurants, and wine-country tourism.

Consider also the Italian leather fashion cluster, which contains well-known shoe companies such as Ferragamo and Gucci as well as a host of specialized suppliers of footwear components, machinery,

Figure 1   Anatomy of the California Wine Cluster

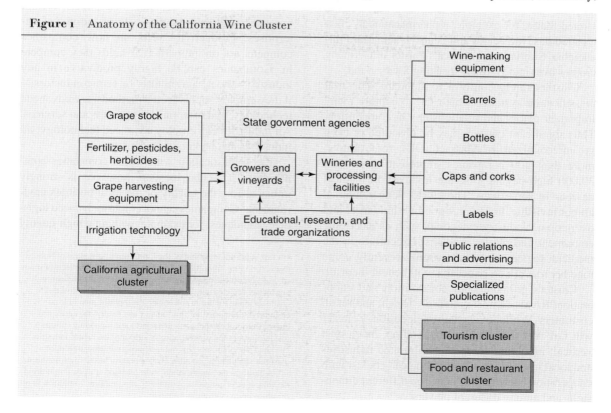

molds, design services, and tanned leather. (See the exhibit "Mapping the Italian Leather Fashion Cluster.") It also consists of several chains of related industries, including those producing different types of leather goods (linked by common inputs and technologies) and different types of footwear (linked by overlapping channels and technologies). These industries employ common marketing media and compete with similar images in similar customer segments. A related Italian cluster in textile fashion, including clothing, scarves, and accessories, produces complementary products that often employ common channels. The extraordinary strength of the Italian leather fashion cluster can be attributed, at least in part, to the multiple linkages and synergies that participating Italian businesses enjoy.

A cluster's boundaries are defined by the linkages and complementarities across industries and institutions that are most important to competition. Although clusters often fit within political boundaries, they may cross state or even national borders. In the United States, for example, a pharmaceuticals cluster straddles New Jersey and Pennsylvania near Philadelphia. Similarly, a chemicals cluster in Germany crosses over into German-speaking Switzerland.

Clusters rarely conform to standard industrial classification systems, which fail to capture many important actors and relationships in competition. Thus significant clusters may be obscured or even go unrecognized. In Massachusetts, for example, more than 400 companies, representing at least 39,000 high-paying jobs, are involved in medical devices in some way. The cluster long remained all but invisible, however, buried within larger and overlapping industry categories such as electronic equipment and plastic products. Executives in the medical devices cluster have only recently come together to work on issues that will benefit them all.

Clusters promote both competition and cooperation. Rivals compete intensely to win and retain customers. Without vigorous competition, a cluster will fail. Yet there is also cooperation, much of it vertical, involving companies in related industries and local institutions. Competition can coexist with cooperation because they occur on different dimensions and among different players.

Clusters represent a kind of new spatial organizational form in between arm's-length markets on the one hand and hierarchies, or vertical integration, on the other. A cluster, then, is an alternative way of organizing the value chain. Compared with market transactions among dispersed and random buyers and sellers, the proximity of companies and institutions in one location—and the repeated exchanges among them—fosters better coordination and trust. Thus clusters mitigate the problems inherent in arm's-length relationships without imposing the inflexibilities of vertical integration or the management challenges of creating and maintaining formal linkages such as networks, alliances, and partnerships. A cluster of independent and informally linked companies and institutions represents a robust organizational form that offers advantages in efficiency, effectiveness, and flexibility.

Why Clusters Are Critical to Competition

Modern competition depends on productivity, not on access to inputs or the scale of individual enterprises. Productivity rests on how companies compete, not on the particular fields they compete in. Companies can be highly productive in any industry—shoes, agriculture, or semiconductors— if they employ sophisticated methods, use advanced technology, and offer unique products and services. All industries can employ advanced technology; all industries can be knowledge intensive.

The sophistication with which companies compete in a particular location, however, is strongly influenced by the quality of the local business environment.[1] Companies cannot employ advanced logistical techniques, for example, without a high-quality

[1] I first made this argument in The Competitive Advantage of Nations (New York: Free Press, 1990). I modeled the effect of the local business environment on competition in terms of four interrelated influences, graphically depicted in a diamond: factor conditions (the cost and quality of inputs); demand conditions (the sophistication of local customers); the context for firm strategy and rivalry (the nature and intensity of local competition); and related and supporting industries (the local extent and sophistication of suppliers and related industries). Diamond theory stresses how these elements combine to produce a dynamic, stimulating, and intensely competitive business environment.

A cluster is the manifestation of the diamond at work. Proximity— the colocation of companies, customers, and suppliers—amplifies all of the pressures to innovate and upgrade.

Figure 2   Mapping the Italian Leather Fashion Cluster

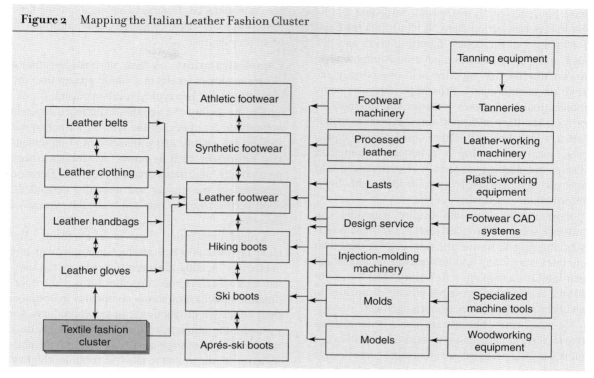

transportation infrastructure. Nor can companies effectively compete on sophisticated service without well-educated employees. Businesses cannot operate efficiently under onerous regulatory red tape or under a court system that fails to resolve disputes quickly and fairly. Some aspects of the business environment, such as the legal system, for example, or corporate tax rates, affect all industries. In advanced economies, however, the more decisive aspects of the business environment are often cluster specific; these constitute some of the most important microeconomic foundations for competition.

Clusters affect competition in three broad ways: first, by increasing the productivity of companies based in the area; second, by driving the direction and pace of innovation, which underpins future productivity growth; and third, by stimulating the formation of new businesses, which expands and strengthens the cluster itself. A cluster allows each member to benefit as if it had greater scale or as if it

had joined with others formally—without requiring it to sacrifice its flexibility.

Clusters and Productivity   Being part of a cluster allows companies to operate more productively in sourcing inputs; accessing information, technology, and needed institutions; coordinating with related companies; and measuring and motivating improvement.

Better Access to Employees and Suppliers   Companies in vibrant clusters can tap into an existing pool of specialized and experienced employees, thereby lowering their search and transaction costs in recruiting. Because a cluster signals opportunity and reduces the risk of relocation for employees, it can also be easier to attract talented people from other locations, a decisive advantage in some industries.

A well-developed cluster also provides an efficient means of obtaining other important inputs. Such a cluster offers a deep and specialized supplier base. Sourcing locally instead of from distant suppliers lowers transaction costs. It minimizes the need for inventory, eliminates importing costs and delays, and—because local reputation is important—lowers the risk that suppliers will overprice or renege on commitments. Proximity improves communications and makes it easier for suppliers to provide ancillary or support services such as installation and debugging. Other things being equal, then, local outsourcing is a better solution than distant outsourcing, especially for advanced and specialized inputs involving embedded technology, information, and service content.

Formal alliances with distant suppliers can mitigate some of the disadvantages of distant outsourcing. But all formal alliances involve their own complex bargaining and governance problems and can inhibit a company's flexibility. The close, informal relationships possible among companies in a cluster are often a superior arrangement.

In many cases, clusters are also a better alternative to vertical integration. Compared with in-house units, outside specialists are often more cost effective and responsive, not only in component production but also in services such as training. Although extensive vertical integration may have once been the norm, a fast-changing environment can render vertical integration inefficient, ineffective, and inflexible.

Even when some inputs are best sourced from a distance, clusters offer advantages. Suppliers trying to penetrate a large, concentrated market will price more aggressively, knowing that as they do so they can realize efficiencies in marketing and in service.

Working against a cluster's advantages in assembling resources is the possibility that competition will render them more expensive and scarce. But companies do have the alternative of outsourcing many inputs from other locations, which tends to limit potential cost penalties. More important, clusters increase not only the demand for specialized inputs but also their supply.

Access to Specialized Information Extensive market, technical, and competitive information accumulates within a cluster, and members have preferred access to it. In addition, personal relationships and community ties foster trust and facilitate the flow of information. These conditions make information more transferable.

Complementarities A host of linkages among cluster members results in a whole greater than the sum of its parts. In a typical tourism cluster, for example, the quality of a visitor's experience depends not only on the appeal of the primary attraction but also on the quality and efficiency of complementary businesses such as hotels, restaurants, shopping outlets, and transportation facilities. Because members of the cluster are mutually dependent, good performance by one can boost the success of the others.

Complementarities come in many forms. The most obvious is when products complement one another in meeting customers' needs, as the tourism example illustrates. Another form is the coordination of activities across companies to optimize their collective productivity. In wood products, for instance, the efficiency of sawmills depends on a reliable supply of high-quality timber and the ability to put all the timber to use—in furniture (highest quality), pallets and boxes (lower quality), or wood chips (lowest quality). In the early 1990s, Portuguese sawmills suffered from poor timber quality because local landowners did not invest in timber management. Hence most timber was processed for use in pallets and boxes, a lower-value use that limited the price paid to landowners. Substantial improvement in productivity was possible, but only if several parts of the cluster changed simultaneously. Logging operations, for example, had to modify cutting and sorting procedures, while sawmills had to develop the capacity to process wood in more sophisticated ways. Coordination to develop standard wood classifications and measures was an important enabling step. Geographically dispersed companies are less likely to recognize and capture such linkages.

Other complementarities arise in marketing. A cluster frequently enhances the reputation of a location in a particular field, making it more likely that buyers will turn to a vendor based there. Italy's strong reputation for fashion and design, for

Figure 3   Mapping Selected U.S. Clusters

Here are just some of the clusters in the United States. A few—Hollywood's entertainment cluster and High Point, North Carolina's household-furniture cluster—are well known. Others are less familiar, such as golf equipment in Carlsbad, California, and optics in Phoenix, Arizona. A relatively small number of clusters usually account for a major share of the economy within a geographic area as well as for an overwhelming share of its economic activity that is "exported" to other locations. Exporting clusters—those that export products or make investments to compete outside the local area—are the primary source of an area's economic growth and prosperity over the long run. The demand for local industries is inherently limited by the size of the local market, but exporting clusters can grow far beyond that limit.

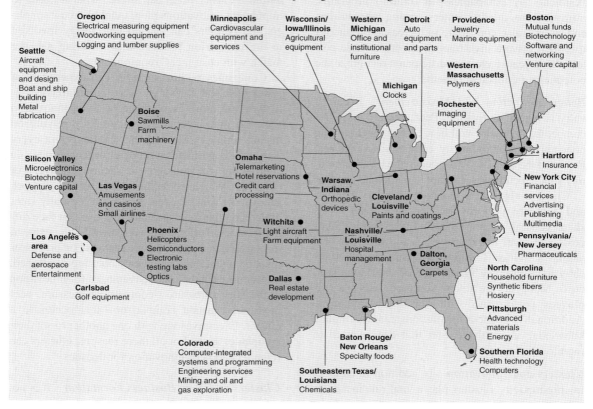

example, benefits companies involved in leather goods, footwear, apparel, and accessories. Beyond reputation, cluster members often profit from a variety of joint marketing mechanisms, such as company referrals, trade fairs, trade magazines, and marketing delegations.

Finally, complementarities can make buying from a cluster more attractive for customers. Visiting buyers can see many vendors in a single trip. They also may perceive their buying risk to

be lower because one location provides alternative suppliers. That allows them to multisource or to switch vendors if the need arises. Hong Kong thrives as a source of fashion apparel in part for this reason.

Access to Institutions and Public Goods Investments made by government or other public institutions—such as public spending for specialized infrastructure or educational programs—can enhance a company's productivity. The ability to recruit employees trained at local programs, for example, lowers the cost of internal training. Other quasi-public goods, such as the cluster's information and technology pools and its reputation, arise as natural by-products of competition.

It is not just governments that create public goods that enhance productivity in the private sector. Investments by companies—in training programs, infrastructure, quality centers, testing laboratories, and so on—also contribute to increased productivity. Such private investments are often made collectively because cluster participants recognize the potential for collective benefits.

Better Motivation and Measurement   Local rivalry is highly motivating. Peer pressure amplifies competitive pressure within a cluster, even among noncompeting or indirectly competing companies. Pride and the desire to look good in the local community spur executives to attempt to outdo one another.

Clusters also often make it easier to measure and compare performances because local rivals share general circumstances—for example, labor costs and local market access—and they perform similar activities. Companies within clusters typically have intimate knowledge of their suppliers' costs. Managers are able to compare costs and employees' performance with other local companies. Additionally, financial institutions can accumulate knowledge about the cluster that can be used to monitor performance.

Clusters and Innovation   In addition to enhancing productivity, clusters play a vital role in a company's ongoing ability to innovate. Some of the same characteristics that enhance current productivity have an even more dramatic effect on innovation and productivity growth.

Because sophisticated buyers are often part of a cluster, companies inside clusters usually have a better window on the market than isolated competitors do. Computer companies based in Silicon Valley and Austin, Texas, for example, plug into customer needs and trends with a speed difficult to match by companies located elsewhere. The ongoing relationships with other entities within the

cluster also help companies to learn early about evolving technology, component and machinery availability, service and marketing concepts, and so on. Such learning is facilitated by the ease of making site visits and frequent face-to-face contact.

Clusters do more than make opportunities for innovation more visible. They also provide the capacity and the flexibility to act rapidly. A company within a cluster often can source what it needs to implement innovations more quickly. Local suppliers and partners can and do get closely involved in the innovation process, thus ensuring a better match with customers' requirements.

Companies within a cluster can experiment at lower cost and can delay large commitments until they are more assured that a given innovation will pan out. In contrast, a company relying on distant suppliers faces greater challenges in every activity it coordinates with other organizations—in contracting, for example, or securing delivery or obtaining associated technical and service support. Innovation can be even harder in vertically integrated companies, especially in those that face difficult trade-offs if the innovation erodes the value of in-house assets or if current products or processes must be maintained while new ones are developed.

Reinforcing the other advantages for innovation is the sheer pressure—competitive pressure, peer pressure, constant comparison—that occurs in a cluster. Executives vie with one another to set their companies apart. For all these reasons, clusters can remain centers of innovation for decades.

Clusters and New Business Formation   It is not surprising, then, that many new companies grow up within an existing cluster rather than at isolated locations. New suppliers, for example, proliferate within a cluster because a concentrated customer base lowers their risks and makes it easier for them to spot market opportunities. Moreover, because developed clusters comprise related industries that normally draw on common or very similar inputs, suppliers enjoy expanded opportunities.

Clusters are conducive to new business formation for a variety of reasons. Individuals working within a cluster can more easily perceive gaps in products or services around which they can build businesses. Beyond that, barriers to entry are lower than elsewhere. Needed assets, skills, inputs, and staff are often readily available at the cluster location, waiting to be assembled into a new enterprise. Local financial institutions and investors, already familiar with the cluster, may require a lower risk premium on capital. In addition, the cluster often presents a significant local market, and an entrepreneur may benefit from established relationships. All of these factors reduce the perceived risks of entry—and of exit, should the enterprise fail.

The formation of new businesses within a cluster is part of a positive feedback loop. An expanded cluster amplifies all the benefits I have described—it increases the collective pool of competitive resources, which benefits all the cluster's members. The net result is that companies in the cluster advance relative to rivals at other locations.

Birth, Evolution, and Decline

A cluster's roots can often be traced to historical circumstances. In Massachusetts, for example, several clusters had their beginnings in research done at MIT or Harvard. The Dutch transportation cluster owes much to Holland's central location within Europe, an extensive network of waterways, the efficiency of the port of Rotterdam, and the skills accumulated by the Dutch through Holland's long maritime history.

Clusters may also arise from unusual, sophisticated, or stringent local demand. Israel's cluster in irrigation equipment and other advanced agricultural technologies reflects that nation's strong desire for self-sufficiency in food together with a scarcity of water and hot, arid growing conditions. The environmental cluster in Finland emerged as a result of pollution problems created by local process industries such as metals, forestry, chemicals, and energy.

Prior existence of supplier industries, related industries, or even entire related clusters provides yet another seed for new clusters. The golf equipment cluster near San Diego, for example, has its roots in southern California's aerospace cluster. That cluster created a pool of suppliers for castings and advanced materials as well as engineers with the requisite experience in those technologies.

New clusters may also arise from one or two innovative companies that stimulate the growth of many others. Medtronic played this role in helping to create the Minneapolis medical-device cluster. Similarly, MCI and America Online have been hubs for growing new businesses in the telecommunications cluster in the Washington, D.C., metropolitan area.

Sometimes a chance event creates some advantageous factor that, in turn, fosters cluster development—although chance rarely provides the sole explanation for a cluster's success in a location. The telemarketing cluster in Omaha, Nebraska, for example, owes much to the decision by the United States Air Force to locate the Strategic Air Command (SAC) there. Charged with a key role in the country's nuclear deterrence strategy, SAC was the site of the first installation of fiber-optic telecommunications cables in the United States. The local Bell operating company (now U.S. West) developed unusual capabilities through its dealings with such a demanding customer. The extraordinary telecommunications capability and infrastructure that consequently developed in Omaha, coupled with less unique attributes such as its central-time-zone location and easily understandable local accent, provided the underpinnings of the area's telemarketing cluster.

Once a cluster begins to form, a self-reinforcing cycle promotes its growth, especially when local institutions are supportive and local competition is vigorous. As the cluster expands, so does its influence with government and with public and private institutions.

A growing cluster signals opportunity, and its success stories help attract the best talent. Entrepreneurs take notice, and individuals with ideas or relevant skills migrate in from other locations. Specialized suppliers emerge; information accumulates; local institutions develop specialized training, research, and infrastructure; and the cluster's strength and visibility grow. Eventually, the cluster broadens to encompass related industries. Numerous case studies suggest that clusters require a decade or more to develop depth and real competitive advantage.[2]

Cluster development is often particularly vibrant at the intersection of clusters, where insights, skills, and technologies from various fields merge, sparking innovation and new businesses. An example from Germany illustrates this point. The country has distinct clusters in both home appliances and household furniture, each based on different technologies and inputs. At the intersection of the two, though, is a cluster of built-in kitchens and appliances, an area in which Germany commands a higher share of world exports than in either appliances or furniture.

Clusters continually evolve as new companies and industries emerge or decline and as local institutions develop and change. They can maintain vibrancy as competitive locations for centuries; most successful clusters prosper for decades at least. However, they can and do lose their competitive edge due to both external and internal forces. Technological discontinuities are perhaps the most significant of the external threats because they can neutralize many advantages simultaneously. A cluster's assets—market information, employees' skills, scientific and technical expertise, and supplier bases—may all become irrelevant. New England's loss of market share in golf equipment is a good example. The New England cluster was based on steel shafts, steel irons, and wooden-headed woods. When companies in California began making golf clubs with advanced materials, East Coast producers had difficulty competing. A number of them were acquired or went out of business.

A shift in buyers' needs, creating a divergence between local needs and needs elsewhere, constitutes another external threat. U.S. companies in a variety of clusters, for example, suffered when energy efficiency grew in importance in most parts of the world while the United States maintained low energy prices. Lacking both pressure to improve

and insight into customer needs, U.S. companies were slow to innovate, and they lost ground to European and Japanese competitors.

Clusters are at least as vulnerable to internal rigidities as they are to external threats. Overconsolidation, mutual understandings, cartels, and other restraints to competition undermine local rivalry. Regulatory inflexibility or the introduction of restrictive union rules slows productivity improvement. The quality of institutions such as schools and universities can stagnate.

Groupthink among cluster participants—Detroit's attachment to gas-guzzling autos in the 1970s is one example—can be another powerful form of rigidity. If companies in a cluster are too inward looking, the whole cluster suffers from a collective inertia, making it harder for individual companies to embrace new ideas, much less perceive the need for radical innovation.

Such rigidities tend to arise when government suspends or intervenes in competition or when companies persist in old behaviors and relationships that no longer contribute to competitive advantage. Increases in the cost of doing business begin to outrun the ability to upgrade. Rigidities of this nature currently work against a variety of clusters in Switzerland and Germany.

As long as rivalry remains sufficiently vigorous, companies can partially compensate for some decline in the cluster's competitiveness by outsourcing to distant suppliers or moving part or all of production elsewhere to offset local wages that rise ahead of productivity. German companies in the 1990s, for example, have been doing just that. Technology can be licensed or sourced from other locations, and product development can be moved. Over time, however, a location will decline if it fails to build capabilities in major new technologies or needed supporting firms and institutions.

Implications for Companies   In the new economics of competition, what matters most is not inputs and scale, but productivity—and that is true in all industries. The term high tech, normally used to refer to fields such as information technology and

---

[2]Selected case studies are described in "Clusters and Competition" in my book On Competition (Boston: Harvard Business School Press, 1998), which also includes citations of the published output of a number of cluster initiatives. Readers can also find a full treatment of the intellectual roots of cluster thinking, along with an extensive bibliography.

biotechnology, has distorted thinking about competition, creating the misconception that only a handful of businesses compete in sophisticated ways.

In fact, there is no such thing as a low-tech industry. There are only low-tech companies—that is, companies that fail to use world-class technology and practices to enhance productivity and innovation. A vibrant cluster can help any company in any industry compete in the most sophisticated ways, using the most advanced, relevant skills and technologies.

Thus executives must extend their thinking beyond what goes on inside their own organizations and within their own industries. Strategy must also address what goes on outside. Extensive vertical integration may once have been appropriate, but companies today must forge close linkages with buyers, suppliers, and other institutions.

Specifically, understanding clusters adds the following four issues to the strategic agenda.

1. Choosing Locations. Globalization and the ease of transportation and communication have led many companies to move some or all of their operations to locations with low wages, taxes, and utility costs. What we know about clusters suggests, first, that some of those cost advantages may well turn out to be illusory. Locations with those advantages often lack efficient infrastructure, sophisticated suppliers, and other cluster benefits that can more than offset any savings from lower input costs. Savings in wages, utilities, and taxes may be highly visible and easy to measure up front, but productivity penalties remain hidden and unanticipated.

More important to ongoing competitiveness is the role of location in innovation. Yes, companies have to spread activities globally to source inputs and gain access to markets. Failure to do so will lead to a competitive disadvantage. And for stable, labor-intensive activities such as assembly and software translation, low factor costs are often decisive in driving locational choices.

For a company's "home base" for each product line, however, clusters are critical. Home base activities—strategy development, core product and process R&D, a critical mass of the most sophisticated production or service provision—create and renew the company's product, processes, and services. Therefore locational decisions must be based on both total systems costs and innovation potential, not on input costs alone. Cluster thinking suggests that every product line needs a home base, and the most vibrant cluster will offer the best location. Within the United States, for example, Hewlett-Packard has chosen cluster locations for the home bases of its major product lines: California, where almost all of the world's leading personal computer and workstation businesses are located, is home to personal computers and workstations; Massachusetts, which has an extraordinary concentration of world-renowned research hospitals and leading medical instrument companies, is home to medical instruments.

As global competition nullifies traditional comparative advantages and exposes companies to the best rivals from around the world, a growing number of multinationals are shifting their home bases to more vibrant clusters—often using acquisitions as a means of establishing themselves as insiders in a new location. Nestlé, for example, after acquiring Rowntree Mackintosh, relocated its confectionary business to York, England, where Rowntree was originally based, because a vibrant food cluster thrives there. England, with its sweet-toothed consumers, sophisticated retailers, advanced advertising agencies, and highly competitive media companies, constitutes a more dynamic environment for competing in mass-market candy than Switzerland did. Similarly, Nestlé has moved its headquarters for bottled water to France, the most competitive location in that industry. Northern Telecom has relocated its home base for central office switching from Canada to the United States—drawn by the vibrancy of the U.S. telecommunications-equipment cluster.

Cluster thinking also suggests that it is better to move groups of linked activities to the same place than to spread them across numerous locations. Co-locating R&D, component fabrication, assembly, marketing, customer support, and even related businesses can facilitate internal efficiencies in sourcing and in sharing technology and information. Grouping activities into campuses also allows companies

Clusters, Geography, and Economic Development

Poor countries lack well-developed clusters; they compete in the world market with cheap labor and natural resources. To move beyond this stage, the development of well-functioning clusters is essential. Clusters become an especially controlling factor for countries moving from a middle-income to an advanced economy. Even in high-wage economies, however, the need for cluster upgrading is constant. The wealthier the economy, the more it will require innovation to support rising wages and to replace jobs eliminated by improvements in efficiency and the migration of standard production to low-cost areas.

Promoting cluster formation in developing economies means starting at the most basic level. Policy-makers must first address the foundations: improving education and skill levels, building capacity in technology, opening access to capital markets, and improving institutions. Over time, additional investment in more cluster-specific assets is necessary.

Government policies in developing economies often unwittingly work against cluster formation. Restrictions on industrial location and subsidies to invest in distressed areas, for example, can disperse companies artificially. Protecting local companies from competition leads to excessive vertical integration and blunted pressure for innovation, retarding cluster development.

In the early stages of economic development, countries should expand internal trade among cities and states and trade with neighboring countries as important stepping stones to building the skills to compete globally. Such trade greatly enhances cluster development. Instead, attention is typically riveted on the large, advanced markets, an orientation that has often been reinforced by protectionist policies restricting trade with nearby markets. However, the kinds of goods developing countries can trade with advanced economies are limited to commodities and to activities sensitive to labor costs.

While it is essential that clusters form, where they form also matters. In developing economies, a large proportion of economic activity tends to concentrate around capital cities such as Bangkok and Bogotá. That is usually because outlying areas lack infrastructure, institutions, and suppliers. It may also reflect an intrusive role by the central government in controlling competition, leading companies to locate near the seat of power and the agencies whose approval they require to do business.

This pattern of economic geography inflicts high costs on productivity. Congestion, bottlenecks, and inflexibility lead to high administrative costs and major inefficiencies, not to mention a diminished quality of life. Companies cannot easily move out from the center, however, because neither infrastructure nor rudimentary clusters exist in the smaller cities and towns. (The building of a tourism cluster in developing economies can be a positive force in improving the outlying infrastructure and in dispersing economic activity.)

Even in advanced economies, however, economic activity may be geographically concentrated. Japan offers a particularly striking case, with nearly 50% of total manufacturing shipments located around Tokyo and Osaka. This is due less to inadequacies in infrastructure in outlying areas than to a powerful and intrusive central government, with its centralizing bias in policies and institutions. The Japanese case vividly illustrates the major inefficiencies and productivity costs resulting from such a pattern of economic geography, even for advanced nations. It is a major policy issue facing Japan.

An economic geography characterized by specialization and dispersion—that is, a number of metropolitan areas, each specializing in an array of clusters—appears to be a far more productive industrial organization than one based on one or two huge, diversified cities. In nations such as Germany, Italy, Switzerland, and the United States, this kind of internal specialization and trade—and internal competition among locations—fuels productivity growth and hones the ability of companies to compete effectively in the global arena.

Figure 4   Mapping Portugal's Clusters

In a middle-income economy like Portugal, exporting clusters tend to be more natural-resource labor intensive.

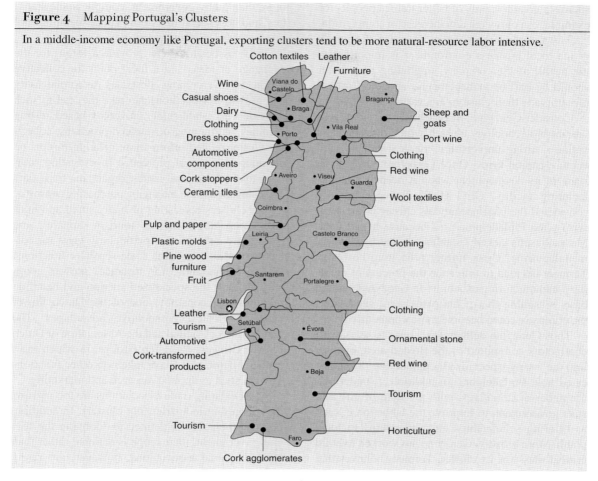

to extend deeper roots into local clusters, improving their ability to capture potential benefits.

2. Engaging Locally. The social glue that binds clusters together also facilitates access to important resources and information. Tapping into the competitively valuable assets within a cluster requires personal relationships, face-to-face contact, a sense of common interest, and "insider" status. The mere colocation of companies, suppliers, and institutions creates the potential for economic value; it does not necessarily ensure its realization.

To maximize the benefits of cluster involvement, companies must participate actively and establish a significant local presence. They must

have a substantial local investment even if the parent company is headquartered elsewhere. And they must foster ongoing relationships with government bodies and local institutions such as utilities, schools, and research groups.

Companies have much to gain by engaging beyond their narrow confines as single entities. Yet managers tend to be wary, at least initially. They fear that a growing cluster will attract competition, drive up costs, or cause them to lose valued employees to rivals or spin-offs. As their understanding of the cluster concept grows, however, managers realize that many participants in the cluster do not compete directly and that the offsetting benefits, such as a greater supply of better trained people, for example, can outweigh any increase in competition.

3. Upgrading the Cluster. Because the health of the local business environment is important to the health of the company, upgrading the cluster should be part of management's agenda. Companies upgrade their clusters in a variety of ways.

Consider Genzyme. Massachusetts is home to a vibrant biotechnology cluster, which draws on the region's strong universities, medical centers, and venture capital firms. Once Genzyme reached the stage in its development when it needed a manufacturing facility, CEO Henri Termeer initially considered the pharmaceuticals cluster in the New Jersey and Philadelphia area because it had what Massachusetts lacked: established expertise in drug manufacturing. Upon further reflection, however, Termeer decided to influence the process of creating a manufacturing capability in Genzyme's home base, reasoning that if his plans were successful, the company could become more competitive.

Thus Genzyme deliberately chose to work with contractors committed to the Boston area, bypassing the many specialized engineering firms located near Philadelphia. In addition, it undertook a number of initiatives, with the help of city and state government, to improve the labor force, such as offering scholarships and internships to local youth. More broadly, Genzyme has worked to build critical mass for its cluster. Termeer believes that Genzyme's success is linked to the cluster's—and that all members will benefit from a strong base of supporting functions and institutions.

4. Working Collectively. The way clusters operate suggests a new agenda of collective action in the private sector. Investing in public goods is normally seen as a function of government, yet cluster thinking clearly demonstrates how companies benefit from local assets and institutions.

In the past, collective action in the private sector has focused on seeking government subsidies and special favors that often distort competition. But executives' long-term interests would be better served by working to promote a higher plane of competition. They can begin by rethinking the role of trade associations, which often do little more than lobby government, compile some statistics, and host social functions. The associations are missing an important opportunity.

Trade associations can provide a forum for the exchange of ideas and a focal point for collective action in overcoming obstacles to productivity and growth. Associations can take the lead in such activities as establishing university-based testing facilities and training or research programs; collecting cluster-related information; offering forums on common managerial problems; investigating solutions to environmental issues; organizing trade fairs and delegations; and managing purchasing consortia.

For clusters consisting of many small and midsize companies—such as tourism, apparel, and agriculture—the need is particularly great for collective bodies to assume scale-sensitive functions. In the Netherlands, for instance, grower cooperatives built the specialized auction and handling facilities that constitute one of the Dutch flower cluster's greatest competitive advantages. The Dutch Flower Council and the Association of Dutch Flower Growers Research Groups, in which most growers participate, have taken on other functions as well, such as applied research and marketing.

Most existing trade associations are too narrow; they represent industries, not clusters. In addition, because their role is defined as lobbying the federal government, their scope is national rather than local. National associations, however, are rarely sufficient to address the local issues that are most important to cluster productivity.

By revealing how business and government together create the conditions that promote growth, clusters offer a constructive way to change the nature of the dialogue between the public and private sectors. With a better understanding of what fosters true competitiveness, executives can start asking government for the right things. The example of MassMEDIC, an association formed in 1996 by the Massachusetts medical-devices cluster, illustrates this point. It recently worked successfully with the U.S. Food and Drug Administration to streamline the approval process for medical devices. Such a step clearly benefits cluster members and enhances competition at the same time.

What's Wrong with Industrial Policy

Productivity, not exports or natural resources, determines the prosperity of any state or nation. Recognizing this, governments should strive to create an environment that supports rising productivity. Sound macroeconomic policy is necessary but not sufficient. The microeconomic foundations for competition will ultimately determine productivity and competitiveness.

Governments—both national and local—have new roles to play. They must ensure the supply of high-quality inputs such as educated citizens and physical infrastructure. They must set the rules of competition—by protecting intellectual property and enforcing antitrust laws, for example—so that productivity and innovation will govern success in the economy. Finally, governments should promote cluster formation and upgrading and the buildup of public or quasi-public goods that have a significant impact on many linked businesses.

This sort of role for government is a far cry from industrial policy. In industrial policy, governments target "desirable" industries and intervene—through subsidies or restrictions on investments by foreign companies, for example—to favor local companies. In contrast, the aim of cluster policy is to reinforce the development of all clusters. This means that a traditional cluster such as agriculture should not be abandoned; it should be upgraded. Governments should not choose among clusters, because each one offers opportunities to improve productivity and support rising wages. Every cluster not only contributes directly to national productivity but also affects the productivity of other clusters. Not all clusters will succeed, of course, but market forces—not government decisions—should determine the outcomes.

Government, working with the private sector, should reinforce and build on existing and emerging clusters rather than attempt to create entirely new ones. Successful new industries and clusters often grow out of established ones. Businesses involving advanced technology succeed not in a vacuum but where there is already a base of related activities in the field. In fact, most clusters form independently of government action—and sometimes in spite of it. They form where a foundation of locational advantages exists. To justify cluster development efforts, some seeds of a cluster should have already passed a market test.

Cluster development initiatives should embrace the pursuit of competitive advantage and specialization rather than simply imitate successful clusters in other locations. This requires building on local sources of uniqueness. Finding areas of specialization normally proves more effective than head-on competition with well-established rival locations.

New Public-Private Responsibilities

Economic geography in an era of global competition, then, poses a paradox. In a global economy—which boasts rapid transportation, high-speed communication, and accessible markets—one would expect location to diminish in importance. But the opposite is true. The enduring competitive advantages in a global economy are often heavily local, arising from concentrations of highly specialized skills and knowledge, institutions, rivals, related businesses, and sophisticated customers. Geographic, cultural, and institutional proximity leads to special access, closer relationships, better information, powerful incentives, and other advantages in productivity and innovation that are difficult to tap from a distance. The more the world economy becomes complex, knowledge based, and dynamic, the more this is true.

Leaders of businesses, government, and institutions all have a stake—and a role to play—in the new economics of competition. Clusters reveal the mutual dependence and collective responsibility of all these entities for creating the conditions for productive competition. This task will require fresh thinking on the part of leaders and the willingness to abandon the traditional categories that drive our thinking about who does what in the economy. The lines between public and private investment blur. Companies, no less than governments and universities, have a stake in education. Universities have a stake in the competitiveness of local businesses. By revealing the process by which wealth is actually created in an economy, clusters open new public-private avenues for constructive action.

Reading 2-2   Managing Risk in an Unstable World

by Ian Bremmer

Countries in turmoil elbow one another off the front page at a dizzying pace: Lebanon follows Ukraine follows Sudan follows Argentina. Companies, meanwhile, fear unpredictable change, even as they seek profit from the opportunities change creates—a freshly privatized industry in Turkey, recently tendered oil blocks in Libya, a new pro-Western government in the former Soviet republic of Ukraine. To help weigh dangers against opportunities, corporations mulling foreign ventures routinely consult economic risk analysts. But basing global investment decisions on economic data without understanding the political context is like basing nutrition decisions on calorie counts without examining the list of ingredients.

Reassuring data on countries' per capita income, growth, and inflation—the bread and butter of economic risk analysis—often obscures potential threats from other sources. Iran's parliament, for example, last year passed legislation that complicates foreign companies' abilities to plant stakes in that country's telecom sector. The 2003 revolution in Georgia altered the strategic calculus for investment in Caspian Sea energy development. The Kremlin's politically motivated prosecution of business tycoon Mikhail Khodorkovsky sent a chill through Russia's oil market. And Brazil's government is pressing both its agencies and its citizens to adopt open-source software, a policy that could inflict some nasty wounds on Microsoft and other technology companies.

These are examples of *political risk,* broadly defined as the impact of politics on markets. Political

risk is influenced by the passage of laws, the foibles of leaders, and the rise of popular movements—in short, all the factors that might politically stabilize or destabilize a country. The significance of any given risk, of course, depends upon the context of the investment decision. A hedge fund manager worries about developments that could move markets tomorrow, while the leader of a corporation building an overseas chemical plant needs a longer view. Strategists evaluating emerging markets must be especially vigilant (in fact, an emerging market may be defined as a state in which politics matters at least as much as economics). But even those businesses active only in developed nations should factor political risk into their planning scenarios.

Most companies are already navigating the choppy waters of globalization, and none, presumably, are sailing blind. But corporate leaders may lack the sophisticated understanding this very complex subject requires. Political risk analysis is more subjective than its economic counterpart and demands that leaders grapple not just with broad, easily observable trends but also with nuances of society and even quirks of personality. And those hard-to-quantify factors must constantly be pieced into an ongoing narrative within historical and regional contexts.

This article will help corporate leaders become better appraisers of information about the myriad shifting influences on global investments. Armed with that understanding, business strategists can minimize risks and seize opportunities far beyond their home shores.

▌ Politics Is Everyone's Business

Corporations with investments in such opaque countries as Zimbabwe, Myanmar, and Vietnam have long understood how political risk affects their bottom lines.

▌ *Ian Bremmer* is the president of Eurasia Group, a political-risk consulting firm, and a senior fellow at the World Policy Institute in New York.

In fact, historically, some of the business world's best political risk analysis has come from multinational corporations, like Royal Dutch/Shell and American International Group (AIG), that have entire departments dedicated to the subject. But today, any company with exposure in foreign markets needs early, accurate information on political developments. There are four principle reasons for this.

First, international markets are more interconnected than ever before. Tremors following a market shock in Argentina are quickly felt in Brazil and Venezuela, but they also rumble through Thailand. In 1997, capital flight from Southeast Asia roiled markets around the world. If China's rapidly growing economy overshoots a soft landing and crashes into recession, the impact on Chile, Russia, India, and the United States will be measurable within hours. China's political decisions today will have dramatic long-term effects on its markets. Companies with exposure anywhere in the world that China does business ignore those decisions at their peril.

Second, for good or ill, the United States is making the world a more volatile place, and that has changed risk calculations everywhere. The attacks on the World Trade Center in New York put foreign affairs and security front and center of federal government policy. Washington has shown its willingness to aggressively preempt threats to American security and national interests. The U.S. military has demonstrated an unprecedented capability to respond to international shocks—and to create them.

Third, the offshoring trend is growing. Businesses shift some operations to countries where labor is cheap—but the labor is cheap for a reason. In countries such as India (an established offshoring destination) and Kenya (an emerging one), living conditions for the working classes can be harsh, and there is greater threat of unrest than in developed countries with their large, relatively prosperous middle classes. Offshoring presents other risks as well. The Chinese government, for example, is already cavalier about intellectual property rights and shows signs of becoming more so. Companies moving manufacturing and other functions there may be hard-pressed to protect some of their most valuable intellectual assets.

Fourth, the world is increasingly dependent for energy on states troubled by considerable political risk—Saudi Arabia, Iran, Nigeria, Russia, and Venezuela among them. As global supply struggles to keep pace with rising demand, political instability in these oil-producing states can quickly produce shocks all over the world.

It is difficult to imagine a business that is not affected by at least one or two of these developments. And corporations' exposure will only grow as supply chains become more global and developing countries increasingly participate in international trade.

What Economics Can't Tell You

Economic risk analysis and political risk analysis address two fundamentally different questions. Economic risk analysis tells corporate leaders whether a particular country *can* pay its debt. Political risk analysis tells them whether that country *will* pay its debt. Two examples illustrate this distinction.

When 35-year-old Sergei Kiriyenko replaced Viktor Chernomyrdin as prime minister in March 1998, Russia's economy seemed to be emerging from post–Soviet era turmoil. Inflation had been reduced to single digits, the economy was growing, and the government appeared committed to a moderate reformist path. Economic analysts saw clear skies.

But political analysts recognized that an obstructionist parliament intended to block Kremlin attempts to tighten fiscal policy and streamline tax collection. They saw that an absence of consensus was producing incoherent monetary policies and that the absentee, alcoholic president wasn't going to enforce discipline on an increasingly chaotic policy-formulation process. When oil prices fell, political analysts underlined the country's lack of fiscal discipline as a cause for immediate concern.

In short, political analysts produced a darker—and more accurate—portrait of Russia's market instability in the period leading up to the financial crisis of 1998. When Russia ultimately defaulted on international debt and devalued the ruble, companies that had studied both economic and political risk weathered the storm with far fewer repercussions than those that had relied on economic analysis alone.

In other instances, political risk analysts have been able to detect the silver linings in economists' dark clouds. The value of Brazilian bonds and currency fell sharply in 2002 when it became clear that Luis Inacio Lula da Silva would be elected that country's president. In earlier campaigns, Lula had criticized the International Monetary Fund and Brazil's fiscal conservatives, whom he accused of widening the gap between rich and poor. Comparisons of Lula with Cuba's Fidel Castro and Venezuelan president Hugo Chávez spooked economic risk analysts, who feared that the election of Brazil's first "leftist" president would produce a politically driven market crisis.

But many political analysts considered such an outcome unlikely. In Lula they saw not an ideologue or a theoretician but a man who made his name as a tough, pragmatic labor negotiator. They observed in his campaign an inclusive, conciliatory electoral strategy. They heard in his speeches a determination not to allow Brazil to fall into the kind of financial crisis that had inflicted so much damage on Argentina. And so they argued that Lula's victory would be more likely to produce political and economic stability. If Lula won, they predicted, his government would enfranchise the poor. And he would keep his campaign promise to reserve an IMF-established percentage of tax revenue for the repayment of debt, instead of spending it on social programs and make-work projects.

The political analysts were right. Lula won the election and kept his promises of fiscal discipline. Within weeks, Brazilian bonds staged a dramatic recovery.

Strength Against Shocks

In both Russia and Brazil, political analysts focused on how a specific leadership change would affect the country's *stability*—the unit of measure for political risk. A nation's stability is determined by two things: political leaders' capacity to implement the policies they want even amidst shocks and their ability to avoid generating shocks of their own. A country with both capabilities will always be more stable than a country with just one. Countries with neither are the most vulnerable to political risk.

Shocks themselves are another important concept in political risk. They can be either internal (demonstrations in Egypt; a transfer of political power in Cuba) or external (thousands of refugees fleeing from North Korea into China; the tsunami in Southeast Asia). The presence of shocks alone, however, is not a sign of instability. Saudi Arabia, for example, has produced countless shocks over the years but has so far ridden out the tremors. It will probably continue to do so, at least in the near term: The nation is built on political and religious fault lines, but its strong authoritarian control and deep pockets allow the Saudi elite to adapt to quite dramatic changes.

Saudi Arabia's relative stability is grounded in its capacity to withstand shocks; other countries depend more on their capacity not to produce them. Kazakhstan's political structure, for example, is less supple and adaptable than that of Saudi Arabia. But the country also stands much further from the epicenter of political earthquakes.

Clearly then, two countries will react differently to similar shocks, depending on how stable they are. Say an election is held and a head of state is chosen but the victory is challenged by a large number of voters, and the nation's highest judicial body must rule on a recount. That happened in the United States in 2000 without any significant implications for the stability of the country or its markets. When similar events erupted in Taiwan in 2003 and Ukraine in 2004, however, demonstrations closed city streets, civil violence threatened, and international observers speculated on the viability of those nations' economies.

The 2000 U.S. elections point to another complicating factor in political risk: the relationship between stability and openness. The United States is stable because it is open—information flows widely, people express themselves freely, and institutions matter more than personalities.

Consequently, the nation weathered its election controversy without a Wall Street panic; investors knew the problem would be resolved and that the outcome would be broadly perceived as legitimate.

But other countries—such as North Korea, Myanmar, and Cuba—are stable because they are closed. What's more, the slightest opening could push the most brittle of these nations into dangerous territory. Twenty minutes' exposure to CNN would reveal to North Korean citizens how outrageously their government lies to them about life outside; the result might be significant unrest. And while there is considerable world pressure on closed countries to open up, the transition from a stable-because-closed state to a stable-because-open state is inevitably marked by instability. Some nations, for instance South Africa, survive that transition. Others, like the Soviet Union, collapse.

Plotting where nations lie on the openness-stability spectrum, and in which direction they are heading, is tricky. And no country poses a greater challenge than China, which appears equally at home on two different points along this range. Politically, China is stable-because-closed; it is a police state with absolute control over public expression. For example, security forces severely restricted media coverage of the recent death of Zhao Ziyang, a relatively progressive politician, in order to prevent the kinds of uprisings sparked by the deaths of Chou En-lai in 1976 and Hu Yaobang in 1989. Economically, however, China is opening at a rapid clip, as diplomats and negotiators globe trot in search of new trade relationships to feed the country's growth.

When a country is politically closed but economically open, something has to give. Whether China's political system will follow its economic trend line or vice versa is a fascinating and hotly contested subject in the political analyst community. (See the sidebar "Why China Keeps Us Up at Night.")

Corporate executives, however, generally focus on more immediate concerns when assessing a country's ripeness for investment. Broadly speaking, decision makers must know three things: How likely is it that a shock will occur? If likely, when will it probably occur? And how high are the stakes if it does?

The greatest risk, not surprisingly, is when shocks are likely, imminent, and have widespread consequences. All three conditions exist in North Korea, which has remained stable only by resisting movement toward market economics and more open government. North Korea's stability is so dependent on Kim Jong Il and the country's military elite that any threat to their safety could destroy the regime and destabilize the entire region very quickly. And the stakes are high because the most valuable products North Korea has to sell—military and nuclear components—tend to produce political shocks.

In other nations, shocks are likely and expected to occur relatively soon, but the stakes for world markets are much lower. Fidel Castro, for example, is 78, and the fate of the revolution after his death is unclear. Castro's hard-line younger brother Raul might assume power, but he is also in his 70s; if he replaces Castro, political uncertainty will build until the next transfer of power. Similarly, if a reformer like Carlos Lage steps forward to begin a process of gradual opening, the release of long-repressed dissent could spark violence. So either outcome will probably produce instability. But because Cuba is not an exporter of nuclear technology, oil, or any other vital resource, the shock's effect on world markets will be minor.

Risk by the Numbers Speculation on the outcomes of these and other scenarios appears in numerous publications, but corporations debating operational or infrastructure investments abroad need more objective, rigorous assessments than those found in the op-ed pages. Companies can either buy political risk services from consultants or, like Shell and AIG, develop the capacity in-house. Either way, a complete and accurate picture of any country's risk requires analysts with strong reportorial skills; timely, accurate data on a variety of social and political trends; and a framework for evaluating the impact of individual risks on stability.

The Analysts   Politics never stops moving, and risk analysts must be able to follow a nation's story as it develops. Usually, that means being on the ground in that country. And in the case of a particularly opaque regime, it can mean being there a very long time. Some information is published in official reports or in the media, but analysts will gather most of their intelligence from primary sources: well-connected journalists in the local and foreign press, current and former midlevel officials, and think tank specialists.

Companies should bear in mind that political analysis is more subjective and consequently more vulnerable to bias than its economic counterpart. One danger is that analysts with their own political opinions may view their research through a particular philosophical scrim. In addition, political analysts will probably have subject-matter—as well as nation-specific—expertise that can color their reports. A Taiwan analyst with a background in security, for example, may overemphasize such risk variables as cross-strait tensions and the growing imbalance of military power between Taiwan and China. An Eastern Europe analyst studying social unrest may insist that demonstrations by pensioners have the largest political impact on the government. As decision makers peruse analysts' reports, they should be alert for any potential bias and correct for it.

The Data   Because of their very nature, political risk variables are more difficult to measure than economic variables (although in some countries, such as China and Saudi Arabia, even the reliability of government-produced economic data is open to question). Politics, after all, is influenced by human behavior and the sudden confluence of events, for which no direct calibrations exist. How do you assign numbers to such concepts as the rule of law?

To accurately quantify political risk, then, analysts need proxies for their variables. Instead of trying to measure the independence of a nation's judiciary, for example, analysts can determine whether judges in a particular country are paid a living wage, whether funded programs exist to inform them about new legislation, and whether—and how often—they are targeted for assassination. Political risk analysts also study the percentage of children who regularly attend school, how police and military salaries compare with criminal opportunities, and how much access to medical care is available in towns with populations of 10,000 to 50,000 people. They look at such statistics as the unemployment rate for people between the ages of 18 and 29 and determine how many of them are in prison. And, of course, they add economic variables to the mix: per capita income, balance of payments, and national debt.

Taken together, this often anecdotal information reveals much about a country's underlying sources of strength or vulnerability. Comparing data from neighboring countries provides a good sense of where shocks from unstable nations might rumble into stable ones. Comparing a single nation's data points over time tells the analyst whether that nation is becoming more stable or less so, and how quickly.

The Framework   Different companies and consultancies will have different methods for measuring and presenting stability data. We at Eurasia Group have developed a tool that incorporates 20 composite indicators of risk in emerging markets. Distributed as part of a strategic relationship with Deutsche Bank, the Deutsche Bank Eurasia Group Stability Index (DESIX) scores risk variables according to both their structural and temporal components. Structural scores highlight long-term underlying conditions that affect stability. They then serve as a baseline for temporal scores, which reflect the impact of policies, events, and developments that occur each month.

The indicators are organized into four equally weighted subcategories: government, society, security, and the economy. Ratings for all four subcategories are aggregated into a single composite stability rating, which is expressed as a number on a scale of zero to 100—from a failed state to a fully institutionalized, stable democracy. (See the exhibits "Political Risk at a Glance" and "Anatomy of India's Political Risk.")

Political Risk at a Glance

Political risk measures the stability of individual countries based on factors grounded in government, society, security, and the economy. Emerging markets are generally in the moderate- to high-stability range. The map shows how some countries scored in March 2005.

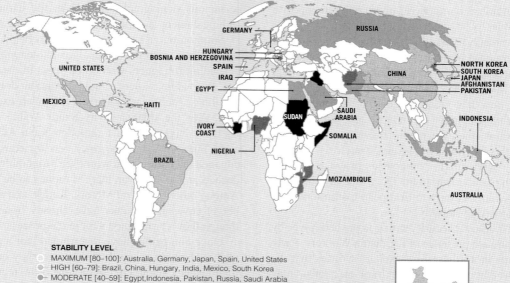

STABILITY LEVEL

- ○ MAXIMUM [80–100]: Australia, Germany, Japan, Spain, United States
- ◔ HIGH [60–79]: Brazil, China, Hungary, India, Mexico, South Korea
- ◑ MODERATE [40–59]: Egypt, Indonesia, Pakistan, Russia, Saudi Arabia
- ◕ LOW [20–39]: Afghanistan, Bosnia and Herzegovina, Mozambique, Nigeria, North Korea
- ● FAILED STATE [0–19]: Haiti, Iraq, Ivory Coast, Somalia, Sudan

Anatomy of India's Political Risk

National stability scores are plotted over time and comprise dozens of measurements, ranging from hard economic data on growth and investment to more amorphous assessments of youth disaffection and corruption. At the beginning of this year, India was hovering between moderate and high stability. (The numbers used to obtain each average have been rounded off.)

FACTORS AFFECTING STABILITY	STABILITY SCORES (0–100)			COMMENTS
	Jan 2005	Feb 2005	Mar 2005	
GOVERNMENT (such as strength of current government, rule of law, and level of corruption)	67	64	62	Political missteps by the government led to poor performance in state elections and strengthened opposition parties.
SOCIETY (such as social tension, youth disaffection, and health, education, and other services)	58	58	58	Low per capita income and literacy levels lead to a low human development index. Simmering social tensions keep the society score low.
SECURITY (such as level of globalization, geostrategic condition, and emergencies and disasters)	53	48	48	Peace talks with Pakistan and China have eased security fears. But a Maoist insurgency in Nepal and continuing Kashmir violence keep the score low.
ECONOMY (such as scal condition, growth and investment, and external sector and debt)	75	75	76	Economic growth and expanding trade keep the numbers healthy. The fiscal deficit remains a worry.
Cumulative National Stability Score	63	61	62	

Source: Deutsche Bank Eurasia Group Stability Index (DESIX), March 2005

Very often, the numbers that make up the stability rating are as interesting as the stability rating itself. Consider Turkey, whose March 2005 stability rating was 60, five points lower than Brazil's and two points higher than Russia's. Within that composite number, components are moving in opposite directions.

Specifically, Turkey's government rating rose as a consequence of the European Union agreement to open accession talks with Ankara in October 2005. Prime Minister Recep Tayyip Erdogan's administration now has greater incentive to continue reforms that strengthen the independence of Turkey's institutions, increase media freedom, and protect the rights of minority groups—such as Turkish Kurds—who might otherwise provoke unrest. Turkish membership in the EU would also bind the country more closely to European institutions, further increasing stability.

Yet Turkey's security rating is pushed lower by the continued presence of Kurdistan Workers' Party militants in northern Iraq. Ankara worries that the Kurds—empowered by the Iraqi elections—may try to regain control of the oil-rich northern Iraqi town of Kirkuk, which would provide the financial basis for an independent Kurdish state. A Kurdish state on Turkey's borders would likely fan separatist flames in that country's own Kurdish population.

Once You Know the Odds

How companies apply such analysis obviously depends upon their industry, strategy, and risk tolerance profile. Of necessity, companies in the energy industry, for example, have demonstrated a high tolerance for risk, relying on mitigation techniques to manage their exposure. By contrast, light manufacturers and midsize companies in industrial supply chains tend to bide their time to see how situations evolve. And pharmaceutical corporations generally shy away from investment when presented with infrastructure or intellectual property risks.

Companies making extended commitments in unstable nations must give top priority to long-term risk—issues related to demographics and natural resources, for example—when making decisions.

In May 2004, Japan's Sumitomo Chemical agreed to a $4.3 billion joint venture with Saudi Aramco to build a major petrochemical plant at Rabigh in Saudi Arabia. The plant isn't scheduled to open until 2008, so Sumitomo is particularly vulnerable to such pernicious demographic trends as the exodus of technical talent and the joblessness of young men.

Sumitomo's risk tolerance is already being tested by an Islamic extremist campaign of kidnapping and beheading foreigners who do business in the country. But while violence and corruption dominate headlines, such near-term risks are much exaggerated. (See the sidebar "Why Saudi Arabia Keeps Us Up at Night.") In fact, although Saudi Arabia—and China, too—may be risky bets for companies engaged in ventures that won't see profitability for a decade, in the short run there is money to be made. Among others, General Motors, Kodak, and a number of investment banks have already done so—though they've stumbled a bit in the process.

Once companies have determined that a particular investment is worth the danger, they can use traditional techniques to mitigate the risk—recruiting local partners, for example, or limiting R&D in nations with leaky intellectual property protection. In addition, a growing number of commercial and government organizations now offer insurance against political risks such as the expropriation of property, political violence, currency inconvertibility, and breach of contract. (Such insurance is expensive, however, because risks are so hard to assess.) Otherwise it's mostly a matter of hedging—locating a factory in Mexico as well as Venezuela, say, so as not to bet the entire Latin America strategy on a single opaque regime.

Finally, it is worth remembering that though instability translates into greater risk, risk is not always a bad thing. Political risk in underdeveloped countries nearly always carries an upside because such nations are so unstable that negative shocks can do little further damage. On the stability ladder, for example, Afghanistan and Cambodia simply don't have far to fall; only favorable external conditions—such as debt relief from the developed world or loans from international institutions—could have much effect on their political stability. For some companies, that could make investments in such countries an attractive part of an enterprise risk portfolio.

Politics has always been inseparable from markets; the world's first transnational trade organizations were moved by the political waves of their time. Today, goods, services, information, ideas, and people cross borders with unprecedented velocity—and the trend is only intensifying. For company leaders seeking profit in places that are socially, culturally, and governmentally alien, the complementary insights of political and economic risk analysts are vital.

Call Outs

Why China Keeps Us Up at Night China bestrides the world of political risk like a colossus. Many experts tout it as the great investment opportunity of the new millennium, but it is also a great unknown. Among the questions political risk analysts are studying: Can China's explosive economic growth survive its corrupt and inefficient political system? Do the country's political leaders agree that preparations for a soft landing to avoid recession are necessary? Would reform that opens its political process make China more stable or less?

China's continued expansion depends on the central government's capacity to handle complex economic transitions and avoid instability. At the same time, the state must juggle huge security, demographic, and political challenges. Imminent agricultural, banking, and urban policy reforms will probably produce even more complex management problems for the country's dysfunctional bureaucracy.

China appears to be inching toward instability as reforms strain the relationships between national and regional leaders, increasing the probability of an economic shock followed by a political one. Complicating matters, China's bureaucracy lacks the administrative control necessary to modulate the pace of an economic slowdown.

Analysts of economic risk tend to base projections for China's growth rates on its past performance. But there are few countries for which past performance is so poor a predictor of future results. With a few notable exceptions, such as the 1989 protests in Tiananmen Square, social unrest in modern-day China has been rare. But the risk of popular unrest is going up as a result of widening income inequality, slowing—although still intense—economic growth, and continuing official abuse and corruption. The urban unemployed and migrant workers could stage protests; rural rebellion over land reclamations and onerous administrative fees could escalate. China's leaders might then clamp down on the media, religious groups, use of the Internet, and other forms of expression and communication. Faced with international criticism, the government could become more antagonistic and dogmatic about issues of concern to the United States and East Asia.

The probability of such events occurring in the short-term is low, but China's risk indicators suggest it is rising.

Why Saudi Arabia Keeps Us Up at Night Saudi Arabia's stability is under fire from religious and secular forces. Islamic extremists hope to undermine the legitimacy of the royal family. Real unemployment is estimated to be between 20% and 25%; frustrated, jobless young men are flocking to mosques and schools where religious leaders thunder against the infidels. Western nations, meanwhile, are calling on the royals to move toward political liberalization. And the flight of expatriates will eventually take its toll on the Saudis' ability to diversify their economy.

Such volatility complicates financial deals—particularly those that take years to assemble—and extends the exposure to political risk over time.

But while companies with long-term investments must worry, short-term investors in Saudi Arabia have less cause for concern. That's because oil money stabilizes the political system, and the royal family can count on those revenues for years to come. Yes, oil supplies are a tempting target for terrorists; but the country's oil infrastructure is isolated from population centers, and redundancies in the pipeline system make it almost impossible to inflict lasting damage with a single blow. In addition, the national oil company has the technology, the trained engineers, and the spare capacity to continue producing significantly more than 9 million barrels per day. Finally, in light of concerns that foreign governments might freeze Saudi assets following September 11, 2001, a great deal of money flowed back into the kingdom, providing the House of Saud with more ready cash.

Clearly, any project in Saudi Arabia that needs a decade to show a profit is deeply problematic. But those willing to brave volatility in the near term may profit from opportunities that more risk-averse companies forgo.

Developing Transnational Strategies:
Building Layers of Competitive Advantage

In this chapter, we discuss how the numerous conflicting demands and pressures described in the first two chapters shape the strategic choices that multinational enterprises (MNEs) must make. In this complex situation, an MNE determines strategy by balancing the motivations for its own international expansion with the economic imperatives of its industry structure and competitive dynamics, the social and cultural forces of the markets that it has entered worldwide, and the political demands of its home- and host-country governments. To frame this complex analysis, in this chapter, we examine how MNEs balance strategic means and ends to build the three required capabilities: global-scale efficiency and competitiveness, multinational flexibility and responsiveness, and worldwide innovation and learning. After defining each of the dominant historic strategic approaches—what we term *classic multinational, international,* and *global strategies*—we explore the emerging transnational strategic model that most MNEs must adopt today. Finally, we describe not only how companies can develop this approach themselves, but also how they can defend against transnational competitors.

The strategies of MNEs at the start of the 21st century were shaped by the turbulent international environment that redefined global competition in the closing decades of the 20th century. It was during that turmoil that a number of different perspectives and prescriptions emerged about how companies could create strategic advantage in their worldwide businesses.

Consider, for example, three of the most influential articles on global strategy published during the 1980s—the decade in which many new trends first emerged.[1] Each is reasonable and intuitively appealing. What soon becomes clear, however, is that their prescriptions are very different and often contradictory, a reality that highlights not only the complexity of the strategic challenge that faced managers in large, worldwide companies but also the confusion of advice being offered to them.

- In one of the most provocative articles of that era, Theodore Levitt argued that effective global strategy was not a bag of many tricks, but the successful practice of just one: product standardization. According to him, the core of a global strategy

---

[1] See Theodeore Levitt, "The Globalization of Markets" *Harvard Business Review* 61, no. 3 (1983), pp. 92–102; T. Hout, M. E. Porter, and E. Rudden, "How Global Companies Win Out," *Harvard Business Review* 60, no. 5 (1982), pp. 98–109; G. Hamel and C. K. Prahalad, "Do You Really Have a Global Strategy?" *Harvard Business Review* 63, no. 4 (1985), pp. 139–49.

lay in developing a standardized product to be manufactured and sold the same way throughout the world.

- In contrast, an article by Michael Porter and his colleagues suggested that effective global strategy required the approach not of a hedgehog, who knows only one trick, but that of a fox, who knows many. These tricks include exploiting economies of scale through global volume, taking preemptive positions through quick and large investments, and managing interdependently to achieve synergies across different activities.
- Gary Hamel and C. K. Prahalad's prescription for a global strategy contradicted Levitt's even more sharply. Instead of a single standardized product, they recommended a broad product portfolio, with many product varieties, so that investments in technologies and distribution channels could be shared. Cross-subsidization across products and markets and the development of a strong worldwide distribution system were at the center of these authors' view of how to succeed in the game of global chess.

As we described in the preceding chapter, what was becoming increasingly clear during the next two decades was that to achieve sustainable competitive advantage, MNEs needed to develop layers of competitive advantage—global-scale efficiency, multinational flexibility, and the ability to develop innovations and leverage knowledge on a worldwide basis. And though each of the different prescriptions focuses on one or another of these different strategic objectives, the challenge for most companies today is to achieve all of them simultaneously.

■ Worldwide Competitive Advantage: Goals and Means

Competitive advantage is developed by taking strategic actions that optimize a company's achievement of these three different and, at times, conflicting goals. In developing each of these capabilities, the MNE can use three very different tools and approaches, which we described briefly in Chapter 1 as the main forces motivating companies to internationalize. It can leverage the scale economies that are potentially available in its different worldwide activities; it can exploit the differences in sourcing and market opportunities among the many countries in which it operates; and it can capitalize on the diversity of its activities and operations to create synergies or develop economies of scope.

The MNE's strategic challenge therefore is to exploit all three sources of global competitive advantage—scale economies, national differences, and scope economies—to optimize global efficiencies, multinational flexibility, and worldwide learning. And thus, the key to worldwide competitive advantage lies in managing the interactions between the different goals and the different means.

■ The Goals: Efficiency, Flexibility, and Learning

Let us now consider each of these strategic goals in a little more detail.

Global Efficiency

Viewing an MNE as an input-output system, we can think of its overall efficiency as the ratio of the value of its outputs to the value of its inputs. In this simplified view of the firm, its efficiency could be enhanced by increasing the value of outputs (i.e., securing

Figure 3-1   The integration–responsiveness framework

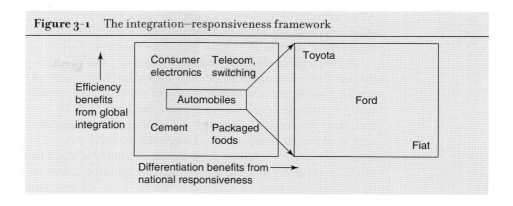

higher revenues), lowering the value of its inputs (i.e., lowering costs), or doing both. This is a simple point but one that is often overlooked: Efficiency improvement is not just cost reduction; it is revenue enhancement as well.

To help understand the concept of global efficiency, we use the global integration–national responsiveness framework first developed by C. K. Prahalad (see Figure 3-1).[2] The vertical axis represents the potential benefits from the global integration of activities—benefits that largely translate into lower costs through scale and scope economies. The horizontal axis represents the benefits of national responsiveness—those that result from the country-by-country differentiation of product, strategies, and activities. These benefits essentially translate into better revenues from more effective differentiation in response to national differences in tastes, industry structures, distribution systems, and government regulations.

As Figure 3-1 illustrates, the framework can be used to understand differences in the benefits of integration and responsiveness at the aggregate level of industries, as well as to identify and describe differences in the strategic approaches of companies competing in the same industry. Also, as the figure indicates, industry characteristics alone do not determine company strategies. In automobiles, for example, Fiat historically pursued a classical multinational strategy, helping establish national auto industries through its joint venture partnerships and host government support in Spain, Poland, and many other countries with state-sponsored auto industries. Toyota, by contrast, succeeded originally by developing products and manufacturing them in centralized, globally scaled facilities in Japan. This sort of strategic choice to focus on the objective of global efficiency (rather than local responsiveness) creates vulnerabilities and challenges, as well as clear benefits.

Multinational Flexibility

A worldwide company faces an operating environment characterized by diversity and volatility. Some opportunities and risks generated by this environment are endemic to all firms; others, however, are unique to companies operating across national borders.

[2]For a detailed exposition of this framework, see C. K. Prahalad and Yves Doz, *The Multinational Mission* (New York: The Free Press, 1987).

A key element of worldwide competitiveness, therefore, is multinational flexibility—the ability of a company to manage the risks and exploit the opportunities that arise from the diversity and volatility of the global environment.[3]

Although there are many sources of diversity and volatility, it is worth highlighting four that we regard as particularly important. First, there are *macroeconomic risks* that are completely outside the control of the MNE, such as changes in prices, factor costs, or exchange rates caused by wars, natural calamities, or economic cycles. Second, there are *political risks* that arise from policy actions of national governments, such as managed changes in exchange rates or interest rate adjustments. Third, there are *competitive risks* arising from the uncertainties of competitors' responses to the MNE's own strategies. And fourth, there are *resource risks,* such as the availability of raw materials, capital, or managerial talent. In all four categories, the common characteristic of the various types of risks is that they vary across countries and change over time. This variance makes flexibility the key strategic management requirement because diversity and volatility create attendant opportunities that must be considered jointly.

In general, multinational flexibility requires management to scan its broad environment to detect changes and discontinuities and then respond to the new situation in the context of the worldwide business. MNEs following this approach exploit their exposure to diverse and dynamic environments to develop strategies—and structures—in more general and more flexible terms so as to be robust to different international environmental scenarios. For example, having a network of affiliated subsidiaries that emphasize global exports rather than individual local markets provides a flexibility to shift production when a particular national market faces an economic crisis.

Worldwide Learning

Most existing theories of the MNE view it as an instrument to extract additional revenues from internalized capabilities. The assumption is that the firm goes abroad to make more profits by exploiting its technology, brand name, or management capabilities in different countries around the world. And most traditional theories assume that the key competencies reside at the MNE's center.

Although the search for additional profits or the desire to protect existing revenues may explain why MNEs come to exist, that does not provide a complete explanation of why some of them continue to grow and flourish. As we suggested in Chapter 1, an alternative view may well be that a key asset of the MNE is the diversity of environments in which it operates. This diversity exposes the MNE to multiple stimuli, allows it to develop diverse capabilities, and provides it with broader learning opportunities than are available to a purely domestic firm. Furthermore, its initial stock of knowledge provides the MNE with strength that allows it to create organizational diversity in the first place. In Chapter 5, we engage in a detailed discussion of the approaches that MNEs use to deliver on the objective of worldwide learning.

---

[3]This issue of multinational flexibility is discussed more fully in Bruce Kogut, "Designing Global Strategies: Profiting from Operating Flexibility," *Sloan Management Review,* Fall 1985, pp. 27–38.

The Means: National Differences, Scale, and Scope Economies

There are three fundamental tools for building worldwide competitive advantage: exploiting differences in sourcing and market potential across countries, exploiting economies of scope, and exploiting economies of scale. In this section, we explore each of these in more depth.

National Differences

In the absence of efficient markets, the fact that different nations have different factor endowments (e.g., an abundance of labor, land, and materials) leads to intercountry differences in factor costs. Because different activities of the firm, such as R&D, production, or marketing, use various factors to different degrees, a firm can gain cost advantages by configuring its value chain so that each activity is located in the country that has the least cost for its most intensively used factor. For example, R&D facilities may be placed in the United Kingdom because of its available supply of high-quality, yet relatively modestly paid, scientists; manufacturing of labor-intensive components may be undertaken in Taiwan to capitalize on the lower-cost, efficient labor force there; and software development could be concentrated in India, where skilled software engineers are paid a fraction of Western salaries. Initially, the "Global Product Concept" at General Electric (GE) was set up to concentrate manufacturing wherever it could be implemented in the most cost-effective way (while still maintaining quality). Over time, however, changes in cost structures, the threat of imitators, and the pursuit of control over the supply chain eventually led the company to move back some of the manufacturing sites to the United States.[4] This highlights the fact that global situations are rarely stable over long periods of time, and that MNE strategy must, above all, be flexible and responsive to changing differences in home and host-country environments.

Market potential varies across countries. According to the International Monetary Fund (IMF), the 10 fastest-growing economies in the years ahead will all be in emerging markets. It is crucial that MNEs be attentive to this trend when developing their strategies. About 40 percent of the growth of the global economy over the next 15 years will be generated in 400 midsized emerging-market cities.[5]

National differences also may exist in output markets. As we have discussed, distribution systems, government regulations, the effectiveness of different promotion strategies, and customer tastes and preferences differ in all these different countries.

In order to exploit national differences, companies may need to reshuffle their business models. For example, the growing middle class in emerging markets will have different needs and priorities than what most of the current business models address.[6] They still may have very basic unmet needs (e.g., refrigeration and clothes washing) that

[4]Jeffrey R. Immelt, "The CEO of General Electric on Sparking an American Manufacturing Renewal," *Harvard Business Review* 90 (2012), pp. 43–46.

[5]Martin Dewhurst, Jonathan Harris, and Suzanne Heywood, "The Global Company's Challenge," *McKinsey Quarterly*, June 2012.

[6]David Court and Laxman Narasimhan, "Capturing the World's Emerging Middle Class," *McKinsey Quarterly* 3 (2010), pp. 12–17.

Figure 3-2   Category Specific Strategies to Help Companies Serve Middle-Class Consumers in Emerging Economies

		Middle-class consumers' needs	
		Local	Global
Middle-class consumers' ability to buy	High	Shape or localize	Create a platform
	Low	Reinvent business model	Target niche

Source: Extracted from David Court and Laxman Narasimhan, 2010. Capturing the world's emerging middle class. *McKinsey Quarterly, Issue* 3, pp. 12–17.

require a different value proposition versus the business model that exists in advanced markets.[7] About 40 percent of the average household income in China and India is spent on food and transportation, whereas in the United States, this figure is 25 percent. For companies operating in emerging economies, addressing such needs is not a matter of transferring their existing business models and adjusting them with small tweaks. Instead, MNEs sometimes need to rethink their business models to solve problems such as accessibility and affordability. To illustrate this point, consider whether consumer needs in emerging economies are basically local or global. Fashion products and personal banking are examples of global needs in these markets, while economy cars and basic and affordable home appliances are examples of local needs. Depending on each of the four categories of needs and consumer combinations shown in Figure 3-2, companies can develop strategies to serve middle-class consumers better in emerging economies.

As we will also see in many of the case examples in this book, a firm can charge higher prices for its output by tailoring its offerings to fit the unique requirements of each national market.

Scale Economies

Microeconomic theory provides a strong basis for evaluating the effect of scale on cost reduction, and the use of scale as a competitive tool is common in industries ranging from roller bearings to semiconductors. Whereas scale is a static concept by itself, there may be dynamic benefits of scale through what has been variously described as the *experience* or *learning effect*. The higher volume that helps a firm exploit scale benefits also allows it to accumulate learning, which leads to progressive cost reduction as the firm moves down its learning curve. So although emerging Korean electronics firms were able to match the scale of their experienced Japanese competitors, it took many years before they could finally compensate for the innumerable process-related efficiencies that the Japanese had learned after decades of operating their global-scale plants.

---

[7]Matthew J. Eyring, Mark W. Johnson, and Hari Nair, "New Business Models in Emerging Markets," *Harvard Business Review* 89 (2011), pp. 88–95.

Table 3-1   Scope Economies in Product and Market Diversification

	Sources of Scope Economies	
	Product Diversification	**Market Diversification**
Shared physical assets	Factory automation with flexibility to produce multiple products (Ford)	Global brand name (Nokia)
Shared external relations	Using common distribution channels for multiple products (Samsung)	Servicing multinational customers worldwide (Citibank)
Shared learning	Shared R& D in computer and communications business (NEC)	Pooling knowledge developed in different markets (Procter & Gamble)

Scope Economies

The concept of scope economies is based on the notion that certain economies arise from the fact that the cost of the joint production (or development or distribution) of two or more products can be less than the cost of producing them separately.[8] Such cost reductions may take place for many reasons—for example, resources such as information or technologies, once acquired for use in producing one item (television sets, for example), can be used without additional cost to produce other items (video players, for instance).

The strategic importance of scope economies arises from a diversified firm's ability to share investments and costs across the same or different value chains—a source of economies that competitors without such internal and external diversity cannot match. Such sharing can take place across segments, products, or markets and may involve the joint use of different kinds of assets (see Table 3-1).

Implicit in each of these tools is the ability to develop an organizational infrastructure that supports it. As we discuss in later chapters, the organizational ability to leverage a global network and value chain will differentiate the winners from the losers.

Mapping Ends and Means: Building Blocks for Worldwide Advantage

Table 3-2 shows a mapping of the different goals and means for achieving worldwide competitiveness. Each goals-means intersection suggests some of the factors that may enhance a company's strategic position. Although the factors are only illustrative, it may be useful to study them carefully and compare them against the proposals of the three academic articles mentioned at the beginning of the chapter. It will become apparent that each author focuses on a specific subset of factors—essentially, some different goals-means combinations—and the differences among their prescriptions can be

---

[8]For a detailed exposition of scope economies, see W. J. Baumol, J. C. Panzer, and R. D. Willig, *Contestable Markets and the Theory of Industry Structure* (New York: Harcourt Brace Jovanovich, 1982).

Table 3-2   Worldwide Advantage: Goals and Means

Strategic Objectives	Sources of Competitive Advantage		
	National Differences	Scale Economies	Scope Economies
Achieving efficiency in current operations	Benefiting from differences in factor costs—wages and cost of capital	Expanding and exploiting potential scale economies in each activity	Sharing of investments and costs across markets and businesses
Managing risks through multinational flexibility	Managing different kinds of risks arising from market- or policy-induced changes in comparative advantages of different countries	Balancing scale with strategic and operational flexibility	Portfolio diversification of risks and creation of options and side bets
Innovation, learning, and adaptation	Learning from societal differences in organizational and managerial processes and systems	Benefiting from experience—cost reduction and innovation	Shared learning across organizational components in different products, markets, or businesses

understood in terms of the differences in the particular aspect of worldwide competitive advantage on which they focus.

International, Multinational, Global, and Transnational Strategies

In Chapter 2, we described how environmental forces in different industries shaped alternative approaches to managing worldwide operations that we described as international, multinational, global, and transnational. We now elaborate on the distinctions among these different approaches, as well as their respective strengths and vulnerabilities in terms of the different goals-means combinations that we have just described.

International Strategy

Companies adopting the broad, international strategy approach focus on creating and exploiting innovations on a worldwide basis, using all the different means to achieve this end. MNEs headquartered in technologically advanced countries with sophisticated markets often adopted this strategic approach but limited it primarily to exploiting home-country innovations to develop their competitive positions abroad. The international product cycle theory that we described in Chapter 1 encompasses both the strategic motivation and competitive posture of these companies: At least initially, their internationalization process relied heavily on transferring new products, processes, or strategies developed in the home country to less-advanced overseas markets.

This approach was common among U.S.-based MNEs such as Kraft, Pfizer, Procter & Gamble (P&G), and GE. Although these companies built considerable strength out of their ability to create and leverage innovation, many suffered from deficiencies of both efficiency and flexibility because they did not develop either the centralized and high-scale operations of companies adopting global strategies or the very high degree of local responsiveness that multinational companies could muster through their autonomous, self-sufficient, and entrepreneurial local operations. This deficiency has led some of the companies in this category to change. Kraft, for example, is aiming to leverage its iconic North American brands in the global snack business through investments in marketing and innovation—hence its efficiency stand. At the same time, its North America–focused grocery business aims to have flexibility and local responsiveness in this line of business.

Multinational Strategy

The multinational strategy approach concentrates primarily on one means (national differences) to achieve most of its strategic objectives. Companies adopting this strategy tend to focus on the revenue side, usually by differentiating their products and services in response to national differences in customer preferences, industry characteristics, and government regulations. This approach leads most multinational companies to depend on local-for-local innovations, a process requiring the subsidiary not only to identify local needs, but also use its own local resources to respond to those needs. Carrying out most activities within each country on a local-for-local basis also allows those adopting a multinational strategy to match costs and revenues on a currency-by-currency basis.

Historically, many European companies such as Unilever, ICI, Philips, and Nestlé followed this strategic model. In these companies, assets and resources were widely dispersed historically, allowing overseas subsidiaries to carry out a wide range of activities, from development and production to sales and services. Their self-sufficiency was typically accompanied by considerable local autonomy. Although such independent national units were unusually flexible and responsive to their local environments, they inevitably suffered problems of inefficiencies and an inability to exploit the knowledge and competencies of other national units. These inefficiencies have led some of these companies to change. The CEO of Unilever, for example, in its 2011 annual report stated: "We are changing the organization. Today, we are more agile, more consumer responsive, and better able to leverage global scale."

Global Strategy

Companies adopting the classic global strategic approach, as we have defined it, depend primarily on developing global efficiency. They use all the different means to achieve the best cost and quality positions for their products.

This strategy has been the classic approach of many Japanese companies such as Toyota, Canon, Komatsu, and Matsushita. As these and similar companies have found, however, such efficiency comes with compromises of both flexibility and learning. For example, concentrating manufacturing to capture global scale also may result in a high level of intercountry product shipments that can raise risks of policy intervention, particularly by host governments in major importer countries. Similarly, companies that centralize R&D for efficiency reasons often find that they are constrained in their ability to capture new developments in countries outside their home markets or to leverage innovations created by foreign subsidiaries in the rest of their worldwide operations. And finally, the concentration (most often through centralization) of activities like R&D and manufacturing to achieve a global scale exposes such companies to high sourcing risks, particularly in exchange rate exposure. As an example, the 2011 earthquake in Japan was so harmful to Canon that it announced two major changes. First, it is pursuing a new three-headquarters system (one each in the United States, Europe, and Japan) to manage its local product developments. Second, it is trying to optimize its global production system, selecting locations using the criterion of lowest ratio of labor cost to total manufacturing cost.

The descriptions that we have presented up to this point regarding multinational versus global strategies have been described in their pure forms. In practice, of course, many firms do adopt a regional strategy, focusing much of their international expansion on the home region, plus perhaps one or two other regions. Toyota, for example, introduced its low-cost Etios model in India in 2012, and then started its global launch by sending the first consignment of 247 units to South Africa.

Transnational Strategy

Beneath each of these three traditional strategic approaches lies some implicit assumptions about how best to build worldwide competitive advantage. The global company assumes that the best-cost position is the key source of competitiveness; the multinational company sees differentiation as the primary way to enhance performance; and the international company expects to use innovations to reduce costs, enhance revenues, or both. Companies adopting the transnational strategy recognize that each of these traditional approaches is partial—that each has its own merits, but none represents the whole truth.

To achieve worldwide competitive advantage, costs and revenues have to be managed simultaneously, both efficiency and innovation are important, and innovations can arise in many different parts of the organization. Therefore, instead of focusing on any subpart of the set of issues shown in Table 3-2, the transnational company focuses on exploiting each and every goals-means combination to develop layers of competitive advantage by exploiting efficiency, flexibility, and learning simultaneously.

To achieve this ambitious strategic approach, however, the transnational company must develop a very different configuration of assets and capabilities than is typical of traditional multinational, international, and global company structures. The global company tends to concentrate all its resources—either in its home country or in low-cost, overseas locations—to exploit the scale economies available in each activity. The multinational company typically disperses its resources among its different national operations to be able to respond to local needs. And the international company tends to centralize those resources that are key to developing innovations, but decentralize others to allow its innovations to be adapted worldwide.

The transnational, however, must develop a more sophisticated and differentiated configuration of assets and capabilities. It first decides which key resources and capabilities are best centralized within the home-country operation, not only to realize scale economies but also to protect certain core competencies and provide the necessary supervision of corporate management. Basic research, for example, is often viewed as such a capability, with core technologies kept at home for reasons of strategic security, as well as competence concentration.

Certain other resources may be concentrated but not necessarily at home—a configuration that might be termed *ex-centralization* rather than *decentralization.* World-scale production plants for labor-intensive products may be built in a low-wage country such as Mexico or Bangladesh. The advanced state of a particular technology may demand concentration of relevant R&D resources and activities in Japan, Germany, or the United States. Such flexible specialization—or *ex-centralization*—combines the benefits of scale economies with the flexibility of accessing low input costs or scarce resources and the responsiveness of accommodating national political interests. This approach can also apply to specific functional activities. For example, Sony relocated its treasury operations to London to improve its access to financial markets. And the Amsterdam-based software company Irdeto recently opened a second headquarters in Beijing to enhance the influence of its managers in the fast-growing Chinese market in the company's decision making processes. To underscore the commitment, the CEO and his family moved to China in 2007.

Some other resources may best be decentralized on a regional or local basis because either potential economies of scale are small or there is a need to create flexibility by avoiding exclusive dependence on a single facility. Local or regional facilities not only may offer protection against exchange rate shifts, strikes, natural disasters, and other disruptions, but also reduce logistical and coordination costs. An important side benefit provided by such facilities is the impact that they can have in building the motivation and capability of national subsidiaries, an impact that can easily make small efficiency sacrifices worthwhile.

Table 3-3 summarizes the differences in the asset configurations that support the different strategic approaches of the various MNE models. We explore these strategy-organizational linkages in more detail in Chapter 4.

Table 3-3   Strategic Orientation and Configuration of Assets and Capabilities in International, Multinational, Global, and Transnational Companies

	International	**Multinational**	**Global**	**Transnational**
Strategic orientation	Exploiting parent-company knowledge and capabilities through worldwide diffusion and adaptation	Building flexibility to respond to national differences through strong, resourceful, and entrepreneurial national operations	Building cost advantages through centralized, global-scale operations	Developing global efficiency, flexibility, and worldwide learning capability simultaneously
Configuration of assets and capabilities	Sources of core competencies centralized, others decentralized	Decentralized and nationally self-sufficient	Centralized and globally scaled	Dispersed, interdependent, and specialized

Worldwide Competitive Advantage: The Strategic Tasks

In the final part of this chapter, we look at how a company can respond to the strategic challenges that we have described. The nature of the task will clearly depend on the company's international posture and history. Companies that are among the major worldwide players in their businesses must focus on defending their dominance while also building new sources of advantage. For companies that are smaller but aspire to worldwide competitiveness, the task is to build the resources and capabilities needed to challenge the entrenched leaders. And, for companies that are focused on their national markets and lack either the resources or the motivation for international expansion, the challenge is to protect their domestic positions from others that have the advantage of being MNEs.

Defending Worldwide Dominance

Over the past decade or so, the shifting external forces that we have described have resulted in severe difficulties—even for those MNEs that had enjoyed strong historical positions in their businesses worldwide.

Typically, most of these companies pursued traditional multinational, international, or global strategies, and their past successes were built on the fit between their specific strategic capability and the dominant environmental force in their industries. In multinational industries such as branded, packaged products in which forces for national responsiveness were dominant, companies such as Unilever developed strong worldwide positions by adopting multinational strategies. In contrast, in global industries like consumer electronics or semiconductor chips, companies such as Matsushita or Hitachi built leadership positions by adopting global strategies.

In the emerging competitive environment, however, these companies no longer could rely on their historic ability to exploit global efficiency, multinational flexibility, or worldwide learning. As an increasing number of industries developed what we have termed *transnational characteristics,* companies faced the need to master all three strategic capabilities simultaneously.

The challenge for the leading companies was to protect and enhance the particular strength they had, while simultaneously building the other capabilities. For many MNEs, the initial response to this new strategic challenge was to try to restructure the configuration of their assets and activities to develop the capabilities that they lacked. For example, global companies with highly centralized resources sought to develop flexibility by dispersing resources among their national subsidiaries; multinational companies, in contrast, tried to emulate their global competitors by centralizing R&D, manufacturing, and other scale-intensive activities. In essence, these companies tried to find a new, better configuration through drastic restructuring of their existing configuration.

Such a zero-based search for the ideal configuration not only led to external problems, such as conflict with host governments over issues like plant closures, but also resulted in trauma inside the company's own organization. The greatest problem with such an approach, however, was that it tended to erode the particular competency that the company already had without effectively adding the new strengths that it sought.

The complex balancing act of protecting existing advantages while building new ones required companies to follow two fairly simple principles. First, they had to concentrate at least as much on defending and reinforcing their existing assets and capabilities as on developing new ones. Their approach tended to be one of building on—and eventually modifying—their existing infrastructure instead of radical restructuring. To the extent possible, they relied on modernizing existing facilities rather than dismantling the old ones and creating new ones.

Second, most successful adaptors looked for ways to compensate for their deficiency or approximate a competitor's source of advantage, rather than trying to imitate its asset structure or task configuration. In searching for efficiency, multinational companies with a decentralized and dispersed resource structure found it easier to develop efficiency by adopting new flexible manufacturing technologies in some of their existing plants and upgrading others to become global or regional sources rather than to close those plants and shift production to lower-cost countries to match the structure of competitive global companies.

Similarly, successful global companies found it more effective to develop responsiveness and flexibility by creating internal linkages between their national sales subsidiaries and their centralized development or manufacturing units, rather than trying to mimic multinational companies by dispersing their resources to each country operation and, in the process, undermining their core strength of efficiency.

Challenging the Global Leader

Over the past two decades, a number of companies have managed to evolve from relatively small national players to major worldwide competitors, challenging the dominance of traditional leaders in their businesses. Dell in the computer industry, Magna in auto parts, Electrolux in the domestic appliances business, and CEMEX in the cement industry are some examples of companies that have evolved from relative obscurity to global visibility within relatively short periods of time.

The actual processes adopted to manage such dramatic transformations vary widely from company to company. Electrolux, for example, grew almost exclusively through acquisitions, whereas Dell built capabilities largely through internal development, and Magna and CEMEX used a combination of greenfield investments and acquisitions. Similarly, whereas Dell built its growth on the basis of cost advantages and logistics capabilities, it expanded internationally because of its direct-sales business model and its ability to react quickly to changes in customer demand.

Despite wide differences in their specific approaches, however, most of these new champions appear to have followed a similar step-by-step approach to building their competitive positions.

Each developed an initial toehold in the market by focusing on a narrow niche—often one specific product within one specific market—and developing a strong competitive position within that niche. That competitive position was built on multiple sources of competitive advantage rather than on a single strategic capability.

Next, they expanded their toehold to a foothold by limited and carefully selected expansion along both product and geographic dimensions and by extending the step-by-step improvement of both cost and quality to this expanded portfolio. Such expansion was typically focused on products and markets that were not of central importance to the established leaders in the business. By staying outside the range of the leaders' peripheral vision, the challenger could remain relatively invisible, thereby building up its strength and infrastructure without incurring direct retaliation from competitors with far greater resources. For example, emerging companies often focused initially on relatively low-margin products, such as small-screen TV sets or subcompact cars.

While developing their own product portfolio, technological capabilities, geographic scope, and marketing expertise, challengers often were able to build up manufacturing volume (and enjoy the resulting cost efficiencies) by becoming original equipment manufacturer (OEM) suppliers to their larger competitors. Although this supply allowed the larger competitor to benefit from the challenger's cost advantages, it also developed the supplying company's understanding of customer needs and marketing strategies in the advanced markets served by the leading companies.

Once these building blocks for worldwide advantage were in place, the challenger typically moved rapidly to convert its low-profile foothold into a strong permanent position in the worldwide business. Dramatic scaling up of production facilities—increasing VCR capacity 30-fold in eight years, as Matsushita did, or expanding computer production 20-fold in seven years, as Acer did a decade later—typically preceded a wave of new product introductions and expansion into the key markets through multiple channels and their own brand names.

Another way that a challenger may pursue rapid transition into a strong international presence is through acquisitions, as Tata Motors did in 2008 by purchasing two iconic British brands, Jaguar and Land Rover, from Ford. The deal included the manufacturing plants, two U.K.-based advanced design centers, national sales companies spanning across the world, as well as the licences of all the property rights.

Protecting Domestic Niches

For reasons of limited resources or other constraints, some national companies may not be able to aspire to such worldwide expansion, though they are not insulated from the impact of global competition. Their major challenge is to protect their domestic niches from worldwide players with superior resources and multiple sources of competitive advantage.[9] This concern is particularly an issue in developing markets such as India and China, where local companies face much larger, more aggressive, and deeper-pocketed competitors.

There are three broad alternative courses of action that can be pursued by such national competitors. The first approach is to defend against the competitor's global advantage. Just as MNE managers can act to facilitate the globalization of industry structure, so their counterparts in national companies can use their influence in the opposite direction. An astute manager of a national company might be able to foil the attempts of a global competitor by taking action to influence industry structure or market

---

[9]For a detailed discussion of such strategies, see N. Dawar and T. Frost, "Competing with Giants: Survival Strategies for Local Companies Competing in Emerging Markets," *Harvard Business Review* 77, no. 2 (1999), pp. 119–30.

conditions to the national company's advantage. These actions might involve influencing consumer preference to demand a more locally adapted or service-intensive product; it could imply tying up key distribution channels; or it might mean preempting local sources of critical supplies. Many companies trying to enter the Japanese market claim to have faced this type of defensive strategy by local firms.

A second strategic option would be to offset the competitor's global advantage. The simplest way to do this is to lobby for government assistance in the form of tariff protections. However, in an era of declining tariffs, this is increasingly unsuccessful. A more ambitious approach is to gain government sponsorship to develop equivalent global capabilities through funding of R&D, subsidizing exports, and financing capital investments. As a "national champion," the company would be able to compete globally, in theory. However, in reality, it is very unusual for such a company to prosper. Airbus Industrie, which now shares the global market for large commercial airplanes with Boeing, is one of the few exceptions—rising from the ashes of other attempts by European governments to sponsor a viable computer company in the 1970s and then to promote a European electronics industry a decade later. Also, GE's lobbying activities in 2009 led to its inclusion in a bailout program of the U.S. government. The protective policy of the government of Canada to support Air Canada against international rivals such as Emirates Airlines and Singaporean Airlines in 2010 is another example of offsetting a competitor's global advantage.

The third alternative is to approximate the competitors' global advantages by linking up in some form of alliance or coalition with a viable global company. Numerous such linkages have been formed, with the purpose of sharing the risks and costs of operating in a high-risk global environment. By pooling or exchanging market access, technology, and production capability, smaller competitors can gain some measure of defense against global giants. For example, Siemens, ICL, and other small computer companies entered into agreements and joint projects with Fujitsu to enable them to maintain viability against the dominant transnational competitor, IBM. Similarly, the Indian telecom company Bharti has established a variety of inbound alliances with foreign firms to create a winning strategy for the Indian market.

Concluding Comments

Although these three strategic responses obviously do not cover every possible scenario, they highlight two important points from this chapter. First, the MNE faces a complex set of options in terms of the strategic levers that it can pull to achieve competitive advantage, and the framework in Table 3-2 helps make sense of those options by separating out means and ends. Second, the competitive intensity in most industries is such that a company cannot just afford to plough its own furrow. Rather, it is necessary to gain competitive parity on all relevant dimensions (efficiency, flexibility, learning, etc.) while also achieving differentiation on one. To be sure, the ability to achieve multiple competitive objectives at the same time is far from straightforward, and as a result, we see many MNEs experimenting with new ways of organizing their worldwide activities. And this organization will be the core issue we will address in the next chapter.

Chapter 3 Readings

- In Reading 3-1, "Managing Differences: The Central Challenge of Global Strategy," Ghemawat introduces a framework to help managers think through their options. The three broad strategies available are aggregation (achieving economies of scale by standardizing regional or global operations), adaptation (boosting market share by customizing processes and offerings to meet local markets' unique needs); and arbitrage (exploiting difference, by such activities as offshoring certain processes to countries with cheaper labor). Each strategy is considered against seven questions.

- In Reading 3-2, "Capturing the World's Emerging Middle Class," Court and Narasimhan emphasize the importance of the emergence of the middle class in emerging economies, a population of close to 2 billion. This group creates a great opportunity for MNEs to gain advantage by addressing their needs. The needs of this group are different, and so are their priorities. After understanding the idiosyncrasies of the middle class, companies will have to introduce new business models to address their specific needs. The types of need (global or local) and consumer characteristics are discussed, and the appropriate strategies are introduced.

- In Reading 3-3, "New Business Models in Emerging Markets," Eyring, Johnson, and Nair argue for the need to rethink the business models for emerging markets. A better way to tap these markets is to consider the existing unmet needs, some of them very basic. Affordability and accessibility for consumers in the middle class is key to the success of new business models in these markets. Depending on the basis on which firms compete (differentiation, or price), the article explains the sequence through which business models are developed. Examples of such business models are presented.

While all three readings in this chapter highlight that although the general concepts of how to build competitive advantage are constant, situations of time and space evolve such that companies need to heed them while developing their strategies. The concept that MNEs should build their capabilities layer by layer, however, holds in all contexts.

Case 3-1   The Global Branding of Stella Artois

Paul W. Beamish and Anthony Goerzen

In April 2000, Paul Cooke, chief marketing officer of Interbrew, the world's fourth largest brewer, contemplated the further development of their premium product, Stella Artois, as the company's flagship brand in key markets around the world. Although the long-range plan for 2000–2002 had been approved, there still remained some important strategic issues to resolve.

A Brief History of Interbrew

Interbrew traced its origins back to 1366 to a brewery called Den Hoorn, located in Leuven, a town just outside of Brussels. In 1717, when it was purchased by its master brewer, Sebastiaan Artois, the brewery changed its name to Artois.

The firm's expansion began when Artois acquired a major interest in the Leffe Brewery in Belgium in 1954, the Dommelsch Brewery in the Netherlands in 1968, and the Brasserie du Nord in France in 1970. In 1987, when Artois and another Belgian brewery called Piedboeuf came together, the merged company was named Interbrew. The

IVEY

Richard Ivey School of Business
The University of Western Ontario

▌ Professors Paul W. Beamish and Anthony Goerzen prepared this case solely to provide material for class discussion. The authors do not intend to illustrate either effective or ineffective handling of a managerial situation. The authors may have disguised certain names and other identifying information to protect confidentiality.

new company soon acquired other Belgian specialty beer brewers, building up the Interbrew brand portfolio with the purchase of the Hoegaarden brewery in 1989 and the Belle-Vue Brewery in 1990.

Interbrew then entered into a phase of rapid growth. The company acquired breweries in Hungary in 1991, in Croatia and Romania in 1994, and in three plants in Bulgaria in 1995. Again in 1995, Interbrew completed an unexpected major acquisition by purchasing Labatt, a large Canadian brewer also with international interests. Labatt had operations in the United States, for example, with the Latrobe brewery, home of the Rolling Rock brand. Labatt also held a substantial minority stake in the second largest Mexican brewer, Femsa Cervesa, which produced Dos Equis, Sol, and Tecate brands. Following this major acquisition, Interbrew went on, in 1996, to buy a brewery in the Ukraine and engaged in a joint venture in the Dominican Republic. Subsequently, breweries were added in China in 1997, Montenegro and Russia in 1998, and another brewery in Bulgaria and one in Korea in 1999.

Thus, through acquisition expenditures of U.S.$2.5 billion in the previous four years, Interbrew had transformed itself from a simple Belgian brewery into one of the largest beer companies in the world. By 1999, the company had become a brewer on a truly global scale that now derived more than 90 per cent of its volume from markets outside Belgium. It remained a privately held company, headquartered in Belgium, with subsidiaries and joint ventures in 23 countries across four continents.

The International Market for Beer

In the 1990s, the world beer market was growing at an annual rate of one to two per cent. In 1998, beer consumption reached a total of 1.3 billion hectolitres (hls). There were, however, great regional differences in both market size and growth rates. Most industry analysts split the world market

Exhibit 1   The World Beer Market in 1998

Region	% of Global Consumption	Growth Index ('98 Vs '92)	Per Capita Consumption
Americas	35.1%	112.6	57
Europe	32.8%	97.7	54
Asia Pacific	27.2%	146.2	11
Africa	4.6%	107.7	8
Middle East/Central Asia	0.4%	116.0	2

Source: Canadean Ltd.

for beer between growth and mature markets. The mature markets were generally considered to be North America, Western Europe and Australasia. The growth markets included Latin America, Asia, Central and Eastern Europe including Russia. Although some felt that Africa had considerable potential, despite its low per capita beer consumption, the continent was not considered a viable market by many brewers because of its political and economic instability (see **Exhibit 1**).

Mature Markets   The North American beer market was virtually stagnant, although annual beer consumption per person was already at a sizeable 83 litres per capita (lpc). The Western European market had also reached maturity with consumption of 79 lpc. Some analysts believed that this consumption level was under considerable pressure, forecasting a decline to near 75 lpc over the medium term. Australia and New Zealand were also considered mature markets, with consumption at 93 lpc and 84 lpc, respectively. In fact, volumes in both markets, New Zealand in particular, had declined through the 1990s following tight social policies on alcohol consumption and the emergence of a wine culture.

Growth Markets   Given that average consumption in Eastern Europe was only 29 lpc, the region appeared to offer great potential. This consumption figure, however, was heavily influenced by Russia's very low level, and the future for the large Russian market was unclear. Further, some markets, such as the Czech Republic that consumed the most beer per person in the world at 163 lpc, appeared to have already reached maturity. Central and South America, on the other hand, were showing healthy growth and, with consumption at an average of 43 lpc, there was believed to be considerable upside. The most exciting growth rates, however, were in Asia. Despite the fact that the market in this region had grown by more than 30 per cent since 1995, consumption levels were still comparatively low. In China, the region's largest market, consumption was only 16 lpc and 20 to 25 lpc in Hong Kong and Taiwan. Although the 1997 Asian financial crisis did not immediately affect beer consumption (although company profits from the region were hit by currency translation), demand in some key markets, such as Indonesia, was reduced and in others growth slowed. The situation, however, was expected to improve upon economic recovery in the medium term.

Beer Industry Structure

The world beer industry was relatively fragmented with the top four players accounting for only 22 per cent of global volume—a relatively low figure as compared to 78 per cent in the soft drinks industry, 60 per cent in tobacco and 44 per cent in spirits. This suggested great opportunities for consolidation, a process that had already begun two decades prior. Many analysts, including those at Interbrew, expected that this process would probably accelerate in the future. The driver behind industry rationalization was the need to achieve economies of scale in production, advertising and distribution. It was widely recognized that the best profit margins were attained either by those with a commanding position in the market or those with a niche position. However, there were several factors that mitigated the trend towards rapid concentration of the brewing industry.

One factor that slowed the process of consolidation was that the ratio of fixed versus variable costs of beer production was relatively high. Essentially, this meant that there was a limited cost savings potential that could be achieved by bringing more operations under a common administration. Real cost savings could be generated by purchasing and then rationalizing operations through shifting production to more efficient (usually more modern) facilities. This approach, however, required large initial capital outlays. As a result, in some markets with "unstable" economies, it was desirable to spread out capital expenditures over a longer period of time to ensure appropriate profitability in the early stages. A second factor that may have had a dampening effect on the trend towards industry consolidation was that local tastes differed. In some cases, beer brands had hundreds of years of heritage behind them and had become such an integral part of everyday life that consumers were often fiercely loyal to their local brew. This appeared to be a fact in many markets around the world.

Interbrew's Global Position

Through Interbrew's acquisitions in the 1990s, the company had expanded rapidly. During this period, the company's total volumes had increased more than fourfold. These figures translated to total beer production of 57.5 million hls in 1998 (when including the volume of all affiliates), as compared to just 14.7 million hls in 1992. Volume growth had propelled the company into the number four position among the world's brewers.

Faced with a mature and dominant position in the declining Belgian domestic market, the company decided to focus on consolidating and developing key markets, namely Belgium, the Netherlands, France and North America, and expansion through acquisition in Central Europe, Asia and South America. Subsequently, Interbrew reduced its dependence

on the Belgian market from 44 per cent in 1992 to less than 10 per cent by 1998 (total volumes including Mexico). Concurrently, a significant milestone for the company was achieved by 1999 when more than 50 per cent of its total volume was produced in growth markets (including Mexico). Interbrew had shifted its volume so that the Americas accounted for 61 per cent of its total volume, Europe added 35 per cent, and Asia Pacific the remaining four per cent.

Taken together, the top 10 markets for beer accounted for 86 per cent of Interbrew's total volume in 1998 (see **Exhibit 2**). The Mexican beer market alone accounted for 37 per cent of total volume in 1998. Canada, Belgium, the United States and the United Kingdom were the next most important markets. However, smaller, growing markets such as Hungary, Croatia, Bulgaria, and Romania had begun to increase in importance.

Adding to its existing breweries in Belgium, France and the Netherlands, Interbrew's expansion strategy in the 1990s had resulted in acquisitions in Bosnia-Herzegovina, Bulgaria, Canada, China, Croatia, Hungary, Korea, Montenegro, Romania, Russia, the Ukraine, the United States, in a joint

Exhibit 2   Interbrew's 1998 Share of the World's Top 10 Markets

Rank	Country	Volume (000 HL)	Market Share
1	USA	3,768	1.6%
2	China	526	0.3%
3	Germany	—	—
4	Brazil	—	—
5	Japan	—	—
6	UK	3,335	5.5%
7	Mexico	21,269	45.0%
8	Spain	—	—
9	South Africa	—	—
10	France	1,915	8.4%
Total		30,813	3.6%

Source: Canadean Ltd.

venture in South Korea, and in minority equity positions in Mexico and Luxembourg. Through these breweries, in addition to those that were covered by licensing agreements in Australia, Italy, Sweden and the United Kingdom, Interbrew sold its beers in over 80 countries.

Interbrew's Corporate Structure

Following the acquisition of Labatt in 1995, Interbrew's corporate structure was divided into two geographic zones: the Americas and Europe/Asia/Africa. This structure was in place until September 1999 when Interbrew shifted to a fully integrated structure to consolidate its holdings in the face of industry globalization. Hugo Powell, formerly head of the Americas division, was appointed to the position of chief executive officer (CEO). The former head of the Europe/Africa/Asia division assumed the role of chief operating officer, but subsequently resigned and was not replaced, leaving Interbrew with a more conventional structure, with the five regional heads and the various corporate functional managers reporting directly to the CEO.

Recent Performance

1998 had been a good year for Interbrew in terms of volume in both mature and growth markets. Overall, sales volumes increased by 11.1 per cent as most of the company's international and local brands maintained or gained market share. In terms of the compounded annual growth rate, Interbrew outperformed all of its major competitors by a wide margin. While Interbrew's 1998 net sales were up 29 per cent, the best performing competitor achieved an increase of only 16 per cent. Of Interbrew's increased sales, 67 per cent was related to the new affiliates in China, Montenegro and Korea. The balance was the result of organic growth. Considerable volume increases were achieved also in Romania (72 per cent), Bulgaria (28 per cent), Croatia (13 per cent), and the United States (14 per cent). While volumes in Western Europe were flat, duty-free sales grew strongly. In the U.S. market, strong progress was made by Interbrew's Canadian and Mexican brands, and Latrobe's Rolling Rock was

successfully relaunched. In Canada, performance was strong, fuelled by a two per cent increase in domestic consumption. Labatt's sales of Budweiser (produced under license from Anheuser Busch) also continued to grow rapidly.

Given that the premium and specialty beer markets were growing quickly, particularly those within the large, mature markets, Interbrew began to shift its product mix to take advantage of this trend and the superior margins it offered. A notable brand success was Stella Artois, for which total global sales volumes were up by 19.7 per cent. That growth came from sales generated by Whitbread in the United Kingdom, from exports, and from sales in Central Europe where Stella Artois volumes took off. The strong growth of Stella Artois was also notable in that it was sold in the premium lager segment. In Europe, Asia Pacific and Africa, Interbrew's premium and specialty beers, which generated a bigger margin, increased as a proportion of total sales from 31 per cent in 1997 to 33 per cent in 1998. This product mix shift was particularly important since intense competition in most markets inhibited real price increases.

Success was also achieved in the United States specialty beer segment where total volume had been growing at nine per cent annually in the 1990s. In 1998, Interbrew's share of this growing market segment had risen even faster as Labatt USA realized increased sales of 16 per cent. The other continuing development was the growth of the light beer segment, which had become over 40 per cent of the total sales. Sales of Labatt's Blue Light, for example, had increased and Labatt Blue had become the number three imported beer in the United States, with volumes up 18 per cent. Latrobe's Rolling Rock brand grew by four per cent, the first increase in four years. Interbrew's Mexican brands, Dos Equis, Tecate and Sol, were also up by 19 per cent.

Following solid volume growth in profitable market segments, good global results were realized in key financial areas. Net profit, having grown for each of the previous six consecutive years, was 7.7 billion Belgian francs (BEF) in 1998, up

43.7 per cent from the previous year. Operating profit also rose 7.9 per cent over 1997, from 14.3 to 15.4 BEF; in both the Europe/Asia/Africa region and the Americas, operating profit was up by 8.5 per cent and 4.9 per cent respectively. Further, Interbrew's EBIT margin was up 58.1 per cent as compared to the best performing competitor's figure of 17.0 per cent. However, having made several large investments in Korea and Russia, and exercising an option to increase its share of Femsa Cerveza in Mexico from 22 per cent to 30 per cent, Interbrew's debt-equity ratio increased from 1.04 to 1.35. As a result, interest payments rose accordingly.

Interbrew also enjoyed good results in volume sales in many of its markets in 1999. Although Canadian sales remained largely unchanged over 1998, Labatt USA experienced strong growth in 1999, with volumes up by 10 per cent. There was a positive evolution in Western European volumes as well, as overall sales were up by 6.5 per cent overall in Belgium, France and the Netherlands. Central European markets also grew with Hungary showing an increase of 9.6 per cent, Croatia up by 5.5 per cent, Romania by 18.9 per cent, Montenegro by 29 per cent, and Bulgaria with a rise of 3.6 per cent in terms of volume. Sales positions were also satisfactory in the Russian and Ukrainian markets. Further, while South Korean sales volume remained unchanged, volumes in China were 10 per cent higher, although this figure was still short of expectations.

Interbrew Corporate Strategy

The three facets of Interbrew's corporate strategy, i.e., brands, markets and operations, were considered the "sides of the Interbrew triangle." Each of these aspects of corporate strategy was considered to be equally important in order to achieve the fundamental objective of increasing shareholder value. With a corporate focus entirely on beer, the underlying objectives of the company were to consolidate its positions in mature markets and improve margins through higher volumes of premium and specialty brands. Further, the company's emphasis on growth was driven by the belief that beer industry rationalization still had some way to go and that

the majority of the world's major markets would each end up with just two or three major players.

Operations Strategy Cross fertilization of best practices between sites was a central component of Interbrew's operations strategy. In the company's two main markets, Belgium and Canada, each brewery monitored its performance on 10 different dimensions against its peers. As a result, the gap between the best and the worst of Interbrew's operations had narrowed decisively since 1995. Employees continuously put forward propositions to improve processes. The program had resulted in significantly lower production costs, suggesting to Interbrew management that most improvements had more to do with employee motivation than with pure technical performance. In addition, capacity utilization and strategic sourcing had been identified as two areas of major opportunity.

Capacity Utilization Given that brewing was a capital-intensive business, capacity utilization had a major influence on profitability. Since declining consumption in mature markets had generated excess capacity, several of Interbrew's old breweries and processing facilities were scheduled to be shut down. In contrast, in several growth markets such as Romania, Bulgaria, Croatia and Montenegro, the opposite problem existed, so facilities in other locations were used more fully until local capacities were increased.

Strategic Sourcing Interbrew had begun to rationalize its supply base as well. By selecting a smaller number of its best suppliers and working more closely with them, Interbrew believed that innovative changes resulted, saving both parties considerable sums every year. For most of the major commodities, the company had gone to single suppliers and was planning to extend this approach to all operations worldwide.

Market Strategy The underlying objectives of Interbrew's market strategy were to increase volume and to lessen its dependence on Belgium and Canada, its two traditional markets. Interbrew dichotomized its market strategy into the mature and growth market segments, although investments were considered wherever opportunities to generate sustainable profits existed. One of the key elements of Interbrew's market strategy was to establish and manage strong market platforms. It was believed that a brand strength was directly related to a competitive and dedicated market platform (i.e., sales and distribution, wholesaler networks, etc.) to support the brand. Further, Interbrew allowed individual country teams to manage their own affairs and many felt that the speed of success in many markets was related to this decentralized approach.

Mature Markets   Interbrew's goals in its mature markets were to continue to build market share and to improve margins through greater efficiencies in production, distribution and marketing. At the same time, the company intended to exploit the growing trend in these markets towards premium and specialty products of which Interbrew already possessed an unrivalled portfolio. The key markets in which this strategy was being actively pursued were the United States, Canada, the United Kingdom, France, the Netherlands and Belgium.

Growth Markets   Based on the belief that the world's beer markets would undergo further consolidation, Interbrew's market strategy was to build significant positions in markets that had long-term volume growth potential. This goal led to a clear focus on Central and Eastern Europe and Asia, South Korea and China in particular. In China, for example, Interbrew had just completed an acquisition of a second brewery in Nanjing. The Yali brand was thereby added to the corporate portfolio and, together with its Jinling brand, Interbrew became the market leader in Nanjing, a city of six million people.

In Korea, Interbrew entered into a 50:50 joint venture with the Doosan Chaebol to operate the Oriental Brewery, producing the OB Lager and Cafri pilsener brands. With this move, Interbrew took the number two position in the Korean beer market with a 36 per cent share and sales of 5.1 million hls. The venture with Doosan was followed in December 1999 by the purchase of the Jinro Coors brewery. This added 2.5 million hls and increased Interbrew's market share to 50 per cent of total Korean volume. Thus, the Interbrew portfolio in Korea consisted of two mainstream pilsener brands, OB Lager and Cass, the two local premium brands, Cafri and Red Rock, and Budweiser, an international premium brand.

In Russia, Interbrew expanded its presence by taking a majority stake in the Rosar Brewery in Omsk, adding the BAG Bier and Sibirskaya Korona brands. Rosar was the leading brewer in Siberia with a 25 per cent regional market share, and held the number four position in Russia. New initiatives were also undertaken in Central Europe with acquisitions of a brewery in Montenegro and the Pleven brewery in Bulgaria, as well as the introduction of Interbrew products into the Yugoslavian market. Finally, although Interbrew had just increased its already significant investment in Mexico's second largest brewer from 22 per cent to 30 per cent, Latin America remained a region of great interest.

Brand Strategy   A central piece of Interbrew's traditional brand strategy had been to add to its portfolio of brands through acquisition of existing brewers, principally in growth markets. Since its goal was to have the number one or two brand in every market segment in which it operated, Interbrew concentrated on purchasing and developing strong local brands. As it moved into new territories, the company's first priority was to upgrade product quality and to improve the positioning of the acquired local core lager brands. In mature markets, it drew on the strength of the established brands such as Jupiler, Belgium's leading lager brand, Labatt Blue, the famous Canadian brand, and Dommelsch, an important brand in the Netherlands. In growth markets, Interbrew supported brands like Borsodi Sor in Hungary, Kamenitza in Bulgaria, Ozujsko in Croatia, Bergenbier in Romania, Jinling in China, and OB Lager in Korea. In addition, new products were launched such as Taller, a premium brand in the Ukraine, and Boomerang, an alternative malt-based drink in Canada.

A second facet of the company's brand strategy was to identify certain brands, typically specialty products, and to develop them on a regional basis across a group of markets. At the forefront of this strategy were the Abbaye de Leffe and Hoegaarden brands and, to a lesser extent, Belle-Vue. In fact, both Hoegaarden and Leffe achieved a leading position as the number one white beer and abbey beer in France and Holland. The Loburg premium pilsener brand also strengthened its position when it was relaunched in France. Further, in Canada, Interbrew created a dedicated organization for specialty beers called the Oland Specialty Beer Company. In its first year of operation, the brands marketed by Oland increased its volumes by over 40 per cent. More specifically, sales of the Alexander Keith's brand doubled and the negative volume trend of the John Labatt Classic brand was reversed. The underlying message promoted by Oland was the richness, mystique and heritage of beer.

To support the regional growth of specialty beers, Interbrew established a new type of café. The Belgian Beer Café, owned and run by independent operators, created an authentic Belgian atmosphere where customers sampled Interbrew's Belgian specialty beers. By 1999, Belgian Beer Cafés were open in the many of Interbrew's key markets, including top selling outlets in New York, Auckland, Zagreb and Budapest, to name a few. The business concept was that these cafés were to serve as an ambassador of the Belgian beer culture in foreign countries. They were intended to serve as vehicles to showcase Interbrew's specialty brands, benefiting from the international appeal of European styles and fashions. Although these cafés represented strong marketing tools for brand positioning, the key factors that led to the success of this concept were tied very closely to the individual establishments and the personnel running them. The bar staff, for example, had to be trained to serve the beer in the right branded glass, at the right temperature, and with a nice foamy head. It was anticipated that the concept of the specialty café would be used to support the brand development efforts of Interbrew's Belgian beers in all of its important markets.

The third facet of Interbrew's brand strategy was to identify a key corporate brand and to develop it as a global product. While the market segment for a global brand was currently relatively small, with the bulk of the beer demand still in local brands, the demand for international brands was expected to grow, as many consumers became increasingly attracted to the sophistication of premium and super-premium beers.

The Evolution of Interbrew's Global Brand Strategy

Until 1997, Interbrew's brand development strategy for international markets was largely *laissez faire*. Brands were introduced to new markets through licensing, export and local production when opportunities were uncovered. Stella Artois, Interbrew's most broadly available and oldest brand, received an important new thrust when it was launched through local production in three of the company's subsidiaries in Central Europe in 1997. This approach was consistent with the company's overall goals of building a complete portfolio in high growth potential markets.

By 1998, however, the executive management committee perceived the need to identify a brand from its wide portfolio to systematically develop into the company's global brand. Although the market for global brands was still small, there were some growing successes (e.g., Heineken, Corona, Fosters and Budweiser) and Interbrew believed that there were several basic global trends that would improve the viability of this class of product over the next couple of decades. First, while many consumers were seeking more variety, others were seeking lower prices. It appeared that the number of affluent and poor consumer segments would increase at the expense of the middle income segments. The upshot of this socioeconomic trend was that eventually all markets would likely evolve in such a way that demand for both premium and economy-priced beers would increase, squeezing the mainstream beers in the middle. A second trend was the internationalization of the beer business. As consumers travelled around the world, consuming global media (e.g., CNN, Eurosport, MTV, international magazines, etc.), global media were expected to become more effective for building brands. A global strategy could, therefore, lead to synergies in global advertising and sponsoring. In addition, the needs of consumers in many markets were expected to converge. As a result of these various factors, Interbrew believed that there would be an increasing interest in authentic, international brands in a growing number of countries. Interbrew had a wide portfolio of national brands that it could set on the international stage. The two most obvious candidates were Labatt Blue and Stella Artois.

The Labatt range of brands included Labatt Blue, Labatt Blue Light and Labatt Ice. To date, however, the exposure of these brands outside of North America had been extremely limited and they were not yet budding global brands. Of the total Labatt Blue volume in 1998, 85 per cent was derived from the Canadian domestic and U.S. markets, with the balance sold in the United Kingdom. The Labatt brands had been introduced to both France and Belgium, and production had been licensed in Italy, but these volumes were minimal. The only real export growth market for Labatt Blue appeared to be the United States, where the brands volume in 1998 was some 23 per cent higher than in 1995, behind only Corona and Heineken in the imported brand segment. The Labatt Ice brand was also sold in a limited number of markets and, after the appeal of this Labatt innovation had peaked, its

total volume had declined by more than 25 per cent since 1996. Total Labatt Ice volume worldwide was just 450,000 hls in 1998, of which 43 per cent was sold in Canada, 33 per cent in the United States, and 21 per cent in the United Kingdom.

Stella Artois as Interbrew's International Flagship Brand

The other potential brand that Interbrew could develop on a global scale was Stella Artois, a brand that could trace its roots back to 1366. The modern version of Stella Artois was launched in 1920 as a Christmas beer and had become a strong market leader in its home market of Belgium through the 1970s. By the 1990s, however, Stella's market position began to suffer from an image as a somewhat old-fashioned beer, and the brand began to experience persistent volume decline. Problems in the domestic market, however, appeared to be shared by a number of other prominent international brands. In fact, seven of the top 10 international brands had experienced declining sales in their home markets between 1995 and 1999 (see **Exhibit 3**).

Stella Artois had achieved great success in the United Kingdom through its licensee, Whitbread, where Stella Artois became the leading premium lager beer. Indeed, the United Kingdom was the largest market for Stella Artois, accounting for 49 per cent of total brand volume in 1998. Stella Artois volume in the U.K. market reached 2.8 million hls in 1998, a 7.6 per cent share of the lager

Exhibit 3   Domestic Sales History of Major International Brands (million hectolitre)

	1995	1996	1997	1998
Budweiser (incl. Bud Light until '98)	69.48	71.10	72.43	40.00
Bud Light	n/a	n/a	n/a	30.00
Heineken	3.87	3.78	3.85	3.78
Becks	1.68	1.71	1.72	1.78
Carlsberg	1.47	1.39	1.31	1.22
Stella Artois	1.08	1.00	0.96	0.92
Fosters	1.48	1.11	1.40	1.43
Kronenbourg	5.65	5.53	5.35	5.60
Amstel	2.30	2.23	2.21	2.18
Corona	12.89	14.09	14.80	15.18

Exhibit 4 1999 World Sales Profile of Stella Artois

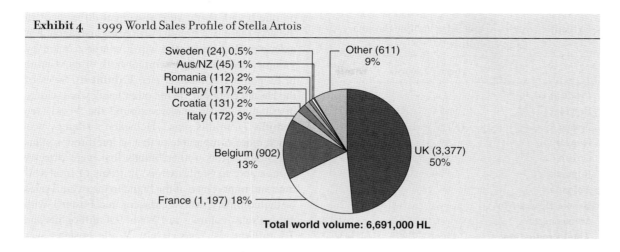

Sweden (24) 0.5%
Aus/NZ (45) 1%
Romania (112) 2%
Hungary (117) 2%
Croatia (131) 2%
Italy (172) 3%

Other (611) 9%

Belgium (902) 13%

France (1,197) 18%

UK (3,377) 50%

Total world volume: 6,691,000 HL

market, and came close to 3.5 million hls in 1999, a 25 per cent increase over the previous year. By this time, over 32,000 outlets sold Stella Artois on draught.

Apart from the United Kingdom, the key markets for Stella Artois were France and Belgium, which together accounted for a further 31 per cent of total brand volume (see **Exhibit 4**). With these three markets accounting for 81 per cent of total Stella Artois volume in 1999, few other areas represented a significant volume base (see **Exhibit 5**). Beyond the top three markets, the largest market for Stella Artois was Italy, where the brand was produced under license by Heineken. Stella Artois volume in Italy had, however, declined slightly to 166,000 hls in 1998. Licensing agreements were also in place in Sweden and Australia, but volume was small.

Stella Artois was also produced in Interbrew's own breweries in Hungary, Croatia and Romania, with very pleasing 1998 volumes of 84,000 hls, 120,000 hls, and 60,000 hls, respectively. After only three years, the market share of Stella Artois in Croatia, for example, had reached four per cent— a significant result, given that the brand was a premium-priced product. In all Central European markets, Stella Artois was priced at a premium; in Hungary, however, that premium was lower than in Croatia and Romania where, on an index comparing

Stella's price to that of core lagers, the indices by country were 140, 260 and 175 respectively.

Promising first results were also attained in Australia and New Zealand. Particularly in New Zealand, through a "seeding" approach, Interbrew and their local partner, Lion Nathan, had realized great success in the Belgian Beer Café in Auckland where the brands were showcased. After only two years of support, Stella Artois volume was up to 20,000 hls, and growing at 70 per cent annually, out of a total premium segment of 400,000 hls. Interbrew's market development plan limited distribution to top outlets in key metropolitan centres and priced Stella Artois significantly above competitors (e.g., 10 per cent over Heineken and 20 per cent over Steinlager, the leading domestic premium lager brand).

The evolution of the brand looked very positive as world volumes for Stella Artois continued to grow. In fact, Stella Artois volume had increased from 3.4 million hls in 1992 to a total of 6.7 million hls in 1999, a rise of 97 per cent. Ironically, the only market where the brand continued its steady decline was in its home base of Belgium. Analysts suggested a variety of reasons to explain this anomaly, including inconsistent sales and marketing support, particularly as the organization began to favor the rising Jupiler brand.

Overall, given Interbrew's large number of local brands, especially those in Mexico with very

Exhibit 5   Stella Artois Sales Volume Summary (ooo Hectolitre)

	1997	1998	1999
Production:			
Belgium	965	921	902
France	1,028	1,110	1,074
Hungary	59	84	117
Croatia	54	120	133
Romania	17	60	112
Bulgaria	—	—	3
Bosnia-Herzegovina	—	—	2
Montenegro	—	—	0
Total Production	**2,123**	**2,295**	**2,343**
License Brewing:			
Italy	162	166	172
Australia	6	11	22
New Zealand	7	11	22
Sweden	29	27	24
Greece	7	7	10
UK	2,139	2,815	3,377
Total Licensed	**2,350**	**3,037**	**3,627**
Export:			
USA	—	—	7
Canada	—	—	5
Other Countries	92	49	202
Duty Free	245	389	507
Total Export	**337**	**438**	**721**
Overall Total	**4,810**	**5,770**	**6,691**

high volumes, total Stella Artois volume accounted for only 10 per cent of total Interbrew volume in 1999 (14 per cent if Femsa volumes are excluded). Interbrew's strategy of nurturing a wide portfolio of strong brands was very different as compared to some of its major competitors. For example, Anheuser-Busch, the world's largest brewer, focused its international strategy almost exclusively on the development of the Budweiser brand. Similarly, Heineken sought to centre its international business on the Heineken brand and, to a lesser extent, on Amstel. While the strategies of Anheuser-Busch and Heineken focused primarily

on one brand, there were also great differences in the way these two brands were being managed. For example, Budweiser, the world's largest brand by volume, had the overwhelming bulk of its volume in its home U.S. market (see **Exhibit 6**). Sales of the Heineken brand, on the other hand, were widely distributed across markets around the world (see **Exhibit 7**). In this sense, Heineken's strategy was much more comparable to that of Interbrew's plans for Stella Artois. Other brands that were directly comparable to Stella Artois, in terms of total volume and importance of the brand to the overall sales of the company, were Carlsberg and Foster's with annual sales volumes in 1998 of 9.4 million hls and 7.1 million hls, respectively. While Foster's was successful in many international markets, there was a heavy focus on sales in the United Kingdom and the United States (see **Exhibit 8**). Carlsberg sales volume profile was different in that sales were more widely distributed across international markets (see **Exhibit 9**).

Stella's Global Launch

In 1998, Interbrew's executive management committee settled on Stella Artois, positioned as the premium European lager, as the company's global flagship brand. In fact, the Interbrew management felt that stock analysts would be favorably disposed to Interbrew having an acknowledged global brand with the potential for a higher corporate valuation and price earnings (P/E) multiple.

As the global campaign got under way, it became clear that the organization needed time to adapt to centralized co-ordination and control of Stella Artois brand marketing. This was, perhaps, not unexpected given that Interbrew had until recently operated on a regional basis; the new centralized Stella brand management approach had been in place only since September 1998. In addition, there were often difficulties in convincing all parties to become part of a new global approach, particularly the international advertising campaign that was the backbone of the global plan for Stella Artois. Belgium, for example, continued with a specific

Exhibit 6   TOP 10 Brewers by International Sales

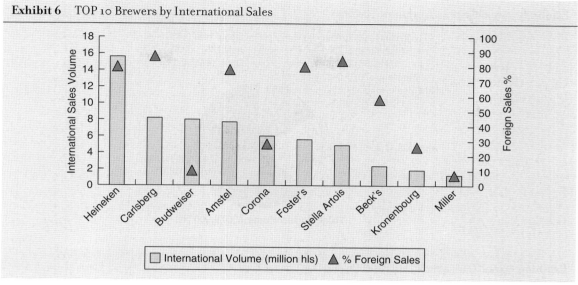

Exhibit 7   1998 Heineken World Sales Profile

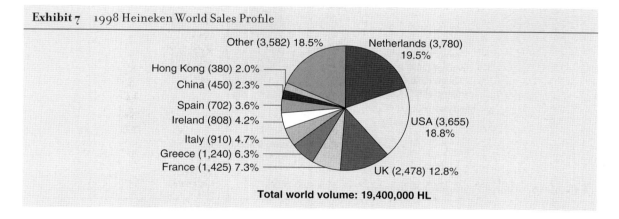

local advertising program that positioned Stella as a mainstream lager in its home market, and in the United Kingdom, Whitbread maintained its "reassuringly expensive" advertising slogan that had already proved to be so successful. For other less-established markets, a global advertising framework was created that included a television concept and a series of print and outdoor executions. This base advertising plan was rolled out in 1999 in 15 markets, including the United States, Canada, Italy, Hungary, Croatia, Bulgaria, Romania, New

Zealand and France (with a slightly changed format) after research suggested that the campaign had the ability to cross borders. The objective of this campaign was to position Stella Artois as a sophisticated European lager. It was intended that Stella Artois should be perceived as a beer with an important brewing tradition and heritage but, at the same time, also as a contemporary beer (see **Exhibit 10**).

In 1998, an accelerated plan was devised to introduce Stella Artois to two key markets within the United States, utilizing both local and corporate

Exhibit 8   1998 Foster's World Sales Profile

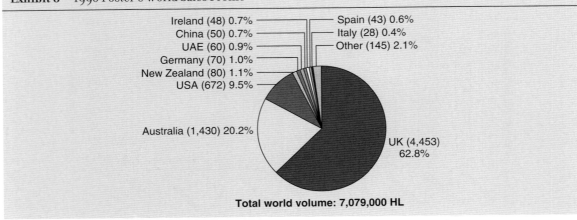

Ireland (48) 0.7%
China (50) 0.7%
UAE (60) 0.9%
Germany (70) 1.0%
New Zealand (80) 1.1%
USA (672) 9.5%
Spain (43) 0.6%
Italy (28) 0.4%
Other (145) 2.1%
Australia (1,430) 20.2%
UK (4,453) 62.8%

Total world volume: 7,079,000 HL

Exhibit 9   1998 Carlsberg World Sales Profile

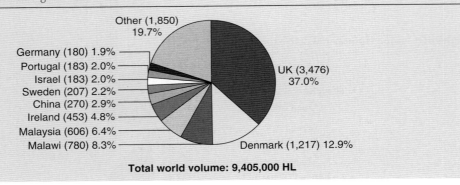

Other (1,850) 19.7%
Germany (180) 1.9%
Portugal (183) 2.0%
Israel (183) 2.0%
Sweden (207) 2.2%
China (270) 2.9%
Ireland (453) 4.8%
Malaysia (606) 6.4%
Malawi (780) 8.3%
UK (3,476) 37.0%
Denmark (1,217) 12.9%

Total world volume: 9,405,000 HL

Exhibit 10   Global Positioning Statement

Brand Positioning

To males, between 21 to 45 years of age, that are premium lager drinkers, Stella Artois is a European premium lager beer, differentially positioned towards the product.

Stella Artois offers a modern, sophisticated, yet accessible drinking experience with an emphasis on the very high quality of the beer supported by the noble tradition of European brewing.

The accent is on the emotional consequence of benefit: a positive feeling of self esteem and sophistication.

Character, Tone of Voice

Sophistication
Authenticity, tradition, yet touch of modernity
Timelessness
Premium quality
Special, yet accessible
Mysticism
European

funding. The U.S. market was believed to be key for the future development of the brand since it was the most developed specialty market in the world (12 per cent specialty market share, growing 10 per cent plus annually through the 1990s), and because of the strong influence on international trends. Thus, Stella Artois was launched in New York City and Boston and was well received by the demanding U.S. consumer and pub owner. Within 1999, over 200 pubs in Manhattan and 80 bars in Boston had begun to sell Stella Artois on tap. To support the heightened efforts to establish Stella Artois in these competitive urban markets, Interbrew's corporate marketing department added several million dollars to Labatt USA's budget for Stella Artois in 2000, with commitments to continue this additional funding in subsequent years.

Current Thinking

Good progress had been made since 1998 when Stella Artois was established as Interbrew's global brand. However, management had revised its expectations for P/E leverage from having a global brand. The reality was that Interbrew would be rewarded only through cash benefits from operational leverage of a global brand. There would be no "free lunch" simply for being perceived as having a global brand. In addition, in an era of tight fiscal management, it was an ongoing challenge to maintain the funding levels required by the ambitious development plans for Stella Artois. As a result, in early 2000 the prevailing view at Interbrew began to shift, converging on a different long-range approach towards global branding. The emerging perspective emphasized a more balanced brand development program, focusing on the highest leverage opportunities.

The experience of other brewers that had established global brands offered an opportunity for Interbrew to learn from their successes and failures. Carlsberg and Heineken, for example, were two comparable global brands that were valued quite differently by the stock market. Both sold over 80 per cent of their total volumes outside their domestic market, and yet Heineken stock achieved a P/E ratio of 32.4 in 1999 versus Carlsberg's figure of only 17.1. According to industry analysts, the driving force behind this difference was that Heineken maintained a superior market distribution in terms of growth and margin (see **Exhibit 11**). The key lesson from examining these global brands appeared to be that great discipline must be applied to focus resources in the right places.

In line with this thinking, a long range marketing plan began to take shape that made use of a series of strategic filters to yield a focused set of attractive opportunities. The first filter that any potential market had to pass through was its long-term

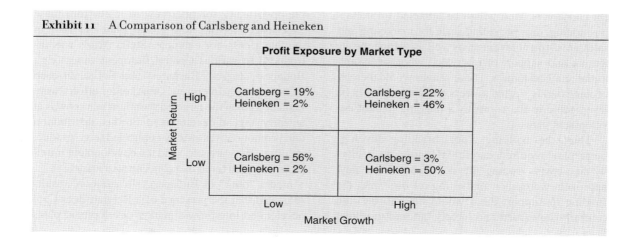

Exhibit 11   A Comparison of Carlsberg and Heineken

Profit Exposure by Market Type

	Market Return	Low Market Growth	High Market Growth
	High	Carlsberg = 19% Heineken = 2%	Carlsberg = 22% Heineken = 46%
	Low	Carlsberg = 56% Heineken = 2%	Carlsberg = 3% Heineken = 50%

volume potential for Stella Artois. This volume had to trace back to a large and/or growing market, the current or potential sizeable premium lager segment (at least five per cent of the total market), and the possibility for Stella Artois to penetrate the top three brands. The second screen was the potential to achieve attractive margins after an initial starting period of approximately three years. The third filter was whether or not a committed local partner was available to provide the right quality of distribution and to co-invest in the brand. The final screen was the determination that success in the chosen focus markets should increase leverage in other local and regional markets. For example, the size and stature of Stella Artois in the United Kingdom was a significant factor in the easy sell-in of Stella Artois into New York in 1999.

Once filtered through these strategic market development screens, the global branding plans for Stella Artois began to take a different shape. Rather than focus on national markets, plans emerged with an emphasis on about 20 cities, some of which Interbrew was already present in (e.g., London, Brussels, New York, etc.). This approach suggested that the next moves should be in such potential markets as Moscow Los Angeles and Hong Kong. Some existing cities would receive focused efforts only when distribution partner issues had been successfully resolved to solidify the bases for sustained long term growth. The major cities that fit these criteria provided the right concentration of affluent consumers, who would be attracted to Stella's positioning, thus providing scale for marketing and sales, investment leverage, as well as getting the attention and support of motivated wholesalers and initial retail customers. These venues would thereby become highly visible success stories that would be leveragable in the company's ongoing market development plans.

Thus, the evolving global branding development plan required careful planning on a city-by-city basis. Among the demands of this new approach were that marketing efforts and the funding to support them would have to be both centrally stewarded and locally tailored to reflect the unique local environments. A corporate marketing group was, therefore, established and was charged with the responsibility to identify top priority markets, develop core positioning and guidelines for local execution, assemble broadly based marketing programs (e.g., TV, print advertising, global sponsorships, beer.com content, etc.), and allocate resources to achieve the accelerated growth objectives in these targeted cities. To ensure an integrated development effort the company brought all pivotal resources together, under the leadership of a global brand development director. In addition to the brand management team, the group included regional sales managers who were responsible for licensed partner management, a customer services group, a Belgian beer café manager, and cruise business management group. Another significant challenge that faced the corporate marketing group was to ensure that all necessary groups were supportive of the new approach. This was a simpler undertaking among those business units that were wholly owned subsidiaries; it was a more delicate issue in the case of licensees and joint ventures. A key element of managing brands through a global organizational structure was that the head office team had to effectively build partnerships with local managers to ensure their commitment.

Fortunately, much of the initial effort to establish Stella Artois as a global brand had been done on a city-by-city basis and, as such, there was ample opportunity for Interbrew to learn from these experiences as the new global plan evolved. In the late 1990s, for example, Stella Artois was introduced to various Central European cities (e.g., Budapest, Zagreb, Bucharest and Sofia). In each of these cities, Interbrew's marketing efforts were launched when the targeted premium market was at an early stage of development. Further, distribution and promotion was strictly controlled (e.g., product quality, glassware, etc.) and the development initiatives were delivered in a concentrated manner (e.g., a media "blitz" in Budapest). In addition, results indicated that the presence of a Belgian Beer Café accelerated Interbrew's market development plans in these new areas. These early successes suggested that brand success could be derived from the careful and concentrated targeting of young adults living in urban centres, with subsequent pull from outlying areas following key city success.

The key lessons of these efforts in Central Europe proved to be very valuable in guiding the market development plan in New York City. In this key North American city, the rollout of Stella Artois was perceived by the analysts as "one of the most promising introductions in New York over the last 20 years" and had generated great wholesaler support and excitement. Among the tactics used to achieve this early success was selective distribution with targeted point of sale materials support. In addition, a selective media campaign was undertaken that included only prestigious outdoor advertising (e.g., a Times Square poster run through the Millennium celebrations). Similarly, the sponsoring strategy focused only on high-end celebrity events, Belgian food events, exclusive parties, fashion shows, etc. Finally, the price of Stella Artois was targeted at levels above Heineken, to reinforce its gold standard positioning. This concerted and consistent market push created an impact that resulted in the "easiest new brand sell" in years, according to wholesalers. The success of this launch also built brand and corporate credibility, paving the way to introductions in other U.S. cities as well as "opening the eyes" of other customers and distribution partners around the world.

To pursue this new global development plan over the next three years, a revised marketing budget was required. Given that the corporate marketing department was responsible for both the development of core programs as well as the selective support of local markets, the budget had to cover both of these key elements. To achieve these ends, total spending was expected to more than double over the next three years.

While great progress had been made on the global branding of Stella Artois, Cooke still ruminated on a variety of important interrelated issues. Among these issues was the situation of Stella Artois in Belgium—would it be possible to win in the "global game" without renewed growth in the home market? What specific aspirations should Interbrew set for Belgium over the next three years? Further, what expectations should Interbrew have of its global brand market development (e.g., volumes, profit levels, number of markets and cities, etc.)? How should global success be measured? With respect to Interbrew's promotional efforts, how likely would it be that a single global ad campaign could be successful for Stella Artois? Was there a particular sponsorship or promotion idea that could be singled out for global leverage? And what role should the Internet play in developing Stella Artois as a true global brand?

Case 3-2   United Cereal: Lora Brill's Eurobrand Challenge

Christopher A. Bartlett and Carole Carlson

Lora Brill, United Cereal's European vice president, was alone in her office early on a cold March morning in 2010. "I've given approval to a dozen big product launches in my career," she thought. "But the implications that this one has for our European strategy and organization make it by far the most difficult I've had to make."

The decision related to Healthy Berry Crunch, a new breakfast cereal that the French subsidiary wanted to launch. But Europe's changing market and competitive conditions had led Brill to consider making this the company's first coordinated multimarket Eurobrand launch. It was a possibility that had surfaced some equally challenging organizational questions. "Well it's only 7 AM," Brill thought to herself, smiling. "I have until my lunch appointment to decide!"

▌ United Cereal: Breakfast Cereal Pioneer

In 2010, United Cereal celebrated its 100th birthday. Established in 1910 by Jed Thomas, an immigrant grocer from England, the company's first product was a packaged mix of cracked wheat, rolled oats, and malt flakes that Thomas sold in his Kalamazoo, Michigan, grocery store. UC, as it was known in the industry, eventually diversified into snack foods, dairy products, drinks and beverages, frozen foods, and baked goods. By 2010 UC was a $9 billion business, but breakfast cereals still accounted for one-third of its revenues and even more of its profits.

UC's Corporate Values, Policies, and Practices
Thomas grew the company with strong set of values that endured through its history, and "commitment, diligence, and loyalty" were watchwords in UC. As a result, it attracted people who wanted to make a career with the company, and it promoted managers from within.

Among its managers United Cereal instilled a strong commitment to "The UC Way," a set of time-tested policies, processes, and practices embedded in iconic company phrases. For example, "Listen to the customer" was a deeply rooted belief that led UC to become a pioneer in the use of consumer research and focus groups. "Spot the trend, make the market" was another iconic phrase reflecting the high value placed on extensive market testing prior to launching new products. Finally, the value of "Honoring the past while embracing the future" led UC to reject the conventional wisdom that processed food brands had fixed life cycles. Through continuous innovation in marketing and product development, many of its products remained market leaders despite being more than half a century old.

United Cereal had a well-earned reputation as an innovator. During its 100-year history, its R&D labs had secured more product and process patents than any other competitor. The company had also pioneered the "brand management" system in the food industry, giving brand managers leadership of cross-functional teams that included manufacturing, marketing, and other functions. Each brand was managed as a profit center and was constantly measured against other brands. Brand managers also competed for R&D and product development resources.

Although this system reduced lateral communication, vertical communication was strong, and top managers were very involved in seemingly mundane brand decisions. For example, advertising copy and label changes could require up to a dozen sign-offs before obtaining final approval at the corporate VP level. "It's due to the high value we attach to our brands and our image," explained a senior executive. "But it's also because we give our brand managers responsibility at a very young age." While the company took few risks (a failed launch could cost millions even in small markets), it balanced deliberate cautiousness with a willingness to invest in products it decided to support. "The competitors can see us coming months ahead and miles away," the senior executives said. "But they know that when we get there, we'll bet the farm."

The Breakfast Cereal Market   Breakfast cereal was in its infancy when UC was founded, but it soon grew to be one of the great food commercialization successes of the 20th century. From the 1890s when Keith Kellogg created corn flakes in his attempt to improve the diet of hospital patients, the industry had grown to achieve worldwide revenues exceeding $21 billion in 2009. The U.S. industry included more than 30 companies with combined annual revenues of $12 billion. But just five players accounted for 80% of sales.

The industry recognized two categories of cereals—hot and ready-to-eat. The latter accounted for 90% of sales in both the United States and Europe. In this highly competitive industry, more than 10% of revenues was spent on advertising and marketing. Profitability also depended on operating efficiently, managing materials costs, and maximizing retail shelf space. Larger companies had significant advantages in purchasing, distribution, and marketing.

In the fight for share, several new-product introductions typically occurred each year. Developing a new brand was time-intensive and expensive, typically taking two to four years. Brand extensions—for example, General Mills's creation of Honey Nut Cheerios—were generally less expensive and less risky due to scale economies that could be leveraged in both production and marketing. But for most U.S. cereal companies, growth was increasingly coming from expansion into new offshore markets, and UC was no exception.

UC's European Operations

United Cereal entered European markets in 1952 by acquiring an English baked goods company. (Its European offices were still in London.) Over the next 30 years, UC expanded its European presence, typically by acquiring an established company with local market distribution, and then growing it by introducing products from the U.S. line. By 2009, Europe accounted for 20% of United Cereal's worldwide sales.

European Industry and Competitive Structure
Europe's $7 billion breakfast cereal market in 2010 had been overlaid on a variety of national tastes and breakfast traditions—cold meats and cheese in the Netherlands, pastries in Greece, bacon and eggs in Britain, and croissants in France. As a result, per capita consumption of cereals varied significantly across markets from 8 kg. a year in the United Kingdom to 0.5 kg. a year in Italy. Channels also varied widely by country, with supermarkets and hypermarkets accounting for more than 80% of grocery sales in Germany, 37% in France, and only 17% in Italy.

U.S.-based companies Kellogg and United Cereal were the largest two competitors in the European market with 26% and 20% share respectively. Cereal Partners, a joint venture between General Mills and Nestlé, ranked third with 17%, and U.K.-based Weetabix trailed these leaders with 7%. Numerous smaller manufacturers divided the remaining 30% of the market.

United Cereal regarded Kellogg as its toughest competitor. Operating through strong national subsidiaries, Kellogg used its volume to lower operating costs and to establish and maintain shelf space. Cereal Partners sold brands that included Cheerios and Shredded Wheat, and leveraged Nestlé's technical expertise and its European retailer relationships to compete. Although Weetabix was a smaller private company, like the bigger competitors, it also relied on strong branding and promotions to gain market share. Smaller competitors tended to hold niche market positions, but often challenged larger players with targeted price promotions.

UC's Europe Strategy and Organization   Major differences across European markets had led United Cereal to establish national subsidiaries, each led by a country manager (CM) who operated with wide latitude to make product and marketing decisions that would maximize the subsidiary's local profit. Based on their market understanding, these CMs usually selected from United Cereal's stable of more than 100 branded products, adapting them to the local situation.

Expecting its CMs to conform to its embedded values, policies, and procedures, United Cereal built its subsidiaries as "mini UC's"—exact replicas of the parent organization staffed by managers well-versed in UC's corporate values and practices. So while CMs were able to customize products, adjust manufacturing processes, and adapt advertising and promotions, they had to do so while respecting the "UC Way."

This approach unleashed CMs' entrepreneurial instincts and led to strong penetration in most national markets. While many products flourished through such local customization, over time, wide differences in product profiles and market strategies became problematic. For example, in the U.K., the Wake Up! instant coffee brand was formulated as a mild to medium roast beverage promoted as "the perfect milk coffee." But in France and Italy it was sold as a dark roast product and advertised as "the instant espresso." And differences in the positioning of Mother Hubbard's Pies resulted in it being offered as a high-end dessert in Germany, while in

the U.K. it was priced aggressively and positioned as "a convenient everyday treat."

Increasing Price and Profit Pressure   Over the preceding decade, the cereal market in Europe had become increasingly competitive. While total grocery sales had remained remarkably stable through the 2008–09 global recession, all manufacturers had seen their product mix shift toward their lower-priced offerings. Market growth slowed to less than 1% annually, and UC experienced growing price and promotion pressure from Kellogg and Cereal Partners in virtually every country in which it operated. As margins came under pressure, achieving lower costs and implementing more efficient processes became vital. (See **Exhibits 1** and **2** for financial performance.)

In this changing landscape, some of UC's historical policies came under the microscope. The company's focus on local products and markets, with its need for significant marketing and product development teams in each country, had led to a situation where sales, general and administrative (SG&A) expenses were 25% higher than in the U.S. operations. Furthermore, due to the high costs of developing and launching new products for single country markets, the pace of major new product introductions had slowed considerably in recent years. Lacking the resources for either large-scale market testing or new product launches, most CMs now favored product extensions over new product introductions, and many increasingly relied on cost reductions in their existing portfolios to maintain profits. It was a situation that raised concerns.

United Cereal Response   The earliest response to these problems had been initiated by Arne Olsen, a Norwegian appointed as UC's European VP in 2002 with a mandate to invigorate the product portfolio and reverse declining profitability. Olsen quickly reorganized R&D, reinforcing the European research facility near UC Europe's headquarters in London. To link these food scientists working on basic issues with the subsidiary-based technologists refining and testing products in local markets, Olsen created a European Technical Team (ETT)

Exhibit 1   United Cereal Selected Financial Results (USD in 000's)

	2007	2008	2009
Sales	8,993,204	9,069,242	9,254,329
COGS	4,226,806	4,271,613	4,445,671
SG&A	2,787,893	2,856,811	2,868,842
Depreciation and amortization	362,500	375,000	370,173
Operating Income	1,616,005	1,565,818	1,569,643
Interest expense	44,120	45,667	46,271
Other income	19,653	22,500	18,508
Income before taxes	1,679,778	1,633,985	1,634,422
Income taxes	410,232	415,450	420,000
Net income	1,269,546	1,218,535	1,214,422
Total Assets	6,313,000	6,215,890	6,300,000
Long-term debt	1,021,300	998,100	1,050,000
Shareholder's equity	1,722,900	1,786,200	1,751,400

Exhibit 2   United Cereal SG&A by Market (dollars in 000's) 2009 Sales and SG&A Expense

	United Cereal	Europe	France
Sales	9,254,329	1,850,866	388,682
SG&A			
Advertising and Other Marketing	1,526,964	378,687	75,737
Product Development	188,815	54,701	5,553
Other SG&A	1,153,063	216,263	46,071
SG&A subtotal	2,868,842	649,651	127,361
SG&A as a % of Sales	31.00%	35.10%	32.77%

for each major product group. Each ETT was composed of the strongest local product development technologists teamed with central R&D scientists to provide overall direction on European product development. To facilitate collaboration, Olsen encouraged transfers between the London team and the country offices, and also strengthened relationships with the R&D labs in Kalamazoo.

In 2004, Olsen expanded this technical program into what he called the "Europeanization Initiative," aimed squarely at product market strategies. His first test was UC's frozen fruit juice line, which had languished for years. He was convinced that there was little difference in tastes for fruit juice

across markets, and that there were significant benefits in standardizing the products as well as their marketing, promotion, and advertising. He transferred a senior manager from Germany to the European headquarters and gave him responsibility to standardize products, develop a coordinated Europewide strategy, and oversee implementation across subsidiaries.

The experiment was a disaster. Local CMs perceived the initiative as a direct challenge to their local autonomy—a belief made worse by the domineering personality of the individual they called the "European Juice Nazi." While they reluctantly implemented his imposed product positioning and advertising directives, they provided minimal support from the local sales forces that remained under their control. Unsurprisingly, the frozen juice category stagnated, and eventually responsibility for juice products was returned to the countries.

In 2006, Olsen was transferred to Kalamazoo in a senior marketing role, and Lora Brill, former UK country manager, became the new European vice president. In the aftermath of the 2008/2009 recession, with continuing pressure on margins, Brill needed to leverage marketing resources—the largest controllable expense in subsidiary budgets. Eventually, she too became convinced that the coordinated European approach that had succeeded in product development could be adapted for product marketing. It was in this context that she began to pursue an idea she referred to as the "Eurobrand" concept. And in 2010, a proposal by the French subsidiary to launch Healthy Berry Crunch offered the possibility of a first test case.

The Healthy Berry Crunch Project

In the late 1990s, aging baby boomers took an increased interest in natural, healthy foods in both the United States and Europe. This created a challenge for cereal companies whose highly processed products were typically high in sugar. In response, some felt that the addition of fruit could provide "a halo of health." The main technical problem was that fruit's moisture content made it difficult to maintain the crispness and shelf life of cereal. But a solution was found in the use of freeze-dried fruits, which also retained their color and shape in a cereal mix.

The French Opportunity   In 2003, Kellogg introduced Special K with freeze-dried strawberries in the U.K., and in 2007 Cereal Partners launched Berry Burst Cheerios. Seeing interest in healthy breakfast foods growing in France, UC's French country manager Jean-Luc Michel felt there could be a market for an organic fruit-based cereal in his market. Although Kellogg's Special K with Strawberries had been launched in France in 2006, to date it was alone in this new segment.

In 2008, Michel started initial product development and testing in France, later involving the ETT to develop detailed specifications. He recommended an organic blueberry-based cereal as a product extension of Healthy Crunch—a UC cereal already positioned in the health-conscious adult segment but experiencing no growth in recent years. He felt the use of blueberries, with their well-known antioxidant qualities, would reinforce the positioning.

In keeping with UC policy, as soon as the product was ready, Michel implemented a full-scale test market in Lyon. (See **Exhibit 3** for test market results.) Results were mixed, with some consumers finding the berries too tart. With the "intention to repurchase" rate below UC's 60% minimum target, an alternate raspberry-based product was developed but proved too expensive to manufacture. So a sweeter blueberry version was taste-tested with focus groups in six French cities. While lacking the validated full test-market data UC policy required, Michel felt focus group data indicating a 64% intention to repurchase was very promising. He was ready to launch:

> It's clearly a big improvement on our initial test market data. But this is a new product concept, so any test only provides a general indication. In a fast-growing category like this, we need to launch now before competitors preempt us. . . . We've been in development and testing for more than a year. We can't wait three months more to mount another full-scale test market. Besides, my budget won't support the $2 million it would cost.

The European Debate   Even before Michel set about obtaining launch approval, Brill was aware of his intention and had begun exploring the idea of launching Healthy Berry Crunch Europewide to test her nascent Eurobrand concept. Her director of finance had estimated that implementing coordinated European product market strategies could result in staff reductions and other savings that would cut product development and marketing costs by 10% to 15% over three years. Since these costs were running above 23% of sales in Europe, the savings could be very significant.

Exhibit 3   Test Market and Consumer Panel Results

Lyon Test Market: September–November 2009

| | Shipments in Stock Taking Units (000's) (volume index) | | | Share % | |
Month	Actual	Target		Actual	Target
September	4.6	1.9		1.5	0.6
October	4.0	2.5		1.3	0.8
November	3.1	4.0		1.0	1.3

Use and Awareness (After 3 months, 188 responses)		Attitude Data (After 3 months, 126 responses: Free sample and purchase users)	
Ever consumed	14	Taste: cereal	65/11[b]
Consumed in past 4 weeks	4	Taste: fruit	49/19
Ever purchased[a]	3	Health aspect	37/4
Purchased past 4 weeks	2	Form, consistency	13/6
Advertising awareness	19		
Brand awareness	28		

Intent to Repurchase (After 3 months: 126 responses from free and sample purchase users)	%
"I plan to repurchase the product in the next three months"	56/26/18[c]

[a]Difference between consumed and purchased data due to free sampling
[b]Number of unsolicited and unduplicated comments Favorable/Unfavorable in user interviews (e.g., among 126 consumers interviewed, 65 commented favorably on the cereal taste and 11 commented negatively).
[c]Percentage split Yes/No/Unsure

Brill next met with Kurt Jaeger, her Division VP responsible for Northern Europe and the person she regarded as Europe's most knowledgeable about breakfast cereal strategy. He was strongly in favor of a coordinated European rollout:

Our strategy of responding to local market differences was right for its time, but not necessarily today. Consumer tastes are converging, old cultural habits are disappearing, and EU regulation of labeling, advertising, and general marketing practices is eroding market differences... I've had my CMs in Germany and Benelux conduct consumer panels on Healthy

Berry Crunch. The samples are small, but it's encouraging that their results are similar to the French panel findings... Our biggest risk is the competition. The PodCafé debacle shows that they are way ahead of us in coordinating European strategy.

The "PodCafé debacle" to which Jaeger referred had occurred following UC's introduction of its innovative PodCafé single-serve coffee pods for home espresso machines in Germany in 2003. But by the time the French subsidiary decided to launch its version in 2006, and Italy the following year, the coffee pod market had become crowded with copycat products, and United Cereal's product was relegated to a third-place share in both of those key markets.

But Jorge Sanchez, the Division VP for Southern Europe to whom Jean-Luc Michel reported, was less enthusiastic about the Eurobrand idea. He told Brill:

> Although Jean-Luc has only been in his CM role for 18 months, I think his enthusiasm for Healthy Berry Crunch is just the kind of entrepreneurial initiative we want from our CM's. But a launch like this will cost at least $20 million in France—10 times my approval level, and twice yours. Frankly, I have real concerns about whether his budget can support it... Even if France goes ahead, my Italian CM tells me he doesn't think he could get shelf space for a specialty cereal. And our struggling Spanish subsidiary is still in recovery from the recession. There's no way they have a budget for a new launch now.

Brill also heard from her old boss, Arne Olsen, who told her that word of the proposed French launch had already reached to Kalamazoo. Olsen thought she should know about a conversation he recently had with the company's executive vice president:

> Lou's an old traditionalist who has spent his whole career here in corporate headquarters, and sees himself as a guardian of the company's values. He told me over lunch that he's worried that Europe is rushing into this launch, shortcutting the product, consumer, and market research that has ensured UC's past successes. His is one of the signatures you'll need to authorize the launch, so I thought you should know his views.

The Organizational Challenge   As she listened to this different advice, Brill was also aware that her decision would be based on organizational as well as strategic considerations. Having witnessed the disastrous European fruit juice strategy years earlier, she was determined to learn from its failure. In meetings with her HR director, she began to develop some alternative organizational proposals.

For some time, she had been planning to expand the responsibilities of her three regional vice presidents. In addition to their current roles supervising subsidiaries by region, she proposed giving each of them Europewide coordinating responsibility for several products. For example, Kurt Jaeger, who was responsible for UC's subsidiaries in Germany, Austria, Switzerland, and Benelux, would also oversee the cross-market coordination of strategy for cereals, snacks, and baked goods. For the first time, the structure would introduce a European perspective to product strategy. But Brill was conscious that she did not want to dilute the responsibility of CMs and clearly described the VPs' new-product roles as advisory. She hoped that the status, position, and experience of these senior managers would ensure that their input would be carefully considered. (**Exhibit 4** shows the proposed organization.)

Conscious that these changes would not be sufficient to implement her Eurobrand concept, Brill began to explore the idea of creating Eurobrand Teams modeled on the European Technical Teams that had proved so effective. The proposed teams would be composed of brand managers from each country subsidiary that sold the product, representatives of the European central functional departments including manufacturing, R&D, purchasing and logistics, and a representative from the appropriate regional division VP's office. They would be chaired by the brand manager of an assigned "lead country," selected based on the individual's experience and the subsidiary's resources, expertise, and strong market position in the brand.

Brill envisioned that European brand strategies would be developed by the relevant Eurobrand Teams rather than by someone at European headquarters. This meant that these teams would decide product formulation, market positioning, packaging, advertising, pricing, and promotions. In her vision, the teams would also be responsible for finding ways to reduce costs and increase brand profitability.

As she tested these ideas with her HR director and others in the London office, the European VP received some positive feedback but also heard some criticisms and concerns. Some wondered whether the CMs might still see this as a challenge to their local authority; others raised the question of whether the allocation of "lead country" roles might not concentrate power in a few large subsidiaries like Germany; and still others questioned whether teams with a dozen or more members would function effectively.

But the strongest pushback Brill received was from James Miller, the Division VP responsible for U.K. and Scandinavian countries. "This all sounds far too complex for me," he told her. "If we're serious about competing as one company in Europe, let's forget about all these teams and just move to a European product structure with someone clearly in charge."

Decision Time   On a cold March morning, Brill arrived in her office at 7 AM and began checking her e-mail. At the top of the inbox was a message from Jean-Luc Michel to Jorge Sanchez with a copy to Brill: "Jorge: One of my sales reps just heard a rumor that Cereal Partners is planning to launch Berry Burst Cheerios in France. It's now two weeks since I submitted my Healthy Berry Crunch launch request. Can you advise when I might expect a decision? Regards, Jean-Luc."

Exhibit 4   Organization Chart

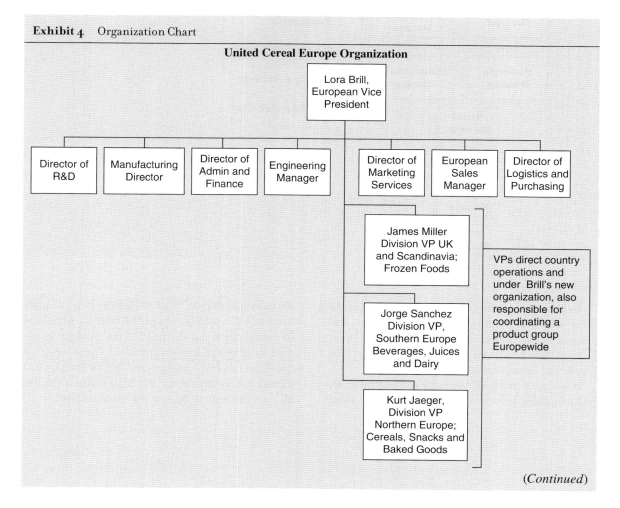

(Continued)

Exhibit 4   Organization Chart (*Continued*)

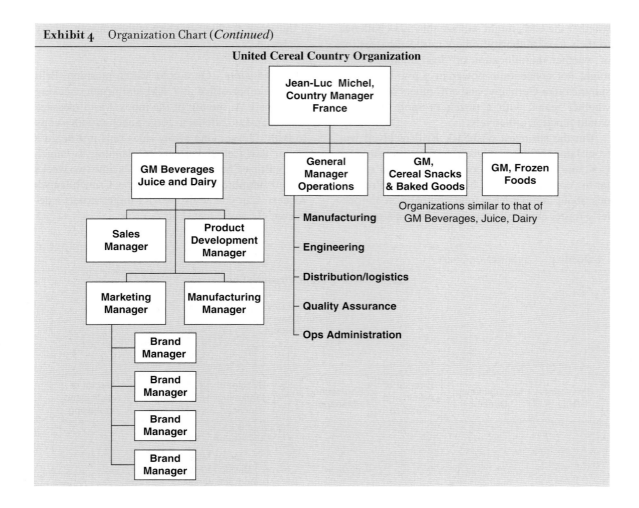

Brill nodded silently as she checked her appointment schedule for the day and saw that Kurt Jaeger had set up a lunch meeting with her for noon. Her assistant had noted on the calendar entry: "Re. Eurobrand launch decision."

It was clear that both men quite reasonably would be looking for answers today. Should she authorize the launch in France? Should Healthy Berry Crunch become UC's first Eurobrand? And if so, what kind of organization did she need to put in place to ensure its effective implementation? These were big questions, and the stakes were high for both United Cereal and for her career. But Brill realized she had all the information. Now it was decision time.

Case 3-3   GE's Imagination Breakthroughs: The Evo Project

Christopher A. Bartlett, Brian J. Hall, and Nicole S. Bennett

As he prepared for the December 2006 meeting with GE's CEO Jeff Immelt, Pierre Comte faced some difficult decisions. Only eight months into his job as chief marketing officer (CMO) of GE's Transportation business, Comte would be presenting Transportation's recommendations on some of the most visible growth initiatives in its locomotive business—projects that had been designated "Imagination Breakthroughs." IBs, as they were called within GE, were new projects with the potential to generate $100 million in new business within two to three years, and were a key part of Immelt's organic growth strategy. At the IB Review, Immelt expected to hear how Transportation was progressing with each of its locomotive IBs and what plans they had for their future.

Within GE Transportation, however, the future of several IBs had been a source of considerable debate, with none more sensitive than the Hybrid locomotive. Launched two years earlier in the belief that it could become a disruptive technology that could redefine the industry, the Hybrid had struggled to develop cost-effective performance, and some of its key sponsors were beginning to wonder if resources should continue to be committed to it. The ongoing debate had resurfaced in November at a growth review meeting in Erie, Pennsylvania, where Transportation's CEO John Dineen asked Comte and Brett BeGole, head of Transportation's Locomotive P&L unit, to describe how they planned to update Immelt on the Hybrid IB. BeGole, an experienced and effective business leader, explained that problems with the cost and performance of batteries had made the project's future highly uncertain. Feeling it was sapping resources from more profitable growth opportunities, he wondered whether it should be sidelined until the technology was further developed.

Comte was uncomfortable with that proposition. He felt that the Hybrid represented a real opportunity for GE to lead fundamental market change, and that sidelining the project could cause it to lose the resources and attention it needed at this critical stage of its development. He also worried about Immelt's reaction, especially since the Hybrid was one of his favorite IB projects. But while he knew that the IB process was designed to encourage risk-taking, Comte also realized that at the end of the day, it had to be commercially viable. In GE, the bottom line always mattered.

As Dineen listened to his direct reports, he understood the source of their differences. BeGole was responsible for the profitability and growth of the Locomotive P&L unit, and would be held accountable for its bottom-line results. But Comte, with his mandate to develop market knowledge and competitive intelligence, had been asked to challenge and stretch the existing organization. Indeed, Dineen recalled telling his new CMO, "Pierre, your job is to make marketing 'the point of the spear'; to take us to places we don't want to go." Now, after listening to the debate, Dineen wondered what

▌ Professors Christopher A. Bartlett and Brian J. Hall and Research Associate Nicole S. Bennett prepared this case. Some company information and data have been disguised for confidentiality. HBS cases are developed solely as the basis for class discussion. Cases are not intended to serve as endorsements, sources of primary data, or illustrations of effective or ineffective management.

Transportation's position on the Hybrid should be in its upcoming IB Review with Immelt.

Immelt Takes Charge: New Demands, New Responses[a]

On Friday, September 7, 2001, 43-year-old Jeff Immelt became GE's ninth CEO in its 109-year history. Four days later, two planes crashed into the World Trade Center towers. In the turmoil that followed, an already fragile post-Internet bubble stock market dropped further, and the subsequent downturn in the economy resulted in a drop in confidence that spread rapidly around the globe.

Despite his many efforts to tighten operations while continuing to grow the business, the new CEO did not have an easy initiation as he tried to deal with the resulting economic downturn, the post-Enron suspicions of large corporations, and the growing global political instability. In 2002, after promising that earnings would grow by double digits, Immelt had to report a modest 7% increase in GE's profits on revenues that were up only 5% on the 2001 sales, which had declined 3% from the prior year. (See **Exhibit 1** for GE financials, 1996–2006.) By the end of 2002, GE's stock was trading at $24, down 39% from a year earlier and 60% from its all-time high of $60 in August 2000. With considerable understatement, Immelt said, "This was not a great year to be a rookie CEO."[1]

Driving Growth: The Strategic Priority   Beyond this immediate market pressure, Immelt was acutely aware that he stood in the very long shadow cast by his predecessor, Jack Welch, under whose leadership GE had generated a total return to shareholders of 23% per annum for 20 years, representing an astonishing $380 billion increase in shareholder wealth over his two decades as CEO. Much of the company's stock price premium was due to the fact that Welch had built GE into a disciplined, efficient machine that delivered on its promise of consistent growth in sales and earnings. The results were

achieved in part through effective operations management that drove a 4% per annum organic growth rate (much of it productivity driven), but primarily through a continuous stream of timely acquisitions and clever deal making. This two-pronged approach had resulted in double-digit revenue and profit increases through most of the 1990s.

But Immelt knew that he could not hope to replicate such a performance by simply continuing the same strategy. The environment in the new millennium had changed too much. The new CEO wanted to use GE's size and diversity as sources of strength and to drive growth by investing in places and in ways that others could not easily follow. He began to articulate a strategy that would rely on technology leadership, commercial excellence, and global expansion to build new business bases that would capitalize on what he described as "unstoppable trends."

Beginning in 2002, he challenged his business leaders to identify these new "growth platforms" with the potential to generate $1 billion in operating profit within the next few years. In response, several opportunities emerged, and the company soon began engaging in new fields such as oil and gas technology, securities and sensors, water technology, Hispanic broadcasting, and consumer finance, all of which were growing at a 15% annual rate. "The growth platforms we have identified are in markets that have above average growth rates and can uniquely benefit from GE's capabilities," said Immelt. "Growth is *the* initiative, *the* core competency that we are building in GE."[2]

Building New Capabilities: Investing in Technology and Marketing

To reposition GE's portfolio to leverage growth, Immelt's team lost little time in acquiring companies such as Telemundo to build a base in Hispanic broadcasting, Interlogix in security systems, BetzDearborn in water-processing services, and Enron Wind in renewable energy. After completing $35 billion worth of acquisitions in 2001 and 2002, GE completed the biggest acquisition year

---

[a] This section summarizes "GE's Growth Strategy: The Immelt Initiative," Harvard Business School Case No. 306-087.
[1] GE 2002 Annual Report, p. 5.

[2] GE 2003 Annual Report, p. 9.

Exhibit 1 GE Financial Performance, 1992–2006 ($ millions)

	2006	2005	2004	2003	2002	2001	2000	1995
General Electric Company & Consolidated Affiliates								
Revenues	163,391	147,956	134,291	113,421	132,226	125,913	129,853	70,028
Earnings from continuing operations	20,666	18,631	16,601	15,589	15,133	14,128	12,735	6,573
Loss from discontinued operations	163	(1,922)	559	2,057	(616)	(444)	0	
Net earnings	20,829	16,711	17,160	14,091	14,629	13,684	12,735	6,573
Dividends declared	10,675	9,647	8,594	7,759	7,266	6,555	5,647	2,838
Earned on average shareowner's equity	19.5%	17.8%	17.9%	20%	25.2%	27.1%	27.5%	23.5%
Per share:								
Net earnings	1.99	1.76	1.59	1.4	1.46	1.41	3.87	3.90
Net earnings—diluted	1.99	1.76	1.59	1.4	1.52	1.37	3.81	
Dividends declared	1.03	0.91	0.82	0.77	0.73	0.66	1.71	1.69
Stock price range[a]	38.49–32.06	37.34–32.67	37.75–28.88	32.43–21.30	41.84–21.40	52.90–28.25	60.5–41.66	73.13–49.88
Total assets of continuing operations	697,239	673,321	750,617	647,834	575,018	495,023	437,006	228,035
Long-term borrowings	260,804	212,281	207,871	170,309	138,570	79,806	82,132	51,027
Shares outstanding—average (in thousands)	10,359,320	10,569,805	10,399,629	10,018,587	9,947,113	9,932,245	3,299,037	1,683,812
Employees at year-end:								
United States	155,000	161,000	165,000	155,000	161,000	158,000	168,000	150,000
Other countries	165,000	155,000	142,000	150,000	154,000	152,000	145,000	72,000
Total employees	319,000	316,000	307,000	305,000	315,000	310,000	313,000	222,000

Source: Compiled from GE annual reports, various years.
[a]Stock price adjusted for stock split in 2000.

in its history in 2003, including two megadeals: $14 billion for media giant Vivendi Universal Entertainment (VUE), and $10 billion for UK-based Amersham, a leader in biosciences.

But Immelt also recognized that he would have to make equally significant internal investments to ensure that his strategy of technology-driven, commercially-oriented global expansion could build on this new growth platform. Within his first six months, he had committed $100 million to upgrade GE's major R&D facility at Niskayuna in upstate New York. Then, in 2002, he authorized a new Global Research Center (GRC) in Shanghai, and in 2003 agreed to build another GRC in Munich, investments involving another $100 million. And despite the slowing economy, he upped the R&D budget 14% to $359 million in 2003. When asked about the increase in spending during such a difficult time for the company, he said, "Organic growth is the driver. Acquisitions are secondary to that. I can't see us go out and pay a start-up $100 million for technology that, if we had just spent $2 million a year for 10 years, we could have done a better job at it. I hate that, I just hate that."[3]

Rather than concentrating primarily on short-term product development as it had in the past, the GRCs' agenda become more oriented toward the long term. R&D also became more focused, with more than 1,000 projects slashed to just 100. Furthermore, the research group identified five very long-term technology areas for special attention, in fields as diverse as nanotechnology, advanced propulsion, and biotechnology. It was a longer-term R&D focus than GE had seen for many years.

The other core competency Immelt wanted to use to drive organic growth was marketing. As an ex-salesman, he had always focused on the customer and felt that an unintended by-product of Welch's obsession with operating efficiency and cost-cutting had been the development of a culture that was too internally focused. He wanted the organization to turn its attention to the marketplace and to bring in a more commercially oriented perspective to its decisions.

In one of Immelt's first appointments, Beth Comstock was named GE's chief marketing officer, a position Welch had abolished decades earlier. (See **Exhibit 2** for the GE's corporate organization chart.) Immelt also redeployed most of GE's large acquisition-oriented corporate business development staff into marketing roles, and asked each of GE's businesses to appoint a VP-level marketing head to develop that capability in the business. Because of the shortage of internal talent, many of these marketing leaders had to be recruited from outside, an uncommon practice at GE.

To provide a forum for these new leaders to monitor and drive the change Immelt wanted, in 2003 he formed a Commercial Council made up of 20 respected commercial leaders drawn from a diverse range of GE businesses. Not all members were corporate officers, or even among the top 600 in GE's Senior Executive Band, but all shared the distinction of being personally selected by the CEO for their innovative thinking. Meeting monthly by phone and quarterly in person, the group used this forum to discuss mega-trends, to identify broad strategies for international growth, and to diffuse best marketing practices rapidly throughout GE. To underline its importance, Immelt chaired the council.

Realigning Personal Competencies: Developing "Growth Leaders" The investment in new capabilities had an immediate impact on GE's management profile. Within Immelt's first two years, the company recruited over 5000 engineers, and among the 175 corporate officers, the number of engineers grew from seven to 21. The same dramatic change was occurring in sales and marketing, and in 2003, the company began a process to increase GE's under-resourced marketing staff by 2000 over the next two years. To help integrate this influx of senior-level marketers into GE's culture and systems, the Experienced Commercial Leadership Program was created.

As big a task as it was, recruiting top talent into these growth-driving functions was less of a

---

[3]Robert Buderi, "GE Finds Its Inner Edison," *Technology Review*, October, 2003, pp. 46–50.

Exhibit 2   GE Corporate Structure

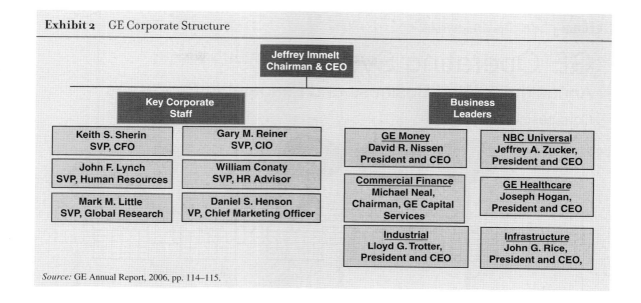

Source: GE Annual Report, 2006, pp. 114–115.

concern to the CEO than the challenge of developing new capabilities in his current management team. While strong in operations and finance, some lacked the skills Immelt felt they would need to succeed in the more entrepreneurial, risk-taking environment he wanted to create. To help define the leadership behaviors that would be required to drive organic growth, the human resources staff researched the competency profiles at 15 large, fast-growth global companies such as Toyota, P&G, and Dell. They concluded that five leadership traits would be key to driving organic growth in GE:

- An external focus
- An ability to think clearly
- Imagination and courage
- Inclusiveness and connection with people
- In-depth expertise

Soon, all courses at GE's Crotonville education center focused on developing these characteristics, and Immelt made it clear that unless managers had these traits or were developing them, they would not be likely to succeed at GE regardless of their past track record. And to underline his commitment to supporting a new generation of "growth leaders," he began making changes to some of GE's well-established norms and practices. For example, to develop leaders with more in-depth market and technological knowledge and domain expertise, Immelt decided to slow the job rotations that had long been central to management development at GE; to build new technological and marketing capabilities rapidly, he accepted the need to recruit from the outside; and to encourage individuals to take risks, and even to fail, Immelt adjusted the evaluation and reward processes that previously had been tied to flawless execution of short-term budget objectives.

Embedding Growth in Processes and Metrics   In classic GE form, all elements of the new organic growth initiative were soon being reinforced in metrics, systems, and processes to ensure that the new objectives received the disciplined follow-up that characterized GE's management style. It was this cycle of tightly linked and mutually supportive systems and processes and that were the backbone of the company's Operating System that supported GE's reputation for clear strategy and a disciplined implementation.

Exhibit 3   GE's Operating System

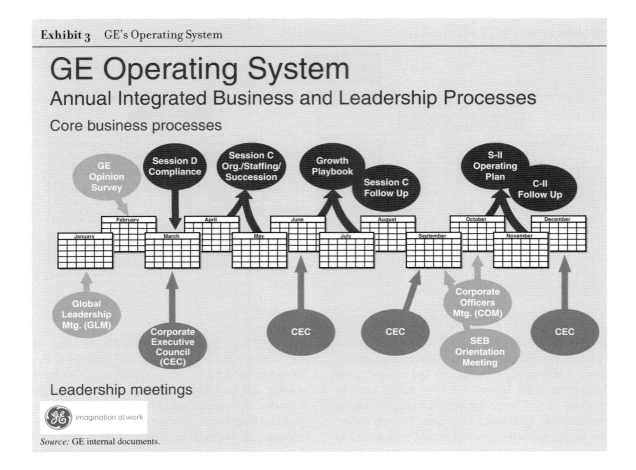

GE Operating System
Annual Integrated Business and Leadership Processes

Core business processes

Leadership meetings

Source: GE internal documents.

At the heart of the Operating System were three core processes that had framed management reviews over many decades—Session C, Session I, and Session II. (See **Exhibit 3** for a graphic representation.) Each was now harnessed to drive the growth agenda. For example, the Session C organization, staffing, and succession reviews each May became a powerful tool to reinforce the recruitment, promotion, and deployment of technological and marketing talent, as well as the development of a new generation of "growth leaders" willing to take risks to build new businesses. Next, in July, Session I (GE's strategy review process that Immelt renamed the Growth Playbook) required each business to drill down on how market trends and

customer needs provided opportunities for them to grow their business organically. And in November's Session II, discussions of the operating budget (driven in the GE model by stretch targets rather than line item expense reviews) made sure that each business's commitments to invest in and deliver on growth projects were not cut back in order to meet short-term performance objectives.

Further, the metrics used in the implementation of each of these systems were also changed to reflect the new growth objectives. For example, individual development reviews and performance evaluations leading up to Session C now evaluated managers against the new growth traits. In the first year, only corporate officers were evaluated;

the following year, the metrics were extended to the 600 in the Senior Executive Band; and by year three, the top 7000 executives were getting feedback and development support around the required growth traits. New metrics in the Session I/Growth Playbook review required managers to develop and defend strategies to achieve Immelt's objective organic growth rate of 5% above GDP growth by doubling GE's organic growth from 4% to 8% annually. And in Session II, a new Net Promoter Score was added to hold managers accountable for a demanding measure of customer loyalty and repurchase.

Imagination Breakthroughs: Engine of Organic Growth   By the end of 2003, Immelt told investors that he had now completed the big investments needed to re-position the company's business platforms for the future. But results were still disappointing, and with both income and revenue barely above the levels of 2000, some observers were beginning to question whether the GE's greatest growth was behind it. Immelt rejected that notion, and saw no reason for GE to slow down as long as it was able to change its approach and emphasize organic growth. "In the late 1990s, we became business traders not business growers," he said. "Today, organic growth is absolutely the biggest task in every one of our companies."[4]

Having spent his first two years repositioning the business portfolio and investing in new organizational capabilities, Immelt now wanted to drive the pursuit of organic growth much deeper into the company. In September 2003, he convened a meeting of marketing directors from each of GE's businesses and challenged to develop by November five proposals for new growth businesses— "Imagination Breakthroughs" he called them, or IBs as they quickly became known. "We have to put growth on steroids," he said. "I want game changers. Take a big swing."[5]

[4]Jeffrey R. Immelt, "Growth As a Process," *Harvard Business Review*, June 2006, p. 64.
[5]Erick Schonfeld, "GE Sees the Light," *Business 2.0*, July 2004, Vol. 5, Iss. 6, pp. 80–86.

Over the next two months, the marketing leaders engaged management of all of GE's businesses to respond to Immelt's challenge. In November, they presented 50 IB proposals to the CEO and a small group of corporate marketing staff who now became the IB Review Committee. Of this initial portfolio, the CEO green-lighted 35, which the businesses were then expected to fund, adapt, and pursue. And Immelt indicated that he intended to monitor progress—personally and closely.

GE Transportation's First IB: The Evo Story

In September 2003, in response to Immelt's request, GE Transportation identified its five potential IBs. Perhaps the most exciting was the Evolution Locomotive, a product already on the shelf as a planned new product introduction, but struggling to get support due to challenges in both its technical development and its market acceptance. The designation of this project as an IB turned a corporate spotlight on its funding and put a supercharger on its commercialization.

Origins of the Evolution Locomotive   GE began serving the North American rail market in 1918, and through numerous cycles over the better part of the next century, the company steadily built a good business selling to North America's six large rail companies. By the mid-1990s, with revenues approaching $2 billion, GE had built a dominant market share, and its AC4400 long-haul locomotive was recognized as the most successful engine on the market. But it was a mature and conservative industry, and an unlikely place to jumpstart an initiative that called for cutting-edge technology, innovation, and risk taking.

In a rare innovative move in the industry, in 1995 GE introduced its much anticipated "super-loco," the AC6000. Touted as the most powerful locomotive on the market, its size and hauling capability were impressive. But within a year of its launch, North American customers were reporting that most of the AC6000's new capabilities were unnecessary or uneconomical. This unfortunate misreading of market needs led to only 207 units of the 6000 being sold over the next five years compared with more than 3,000 classic AC4400 locomotives in the same period.[6] Worse, many of those that were sold either failed to deliver on their promised cost-benefit performance or had reliability problems. The AC6000 locomotive was eventually discontinued and became a black eye on GE's otherwise strong record in the industry.

Meanwhile, in December 1997, Environmental Protection Agency (EPA) upset the predictable rail market by announcing strict emissions requirements for all new locomotives to be put in service after January 1, 2005. The regulations posed serious engineering challenges and a major commercial risk for locomotive manufacturers whose safest response was to modify existing models to meet the new standards. While most companies chose to follow this conservative strategy, GE engineers committed to a riskier and more expensive approach of designing a completely new platform able to meet future emissions standards while also keeping fuel costs down.

Over the following three years, engineers in Erie and at the Global Research Center in Niskayuna worked to redefine the paradigm of locomotive design by eliminating the traditional tradeoff between fuel efficiency and emissions. The result was the Evolution Locomotive (quickly dubbed the Evo) which used a revolutionary engine combined with a patented cooling system to achieve 3% to 5% fuel savings while generating 40% less emissions than the previous generation. It also incorporated a locomotive control system enhancement that managed the speed and throttle settings to minimize fuel consumption and/or emissions, taking into account train composition, terrain, track conditions, train dynamics, and weather, without negatively impacting the train's arrival time.

Although this radical new engine represented a clear technical advancement, the decision to take it from design to production was a gamble. Because locomotives delivered before January 1, 2005 were exempt from the new regulations, some predicted that there would be a spike in demand for old models in 2004, leaving little market for the Evo in 2005. Indeed, the sales force reported that most customers were wary about making early commitments to meet the new requirements. But the believers on the GE team argued that the Evo could deliver real savings in fuel and labor, areas in which costs were mounting rapidly in the industry. In a major bet, in 2002 GE committed to building its Evolution locomotive. (See **Exhibit 4** for a photo and basic specifications for the Evo.)

Evo Becomes an IB   The earlier AC6000 product failure coupled with the looming change in environmental regulations in the industry put the locomotive business leaders in Erie under intense pressure to prove to the CEO that they could grow their mature business organically. When Immelt announced his quest for $100 million Imagination Breakthroughs, it was clear that the Evo would be a "make or break" project. Despite the continuing uncertainty around its market potential, the Evo became the centerpiece of Transportation's presentation in its first IB Review with Immelt. The CEO was immediately taken by the project's potential and told the sponsoring managers that he would be monitoring progress in regular review meetings that he planned to conduct monthly with those responsible for IBs.

True to his word, Immelt conducted reviews of several businesses' IBs every month. This meant that every six months or so, those directly responsible for Evo—the P&L leader, the technology leader, and/or the marketing leader—met with him to describe progress and outline next steps for their project. As the team soon learned, PowerPoint presentations were strictly prohibited in these meetings. To encourage an atmosphere of discussion and debate, presenters were allowed no more than one page of documentation for each IB. Although the meetings were small and informal, the managers were not necessarily relaxed. They knew that

---

[6]"US loco market still a two-horse race," *Railway Gazette International*, July 1, 2006.

Exhibit 4   Evolution Locomotive Product Specifications

Evolution Series Technology Bears Close Inspection, By Accounting as Well as Engineering.

Overcoming obstacles with technological innovation is meaningless if that technology isn't economically viable for everyday use. That's why every component in an Evolution Series locomotive is proven to meet the demands of those who operate them as well as those who pay for them.

Nowhere is this more evident than with the GEVO-12 engine. The heart of the Evolution Series locomotives, the 45-degree, 12-cylinder, 4-stroke, turbocharged GEVO-12 engine produces the some 4,400 HP as its 16-cylinder predecessor. And it does it with greater fuel efficiency, lower emissions, and extended overhaul intervals. Enhanced cooling and higher-strength materials dramatically improve reliability and allow for future increases in power and efficiency.

❶	❷	❸	❹	❺	❻
Smart Displays Several add-on black boxes are eliminated with a new computer display combination, enhancing both reliability and operator ergonomics.	**Enhanced Microprocessor Controls** Upgraded components and software improve wheel slip/slide control and reliability while providing more comprehensive and simplified diagnostics. Open architecture enables easier integration of software and third-party devices.	**"HiAd" Trucks** Low weight transfer, an improved microprocessor wheel slip/slide system, and single inverter per motor, combine to optimize adhesion under all rail conditions. Design simplicity and 10-year overhaul intervals significantly reduce maintenance costs.	**Low-Slip, High-Performance AC Traction Motors** Get a full 166,000 lbs. (AC) of continuous tractive effort and up to 198,000 lbs. (AC) starting tractive effort from a 6-axle locomotive. Integral pinion design eliminates slippage, extending pinion life to 2 million miles. Million-mile motor overhaul intervals further reduce maintenance costs.	**Superior Dynamic Braking** Evolution Series locomotives feature up to 117,000 lbs. (AC) of braking effort, utilizing the proven grids and blowers from our current production AC 4400 & Dash 9. Braking grids are also completely isolated for greater reliability and simplified maintenance.	**Air-Cooled Inverters** No coolant. No environmental concerns. A single air-cooled inverter per traction motor provides individual axle control that improves wheel slip/slide, increases mission reliability, maximizes tractive effort, and improves transmission efficiency.

Exhibit 4   Evolution Locomotive Product Specifications (*Continued*)

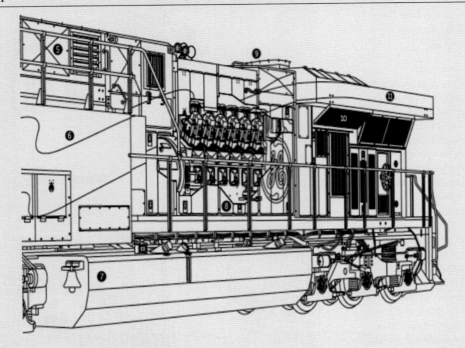

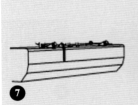

7

High-Impact Fuel Tank

This tank exceeds AAR S-5506 with thickened, reinforced walls and

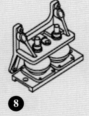

8

baffles for even greater puncture resistance.

Isolation Mounts

Smoother, Quieter, New isolation mounts on the engine and alternator significantly improve operator environment

9

with reduced cab noise and vibration.

Emissions

"Environmentally compatible" is more than a buzzword for Evolution Series locomotives. Advanced electronic fuel injection, air-to-air cooling, adaptive controls, and GEVO-12 engine technology combine to reduce

10

emissions by over 40 percent.

Air-To-Air Intercooler

Manifold Air Temperature (MAT) is greatly reduced with the new hybrid cooling system and air-to-air intercooler. The lower MAT enables emissions compliance while

11

simultaneously improving fuel efficiency.

Spilt Cooling

The proven Split Cooling radiator system reduces engine-air-inlet temperatures and cools the engine oil for increased reliability and longer engine-bearing life.

Source: Evolution Locomotive brochure, GE Transportation website: http://www.getransportation.com/na/en/evolution.html.

Exhibit 5   IB Review Preparation: Sample Questions

The following are a few of the questions given to IB teams to help them prepare for reviews:

Market Opportunity

- Can you start with the answer: Where would you like to be and why?
- How does this fit in your strategy?
- What does it take to be good at this?
- How does technology play a role here? Does it give us an advantage?

Competition

- Is anyone else doing this? Who is best at this?
- How we placed vis-à-vis the competition?
- How many others have tried this? Have they succeeded or failed?
- Do our competitors make money at this?

Pricing

- How much would we make on this product?
- How much would the customer pay for this product?
- How do we price it correctly?
- Why aren't we charging a higher price?

Resources

- Where do we have in-house expertise?
- Are you working with any other GE business on this?
- How do we use GE Financial Services as a weapon?
- What resources do we need to hit the growth target? A doubling/tripling of resources?

Go to Market

- What is standing in our way in order to execute this well?
- Is there a way to tap into global suppliers to fill the global pipeline?
- What is the value proposition? How would you differentiate?
- How will you build capability?

Source: GE internal documents.

---

questioning would be intense, and were advised to be prepared to discuss a range of sample questions. (See **Exhibit 5** for a preparatory list.) So meeting the CEO (supported by just a few of his corporate marketing staff), created some nervous tension. As one manager reflected, "Do you really want to be the only business that shows no imagination or, compared to other business's IBs being presented, has no breakthrough?"

Managers came to IB Review meetings armed with extensive market information, the result of a rigorous analytical process called CECOR that was being rolled out by the corporate marketing group to help business-level marketing teams systematize analysis to support the IB process.[b] (See **Exhibit 6** for an outline of the CECOR process and tools.)

---

[b]CECOR stood for Calibrate, Explore, Create, Organize, and Realize, an analytical process that the corporate marketing group had developed. It was supported by a portfolio of tools borrowed from a variety of sources including the consulting groups Bain and McKinsey, which had proved helpful in doing market segmentation, customer analysis, competitive analysis, etc.

Exhibit 6   CECOR Tool Kit

CECOR Framework
Identifying questions to ask and tools to apply

C CALIBRATE	**E** EXPLORE	**C** CREATE	**O** ORGANIZE	**R** REALIZE
➤ What industry are you in? ➤ Who are the customers and what do they need?	➤ What are our potential avenues of growth? ➤ Which ones will you target?	➤ What are our best ideas? ➤ What is the customer value?	➤ Is the go-to-market plan aligned with the value proposition? ➤ Are you prepared to implement?	➤ Will you meet your revenue and income plans? ➤ How will you measure customer and GE impact?

Tools

• Five Forces • Market Maps • Profit Pools • Value Chain	• Customer Experience Grid • Segmentation • Competitive Assessment • Targeting	• Capability Assessment • Ideation Sessions • Positioning	• Conjoint Analysis • Value Proposition • Value Based Pricing • Branding	• Go-to-Market Plan • Continuous Feedback (VoC) • Impact Metrics

GE imagination at work

CECOR's fit in GE's operating rigor

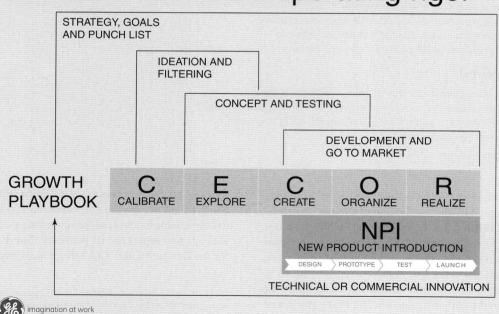

GE imagination at work

Source: GE internal documents.

Because of Immelt's understanding of the issues and his direct, in-depth questioning, some began calling the IB Review meetings the "Committee of One."

In the glare of the IB spotlight, the Evo product management and sales team found themselves under increased pressure to perform. But discussions with customers revealed that GE was still "paying for sins of the past," as one salesman put it, and the team concluded that it would not be able to sell the Evo's value proposition from a piece of paper and a set of specifications. After the failure of the AC6000, customers wanted solid evidence of the benefits being promised.

In a leap of faith, GE Transportation took the financial risk of committing $100 million to build 50 Evo units, which they then planned to lease to customers for a nominal fee. The locomotives were to be carried on GE's books, but would be operated by customers and used on their North American lines. The goal was to log five million miles before the 2005 launch, thereby regaining customers' trust by proving the engine's reliability and the value of the technological advancements.

Preparing to Launch: The Agony ...   In early 2004, vague concerns about Evo began turning to panic. A year into the leasing plan, the sales team did not have a single firm order. Sales reps were getting positive feedback about performance of the leased Evos, but customers were still reluctant to make the capital expenditure. Transportation's November SII Budget Review for Evo had been grim: worst-case scenarios projected sales of only 30 or 50 locomotives out of a total 2005 capacity of 600 Evos. It was a performance that would result in significant losses. While some felt that GE might have to offer the Evo at an attractive initial price to attract sales, Immelt challenged that assumption. At IB Review meetings, he was pushing the team in the opposite direction, urging them to focus on how to price the soon-to-be-launched product to capture its full value.

Because the Evo offered significant economic savings to the railroads over its lifecycle, Immelt asked why it could not be sold at a premium over

the previous model. Discussion about the impact of rising energy costs in the IB Review meetings spilled over into detailed market and product analysis in Growth Playbook sessions. These meetings with Immelt were very different from the Session I strategy reviews over which Welch had presided. Where Welch had been cost and efficiency-driven, Immelt was focused on the market value of technological advancements like the Evo. "In a deflationary world, you could get margin by working productivity," Immelt said. "Now you need marketing to get a price."[7]

As a result of these discussions, the IB team refined Evo's value story to focus on its lifecycle costs, and decided to reflect the Evo's significant performance improvements in a 10% price premium. Knowing that this decision would cause anxiety within the sales ranks, Dave Tucker, Transportation's VP of Global Sales, turned the annual January sales meeting in Coco Beach, Florida into a call to arms for the Evo. Despite having a single firm order, in the opening session he announced that by June the sales team needed to sell out the factory—and at a significant price premium over the previous model. "It scared the hell out of the sales force," Tucker recalled. "Frankly, we had never had a step-function increase in pricing like that."

Tucker challenged his sales force to come up with the means to implement the plan. In addition to worries about the expected customer reaction, some expressed concerns about the likely response of a key competitor who had not made the same upfront investment. But the marketing group's analysis suggested that rising oil prices, increased rail traffic, and tightening emission standards could make customers more open to Evo's benefits. After several days of joint discussions with marketing and product management, the sales force hit the streets committed to booking orders at the new price.

Implementing the Launch:... The Ecstasy   Over the following months, the sales team went back to its customers, emphasizing value to

[7]Jeffrey R. Immelt, "Growth As a Process," *Harvard Business Review*, June 2006, p. 64.

convince them that Evo was worth its price premium. As if responding to a cue, oil prices continued to rise—from $32 a barrel in January 2004, to $40 by June, and $50 by October. At the same time, driven by surging Chinese imports entering the U.S. on the West Coast, transcontinental rail traffic was booming. And state regulatory bodies' demands were making emissions an industry-wide concern. The marketing analyses had proved correct: customers were ready for the Evo.

By the launch date on January 1, 2005, not only was Evo's entire 2005 production sold out, product was on backorder through much of 2006. Despite earlier concerns about a risk of a temporary drop in market share, industry experts estimated that GE maintained or increased its 70% share through the launch and outsold its competition by three to one in the U.S. market during 2005.[8] By mid-2006, there was a backlog of 1500 locomotives, representing two years of production capacity. The early success of the Evo continued into 2007, with all-time highs in deliveries surpassing records set just one year earlier. The Evo had become a posterchild IB success story.

Managing the IB Lifecycle: Raising the Evo Babies

When John Dineen became CEO of GE Transportation in the summer of 2005, Evo was well on its way to being one of the outstanding IB successes. But Dineen made it clear that he wanted to drive even more growth from this old-line, mature portfolio of businesses. To emphasize that objective, he reinforced Immelt's annual corporate Growth Playbook process by creating a Growth Council, to which he invited his entire management team to engage in a monthly review of growth initiatives in each of Transportation's businesses. His objective was to build a growth agenda into the pulse of the business and make it part of the ongoing management discussion.

[8]From GE press documents. "Ecomagination: The Hybrid Locomotive," www.ge.com.

Birth of an Evo Baby: The Global Modular Locomotive Acknowledging that the slow-growth domestic markets already dominated by GE were unlikely to be the major source of new business, Dineen emphasized the opportunities for international expansion. Responding to that challenge, Tim Schweikert, general manager of the Locomotive P&L unit, began to explore with his team the challenge of breaking into the global locomotive market. They soon identified the hurdles they would have to clear in order to sell internationally. First, because railway gauge width, weight limits, and clearance requirements varied widely by country, the team decided that there could be no standardized "global locomotive." Furthermore, the number of locomotives called for in most international tenders (as few as 10 or 15) made the huge upfront investment in engineering a major cost barrier. And finally, because governments were typically the operators of railways, the selling process usually involved complex political negotiations.

Recognizing all of these constraints, Schweikert and his team developed a product concept that it termed the Global Modular Locomotive (GML), a design developed around a set of standard components that could be built to different national requirements using a Lego-like construction approach. With great excitement, they took their idea to Dineen's monthly Growth Council where it was endorsed as a candidate for Immelt's IB Review. Presenting their ideas in this forum in September 2005, the locomotive team preempted Immelt's opening question by identifying GML's three value-creating objectives: to reduce the response time in international tender processing, to reduce the amount spent on nonrecurring engineering, and to reduce the time between the order and the sale. After further probing questions, Immelt congratulated them and approved GML as an IB.

To help Schweikert implement the new IB project, Dineen assigned Gokhan Bayhan to the role of marketing leader for the Locomotive P&L unit. The move was part of a larger strategy of transferring recognized talent into the fledgling business marketing roles. "We took some of our best people from our commercial and engineering organization and put them into these roles," said Dineen. "As soon as you start doing that, the rest of the organization realizes it's important. Initially, we had to draft people and assure them that the move was going to be good for their careers. But it was hard. Every bone in their body was telling them not to do it because there was no track record." (See **Exhibit 7** for GE Transportation's organization chart.)

Because Bayhan had earlier worked on a locomotive modernization contract that GE had won to overhaul and rebuild 400 locomotives for the state-owned railway in Kazakhstan, he decided this was a perfect place to explore GML's potential. Soon, he and the sales team were talking to government contacts about the new concept and about the opportunity for GE to help them expand and modernize their railway system to meet the needs of Kazakhstan's fast-growing China trade.

The disciplined process of analyzing the market opportunities and customer needs was part of the marketing group's responsibility. But because this analysis was a new element in the existing process of bringing a product to market, gaining acceptance was not always easy, as Bayhan explained:

> The relationships between product management, sales, and engineering were well established, so a lot of marketing team members had difficulty breaking into that process, and taking on a role that didn't exist before. It was hardest for those from the outside, and they were the majority. It helped that I'd been in the organization in various product management and finance roles because it allowed me to use my access and credibility to contribute a marketing point of view. But lots of others had a hard time with it.

Meanwhile, as sales, engineering, and marketing worked together to test and approve the GML concept, a major boost to the effort occurred in December 2005 when the company announced that it had received an order for 300 GML locomotives from the Chinese railway. In October, Schweikert, who had been close to the Chinese negotiations, was transferred from his position in Erie to become head of GE transportation in China, not only to oversee this important contract, but to use it to expand GE's penetration into this huge market.

Making Marketing Mainstream As the role and impact of the marketing function grew within Transportation, Dineen accelerated his efforts to find a head of marketing who could not only accelerate existing marketing efforts, but could also provide the function with greater access and influence at the most senior levels of discussion in the company. Finally, in early 2006, he found the person he felt could fill the role. Pierre Comte became chief marketing officer of GE Transportation in May 2006. Surprisingly, although he had a strong commercial background built up through an international career, he did not come from a traditional marketing background. Most recently he had run the rail signaling business at a major European transportation company. But to Dineen, he seemed an ideal fit—someone with relevant industry expertise, good frontline experience, and a strong enough personality to deal credibly with his P&L leaders, and understand their pressures and constraints.

In his first meeting with his new CMO, Dineen told Comte to "create a crisis around growth." But Comte realized he would first have to convince his bottom-line-driven peers that he could help them:

> When you run a $2 billion Locomotive P&L that's doing great, you don't have a pressing need to reinvent yourself and your business. The role of the marketing group is to push the P&L leaders to revisit their portfolios. But they won't listen to chart makers or theoreticians. So I spent three months telling them, "I'm like you, I'm a business guy; I've lived in Asia and Europe. I've run a P&L with a couple of thousand people reporting to me. I know that the last thing you want is another headquarters guy giving you more work to do. I'm not going to do that. I'm here to help you make your P&Ls bigger, stronger."

Under Comte, the new marketing team began to take a more active role in the business, a role that became more and more evident as the Evo offshoot businesses started to grow. The contributions that Gokhan Bayhan made to the redefinition of GML provided a classic example.

Exhibit 7 GE Transportation Organizational Chart

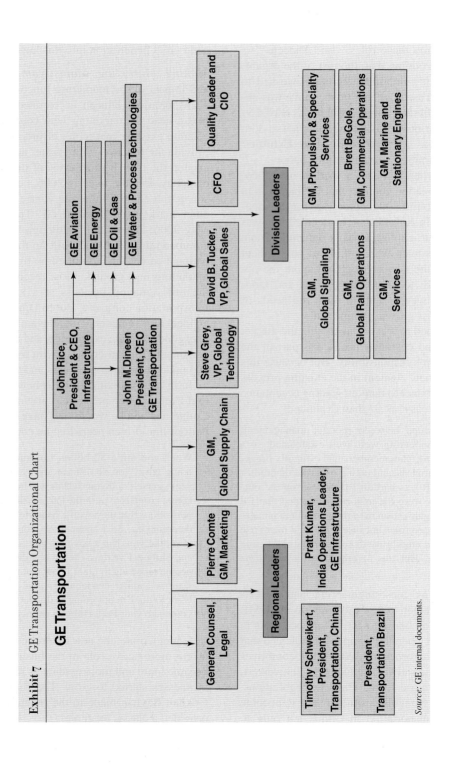

GE Transportation

John Rice, President & CEO, Infrastructure

- GE Aviation
- GE Energy
- GE Oil & Gas
- GE Water & Process Technologies

John M. Dineen, President, CEO GE Transportation

General Counsel, Legal	Pierre Comte GM, Marketing	GM, Global Supply Chain	Steve Grey, VP, Global Technology	David B. Tucker, VP, Global Sales	CFO

Quality Leader and CIO

Regional Leaders

- Timothy Schweikert, President, Transportation, China
- Pratt Kumar, India Operations Leader, GE Infrastructure
- President, Transportation Brazil

Division Leaders

- GM, Global Signaling
- GM, Propulsion & Specialty Services
- GM, Global Rail Operations
- Brett BeGole, GM, Commercial Operations
- GM, Services
- GM, Marine and Stationary Engines

Source: GE internal documents.

The Baby Grows into a Family   In April 2006, as members of the locomotive management team sat down to prepare for their presentation to Immelt at Transportation's Growth Playbook/Session I review in June, some of the initial ideas behind the GML concept were beginning to seem questionable. Doubts were being expressed by people from project management, marketing, and engineering about whether the GML's Lego design would work in practice. To resolve the concerns, Brett BeGole, Schweikert's replacement as global operations general manager for the Locomotive P&L unit, commissioned a "Tiger Team" of six people from engineering, product management, and marketing and gave them two weeks to recommend what changes, if any, should be made to the GML concept.

Much of the team's work was based on a rigorous analysis of a rich set of data on customers, competitors, and market trends that Gokhan Bayhan had assembled. Using CECOR tools including a customer needs analysis, a competitive response analysis, and a market segmentation map, Bayhan presented Steve Gray, his engineering counterpart on the Tiger Team, a rich picture of the critical technical and quality elements that customers were demanding.

After an intense two weeks of analysis, the team came to the conclusion that the GML concept was too complex and too expensive to serve the market efficiently. Instead, they proposed that GML's modular approach be replaced by a platform concept that defined five different families of locomotives, which together would serve 85% to 90% of the global market demand. Three of the five platforms to be developed were based on the Evo engine, while the two other family members would use another engine still under development.

The Tiger Team's recommendations were presented at Transportation's Growth Council in May, where Dineen backed their recommendation by committing to invest in the development engineering required for the Global Locomotive Families (GLF) ahead of any orders being received. It was a major change in practice for the business. With strong analysis and data to support the team's proposal and a clear commitment to invest in it, the new

GLF concept was quickly accepted and supported in July's Growth Playbook /Session I review with Immelt and became one of Transportation's official IBs.

The concept was soon validated when, in September of 2006, the Kazakhstan Railway placed an order for 310 locomotives; soon after, GE received an additional large order from a mining company in Australia; and before year's end it won a tender for 40 more locomotives in Egypt. Bayhan described it as the industry's "perfect storm":

> The big driver was what we call the "China Effect." Our analysis showed how increased trade with China is driving a big surge in demand for all forms of transportation. Around the world, GDP is growing, industrialization is happening, and the China Effect is spreading to other countries. And we were right there when it happened with a good understanding of the customers' needs and the newest technology to meet them. So we were able to respond to the perfect storm with a great product, the right commercial strategy, and perfect market timing.

Like the China order nine months earlier, the big Kazakhstan order came with a condition that after building the first 10 locomotives in Erie, GE would commit to transferring the assembly operation to Kazakhstan in the second half of 2008. The facility would assemble kits shipped from Erie and would become the regional source for locomotives sold to other countries in the CIS (the Commonwealth of Independent States, consisting of 11 former Soviet Republics in Eurasia). It was part of GE's "In Country, For Country" international strategy, and a matter of great pride for the country's prime minister, who proudly announced that Kazakhstan had locomotives with the same technology as the U.S. models.

The Morphing Continues: The New Regional Strategy   As the locomotive contract negotiations were being finalized, they provided a convenient market entrée to other parts of GE's transportation business. In particular, the sales and marketing people from the Services and Signaling P&Ls began using the Locomotive team's contacts to introduce their own products and services. For example, Transportation's Service P&L planned to link any new locomotive sales with a service contract to renew and refurbish worn components locally rather than replacing them with imported new parts. Not only could they promise to save the customer money, they could offer to transfer technology and bring employment to the country.

As initiatives such as this became the norm in markets where locomotive contracts had been signed, the management team of the Locomotive P&L began to explore whether an integrated regional approach to growth might be a more effective business model than the product-based Global Families approach. It was an approach that Comte believed had great value. As he grew the Transportation marketing staff from 14 people to 32, he began moving a significant number of them out of Erie and into the field where they could be closer to the customer. As part of a new geographic-based capability, he deployed seven Regional Marketing Strategists, each of whom built

his own local capabilities to support Transportation's regional general managers. (See **Exhibit 8** for Transportation's marketing organization.)

In December 2006, when the message came down that the Commercial Council would like to see businesses submitting more IB proposals for new emerging countries, it gave support to the growing notion that there was a need to reconfigure the global locomotive IB project once again. One proposal was to morph the major thrust of the GLF project into three integrated regional IBs—one for China, one for Russia/CIS, and one for India—each responsible for driving growth by developing its market for an integrated package of GE locomotives, signals, services, etc. It was an intriguing idea with the potential to roll out to other regions, but would mark the third iteration of this IB in its young, less than 18 month life. Some were concerned that it might seem like project churning.

Exhibit 8   Comte's Marketing Organization

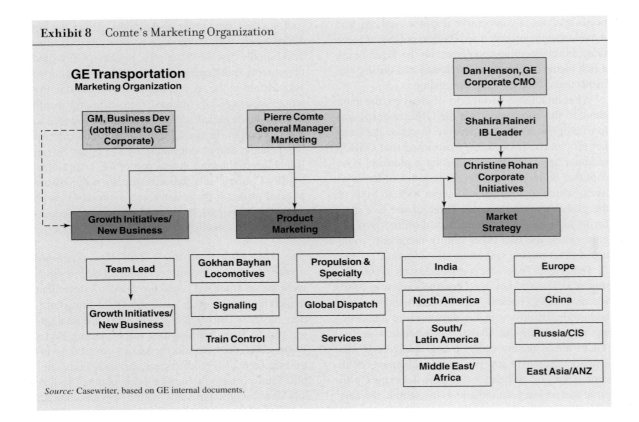

Source: Casewriter, based on GE internal documents.

The Hybrid Engine Dilemma: To Be or Not to Be?

At the same December IB Review, the Transportation business was also scheduled to present its latest plans for the Hybrid Locomotive IB. As the entire management team understood, almost three years earlier the Hybrid had captured Immelt's attention as a perfect candidate to fit into the company's just-announced Ecomagination program committed to environmentally responsive innovation. Indeed, it had been the CEO's suggestion to elevate the research on the Hybrid engine and to give it IB status. As he had publicly stated, the Hybrid Locomotive represented "the right solution for the customer, for the market, for the environment, and for GE."

The plans for the Hybrid were centered on a diesel-electric engine that would capture the energy generated during braking and store it in a series of sophisticated batteries. That stored energy could then be used on demand, reducing fuel consumption by as much as 15% and emissions by as much as 50% compared with freight locomotives already in service.[8] But as the concept was translated into a product, it became clear that the battery technology at the core of its design was not able to achieve the proposed customer benefits or provide them at a cost that would make the project economical. As a result, three years into the program, there was no clear evidence that the Hybrid IB would be able to meet any of its original stated objectives—to add value to the customer, to provide returns to GE, and to allow access to new markets. This led some to suggest that the Hybrid should join of the lapsed IBs that had been declared "worthwhile experiments that did not work out."

At Transportation's monthly Growth Council preparing for Immelt's December IB Review, Dineen, BeGole, and Comte explored the options. BeGole argued that with all the opportunities available in other product-line extensions and geographic expansions, the opportunity cost of the Hybrid project was very high. Specifically, he explained that because of his limited finances and engineering resources (particularly the latter), committing to this option would mean postponing the

rollout of some of the promising new international regional platforms for Evo.

On the other hand, as Compte reminded the team, the long-term trend away from fossil fuels and toward alternative energy meant that eventually GE would have to develop hybrid technology. Knowing Immelt's commitment to the Hybrid project, Compte asked whether the team had done enough to understand how customer value could be created in different segments, to explore alternative technological solutions, or to pursue other sources of funding. On the last point, he explained that while his marketing organization had located some potential government funding for hybrid development, they had not applied for funds since this was not GE's normal approach to project financing. In response to questioning, however, Compte acknowledge that even with such additional funds, investing in the Hybrid would mean diverting resources from other growth prospects that seemed more immediately promising.

As Dineen summarized the discussions, he posed three alternative scenarios that could be presented at the December IB Review:

- The first option would be to explain that while the project as currently defined appeared to have very limited to short- to medium-term commercial viability, the business would commit to it as an IB and continue to explore alternative ways to make it successful.
- The second approach would be to acknowledge the Hybrid's long-term potential, but suggest that it be placed on hold as an IB, perhaps by transferring primary responsibility to the Global Research Center to work on the battery technology in collaboration with various GE businesses—including Transportation—that had an interest in its development.
- The final alternative would be to recommend that the company acknowledge the fact that after three years of hard work on Hybrid, neither the technology development nor the market acceptance of the concept had indicated that it could be a viable commercial proposition in the foreseeable future, and therefore that it be dropped as an IB.

---

[8]For a detailed exposition of scope economies, see W. J. Baumol, J. C. Panzer, and R. D. Willig, *Contestable Markets and the Theory of Industry Structure* (New York: Harcourt Brace Jovanovich, 1982).

As the management team talked through these options, they tried to balance the best interest of the business with what Immelt was likely to believe was in the best interests of the company. With 83 IBs now approved, and 35 already launched and generating more than $2 billion in additional revenues, the CEO and felt that the process of generating organic growth was established. But that did not mean that he was becoming less involved. He personally tracked every IB, and focused even more intently on those that had caught his attention—like the Hybrid Locomotive. But in true GE fashion, he also held each business responsible for its current performance. As Transportation's management team realized, determining the Hybrid's future was a tough and vital decision that it must now make.

Reading 3-1   Managing Differences: The Central Challenge of Global Strategy

by Pankaj Ghemawat

When it comes to global strategy, most business leaders and academics make two assumptions: first, that the central challenge is to strike the right balance between economies of scale and responsiveness to local conditions, and second, that the more emphasis companies place on scale economies in their worldwide operations, the more global their strategies will be.

These assumptions are problematic. The main goal of any global strategy must be to manage the large differences that arise at borders, whether those borders are defined geographically or otherwise. (Strategies of standardization and those of local responsiveness are both conceivably valid responses to that challenge—both, in other words, are global strategies.) Moreover, assuming that the principal tension in global strategy is between scale economies and local responsiveness encourages companies to ignore another functional response to the challenge of cross-border integration: arbitrage. Some companies are finding large opportunities for value creation in exploiting, rather than simply adjusting to or overcoming, the differences they encounter at the borders of their various markets. As a result, we increasingly see value chains spanning multiple countries. IBM's CEO, Sam Palmisano, noted in a recent *Foreign Affairs* article that an estimated 60,000 manufacturing plants were built by foreign firms in China alone between 2000 and 2003. And trade in IT-enabled services—with India accounting for more than half of IT and business-process offshoring in 2005—is finally starting to have a measurable effect on international trade in services overall.

In this article, I present a new framework for approaching global integration that gets around the problems outlined above. I call it the AAA Triangle. The three A's stand for the three distinct types of global strategy. *Adaptation* seeks to boost revenues and market share by maximizing a firm's local relevance. One extreme example is simply creating local units in each national market that do a pretty good job of carrying out all the steps in the supply chain; many companies use this strategy as they start

▌ **Pankaj Ghemawat** is the Anselmo Rubiralta Professor of Global Strategy at IESE Business School in Barcelona, Spain, and the Jaime and Josefina Chua Tiampo Professor of Business Administration at Harvard Business School in Boston. He is the author of "Regional Strategies for Global Leadership" (HBR December 2005) and the forthcoming book *Redefining Global Strategy: Crossing Borders in a World Where Differences Still Matter,* which will be published in September 2007 by Harvard Business School Press.

expanding beyond their home markets. *Aggregation* attempts to deliver economies of scale by creating regional or sometimes global operations; it involves standardizing the product or service offering and grouping together the development and production processes. *Arbitrage* is the exploitation of differences between national or regional markets, often by locating separate parts of the supply chain in different places—for instance, call centers in India, factories in China, and retail shops in Western Europe.

Because most border-crossing enterprises will draw from all three A's to some extent, the framework can be used to develop a summary scorecard indicating how well the company is globalizing. However, because of the significant tensions within and among the approaches, it's not enough to tick off the boxes corresponding to all three. Strategic choice requires some degree of prioritization—and the framework can help with that as well.

Understanding the AAA Triangle

Underlying the AAA Triangle is the premise that companies growing their businesses outside the home market must choose one or more of three basic strategic options: adaptation, aggregation, and arbitrage. These types of strategy differ in a number of important ways, as summarized in the exhibit "What Are Your Globalization Options?"

The three A's are associated with different organizational types. If a company is emphasizing adaptation, it probably has a country-centered organization. If aggregation is the primary objective, cross-border groupings of various sorts—global business units or product divisions, regional structures, global accounts, and so on—make sense. An emphasis on arbitrage is often best pursued by a vertical, or functional, organization that pays explicit attention to the balancing of supply and demand within and across organizational boundaries. Clearly, not all three modes of organizing can take precedence in one organization at the same time. And although some approaches to corporate organization (such as the matrix) can combine elements of more than one pure mode, they carry costs in terms of managerial complexity.

Most companies will emphasize different A's at different points in their evolution as global enterprises, and some will run through all three. IBM is a case in point. (This characterization of IBM and those of the firms that follow are informed by interviews with the CEOs and other executives.) For most of its history, IBM pursued an adaptation strategy, serving overseas markets by setting up a mini-IBM in each target country. Every one of these companies performed a largely complete set of activities (apart from R&D and resource allocation) and adapted to local differences as necessary. In the 1980s and 1990s, dissatisfaction with the extent to which country-by-country adaptation curtailed opportunities to gain international scale economies led to the overlay of a regional structure on the mini-IBMs. IBM aggregated the countries into regions in order to improve coordination and thus generate more scale economies at the regional and global levels. More recently, however, IBM has also begun to exploit differences across countries. The most visible signs of this new emphasis on arbitrage (not a term the company's leadership uses) are IBM's efforts to exploit wage differentials by increasing the number of employees in India from 9,000 in 2004 to 43,000 by mid-2006 and by planning for massive additional growth. Most of these employees are in IBM Global Services, the part of the company that is growing fastest but has the lowest margins—which they are supposed to help improve, presumably by reducing costs rather than raising prices.

Procter & Gamble started out like IBM, with mini-P&Gs that tried to fit into local markets, but it has evolved differently. The company's global business units now sell through market development organizations that are aggregated up to the regional level. CEO A.G. Lafley explains that while P&G remains willing to adapt to important markets, it ultimately aims to beat competitors—country-centered multinationals as well as local companies—through aggregation. He also makes it clear that arbitrage is important to P&G (mostly through outsourcing) but takes a backseat to both adaptation and aggregation: "If it touches the customer, we don't outsource it." One obvious reason is that the scope for labor arbitrage in the fast-moving consumer goods industry may be increasing but is still much less substantial overall than in, say, IT services. As these examples show, industries vary in terms of the headroom they offer for each of the three A strategies.

Even within the same industry, firms can differ sharply in their global strategic profiles. For a paired example that takes us beyond behemoths from advanced countries, consider two of the leading IT services companies that develop software in India: Tata Consultancy Services, or TCS, and Cognizant Technology Solutions. TCS, the largest such firm, started exporting software services from India more than 30 years ago and has long stressed arbitrage. Over the past four years, though, I have closely watched and even been involved in its development of a network delivery model to aggregate within and across regions. Cognizant, the fourth largest, also started out with arbitrage and still considers that to be its main strategy but has begun to invest more heavily in adaptation to achieve local presence in the U.S. market in particular. (Although the company is headquartered in the United States, most of its software development centers and employees are in India.)

The AAA Triangle allows managers to see which of the three strategies—or which combination—is likely to afford the most leverage for their companies or in their industries overall. Expense items from businesses' income statements provide rough-and-ready proxies for the importance of each of the three A's. Companies that do a lot of advertising will need to adapt to the local market. Those that do a lot of R&D may want to aggregate to improve economies of scale, since many R&D outlays are fixed costs. For firms whose operations are labor intensive, arbitrage will be of particular concern because labor costs vary greatly from country to country. By calculating these three types of expenses as percentages of sales, a company can get a picture of how intensely it is pursuing each course. Those that score in the top decile of companies along any of the three dimensions—advertising intensity, R&D

intensity, or labor intensity—should be on alert. (See the exhibit "The AAA Triangle" for more detail on the framework.)

How do the companies I've already mentioned look when their expenditures are mapped on the AAA Triangle? At Procter & Gamble, businesses tend to cluster in the top quartile for advertising intensity, indicating the appropriateness of an adaptation strategy. TCS, Cognizant, and IBM Global Services are distinguished by their labor intensity, indicating arbitrage potential. But IBM Systems ranks significantly higher in R&D intensity than in labor intensity and, by implication, has greater potential for aggregation than for arbitrage.

From A to AA

Although many companies will (and should) follow a strategy that involves the focused pursuit of just one of the three A's, some leading-edge companies—IBM, P&G, TCS, and Cognizant among them—are attempting to perform two A's particularly well. Success in "AA strategies" takes two forms. In some cases, a company wins because it actually beats competitors along both dimensions at once. More commonly, however, a company wins because it manages the tensions between two A's better than its competitors do.

The pursuit of AA strategies requires considerable organizational and material innovation. Companies must do more than just allocate resources and monitor national operations from headquarters. They need to deploy a broad array of integrative devices, ranging from the hard (for instance, structures and systems) to the soft (for instance, style and socialization). Let's look at some examples.

Adaptation and Aggregation   As I noted above, Procter & Gamble started out with an adaptation strategy. Halting attempts at aggregation across Europe, in particular, led to a drawn-out, function-by-function installation of a matrix structure throughout the 1980s, but the matrix proved unwieldy. So in 1999, the new CEO, Durk Jager, announced the reorganization mentioned earlier, whereby global business units (GBUs) retained

What Are Your Globalization Options?

When managers first hear about the broad strategies (adaptation, aggregation, and arbitrage) that make up the AAA Triangle framework for globalization, their most common response by far is "Let's do all three" But it's not that simple. A close look at the three strategies reveals the differences—and tensions—among them. Business leaders must figure out which elements will meet their companies' needs and prioritize accordingly.

	ADAPTATION	AGGREGATION	ARBITRAGE
Competitive Advantage Why should we globalize at all?	To achieve local relevance through national focus while exploiting some economies of scale	To achieve scale and scope economies through international standardization	To achieve absolute economies through international specialization
Configuration Where should we locate operations overseas?	Mainly in foreign countries that are similar to the home base, to limit the effects of cultural, administrative, geographic, and economic distance		In a more diverse set of countries, to exploit some elements of distance
Coordination How should we connect international operations?	By country, with emphasis on achieving local presence within borders	By business, region, or custom, with emphasis on horizontal relationships for cross-border economies of scale	By function, with emphasis on vertical relationships, even across organizational boundaries
Controls What types of extremes should we watch for?	Excessive variety or complexity	Excessive standardization, with emphasis on scale	Narrowing spreads
Change Blockers Whom should we watch out for internally?	Entrenched country chiefs	All-powerful unit, regional, or account heads	Heads of key functions
Corporate Diplomacy How should we approach corporate diplomacy?	Address issues of concern, but proceed with discretion, given the emphasis on cultivating local presence	Avoid the appearance of homogenization or hegemonism (especially for U.S. companies); be sensitive to any backlash	Address the exploitation or displacement of suppliers, channels, or intermediaries, which are potentially most prone to political disruption
Corporate Strategy What strategic levers do we have?	Scope selection Variation Decentralization Partitioning Modularization Flexibility Partnership Recombination Innovation	Regions and other country groupings Product or business Function Platform Competence Client industry	Cultural (country-of-origin effects) Administrative (taxes, regulations, security) Geographic (distance, climate differences) Economic (differences in prices, resources, knowledge)

ultimate profit responsibility but were complemented by geographic market development organizations (MDOs) that actually ran the sales force
(shared across GBUs) and went to market.

The result? All hell broke loose in multiple areas,
including at the key GBU/MDO interfaces. Jager
departed after less than a year. Under his successor,
Lafley, P&G has enjoyed much more success, with
an approach that strikes more of a balance between
adaptation and aggregation and allows room for differences across general business units and markets.
Thus, its pharmaceuticals division, with distinct distribution channels, has been left out of the MDO
structure; in emerging markets, where market development challenges loom large, profit responsibility
continues to be vested with country managers. Also
important are the company's decision grids, which
are devised after months of negotiation. These define protocols for how different decisions are to be
made, and by whom—the general business units
or the market development organizations—while
still generally reserving responsibility for profits
(and the right to make decisions not covered by the
grids) for the GBUs. Common IT systems help with
integration as well. This structure is animated by an
elaborate cycle of reviews at multiple levels.

Such structures and systems are supplemented
with other, softer tools, which promote mutual understanding and collaboration. Thus, the GBUs'
regional headquarters are often collocated with the
headquarters of regional MDOs. Promotion to the
director level or beyond generally requires experience on both the GBU and the MDO sides of the
house. The implied crisscrossing of career paths
reinforces the message that people within the two
realms are equal citizens. As another safeguard
against the MDOs' feeling marginalized by a lack
of profit responsibility, P&G created a structure—
initially anchored by the vice chairman of global
operations, Robert McDonald—to focus on their
perspectives and concerns.

Aggregation and Arbitrage In contrast to
Procter & Gamble, TCS is targeting a balance between
aggregation and arbitrage. To obtain the benefits of aggregation without losing its traditional arbitrage-based

competitive advantage, it has placed great emphasis
on its global network delivery model, which aims to
build a coherent delivery structure that consists of
three kinds of software development centers:

- The global centers serve large customers and
  have breadth and depth of skill, very high scales,
  and mature coding and quality control processes. These centers are located in India, but some
  are under development in China, where TCS
  was the first Indian software firm to set up shop.
- The regional centers (such as those in Uruguay,
  Brazil, and Hungary) have medium scales, select capabilities, and an emphasis on addressing
  language and cultural challenges. These centers
  offer some arbitrage economies, although not
  yet as sizable as those created by the global
  centers in India.
- The nearshore centers (such as those in Boston
  and Phoenix) have small scales and focus on
  building customer comfort through proximity.

In addition to helping improve TCS's economics in a number of ways, a coherent global delivery
structure also seems to hold potential for significant international revenue gains. For example, in
September 2005, TCS announced the signing of
a five-year, multinational contract with the Dutch
bank ABN AMRO that's expected to generate
more than €200 million. IBM won a much bigger
deal from ABN AMRO, but TCS's deal did represent the largest such contract ever for an Indian
software firm and is regarded by the company's
management as a breakthrough in its attempts to
compete with IBM Global Services and Accenture.
According to CEO S. Ramadorai, TCS managed to
beat out its Indian competitors, including one that
was already established at ABN AMRO, largely
because it was the only Indian vendor positioned
to deploy several hundred professionals to meet the
application development and maintenance needs of
ABN AMRO's Brazilian operations.

Arbitrage and Adaptation Cognizant has taken
another approach and emphasized arbitrage and adaptation by investing heavily in a local presence in

The AAA Triangle

The AAA Triangle serves as a kind of strategy map for managers. The percentage of sales spent on advertising indicates how important adaptation is likely to be for the company; the percentage spent on R&D is a proxy for the importance of aggregation; and the percentage spent on labor helps gauge the importance of arbitrage. Managers should pay attention to any scores above the median because, most likely, those are areas that merit strategic focus. Scores above the 90th percentile may be perilous to ignore.

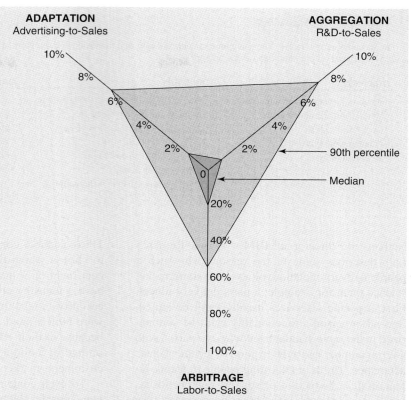

Median and top-decile scores are based on U.S. manufacturing data from Compustat's Global Vantage database and the U.S. Census Bureau. Since the ratios of advertising and R&D to sales rarely exceed 10%, those are given a maximum value of 10% in the chart.

its key market, the United States, to the point where it can pass itself off as either Indian or U.S.-based, depending on the occasion.

Cognizant began life in 1994 as a captive of Dun & Bradstreet, with a more balanced distribution of power than purely Indian firms have. When Cognizant spun off from D&B a couple of years later, founder Kumar Mahadeva dealt with customers in the United States, while Lakshmi Narayanan (then COO, now vice chairman) oversaw delivery out of India. The company soon set up a two-in-a-box structure, in which there were always two global leads for each project—one in India and one in the United States—who were held jointly accountable and were compensated in the same way. Francisco D'Souza, Cognizant's CEO, recalls that it took two years to implement this structure and

even longer to change mind-sets—at a time when there were fewer than 600 employees (compared with more than 24,000 now). As the exhibit "Cognizant's AA Strategy" shows, two-in-a-box is just one element, albeit an important one, of a broad, cross-functional effort to get past what management sees as the key integration challenge in global offshoring: poor coordination between delivery and marketing that leads to "tossing stuff over the wall."

Not all of the innovations that enable AA strategies are structural. At the heart of IBM's recent arbitrage initiatives (which have been added to the company's aggregation strategy) is a sophisticated matching algorithm that can dynamically optimize people's assignments across all of IBM's locations—a critical capability because of the speed with which "hot" and "cold" skills can change. Krisha

Cognizant's AA Strategy

Cognizant is experimenting with changes in staffing, delivery, and marketing in its pursuit of a strategy that emphasizes both adaptation and arbitrage.

STAFFING	DELIVERY	MARKETING
• Relatively stringent recruiting process • More MBAs and consultants • More non-Indians • Training programs in India for acculturation	• Two global leads—one in the U.S., one in India—for each project • All proposals done jointly (between India and the U.S.) • More proximity to customers • On-site kickoff teams • Intensive travel, use of technology	• Joint Indian—U.S. positioning • Use of U.S. nationals in key marketing positions • Very senior relationship managers • Focus on selling to a small number of large customers

Nathan, the director of IBM's Zurich Research Lab, describes some of the reasons why such a people delivery model involves much more rocket science than, for example, a parts delivery model. First, a person's services usually can't be stored. Second, a person's functionality can't be summarized in the same standardized way as a part's, with a serial number and a description of technical characteristics. Third, in allocating people to teams, attention must be paid to personality and chemistry, which can make the team either more or less than the sum of its parts; not so with machines. Fourth, for that reason and others (employee development, for instance), assignment durations and sequencing are additionally constrained. Nathan describes the resultant assignment patterns as "75% global and 25% local." While this may be more aspirational than actual, it is clear that to the extent such matching devices are being used more effectively for arbitrage, they represent a massive power shift in a company that has hitherto eschewed arbitrage.

The Elusive Trifecta

There are serious constraints on the ability of any one organization to use all three A's simultaneously with great effectiveness. First, the complexity of doing so collides with limited managerial bandwidth. Second, many people think an organization should have only one culture, and that can get in the way of hitting multiple strategic targets.

Third, capable competitors can force a company to choose which dimension it is going to try to beat them on. Finally, external relationships may have a focusing effect as well. For instance, several private-label manufacturers whose businesses were built around arbitrage have run into trouble because of their efforts to aggregate as well as arbitrage by building up their own brands in their customers' markets.

To even contemplate a AAA strategy, a company must be operating in an environment in which the tensions among adaptation, aggregation, and arbitrage are weak or can be overridden by large scale economies or structural advantages, or in which competitors are otherwise constrained.

Consider GE Healthcare (GEH). The diagnostic-imaging industry has been growing rapidly and has concentrated globally in the hands of three large firms, which together command an estimated 75% of revenues in the business worldwide: GEH, with 30%; Siemens Medical Solutions (SMS), with 25%; and Philips Medical Systems (PMS), with 20%.[1] This high degree of concentration is probably related to the fact that the industry ranks in the 90th percentile in terms of R&D intensity. R&D

[1]Figures are for 2005. Otherwise, the account is largely based on Tarun Khanna and Elizabeth A. Raabe, "General Electric Healthcare, 2006" (HBS case no. 9-706-478); D. Quinn Mills and Julian Kurz, "Siemens Medical Solutions: Strategic Turnaround" (HBS case no. 9-703-494); and PankajGhemawat, "Philips Medical Systems in 2005" (HBS case no. 9-706-488).

expenditures are greater than 10% of sales for the "big three" competitors and even higher for smaller rivals, many of whom face profit squeezes. All of this suggests that the aggregation-related challenge of building global scale has proven particularly important in the industry in recent years.

GEH, the largest of the three firms, has also consistently been the most profitable. This reflects its success at aggregation, as indicated by the following:

Economies of Scale   GEH has higher total R&D spending than SMS or PMS, greater total sales, and a larger service force (constituting half of GEH's total employee head count)—but its R&D-to-sales ratio is lower, its other expense ratios are comparable, and it has fewer major production sites.

Acquisition Capabilities   Through experience, GEH has become more efficient at acquiring. It made nearly 100 acquisitions under Jeffrey Immelt (before he became GE's CEO); since then, it has continued to do a lot of acquiring, including the $9.5 billion Amersham deal in 2004, which moved the company beyond metal boxes and into medicine.

Economies of Scope   The company strives, through Amersham, to integrate its biochemistry skills with its traditional base of physics and engineering skills; it finances equipment purchases through GE Capital.

GEH has even more clearly outpaced its competitors through arbitrage. Under Immelt, but especially more recently, it has moved to become a global product company by migrating rapidly to low-cost production bases. Moves have been facilitated by a "pitcher-catcher" concept originally developed elsewhere in GE: A "pitching team" at the existing site works closely with a "catching team" at the new site until the latter's performance is at least as strong as the former's. By 2005, GEH was reportedly more than halfway to its goals of purchasing 50% of its materials directly from low-cost countries and locating 60% of its manufacturing in such countries.

In terms of adaptation, GEH has invested heavily in country-focused marketing organizations,

coupling such investments relatively loosely with the integrated development-and-manufacturing back end, with objectives that one executive characterizes as being "more German than the Germans." It also boosts customer appeal with its emphasis on providing services as well as equipment—for example, by training radiologists and providing consulting advice on post-image processing. Such customer intimacy obviously has to be tailored by country. And recently, GEH has cautiously engaged in some "in China, for China" manufacture of stripped-down, cheaper equipment aimed at increasing penetration there.

GEH has managed to use the three A's to the extent that it has partly by separating the three and, paradoxically, by downplaying the pursuit of one of them: adaptation. This is one example of how companies can get around the problem of limited managerial bandwidth. Others range from outsourcing to the use of more market or marketlike

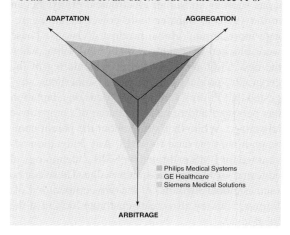

**AAA Competitive Map
for Diagnostic Imaging**

Philips Medical Systems, the smallest of the big three diagnostic-imaging firms, historically emphasized adaptation but has recently placed some focus on aggregation. Siemens Medical Solutions emphasizes aggregation and uses some arbitrage. The most successful of the three, GE Healthcare, beats each of its rivals on two out of the three A's.

mechanisms, such as internal markets. GEH's success has also depended on competitors' weaknesses. In addition to facing a variety of size-related and other structural disadvantages relative to GEH, SMS and particularly PMS have been slow in some respects—for instance, in shifting production to low-cost countries. For all these reasons, the temptation to treat the GEH example as an open invitation for everyone to pursue all three A's should be stubbornly resisted.

Besides, the jury is still out on GEH. Adapting to the exceptional requirements of potentially large but low-income markets such as China and India while trying to integrate globally is likely to be an ongoing tension for the company. What's more, GEH isn't clearly ahead on all performance dimensions: SMS has focused more on core imaging, where it is seen as the technological leader.

Developing a AAA Strategy

Let's now consider how a company might use the AAA Triangle to put together a globally competitive strategy. The example I'll use here will be PMS, the smallest of the big three diagnostic-imaging firms.

At a corporate level, Philips had long followed a highly decentralized strategy that concentrated significant power in the hands of country managers and emphasized adaptation. Under pressure from more aggregation-oriented Japanese competitors in areas such as consumer electronics, efforts began in the 1970s to transfer more power to and aggregate more around global product divisions. These were blocked by country chiefs until 1996, when the new CEO abolished the geographic leg of the geography-product matrix. It is sometimes suggested that Philips's traditional focus on adaptation has persisted and remains a source of competitive advantage. While that's true about the parent company, it isn't the case for PMS. Any adaptation advantage for PMS is limited by SMS's technological edge and GEH's service-quality edge. These can be seen as global attributes of the two competitors' offerings, but they also create customer lock-in at the local level.

More generally, any adaptation advantage at PMS is more than offset by its aggregation disadvantages. PMS's absolute R&D expenditures are one-third lower than those of GEH and one-quarter lower than those of SMS, and PMS is a much larger part of a much smaller corporation than its rivals are. (Philips's total acquisition war chest at the corporate level was recently reported to be not much larger than the amount that GEH put down for the Amersham acquisition alone.) In addition, PMS was stitched together out of six separate companies in a series of acquisitions made over three years to improve the original and aging X-ray technology. It is somewhat surprising that this attempt has worked as well as it has in a corporation without much acquisition experience to fall back on—but there have also clearly been negative aftereffects. Most dramatically, PMS paid more than €700 million in 2004 related to past acquisition attempts—one consummated, another considered—nearly wiping out its reported earnings for that year, although profitability did recover nicely in 2005.

PMS's preoccupation (until recently) with connecting its disparate parts is also somewhat to blame for the company's lack of progress on the arbitrage front. PMS has trailed not only its rivals but also other Philips divisions in moving manufacturing to low-cost areas, particularly China. Although Philips claims to be the largest Western multinational in China, PMS did not start a manufacturing joint venture there until September 2004, with the first output for the Chinese market becoming available in 2005 and the first supplies for export in 2006. Overall, PMS's sourcing levels from low-cost countries in 2005 were comparable to levels GEH achieved back in 2001, and they lagged SMS's as well.

Insights on positioning relative to the three A's can be pulled together into a single map, as shown in the exhibit "AAA Competitive Map for Diagnostic Imaging." Assessments along these lines, while always approximate, call attention to where competitors are actually located in strategy space; they also help companies visualize trade-offs across different A's. Both factors are important in thinking through where and where not to focus the organization's efforts.

How might this representation be used to articulate an action agenda for PMS? The two most obvious strategy alternatives for PMS are AA strategies: adaptation-aggregation and adaptation-arbitrage.

Adaptation-aggregation comes closest to the strategy currently in place. However, it is unlikely to solve the aggregation-related challenges facing PMS, so it had better offer some meaningful extras in terms of local responsiveness. PMS could also give up on the idea of creating a competitive advantage and simply be content with achieving average industry profitability, which is high: The big three diagnostic-imaging companies (which also account for another profitable global triopoly, in light bulbs) are described as "gentlemanly" in setting prices. Either way, imitation of bigger rivals' large-scale moves into entirely new areas seems likely to magnify, rather than minimize, this source of disadvantage. PMS does appear to be exercising some discipline in this regard, preferring to engage in joint ventures and other relatively small-scale moves rather than any Amersham-sized acquisitions.

The adaptation-arbitrage alternative would aim not just at producing in low-cost locations but also at radically reengineering and simplifying the product to slash costs for large emerging markets in China, India, and so forth. However, this option does not fit with Philips's heritage, which is not one of competing through low costs. And PMS has less room to follow a strategy of this sort because of GEH's "in China, for China" product, which is supposed to cut costs by 50%. PMS, in contrast, is talking of cost reductions of 20% for its first line of Chinese offerings.

If PMS found neither of these alternatives appealing—and frankly, neither seems likely to lead to a competitive advantage for the company—it could try to change the game entirely. Although PMS seems stuck with structural disadvantages in core diagnostic imaging compared with GEH and SMS, it could look for related fields in which its adaptation profile might have more advantages and fewer disadvantages. In terms of the AAA Triangle, this would be best thought of as a lateral shift

to a new area of business, where the organization would have more of a competitive advantage. PMS does seem to be attempting something along these lines—albeit slowly—with its recent emphasis on medical devices for people to use at home. As former Philips CFO Jan Hommen puts it, the company has an advantage here over both Siemens and GE: "With our consumer electronics and domestic appliances businesses, we have gained a lot of experience and knowledge." The flip side, though, is that PMS starts competing with large companies such as Johnson & Johnson. PMS's first product of this sort—launched in the United States and retailing for around $1,500—is a home-use defibrillator. Note also that the resources emphasized in this strategy—that is, brand and distribution—operate at the local (national) level. So the new strategy can be seen as focusing on adaptation in a new market.

What do these strategic considerations imply for integration at PMS? The company needs to continue streamlining operations and speed up attempts at arbitrage, possibly considering tools such as the pitcher-catcher concept. It needs to think about geographic variation, probably at the regional level, given the variation in industry attractiveness as well as PMS's average market share across regions. Finally, it needs to enable its at-home devices business to tap Philips's consumer electronics division for resources and capabilities. This last item is especially important because, in light of its track record thus far, PMS will have to make some early wins if it is to generate any excitement around a relaunch.

Broader Lessons

The danger in discussions about integration is that they can float off into the realm of the ethereal. That's why I went into specifics about the integration challenges facing PMS—and it's why it seems like a good idea to wrap this article up by recapitulating the general points outlined.

Focus on One or Two of the A's   While it is possible to make progress on all three A's—especially for a firm that is coming from behind—companies (or, often more to the point, businesses or divisions) usually have to focus on one or at most two A's in trying to build competitive advantage. Can your organization agree on what they are? It may have to shift its focus across the A's as the company's needs change. IBM is just one example of a general shift toward arbitrage. But the examples of IBM, P&G, and, in particular, PMS illustrate how long such shifts can take—and the importance, therefore, of looking ahead when deciding what to focus on.

Make Sure the New Elements of a Strategy Are a Good Fit Organizationally   While this isn't a fixed rule, if your strategy does embody nontrivially new elements, you should pay particular attention to how well they work with other things the organization is doing. IBM has grown its staff in India much faster than other international competitors (such as Accenture) that have begun to emphasize India-based arbitrage. But quickly molding this workforce into an efficient organization with high delivery standards and a sense of connection to the parent company is a critical challenge: Failure in this regard might even be fatal to the arbitrage initiative.

Employ Multiple Integration Mechanisms   Pursuit of more than one of the A's requires creativity and breadth in thinking about integration mechanisms. Given the stakes, these factors can't be left to chance. In addition to IBM's algorithm for matching people to opportunities, the company has demonstrated creativity in devising "deal hubs" to aggregate across its hardware, software, and services businesses. It has also reconsidered its previous assumption that global functional headquarters should be centralized (recently, IBM relocated its procurement office from Somers, New York, to Shenzhen, China). Of course, such creativity must be reinforced by organizational structures, systems, incentives, and norms conducive to integration, as at P&G. Also essential to making such integration work is an adequate supply of leaders and succession candidates of the right stripe.

Think About Externalizing Integration   Not all the integration that is required to add value across borders needs to occur within a single organization.

IBM and other firms illustrate that some externalization is a key part of most ambitious global strategies. It takes a diversity of forms: joint ventures in advanced semiconductor research, development, and manufacturing; links to and support of Linux and other efforts at open innovation; (some) outsourcing of hardware to contract manufacturers and services to business partners; IBM's relationship with Lenovo in personal computers; customer relationships governed by memoranda of understanding rather than detailed contracts. Reflecting this increased range of possibilities, reported levels of international joint ventures are running only one-quarter as high as they were in the mid-1990s, even though more companies are externalizing operations. Externalization offers advantages not just for outsourcing noncore services but also for obtaining ideas from the outside for core areas: for instance, Procter & Gamble's connect-and-develop program, IBM's innovation jams, and TCS's investments in involving customers in quality measurement and improvement.

Know When Not to Integrate   Some integration is always a good idea, but that is not to say that more integration is always better. First of all, very tightly coupled systems are not particularly flexible. Second, domain selection—in other words, knowing what not to do as well as what to do—is usually considered an essential part of strategy. Third, even when many diverse activities are housed within one organization, keeping them apart may be a better overall approach than forcing them together in, say, the bear hug of a matrix structure. As Lafley explains, the reason P&G is able to pursue arbitrage up to a point as well as adaptation and aggregation is that the company has deliberately separated these functions into three kinds of subunits (global business units, market development organizations, and global business shared services) and imposed a structure that minimizes points of contact and, thereby, friction.

• • •

For most of the past 25 years, the rhetoric of globalization has been concentrated on markets. Only recently has the spotlight turned to production, as firms have become aware of the arbitrage opportunities available through offshoring. This phenomenon appears to have outpaced strategic thinking about it. Many academic writings remain focused on the globalization (or nonglobalization) of markets. And only a tiny fraction of the many companies that engage in offshoring appear to think about it strategically: Only 1% of the respondents to a recent survey conducted by Arie Lewin at Duke University say that their company has a corporatewide strategy in this regard. The AAA framework provides a basis for considering global strategies that encompasses all three effective responses to the large differences that arise at national borders. Clearer thinking about the full range of strategy options should broaden the perceived opportunities, sharpen strategic choices, and enhance global performance.

A Supplemental Note from the Author

The fundamental strategic choice traditionally emphasized in the literature on international strategy concerns the extent to which a company stresses global integration and standardization versus differentiation and responsiveness to national or local markets. Focus on this choice can be traced at least as far back as John Fayerweather's discussion of the tension between pressures for unification within companies and the fragmentation that different national environments can create. C.K. Prahalad and Yves Doz, among others, elaborated this tension into the widely cited trade-off between global integration and national responsiveness. However, Prahalad and Doz also resisted the idea of multinationals embracing just one facet or the other: They stressed the existence of contexts in which it was necessary to be multifocal—that is, to manage both dimensions well (enough).

Even so, Prahalad and Doz continued to respect the basic integration-responsiveness trade-off. Subsequently, Chris Bartlett and Sumantra Ghoshal argued that companies could transcend the trade-off, or become *transnationals,* by performing three functions well—transferring knowledge internationally as well as building a local presence and centralizing global-scale operations—rather than just the two proposed by Prahalad and Doz. Note the emphasis on differences in knowledge—but *not* other kinds of international differences—in Bartlett and Ghoshal's formulation. Bartlett and Ghoshal's proposal also significantly increased the amount of organizational complexity required: While Prahalad and Doz were able to recommend matrix structures for multifocal businesses, nothing as clear-cut could be specified for transnationals.

Christopher A. Bartlett and Sumantra Ghoshal, *Managing Across Borders: The Transnational Solution* (Harvard Business School Press, 1989).

C.K. Prahalad and Yves L. Doz, *The Multinational Mission: Balancing Local Demands and Global Vision* (Free Press, 1987).

John Fayerweather, *International Business Management: A Conceptual Framework* (McGraw-Hill, 1969).

Yves L. Doz, "Strategic Management in Multinational Companies," *Sloan Management Review,* Winter 1980.

Reading 3-2   Capturing the World's Emerging Middle Class

David Court and Laxman Narasimhan

Multinational companies need new "scale at speed" approaches to penetrate the developing world's increasingly prosperous consumer markets.

The Rapidly Growing Ranks of middle-class consumers span a dozen emerging nations, not just the fast-growing BRIC countries,[1] and include almost two billion people, spending a total of $6.9 trillion annually. Our research suggests that this figure will rise to $20 trillion during the next decade—about twice the current consumption in the United States.

These new spenders offer an opportunity for early winners to gain lasting advantages, just as companies in Europe and the United States did at similar points in their development. In 17 product categories in the United States, for example, we found that the market leader in 1925 remained the number-one or number-two player for the rest of the century. These companies include Kraft Foods (Nabisco), which led in biscuits; Del Monte Foods, in canned fruit; and Wrigley, in chewing gum.

Despite having strong global brands, multinational companies face challenging competition in emerging markets, as these economies already boast aggressive local players that have captured a significant portion of spending. Chinese beverage maker Hangzhou Wahaha, for example, has built a $5.2 billion business against global competitors such as Coca-Cola and PepsiCo by targeting rural

▋ David Court is a director in McKinsey's Dallas office, and Laxman Narasimhan is a director in the Delhi office.
▋ Copyright © 2010 McKinsey & Company. All rights reserved. We welcome your comments on this article. Please send them to quarterly_comments@ mckinsey.com.
▋ *The authors would like to acknowledge the contributions of Georges Desvaux, Vinay Dixit, Martin Elling, John Forsyth, Prashant Gandhi, Trond Riiber Knudsen, Vikram Vaidyanathan, and Ireena Vittal to this article.*
▋ [1]Brazil, Russia, India, and China.

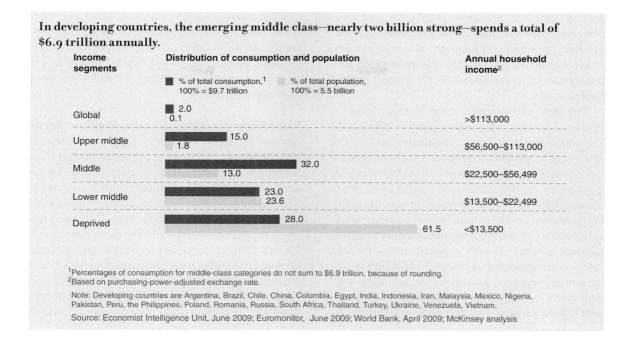

In developing countries, the emerging middle class—nearly two billion strong—spends a total of $6.9 trillion annually.

Income segments	Distribution of consumption and population	Annual household income[2]

- ■ % of total consumption,[1] 100% = $9.7 trillion
- ▨ % of total population, 100% = 5.5 billion

Income segments	% consumption	% population	Annual household income[2]
Global	2.0	0.1	>$113,000
Upper middle	15.0	1.8	$56,500–$113,000
Middle	32.0	13.0	$22,500–$56,499
Lower middle	23.0	23.6	$13,500–$22,499
Deprived	28.0	61.5	<$13,500

[1]Percentages of consumption for middle-class categories do not sum to $6.9 trillion, because of rounding.
[2]Based on purchasing-power-adjusted exchange rate.

Note: Developing countries are Argentina, Brazil, Chile, China, Colombia, Egypt, India, Indonesia, Iran, Malaysia, Mexico, Nigeria, Pakistan, Peru, the Philippines, Poland, Romania, Russia, South Africa, Thailand, Turkey, Ukraine, Venezuela, Vietnam.

Source: Economist Intelligence Unit, June 2009; Euromonitor, June 2009; World Bank, April 2009; McKinsey analysis

areas, filling product gaps that meet local needs, keeping costs low, and appealing to patriotism.

Further complicating matters is the fact that the multinationals' business models are based on practices established in the markets of the developed world, where the game is won slowly by finding cost savings and making product improvements that capture single percentage points of market share over time. Among emerging markets, perhaps only China can provide enough short-term growth to justify that strategy. Meeting the needs of most consumers in emerging markets requires a different course, which often elicits anguished cries in the corridors of the multinationals: "You want me to change my business model and go across the world for $50 million in revenue?" It's an understandable lament for executives who not only fear ending up with little to show for their efforts but also are wary of the battles already under way among emerging-market champions.

While there are multiple approaches to capturing emerging-market consumers, the two critical factors are speed and scale. Our experience suggests that one way multinationals can quickly gain the scale they need is to identify clusters of similar consumers across multiple markets. That approach allows these companies to build revenue and profit streams that are collectively material and justify significant, ongoing capital investments to fuel growth. Another tack is to work at a more local level, gaining scale in specific regions and categories by teaming up with deeply knowledgeable on-the-ground partners. They can help not only in product development but also in distribution and market positioning—the crucial final steps to reaching highly local consumer markets.

All of this is easier said than done, of course, because consumers in emerging markets are extremely diverse. In some ways, they resemble those in developed nations: they are aware of and have a fondness for brands and want access to a variety of products at different prices, including products they aspire to but can't currently afford. Yet their tastes are often localized, and while they are middle-class in regional terms,[2] they are still not wealthy

[2]We define *emerging middle-class consumers* as those with yearly incomes of $13,500 to $113,000, in purchasing-power-parity terms.

enough to replace products regularly, because their percentage of truly discretionary income is lower: in China and India, for example, about 40 percent of average household income is spent on food and transportation, compared with 25 percent in the United States.

The best way to make sense of this picture is to take a granular view using product categories. For individual categories, multinationals should first identify whether consumer needs in emerging markets are fundamentally global or local. A good proxy for this issue is the similarity of product offerings across geographies, as shown on the horizontal axis of the exhibit below. Second, multinationals can assess the consumer's ability to afford a given product. Useful approximations include category penetration and product availability in key developing markets, as well as the willingness of consumers to "stretch" to buy less-affordable products. By developing a perspective on whether and

to what extent consumer tastes are global or local and combining that with a clear view on the affordability and accessibility of a given product, multinationals can go a long way toward determining the strategies and business models that will allow them to gain scale quickly.

Identifying Consumers with Similar Needs Across Markets The first category, at the top right of the matrix, comprises products and services for which consumer needs are quite similar across geographies and affordability is not a constraint. There is little need to create marketing plans to roll out such products in different countries, one after another: we've found that it's most efficient to identify similar consumer segments across countries and to build scalable business models for each cluster. Examples of products in this category include personal banking, mobile communications, consumer electronics, and pharmaceuticals, which

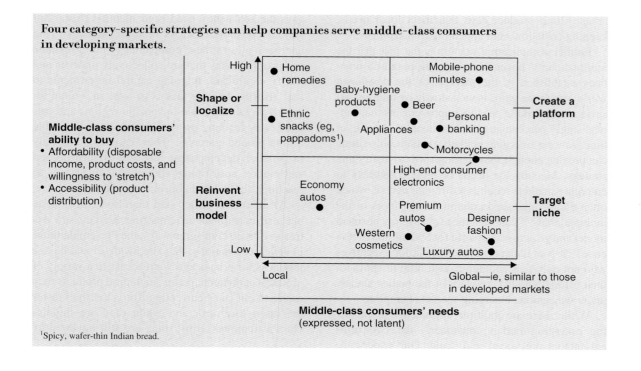

Four category-specific strategies can help companies serve middle-class consumers in developing markets.

¹Spicy, wafer-thin Indian bread.

have similar industry structures, rates of consumer adoption, and socioreligious factors across geographies.

A leading multinational retail bank's marketing team, for example, used longitudinal consumer data to identify five clusters across multiple Asian countries. These segments included one of conservative users very loyal to their local banks (in India, Indonesia, the Philippines, and Taiwan) and another of remote-channel users who were highly price sensitive (in Hong Kong, Singapore, and South Korea). The bank successfully designed and implemented a specific product and channel strategy for each of these five segments across countries.

Targeting Premium Consumers in Product Niches   The category on the bottom right of the matrix comprises emerging-market consumers who have the means to buy products and services that are widely available or even mass market in the developed world. (For the vast majority of the emerging middle class, however, these products and services are neither affordable nor accessible—they are premium items.) While we forecast that less than 3 percent of total emerging-market households will be in this bottom-right category in 2025, their prosperity and the fact that their behavior resembles that of consumers in the developed world has historically made this category appealing to multinationals.

Capturing the loyalty of these consumers and, as they develop new needs, upgrading them is the key. Since emerging-market consumers want value—even in this category—companies should offer products at "mass premium" price points. Consumer electronics manufacturer LG has found that people in many developing markets are more willing to pay for better service than are their counterparts in the developed world. The company launched a premium offering that not only gives consumers a full-time contact person who acts as a go-between with LG and monitors the health of products but also guarantees maintenance visits within 6 hours (compared with the normal 24-hour commitment).

Shaping the Market by Localizing   The third category, on the top left of the matrix, comprises affordable and accessible products, such as low-cost snacks and highly localized baby-care hygiene products.

In this category, there's clear merit in evaluating how companies can scale up across markets, even if needs are local. One approach is to shape the market through minor product enhancements and sharper positioning that encourages consumers to shift toward more globally convergent offerings over time and allows companies to enjoy greater economies of scale and lower delivery costs. In India, for example, PepsiCo successfully shaped the snack market by creating a new platform, called Kurkure, for younger consumers. The product feels entirely local, though it is packaged and distributed by Frito-Lay.

Other strategies for penetrating this affordable, accessible, and local market are to use celebrity endorsements and to leverage local knowledge, either selectively, in areas such as distribution, or through more comprehensive alliances. The partnership between Norwegian telecommunications company Telenor and Bangladesh's Grameen Telecom, for example, resulted in the creation, in 1997, of Grameen Phone, now the country's largest mobile operator.

Reinventing the Business Model   The final category, on the bottom left of the matrix, represents products and services for which needs are (and will probably remain) very local and affordability is a challenge. In this segment, the potential available market share is high, though the market looks small, since consumers often substitute cheaper products, from adjacent categories, that satisfy similar needs rather than buy a higher-priced global product. The first step for multinationals is to define the market by measuring current total consumption, examining product alternatives that satisfy similar needs, and studying potential spending likely to be unlocked once incomes grow. Companies then need to make their products more affordable and accessible, looking at everything from capital expenditures to product features to distribution. There's real value in working with local players to drive product, distribution, and sales innovations in that "last mile" before reaching consumers.

Beer manufacturer SABMiller, for example, decided it could not achieve price points that would spur demand in Africa without changing its business model. It retooled its factories for cheaper, locally sourced ingredients (such as cassava and sugar rather than barley and maize) and used local distributors to ensure the availability of its products. The result: lower prices, growing demand, and significant increases in market share across several African countries.

• • •

Traditional approaches in which companies enter markets one by one and focus on a handful of brand and market combinations will not meet the challenges of the developing world's large and growing body of middle-class consumers. Companies need to become adept at building and sharing customer information across markets and more willing to work with others to gain scale quickly. In some regions, such as Africa, multinationals may even need to work with the public and social sector to ensure that consumers have adequate income to generate demand.

Structural changes might also be required. Because multinationals may have to adopt different business models by market, category, and brand, they need flexible and responsive organizations. Cisco, for example, has created a second world headquarters, in India, to spearhead its push into the country, while other companies are establishing centers of excellence to identify, recruit, and develop staff that can be deployed locally. Using local vendors is critical to running a lean operation: many multinationals have found, for example, that capital outlays in emerging markets are often only 30 percent of those required for a factory in the West if they use local resources for plant and process engineering and to execute projects.

Finally, companies need to be aware of perhaps the biggest bottleneck to seizing the emerging middle-class opportunity: talent. Relying excessively on expatriates is likely to stifle an organization's ability to scale up adequately across markets—there simply won't be enough staff. We believe that building talent academies inside companies to accelerate leadership development is a good step. Yet the rapid growth in many emerging markets may make traditional "grow your own" or "hire from within" approaches manifestly inadequate to meet staffing needs. By addressing these structural and operational imperatives and identifying the best approaches to achieve the scale needed to serve the growing middle class, multinationals can meet their high expectations for international growth.

Reading 3-3 New Business Models in Emerging Markets

by Matthew J. Eyring, Mark W. Johnson, and Hari Nair

Right now more than 20,000 multinationals are operating in emerging economies. According to the *Economist,* Western multinationals expect to find 70% of their future growth there—40% of it in China and India alone. But if the opportunity is huge, so are the obstacles to seizing it. On its 2010 Ease of Doing Business Index, the World Bank ranked China 89th, Brazil 129th, and India 133rd out of 183 countries. Summarizing the bank's conclusions, the *Economist* wrote, "The only way that companies can prosper in these markets is to cut costs relentlessly and accept profit margins close to zero."

Yes, the challenges are significant. But we couldn't disagree more with that opinion. We have seen the opportunities of the future on a street corner in Bangalore, in a small city in central India, in a village in Kenya—and they don't require companies to forgo profits. On the surface, nothing could be more prosaic: a laundry, a compact fridge, a money-transfer service. But look closely at the businesses behind these offerings and you will find the frontiers of business model innovation. These novel ventures reveal a way to help companies escape stagnant demand at home, create new and profitable revenue streams, and find competitive advantage.

▌ **Matthew J. Eyring** (meyring@innosight.com) is the president of Innosight, a strategic innovation consulting and investment firm with offices in Boston, Singapore, and India.

▌ **Mark W. Johnson** (mjohnson@innosight.com) is the chairman of Innosight and the author of *Seizing the White Space: Business Model Innovation for Growth and Renewal* (Harvard Business Review Press, 2010).

▌ **Hari Nair** (hnair@innosight.com) is a venture partner in India at Innosight's business-building arm, Innosight Labs.

That may sound overly optimistic, given the difficulty Western companies have had entering emerging markets to date. But we believe they've struggled not because they can't create viable offerings but because they get their business models wrong. Many multinationals simply import their domestic models into emerging markets. They may tinker at the edges, lowering prices—perhaps by selling smaller sizes or by using lower-cost labor, materials, or other resources. Sometimes they even design and manufacture their products locally and hire local country managers. But their fundamental profit formulas and operating models remain unchanged, consigning these companies to selling largely in the highest income tiers, which in most emerging markets aren't big enough to generate sufficient returns.

What's often missing from even the savviest of these efforts is a systematic process for reconceiving the business model. For more than a decade, through research and our work in both mature and emerging markets, we have been developing our business model innovation and implementation process (see "Reinventing Your Business Model," HBR December 2008, and "Beating the Odds When You Launch a New Venture," HBR May 2010). At its most basic level, the process consists of three steps: *Identify an important unmet job* a target customer needs done; *blueprint a model* that can accomplish that job profitably for a price the customer is willing to pay; and carefully *implement and evolve the model* by testing essential assumptions and adjusting as you learn.

Start in the Middle

Established companies entering emerging markets should take a page from the strategy of start-ups, for which all markets are new: Instead of looking for additional outlets for existing offerings, they should identify unmet needs—"the jobs to be done" in our terminology—that can be fulfilled at a profit. Emerging markets teem with such jobs. Even the basic needs of their large populations may not yet have been met. In fact, the challenge lies less in finding jobs than in settling on the ones most appropriate for your company to tackle.

Many companies have already been lured by the promise of profits from selling low-end products and services in high volume to the very poor in emerging markets. And high-end products and services are widely available in these markets for the very few who can afford them: You can buy a Mercedes or a washing machine, or stay at a nice hotel, almost anywhere in the world. Our experience suggests a far more promising place to begin: between these two extremes, in the vast middle market. Consumers there are defined not so much by any particular income band as by a common circumstance: Their needs are being met very poorly by existing low-end solutions, because they cannot afford even the cheapest of the high-end alternatives. Companies that devise new business models and offerings to better meet those consumers' needs affordably will discover enormous opportunities for growth.

Take, for example, the Indian consumer durables company Godrej & Boyce. Founded in 1897 to sell locks, Godrej is today a diversified manufacturer of everything from safes to hair dye to refrigerators and washing machines. In workshops we conducted with key managers in the appliances division, refrigerators emerged as a high-potential area: Because of the cost both to buy and to operate them, traditional compressor-driven refrigerators had penetrated only 18% of the market.

The first thing these managers wanted to know, naturally enough, was "Could Godrej provide a cheaper, stripped-down version of our higher-end refrigerator?" We asked them to consider instead the key needs of those with poor or no refrigeration. Did they know what those consumers really wanted? In a word, no. A small team was assigned to conduct detailed observations, open-ended interviews, and video ethnography to illuminate the job to be done for that untapped market.

The semiurban and rural people the team observed typically earned 5,000 to 8,000 rupees (about $125 to $200) a month, lived in single-room dwellings with four or five family members, and changed residences frequently. Unable to afford conventional refrigerators in their own homes, they were making do with communal, usually secondhand ones.

The shared fridges weren't meeting these people's needs very well, but not for the reasons one might expect. The observers found that they almost invariably contained only a few items. Their users tended to shop daily and buy small quantities of vegetables and milk. Electricity was unreliable, putting even the little food they did want to preserve at risk. What's more, although they wanted to cool their drinking water, making ice wasn't a job for which these people would "hire" a refrigerator.

The team concluded that what this group needed to do was to stretch one meal into two by preserving leftovers and to keep drinks cooler than room temperature—a job markedly different from the one higher-end refrigerators do, which is to keep a large supply of perishables on hand, cold or frozen. Clearly, there was no reason to spend a month's salary on a conventional refrigerator and pay steep electricity prices to get the simpler job done. And just as clearly, the solution wasn't a cheaper conventional fridge. Here was an opportunity to create a fundamentally new product for the underserved middle market.

Targeting this market has two great advantages. First, it's easier to upgrade the solution to a job people are already trying to do than to create sufficient customer demand where none yet exists—as would-be vendors of purified water and other seemingly essential offerings have found to their dismay. Second, it's easier to reach people who are already spending money to get their jobs done. That's essentially what Ratan Tata did with the $2,500 Nano. He didn't ask, "How can I get people who've never bought any form of transportation to buy a car?" He asked, "How can I produce a better alternative for people who hire motor scooters to transport their families?" The goal is to redirect existing demand by offering a clear path from an unsatisfactory solution to a better one.

Offer Unique Benefits for Less

To redirect demand, your customer value proposition (CVP) must solve a problem more effectively, simply, accessibly, or affordably than the alternatives. In developing markets, we have found, the components of a CVP that matter most are affordability and access. Let's look at each in turn.

Affordability Western companies know that they need to come up with lower-cost offerings in emerging markets, but they too often limit themselves to providing less for less. In 2001, for instance, a 300 ml bottle of Coke cost 10 rupees—a day's wages, on average, and a luxury the company estimated only 4% of the population could afford. To reach the other 96%, it introduced a 200 ml bottle and cut the price in half, shaving margins to make Coke more competitive with common alternatives such as lemonade and tea.

In our experience, though, a far more robust approach to creating an affordable emerging market offering is to trade off expensive features and functions that people don't need for less-expensive ones they do need. To get that right requires a clear understanding of the context in which the offering will be sold—which calls for further fieldwork, preferably of a collaborative rather than a merely observational kind. This is good product-development advice in any market. In fact, it applies to indigenous players operating close to home, like Godrej, as well as to Western companies confronting the unfamiliar.

Godrej's team designed and built a prototype cooling unit from the ground up and tested it in the field with consumers. Then, in February 2008, more than 600 women in Osmanabad, a city in India's Marathwada region, gathered to participate in a cocreation event. Working with the original prototypes and several others that had followed, they collaborated with Godrej on every aspect of the product's design. They helped plan the interior arrangements, made suggestions for the lid, and provided insights on color (eventually settling on candy red).

The result was the ChotuKool ("little cool"), a top-opening unit that, at 1.5 × 2 feet and with a

The final design for the Chotukool ("little cool") emerged from a cocreation event in Osmanabad, India, in which more than 600 local women participated.

capacity of 43 liters, has enough room for the few items users want to keep fresh for a day or two. With only 20 (rather than the usual 200) parts, it has no compressor, cooling tubes, or refrigerant. Instead it uses a chip that cools when a current is applied and a fan like those that prevent desktop computers from overheating. Its top-opening design keeps most of the cold air inside when the lid is opened. It uses less than half the energy of a conventional refrigerator and can run on a battery during the power outages that are common in rural villages. At just 7.8 kilograms, it's highly portable, and at $69, it costs half what the most basic refrigerator does. Because it's the right size for the job, easier to move, and more reliable in a power outage than a conventional fridge, it surpasses the higher-end offering on the performance measures that matter most to these consumers.

Access It's not surprising that portability is important to potential ChotuKool customers, given that they move frequently. And because populations in emerging markets tend to be dispersed, obtaining goods and services can be more difficult than in the West. This creates opportunities for companies that solve challenges of access.

In Kenya, for example, banking services are scarce and transferring money is complicated and expensive. Without access to traditional services, many people must use unsafe alternatives such as *hawala*—an unregulated network of brokers operating on the honor system—or transport cash by bus. The UK-based Vodafone solved this problem by developing a secure, low-cost mobile money-transfer service. Called M-PESA (*M* for "mobile" and *PESA* from the Swahili word for "money"), the system is operated by Safaricom, Kenya's leading mobile network.

Customers register free with an authorized M-PESA agent—typically a Safaricom dealer, but sometimes a gas station, food market, or other local shop. Once registered, they can deposit or withdraw cash at the agent or transfer money electronically to any mobile phone user, even if the recipient is not a Safaricom subscriber. They can also buy Safaricom airtime for themselves or other subscribers. Customers pay a flat fee of about US 40 cents for person-to-person transfers, 33 cents for withdrawals under $33, and 1.3 cents for balance inquiries. Vodafone (which owns a significant stake in Safaricom) manages individual customer accounts on its server, and Safaricom deposits its customers' balances in pooled accounts in two regulated banks, so their full value is backed by highly liquid assets.

Since its launch, in March 2007, the service has acquired more than 9 million customers—40% of Kenya's adult population. As of June 2010, the *Economist* reported, M-PESA customers could conduct transactions at some 17,900 retail outlets, more than half of them in rural areas. That figure dwarfs the total number of bank branches, post offices, and Post Banks—which is only about 840 nationwide.

Spurred by the success of its original offerings, the service has expanded to include bill payment, business-to-customer payments such as paychecks and microfinance loan disbursements, delivery of humanitarian aid, and international money transfers. After just three years M-PESA accounted for 9% of Safaricom's total revenue. More important, it has become the engine driving the company's profits, which have shifted dramatically from voice to data traffic. Vodafone has launched similar services in Tanzania, Afghanistan, and South Africa and plans to introduce them in Egypt, Fiji, and Qatar as well.

Failure to address the access challenge is an important reason that so many companies have little success adapting their current models to emerging markets. Time and again, the increased volume they hope will offset slimmer profit margins doesn't in fact result in profits, because the costs of serving far-flung customers in infrastructure-poor developing countries are just too high. But companies that, like Vodafone, devise novel approaches may find them to be widely applicable in many markets.

Integrate the Elements

Business models can be conceived in a variety of ways. Our approach focuses on the basics and also on factors that make it difficult to move from an existing model to a new one—margin requirements, overhead, and "resource velocity" (the capacity to generate a given volume of business within a specific time frame). It has four parts: the customer value proposition, a profit formula, key processes, and key resources the company must use to deliver the CVP repeatedly and at scale. Creating competitive advantage lies in integrating these elements to produce value for both the customer and the company. That's easy to say but devilishly hard to do. Mapping the traditional functions of your company to these broad categories will show you how much you'd have to change to integrate those functions into a new business model (see the exhibit "Building a New Model").

Once you've devised a CVP for your proposed offering, consider the basis on which you compete—differentiation or price. Offerings that compete on differentiation require that you ask, "What do I have to do to produce this?" which leads you counterclockwise around the model, looking first at what resources and processes are needed, the cost of which (both fixed and variable) will determine what price can deliver the desired profit margin. That's what Whole Foods did when it created a new market for organic foods. Costs drove prices.

For offerings that compete on the basis of price, you move clockwise around the model, again starting with the CVP, but next setting the price, devising a rough cost structure, and then determining what processes and resources (often radically different from those in your current model) are needed to meet your price requirements. Because affordability is so critical in emerging markets, the decision journey is almost invariably clockwise. Innovators start with a revenue model—"We think we can sell this offering to X number of people at price Y"—and then devise the cost structure required to deliver a certain unit margin. Becoming profitable at that margin means operating at a certain resource velocity, which in turn drives decisions about how to organize operations, what materials to use, and other questions.

More often than not, this exercise reveals that a company can't meet its profit goals in emerging markets merely by reducing variable costs in its current profit formula and that a viable model will require changes to fixed costs or overhead as well. That's what Ratan Tata discovered when he set out to produce his $2,500 car. He couldn't just send the car down the production line and somehow spend less to make it. He needed to reduce fixed costs by designing a car with far fewer parts and changing assembly methods and other key processes. Implementing models that require changes in overhead, margins, or resource velocity tends to be problematic for incumbent companies, which is why it's not surprising that start-ups so often have the edge in bringing to market offerings that require new ways to turn a profit. An open mind is perhaps the most important asset anyone can bring to emerging markets. We learned that lesson when we set out to solve a basic but knotty cleaning problem for a vast group of frustrated consumers.

Village Laundry Service—which was founded by our company and uses the Chamak brand—was aimed squarely at the emerging middle market. In India people who can't afford a washing machine but want an alternative to laborious washing by hand after a long day's work have unappealing choices: They can patronize a *dhobi* (a traditional washing person), or they can take their clothes to a neighborhood laundry or dry-cleaning establishment. The dhobis are cheap, but they use any available water, which can be unhygienic. They slap the clothes against rocks to clean them, which wears down the fabrics, and they don't compensate customers for damage. Turnaround time is five to seven days. A laundry or dry cleaner can do the job in four or five days, generally returns the clothes in good shape, and makes amends if something goes wrong. A laundry may or may not use clean water, however, and both are far more expensive than a dhobi.

In early 2009 we ventured into several parts of India, from urban slums to rural villages, conducting interviews and immersing ourselves in the lives of the people who faced this frustrating choice. What, exactly, was the job to be done? What sort of laundry service would these customers hire? We discovered several things: The job wasn't to make it affordable for them to clean their clothes the way rich people did; it was to replicate the advantage of a home washer and dryer at a price they could afford. It wouldn't be sufficient to get the clothes back in four days—they'd have to be ready within 24 hours, and at a price well below the laundry's or dry cleaner's. And they'd have to be easy to pick up at a nearby location.

With those requirements clearly in mind, we examined all parts of the business model to come up with an inventive way of extending access while keeping costs low. We immediately realized that it would be hard to create a profitable business that placed many traditional self-service laundries across a town, because demand was unpredictable and up-front capital investment and rental deposits would be high. Our solution: Portable seven-foot-square kiosks, each holding an efficient front-loading washer and a dryer, which can be placed wherever there is heavy foot traffic. Customers drop off their clothes to be washed, dried, and ironed, all within 24 hours. The kiosk's small footprint minimizes rents, and its independent water supply, delivered through a fixed contract, is both less expensive and more reliable than the public utility connection. Covered with ads for the Chamak brand, the kiosks also serve as billboards, reducing the need for paid advertising. We keep transaction costs low through an innovative point-of-sale system, made up of a cell phone linked to a Bluetooth printer and report server, which prints receipts, tracks orders, and captures data on business volume.

After much experimentation, we developed standard procedures for staffing and running the kiosks, including tests to gauge potential operators' aptitude and commitment; simple picture-based operating instructions (much like those used in fast-food restaurants) to ensure consistent service; and a scorecard for traffic level, customer satisfaction, marketing effectiveness, and other variables, allowing us to predict the chances of success at each location and to make operations replicable and scalable.

It is this innovative marriage of a novel solution with all the other elements of the business model that makes Chamak's services affordable and profitable. The model allows the company to charge 40 rupees (about $1) per kilogram of clothing—little more than what dhobis charge and significantly less than what professional laundries and dry cleaners do (sometimes 90 rupees per garment). Village Laundry Service currently has 5,000 customers patronizing some 20 booths in Mumbai, Bangalore, and Mysore. The company expects to reach break-even in late 2011. Of course, as with any new business, how Village Laundry Service performs over the long term will depend on a number of hard-to-predict factors.

From Blueprint to Operating Business

Testing and implementing the business model blueprint in emerging markets is as much an art as a science. Having a cadre of global "experts" study the market for months and create a plan that is then handed over to the local team for execution simply doesn't work. Quick adjustments based on early lessons learned on the ground trump the best and most detailed strategic plan developed before the fact.

M-PESA succeeded in part because Kenya's banking regulator permitted Safaricom to test various business models from the very beginning. Safaricom made the most of the opportunity. It started in 2004 by experimenting with 500 customers and a system designed to allow them to repay micro-loans. As the company market-tested this concept,

it discovered a more-compelling value proposition—namely, a way for urban workers to transfer funds to friends and family members in rural areas. That fundamental insight was the basis on which subsequent services were built, and since M-PESA's commercial launch, its simple but powerful branding message has been "Send money home."

This doesn't mean that expertise is unimportant when launching a new business in an emerging market. But we've found that agile functional expertise is the most critical kind, because the uncertainties in emerging markets are so great. A broad network of resources—including responsive advertising agencies, companies that can produce prototypes on demand, financial service advisers who understand local regulatory guidelines, and a healthy bench of local entrepreneurs to execute the plan—is essential.

The ability to conduct rapid experiments inexpensively and use what you learn from them to hone the business model is essential to success. It allows you to make course corrections before you commit to major operational or strategic investments. Recently a company we incubated was looking to launch a men's grooming business but was uncertain about demand. Rather than commission an expensive 10-city quantitative research study, we rented a small air-conditioned truck and created a mini hair salon on wheels, outfitted with a barber's chair, scissors and other implements, and a mirror. For two weeks we drove the truck around the streets of Bangalore to gauge demand and test various pricing scenarios at various locations. The experiment, which cost all of $3,000, provided essential answers that no survey could have and demonstrated the business potential for an affordable and convenient Supercuts-like business for men. The company changed from a roving barbershop model to a kiosk-based model and is considering offering additional services, such as facials and skin lightening, that many customers desire.

Ultimately, the potential for such business model innovations, as for many other disruptive innovations, may extend far beyond the markets for which they were created. G. Sunderraman, the vice president of corporate development at Godrej, sees the ChotuKool as a new growth platform. Unit sales are projected to reach 10,000 in the first year and 100,000 by the end of the second. If Godrej considered the ChotuKool to be simply a no-frills refrigerator for the middle market, it might be content with a moderate penetration rate. But the company's managers regard it as a new product category, based on new technology, that has the potential to perform jobs for people at many income levels. In areas with frequent power outages, the owners of conventional refrigerators might want an inexpensive and reliable backup. Small shops, offices, and manufacturing sites might use it to maintain a supply of cool drinks. Higher-income customers—perhaps in developed economies as well—might use it in their bedrooms, their cars, or their boats. When the technology improves, Godrej believes, it can enter mainstream markets as

ChotuKool changes consumers' expectations about refrigerator prices and performance and addresses a need that previously went unmet.

Many companies view emerging markets as one large foothold market, and in this they are right. Classic disruptive innovation theory holds that, ideally, innovations should first be introduced in markets where the alternatives fall short on some dimension (typically price) or are utterly unavailable. Emerging markets fit that bill in spades. They are excellent arenas for trying out product innovations far from competitors' prying eyes. But we are convinced that a much greater opportunity lies in viewing these markets not as one vast lab for *product* R&D but as unique environments filled with poorly done jobs that could be creatively addressed with *business model* R&D. Creating new business models will give your company a more enduring competitive advantage.

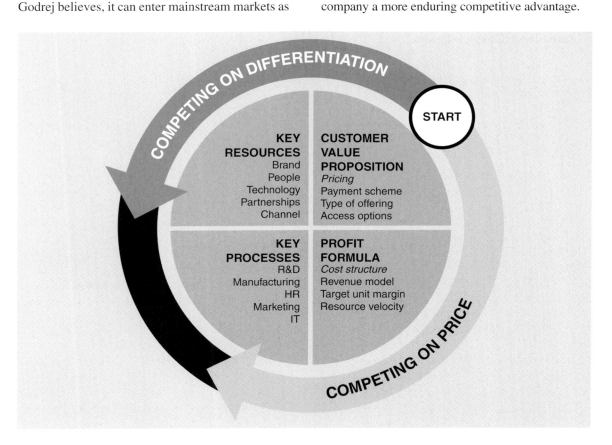

Building a New Model

Business models must integrate four elements: the customer value proposition (CVP), the profit formula, key processes, and key resources. Developing new business models always begins with devising a new CVP. Models designed to compete on differentiation next establish the resources and processes needed to deliver the CVP, the cost of which determines the price required in the profit formula. Models designed to compete on price proceed in the opposite way, establishing first the offering's price, then the cost structure, and finally the processes and resources required.

Four Ways to Uncover Unmet Needs

1. **Study what your customers are doing with your product.** Be aware that, as Peter Drucker famously said, "The customer rarely buys what the business thinks it sells him."

2. **Look at the alternatives to your offerings that consumers buy.** Investigate a wide range of substitutes for your products, not just what your competitors make.

3. **Watch for compensating behaviors.** Discover what jobs people are satisfying poorly.

4. **Search for explanations.** Uncover the root causes of consumers' behavior by asking what people are trying to accomplish with the goods and services they use.

Developing a Transnational Organization:
Managing Integration, Responsiveness, and Flexibility

Having discussed how multinational enterprises (MNEs) need to develop strategies that find the right balance among pressures to achieve global efficiency, national responsiveness, and worldwide innovation and learning, we now focus our attention on the kind of organizations that they must build to manage these often-conflicting strategic tasks. In this chapter, we begin by suggesting that this balance requires MNEs not only to understand the nature of their present and future strategic tasks, but also to appreciate their embedded organizational capabilities—something we call a company's "administrative heritage." It is only through such an understanding that they will be able to build transnational organizations that incorporate the multidimensional and flexible capabilities demanded by transnational strategies. This task involves more than a search for an ideal structural solution. Using a biological analogy, we describe the attributes of a transnational organization that must be built—its structure (anatomy), its processes, (physiology), and its culture (psychology). In the final section of the chapter, we examine the processes necessary to build such organizational capabilities.

In preceding chapters, we described how changes in the international operating environment have forced MNEs to respond simultaneously to the strategic need for global efficiency, national responsiveness, and worldwide learning. Implementing such a complex, three-pronged strategic objective would be difficult under any circumstances, but the very act of "going international" multiplies a company's organizational complexity.

Most domestic companies find it difficult enough to balance business units with corporate staff functions, so the thought of adding a geographically oriented management dimension can be daunting. It implies maintaining a three-way balance of perspectives and capabilities among organizational units responsible for the MNE's businesses, functions, and regions. The difficulty is increased further because the resolution of tensions among those three different management groups must be accomplished in an organization whose operating units are divided by distance and time and whose key members are separated by barriers of culture and language.

Beyond Structure: "Fit"

Because the choice of a basic organizational structure has such a powerful influence on the management process in an MNE, historically much of the attention of managers and researchers alike was focused on trying to find which formal structure provided the

Figure 4-1   Stopford and Wells's International Structural Stages model

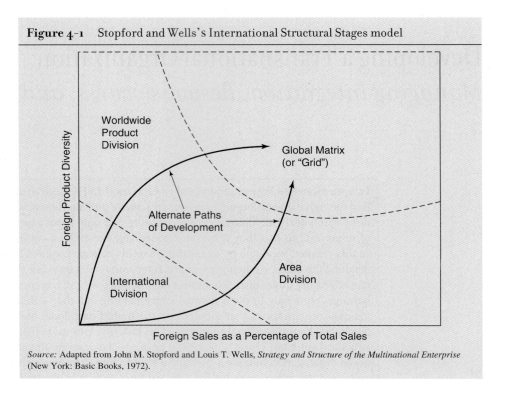

Source: Adapted from John M. Stopford and Louis T. Wells, *Strategy and Structure of the Multinational Enterprise* (New York: Basic Books, 1972).

right "fit" in various conditions. The most widely recognized early study on this issue was Stopford and Wells's research on the 187 largest U.S.-based MNEs.[1] Their work resulted in a "stages model" of international organization structure that defined two variables to capture the strategic and administrative complexity most companies faced as they expanded abroad: the number of products sold internationally ("foreign product diversity" in Figure 4-1) and the importance of international sales to the company ("foreign sales as a percentage of total sales"). Plotting the structural changes made by the sample companies, Stopford and Wells found that these MNEs adopted different organizational structures at different stages of international expansion, leading them to develop their International Structural Stages model.

According to this model, in the early stages of foreign expansion, MNEs typically managed their overseas operations through an international division. Subsequently, those companies that expanded abroad by entering more countries with a limited range of products typically adopted an area structure (e.g., European region or Asia-Pacific region). Other companies that expanded by increasing their foreign product diversity in fewer countries tended to adopt a worldwide product division structure (e.g., chemicals division or plastics division). Finally, when both foreign sales and foreign product

[1]Stopford's research is described in John M. Stopford and Louis T. Wells, *Managing the Multinational Enterprise* (New York: Basic Books, 1972).

diversity were high, companies tended to organize around some form of global matrix in which the manager of the chemicals business in France might report simultaneously to the company's European regional head and the global chemicals division president at corporate headquarters.

Although these ideas were presented as a descriptive model rather than a normative ideal, and despite the fact that the global matrix was a new organizational form that had been adopted by relatively few companies, consultants and managers soon began to apply the model prescriptively and a new generation of international organizations was created. In the process, the debate was often reduced to generalized discussions of the comparative value of product- versus geography-based structures and to simplistic choices between "centralization" and "decentralization."

Confronted with increasing complexity, diversity, and change in the 1980s and 1990s, managers in many worldwide companies looked for an ideal structure that would allow them to manage their large, complex international operations. Conventional wisdom provided a ready solution: the global matrix. For a while, it seemed as if the old adage "structure follows strategy" had been replaced by "structure follows fashion." But for most companies, the results of the reorganizations were disappointing. The promised land of the global matrix turned out to be an organizational quagmire from which they were forced to retreat.

Failure of the Matrix

In theory, the solution should have worked. Having frontline managers report simultaneously to different organizational groups (e.g., the French chemicals manager in the preceding example) should have enabled companies to resolve the conflict built into MNEs' strategy and operations. Theoretically, such a multidimensional organization should have allowed companies to maintain a balance between centralized efficiency and local responsiveness, for example. And the matrix's multiple channels of communication and control promised the ability to transmit and resolve diverse management perspectives. The reality turned out to be otherwise, however, and the history of companies that built formal global matrix structures—Citibank, Nestlé, Xerox, IBM, Shell, and ABB among the most prominent—was an unhappy one.

Dow Chemical, a pioneer of the global matrix organization, was also one of the first to abandon it, returning clear lines of responsibility to its geographic managers. And after spending more than a decade serving as the classic example of a global matrix through the 1990s, ABB abandoned the structure in 2002. So too did scores of other companies that tried to manage their worldwide activities through a structure that most often seemed to result in complex and rather bureaucratic processes and relationships.

Dual reporting led to conflict and confusion on many levels: the proliferation of channels created informational logjams, conflicts could be resolved only by escalating the problem, and overlapping responsibilities resulted in turf battles and a loss of accountability. In short, by forcing all issues through the dual chains of command, the matrix amplified the differences in perspectives and interests so that even a minor difference could become the subject of heated disagreement and debate. Separated by barriers of distance, time, language, and culture, managers found it virtually impossible to clarify the resulting confusion and resolve the conflicts. As a result, in company after company, the initial appeal of the global matrix structure quickly faded into the recognition that a different solution was required.

Building Organizational Capability

The basic problem underlying a company's search for a structural fit was that it focused on only one organizational variable—formal structure. This single tool proved unequal to the job of capturing the complexity of the strategic tasks facing most MNEs.

First, the emphasis on making either-or choices between product-based versus geographically based structures often forced managers to ignore the multiple demands in their external environment. Second, the focus on structure led to the definition of a static set of roles, responsibilities, and relationships in a strategic task environment that was dynamic and rapidly evolving. And third, restructuring efforts often proved harmful, as organizations were often bludgeoned into a major realignment of these roles, responsibilities, and relationships by overnight changes in structure.

As it became increasingly difficult to find structures that fit their more complex strategies, managers have begun to recognize that formal structure is a powerful but blunt instrument of strategic change. To develop the vital multidimensional and flexible capabilities required by today's MNE, a company must reorient its managers' thinking and reshape its core decision-making capabilities. In doing so, the company's entire management process—including its administrative systems, communication channels, decision-making forums, and interpersonal relationships—becomes the means for managing such change. In short, rather than imposing a structure that defines formal responsibilities, the challenge facing MNEs today is to develop an organization with an appropriate internal network of relationships.

As a first step in exploring some of the more subtle and sophisticated tools, we now examine how *administrative heritage*—a company's history and its embedded management culture—influences its organization and its ability and willingness to change. It is a concept to which we have already alluded in previous chapters when we acknowledged that an MNE's management mentality and strategic posture may have been shaped by different motivations for international expansion, historical and cultural factors, and different external industry forces. History matters—even in shaping how MNEs think about their organizations.

Administrative Heritage

Whereas industry analysis can reveal a company's competitive challenges and market needs, its ability to meet those external opportunities and threats will be greatly influenced—sometimes positively, sometimes negatively—by its existing internal world. Its ability to respond will be shaped by its in-place configuration and resource distribution, its historical definition of management responsibilities, and its ingrained organizational norms, for example. In short, a company's organization is shaped not only by current external task demands but also by past internal structures and management biases. In particular, each company is influenced by the path by which it developed (its organizational history) and the values, norms, and practices of its management (its management culture). Collectively, these factors constitute what we call a company's *administrative heritage*.

Administrative heritage can be one of the company's greatest assets providing the underlying source of its core competencies. At the same time, it can also be a significant liability because it embeds attitudes that may resist change and thereby prevents realignment. As managers in many companies have learned, unlike strategic plans that can be scrapped and redrawn overnight, there is no such thing as a zero-based organization. Companies are, to a significant extent, captives of their past, and any organizational transformation has to focus at least as much on where the company is coming from—its administrative heritage—as on where it wants to go.

The importance of a company's administrative heritage can be illustrated by contrasting the development of a typical European MNE whose major international expansion occurred in the decades of the 1920s and 1930s, a typical American MNE that expanded abroad in the 1950s and 1960s, and a typical Japanese company that made its main overseas thrust in the 1970s and 1980s. Even when these companies were in the same industry, their different heritages usually led them to adopt very different strategic and organizational models.

This will undoubtedly be true of a new generation of MNEs that are now expanding from developing countries like China, India, and Brazil. Their strategic posture, their organizational framework, and their management mentalities are being shaped by the cultural norms of their home countries and the global environment into which they are expanding. And if the following description of the current generation of leading MNEs is a predictor, the unique administrative heritage of the next generation of MNEs will shape the way they operate for decades to come.

Decentralized Federation

Expanding abroad in a pre-World War II era of rising tariffs and discriminatory legislation, the typical European company was forced to build local national production facilities to compete effectively with competitors in that country. With their own local plants, national subsidiaries of MNEs were able to modify products and marketing approaches to meet widely differing local market needs. The increasing independence of these self-sufficient national units was reinforced by the communication barriers that existed in that era, limiting headquarters' ability to intervene in the management of the company's spreading worldwide operations.

This configuration of widely distributed assets and delegated responsibility fit well with the management norms and practices that existed in many European companies at that time. Many European companies, particularly those from the United Kingdom, the Netherlands, and France, had developed an internal culture that emphasized personal relationships (an "old boys' network") rather than formal structures, and financial controls more than operational controls. This management style tended to reinforce these companies' willingness to delegate more operating independence and strategic freedom to their foreign subsidiaries. Highly autonomous national companies were often managed as a portfolio of offshore investments rather than as a single international business.

The resulting organization pattern was a loose federation of independent national subsidiaries, each focused primarily on its local market. As a result, many of these companies, including classic European MNEs like Philips, Unilever, and Nestlé, adopted what we have described in previous chapters as the *multinational strategy* and managed it through a *decentralized federation* organization model, as represented in Figure 4-2(a).

Coordinated Federation

U.S. companies, many of which enjoyed their fastest international expansion in the 1950s and 1960s, developed in very different circumstances. The strength of companies such as General Electric (GE), Pfizer, and Procter & Gamble (P&G) lay in the new technologies and management processes they had developed through being located in the United States—at that time, the world's largest, richest, and most technologically advanced market. After World War II, their foreign expansion focused primarily on leveraging this strength, giving rise to the international product cycle theory discussed in Chapter 1.

Reinforcing this strategy was a professional managerial culture in most U.S.-based companies that contrasted with the "old boys' network" that typified the European companies' processes. The U.S. management approach was built on a willingness to delegate responsibility while retaining overall control through sophisticated management systems and specialist corporate staffs. Foreign subsidiaries were often free to adapt products or strategies to reflect market differences, but their dependence on the parent company for new products, processes, and ideas dictated a great deal more coordination and control by headquarters than did the decentralized federation organization. This relationship was facilitated by the existence of formal systems and controls in the headquarters-subsidiary link.

The main handicap that such companies faced was that parent-company management often adopted a parochial and even superior attitude toward international operations, perhaps because of the assumption that new ideas and developments all came from the parent. Despite corporate management's increased understanding of its overseas markets, it often seemed to view foreign operations as appendages whose principal purpose was to leverage the capabilities and resources developed in the home market.

Nonetheless, the approach was highly successful in the postwar decades, and many U.S.-based companies adopted what we have described as the *international strategy* and the *coordinated federation* organizational model shown in Figure 4-2(b).

Centralized Hub

In contrast to both the European and the American models, the Japanese companies that made their major impact on the international economy in the 1970s and 1980s faced a greatly altered external environment and operated with very different internal norms and values. With limited prior overseas exposure, Japanese MNEs like Sony, Toyota, and Komatsu typically chose not to match the well-established local marketing capabilities and facilities of their European and U.S. competitors. (Indeed, well-established Japanese trading companies often provided them an easier means of entering foreign markets—namely, exporting.) However, the rapid postwar growth of the Japanese economy gave such companies new, efficient, and scale-intensive plants that became major assets as they expanded into a global environment of declining trade barriers.

Figure 4-2   Organizational configuration models

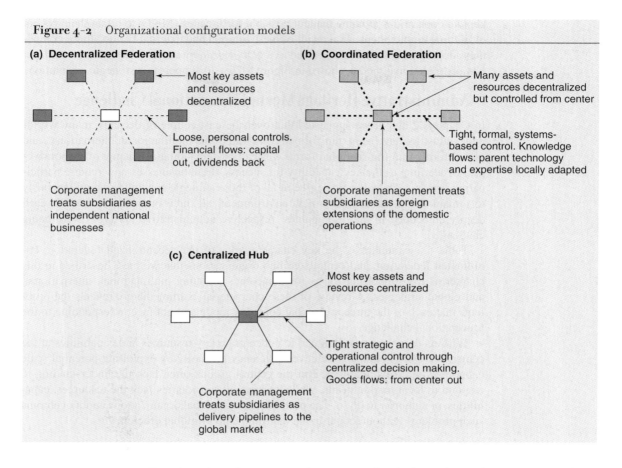

Together, these factors gave these companies the incentive to develop a competitive advantage at the upstream end of the value-added chain. Their competitive strategy emphasized cost advantages and quality assurance, both of which demanded tight control over product development, procurement, and manufacturing. When forced to do so, these Japanese-based MNEs moved some assembly operations offshore, but most kept the major value-adding and strategic activities at home. This centrally controlled, export-based internationalization strategy represented a perfect fit with the external environment and companies' competitive capabilities.

Such an approach also fit the cultural background and organizational values that were part of the deeply embedded administrative heritage of these emerging Japanese MNEs. At the foundation were strong national cultural norms that emphasized group behavior and valued interpersonal harmony as reflected in management practices such as *nemawashi* (consensus building) and *ringi* (shared decision making).

By keeping primary decision making and control at the center, the Japanese company could retain its culturally dependent management system that was so communications-intensive and people-dependent. In addition, international growth that kept key operations at home made it possible for Japanese MNEs to retain their system of lifetime employment. As a result of these internal and external factors, these companies adopted what we have described as a *global strategy* and developed the *centralized hub* organizational model, shown in Figure 4-2(c), to support this strategic orientation.

Administrative Heritage Meets Transnational Challenge

In Chapters 2 and 3, we suggested that over the past couple of decades, many worldwide industries have been transformed from traditional multinational, international, and global forms into transnational forms. Instead of demanding efficiency *or* responsiveness *or* learning as the key capability for success, these businesses now require participating firms to achieve some degree of all of those strategic capabilities simultaneously to remain competitive. In this new environment, all three organization models each deeply embedded in their companies' respective administrative heritages were being challenged.

Table 4-1 summarizes the key characteristics of the decentralized federation, coordinated federation, and centralized hub organizations that we have described in this chapter as the supporting forms for companies pursuing multinational, international, and global strategies. A review of these characteristics immediately reveals the problems that each of the three archetypal company models might face in responding to the transnational challenge.

With its organizations designed to concentrate key resources and capabilities at the center, the *global* company achieves efficiency primarily by exploiting potential scale economies in all its activities. But the central groups often lack the understanding to respond to local market needs, while its national subsidiaries lack the resources, capabilities, or authority to do so. The problem is that a global organization cannot overcome such problems without jeopardizing its trump card of global efficiency.

Table 4-1   Organizational Characteristics of Decentralized Federation, Coordinated Federation, and Centralized Hub Organizations

	Decentralized Federation	**Coordinated Federation**	**Centralized Hub**
Strategic approach	Multinational	International	Global
Key strategic capability	National responsiveness	Transfer home country innovations abroad	Global-scale efficiency
Configuration of key assets and capabilities	Predominantly decentralized and nationally self-sufficient	Core innovative capabilities centralized; adaptive capabilities decentralized	Predominantly centralized and globally scaled
Role of overseas operations	Sensing and exploiting local opportunities	Adapting and leveraging parent-company competencies	Implementing parent-company strategies
Development and diffusion of most key knowledge	Developed and retained within each unit	Developed at the center and transferred to overseas units	Developed and retained at the center

The classic organizational form or *multinational* company suffers from other limitations. Although its dispersed resources and decentralized decision-making authority allow its national subsidiaries to respond to local needs, the resulting fragmentation of activities leads to inefficiency. Worldwide learning also suffers, because knowledge is not consolidated and does not flow freely across national boundaries. As a result, local innovations often represent little more than the efforts of subsidiary management to protect its turf and autonomy or reinventions of the wheel caused by blocked communication or the not-invented-here (NIH) syndrome.

And while the *international* company's organization is designed to allow it to leverage the knowledge and capabilities of the parent company, its resource configuration and operating systems make it less efficient than the global company and less responsive than the multinational company.

The Transnational Organization

As MNEs recognized these limitations imposed by their administrative heritage, many began trying to match the capabilities of their competitors while simultaneously protecting their existing sources of competitive advantage. Those that succeeded gradually developed the characteristics of what we describe as transnational organizations.

Three important organizational characteristics characterize this emerging form of cross-border organization and distinguish it from its multinational, international, or global counterparts: transnational organizations have decision-making roles and responsibilities that legitimize multiple diverse management perspectives, a structure based on assets and capabilities that are both distributed and interdependent, and internal integrative processes that are robust and flexible. In this section, we will describe and illustrate each of these core characteristics.

Multidimensional Perspectives

An MNE cannot respond effectively to strategic demands that are diverse and changeable through an organization that is one-dimensional and static. The transnational company must create the multidimensional ability to sense and analyze these diverse and often conflicting opportunities, pressures, and demands. Strong *national subsidiary management* is needed to sense and represent the changing needs of local consumers and the increasing pressures from host governments; capable *global business management* is required to track the strategy of global competitors and provide the coordination necessary to respond appropriately; and influential *worldwide functional management* is needed to concentrate corporate knowledge, information, and expertise and facilitate its transfer among organizational units.

Unfortunately, in many companies, power is concentrated with the management group that has historically had responsibility for the company's principal critical strategic task—often at the cost of the influence of groups representing other needs. For example, in companies pursuing a *multinational* strategy, key decisions were usually dominated by the country management, the group that made the most critical contribution to achieving national responsiveness. In *global* companies, managers running the worldwide business divisions were typically the most influential because they played the key role in the company's efforts to seek global efficiency. And in *international* companies, functional management groups often came to assume this position of dominance because of their roles in building, accumulating, and transferring the company's knowledge and capabilities in technology, marketing, and other specialist fields.

In *transnational* companies, however, such biases in the decision-making process are offset through a conscious effort to build up the capability, credibility, and influence of the less powerful management groups while protecting the morale and expertise of the dominant group. The objective is to create a multidimensional organization in which all three management groups have a seat at the table.

Companies that are born into today's environment of multiple conflicting demands—web-based firms like Amazon, for example, or MNEs launched into the world from emerging economies, like the Chinese appliance company Haier—typically are creating such organizations from the beginning. But as the "Philips versus Matsushita: The Competitive Battle Continues" case that follows this chapter will show, existing MNEs with deeply embedded administrative heritages can spend decades struggling to develop such balanced multidimensional management perspectives.

Distributed, Interdependent Capabilities

It's one thing to ensure that multidimensional management perspectives are represented. It's quite another to be able to respond to the diverse opportunities and demands that they bring to their seat at the table. To do this requires an organizational model where the assets, resources, and capabilities are arranged in ways that are very different from the global organization's centralized hub configuration or the multinational organization's decentralized federation of independent operations.

Recognizing that centralization is not the only way to achieve efficiency, transnational organizations ensure that selected units located either in the home country or abroad achieve global scale by specializing their activities. They do this by identifying their most effective manufacturing operations and making them the company's regional or global source for a given product or expertise. They also tap into important technological advances and market developments wherever they are occurring, engaging and harnessing the most effective product development and marketing groups in national units to become centers of excellence or lead country marketing operations.

One major consequence of such a distribution of specialized assets and responsibilities is that the interdependence of worldwide units automatically increases. For example, in an evolved transnational organization such as GE, an opportunity for a diesel engine for a specialized mining application may first be sensed by the company's Australian subsidiary, developed through a collaboration between corporate R&D and GE's German technical group, jointly produced by the South Korean and Mexican manufacturing operations, and rolled out into the global marketplace through the company's subsidiaries worldwide.

In such an organization, simple structural configurations like the decentralized federation, coordinated federation, or centralized hub are inadequate for the task facing the transnational corporation. What is needed is a structure that we term the *integrated network* (see Figure 4-3). In this structure, management regards each of the worldwide units as a source of ideas, skills, capabilities, knowledge, and expertise that can be harnessed for the benefit of the total organization. Efficient local plants may be converted

Figure 4-3   Integrated network model

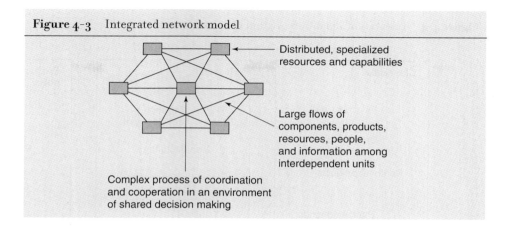

into regional or global production centers; innovative national or regional development labs may be designated the company's "centers of excellence" for a particular product or process development; and creative subsidiary marketing groups may be given a lead role in developing worldwide marketing strategies for certain products or businesses.

Flexible Integrative Process

Finally, the transnational organization requires a management process that can resolve the diversity of interests and integrate the dispersed assets and resources that we just described. In doing so, it cannot be bound by a symmetrical organizational process that defines the task in such traditionally simplistic terms as centralization versus decentralization. The reason is simple: the benefits to be gained from central control of worldwide research or manufacturing activities may be much more important than those related to the global coordination of the sales and service functions. The need for functional coordination also varies by business and by geographic area. Aircraft engine companies clearly need central control of more decisions than multinational food packagers, and operations in developing countries may need more support from the center than those in advanced countries. Furthermore, all such coordination needs to be able to change over time.

In short, the transnational organization recognizes that there is not a single static management model that it can apply universally. It acknowledges that the management process must be able to change from product to product, from country to country, and even from decision to decision. Elaborating on the integration-responsiveness framework that we developed in Chapter 3, we illustrate such a distribution of roles and responsibilities in Figure 4-4, with an example from Unilever. As the figure demonstrates, Unilever's chemicals business is managed in a much more globally integrated way that its packaged food business. And even within the detergent business, R&D is managed more centrally than marketing, which in turn manages its product policy decisions more centrally that its promotions policies.

Figure 4-4   Integration and differentiation needs at Unilever

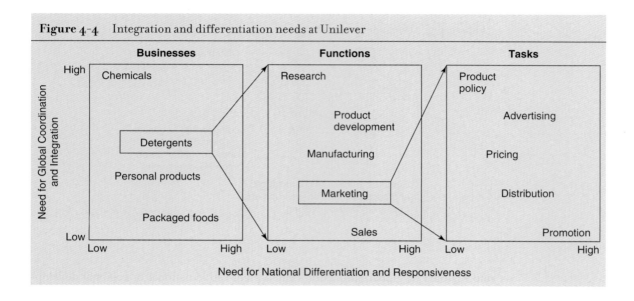

The implied distribution of roles and responsibilities requires the development of rather sophisticated and subtle decision-making machinery based on three interdependent management processes. The first is a focused and constrained escalation process that allows top management to intervene directly in key decision content. This carefully managed form of *centralization* may be appropriate for major resource allocation commitments, for example. The second is a process in which management uses its ability to structure individual roles and administrative systems to influence specific decisions. This *formalization* process is typically used for decisions involving repetitive or routine activities like setting transfer prices. The third is a self-regulatory capability in which top management's role is to establish a broad culture and set of relationships that provide a supportive organizational context for delegated decisions. This is a sophisticated management process driven by *socialization* and is most effective in decisions that require the effective use of the large amounts of information, knowledge, and expertise that resides in the dispersed activities of the transnational organization.

Building a Transnational Organization: Beyond Structure

The kind of organization that we have described as a transnational clearly represents something quite different from its predecessors—the multinational, international, and global organizations. Building such an organization requires much more than choosing between a product or a geographic organization structure; managing it implies much more than centralizing or decentralizing decisions. So what exactly is involved in building a transnational organization?

At the beginning of this chapter, we saw that the classic structural stages model no longer provides a helpful description of international organization development. To describe the transnational organization, we need a different way to frame the more complex and subtle array of characteristics and capabilities that we have described in the preceding paragraphs. The simple framework that we adopt here describes the organization in terms of a physiological model. This allows us to hypothesize that any effective organization must be framed by a strong anatomy (the formal structure of its assets, resources, and responsibilities) complemented by a robust, functioning physiology (the organization's systems and decision processes) and an appropriate, healthy psychology (the organization's culture and management mentality).

Using this model, we will now describe the different tools and processes used to build and manage the transnational organization.

Structuring the Organizational Anatomy

As we have seen, the traditional approach to MNE organization problems has been defined in macro-structural terms that focused on simple but rather superficial choices, such as the classic "product versus geography" structural debate. In a transnational organization, however, managers must also develop supporting structures that both supplement and counterbalance the embedded power of their dominant line managers.

Having carefully defined the roles and responsibilities of their geographic, functional, and product management groups (recognizing that those may vary business by business, as illustrated in Figure 4-4), the next challenge is to ensure that particularly those without line authority have appropriate access to and influence in the management process. Microstructural tools such as cross-unit teams, task forces, or committees can create supplemental decision-making forums that allow non-line managers to have significant influence, and even to assume responsibility in a way that is not possible in classic one-dimensional organizations. So, in the example illustrated in Figure 4-4, while the detergent product manager may have formal line authority for worldwide pricing, decisions may be set in consultation with geographic managers who may negotiate flexibility for their regions or countries based on local competitive situations.

Where task forces and consultative committees were once considered ad hoc, quick-fix devices, companies building transnational organizations use them as legitimate, ongoing structural tools through which top management can fine-tune or rebalance the basic structure. To stretch our anatomical analogy, if the formal line structure is the organization's backbone, the non-line groups represent its rib cage, and these microstructural structural overlays like teams and task forces provide the muscle, tendons, and cartilage that give the organizational skeleton its flexibility.

Building the Organizational Physiology

One of the key roles of management is to develop the communication channels through which the organization's decision-making process operates. By adapting the various administrative systems, communication channels, and informal relationships, management can shape the volume, content, and direction of information flows that provide the lifeblood of all management processes. It is this flow of information that defines the organizational physiology—its veins, arteries, and airways.

Many researchers have shown the strong link between the complexity and uncertainty of the tasks to be performed and the need for information. In an integrated network configuration, task complexity and uncertainty are very high. Operating in such a multidimensional, interdependent system requires large volumes of information to be gathered, exchanged, and processed, so the role of formal information, planning, reporting and control systems is vital. But formal systems alone cannot support the huge information processing needs, and companies are forced to look beyond their traditional tools and conventional systems.

For years, managers have recognized that a great deal of information exchange and even decision making occurs through the organization's innumerable informal channels and relationships. Yet this part of the management process has often been dismissed as either unimportant ("office gossip" or "rumor mill") or unmanageable ("disruptive cliques" or "unholy alliances"). In the management of transnational organizations, such biases need to be reexamined. Because organizational units are widely separated and information is scarce, not only is it more important for managers of international operations to exert some control and influence over informal systems, it is also more feasible for them to do so.

Getting started is often remarkably easy, requiring managers to do little more than use their daily involvement in the ongoing management processes to shape the nature and quality of communications patterns and relationships. The easiest place to start is to recognize, legitimize, and reinforce existing informal relationships that have the potential to contribute to the corporate objective. These can then be consciously influenced by adjusting the frequency and agenda of management trips and corporate meetings (a good way to focus and diffuse information), the pattern of committee assignments (an effective way of building relationships and shaping decisions), and the track of people's career development (a powerful way to reinforce and reward flexibility and collaboration).

Developing the Organizational Psychology

In addition to an anatomy and a physiology, each organization also has a psychology—a set of explicit or implicit corporate values and shared beliefs—that greatly influences the way that its members act. Particularly when employees come from a variety of different national backgrounds, management cannot assume that all will share common values and relate to common norms. Furthermore, in an operating environment in which managers are separated by distance, language, and time barriers, shared management understanding is often a much more powerful tool than formal structures and systems for coordinating diverse activities.

Of the numerous tools and techniques that can affect an organization's psychology, our review of transnational organizations has highlighted three that are particularly important. The first is the need for a clear, shared understanding of the company's mission and objectives. Classic models range from Google's mission, "to organize the world's information and make it universally accessible and useful," to Konosuke Matsushita's mission, "to create material abundance by providing goods as plentiful and inexpensive as tap water"—a mission that he translated into a 250-year plan broken into ten 25-year goals!

The second important tool is the visible behavior and public actions of senior management. Particularly in a transnational organization in which other signals may be diluted or distorted, top management's actions speak louder than words and tend to have a powerful influence on the company's culture. They represent the clearest role model of behavior and a signal of the company's strategic and organizational priorities. When Cisco's CEO John Chambers decided to increase the company's commitment to its internationalization strategy, he established a major corporate center in India, which he called Globalization Center East. He dispatched Wim Elfrink, Cisco's number two executive, to go to India and personally take charge of the proposed 3,000-person operation. Elfrink was also named the company's chief globalization officer. This very significant transfer of corporate resources was a clear message to the organization that Cisco was very committed to its internationalization strategy.

The third and most commonly used set of tools for modifying organizational psychology in the transnational organization is nested in the company's personnel policies, practices, and systems. A company can develop a multidimensional and flexible organization process only if its personnel systems develop and reinforce the appropriate kinds of people. At Eli Lilly, the recruiting and promotion policies emphasize the importance of good interpersonal skills and flexible, nonparochial personalities; its career path management is used not only to develop necessary management skills and expertise, but also to broaden individual perspectives and interpersonal relationships; and its measurement and reward systems are explicitly designed to reinforce the thrust of organization-building efforts and cultural values.

Although the process of adapting an organization's culture, values, or beliefs is slow and the techniques are subtle, this tool plays a particularly important role in the development of a transnational organization because change in the organizational anatomy and physiology without complementary modifications to its psychology can lead to severe organizational problems.

Managing the Process of Change

As they adapted their worldwide operations, managers in some companies assumed that organizational change could be driven by changes in the formal structure. One of the most dramatic examples was Westinghouse's reorganization of its operations. Dissatisfied with its worldwide product organization, top management assigned a team of executives to study the company's international organization problems for 90 days. Its proposal that Westinghouse adopt a global matrix was accepted, and the team was then given three months to "install the new structure." We saw a similar approach at P&G, when it adopted its Organization 2005 and then, with little input or discussion, rolled out the radical structural change worldwide.

Such examples are far from unusual—literally hundreds of other companies have done something similar. The managers involved seemed to assume that by announcing changes in formal roles and reporting relationships (the organization's anatomy), they would force changes in the organizational relationships and decision processes (its physiology), which in turn would reshape the way individual managers think and act (its psychology). This model of the process of organizational change is illustrated in Figure 4-5.

But such an approach loses sight of the real organization behind the boxes and lines on the chart. The boxes that are casually shifted around represent people with abilities, motivations, beliefs, and interests, not just formal positions with specified roles. The

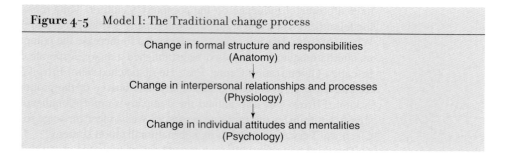

Figure 4-5   Model I: The Traditional change process

Change in formal structure and responsibilities
(Anatomy)

Change in interpersonal relationships and processes
(Physiology)

Change in individual attitudes and mentalities
(Psychology)

Figure 4-6   Model II: The emerging change process

Change in individual attitudes and mentalities

Change in interpersonal relationships and processes

Change in formal structure and responsibilities

lines that are redrawn are not just formal reporting channels, but interpersonal relationships that may have taken years to develop. As a result, trying to force changes in organizational processes and management mentality by altering the formal structure can have a high cost. The new relationships defined in the reorganized structure often will take months to establish at the most basic level and a year or more to become truly effective. Developing new individual attitudes and behaviors will take even longer because many employees will be frustrated, alienated, or simply unequal to the new job requirements.

More-sophisticated MNEs tend to adopt a very different approach that relies more on personnel assignments that process adjustments as important mechanisms of organizational change. Building on the informal relationships that dominated their earlier management processes, these companies often use assignments and transfers to forge interpersonal links, build organizational cohesion, and develop policy consistency. And in some companies (particularly those from Asian countries) enormous emphasis is placed on socializing the individual into the organization and shaping his or her attitudes to conform to overall corporate values. Organizational change in these companies is often driven more by intensive education programs than by reconfigurations of the structure or systems.

Although the specific change process and sequence must vary from one company to the next, the overall change process adopted in these companies is very different from the process driven by structural realignment. Indeed, the sequence is often the reverse. The first objective is to influence the understanding and perceptions of key individuals. Then follows a series of changes aimed at modifying the communication flows and decision-making processes. Only in a final stage are the changes consolidated and confirmed by structural realignment. This process is represented by the model in Figure 4-6.

Of course, these two models of organizational change are both gross over simplifications of the process. But they do serve to highlight the key message that organizations are shaped and defined by more than their formal structures, and as a result, organizational change must involve more than simply redrawing the organization chart.

All change processes inevitably involve substantial overlap of changes to the organizational anatomy, physiology, and psychology; the two sequences merely reflect differences in the relative emphasis on each set of tools during the process. Although the more gradual change process is much less organizationally traumatic, in times of crisis—chronic poor performance, a badly misaligned structure, or a major structural change in the environment, for example—radical restructuring may be necessary to achieve rapid and sweeping change. For most organizations, however, dramatic structural change is highly traumatic and can distract managers from their external tasks as they focus on the internal realignment. Fortunately, most change processes can be managed in a more evolutionary manner, focusing first on the modification of individual perspectives and interpersonal relationships before tackling the formal redistribution of responsibilities and power.

The Transnational Organization in Transition

During the past decade or so, political, competitive, and social pressures have reinforced the need for MNEs to create organizations that can sense and respond to complex, yet often conflicting, demands. So as more and more companies confront the need to build worldwide organizations that are both multidimensional and flexible, the form of the transnational organization they are creating continues to adapt. Among the most widespread transnational organizational trends that we have observed in recent years are disenchantment with formal matrix structures, the redefinition of primary organizational dimensions, and the changing role of functional management in transnationals.

Disenchantment with Formal Matrix Structures

As an increasing number of managers recognized the need to develop the multidimensional organizational capabilities that characterize a transnational organization, the initial reaction of many was to impose the new model through a global matrix structure.

Widespread press coverage of ABB's decade-long global expansion through such an organization encouraged some to believe that this structure was the key to exploiting global scale efficiencies while responding to local market needs. But as many soon discovered, the strategic benefits provided by such a complex organization came at an organizational cost.

Although some companies were able to create the culture and process vital to the success of the matrix structure—in ABB's case, they supported the company's ambitious global expansion for more than a decade—others were much less successful. One such failure was P&G's much publicized Organization 2005, referred to briefly above. This radical structural change boldly imposed a global product structure over the company's historically successful geographic organization. The resulting global matrix was installed worldwide, creating problems that eventually cost CEO Durk Jager his job.

But despite continuing nervousness about the global matrix structure, most MNEs still recognize the need to create multidimensional and flexible organizations. The big lesson of the 2000s was that such organizations are best built by developing overlaid processes and supportive cultures, not just by formalizing multiple reporting relationships. A.G. Lafley, the CEO who succeeded Jager at P&G, put it well when he said, "We built this new house, then moved in before the plumbing and wiring were connected. You cannot change organization with structure alone." Or in the terms that we have used, changes in an organization's anatomy must be supplemented with changes to its physiology and psychology.

Redefinition of Key Organization Dimensions

Historically, the dominant dimensions around which most MNEs built their worldwide operations had business or product management on one side and country or regional management on the other. But in the past decade or so, the global customer dimension is becoming increasingly important in many worldwide organizations.

The pressure to create such customer-driven organizations grew gradually in the new millennium. First, as global customers began demanding uniform prices and service levels from their suppliers, MNEs were forced to respond by creating dedicated global account managers who would take responsibility for all sales to customers around the world. Then, as customers expected increasing levels of value-added services, companies began to shift from "selling products" to "providing solutions."

These and similar forces led to the creation of transnational organizations in which front-end, customer-facing units bundled products from back-end, product-driven units. A good example of this was IBM's Global Services Organization, one of the most successful customer-facing organizations, which grew rapidly because of its ability to supply customers whose operations often spread around the globe with a combination of IBM's products, consulting services, and often an additional package of related, outsourced products and services.

Changing the Functional Management Role

In transnational organizations built around business, geography, and, more recently, the customer, the functional managers responsible for finance, human resources, logistics, and other cross-business and cross-organizational specialties were often relegated to secondary staff roles. However, with the expansion of the information-based, knowledge-intensive service economy, the resources and expertise that resided in these specialized functions became increasingly important sources of competitive advantage. As a result, recent years have seen their roles become progressively more central in many transnational organizations.

Managers of finance, HR, and IT functions gained importance because of their control of the scarce strategic resources that were so critical to capture and leverage on a worldwide basis. With the globalization of financial markets in the global financial crisis of 2008/2009, the finance function was often able to play an essential role in lowering the cost of capital and managing cross-border risk exposure. Just as dramatic has been the role of the HR experts, as MNEs tapped into scarce knowledge and expertise outside the home country and leveraged it for global competitive advantage. Similarly, the emergence of the chief knowledge officer role reflects the importance that many companies are placing on the organization's ability to capture and leverage valuable information, best practices, and scarce knowledge and expertise wherever it exists in the company.

Again, this trend is creating a need for transnational companies to create organizational overlays supplemented by new channels of communication and forums of decision making that enable managers to develop and leverage the company's competitive advantage through its sophisticated organizational capabilities. The form and function of the transnational organization continues to adapt as MNE managers seek new ways to develop and deliver layers of competitive advantage.

Concluding Comments

In this chapter, we have looked at the organizational capabilities that the MNE must build to operate effectively in today's fast-changing global business environment. The strategic challenge, as we have described it, requires the MNE to optimize global efficiency, national responsiveness, and worldwide learning simultaneously. To address this complex and conflicting set of demands, a new form of organization is required, which we call the *transnational*. The transnational is characterized by its legitimization of multidimensional perspectives, its distributed and interdependent capabilities, and its flexible integrative processes. It is a model that is increasingly becoming mainstream.

Chapter 4 Readings

- Reading 4-1, "Organizing for an Emerging World," draws on the lessons learned by McKinsey organizational consultants as they worked with companies expanding into emerging markets. They address questions of how to adjust structure to support growth in emerging markets, how to find a productive balance between standardized global and diverse local processes, where to locate the corporate center and what to do there, and how to deploy knowledge and skills effectively around the world by getting the right people to communicate with each other.
- In Reading 4-2, "Have You Restructured for Global Success?" the authors emphasize the importance of creating organizations that are not only able to manage existing operations in developed countries, but also have the ability to capture the energy, ambition, and optimism that they often unleash in the developing world. They propose the creation of a T-shaped organization that allows the MNE to "walk the tightrope" between these different organizational needs.
- Reading 4-3, "Matrix Management: Not a Structure, a Frame of Mind" is a classic article that emphasizes the need to focus less on the search for an ideal organization structure and more on developing the abilities, behavior, and performance of individual managers.

In different ways, each of these readings underscores the need to build an organization that balances global integration, national responsiveness, and worldwide learning.

Case 4-1   Philips versus Matsushita: The Competitive Battle Continues

Christopher A. Bartlett

Throughout their long histories, N.V. Philips (Netherlands) and Matsushita Electric (Japan) had followed very different strategies and emerged with very different organizational capabilities. Philips built its success on a worldwide portfolio of responsive national organizations while Matsushita based its global competitiveness on its centralized, highly efficient operations in Japan.

During the first decade of the 21st century, however, both companies experienced major challenges to their historic competitive positions and organizational models. Implementing yet another round of strategic initiatives and organizational restructurings, the CEOs at both companies were taking their respective organizations in very different directions. At the end of the decade, observers wondered how the changes would affect their long-running competitive battle.

Philips: Background

In 1892, Gerard Philips and his father opened a small light-bulb factory in Eindhoven, Holland. When their venture almost failed, they recruited Gerard's brother, Anton, an excellent salesman and

manager. By 1900, Philips was the third largest light-bulb producer in Europe.

Technological Competence and Geographic Expansion   While larger electrical products companies were racing to diversify, Philips made only light-bulbs. This one-product focus and Gerard's technological prowess enabled the company to create significant innovations. Company policy was to scrap old plants and use new machines or factories whenever advances were made in new production technology. Anton wrote down assets rapidly and set aside substantial reserves for replacing outdated equipment. Philips also became a leader in industrial research, creating physics and chemistry labs to address production problems as well as more abstract scientific ones. The labs developed a tungsten metal filament bulb that was a great commercial success and gave Philips the financial strength to compete against its giant rivals.

Holland's small size soon forced Philips to look aboard for enough volume to mass produce. In 1899, Anton hired the company's first export manager, and soon the company was selling into such diverse markets as Japan, Australia, Canada, Brazil, and Russia. In 1912, as the electric lamp industry began to show signs of overcapacity, Philips started building sales organizations in the United States, Canada, and France. All other functions remained highly centralized in Eindhoven. In many foreign countries Philips created local joint ventures to gain market acceptance.

In 1919, Philips entered into the Principal Agreement with General Electric, giving each company the use of the other's patents, while simultaneously dividing the world into "three spheres of influence." After this time, Philips began evolving from a highly centralized company, whose sales were conducted through third parties, to a decentralized sales organization with autonomous marketing companies in 14 European countries, China, Brazil, and Australia.

During this period, the company also broadened its product line significantly. In 1918, it began producing electronic vacuum tubes; eight years later its first radios appeared, capturing a 20% world market share within a decade; and during the 1930s, Philips began producing X-ray tubes. The Great Depression brought with it trade barriers and high tariffs, and Philips was forced to build local production facilities to protect its foreign sales of these products.

Philips: Organizational Development

One of the earliest traditions at Philips was a shared but competitive leadership by the commercial and technical functions. Gerard, an engineer, and Anton, a businessman, began a subtle competition where Gerard would try to produce more than Anton could sell and vice versa. Nevertheless, the two agreed that strong research was vital to Philip's survival.

During the late 1930s, in anticipation of the impending war, Philips transferred its overseas assets to two trusts, British Philips and the North American Philips Corporation; it also moved most of its vital research laboratories to Redhill in Surrey, England, and its top management to the United States. Supported by the assets and resources transferred abroad, and isolated from their parent, the individual country organizations became more independent during the war.

Because waves of Allied and German bombing had pummeled most of Philip's industrial plant in the Netherlands, the management board decided to build the postwar organization on the strengths of the national organizations (NOs). Their greatly increased self-sufficiency during the war had allowed most to become adept at responding to country-specific market conditions—a capability that became a valuable asset in the postwar era. For example, when international wrangling precluded any agreement on three competing television transmission standards (PAL, SECAM, and NTSC), each nation decided which to adopt.

Furthermore, consumer preferences and economic conditions varied: in some countries, rich, furniture-encased TV sets were the norm; in others, sleek, contemporary models dominated the market. In the United Kingdom, the only way to penetrate the market was to establish a rental business; in richer countries, a major marketing challenge was overcoming elitist prejudice against television. In this environment, the independent NOs had a great advantage in being able to sense and respond to the differences.

Eventually, responsiveness extended beyond adaptive marketing. As NOs built their own technical capabilities, product development often became a function of local market conditions. For example, Philips of Canada created the company's first color TV; Philips of Australia created the first stereo TV; and Philips of the United Kingdom created the first TVs with teletext.

While NOs took major responsibility for financial, legal, and administrative matters, fourteen product divisions (PDs), located in Eindhoven, were formally responsible for development, production, and global distribution. (In reality, the NOs' control of assets and the PDs' distance from the operations often undercut this formal role.) The research function remained independent and, with continued strong funding, set up eight separate laboratories in Europe and the United States.

While the formal corporate-level structure was represented as a type of geographic/product matrix, it was clear that NOs had the real power. They reported directly to the management board, which Philips enlarged from four members to 10 to ensure that top management remained in contact with the highly autonomous NOs. Each NO also regularly sent envoys to Eindhoven to represent its interests. Top management, most of whom had careers that included multiple foreign tours of duty, made frequent overseas visits to the NOs. In 1954, the board established the International Concern Council to formalize regular meetings with the heads of all major NOs.

Within the NOs, management structure mimicked the legendary joint technical and commercial leadership of the two Philips brothers. Most were led by a technical manager and a commercial manager. In some locations, a finance manager filled out the top management triad that typically reached key decisions collectively. This cross-functional coordination capability was reflected down through the NOs in front-line product teams, product-group-level management teams, and at the senior management committee of the NOs' top commercial, technical, and financial managers.

The overwhelming importance of foreign operations to Philips, the commensurate status of the NOs within the corporate hierarchy, and even the cosmopolitan appeal of many of the offshore subsidiaries' locations encouraged many Philips managers to take extended foreign tours of duty, working in a series of two- or three-year posts. This elite group of expatriate managers identified strongly with each other and with the NOs as a group and had no difficulty representing their strong, country-oriented views to corporate management.

Philips: Attempts at Reorganization

In the late 1960s, the creation of the European Common Market eroded trade barriers and diluted the rationale for independent country subsidiaries. New transistor-based technologies demanded larger production runs than most national plants could justify, and many of Philips' competitors were moving production of electronics to new facilities in low-wage areas in Asia and South America.

Simultaneously, Philips' ability to bring its innovative products to market began to falter, and in the 1960s it watched Japanese competitors capture the mass market for audiocassettes and microwave ovens, two technologies it had invented. A decade later, it had to abandon its V2000 videocassette format—superior technically to Sony's Beta or Matsushita's VHS—when North American Philips decided to outsource a VHS product which it manufactured under license from Matsushita.

Over the next four decades, seven chairmen experimented with reorganizing the company to deal with its growing problems. Yet, in 2009, Philips'

financial performance remained poor and its global competitiveness was still in question. (See **Exhibits 1** and **2.**)

Van Reimsdijk and the Yellow Booklet Concerned about what one magazine described as "continued profitless progress," newly appointed CEO Hendrick van Riemsdijk created an organization committee to prepare a policy paper on the division of responsibilities between the PDs and the NOs. In 1971, their report, dubbed the "Yellow Booklet," outlined the disadvantages of Philips' matrix organization in 1971: "Without an agreement [defining the relationship between national organizations and product divisions], it is impossible to determine in any given situation which of the two parties is responsible... As operations become increasingly complex, an organizational form of this type will only lower the speed of reaction of an enterprise."

On the basis of this report, van Reimsdijk proposed rebalancing the managerial relationships between PDs and NOs—"tilting the matrix towards the PDs" in his words—to allow Philips to decrease the number of products marketed, build scale by concentrating production, and increase the product flows across NOs. He proposed closing the least efficient local plants and converting the best into International Production Centers (IPCs), each supplying many NOs. In so doing, van Reimsdijk hoped that PD managers would gain control over manufacturing operations. Due to the political and organizational difficulty of closing local plants, however, implementation was slow.

Rodenberg and Dekker: "Tilting the Matrix" In the late 1970s, van Riemsdijk's successor, Dr. Rodenburg, continued his thrust. Several IPCs were established, but the NOs seemed as powerful and independent as ever. He furthered matrix simplification by replacing the dual commercial and technical leadership with single management at both the corporate and national organizational levels. Yet the power struggles continued.

Upon becoming CEO in 1982, Wisse Dekker outlined a new initiative. Aware of the cost advantage

Exhibit 1   Philips Group Summary Financial Data, 1970–2008 (Reported in millions of Dutch Guilders (F) to 1996; Euros (€) after 1997)

	2008	2000	1990	1980	1970
Net sales	€26,385	€37,862	F55,764	F36,536	F15,070
Income from operations (excluding restructuring)	NA	NA	2,260	1,577	1,280
Income from operations (including restructuring)	551	3,022	−2,389	NA	NA
As a percentage of net sales	2.1%	8.0%	−4.3%	4.3%	8.5%
Income after taxes	NA	NA	F−4,447	F532	F446
Net income from normal business operations	−178	9,577	−4,526	328	435
Stockholders' equity (common)	16,267	15,847	11,165	12,996	6,324
Return on stockholders' equity	−1.0%	60.4%	−30.2%	2.7%	7.3%
Distribution per common share, per value F10 (in guilders)	€0.7	€0.36	F0.0	F1.80	F1.70
Total assets	33,048	38,541	51,595	39,647	19,088
Inventories as a percentage of net sales	12.8%	13.9%	20.7%	32.8%	35.2%
Outstanding trade receivables in month's sales	1.9	1.6	1.6	3.0	2.8
Current ratio	1.2	1.2	1.4	1.7	1.7
Employees at year-end (in thousands)	121	219	273	373	359
Selected data in millions of dollars:					
Sales	$36,868	$35,564	$33,018	$16,993	$4,163
Operating profit	770	2,838	1,247	734	NA
Pretax income	155	9,587	−2,380	364	NA
Net income	−260	9,078	−2,510	153	120
Total assets	46,169	35,885	30,549	18,440	5,273
Shareholders' equity (common)	22,697	20,238	6,611	6,044	1,747

Note: Exchange rate

Guilder/Dollar	1970	3.62
	1980	2.15
	1990	1.68
Euro/Dollar	2000	0.94
	2008	1.40

Sources: Annual reports; Standard & Poor's Compustat®; Moody's Industrial and International Manuals.

of Philips' Japanese counterparts, he closed inefficient operations—particularly in Europe where 40 of the company's more than 200 plants were shut. He focused on core operations by selling peripheral businesses such welding, energy cables, and furniture making, while simultaneously acquiring an interest in Grundig and Westinghouse's North American lamp activities.

He also continued to "tilt the matrix," giving PDs product management responsibility, but leaving NOs responsible for local profits. And he allowed NOs to input into product planning, but gave

Exhibit 2 Philips Group, Sales by Product and Geographic Segment, 1985–2003 (Reported in millions of Dutch Guilders (F) to 1996; Euros (€) after 1997)

	2003		2000		1995		1990		1985	
Net Sales by Product Segment:										
Lighting	€4,634	16%	€5,051	13%	F8,353	13%	F7,026	13%	F7,976	12%
Consumer electronics	9,415	33	14,681	39	22,027	34	25,400	46	16,906	26
Domestic appliances	2,183	7	2,107	6	—		—		6,664	10
Professional products/Systems	—		—		11,562	18	13,059	23	17,850	28
Components/Semiconductors	3,984	14%	10,440	28	10,714	17	8,161	15	11,620	18
Software/Services	—		—		9,425	15	—		—	
Medical systems/Health care	6,138	21	3,030	8	—		—		—	
Origin	—		716	2	—		—		—	
Miscellaneous	4,455	15	1,831	5	2,381	4	2,118	4	3,272	5
Total	28,627	100%	37,862	100%	64,462	100%	F55,764	100%	F64,266	100%
Operating Income by Sector:										
Lighting	591		668	16%	983	24%	419	18%	F910	30%
Consumer electronics	254		374	9	167	4	1,499	66	34	1
Domestic appliances	407		287	7	—		—		397	13
Professional products/Systems	—		—		157	4	189	8	1,484	48
Components/Semiconductors	–336		1,915	45	2,233	55	–43	–2	44	1
Software/Services	—		—		886	22	—		—	
Medical systems	441		169	4	—		—		—	
Origin	—		1,063	25	—		—		—	
Miscellaneous	–845		–113	–3	423	10	218	10	200	7
Increase not attributable to a sector	—		–82	–2	(805)	(20)	–22	–1	6	0
Total	513		4,280	100%	4,044	100%	2,260	100%	F3,074	100%

Notes: Totals may not add due to rounding.
Product sector sales after 1988 are external sales only; therefore, no eliminations are made; sector sales before 1988 include sales to other sectors; therefore, eliminations are made.
Data are not comparable to consolidated financial summary due to restating.
Source: Annual reports.

global PDs the final decision on long-range direction. Still sales declined and profits stagnated.

Van der Klugt's Radical Restructuring When Cor van der Klugt succeeded Dekker as chairman in 1987, Philips had lost its long-held consumer electronics leadership position to Matsushita, and was one of only two non-Japanese companies in the world's top ten. Its net profit margins of 1% to 2% not only lagged behind General Electric's 9%, but even its highly aggressive Japanese competitor's slim 4%. Van der Klugt set a profit objective of 3% to 4% and made beating the Japanese companies a top priority.

As van der Klugt reviewed Philips' strategy, he designated various businesses as core (those that shared related technologies, had strategic importance, or were technical leaders) and non-core (stand-alone businesses that were not targets for world leadership and could eventually be sold if required). Of the four businesses defined as core, three were strategically linked: components, consumer electronics, and telecommunications and data systems. The fourth, lighting, was regarded as strategically vital because its cash flow funded development. The non-core businesses included domestic appliances and medical systems which van der Klugt spun off into joint ventures with Whirlpool and GE, respectively.

In continuing efforts to strengthen the PDs relative to the NOs, van der Klugt restructured Philips around the four core global divisions rather than the former 14 PDs. This allowed him to trim the management board, appointing the displaced board members to a new policy-making Group Management Committee. Consisting primarily of PD heads and functional chiefs, this body replaced the old NO-dominated International Concern Council. Finally, he sharply reduced the 3,000-strong headquarters staff, reallocating many of them to the PDs.

To link PDs more directly to markets, van der Klugt dispatched many experienced product-line managers to Philips' most competitive markets. For example, management of the digital audio tape and electric-shaver product lines were relocated to Japan, while the medical technology and domestic appliances lines were moved to the United States.

Such moves, along with continued efforts at globalizing product development and production efforts, required that the parent company gain firmer control over NOs, especially the giant North American Philips Corp. (NAPC). Although Philips had obtained a majority equity interest after World War II, it was not always able to make the U.S. company respond to directives from the center, as the V2000 VCR incident showed. To prevent replays of such experiences, in 1987 van der Klugt repurchased publicly owned NAPC shares for $700 million.

Reflecting the growing sentiment among some managers that R&D was not market oriented enough, van der Klugt halved spending on basic research to about 10% of total R&D. To manage what he described as "R&D's tendency to ponder the fundamental laws of nature," he made the R&D budget the direct responsibility of the businesses being supported by the research. This required that each research lab become focused on specific business areas (see **Exhibit 3**).

Finally, van der Klugt continued the effort to build efficient, specialized, multi-market production facilities by closing 75 of the company's 420 remaining plants worldwide. He also eliminated 38,000 of its 344,000 employees—21,000 through divesting businesses, shaking up the myth of lifetime employment at the company. He anticipated that all these restructurings would lead to a financial recovery by 1990. Unanticipated losses for that year, however—more than 4.5 billion Dutch guilders ($2.5 billion)—provoked a class-action law suit by angry American investors, who alleged that positive projections by the company had been misleading. In a surprise move, on May 14, 1990, van der Klugt and half of the management board were replaced.

Timmer's "Operation Centurion" The new president, Jan Timmer, had spent most of his 35-year Philips career turning around unprofitable businesses. Under the banner "Operation Centurion," he lost no time in launching an initiative that cut headcount by 68,000 or 22% over the next 18 months, earning Timmer the nickname "The

Exhibit 3   Philips Research Labs by Location and Specialty, 1987

Location	Size (staff)	Specialty
Eindhoven, The Netherlands	2,000	Basic research, electronics, manufacturing technology
Redhill, Surrey, England	450	Microelectronics, television, defense
Hamburg, Germany	350	Communications, office equipment, medical imaging
Aachen, W. Germany	250	Fiber optics, X-ray systems
Paris, France	350	Microprocessors, chip materials, design
Brussels	50	Artificial intelligence
Briarcliff Manor, New York	35	Optical systems, television, superconductivity, defense
Sunnyvale, California	150	Integrated circuits

Source: Philips, in *Business Week,* March 21, 1988, p. 156.

Butcher of Eindhoven." Because European laws required substantial compensation for layoffs—Eindhoven workers received 15 months' pay, for example—the first round of 10,000 layoffs alone cost Philips $700 million. To spread the burden around the globe, Timmer asked his PD managers to negotiate cuts with NO managers. But according to one report, country managers were "digging in their heels to save local jobs." Nonetheless, cuts came—many from overseas operations.

To focus resources further, Timmer sold off various businesses including integrated circuits to Matsushita, minicomputers to Digital, defense electronics to Thomson and the remaining 53% of appliances to Whirlpool. Yet profitability was still well below the modest 4% on sales he promised. In particular, consumer electronics lagged with slow growth in a price-competitive market. The core problem was identified by a 1994 McKinsey study that estimated that value added per hour in Japanese consumer electronic factories was still 68% above that of European plants.

After three years of cost-cutting, in early 1994 Timmer finally presented a new growth strategy to the board. His plan was to expand software, services, and multimedia to become 40% of revenues by 2000. He was betting on Philips' legendary innovative capability to restart the growth engines. He hired Hewlett-Packard's director of research and encouraged him to focus on developing 15 core technologies. The list, which included interactive compact disc (CD-i), digital compact cassettes (DCC), high definition television (HDTV), and multimedia software, was soon dubbed "the president's projects." Over the next few years, Philips invested over $2.5 billion in these technologies. But the earlier divestment of some of the company's truly high-tech businesses and a 37% cut in R&D personnel left it with few who understood the technology of the new priority businesses.

By 1996, it was clear that Philips' analog HDTV technology would not become industry standard, that its DCC gamble had lost out to Sony's Minidisc, and that CD-i was a marketing failure. And while costs in Philips were lower, so too was morale, particularly among middle management. Critics claimed that the company's drive for cost-cutting and standardization had led it to ignore new worldwide market demands for more segmented products and higher consumer service.

Boonstra's Reorganization When Timmer stepped down in October 1996, the board replaced him with a radical choice for Philips—an outsider whose expertise was in marketing and Asia rather than technology and Europe. Cor Boonstra was a 58-year-old Dutchman whose years as CEO of Sara Lee, the U.S. consumer products firm, had earned him a reputation as a hard-driving marketing genius. Joining Philips in 1994, he headed the Asia

Pacific region and the lighting division before being tapped as CEO.

Unencumbered by tradition, he announced strategic sweeping changes designed to reach his goal of increasing return on net assets from 17% to 24% by 1999. "There are no taboos, no sacred cows," he said. "The bleeders must be turned around, sold, or closed." Within three years, he had sold off 40 of Philips' 120 major businesses—including such well known units as Polygram and Grundig.

Promising to transform a structure he described as "a plate of spaghetti" into "a neat row of asparagus," he then initiated a major worldwide restructuring. "How can we compete with the Koreans?" he asked. "They don't have 350 companies all over the world. Their factory in Ireland covers Europe and their manufacturing facility in Mexico serves North America. We need a more structured and simpler manufacturing and marketing organization to achieve a cost pattern in line with those who do not have our heritage. This is still one of the biggest issues facing Philips."

Within a year, 3,100 jobs were eliminated in North America and 3,000 employees were added in Asia Pacific, emphasizing Boonstra's determination to shift production to low-wage countries and his broader commitment to Asia. And after three years, he had closed 100 of the company's 356 factories worldwide. At the same time, he replaced the company's 21 PDs with 7 divisions, but shifted day-to-day operating responsibility to 100 business units, each responsible for its profits worldwide. It was a move designed to finally eliminate the old PD/NO matrix. Finally, in a move that shocked most employees, he announced that the 100-year-old Eindhoven headquarters would be relocated to Amsterdam with only 400 of the 3,000 corporate positions remaining.

By early 1998, he was ready to announce his new strategy. Despite early speculation that he might abandon consumer electronics, he proclaimed it as the center of Philips' future. Betting on the "digital revolution," he planned to focus on established technologies such as cellular phones (through a joint venture with Lucent), digital TV, digital videodisc, and web TV. Furthermore, he committed major resources to marketing, including a 40% increase in advertising to raise awareness and image of the Philips brand and deemphasize most of the 150 other brands it supported worldwide—from Magnavox TVs to Norelco shavers to Marantz stereos.

While not everything succeeded (the Lucent cell phone JV collapsed after nine months, for example), overall performance improved significantly in the late 1990s. By 2000, Boonstra was able to announce that he had achieved his objective of a 24% return on net assets.

Kleisterlee's Refocusing   By the time the Boonstra stepped down in May 2001, however, a global "tech wreck" recession had begun, resulting in what Fortune described as "a tidal wave of red ink" to greet the new CEO, Gerard Kleisterlee, a 54-year-old career Philips man. With the share price in free fall from $60 in 2001 to $13 in 2002, Kleisterlee faced what he described as "the biggest losses in the history of the company."

Moving quickly, the new CEO began restructuring the company, announcing the outsourcing of Philips mobile phone production to CEC of China, and the production of VCRs to Japan's Funai Electric. But it was not sufficient to prevent a 2001 loss of €2.6 billion compared to a €9.6 billion profit in 2000. So, over the next few years, he continued to outsource production of TVs, CD players, and components, while simultaneously moving the remaining in-house production to low-cost countries like China, Poland, or Mexico. He also sold off several businesses including most components, mobile phones, audio, and even the core semiconductor business. Within four years he had removed more than one in four Philips employees, reducing headcount by 60,000.

But Kleisterlee felt he faced a bigger challenge. "Phillips never really had any kind of strategy," he conceded. "If our engineers could make it, we would try to sell it . . . In 2001, we were still focused on a broad range of volatile, high-volume products like consumer electronics, semiconductors, and components. Now we are trying to create a company that generates value in a more predictable way with a portfolio that is less volatile."

The shape of that new portfolio soon became clear. Using funds generated by selling businesses, Kleisterlee began acquiring companies in the high-growth medical and lighting segments, and began referring to Philips as "a lifestyle company" centered on health and well-being. "We came to the conclusion that the thing that holds everything together is not the fact that we made our own components and semiconductors. It's the fact that we have a common mission," he said.

A business once at the center of Philips portfolio now had a new role. "Consumer electronics is a very, very small leftover part in our lifestyle portfolio," he explained. "That business is too big a battle to fight now. We plan to be the Dell of consumer electronics, making less and marketing more. That means that we will be focused on product development, brand, and channel management."

So while Phillips continued to create innovations for its TVs, it focused them on its high-definition plasma and LCD sets with breakthroughs like Pixel Plus 2, a digital technology that refined the incoming signal to produce sharper pictures with more vivid color. But in addition to technological breakthroughs, R&D was also focused on more basic products for developing markets—hand-crank radios, high powered mixers designed for exotic foods, and irons with dust tolerant thermostats.

Phillips approach to marketing was also changing. In the developed world, it slashed the number of retail chains it serviced from 600 to 200, focusing particularly on seven giants like Wal-Mart, Tesco, and Carrefour. But in developing countries, it took a different approach. For example in India, its strategy was to sell its adapted low-end products through 35,000 village stores.

Kleisterlee explained how his adaptive product-market strategy worked: "In India, we have vans with diagnostic and lab equipment, equipped with a satellite video link to a top hospital. Instead of making long trips to a city hospital, people can now get cheaper, more convenient treatment where they

live." With 700 million people in rural India, the company felt it had a great opportunity.

By 2008, Kleisterlee was ready to confirm his new focused strategy in the organization structure. Having earlier cut the number of divisions to five (there have been 14 as recently as 1995), in early 2008, he defined just three—healthcare, lighting, and consumer lifestyle. "We have to organize around markets," he said. "We're going to organize from the outside in."

But competition in consumer electronics remained brutal, especially in a growing global recession. In late 2008, Philips licensed Funai to make and market TVs under the Philips name in North America. A few months later, it extended that license to cover other markets as well as products such as DVDs, home theater, Blu-Ray, and other products. "We spent the 1980s and 1990s restructuring and trying to find our way," Kleisterlee said. "My goal is to leave behind a company on a successful part to steady, profitable growth." Some wondered whether he had found that path.

Matsushita: Background

In 1918, 23 year old Konosuke Matsushita (or "KM" as he was affectionately known), invested ¥100 to start production of double-ended sockets in his modest home. The company grew rapidly, expanding into battery-powered lamps, electric irons, and radios. On May 5, 1932, Matsushita's 14th anniversary, KM announced to his 162 employees a 250-year corporate plan, broken into 25-year sections, each to be carried out by successive generations. His plan was codified in a company creed and in the "Seven Spirits of Matsushita" (see **Exhibit 4**), which provided the basis of the "cultural and spiritual training" all new employees received on joining the company.

In the post-war boom, Matsushita introduced a flood of new products: TV sets in 1952; transistor radios in 1958; color TVs, dishwashers, and electric ovens in 1960. Capitalizing on its broad line of 5,000 products, the company opened 25,000 domestic retail outlets—40% of appliance stores in Japan in the late 1960s. These not only assured sales

Exhibit 4   Matsushita Creed and Philosophy (Excerpts)

Creed

Through our industrial activities, we strive to foster progress, to promote the general welfare of society, and to devote ourselves to furthering the development of world culture.

Seven Spirits of Matsushita

Service through Industry
Fairness
Harmony and Cooperation
Struggle for Progress
Courtesy and Humility
Adjustment and Assimilation
Gratitude

KM's Business Philosophy (Selected Quotations)

"The purpose of an enterprise is to contribute to society by supplying goods of high quality at low prices in ample quantity."

"Profit comes in compensation for contribution to society. . . . [It] is a result rather than a goal."

"The responsibility of the manufacturer cannot be relieved until its product is disposed of by the end user."

"Unsuccessful business employs a wrong management. You should not find its causes in bad fortune, unfavorable surroundings or wrong timing."

"Business appetite has no self-restraining mechanism. . . . When you notice you have gone too far, you must have the courage to come back."

Source: Christopher A. Bartlett, "Matsushita Electric Industrial (MEI) in 1987," HBS No. 388-144 (Boston: Harvard Business School Publishing, 1988) p. 17.

volume, but also gave the company direct access to market trends. When post-war growth slowed, however, product line expansion and an excellent distribution system no longer insured growth, and the company looked to export markets.

The Organization's Foundation: Divisional Structure   Plagued by ill health, KM began to delegate more than was typical in Japanese companies. In 1933, Matsushita became the first Japanese company to adopt a divisional structure. In addition to creating a "small business" environment, the structure generated internal competition that spurred each business to drive growth by leveraging its technology to develop new products. But after the innovating division had earned substantial profits on its new product, the "one-product-one-division" policy was to spin it off as a new division to maintain the "hungry spirit."

Management provided each division with funds to establish largely self-sufficient development, production, and marketing capabilities. Corporate treasury operated like a commercial bank, reviewing divisions' loan requests for which it charged slightly higher-than-market interest, and accepting interest-bearing deposits on their excess funds. Divisional profitability was determined after deductions for central services and interest on internal borrowings. Each division paid 60% of earnings to headquarters and financed working capital and fixed asset needs from the retained 40%. Transfer prices were based on the market and settled through the treasury on normal commercial terms. KM expected uniform performance across the company's 36 divisions, and division managers whose operating profits fell below 4% of sales for two successive years were replaced.

While basic technology was developed in a central research laboratory (CRL), product development and engineering occurred in each of the product divisions. Matsushita intentionally underfunded the CRL, forcing it to compete for additional funding from the divisions. Annually, the CRL publicized its major research projects to the product divisions, which then provided funding for CRL to develop technology for marketable applications. Rarely the innovator, Matsushita was usually very fast to market—earning it the nickname "Manishita," or copycat.

Matsushita: Internationalization

Although the establishment of overseas markets was a major thrust of the second 25 years in the 250-year plan, in an overseas trip in 1951 KM had been unable to find any American company willing to collaborate with Matsushita. The best he could do was a technology exchange and licensing agreement with Philips. Nonetheless, the push to internationalize continued.

Expanding Through Color TV   In the 1950s and 1960s, trade liberalization and lower shipping allowed Matsushita to build a healthy export business with its black and white TV sets. In 1953, the company opened its first overseas branch office—the Matsushita Electric Corporation of America (MECA). With neither a distribution network nor a strong brand, the company had to resort to selling through mass merchandisers and discounters under their private brands.

During the 1960s, pressure from national governments in developing countries led Matsushita to open plants Southeast Asia and Central and South America. As manufacturing costs in Japan rose, the company shifted more basic production to these low-wage countries, but almost all high-value components and subassemblies remained in its scale-intensive Japanese plants. By the 1970s, political pressure forced Matsushita to establish assembly operations in the Americas and Europe. In 1972, it opened a plant in Canada; in 1974, it bought Motorola's TV business in the United States; and in 1976, it for him built a plant in Wales to supply the European Common Market.

Building Global Leadership Through VCRs   The birth of the videocassette recorder (VCR) propelled Matsushita into first place in the consumer electronics industry during the 1980s. Recognizing the potential mass-market appeal of the professional broadcast VCR first developed in 1956 by Californian company Ampex, Matsushita began developing the technology. It launched its commercial broadcast video recorder in 1964, and two years later, introduced a consumer version.

Subsequently, a battle over VCR format developed. In 1975, Sony introduced the technically superior "Betamax" format, and in 1976, JVC launched a competing "VHS" format. Under pressure from MITI, Japan's industrial planning ministry, Matsushita agreed to give up its own format and adopt the VHS standard. During its 20 years of development, Matsushita's research team lived the VCR product cycle, moving from CRL to the product division's development labs, and eventually to the plants producing VCRs.

Between 1977 and 1985, Matsushita increased VCR capacity 33-fold to 6.8 million units, not only to meet its own needs, but also those of OEM customers like GE, RCA, Philips, and Zenith, who decided to forego self-manufacture and outsource to the low-cost Japanese. Increased volume enabled Matsushita to slash prices 50% within five years of launch. In parallel, the company licensed the VHS format to other manufacturers, including Hitachi, Sharp, Mitsubishi and, eventually, Philips. By the mid-1980s, VCRs accounted for 30% of Matsushita's sales and 45% of its profits.

Changing Systems and Controls   In the mid-1980s, Matsushita's growing number of overseas companies reported to the parent in one of two ways: wholly owned, single-product global plants reported directly to the appropriate product division, while overseas sales and marketing subsidiaries and overseas companies producing a broad product line for local markets reported to Matsushita Electric Trading Company (METC), a separate legal entity. (See **Exhibit 5** for METC's organization.)

Throughout the 1970s, product divisions maintained strong operating control over their offshore operations. They had plant and equipment designed by the parent company, followed manufacturing procedures dictated by the center, and used materials from Matsushita's domestic plants. By the 1980s, increased local sourcing gradually weakened the divisions' direct control, so instead of controlling inputs, they began to monitor output—quality and productivity levels for example.

Headquarters-Subsidiary Relations   Although METC and the product divisions set detailed sales and profits targets for their overseas subsidiaries, they told local managers they had autonomy on how to achieve them. But as "Mike" Matsuoko, president of the European source in Cardiff, Wales emphasized, failure forfeited freedom: "Losses

Exhibit 5   Organization of METC, 1985

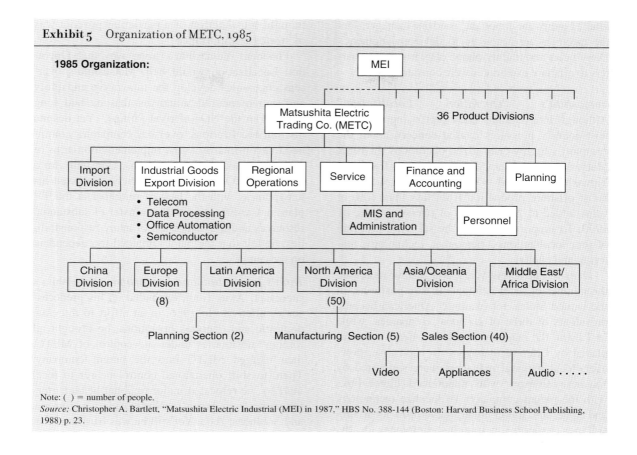

Note: ( ) = number of people.
Source: Christopher A. Bartlett, "Matsushita Electric Industrial (MEI) in 1987," HBS No. 388-144 (Boston: Harvard Business School Publishing, 1988) p. 23.

show bad health and invite many doctors from Japan who provide advice and support."

In the mid-1980s, Matsushita had over 700 expatriate Japanese managers and technicians on foreign assignment for four to eight years, primarily to play a "vital communication role." Explained one senior executive, "Even if a local manager speaks Japanese, he would not have the long experience that is needed to build relationships and understand our management processes."

Expatriate managers were located throughout foreign subsidiaries, but there were a few positions that were almost always reserved for them. The most visible were subsidiary general managers whose main role was to translate Matsushita philosophy abroad. Expatriate accounting managers

were expected to "mercilessly expose the truth" to corporate headquarters; and Japanese technical managers were sent to transfer product and process technologies and provide headquarters with local market information. These expatriates maintained relationships with senior colleagues in their divisions, who acted as career mentors, evaluated performance (with some input from local managers), and provided expatriates with information about parent company developments.

Subsidiary general managers visited Osaka at least two or three times each year—some as often as every month. Corporate managers reciprocated these visits, and on average, major operations hosted a headquarters manager each day of the year. Face-to-face meetings were considered vital: "Figures are important," said one manager, "but the meetings are necessary to develop judgment." Daily faxes and nightly phone calls from headquarters to offshore expatriates were considered vital.

Yamashita's "Operation Localization"
Although international sales kept rising, growing host country pressures caused concern about the company's highly centralized operations. In 1982, Matsushita's newly appointed president Toshihiko Yamashita launched "Operation Localization" to boost offshore production from less than 10% of value-added to 25%, or half of overseas sales, by 1990. To support the target, he set out a program of four localizations—personnel, technology, material, and capital.

Over the next few years, Matsushita increased the number of local nationals in key positions. In the United States, for example, American became presidents of three of six local companies, while in Taiwan the majority of division heads were replaced by Chinese managers. In each case, however, local national managers were supported by Japanese advisors who maintained direct links with the parent company. To localize technology and materials, the company developed local subsidiaries' expertise in sourcing equipment locally, modifying designs to local requirements, incorporating local components, and adapting corporate processes and technologies to accommodate the changes. And by the mid-1980s, offshore production subsidiaries were free to buy minor supplies from local vendors, but still had to buy key components from internal sources.

One of the most successful innovations was to give overseas sales subsidiaries more choice over the products they sold. Each year the company held a two-week internal merchandising show and product planning meeting where product divisions exhibited the new lines. Here, foreign subsidiary managers negotiated for changes in product features, quantities, and even prices for products they felt would better meet their local needs. Product division managers, however, could overrule the sales subsidiary if they

thought introduction of a particular product was of strategic importance.

President Yamashita's hope was that Operation Localization would help Matsushita's overseas companies develop the innovative capability and entrepreneurial initiatives that he had long admired in the NOs of rival Philips.[1] Yet despite his four localizations, overseas companies continued to act primarily as the implementation arms of Japanese-based product divisions. Unusually for a Japanese CEO, Yamashita publicly expressed his unhappiness with the lack of initiative at the TV plant in Cardiff. Despite the transfer of substantial resources and the delegation of many responsibilities, he felt that the plant remained too dependent on the center.

Tanii's Integration and Expansion Yamashita's successor, Akio Tanii, expanded on his predecessor's initiatives. In 1986, in an effort to integrate domestic and overseas operations, he brought all foreign subsidiaries under the control of METC, then merged METC into the parent company. Then, to shift operational control nearer to local markets, he relocated major regional headquarters functions from Japan to North America, Europe, and Southeast Asia. Yet still he was frustrated that the overseas subsidiary companies acted as little more than the implementing agents of the Osaka-based product divisions.

Through all these changes, however, Matsushita's worldwide growth continued, generating huge reserves. With $17.5 billion in liquid financial assets at the end of 1989, the company was referred to as the "Matsushita Bank." Frustrated by their inability to develop innovative overseas companies, top management decided to buy them. To obtain a software source for its hardware businesses, in 1991 the company acquired MCA, the U.S. entertainment

---

[1]Past efforts to develop such capabilities abroad had failed. For example, when Matsushita acquired Motorola's TV business in the United States, the U.S. company's highly innovative technology group atrophied as American engineers resigned in response to what they felt to be excessive control from Japan's highly centralized R&D operations.

giant, for $6.1 billion. Within a year, however, Japan's bubble economy had burst, and almost overnight, Tanii had to shift the focus from expansion to cost containment. Despite his best efforts, the problems ran too deep. With 1992 profits less than half their 1991 level, the board took the unusual move of forcing Tanii to resign in February 1993.

Morishita's Challenge and Response   At 56, Yoichi Morishita was the most junior of the company's executive vice presidents when he was tapped as the new president. In a major strategic reversal, he sold 80% of MCI to Seagram, booking a $1.2 billion loss on the transaction. Over the following 18 months, under the slogan "simple, small, speedy and strategic," he then moved 6,000 staff to operating jobs.

Yet the company continued to struggle. Japan's domestic market for consumer electronics collapsed—from $42 billion in 1989 to $21 billion in 1999. And the rise of new competition—from Korea, then China—created a global glut, then a price collapse. With a strong yen making its exports uncompetitive, Matsushita's product divisions shifted production offshore, mostly to low-cost countries like China and Malaysia. By the end of the decade, its 160 factories outside Japan employed 140,000 people—about the same number of employees as in its 133 plants in Japan. Yet management seemed unwilling to close inefficient Japanese plans or lay off staff with the commitment of lifetime employment. Despite Morishita's promises, internal resistance prevented his implementation of much of the promised radical change.

In the closing years of the decade, Morishita began emphasizing the need to develop technology and innovation offshore. Concerned that only 250 of the company's 3,000 R&D scientists and engineers were located outside Japan, he began investing in R&D partnerships and technical exchanges, particularly in emerging fields. For example, an 1998, he signed a joint R&D agreement with the Chinese Academy of Sciences, China's leading research organization. Later that year, he announced the establishment of the Panasonic Digital Concepts Center in California. Its mission was to act as a venture fund and an incubation center for the new ideas and technologies emerging in Silicon Valley. To some it was an indication that Matsushita had given up trying to generate new technology and business initiatives from its own overseas companies.

Nakamura's Transformation   In June 2000, Kunio Nakamura, the 38-year veteran who had headed MEI's North American operations was named president. Operating profits were 2.2% of sales, with consumer electronics generating only 0.4% due to losses in the TV and VCR divisions. Just as Morishita had promised seven years earlier, the new CEO vowed to raise operating margins to 5% in three years.

By December, Nakamura was ready to announce his first three-year plan dubbed "Value Creation 21" or VC 21. Its main objective was to build a "super manufacturing company" on three foundations: a strong technology-based components business, a flexible and responsive manufacturing capability, and customer-oriented, solutions-based businesses. The new CEO emphasized the need to retain Matsushita's fully integrated value chain, justifying it with a "smile curve" which promised high returns in both upstream components and downstream services and solutions to offset lower returns in the highly competitive consumer electronics products in the middle of the value chain.

At the core of VC 21 was a plan to close inefficient scale-driven plants and concentrate production in Manufacturing Centers, facilities transformed from old mass production assembly lines to modern flexible manufacturing cells. The transformation would be implemented first in Japanese mother plants, and then rolled out to the 170 plants it had worldwide.

Furthermore, as part of a plan to replace Matsushita's historic fragmented and compartmentalized structure with a "flat web-based organization", Nakamura separated plants from product divisions which now had to source their products from non-captive and non-exclusive Manufacturing

Centers. Sales and marketing was also stripped from the once powerful product divisions, and absorbed in one of two global marketing organizations, one for appliances and the other for consumer electronics. "It was a cultural revolution," said one manager.

But the strong financial performance Nakamura had assumed would support his plan, disappeared with the "tech wreck" recession of 2001, resulting in Matsushita's first quarterly loss in its history. The CEO and immediately announced five

emergency measures to reverse the situation. In one bold move, the company dropped its lifetime employment practice and offered early retirement to 18,000 employees. Over 13,000 accepted, not only reducing costs, but also allowing a new generation of managers to emerge. In total, the domestic workforce was cut by 25,000, and 30 inefficient plants were closed.

Despite these efforts, in March 2002 Matsushita announced an operating loss of ¥199 billion

Exhibit 6   Matsushita, Summary Financial Data, 1970–2000[a]

	2008	2000	1995	1990	1985	1980	1975	1970
In billions of yen and percent:								
Sales	¥9,069	¥7,299	¥6,948	¥6,003	¥5,291	¥2,916	¥1,385	¥932
Income before tax	527	219	232	572	723	324	83	147
As % of sales	5.8%	3.0%	3.3%	9.5%	13.7%	11.1%	6.0%	15.8%
Net income	¥282	¥100	¥90	¥236	¥216	¥125	¥32	¥70
As % of sales	3.1%	1.4%	1.3%	3.9%	4.1%	4.3%	2.3%	7.6%
Cash dividends (per share)	¥35.00	¥14.00	¥13.50	¥10.00	¥ 9.52	¥7.51	¥6.82	¥6.21
Total assets	7,443	7,955	8,202	7,851	5,076	2,479	1,274	735
Stockholders' equity	3,742	3,684	3,255	3,201	2,084	1,092	573	324
Capital investment	503	355	316	355	288	NA	NA	NA
Depreciation	320	343	296	238	227	65	28	23
R&D	554	526	378	346	248	102	51	NA
Employees (units)	305,828	290,448	265,397	198,299	175,828	107,057	82,869	78,924
Overseas employees	170,265	143,773	112,314	59,216	38,380	NA	NA	NA
As % of total employees	56%	50%	42%	30%	22%	NA	NA	NA
Exchange rate (fiscal period end; ¥/$)	100	103	89	159	213	213	303	360
In millions of dollars:								
Sales	$90,949	$68,862	$78,069	$37,753	$24,890	$13,690	$4,572	$2,588
Operating income before depreciation	8,424	4,944	6,250	4,343	3,682	1,606	317	NA
Operating income after depreciation	NA	1,501	2,609	2,847	2,764	1,301	224	NA
Pretax income	4,263	2,224	2,678	3,667	3,396	1,520	273	408
Net income	2,827	941	1,017	1,482	1,214	584	105	195
Total assets	74,648	77,233	92,159	49,379	21,499	11,636	4,206	2,042
Total equity	37,530	35,767	36,575	20,131	10,153	5,129	1,890	900

[a]Data prior to 1987 are for the fiscal year ending November 20; data 1988 and after are for the fiscal year ending March 31.
Sources: Annual reports; Standard & Poor's Compustat®; Moody's Industrial and International Manuals.

Exhibit 7   Matsushita, Sales by Product and Geographic Segment, 1985–2000 (billion yen)

	2008	2000		1995		FY 1990		FY 1985	
By Product Segment:									
Audio, Video, Communications Networks	¥4,319	—	—	—	—	—	—	—	—
Video and Audio Equipment	—	¥1,706	23%	¥1,827	26%	¥2,159	36%	¥2,517	48%
Electronic components	—	—	—	893	13	781	13	573	11
Home appliances and household equipment	1,316	1,306	18	—	—	—	—	—	—
Home appliances	—	—	—	916	13	802	13	763	14
Communication and industrial equipment	—	—	—	1,797	26	1,375	23	849	16
Batteries and kitchen-related equipment	—	—	—	374	4	312	5	217	4
Information and communications equipment	—	2,175	28	—	—	—	—	—	—
Industrial equipment	—	817	11	—	—	—	—	—	—
Components	1,399	1,618	21	—	—	—	—	—	—
Others	123	—	—	530	8	573	10	372	7
Total	¥9,069	¥7,682	100%	¥6,948	100%	¥6,003	100%	¥5,291	100%
By Geographic Segment:									
Domestic	¥6,789	¥3,698	51%	¥3,455	50%	¥3,382	56%	¥2,659	50%
Overseas	5,404	3,601	49	3,493	50	2,621	44	2,632	50
Corporate	(3,120)								

Note: Total may not add due to rounding.
Source: Annual reports.

($1.7 billion), and an even more shocking loss of ¥428 billion ($3.7 billion) including restructuring charges. Calling the situation "an intolerable social evil", Nakamura committed to delivering profit of ¥100 billion the next year. He told his executives that because implementation of his emergency measures had not been satisfactory, he was launching a management improvement initiative. He challenged them to deliver "a V-shaped recovery" driven by V-Products—innovative, customer-focused products launched rapidly into global markets, at competitive prices. He focused 70% of investments on consumer electronics and semiconductors, urging his managers to move past Matsushita's reputation for slow innovation and imitation. "In the digital age, there is no room for imitators," he said.

To eliminate the internal competitiveness he felt that had constrained the turnaround, he grouped all businesses into one of three closely linked domains—Digital Networks (primarily consumer electronics, mobile phones, and telecom), Home Appliances (including lighting and environmental systems), and Components (with semiconductors, batteries, and motors.)

In March 2004, at the end of the three year "VC 21" plan, the company reported a profit of ¥185 billion ($1.9 billion) on sales of ¥7,500 billion ($72 billion). As impressive as the result was, it was still less than half of the promised 5% operating margin. So Nakamura announced a new three-year plan called "Leap Ahead 21" with a 5% objective for 2007 as an interim step on the way to 10% by 2010.

Ohtsubo's Inheritance In April 2006, after announcing operating profits of $3.6 billion, Nakamura announced that he would step down as CEO in June. Spontaneously, analysts at the presentation gave him a standing ovation, a unique event in reserved Japan. His successor, Eumio Ohtsubo, previously head the consumer electronics business, embraced Nakamura's commitment to surpass Samsung's 9.4% operating margin by 2010.

Having led effort making Matsushita the world's leading plasma TV maker, Ohtsubo committed to dominating the fast-growing flatscreen market by investing Its $1.3 billion cash balance in focused R&D and more efficient global production. He wanted to build an ability to develop, manufacture, and launch superior new products twice a year, globally. "We will absolutely not be beaten in the flat-panel TV business," he said.

In January 2008, he surprised many when he announced the change in the company's name from Matsushita to Panasonic, reflecting the name of the company's best-known brand. It was part of Ohtsubo's efforts to grow overseas revenues from less than 50% to 60% by 2010. Still, with Panasonic in 78th place on the Interbrand survey of the world brand recognition, he had a way to go.

But any talk about foreign sales growth evaporated when the global financial crisis struck in 2008. In the December quarter, company sales slid 20%, while operating profit plunged 84%. Immediately Ohtsubo initiated a review of the company's 170 overseas plants, vowing to shut down any with operating profit of less than 3%, or declining sales over three years. The review resulted in the closure of 27 plants, and the lay off 15,000 workers. But the global crisis hit hard, and with restructuring charges and write-offs, the company projected a $4.2 billion loss for the full year ending in March 2009. The carefully laid plans for $90 billion in revenues and 10% operating margin by 2010 were vanishing dreams.

Case 4-2   ECCO A/S–Global Value Chain Management

Bo Bernhard Nielsen, Torben Pedersen, and Jacob Pyndt

Despite the summer, the weather was hazy on that day in May 2004 as the airplane took off from Hongqiao International Airport, Shanghai. The plane was likely to encounter some turbulence on its way to Copenhagen Airport in Denmark. The chief operations officer (COO) of the Danish shoe manufacturer ECCO A/S (ECCO), Mikael Thinghuus, did not particularly enjoy bumpy flights, but the rough flight could not overshadow the confidence and optimism he felt after his visit to Xiamen in southeast China. This was his third visit in three months.

During 2003/2004, ECCO spent substantial resources on analyzing where to establish production facilities in China. On this trip, together with Flemming Brønd, the production director in China, Thinghuus had finalized negotiations with Novo Nordisk Engineering (NNE). NNE possessed valuable experience in building factories in China, experience gained through their work for Novozymes and Novo Nordisk. Now everything seemed to be in place. Construction was to begin in August,

Richard Ivey School of Business
The University of Western Ontario

machines would be installed in January 2005, and the first pair of shoes would be leaving the factory by the end of March 2005 if all went well. The plan was to build five closely connected factories over the next four years with a total capacity of five million pairs of shoes per year, serving both export needs and the Chinese market, which was expected to grow in the future.

Thinghuus felt relieved. He was confident that the massive investments in China would serve as a solid footstep on a fast growing market and provide a unique export platform to the global shoe market. However, he could not rest on his laurels. The massive investment in China was an integrated part of ECCO's continuous attempt to optimize various activities in the value chain. Operating five distinct factories in Portugal, Slovakia, Indonesia, Thailand and shortly in China combined with a declared vision of integrating the global value chain, the task at hand was certainly complicated. Moreover, ECCO had one tannery located in the Netherlands and two located adjacent to shoe production facilities in Indonesia and Thailand. These tanneries enabled ECCO to maintain control of leather processing and ensure the quality of the leather utilized in ECCO's shoe manufacturing.

Introducing ECCO

It has always been our philosophy that quality is the only thing that endures. That is why we constantly work to create the perfect shoe—so good that you forget you are wearing it. It has to be light and solid, designed on the basis of the newest technology and knowledge about comfort and materials. ECCO have to be the world's best shoes—shoes with internal values.

Karl Toosbuy, founder

With the simple slogan "A perfect fit—a simple idea," Karl Toosbuy founded ECCO in Bredebro, Denmark in 1963. Inspired by the open and harsh landscape of southern Jutland, Toosbuy presented ECCO as a company with a passion for pleasant walking. Today, after more than 40 years of craftsmanship and dedication to uncompromised quality, ECCO remains extremely committed to comfort, design and a perfectly fitting shoe with the goal of constantly developing shoes that are pleasant to walk in regardless of the weather conditions. The company's vision is to be the "most wanted brand within innovation and comfort footwear—a position that only can be attained by constantly and courageously researching new paths, investing in employees, in our core competencies of product development and production technology."[1]

ECCO aimed at producing the world's most comfortable and modern footwear for work and leisure. Footwear for work, leisure and festive occasions had to be designed and constructed with uncompromising attention to customer comfort. Evidently, trends in the market in terms of fashion and elegance were important, but usability was ECCO's highest design priority. As Søren Steffensen, executive vice-president, stated: "ECCO is not a fashion brand and it never will be. We do not sell shoes where the brand name is the most important and quality is a secondary consideration. Primarily, we sell high-quality shoes and that is where we seek recognition."[2]

Products and Markets   The ECCO group produces various types of shoes including casual and outdoor shoes for men, ladies, and children, as well as semi-sport shoes, for two different seasons—spring/summer and autumn/winter. In 2004, the sales split between the different categories was children 11 per cent, ladies 47 per cent, men 30 per cent, and sport 12 per cent. The sport division produced outdoor, walking, running and golf shoes. ECCO's golf shoes category had experienced particularly significant growth. ECCO's development of golf shoes had started as a joke between Toosbuy and Dieter Kasprzak, chief executive officer (CEO), on the golf course 10 years ago. In 2004, the

joke turned into 300,000 pairs sold, sponsorships of international golfers like Thomas Bjørn and Colin Montgomerie, and numerous endorsements in independent tests of golf equipment in the United States. Having tested ECCO's golf shoes, Rankmark, an American company conducting objective tests and analyzes of golf products, stated that "ECCO Golf Footwear was preferred by more than 90 per cent of golfers over their current brands."

In 2004, ECCO exported more than 90 per cent of its production, with the United States, Germany and Japan being the main markets. ECCO's international profile was reflected in the workforce composition. In the same year, ECCO employed 9,657 employees of which 553 were located in Denmark. The company worked constantly on creating new markets, particularly in Asia and Central and Eastern Europe. The North American market—the United States and Canada—was of great importance to ECCO. In 2004, the company's American operations attained 17 per cent growth in sales when compared to 2003. That year, the American operations accounted for DKK 875 million in revenue, roughly 26 per cent of ECCO's total sales.[3] The American subsidiary had streamlined its vendorship, cutting the number from 1,200 in 2002 to 1,000 in 2004, yet the remaining dealers had purchased a higher volume. In addition, ECCO increased its number of partnerships by 18 to 34 in 2004. The American market was lucrative as shoes were selling at high prices. Men's shoes typically cost between US$150 and US$450 and the highly successful golf shoes were sold for between US$200 and US$400. The majority of ECCO's sales in North America went through exclusive department stores, such as Nordstrom's and Dillard's.

Finance and Ownership Structure

During the period from 1999 to 2003, ECCO experienced stagnating productivity and declining operating margins (see **Exhibit 1**). For instance, the operating margin fell from 15 per cent in 2000 to five per cent in 2002. Moreover, company debts

---

[1]http://www.ecco.com/int/en/aboutus/index.jsp, accessed April 2005.
[2]*Berlingske News Magazine,* March 7, 2004.

[3]*Børsen,* December 22, 2004.

Exhibit 1   ECCO's Financial Highlights 1999 to 2004

ECCO's consolidated financial highlights and key ratios 1999–2004

(DKK million)	1999	2000	2001	2002	2003	2004
Net revenue	2,552	2,836	3,216	3,360	3,169	3,394
Profit before amortization and depreciation	409	560	416	343	370	448
Amortization and depreciation	−106	−143	−167	−187	−189	−181
Profit before financials	302	416	249	156	182	267
Net financials	−25	−112	−93	−73	−61	−61
Profit before tax	277	305	156	82	120	206
Group profit	195	216	123	60	71	164
Profit for the year	185	208	115	51	62	151
Key ratios (%)						
Operating margin	11.9	14.7	7.8	4.6	5.7	7.9
Return on assets	11.7	10.6	5	2.8	4.3	7
ROIC	12.7	14.5	8.1	5.3	6.5	9.1
Investment ratio	3.3	2.2	1.5	1.2	1.2	1.2
Return on equity	28.9	25.7	12.4	5.3	6.5	15.2
Solvency ratio	30.9	31.1	31.4	33	34.1	35.1
Liquidity ratio	1.8	1.9	2.1	2	1.9	2
Pairs of shoes sold (millions)	9.160	9.603	10.14	10.65	11.22	12.04
Number of employees (2004)	8,290	8,853	9,087	8,839	9,388	9,657
Sold shoes per employee	**1,104**	**1,084**	**1,116**	**1,205**	**1,195**	**1,247**

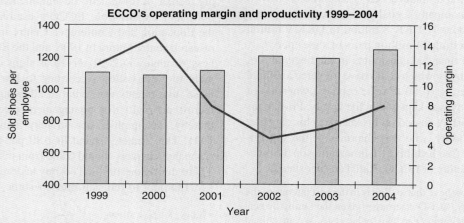

ECCO's operating margin and productivity 1999–2004

Source: ECCO annual reports 1999–2004.

Exhibit 2   Composition of Management Board as of 2004

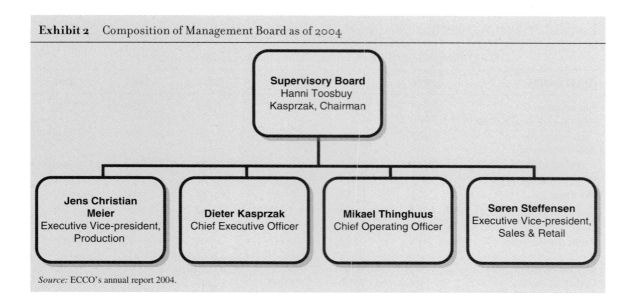

Source: ECCO's annual report 2004.

increased from DKK 1 billion to DKK 2 billion following investments in expansion and inventories. In response to these negative trends, ECCO launched strategic initiatives to streamline logistics, focus on more modern shoes and facilitate monitoring of the market. 2004 brought signs of improvement as the company achieved earnings of DKK 150 million and lifted its operating margin to eight per cent. The reduction of stock had a particularly notable effect on the 2004 result, further freeing up capital to finance ECCO's ambitious growth plan. The company's goal was to increase revenue to approximately DKK 8 billion to DKK 9 billion by 2013, selling 24 million pairs of shoes per year.

Despite financial constraints in the beginning of the 21st century which could have triggered an Initial public offering (IPO) to raise capital, ownership of the company was kept within the family. Prior to his death, Toosbuy passed on his shares to his daughter Hanni Toosbuy, who was chairman of the supervisory board (see **Exhibit 2**). Commenting on the ownership structure of ECCO, Karl Toosbuy stated:

> I do not believe that an IPO is in the best interest of the company. ECCO is stronger given the family ownership. The family can take higher risks. We are able to

allocate. In many cases, we do not have the time to investigate things as profoundly as a listed company ought to do. Yet, we are sure that what we want is the right thing. Then we act instead of waiting.[4]

Organizational Developments   Operating on a global scale required employees with international mindsets and good adaptability skills. Since its inception ECCO had given high priority to the continuous education and training of its employees. The company invested aggressively in vocational training, career development, developmental conversations and expatriation. ECCO's establishment of the Education and Conference Centre in 1994, the research centre Futura in 1996, and the ECCO Business Academy in 2001 served as signs of commitment to these issues. According to Karl Toosbuy, these investments were vital to allowing ECCO to recruit internally for management positions and, thereby, accomplish his strategy announced in 1991. This strategy stated that 80 per cent of the company's leaders should come from inside ECCO. Twice during the 1990s, Toosbuy had stepped down as CEO only to reinstall himself some years later,

[4]*Børsen*, February 20, 1998.

underpinning the importance of knowing the company inside-out and adapting to ECCO's culture.

Despite the founder's intention of internal recruitment for management positions, on two recent occasions this ambition could not be met. In 2001, ECCO hired Søren Steffensen in the position as sales and marketing director. Coming from a position as retail director in the Danish fashion clothing company, Carli Gry, he had a reputation of knowing every shopping corner in Europe and was an efficient negotiator. In addition, Mikael Thinghuus took over the position of chief operating officer (COO) in 2003, having held positions at IBM and the East Asiatic Company. The third member of the executive committee was Jens Christian Meier, executive vice-president, who had spent most of his career within shoe manufacturing. He actually initiated his career at ECCO, continued at Clarks, and then moved on to Elefanten Shoes as managing director before returning to ECCO. His main responsibilities lay within the fields of logistics, sourcing and handling ECCO's production facilities. When Karl Toosbuy died in June 2004, his son-in-law, Dieter Kasprzak, became CEO. Kasprzak had spent 23 years with ECCO, primarily as the director of design and product development. Whereas Toosbuy was known for his abilities to develop unique production techniques, Kasprzak was a designer by trade and was much more involved in product development and branding. The death of Toosbuy triggered considerations about future development becoming more market oriented. Thinghuus commented: "Evidently, we may learn something from the marketing oriented firms [Nike, Reebok and Adidas]. We should aim at becoming better at telling what we stand for. We cannot expect that our unique production technology will last an eternity."[5]

ECCO's Global Value Chain

ECCO maintained focus on the entire value chain or from "cow to shoe" as the company liked to put it. ECCO bought raw hides and transformed these

into various kinds of leather usable in shoe manufacturing. Leather constituted the main material in shoe uppers which were produced at ECCO's production sites (see **Exhibits 3** and **4**). The company owned several tanneries in the Netherlands, Thailand (opened in 1999) and Indonesia, which supplied leather to ECCO's factories all over the world. ECCO's 2001 acquisition of the largest tannery in the Netherlands, followed by a tannery and leather research centre in 2002, made it possible to access leading expert knowledge about tanning. ECCO's Dutch tannery manufactured around 3,500 rawhides a day, corresponding to approximately one million cows per year. Apart from providing ECCO's factories with "wetblue" (see **Exhibit 3**), the development and research centre's main task was to explore less polluting tanning methods and experiment with various kinds of leather for the coming generation of ECCO shoes. The centre employed 15 specialists who were also responsible for training employees from Thailand and Indonesia, allowing new technology and improved tannery methods to be disseminated. ECCO was among the five largest producers of leather worldwide. The majority of the rawhides originated from Germany, France, Denmark and Finland. Apart from supplying leather to its shoe factories around the world, it also sold leather to the auto and furniture industries. Explaining ECCO's tanning activities, Toosbuy commented: "To us, it is a matter of the level of ambition. We make high demands on quality and lead times—higher than any of our suppliers have been able to accommodate. In essence, we really do not have an alternative to being self-sufficient."[6]

In addition, the plan was to set up a tannery in conjunction with the factories in China. ECCO's strategy was quite unique, as most of its competitors had phased out in-house production. Companies like Clarks and Timberland had followed Nike's marketing oriented business model by outsourcing the production to a large extent. These companies were described as branded marketers,

[5]*Berlingske News Magazine,* March 7, 2004.

[6]*Jyllands-Posten,* May 22, 2002.

Exhibit 3   ECCO's Value Chain and Explanation of Tannery Operation

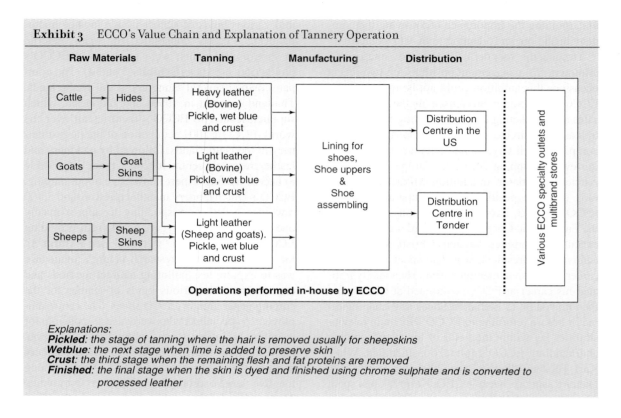

Explanations:
Pickled: the stage of tanning where the hair is removed usually for sheepskins
Wetblue: the next stage when lime is added to preserve skin
Crust: the third stage when the remaining flesh and fat proteins are removed
Finished: the final stage when the skin is dyed and finished using chrome sulphate and is converted to
          processed leather

i.e., manufacturers without factories, who only design and market their goods. While Timberland produced approximately 10 per cent of its shoes in-house, Clarks had completely outsourced its production. ECCO, by contrast, produced 80 per cent of its shoes in-house. The remaining 20 per cent were outsourced as these shoes (for instance, ladies' shoes with thin soles and certain types of sport shoes) contained specific features that would not benefit from ECCO's "direct injected" technology.

ECCO's production process could be divided into five strategic roles or phases: full-scale, benchmarking, ramp-up, prototype and laboratory production. The objectives of full-scale production were to uphold demand, quality and operational reliability, and still produce high volumes. Benchmarking production, on the other hand, strove to retain knowledge and competencies in terms of opportunities for improvements and production cost

structure. ECCO had full-scale production units in Portugal, Indonesia, Thailand, Slovakia and China (in operation from March 2005). A logical consequence of ECCO's control of their value chain was that benchmarking served more to evaluate such aspects as the production unit in Portugal, *vis-à-vis* the plant in Slovakia, than to establish parameters upon which to evaluate external partners. The ramp-up process encompassed the set-up for the production system at large, such as running an assembly system based on new technology. While the newest technology came from Bredebro, Denmark, the actual establishment of the production system, including the streamlining of processes and the specific volumes of various kinds of materials, took place in ECCO's foreign production units. The development of new products, prototypes and laboratory production technologies, was carried out at ECCO's production site in Denmark. In particular,

Exhibit 4   Converting Skin and Hides into Leather

Steps in leather production

The production of leather from hides and skins involves the treatment of raw materials, i.e., the conversion of the raw hide or skin, a putrecible material, into leather, a stable material. This material is obtained after passing through the different treatment and processing steps described in points 1 to 4. The production processes in a tannery can be divided into four main categories, though the processes employed in each of these categories may change, depending on the raw material used and the final goods that are to be produced.

1. Hides and Skins Storage and Beam-house Operations

Upon delivery, hides and skins can be sorted, trimmed, cured (when the raw material cannot be processed immediately) and stored pending operations in the beam house. The following processes are typically carried out in the beam house of a tannery: soaking, de-haring, liming, fleshing (mechanical scraping off of the excessive organic material) and splitting (mechanically splitting regulates the thickness of hides and skins, splitting them horizontally into a grain layer, and, if the hide is thick enough, a flesh layer).

2. Tannery Operations

Typically the following processes are carried out in the tannery: de-liming, bating, pickling and tanning. Once pickling has been carried out to reduce the pH of the pelt prior to tanning, pickled pelts, i.e., sheepskins can be traded. In the tanning process the collagen fibre is stabilized by the tanning agents so that the hide (the raw material) is no longer susceptible to putrefaction. The two main categories of tanning agents are minerals (trivalent chromium salts) and vegetable (quebracho and mimosa). The tanned hides and skins, once they have been converted to a non-putrescible material called leather, are tradable as intermediate products (wetblue). However, if leather is to be used to manufacture consumer products, it needs further processing and finishing.

3. Post-Tanning Operations

Post-tanning operations generally involve washing out the acids that are still present in the leather following the tanning process. According to the desired leather type to be produced the leather is retanned (to improve the feel and handle of leathers), dyed with water-soluble dyestuffs (to produce even colours over the whole surface of each hide and skin), fat liquored (leathers must be lubricated to achieve product-specific characteristics and to re-establish the fat content lost in the previous procedures) and finally dried. After drying, the leather may be referred to as crust, which is a tradable intermediate product. Operations carried out in the beam house, the tannery, and the post-tanning areas are often referred to as wet processing, as they are performed in processing vessels filled with water to which the necessary chemicals are added to produce the desired reaction. After post-tanning the leather is dried and subsequent operations are referred to as dry processing. Typically, hides and skins are traded in the salted state, or, increasingly, as intermediate products, particularly in the wetblue condition for bovine hides and the pickled condition for ovine skins.

4. Finishing Operations

The art of finishing is to give the leather as thin a finish as possible without harming the known characteristics of leather, such as its look and its ability to breathe. The aim of this process is to treat the upper (grain) surface to give it the desired final look. By grounding (applying a base coat to leather to block pores before applying the true finish coats), coating, seasoning, embossing (to create a raised design upon a leather surface by pressure from a heated engraved plate or roller) and ironing (to pass a heated iron over the grain surface of the leather to smooth it and/or to give it a glossy appearance) the leather will have, as desired by fashion, a shiny or matt, single or multi-coloured, smooth or clearly grained surface. The overall objective of finishing is to enhance the appearance of the leather and to provide the appropriate performance characteristics in terms of colour, gloss, and handling, among others.

Source: A Blueprint for the African Leather Industry—a development, investment and trade guide for the leather industry in Africa, UNIDO 2004, p. 17.

ECCO's research centre, Futura in Tønder, Denmark, experimented with new materials, processes and technologies. Over the years ECCO had seen a sharp division of tasks between Denmark and various foreign production sites. Earlier operations in Denmark had encompassed all design, prototype, ramp-up, quality control, branding, marketing and most research and development (R&D) aspects, while ECCO foreign plants performed volume production. For instance, ECCO had split up R&D activities relocating many activities to the production sites, which evidently were more in touch with ECCO's R&D efforts from a practical perspective. The R&D activities conducted at the production sites revolved around support for the production process and optimization of materials.

ECCO's full-scale production process involved both manual labor and capital-intensive machinery. Normally, the uppers were cut by hydraulic presses called clicking machines, although at times hand cutting was used in the manufacture of shoes made of fine leather (see **Exhibit 5**). The upper was then attached to the insole with adhesives, tacks, and staples. Applying advanced machinery, the uppers were then placed in an injection-molding machine where the shoe bottom, including the outsole and heel, was attached to the uppers under very high pressure. Lastly, each pair of shoes went through the finishing process using various operations such as bottom securing and edge trimming which improved the durability and appearance of the shoe. According to ECCO's estimates, each pair of shoes comprised approximately 30 minutes of manual labor.

ECCO's tannery operations revolved around similar phases including prototype, laboratory and ramp-up production of leather, which took place in the Netherlands. The full-scale processing of leather took place in tanneries in Indonesia and Thailand. ECCO's maintaining ownership of the tannery operations not only reflected the company's commitment to quality but also illustrated a high level of ambition and confidence. ECCO's profound belief that "we cannot get the best quality if we do not do it ourselves," as often stated by Toosbuy, still permeated the company's business philosophy in 2005.

Although design and product development processes were generally conducted by the head office in Bredebro, Denmark, at times the division between the different phases was not clear-cut. For instance, the design and development of shoe uppers happened with the strong involvement of the subsidiary in Indonesia in order to transform the design into high-quality, comfortable shoe uppers. Prior to beginning actual production for the next season, the subsidiary in Indonesia was required to make production samples. ECCO's marketing team would screen the samples to forecast volumes and style of production. Based on the sales forecast headquarters would allocate production orders among its network of subsidiaries and licensees. The production of shoe uppers itself generally involved significant manual work. When the shoe uppers were completed they were shipped by sea to another group's facilities for subsequent processing according to the allocation set by headquarters. Finished shoes were distributed via the group's distribution centre and sales agents.

ECCO's distribution system was also vital to its business. ECCO had two main distribution centres; one in the United States and one in Tønder, Denmark. The latter was expanded in 2001 with four additional warehouses totaling 9,000 square meters, doubling the capacity from one million to two million pairs of shoes. The majority of ECCO's shoe production went through Tønder, however, over the last years only between six and nine per cent of total production was actually sold on the Danish market. The consolidation of distribution in Tønder also involved the closure of ECCO's distribution centre in Brøndby, Denmark and the warehouse in Bredebro, Denmark. The majority of shoe shipments arrived through the harbor of Aarhus, Denmark but ECCO also utilized vans for transportation and freight planes in urgent cases. Through the use of a bar code system the distribution centre was able to ship 60,000 pairs of shoes per day by lorry to 25 countries. Shoes for markets outside Europe were shipped by sea.

Recent developments within the shoe business had resulted in retailers ordering a larger proportion

Exhibit 5   Illustration of Different Components in the Construction of ECCO's Walkathon Shoe

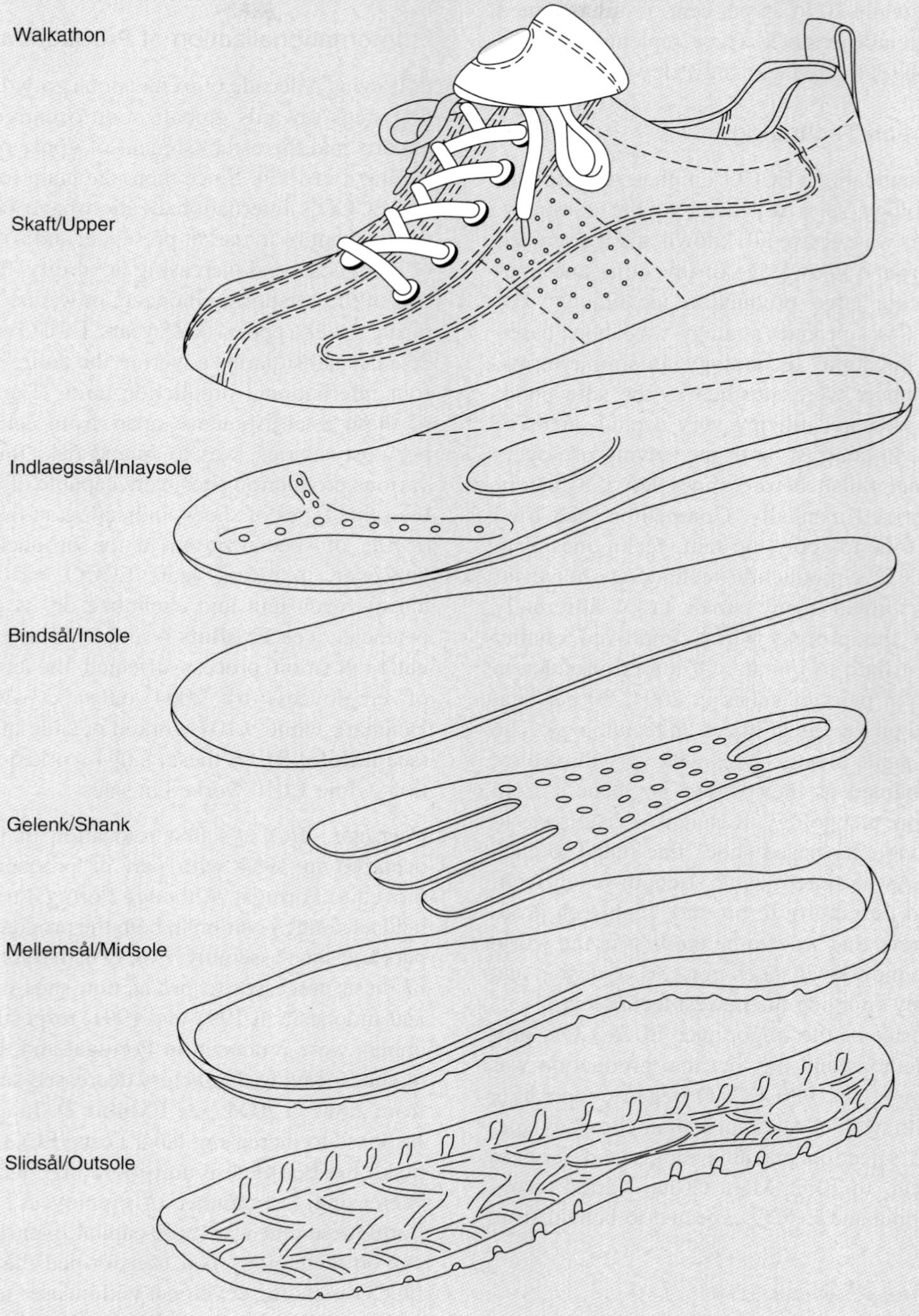

Walkathon

Skaft/Upper

Indlaegssål/Inlaysole

Bindsål/Insole

Gelenk/Shank

Mellemsål/Midsole

Slidsål/Outsole

Source: ECCO internal illustration

of shoes in advance. Retailers typically ordered 75 to 80 per cent of ECCO's production in advance of the season, while 20 to 25 per cent of orders aimed to fill up a retailer's stock. These replenishment orders had to be delivered with only a few days' notice.

Production Technology

Since its foundation, ECCO emphasized production technology as a key asset to the company. The founder was, above all, known and recognized for his profound knowledge of inventing and fine-tuning cutting edge production techniques. The core of ECCO's product strategy was shoes based on "direct injection" technology. In simple terms, the shoe uppers were attached to the sole under very high pressure utilizing very capital-intensive machinery. In contrast, both the sewing of uppers and the final finish before shoes left the factory were performed manually. Competitors had tried for a long time to apply the same techniques or to license ECCO's production techniques, however, ECCO performed many small tasks differently throughout the process which improved quality and made it hard to imitate. Of a total production of 12 million pairs of shoes in 2004, 80 per cent were based on the direct injection technology. The remaining pairs, mostly shoes with very thin soles, were outsourced as they would not benefit from ECCO's core technology. Kasprzak's vision was to make individually based shoes fine-tuned to each customer. As he stated: "Our strength is our technology and our ability to produce high-tech products. I believe that we can be the first in the world to produce individual shoes in terms of design and instant fit by applying the newest technology."[7]

As a result of the importance of ECCO's production methods and the fact that production was kept in-house, in 1980 ECCO began cooperating closely with Main Group, an Italian company specialized in injection machine molds and services for footwear. In 2002, Main Group started operations in China and ECCO expected to benefit from

cheaper Main Group machines when initiating its production in China in spring 2005.

Internationalization of Production

Following a decade of tremendous growth ECCO's first steps towards globalization occurred through exports and the establishment of upper production in Brazil in 1974. Since then, the main forces driving ECCO's internationalization have been i) establishment of a market presence, and ii) reduction of labor costs and increasing flexibility. ECCO was one of the offshoring pioneers in Danish manufacturing. Over a period of 25 years, ECCO established 26 sales subsidiaries covering the entire world and four international production units. The objective of these establishments, apart from achieving labor cost savings, was to spread risk. Initially, the various production sites were capable of producing the same types of shoes, indicating an insignificant degree of specialization in the production units. However, in recent years ECCO had strived to narrow each unit and capitalize on its core competencies (see **Exhibits 6** and **7**). The early internationalization process affected the composition of employees—by 2004 only 553 worked in Denmark while 9,104 worked outside of Denmark (see **Exhibit 8**). Of these, 8,094 worked in production, while 1,010 worked in sales.

Portugal   ECCO's first relocation of production occurred in 1984 with part of production being moved to Portugal. Although Portugal traditionally held a leading position in both the production of uppers and shoe assembly, ECCO then relocated some of these processes to production sites in Thailand and Indonesia in 1993 and 1991, respectively. Few uppers were produced in Portugal and the number of shoes leaving the factory decreased substantially from 2000 to 2004 (see **Exhibit 7**). In addition, in response to increasing labor costs, ECCO strove to make the Portuguese unit more high-tech, thereby decreasing the number of employees. While the Portuguese unit was more capital intensive, the focus on technology had transformed the plant into ECCO's leading developer within laser-technology.

[7]*Berlingske Tidende*, September 5, 2004.

Exhibit 6   ECCO's Production Output Worldwide 2000–2004

	2004	2003	2002	2001	2000
Bredebro, Denmark (1963)					
Activity: Shoe factory. Development and preparation of new articles and prototype testing. No. of employees: 124					
- Uppers produced (pairs)	3,805	3,720	4,482	5,281	—
- Shoes produced (pairs)	20,577	38,000	211,413	478,674	800,605
Santa Maria da Feria, Portugal (1984)					
Activity: Shoe factory. Production of uppers and shoes. No. of employees: 720					
- Uppers produced (pairs)	20,737	79,690	241,961	438,299	535,200
- Shoes produced (pairs)	2,649,178	2,442,395	2,590,327	3,769,754	4,150,000
Surabaya, Indonesia (1991)					
Activity: Tannery and shoe factory. Production of wetblue, crust, leather, uppers and shoes. No. of employees: 3554					
- Wetblue produced (ft²)	18,249,560	15,970,001	15,338,582	8,432,162	11,134,743
- Leather produced (ft²)	15,098,971	14,062,152	12,048,197	15,566,070	15,104,307
- Uppers produced (pairs)	5,326,300	4,664,023	4,063,840	3,968,559	3,750,000
- Shoes produced (pairs)	246,018	29,119	—	—	220,000
Ayudhthaya, Thailand (1993)					
Activity: Tannery and shoe factory. Production of crust, leather, uppers and shoes. No. of employees: 2775					
- Leather produced (ft²)	10,095,425	9,138,590	8,046,037	8,291,589	5,800,000
- Uppers produced (pairs)	3,237,054	2,868,227	2,708,639	2,891,591	3,150,000
- Shoes produced (pairs)	3,910,382	3,319,623	3,264,747	3,102,710	3,200,000
Martin, Slovakia (1998)					
Activity: Shoe factory. Production of uppers and shoes. No. of employees: 824					
- Uppers produced (pairs)	163,297	259,136	792,473	287,694	130,000
- Shoes produced (pairs)	2,771,025	2,265,312	1,974,408	1,657,498	1,500,000
Dongen, The Netherlands (2001)					
Activity: Tannery. Production of wetblue. Leather and development centre. Acquired by ECCO in 2001. No. of employees: 79					
- Wetblue produced (ft²)	19,931,818	26,704,106	30,886,062	23,686,640	

Source: ECCOs environmental report 2004

Indonesia The Indonesian production unit, opened in 1991, specialized in producing shoe uppers for the ECCO group, while the finishing processes, such as attaching shoe uppers to soles, were undertaken in other facilities of the group. The production unit in Indonesia satisfied approximately 40 to 50 per cent of the group's shoe upper demand. In shoe production, the main materials required were rawhides (procured locally as well as imported) that were processed into semi-finished and finished leather. Other materials required for production included reinforcement, yarn and accessories. Apart from the leather, the majority of the materials (70 to 80 per cent) were obtained from European suppliers, in particular granulate and Gore-Tex. Procurement of raw material took eight weeks

Exhibit 7   ECCO's Production Output Worldwide 2000–2004

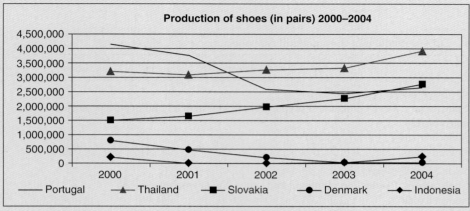

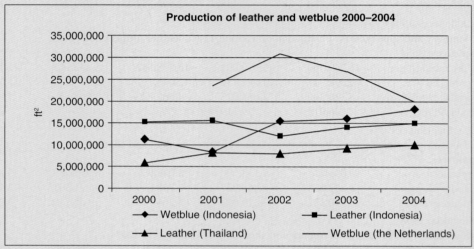

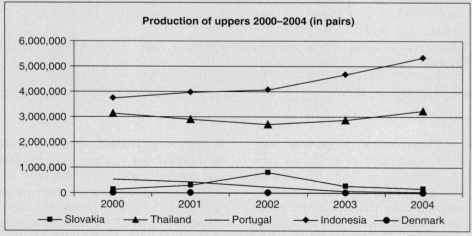

Source: ECCO annual report, various issues

Exhibit 8   Employee Statistics—Geographical Composition 1980–2004

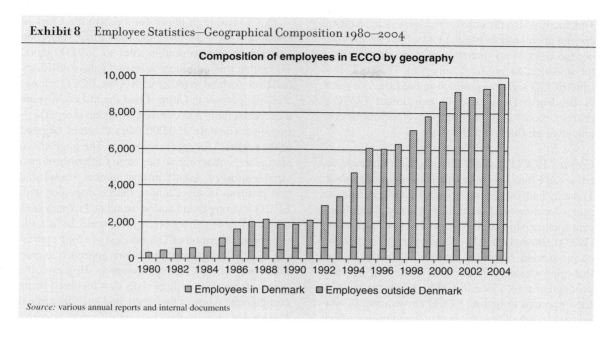

Composition of employees in ECCO by geography

□ Employees in Denmark   ▨ Employees outside Denmark

Source: various annual reports and internal documents

from the placement of the order until materials were ready to be shipped, and another five weeks for sea shipment.

Thailand   ECCO's production facility in Thailand, opened in 1993, encompassed both tannery and assembling facilities. In 2004, the site produced roughly 37 per cent of the uppers, primarily for shoe assembly in Thailand where 40 per cent of total unit volume was produced. ECCO's production site in Thailand was rather successful in terms of output, employee satisfaction and size. Over the years, the number of employees increased substantially and annual employee turnover was less than seven per cent. Moreover, the Thais had a good eye for small details and were able to deliver first class workmanship. These characteristics led ECCO to concentrate the production of its most complicated shoes in Thailand, including golf shoes and its advanced trekking boots.

Slovakia   Opened in 1998, ECCO's production unit in Slovakia primarily assembled shoes and, to a lesser extent, uppers. The plant employed 824 people in 2004 and produced shoes primarily within the men's segment. The underlying rationale

for setting up production in Slovakia, apart from lower labor costs, was the country's proximity to promising markets like Russia and Poland. Prior to entering Slovakia, Toosbuy stated: "We need bigger production capacity and quicker deliveries. Our goal is to increase production capacity by 15 per cent per year. One of our challenges associated with production in Asia is the three to four week transportation time."[8] Years later, ECCO's executive production director, Flemming Brønd, added:

> Shoe manufacturing is labor intensive, thus the wage level is of paramount importance. We already had a factory in Portugal yet we were searching for an optimal location for a new plant in Europe as labor costs were raising in Portugal. We have the majority of our uppers flown in from Indonesia and India after which the shoes are assembled. Although we automated the assembly process by using robots, we still needed skilled labor to handle the machines.[9]

Having established production facilities in Slovakia, ECCO set up a production network in close proximity to the company's major markets.

[8]*Berlingske Tidende,* February 2, 1998.
[9]*Jyllands-Posten,* December 12, 2003.

This facility also provided some leeway in terms of driving up volume between plants, thereby alleviating the risks of an interruption in production due, for instance, to political unrest in Thailand. Despite ECCO's global production facilities the plant in Bredebro, Denmark still constituted ECCO's primary model in terms of the development of cutting edge production technology.

China ECCO's establishment of production facilities in China was by no means a spontaneous act. Toosbuy had, on various occasions, visited China to assess locations and the timing of entry. China's recent membership of the World Trade Organization (WTO) allowed for 100 per cent foreign ownership of production sites. This, combined with the fact that approximately 50 per cent of the world's shoe production took place in China, made the country too important to ignore. ECCO chose a site in Xiamen just north of the province of Guangdong, which Kasprzak described as "a smaller yet dynamic community where we have been very well received and provided good and competent service from the local authorities." The plan was to build five factories over the next five years, as well as a very advanced tannery including a beam house to convert rawhides. Total investment including tanneries would amount to approximately DKK 500 million. When realized, the Chinese production site would become ECCO's largest worldwide, delivering some five million pairs of shoes annually. Although mostly targeted for export, one of the factories would serve the Chinese market exclusively. ECCO expected to employ around 3,000 people in China.

Although low labor costs and taxes were considered, access to local manpower was the decisive factor when establishing operations in China. "Taxes are more or less the same in different zones so it did not influence our location decision as such. On the other hand it was important to us that Xiamen could provide local employees who we can train and keep for a longer period of time which is definitely not the case in other places in China."[10]

[10]Assistant General Manager, Morten Bay Jensen.

ECCO had high hopes for sales to the Chinese consumers as well. Over the next three years, the company hoped to double sales to 500,000 pairs. To realize this ambition, a formal sales subsidiary had been formed together with Aibu, ECCO's long-standing partner in China. Over the last eight years their partnership had evolved from one shop to selling approximately 250,000 pairs of shoes targeted at the segment for exclusive shoes. The plan was to strengthen collaborative ties even further through a combination of Aibu's unique market knowledge and position in the Chinese market together with ECCO's strong brand and accumulated experiences with positioning shoes on a global scale. In fact, the experience from other Danish design icons operating in China suggested a network approach to gain the loyalty of the Chinese consumers. However, the approach was not without risks as it involved being complaisant while at the same time keeping critical knowledge close to the chest until formal contracts had been signed. During 2003/2004, ECCO had been plagued by Chinese manufacturers copying the ECCO design. According to Søren Steffensen, executive vice-president of sales, every single case was pursued and handled by a special unit of attorneys at ECCO whose primary task was to protect the company's brand and design.

The Competitive Landscape

Generally, the market for lifestyle casual footwear was highly competitive and subject to changes in consumer preferences. Fierce competition had sparked investments in both cost optimization and new technologies. First, the quest for competitive pricing had driven the search for new ways of producing and assembling in order to lower costs and reduce time to market. Operations were streamlined and formerly manual processes were automated. Second, incumbents invested in new technology, improved customer service, and market knowledge.

Traditionally, the footwear industry had been fragmented yet in recent years the distinction between athletic and lifestyle casual footwear blurred. Financially strong athletic shoe companies, like Nike and Reebok, competed directly with some of

ECCO's products. On the other hand, ECCO's expansion into such new segments as golf shoes gave rise to new competitors. In addition, the industry felt increasing pressure from retailers that had established products under private labels. As a consequence of the fuzzy boundaries between different footwear product categories and geographical regions, pinpointing ECCO's competitors was a challenge. However, ECCO itself regarded Geox, Clarks and Timberland as its main competitive threats worldwide (see **Exhibit 9**).

Geox   By all measures the Italian shoemaker Geox constituted a competitive threat to ECCO's operations in the casual lifestyle footwear segment. Founded in 1994 by the Italian entrepreneur Mario Moretti Polegato, Geox achieved impressive growth rates, increasing sales from €147.6 million in 2001 to €340.1 million in 2004, corresponding to a compound annual growth rate (CAGR) of

32 per cent. The success of Geox was based on perforated rubber soles in which a special waterproof and breathable membrane was inserted, allowing the vapor from perspiration to leave but still preventing water from entering the shoe—a technology protected by over 30 patents. Geox's headquarters and R&D facilities were located in the centre of a large shoe-making area northwest of Venice—Montebelluna. Geox had its own production facilities in Slovakia and Romania and outsourced to manufacturers in China, Vietnam and Indonesia. The entire production process and logistics were closely monitored in-house from headquarters in Italy.

In terms of distribution, Geox operated with a business model similar to ECCO's. The company's shoes were sold in more than 60 countries through a worldwide distribution network of more than 230 single-brand Geox Shop stores and about 8,000 multi-brand points of sale.

Exhibit 9   Global Sales of Lifestyle Casual Footwear Brand Sales (In US$ Million) 2002–2003

Rank	Company	2002	2003	% Change
1	Clarks	1,399	1,534	9.6%
		29.2%	29.6%	
2	ECCO	502	590	17.5%
		10.5%	11.4%	
3	Rockport	385	361	6.2%
		8.0%	7.0%	
4	Geox	208	329	58.2%
		4.3%	6.3%	
5	Birkenstock	270	300	11.1%
		5.6%	5.8%	
6	Bass	275	285	3.6%
		5.7%	5.5%	
7	Caterpillar	209	210	0.5%
		4.4%	4.0%	
8	Doc Martens	295	195	−34.0%
		6.2%	3.8%	
	Others	1,252	1,383	
		26.1%	26.7%	
	Total	**$4,795**	**$5,187**	**8.2%**

Note: Timberland is not included in the table. The company offers footwear across different categories including rugged footwear and athletic footwear as well as casual lifestyle footwear.

Geox had global ambitions. The company still had a strong penetration in the Italian market, which generated approximately 55 per cent of sales. International sales were gaining momentum, however, comprising 45 per cent in 2004, with Germany, France, Iberia (Spain and Portugal) and the United States being the largest markets. Geox increased sales by 250 per cent from 2002 (US$4 million) to 2003 (US$14 million) in the very competitive American market. As a comparison, ECCO grew only 4.5 per cent in this market with

sales of US$115 million in 2003 (see **Exhibit 10**). Although extremely successful, Geox planned to enter clothing in order to circumvent sudden shifts in consumer tastes.

Clarks   Clarks, the English shoemaker, was the biggest player within the casual lifestyle footwear segment achieving global sales of US$1,534 million in 2003 (see **Exhibit 9**). Since its humble beginnings in 1825, Clarks had grown into a global shoemaker producing 35 million pairs and offering

Exhibit 10   U.S. Sales of Lifestyle Casual Footwear Brand Sales (In US$ Million) 2002–2003

Rank	Company	2002	2003	% Change
1	Clarks	339 *18.8%*	375 *21.5%*	*10.6%*
2	Rockport	291 *16.2%*	266 *15.2%*	*−8.6%*
3	Bass	258 *14.3%*	265 *15.2%*	*2.7%*
4	Doc Martens	195 *10.8%*	127 *7.3%*	*−34.9%*
5	ECCO	110 *6.1%*	115 *6.6%*	*4.5%*
6	Birkenstock	110 *6.1%*	80 *4.6%*	*−27.3%*
7	Dansko	62 *3.4%*	71 *4.1%*	*14.5%*
8	Mephisto	55 *3.1%*	55 *3.1%*	*0.0%*
9	Sperry	49 *2.7%*	53 *3.0%*	*8.2%*
10	Josef Seibel	33 *1.8%*	35 *2.0%*	*6.1%*
11	Caterpillar	33 *1.8%*	30 *1.7%*	*−9.1%*
12	Sebago	20 *1.1%*	16 *0.9%*	*−20.0%*
13	Geox	4 *0.2%*	14 *0.8%*	*250.0%*
14	Stonefly	10 *0.6%*	11 *0.6%*	*10.0%*
15	FinnComfort	10 *0.6%*	11 *0.6%*	*10.0%*
	Others	220 *12.2%*	224 *12.8%*	
	Total	**$1,799**	**$1,748**	*−2.8%*

Source: JP Morgan—Apparel and Footwear Yearbook 2003

a wide product portfolio under the slogan "from career wear to weekend wear." Clark's product portfolio included casual, dress casual, boots and sandals. Central to various categories were Clark's widely used technical features like "active air" (an air-cushioning technology) and "waterproof" (impermeable membrane sewn inside the boot), which sought to improve comfort, performance and versatility.

Clarks, like other shoe manufacturers, had vigorously sought lower labor costs in response to fierce competition. The company once had 15 plants across the United Kingdom but by 2005 only one small factory with 37 employees remained in Millom, Cumbria. The most recent closure occurred in early 2005 when the company shifted production to independent factories in Vietnam, Romania and China. According to company spokesman John Keery, this move was vital to ensuring that the business remained financially viable. As he stated: "The cost of manufacturing in the UK has increased over the last 20 years and we have been able to source our shoes cheaper in the Far East."[11] Based on cost considerations, availability of materials and capacity issues within individual countries, Clarks sourced shoes from 12 different manufacturers located primarily in Asia. Clarks kept less than one per cent of its production in-house. By using many independent manufacturers, Clarks was exposed to a variety of technologies, materials and shoemaking techniques and thus could access various types of expertise. However, monitoring material standard and product quality was an enormous task.

Timberland   Founded in Boston in 1918 by Nathan Swartz, Timberland designed, marketed and distributed under the Timberland® and Timberland PRO® brands. Their products included footwear and apparel and accessories products for men, women and children. Having introduced the

waterproof boot based on injection-molding technology in 1973, Timberland's primary strength resided within the outdoor boot category, which competed with ECCO's outdoor and sport product categories. In 1978 and 1979, Timberland added casual and boat shoes to its line to become more than just a boot company. In the eighties, the company strived to be recognized as a lifestyle brand and entered Italy as the first international market. During the 1990s, Timberland introduced kids' footwear and launched the Timberland PRO® series designed for maximum surface contact and targeted at skilled tradesmen and working professionals.

Timberland's 2003 total revenue of US$1.328 million was comprised of footwear (76.7 per cent) and apparel and accessories (23.3 per cent), making Timberland twice the size of ECCO in terms of product sales. Despite the company's late appearance in international markets, international sales comprised 38.5 per cent of total generated revenue—up from 29.5 per cent in 2001. Timberland's products in the United States and internationally were sold through independent retailers, department stores, athletic stores, Timberland specialty stores and factory outlets dedicated exclusively to Timberland products. In Europe, products were sold mostly through franchised retail stores.

In terms of manufacturing, Timberland operated production facilities in Puerto Rico and the Dominican Republic. Contrary to ECCO, which on average produced 80 per cent of its shoes in-house, Timberland manufactured only 10 per cent of total unit volume with the remainder of the footwear production being performed by independent manufactures in China, Vietnam and Thailand. Timberland believed that attaining some internal manufacturing capabilities, such as refined production techniques, planning efficiencies and lead time reduction, might prove beneficial when collaborating with manufactures in Asia. To facilitate this collaboration, Timberland set up a quality management group to develop, review and update the company's quality and production standards in

---

[11] www.bbc.co.uk/somerset/content/articles/2005/01/10/clarks_feature.shtml, accessed March 2005.

Bangkok, Zhu Hai, Hong Kong and Ho Chi Minh City (Saigon).

In terms of leather supplies, Timberland purchased from an independent web of 60 suppliers who were subject to rigid quality controls. This required substantial resources in order to scrutinize and monitor the supplier network. Analysts argued that Timberland was vulnerable to price increases on raw materials. Gross margins were negatively affected by increases in the cost of leather as selling prices did not increase proportionally. Shoe manufacturers like Timberland found it difficult to pass on the extra cost to the consumer. In order to diminish the effect of increasing prices for leather and other materials, Timberland was forced to closely monitor the market prices and interact closely with suppliers to achieve maximum price stability. By 2003, 10 suppliers provided approximately 80 per cent of Timberland's leather purchases.

As the plane approached Copenhagen Airport, Mikael Thinghuus recalled a management board meeting prior to his visit to China. Several viewpoints concerning ECCO's future strategy had been presented and, while no one discredited ECCO's unique production assets, there was a sentiment that advantages accruing from world-class production technologies could not be sustained forever. "We are not going to exist in 20 years time if we cannot excite and cast a spell over our customers," one member of the committee commented. Another added: "We do not operate marketing budgets of the same magnitude as the big fashion brands. But our shoes are produced with an unconditional commitment to quality and our history is truly unique. We need to be better at telling that story." Thinghuus was pondering:

> "We need to be more concrete about the process towards market orientation. How can we relate better to our customers while at the same time being able to exploit efficiencies from a global value chain? Integrated or not. And what about entering new markets? The recent market expansion in China was just the beginning. Long term outlook seemed favorable. Yet, was it feasible to invest in new markets, increase marketing efforts, and optimize a global value chain—all at the same time?"

Irrespective of the outcome of these thoughts, it was pivotal to consider how strategic initiatives would go hand in hand with ECCO's philosophy of integrating the value chain from cow to shoe.

Case 4-3 Lundbeck Korea: Managing an International Growth Engine

Michael Roberts

Early in 2005, Michael Andersen, vice president of Lundbeck—a leading central nervous system (CNS) pharmaceutical company in Denmark, questioned whether he should rethink Lundbeck's reporting structure in Asia. In particular, the Korean subsidiary was experiencing very strong growth and Andersen wondered whether Lundbeck Korea would achieve its full potential if it remained part of Lundbeck Asia, the regional group, or whether it would be better to have the managers at Lundbeck Korea report directly to him in Copenhagen.

Korea had proven itself to be a rising star among Lundbeck's overseas subsidiaries, and the staff in Korea, led by country manager Jin-Ho Jun (Jun), wanted more independence to chart their own path. The Korean subsidiary's performance had far exceeded what was projected in the original business plan. It had grown from one employee in 2002 to over 50 employees in 2005, and had sales of KRW25 billion (approximately US$22 million). Given the current success, Andersen wondered whether the current reporting structure was still appropriate.

IVEY

Richard Ivey School of Business
The University of Western Ontario

The decision was not to be taken lightly; while the Korean division, under the leadership of Jun, was experiencing enormous growth, it was only barely three years in the making. In addition, while normal and expected in a recently established subsidiary, Lundbeck Korea was still not a profitable business unit. Since most of the other Asian countries were part of the Asia division, Andersen also had to think about how this would affect Lundbeck's regional and worldwide organizational reporting norms; in particular, he was concerned about the Chinese subsidiary. While making adjustments to reporting structures was a normal part of doing business for Lundbeck, Andersen had not anticipated that he would be considering this decision so soon for Korea.

The CNS Landscape

However, these markets were fairly stable and generally experienced low single-digit growth. **Exhibit 1** is a list of the top pharmaceutical markets. The major CNS pharmaceutical markets by country were: United States, 59%; Germany, 5%; Japan, 4%; France, 4%; United Kingdom, 4%; Spain, 3%; Italy, 2%; South Korea, 1.5%. The bulk of the remaining 19 per cent of the CNS market came from emerging economies such as Brazil, China, India, and South Korea. While the market for CNS drugs in these emerging economies was much smaller, the rate of growth in many of these countries was in excess of 15 per cent per year.[1]

The global industry for CNS pharmaceuticals was about $93 billion in 2005. CNS diseases are serious and life-threatening and affect the quality of life of patients as well as of their relatives. Over the

---

[1]B. Nehru, *The CNS Market Outlook to 2012*, Business Insights Ltd, London, United Kingdom, 2007, p. 59.

Exhibit 1   Top Pharmaceutical Markets, 2005

Country	Pharmaceutical Market Size (billions USD)	Population (millions USD)	Lundbeck Functions
United States	270.2	307.2	Sales/Research
Japan	76.2	127.1	—
Germany	43.9	82.3	Sales
France	39.1	64.1	Sales
United Kingdom	31.3	61.1	Sales
Italy	24.3	58.1	Sales/Research
China	20.4	1,338.6	Sales
Canada	16.3	33.5	Sales
India	9.3	1,166.1	Sales
South Korea	7.9	48.5	Sales
Russia	7.9	140.0	Sales
Turkey	7.5	76.8	Sales
. . .	—	—	. . .
Denmark	2.6	5.5	Sales/Research/Production

Source: Business Monitor International, "Pharmaceutical Market Statistics: Statistics for 2005," London, United Kingdom, 2009.

past 50 years, new pharmaceuticals had revolutionized treatment options, but there remained a large unmet need for new and innovative therapeutics.

Overall, the industry was marked by intense competition from both rival branded pharmaceutical firms and generic competitors. In most markets, branded pharmaceuticals were given a number of years of exclusivity—a period in which no generic version of the drug can be sold. However, these periods of exclusivity varied greatly by country. Patent protection could range from no protection to 20 years of exclusivity. In most developed markets, for example the United States, exclusivity began at the time the drug was patented; in other markets, for instance South Korea, it began when the drug was launched. The laws and regulations around granting exclusivity also varied by country, and were often heavily influenced by political concerns. Regardless of the region, when the exclusivity periods run out, the price of a drug drops dramatically. The revenues from Eli Lilly's anti-depressant drug Prozac, for example, fell by over 80 per cent following the

loss of its patent protection at the end of the 1990s.[2] While the decrease in revenues from this drug could also be attributed to new branded pharmaceuticals entering the anti-depressant market, the significance of loss of patent protection cannot be overstated.

Almost 60 per cent of the total market sales in the CNS industry came from the nine largest firms (Johnson & Johnson, 11%; Glaxo Smith Kline, or GSK, 9%; Pfizer, 8%; Lilly, 7%; Sanofi-Aventis, 5%; Novartis, 5%; Astra Zeneca, 5%; Wyeth, 5%; Forest Labs, 3%). Lundbeck held 2%. In this industry, sales growth was highly dependent on the successful introduction of a new patented drug, and sales declines were most often a result of a patent expiration. A firm's revenue was often disproportionally dominated by one blockbuster drug—a drug that dominates a class of drugs. For example, Johnson & Johnson generated 41 per cent of its revenue from the blockbuster schizophrenia drug Risperdal.[3]

Depending on the country, buyers of pharmaceuticals could be national health services, private

[2]B. Massingham, *CNS Market Outlook to 2000,* Business Insights Ltd, London, United Kingdom, 2000.

[3]B. Nehru, op.cit., p. 15.

Exhibit 2 Leading Anti-Depressants and Alzheimers Disease Medications in the Global CNS Market, 2005

Brand	Company	Generic	Class	Sales (millions USD)	Share (%)	Expected Growth (%) 2006	2012 (per/y)	Patent Expiry
Anti-Depressants								
Effexor	Wyeth	venlafaxine	SNRI	3,830	20.1	3.0	−20.4	2007
Lexapro	Lundbeck/ Forest	escitalopram	SSRI	2,455**	12.9	19.0	8.4	2011
Zoloft	Pfizer	sertraline	SSRI	3,641	19.2	−34.0	−32.6	expired
Wellbutrin	GSK	bupropion	Other	1,605	8.4	22.0	—*	—
Yentreve	Lilly	duloxetine	SNRI	684	3.6	95.0	23.9	2013
Seroxat	GSK	paroxetine	SSRI	819	4.3	−13.0	−28.3	expired
Prozac	Lilly	fluoxetine	SSRI	408	2.1	−21.0	−34.7	expired
Remeron	Organon	mirtazapine	Other	351	1.8	−15.0	—	—
Others				5,220	27.5	−3.0	−2.7	
Total				19,013	100.0	3.5	1.5	
Alzheimers Medications								
Aricept	Pfizer	donepezil	CI	2,215	54.9	13.5	−5.5	2010
Namenda	Forest	memantine	NMDAA	482	11.9	35.7	24.6	2014
Exelon	Novartis	rivastigmine	CI	496	12.3	5.6	−0.9	2012
Reminyl	J&J	galantamine	CI	490	12.1	6.7	−16.7	2008
Ebixa	Lundbeck	memantine	NMDAA	189	4.7	29.7	.6	2010
Akatinol	Lundbeck	memantine	NMDAA	60	1.5	13.2	−11.5	2008
Axura	Merz	memantine	NMDAA	22	0.5	35.6	7.2	2008
Prometax	Novartis	rivastigmine	CI	25	0.6	5.3	4.0	2012
Other				57	1.4	29.1	98	
Total				4,036	100	15.4	13.1	

* — is used to indicate that no information is available
** of which Lundbeck is 863
Source: Modified from B. Nehru, *The CNS Market Outlook to 2012*, Business Insights Ltd, London, United Kingdom, 2007.

insurance companies, or individuals. However, in general, decisions about prescribing drugs were made by practitioners (i.e. doctors, etc.).[4] Psychiatrists represented the largest group of practitioners in the CNS industry. Since doctors were the ultimate decision makers, the buyer had little direct product choice. However, the type of buyer system greatly affected the potential market size and price

that could be charged for the product. The presence of a national health service that covered prescription drugs, for example, could greatly expand the market, but government pressure could potentially lower prices per unit.

Key Products

The largest class of drugs in the CNS market was comprised of anti-depressants, which represented almost 20 per cent of the total market. Depression is a genuine physical condition and affects

[4]*Datamonitor,* "Global Pharmaceuticals, Biotechnology & Life Sciences: Industry Profile," New York, New York, 2009.

approximately 10 per cent of the global population.[5] "Bad" mood, loss of energy, feelings of worthlessness, difficulty concentrating, and even thoughts of suicide are just some of the many symptoms.

The market for anti-depressants was $19 billion in 2005 (see **Exhibit 2**). However, the market segment was due to have very poor growth rates over the next several years because of the large influx of generic drugs in selective serotonin reuptake inhibitors (SSRIs), the largest class of anti-depressant drugs. SSRIs, which made up more than 50 per cent of the anti-depressant market segment, were a class of compounds typically used in the treatment of depression, anxiety disorders, personality disorders, and some cases of insomnia. In particular, sales of Zoloft by Pfizer were expected to decrease by one third in 2006 due to the expiration of its patent in the U.S. market. This left only three products with patent protection: Effexor by Wyeth, Lexapro by Lundbeck, and Yentreve by Lilly.[6] Overall, this class of drugs was only forecasted to growth by 1.5 per cent a year until 2012.

New growth in the CNS market was driven by drugs for Alzheimer's disease (AD). Over the last few years, this class of drugs experienced growth rates upwards of 15 per cent per year.[7] The market for AD medications was $4 billion in 2005, and was expected to see growth of more than 15 per cent in 2006. **Exhibit 2** gives an overview of the AD medication market. The future of AD medication was in the NMDA receptor antagonist class of drugs, which was expected to grow by over 30 per cent in 2006. The drugs in this class were all derivatives of memantine. There were three memantine-based drugs on the market; however, they were not in direct competition with each other as they were a result of shared development and licensing. Forest Labs marketed Namenda in the United States; Merz sold Axura in Germany; and Lundbeck marketed Ebixa in the rest of Europe. Memantine was an important medication because it was the only pharmaceutical available for moderate and severe forms of AD. Since most AD patients lived long enough to experience all stages of the disease, memantine filled a crucial role in AD therapy. There were no threats of generics to memantine until after 2008. Overall, this class of drugs was forecasted to grow by 13.1 per cent a year until 2012.[8]

The Asian Market

At $97.4 billion in 2005, the pharmaceutical market in Asia represented approximately 20 per cent of the global pharmaceutical industry. The Asia pharmaceutical market had a growth rate of about 6.4 per cent a year which was forecasted to remain steady for the next several years. However, some markets throughout Asia were vastly different from others. For example, the largest market in Asia was Japan, which accounted for 55 per cent of the entire market but only had a growth rate of 2.4 per cent a year. China, on the other hand, accounted for 17.5 per cent of the pharmaceutical market, with a growth rate in excess of 20 per cent per year. The other major markets in Asia were South Korea and India, representing 8.3 per cent and 8.1 per cent of the market, respectively. Excluding Japan, the other Asian markets grew at an average rate of 11.3 per cent per year. The CNS market represented nine per cent of the total pharmaceutical market in Asia for a total of $8.7 billion.[9]

The payer systems also varied greatly throughout Asia. Japan had a combination of government insurance and private employer-based insurance. Hong Kong and Singapore had a combination of private pay and private insurance programs. South Korea had a fully government-funded national insurance for pharmaceutical prescriptions. China, Thailand, and Malaysia had virtually no group or collective programs and most costs for pharmaceuticals were paid by individuals.

[5]B. Nehru, op.cit., p. 33.

[6] Ibid., p. 53.

[7]Ibid., pp. 58–60.

[8]Ibid., pp. 94–98.

[9]*Datamonitor,* "Pharmaceuticals in Asia-Pacific," New York, New York, 2008, p. 9.

Exhibit 3   Lundbeck Financial Highlights, 2005

	DKK millions	USD millions
Revenue	9,070	1,513
Profit from operations	2,174	363
Finance income, net	17	3
Profit before tax	2,156	360
Net profit	1,457	243
		0
Cash flows from operating activities	2,074	346
		0
Total assets	11,560	1,928
Capital and reserves	7,437	1,240
EBIT margin (%)	24	
Return on equity (%)	19.3	
Earnings per share (EPS) (DKK)	6.52	1.1
Earnings per share-diluted (DEPS) (DKK)	6.5	1.1
Cash flow per share (DKK)	9.2	1.5

Revenue by Product and Region	Product	Region	Product	Region
Europe		4,680		781
Cipralex®/Lexapro®	1,963		327	
Ebixa®	933		156	
Azilect®	6		1	
Other pharmaceuticals	1,777		296	
United States		2,618		437
Income from Cipralex®/Lexapro®	2,552		426	
Other pharmaceuticals	66		11	
International Markets*		1,539		257
Cipralex®/Lexapro®	662		110	
Ebixa®	172		29	
Azilect®	0		0	
Other pharmaceuticals	706		118	
Other revenue		232		39
Total group revenue		9,070		1,513

*Asia, Australia, Africa, Americas, Canada, Middle East
*Estimated on the 2005 annual DKK/USD exchange rate of 5.996475
Source: Company documents.

Lundbeck

Lundbeck was an international CNS pharmaceutical company headquartered in Denmark. Founded as a trading company in 1915 by Hans Lundbeck, the company had evolved into a global CNS pharmaceutical firm. In 2005, Lundbeck earned over $240 million in operating profits from over $1.5 billion in sales. Lundbeck conducted research on, developed, manufactured, marketed, sold, and distributed pharmaceuticals for the treatment of neurological disorders, including depression, schizophrenia, Alzheimer's disease, Parkinson's disease and insomnia.

Lundbeck employed 5,500 people worldwide, 2,100 of whom were based in Denmark. It manufactured its products in Denmark and Italy, and had research facilities in Denmark and the United States. Lundbeck's drugs were registered for sale in more than 90 countries, and it had its own independent sales forces in 55 countries. For Lundbeck's financial highlights in 2005 (see **Exhibit 3**).

Lundbeck was a research-intensive company, structured to be constantly producing the next generation of drugs. The primary mission of the company was to undertake the tasks of improving the quality of life for persons with a psychiatric or neurological disorder, and to work intensely to find and develop new and improved drugs. It employed a total of 1,100 specialists in its R&D units, which consumed more than 20 per cent of annual revenues.

Strategic Drivers

Lundbeck's strategy was driven by four principles: specialization, speed, integration, and results.[10]

Specialization: Unlike many of its competitors, Lundbeck specialized exclusively in the CNS pharmaceutical area. Moreover, the strategy of specialization had been extended to include all aspects of its business. Thus, Lundbeck's goal was to focus and streamline its key products, simplify its processes and business procedures, and focus on long-term growth in the CNS industry. To do this, Lundbeck focused on marketing and distributing its new and innovative products. Lundbeck tried to balance innovative activities while maintaining a competitive cost structure.

Speed: Lundbeck's strategy was to use its small size as an advantage. The goal was to maintain short decision-making processes in order to respond quickly to the demands of a highly competitive market. That being said, Lundbeck set up strong control systems to ensure that the company was able to balance its results-focused mindset with exposure to risk and the need to maintain ethical business practices. Lundbeck used its small size to flexibly respond to risks at all stages in the value

chain. Some of the key risks that it identified at the sales and marketing level included generic competition; adherence to ethical sales and marketing practices; and risks associated with product liability. Its intention was to structure its organization to control and respond quickly to any new threat.

Integration: Lundbeck's goal was to continue to become a global pharmaceutical firm. In order to achieve that, it sought to continue to develop strong competencies through the entire value chain of the pharmaceuticals market, from knowledge and control of research to the development of new pharmaceuticals, production, marketing and sales. However, it did not believe that it had to do everything in-house or at home in Denmark. As the firm grew in its global competency, it planned to seek new locations and partners for any aspect of the value chain that could offer better value in terms of quality, price, commodities, and labour.

Results: Lundbeck intended to provide continuous short-term and long-term value to its shareholders. In 1999, Lundbeck's shares were listed on the Copenhagen Stock Exchange. The Lundbeck Foundation, which distributed $40 million to $50 million each year in grants to the scientific community for various types of research, owned about 70 per cent of the shares in Lundbeck, while the remaining 30 per cent were traded on the stock exchange. Lundbeck's semi-private ownership by the Lundbeck Foundation was a long-term strength for the company because this ownership structure gave the firm greater flexibility than most of its competitors to re-invest its current profits for long-term growth.[11]

Lundbeck's leading products were Lexapro and Ebixa. Lexapro represented 57.1 per cent of Lundbeck's revenues and Ebixa represented 12.2 per cent. Lexapro was one of the world's most often prescribed SSRIs for the treatment of depression and anxiety disorders. Lexapro was launched in 2002 and was marketed globally by Lundbeck and its partners. Unlike most other SSRIs on the market, which had lost patent protection or would

---

[10]Company documents.

[11]*Datamonitor*, "H. Lundbeck A/S," New York, New York, 2009, p. 16.

lose protection over the next year or two, Lexapro would have patent protection until 2011. Lexapro could expect growth of more than 20 per cent per year until 2011, when its sales would drop off dramatically. Lexapro was a next-generation drug launched to replace the drug Cipram (citalopram), which had lost its patent protection in major markets. However, Lexapro had proven to be superior to Cipram in controlling many disorders.

Ebixa was Lundbeck's memantine drug for the treatment of AD. This drug was certain to be a major growth engine for Lundbeck. However, due to licensing agreements with Merz and Forest, Lundbeck was prohibited from marketing the drug in Germany or the United States. Lundbeck anticipated that growth in 2006 would be in excess of 25 per cent. Ebixa was forecasted to have strong growth until 2010, when it would lose patent protection.

Lundbeck Asia

Lundbeck products had been available in many Asian countries since the early 1990s. In the past, Lundbeck chose to licence its product for sales and distribution by local pharmaceutical firms. As a result, several of Lundbeck's key products for depression and Alzheimer's had become well known throughout Asia, and had been used as primary psychiatric medications. Seeing the importance of Asia for its long-term growth, Lundbeck decided in the late 1990s to set up wholly owned subsidiaries in each of its markets in Asia and gradually retake its licenses. Before this time, Lundbeck had no standalone subsidiaries in Asia. So, controlling its own distribution, sales, and marketing would allow Lundbeck to integrate the Asian markets into the Lundbeck strategy of specialization, speed, integration, and results. By the early 2000s, Lundbeck had established subsidiaries in most Asian markets.

The Asian subsidiaries were joined together as part of a regional group headquartered in Hong Kong, called Lundbeck Asia. In total, Lundbeck Asia consisted of eight country subsidiaries: China,

Hong Kong, Indonesia, Malaysia, Pakistan, the Philippines, Singapore, and Thailand. Due to unfavourable market conditions, Lundbeck did not initially establish any successful distribution channels in South Korea.

Lundbeck established a subsidiary in Japan, but had not been able to generate any sales there. The complexity of the regulations surrounding exclusivity rights in Japan made it very difficult for Lundbeck to market its drugs in the Japanese market. One of the biggest hurdles was that Japanese regulators required that the data used in the application documentation for exclusivity be gathered in Japan.

The purpose of Lundbeck Asia was to provide control, support, guidance, and direction for the Lundbeck subsidiaries in the region. The management team consisted of regional vice president Asif Rajar, plus a regional product manager, a regional finance officer, and a regional regulatory affairs officer. The management at Lundbeck Asia was tasked with implementing Lundbeck's strategy in Asia and ensuring that it be executed appropriately in each country. Since Lundbeck was just entering these markets, the regional management was also charged with developing a sense of corporate identity and pride.

The Korean Pharmaceutical Market

In 2005, the South Korean pharmaceutical market was the 11th largest in the world (see **Exhibit 1**). The past 10 years had been revolutionary for the Korean pharmaceutical market because the prescription drug market in Korea was quite underdeveloped prior to 2001. Without a doctor's prescription, pharmacists were able to dispense any medicine that was legal for sale. Thus, existing medications were available from pharmacists upon request. However, beginning in 2001, Korea divided pharmaceuticals into prescription only and over-the-counter (OTC) medication. This caused a surge in the prescription drug market.

After the Asian financial meltdown in 1997 (known in Korea as the IMF crisis—because the Korean government needed to secure large loan agreements from the International Monetary Fund), the Korean government began a process of opening up markets to foreign multinational enterprises (MNEs). Before 2000, any MNE wishing to enter the Korean pharmaceutical market needed to have a joint venture with a Korean company. In addition, prior to 2000, it would have been very difficult for a pharmaceutical firm to establish a subsidiary in Korea unless it was prepared to establish production facilities. While not an absolute legal requirement, a firm that was trying to sell imported medicine could expect to receive very unfair treatment from regulators, price boards, and practitioners.

CNS Pharmaceuticals in Korea

Even though the market share for treatment of CNS disorders was growing fast, it was still quite small compared to the rest of the Korean pharmaceutical market. This was because mental disorders were not given high legitimacy in Asian societies like Korea; thus, there were limited resources for treating people who suffered from mental illness. Instead, Korean society gave priority and medical resources to physically life-threatening diseases such as cancer and heart disease.

There were stigmas surrounding mental disorders everywhere in the world, but in South Korea these were very pronounced. Only a few years earlier, anyone with depression would have tried to conceal it. However, this had begun to change in 2005 after the son of a well-known businessman committed suicide and it was publicly announced that he had suffered from depression. The situation repeated itself soon after, when a very popular Korean film actress committed suicide. These incidents sent shock waves through society. The Korean people simply could not comprehend how someone with so much success could possibly take their own life. However, these unfortunate situations led to a greater public discourse on, and improved understanding of, mental illness. As such, Korean society had begun to experience greater openness around depression during the last five years.

In 2001, when the Korean pharmaceutical market was divided into prescription only and over-the-counter (OTC) medication, the government insurance policy began to pay for CNS prescription medication. The CNS industry began to see market increases of 30 to 40 per cent per year, making CNS medications a nearly three quarters of a billion dollar industry by 2005.[12] Growth estimations were projected to continue at the same pace for the next several years. In an established market, such as the United States or Western Europe, sales had the potential for growing at one or two per cent per year.

Lundbeck Korea

While many of the big pharmaceutical companies had entered the Korean market, to Lundbeck, Korea did not seem like a significant market in the 1990s. Moreover, Lundbeck had centralized production, and it was not prepared to allow production outside of Denmark or Italy just to enter a very small market. In fact, in 1996, one of Lundbeck's key drugs, Cipram, was licensed to a Korean firm and registered for sale; however, it was never marketed because of the requirement to have the drug manufactured in Korea.

Lundbeck Korea was established in March 2002, after Lundbeck could justify the establishment of a subsidiary based on developments in the Korean market. The original plan was to establish the Korean and Japanese subsidiaries as one unit separate from the rest of Asia. However, immediately after Lundbeck Korea was established, the executives in Copenhagen chose to have the managers in Lundbeck Korea report to Lundbeck Asia, the regional headquarters. Jin-Ho Jun was hired as the country manager of Korea. Jun reported directly to Rajar in Hong Kong, who reported to Andersen in Copenhagen.

---

[12]Calculated based on available data.

Even though Lundbeck was a small actor in the South Korean market, it quickly established a strong reputation. Lundbeck worked primarily with the hospitals because Koreans generally preferred to seek treatment at hospitals rather than private clinics. They considered the medical staff to be more competent at major hospitals and saw major hospitals as having superior facilities and equipment. With a few exceptions, major hospitals were generally part of large university systems.

Jin-Ho Jun

Jun had the two essential qualities that Lundbeck needed to help establish its subsidiary in this unfamiliar market: he had almost fifteen years of experience in the CNS market in Korea, which made him a local expert; and he had spent most of his career working for multi-national pharmaceutical companies. This gave him the global mindset needed to carry out Lundbeck's strategies and corporate policies. Jun began working for the German multinational pharmaceutical company Bayer in 1990 as a CNS product manager. He was quite successful and was promoted to strategic product manager in 1996. In 1999, he left Bayer to work at an American MNE, Eli Lilly, as its product manager of neuroscience and eventually as its senior product manager. At Bayer and Lilly, Jun developed a deep and rich knowledge of the Korean CNS pharmaceutical market.

Perhaps even more importantly, especially in Korea, Jun developed a very good network of relationships with the top Korean psychiatrists. He devoted considerable time and effort to ensuring high-quality relationships with these important opinion leaders. This was not an easy or painless endeavour. In Korea, good relationships were built up over time, and involved numerous hours eating and socializing during evening social gatherings. To establish the quality of network that Jun had achieved, a person must be willing to sacrifice a great deal of family time. These social meetings were a very important forum for professional discussions and sales pitches.

The State of Local Management

To Jun's mind, choosing how much control and supervision to place on local managers was always tricky in Korea. Sitting in on meetings as a junior manager, he repeatedly heard the Korean managers explain with great frustration to the regional and headquarters managers that the non-Korean managers did not understand the uniqueness of the Korean market. On the other hand, it was difficult for the parent company managers to trust the Korean managers: the educational backgrounds, communication skills, and global knowledge of the Korean managers were usually inferior to those of their foreign counterparts. While their local knowledge was essential, they did not have the necessary management skills. However, because of foreign managers' imperfect knowledge of the Korean market, they were apt to make strategic miscalculations.

In 2005, Jun knew that the Korean pharmaceutical market had become similar to markets in other developed nations. Local knowledge and skills, while still important, were not quite as important as they were 20 years earlier. Meanwhile, Korean managers' communication skills, management skills, and global knowledge needed to succeed in an MNE were much more sophisticated than they were 20 years ago. As a consequence, Jun believed that Korean subsidiaries now required less supervision and control.

Asif Rajar

Being part of Lundbeck Asia had advantages for Lundbeck Korea. Asif Rajar helped establish Lundbeck Korea. Located in Hong Kong, he could easily maintain tight control over the Asian operation. Rajar had extensive experience with Lundbeck throughout Asia, spending many years with Lundbeck in Thailand, Indonesia and other Southeast Asian countries. Though he was a Swiss citizen through marriage, Rajar was originally from Pakistan, giving him a background with both a European and Asian mindset. He was bright and well educated, having achieved his MBA from a top business school in the

United States, where he was now often invited to give guest lectures.

Rajar was very active in helping the Asian country managers run their businesses, and was enjoying very good success. He involved himself in all areas of planning and even took the time to interview candidates for important staff positions before the country manager hired them. Rajar requested that all decisions be cleared with him, and involved himself quite heavily in the strategic plans of the subsidiaries under his control. As regional vice president, Rajar was focused on implementing Lundbeck's strategy in Asia. His success was measured on how well he was able to execute that strategy and grow the Asia region.

Rajar's goals were to launch and market Lundbeck's newest and most innovative products; to control costs and preserve resources; to create effective communication channels between the corporate office and Lundbeck's customers (doctors, regulators, and patients) in order to respond quickly to their needs; to reduce risks by ensuring that all ethical standards were being followed; and to have an understanding of the strengths and weaknesses of each of his markets.

Rajar was a very direct communicator and provided very clear guidelines to Jun. His expectations were unambiguous and he was able to illustrate a comprehensible path for Lundbeck Korea that followed the Lundbeck strategy. Before Jun sent any report or proposal to the head office, Rajar took the time to review the reports and provide Jun with feedback and suggestions. Rajar provided active assistance to Jun on how to communicate with the management team in Copenhagen. Because Rajar had extensive experience in management, his guidance was indispensable. He was also adept at paying attention to the details of local business. Rajar also organized extremely helpful meetings and conferences for the Asian country managers. Rajar facilitated meetings where country managers could share their best practices and discuss ways of developing local programs and handling difficult situations. Through these meetings, the Lundbeck Asia managers gained a sense of association and

pride in being part of Lundbeck. Overall, Rajar was a good coach and mentor and was a significant player in the creation and execution of the business plan for Lundbeck Korea.

The First Lundbeck Product in Korea: Cipram

Lundbeck began by marketing Cipram, the forerunner of Lexapro, in the newly established Korean subsidiary in 2002. For the purpose of distributing and marketing Cipram, Lundbeck entered into a sales alliance with Whanin, a local Korean firm, by establishing a separate business unit. Each firm agreed to invest an increasing number of resources into the Cipram business unit each year. However, this business unit was only established for the marketing of Cipram. If Lundbeck were to launch a different class of drugs, it would do so on its own or under a separate arrangement.

The launching of Cipram was Lundbeck Korea's first of many successful attempts to debunk local myths. Initially, many industry leaders doubted the success of Cipram, as it would be the fifth SSRI in the market. Since the other four products were well established and better priced, there was little chance for the launch of Cipram to be successful. However, within three years, Lundbeck was able to capture almost 8.3 per cent of the highly competitive and generic-filled market with Cipram, thereby making Lundbeck Korea a major market player. As a comparison, the other major anti-depressant medications in the Korean market in 2005 were Seroxat (12 per cent of market share), Effexor (11 per cent), and Paxil CR (five per cent). The rest of the market was dominated by generics. This initial success allowed Jun to gain an upper hand that gave Lundbeck an advantage in future contract negotiations with the local partner.

The Launch of Ebixa

Ebixa was the only medication available for the treatment of severe stages of Alzheimer's. All other drugs on the market only targeted mild and moderate cases. Since most Alzheimer's patients would enter the severe stage long before they died of the disease, Ebixa was an important medication. In most markets, Lundbeck sold Ebixa as a new product; and in fact, Ebixa had been registered many years ago by a Korean pharmaceutical firm, but unfortunately it was poorly promoted in the Korean market.

Since Ebixa had been registered many years earlier, the price set by the government insurance regulator was very low, in fact well below the current production cost. Jun and his staff combined Lundbeck's competencies with their understanding of the local market. The normal way to convince the insurance regulator to increase the price of a drug was to hire a large law firm and have lawyers present clear and convincing arguments. However, this rarely worked, and so after consultation with an old colleague who was familiar with the politics of medical insurance pricing, Jun chose a different approach. He decided to put Lundbeck's highly specialized knowledge and small size to work by developing personal contacts with members of the regulatory body to win over both their hearts and their minds. Though, of course, Jun and his staff needed to provide persuasive evidence, they decided that they would also try to win the members over with emotional arguments. Jun argued that:

> Since Korean society is still a Confucian society, we have a very high regard for elder members of society. So, we met the key people and told them that this is the only medicine that can help severe Alzheimer patients. We asked them to imagine if their mother, father or close relative had Alzheimer's. Would you want them to be without medication when they entered the severe state? In this way, we convinced them that the product was necessary, and since it was the only available product on the market, it should have a price equal to other Alzheimer medications.

In the end, they were able to successfully argue for a substantially greater price for Ebixa. By opening up this new market, the Ebixa case demonstrated to Jun that local expertise played a significant role in achieving an unprecedented success in the industry.

The Lexapro Launch: A Conflict of Strategy

Lundbeck focused on streamlining its key products, and on long-term growth in the CNS industry. This included marketing the new and most innovative products. As part of bringing Lundbeck Asia into step with the rest of the Lundbeck group, Rajar believed that it was important that all the subsidiaries kept up to date with Lundbeck's product offerings. Jun's position was somewhat different; he believed that Lundbeck Korea should simply pursue the path that maximized revenue in Korea.

These diverging perspectives became apparent when Lundbeck introduced Lexapro to replace Cipram. The corporate strategy was to launch a switch-over campaign, which involved convincing doctors to stop prescribing a particular drug and switch to that drug's "next generation" product. By 2005, Rajar felt that Lundbeck Asia was ready to participate in this switch-over campaign. Since Cipram had been launched and promoted by local firms for several years in most of the other countries in the Asia region, the brand was well known.

In contrast, Cipram had only just been introduced in Korea. Thus, in the Korean market it was a new drug, which made the Korean situation different in two ways. First, Lundbeck Korea was just beginning to build the brand awareness in Korea; and second, since Cipram had just been launched in Korea, Cipram still had four years in which generic copies could not be introduced into the market. To avoid sending confusing signals to doctors, sales reps and other stakeholders, and to capture the benefits from the exclusivity period, Jun proposed a special Korea strategy. He believed Lundbeck Korea should continue to sell Cipram until the brand was fully established and then introduce Lexapro.

Rajar disagreed. He argued that a generic company might register a generic version of Lexapro. If it did, the generic brand would be the original and Lexapro would become the generic in the Korean market. Jun's team argued that such a possibility would be highly improbable in Korea due to the data that would have to be gathered and presented to the regulatory board. Rajar retorted that while it might be improbable, it was not impossible. As long as any possibility remained, he would not allow it.

Jun, rightly or wrongly, felt that Rajar was using the possibility of a generic brand entering the market as an excuse not to allow Korea to pursue an independent strategy. According to Jun, what Rajar really seemed to be saying was that Korea was part of Lundbeck and the launching of Lexapro was part of the corporate strategy. Lundbeck's strategy of specialization was to promote its newest and most innovative drugs. The tension was clear; Rajar, as regional vice president, was focused on developing a strong Asia market that was integrated into the Lundbeck strategy. Jun, as the country manager of Korea, wanted to build Lundbeck Korea and maximize long-term growth and profits in Korea.

Rajar was the regional boss, and his preference was to put Lexapro on the market as soon as possible. Thus, assuming Lexapro passed all government regulations in a timely manner, it would be launched in Korea in early 2006. The result would be that Jun would face an uphill battle in his switch-over campaign. Since they had only been prescribing it for a few years, many Korean psychiatrists were still very happy with Cipram. The Whanin representatives were upset because they saw Cipram as having good margins and consistent sales. They were not interested in introducing an entirely new product when they were making money on the old one. However, the decision was made final. While this may have been the most visible sign of conflict between Jun and Rajar, there was a growing number of issues that Jun felt Lundbeck Asia was not handling in the best interests of Korea. He felt strongly that Korea was quite different from other countries in the region.

Conflict in the Placement of Marketing Resources

Jun had dedicated an enormous amount of his staff's time and energy on building relationships with the country's top psychiatrists in the CNS industry rather than the more common approach of marketing to a broader base of practitioners. In Jun's opinion, the management of these key opinion leaders was quite important. "Korea is a very hierarchical society. Also, since we only have one culture, we have very strong barriers to becoming influential and powerful; however, once you overcome those barriers you gain extremely high credibility and power in the market." He felt that there was no sense targeting the lower tier of doctors until he had the support of the opinion leaders. A positive endorsement from these doctors would be more effective than any other marketing campaign.

Rajar was keen to make certain that resources were not wasted, costs were controlled and that marketing and business practices were perceived to be beyond reproach. Thus, Rajar believed that this type of selective marketing was risky. A broader marketing approach had worked well in the other Asian markets, and Rajar was not convinced that Korea was much different because other Asian societies were also quite hierarchal. Rajar continued to ask Jun how Lundbeck could justify spending significant amounts of money to target so few individuals. Rajar insisted that Jun should use these resources to fund other programs. He wanted Jun to integrate his approach into the established Lundbeck approach.

In addition, Rajar felt that the client entertainment that occurred in the Korean subsidiary was excessive, and as such a poor business practice. He certainly did not feel that there was a need to spend so much time eating, drinking, and going to karaoke bars with the top doctors. In contrast, Jun felt that Rajar needed to be more open-minded to the Korean situation:

> Rajar didn't understand the importance of our entertainment culture. In Korea, social events generally consist of a main meal in a restaurant, followed by drinking in a bar or pub, and then topped off with a visit to the karaoke bar. Usually when he was in town, he went home after dinner. However, this is our culture and he needed to understand it. When he went

home early, it made a poor impression on the people with whom I was trying to build relationships. In Korean culture, togetherness and harmony are very important, but I don't think he understood this.

In terms of cultural understanding, Jun recalled giving a doctor a few small gifts with the Lundbeck logo imprinted on them. The doctor thanked him and told him that the current sales representatives from other foreign companies were so restricted by their global ethical regulations that they could not even bring small gifts. Jun and the doctor agreed that these regulations reflected a poor appreciation for the Korean culture, where it is expected and customary to bring gifts.

Jun's Car and Its Effect on Lundbeck's Image

Jun also recalled a story that to him represented the cultural tension that existed with his relationship with Lundbeck Asia and Rajar. For Jun, this was a microcosm of how difficult it was being controlled by the regional office.

> When I first started as Lundbeck Korea country manager, the person who hired me asked me what kind of car I wanted. I thought about it carefully because it is very important in Korea to match your car with your status—too low of a car and you will not be respected, too high of a car and you will look arrogant. Since I was young and the country manager of a newly established subsidiary, I felt that I needed to be quite modest. The original boss allowed me enough budget to get a stylish midsize car with a 2.5 litre engine. However, I thought that was a little too much for me, so I got one with a smaller engine on a three year lease. Then, in 2005, I had to renew the car. So, I proposed to Rajar that I get a car that was not too high end, but something better than I had been driving. I didn't want anything too fancy; however, as an important symbol to show that our company was growing, I believed that I should have a car of above average status. The symbolism is quite important—my customers really notice this type of thing, so it is important for doing business. So, I proposed that I get a full-size sedan. But he thought that was unnecessary and told me that status is not important and that I

should break that type of thinking; however, I cannot change the importance that Koreans place on symbolism. He wanted me to provide him every detail on the cars that I was considering and then insisted I buy a car of similar status as the one I had been driving. When I went out to entertain the opinion leaders, they commented on my car. This was not good for our business. It made it harder for me to gain their respect. Everyone might think this is a small thing, but it is not. It really discourages the local manager and is bad for the company's image.

Lundbeck's Strategy Interpreted by Jun for Korea

Jun believed that he had a very clear understanding of Lundbeck's core strategy. Integrating the uniqueness of Korea with the global beliefs of Lundbeck had always been his goal. In every room in the Lundbeck Korea office was a poster from headquarters that highlighted the strategy of Lundbeck. Jun's goal was to find a balance between integrating local expertise with the overall strategy of Lundbeck.

Jun believed that in order to convince the Korean medical profession and government regulators that Lundbeck's products were substantially more valuable than the products offered by the general pharmaceutical firms and the generic producers, the staff would have to mirror the specialization of the company. So, from the beginning, all key people in Lundbeck Korea were required to have a CNS background. This gave Lundbeck instant credibility and allowed it to quickly establish a foundation in the CNS field. Jun believed that this expertise was the basis for Lundbeck Korea's major achievements.

In respect to speed, he understood that in the Korean market, response times were important. Abandoning the traditional hierarchical organizational structures that were prevalent in Korean firms, Lundbeck Korea established a lean organization with straight reporting lines. Jun believed that this agility in the market was one of Lundbeck's advantages over bigger competitors. It allowed Lundbeck to hear customer demand quickly, discuss options immediately, and implement decisions swiftly.

In respect to integration, Lundbeck's Korean partner Whanin had a very different set of competencies, organizational structure, and business philosophy. As such, it would have been very easy for Lundbeck Korea and Whanin to be constantly butting heads. Do they follow the Lundbeck way or the Whanin way? Using a spirit of integration, Jun chose to avoid this conflict by having each group focus its energies where it had a competitive advantage.

In respect to results, by maintaining focus on the results, Lundbeck Korea easily surpassed the business case set for it. Jun argued that Lundbeck Korea "have been able to constantly add value every year. The key is that we generate better results and add value in everything we do." Lundbeck Korea focused its energies on projects and activities that generated the most income.

The Decision

The question for Andersen, vice president for Lundbeck, was how to move Lundbeck Korea forward. He believed that Rajar had done a very good job implementing Lundbeck's strategy in the Asian markets. In fact, under Rajar's leadership Korea had emerged, in Andersen's opinion, as the market with the most potential. Lundbeck Korea had good protection from generics, a strong government insurance program for reimbursement, decent pricing on its products, a large and growing market, and a highly innovative staff. Rajar had done a very good job at running a tight ship—he focused on control, cost effectiveness, knowledge transfer, and instilling ethical business practices, which are all important roles for a regional manager. However, Andersen wondered if Rajar was putting too little emphasis on developing new and unique opportunities. The question for Andersen was whether Jun would blossom without the controls or whether the lack of guidance would hinder his development. In addition, as the goal was to integrate all aspects of the value chain, Andersen certainly did not want Korea to be off in its own little world.

In addition, there seemed to be a conflict of personalities. In several meetings, Andersen had sensed poor chemistry between Jun and Rajar. He could not exactly put his finger on it, and it was impossible for him to get Jun to open up about this. Andersen believed that an individual's strengths and weaknesses were part of the strategic decision process. Moreover, he wondered whether Lundbeck Korea might blossom under less strict management and at the same time benefit from a direct relationship with the headquarters functions in Copenhagen. Finally, Andersen wanted to find a way to create more focus on Korea in headquarters.

Of course, no decision is made in a vacuum. The Chinese subsidiary, which had been part of the Lundbeck Asia division for many years, was also growing rapidly. Even though China was in a different position than Korea, would the Chinese managers expect the same treatment? And should they receive it? Also, Andersen had to consider his key person in Asia, Asif Rajar. How would he react to having one of his fastest growing units taken away from him?

Case 4-4   Kent Chemical: Organizing for International Growth

Christopher A. Bartlett and Laura Winig

In July 2008, Luis Morales, president of Kent Chemical International (KCI), the international arm of Kent Chemical Products (KCP), balanced a computer on his lap, trying to merge the organizational charts of his KCI worldwide operations with KCP's domestic businesses. After his third attempt, the two charts finally shared the screen. He had achieved digital success, but as he looked at a chart that reminded him of a multiheaded hydra, Morales was not convinced he had found a real-life solution.

Over the past two years, the KCI president had been searching for a way to better coordinate his fast-growing international operations with Kent's domestic core. Two previous reorganizations had not achieved that objective, and now the global economy looked as if it were headed for a recession. If he was to recommend another restructuring, Morales knew it would have to be successful.

Kent Chemical Products: The Company and Its Businesses

Kent was established in 1917 as a rubber producer, and its historical roots were still evident. The founding Fisher family owned 10% of the stock and was still the largest stockholder; family members held a

few key positions; and corporate headquarters remained in Kent, Ohio, a town outside Akron.

During the 1940s, Kent had diversified into plastics and, as that market soared, expanded through acquisitions to become one of the country's largest producers and marketers of plastic additives and other specialty chemicals. Responding to postwar opportunities, KCP opened a research laboratory in 1953, harnessing technology-based research to drive product development. By the 2000s, Kent had become a leading global specialty-chemical company, with 2007 revenues of $2.2 billion. (See **Exhibit 1** for summary financials.) It held minority and majority stakes in more than two dozen businesses in the U.S. and overseas, employed 4,200 people including 1,200 offshore, operated 30 manufacturing facilities in 13 countries, and sold its products in almost 100 countries.

Kent offered a wide range of products from specialty lubricants to polymer additives, focusing on niche-market needs in the construction, electronics, medical products, and consumer industries. The range was managed through six business divisions, three of which had significant international sales.

Consumer Products   Grease-B-Gone, the company's first major consumer product, was introduced in 1966 and became the leading de-greaser in the U.S. First targeted at the auto engine market, the brand had expanded into a range of specially formulated products designed for high-margin niche household applications such as oven, barbeque, and stainless steel cleaners. KCP subsequently introduced other specialty household product's including drain openers, rust removers, and eco-friendly surface cleaners.

In the U.S., these products were distributed primarily through independent retailers and buying groups in the hardware and do-it-yourself sectors.

Exhibit 1   Kent Chemical: Summary of Financial Data, 2003–2007 ($ millions)

	2007	2006	2005	2004	2003
Consolidated Statements of Income					
Net sales	$2,238	$2,072	$1,937	$1,810	$1,628
Cost of sales	1,700	1,440	1,339	1277	1,150
	538	632	598	533	478
Selling, general, and administrative expenses	320	305	295	263	248
Research and development expenses	90	84	82	77	68
	410	389	377	340	316
Income from operations	128	243	221	193	162
Royalty, interest, and dividend income	33	51	44	49	47
Interest expense	−38	−44	−23	−30	−22
Other income (deductions)	−2	−20	−3	−3	−1
Taxes on income	−50	−110	−115	−96	−88
Income before minority interest and equity earnings	71	120	124	113	98
Minority interest earnings (losses) of subsidiaries	5	−1	−3	6	0
Earnings of associated companies	20	21	28	34	40
Net income	$ 96	$ 140	$ 149	$ 154	$ 128
Kent Chemical International contributions to corporate results (Unaudited)					
Net sales	$ 598	$ 578	$ 466	$ 402	$ 322
Net income	$ 24	$ 38	$ 37	$ 33	$ 23

Outside the U.S., consumer sales outlets and retail distribution channels varied by country. In Brazil, for example, Kent sold through distributors to small independent outlets; in France a direct sales force sold to national chains. And while consumer preferences in the U.S. were largely homogeneous, overseas the product's packaging, container size, aesthetics (scent, color, etc.), and even active ingredients could vary from one country to the next.

About one-third of this business's $522 million worldwide sales were outside the U.S., with strong local and regional competitors in each offshore market. General household products were produced in the company's large, multiproduct mixing and packing plants in markets from France to Brazil to New Zealand. However, the only non-U.S. facility able to produce the specially formulated, aerosol-packaged *Grease-B-Gone* line was in France, in a single-product plant built in 1990.

Fire Protection Products   Kent entered the fire protection business in the 1950s by acquiring a company that had developed fire retardant chemicals for the apparel industry. Subsequently, Kent's R&D lab developed other fire retardants for the electronics, building, and transport industries. Then, following the 1967 fire that claimed the lives of three Apollo astronauts, government-funded research led Kent to develop a line of foams, chemicals, and gases, thereby allowing it to enter the larger fire control market segment.

By 2008, fire retardants were mature commodities, but the fire control segment was a large, fast-growing and increasingly specialized field, requiring big investments in R&D to keep pace. The latter product line was sold to both fire control systems companies and original equipment manufacturers (OEMs) in the electronics, building, and oil refining industries. Intense price competition particularly in the retardant segment, caused Kent to focus on reducing production costs.

Outside the U.S., fire retardants were produced by former Kent licensees, FireGard plc in England and SicherFeuer AG in Germany, both with long histories in the industry. Fire protection regulations varied by country, so the chemical agents Kent produced in its four plants around the world often had to be adapted to local markets. A few multinational customers accounted for the majority of Kent's $210 million in worldwide sales, 45% of which came from international markets. As the number-three competitor worldwide, Kent faced pressure from both local and global companies.

Medical Plastics   In the 1960s, Kent collaborated with a major hospital supply company to develop a non-leaching, sterilizable plastic that won the U.S. Food and Drug Administration approval to hold intravenous solutions. That partnership created plastic IV bags that gradually replaced the ubiquitous glass bottles hanging over hospital beds around the world. Building on that reputation, Kent became a leading supplier of plastics for medical applications. Over subsequent decades it developed special formulations for everything from surgical instruments to implantable devices to replacement joints.

Its customers were large global hospital supply and medical device companies with which it worked in partnership to develop specialized plastics for targeted applications. In addition to properties such as biocompatibility, self-lubrication, and non-toxicity, these plastics also had to retain those characteristics under sterilization-imposed conditions of extreme temperature and moisture.

Kent's growing line of medical products had been developed entirely in the company's Ohio R&D labs and manufactured in one of two specialized plants in California and the Netherlands. Overseas sales accounted for about 35% of the business's $625 million global revenue.

Kent Chemical International: Going Global for Growth

For many years, Kent's overseas operations were seen as a source of incremental sales through exports, licensing agreements, and minority joint ventures (JVs). That view changed in 1998, when Ben Fisher, KCP's newly appointed CEO, announced that a more strategic approach to global expansion would be his top priority: "Our goal is to remake Kent from a U.S. company dabbling in international markets to one that develops, manufactures, and sells worldwide."

Old Root Stock, New Growth   To implement his vision of a globally integrated company, Fisher named Luis Morales to head the revitalized international division. Morales was a 22-year Kent veteran who had joined its Mexican subsidiary in sales, risen to become country manager, then moved to Ohio to run KCP's Consumer Products division. He had a reputation as a smart, hardworking team player who liked to win.

Morales began implementing the global integration strategy by taking majority interests in Kent's 15 offshore JVs, acquiring other overseas companies, and generally expanding global presence. The subsequent rapid international sales growth—from $139 million in 1999 (11% of total revenue) to $598 million in 2007 (27% of revenue)—was managed through Kent's International division. That division reported to Morales through three regional directors—for Europe, Middle East, and Africa (EMEA); Central and South America; and Asia-Pacific—all located in Kent, Ohio. (See **Exhibit 2**.)

Historically, regional directors had managed subsidiary and JV managers in 22 countries with a light touch encouraging them to optimize their local positions. Because Kent was a minority shareholder of many of these companies, its financial and operating controls were often limited. But strong informal links ensured the necessary financial and technological support. "For decades we'd provided them support, and they had sent us dividends," Morales said.

The entrepreneurial independence of offshore entities was often complicated by long competitive histories. Morales acknowledged that the regional directors' post-acquisition task of coordinating activities and integrating operations was extremely difficult. "For example, FireGard and SicherFeuer had been competitors for decades," he said. "Even after we took minority positions, they refused to

Exhibit 2   KCP International Division Organizational Chart, 2000

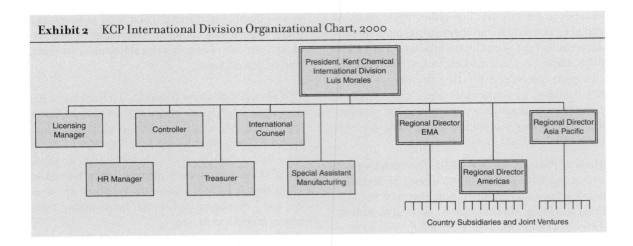

cooperate or even to coordinate activities. In fact, it's only in the last couple of years that we've finally begun to get many of our own subsidiaries to stop exporting into each other's markets."

Even after Kent took majority positions, establishing control often proved to be difficult. In 2000, the EMEA regional manager relocated his staff to Hamburg. "We needed to work more closely with local companies to rationalize overlapping activities and duplicative operations," he said. "But relocating didn't solve the problem. When my staff tried to consolidate redundant European manufacturing, for example, local managers with 20 or 30 years' experience in their markets ran circles around them. It soon became clear that most of the regional staff simply lacked the market knowledge and detailed technical expertise to counter the country subsidiaries' strong pushback."

New Strategies, New Stresses   As overseas operations grew, Morales became concerned that his organization was not adapting well to changing pressures and demands. His first concern was the impact of new systems. As Kent acquired majority positions, corporate reporting systems had been added to allow operations to be controlled and financial reports consolidated. But these changes had caused strains. "Having the data sometimes tempted my staff to second-guess local country

managers," admitted Morales. "The subsidiaries felt that we set arbitrary financial targets that were out of touch with their market realities. Despite our good intentions, I think the country managers were often right."

Capital allocation had also become more complex. Subsidiaries now had to complete capital requests that were first reviewed by a regional manager, then by Morales, and often at the corporate level. In the process, relations between subsidiaries and their U.S. technical contacts shifted. A country manager explained: "Our U.S. colleagues used to consult with us on our projects, but once they were involved in evaluating the funding decisions, they became more critical and less collaborative."

Morales's second concern was that overseas subsidiaries' long history of independence led managers to protect their self-interests. "When the Korean subsidiary wanted to manufacture fire retardants for its electronics customers, its plans challenged the German subsidiary that had been exporting retardants to Korea for years," he said. "When we began trying to integrate the strategies of our overseas operations, conflicts like this regularly reached my desk for resolution."

Parochial attitudes also blocked technology transfer when the informal relationships that had long linked offshore operations with U.S. technical experts were replaced by the more-formal structures that growth had required. Berthold Hugel, SicherFeuer's general manager, explained:

> As we grew, a U.S.-based technical manager was appointed to the regional director's staff as our liaison with domestic divisions. Perhaps he just lacked good contacts, but we were never properly connected. So I sent an English-speaking SicherFeuer employee to Ohio to serve as our technical link. But he had no clout, so that didn't work either. Finally, I decided that the only way to get technical help and to learn what new products were being developed was for me personally to travel to Kent headquarters every 60 days. So that's what I did.

Frustration about links between geographic and product organizations also existed in the U.S. divisions, as reflected in the comments of Jack Davies, the VP responsible for Fire Protection:

> We had developed this great new halogenated flame retardant product that was selling great in the U.S., but it was stalled in Europe. The U.K. subsidiary told me that their project-appropriation request had been blocked by corporate. I discovered that someone in the controller's office was withholding approval as a lever to force the U.K. to bring its receivables under control. It wasn't my responsibility, but I stepped in to put a stop to it.

The third problem worrying Morales was that even within his international division, the regional organization had difficulty coordinating issues with global implications. In the Medical Plastics business for example, most of KCP's customers were multinational hospital supply and medical device companies. So when the Brazilian subsidiary unilaterally reduced prices on its line of general purpose polycarbonates as a loss leader to sell more of the expensive, technical medical products, the pricing impact was felt throughout Kent's worldwide medical plastics business.

The issue highlighted the fact that nobody was coordinating price, product, or sourcing decisions globally. "Worse still, because the international division had a regional rather than a product-based structure, our global product-development needs and priorities were seldom communicated to the research group," said Morales. "And since our R&D efforts respond to specific problems or identified applications, they rarely focused on offshore opportunities or needs."

The 2006 Reorganization: Bridging Gaps with GBDs

In June 2006, when CEO Ben Fisher also became Kent's board chairman, he used the occasion to announce a major reorganization. Angela Perri, who had joined KCP 20 years earlier as a PhD scientist in the R&D lab, was named president of the U.S. businesses. Perri was a capable, hard-driving, ambitious executive who most recently had run the U.S. Medical Plastics division.

Simultaneously, Peter Fisher, Ben's 35-year-old son was named vice chairman with responsibility for all corporate staffs and the international operations. Peter had joined Kent in sales before heading the Consumer Products division for the past four years. Under the new organization, the International division became Kent Chemical International (KCI), a separate legal entity structured as a subsidiary of KCP. Both Angela Perri and Peter Fisher reported to the chairman. (See **Exhibit 3.**)

Morales hoped the reorganization would improve domestic/international relations. "Historically, all vital communication between us occurred either at top levels or on the front lines," he said. "At my level, I'd negotiate funding decisions, and in the trenches relationships between U.S.-based technical experts and international plant managers got things done." But as overseas operations grew, Morales had become stretched thin as KCI's principal top-level contact. And the advice and support that had long flowed freely to the front lines was now provided slowly, reluctantly, and often accompanied by an invoice for intercompany charges. "The regional directors should have provided the extra link with the domestic divisions. But they never had the status or power of product division managers, who were all KCP vice presidents," said Morales.

To respond to these problems, Morales in 2006 appointed three global business directors (GBDs), each with a long, successful U.S. career before

Exhibit 3 Kent Chemical Products Organizational Chart, 2006

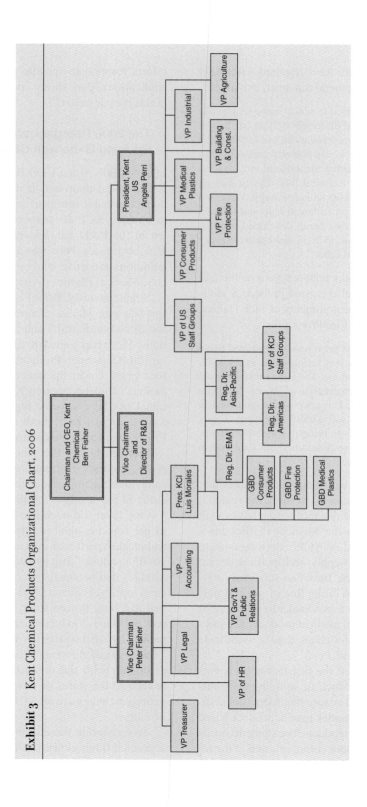

moving to KCI. The GBDs would be responsible for the three lines of business within KCI, and although the new roles were not well defined, they were announced as VP-level positions reporting directly to Morales. Each GBD assembled a staff of 3 to 6 product or project managers and began defining their roles and setting priorities.

The consumer-products GBD was a 25-year Kent veteran of senior sales management in KCP's Consumer Products division. Before this appointment, he had run a small domestic JV. He explained his understanding of the new role: "I'm trying to inject consumer-oriented thinking into our overseas subsidiaries. I don't care if they see my role as advisory or directive, as long as they do what needs to be done. They have to realize they're part of a global company now." Responding to his mandate to "sort things out," particularly within EMEA, he saw his first priority as determining why the *Grease-B-Gone* line had not sold as well in Europe as it had in the U.S.—and then to fix it.

A second GBD was given responsibility for fire protection products. He had 10 years of international sales experience, and four as manager of market planning in the Fire Protection division. "I'll need to assume worldwide technology control and marketing responsibility," he said. "The way I see it, regional managers should be mainly responsible for production and government relations."

The third GBD, an engineer and 15-year KCP veteran, was assigned to medical plastics. She saw her role as a strategic planner linking the U.S., regional, and subsidiary managers. "To be effective, the regional managers will have to maintain authority over their operations," she said. "I can be most useful by helping to integrate the international and domestic parts of our operation."

After just a few months, the GBDs were faltering. "The subsidiaries saw GBDs as interlopers, but some more than others," said Morales. "The medical-plastics GBD was appreciated because she provided useful worldwide business coordination. But the consumer-products GBD was a disaster. Subsidiaries felt he interfered in local issues where he had neither experience nor understanding."

Many reasons were offered for KCI's post-reorganization problems. The EMEA regional director thought the new structure just strained the existing organization's time and resources. "We wanted to integrate our businesses globally, but the GBDs didn't know what their role was, and as regional directors, we weren't clear about how to work with them," he said. "So we ended up in a lot of meetings that took us away from dealing with important day-to-day matters."

Morales felt the main problem was the GBD's inability to provide a link to the domestic product divisions and assume the conflict-resolution roles he had been playing. "Despite years of service, the GBDs lacked the credibility and power to get things done. And some of the domestic managers didn't help. They just seemed to want control over the fast growth overseas businesses," he said.

Jack Davies, the VP responsible for the Fire Protection division had a different view. He felt the problem lay in the people appointed as GBDs. "I don't think there was a single vice president in the domestic corporation who saw them as equals," he said.

The 2007 Adaptation: World Boards

By mid-2007, it was clear that the GBD concept was struggling. After long discussions with Morales about more-effective means to integrate KCI with KCP, Peter Fisher developed the idea to support GBDs with world boards. They would be composed of managers from the domestic and international organizations, with geographic, product, and functional expertise all represented. These boards would be responsible for developing strategies for the global businesses.

In June 2007, Peter Fisher presented the concept to a meeting of the company's top 150 managers:

> The GBDs are serving an important function linking our U.S. and international operations. But they can't manage this vital role by themselves. To provide support, we are introducing world boards to help each business advance its global strategy and integrate its worldwide operations. They are not meant to replace local management. Their role will be as planners,

reviewers, and communicators, not managers or controllers. They offer us an opportunity to work together and share responsibility for ensuring that our global businesses succeed.

A world board was formed for each of the company's three major worldwide businesses. Each was instructed to provide worldwide marketing and operations planning, optimize global sourcing, develop technology on a global scale, make investment recommendations, and build international management capabilities. Although they determined their own membership, they typically included the head of the U.S. product division, the division's technical and marketing staff members, key country general managers, and their appropriate product managers. The GBD served as board chair, providing him or her with a forum to involve the domestic division managers in the international business, and to give regional and subsidiary managers a link to the parent company.

The fire protection world board got off to a strong start and generally met the stated objectives. "It works because the business has opportunities and problems with worldwide implications," said Berthold Hugel, the former German subsidiary general manager who was named Fire Protection GBD in 2007. "Also, before each board meeting, Jack Davies (the domestic division VP) and I sit down and work through all the issues so that the discussions never become politicized."

The other two world boards did not fare as well. The medical plastics board became a platform for discussion but rarely reached agreement or decided on action. And despite Peter Fisher's personal intervention, the consumer products board met only twice, then quietly disbanded. "We couldn't even agree on what issues needed to be managed locally or globally," said the new Consumer GBD.

Reflecting on the experience, Morales felt that the negative reaction to the 2006 GBD concept had made managers hesitate to embrace the world boards. "Some of my country and regional managers felt threatened and thought this was the first step in dismantling the regional organizations. And many

domestic managers thought it was just a way to give our struggling GBDs more power," he said. He also noted that in order to succeed, all board members—GBDs, domestic division managers and country managers—had to be open, cooperative, rational team players, even when their interests were not being served. "The model requires practically perfect managers," he said.

Peter Fisher had a different view. "To accommodate all interests, some world boards had more than 20 members. They had just become too large and unwieldy. There were too many competing priorities, so the big issues were never addressed. And, frankly, many domestic division managers were blocking progress and trying to control the global business directly," he said.

From Perri's point of view, the domestic organization would have been more supportive if key managers had been consulted when the world boards were formed. "Peter and Luis expected the division managers to be involved and supportive. But I was never asked my opinion about the world boards' structure or activities, and frankly I didn't altogether agree with the concept," she said.

Back to the Drawing Board: Another Change?

In March 2008, with the world boards concept struggling and strains in international/domestic relationships, Perri met with Morales and Peter Fisher to discuss possible solutions. Perri was blunt. "We're a science-based company," she said. "Our competitive advantage is in using our scientific expertise to develop products. So it's a real problem that we have barriers between the scientific resources that I manage and the international markets that you control. We really need to fix this."

Peter Fisher responded. "I agree that our technological capability is a huge asset, Angela," he said. "But let's acknowledge that Kent's domestic growth has plateaued. So the company's future relies on our ability to expand into international markets. We need an organizational solution that empowers rather than subjugates our international presence."

The Consultants' Proposal Recognizing the need to find a solution, the three senior executives contacted Sterling Partners, a respected international management consulting firm, to help them sort through the issue. For a fee of $1.8 million, a team of four consultants worked with four Kent managers to gather information on the industry context, Kent's competitive position, and the strategic objectives of each of its global businesses. After analyzing these data, they prepared recommendations that they hoped would convince Kent chairman Ben Fisher, a longtime skeptic of both outside consultants and complex organizational structures.

The consultants concluded that one of the company's main problems was that it had been imposing uniform organizational solutions on a strategically diverse portfolio. Because each business had a different mix of global imperatives and local demands, they suggested taking a more tailored approach. In summary, their detailed report of analysis and conclusions found:

- The consumer product line's key strategic need was for locally adapted marketing programs to respond to local consumer needs, distribution channel differences, and competition that varied by country. While the aerosol-based *Grease-B-Gone* line was sourced regionally, locally tailored general household products were usually produced in national mixing plants. The report suggested a business that should be predominantly managed locally and regionally.
- The consultants placed the medical plastics business at the other end of the local–global spectrum. Here the key success factor was the central R&D input required to develop new products and technologies. Manufacturing occurred in two specialized globally scaled plants where quality was tightly controlled. Customers were primarily multinational companies with worldwide operations. These factors indicated a business that needed global control.
- Fire control products fell between these extremes. Because R&D was important for innovation, global coordination was critical. But fire prevention was a highly regulated industry in which

relationships with national regulatory bodies and control agencies were critical. While some customers were multinational corporations, many smaller national and regional customers (and competitors) were also significant. Product sourcing was largely regional.

Under the Fisher family's mandate that Kent not be broken up, the consultants recommended that the company evolve to a more differentiated organization using a tool they termed a "decision matrix." The tool's purpose was to expand on their analysis by defining core decisions business by business and then creating a process to analyze how they should be decided. This process would involve assembling the key business, geographic, and functional managers from each business and engaging them in discussions about the decisions. The discussions would be facilitated by a consultant.

As a model, the consultants had prepared a set of blank fire protection decision-matrix forms. The one for resource-allocation decisions for the European fire protection business is shown in **Exhibit 4.** This completed form identifies that multiple players would be responsible to provide input (IP), offer business or technical concurrence (BC or TC), and make recommendations (R). But it clarifies that the final decision (D) on product development would be made by the Fire Protection division VP.

Ten similar sheets listed decisions relating to strategy development, budget preparation, marketing decisions, etc. In all, 62 European fire protection decisions were identified for review. As the next step, the consultants proposed that the executive team authorize a trial run of facilitated discussions with European fire protection managers to complete these forms.

A Brewing Storm, A Key Decision Although many senior Kent managers found the report convincing, others were worried it was too complex. Some regional managers argued that the company should just revert to the geographic structure that had allowed it to grow. But several domestic managers felt the time had come to simplify the structure by giving them worldwide business responsibility.

Exhibit 4 Decision Matrix for Resource-Allocation Decisions on the European Fire Protection Business

Resource Allocation	KCI: Fire Protection					European Fire Protection — Firegard plc						European Fire Protection — SicherFeuer AG					KCP Fire Protection Division (Ohio)				Corporate Staffs						
	Regional Director EMEA	GBD Fire Protection	Controller	Special Asst. Manufacturing	Human Resources Manager	FireSafe GM	Division Manager, Fire Protection	Plant Controller	Production Manager	Sales and Marketing Manager	Technical Director	Sicher-Feuer General Manager	Production Manager	Technical Manager	Financial Manager	General Sales Manager	KCP VP Fire Protection	Business Development Manager	Manufacturing/Engineering Manager	Controller	Treasurer	Controller	Manufacturing	Industrial Relations	Human Resources	Government & Public Relations	Legal
1. Recommend allocation of resources to major new product development programs	R	R	IP	R	R	BC	R	IP	R	R	IP	BC	R	C		IP	D	R	IP	IP		TC	TC		IP/TC		TC
2. Recommend allocation of resources to major process development programs	R	IP	IP	R	IP	BC	R	IP	R	IP	IP	BC	R	C		IP	D	IP	R	IP		TC	R/TC		IP/TC		C
3. Recommend allocation of resources for major cost reduction programs	R	IP	IP	R	R	BC	R	R	R	IP	R	BC	R	C		IP	D	IP	R	IP		TC	R/TC		IP/TC		
4. Determine need, location, and timing for adding or reducing manufacturing capacity	D*	IP	IP	R		D*	R	IP	R	IP	IP	D*	R	R	IP	IP	D*	IP	R	IP		TC	R	IP/TC	IP/TC		TC
5. Decide management of production workforce (expansion, contraction, assignment)	C	IP		D		D	R					D	R				C									C**	TC**
6. Decide on inter-region sourcing	R	IP	IP	R		BC	R	IP	IP	IP	IP	R	R	IP	IP	IP	D	IP	R	IP	TC	TC	IP			C	C
7. Decide who maintains existing technologies	R	IP		R		BC	R	IP	IP	IP	IP	BC	R	R	R	IP	D	IP	R	IP			R/TC				

* Joint decision
** For U.S. decisions only
D = Decides; A = Approves; R = Recommends; BC = Business concurrence; TC = Technical concurrence; C = Concurs; I = Initiates; IP = Inputs.

While digesting the Sterling report, top management was also focused on the global economy. Its 2007 results had been down 30% from the previous year, and 2008 was beginning to look worse. With an ongoing subprime mortgage crisis in the U.S., some felt a global economic downturn was brewing.

Morales knew that the time had come to make his recommendation. Conscious he had two strikes against him on organizational change, he knew that his proposal not only had to resolve the company's organizational problems, but it also had to do so within a skeptical organization operating in a threatening global economic environment. It was probably the biggest decision of his career.

Reading 4-1   Organizing for an Emerging World

Toby Gibbs, Suzanne Heywood, and Leigh Weiss

The problem
Rising complexity is making global organizations more difficult to manage.

Why it matters
Organizational friction can hamper growth, especially in emerging markets; undermine strategic decision making; and make it harder to manage costs, people, and risks.

What to do about it
Revisit the case for regional organizational layers and consider grouping activities according to nongeographic criteria, such as growth goals.

Streamline processes without standardizing more than is necessary, force-fitting rigid technology solutions, or creating overly detailed rules.

Consider moving the corporate center (or creating a "virtual headquarters") closer to high-growth markets, and ensure a constant flow of talent between the business units and the center.

Find out how and why people share information, and then decide which connections to drop, keep, or add.

As global organizations expand, they get more complicated and difficult to manage. For evidence, look no further than the interviews and surveys we recently conducted with 300 executives at 17 major global companies. Fewer than half of the respondents believed that their organizations' structure created clear accountabilities, and many suggested that globalization brings, as one put it, "cumulative degrees of complexity."

However, our research and experience in the field suggest that even complex organizations can be improved to give employees around the world the mix of control, support, and autonomy they need to do their jobs well. What's more, redesigning an organization to suit its changing scale and scope can do much to address the challenges of managing strategy, costs, people, and risk on a global basis.

Our goal in this article isn't to provide a definitive blueprint for the global organization of the future (there's no such thing), but rather to offer multinationals fresh ideas on the critical organizational-design questions facing them today: how to adjust

The authors would like to acknowledge the contributions of Gregor Jost and Roni Katz to the development of this article.

▌ Toby Gibbs and Suzanne Heywood are principals in McKinsey's London office; Leigh Weiss is a senior expert in the Boston office.

structure to support growth in emerging markets, how to find a productive balance between standardized global and diverse local processes, where to locate the corporate center and what to do there, and how to deploy knowledge and skills effectively around the world by getting the right people communicating with each other—and no one else.

Rethinking Boundaries

Global organizations have long sought to realize scale benefits by centralizing activities that are similar across locations and tailoring to local markets any tasks that need to differ from country to country. Today, as more and more companies shift their weight to emerging markets, boundaries between those activities are changing for many organizations.

At some point, they will need to adapt their structures and processes to acknowledge this boundary shift, whose nature will vary across and within companies, depending on their industry, focus, and history. In one recent case, an international publishing company created global "verticals" comprising people who work on content and delivery technology for similar publications around the world. But it was careful to leave all sales and marketing operations in the hands of local country managers, because in publishing these activities can succeed only if they are tailored to local markets. In the case of IBM in Asia, the company has globalized its business services but left the businesses local.

IBM's Experience in Asia   IBM's vice president of global strategy for growth markets, Michael Cannon-Brookes, described to us the structural redesign of the company. Shortly after the start of the new millennium, its leaders realized that having each country operation in Asia run a complete suite of business services to support different product brands no longer made sense; there was simply too much duplication of effort. In each country market, these leaders identified 11 services with common features in functional areas: supply chain, legal, communications, marketing, sales management, HR, and finance. Each function was assigned

a global "owner" with the task of consolidating and refining operations to support businesses in the region's different countries. The company then assessed which essential elements of each function to keep and which redundant (or potentially redundant) elements to eliminate.

From these assessments grew the "globally integrated enterprise model," which evolved into an entirely new structure for IBM's global operations. "Instead of taking people to where the work is, you take work to where the people are," says Cannon-Brookes. IBM sought out pools of competitive talent with the skills required to perform each service at different cost points. Then it built teams of specialists geographically close to the relevant pool to meet the region's needs in each service. So now, for instance, IBM's growth market operations are served by HR specialists in Manila, accounts receivable are processed in Shanghai, accounting is done in Kuala Lumpur, procurement in Shenzhen, and the customer service help desk is based in Brisbane. Globalizing functions that were previously country based has been a huge corporate-wide undertaking for IBM.

"This is a cultural transformation," says Cannon-Brookes. "Changing organization charts can take a few mouse clicks. Changing business processes can take months. Changing a culture and the way employees adapt to new ways of working takes years."

A Complex Calculus   To repeat, though, no company's restructuring should be viewed as a blueprint for that of another. On the one hand, the importance of regional layers seems to be growing for companies in sectors such as pharmaceuticals and consumer goods. Regional centers of excellence in these sectors often are cost effective. Brand and product portfolios often differ significantly between regional outposts and the traditional core, and greater regional muscle can make it easier to pull local perspectives into global product-innovation efforts.

On the other hand, we've seen companies conclude that the traditional role of their regional layers—as "span breakers" helping distant corporate leaders to gather data and distill strategically important information—is becoming obsolescent as information technology makes analyzing, synthesizing, and exchanging information so much easier. Today's faster data exchanges, along with faster travel and video conferencing, make it feasible for some organizations to group their units by criteria other than physical proximity—for example, similar growth rates or strategies. (For more on the role of technology in managing global organizations, see sidebar, "Technology as friend or foe?")

That's led some companies to reduce regional layers to teams of ten or fewer members. Those teams might focus on managing people strategy in a region or on gathering high-level business intelligence that feeds into regional-strategy setting—for example, spotting regional, country, and competitive risks and opportunities. Wafer-thin regional layers have the added benefit of curbing "shadow" functional structures (in HR, marketing, and so forth), which tend to sprout unplanned in larger regional organizations. Although these structures are not clearly visible to the corporate center, they add considerable cost and complexity.

Process Pointers   As IBM's experience illustrates, executives evaluating the structure of their companies will often be drawn into considering which processes should be global or local. That's sensible: in our survey of more than 300 executives at global companies, processes emerged as one of the 3 weakest aspects of organization, out of 12 we explored. Some companies have far too many processes—nearly a third of the surveyed executives said that their companies would be more effective globally with fewer standard ones. Some companies, especially if they grew by M&A, don't know how many processes they have or what those processes are. And, most important, few can distinguish standard processes that create value from those that don't or can identify the value drivers of worthwhile standard processes.

For managers grappling with these issues, here are some ideas that have proved valuable in practice:

- *Don't standardize more than is necessary.* For example, businesses and regions should be allowed to choose their own locally relevant key performance indicators to track, on top of the four or five KPIs used in the global process for setting annual targets.
- *Fit technology to the process, not vice versa.* Standard screen-based processes may ensure global compliance in an instant but can lock in globalized costs, too. Before making huge investments in technology to standardize a process, businesses must be sure they can realize the expected return.
- *Prefer standard principles to detailed rules for local processes.* For instance, to hire an assistant in a new location, managers need only a set of global fair-hiring principles, not chapter and verse on how to hire.
- *Listen to voices from all the functions that are—or should be—involved in making a process better and make sure those people can continue communicating with each other.* Standard processes, by themselves, are not enough to capture all of the potential value from a company's global footprint: ongoing communication between people who influence and execute processes helps to capture more of it.
- *Implement new processes from the top.* Consultation on design is important, but business leaders may eventually need to cut the talk and mandate a new process. Unfashionable command-and-control methods can be appropriate in this sphere because, as one executive explained, "Locations aren't nearly as different as they think they are."

Lightening the Corporate Heart

Over the past decade, corporate centers have been slimming down. Many have shed their traditional roles of providing the business units with shared backbone services. Similarly, some companies have found locations other than the corporate headquarters for centers of excellence on, among other things, innovation or customer insights and sometimes host them within one business for the benefit of all. This leaves slim corporate centers free to focus on their perennial headquarters roles:

Technology as Friend or Foe?

Inexpensive electronic and voice communications, video-conferencing, technology-enabled workflows, and, most recently, social-networking technologies have transformed connectivity and knowledge sharing within complex global organizations. Aditya Birla's HR director, Santrupt Misra, says, "Our use of ICT [information and communications technology] has really helped us become global. For example, we acquired Colombian Chemicals six months ago, and the first thing we established is . . . connectivity between them and our locations elsewhere so they have access to our portal, our knowledge, our e-learning, and every other support." The company puts out regular live webcasts aimed at all employees and their families. It also makes all internal vacancies visible to all employees, to foster the sense of belonging to a community that is local and global at the same time. Similarly, IBM's internal Beehive Web site helps employees to connect with peers they meet on interdepartmental projects or meetings, to brainstorm for current and new projects, and to approach higher-ranking people they wouldn't normally have contact with to share ideas and ask for advice.[1]

Yet fewer than one-third of the more than 300 global executives we surveyed and interviewed believed that their companies were getting the most out of information and communications technology. For all its benefits, it sometimes creates challenges such as the following.

[1]For more, see Joan M. DiMicco, et al., *Research on the Use of Social Software in the Workplace*, Conference on Computer Supported Cooperative Work (CSCW), San Diego, California, November 2008; and Karl Moore and Peter Neely, "From social networks to collaboration networks: The next evolution of social media for business," Forbes.com, September 15, 2011.

Exacerbating pressure A senior executive at one company's central site in China says he regularly works a "second shift" on conference calls when he should be asleep—not good for him or the company in the long term. Jesse Wu, worldwide chairman of Johnson & Johnsons consumer group, observes, "Many people in New York like to have global calls on a Friday morning, so they can get everything clear before the weekend. However, that's Friday evening in Asia, thus unnecessarily affecting a colleague's family life on the other side of the world." Company leaders have to model the time zone sensitivity on which a healthy global organization depends.

Locking in complexity Computerized forms can instantly standardize a process around the world, but once that process is locked in, technology can make changing it complicated and expensive. One global retailer, for example, generated significant value by standardizing supply chain processes in its home market and then adapted and extended the system to its operations overseas. Whenever overseas operations wanted to tweak their local procedures, a change to the global IT system was involved, making such small but necessary changes very costly.

Elevating issues indiscriminately One leader of a global company based in an emerging market notes: "With the growth of ICT, we have become more headquarters-centric. This hasn't been a deliberate policy; it's just that people in the distant territories have found ICT an easy way to kick the ball upstairs."

While these are avoidable problems, they underscore the fact that technology is not a panacea for companies facing organizational challenges. Rather, its creative deployment should reinforce—and be supported by—a company's organizational design.

---

upholding the organization's values, developing corporate strategy, and managing the portfolio of businesses and their individual performance in line with those values and strategies.[1]

However, even a newly focused corporate center can struggle to grasp just how diverse a company's

[1]For more on the role of the corporate center in establishing strategic direction, see Stephen Hall, Bill Huyett, and Tim Koller, "The power of an independent corporate center," mckinseyquarterly.com, March 2012.

markets have become and how fast they are changing: one group based in the United States accepted 2 percent growth targets from its local managers in India because the US market was growing by only 1 percent a year. But the Indian economy was growing much faster, so precious market share was lost.

Corporate centers are likely to make better strategic calls if they move closer to the action. Locating headquarters in a growth market also sends a clear signal about company priorities to current and future employees, as well as to investors, customers, and other external stakeholders. However, a lot of corporate centers can't or won't move in their entirety, for reasons of history, convenience, or legal constraints. So we see a growing number of companies creating a global "virtual headquarters," in which vision-setting and-coordinating activities and centers of excellence are placed in different areas around the world: global procurement may be located in a geography quite different from that of, say, global talent. Thus companies can move headquarters activities closer to high-priority markets without having to shut up the home headquarters.

For instance, ABB has shifted the global base of its robotics business from Detroit to Shanghai, where it has built a robotics R&D center and production line in response to expected demand for robots in Asia. Other firms are going for a split center, with a site in a mature market and another in an emerging one. US technology company Dell, for instance, has set up a functional headquarters in Singapore in pursuit of greater financial, operational, and tax efficiency. The US oil and gas company Halliburton created a second headquarters, in Dubai, to speed up decision making by putting it closer to major customers.

Who should staff the lighter corporate center? To cross-pollinate ideas and knowledge, a headquarters ideally needs to attract but not retain talent. Picture it as the beating heart of the organization, pumping high-potential staff to and from the business units and replenishing each person with the oxygen of learning. Given the right HR mechanisms, a headquarters could do without any permanent staff except the CEO and his or her direct reports; other executives could have fixed-term appointments and then return to a business unit or function. The diversity of the corporate center's constant flow of staff would then naturally reflect a company's international reach and strengths.

Coordinating Communication

Having the right structures and processes to enable growth and reduce complexity is a triumph in itself.

But even the best-structured organization with the most carefully designed processes may falter without the right linkages between them. By the same token, two-thirds of the executives at global companies we recently surveyed said that their ability to create internal links was a source of strength.

To get the best from modern communications and a global network of contacts, managers should focus their communications, both regular and intermittent, on contacts that really matter to their jobs. Leaders can help by making it easier for their people to forge the kind of Web-based connections and communities of interest that spread knowledge quickly. But they also must protect managers from the need to spend a lot of time in conversations and meetings where agendas and decision rights are so hazy that they can't get their jobs done.

Taking Stock   Understanding the number and value of the communications that managers participate in is a first step in finding the sweet spot. A variety of tools are available to help. They include interviews with employees; social-network analyses, which map the frequency and effectiveness of communications; and employee surveys that review connections among a company's major business, functional, and geographic units to find out why they're sharing information, the importance of the information they get to meeting their performance or strategic goals, and how effectively they share it.

Leaders of a global oil and gas company, for example, understood that operations personnel weren't sharing best practices well, because a quick review showed that the company had dozens of ways to operate a given rig. Managers also knew that workers facing problems in the field (such as equipment breakages or uncertainty about the local terrain) didn't know how to get expert help quickly and effectively. A social-network analysis of how information flowed between field workers and technical experts identified three problems. First, field workers tended to reach out only to those technical experts with whom they had strong personal relationships. Also, experts did not reach out unasked to field workers to share best practices. Finally, only when staff moved between sites—as when a

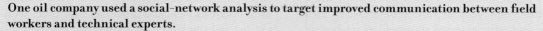

One oil company used a social-network analysis to target improved communication between field workers and technical experts.

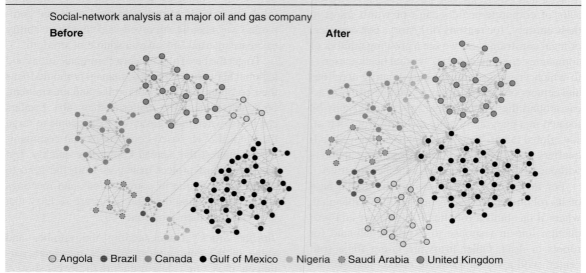

Social-network analysis at a major oil and gas company

Before   **After**

○ Angola ● Brazil ● Canada ● Gulf of Mexico ● Nigeria ✦ Saudi Arabia ● United Kingdom

group went from Angola to the Gulf of Mexico—did field workers from different sites share best practices among themselves.

Strengthening the Right Connections Once people understand the number and nature of their connections and communications, they can decide which to drop, keep, or add. In companies where a lot of people seem to lose time on too many linkages, the leaders' reflex response is often to clarify links by changing the structure—for example, adding reporting lines or new dimensions to the organizational matrix. But these make the organization more complex and costly to manage; dual reporting lines will almost certainly double an executive's administrative burden, to take only the most obvious example.

Better solutions can come from considering a wider range of linkage mechanisms, their different strategic purposes, and what must be in place to make them work. For example, coaching or mentoring links transfer knowledge across an organization and build future leaders. They require strong, personal, and frequent interactions based on trust. Other knowledge transfer connections, such as those for sharing documents, can be weaker, impersonal, and less frequent. Although these kinds of relationships deliver important gains, they do not have to be formally enshrined in a structure or process.

If people have too few contacts (as at the oil company) or contacts in the wrong places, managers with a particular area of responsibility will have to identify who needs knowledge in that area, who has it, and how best to connect them. One way companies can foster strong personal ties is to designate someone to nurture them until they flourish unaided. When researchers analyzed social networks and e-mails among teams developing aerodynamic components for Formula 1 racing cars, they found that teams that designated someone to keep in touch with peers working on related products across geographies were 20 percent more productive than teams whose managers interacted less often.[2]

The oil company above transferred some field workers to peer teams elsewhere. That move forged

[2]Jacomo Corbo and Gary Pisano, *The Impact of Information Networks on Productivity*, Circuits of Profit conference, Budapest, June 20, 2011.

global connections and expanded the collective expertise on which each field worker could draw. New networks blossomed (exhibit) and quickly showed results: within a year, productivity rose by 10 percent, while costs related to poor quality fell by two-thirds.

• • •

Structure, processes, and linkages are interrelated: it's easier to avoid duplication in organizational structures when a company gets the balance right among global, regional, and local processes—and vice versa. Clear structures and processes also clarify roles, helping to focus communications, while structure and process problems can undermine the effectiveness of managers' global networks and communications. Focusing on some of the points where structure, processes, and communications intersect, and engaging all the stakeholders involved to work on those critical junctions, can release benefits that ripple across organizations.

Reading 4-2   Have You Restructured for Global Success?

by Nirmalya Kumar and Phanish Puranam

Two summers ago, Frits van Paasschen, the CEO of Starwood Hotels, was talking to his wife, Laura, about China. With 70 properties in operation there and 80 more being built, the People's Republic had just become Starwood's second-largest market, after the United States. Van Paasschen jokingly said, "It's almost like we should move our headquarters there." Laura's response, in a nutshell: Perhaps you should.

A year later, van Paasschen did just that—for a month. From June 8 to July 11, 2011, Starwood's eight-member top management team worked out of Shanghai, doing business 12 hours ahead of, rather than behind, the company's official White Plains, New York, headquarters. Starwood now plans to shift its base for a month every year to fast-growing markets such as Brazil, Dubai, and India. The end result of these relocations remains unclear: They may prove to be symbolic, they could be learning moments, or they might portend a permanent move of Starwood's headquarters. Today they epitomize the mounting pressures on multinational companies' organizational structures.

As emerging markets grew explosively in the first decade of the 21st century, multinationals raced to develop new strategies. However, changes in their organizational structures have been slow to follow, and people and processes are coping—but badly. Corporations are trying to shoehorn global operations into existing structures, which is in part why so many are unable to realize the full potential of emerging markets. In fact, 95% of senior executives say that they doubt their companies have the right operating model (of which structure is a key component) for today's world, according to a 2011 Accenture study. Organizational redesigns are complicated and politically messy, however, so responses have ranged from outright denial to grudging acceptance; only a few companies are actually trying to fix the problem.

The pressures on multinational structures seem likely to intensify. Businesses are increasingly seeking not just suppliers and raw materials in emerging markets such as China and India, but also customers. The recent recession has served as a catalyst: Many Western companies believe they have focused too much and for too long on the

Nirmalya Kumar is a professor of marketing, and Phanish Puranam is a professor of strategy and entrepreneurship, at London Business School. They are the codirectors of the schools Aditya Birla India Centre and the coauthors of *India Inside: The Emerging Innovation Challenge to the West* (Harvard Business Review Press, forthcoming in 2011)

Why Existing Structures Are Deficient

Figuring out how to manage product lines, regions, and functions has been a perennial problem for multinational companies. Most started out by forming international sales divisions with country-specific subunits at home and by locating only customer-facing (or front-end) processes in each country.

Several companies later adopted transnational structures in order to exploit location-specific advantages in countries far from their home base. Each country's operations specialized in part of the value chain (for instance, Germany focused on product engineering and Mexico on manufacturing) or, sometimes, product lines (Japan developed CT scanners, for example, and Europe X-ray machines).

Other corporations have adopted matrix structures; the axes of the matrix may be products, businesses, functions, or regions. At companies such as ABB and Unilever, managers in an emerging market may have one reporting relationship for product lines and another for functions or regions. One or the other of those relationships tends to dominate in practice, despite their equal importance in theory.

What Kind of Multinational Structure Fits Your Company? This two-part diagnostic tool can help you calibrate, on scales ranging from 1 to 5, how geographically clustered or dispersed the key capabilities of your businesses are—and gauge whether your organization can collaborate seamlessly across geographies. Plot the two scores on the graph (right) to identify an appropriate global structure for your company.

A. How geographically clustered or dispersed are the skills, capabilities, and resources needed for your businesses to operate?

Highly Clustered: Most are found in one region, often the home region. SCORE 1

Example: Sharp historically has done most of its R&D and manufacturing in Japan. It set up sales units abroad only during the early stages of its international expansion.

Moderately Clustered: Most are found in one region, although different regions may possess advantages for different functions. SCORE 3

Example: Many consumer goods companies today locate manufacturing in Asia, but R&D and product design remain in the U.S.

Highly Distributed: Most are spread across multiple regions. SCORE 5

Example: When GE develops new jet engines, it relies on its China unit to design for manufacture, its India unit for analytics and materials science, and its German labs for wind-tunnel testing.

Score for A: _

B. How competent are people in your organization at working closely across geographies?

Not Very Competent: Effectiveness is confined within specific geographies, functions, and product divisions. SCORE 1

Symptoms: Large technical and cultural differences exist within functions. IT systems don't permit effective collaboration. Resistance to rotating people across countries is strong.

Moderately Competent: People are somewhat effective at working across geographies, functions, and product divisions. SCORE 3

Symptoms: Some but not all of the key ingredients—common language and organizational culture, IT systems that allow remote collaboration, and rotation of employees—are in place.

Highly Competent: People are adept at working across geographies, functions, and product divisions. SCORE 5

Symptoms: Most or all of the key ingredients of collaboration are in place.

Score for B: _

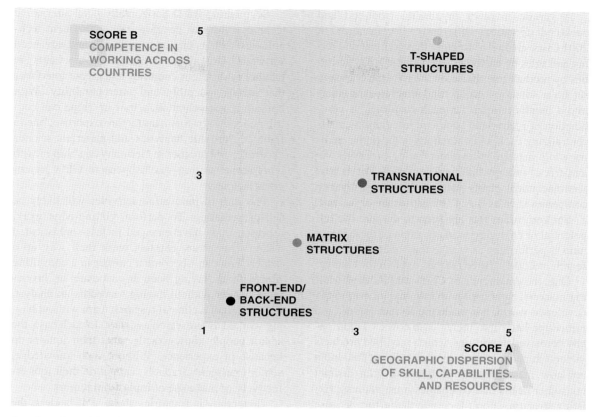

developed world. Moreover, multinational corporations are scouting for new products and services in developing countries—not just to break into them, but also to kick-start growth at home by offering more value for less money. GE's recent "reverse innovation" success with its MAC 400 and 400i portable electrocardiography machines in India, for example, may seem simple, but most companies struggle to develop such innovations in developing countries or to transplant locally developed innovations worldwide. Such efforts sorely challenge established structures and processes.

At the same time, the nature of innovation is becoming more global because of technological advances. Organizations are figuring out how to break up and distribute, across nations and locations, tightly integrated tasks once performed at only a single site. This global division of R&D facilitates intrafunctional specialization among countries.

The advantages include conducting work where the best expertise exists, at the lowest possible cost; exploiting time zone variation to operate 24/7; and mitigating risks by building redundancies across locations. The management dilemmas are, of course, substantial: How do you choose which processes to distribute and where to relocate them? How do you reintegrate them across borders? How do you get people to work effectively across organizational, national, cultural, and time zone barriers?

What's emerging is a new structure, which we call the *T-shaped country organization*. It helps to localize customer-facing operations even as it distributes back-end activities across countries. Showing the way are companies, such as GE, Intel, and AstraZeneca, that are adapting ideas from the Indian IT-offshoring industry and, in the process, rewriting the way corporations should think about structures.

A variant involves organizing front-end and back-end operations differently. For instance, in 2001 Cisco created a structure that grouped marketing and sales by customer segment but R&D activities by product line. Between the two, the company set up a solutions group that integrated products into a bundle tailored for each customer. A combination of matrix and back-end integration entails centralizing back-end operations in the home country while managing customer-facing processes via a matrix of product lines and countries. That's how pharmaceutical giants such as Pfizer and tobacco companies such as B.A.T. Industries are organized.

For companies that are keen to tap into the full potential of emerging markets, none of these structures is performing as well as they once did, our research indicates. Three reasons explain the change:

One, the emergence of China and India as leading markets, combined with minimal growth in the developed world, has made the former "stars" and turned the latter into mere "cash cows." Traditionally perceived as add-ons, whose modified products yielded supplementary revenue, China and India are now major sources of demand, with distinct consumer needs that companies must address. Existing structures don't facilitate that effort because the balance they strike among products, businesses, functions, and regions is no longer adequate in these two markets.

Two, China and India are becoming sources of talent for developing new products and processes. This trend has resulted in the global segmentation of R&D and in intra-functional specialization among countries, as mentioned earlier. Corporations can segment R&D vertically into distinct processes that capture customer requirements; generate product specifications; search for technological solutions to meet those specifications; prototype results; and then engineer for manufacture. For instance, Microsoft's product development team in Hyderabad, India, develops software according to specifications from its U.S. counterparts in Redmond, Washington. That kind of vertical segmentation requires temporal sequencing of each step in the process.

Segmenting R&D horizontally is an alternative technique used to develop multicomponent technologies such as engines, hardware, and advanced software. Organizations design components in parallel in different countries and create interfaces that enable assembly and interoperability. With horizontal segmentation, a unit in China can contribute its design-for-manufacture expertise; one in India can provide analytics and materials science expertise; and another in Germany can chip in with wind-tunnel testing—as happens in GE's jet engines business.

The shift of innovation activities will likely be self-perpetuating. To perform cutting-edge work, a person must have engaged in less-sophisticated tasks earlier. New entrants work their way up a ladder. You can't become a partner in a consulting firm without having been an associate, an investment banker without having served as an analyst, or the head of a clinical research team without having worked as a research assistant. In each case, the senior people know exactly what their juniors do because of experience. Without such knowledge, senior managers, arguably, cannot do their jobs effectively or make use of input from juniors.

Geography is fracturing these skill ladders; the lowest rungs for many jobs are now located in developing countries. With those rungs having moved out of the West or having become less remunerative, Western students are less likely to invest in climbing them. The limited availability of talent will, in turn, reinforce the trend of moving the lower rungs of the skill ladder offshore, and so on. To be clear, we are not arguing that Silicon Valley will collapse or that R&D centers in the West are likely to shut down anytime soon. But companies deciding whether to open a new R&D lab in New Jersey or Basel, Switzerland, will increasingly need to justify why they shouldn't do so in Beijing or Hyderabad, where talent is relatively plentiful and cheaper. The locations multinationals choose for developing their innovation capabilities are likely to change dramatically in the future.

Three, the assumption that multinational corporations' intellectual leadership should come only from developed markets persists. After all, they used to be the largest and the most profitable markets. Despite the lip service paid to globalization nowadays, estimates suggest that fewer than 15% of *Fortune* Global 500 companies have a CEO from outside their bases. Organizational cultures, too, reflect developed nations' dominance in intellectual leadership: Think of American creativity at Apple, German reliability at Daimler, Norwegian egalitarianism at Telenor, and so on.

But change is becoming necessary. If China and India turn out to be both a company's largest markets and its major sources of innovation, something has to give. Few multinationals can escape the "Asianization" of their top management teams. As leadership composition changes, the political center of gravity also will shift eastward. Unless corporations adapt to the new loci of innovation and growth, which will change the organizational fabric, they are unlikely to grow as fast as rivals will.

Falling into the Gaps

These tectonic forces are together opening a set of gaps between multinational companies' ambitions and achievements in emerging markets.

The Passion Gap Multinational companies' subsidiaries in China and India frequently complain about top managements' lack of commitment to their markets. Senior executives may pay lip service to growth in China and India, and may visit them frequently, but Asian countries are high-context cultures where executives and investors seek signs that are more tangible than public appearances and pronouncements. Cultural barriers often make local managers suspect that the global leadership isn't excited by foreign markets. They may be right: According to upper echelon theory, the composition of top management teams affects companies' strategic choices. For example, if several senior executives have backgrounds in finance, the company is more likely to rely on M&A. Conversely, the lack of emerging-market experience at the top tends to limit the commitment to developing countries.

The Ambition Gap Most multinational corporations are headquartered in nations whose economies grow today, at most, between 1% and 3% a year. Their CEOs are delighted when overseas subsidiaries deliver double-digit sales growth, but Chinese and Indian entrepreneurs would deem it unacceptable just to reach that threshold. They demand—and invest aggressively to achieve— at least 25% growth year after year. By contrast, Western companies prefer to report revenues and earnings to Wall Street as per their forecasts, which are usually conservative. In addition, many companies refuse to make significant overseas investments simply because short-term profits and management bonuses may suffer.

The Value-Proposition Gap Most Chinese and Indian customers are constrained by low incomes and budgets, forcing Western companies to revise their business models and, sometimes, reinvent them completely. Local entrepreneurs, trying to ramp up businesses quickly, are short of capital, too: They often have to pay annual interest rates on borrowings of about 15% (China is an exception), compared with 5% in the developed world. The high cost of capital has led some Indian companies to develop unique business models. For instance, Bharti Airtel outsources IT infrastructure and customer services; buys network capacity instead of equipment; and has merged its infrastructure with that of rivals, thereby limiting the investment required to scale up. Many Western companies find it tough to make inroads against local competitors that have adapted well to these conditions.

The Product Line Gap Many transnational giants have not pushed their R&D operations to innovate for the great mass of middle-market consumers in developing countries, or tried to tailor products to local preferences, or even localized their marketing activities. For example, how does BMW's tag line, "The ultimate driving machine," translate in China, where BMWs are usually driven by chauffeurs? How do luxury companies change their product lines from the understated markers of status that are popular in the West to the "bling" that many emerging-market consumers covet? A few Western companies do develop products exclusively for China and India, but most are content to skim the surface of these markets' potential.

The Two Strokes of the T-Shaped Structure

Multinational subsidiaries in emerging markets must reorganize themselves so that they can cope better with two sets of pressures. On the customer side, they need to move faster, make more decisions locally, and alter the incentives and career opportunities offered to employees. In other words, their front-end operations must become highly localized. Given the size of emerging markets like China and India, a high level of localization doesn't preclude economies of scale.

On the back end of the value chain, transnational companies should use emerging markets as platforms for globally segmented innovation, manufacturing, and offshore services. They must break up operations such as product development and R&D, relocate them, possibly across several countries, and integrate them across the world. The issue is no longer simply whether to integrate a subsidiary or give it more autonomy; the answer will depend on whether you're talking about front-end or back-end processes.

These imperatives demand new responses. Companies must let front-end, or customer-facing, processes in emerging markets enjoy greater autonomy. Back-end processes, particularly product development and R&D, need not be collocated; they could be broken up and integrated across countries to foster global development and manufacturing, not just sharing of ideas. That dual approach yields a T-shaped form: The horizontal stroke represents linkages across countries; the vertical stroke illustrates the need for depth within each country. A T-shaped structure is thus a response to the fact that emerging markets are increasingly becoming lead markets as well as talent pools.

The T-shaped country structure can be seen as an extension of the transnational structure, with one difference: It distributes parts of functions—not entire functions—geographically, which requires unprecedented integration across countries. This differs from the avoidance of duplication across geographies or "nice to have" horizontal exchanges of best practices. Each country unit will have its own area of expertise, and all areas will be necessary for developing new products and services. In each country, the horizontal and vertical strokes of the "T" will be connected loosely. For instance, in India the global R&D centers of companies such as Intel, GE, and Microsoft have a few projects to develop products for local customers, but most of the work supports global product development.

Past research has shown that companies can use two complementary approaches to coordinate processes across geographies: separation and integration. Separation entails isolating the activities in each country and minimizing interactions among countries. Partitioning work in this way allows companies to divide tasks across the globe and exploit local skills. For example, GE's John F Welch Technology Centre, in Bangalore, embodies GE's worldwide capability for computational modeling, and AstraZeneca's unit in Bangalore specializes in tropical medicine. Setting up such centers of expertise means that work can proceed largely independently across locations.

When these spatially distributed pieces of specialist work can't be completely black-boxed, they must be integrated. One approach involves building formal channels for coordination. These include assigning integration roles (such as that of program manager), locating some employees physically close to others, and opening direct channels of communication to help bridge distances. Ensuring that people speak the same "language" (and that doesn't mean English) augments the efficacy of these channels. At GE, design engineers from R&D centers around the world collaborate effectively because, as a senior GE Bangalore manager puts it, "We all speak the language of Six Sigma."

Companies can also use tacit coordination—in other words, without extensive communication—for the same purpose. This relies on shared decision-making procedures, a common vocabulary, and the ability to observe work as it happens across locations. Research has shown that some companies have figured out how to let software engineers in different locations coordinate their iterative programming and bug-fixing activities without communicating in detail. The engineers draw instead on the knowledge they share—which comes from common training and the use of workflow software—to anticipate colleagues' responses to problems. Even when the engineers had poor substitutes for face-to-face interactions (such as webcams, telephone, and e-mail), they successfully managed cognitive collocation. A senior scientist at AstraZeneca's Bangalore unit told us, "When people share the same understanding about work procedures, data, methods, and the underlying science, the need to pick up the phone and ask a question doesn't arise too often."

The soft factors underlying the mutual understanding shared by geographically dispersed teams have hard consequences, in that they limit the need for travel and prevent coordination failures. Here's how Guillermo Wille, who used to head GE's Bangalore R&D campus, summarized the challenge: "People usually don't trust their counterparts who are sitting 11,000 miles away. If you think about it, though, few companies have the luxury of having all their technologists sitting in one building . . . The behavioral reality is that if people are sitting in different buildings, they already pick up the phone or communicate through computers. If you understand that, and have created a culture of treating your teams in the next building or those 11,000 miles away the same, you have it. The only caveat is the time difference, which generates issues in work/life balance. That's the problem you face."

Challenges for Top Teams

Amid the focus on structure, it's easy to forget that leaders are the people who make organizations tick globally. The rise of emerging markets has major implications for how top management teams are configured, where they sit physically, and how they operate culturally.

"Re-peopling" the Leadership Tier   Multinational companies will increasingly have to move people from emerging markets, especially Chinese and Indian managers, into leadership positions. Companies in financial services, consulting, and technology, where opportunities have migrated quickly to China and India, have been among the first to do so. As a bridging mechanism, companies like P&G rotate non-U.S. executives in and out of headquarters. Many corporations, including P&G and Unilever, have asked the China and India heads to report directly to the worldwide CEO or have accorded them the status of regional heads. Samsung's China CEO, for instance, is regarded as one of the company's top three executives worldwide.

Redrawing HQ Geography   Before Asian managers enter the C-suite, Western companies may move closer to China and India. In 2006 McDonald's located its Asia head to China—its first regional head outside Oak Brook, Illinois. IBM created a growth-markets headquarters in 2008, based in Shanghai and responsible for Asia (non-Japan), Latin America, Russia, Eastern Europe, the Middle East, and Africa. In 2009 HSBC's then-CEO, Michael Geoghegan, moved from London to Hong Kong to focus on emerging markets, and GM moved the responsibility for global purchasing from Detroit to Shanghai. In 2011 Bayer shifted the base of its general medicines division to Beijing. And GE's health care unit, the world's biggest manufacturer of medical-imaging machines, is moving the headquarters of the 115-year-old business from Waukesha, Wisconsin, to Beijing. When Irdeto set up dual headquarters in Hoofddorp, the Netherlands, and in Beijing, the CEO moved to China with his family. In the not-too-distant future, some multinational companies may toy with the idea of splitting headquarters functions, with compliance staying in the West but intellectual leadership moving to Asia—permanently.

Recognizing Cultural Shifts   Not surprisingly, the rise of China and India is leading to discontent among some multinational companies' senior executives who work in developed countries, which still account for most of their profits. However, these markets are growing slowly, competition is intensifying, and profit margins are falling. Besides, as a senior executive at the energy and water company Nalco recently noted, companies often have to dismantle something in mature markets to build elsewhere. Before Western executives start packing their bags for emerging markets, they must realize that expat managers may not always be welcomed: They're expensive, often unable to speak the local language, and lack local networks. On the other hand, expats are likely to be more valued in back-end functions such as R&D and product development, where global segmentation requires intracompany networks and deep technical knowledge.

No organizational design is perfect or permanent. Smart executives recognize that they must make trade-offs that are appropriate to the economic climate, competitive context, and corporate history. The challenge for CEOs is to let the energy, ambition, and optimism they sense in China and India coexist with their developed-market units. Local subsidiaries, frustrated by the shackles that HQ places on them, are increasingly demanding that the worldwide leadership move to emerging markets, defer to them, or get out of the way. Deploying the T-shaped country organization can help companies to walk the tightrope between their operations in developed and rapidly developing countries, to knit people across countries, and to thereby create global competitive advantage.

Reading 4-3   Matrix Management: Not a Structure, a Frame of Mind

Christopher A. Bartlett and Sumantra Ghoshal

Top-level managers in many of today's leading corporations are losing control of their companies. The problem is not that they have misjudged the demands created by an increasingly complex environment and an accelerating rate of environmental change, nor even that they have failed to develop strategies appropriate to the new challenges. The problem is that their companies are organizationally incapable of carrying out the sophisticated strategies they have developed. Over the past 20 years, strategic thinking has far outdistanced organizational capabilities.

All through the 1980s, companies everywhere were redefining their strategies and reconfiguring their operations in response to such developments

▌*Christopher A. Bartlett is a professor of general management at the Harvard Business School, where he is also chairman of the International Senior Management program. Sumantra Ghoshal is an associate professor who teaches business policy at the European Institute of Business Administration (INSEAD) in Fontainebleau, France. This article is based on their recent book,* Managing Across Borders: The Transnational Solution *(Harvard Business School Press, 1989).*

as the globalization of markets, the intensification of competition, the acceleration of product life cycles, and the growing complexity of relationships with suppliers, customers, employees, governments, even competitors. But as companies struggled with these changing environmental realities, many fell into one of two traps—one strategic, one structural.

The strategic trap was to implement simple, static solutions to complex and dynamic problems. The bait was often a consultant's siren song promising to simplify or at least minimize complexity and discontinuity. Despite the new demands of overlapping industry boundaries and greatly altered value-added chains, managers were promised success if they would "stick to their knitting." In a swiftly changing international political economy, they were urged to rein in dispersed overseas operations and focus on the triad markets, and in an increasingly intricate and sophisticated competitive environment, they were encouraged to choose between alternative generic strategies—low cost or differentiation.

Yet the strategic reality for most companies was that both their business and their environment really *were* more complex, while the proposed solutions were often simple, even simplistic. The traditional telephone company that stuck to its knitting was trampled by competitors who redefined their strategies in response to new technologies linking telecommunications, computers, and office equipment into a single integrated system. The packaged-goods company that concentrated on the triad markets quickly discovered that Europe, Japan, and the United States were the epicenters of global competitive activity, with higher risks and slimmer profits than more protected and less competitive markets such as Australia, Turkey, and Brazil. The consumer electronics company that adopted an either-or generic strategy found itself facing competitors able to develop cost and differentiation capabilities at the same time.

In recent years, as more and more managers recognized oversimplification as a strategic trap, they began to accept the need to manage complexity rather than seek to minimize it. This realization, however, led many into an equally threatening organizational trap when they concluded that the best response to increasingly complex strategic requirements was increasingly complex organizational structures.

The obvious organizational solution to strategies that required multiple, simultaneous management capabilities was the matrix structure that became so fashionable in the late 1970s and the early 1980s. Its parallel reporting relation-ships acknowledged the diverse, conflicting needs of functional, product, and geographic management groups and provided a formal mechanism for resolving them. Its multiple information channels allowed the organization to capture and analyze external complexity. And its overlapping responsibilities were designed to combat parochialism and build flexibility into the company's response to change.

In practice, however, the matrix proved all but unmanageable—especially in an international context. Dual reporting led to conflict and confusion; the proliferation of channels created informational logjams as a proliferation of committees and

reports bogged down the organization; and overlapping responsibilities produced turf battles and a loss of accountability. Separated by barriers of distance, language, time, and culture, managers found it virtually impossible to clarify the confusion and resolve the conflicts.

In hindsight, the strategic and structural traps seem simple enough to avoid, so one has to wonder why so many experienced general managers have fallen into them. Much of the answer lies in the way we have traditionally thought about the general manager's role. For decades, we have seen the general manager as chief strategic guru and principal organizational architect. But as the competitive climate grows less stable and less predictable, it is harder for one person alone to succeed in that great visionary role. Similarly, as formal, hierarchical structure gives way to networks of personal relationships that work through informal, horizontal communication channels, the image of top management in an isolated corner office moving boxes and lines on an organization chart becomes increasingly anachronistic.

Paradoxically, as strategies and organizations become more complex and sophisticated, top-level general managers are beginning to replace their historical concentration on the grand issues of strategy and structure with a focus on the details of managing people and processes. The critical strategic requirement is not to devise the most ingenious and well-coordinated plan but to build the most viable and flexible strategic process; the key organizational task is not to design the most elegant structure but to capture individual capabilities and motivate the entire organization to respond cooperatively to a complicated and dynamic environment.

Building an Organization

Although business thinkers have written a great deal about strategic innovation, they have paid far less attention to the accompanying organizational challenges. Yet many companies remain caught in the structural-complexity trap that paralyzes their ability to respond quickly or flexibly to the new strategic imperatives.

For those companies that adopted matrix structures, the problem was not in the way they defined the goal. They correctly recognized the need for a multi-dimensional organization to respond to growing external complexity. The problem was that they defined their organizational objectives in purely structural terms. Yet the term *formal structure* describes only the organization's basic anatomy. Companies must also concern themselves with organizational physiology—the systems and relationships that allow the lifeblood of information to flow through the organization. They also need to develop a healthy organizational psychology—the shared norms, values, and beliefs that shape the way individual managers think and act.

The companies that fell into the organizational trap assumed that changing their formal structure (anatomy) would force changes in interpersonal relationships and decision processes (physiology), which in turn would reshape the individual attitudes and actions of managers (psychology).

But as many companies have discovered, reconfiguring the formal structure is a blunt and sometimes brutal instrument of change. A new structure creates new and presumably more useful managerial ties, but these can take months and often years to evolve into effective knowledge-generating and decision-making relationships. And because the new job requirements will frustrate, alienate, or simply overwhelm so many managers, changes in individual attitudes and behavior will likely take even longer.

As companies struggle to create organizational capabilities that reflect rather than diminish environmental complexity, good managers gradually stop searching for the ideal structural template to impose on the company from the top down. Instead, they focus on the challenge of building up an appropriate set of employee attitudes and skills and linking them together with carefully developed processes and relationships. In other words, they begin to focus on building the organization rather than simply on installing a new structure.

Indeed, the companies that are most successful at developing multi-dimensional organizations begin at the far end of the anatomy-physiology-psychology sequence. Their first objective is to alter the organizational psychology—the broad corporate beliefs and norms that shape managers' perceptions and actions. Then, by enriching and clarifying communication and decision processes, companies reinforce these psychological changes with improvements in organizational physiology. Only later do they consolidate and confirm their progress by realigning organizational anatomy through changes in the formal structure.

No company we know of has discovered a quick or easy way to change its organizational psychology to reshape the understanding, identification, and commitment of its employees. But we found three principal characteristics common to those that managed the task most effectively:

1. They developed and communicated a clear and consistent corporate vision.
2. They effectively managed human resource tools to broaden individual perspectives and to develop identification with corporate goals.
3. They integrated individual thinking and activities into the broad corporate agenda by a process we call co-option.

Building a Shared Vision

Perhaps the main reason managers in large, complex companies cling to parochial attitudes is that their frame of reference is bounded by their specific responsibilities. The surest way to break down such insularity is to develop and communicate a clear sense of corporate purpose that extends into every corner of the company and gives context and meaning to each manager's particular roles and responsibilities. We are not talking about a slogan, however catchy and pointed. We are talking about a company vision, which must be crafted and articulated with clarity, continuity, and consistency. We are talking about clarity of expression that makes company objectives understandable and meaningful; continuity of purpose that underscores their enduring importance; and consistency of application across business units and geographical boundaries that ensures uniformity throughout the organization.

Clarity   There are three keys to clarity in a corporate vision: simplicity, relevance, and reinforcement. NEC's integration of computers and communications—C&C—is probably the best single example of how simplicity can make a vision more powerful. Top management has applied the C&C concept so effectively that it describes the company's business focus, defines its distinctive source of competitive advantage over large companies like IBM and AT&T, and summarizes its strategic and organizational imperatives.

The second key, relevance, means linking broad objectives to concrete agendas. When Wisse Dekker became CEO at Philips, his principal strategic concern was the problem of competing with Japan. He stated this challenge in martial terms—the U.S. had abandoned the battlefield; Philips was now Europe's last defense against insurgent Japanese electronics companies. By focusing the company's attention not only on Philips's corporate survival but also on the protection of national and regional interests, Dekker heightened the sense of urgency and commitment in a way that legitimized cost-cutting efforts, drove an extensive rationalization of plant operations, and inspired a new level of sales achievements.

The third key to clarity is top management's continual reinforcement, elaboration, and interpretation of the core vision to keep it from becoming obsolete or abstract. Founder Konosuke Matsushita developed a grand, 250- year vision for his company, but he also managed to give it immediate relevance. He summed up its overall message in the "Seven Spirits of Matsushita," to which he referred constantly in his policy statements. Each January he wove the company's one-year operational objectives into his overarching concept to produce an annual theme that he then captured in a slogan. For all the loftiness of his concept of corporate purpose, he gave his managers immediate, concrete guidance in implementing Matsushita's goals.

Continuity   Despite shifts in leadership and continual adjustments in short-term business priorities, companies must remain committed to the same core set of strategic objectives and organizational values. Without such continuity, unifying vision might as well be expressed in terms of quarterly goals.

It was General Electric's lack of this kind of continuity that led to the erosion of its once formidable position in electrical appliances in many countries. Over a period of 20 years and under successive CEOs, the company's international consumer-product strategy never stayed the same for long. From building locally responsive and self-sufficient "mini-GEs" in each market, the company turned to a policy of developing low-cost offshore sources, which eventually evolved into a de facto strategy of international outsourcing. Finally, following its acquisition of RCA, GE's consumer electronics strategy made another about-face and focused on building centralized scale to defend domestic share. Meanwhile, the product strategy within this shifting business emphasis was itself unstable. The Brazilian subsidiary, for example, built its TV business in the 1960s until it was told to stop; in the early 1970s, it emphasized large appliances until it was denied funding, then it focused on housewares until the parent company sold off that business. In two decades, GE utterly dissipated its dominant franchise in Brazil's electrical products market.

Unilever, by contrast, made an enduring commitment to its Brazilian subsidiary, despite volatile swings in Brazil's business climate. Company chairman Floris Maljers emphasized the importance of looking past the latest political crisis or economic downturn to the long-term business potential. "In those parts of the world," he remarked, "you take your management cues from the way they dance. The samba method of management is two steps forward then one step back." Unilever built—two steps forward and one step back—a profitable $300 million business in a rapidly growing economy with 130 million consumers, while its wallflower competitors never ventured out onto the floor.

Consistency   The third task for top management in communicating strategic purpose is to ensure that everyone in the company shares the same vision. The cost of inconsistency can be horrendous. It always produces confusion and, in extreme cases, can lead to total chaos, with different units of the organization pursuing agendas that are mutually debilitating.

Philips is a good example of a company that, for a time, lost its consistency of corporate purpose. As a legacy of its wartime decision to give some overseas units legal autonomy, management had long experienced difficulty persuading North American Philips (NAP) to play a supportive role in the parent company's global strategies. The problem came to a head with the introduction of Philips's technologically first-rate videocassette recording system, the V2000. Despite considerable pressure from world headquarters in the Netherlands, NAP refused to launch the system, arguing that Sony's Beta system and Matsushita's VHS format were too well established and had cost, feature, and system-support advantages Philips couldn't match. Relying on its legal independence and managerial autonomy, NAP management decided instead to source products from its Japanese competitors and market them under its Magnavox brand name. As a result, Philips was unable to build the efficiency and credibility it needed to challenge Japanese dominance of the VCR business.

Most inconsistencies involve differences between what managers of different operating units see as the company's key objectives. Sometimes, however, different corporate leaders transmit different views of overall priorities and purpose. When this stems from poor communication, it can be fixed. When it's a result of fundamental disagreement, the problem is serious indeed, as illustrated by ITT's problems in developing its strategically vital System 12 switching equipment. Continuing differences between the head of the European organization and the company's chief technology officer over the location and philosophy of the development effort led to confusion and conflict throughout the company. The result was disastrous. ITT had difficulty transferring vital technology across its own unit boundaries and so was irreparably late introducing this key product to a rapidly changing global market. These problems eventually led the company to sell off its core telecommunications business to a competitor.

But formulating and communicating a vision—no matter how clear, enduring, and consistent—cannot succeed unless individual employees understand and accept the company's stated goals and objectives. Problems at this level are more often related to receptivity than to communication. The development of individual understanding and acceptance is a challenge for a company's human resource practices.

Developing Human Resources

While top managers universally recognize their responsibility for developing and allocating a company's scarce assets and resources, their focus on finance and technology often overshadows the task of developing the scarcest resource of all—capable managers. But if there is one key to regaining control of companies that operate in fast-changing environments, it is the ability of top management to turn the perceptions, capabilities, and relationships of individual managers into the building blocks of the organization.

One pervasive problem in companies whose leaders lack this ability—or fail to exercise it—is getting managers to see how their specific responsibilities relate to the broad corporate vision. Growing external complexity and strategic sophistication have accelerated the growth of a cadre of specialists who are physically and organizationally isolated from each other, and the task of dealing with their consequent parochialism should not be delegated to the clerical staff that administers salary structures and benefit programs. Top managers inside and outside the human resource function must be leaders in the recruitment, development, and assignment of the company's vital human talent.

Recruitment and Selection   The first step in successfully managing complexity is to tap the full range of available talent. It is a serious mistake to permit historical imbalances in the nationality or functional background of the management group to constrain hiring or subsequent promotion. In today's global marketplace, domestically oriented recruiting limits a company's ability to capitalize on its worldwide pool of management skill and biases its decision-making processes.

After decades of routinely appointing managers from its domestic operations to key positions in overseas subsidiaries, Procter & Gamble realized that the practice not only worked against sensitivity to local cultures—a lesson driven home by several marketing failures in Japan—but also greatly under-utilized its pool of high-potential *non-American* managers. (Fortunately, our studies turned up few companies as shortsighted as one that made overseas assignments on the basis of *poor* performance, because foreign markets were assumed to be "not as tough as the domestic environment.")

Not only must companies enlarge the pool of people available for key positions, they must also develop new criteria for choosing those most likely to succeed. Because past success is no longer a sufficient qualification for increasingly subtle, sensitive, and unpredictable senior-level tasks, top management must become involved in a more discriminating selection process. At Matsushita, top management selects candidates for international assignments on the basis of a comprehensive set of personal characteristics, expressed for simplicity in the acronym SMILE: specialty (the needed skill, capability, or knowledge); management ability (particularly motivational ability); international flexibility (willingness to learn and ability to adapt); language facility; and endeavor (vitality, perseverance in the face of difficulty). These attributes are remarkably similar to those targeted by NEC and Philips, where top executives also are involved in the senior-level selection process.

Training and Development   Once the appropriate top-level candidates have been identified, the next challenge is to develop their potential. The most successful development efforts have three aims that take them well beyond the skill-building objectives of classic training programs: to inculcate a common vision and shared values; to broaden management perspectives and capabilities; and to develop contacts and shape management relationships.

To build common vision and values, white-collar employees at Matsushita spend a good part of their first six months in what the company calls "cultural and spiritual training." They study the company credo, the "Seven Spirits of Matsushita," and the philosophy of Konosuke Matsushita. Then they learn how to translate these internalized lessons into daily behavior and even operational decisions. Culture-building exercises as intensive as Matsushitas are sometimes dismissed as innate Japanese practices that would not work in other societies, but in fact, Philips has a similar entry-level training practice (called "organization cohesion training"), as does Unilever (called, straight-forwardly, "indoctrination").

The second objective—broadening management perspectives—is essentially a matter of teaching people how to manage complexity instead of merely to make room for it. To reverse a long and unwieldy tradition of running its operations with two- and three-headed management teams of separate technical, commercial, and sometimes administrative specialists, Philips asked its training and development group to de-specialize top management trainees. By supplementing its traditional menu of specialist courses and functional programs with more intensive general management training, Philips was able to begin replacing the ubiquitous teams with single business heads who also appreciated and respected specialist points of view.

The final aim—developing contacts and relationships—is much more than an incidental by-product of good management development, as the comments of a senior personnel manager at Unilever suggest: "By bringing managers from different countries and businesses together at Four Acres [Unilever's international management-training college], we build contacts and create bonds that we could never achieve by other means. The company spends as much on training as it does on R&D not only because of the direct effect it has on upgrading skills and knowledge but also because it plays a central role in indoctrinating managers into a Unilever club where personal relationships and informal contacts are much more powerful than the formal systems and structures."

Career-Path Management   Although recruitment and training are critically important, the most effective companies recognize that the best way to develop new perspectives and thwart parochialism in their managers is through personal experience. By moving selected managers across functions, businesses, and geographic units, a company encourages cross-fertilization of ideas as well as the flexibility and breadth of experience that enable managers to grapple with complexity and come out on top.

Unilever has long been committed to the development of its human resources as a means of attaining durable competitive advantage. As early as the 1930s, the company was recruiting and developing local employees to replace the parent-company managers who had been running most of its overseas subsidiaries. In a practice that came to be known as "-ization," the company committed itself to the Indianization of its Indian company, the Australization of its Australian company, and so on.

Although delighted with the new talent that began working its way up through the organization, management soon realized that by reducing the transfer of parent-company managers abroad, it had diluted the powerful glue that bound diverse organizational groups together and linked dispersed operations. The answer lay in formalizing a second phase of the -ization process. While continuing with Indianization, for example, Unilever added programs aimed at the "Unileverization" of its Indian managers.

In addition to bringing 300 to 400 managers to Four Acres each year, Unilever typically has 100 to 150 of its most promising overseas managers on short- and long-term job assignments at corporate headquarters. This policy not only brings fresh, close-to-the-market perspectives into corporate decision making but also gives the visiting managers a strong sense of Unilever's strategic vision and organizational values. In the words of one of the expatriates in the corporate offices, "The experience initiates you into the Unilever Club and the clear norms, values, and behaviors that distinguish our people—so much so that we really believe we can spot another Unilever manager anywhere in the world."

Furthermore, the company carefully transfers most of these high-potential individuals through a variety of different functional, product, and geographic positions, often rotating every two or three years. Most important, top management tracks about 1,000 of these people—some 5% of Unilever's total management group—who, as they move through the company, forge an informal network of contacts and relationships that is central to Unilever's decision-making and information-exchange processes.

Widening the perspectives and relationships of key managers as Unilever has done is a good way of developing identification with the broader corporate mission. But a broad sense of identity is not enough. To maintain control of its global strategies, Unilever must secure a strong and lasting individual commitment to corporate visions and objectives. In effect, it must co-opt individual energies and ambitions into the service of corporate goals.

Co-Opting Management Efforts

As organizational complexity grows, managers and management groups tend to become so specialized and isolated and to focus so intently on their own immediate operating responsibilities that they are apt to respond parochially to intrusions on their organizational turf, even when the overall corporate interest is at stake. A classic example, described earlier, was the decision by North American Philips's consumer electronics group to reject the parent company's VCR system.

At about the same time, Philips, like many other companies, began experimenting with ways to convert managers' intellectual understanding of the corporate vision—in Philips's case, an almost evangelical determination to defend Western electronics against the Japanese—into a binding personal commitment. Philips concluded that it could co-opt individuals and organizational groups into the broader vision by inviting them to contribute to the corporate agenda and then giving them direct responsibility for implementation.

In the face of intensifying Japanese competition, Philips knew it had to improve coordination in its consumer electronics among its fiercely independent national organizations. In strengthening the central product divisions, however, Philips did not want to deplete the enterprise or commitment of its capable national management teams.

The company met these conflicting needs with two cross-border initiatives. First, it created a top-level World Policy Council for its video business that included key managers from strategic markets—Germany, France, the United Kingdom, the United States, and Japan. Philips knew that its national companies' long history of independence made local managers reluctant to take orders from Dutch headquarters in Eindhoven—often for good reason, because much of the company's best market knowledge and technological expertise resided in its offshore units. Through the council, Philips co-opted their support for company decisions about product policy and manufacturing location.

Second, in a more powerful move, Philips allocated global responsibilities to units that previously had been purely national in focus. Eindhoven gave NAP the leading role in the development of Philips's projection television and asked it to coordinate development and manufacture of all Philips television sets for North America and Asia. The change in the attitude of NAP managers was dramatic.

A senior manager in NAP's consumer electronics business summed up the feelings of U.S. managers: "At last, we are moving out of the dependency relationship with Eindhoven that was so frustrating to us." Co-option had transformed the defensive, territorial attitude of NAP managers into a more collaborative mind-set. They were making important contributions to global corporate strategy instead of looking for ways to subvert it.

In 1987, with much of its TV set production established in Mexico, the president of NAP's consumer electronics group told the press, "It is the commonality of design that makes it possible for us to move production globally. We have splendid cooperation with Philips in Eindhoven." It was a statement no NAP manager would have made a few years earlier, and it perfectly captured how effectively Philips had co-opted previously isolated, even adversarial, managers into the corporate agenda.

The Matrix in the Manager's Mind

Since the end of World War II, corporate strategy has survived several generations of painful transformation and has grown appropriately agile and athletic. Unfortunately, organizational development has not kept pace, and managerial attitudes lag even farther behind. As a result, corporations now commonly design strategies that seem impossible to implement, for the simple reason that no one can effectively implement third-generation strategies through second-generation organizations run by first-generation managers.

Today the most successful companies are those where top executives recognize the need to manage the new environmental and competitive demands by focusing less on the quest for an ideal structure and more on developing the abilities, behavior, and performance of individual managers. Change succeeds only when those assigned to the new transnational and interdependent tasks understand the overall goals and are dedicated to achieving them.

One senior executive put it this way: "The challenge is not so much to build a matrix structure as it is to create a matrix in the minds of our managers." The inbuilt conflict in a matrix structure pulls managers in several directions at once. Developing a matrix of flexible perspectives and relationships within each manager's mind, however, achieves an entirely different result. It lets individuals make the judgments and negotiate the trade-offs that drive the organization toward a shared strategic objective.

Creating Worldwide Innovation and Learning:
Exploiting Cross-Border Knowledge Management

In the information-based, knowledge-intensive economy of the 21st century, multinational enterprises (MNEs) are not competing only in terms of their traditional ability to access new markets and arbitrage factor costs. Today, the challenge is to build transnational organizations that can sense an emerging consumer trend in one country, link it to a new technology or capability that it has in another, develop a creative new product or service in a third, then diffuse that innovation rapidly around the world. This transnational innovation process is much more sophisticated than the more traditional "center-for-global" and "local-for-local" approaches that have been the dominant form of cross-border innovation in the past. In this chapter, we describe the traditional and the emerging models of cross-border innovation, as well as the nature of the organizational capabilities that must be developed to make them effective. The chapter concludes with a closer examination of the characteristics of the transnational organization that allow the MNE to supplement its traditional ability to manage international flows of financial capital with an equal facility to develop and manage cross-border flows of human and intellectual capital.

In Chapter 3, we described how MNEs competing in today's global competitive environment are being required to build layers of competitive advantage—the ability to capture global scale efficiencies, local market responsiveness, and worldwide learning capability. As these companies found ways to match one another in the more familiar attributes of global scale efficiency and local responsiveness, competitive battles among leading-edge MNEs (particularly those in knowledge-intensive industries such as telecommunications, biotechnology, pharmaceuticals, etc.) have shifted to their ability to link and leverage their worldwide resources and capabilities to develop and diffuse innovation.[1]

The trend is reflected in the fact that R&D expenditure globally more than doubled in real terms between 1992 and 2010. Unsurprisingly, worldwide patent applications have grown from 922,000 in 1985 to almost 2 million in 2010. In the same period, trademark applications also increased worldwide from about 1 million in 1985 to 3.6 million in 2010. Among U.S. companies, this fast-growing investment in knowledge-based assets is reflected in the value of intangible assets (i.e. *not* fixed assets such as plant and

---

[1]Throughout this chapter, when we talk about innovation, we are not only referring to the creation of technology-based new products or services, but also to innovations that come from organizational effectiveness breakthroughs, pioneering marketing strategies, state-of-the-art manufacturing processes, or logistical innovations.

equipment or current assets like inventory) of the average S&P 500 company, which has risen from 32 percent of the total value in 1985 to 68 percent in 1995, and to over 80 percent today.

All of this is changing the way companies regard their international operations. Particularly in previous decades, MNEs often regarded their stock of domestically accumulated knowledge and expertise as an asset they could sell into foreign markets. This was particularly true of the U.S.-based MNEs that followed the early "international" strategy that we described in Chapter 3. For example, in the 1960s, RCA decided that its most appropriate strategy of international expansion was to license its leading-edge technology. By treating the global market just as an opportunity to generate incremental revenue, rather than a source of innovation and learning, the company soon found that after its licensees had learned what they could, they quickly caught up with and then overtook RCA in creating new innovative products more adapted to the global market.

In today's competitive environment, no company can assume that it can accumulate world-class knowledge and expertise by focusing only on its home-country environment, or that it can succeed just by tweaking its domestic product line. So while Qualcomm, the world leader in mobile and wireless technologies, may appear to be like RCA in licensing its technology as a core element of its international expansion, its strategy is very different. By licensing essentially every company in the telecom industry worldwide, Qualcomm generates over a third of its total revenue from royalty-based licensing agreements. But almost a quarter of its total revenue is plowed back into R&D at its major research centers in the United States, Germany, China, India, Republic of Korea, and the United Kingdom. In each of these countries, the company actively recruits the brightest technologists, monitors technological and competitive developments, collaborates with leading university researchers, and develops products in partnership with its global customers. In short, Qualcomm is using its worldwide presence to maintain and expand its innovative lead.

The ability to develop and rapidly diffuse innovations around the world is vital, and in this challenge, overseas operations need to take on important new roles. In addition to their traditional roles, all offshore sales subsidiaries, manufacturing operations and R&D centers must become the sensors of new market trends or technological developments, they must be able to attract scarce talent and expertise, and they must be able to act collectively with the company and other offshore units to exploit the resulting innovations worldwide, regardless of where they originated.

Yet developing this capability to create, leverage, and apply knowledge worldwide is not a simple task for most MNEs. Although people are innately curious and naturally motivated to learn from one another, most modern corporations are constructed in a way that constrains and sometimes kills this natural human instinct. In this chapter, we focus on one of the most important current challenges facing MNE management: how to capture, develop, leverage, and exploit knowledge to support effective worldwide innovation and learning.

Traditional Innovation: Central and Local Models

Traditionally, MNEs' innovative capabilities were dominated by one of two classic processes. In what we describe as the *center-for-global* innovation model, the new opportunity was sensed in the home country; the centralized resources and capabilities of the parent company were brought in to create the new product or process, usually in the main R&D center; and implementation involved driving the innovation through subsidiaries whose role it was to introduce that innovation to their local market. Classic examples of this model would be Pfizer's R&D that led to the development and eventual worldwide introduction of Viagra, or Komatsu's international rollout of its line of heavy construction equipment designed and developed in Japan.

In contrast, what we call *local-for-local* innovation relies on subsidiary-based knowledge development. Responding to perceived local opportunities, subsidiaries use their own resources and capabilities to create innovative responses that are then implemented in the local market. Unilever's development of a detergent bar in response to the Indian market's need for a product suitable for stream washing is a good illustration of the process, as is Philippines-based Jollibee's strategy of adapting its fast-food products to the local market preferences of each country that it entered.

As MNEs relying on each of these sources of innovation competed for market share, the more sophisticated tried to develop elements of both models. But the tension between the knowledge management processes supporting each usually meant that one philosophy and set of practices ended up dominating. Not surprisingly, center-for-global innovation tends to dominate in companies that we describe as global or international, whereas local-for-local processes fit more easily into the multinational strategic model.

Regardless of which model dominated, the first challenge facing all these companies was to overcome the limitations and vulnerabilities built into their dominant process of cross-border innovation. In the following paragraphs, we will outline how the most effective MNEs did this. But as we will see in a later section of the chapter, even the best-managed central and local innovation processes were rarely sufficient, particularly for companies in fast-changing, knowledge-intensive industries like electronics, biotechnology, and communications. These MNEs required an entirely different set of skills to master what we will call *transnational innovation capability*. First, however, let's review how companies learned to make their traditional models of cross-border innovation effective.

Making Central Innovations Effective

The key strength on which many Japanese companies built their global leadership positions in a diverse range of businesses, from automobiles to zippers, lay in the effectiveness of their center-for-global innovations. This is not to say that many of them did not use other modes, but in general, the Japanese became the champions of centralized innovation and have remained so. In a subsequent wave of international expansion, many Korean MNEs followed their example.

Over time, these companies learned that the greatest risk of center-for-global innovation is market insensitivity and the accompanying resistance of local subsidiary managers to what they may view as inappropriate new products and processes. As a result, the most successful companies developed three important capabilities that are key to managing the center-for-global process: gaining the input of subsidiaries into centralized activities, ensuring that all functional tasks are linked to market needs, and integrating value chain functions by managing the transfer of responsibilities across development, production, and marketing, for example.

Gaining Subsidiary Input: Multiple Linkages

The most important problems facing a company with highly centralized operations are that those at the center may not understand market needs, and those in the subsidiaries required to implement a central innovation may not be committed to it. Both problems are best addressed by building multiple linkages between headquarters and overseas subsidiaries, not only to give headquarters managers a better understanding of country-level needs and opportunities, but also to offer subsidiary managers greater access to and involvement in centralized decisions and tasks.

For example, the Japanese electronics company Sharp has radically increased the number of linkages that it has between headquarters and subsidiaries and no longer tries to focus them through a single point of contact for the sake of efficiency. Instead, this company now consciously works to preserve the different perspectives, priorities, and even prejudices of its diverse groups worldwide, and then ensure that they have linkages to those in the corporate headquarters who can represent and defend their views best. Such an approach has helped it grow its foreign sales from 34 percent of total revenue in 2000 to 56 percent a decade later. And the innovations driving such growth were sometimes as simple as putting thicker, more durable insulation on the electrical cords of TV sets sold in rural China so that mice could not chew through them.

Responding to National Needs: Market Mechanisms

Like many other MNEs, Panasonic (formerly Matsushita) has created an integrative process to ensure that headquarters managers responsible for R&D, manufacturing, and marketing are not sheltered from the constraints and demands felt by managers on the front lines of the operations. A key element in achieving this difficult organizational task is the company's use of internal "market mechanisms" to direct and regulate central activities.

For example, approximately half of Panasonic's total research budget is allocated to corporate R&D; the rest is dedicated to the product divisions. The purpose of the split budget is to create a context in which technology-driven and market-led ideas can compete for attention. Each year, the various corporate research laboratories hold exhibitions to highlight research projects that they want to undertake. The divisions identify projects of interest and indicate their willingness to support them with requisite funds and other resources. But how do the product division's developers know which projects to support? Each year, they hold internal merchandise meetings at which their overseas subsidiaries negotiate for the features and prices of the products that they would be willing to purchase in the coming year. The internal market connects consumer demand to technological innovation.

Managing Responsibility Transfer: Personnel Flow

When parent company units take the lead role in the development and manufacture of new products and processes, integration across research, manufacturing, and marketing is much more difficult than in local-for-local innovation processes. This is because the latter processes are greatly facilitated by the smaller size and closer proximity of the units responsible for cross-functional coordination. In centralized organizations, alternative means to integrate the different tasks must be constructed carefully.

At Panasonic, the integrative systems rely heavily on the transfer of people. The career paths of research engineers are structured to ensure that many of them spend about five to eight years in the central research laboratories engaged in pure research before moving on to the product divisions, typically in applied research and development. In a later stage of their careers, many move into a direct operational function, such as production or marketing, where they often take line management positions. Typically, an engineer will transition from one department to the next at the same time as the transfer of the major project on which he or she has been working, thereby ensuring that specific knowledge about the project moves with the individual.

Another mechanism for cross-functional integration in Panasonic works in the opposite direction. Wherever possible, the company tries to identify the manager who will head the production task for a new product under development and then makes that person a full-time member of the research team from the initial stage of the development process. This system not only injects direct production expertise into the development team, but also facilitates the transfer of the project after the design is completed.

Making Local Innovations Efficient

If the classic global companies are the champions of central innovation, the archetypal multinational companies are often masters at managing local innovations. But these companies have to deal with the fact that local-for-local innovations often suffer from needless differentiation and "reinvention of the wheel" caused by resource-rich subsidiaries trying to protect their independence and autonomy.

Of the many ways companies have dealt successfully with these problems, three abilities proved to be most significant: to empower local management in national subsidiaries, to establish effective mechanisms for linking these local managers to corporate decision-making processes, and to force tight, cross-functional integration within each subsidiary.

Empowering Local Management

Perhaps the most important factor supporting local innovation is the dispersal of the organizational assets and resources and the delegation of authority that must accompany it. These twin prerequisites provide the tools for country-level organizations to take the initiative in creating new products or processes. Companies like Unilever and Philips, with their well-established decentralized federation organizations, had little difficulty in creating such local-for-local innovation. (Recall Hindustan Unilever's detergent bar for stream washing.) But many others wanting to achieve similar capabilities have had to jump-start this process by transferring assets and resources and empowering their subsidiary operations.

When U.S. agricultural machinery manufacturer John Deere found its significant market position in India being challenged by local competitor Mahindra and Mahindra, management decided that it needed a more locally tailored product line. The company created a technology center in Pune, India, staffed by 2,000 technical employees who were focused on the needs of cost-conscious Indian farmers. The subsequent creation of the smaller, simpler 5003 tractor series, developed specifically for those local needs, resulted in the turnaround of the company's share of this large and important agricultural equipment market.

Linking Local Managers to Corporate Decision-Making Processes

Whereas local resources and autonomy make it feasible for subsidiary managers to be creative and entrepreneurial, linkages to corporate decision-making processes are necessary to make these local-for-local tasks effective for the company as a whole. That certainly was true for John Deere's Indian technology group, which was closely linked to the company's main technical center in Moline, Illinois, through the many development teams on which they worked collaboratively.

In many European companies, a cadre of entrepreneurial expatriates has long played a key role in developing and maintaining such linkages. At Philips, for example, many of the best managers spend much of their careers in national operations, working for three to four years in a series of subsidiaries—jobs that are often much larger and have higher status than those available in the small, home-country market of the Netherlands.

Not surprisingly, such a career assignment pattern has an important influence on managerial attitudes and organizational relationships. The expatriate managers tend to identify strongly with the national organization's point of view, and this shared identity creates a strong bond and distinct subculture within the company. In contrast, Panasonic has been able to generate very little interaction among its expatriate managers, who tend to regard themselves as parent-company executives temporarily on assignment in a foreign company.

Integrating Subsidiary Functions

Finally, the local innovativeness of decentralized federation organizations is enhanced when there is strong cross-functional integration within each national operation. Most Philips subsidiaries use integration mechanisms at three organizational levels. For each project, there is what Philips calls an "article team" consisting of relatively junior managers from the commercial and technical functions. It is the responsibility of this team to evolve product policies and prepare annual sales plans and budgets.

At the product level, cross-functional coordination is accomplished through a product group team of technical and commercial representatives, which meets to review results, suggest corrective actions, and resolve any interfunctional differences. Restraining control and conflict resolution to this level facilitates sensitive and rapid responses to initiatives and ideas generated at the local level.

The highest subsidiary-level coordination forum is the senior management committee (SMC), which consists of the top commercial, technical, and financial managers in the subsidiary. Acting essentially as a local board, the SMC coordinates efforts among the functional groups and ensures that the national operation retains primary responsibility for its own strategies and priorities. Each of these three forums facilitates local initiative by encouraging that issues be resolved without escalation for approval or arbitration.

Transnational Innovation: Locally Leveraged, Globally Linked

In recent years, the traditional models that shaped cross-border innovation have evolved into two new processes: transnational innovation models that we describe as locally leveraged and globally linked.

Locally leveraged innovation involves ensuring that the special resources and capabilities of each national subsidiary are available not only to that local entity, but also to other MNE units worldwide. For example, the world's best-selling phone, the Nokia 1100, was developed in 2003 specifically for the Indian market. Priced between $10 and $20, it did not feature a camera, but it did have a built-in flashlight, which was a popular feature with rural buyers. Following its great success in the Indian market, Nokia realized that the 1100's robust construction, dust-proof keypad, and water-resistant grip made it ideal for other markets. Over the next seven years, the company sold more than 250 million units through Nokia's sales subsidiaries in various developing countries worldwide.

Globally linked innovation pools the resources and capabilities of many different units—typically at both the parent company and the subsidiary level—to create and manage an activity jointly. It allows the company to take market intelligence developed in one part of the organization, perhaps link it to specialized expertise located in a second entity and a scarce resource in a third, and then eventually diffuse the new product or proposal worldwide.

An example of globally linked innovation occurred when P&G wanted to launch an improved liquid laundry detergent and deliberately decided to draw on the diverse technological capabilities being applied separately to products it sold in Europe, Japan, and the United States. Because the Japanese often do their laundry in cold water, researchers in Japan developed a more robust surfactant (the ingredient that removes greasy stains). Meanwhile, the Europeans had been working on a liquid detergent with bleach substitutes, water softeners, and enzymes that would work in their high-temperature, front-loading washers. These innovations were combined with a new generation of builders developed in the United States to prevent the redisposition of dirt. The result was a global, heavy-duty liquid detergent, introduced as Improved Liquid Tide in the United States, Liquid Ariel in Europe, and Liquid Cheer in Japan.

Although these two transnational innovation processes are becoming more widespread, they have supplemented rather than replaced the traditional center-for-global and local-for-local innovation processes that are so well embedded in many MNEs. In a competitive environment, most companies recognize the need to engage their resources and capabilities in as many ways as they can. The challenge is to build an organization that can facilitate all four processes of cross-border innovation and learning simultaneously, which requires that it understand not only the power of each but also the limitations.

Making Transnational Processes Feasible

Building a portfolio of innovative processes to drive worldwide learning requires that companies overcome two related but different problems. Not only must they avoid the various pitfalls associated with each process, they must also find ways to overcome the organizational contradictions among them as they try to manage all the sources of innovation simultaneously.

In many MNEs, three simplifying assumptions traditionally have blocked the organizational capabilities necessary for managing such multifaceted and often contradictory operations. The drive to reduce organizational and strategic complexity made these assumptions extremely widespread among large MNEs:

- An often-implicit assumption that roles of organizational units responsible for very different businesses, functions, and national operations should be uniform and symmetrical.
- An assumption, conscious or unconscious, that headquarters-subsidiary relationships should be based on clear and unambiguous patterns of dependence or independence.
- An assumption that corporate management has a responsibility to exercise decision making and control uniformly.

Companies that are most successful in developing transnational innovations challenge these assumptions. Instead of treating all businesses, functions, and subsidiaries the same way, they systematically differentiate tasks and responsibilities. Instead of seeking organizational clarity by basing relationships on dependence or independence, they build and manage interdependence among the different units of the companies. And instead of considering control their key task, corporate managers search for complex mechanisms to coordinate and coopt the differentiated and interdependent organizational units into sharing a vision of the company's strategic tasks.

From Symmetry to Differentiation

Like many other companies, Unilever built its international operations with an implicit assumption of organizational symmetry. Managers of diverse local *businesses,* with products ranging from packaged foods to chemicals and detergents, all reported to strongly independent national subsidiary managers, who in turn reported through regional directors to the board. But as management began to recognize the need to capture potential economies across national boundaries and transfer learning worldwide, product coordination groups were formed at the corporate center and soon encompassed all businesses.

As this change progressed, however, there was a recognition that different businesses faced different demands for integration and responsiveness. Whereas cross-country standardization, coordination, and integration paid high dividends in the chemical and detergent businesses, for example, important differences in local tastes and national cultures impeded the same degree of standardization, coordination, and integration in its branded packaged foods business.

As Unilever tackled the challenge of managing some businesses in a more globally (or at least regionally) coordinated manner, it also confronted the question of what *functions* to coordinate. Historically, most national subsidiaries chose to develop, manufacture, and market products that they thought appropriate. Over time, however, decentralization of all functional responsibilities became increasingly difficult to support.

For the sake of cost control and competitive effectiveness, Unilever recognized that it needed to break with tradition. For example, it began centralizing European product development and purchasing but was less compelled to pull local sales and promotional responsibilities to the center.

In addition to differentiating the way that they managed their various businesses and functions, most companies eventually recognized the importance of differentiating the management of diverse *geographic* operations. Although various national subsidiaries operated with very different external environments and internal constraints, in many MNEs, country operations in Sydney, Singapore, and Shanghai reported through the same channels, were managed by standardized planning and control systems, and worked under a set of common and generalized subsidiary mandates.

Recognizing that such symmetrical treatment could constrain strategic capabilities, most sophisticated MNEs eventually made changes. At Unilever, for example, Europe's highly competitive markets and closely linked economies led management to increase the role of European product coordinators gradually until at last, they had direct line responsibility for all operating companies in their businesses. In Latin America, however, national subsidiary managers maintained their historic line management role, and product coordinators acted only as advisers. Unilever has thus moved in sequence from a symmetrical organization managed through a uniformly decentralized federation to a much more differentiated one: differentiating first by product, then by function, and finally by geography.

From Dependence or Independence to Interdependence

As we described in Chapter 4, national subsidiaries in decentralized federation organizations enjoyed considerable independence from the headquarters, whereas those in centralized hub organizations remained strongly dependent on the parent company for resources and capabilities. But the emerging strategic demands—including the need to develop transnational innovation and learning capabilities—make organizational models based on such simple interunit dependence or independence inappropriate. Increasingly, this means they must build the interdependent relationships that are at the heart of the transnational, integrated-network organization.

However, it is not easy to change relationships that have developed over a long period of time and have a history of their own. Most companies found that attempts to improve interunit collaboration by adding layer upon layer of administrative mechanisms to foster greater cooperation were disappointing. Independent units feigned compliance while fiercely protecting their independence, and dependent units discovered that the new cooperative spirit bestowed little more than the right to agree with those on whom they depended.

For an effective interdependent organization to exist, two requirements must be satisfied. First, the company must develop the interdependent configuration of dispersed and specialized resources that we described as an integrated network in Chapter 4. Such an organization model can frame the new roles and responsibilities necessary for worldwide innovation and learning. In this organization, all country subsidiary companies will take on sensing and scanning roles to detect the consumer trends, technological advances, or competitive activities that may trigger a new opportunity or threat. Typically, such information would be fed to those officers or units in the network with primary responsibility for the particular product or technology—a global product manager, a lead country subsidiary, or a center of excellence development operation.

Second, the innovative transnational organization must build interunit integration mechanisms to ensure that task interdependencies lead to the benefits of synergy rather than the paralysis of conflict. Above all else, interunit cooperation requires good interpersonal relations among managers in different units—the headquarters-based business manager must work effectively with the center of excellence technician and the lead country marketing specialist, for example.

The experiences of Ericsson, the Swedish telecommunications company, suggest that the movement of people is one of the strongest mechanisms for breaking down local dogmas. Ericsson achieved this with a longstanding policy of transferring large numbers of people back and forth between headquarters and subsidiaries. Whereas its Japanese competitor NEC may transfer a new technology through a few key managers sent on temporary assignment, Ericsson will send a team of 50 or 100 engineers and managers for a year or two; whereas NEC's flow is primarily from headquarters to subsidiary, Ericsson's is a balanced two-way flow, in which people come to the parent company to both learn and provide their expertise; and whereas NEC's transfers are predominantly Japanese, Ericsson's multidirectional process involves all nationalities.

However, any organization in which there are shared tasks and joint responsibilities requires additional decision-making and conflict-resolution forums. In Ericsson, the often-divergent objectives and interests of the parent company and the local subsidiary are exchanged in the national company's board meetings. Unlike many companies, whose local boards are designed solely to satisfy national legal requirements, Ericsson uses its local boards as legitimate forums for communicating objectives, resolving differences, and making decisions.

From Simple Control to Flexible Coordination

The simplifying assumptions of organizational symmetry and dependence (or independence) allowed the management processes in many companies to be dominated by simple controls—tight operational controls in subsidiaries that depend on the center, or a looser system of administrative controls in decentralized units. But when companies began to challenge the assumptions underlying organizational roles and relationships (for example, when subsidiaries began to take innovative roles that required more collaborative behavior), they found that they also needed to adapt their management processes. The growing interdependence of organizational units strained the simple control-dominated systems and underlined the need to supplement existing processes with more subtle and sophisticated ones.

As MNEs began exploring transnational innovation opportunities simultaneously, they became more diverse and more interdependent. This meant that there was an explosion in the number of issues that had to be linked, reconciled, or integrated. But the costs of coordination are high, in both financial and human terms, and coordinating capabilities are always limited. Still, because a company's administrative heritage often shaped its behavior, most MNEs tended to concentrate on a primary means of coordination and control—"the company's way of doing things."

Then, additional coordination needs required by transnational innovation processes forced many MNEs to develop a coordination system that best fits the needs of various functions and tasks. In doing so, they recognized the need to coordinate some different flows among the organizational units involved in the execution of each task.

Three flows are the lifeblood of any organization but are of particular importance in a transnational company. The first is the flow of goods: the complex interconnections through which companies source their raw materials and other supplies, link the flows of components and subassemblies, and distribute finished goods. The second is the flow of resources, which encompasses not only the allocation of capital and repatriation of dividends, but also the movement of personnel and technological resources throughout the system. The third is the flow of valuable information and knowledge—from raw data and analyzed information to accumulated knowledge and embedded expertise—that companies must diffuse throughout the worldwide network of national units.

It can be very difficult to coordinate the flows of *goods* in a complex integrated network of interdependent operations. But in most companies, this coordination process can be managed effectively at lower levels of the organization through clear procedures and strong systems. For example, within its network of manufacturing plants in different countries, Ericsson learned to coordinate product and material flows by standardizing as many procedures as possible and formalizing the logistics control. In other words, the flow of goods is best achieved through the *formalization* of management processes

It is more difficult to coordinate flows of financial, human, and technological *resources*. Allocation of these scarce resources represents the major strategic choices the company makes; therefore, they must be controlled at the corporate level. We have described the transnational company as an organization of diverse needs and perspectives, many of which conflict and all of which are changing. In such an organization, only managers with an overview of the total situation can make critical decisions about the funding of projects, the sharing of scarce technological resources, and the allocation of organizational skills and capabilities. Managing the flow of resources is a classic example of the need for coordination by *centralization*.

Perhaps the most difficult task is to coordinate the huge flow of strategic information and proprietary *knowledge* required to operate a transnational organization. Much of the most valuable parts of this increasingly vital asset exist in the form of tacit knowledge and embedded expertise. This makes it impossible to coordinate through formal systems or centralized controls. The most effective way to ensure that worldwide organizational units analyze their diverse environments appropriately is to sensitize local managers to broader corporate objectives and priorities, ensuring that they are exposed to the relevant knowledge of values through frequent contacts, or by creating organizational forums that allow for the free exchange of information and foster cross-unit learning. In short, the *socialization* process is the classic solution for the coordination of information flows.

Figure 5-1   Mobilizing knowledge

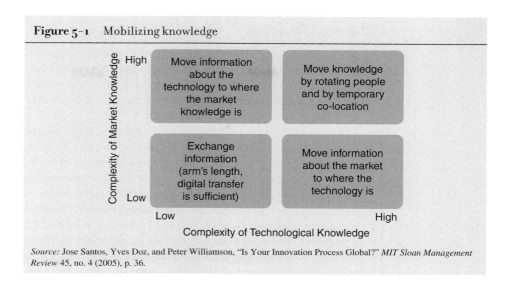

Source: Jose Santos, Yves Doz, and Peter Williamson, "Is Your Innovation Process Global?" *MIT Sloan Management Review* 45, no. 4 (2005), p. 36.

Naturally, none of these broad characterizations of the fit between flows and processes is absolute, and companies use a variety of coordinative mechanisms to manage all three flows. For example, goods flows may be centrally coordinated for products under allocation, when several plants operate at less than capacity, or if the cost structures or host government demand change. And as information flows become routine, they can be coordinated through formalization if appropriate management information systems have been installed.

Realistically, a one-size-fits-all approach to capturing the benefits of innovation will not work in a large MNE. As Figure 5-1 suggests, the most effective way to exploit the knowledge within an organization depends on the complexity of the technology itself and the understanding of the focal market. In practice, the best way to capture innovation is sometimes to move people, and sometimes to move or exchange the information.

Concluding Comments

The approaches to innovation in MNEs have changed considerably. Whereas MNEs once relied on simple models of centralized or localized innovation, the vast majority now find it necessary to build their innovation processes around multiple operating units and geographically disparate sources of knowledge. In this chapter, we identified three generic approaches to innovation, and for each, we identified its typical limitations and the approaches that MNEs can use to overcome them. To be clear, there is no single right way of managing the innovation process in an MNE; each company has its own unique administrative heritage that it cannot and should not disavow. Nonetheless, it is possible to identify certain principles—around the differentiation of roles, interdependence of units, and modes of control—that underpin the development of an effective transnational organization.

Chapter 5 Readings

- In Reading 5-1, "Building Effective R&D Capabilities Abroad," Kuemmerle considers the importance of articulating each foreign R&D site's primary objective, either as a home-base-augmenting laboratory site or a home-base-exploiting laboratory site. He then discusses the three phases associated with each: choosing a location, ramping up, and maximizing lab impact.
- In Reading 5-2, "How to Build Collaborative Advantage," Hansen and Nohria propose that collaboration can be an MNC's source of competitive advantage, especially in an environment where new economies of scope are based on the ability of business units, subsidiaries, and functional departments within the company to collaborate by sharing knowledge and jointly developing new products and services.
- In Reading 5-3, "How GE Is Disrupting Itself," General Electric (GE) CEO Jeff Immelt, along with academics Govindarajan and Trimble, describe how GE has learned to master a process of reverse innovation that allows it to bring low-end products created for emerging markets into wealthy markets. It is an innovation process that is increasingly necessary to compete against the emerging giants from developing countries.

All three of these readings underscore the value in exploiting cross-border knowledge management to create worldwide innovation and learning for competitive advantage.

Case 5-1 Applied Research Technologies, Inc.: Global Innovation's Challenges

Christopher A. Bartlett and Heather Beckham

On June 5, 2006, Peter Vyas paced his office as he grappled with a request for $2 million to re-launch a mini water-oxidation product. Despite two failures to bring this product to market over the past

HBS Professor Christopher A. Bartlett and Heather Beckham prepared this case solely as a basis for class discussion and not as an endorsement, a source of primary data, or an illustration of effective or ineffective management. This case, though based on real events, is fictionalized, and any resemblance to actual persons or entities is coincidental. There are occasional references to actual companies in the narration.

three years, his team was confident this latest iteration was a winner.

For Vyas, general manager of the Filtration Unit of Applied Research Technologies (ART), the request presented a major challenge. He recognized that his team had worked tirelessly to make this project a reality and strongly believed they were now headed in the right direction. But he also understood that the Filtration Unit's track record of failure during this product's development had hurt its credibility. If he supported the proposal, he knew he would be putting on the line not only his own personal credibility but also that of the entire unit.

Due to the project's size, final approval would be made by Vyas's boss, Cynthia Jackson—the newly appointed vice president of ART's Water Management Division. Jackson was acutely aware of the mounting losses in the Filtration Unit, and she had already devoted a significant amount of time trying to get them back on track. She had confided to one of her colleagues:

> When I took on this assignment, I was told my first task was to "fix" the Filtration Unit. The unit only had one revenue-generating product line and had failed to bring a profitable new product to market in five years. It was clear that I was expected to either turn it around or shut it down.
>
> I'm trying to protect them and ensure they get support, but my initial feeling is if they are to survive, they must become much more disciplined. They seem to be making progress on that front, but in all honesty, I sometimes wonder if it is time to cut our losses and initiate a harvest strategy for the unit.

Applied Research Technologies, Inc.

ART was one of the technology world's emerging giants. The company had grown through the merger and acquisition of numerous technology-based industrial companies, acquired in the LBO buyout waves of the 1980s and 1990s.

By 2006, ART consisted of a portfolio of about 60 business units, each of which operated as a profit center. Total corporate revenue was $11 billion in 2006.[1] Major divisions in the corporation included Healthcare (medical diagnostic equipment), Industrial Automation (robotics), Energy (extraction, conversion, and transportation solutions for the oil and gas industry—including the Water Management Division), and HVAC (Heating Ventilation and Air Conditioning, including climate control solutions for residential, commercial, and industrial markets). **Exhibit 1** shows the organization structure of the company.

The company's success had been built on its innovative and entrepreneurial culture, coupled with a decentralized management philosophy. ART's

vision statement, proudly displayed in almost every office and cubicle, stated: "We aim to change the world through innovation, and to grow our place in it through entrepreneurship."

Culture and Practices   ART was dedicated to supporting innovation not only with funding (the company's R&D spending was double the rate for U.S. industrial companies), but also in its practices, several of which were deeply embedded in the company's culture. ART encouraged employees to spend a half day each week "experimenting, brainstorming, and thinking outside the box." It was a practice that the company's visionary founder and current CEO, David Hall, referred to as "tinker time." He explained the concept:

> Innovation and entrepreneurship are the twin engines driving this company. It's the reason we've ingrained "tinker time" in our culture ... I expect all our managers, and particularly those on the front line, to create, promote, and back promising ideas. But we understand that when you go for the big leap, you won't always clear the bar. So there is no shame in failure when you are stretching for big objectives. Around here we routinely celebrate what we call "worthy attempts"—even when they are unsuccessful.

Knowledge sharing and dissemination was another key part of ART's business philosophy, and despite the high level of decentralization and profit accountability, technology and human capital were both widely shared among divisions. For example, experts in one division routinely served as advisors on project committees for other divisions, and it was not uncommon for employees to go "on loan" to help another unit with a promising product idea or technology.

The company also moved quickly to bring products to market. If an idea showed promise, funding was usually available for small "beta batch" productions, which often allowed market testing to achieve what was called "proof of concept" within ART. Once an innovation was proven, significant investment was quickly put behind it.

Objectives and Priorities   To infuse discipline into its decentralized organization, ART's top

---

[1] Of that total, Water Management Division sales were $560 million and Filtration Unit sales were $38 million.

Exhibit 1   ART Organization with Filtration Unit Detail

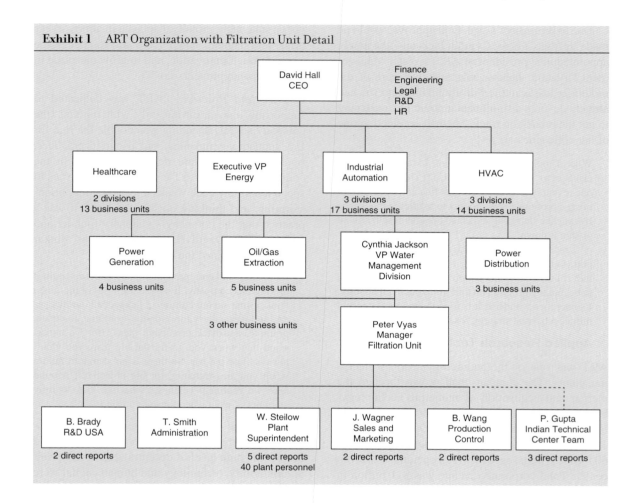

management set highly aggressive performance objectives and tied executive compensation tightly to them. In 2006, as in any other year, each division was expected to deliver sales growth of 10%, pretax margins of 15%, and return on invested capital of 20%, referred to as the "10/15/20 Target." The belief that innovative products were the source of the company's ongoing competitive advantage was reflected in a companywide metric requiring 30% of each division's total sales come from products developed in the last four years.[2]

[2]Hall had recently increased this target from 25% of each unit's sales from products developed in the last five years.

Hall also continually emphasized that to be competitive, ART had to shorten the life cycle between a new technology's conception and its commercialization. In response, the company had introduced the "Fast Track Pipeline," a program that focused on the highest priority projects by providing them with additional resources and management attention. ART currently had 67 such projects in the pipeline, six in the Water Division, but none in the Filtration Unit. (The mini oxidation unit had not been identified as a "Fast Track" project).

In the late 1990s, Hall began pushing to grow ART's global presence. "It's important not just to expand our market access, but also to broaden our talent access," he insisted. "Innovation and entrepreneurship know no national boundaries." In the quest to meet this challenge "to attract the best and the brightest wherever they live," in 2000, the corporate R&D group opened the India Technical Center (ITC)—a substantial operation that Hall hoped would become a model for other R&D centers he planned to open up around the globe.

The Filtration Business Unit

The Filtration Unit was part of a business ART acquired from an oil and gas services company in 1996. Its core product line was in mobile water treatment that allowed oil and gas exploration companies to meet government water recycling requirements at well heads and drilling sites. These products were still the unit's core line, but in the late 1990s, new competition from Chinese manufacturers had led to a commoditization of the business and an erosion of margins. ART's newly acquired filtration business had tried to develop the next generation of products and technologies, but after two high-profile new product failures, the unit had lost confidence. By 2006, it was losing about $6 million annually.

New Management, New Energy   In a promotion from his role as a lab manager in the HVAC Division, the 32-year-old Vyas had assumed the role of business manager for the Filtration Unit in June 2001. He immediately confronted the unit's twin organizational problems of low morale and growing turnover, and in his first year, rebuilt the team by carefully selecting entrepreneurial-minded individuals to fill the vacancies left by turnover in the unit. One of his key recruits was Janice Wagner, whom he knew from her five years as a marketing manager in the HVAC Division. She was excited to join a unit that had an opportunity to develop a new business from scratch.

Convinced that survival depended on innovative growth, Vyas appointed a technology evaluation team early in his tenure, charging them with the responsibility to focus on technologies with the

potential to turn the unit around. In one of his first reviews with that team, Vyas learned that for almost a year, the filtration unit had been working with ITC technicians on an exciting new technology the young Indian team had developed based on a license obtained from a Delhi-based start-up company. Developed as a potential solution to the widespread Third World problem of obtaining clean water in remote regions, this small-scale oxidation system was thought to have application in many less-developed markets. But in an effort to cut costs, the filtration unit's previous management had decided to abandon the collaboration a year earlier.

After reviewing the technology, Vyas became convinced that this had been a mistake and encouraged his evaluation team to pursue the project. Working closely with the ITC technologists, the team concluded that the oxidation technology was the most promising opportunity in their portfolio, and recommended developing a small-scale oxidation system that enabled waste-water disinfection in small batches. "We were so excited by that decision," said Div Verma, the ITC technologist in charge of the project. "We believe this project can make a huge difference to the lives of millions."

Motivated by the support they received, the ITC technicians developed a promising initial design. Without bulky equipment (the equipment was a 26-inch cube) or an electrical power source (it utilized battery power), this small system could transform waste water into potable water without chemicals in minutes. A single unit had the capacity to process approximately 2,000 liters of contaminated water per day. With pride, they took their design to Vyas.

But Vyas wanted to understand the business opportunity and asked Wagner to prepare a brief overview. Wagner learned that only about 2.5% of the world's water was fresh, and most of that was frozen. Population growth, industrial development, and agricultural expansion were all putting pressure on fresh-water supplies in both developed and developing countries. Indeed, the World Resources Institute found that demand for water was growing at twice the rate of the population. As a result, the World Health Organization estimated that over 1.1 billion people lacked access to clean water, and that 2.4 billion lacked access to basic sanitation. The research also revealed that water-borne diseases accounted for 80% of infections in the developing world, and in 2002, 3.1 million deaths occurred (90% children) as a result of diarrheal diseases and malaria. As countries such as India and China industrialized, they used more fresh water and added more pollution to existing water sources.

Wagner concluded that the scarcity of clean water was reaching crisis levels in developing nations, and that the mini-oxidation system could help avert some of the catastrophic effects. But she also reported comparable R&D efforts also underway in the government and private sectors in China and Europe, and that several companies in the United States and Canada were researching the technology. Nevertheless, her analysis suggested the ITC team's product was further along and probably superior to anything else in the space.

New Opportunities, New Initiatives   Vyas decided to pursue the project and convinced the VP of Corporate R&D who had ITC oversight to allow the three ITC technologists working on it to become members of his technical team—a move that would allow them to focus on developing commercial designs for the oxidation technology. Simultaneously, he asked Wagner to do a first-cut market assessment to identify potential opportunities for the technology. Over the next few weeks, through focus groups and interviews with potential customers, she uncovered several promising applications. (See **Exhibit 2**).

But while the market research was exciting, progress in bringing a product to market proved to be slow and difficult. From January 2003 to February 2006, the technology team coordinated with separate manufacturing and marketing teams located in the United States to work through two complete cycles of product development, beta batch productions, and test marketing of two different versions of the mini-oxidation system. Both

---

Exhibit 2   Wagner's List of Potential Markets

Developing Nations
- Provide potable water solutions for areas with unsafe drinking water

U.S. Residential
- Landscape irrigation
- Pools
- In-house water recirculation for non-drinking purposes (e.g., laundry, dishwashers, etc.)

U.S. Commercial
- Restaurants
- Grocery stores
- Laundromats
- Linen/Uniform companies
- Farms
- Landscape irrigation

U.S. and Overseas Emergency Units
- Disaster relief
- Military

---

failed due to what were subsequently revealed to be defects in the design and lack of interest in the marketplace.

The first-generation product was aimed at the application for which the technology was originally developed—to provide developing nations with safe drinking water. Largely supported by foreign aid, the mini-oxidation system was field-tested by representatives from funding agencies. Unfortunately, the output water had a detectable odor which the funders found unacceptable. Despite assurances that ITC technicians could fix the problem, the trials failed to convert into orders.

The team decided to refocus a second-generation product on specialized applications in Western countries where funding was more available. The plan was to develop a slightly modified version of the product and aim it at a potential market for military use and NGO disaster relief activities that Wagner had identified in her initial analysis. This decision was enormously disappointing to the

Indian technologists who had developed the initial prototypes, and Vyas had to work hard to keep them on board. The second-generation product fixed the odor problem, but field trials showed that the solution caused the unit to consume too much power, requiring frequent battery replacement. Once again, no orders were forthcoming.

While these trials were occurring, the filtration unit's small R&D team in the United States persuaded Vyas to allow them to work with corporate R&D on an entirely new version of the product that would utilize ultrasound waves for water disinfection. High frequency vibrations were shown to control the growth of algae, organic waste, and bacteria such as E. coli. Market applications for this technology included treatment for clean water storage receptacles, public/private ponds, fish tanks, and ballast water. However, in 2006 this technology was still in the earliest stages of research and testing.

New Oversight, New Discipline In January 2006, just as Vyas and the rest of the mini-oxidation team were launching their second-generation system, Cynthia Jackson was appointed vice president of the Water Management Division. Jackson's attention was soon drawn to the troubled Filtration Unit which she felt needed to put much more rigor into the planning and analysis that supported their product development activities. According to Jackson:

> Peter Vyas seems to be an excellent talent manager. He was able to recruit and retain good people to his unit, and then build them into highly motivated teams on two different continents. He's also shown himself to be an outstanding advocate for the group's ideas—skilled at managing upward, gaining support, and running interference so his team can concentrate on the task at hand. And I'm aware that the company has high hopes for the Filtration Unit, but the results just are not there.
>
> In my view, the unit lacks discipline. They had a promising technology that was in search of a market, but had not done the work to nail down either. In the first meeting I had with them I explained that they would be developing any future proposals using a rigorous three-phase process linking market analysis and technological development to business planning.

In her first meeting with Vyas, Jackson also made it clear that the unit's continued existence was in jeopardy if they did not turn things around.

Mini-Oxidation's Third Launch Attempt

To coordinate the third launch of the mini-oxidation system, Vyas assembled a single six-person development team with representatives from various functions located in the United States and India. Because Janice Wagner had demonstrated strong project management skills, Vyas named her as the team leader. (**Exhibit 3** details committee membership.) From the outset, the team was highly committed to the product and worked tirelessly to complete Jackson's three-phase process.

Phase 1: General Product Concept and Market Analysis Wagner took the lead in preparing the Phase 1 requirement "to develop a general product concept supported by market research." Having learned that the unit lacked the expertise to sell to developing markets, governments, and NGOs, she decided to focus additional research on U.S. data that seemed to indicate strong potential for a residential water purification system. She also decided to see if opportunities might exist in domestic agricultural applications.

Exhibit 3 ART Mini Water Oxidation System—Development Committee Team Structure

New Product Introduction Team Members	
D. Verma	Laboratory Leader—Indian Technical Center
R. Patel	Product Development—Indian Technical Center
B. Wang	Manufacturing
H. Lewis	Quality Assurance
J. Wagner	Marketing (TEAM LEADER)
T. Smith	Project Administration
C. Cortez[a]	HVAC Division Representative
G. Steinberg[a]	Healthcare Division Representative

[a]Member from another unit of ART added in Phase 2

According to the Palmer Drought Index from April of 2006, 26% of the United States was considered in moderate to extreme drought conditions, and Wagner's research showed that low rainfall, high wind, and rapid population growth in the Western and Southeastern regions of the country caused a major water scarcity problem for these areas. The resulting government-imposed water restrictions often led to severe limitations or outright bans of water used in residential landscape irrigation. Because re-use of waste water would serve conservation efforts while preserving residential landscaping, Wagner felt that the mini-oxidation system offered a perfect solution for the needs of homeowners in these drought-stricken areas. In addition, since the product would be used for irrigation and not for drinking water, the disinfection quality could be lowered and energy consumption would therefore be reduced compared to past product iterations.

Wagner's research on the U.S. water industry indicated that the domestic water-treatment equipment market generated sales of over $9 billion. (**Exhibit 4** provides selected data from the research.) Residential water treatment -products ranged from water filters that reduced sediment, rust, and chlorine odor (average retail price $50) to systems that provided more comprehensive household water purification (retail price $1,500 to $3,000). The research also showed that in-ground sprinkler systems cost between $1,800 and $4,000, and after conducting some industry interviews and focus groups, Wagner felt this was a good barometer of what a homeowner was willing to pay for a lush, green lawn.

After discussing the product concept with the development committee members, the team decided to recommend a retail price of $2,000 ($1,000 wholesale price) for a residential irrigation mini-oxidation system (RIMOS) capable of supporting a

Exhibit 4   Market Research: Summary Data

The U.S. Water Industry (Revenues in millions)[a]

Water Treatment Equipment	$9,110
Delivery Equipment	$11,660
Chemicals	$4,020
Contract Operations	$2,350
Consulting/Engineering	$7,460
Maintenance Services	$1,780
Instruments and Testing	$1,400
Wastewater Utilities	$34,130
Drinking Water Utilitiess	$35,070
Total U.S. Water Industry	**$106,980**

U.S. Residences (2000 Census)

Total Housing Units	116 million
Single-Family Detached Homes	70 million

Drought Indicators (Palmer Drought Index 4/10/2006)

% of the continuous U.S. in severe to extreme drought	13%
% of the continuous U.S. in moderate to extreme drought	26%

Note: Mini-Oxidation Systems are a "new-to-the-world" product with unknown market potential.
[a]*Source:* Adapted from the Environmental Business Journal, 2006.

10,000 square-foot lawn. Pricing for an agricultural irrigation large oxidation system (AILOS) would be significantly less on a per-acre basis, with details to be developed only after further research had been done. Wagner and Vyas compiled the data and product concept information in a formal proposal for Jackson to approve.

Jackson responded to the team's Phase 1 proposal with a flurry of questions and challenges. She highlighted the sparseness of concrete market numbers and their lack of data on target markets. And when the team floated the idea of designing a larger-scale agricultural version of the system, she asked them to think about whether that would stretch resources too thin. With the whole company under pressure to trim budgets, Jackson asked the team to consider reducing the project's costs by eliminating either the RIMOS or AILOS product. After some discussion, Vyas and his team agreed to focus future product development and marketing efforts on the RIMOS product for the U.S. market.

Phase 2: Technical Specifications and Prototype

Having won the approval of Phase 1, the team was now ready to begin the second phase of Jackson's product development process. This involved designing actual product specifications and determining how to do this within the $1,000 wholesale price point that the group had determined was appropriate. A working prototype was also to be created as part of this phase.

The team relied heavily on ITC expertise to adapt the existing product originally designed to provide potable water in remote locations, to one capable of processing wastewater for lawn irrigation. During this phase, several misunderstandings surfaced between team members in the United States and India. For example, Wagner became concerned when the Indian team repeatedly missed design deadlines she had requested. When she confronted Div Verma, the lab leader responsible for the project, he responded tersely:

> Peter told us he wanted the new design to be flawless. I take that as my number one priority. We can't meet this deliverable without proper testing. Why is everything so rushed with you? If we don't have a perfect design, then we run the risk of failing a third time and that is not acceptable. My team will not provide designs for a prototype until we are sure that all the bugs have been worked out. We don't want to be involved in another failure.

Emphasizing the mandate to move quickly while ensuring product quality, Vyas mediated the disagreement by crafting a compromise that gave the Indian technical team a formal schedule allowing them two weeks of extra testing time. "I felt there was a mix of disappointment and pride that had to be dealt with," said Vyas. "I also told Div that this third generation product would give us the credibility to return to the developing world project." Once the prototype was finished, the final designs and specs were again submitted for review.

Jackson was impressed by the attention to detail in this latest iteration, but wanted to ensure that the team was fully utilizing the internal expertise available at ART. With Jackson's help, Vyas tapped engineers and manufacturing managers from the HVAC and Healthcare Divisions who had expertise his team was lacking. He invited them to join his development team, and they quickly became deeply engaged in the project. They identified several design changes and production specifications that increased efficiency and lowered manufacturing costs.

Phase 3: Business Plan

The development of the business plan was the most difficult phase for Vyas and his team. They were unaccustomed to creating complex sales forecast models and cost estimates. But eventually they developed a detailed product concept, marketing approach, and manufacturing strategy for RIMOS, as well as sales forecasts, cost projections, and expense estimates. They also acknowledged that they still believed there was a significant market in water treatment for the developing world and in emergency relief work, but these future options had not been included in the current forecasts or business plan. They hoped to explore these with the help of the Oil and Gas Division which had excellent international contacts.

Exhibit 5   Summary Sales and Profit Forecast for RIMOS

	2007	2008	2009	2010	2011
Forecast Sales ($ millions)	$5.45	$7.08	$8.86	$10.89	$13.07
Forecast Operating Income (%)	10%	15%	20%	20%	20%

Exhibit 6   Summary Risk Analysis and Risk Mitigation for RIMOS

Risk	Level	Plan
May not gain market acceptance	High	–Ensure HVAC distribution support –Highlight ART name –Supplement marketing budget for product launch
Product design flaws	Medium	–Monitor beta batch closely
Price point too high	Medium	–Quantify customer savings from increased water efficiency –Provide sales training to distributors
Emerging competition	Low	–Get to market first –Leverage ART global presence, technical support, supplier relationships, and distribution network

Jackson challenged the team's pro forma financials which she felt lacked the data to support their assumptions. She asked the team to perform additional due diligence and to justify their assumptions. She also pushed back on the projected sales assumptions and suggested that the pro forma financials needed to be stress-tested. But after testing the analysis, Wagner felt her research was sound and was adamant about the size of the opportunity and their ability to capture the market. Vyas stood by Wagner and also defended the financial data which he felt had been carefully developed by the manufacturing and technology experts. **Exhibit 5** summarizes the team's sales and operating margin forecasts.

The team acknowledged that its assumptions relied on the ability to gain access to the HVAC Group's Residential Market Division. As Wagner pointed out, ART's norms encouraged them to take advantage of these types of synergies, and they had good contacts in the division. However, the HVAC Residential Market Division's senior executives had full discretion regarding the products distributed through its channels, and they had not yet made a formal decision about RIMOS.

Jackson also expressed her concerns with the $2,000 retail price point and pushed Vyas to clearly identify the risks associated with the plan. After further consideration, the team developed a risk assessment and response matrix, which they included in the business plan (**Exhibit 6**). The business plan revealed the need for $2 million in funding for beta batch production of RIMOS and the marketing budget to support its distribution and promotion.

Toward a Decision: Go or No Go?

An hour after receiving the investment proposal from his team, Vyas was still pacing back and forth trying to decide whether to support or reject their request for the $2 million in funding for RIMOS. He knew his development team was absolutely convinced it could succeed, but he also realized that the unit's existence and even his own career were being openly questioned.

Two floors above Vyas's office, Jackson was also contemplating the RIMOS project. Having heard through the company grapevine that a funding request had been submitted to Vyas, she began to think about how she would handle the request if it was sent up to her. She had heard rumblings from other managers in her division that the Filtration Unit was a drain on division resources and that it was time to pull the plug on any additional funding.

As a newly promoted division VP, Jackson understood that her actions would be closely watched. She wanted to make sure she did not drop the ball.

Case 5-2   P&G Japan: The SK-II Globalization Project

Christopher A. Bartlett

In November 1999, Paolo de Cesare was preparing for a meeting with the Global Leadership Team (GLT) of P&G's Beauty Care Global Business Unit (GBU) to present his analysis of whether SK-II, a prestige skin care line from Japan, should become a global P&G brand. As president of Max Factor Japan, the hub of P&G's fast-growing cosmetics business in Asia, and previous head of its European skin care business, de Cesare had considerable credibility with the GLT. Yet, as he readily acknowledged, there were significant risks in his proposal to expand SK-II into China and Europe.

Chairing the GLT meeting was Alan ("A. G.") Lafley, head of P&G's Beauty Care GBU, to which de Cesare reported. In the end, it was his organization—and his budget—that would support such a global expansion. Although he had been an early champion of SK-II in Japan, Lafley would need strong evidence to support P&G's first-ever proposal to expand a Japanese brand worldwide. After all, SK-II's success had been achieved in a culture where the consumers, distribution channels, and competitors were vastly different from those in most other countries.

Another constraint facing de Cesare was that P&G's global organization was in the midst of the bold but disruptive Organization 2005 restructuring program. As GBUs took over profit responsibility historically held by P&G's country-based organizations, management was still trying to negotiate their new working relationships. In this context, de Cesare, Lafley, and other GLT members struggled to answer some key questions: Did SK-II have the potential to develop into a major global brand? If so, which markets were the most important to enter now? And how should this be implemented in P&G's newly reorganized global operations?

P&G's Internationalization: Engine of Growth

De Cesare's expansion plans for a Japanese product was just the latest step in a process of internationalization that had begun three-quarters of a century earlier. But it was the creation of the Overseas Division in 1948 that drove three decades of rapid expansion. Growing first in Europe, then Latin America and Asia, by 1980 P&G's operations in 27 overseas countries accounted for over 25% of its $11 billion worldwide sales. (**Exhibit 1** summarizes P&G's international expansion.)

Exhibit 1   P&G's Internationalization Timetable

Year	Markets Entered
1837–1930	United States and Canada
1930–1940	United Kingdom, Philippines
1940–1950	Puerto Rico, Venezuela, Mexico
1950–1960	Switzerland, France, Belgium, Italy, Peru, Saudi Arabia, Morocco
1960–1970	Germany, Greece, Spain, Netherlands, Sweden, Austria, Indonesia, Malaysia, Hong Kong, Singapore, Japan
1970–1980	Ireland
1980–1990	Colombia, Chile, Caribbean, Guatemala, Kenya, Egypt, Thailand, Australia, New Zealand, India, Taiwan, South Korea, Pakistan, Turkey, Brazil, El Salvador
1990–2000	Russia, China, Czech Republic, Hungary, Poland, Slovak Republic, Bulgaria, Belarus, Latvia, Estonia, Romania, Lithuania, Kazakhstan, Yugoslavia, Croatia, Uzbekistan, Ukraine, Slovenia, Nigeria, South Africa, Denmark, Portugal, Norway, Argentina, Yemen, Sri Lanka, Vietnam, Bangladesh, Costa Rica, Turkmenistan

Source: Company records.

Local Adaptiveness Meets Cross-Market Integration   Throughout its early expansion, the company adhered to a set of principles set down by Walter Lingle, the first vice president of overseas operations. "We must tailor our products to meet consumer demands in each nation," he said. "But we must create local country subsidiaries whose structure, policies, and practices are as exact a replica of the U.S. Procter & Gamble organization as it is possible to create." Under the Lingle principles, the company soon built a portfolio of self-sufficient subsidiaries run by country general managers (GMs) who grew their companies by adapting P&G technology and marketing expertise to their knowledge of their local markets.

Yet, by the 1980s, two problems emerged. First, the cost of running all the local product development labs and manufacturing plants was limiting profits. And second, the ferocious autonomy of national subsidiaries was preventing the global rollout of new products and technology improvements. Local GMs often resisted such initiatives due to the negative impact they had on local profits, for which the country subsidiaries were held accountable. As a result, new products could take a decade or more to be introduced worldwide.

Consequently, during the 1980s, P&G's historically "hands-off" regional headquarters became more active. In Europe, for example, Euro Technical Teams were formed to eliminate needless country-by-country product differences, reduce duplicated development efforts, and gain consensus on new-technology diffusion. Subsequently, regionwide coordination spread to purchasing, finance, and even marketing. In particular, the formation of Euro Brand Teams became an effective forum for marketing managers to coordinate regionwide product strategy and new product rollouts.

By the mid-1980s, these overlaid coordinating processes were formalized when each of the three European regional vice presidents was also given coordinative responsibility for a product category. While these individuals clearly had organizational influence, profit responsibility remained with the country subsidiary GMs. (See **Exhibit 2** for the 1986 European organization.)

Birth of Global Management   In 1986, P&G's seven divisions in the U.S. organization were broken into 26 product categories, each with its own product development, product supply, and sales and marketing capabilities. Given the parallel development of a European category management structure, it was not a big leap to appoint the first

Exhibit 2   P&G European Organization, 1986

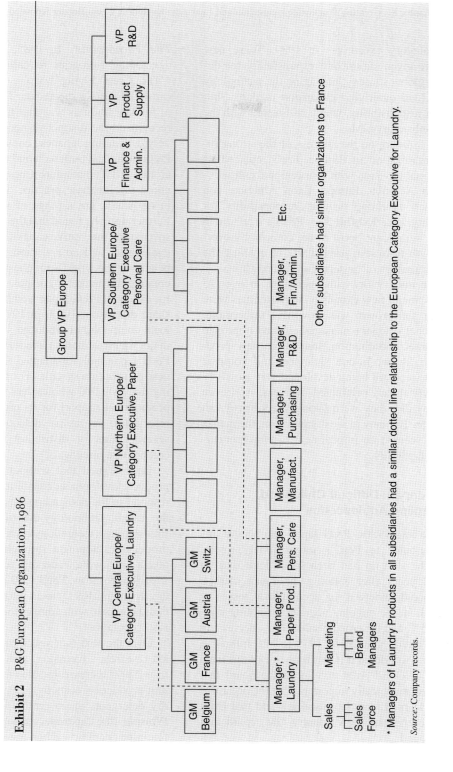

* Managers of Laundry Products in all subsidiaries had a similar dotted line relationship to the European Category Executive for Laundry.

Source: Company records.

397

global category executives in 1989. These new roles were given significant responsibility for developing global strategy, managing the technology program, and qualifying expansion markets—but not profit responsibility, which still rested with the country subsidiary GMs.

Then, building on the success of the strong regional organization in Europe, P&G replaced its International Division with four regional entities—for North America, Europe, Latin America, and Asia—each assuming primary responsibility for profitability. (See **Exhibit 3** for P&G's structure in 1990.) A significant boost in the company's overseas growth followed, particularly in opening the untapped markets of Eastern Europe and China.

By the mid-1990s, with operations in over 75 countries, major new expansion opportunities were shrinking and growth was slowing. Furthermore, while global category management had improved cross-market coordination, innovative new products such as two-in-one shampoo and compact detergent were still being developed very slowly—particularly if they originated overseas. And even when they did, they were taking years to roll out worldwide. To many in the organization, the matrix structure seemed an impediment to entrepreneurship and flexibility.

P&G Japan: Difficult Childhood, Struggling Adolescence

Up to the mid-1980s, P&G Japan had been a minor contributor to P&G's international growth. Indeed, the start-up had been so difficult that, in 1984, 12 years after entering the Japan market, P&G's board reviewed the accumulated losses of $200 million, the ongoing negative operating margins of 75%, and the eroding sales base—decreasing from 44 billion yen (¥) in 1979 to ¥26 billion in 1984—and wondered if it was time to exit this market. But CEO Ed Artzt convinced the board that Japan was strategically important, that the organization had learned from its mistakes—and that Durk Jager, the energetic new country GM, could turn things around.

The Turnaround In 1985, as the first step in developing a program he called "Ichidai Hiyaku" ("The Great Flying Leap"), Jager analyzed the causes of P&G's spectacular failure in Japan. One of his key findings was that the company had not recognized the distinctive needs and habits of the very demanding Japanese consumer. (For instance, P&G Japan had built its laundry-detergent business around All Temperature Cheer, a product that ignored the Japanese practice of doing the laundry in tap water, not a range of water temperatures.) Furthermore, he found that the company had not respected the innovative capability of Japanese companies such as Kao and Lion, which turned out to be among the world's toughest competitors. (After creating the market for disposable diapers in Japan, for example, P&G Japan watched Pampers' market share drop from 100% in 1979 to 8% in 1985 as local competitors introduced similar products with major improvements.) And Jager concluded that P&G Japan had not adapted to the complex Japanese distribution system. (For instance, after realizing that its 3,000 wholesalers were providing little promotional support for its products, the company resorted to aggressive discounting that triggered several years of distributor disengagement and competitive price wars.)

Jager argued that without a major in-country product development capability, P&G could never respond to the demanding Japanese consumer and the tough, technology-driven local competitors. Envisioning a technology center that would support product development throughout Asia and even take a worldwide leadership role, he persuaded his superiors to grow P&G's 60-person research and development (R&D) team into an organization that could compete with competitor Kao's 2,000-strong R&D operation.

Over the next four years, radical change in market research, advertising, and distribution resulted in a 270% increase in sales that, in turn, reduced unit production costs by 62%. In 1988, with laundry detergents again profitable and Pampers and Whisper (the Japanese version of P&G's Always feminine napkin) achieving market leadership,

Exhibit 3 P&G's Worldwide Organizational Structure, 1990

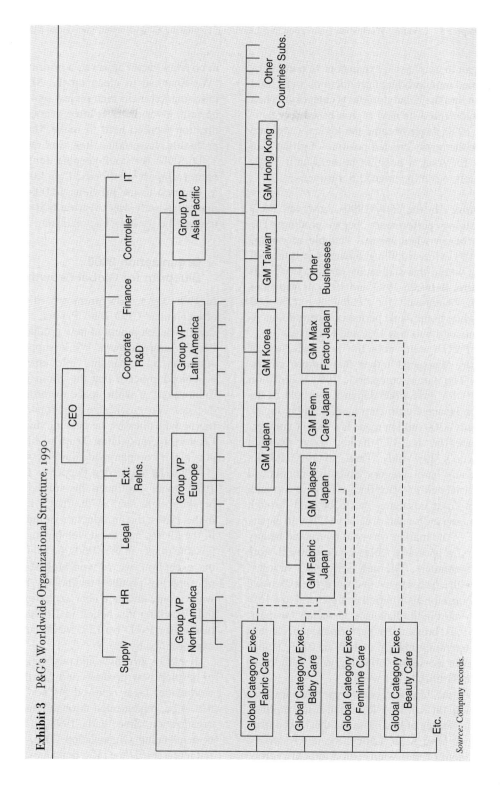

Source: Company records.

Jager began to emphasize expansion. In particular, he promoted more product introductions and a bold expansion into the beauty products category. When P&G implemented its new region-based reorganization in 1990, Jager became the logical candidate to assume the newly created position of group vice president for Asia, a position he held until 1991, when he left to run the huge U.S. business.

The Relapse   In the early 1990s, however, P&G Japan's strong performance began eroding. The problems began when Japan's "bubble economy" burst in 1991. More troubling, however, was the fact that, even within this stagnating market, P&G was losing share. Between 1992 and 1996 its yen sales fell 3% to 4% annually for a cumulative 20% total decline, while in the same period competitor Unicharm's annual growth was 13% and Kao's was 3%.

Even P&G's entry into the new category of beauty care worsened rather than improved the situation. The parent company's 1991 acquisition of Max Factor gave P&G Japan a foothold in the $10 billion Japanese cosmetics market. But in Japan, sales of only $300 million made it a distant number-five competitor, its 3% market share dwarfed by Shiseido's 20% plus. Then, in 1992 P&G's global beauty care category executive announced the global launch of Max Factor Blue, a top-end, self-select color cosmetic line to be sold through general merchandise and drug stores. But in Japan, over 80% of the market was sold by trained beauty counselors in specialty stores or department store cosmetics counters. The new self-select strategy, coupled with a decision to cut costs in the expensive beauty-counselor distribution channel, led to a 15% decline in sales in the Japanese cosmetics business. The previous break-even performance became a negative operating margin of 10% in 1993. Things became even worse the following year, with losses running at $1 million per week.

In 1994, the Japanese beauty care business lost $50 million on sales of less than $300 million. Among the scores of businesses in the 15 countries reporting to him, A. G. Lafley, the newly arrived vice president of the Asian region, quickly zeroed

in on Max Factor Japan as a priority problem area. "We first had to clean up the Max Factor Blue mass-market mess then review our basic strategy," he said. Over the next three years, the local organization worked hard to make Max Factor Japan profitable. Its product line was rationalized from 1,400 SKUs (or stock-keeping units) to 500, distribution support was focused on 4,000 sales outlets as opposed to the previous 10,000, and sales and marketing staff was cut from 600 to 150. It was a trying time for Max Factor Japan.

Organization 2005: Blueprint for Global Growth

In 1996 Jager, now promoted to chief operating officer under CEO John Pepper, signaled that he saw the development of new products as the key to P&G's future growth. While supporting Pepper's emphasis on expanding into emerging markets, he voiced concern that the company would "start running out of white space towards the end of the decade." To emphasize the importance of creating new businesses, he became the champion of a Leadership Innovation Team to identify and support major companywide innovations.

When he succeeded Pepper as CEO in January 1999, Jager continued his mission. Citing P&G breakthroughs such as the first synthetic detergent in the 1930s, the introduction of fluoride toothpaste in the 1950s, and the development of the first disposable diaper in the 1960s, he said, "Almost without exception, we've won biggest on the strength of superior product technology... But frankly, we've come nowhere near exploiting its full potential." Backing this belief, in 1999 he increased the budget for R&D by 12% while cutting marketing expenditures by 9%.

If P&G's growth would now depend on its ability to develop new products and roll them out rapidly worldwide, Jager believed his new strategic thrust had to be implemented through a radically different organization. Since early 1998 he and Pepper had been planning Organization 2005, an initiative he felt represented "the most dramatic change to P&G's

structure, processes, and culture in the company's history." Implementing O2005, as it came to be called, he promised would bring 13% to 15% annual earnings growth and would result in $900 million in annual savings starting in 2004. Implementation would be painful, he warned; in the first five years, it called for the closing of 10 plants and the loss of 15,000 jobs—13% of the worldwide workforce. The cost of the restructuring was estimated at $1.9 billion, with $1 billion of that total forecast for 1999 and 2000.

Changing the Culture   During the three months prior to assuming the CEO role, Jager toured company facilities worldwide. He concluded that P&G's sluggish 2% annual volume growth and its loss of global market share was due to a culture he saw as slow, conformist, and risk averse. (See **Exhibit 4** for P&G's financial performance.) In his view, employees were wasting half their time on "non-value-added work" such as memo writing, form filling, or chart preparation, slowing down decisions and making the company vulnerable to more nimble competition. (One observer described P&G's product development model as "ready, aim, aim, aim, aim, fire.") He concluded that any organizational change would have to be built on a cultural revolution.

With "stretch, innovation, and speed" as his watchwords, Jager signaled his intent to shake up norms and practices that had shaped generations of highly disciplined, intensely loyal managers often referred to within the industry as "Proctoids." "Great ideas come from conflict and dissatisfaction with the status quo," he said. "I'd like an organization where there are rebels." To signal the importance of risk taking and speed, Jager gave a green light to the Leadership Innovation Team to implement a global rollout of two radically new products: Dryel, a home dry-cleaning kit; and Swiffer, an electrostatically charged dust mop. Just 18 months after entering their first test market, they were on sale in the United States, Europe, Latin America, and Asia. Jager promised 20 more new products over the next 18 months. "And if you are worried about oversight," he said, "I am the portfolio manager."

Changing the Processes   Reinforcing the new culture were some major changes to P&G's traditional systems and processes. To emphasize the need for greater risk taking, Jager leveraged the performance-based component of compensation so that, for example, the variability of a vice president's annual pay package increased from a traditional range of 20% (10% up or down) to 80% (40% up or down). And to motivate people and align them with the overall success of the company, he extended the reach of the stock option plan from senior management to virtually all employees. Even outsiders were involved, and P&G's advertising agencies soon found their compensation linked to sales increases per dollar spent.

Another major systems shift occurred in the area of budgets. Jager felt that the annual ritual of preparing, negotiating, and revising line item sales and expenses by product and country was enormously time wasting and energy sapping. In future, they would be encouraged to propose ambitious stretch objectives. And going forward, Jager also argued to replace the episodic nature of separate marketing, payroll, and initiative budgets with an integrated business planning process where all budget elements of the operating plan could be reviewed and approved together.

Changing the Structure   In perhaps the most drastic change introduced in O2005, primary profit responsibility shifted from P&G's four regional organizations to seven global business units (GBUs) that would now manage product development, manufacturing, and marketing of their respective categories worldwide. The old regional organizations were reconstituted into seven market development organizations (MDOs) that assumed responsibility for local implementation of the GBUs' global strategies.[1] And transactional activities such as accounting, human resources, payroll, and much of IT were coordinated through a global business service unit (GBS). (See **Exhibit 5** for a representation of the new structure.)

---

[1] In an exception to the shift of profit responsibility to the GBUs, the MDOs responsible for developing countries were treated as profit centers.

Exhibit 4 P&G Select Financial Performance Data, 1980–1999

Annual Income Statement ($ millions)	June 1999	June 1998	June 1997	June 1996	June 1995	June 1990	June 1985	June 1980
Sales	38,125	37,154	35,764	35,284	33,434	24,081	13,552	10,772
Cost of Goods Sold	18,615	19,466	18,829	19,404	18,370	14,658	9,099	7,471
Gross Profit	19,510	17,688	16,935	15,880	15,064	9,423	4,453	3,301
Selling, General, and Administrative Expense	10,628	10,035	9,960	9,707	9,632	6,262	3,099	1,977
of which:								
Research and Development Expense	1,726	1,546	1,469	1,399	1,148	693	400	228
Advertising Expense	3,538	3,704	3,466	3,254	3,284	2,059	1,105	621
Depreciation, Depletion, and Amortization	2,148	1,598	1,487	1,358	1,253	859	378	196
Operating Profit	6,734	6,055	5,488	4,815	4,179	2,302	976	1,128
Interest Expense	650	548	457	493	511	395	165	97
Non-Operating Income/Expense	235	201	218	272	409	561	193	51
Special Items	−481	0	0	75	−77	0	0	0
Total Income Taxes	2,075	1,928	1,834	1,623	1,355	914	369	440
Net Income	3,763	3,780	3,415	3,046	2,645	1,554	635	642
Geographic Breakdown: Net Sales								
Americas	58.4%	54.7%	53.8%	52.9%	55.1%	62.5%	75.4%	80.9%
United States								
Europe, Middle East, and Africa	31.9%	35.1%	35.3%	35.2%	32.9%	39.9%	22.3%	22.4%
International								
Asia	9.7%	10.2%	10.9%	11.9%	10.8%			
Corporate					1.2%	−2.1%	2.3%	−3.3%
Number of Employees	110,000	110,000	106,000	103,000	99,200	94,000	62,000	59,000

Abbreviated Balance Sheet ($ millions)	June 1999	June 1998	June 1997	June 1996	June 1995	June 1990	June 1985	June 1980
ASSETS								
Total Current Assets	11,358	10,577	10,786	10,807	10,842	7,644	3,816	3,007
Plant, Property & Equipment, net	12,626	12,180	11,376	11,118	11,026	7,436	5,292	3,237
Other Assets	8,129	8,209	5,382	5,805	6,257	3,407	575	309
TOTAL ASSETS	32,113	30,966	27,544	27,730	28,125	18,487	9,683	6,553
LIABILITIES								
Total Current Liabilities	10,761	9,250	7,798	7,825	8,648	5,417	2,589	1,670
Long-Term Debt	6,231	5,765	4,143	4,670	5,161	3,588	877	835
Deferred Taxes	362	428	559	638	531	1,258	945	445
Other Liabilities	2,701	3,287	2,998	2,875	3,196	706	0	0
TOTAL LIABILITIES	20,055	18,730	15,498	16,008	17,536	10,969	4,411	2,950
TOTAL EQUITY	12,058	12,236	12,046	11,722	10,589	7,518	5,272	3,603
TOTAL LIABILITIES & EQUITY	32,113	30,966	27,544	27,730	28,125	18,487	9,683	6,553

Exhibit 5 P&G Organization, 1999 (Post O2005 Implementation)

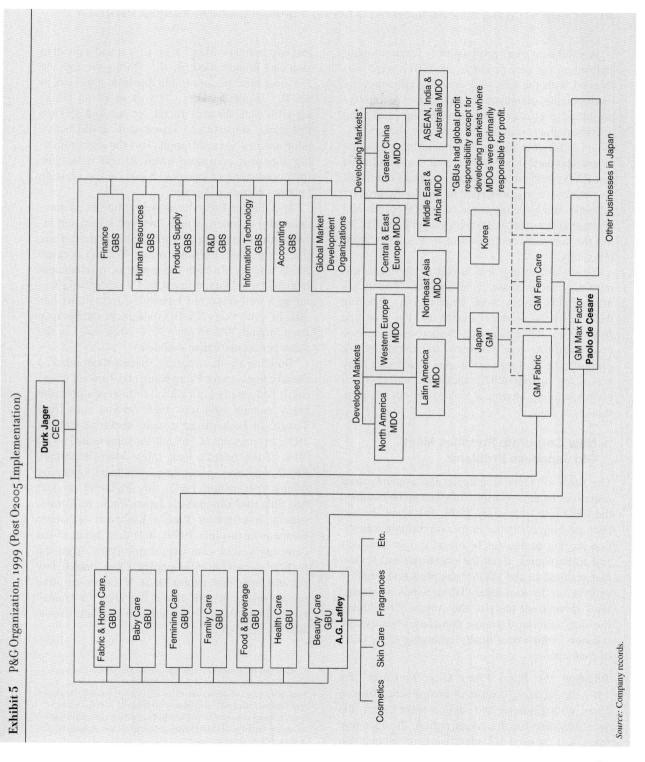

Source: Company records.

Beyond their clear responsibility for developing and rolling out new products, the GBUs were also charged with the task of increasing efficiency by standardizing manufacturing processes, simplifying brand portfolios, and coordinating marketing activities. For example, by reducing the company's 12 different diaper-manufacturing processes to one standard production model, Jager believed that P&G could not only reap economies but might also remove a major barrier to rapid new-product rollouts. And by axing some of its 300 brands and evaluating the core group with global potential, he felt the company could exploit its resources more efficiently.

The restructuring also aimed to eliminate bureaucracy and increase accountability. Overall, six management layers were stripped out, reducing the levels between the chairman and the front line from 13 to 7. Furthermore, numerous committee responsibilities were transferred to individuals. For example, the final sign-off on new advertising copy was given to individual executives, not approval boards, cutting the time it took to get out ads from months to days.

New Corporate Priorities Meet Old Japanese Problems

The seeds of Jager's strategic and organizational initiatives began sprouting long before he assumed the CEO role in January 1999. For years, he had been pushing his belief in growth through innovation, urging businesses to invest in new products and technologies. Even the organizational review that resulted in the O2005 blueprint had begun a year before he took over. These winds of change blew through all parts of the company, including the long-suffering Japanese company's beauty care business, which was finally emerging from years of problems.

Building the Base: From Mass to Class   By 1997 the Japanese cosmetics business had broken even. With guidance and support from Lafley, the vice president for the Asian region, the Japanese team had focused its advertising investment on just two brands—Max Factor Color, and a prestige skin care brand called SK-II.[2] "Poring through the Japanese business, we found this little jewel called SK-II," recalled Lafley. "To those of us familiar with rich Western facial creams and lotions, this clear, unperfumed liquid with a distinctive odor seemed very different. But the discriminating Japanese consumer loved it, and it became the cornerstone of our new focus on the prestige beauty-counselor segment."

Max Factor Japan began rebuilding its beauty-counselor channels, which involved significant investments in training as well as counter design and installation (see **Exhibits 6** and **7**). And because SK-II was such a high margin item, management launched a bold experiment in TV advertising featuring a well-respected Japanese actress in her late 30s. In three years SK-II's awareness ratings rose from around 20% to over 70%, while sales in the same period more than doubled.

Building on this success, management adapted the ad campaign for Hong Kong and Taiwan, where SK-II had quietly built a loyal following among the many women who took their fashion cues from Tokyo. In both markets, sales rocketed, and by 1997, export sales of $68 million represented about 30% of the brand's total sales. More important, SK-II was now generating significant operating profits. Yet within P&G, this high-end product had little visibility outside Japan. Paolo de Cesare, general manager of P&G's European skin care business in the mid-1990s, felt that, because the company's skin care experience came from the highly successful mass-market Olay brand, few outside Japan understood SK-II. "I remember some people saying that SK-II was like Olay for Japan," he recalled. "People outside Japan just didn't know what to make of it."

[2]SK-II was an obscure skin care product that had not even been recognized, much less evaluated, in the Max Factor acquisition. Containing Pitera, a secret yeast-based ingredient supposedly developed by a Japanese monk who noticed how the hands of workers in sake breweries kept young looking, SK-II had a small but extremely loyal following. Priced at ¥15,000 ($120) or more per bottle, it clearly was at the top of the skin care range.

Exhibit 6   Beauty Counselor Work Flow

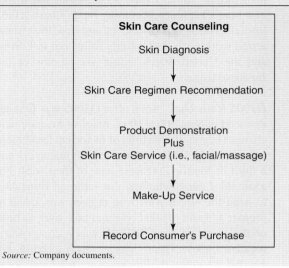
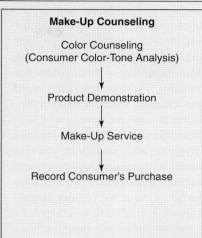

Skin Care Counseling

Skin Diagnosis

↓

Skin Care Regimen Recommendation

↓

Product Demonstration
Plus
Skin Care Service (i.e., facial/massage)

↓

Make-Up Service

↓

Record Consumer's Purchase

Make-Up Counseling

Color Counseling
(Consumer Color-Tone Analysis)

↓

Product Demonstration

↓

Make-Up Service

↓

Record Consumer's Purchase

Source: Company documents.

Exhibit 7   In-Store SK-II Counter Space

Source: Company documents.

Responding to the Innovation Push   Meanwhile, Jager had begun his push for more innovation. Given his firmly held belief that Japan's demanding consumers and tough competitors made it an important source of leading-edge ideas, it was not surprising that more innovative ideas and initiatives from Japan began finding their way through the company. For example, an electrostatically charged cleaning cloth developed by a Japanese competitor became the genesis of P&G's global rollout of Swiffer dry mops; rising Japanese sensitivity to hygiene and sanitation spawned worldwide application in products such as Ariel Pure Clean ("beyond whiteness, it washes away germs"); and dozens of other ideas from Japan—from a waterless car-washing cloth to a disposable stain-removing pad to a washing machine-based dry-cleaning product—were all put into P&G's product development pipeline.

Because Japanese women had by far the highest use of beauty care products in the world, it was natural that the global beauty care category management started to regard Max Factor Japan as a potential source of innovation. One of the first worldwide development projects on which Japan played a key role was Lipfinity, a long-lasting lipstick that was felt to have global potential.

In the mid-1990s, the impressive but short-lived success of long-lasting lipsticks introduced in Japan by Shiseido and Kenebo reinforced P&G's own consumer research, which had long indicated the potential for such a product. Working with R&D labs in Cincinnati and the United Kingdom, several Japanese technologists participated on a global team that developed a new product involving a durable color base and a renewable moisturizing second coat. Recognizing that this two-stage application would result in a more expensive product that involved basic habit changes, the global cosmetics category executive asked Max Factor Japan to be the new brand's global lead market.

Viewing their task as "translating the breakthrough technology invention into a market-sensitive product innovation," the Japanese product management team developed the marketing approach—concept, packaging, positioning, communications strategy, and so on—that led to the new brand, Lipfinity, becoming Japan's best-selling lipstick. The Japanese innovations were then transferred worldwide, as Lipfinity rolled out in Europe and the United States within six months of the Japanese launch.

O2005 Rolls Out   Soon after O2005 was first announced in September 1998, massive management changes began. By the time of its formal implementation in July 1999, half the top 30 managers and a third of the top 300 were new to their jobs. For example, Lafley, who had just returned from Asia to head the North American region, was asked to prepare to hand off that role and take over as head of the Beauty Care GBU. "It was a crazy year," recalled Lafley. "There was so much to build, but beyond the grand design, we were not clear about how it should operate."

In another of the hundreds of O2005 senior management changes, de Cesare, head of P&G's European skin care business, was promoted to vice president and asked to move to Osaka and head up Max Factor Japan. Under the new structure he would report directly to Lafley's Beauty Care GBU and on a dotted-line basis to the head of the MDO for Northeast Asia.

In addition to adjusting to this new complexity where responsibilities and relationships were still being defined, de Cesare found himself in a new global role. As president of Max Factor Japan he became a member of the Beauty Care Global Leadership Team (GLT), a group comprised of the business GMs from three key MDOs, representatives from key functions such as R&D, consumer research, product supply, HR, and finance, and chaired by Lafley as GBU head. These meetings became vital forums for implementing Lafley's charge "to review P&G's huge beauty care portfolio and focus investment on the top brands with the potential to become global assets." The question took on new importance for de Cesare when he was named global franchise leader for SK-II and asked to explore its potential as a global brand.

A New Global Product Development Process
Soon after arriving in Japan, de Cesare discovered that the Japanese Max Factor organization was increasingly involved in new global product development activities following its successful Lipfinity role. This process began under the leadership of the Beauty Care GLT when consumer research identified an unmet consumer need worldwide. A lead research center then developed a technical model of how P&G could respond to the need. Next, the GLT process brought in marketing expertise from lead markets to expand that technology "chassis" to a holistic new-product concept. Finally, contributing technologists and marketers were designated to work on the variations in ingredients or aesthetics necessary to adapt the core technology or product concept to local markets.

This global product development process was set in motion when consumer researchers found that, despite regional differences, there was a worldwide opportunity in facial cleansing. The research showed that, although U.S. women were satisfied with the clean feeling they got using bar soaps, it left their skin tight and dry; in Europe, women applied a cleansing milk with a cotton pad that left their skin moisturized and conditioned but not as clean as they wanted; and in Japan, the habit of using foaming facial cleansers left women satisfied with skin conditioning but not with moisturizing. Globally, however, the unmet need was to achieve soft, moisturized, clean-feeling skin, and herein the GBU saw the product opportunity—and the technological challenge.

A technology team was assembled at an R&D facility in Cincinnati, drawing on the most qualified technologists from its P&G's labs worldwide. For example, because the average Japanese woman spent 4.5 minutes on her face-cleansing regime compared with 1.7 minutes for the typical American woman, Japanese technologists were sought for their refined expertise in the cleansing processes and their particular understanding of how to develop a product with the rich, creamy lather.

Working with a woven substrate technology developed by P&G's paper business, the core technology team found that a 10-micron fiber, when woven into a mesh, was effective in trapping and absorbing dirt and impurities. By impregnating this substrate with a dry-sprayed formula of cleansers and moisturizers activated at different times in the cleansing process, team members felt they could develop a disposable cleansing cloth that would respond to the identified consumer need. After this technology "chassis" had been developed, a technology team in Japan adapted it to allow the cloth to be impregnated with a different cleanser formulation that included the SK-II ingredient, Pitera. (See **Exhibit 8** for an overview of the development process.)

A U.S.-based marketing team took on the task of developing the Olay version. Identifying its consumers' view of a multistep salon facial as the ultimate cleansing experience, this team came up with the concept of a one-step routine that offered the benefits of cleansing, conditioning, and toning— "just like a daily facial." Meanwhile, another team had the same assignment in Japan, which became the lead market for the SK-II version. Because women already had a five- or six-step cleansing routine, the SK-II version was positioned not as a "daily facial" but as a "foaming massage cloth" that built on the ritual experience of increasing skin circulation through a massage while boosting skin clarity due to the microfibers' ability to clean pores and trap dirt. (See **Exhibit 9** for illustration of the Foaming Massage Cloth with other core SK-II products.)

Because of its premium pricing strategy, the SK-II Foaming Massage Cloth was packaged in a much more elegant dispensing box and was priced at ¥6,000 ($50), compared to $7 for the Olay Facial Cloth in the United States. And Japan assigned several technologists to the task of developing detailed product performance data that Japanese beauty magazines required for the much more scientific product reviews they published compared to their Western counterparts. In the end, each market ended up with a distinct product built on a common technology platform. Marketing expertise was also shared—some Japanese performance analysis and

Exhibit 8   Representation of Global Cleansing Cloth Development Program

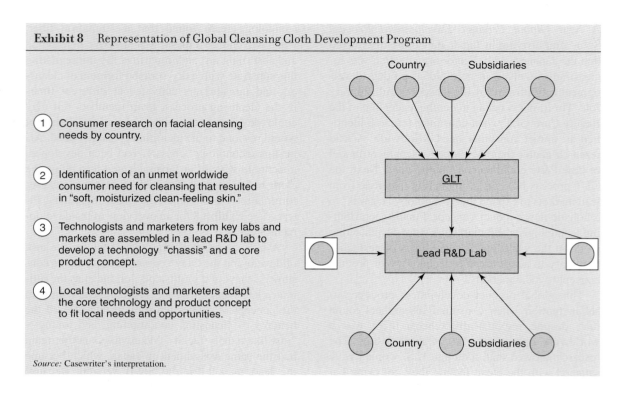

1 Consumer research on facial cleansing needs by country.

2 Identification of an unmet worldwide consumer need for cleansing that resulted in "soft, moisturized clean-feeling skin."

3 Technologists and marketers from key labs and markets are assembled in a lead R&D lab to develop a technology "chassis" and a core product concept.

4 Local technologists and marketers adapt the core technology and product concept to fit local needs and opportunities.

Source: Casewriter's interpretation.

data were also relevant for the Olay version and were used in Europe, for example—allowing the organization to leverage its local learning.

The SK-II Decision: A Global Brand?

After barely six months in Japan, de Cesare recognized that he now had three different roles in the new organization. As president of Max Factor Japan, he was impressed by the turnaround this local company had pulled off and was optimistic about its ability to grow significantly in the large Japanese beauty market. As GLT member on the Beauty Care GBU, he was proud of his organization's contribution to the GBU-sponsored global new-product innovation process and was convinced that Japan could continue to contribute to and learn from P&G's impressive technology base. And now as global franchise leader for SK-II, he was excited by the opportunity to explore whether the brand could break into the $9 billion worldwide

prestige skin care market. (See **Exhibit 10** for prestige market data.)

When he arrived in Japan, de Cesare found that SK-II's success in Taiwan and Hong Kong (by 1999, 45% of total SK-II sales) had already encouraged management to begin expansion into three other regional markets—Singapore, Malaysia, and South Korea. But these were relatively small markets, and as he reviewed data on the global skin care and prestige beauty markets, he wondered if the time was right to make a bold entry into one or more major markets. (See **Exhibits 11** and **12** for global skin-care market and consumer data.)

As he reviewed the opportunities, three alternatives presented themselves. First, the beauty care management team for Greater China was interested in expanding on SK-II's success in Taiwan and Hong Kong by introducing the brand into mainland China. Next, at GLT meetings de Cesare had discussed with the head of beauty care in

Exhibit 9   Illustration of Part of SK-II Product Line

pitera soak

FACIAL TREATMENT ESSENCE
Skin Balancing Essence

The heart of the SK-II range, the revolutionary **Facial Treatment Essence** is the second point in your Ritual. This unique Pitera-rich product helps boost moisture levels to improve texture and clarity for a more beautiful, glowing complexion.

Women are so passionate about **Facial Treatment Essence** that they describe it as their 'holy' water. It contains the most concentrated amount of Pitera of all our skincare products—around 90% pure SK-II Pitera. It absorbs easily and leaves your skin looking radiant, with a supple, smooth feel.

FOAMING MASSAGE CLOTH
Purifying Cleansing Cloth

These innovative **Foaming Massage Cloths** leave your skin feeling smooth and velvety. A single sheet offers the outstanding effects of a cleanser, facial wash and massage. It gently washes away impurities, excess oil and non-waterproof eye make-up, leaving

FACIAL TREATMENT CLEAR LOTION
Clear Purifying Lotion

For a perfectly conditioned and ultra-fresh skin, use the **Facial Treatment Clear Lotion** morning and evening after cleansing your face and neck. The final part of your cleansing process, this Lotion helps remove residual impurities and

Source: Company brochure.

Europe the possibilities of bringing SK-II into that large Western market. His third possibility—really his first option, he realized—was to build on the brand's success in SK-II's rich and proven home Japanese market.

The Japanese Opportunity Japanese women were among the most sophisticated users of beauty products in the world, and per capita they were the world's leading consumers of these products. Despite its improved performance in recent years, Max Factor

Exhibit 10   Global Prestige Market: Size and Geographic Split

Global Prestige Market: 1999 (Fragrances, Cosmetics, Skin) = $15 billion at retail level (of which approximately 60% is skin care)

United States	26%
Canada	2
Asia/Pacifica[a]	25
United Kingdom	5
France	5
Germany	5
Rest of Europe	16
Rest of World	16

[a]Japan represented over 80% of the Asia/Pacific total.
Source: Company data.

Exhibit 11   Global Skin Care Market Size: 1999

Skin Care (Main market and prestige)

Region/Country	Retail Sales ($ million)	Two-Year Growth Rate
Western Europe	8,736	7%
France	2,019	7
Germany	1,839	14
United Kingdom	1,052	17
North America	6,059	18
United States	5,603	18
Asia/Pacific	11,220	2
China	1,022	28
Japan	6,869	6
South Korea	1,895	9
Taiwan	532	18
Hong Kong	266	6

Source: Company data.

Exhibit 12   Skin Care and Cosmetics Habits and Practices: Selected Countries

Product Usage (% Past 7 Days)	United States[a]	Japan[a]	China[b]	United Kingdom[a]
Facial Moisturizer—Lotion	45%	95%	26%	37%
Facial Moisturizer—Cream	25	28	52	45
Facial Cleansers (excluding Family Bar Soap)	51	90	57	41
Foundation	70	85	35	57
Lipstick	84	97	75	85
Mascara	76	27	13	75

[a]Based on broad, representative sample of consumers.
[b]Based on upper-income consumers in Beijing City.
Source: Company data.

Japan claimed less than a 3% share of this $10 billion beauty product market. "It's huge," boasted one local manager. "Larger than the U.S. laundry market."

Although SK-II had sales of more than $150 million in Japan in 1999, de Cesare was also aware that in recent years its home market growth had slowed. This was something the new manager felt he could change by tapping into P&G's extensive technological resources. The successful experience of the foaming massage cloth convinced him that

there was a significant opportunity to expand sales by extending the SK-II line beyond its traditional product offerings. For example, he could see an immediate opportunity to move into new segments by adding anti-aging and skin-whitening products to the SK-II range. Although this would take a considerable amount of time and effort, it would exploit internal capabilities and external brand image. Compared to the new-market entry options, investment would be quite low.

An exciting development that would support this home market thrust emerged when he discovered that his SK-II technology and marketing teams had come together to develop an innovative beauty imaging system (BIS). Using the Japanese technicians' skills in miniaturization and software development, they were working to create a simplified version of scientific equipment used by P&G lab technicians to qualify new skin care products by measuring improvements in skin condition. The plan was to install the modified BIS at SK-II counters and have beauty consultants use it to boost the accuracy and credibility of their skin diagnosis. The project fit perfectly with de Cesare's vision for SK-II to become the brand that solved individual skin care problems. He felt it could build significant loyalty in the analytically inclined Japanese consumer.

With the company's having such a small share of such a rich market, de Cesare felt that a strategy of product innovation and superior in-store service had the potential to accelerate a growth rate that had slowed to 5% per annum over the past three years. Although Shiseido could be expected to put up a good fight, he felt SK-II should double sales in Japan over the next six or seven years. In short, de Cesare was extremely excited about SK-II's potential for growth in its home market. He said: "It's a fabulous opportunity. One loyal SK-II customer in Japan already spends about $1,000 a year on the brand. Even a regular consumer of all P&G's other products—from toothpaste and deodorant to shampoo and detergent—all together spends nowhere near that amount annually."

The Chinese Puzzle   A very different opportunity existed in China, where P&G had been operating only since 1988. Because of the extraordinarily low prices of Chinese laundry products, the company had uncharacteristically led with beauty products when it entered this huge market. Olay was launched in 1989 and, after early problems, eventually became highly successful by adopting a nontraditional marketing strategy. To justify its price premium—its price was 20 to 30 times the price of local skin care products—Shivesh Ram,

the entrepreneurial beauty care manager in China, decided to add a service component to Olay's superior product formulation. Borrowing from the Max Factor Japan model, he began selling through counters in the state-owned department stores staffed by beauty counselors. By 1999, Olay had almost 1,000 such counters in China and was a huge success.

As the Chinese market opened to international retailers, department stores from Taiwan, Hong Kong, and Singapore began opening in Beijing and Shanghai. Familiar with Olay as a mass-market brand, they questioned allocating it scarce beauty counter space alongside Estee Lauder, Lancôme, Shiseido, and other premium brands that had already claimed the prime locations critical to success in this business. It was at this point that Ram began exploring the possibility of introducing SK-II, allowing Olay to move more deeply into second-tier department stores, stores in smaller cities, and to "second-floor" cosmetics locations in large stores. "China is widely predicted to become the second-largest market in the world," said Ram. "The prestige beauty segment is growing at 30 to 40% a year, and virtually every major competitor in that space is already here."

Counterbalancing Ram's enthusiastic proposals, de Cesare also heard voices of concern. Beyond the potential impact on a successful Olay market position, some were worried that SK-II would be a distraction to P&G's strategy of becoming a mainstream Chinese company and to its competitive goal of entering 600 Chinese cities ahead of Unilever, Kao, and other global players. They argued that targeting an elite consumer group with a niche product was not in keeping with the objective of reaching the 1.2 billion population with laundry, hair care, oral care, diapers, and other basics. After all, even with SK-II's basic four-step regimen, a three-month supply could cost more than one month's salary for the average woman working in a major Chinese city.

Furthermore, the skeptics wondered if the Chinese consumer was ready for SK-II. Olay had succeeded only by the company's educating its customers to move from a one-step skin care process—washing with bar soap and water—to a three-step cleansing and moisturizing process. SK-II relied on women developing at least a four- to six-step regimen, something the doubters felt was unrealistic. But as Ram and others argued, within the target market, skin care practices were quite developed, and penetration of skin care products was higher than in many developed markets.

Finally, the Chinese market presented numerous other risks, from the widespread existence of counterfeit prestige products to the bureaucracy attached to a one-year import-registration process. But the biggest concern was the likelihood that SK-II would attract import duties of 35% to 40%. This meant that even if P&G squeezed its margin in China, SK-II would have to be priced significantly above the retail level in other markets. Still, the China team calculated that because of the lower cost of beauty consultants, the product could still be profitable. (See **Exhibit 13** for cost estimates.)

Despite the critics, Ram was eager to try, and he responded to their concerns: "There are three Chinas—rural China, low-income urban China, and sophisticated, wealthy China concentrated in Shanghai, Beijing, and Guangzhou. The third group is as big a target consumer group as in many developed markets. If we don't move soon, the battle for that elite will be lost to the global beauty care powerhouses that have been here for three years or more."

Ram was strongly supported by his regional beauty care manager and by the Greater China MDO president. Together, they were willing to experiment with a few counters in Shanghai, and if successful, to expand to more counters in other major cities. Over the first three years, they expected to generate $10 million to $15 million in sales, by which time they expected the brand to break even. They estimated the initial investment to build counters, train beauty consultants, and support the introduction would probably mean losses of about 10% of sales over that three-year period.

The European Question   As he explored global opportunities for SK-II, de Cesare's mind kept returning to the European market he knew so well. Unlike China, Europe had a relatively large and sophisticated group of beauty-conscious consumers who already practiced a multistep regimen using various specialized skin care products. What he was unsure of was whether there was a significant group willing to adopt the disciplined six- to eight-step ritual that the most devoted Japanese SK-II users followed.

The bigger challenge, in his view, would be introducing a totally new brand into an already crowded field of high-profile, well-respected competitors including Estee Lauder, Clinique, Lancôme, Chanel, and Dior. While TV advertising had proven highly effective in raising SK-II's awareness and sales in Japan, Taiwan, and Hong Kong, the cost

Exhibit 13   Global SK-II Cost Structure (% of net sales)[a]

FY1999/2000	Japan	Taiwan/ Hong Kong	PR China Expected	United Kingdom Expected
Net sales	100%	100%	100%	100%
Cost of products sold	22	26	45	29
Marketing, research, and selling/ administrative expense	67	58	44	63
Operating income	11	16	11	8

[a]Data disguised.
Source: Company estimates.

of television—or even print—ads in Europe made such an approach there prohibitive. And without any real brand awareness or heritage, he wondered if SK-II's mystique would transfer to a Western market.

As he thought through these issues, de Cesare spoke with his old boss, Mike Thompson, the head of P&G's beauty business in Europe. Because the Max Factor sales force sold primarily to mass-distribution outlets, Thompson did not think it provided SK-II the appropriate access to the European market. However, he explained that the fine-fragrance business was beginning to do quite well. In the United Kingdom, for example, its 25-person sales force was on track in 1999 to book $1 million in after-tax profit on sales of $12 million. Because it sold brands such as Hugo Boss, Giorgio, and Beverly Hills to department stores and Boots, the major pharmacy chain, its sales approach and trade relationship was different from the SK-II model in Japan. Nevertheless, Thompson felt it was a major asset that could be exploited.

Furthermore, Thompson told de Cesare that his wife was a loyal SK-II user and reasoned that since she was a critical judge of products, other women would discover the same benefits in the product she did. He believed that SK-II provided the fine-fragrance business a way to extend its line in the few department stores that dominated U.K. distribution in the prestige business. He thought they would be willing to give SK-II a try. (He was less optimistic about countries such as France and Germany, however, where prestige products were sold through thousands of perfumeries, making it impossible to justify the SK-II consultants who would be vital to the sales model.)

Initial consumer research in the United Kingdom had provided mixed results. But de Cesare felt that while this kind of blind testing could provide useful data on detergents, it was less helpful in this case. The consumers tested the product blind for one week, then were interviewed about their impressions. But because they lacked the beauty counselors' analysis and advice and had not practiced the full skin care regimen, he felt the results did not adequately predict SK-II's potential.

In discussions with Thompson, de Cesare concluded that he could hope to achieve sales of $10 million by the fourth year in the U.K. market. Given the intense competition, he recognized that he would have to absorb losses of $1 million to $2 million annually over that period as the start-up investment.

The Organizational Constraint   While the strategic opportunities were clear, de Cesare also recognized that his decision needed to comply with the organizational reality in which it would be implemented. While GBU head Lafley was an early champion and continuing supporter of SK-II, his boss, Jager, was less committed. Jager was among those in P&G who openly questioned how well some of the products in the beauty care business—particularly some of the acquired brands—fit in the P&G portfolio. While he was comfortable with high-volume products like shampoo, he was more skeptical of the upper end of the line, particularly fine fragrances. In his view, the fashion-linked and promotion-driven sales models of luxury products neither played well to P&G's "stack it high, sell it cheap" marketing skills nor leveraged its superior technologies.

The other organizational reality was that the implementation of O2005 was causing a good deal of organizational disruption and management distraction. This was particularly true in Europe, as Thompson explained:

> We swung the pendulum 180 degrees, from a local to a global focus. Marketing plans and budgets had previously been developed locally, strongly debated with European managers, then rolled up. Now they were developed globally—or at least regionally—by new people who often did not understand the competitive and trade differences across markets. We began to standardize and centralize our policies and practices out of Geneva. Not surprisingly, a lot of our best local managers left the company.

One result of the O2005 change was that country subsidiary GMs now focused more on maximizing sales volume than profits, and this had put the beauty care business under significant budget pressure. Thompson explained the situation in Europe in 1999:

> One thing became clear very quickly: It was a lot easier to sell cases of Ariel [detergent] or Pampers [diapers] than cases of cosmetics, so guess where the sales force effort went? At the same time, the new-product pipeline was resulting in almost a "launch of the month," and with the introduction of new products like Swiffer and Febreze, it was hard for the MDOs to manage all of these corporate priorities… Finally, because cosmetics sales required more time and effort from local sales forces, more local costs were assigned to that business, and that has added to profit pressures.

Framing the Proposal   It was in this context that de Cesare was framing his proposal based on the global potential of SK-II as a brand and his plans to exploit the opportunities he saw. But he knew Lafley's long ties and positive feelings towards SK-II would not be sufficient to convince him. The GBU head was committed to focusing beauty care on the core brands that could be developed as a global franchise, and his questions would likely zero in on whether de Cesare could build SK-II into such a brand.

Case 5-3   McKinsey & Company: Managing Knowledge and Learning

Christopher A. Bartlett

In April 1996, halfway through his first three-year term as managing director of McKinsey & Company, Rajat Gupta was feeling quite proud as he flew out of Bermuda, site of the firm's second annual Practice Olympics. He had just listened to twenty teams outlining innovative new ideas they had developed out of recent project work, and, like his fellow senior partner judges, Gupta had come away impressed by the intelligence and creativity of the firm's next generation of consultants.

But there was another thought that kept coming back to the 47 year old leader of this highly successful $1.8 billion consulting firm (See **Exhibit 1** for

a twenty year growth history). If this represented the tip of McKinsey's knowledge and expertise iceberg, how well was the firm doing in developing, capturing, and leveraging this asset in service of its clients worldwide? Although the Practice Olympics was only one of several initiatives he had championed, Gupta wondered if it was enough, particularly in light of his often stated belief that "knowledge is the lifeblood of McKinsey."

▌ The Founders' Legacy[1]

Founded in 1926 by University of Chicago professor, James ("Mac") McKinsey, the firm of "accounting and engineering advisors" that bore his name grew rapidly. Soon Mac began recruiting experienced executives, and training them in the integrated approach he called his General Survey outline. In Saturday morning sessions he would lead consultants through an "undeviating sequence" of

▌ [1]The Founders' Legacy section draws on Amar V. Bhide, "Building the Professional Firm: McKinsey & Co., 1939–1968," HBS Working Paper 95–010.

Exhibit 1   McKinsey & Company: 20 Year Growth Indicators

Year	# Office Locations	# Active Engagements	Number of CSS[a]	Number of MGMs[b]
1975	24	661	529	NA
1980	31	771	744	NA
1985	36	1823	1248	NA
1990	47	2789	2465	348
1991	51	2875	2653	395
1992	55	2917	2875	399
1993	60	3142	3122	422
1994	64	3398	3334	440
1995	69	3559	3817	472

[a]CSS = Client Service Staff (All professional consulting staff).
[b]MGM = Management Group Members (Partners and directors).
Source: Internal McKinsey & Company documents.

analysis—goals, strategy, policies, organization, facilities, procedures, and personnel—while still encouraging them to synthesize data and think for themselves.

In 1932, Mac recruited Marvin Bower, a bright young lawyer with a Harvard MBA, and within two years asked him to become manager of the recently opened New York office. Convinced that he had to upgrade the firm's image in an industry typically regarded as "efficiency experts" or "business doctors," Bower undertook to imbue in his associates the sense of professionalism he had experienced in his time in a law partnership. In a 1937 memo, he outlined his vision for the firm as one focused on issues of importance to top-level management, adhering to the highest standards of integrity, professional ethics, and technical excellence, able to attract and develop young men of outstanding qualifications, and committed to continually raising its stature and influence. Above all, it was to be a firm dedicated to the mission of serving its clients superbly well.

Over the next decade, Bower worked tirelessly to influence his partners and associates to share his vision. As new offices opened, he became a strong advocate of the One Firm policy that required all consultants to be recruited and advanced on a firm-wide basis, clients to be treated as McKinsey & Company responsibilities, and profits to be shared from a firm pool, not an office pool. And through dinner seminars, he began upgrading the size and quality of McKinsey's clients. In the 1945 New Engagement Guide, he articulated a policy that every assignment should bring the firm something more than revenue—experience or prestige, for example.

Elected Managing Partner in 1950, Bower led his ten partners and 74 associates to initiate a series of major changes that turned McKinsey into an elite consulting firm unable to meet the demand for its services. Each client's problems were seen as unique, but Bower and his colleagues firmly believed that well trained, highly intelligent generalists could quickly grasp the issue, and through disciplined analysis find its solution. The firm's extraordinary domestic growth through the 1950s provided a basis for international expansion that accelerated the rate of growth in the 1960s. Following the opening of the London Office in 1959, offices in Geneva, Amsterdam, Düsseldorf, and Paris followed quickly. By the time Bower stepped down as Managing Director in 1967, McKinsey was a well-established and highly respected presence in Europe and North America.

A Decade of Doubt

Although leadership succession was well planned and executed, within a few years, McKinsey's growth engine seemed to stall. The economic turmoil of the oil crisis, the slowing of the divisionalization process that had fueled the European expansion, the growing sophistication of client management, and the appearance of new focused competitors like Boston Consulting Group (BCG) all contributed to the problem. Almost overnight, McKinsey's enormous reservoir of internal self-confidence and even self-satisfaction began to turn to self-doubt and self-criticism.

Commission on Firm Aims and Goals   Concerned that the slowing growth in Europe and the U.S. was more than just a cyclical market downturn, the firm's partners assigned a committee of their most respected peers to study the problem and make recommendations. In April 1971, the Commission on Firm Aims and Goals concluded that the firm has been growing too fast. The authors bluntly reported, "Our preoccupation with the geographic expansion and new practice possibilities has caused us to neglect the development of our technical and professional skills." The report concluded that McKinsey had been too willing to accept routine assignments from marginal clients, that the quality of work done was uneven, and that while its consultants were excellent generalist problem solvers, they often lacked the deep industry knowledge or the substantive specialized expertise that clients were demanding.

One of the Commission's central proposals was that the firm had to recommit itself to the continuous development of its members. This meant that growth would have to be slowed and that the associate to MGM ratio be reduced from 7 to 1 back to 5 or 6 to 1. It further proposed that emphasis be placed on the development of what it termed "T-Shaped" consultants—those who supplemented a broad generalist perspective with an in-depth industry or functional specialty.

Practice Development Initiative   When Ron Daniel was elected Managing Director (MD) in 1976—the fourth to hold the position since Bower had stepped down nine years earlier—McKinsey was still struggling to meet the challenges laid out in the Commission's report. As the head of the New York office since 1970, Daniel had experienced first-hand the rising expectations of increasingly sophisticated clients and the aggressive challenges of new competitors like BCG. In contrast to McKinsey's local office-based model of "client relationship" consulting, BCG began competing on the basis of "thought leadership" from a highly concentrated resource base in Boston. Using some simple but powerful tools, such as the experience curve and the growth-share matrix, BCG began to make strong inroads into the strategy consulting market. As McKinsey began losing both clients and recruits to BCG, Daniel became convinced that his firm could no longer succeed pursuing its generalist model.

One of his first moves was to appoint one of the firm's most respected and productive senior partners as McKinsey's first full-time director of training. As an expanded commitment to developing consultants' skills and expertise became the norm, the executive committee began debating the need to formally updating the firm's long-standing mission to reflect the firm's core commitment not only to serving its clients but also to developing its consultants. (**Exhibit 2.**)

But Daniel also believed some structural changes were necessary. Building on an initiative he and his colleagues had already implemented in the New York office, he created industry-based Clientele Sectors in consumer products, banking, industrial goods, insurance, and so on, cutting across the geographic offices that remained the primary organizational entity. He also encouraged more formal development of the firm's functional expertise in areas like strategy, organization and operations where knowledge and experience were widely diffused and minimally codified. However, many—including Marvin Bower—expressed concern that any move towards a product driven approach could damage McKinsey's distinctive advantage of its local office presence which gave partners strong connections with the business community, allowed

Exhibit 2	McKinsey's Mission and Guiding Principles (1996)

McKinsey Mission

To help our clients make positive, lasting, and substantial improvements in their performance and to build a great Firm that is able to attract, develop, excite, and retain exceptional people.

Guiding Principles

Serving Clients

Adhere to professional standards
Follow the top management approach
Assist the client in implementation and capability building
Perform consulting in a cost effective manner

Building the Firm

Operate as one Firm
Maintain a meritocracy
Show a genuine concern for our people
Foster an open and nonhierarchical working atmosphere
Manage the Firm's resources responsibly

Being a Member of the Professional Staff

Demonstrate commitment to client service
Strive continuously for superior quality
Advance the state of the art management
Contribute a spirit of partnership through teamwork and collaboration
Profit from the freedom and assume the responsibility associated with self-governance
Uphold the obligation to dissent

teams to work on site with clients and facilitated implementation. It was an approach that they felt contrasted sharply with the "fly in, fly out" model of expert-based consulting that BCG ran from its Boston hub.

Nonetheless, Daniel pressed ahead. Having established industry sectors, the MD next turned his attention to leveraging the firm's functional expertise. He assembled working groups to develop knowledge in two areas that were at the heart of McKinsey's practice—strategy and organization. To head up the first group, he named Fred Gluck, a director in the New York office who had been outspoken in urging the firm to modify its traditional generalist approach. In June 1977, Gluck invited a "Super Group" of younger partners with strategy expertise to a three day meeting to share ideas and develop an agenda for the strategy practice. One described the meeting:

> We had three days of unmitigated chaos. Someone from New York would stand up and present a four-box matrix. A partner from London would present a nine-box matrix. A German would present a 47 box matrix. It was chaos... but at the end of the third day some strands of thought were coming together.

At the same time, Daniel asked Bob Waterman who had been working on a Siemens-sponsored study of "excellent companies" and Jim Bennett, a respected senior partner to assemble a group that could articulate the firm's existing knowledge in the organization arena. One of their first recruits was an innovative young Ph.D. in organizational theory named Tom Peters.

Revival and Renewal

By the early 1980s, with growth resuming, a cautious optimism returned to McKinsey for the first time in almost a decade.

Centers of Competence   Recognizing that the activities of the two practice development projects could not just be a one-time effort, in 1980 Daniel asked Gluck to join the central small group that comprised the Firm Office and focus on the knowledge building agenda that had become his passion. Ever since his arrival at the firm from Bell Labs in 1967, Gluck had wanted to bring an equally stimulating intellectual environment to McKinsey. Against some strong internal resistance, he set out to convert his partners to his strongly held beliefs—that knowledge development had to be a core, not a peripheral firm activity; that it needed to be ongoing and institutionalized, not temporary and project based; and that it had to be the responsibility of everyone, not just a few.

To complement the growing number of Clientele Industry Sectors, he created 15 Centers of Competence (virtual centers, not locations) built around existing areas of management expertise like strategy, organization, marketing, change management, and systems. In a 1982 memo to all partners, he described the role of these centers as two-fold: to help develop consultants and to ensure the continued renewal of the firm's intellectual resources. For each Center, Gluck identified one or two highly motivated, recognized experts in the particular field and named them practice leaders. The expectation was that these leaders would assemble from around the firm, a core group of partners who were active in the practice area and interested in contributing to its development. (See **Exhibit 3** for the 15 Centers and 11 Sectors in 1983.)

To help build a shared body of knowledge, the leadership of each of the 15 Centers of Competence began to initiate activities primarily involving the core group and, less frequently, the members of the practice network. A partner commented on Gluck's commitment to the centers:

> Unlike industry sectors, the centers of competence did not have a natural, stable client base, and Fred had to work hard to get them going. . . . He basically told the practice leaders, "Spend whatever you can—the cost is almost irrelevant compared to the payoff." There was no attempt to filter or manage the process, and the effect was "to let a thousand flowers bloom."

Gluck also spent a huge amount of time trying to change an internal status hierarchy based largely on the size and importance of one's client base. Arguing that practice development ("snowball making" as it became known internally) was not less "macho" than client development

Exhibit 3   McKinsey's Emerging Practice Areas: Centers of Competence and Industry Sectors, 1983

Centers of Competence	Clientele Sectors
Building Institutional Skills	Automotive
Business Management Unit	Banking
Change Management	Chemicals
Corporate Leadership	Communications and Information
Corporate Finance	Consumer Products
Diagnostic Scan	Electronics
International Management	Energy
Integrated Logistics	Health Care
Manufacturing	Industrial Goods
Marketing	Insurance
Microeconomics	Steel
Sourcing	
Strategic Management	
Systems	
Technology	

("snowball throwing"), he tried to convince his colleagues that everyone had to become snowball makers *and* snowball throwers. In endless discussions, he would provoke his colleagues with barbed pronouncements and personal challenges: "Knowing what you're talking about is not necessarily a client service handicap" or "Would you want your brain surgery done by a general practitioner?"

Building a Knowledge Infrastructure As the firm's new emphasis on individual consultant training took hold and the Clientele Sectors and Centers of Competence began to generate new insights, many began to feel the need to capture and leverage the learning. Although big ideas had occasionally been written up as articles for publication in newspapers, magazines or journals like *Harvard Business Review,* there was still a deep-seated suspicion of anything that smacked of packaging ideas or creating proprietary concepts or standard solutions.

Such reluctance to document concepts had long constrained the internal transfer of ideas and the vast majority of internally developed knowledge was never captured.

This began to change with the launching of the McKinsey Staff Paper series in 1978, and by the early 1980s the firm was actively encouraging its consultants to publish their key findings. The initiative got a major boost with the publication in 1982 of two major bestsellers, Peters and Waterman's *In Search of Excellence* and Kenichi Ohmae's *The Mind of the Strategist*. But books, articles, and staff papers required major time investments, and only a small minority of consultants made the effort to write them. Believing that the firm had to lower the barrier to internal knowledge communication, Gluck introduced the idea of Practice Bulletins, two page summaries of important new ideas that identified the experts who could provide more detail. A partner elaborated:

> The Bulletins were essentially internal advertisements for ideas and the people who had developed them. We tried to convince people that they would help build their personal networks and internal reputations.... Fred was not at all concerned that the quality was mixed, and had a strong philosophy of letting the internal market sort out what were the really big ideas.

Believing that the firm's organizational infrastructure needed major overhaul, in 1987 Gluck launched a Knowledge Management Project. After five months of study, the team made three recommendations. First, the firm had to make a major commitment to build a common database of knowledge accumulated from client work and developed in the practice areas. Second, to ensure that the data bases were maintained and used, they proposed that each practice area (Clientele Sector and Competence Center) hire a full time practice coordinator who could act as an "intelligent switch" responsible for monitoring the quality of the data and for helping consultants access the relevant information. And finally, they suggested that the firm expand its hiring practices and promotion

policies to create a career path for deep functional specialists whose narrow expertise would make them more I-shaped than the normal profile of a T-shaped consultant.

The task of implementing these recommendations fell to a team led by Bill Matassoni, the firm's director of communications and Brook Manville, a newly recruited Yale Ph.D. with experience with electronic publishing. Focusing first on the Firm Practice Information System (FPIS), a computerized data base of client engagements, they installed new systems and procedures to make the data more complete, accurate, and timely so that it could be accessed as a reliable information resource, not just an archival record. More difficult was the task of capturing the knowledge that had accumulated in the practice areas since much of it had not been formalized and none of it had been prioritized or integrated. To create a computer based Practice Development Network (PDNet), Matassoni and Manville put huge energy into begging, cajoling and challenging each practice to develop and submit documents that represented their core knowledge. After months of work, they had collected the 2,000 documents that they believed provided the critical mass to launch PDNet.

At the last minute, Matassoni and his team also developed another information resource that had not been part of the study team's recommendations. They assembled a listing of all firm experts and key document titles by practice area and published it in a small book, compact enough to fit in any consultant's briefcase. The Knowledge Resource Directory (KRD) became the McKinsey Yellow Pages and found immediate and widespread use firm-wide. Although the computerized data bases were slow to be widely adopted, the KRD found almost immediate enthusiastic acceptance.

Making the new practice coordinator's position effective proved more challenging. Initially, these roles were seen as little more than glorified librarians. It took several years before the new roles were filled by individuals (often ex-consultants) who were sufficiently respected that they could not only act as consultants to those seeking information about their area of expertise, but also were able to impose the discipline necessary to maintain and build the practice's data bases.

Perhaps the most difficult task was to legitimize the role of a new class of I-shaped consultants—the specialist. The basic concept was that a professional could make a career in McKinsey by emphasizing specialized knowledge development rather than the broad based problem solving skills and client development orientation that were deeply embedded in the firm's value system. While several consultants with deep technical expertise in specialties like market research, finance or steel making were recruited, most found it hard to assimilate into the mainstream. The firm seemed uncomfortable about how to evaluate, compensate or promote these individuals, and many either became isolated or disaffected. Nonetheless, the partnership continued to support the notion of a specialist promotion track and continued to struggle with how to make it work.

Matassoni reflected on the changes:

> The objective of the infrastructure changes was not so much to create a new McKinsey as to keep the old "one firm" concept functioning as we grew… Despite all the talk of computerized data bases, the knowledge management process still relied heavily on personal networks, old practices like cross-office transfers, and strong "One Firm" norms like helping other consultants when they called. And at promotion time, nobody reviewed your PD documents. They looked at how you used your internal networks to have your ideas make an impact on clients.

Managing Success

By the late 1980s, the firm was expanding rapidly again. In 1988, the same year Fred Gluck was elected managing director, new offices were opened in Rome, Helsinki, Sao Paulo, and Minneapolis bringing the total to 41. The growing view amongst the partners, however, was that enhancing McKinsey's reputation as a thought leader was at least as important as attracting new business.

Refining Knowledge Management   After being elected MD, Gluck delegated the practice development role he had played since 1980 to a newly constituted Clientele and Professional Development Committee (CPDC). When Ted Hall took over leadership of this committee in late 1991, he felt there was a need to adjust the firm's knowledge development focus. He commented:

> By the early 1990s, too many people were seeing practice development as the creation of experts and the generation of documents in order to build our reputation. But knowledge is only valuable when it is between the ears of consultants and applied to clients' problems. Because it is less effectively developed through the disciplined work of a few than through the spontaneous interaction of many, we had to change the more structured "discover-codify-disseminate" model to a looser and more inclusive "engage-explore-apply-share" approach. In other words, we shifted our focus from developing knowledge to building individual and team capability.

Over the years, Gluck's philosophy "to let 1,000 flowers bloom" had resulted in the original group of 11 sectors and 15 centers expanding to become what Hall called "72 islands of activity," (Sectors, Centers, Working Groups, and Special Projects) many of which were perceived as fiefdoms dominated by one or two established experts. In Hall's view, the garden of 1,000 flowers needed weeding, a task requiring a larger group of mostly different gardeners. The CPDC began integrating the diverse groups into seven sectors and seven functional capability groups (See **Exhibit 4**). These sectors and groups were led by teams of five to seven partners (typically younger directors and principals) with the objective of replacing the leader-driven knowledge creation and dissemination process with a "stewardship model" of self-governing practices focused on competence building.

Client Impact   With responsibility for knowledge management delegated to the CPDC, Gluck began to focus on a new theme—client impact. On being elected managing director, he made this a central theme in his early speeches, memos, and his first

Exhibit 4   Group Framework for Sectors and Centers

Functional Capability Groups	**Clientele Industry Sectors**

Corporate Governance and Leadership
- Corporate organization
- Corporate management processes
- Corporate strategy development
- Corporate relationship design and management
- Corporate finance
- Post-merger management

Organization (OPP/MOVE)
- Corporate transformation design and leadership
- Energizing approaches
- Organization design and development
- Leadership and teams
- Engaging teams

Information Technology/Systems
- To be determined

Marketing
- Market research
- Sales force management
- Channel management
- Global marketing
- Pricing
- Process and sector support

Operations Effectiveness
- Integrated logistics
- Manufacturing
- Purchasing and supply management

Strategy
- Strategy
- Microeconomics
- Business dynamics
- Business planning processes

Cross Functional Management
- Innovation
- Customer satisfaction
- Product/technology development and commercialization
- Core process redesign

Financial Institutions
- Banking
- Insurance
- Health care payer/provider

Consumer
- Retailing
- Consumer industries
- Media
- Pharmaceuticals

Energy
- Electrical utilities
- Petroleum
- Natural gas
- Other energy

Basic Materials
- Steel
- Pulp and paper
- Chemicals
- Other basic materials

Aerospace, Electronics, and Telecom
- Telecom
- Electronics
- Aerospace

Transportation

Automotive, Assembly, and Machinery
- Automotive
- Assembly

Source: Internal McKinsey & Company document.

All Partners Conference. He also created a Client Impact Committee, and asked it to explore the ways in which the firm could ensure that the expertise it was developing created positive measurable results in each client engagement.

One of the most important initiatives of the new committee was to persuade the partners to redefine the firm's key consulting unit from the engagement team (ET) to the client service team (CST). The traditional ET, assembled to deliver a three or four month assignment for a client was a highly efficient and flexible unit, but it tended to focus on the immediate task rather than on the client's long term need. The CST concept was that the firm could add long-term value and increase the effectiveness of individual engagements if it could unite a core of individuals (particularly at the partner level) who were linked across multiple ETs, and commit them to working with the client over an extended period. The impact was to broaden the classic model of a single partner "owning" a client to a group of partners with shared commitment to each client.

In response to concerns within the partnership about a gradual decline in associates' involvement in intellectual capital development, the CPDC began to emphasize the need for CSTs to play a central role in the intellectual life of McKinsey. (See **Exhibit 5** for a CPDC conceptualization.) Believing that the CSTs (by 1993 about 200 firm-wide) represented the real learning laboratories, the CPDC sent memos to the new industry sector and capability group leaders advising them that their practices would be evaluated by their coverage of the firm's CSTs. They also wrote to all consultants emphasizing the importance of the firm's intellectual development and their own professional development, for which they had primary responsibility. Finally, they assembled data on the amount of time consultants were spending on practice and professional development by office, distributing the widely divergent results to partners in offices worldwide.

Exhibit 5   CPDC Proposed Organizational Relationships

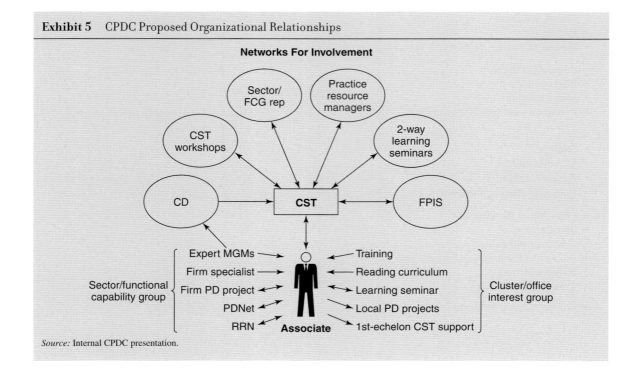

Source: Internal CPDC presentation.

Developing Multiple Career Paths   Despite (or perhaps because of) all these changes, the specialist consultant model continued to struggle. Over the years, the evaluation criteria for the specialist career path had gradually converged with the mainstream generalist promotion criteria. For example, the specialist's old promotion standard of "world-class expertise" in a particular field had given way to a more pragmatic emphasis on client impact; the notion of a legitimate role as a consultant to teams had evolved to a need for specialists to be "engagement director capable"; and the less pressured evaluation standard of "grow or go" was replaced by the normal associate's more demanding "up or out" requirement, albeit within a slightly more flexible timeframe.

Although these changes had reduced the earlier role dissonance—specialists became more T shaped—it also diluted the original objective. While legitimizing the two client service staff tracks, in late 1992 the Professional Personnel Committee decided to create two career paths for client service support and administrative staff. The first reaffirmed a path to partnership for practice-dedicated specialists who built credibility with clients and CSTs through their specialized knowledge

and its expert application. Their skills would have them in high demand as consultants to teams (CDs) rather than as engagement directors (EDs). The second new option was the practice management track designed to provide a career progression for practice coordinators, who had a key role in transferring knowledge and in helping practice leaders manage increasingly complex networks. Valuable administrators could also be promoted on this track. (See **Exhibit 6** for an overview.)

Yet despite the announcement of the new criteria and promotion processes, amongst associates and specialists alike there was still some residual confusion and even skepticism about the viability of the specialist track to partnership. As he dealt with this issue, Gluck kept returning to his long term theme that, "it's all about people," even suggesting people development was the company's primary purpose:

> There are two ways to look at McKinsey. The most common way is that we are a client service firm whose primary purpose is to serve the companies seeking our help. That is legitimate. But I believe there is an even more powerful way for us to see ourselves. We should begin to view our primary purpose as building

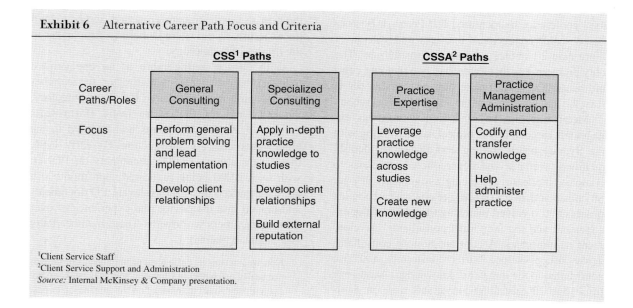

Exhibit 6   Alternative Career Path Focus and Criteria

Career Paths/Roles	CSS[1] Paths		CSSA[2] Paths	
	General Consulting	Specialized Consulting	Practice Expertise	Practice Management Administration
Focus	Perform general problem solving and lead implementation Develop client relationships	Apply in-depth practice knowledge to studies Develop client relationships Build external reputation	Leverage practice knowledge across studies Create new knowledge	Codify and transfer knowledge Help administer practice

[1]Client Service Staff
[2]Client Service Support and Administration
Source: Internal McKinsey & Company presentation.

a great institution that becomes an engine for producing highly motivated world class people who in turn will serve our clients extraordinarily well.

Knowledge Management on the Front

To see how McKinsey's evolving knowledge management processes were being felt by those on the firm's front lines, we will follow the activities of three consultants working in three diverse locations and focused on three different agendas.

Jeff Peters and the Sydney Office Assignment

John Stuckey, a director in McKinsey's Sydney office felt great satisfaction at being invited to bid for a financial services growth strategy study for one of Australia's most respected companies. Yet the opportunity also created some challenges. As in most small or medium sized offices, most consultants in Sydney were generalists. Almost all with financial industry expertise had been "conflicted out" of the project due to work they had done for competing financial institutions in Australia.

Stuckey immediately began using his personal network to find how he might tap into McKinsey's worldwide resources for someone who could lead this first engagement for an important new client. After numerous phone calls and some lobbying at a directors' conference he identified Jeff Peters, a Boston-based senior engagement manager and veteran of more than 20 studies for financial institutions. The only problem was that Peters had two ongoing commitments that would make him unavailable for at least the first six weeks of the Australian assignment.

Meanwhile, Stuckey and Ken Gibson, his engagement director on the project, were working with the Sydney office staffing coordinator to identify qualified, available and nonconflicted associates to complete the team. Balancing assignments of over 80 consultants to 25 ongoing teams was a complex process that involved matching the needs of the engagement and the individual consultants' development requirements. A constant flow of consultants across offices helped buffer constraints, and also contributed to the transfer of knowledge. At any one time 15 to 25 Australian consultants were on short- or long-term assignments abroad, while another 10 to 15 consultants from other offices were working in Australia. (Firm-wide, nearly 20% of work was performed by consultants on inter-office loans.)

They identified a three person team to work with Peters. John Peacocke was a New Zealand army engineer with an MBA in finance from Wharton and two years of experience in McKinsey. Although he had served on a four-month study for a retail bank client in Cleveland, since returning to Australia he had worked mostly for oil and gas clients. Patty Akopiantz was a one-year associate who had worked in investment banking before earning an MBA at Harvard. Her primary interest and her developing expertise was in consumer marketing. The business analyst was Jonathan Liew, previously an actuary who was embarking on his first McKinsey assignment.

With Peters' help, Stuckey and Gibson also began assembling a group of internal specialists and experts who could act as consulting directors (CDs) to the team. James Gorman, a personal financial services expert in New York agreed to visit Sydney for a week and to be available for weekly conference calls; Majid Arab, an insurance industry specialist committed to a two-week visit and a similar "on-call" availability; Andrew Doman, a London-based financial industry expert also signed on as a CD. Within the Sydney office, Charles Conn, a leader in the firm's growth strategies practice, agreed to lend his expertise, as did Clem Doherty, a firm leader in the impact of technology.

With Gibson acting more as an engagement manager than an engagement director, the team began scanning the Knowledge Resource Directory, the FPIS and the PDNet for leads. (Firm-wide, the use of PDNet documents had boomed in the eight years since its introduction. By early 1996, there were almost 12,000 documents on PDNet, with over 2,000 being requested each month.) In all, they tracked down 179 relevant PD documents and tapped into the advice and experience of over 60 firm members worldwide. Team member Patty Akopiantz explained:

> Ken was acting as engagement manager, but he was not really an expert in financial services, so we were even more reliant than usual on the internal network. Some of the ideas we got off PDNet were helpful,

but the trail of contacts was much more valuable ... Being on a completely different time zone had great advantages. If you hit a wall at the end of the day, you could drop messages in a dozen voicemail boxes in Europe and the United States. Because the firm norm is that you respond to requests by colleagues, by morning you would have seven or eight new suggestions, data sources, or leads.

At the end of the first phase, the team convened an internal workshop designed to keep client management informed, involved, and committed to the emerging conclusions. Out of this meeting, the team was focused on seven core beliefs and four viable options that provided its agenda for the next phase of the project. It was at this point that Peters was able to join the team:

By the time I arrived, most of the hard analysis had been done and they had been able to narrow the focus from the universe to four core options in just over a month. It was very impressive how they had been able to do that with limited team-based expertise and a demanding client... With things going so well, my main priority was to focus the team on the end product. Once we got a clear logical outline, I assigned tasks and got out of the way. Most of my time I spent working on the client relationship... It was great learning for John and Patty, and both of them were ready to take on a management role in their next engagements.

In November, the team presented its conclusions to the board, and after some tough questioning and challenging, they accepted the recommendations and began an implementation process. The client's managing director reflected on the outcome:

We're a tough client, but I would rate their work as very good. Their value added was in their access to knowledge, the intellectual rigor they bring, and their ability to build understanding and consensus among a diverse management group ... If things don't go ahead now, it's our own fault.

John Stuckey had a little different post-engagement view of the result:

Overall, I think we did pretty good work, but I was a bit disappointed we didn't come up with a radical breakthrough... We leveraged the firm's knowledge

base effectively, but I worry that we rely so much on our internal expertise. We have to beware of the trap that many large successful companies have fallen into by becoming too introverted, too satisfied with their own view of the world.

Warwick Bray and European Telecoms   After earning his MBA at Melbourne University, Warwick Bray joined McKinsey's Melbourne office in 1989. A computer science major, he had worked as a systems engineer at Hewlett Packard and wanted to leverage his technological experience. For two of his first three years, he worked on engagements related to the impact of deregulation on the Asia-Pacific telecommunications industry. In early 1992, Bray advised his group development leader (his assigned mentor and adviser) that he would be interested in spending a year in London. After several phone discussions the transfer was arranged, and in March the young Australian found himself on his first European team.

From his experience on the Australian telecom projects, Bray had written a PD document, "Negotiating Interconnect" which he presented at the firm's annual worldwide telecom conference. Recognizing this developing "knowledge spike," Michael Patsalos-Fox, telecom practice leader in London, invited Bray to work with him on a study. Soon he was being called in as a deregulation expert to make presentations to various client executives. "In McKinsey you have to earn that right," said Bray. "For me it was immensely satisfying to be recognized as an expert."

Under the leadership of Patsalos-Fox, the telecom practice had grown rapidly in the United Kingdom. With deregulation spreading across the continent in the 1990s, however, he was becoming overwhelmed by the demands for his help. Beginning in the late 1980s, Patsalos-Fox decided to stop acting as the sole repository for and exporter of European telecom information and expertise, and start developing a more interdependent network. To help in this task, he appointed Sulu Soderstrom, a Stanford MBA with a strong technology background, as full-time practice coordinator. Over the next few years she played a key role in creating the administrative glue that bonded together telecom practice groups in offices throughout Europe. Said Patsalos-Fox:

> She wrote proposals, became the expert on information sources, organized European conferences, helped with cross-office staffing, located expertise and supported and participated in our practice development work. Gradually she helped us move from an "export"-based hub and spokes model of information sharing to a true federalist-based network.

In this growth environment and supported by the stronger infrastructure, the practice opportunities exploded during the 1990s. To move the knowledge creation beyond what he described as "incremental synthesis of past experience," Patsalos-Fox launched a series of practice-sponsored studies. Staffed by some of the practice's best consultants, they focused on big topics like "The Industry Structure in 2005," or "The Telephone Company of the Future." But most of the practice's knowledge base was built by the informal initiatives of individual associates who would step back after several engagements and write a paper on their new insights. For example, Bray wrote several well-received PD documents and was enhancing his internal reputation as an expert in deregulation and multimedia. Increasingly he was invited to consult to or even join teams in other parts of Europe. Said Patsalos-Fox:

> He was flying around making presentations and helping teams. Although the internal audience is the toughest, he was getting invited back. When it came time for him to come up for election, the London office nominated him but the strength of his support came from his colleagues in the European telecom network.

In 1996, Patsalos-Fox felt it was time for a new generation of practice leadership. He asked his young Australian protégé and two other partners—one in Brussels, one in Paris—if they would take on a co-leadership role. Bray reflected on two challenges he and his co-leaders faced. The first was to make telecom a really exciting and interesting practice so it could attract the best associates. "That meant taking on the most interesting work, and

running our engagements so that people felt they were developing and having fun," he said.

The second key challenge was how to develop the largely informal links among the fast-growing European telecom practices. Despite the excellent job that Soderstrom had done as the practice's repository of knowledge and channel of communication, it was clear that there were limits to her ability to act as the sole "intelligent switch." As a result, the group had initiated a practice-specific intranet link designed to allow members direct access to the practice's knowledge base (PD documents, conference proceedings, CVs, etc.), its members' capabilities (via home pages for each practice member), client base (CST home pages, links to client web sites), and external knowledge resources (MIT's Multimedia Lab, Theseus Institute, etc.). More open yet more focused than existing firm-wide systems like PDNet, the Telecom Intranet was expected to accelerate the "engage-explore-apply-share" knowledge cycle.

There were some, however, who worried that this would be another step away from "one firm" towards compartmentalization, and from focus on building idea-driven personal networks towards creating data-based electronic transactions. In particular, the concern was that functional capability groups would be less able to transfer their knowledge into increasingly strong and self-contained industry-based practices. Warwick Bray recognized the problem, acknowledging that linkages between European telecom and most functional practices "could be better":

> The problem is we rarely feel the need to draw on those groups. For example, I know the firm's pricing practice has world-class expertise in industrial pricing, but we haven't yet learned how to apply it to telecom. We mostly call on the pricing experts within our practice. We probably should reach out more.

Stephen Dull and the Business Marketing Competence Center   After completing his MBA at the University of Michigan in 1983, Stephen Dull spent the next five years in various consumer marketing jobs at Pillsbury. In 1988, he was contacted by an executive search firm that had been retained by McKinsey to recruit potential consultants in consumer marketing. Joining the Atlanta office, Dull soon discovered that there was no structured development program. Like the eight experienced consumer marketing recruits in other offices, he was expected to create his own agenda.

Working on various studies, Dull found his interests shifting from consumer to industrial marketing issues. As he focused on building his own expertise, however, Dull acknowledged that he did not pay enough attention to developing strong client relations. "And around here, serving clients is what really counts," he said. So, in late 1994—a time when he might be discussing his election to principal—he had a long counseling session with his group development leader about his career. The GDL confirmed that he was not well positioned for election, but proposed another option. He suggested that Dull talk to Rob Rosiello, a principal in the New York office who had just launched a business-to-business marketing initiative within the marketing practice. Said Dull:

> Like most new initiatives, "B to B" was struggling to get established without full-time resources, so Rob was pleased to see me. I was enjoying my business marketing work, so the initiative sounded like a great opportunity.... Together, we wrote a proposal to make me the firm's first business marketing specialist.

The decision to pursue this strategy was not an easy one for Dull. Like most of his colleagues, he felt that specialists were regarded as second-class citizens—"overhead being supported by real consultants who serve clients," Dull suggested. But his GDL told him that recent directors meetings had reaffirmed the importance of building functional expertise, and some had even suggested that 15%–20% of the firm's partners should be functional experts within the next five to seven years. (As of 1995, over 300 associates were specialists, but only 15 of the 500 partners.) In April 1995, Dull and Rosiello took their proposal to Andrew Parsons and David Court, two leaders of the Marketing practice. The directors suggested a mutual trial of the concept until the end of the year and offered to provide Dull the support to commit full time to developing the B to B initiative.

Dull's first priority was to collect the various concepts, frameworks and case studies that existed within the firm, consolidating and synthesizing them in several PD documents. In the process, he and Rosiello began assembling a core team of interested contributors. Together, they developed an agenda of half a dozen cutting-edge issues in business marketing— segmentation, multi-buyer decision making and marketing partnerships, for example—and launched a number of study initiatives around them. Beyond an expanded series of PD documents, the outcome was an emerging set of core beliefs, and a new framework for business marketing.

The activity also attracted the interest of Mark Leiter, a specialist in the Marketing Science Center of Competence. This center, which had developed largely around a group of a dozen or so specialists, was in many ways a model of what Dull hoped the B to B initiative could become, and having a second committed specialist certainly helped.

In November, another major step to that goal occurred when the B to B initiative was declared a Center of Competence. At that time, the core group decided they would test their colleagues' interest and their own credibility by arranging an internal conference at which they would present their ideas. When over 50 people showed up including partners and directors from four continents, Dull felt that prospects for the center looked good.

Through the cumulative impact of the PD documents, the conference and word of mouth recommendations, by early 1996 Dull and his colleagues were getting more calls than the small center could handle. They were proud when the March listing of PDNet "Best Sellers" listed BtoB documents at numbers 2, 4 and 9 (See **Exhibit 7**). For Dull, the resulting process was enlightening:

> We decided that when we got calls we would swarm all over them and show our colleagues we could really add value for their clients.... This may sound strange—even corny—but I now really understand why this is a profession and not a business. If I help a partner serve his client better, he will call me back. It's all about relationships, forming personal bonds, helping each other.

Exhibit 7 PDNet "Best Sellers": March and Year-to-Date, 1996

	Number Requested	Title, Author(s), Date, PDNet #	Functional Capability Group/Sector
March 1996	21	**Developing a Distinctive Consumer Marketing Organization** *Nora Aufreiter, Theresa Austerberry, Steve Carlotti, Mike George, Liz Lempres (1/96, #13240)*	Consumer Industries/ Packaged Goods; Marketing
	19	**VIP: Value Improvement Program to Enhance Customer Value in Business to Business Marketing** *Dirk Berensmann, Marc Fischer, Heiner Frankemölle, Lutz-Peter Pape, Wolf-Dieter Voss (10/95, #13340)*	Marketing; Steel
	16	**Handbook For Sales Force Effectiveness—1991 Edition** *(5/91, #6670)*	Marketing
	15	**Understanding and Influencing Customer Purchase Decisions in Business to Business Markets** *Mark Leiter (3/95, #12525)*	Marketing
	15	**Channel Management Handbook** *Christine Bucklin, Stephen DeFalco, John DeVincentis, John Levis (1/95, #11876)*	Marketing
	15	**Platforms for Growth in Personal Financial Services (PFS201)** *Christopher Leech, Ronald O'Hanley, Eric Lambrecht, Kristin Morse (11/95, #12995)*	Personal Financial Services
	14	**Developing Successful Acquisition Programs To Support Long-Term Growth Strategies** *Steve Coley, Dan Goodwin (11/92, #9150)*	Corporate Finance
	14	**Understanding Value-Based Segmentation** *John Forsyth, Linda Middleton (11/95, #11730)*	Consumer Industries/ Packaged Goods; Marketing
	14	**The Dual Perspective Customer Map for Business to Business Marketing** *(3/95, #12526)*	Marketing
	13	**Growth Strategy—Platforms, Staircases and Franchises** *Charles Conn, Rob McLean, David White (8/94, #11400)*	Strategy
Cumulative Index (January–March)	54	**Introduction to CRM (Continuous Relationship Marketing)—Leveraging CRM to Build PFS Franchise Value (PFS221)** *Margo Geogiadis, Milt Gillespie, Tim Gokey, Mike Sherman, Marc Singer (11/95, #12999)*	Personal Financial Services
	45	**Platforms for Growth in Personal Financial Services (PFS201)** *Christopher Leech, Ronald O'Hanley, Eric Lambrecht, Kristin Morse (11/95, #12995)*	Personal Financial Services
	40	**Launching a CRM Effort (PFS222)** *Nick Brown, Margo Georgiadis (10/95, #12940)*	Marketing
	38	**Building Value Through Continuous Relationship Marketing (CRM)** *Nick Brown, Mike Wright (10/95, #13126)*	Banking and Securities
	36	**Combining Art and Science to Optimize Brand Portfolios** *Richard Benson-Armer, David Court, John Forsyth (10/95, #12916)*	Marketing; Consumer Industries/Packaged Goods
	35	**Consumer Payments and the Future of Retail Banks (PA202)** *John Stephenson, Peter Sands (11/95, #13008)*	Payments and Operating Products
	34	**CRM (Continuous Relationship Marketing) Case Examples Overview** *Howie Hayes, David Putts (9/95, #12931)*	Marketing
	32	**Straightforward Approaches to Building Management Talent** *Parke Boneysteele, Bill Meehan, Kristin Morse, Pete Sidebottom (9/95, #12843)*	Organization
	32	**Reconfiguring and Reenergizing Personal Selling Channels (PFS213)** *Patrick Wetzel, Amy Zinsser (11/95, #12997)*	Personal Financial Services
	31	**From Traditional Home Banking to On-Line PFS (PFS211)** *Gaurang Desai, Brian Johnson, Kai Lahmann, Gottfried Leibbrandt, Paal Weberg (11/95, #12998)*	Personal Financial Services

Source: Month By Month (McKinsey's internal staff magazine).

While Dull was pleased with the way the new center was gaining credibility and having impact, he was still very uncertain about his promotion prospects. As he considered his future, he began to give serious thought to writing a book on business to business marketing to enhance his internal credibility and external visibility.

A New MD, A New Focus

In 1994, after six years of leadership in which firm revenue had doubled to an estimated $1.5 billion annually, Fred Gluck stepped down as MD. His successor was 45 year old Rajat Gupta, a 20 year McKinsey veteran committed to continuing the emphasis on knowledge development. After listening to the continuing debates about which knowledge development approach was most effective, Gupta came to the conclusion that the discussions were consuming energy that should have been directed towards the activity itself. "The firm did not have to make a choice," he said. "We had to pursue *all* the options." With that conclusion, Gupta launched a four-pronged attack.

First, he wanted to capitalize on the firm's long term investment in practice development driven by Clientele Industry Sectors and Functional Capability Groups and supported by the knowledge infrastructure of PDNet and FPIS. But he also wanted to create some new channels, forums, and mechanisms for knowledge development and organizational learning.

Then, building on an experiment begun by the German office, Gupta embraced a grass-roots knowledge-development approach called Practice Olympics. Two- to six-person teams from offices around the world were encouraged to develop ideas that grew out of recent client engagements and formalize them for presentation at a regional competition with senior partners and clients as judges. The twenty best regional teams then competed at a firm-wide event. Gupta was proud that in its second year, the event had attracted over 150 teams and involved 15% of the associate body.

Next, in late 1995 the new MD initiated six special initiatives-multi-year internal assignments led by senior partners that focused on emerging issues that were of importance to CEOs. The initiatives tapped both internal and external expertise to develop "state-of-the-art" formulations of each key issue. For example, one focused on the shape and function of the corporation of the future, another on creating and managing strategic growth, and a third on capturing global opportunities. Gupta saw these initiatives as reasserting the importance of the firm's functional knowledge yet providing a means to do longer term, bigger commitment, cross-functional development.

Finally, he planned to expand on the model of the McKinsey Global Institute, a firm-sponsored research center established in 1991 to study implications of changes in the global economy on business. The proposal was to create other pools of dedicated resources protected from daily pressures and client demands, and focused on long term research agendas. A Change Center was established in 1995 and an Operations Center was being planned. Gupta saw these institutes as a way in which McKinsey could recruit more research-oriented people and link more effectively into the academic arena.

Most of these initiatives were new and their impact had not yet been felt within the firm. Yet Gupta was convinced the direction was right:

> We have easily doubled our investment in knowledge over these past couple of years. There are lots more people involved in many more initiatives. If that means we do 5–10% less client work today, we are willing to pay that price to invest in the future. Since Marvin Bower, every leadership group has had a commitment to leave the firm stronger than it found it. It's a fundamental value of McKinsey to invest for the future of the firm.

Future Directions   Against this background, the McKinsey partnership was engaged in spirited debate about the firm's future directions and priorities. The following is a sampling of their opinions:

> I am concerned that our growth may stretch the fabric of the place. We can't keep on disaggregating our units to create niches for everyone because we have exhausted the capability of our integrating mechanisms. I believe our future is in developing around

CSTs and integrating across them around common knowledge agendas.

Historically, I was a supporter of slower growth, but now I'm convinced we must grow faster. That is the key to creating opportunity and excitement for people, and that generates innovation and drives knowledge development... Technology is vital not only in supporting knowledge transfer, but also in allowing partners to mentor more young associates. We have to be much more aggressive in using it.

There is a dark side to technology—what I call technopoly. It can drive out communication and people start believing that e-mailing someone is the same thing as talking to them. If teams stop meeting as often or if practice conferences evolve into discussion forums on Lotus Notes, the technology that has supported our growth may begin to erode our culture based on personal networks.

I worry that we are losing our sense of village as we compartmentalize our activities and divide into specialties. And the power of IT has sometimes led to information overload. The risks is that the more we spend searching out the right PD document, the ideal framework, or the best expert, the less time we spend thinking creatively about the problem. I worry that as we increase the science, we might lose the craft of what we do.

These were among the scores of opinions that Rajat Gupta heard since becoming MD. His job was to sort through them and set a direction that would "leave the firm stronger than he found it."

Reading 5-1   Building Effective R&D Capabilities Abroad

by Walter Kuemmerle

An increasing number of companies in technologically intensive industries such as pharmaceuticals and electronics have abandoned the traditional approach to managing research and development and are establishing global R&D networks in a noteworthy new way. For example, Canon is now carrying out R&D activities in 8 dedicated facilities in 5 countries, Motorola in 14 facilities in 7 countries, and Bristol-Myers Squibb in 12 facilities in 6 countries. In the past, most companies—even those with a considerable international presence in terms of sales and manufacturing—carried out the majority of their R&D activity in their home countries. Conventional wisdom held that strategy development and R&D had to be kept in close geographical proximity. Because strategic decisions were made primarily at corporate headquarters, the thinking went, R&D facilities should be close to home.

But such a centralized approach to R&D will no longer suffice—for two reasons. First, as more and more sources of potentially relevant knowledge emerge across the globe, companies must establish a presence at an increasing number of locations to access new knowledge and to absorb new research results from foreign universities and competitors into their own organizations. Second, companies competing around the world must move new products from development to market at an ever more

▌ **Walter Kuemmerle** is an assistant professor at the Harvard Business School in Boston, Massachusetts, where he teaches technology and operations management, as well as entrepreneurial finance. His research focuses on the technology strategies of multinational companies, patterns of strategic interaction between small and large companies, and foreign direct investment.

Laboratory Sites Abroad in 1995

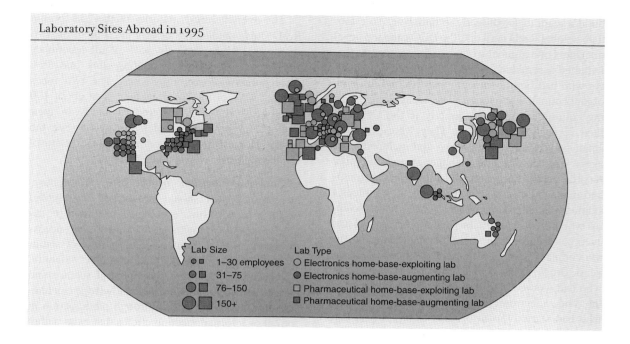

Lab Size
- ● ■ 1–30 employees
- ● ■ 31–75
- ● ■ 76–150
- ● ■ 150+

Lab Type
- ○ Electronics home-base-exploiting lab
- ◐ Electronics home-base-augmenting lab
- □ Pharmaceutical home-base-exploiting lab
- ■ Pharmaceutical home-base-augmenting lab

rapid pace. Consequently, companies must build R&D networks that excel at tapping new centers of knowledge and at commercializing products in foreign markets with the speed required to remain competitive. And more and more, superior manufacturers are doing just that. (See the exhibit "Laboratory Sites Abroad in 1995.")

In an ongoing study on corporate strategy and the geographical dispersion of R&D sites, I have been examining the creation of global research networks by 32 U.S., Japanese, and European multinational companies.[1] The most successful companies in my study brought each new site's research productivity up to full speed within a few years and quickly transformed knowledge created there into innovative products. I found that establishing networks of such sites poses a number of new, complex managerial challenges. According to my research, managers of the most successful R&D networks understand the new dynamics of global R&D, link corporate strategy to R&D strategy, pick the appropriate sites, staff them with the right people, supervise the sites during start-up, and integrate the activities of the different foreign sites so that the entire network is a coordinated whole.

Adopting a Global Approach to R&D

Adopting a global approach to R&D requires linking R&D strategy to a company's overall business strategy. And that requires the involvement of managers at the highest levels of a company.

Creating a Technology Steering Committee   The first step in creating a global R&D network is to

[1]In a systematic effort to analyze the relationship of global strategy and R&D investments in technologically intensive industries, I have been collecting detailed data on all dedicated laboratory sites operated by 32 leading multinational companies. The sample consists of 10 U.S., 12 Japanese, and 10 European companies. Thirteen of the companies are in the pharmaceutical industry, and 19 are in the electronics industry. Data collection includes archival research, a detailed questionnaire, and in-depth interviews with several senior R&D managers in each company. Overall, these companies operate 238 dedicated R&D sites, 156 of them abroad. About 60% of the laboratory sites abroad were established after 1984. I have used this sample, which is the most complete of its kind, as a basis for a number of quantitative and qualitative investigations into global strategy, competitive interaction, and R&D management.

build a team that will lead the initiative. To establish a global R&D network, the CEOs and top-level managers of a number of successful companies that I studied assembled a small team of senior managers who had both technical expertise and in-depth organizational knowledge. The technology steering committees reported directly to the CEOs of their respective companies. They were generally small—five to eight members—and included managers with outstanding managerial and scientific records and a range of educational backgrounds and managerial responsibilities. The committees I studied included as members a former bench scientist who had transferred into manufacturing and had eventually become the head of manufacturing for the company's most important category of therapeutic drugs; a head of marketing for memory chips who had worked before in product development in the same electronics company; and an engineer who had started out in product development, had moved to research, and eventually had become the vice president of R&D. Members of these committees were sufficiently senior to be able to mobilize resources at short notice; and they were actively involved in the management and supervision of R&D programs. In many cases, members included the heads of major existing R&D sites.

Categorizing New R&D Sites.   In selecting new sites, companies find it helpful first to articulate each site's primary objective. (See the exhibit "Establishing New R&D Sites.") R&D sites have one of two missions. The first type of site—what I call a *home-base-augmenting site*—is established in order to tap knowledge from competitors and universities around the globe; in that type of site, information flows *from* the foreign laboratory *to* the central lab at home. The second type of site—what I call a *home-base-exploiting site*—is established to support manufacturing facilities in foreign countries or to adapt standard products to the demand there; in that type of site, information flows *to* the foreign laboratory *from* the central lab at home. (See the exhibit "How Information Flows Between Home-Base and Foreign R&D Sites.")

The overwhelming majority of the 238 foreign R&D sites I studied fell clearly into one of the two categories. Approximately 45% of all laboratory sites were home-base-augmenting sites, and 55% were home-base-exploiting sites. The two types of sites were of the same average size: about 100 employees. But they differed distinctly in their strategic purpose and leadership style.[2] (See the insert "Home-Base-Augmenting and Home-Base-Exploiting Sites: Xerox and Eli Lilly.")

Choosing a Location for the Site   Home-base-augmenting sites should be located in regional clusters of scientific excellence in order to tap new sources of knowledge. Central to the success of corporate R&D strategy is the ability of senior researchers to recognize and combine scientific advancements from different areas of science and technology. Absorbing the new knowledge can happen in a number of ways: through participation in formal or informal meeting circles that exist within a geographic area containing useful knowledge (a knowledge cluster), through hiring employees from competitors, or through sourcing laboratory equipment and research services from the same suppliers that competitors use.

For example, the Silicon Valley knowledge cluster boasts a large number of informal gatherings of experts as well as more formal ways for high-tech companies to exchange information with adjacent universities, such as industrial liaison programs with Stanford University and the University of California at Berkeley. In the field of communication technology, Siemens, NEC, Matsushita, and Toshiba all operate laboratory sites near Princeton University and Bell Labs (now a part of Lucent Technologies) to take advantage of the expertise

[2]My research on global R&D strategies builds on earlier research on the competitiveness of nations and on research on foreign direct investment, including Michael E. Porter, *The Competitive Advantage of Nations* (New York: The Free Press, 1990), and Thomas J. Wesson, "An Alternative Motivation for Foreign Direct Investment" (Ph.D. dissertation, Harvard University, 1993). My research also builds on an existing body of knowledge about the management of multinational companies. See, for example, Christopher A. Bartlett and Sumantra Ghoshal, *Managing Across Borders* (New York: The Free Press, 1989).

Establishing New R&D Sites

Types of R&D Sites	Phase 1 Location Decision	Phase 2 Ramp–Up Period	Phase 3 Maximizing Lab Impact
Home-Base-Augmenting Laboratory Site Objective of establishment: absorbing knowledge from the local scientific community, creating new knowledge, and transferring it to the company's central R&D site	–Select a location for its scientific excellence –Promote cooperation between the company's senior scientists and managers	–Choose as first laboratory leader a renowned local scientist with international experience—one who understands the dynamics of R&D at the new location –Ensure enough critical mass	–Ensure the laboratory's active participation in the local scientific community –Exchange researchers with local university laboratories and with the home-base lab
Home-Base-Exploiting Laboratory Site Objective of establishment: commercializing knowledge by transferring it from the company's home base to the laboratory site abroad and from there to local manufacturing and marketing	–Select a location for its proximity to the company's existing manufacturing and marketing locations –Involve middle managers from other functional areas in start-up decisions	–Choose as first laboratory leader an experienced product-development engineer with a strong company-wide reputation, international experience, and knowledge of marketing and manufacturing	–Emphasize smooth relations with the home-base lab –Encourage employees to seek interaction with other corporate units beyond the manufacturing and marketing units that originally sponsored the lab

How Information Flows Between Home-Base and Foreign R&D Sites

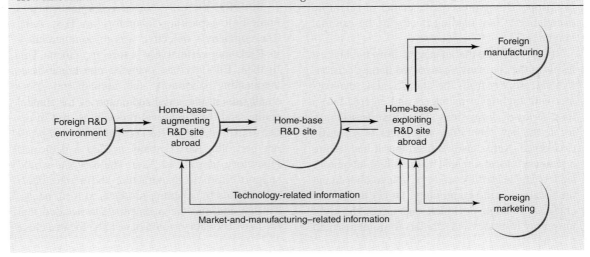

Home-Base-Augmenting and Home-Base-Exploiting Sites: Xerox and Eli Lilly

The particular type of foreign R&D site determines the specific challenges managers will face. Setting up a *home-base-augmenting site*—one designed to gather new knowledge for a company—involves certain skills. And launching a *home-base-exploiting site*—one established to help a company efficiently commercialize its R&D in foreign markets—involves others. The cases of Xerox and Eli Lilly present an instructive contrast.

Xerox established a home-base-augmenting laboratory in Grenoble, France. Its objective: to tap new knowledge from the local scientific community and to transfer it back to its home base. Having already established, in 1986, a home-base-augmenting site in Cambridge, England, Xerox realized in 1992 that the research culture in continental Western Europe was sufficiently different and complementary to Great Britain's to justify another site. Moreover, understanding the most advanced research in France or Germany was very difficult from a base in Great Britain because of language and cultural barriers. One senior R&D manager in the United States notes, "We wanted to learn firsthand what was going on in centers of scientific excellence in Europe. Being present at a center of scientific excellence is like reading poetry in the original language."

It was essential that managers from the highest levels of the company be involved in the decision-making process from the start. Senior scientists met with high-level managers and entered into a long series of discussions. Their first decision: to locate the new laboratory at a center of scientific excellence. Xerox also realized that it had to hire a renowned local scientist as the initial laboratory leader. The leader needed to be able to understand the local scientific community, attract junior scientists with high potential, and target the right university institutes and scholars for joint research

projects. Finally, Xerox knew that the laboratory would have an impact on the company's economic performance only if it had the critical mass to become an accepted member of the local scientific community. At the same time, it could not become isolated from the larger Xerox culture.

Xerox considered a number of locations and carefully evaluated such aspects as their scientific excellence and relevance, university liaison programs, licensing programs, and university recruiting programs. The company came up with four potential locations: Paris, Grenoble, Barcelona, and Munich. At that point, Xerox also identified potential laboratory leaders. The company chose Grenoble on the basis of its demonstrated scientific excellence and hired as the initial laboratory leader a highly regarded French scientist with good connections to local universities. Xerox designed a facility for 40 researchers and made plans for further expansion. In order to integrate the new laboratory's scientists into the Xerox community, senior R&D management in Palo Alto, California, allocated a considerable part of the initial laboratory budget to travel to other Xerox sites and started a program for the temporary transfer of newly hired researchers from Grenoble to other R&D sites. At the same time, the Grenoble site set out to integrate itself within the local research community.

In 1989, Eli Lilly considered establishing a home-base-exploiting laboratory in East Asia. The company's objective was to commercialize its R&D more effectively in foreign markets. Until then, Eli Lilly had operated one home-base-augmenting laboratory site abroad and some small sites in industrialized countries for clinical testing and drug approval procedures. But in order to exploit Lilly's R&D capabilities and product portfolio, the company needed a dedicated laboratory site in East Asia. The new site would support efforts to manufacture and market pharmaceuticals by adapting products to local needs. To that end, the management team decided that the new laboratory would have to be located close to relevant markets and existing corporate facilities. It also determined that the initial laboratory leader would have to be an experienced manager from Lilly's home base—a manager with a deep understanding of both the company's local operations and its overall R&D network.

The team considered Singapore as a potential location because of its proximity to a planned Lilly manufacturing site in Malaysia. But ultimately it decided that the new home-base-exploiting laboratory would have the strongest impact on Lilly's sales if it was located in Kōbe, Japan. By establishing a site in the Kōbe-Osaka region—the second-largest regional market in Japan and one that offered educational institutions with high-quality scientists—Lilly would send a signal to the medical community there that the company was committed to the needs of the Japanese market. Kōbe had another advantage: Lilly's corporate headquarters for Japan were located there, and the company was already

running some of its drug approval operations for the Japanese market out of Kōbe. The city therefore was the logical choice.

The team assigned an experienced Lilly researcher and manager to be the initial leader of the new site. Because he knew the company inside and out—from central research and development to international marketing—the team reasoned that he would be able to bring the new laboratory up to speed quickly by drawing on resources from various divisions within Lilly. In order to integrate the new site into the over-all company, some researchers from other Lilly R&D sites received temporary transfers of up to two years to Kōbe, and some locally hired researchers were temporarily transferred to other Lilly sites. It took about 30 months to activate fully the Kōbe operation—a relatively short period. Today the site is very productive in transferring knowledge from Lilly's home base to Kōbe and in commercializing that knowledge throughout Japan and Asia.

located there. For similar reasons, a number of companies in the same industry have established sites in the Kanto area surrounding Tokyo. Texas Instruments operates a facility in Tsukuba Science City, and Hewlett-Packard operates one in Tokyo.

After a company has picked and established its major R&D sites, it might want to branch out. It might selectively set up secondary sites when a leading competitor or a university succeeds in building a critical mass of research expertise in a more narrowly defined area of science and technology outside the primary cluster. In order to benefit from the resulting miniclusters of expertise, companies sometimes establish additional facilities. For that reason, NEC operates a small telecommunications-oriented R&D facility close to a university laboratory in London, and Canon operates an R&D facility in Rennes, France, close to one of France Telecom's major sites.

Home-base-exploiting sites, in contrast, should be located close to large markets and manufacturing

facilities in order to commercialize new products rapidly in foreign markets. In the past, companies from industrialized countries located manufacturing facilities abroad primarily to benefit from lower wages or to overcome trade barriers. Over time, however, many of those plants have taken on increasingly complex manufacturing tasks that require having an R&D facility nearby in order to ensure the speedy transfer of technology from research to manufacturing. A silicon-wafer plant, for example, has to interact closely with product development engineers during trial runs of a new generation of microchips. The same is true for the manufacture of disk drives and other complex hardware. For that reason, Hewlett-Packard and Texas Instruments both operate laboratories in Singapore, close to manufacturing facilities.

The more complex and varied a manufacturing process is, the more often manufacturing engineers will have to interact with product development engineers. For example, in the case of one of

Toshiba's laptop-computer-manufacturing plants, a new model is introduced to the manufacturing line every two weeks. The introduction has to happen seamlessly, without disturbing the production of existing models on the same line. In order to predict and remedy bugs during initial production runs, development engineers and manufacturing engineers meet several times a week. The proximity of Toshiba's laptop-development laboratory to its manufacturing plant greatly facilitates the interaction.

Establishing a New R&D Facility

Whether establishing a home-base-augmenting or a home-base-exploiting facility, companies must use the same three-stage process: selecting the best laboratory leader, determining the optimal size for the new laboratory site, and keeping close watch over the lab during its start-up period in order to ensure that it is merged into the company's existing global R&D network and contributes sufficiently to the company's product portfolio and its economic performance.

Selecting the Best Site Leader   Identifying the best leader for a new R&D site is one of the most important decisions a company faces in its quest to establish a successful global R&D network. My research shows that the initial leader of an R&D site has a powerful impact not only on the culture of the site but also on its long-term research agenda and performance. The two types of sites require different types of leaders, and each type of leader confronts a particular set of challenges.

The initial leaders of home-base-augmenting sites should be prominent local scientists so that they will be able to fulfill their primary responsibility: to nurture ties between the new site and the local scientific community. If the site does not succeed in becoming part of the local scientific community quickly, it will not be able to generate new knowledge for the company. In addition to hiring a local scientist, there are a variety of other ways to establish local ties. For example, Toshiba used its memory-chip joint venture with Siemens to

develop local ties at its new R&D site in Regensburg, Germany. The venture allowed Toshiba to tap into Siemens's dense network of associations with local universities. In addition, it helped Toshiba develop a better understanding of the compensation packages required to hire first-class German engineering graduates. Finally, it let the company gain useful insights into how to establish effective contract-research relationships with government-funded research institutions in Germany.

In contrast, the initial leaders of home-base-exploiting sites should be highly regarded managers from within the company—managers who are intimately familiar with the company's culture and systems. Such leaders will be able to fulfill their primary responsibility: to forge close ties between the new lab's engineers and the foreign community's manufacturing and marketing facilities. Then the transfer of knowledge from the company's home base to the R&D site will have the maximum impact on manufacturing and marketing located near that site. When one U.S. pharmaceutical company established a home-base-exploiting site in Great Britain, executives appointed as the initial site leader a manager who had been with the company for several years. He had started his career as a bench scientist first in exploratory research, then in the development of one of the company's blockbuster drugs. He had worked closely with marketing, and he had spent two years as supervisor of manufacturing quality at one of the company's U.S. manufacturing sites. With such a background, he was able to lead the new site effectively.

However, the best candidates for both home-base-augmenting and home-base-exploiting sites share four qualities: they are at once respected scientists or engineers and skilled managers; they are able to integrate the new site into the company's existing R&D network; they have a comprehensive understanding of technology trends; and they are able to overcome formal barriers when they seek access to new ideas in local universities and scientific communities.

Appointing an outstanding scientist or engineer who has no management experience can be disastrous. In one case, a leading U.S. electronics company decided to establish a home-base-augmenting site in the United Kingdom. The engineer who was appointed as the first site leader was an outstanding researcher but had little management experience outside the company's central laboratory environment. The leader had difficulties marshaling the necessary resources to expand the laboratory beyond its starting size of 14 researchers. Furthermore, he had a tough time mediating between the research laboratory and the company's product development area. Eleven of the 14 researchers had been hired locally and therefore lacked deep ties to the company. They needed a savvy corporate advocate who could understand company politics and could promote their research results within the company. One reason they didn't have such an advocate was that two of the three managers at the company's home base—people who had promoted the establishment of the new R&D lab—had quit about six months after the lab had opened because they disagreed about the company's overall R&D strategy. The third manager had moved to a different department.

In an effort to improve the situation, the company appointed a U.S. engineer as liaison to the U.K. site. He realized that few ideas were flowing from the site to the home base; but he attributed the problem to an inherently slow scientific-discovery process rather than to organizational barriers within the company. After about two years, senior management finally replaced the initial laboratory leader and the U.S. liaison engineer with two managers—one from the United Kingdom and one from the United States. The managers had experience overseeing one of the company's U.S. joint ventures in technology, and they also had good track records as researchers. Finally, under their leadership, the site dramatically increased its impact on the company's product portfolio. In conjunction with the increase in scientific output, the site grew to its projected size of 225 employees and is now highly productive.

In the case of both types of sites, the ideal leader has in-depth knowledge of both the home-base

culture and the foreign culture. Consider Sharp's experience. In Japan, fewer corporate scientists have Ph.D.'s than their counterparts in the United Kingdom; instead they have picked up their knowledge and skills on the job. That difference presented a management challenge for Sharp when it established a home-base-augmenting facility in the United Kingdom. In order to cope with that challenge, the company hired a British laboratory leader who had previously worked as a science attaché at the British embassy in Japan. In that position, he had developed a good understanding of the Japanese higher-education system. He was well aware that British and Japanese engineers with different academic degrees might have similar levels of expertise, and, as a result, he could manage them better.

The pioneer who heads a newly established home-base-augmenting or home-base-exploiting site also must have a broad perspective and a deep understanding of technology trends. R&D sites abroad are often particularly good at combining knowledge from different scientific fields into new ideas and products. Because those sites start with a clean slate far from the company's powerful central laboratory, they are less plagued by the "not-invented-here" syndrome. For example, Canon's home-base-augmenting laboratory in the United Kingdom developed an innovative loudspeaker that is now being manufactured in Europe for a worldwide market. Senior researchers at Canon in Japan acknowledge that it would have been much more difficult for a new research team located in Japan to come up with the product. As one Canon manager puts it, "Although the new loudspeaker was partially based on knowledge that existed within Canon already, Canon's research management in Japan was too focused on existing product lines and would probably not have tolerated the pioneering loudspeaker project."

Finally, leaders of new R&D sites need to be aware of the considerable formal barriers they might confront when they seek access to local universities and scientific communities. These barriers are often created by lawmakers who want to protect a nation's intellectual capital. Although for-eign companies do indeed absorb local knowledge and transfer it to their home bases—particularly in the case of home-base-augmenting sites—they also create important positive economic effects for the host nation. The laboratory leader of a new R&D site needs to communicate that fact locally in order to reduce existing barriers and prevent the forma-tion of new ones.

Determining the Optimal Size of the New R&D Site

My research indicates that the optimal size for a new foreign R&D facility during the start-up phase is usually 30 to 40 employees, and the best size for a site after the ramp-up period is about 235 employees, including support staff. The optimal size of a site depends mainly on a company's track record in international management. Companies that already operate several sites abroad tend to be more successful at establishing larger new sites.

Companies can run into problems if their for-eign sites are either too small or too large. If the site is too small, the resulting lack of critical mass produces an environment in which there is little cross-fertilization of ideas among researchers. And a small R&D site generally does not command a sufficient level of respect in the scientific com-munity surrounding the laboratory. As a result, its researchers have a harder time gaining access to informal networks and to scientific meetings that provide opportunities for an exchange of knowl-edge. In contrast, if the laboratory site is too large, its culture quickly becomes anonymous, research-ers become isolated, and the benefits of spreading fixed costs over a larger number of researchers are outweighed by the lack of cross-fertilization of ideas. According to one manager at such a lab, "Once people stopped getting to know one another on an informal basis in the lunchroom of our site, they became afraid of deliberately walking into one another's laboratory rooms to talk about research and to ask questions. Researchers who do not know each other on an informal basis are often hesitant to ask their colleagues for advice: they are afraid to reveal any of their own knowledge gaps. We

realized that we had crossed a critical threshold in size. We subsequently scaled back somewhat and made an increased effort to reduce the isolation of individual researchers within the site through com-munication tools and through rotating researchers among different lab units at the site."

Supervising the Start-Up Period

During the initial growth period of an R&D site, which typi-cally lasts anywhere from one to three years, the culture is formed and the groundwork for the site's future productivity is laid. During that period, se-nior management in the home country has to be in particularly close contact with the new site. Although it is important that the new laboratory develop its own identity and stake out its fields of expertise, it also has to be closely connected to the company's existing R&D structure. Newly hired scientists must be aware of the resources that exist within the company as a whole, and scientists at home and at other locations must be aware of the opportunities the new site creates for the company as a whole. Particularly during the start-up period, senior R&D managers at the corporate level have to walk a fine line and decide whether to devote the most resources to connecting the new site to the company or to supporting ties between the new site and its local environment.

To integrate a new site into the company as a whole, managers must pay close attention to the site's research agenda and create mechanisms to in-tegrate it into the company's overall strategic goals. Because of the high degree of uncertainty of R&D outcomes, continuous adjustments to research agendas are the rule. What matters most is speed, both in terms of terminating research projects that go nowhere and in terms of pushing projects that bring unexpectedly good results.

The rapid exchange of information is essential to integrating a site into the overall company during the start-up phase. Companies use a number of mecha-nisms to create a cohesive research community in spite of geographic distance. Hewlett-Packard regularly organizes an in-house science fair at which teams of researchers can present projects and prototypes to one another. Canon has a program that lets researchers from home-base-augmenting sites request a temporary transfer to home-base-exploiting sites. At Xerox, most sites are linked by a sophisticated information system that allows senior R&D managers to determine within minutes the current state of research projects and the number of researchers working on those projects. But nothing can replace face-to-face contact between active researchers. Maintaining a global R&D network requires personal meetings, and therefore many researchers and R&D managers have to spend time visiting not only other R&D sites but also specialized suppliers and local universities affiliated with those sites.

Failing to establish sufficient ties with the company's existing R&D structure during the start-up phase can hamper the success of a new foreign R&D site. For example, in 1986, a large foreign pharmaceutical company established a biotechnology research site in Boston, Massachusetts. In order to recruit outstanding scientists and maintain a high level of creative output, the company's R&D management decided to give the new laboratory considerable leeway in its research agenda and in determining what to do with the results—although the company did reserve the right of first refusal for the commercialization of the lab's inventions. The new site was staffed exclusively with scientists handpicked by a newly hired laboratory leader. A renowned local biochemist, he had been employed for many years by a major U.S. university, where he had carried out contract research for the company. During the start-up phase, few of the company's veteran scientists were involved in joint research projects with the site's scientists—an arrangement that hindered the transfer of ideas between the new lab and the company's other R&D sites. Although the academic community now recognizes the lab as an important contributor to the field, few of its inventions have been patented by the company, fewer have been targeted for commercialization, and none have reached the commercial stage yet. One senior scientist working in the lab commented that ten years after its creation, the lab had become so much of an "independent animal" that it would take a lot of carefully balanced guidance from the company

to instill a stronger sense of commercial orientation without a risk of losing the most creative scientists.

There is no magic formula that senior managers can follow to ensure the success of a foreign R&D site during its start-up phase. Managing an R&D network, particularly in its early stages, is delicate and complex. It requires constant tinkering—evaluation and reevaluation. Senior R&D managers have to decide how much of the research should be initiated by the company and how much by the scientist, determine the appropriate incentive structures and employment contracts, establish policies for the temporary transfer of researchers to the company's other R&D or manufacturing sites, and choose universities from which to hire scientists and engineers.

Flexibility and experimentation during a site's start-up phase can ensure its future productivity. For example, Fujitsu established a software-research laboratory site in San Jose, California, in 1992. The company was seriously thinking of establishing a second site in Boston but eventually reconsidered. Fujitsu realized that the effort that had gone into establishing the San Jose site had been greater than expected. Once the site was up and running, however, its productive output also had been higher than expected. Furthermore, Fujitsu found that its R&D managers had gained an excellent understanding of the R&D community that created advanced software-development tools. Although initially leaning toward establishing a second site, the managers were flexible. They decided to enlarge the existing site because of its better-than-expected performance as well as the limited potential benefits of a second site. The San Jose site has had a major impact on Fujitsu's software development and sales—particularly in Japan but in the United States, too. Similarly, at Alcatel's first foreign R&D site in Germany, senior managers were flexible. After several months, they realized that the travel-and-communications budget would have to be increased substantially beyond initial projections in order to improve the flow of knowledge from the French home base. For instance, in the case of a telephone switchboard project, the actual number of business trips between the two sites was nearly twice as high as originally projected.

Integrating the Global R&D Network

As the number of companies' R&D sites at home and abroad grows, R&D managers will increasingly face the challenging task of coordinating the network. That will require a fundamental shift in the role of senior managers at the central lab. Managers of R&D networks must be global coordinators, not local administrators. More than being managers of people and processes, they must be managers of knowledge. And not all managers that a company has in place will be up to the task.

Consider Matsushita's R&D management. A number of technically competent managers became obsolete at the company once it launched a global approach to R&D. Today managers at Matsushita's central R&D site in Hirakata, Japan, continue to play an important role in the research and development of core processes for manufacturing. But the responsibility of an increasing number of senior managers at the central site is overseeing Matsushita's network of 15 dedicated R&D sites. That responsibility includes setting research agendas, monitoring results, and creating direct ties between sites.

How does the new breed of R&D manager coordinate global knowledge? Look again to Matsushita's central R&D site. First, high-level corporate managers in close cooperation with senior R&D managers develop an overall research agenda and assign different parts of it to individual sites. The process is quite tricky. It requires that the managers in charge have a good understanding of not only the technological capabilities that Matsushita will need to develop in the future but also the stock of technological capabilities already available to it.

Matsushita's central lab organizes two or three yearly off-site meetings devoted to informing R&D scientists and engineers about the entire company's current state of technical knowledge and capabilities. At the same meetings, engineers who have moved from R&D to take over manufacturing and marketing responsibilities inform R&D members about trends in Matsushita's current and potential future markets. Under the guidance of senior project managers, members from R&D, manufacturing, and marketing determine

timelines and resource requirements for specific home-base-augmenting and home-base-exploiting projects. One R&D manager notes, "We discuss not only why a specific scientific insight might be interesting for Matsushita but also how we can turn this insight into a product quickly. We usually seek to develop a prototype early. Prototypes are a good basis for a discussion with marketing and manufacturing. Most of our efforts are targeted at delivering the prototype of a slightly better mousetrap early rather than delivering the blueprint of a much better mousetrap late."

To stimulate the exchange of information, R&D managers at Matsushita's central lab create direct links among researchers across different sites. They promote the use of videoconferencing and frequent face-to-face contact to forge those ties. Reducing the instances in which the central lab must act as mediator means that existing knowledge travels more quickly through the company and new ideas percolate more easily. For example, a researcher at a home-base-exploiting site in Singapore can communicate with another researcher at a home-base-exploiting site in Franklin Park, Illinois, about potential new research projects much more readily now that central R&D fosters informal and formal direct links.

Finally, managers at Matsushita's central lab constantly monitor new regional pockets of knowledge as well as the company's expanding network of manufacturing sites to determine whether the company will need additional R&D locations. With 15 major sites around the world, Matsushita has decided that the number of sites is sufficient at this point. But the company is ever vigilant about surveying the landscape and knows that as the landscape changes, its decision could, too.

As more pockets of knowledge emerge worldwide and competition in foreign markets mounts, the imperative to create global R&D networks will grow all the more pressing. Only those companies that embrace a global approach to R&D will meet the competitive challenges of the new dynamic. And only those managers who embrace their fundamentally new role as global coordinators and managers of knowledge will be able to tap the full potential of their R&D networks.

Reading 5-2   How GE Is Disrupting Itself

by Jeffrey R. Immelt, Vijay Govindarajan, and Chris Trimble

The Idea in Brief

- The model that GE and other industrial manufacturers have followed for decades—developing high-end products at home and adapting them for other markets around the world—won't suffice as growth slows in rich nations.

- To tap opportunities in emerging markets and pioneer value segments in wealthy countries, companies must learn reverse innovation: developing products in countries like China and India and then distributing them globally.

- While multinationals need both approaches, there are deep conflicts between the two. But those conflicts can be overcome.

- If GE doesn't master reverse innovation, the emerging giants could destroy the company.

In May 2009, General Electric announced that over the next six years it would spend $3 billion to create at least 100 health-care innovations that would substantially lower costs, increase access, and improve quality. Two products it highlighted at the time—a $1,000 handheld electrocardiogram device and a portable, PC-based ultrasound machine that sells for as little as $15,000—are revolutionary, and not just because of their small size and low price. They're also extraordinary because they originally were developed for markets in emerging economies (the ECG device for rural India and the ultrasound machine for rural China) and are now being sold in the United States, where they're pioneering new uses for such machines.

Jeffrey R. Immelt is chairman and chief executive officer of General Electric. Vijay Govindarajan (vg@dartmouth.edu) is the Earl C. Daum 1924 Professor of International Business and director of the Center for Global Leadership at the Tuck School of Business at Dartmouth and is professor in residence and chief innovation consultant at GE. Chris Trimble (chris.trimble@dartmouth.edu) is on the faculty of Tuck and consults to GE.

We call the process used to develop the two machines and take them global *reverse innovation,* because it's the opposite of the *glocalization* approach that many industrial-goods manufacturers based in rich countries have employed for decades. With glocalization, companies develop great products at home and then distribute them worldwide, with some adaptations to local conditions. It allows multinationals to make the optimal trade-off between the global scale so crucial to minimizing costs and the local customization required to maximize market share. Glocalization worked fine in an era when rich countries accounted for the vast majority of the market and other countries didn't offer much opportunity. But those days are over—thanks to the rapid development of populous countries like China and India and the slowing growth of wealthy nations.

GE badly needs innovations like the low-cost ECG and ultrasound machines, not only to expand beyond high-end segments in places like China and India but also to preempt local companies in those countries—the emerging giants—from creating similar products and then using them to disrupt GE in rich countries. To put it bluntly: If GE's businesses are to survive and prosper in the next decade, they must become as adept at **reverse innovation** as they are at **glocalization.** Success in developing countries is a prerequisite for continued vitality in developed ones.

The problem is that there are deep conflicts between glocalization and reverse innovation. And the company can't simply replace the first with the second, because glocalization will continue to dominate strategy for the foreseeable future. The two models need to do more than coexist; they need to cooperate. This is a heck of a lot easier said than done since the centralized, product-focused structures and practices that have made multinationals so successful at glocalization actually get in the way of reverse innovation, which requires a decentralized, local-market focus.

Almost all the people and resources dedicated to reverse innovation efforts must be based and managed in the local market. These local growth teams need to have P&L responsibility; the power to decide which products to develop for their markets and how to make, sell, and service them; and the right to draw from the company's global resources. Once products have proven themselves in emerging markets, they must be taken global, which may involve pioneering radically new applications, establishing lower price points, and even using the innovations to cannibalize higher-margin products in rich countries. All of those approaches are antithetical to the glocalization model. This article aims to share what GE has learned in trying to overcome that conflict.

Why Reverse Innovation Is So Important   Glocalization is so dominant today because it has delivered. Largely because of glocalization, GE's revenues outside the United States soared from $4.8 billion, or 19% of total revenues, in 1980, to $97 billion, or more than half of the total, in 2008.

The model came to prominence when opportunities in today's emerging markets were pretty limited—when their economies had yet to take off and their middle or low-end customer segments didn't exist. Therefore, it made sense for multinational manufacturers to simply offer them modifications of products for developed countries. Initially, GE, like other multinationals, was satisfied with the 15% to 20% growth rates its businesses enjoyed in developing countries, thanks to glocalization.

Then in September 2001 one of the coauthors of this piece, Jeff Immelt, who had just become GE's CEO, set a goal: to greatly accelerate organic growth at the company and become less dependent on acquisitions. This made people question many things that had been taken for granted, including the glocalization strategy, which limited the company to skimming the top of emerging markets. A rigorous analysis of GE's health-care, power-generation, and power-distribution businesses showed that if they took full advantage of opportunities that

glocalization had ignored in heavily populated places like China and India, they could grow two to three times faster there. But to do that, they'd have to develop innovative new products that met the specific needs and budgets of customers in those markets. That realization, in turn, led GE executives to question two core tenets of glocalization:

Assumption 1: Emerging economies will largely evolve in the same way that wealthy economies did.   The reality is, developing countries aren't following the same path and could actually jump ahead of developed countries because of their greater willingness to adopt breakthrough innovations. With far smaller per capita incomes, developing countries are more than happy with high-tech solutions that deliver decent performance at an ultralow cost—a 50% solution at a 15% price. And they lack many of the legacy infrastructures of the developed world, which were built when conditions were very different. They need communications, energy, and transportation products that address today's challenges and opportunities, such as unpredictable oil prices and ubiquitous wireless technologies. Finally, because of their huge populations, sustainability problems are especially urgent for countries like China and India. Because of this, they're likely to tackle many environmental issues years or even decades before the developed world.

All this isn't theory. It's already happening. Emerging markets are becoming centers of innovation in fields like low-cost health-care devices, carbon sequestration, solar and wind power, biofuels, distributed power generation, batteries, water desalination, microfinance, electric cars, and even ultra-low-cost homes.

Assumption 2: Products that address developing countries' special needs can't be sold in developed countries because they're not good enough to compete there.   The reality here is, these products can create brand-new markets in the developed world—by establishing dramatically lower price points or pioneering new applications.

Consider GE's health-care business in the United States. It used to make most of its money on premium **computed tomography** (CT) and **magnetic resonance** (MR) imaging machines. But to succeed in the era of broader access and reduced reimbursement that President Obama hopes to bring about, the business will probably need to increase by 50% the number of products it offers at lower price points. And that doesn't mean just cheaper versions of high-tech products like imaging machines. The company also must create more offerings like the heated bassinet it developed for India, which has great potential in U.S. inner cities, where infant deaths related to the cold remain high.

And let's not forget that technology often can be improved until it satisfies more demanding customers. The **compact ultrasound**, which can now handle imaging applications that previously required a conventional machine, is one example. (See "Reverse Innovation in Practice.") Another is an aircraft engine that GE acquired when it bought a Czech aerospace company for $20 million. GE invested an additional $25 million to further develop the engine's technology and now plans to use it to challenge Pratt & Whitney's dominance of the **small turboprop** market in developed countries. GE's cost position is probably half of what Pratt's is.

Reverse Innovation in Practice

Preempting the Emerging Giants   Before the financial crisis plunged the world into a deep recession, GE's leaders had been looking to emerging markets to help achieve their ambitious growth objectives. Now they're counting on these markets even more because they think that after the downturn ends, the developed world will suffer a prolonged period of slow growth—1% to 3% a year. In contrast, annual growth in emerging markets could easily reach two to three times that rate.

Ten years ago when GE senior managers discussed the global marketplace, they talked about "the U.S., Europe, Japan, and the rest of the world." Now they talk about "resource-rich regions," such as the Middle East, Brazil, Canada, Australia, and Russia, and "people-rich regions," such as China and India. The "rest of world" means the U.S., Europe, and Japan.

To be honest, the company also is embracing reverse innovation for defensive reasons. If GE doesn't come up with innovations in poor countries and take them global, new competitors from the developing world—like Mindray, Suzlon, Goldwind, and Haier—will.

In GE's markets the Chinese will be bigger players than the Indians will. The Chinese have a real plan to become a major global force in transportation and power generation. GE Power Generation is already regularly running into Chinese enterprises as it competes in Africa, which will be an extremely important region for the company. One day those enterprises may compete with GE in its own backyard.

That's a bracing prospect. GE has tremendous respect for traditional rivals like Siemens, Philips, and Rolls-Royce. But it knows how to compete with them; they will never destroy GE. By introducing products that create a new price-performance paradigm, however, the emerging giants very well could. Reverse innovation isn't optional; it's oxygen.

A Clash of Two Models   Glocalization has defined international strategy for three decades. All the currently dominant ideas—from Christopher A. Bartlett and SumantraGhoshal's **"transnational" strategy** to PankajGhemawat's **"adaptation-aggregation"** trade-off—fit within the glocalization framework. Since organization follows strategy, it's hardly surprising that glocalization also has molded the way that multinationals are structured and run.

GE is a case in point. For the past 30 years, its organization has evolved to maximize its effectiveness at glocalization. Power and P&L responsibility were concentrated in global business units headquartered in the developed world. The major business functions—including R&D, manufacturing, and marketing—were centralized at headquarters. While some R&D centers and manufacturing

Reverse Innovation in Practice

1 ORIGINAL PRODUCT

In the 1990s GE served the Chinese ultrasound market with machines developed in the U.S. and japan.

CONVENTIONAL ULTRASOUND 2002 PRICE

$100K AND UP

TYPICAL CUSTOMERS
Sophisticated hospital imaging centers

TYPICAL USES
- Cardiology (such as mea-suring the size of passages or blood flow in the heart)
- Obstetrics (monitoring fetal health)
- General radiology (assessing prostate health, for example)

But the expensive, bulky devices sold poorly in China.

2 THE EMERGING MARKET DISRUPTION

In 2002 a local team in China leveraged GE's global resources to develop a cheap, portable machine using a laptop computer enhanced with a probe and sophisticated software.

PORTABLE ULTRASOUND 2002 PRICE

$30K–$40k

TYPICAL CUSTOMERS
- China: Rural clinics
- U.S.: Ambulance squads and emergency rooms

TYPICAL USES
- China: Spotting enlarged livers and galibladder stones
- U.S.: In emergency rooms to identify ectopic pregnancies; at accident sites to check for fluid around the heart; in operating rooms to place catheters for anesthesis

2007 PRICE

$15K

In 2007 the team launched a dramatically cheaper model. Sales in China took off.

3 THE NEW GLOBAL MARKET

PORTABLE ULTRASOUND GLOBAL REVENUES

$4M
2002

2008
$278M

PORTABLE ULTRASOUND 2009 PRICE

$15K–$100k

CONVENTIONAL ULTRASOUND 2009 PRICE

$100K–$350k

Thanks to technology advances, higher-priced PC-based models can now perform radiology and obstetrics functions that once required a conventional machine.

operations were moved abroad to tap overseas talent and reduce costs, they focused mainly on products for wealthy countries.

While this approach has enormous advantages, it makes reverse innovation impossible. The experiences of Venkatraman Raja, the head of GE Healthcare's business in India, illustrate why.

GE Healthcare sells an x-ray imaging product called a surgical C-arm, which is used in basic surgeries. A high-quality, high-priced product designed for hospitals in wealthy countries, it has proven tough to sell in India. Raja saw the problem and made a proposal in 2005. He wanted to develop, manufacture, and sell a simpler, easier-to-use, and substantially cheaper product in India. His proposal made sense, and yet, to no one's surprise, it was not approved.

If you were a leader of a GE operation in a developing country, as Raja was, here's what you were up against: Your formal responsibilities included neither general management nor product development. Your responsibility was to sell, distribute, and service GE's global products locally and provide insights into customers' needs to help the company adapt its offerings. You were expected to grow revenues by 15% to 20% a year and make sure that costs increased at a much slower rate, so that margins rose. You were held rigidly accountable for delivering on plan. Just finding the time for an extracurricular activity like creating a proposal for a product tailored to the local market was challenging.

That was nothing, however, compared with the challenge of the next step: selling your proposal internally. Doing so required getting the attention of the general manager at headquarters in the United States, who sat two or more levels above your immediate boss and was far more familiar with a world-renowned medical center in Boston than a rural clinic outside Bangalore. Even if you got the meeting, you'd have limited time to make your case. (India accounted for just 1% of GE's revenues at the time and occupied roughly the same mindshare of managers with global responsibility.)

If you were extremely persuasive, you might be invited to share the proposal with others. But when you visited the head of global manufacturing, you'd have to counter arguments that a simple, streamlined global product line was much more efficient than custom offerings. When you visited the head of marketing, you'd have to deal with fears that a lower-priced product would weaken the GE brand and cannibalize existing sales. When you met with the head of finance, you'd have to wrestle with concerns that lower-priced products would drag down overall margins. And when you visited the head of global R&D, you'd have to explain why the energies of GE's scientists and engineers—including those in technology centers in emerging markets—should be diverted from projects directed at its most sophisticated customers, who paid top dollar.

Even if you gained support from each of these executives and got the proposal off the ground, you'd still have to compete for capital year after year against more certain projects with shorter-term payoffs. Meanwhile, of course, you'd still have to worry about making your quarterly numbers for your day job.

It was little wonder that successful efforts to develop radically new products for poor countries were extremely rare.

Shifting the Center of Gravity Obviously, changing long-established structures, practices, and attitudes is an enormous task. As is the case in any major change program, the company's top leaders have to play a major role.

To do so, they must investigate firsthand the size of the opportunity and how it could be exploited and encourage the teams running the corporation's businesses to do the same. As GE's CEO, Jeff goes to China and India two times a year. When he's in, say, China, he'll spend a day at GE's research center in Shanghai and then meet separately with dozens of people in the company's local business operations and just let them talk about what they're working on, what their cost points are, who their competitors are, and so on. On such visits, he has realized that there's a whole realm of technology that the company should be applying faster.

While in China, Jeff will also talk with government leaders, including Premier Wen Jiabao. Wen has told Jeff about his plans to develop China's economy and how making health care affordable for all citizens fits into that. It takes a conversation like that to fully appreciate the opportunities in China.

In India, Jeff will have dinner with the CEOs of Indian companies. At one dinner Anand Mahindra talked about how his company, Mahindra & Mahindra, was making life miserable for John Deere in India with a tractor that cost half the price of Deere's but was still enormously profitable. Such discussions drive home the point that you can make a lot of money in India if you have the right business models.

So the job of the CEO—of any senior business leader, for that matter—is to connect all the dots and then act as a catalyst. It's to give initiatives special status and funding and personally monitor them on a monthly or quarterly basis. And perhaps most important in the case of reverse innovation, it's to push your enterprise to come up with the new organizational form that will allow product and business-model innovation to flourish in emerging markets.

A Homegrown Model   To develop that new organizational form, GE did what it has always done: learn from other companies' experiences but also try to find an internal group that somehow had managed to overcome the hurdles and achieve success. During their annual strategy review, the company's leaders spotted one in the ultrasound unit of GE Healthcare.

GE Healthcare's primary business is high-end medical-imaging equipment. By the late 1980s it had become clear that a new technology—ultrasound—had a bright future. Ultrasound machines, like the other imaging devices, were typically found in sophisticated imaging centers in hospitals. While they delivered lower quality than CT or MR scanners, they did so at much lower cost. The company aimed to be number one in ultrasound.

Over the next decade, GE Healthcare expanded its presence in the market. It built an R&D facility for developing new ultrasound products near its headquarters, in Milwaukee, and made acquisitions and entered into joint ventures around the world. It competed in all three of the primary market segments—obstetrics, cardiology, and general radiology—by launching premium products that employed cutting-edge technologies. By 2000, GE Healthcare had established solid market positions in rich countries around the world.

The results in developing countries, by contrast, were disappointing. By 2000, with the help of a joint venture partner in China, GE saw the problem: In wealthy countries performance mattered most, followed by features; in China price mattered most, followed by portability and ease of use.

The priorities weren't the same because the health-care infrastructure of China was so different from that of rich countries. More than 90% of China's population relied (and still relies) on poorly funded, low-tech hospitals or basic clinics in rural villages. These facilities had no sophisticated imaging centers, and transportation to urban hospitals was difficult, especially for the sick. Patients couldn't come to the ultrasound machines; the ultrasound machines, therefore, had to go to the patients.

There was no way that GE could meet that need by simply scaling down, removing features from, or otherwise adapting its existing ultrasound machines, which were large, bulky, expensive, and complex. It needed a revolutionary product.

In 2002, the company launched its first compact ultrasound, which combined a regular laptop computer with sophisticated software. It sold for as low as $30,000. In late 2007, GE introduced a model that sold for as low as $15,000, less than 15% of the cost of GE's high-end ultrasound machines. Of course, its performance was not as high, but it was nonetheless a hit in rural clinics, where doctors used it for simple applications, such as spotting enlarged livers and gallbladders and stomach irregularities. The software-centric design also made it easy to adjust the machine—for example, to improve the interfaces—after observing how doctors worked with it. Today the portable machine is the growth engine of GE's ultrasound business in China.

Even more exciting, the innovation has generated dramatic growth in the developed world by pioneering new applications where portability is critical or space is constrained, such as at accident sites, where the compacts are used to diagnose problems like pericardial effusions (fluid around the heart); in emergency rooms, where they are employed to identify conditions such as ectopic pregnancies; and in operating rooms, where they aid anesthesiologists in placing needles and catheters.

Six years after their launch, portable ultrasounds were a $278 million global product line for GE, one that was growing at 50% to 60% a year before the worldwide recession hit. Someday every general practitioner may carry both a stethoscope and a compact ultrasound device embedded in his or her PDA.

The products owe their successful development to an organizational anomaly in GE: the existence of multiple ultrasound business units. Although the three primary segments of the ultrasound business are vastly different, GE's initial instinct was to follow the glocalization model when it built the business—that is, to create a single integrated global organization. In 1995, however, Omar Ishrak, a newcomer who had been hired to lead the business, saw that meshing operations would reduce them to a common denominator that served nobody well. He decided to run the business as three independent business units with their own P&L responsibility, all reporting to him.

When the compact ultrasound effort began in China, Ishrak saw that the new business would have little in common with the three units, which were focused on premium products. So instead, he created a fourth independent unit, based in Wuxi, China. It evolved the local growth team (LGT) model, which is based on five critical principles.

1. **Shift power to where the growth is.** Without autonomy, the LGTs will become pawns of the global business and won't be able to focus on the problems of customers in emerging markets. Specifically, they need the power to develop their own strategies, organizations, and products. Ishrak understood this and gave such broad authority to Diana Tang and J.K. Koo, the leaders of GE's ultrasound effort in China. The pair of GE veterans had deep experience in the ultrasound business, expertise in biomedical engineering and general management, and lengthy careers in Asia.

2. **Build new offerings from the ground up.** Given the tremendous gulfs between rich countries and poor ones in income, infrastructure, and sustainability needs, reverse innovation must be zero-based. These wide differences cannot be spanned by adapting global products.

   The compact ultrasound was built from scratch, although it drew heavily from an existing R&D effort. In the late 1990s, in a product-development center in Israel, GE had started to experiment with a revolutionary new architecture—one that shifted most of the muscle inside an ultrasound machine from the hardware to the software. Instead of a large box full of custom hardware, the scientists and engineers involved in the project envisioned a standard high-performance PC, special peripherals such as an ultrasound probe, and sophisticated software.

   The concept generated little excitement in GE Healthcare at the time because it could not come close to matching the performance of the business's premium products. But Ishrak quickly saw the value of the new architecture in developing countries. He encouraged the team in China to pursue the concept further. The resulting compact ultrasound based on a laptop computer hit the mark in China.

3. **Build LGTs from the ground up, like new companies.** Zero-based innovation doesn't happen without zero-based organizational design. GE's organizational "software"—its hiring practices, reporting structures, titles, job descriptions, norms for working relationships, and power balances between functions—all evolved to support glocalization. LGTs need to rewrite the software.

   Tang and Koo constructed a business unit that managed a complete value chain: product development, sourcing, manufacturing, marketing, sales, and service. By recruiting locally, they were able to find most of the expertise they needed—including engineers with deep knowledge of miniaturization and low-power consumption and a commercialization team well versed in health care in rural China.

The LGT also decided that dealers—rather than the direct sales force used by the premium ultrasound units—were the only cost-effective way to reach China's vast and fragmented rural markets and third-tier cities. And instead of relying on GE Healthcare's global customer-support and replacement-parts organizations, it built in-country teams that could provide quicker and less costly service.

4. **Customize objectives, targets, and metrics.** Innovation endeavors are, by nature, uncertain. It's more important to learn quickly by efficiently testing assumptions than to hit the numbers. So the relevant metrics and standards for LGTs—the ones that resolve the critical unknowns—are rarely the same as those used by the established businesses.

The ultrasound LGT knew that doctors in rural China were less familiar with ultrasounds than doctors in cities. But the team didn't know how much experience rural doctors had with the technology or what features would meet their needs. So it set out to learn how doctors reacted to the machines and what the obstacles to their adoption were. The team discovered that ease of use, especially in primary-care screenings, where doctors test for common local conditions, was even more crucial than anticipated. In response, the new business emphasized training, offered online guides, designed simpler keyboards, created built-in presets for certain tasks, and tracked customer satisfaction to gauge success.

Ishrak was careful to use different criteria to evaluate the performance of the LGT in China. For example, because the government approval process for new product releases is less intricate in China, he set much shorter product-development cycles than were common in wealthy countries. He also agreed to allow the size of the local service organization to deviate from the GE Healthcare's global standards. Since salaries are lower and service is more demanding in China, a bigger staff relative to the number of installed machines made sense.

5. **Have the LGT report to someone high in the organization.** LGTs cannot thrive without strong support from the top. The executive overseeing the LGT has three critical roles: mediating conflicts between the team and the global business, connecting the team to resources such as global R&D centers, and helping take the innovations that the team develops into rich countries. Only a senior executive in the global business unit, or even its leader, can accomplish all of that.

Even when it was tiny, the LGT in China reported directly to Ishrak. Because GE Healthcare had an ambitious product-development agenda for rich countries when the compact project was launched, the LGT's engineers might easily have been redirected to other projects if Ishrak hadn't shielded the team. He protected and even expanded the team's resources. By 2007 its number of engineers had grown from 13 to 70 and its total payroll had increased from 132 to 339. Ishrak also personally made sure that the team got the expertise it needed from other parts of GE, such as three highly respected development engineers from Israel, Japan, and South Korea. They worked full-time on the project and got it extra support from GE's R&D centers around the world.

Ishrak included the China LGT in the company's Ultrasound Council, a group of ultrasound executives and market and technology experts who meet for two days three times a year. At the meeting they share knowledge and insights and agree on which major projects to pursue. The council was instrumental in moving knowledge and technology into China.

Finally, Ishrak played a critical role in building a global market for the portable ultrasound. He identified potential new applications in the developed world and saw to it that the three units that sold the premium products aggressively pursued those opportunities.

· · ·

GE now has more than a dozen local growth teams in China and India. In the midst of a severe global recession, GE's businesses in China will grow 25% this year—largely because of LGTs. It's way too early to declare victory, however. Progress has been uneven. While some businesses—notably, health care and power generation and distribution—have taken the ball and run with it, others have been less enthusiastic. And though GE's R&D centers in China and India have increased their focus on the problems of developing countries, the vast majority of their resources are still devoted to initiatives for developed ones. So there is still a long way to go.

It's still necessary for the company's top executives to monitor and protect local efforts and make sure they get resources. It's still necessary to experiment with people transfers, organizational structures, and processes to see what works. The biggest experiment is about to come: To speed progress in India, GE is creating a separate P&L that will include all GE businesses in that country and giving the new unit considerable power to tap GE's global R&D resources. It will be headed by a senior vice president who will report to a vice chairman. That's anathema in a company used to a matrix in which product comes first and country second. Nonetheless, the company is going to try it and see if it can create new markets. GE has to learn how to operate on a different axis.

The resistance to giving India its own P&L reflects what is perhaps GE's biggest challenge: changing the mind-set of managers who've spent their careers excelling at glocalization. Even the exemplars have a rich-country bias. In a recent conversation with Jeff, one such manager—the head of a major business that's doing well in India and China—still seemed preoccupied with problems beyond his control in the U.S. "I don't even want to talk to you about your growth plans for the U.S.," Jeff responded. "You've got to triple the size of your Indian business in the next three years. You've got to put more resources, more people, and more products in there, so you're deep in that market and not just skimming the very top. Let's figure out how to do it." That's how senior managers have to think.

Reading 5-3 How to Build Collaborative Advantage

Morten T. Hansen and Nitin Nohria

For many years, multinational corporations could compete successfully by exploiting scale and scope

For multinationals, it is increasingly difficult to maintain competitive advantage on the basis of the traditional economies of scale and scope. Future advantage will go to those that can stimulate and support interunit collaboration to leverage their dispersed resources.

Morten T. Hansen is an associate professor of entrepreneurship at INSEAD in Fontainebleau, France.

Nitin Nohria is Richard P. Chapman Professor of Business Administration at Harvard Business School in Boston. They can be reached at morten.hansen@insead.edu and nnohria@hbs.edu.

Reprint 46105. For ordering information, see page 1.

economies or by taking advantage of imperfections in the world's goods, labor and capital markets. But these ways of competing are no longer as profitable as they once were. In most industries, multinationals no longer compete primarily with companies whose boundaries are confined to a single nation. Rather, they go head-to-head with a handful of other giants that are comparable in size, in their access to international resources and in worldwide market position. Against such global competitors, it is hard to sustain an advantage based on traditional economies of scale and scope.

Consider the oil industry. The industry is dominated by a handful of global players such as

ExxonMobil, BP, Shell and ChevronTexaco. They each have global exploration, refining and distribution operations, leaving little room for any company to gain competitive advantage with economies of scale. Similarly, they each have brands that are more or less equally well recognized the world over, reducing opportunities for a company to seize competitive advantage with an economy of scope based on its brand power. Such relative parity among multinational corporations can also be observed in consumer electronics, information technology, pharmaceuticals, banking, professional services and even retailing.

Under these circumstances, MNCs must seek new sources of competitive advantage. While multinationals in the past realized economies of scope principally by utilizing physical assets (such as distribution systems) and exploiting a company-wide brand, the new economies of scope are based on the ability of business units, subsidiaries and functional departments within the company to collaborate successfully by sharing knowledge and jointly developing new products and services.[1] Multinationals that can stimulate and support collaboration will be better able to leverage their dispersed resources and capabilities in subsidiaries and divisions around the globe.

Collaboration can be an MNC's source of competitive advantage because it does not occur automatically—far from it. Indeed, several barriers impede collaboration within complex multi-unit organizations. And in order to overcome those barriers, companies will have to develop distinct organizing capabilities that cannot be easily imitated.

Interunit collaboration is not only difficult to achieve but also poorly understood. However, a framework that links managerial action, barriers to interunit collaboration, and value creation in MNCs can help managers "unpack" the concept. The framework conceptualizes collaboration as a set of management levers that reduce four specific barriers to collaboration, leading in turn to several types of value creation. (See "A Framework for Creating Value Through Interunit Collaboration," p. 25.) It makes most sense to explain the three elements of the framework in reverse order, beginning with value creation.

Value Creation from Interunit Collaboration

A company should not collaborate across units for collaboration's sake alone, of course, but only if it can reap economic benefits by doing so. The potential varies by company; for instance, a firm with many related businesses or country subsidiaries stands to benefit more than a loose conglomerate of businesses. And the type of benefits will vary, too, from among five major categories:

- Cost savings through the transfer of best practices;
- Better decision making as a result of advice obtained from colleagues in other subsidiaries;
- Increased revenue through the sharing of expertise and products among subsidiaries;
- Innovation through the combination and cross-pollination of ideas; and
- Enhanced capacity for collective action that involves dispersed units.

To concretely grasp the notion of collaboration in a multinational company, consider the case of BP Plc, which has operations in more than 100 countries.[2] Over the last decade, senior executives of this oil and gas giant have transformed the company from a collection of individual fiefdoms into a vast collaborative organization with significant improvements in costs, efficiency and revenues as a result.

Several major initiatives were implemented to foster collaboration between business units and

[1]See B. Kogut and U. Zander, "Knowledge of the Firm, Combinative Capabilities, and the Replication of Technology," Organization Science 3, no. 3 (1992): 383–397; C. Hill, "Diversification and Economic Performance: Bringing Structure and Corporate Management Back Into the Picture," in "Fundamental Issues in Strategy," eds. R. Rumelt, D.Schendel and D. Teece (Boston: Harvard Business School Press, 1995), 297–322; and J. Nahapiet and S. Ghoshal, "Social Capital, Intellectual Capital and the Organizational Advantage," Academy of Management Review 23, no. 2 (April 1998): 242–266.

country operations. Responsibility for resource allocation, for example, was taken away from individual units and handed to groups of peers—business-unit heads running similar businesses. This approach effectively forced the peers to work together to optimize the allocations for the group as a whole rather than for individual units. The company also developed "peer assist" and "peer challenge" processes, whereby managers and engineers in one unit can ask for technical and help from other units, including technical expertise and problem-solving advice. Engineers in a typical business unit spend about 5% of their time on peer assists. Peer assists are supported by several electronic knowledge-management systems as well as videoconferencing technology. And strong personal relationships also have developed as a result of the frequent rotation of managers among units and country operations.

BP also changed its promotion and reward systems. Managers undergo a 360-degree feedback process that includes reviews from peers, and managers who do not collaborate effectively throughout the organization suffer when they are being considered for promotion. In addition, 30% to 50% of bonuses for senior managers are contingent on the performance of the firm as a whole. Naturally, BP's executives continue to change these practices as the company evolves, but the fundamental idea of creating additional value through interunit collaboration remains at the center of the company's organizational model.

These changes have produced real, measurable results at BP. For example, there have been cost savings through the transfer of best practices: A business-unit head in the United States sought to improve the inventory turns of service stations. Tapping the expertise of her peer group, she obtained

knowledge of best practices from operations in the United Kingdom and the Netherlands, leading to a 20% decrease in working capital needed by U.S. service stations. Better decision making was a second result: Another unit head used a peer assist to receive input from six people in other units who had expertise in ordering oil tankers. After several meetings in which the peers advised the unit head's team, the unit bought three tankers and took options on another three. Revenue also grew: During the development of an acetic acid plant in Western China, more than 75 people from various units flew to China to assist the core project team, enabling BP to finish the project on time and to realize revenues from the plant earlier than planned. There was crosspollination of ideas: Managers from 15 units met to brainstorm e-commerce initiatives, and 150 new ideas were implemented. Finally, BP benefited from collective action: The company used peer groups to integrate ahead of schedule its acquisitions of Amoco Corp. and later Atlantic Richfield Co.

To obtain these important benefits, BP had to overcome barriers to collaboration between units, as all companies must do to realize similar creation of value.

Four Barriers to Interunit Collaboration

Although recent research on basic drivers of human action suggests that cooperation may be a natural human tendency, collaboration at multinationals does not just happen on its own.[3] Companies often erect barriers that prevent individuals from engaging in collaborative activities that they might otherwise have undertaken. The first task, then, is to identify the barriers and their causes. The results from a survey of managers in 107 companies suggest that four barriers are prevalent in multinationals.[4] (See "About the Research.") While all four barriers to collaboration may be high in some

[2]For an in-depth look at BP on this issue, see S.E. Prokesch, "Unleashing the Power of Learning: An Interview With British Petroleum's John Browne," Harvard Business Review 75, no. 5 (September–October 1997): 146–168; and M.T. Hansen and B. Von Oetinger, "Introducing T-Shaped Managers: Knowledge Management's Next Generation," Harvard Business Review 79, no. 3 (March 2001): 106–116. The section on BP in the text draws on the latter article.

[3]See P.R. Lawrence and N. Nohria, "Driven: How Human Nature Shapes Our Choices" (San Francisco: Jossey-Bass, 2002).

[4]This section draws on M. Hansen, "Turning the Lone Star Into a Real Team Player," Financial Times, Aug. 7, 2002, 11–13.

About the Research

We conducted a survey of executives in 107 companies in the manufacturing, retail, consumer-goods, health-care, professional-services, financial and high-tech industries. On a scale of 1 to 100, executives were asked to rate the extent to which they agreed or disagreed with statements aimed at determining the degree of collaboration existing within their firms and to what extent they were using management levers to encourage collaboration. On the basis of a factor analysis of the survey data, management levers that can reduce any of the barriers to collaboration were found to fall into three broad categories: leadership behaviors, shared values and goals; human resources procedures; and lateral cross-unit mechanisms. Although based on subjective assessments of benefits, the data suggest that companies enjoy economic benefits from interunit collaboration when senior executives are able to reduce the four barriers. There was a strong negative association between executives' perceptions of the presence of the four barriers in their companies and their perceptions of the benefits from the five sources of value—the higher the perceived barriers, the lower the perceived value creation. In addition, we interviewed managers from more than 30 companies and conducted several in-depth case studies in companies such as BP Plc and Intuit Inc.

multinationals, other companies face only one or two. It is therefore paramount to first diagnose which barriers cause a problem.

First Barrier: Unwillingness to Seek Input and Learn from Others   For several reasons, employees in one unit may close themselves off to help from those in others. Sometimes it is the norm in a unit that people are expected to fix their own problems. In other cases, formal and informal reward systems may give more credit for heroic individual efforts than for collaborative efforts. Some employees may simply believe that others have nothing to teach them. They may have developed what social psychologists call an in-group bias, in which they overvalue their own group and undervalue non-members.[5] As in-group members spend time with one another to the exclusion of outsiders, they necessarily restrict the influx of new viewpoints and reinforce their own commonly held beliefs.[6] As a result, they become prone to the not-invented-here syndrome, in which ideas, knowledge and inventions developed outside their own group are rejected.[7]

Consider this experience in Hewlett-Packard Co.'s European operations a few years ago. HP executives had created a new internal benchmarking system that compared the times to process computer orders at factories in various countries. Although the system revealed several underperforming country operations, the managers with worse processing times were not willing to contact and visit the best performers, partly because they did not believe that others could teach them useful practices and partly because they viewed their problems as unique (they were not). Only when senior managers intervened did the necessary collaboration between country operations take place.

[5]See, for example, M.B. Brewer, "Ingroup Bias in the Minimal Intergroup Situation: A Cognitive Motivational Analysis," Psychological Bulletin 86 (1979): 307-324; and H. Tajfel and J.C. Turner, "The Social Identity Theory of Intergroup Behavior," in "Psychology of Intergroup Relations," 2nd ed., eds. S. Worchel and W.G. Austin (Chicago: Nelson Hall Publishers, 1986), 7–24.

[6]See P.J. Oakes, S.A. Haslam, B. Morrison and D. Grace, "Becoming an In-Group: Reexamining the Impact of Familiarity on Perceptions of Group Homogeneity," Social Psychology Quarterly 58, no. 1 (March 1995): 52–60; and D.A. Wilder, "Reduction of Intergroup Discrimination Through Individuation of the Out-Group," Journal of Personality & Social Psychology 36 (1978): 1361–1374.

[7]See R.H. Hayes and K.B. Clark, "Exploring the Sources of Productivity Differences at the Factory Level" (New York: Wiley, 1985); and R. Katz and T.J. Allen, "Investigating the Not Invented Here (NIH) Syndrome: A Look at the Performance, Tenure and Communication Patterns of 50 R&D Project Groups," in "Readings in the Management of Innovation," 2nd ed., M.L. Tushman and W.L. Moore, eds. (New York: HarperCollins Publishers, 1988), 293–309.

Short of such after-the-fact intervention, management can use several levers to attenuate this problem. At BP, senior executives keep a close eye on the extent to which business-unit managers ask for peer assists and will intervene if someone is not seeking enough help.[8] More direct help comes through peer challenges, in which peers lend on-the-scene support to help a unit improve in specific areas. Another fundamental lever is recruitment— hiring people who have a natural inclination and the confidence to ask for help. At an international chain of up-market restaurants in the United States, prospective staff members are asked, "What obstacles have you faced in a previous job that prevented you from doing a quality job, and how did you overcome those obstacles?" The company is looking for people who asked for help, communicated a problem to others and didn't try to be a hero by fixing it alone.

Second Barrier: Inability to Seek and Find Expertise   Even when employees are willing to seek help in other business units or country subsidiaries, they may not be able to find it or to search efficiently so that the benefits outweigh the costs of searching.[9] In large and dispersed MNCs, this needle-in-a-haystack problem can become a significant barrier to collaboration: Somewhere in the company someone often knows the answer to a problem, but it is nearly impossible to connect the person who has the expertise with the person who needs it.

Databases and electronic search engines can help. In most management-consulting companies, for instance, consultants upload sanitized documents containing their finished work into databases; others in the firm can then access the documents and contact the consultants who did the original work.[10] Another way to help people find expertise

is to create transparent benchmarking systems. Netherlands-based Ispat International N.V., one of the largest steel companies in the world, has a system that performs costing at the plant level and allows managers to compare all their operating units in the world on many dimensions. For instance, one manager found that his furnace maintenance costs were higher than those of other plants, prompting him to contact the most cost-efficient plants in this area for help.

Technology has its limits, however. Expert directories go out of date and do not fully capture what each person knows. More important, they do not allow for creative combinations of ideas and individuals. Companies may therefore need to cultivate "connectors," that is, people who know where experts and ideas reside and who can connect people who do not know each other. Connectors tend to be long-tenured employees who have worked in many different areas in the company and hence have an extensive personal network.

A manager in GlaxoSmithKline Plc, for example, created substantial value for his company by connecting two country managers who did not know each other. A few years ago, an area director in Singapore received a phone call from the company's managing director in the Philippines, who was looking for new product opportunities that could be introduced in his country. Acting on a hunch that there might be an opportunity in India, the area director set up a meeting with the managing director in Bombay. During his visit, the managing director from the Philippines saw that the Indian product developers were creating line extensions in the area of tuberculosis medication—not a major field in the company worldwide but one that is highly relevant in developing countries. The visit to the lab sparked a joint effort between the teams in India and Philippines, resulting in a modified TB medication and several other line extensions for the Philippine market.

[8]See also S. Ghoshal and L. Gratton, "Integrating the Enterprise," MIT Sloan Management Review 44, no. 1 (fall 2002): 31–38.

[9]See M.T. Hansen, "The Search-Transfer Problem: The Role of Weak Ties in Sharing Knowledge Across Organization Subunits," Administrative Science Quarterly 44, no. 1 (March 1999): 82–111; and M.T. Hansen and B. Lovas, "How Do Multinational Companies Leverage Technological Competencies? Moving From Single to Interdependent Explanations," Strategic Management Journal, in press.

[10]For more details on knowledge management in management-consulting companies, see M.T. Hansen, N. Nohria and T. Tierney, "What's Your Strategy for Managing Knowledge?" Harvard Business Review 77, no. 2 (March-April, 1999): 106–116.

A Framework for Creating Value Through Interunit Collaboration

The matrix in the center lists the four major barriers impeding collaboration between units in a global company. Those barriers can be hurdled, however, by using several management levers, and the end result will be newly created value in various forms.

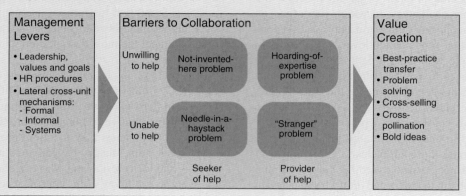

The area director, acting as a connector, was in effect an entrepreneur who saw an opportunity for value creation based on the combination of talent, ideas and expertise from two country subsidiaries.

Third Barrier: Unwillingness to Help   In some cases, the problem lies with the potential provider of help, not the seeker. Some employees are reluctant to share what they know—or refuse to help outright—leading to a hoarding-of-expertise problem.[11] Competition between subsidiaries can undermine people's motivation to cooperate.[12] When two subsidiaries are selling products to the same markets and seeking to develop similar technologies, employees will hesitate to help people in the competing unit. Paradoxically, the emphasis on performance management over the past decade has also fueled this problem. As employees are pressured to perform, they feel that they don't have the

time to help others or they just don't care; all that matters is delivering their own numbers. While this focus on individual performance is clearly important, executives also need to create a counterbalancing force by developing incentives aimed at fostering cooperation and a shared identity among employees.

Unwillingness to help is a significant problem in many investment banks, where bankers chase their own opportunities. When John Mack took over Morgan Stanley Group Inc. in the early 1990s, he set out to create a more collaborative culture and changed the promotion criteria.[13] "Lone stars"—those who delivered great results but did not assist others—would not be promoted. To attain the coveted position of managing director, Morgan Stanley's bankers had to demonstrate both individual performance and their contributions to others. To measure this, executives

[11]See A.K. Gupta and V. Govindarajan, "Knowledge Flows Within Multinational Corporations," Strategic Management Journal 21 (April 2000): 473–496.

[12]See W. Tsai, "Social Structure of 'Coopetition' Within a Multiunit Organization: Coordination, Competition and Intraorganizational Knowledge Sharing," Organization Science 13, no. 2 (March–April 2002): 179–190.

[13]For a detailed description of these changes at Morgan Stanley, see M.D. Burton, T.J. DeLong and K. Lawrence, "Morgan Stanley: Becoming a 'One-Firm' Firm," Harvard Business School case no. 9-400-043 (Boston: Harvard Business School Publishing, 1999); and M.D. Burton, "The Firmwide 360-Degree Performance Evaluation Process at Morgan Stanley," Harvard Business School case no. 9-498-053 (Boston: Harvard Business School Publishing, 1998).

A Road Map to Building Collaborative Advantage in Your Company

The tools below can help a manager identify the mix of barriers to collaboration present in a company and the appropriate choice of levers for that specific situation. Any organizational unit of analysis (the entire company, a business unit, a country subsidiary, a functional department) can be selected and the extent of the barriers within that unit assessed.

1. Which barriers to collaboration are present in your organizational unit?
Assess your unit from 1 (not at all) to 100 (to a large extent):

First Barrier: Unwillingness to seek input and learn from others	Enter 1–100

1. Even when they need help, our employees are not willing to seek input from outside their organizational unit.
2. When faced with problems, employees in our unit strive to solve them by themselves without asking for help from outsiders.
3. There is a prevailing attitude in our unit that people ought to fix their own problems and not rely on help from others outside the unit.

Total of responses to questions 1 to 3

Second Barrier: Inability to seek and find expertise

4. Our employees often complain about the difficulty they have locating colleagues who possess the information and expertise they need.
5. Experts in our company are very difficult to locate.
6. Our employees have great difficulties finding the documents and information they need in the company's databases and knowledge-management systems.

Total of responses to questions 4 to 6

Third Barrier: Unwillingness to help

7. Our people keep their expertise and information to themselves and do not want to share it across organizational units.
8. Our employees do not share their expertise and information for fear of becoming less valuable.
9. Our employees seldom return phone calls and e-mails when asked for help.

Total of responses to questions 7 to 9

Fourth Barrier: Inability to work together to transfer knowledge

10. Our employees have not learned to work together effectively across organizational units to transfer tacit knowledge.
11. Employees from different organizational units are not used to working together and find it hard to do so.
12. Our employees find it difficult to work across units to transfer complex technologies and best practices.

Total of responses to questions 10 to 12

Check the categories that best correlate to your sum of responses for each of the barriers. The table benchmarks the level of barriers in your organizational unit against a sample of 107 companies.

	Lowest quartile (lowest barriers) Implication: Barrier is not a problem	Second lowest quartile Implication: Barrier might cause some problems	Median Implication: Barrier might cause some problems	Second highest quartile Implication: Barrier is a problem	Highest quartile (highest barriers) Implication: Barrier is a big problem
First Barrier: Unwillingness to seek input and learn from others	Scores between 3 and 105	106–159	160	161–200	201–300
Second Barrier: Inability to seek and find expertise	3–90	91–134	135	136–180	181–300
Third Barrier: Unwillingness to help	3–60	61–99	100	101–140	141–300
Fourth Barrier: Inability to work together to transfer knowledge	3–110	111–167	168	169–210	211–300

2. Which management levers should you use to reduce barriers to collaboration?

Your scores above indicate which barrier(s) need to be reduced in your organizational unit. This table shows the management levers that are most appropriate for each of the barriers (marked with a ✓).

	First Barrier: Unwilling to seek input	Second Barrier: Unable to find expertise	Third Barrier: Unwilling to help	Fourth Barrier: Unable to transfer knowledge
Demonstration of leadership behaviors	✓		✓	
Articulation of shared value related to teamwork	✓		✓	
Development of unifying goal	✓		✓	
HR Procedures	✓		✓	
—Recruitment	✓		✓	
—Promotion	✓		✓	
—Compensation				
Informal networks		✓		✓
—Connectors				
—Strong professional relationships				
Formal lateral mechanisms (for example, cross-unit groups)				✓
Information systems		✓		
—Knowledge-management databases		✓		
—Benchmark systems				

put in place a 360-degree review procedure in which peers and subordinates were asked to evaluate a person's contributions beyond his or her department. Not surprisingly, behavior changed; cooperation within the company became much more prevalent. This system also helped break down some of the barriers to collaboration across geographic boundaries. Bankers from Europe, Asia and the United States became more willing to serve global clients collectively rather than chasing the local business of such clients in each country.

Fourth Barrier: Inability to Work Together and Transfer Knowledge   Finally, sometimes people are willing to work together but can't easily transfer what they know to others because of the "stranger" problem. In this case, the nature of the knowledge in question requires that people already have relationships in order to understand each other. For example, when knowledge is tacit, it is difficult to explain its content and nuances to others, who in turn may find it hard to understand, thereby making the tasks of modifying and incorporating it into their own local conditions difficult, too. The same problem crops up with knowledge that is viewed as specific to a context or a culture.[14] Because of these difficulties, transferring tacit or specific knowledge is likely to be more cumbersome, take longer and thus be more costly than transferring explicit or general knowledge.

These problems can be alleviated if the two parties to a transfer have developed a strong professional relationship. In that case, they are likely to have developed a shared communication frame in which each party understands how the other uses subtle phrases and explains difficult concepts. In the absence of such relations, strangers are likely to find it difficult to work together effectively. For example, in a study of time-to-market performance of new product-development projects in a global high-tech company, it was discovered that project engineers who worked with counterparts

from other divisions or subsidiaries took 20% to 30% longer to complete their projects when close personal relationships between them did not exist beforehand. The engineers found it hard to articulate, understand and absorb complex technologies that were transferred between organizational units. Even though they were motivated to cooperate, they were slowed down by the need to learn to work together during the project.

> As leaders signal the importance of collaboration by working together among themselves, employees are more likely to be motivated to seek and provide help.

To alleviate the stranger problem, executives can work to establish relationships between employees from different subsidiaries—but they must do so before specific collaborative events are launched. One of the most effective mechanisms is to rotate people through jobs at different units and subsidiaries. Employees who move to other places temporarily to work on assignments often develop strong bonds with colleagues in those locations. When people are back working in their original sites, those bonds are especially important to the success of cross-unit projects.

Management Levers to Promote Collaboration

Potential management levers that can reduce the barriers fall into three broad categories: leadership, values and goals; human resources procedures; and lateral cross-unit mechanisms. The latter category can in turn be divided into information systems, informal networks and formalized lateral mechanisms. Each mix of barriers in a company requires a specific mix of management levers to foster collaboration across business units, subsidiaries and departments. (See "A Road Map to Building Collaborative Advantage in Your Company," p. 26.) It's important to carefully choose and implement a management lever or levers that will reduce a specific barrier.

Leadership, Values and Goals   These levers reduce people's unwillingness to seek and provide help. As leaders signal the importance of

---

[14] See M. Haas, "Acting on What Others Know: Distributed Knowledge and Team Performance" (unpublished Ph.D. diss., Harvard University, 2002).

collaboration by working together among themselves, articulating the shared values related to teamwork and developing unifying goals, employees are more likely to be motivated to seek and provide help.

Some companies have been particularly good at articulating powerful goals that stop myopic unit-focused behaviors and motivate people to work across company units to realize them. In 1990, Sam Walton said that Wal-Mart Stores Inc. should reach $125 billion in sales by 2000, up from $32 billion at the time. Nike Inc. wanted to "Crush Adidas," its main rival in the athletic shoes industry in the 1960s. Over the past few years employees at Airbus S.A.S. have informally aspired to beating Boeing Co. In the late 1990s, Starbucks Corp. articulated the very ambitious goal of establishing itself as "the most recognized and respected brand in the world."[15] Such goals both stretch and unify an organization's employees; they cannot be reached unless everyone stops pursuing self-promoting, narrow-minded goals and becomes motivated to pull together by seeking and providing help across units.

Levers involving leadership, values and goals, however, do not affect the people's ability to find help and work together. A leader who preaches collaboration may motivate the troops but cannot by words alone help them locate experts or enable employees to work well together. Leadership behaviors and the articulation of shared values and goals are necessary but not sufficient conditions for effective collaboration in MNCs.

Human Resources Procedures   Recruitment and promotion criteria also reduce unwillingness to seek or provide help. By selecting job candidates who have an inclination to search for and offer help, an organization will over time be populated with people who thrive on cooperative work. Likewise, making demonstrated collaborative behaviors a criterion for promotion to senior positions in a

company ensures that the top team will, over time, be composed of leaders who exhibit collaborative behaviors. In addition, having such a promotion criterion sends a powerful signal to employees vying for leadership positions; those who do not have the inclination to collaborate are likely to leave a company that enforces the rule consistently. Finally, compensating employees based on their collaborative behaviors is also a useful lever.

To make the promotion and compensation levers work, a company needs to change its annual performance criteria. Intuit Inc., the financial-software company, has implemented an annual performance system in which employees are evaluated on two questions: "What was accomplished?" and "How were the goals accomplished?"[16] The "how" part evaluates an employee's collaborative efforts across functions and business units in reaching those goals. An employee who did not collaborate enough will receive a lower mark for the year, even if he reached the individual goals.

Lateral Cross-Unit Mechanisms   If the problem is the inability to find help, then the most effective levers tend to be these three: the cultivation of connectors; the development of electronic yellow pages that list experts by area; and the development of benchmark systems that allow employees to identify best practices in the company. If the problem is the inability to work together to transfer knowledge, an effective lever is the cultivation of strong professional relationships between employees from different units and the development of formal cross-unit groups and committees that structure regularly occurring interactions. These provide a forum for people to get to know one another and develop personal bonds that facilitate sharing.

While all four barriers to collaboration may be high in some MNCs, other companies face only one or two. It is therefore paramount to first diagnose

---

[15]For an in-depth look at inspiring common goals, see J. Collins and J. Porras, "Building Your Company's Vision," Harvard Business Review 74, no. 5 (September-October 1996): 65–77.

[16]See M.T. Hansen and C. Darwall, 2003, "Intuit Inc.: Transforming an Entrepreneurial Company Into a Collaborative Organization," Harvard Business School case 9-403-064 (Boston: Harvard Business School Publishing, 2003).

which barriers cause a problem. For example, if the problem is an inability to find help, putting in a knowledge-management or benchmarking system would be appropriate, but changing HR procedures would not—if people cannot find experts, it makes no sense to make promotion contingent on doing so. In contrast, if the problem is a widespread not-invented-here syndrome, changing the HR procedures should help, but a new knowledge-management system is unlikely to have any effect on employees who will not seek help or who hoard what they know.

Potential Downsides of Collaboration

While collaboration can create substantial value, it also has a downside that executives need to manage. One pitfall is that it can easily be overdone. Prompted by collaboration initiatives, employees may begin to participate in all kinds of meetings in which nothing of substance is accomplished. Such unproductive collaboration will undermine overall company performance. For example, when executives were just beginning to develop collaborative behaviors within BP, employees started to form an unforeseen number of cross-unit networks. An audit within the oil exploration business alone identified several hundred of these networks, including one on helicopter utilization. According to John Leggate, who ran several business units during that time, "People always had a good reason to meet, but increasingly we found that people were flying around the world and simply sharing ideas without always having a strong focus on the bottom line." BP's executives had to reduce the number of networks and limit interunit meetings to those focused on getting specific results.

Management levers to create a collaborative organization must be counterbalanced with performance management of each individual and business unit, including a clear specification of who's responsible for what. At BP, each manager has an individual performance contract that is coupled with clear expectations for participating across the organization. These managers have a "T-shaped" role—while their primary responsibility is to deliver results for their own business unit or country

subsidiary (the vertical part of the T), their other responsibility is to seek help and to aid others (the horizontal part of the T). This dual role is difficult to carry out well and is a source of stress. Effective T-shaped managers tend to be good at prioritizing and delegating to subordinates. While those are attributes of any good manager, they are especially important in MNCs that require their managers to be effective along both dimensions of the T.

The Central Role of Collaboration

How one views the importance of collaboration relates directly to ideas about the purpose of any corporation and the reason for its existence. In the standard economic argument, firms arise when markets fail.[17] In consonance with that view, market failures in the exchange of goods, people and knowledge across geographic boundaries have long occupied center stage in economic theories of the multinational enterprise.[18] When global markets were relatively underdeveloped and prone to failure, this view made a legitimate contribution to our understanding. But now that global markets have become much more developed and relatively more efficient, it is time to consider an equally long-standing conception of why firms exist.[19]

In the alternative view, firms come into being in order to enable human beings to achieve collaboratively what they could not achieve alone. If one accepts this as the true purpose of any organization, then the main focus of executives' attention should be on how to foster collaboration within their companies. Especially in an era when advantages based on traditional economies of scale and scope are rapidly diminishing, the successful exploitation of collaborative possibilities may hold the key for multinationals seeking to gain or maintain leads over their rivals.

[17]See R.H. Coase, "The Nature of the Firm," Econometrica 4 (1937): 386–405.

[18]See R.E. Caves, "Multinational Enterprise and Economic Analysis (Cambridge, United Kingdom: Cambridge University Press, 1982).

[19]See C. Barnard, "The Functions of the Executive" (Cambridge, Massachusetts: Harvard University Press, 1939).

Engaging in Cross-Border Collaboration:
Managing Across Corporate Boundaries

As we saw in the last chapter, in the international business environment of the 21st century, few companies have all the resources and capabilities they need to develop the kind of multidimensional strategies and adaptive organizational capabilities that we have described. Increasingly, they must collaborate not only with research collaborators, but also with their suppliers, distributors, customers, agents, licensors, joint venture partners, and others to meet the needs of the increasingly complex global environment. This requirement implies that today's multinational enterprises (MNEs) must develop the skills to not only manage assets and resources under their own direct control, but also span their corporate boundaries and capture vital capabilities in the partnerships and alliances that are central to the strategic response capability of so many companies. After exploring the motivation for entering into such partnerships, we examine some of the costs and risks of collaboration before discussing the organizational and managerial skills required to build and manage these boundary-spanning relationships effectively.

Historically, the strategic challenge for a company has been viewed primarily as protecting potential profits from erosion. Such erosion of profits could be caused not only by the actions of competitors, but also by the bargaining powers of customers, suppliers, and governments. The key challenge facing a company was assumed to be its ability to maintain its independence by maintaining strong control over its activities. Furthermore, this strategic approach emphasized the defensive value of making other entities depend on it by capturing critical resources, building switching costs, and exploiting other vulnerabilities.[1]

This view of strategy subsequently underwent a sea change. The need to pursue multiple sources of competitive advantage simultaneously (as we discussed in detail in Chapter 3) led to the need for building not only an interdependent and integrated network organization within the company (Chapter 4), but also collaborative relationships with other firms, be they competitors, customers, suppliers, or a variety of other institutions.

This important shift in strategic perspective was triggered by a variety of factors, including rising R&D costs, shortened product life cycles, growing barriers to market entry, increasing needs for global-scale economies, and the expanding importance of global standards. Such dramatic changes led managers to recognize that many of

---

[1]For the most influential exposition of this view, see Michael E. Porter, *Competitive Strategy* (New York: Free Press, 1980).

the human, financial, and technological resources that they required to compete effectively lay beyond their boundaries and were sometimes—for political or regulatory reasons—not for sale. In response, many shifted their strategic focus away from an all-encompassing obsession with preempting competition to a broader view of building competitive advantage through selective, often simultaneous reliance on both collaboration and competition.

The previously dominant focus on value appropriation that characterized all dealings across a company's organizational boundary changed to the simultaneous consideration of both value creation and value appropriation. Instead of trying to enhance their bargaining power over customers, companies began to build partnerships with them, thereby bolstering the customer's competitive position and, at the same time, leveraging their own competitiveness and innovative capabilities.

However, perhaps the most visible manifestation of this growing role of collaborative strategies appears in the phenomenon often described as *strategic alliances:* the increasing propensity of MNEs to form cooperative relationships with their competitors. The Strategic Alliance Program implemented by Unisys provides a good illustration of this concept. Unisys is a global information technology company whose Alliance Program has positioned it to develop strategic relationships with other global leaders in its industry, including Microsoft, SAP, Oracle, EMC, Cisco, Dell, Intel, and IBM. As the company describes it, "Our alliances allow us to innovate, develop new technologies, and offer clients cutting-edge products and services."

Although our analysis of the causes and consequences of such collaborative strategies in this chapter focuses on the phenomenon of strategic alliances among global companies, some of our arguments can be applied to a broader range of cooperative relations, including those with customers, suppliers, and governments. We begin with a discussion of the key motivations for forming strategic alliances.

Why Strategic Alliances?

The term *strategic alliance* currently is used to describe a variety of interfirm cooperation agreements, ranging from shared research to formal joint ventures and minority equity participation (see Figure 6-1).

The key challenges surrounding the management of the various types of alliances detailed in Figure 6-1 will vary. In some cases, it may relate to the "fairness" of management or technology payments; in others, it may be related to where the organizational problems typically will arise. Every form of alliance has predictable strengths and weaknesses, because each form is intended and/or designed for particular circumstances.

Many firms worldwide, including many industry leaders, are increasingly involved in strategic alliances. Furthermore, several surveys suggest that such partnerships may be distinguished from traditional foreign investment joint ventures in important ways.

Classically, traditional joint ventures were formed between a senior multinational headquartered in an industrialized country and a junior local partner in a less-developed or less-industrialized country. The primary goal that dominated their formation was to gain new market access for existing products. In this classic contractual agreement, the senior partner provided existing products, while the junior partner provided the local

Figure 6-1   Range of Strategic Alliances

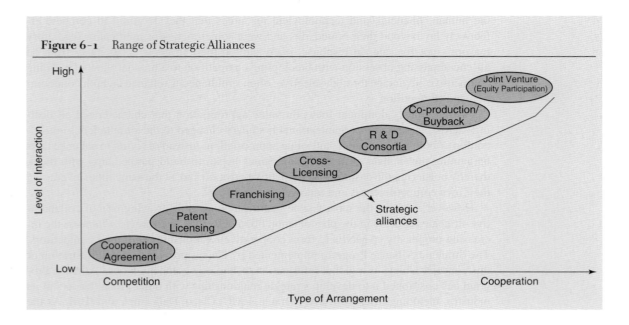

marketing expertise, the means to overcome any protectionist barriers, and the governmental contacts to deal with national regulations. Both partners benefited: The multinational increased its sales volume, and the local firm gained access to new products and often learned important new skills from its partner.

In contrast, the scope and motivations for the modern form of strategic alliances are clearly broadening. There are three trends that are particularly noteworthy. First, present-day strategic alliances are frequently between firms in industrialized countries. Second, the focus is often on the creation of new products and technologies rather than the distribution of existing ones. Third, present-day strategic alliances are often forged for only short periods of time.

All these characteristics mean that the new forms of strategic alliances expand the strategic importance of cooperation considerably beyond that which existed for classic joint ventures, and the opportunity for competitive gain and loss through partnering today is substantial. In the following sections, we discuss in more detail why this form of business relationship has become so important by focusing on five key motivations that are driving the formation of strategic alliances: technology exchange, global competition, industry convergence, economies of scale, and alliances as an alternative to merging.

Technology Exchange

As we discussed in some detail in Chapter 5, technology transfer or R&D collaboration is a major objective of many strategic alliances. The reason that technological exchange is such a strong driver of alliances is simple: As more and more breakthroughs and major innovations are based on interdisciplinary and inter-industry advances, the formerly clear boundaries between different industrial sectors and technologies become blurred. As a result, the necessary capabilities and resources are often beyond the scope of a single firm, making it increasingly difficult to compete effectively on the strength of one's own internal R&D efforts. The need to collaborate is intensified further by shorter product life cycles that increase both the time pressure and risk exposures, while reducing the potential payback of massive R&D investments.

Not surprisingly, technology-intensive sectors such as telecommunications, information technology, electronics, pharmaceuticals, and specialty chemicals have become the central arenas for major and extensive cooperative agreements. Companies in these industries face an environment of accelerating change, short product life cycles, small market windows, and multiple vertical and lateral dependencies in their value chains. Because interfirm cooperation has provided solutions to many of these strategic challenges, much of the technological development in these industries is being driven by some form of R&D partnership.

Even mainstream industrial MNEs have employed strategic alliances to meet the challenge of coordinating and deploying discrete pools of technological resources without sacrificing R&D and commercialization scale advantages. For example, three major energy corporations, General Electric (GE), ConocoPhillips and NRG Energy recently formed a joint venture designed to facilitate investment in and commercial collaboration with innovative energy technology companies developing leading-edge technologies such as solar photovoltaic, clean coal, and non-food biofuels, primarily in North America, Europe, and Israel. Kevin Skillern, managing director of GE's Energy Financial Services division, commented, "Partnering with major energy companies such as NRG and ConocoPhillips enables us to pool our financial resources and technological expertise." Mark Little, senior vice-president of GE Global Research, said, "This joint venture will build on our long history of innovation and expand our network of collaborators to speed the invention, development, and commercialization of new technologies."

Global Competition

A widespread perception has emerged that global competitive battles will increasingly be fought between teams of players aligned in strategic partnerships. In 2010, shortly after the triumvirate of major airline alliances (Star Alliance, Sky Team, and OneWorld) celebrated their 10-year anniversaries, Richard Branson announced that the Virgin Group's constituent airlines—Virgin Atlantic, Virgin America, and Virgin Australia—would be integrated into a quality alliance designed to compete with the "monster monopolies."

Particularly in industries in which there is a dominant worldwide market leader, joint ventures, strategic alliances, and networks allow coalitions of smaller partners to compete more effectively against a global "common enemy" rather than against one another. For example, the 2011 joint venture between China's Lenovo and Japan's NEC was designed to enable Lenovo to challenge the market leadership of the three firms that have traditionally dominated global PC sales (Hewlett-Packard, Dell, and Acer), while sustaining NEC's leadership in the Japanese PC market. Previous to the formation of the joint venture, Lenovo had been unable to unseat the leaders in the global PC industry and had been unable to penetrate the sizeable Japanese PC market.

Industry Convergence

Many high-technology industries are converging and overlapping in a way that seems destined to create a huge competitive traffic jam. Producers of computers, telecommunications, and components are merging, biological and chip technologies are intersecting, and advanced materials applications are creating greater overlaps in diverse applications from the aerospace to the automotive industry. Again, the preferred solution has been to create cross-industry alliances.

Furthermore, strategic alliances are sometimes the only way to develop the complex and interdisciplinary skills necessary in the time frame required. Alliances become a way of shaping competition by reducing competitive intensity, excluding potential entrants and isolating particular players, and building complex integrated value chains that can act as barriers to those who choose to go it alone.

Nowhere are the implications of this cross-industry convergence and broad-based collaboration clearer than in the case of high-definition television (HDTV). As with many other strategically critical technologies of the future—biotechnology, superconductivity, advanced ceramics, and artificial intelligence, for example—HDTV not only dwarfs previous investment requirements but extends beyond the technological capabilities of even the largest and most diversified MNEs. As a result, the development of this important industry segment has been undertaken almost exclusively by country-based, cross-industry alliances of large powerful companies. In Japan, companies allied to develop the range of products necessary for a system offering. At the same time, a European HDTV consortium banded together to develop a competitive system. But in the United States, the legal and cultural barriers that prevented companies from working together in such partnerships threatened to compromise U.S. competitiveness in this major industry.

Economies of Scale and Reduction of Risk

There are several ways that strategic alliances and networks allow participating firms to reap the benefits of scale economies or learning—advantages that are particularly interesting to smaller companies trying to match the economic benefits that accrue to the largest MNEs. First, partners can pool their resources and concentrate their activities not only to raise the scale of activity, but also to increase the rate of learning within the alliance compared to what each firm could achieve operating separately. Second, alliances enable partners to share and leverage the specific strengths and capabilities of all the other participating firms. Third, trading different or complementary resources among companies can result in mutual gains and save each partner the high cost of duplication.

While partnering has proven to be particularly useful for smaller firms that pursue rapid growth with limited resources, even the very largest MNEs have recognized the investment and growth benefits associated with partnering with other companies rather than "going it alone." For example, as part of Dow Chemical's effort to shift its focus toward the Middle East, the company implemented an "asset-light strategy," which resulted in the firm divesting many capital-intensive operations in favor of investing in a greater number of joint ventures with chemical firms situated in the growing emerging markets of the Middle East. David Kepler, Dow's chief information officer, commented that "we are doing much more partnering because of the large capital size of these investments." One industry analyst who agrees with Dow's strategy noted that "the projects are so big and capital intensive that even Dow ... doesn't have the capital to undertake them on its own," while another analyst observed, "By splitting the investment cost with a partner, Dow can invest in larger projects than it could alone, thereby adding shareholder value ... the risk of the investment is shared and Dow can achieve quicker growth."

One company activity that is especially motivated by the risk-sharing opportunities of such partnerships is R&D, where product life cycles are shortening and technological complexity is increasing. At the same time, R&D expenses are being driven sharply higher by personnel and capital costs. Because none of the participating firms bears the full risk and cost of the joint activity, alliances are often seen as an attractive risk-hedging mechanism.

One alliance driven by these motivations is the Renault-Nissan partnership. These two companies came together in 1999, with Renault taking a 36 percent share in Nissan and installing Carlos Ghosn as its chief operating officer. Although Nissan's perilous financial position was evidently a key factor in the decision to bring in a foreign partner, the underlying driver of the alliance was the need—on both sides—for greater economies of scale and scope to achieve competitive parity with General Motors (GM), Ford, and Toyota. The alliance led to a surprisingly fast turnaround of Nissan's fortunes, largely through Ghosn's decisive leadership, and, subsequently, to a broad set of projects to deliver synergies in product development, manufacturing, and distribution. Although still much smaller than GM or Ford, Renault-Nissan now is believed to be one of the long-term surviving players in the global automobile industry. In the first half of fiscal 2008, Nissan sales grew significantly, despite overall industry decline in the largest global markets.

More recently, BMW and PSA Peugeot Citroen formed their BMW Peugeot Citroen Electrification joint venture to develop and manufacture electric- and hybrid-vehicle components. The companies invested 100 million euros and hired 400 employees to work at a joint R&D center in order to develop more fuel-efficient automotive technologies. The joint venture's managing director, Jean Leflour, speculated, "We will set new standards for tomorrow's clean mobility with our agility, efficiency, and world class know-how in electrification systems." The joint venture was structured to create an open technology platform that would enable the joint venture to integrate suppliers into the development and purchasing processes once manufacturing commences in 2015.

Forming Alliances as an Alternative to Merging

Finally, there remain industry sectors in which political, regulatory, and legal constraints limit the extent of cross-border mergers and acquisitions. In such cases, companies often create alliances not because they are inherently the most attractive organizational form, but because they represent the best available alternative to a merger.

The classic examples of this phenomenon occur in the airline and telecommunications industries. Many countries still preclude foreign ownership in these industries. But a simple analysis of the economics of the industry—in terms of potential economies of scale, concentration of suppliers, opportunities for standardization of services, and competitive dynamics—would highlight the availability of substantial benefits from global integration. So as a means of generating at least some of the benefits of global integration (but not breaking the rules against foreign ownership), most major airlines have formed marketing and code-sharing partnerships, including the aforementioned Star Alliance and OneWorld, and many telecom companies have formed telecommunications alliances.

Alliances of this type often lead to full-scale global integration if restrictions on foreign ownership are lifted. For example, as the telecommunications industry was gradually deregulated during the 1990s, alliances such as Concert and Unisource gave way to the emergence of true multinational players such as Verizon, Vodafone, Telefonica, France Telecom, and Deutsche Telekom. Firms may prefer to engage in longer-term partnership relationships rather than merge. The inception of the BMW PSA Peugeot Citroen Electrification joint venture followed the successful operation of a separate, 10-year joint venture in which BMW and PSA Peugeot Citroen developed and manufactured 1.8 million fuel engines for the MINI, Peugeot, and Citroen car brands.

The Risks and Costs of Collaboration

Because of these different motivations, there was an initial period of euphoria during which partnerships were seen as the panacea for most of MNEs' global strategic problems and opportunities. The euphoria of the 1980s to form relationships was fueled by two fashionable management concepts of the period: "triad power"[2] and "stick to your knitting."[3]

The triad power concept emphasized the need to develop significant positions in three key markets (the United States, Western Europe, and Japan) as a prerequisite for competing in global industries. Given the enormous costs and difficulties of accessing any one of these developed and highly competitive markets independently, many companies with unequal legs on their geographic stool regarded alliances as the only feasible way to develop this triadic position.

The stick-to-your-knitting prescription in essence urged managers to disaggregate the value chain and focus their investments, efforts, and attention on only those tasks in which the company had a significant competitive advantage. Other operations were to be externalized through outsourcing or alliances. The seductive logic of both arguments, coupled with rapidly evolving environmental demands, led to an explosion in the formation of such alliances.

Since then, the experience that companies gathered through such collaborative ventures highlighted some of the costs and risks of such partnerships. Some risks arise from the simultaneous presence of both collaborative and competitive aspects in

[2]See Kenichi Ohmae, *Triad Power* (New York: Free Press, 1985).
[3]This idea is one of the lessons developed in the highly influential book by Thomas Peters and Robert Waterman, *In Search of Excellence* (New York: Harper & Row, 1982).

the relationships. Others arise from the higher levels of strategic and organizational complexity involved in managing cooperative relationships outside the company's own boundaries.

The Risks of Competitive Collaboration

Some strategic alliances—including some of the most visible—involve partners who are fierce competitors outside the specific scope of the cooperative venture. Such relationships create the possibility that the collaborative venture might be used by one or both partners to develop a competitive edge over the other, or at least that the benefits from the partnership will be asymmetrical for the two parties, which might change their relative competitive positions. There are several factors that might cause such asymmetry.

A partnership is often motivated by the desire to join and leverage complementary skills and resources. The partners may have access to very different resources and capabilities that could be combined to create new businesses or products. For example, Virgin Mobile India was formed to leverage Tata Teleservices' Code Division Multiple Access (CDMA) mobile technology network and Virgin Mobile's brand and marketing capabilities to target India's youth market for mobile telephone services. Such an arrangement for competency pooling inevitably entails the possibility that, in the course of the partnership, one of the partners will learn and internalize the other's skills while carefully protecting its own, thereby creating the option of discarding the partner and appropriating all the benefits created by the partnership. This possibility becomes particularly salient when the skills and competencies of one partner are tacit and deeply embedded in complex organizational processes (and thereby difficult to learn or emulate), whereas those of the other partner are explicit and embodied in specific individual machines or drawings (and thereby liable to relatively easy observation and emulation).

When General Foods entered into a partnership with Ajinimoto, the Japanese food giant, it agreed to make available its advanced processing technology for products such as freeze-dried coffee. In return, its Japanese partner would contribute its marketing expertise to launch the new products on the Japanese market. After several years, however, the collaboration deteriorated and was eventually dissolved after Ajinomoto absorbed the technology transfer, and its management believed that it was no longer learning from its U.S. partner. Unfortunately, General Foods had not done such a good job learning about the Japanese market, and it left the alliance with some bitterness.

Another predatory tactic might involve capturing investment initiative to use the partnership to erode the other's competitive position. In this scenario, the company ensures that it, rather than the partner, makes and keeps control over the critical investments. Such investments can be in the domain of product development, manufacturing, marketing, or wherever the most strategically vital part of the business value chain is located. Through these tactics, the aggressive company can strip its partner of the necessary infrastructure for competing independently and create one-way dependence in the collaboration that can be exploited at will.

Although they provide lively copy for magazine articles, such Machiavellian intentions and actions remain the exception, and the vast majority of cross-company collaborations are founded and maintained on a basis of mutual trust and shared commitment.

Yet even the most carefully constructed strategic alliances can become problematic. Although many provide short-term solutions to some strategic problems, they also serve to hide the deeper and more fundamental deficiencies that cause those problems. The short-term solution takes the pressure off the problem without solving it, and makes the company highly vulnerable when the problem finally resurfaces, usually in a more extreme and immediate form.

Furthermore, because such alliances typically involve task sharing, each company almost inevitably trades off some of the benefits of "learning by doing" the tasks that it externalizes to its partner. Thus, even in the best-case scenario of a partnership that meets all expectations, the very success of the partnership leads to some benefits for each partner and therefore to some strengthening of a competitor. Behind the success of the alliance, therefore, lies the ever-present possibility that a competitor's newly acquired strength will be used against its alliance partner in some future competitive battle.[4] Consider the example of Shanghai Automotive Industry Corp. (SAIC), one of China's largest state-owned enterprises. In April 2006, it announced that it was going to start producing a car under its own name. Up to that time, SAIC had been operating large joint ventures for many years with both Volkswagen and GM for the Chinese market. Under Chinese law, foreign companies wishing to produce automobiles in China must have a local partner who owns at least 50 percent of the business. Henceforth, the Volkswagen and GM joint ventures with SAIC would be competing with SAIC's wholly owned subsidiary. According to the China Association of Automobile Manufacturers, in 2011, SAIC's delivery of 3.6 million units made it the leading Chinese-based automaker in terms of output volume.

Finally, there is the risk that collaborating with a competitor might be a precursor to a takeover by one of the firms. Carlsberg's Baltic Beverages joint venture with Scottish & Newcastle (S&N) was created in 2002 to target the Russian and other emerging Eastern European beer markets. Eventually, Carlsberg sought to pursue these markets without its joint venture partner. However, a "shotgun clause" in the joint venture agreement required either partner to offer its shares in Baltic Beverages to the other partner in the event that either wanted to exit the joint venture. In court filings, S&N alleged that Carlsberg was attempting to circumvent the clause when Carlsberg announced in 2007 the formation of a consortium with Heineken in order to finance the hostile acquisition of S&N. Ultimately, Carlsberg's attempted acquisition of S&N was successful, and Carlsberg assumed ownership of S&N's share.

The Cost of Strategic and Organizational Complexity

Cooperation is difficult to attain even in the best of circumstances. One of the strongest forces facilitating such behavior within a single company's internal operations is the understanding that the risks and rewards ultimately accrue to the company's own accounts and therefore, either directly or indirectly, to the cooperating participants. This basic motivation is diluted in strategic alliances. Furthermore, the scope of most alliances and the environmental uncertainties that they inevitably face often prevent a clear

---

[4]These potential risks of competitive collaboration are discussed in Gary Hamel, Yves L. Doz, and C. K. Prahalad, "Collaborate with Your Competitor—and Win," *Harvard Business Review,* January/February 1989.

understanding of the risks that might be incurred or rewards that might accrue in the course of the partnership's evolution. As a result, cooperation in the context of allocated risks and rewards and divided loyalties inevitably creates additional strategic and organizational complexity that involves additional costs to manage.

International partnerships bring together companies that are often products of different economic, political, social, and cultural systems. Such differences in the administrative heritages of the partner companies, each of which brings its own strategic mentality and managerial practices to the venture, further exacerbate the organizational challenge. For example, tensions between Xerox and Fuji Xerox—a successful but often troubled relationship—were as much an outgrowth of the differences in the business systems in which each was located as of the differences in the corporate culture between the U.S. company and its Japanese joint venture. Similarly, the tumultuous eight-year joint venture relationship between Italy's Fiat and China's Nanjing Automotive was presided over by no fewer than four different CEOs, who terminated seven different sales and marketing heads before the joint venture was dissolved.

Organizational complexity also contributes to added difficulties, due to the very broad scope of operations typical of many strategic alliances. As we have described, one of the distinguishing characteristics of present-day alliances is that they often cover a broad range of activities. This expansion of scope requires partners not only to manage the many areas of contact within the alliance but also to coordinate the different alliance-related tasks within their own organizations. And the goals, tasks, and management processes for the alliance must be constantly monitored and adapted to changing conditions.

Building and Managing Collaborative Ventures

As we have described in the preceding sections, alliances are neither conventional organizations with fully internalized activities nor well-specified transaction relationships through which externalized activities may be linked by market-based contracts. Instead, they combine elements of both. The participating companies retain their own competitive strategies and performance expectations, as well as their national, ideological, and administrative identities. But to obtain the required benefits of a partnership, diverse organizational units in different companies and different countries must coordinate their activities effectively and flexibly.

There are numerous reasons that such collaborative ventures inevitably present some significant management challenges: strategic and environmental disparities among the partners, lack of a common experience and perception base, difficulties in interfirm communication, conflicts of interest and priorities, and inevitable personal differences among the individuals who manage the interface. As a result, although it is clear to most managers that strategic alliances can provide great benefits, they also realize that there is a big difference between establishing alliances and making them work.

The challenge can be considered in two parts, reflecting the pre-alliance tasks of analysis, negotiation, and decision making and the post-alliance tasks of coordination, integration, and adaptation.

Building Cooperative Ventures

The quality of the pre-alliance processes of partner selection and negotiation influences the clarity and reciprocity of mutual expectations from the alliance. There are three aspects of the pre-alliance process to which managers must pay close attention if the alliance is to have the best possible chance of success: partner selection, escalating commitment, and alliance scope.[5]

Partner Selection: Strategic and Organizational Analysis

The process of analyzing a potential partner's strategic and organizational capabilities is an important yet difficult pre-alliance task. Several factors impede the quality of the choice-making process.

The most important constraint lies in the availability of information required for an effective evaluation of the potential partner. Effective pre-alliance analysis needs data about the partner's relevant physical assets (e.g., the condition and productivity of plants and equipment), as well as less tangible assets (e.g., strength of brands, quality of customer relationships, and level of technological expertise) and organizational capabilities (e.g., managerial competence, employee loyalty, and shared values). The difficulty of obtaining such information in the short time limits in which most alliances are finalized is complicated further by the barriers of cultural and physical distance that MNEs must also overcome.

The pressures of time and distance sometimes result in suboptimal partner selection. As Figure 6-2 suggests, there is no real upside to selecting a partner who is competent but with whom you may not be comfortable working. Nor, however, should partners be selected on the basis of comfort rather than competence.

A key lesson emerging from the experience of most strategic alliances is that changes in each partner's competitive positions and strategic priorities have crucial effects on the viability of the alliance over time. Even if the strategic trajectories of two companies cross at a particular point in time, creating complementarities and the potential for a partnership, their paths may be so divergent as to make such complementarities too transient for the alliance to have any lasting value. Case 6-3, about Eli Lilly in India, explores whether the Eli Lilly–Ranbaxy joint venture still meets each partner's strategic objectives, 15 years after it was established.

Although it is difficult enough to make a static assessment of a potential partner's strategic and organizational capabilities, it is almost impossible to make an effective pre-alliance analysis of how those capabilities are likely to evolve over time. This challenge may be more pronounced where partnerships are formed between developed market and developing market firms. For example, John Hopkins Medicine International, a nonprofit organization, partners with governments, insurance firms, other charitable foundations, and health care companies to develop and operate state-of-the-art medical facilities worldwide.[6] The organization's CEO, Steven J. Thompson, has suggested that

---

[5]The pre-alliance process is in many ways similar to a pre-acquisition process and shares the same needs. See David B. Jemison and Sim B. Sitkin, "Acquisitions: The Process Can Be a Problem," *Harvard Business Review,* 2 (1986), pp. 107–14.

[6]Steven J. Thompson, "The Perils of Partnering in Developing Markets," *Harvard Business Review,* June (2012).

Figure 6-2   Partner Selection: Comfort vs. Competence

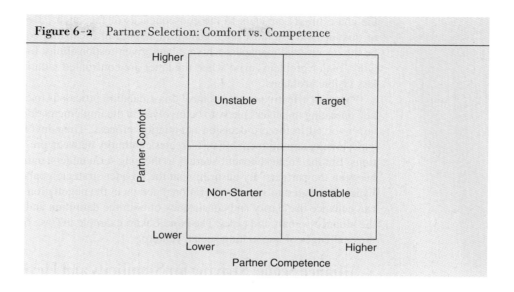

partnering with developing market firms poses a unique set of challenges, including the incessant conflict between a partner's local market culture and best practices in Western medicine, as well the risk that developing market partners are more concerned with securing healthy financial returns than with being committed to the goal of delivering sustainable quality in developing market medical services. To mitigate against these risks, Thompson advises firms that seek to engage with developing market partners to assess their potential partner's willingness to commit resources, to work with the partner through a project or business planning process, and to ensure that both partners can reach a clear understanding of the potential project, as well as agreeing to realistic expectations for the project.

There probably is no solution to this problem of how a potential partner's capabilities are likely to evolve over time, but companies that recognize alliances as a permanent and important part of their future organization have made monitoring their partners an ongoing process rather than an ad hoc one. Some have linked such activities to their integrated business intelligence system, which was set up to monitor competitors. By having this group not only analyze competitors' potential strategies but also assess their value as acquisition or alliance candidates, these companies find themselves much better prepared when a specific alliance opportunity arises.

Escalating Commitment: Thrill of the Chase

The very process of alliance planning and negotiations can cause unrealistic expectations and wrong choices. In particular, some managers involved in the process can build up a great deal of personal enthusiasm and expectations in trying to sell the idea of the alliance within their own organization. This escalation process is similar to a process observed in many acquisition decisions where, in one manager's words, "The thrill of the chase blinds pursuers to the consequences of the catch." Because the champions of this idea—those most often caught in a spiral of escalating commitment—may not be the operational managers who are later given responsibility for making the alliance work, major problems arise when the latter are confronted with inevitable pitfalls and less visible problems.

The most effective way to control this escalation process is to ensure that at least the key operating managers likely to be involved in the implementation stage of the alliance are involved in the pre-decision negotiation process. Their involvement not only ensures greater commitment but also creates continuity between pre- and post-alliance actions. But the greatest benefit accrues to the long-term understanding that must develop between the partners. By ensuring that the broader strategic goals that motivate the alliance are related to specific operational details in the negotiation stage, the companies can enhance the clarity and consistency of both the definition and the understanding of the alliance's goals and tasks. The Nora Sakari example in Case 6-2 considers in detail the challenges of negotiating such a venture.

Alliance Scope: Striving for Simplicity and Flexibility

All too often, in an effort to show commitment at the time of the agreement, partners press for broad and all-encompassing corporate partnerships and equity participation or exchange. Yet a key to successful alliance building lies in defining as simple and focused a scope for the partnership as is adequate to get the job done, but to retain at the same time the possibility to redefine and broaden the scope if needed. Alliances that are more complex also require more management attention to succeed and tend to be more difficult to manage.

Three factors add to the management complexity of a partnership: complicated cross-holdings of ownership or equity, the need for cross-functional coordination or integration, and breadth in the number and scope of joint activities. Before involving any alliance in such potentially complicated arrangements, management should ask: "Are these conditions absolutely necessary, given our objectives?" If a simple original equipment manufacturer (OEM) arrangement can suffice, it is not only unnecessary to enter into a more committed alliance relationship but also is undesirable, because the added complexity will increase the likelihood of problems and difficulties in achieving the objectives of the partnership.

At the same time, it might be useful to provide some flexibility in the terms of the alliance for renegotiating and changing the scope, if and when necessary. Even when a broad-based and multifaceted alliance represents the ultimate goal, many companies have found it preferable to start with a relatively simple and limited partnership whose scope is expanded gradually as both partners develop a better understanding of and greater trust in each other's motives, capabilities, and expectations.

Multinationals are increasingly relying upon highly flexible and globally oriented interorganizational networks to supplement their more traditional dyadic alliances and partnerships. For example, Proctor & Gamble (P&G) recognized that that it was unable to sustain high revenue growth by continuing to rely on an innovation model that relied on internally networking its business units. As a result, the firm shifted its R&D model and mandated that 50 percent of its innovations should be acquired from a worldwide network of external engineers and scientists. Larry Huston, P&G's vice president for innovation and knowledge, and Nabil Sakkab, the firm's president for corporate R&D, acknowledged that "we needed to change how we defined, and perceived, our R&D organization—from 7,500 people inside [the company] to 7,500 plus 1.5 million (P&G's estimate of the number of qualified scientists and engineers worldwide), with a permeable boundary between them. It was against this backdrop that we created our 'connect and develop' innovation model. With a clear sense of consumers' needs, we could identify promising ideas throughout the world and apply our own R&D, manufacturing, marketing, and purchasing capabilities to them to create better and cheaper products, faster."[7]

Managing Cooperative Ventures

Although the pre-alliance analysis and negotiation processes are important, a company's ability to manage an ongoing relationship also tends to be a key determining factor for the success or failure of an alliance. Among the numerous issues that influence a company's ability to manage a cooperative venture, there are three that appear to present the greatest challenges: managing the boundary, managing knowledge flows, and providing strategic directions.

Managing the Boundary: Structuring the Interface

There are many different ways in which the partners can structure the boundary of an alliance and manage the interface between this boundary and their own organizations. At one extreme, an independent legal organization can be created and given complete freedom to manage the alliance tasks. Alternatively, the alliance's operations can be managed by one or both parents with more substantial strategic, operational, or administrative controls. In many cases, however, the creation of such a distinct entity is not necessary, and simpler, less bureaucratic governance mechanisms such as joint committees may be enough to guide and supervise shared tasks. Also, given the potentially enormous breadth in the scope of activities (see Figure 6-3), it may be more practical to start with a limited agreement. It is always easier to gain a partner's agreement to expand than to contract an alliance's terms of reference.**Figure 6-3**   Scope of activity

The choice among alternative boundary structures depends largely on the scope of the alliance. When the alliance's tasks are characterized by extensive functional interdependencies, there is a need for a high level of integration in the decision-making process related to those shared tasks. In such circumstances, the creation of a separate entity is often the only effective way to manage such dense interlinkages. In contrast, an alliance between two companies with the objective of marketing each other's existing products in noncompetitive markets may need only a few simple rules that govern marketing parameters and financial arrangements and a single joint committee to review the outcomes periodically.

---

[7]Larry Huston and Nabil Sakkab, "Connect and Develop: Inside Proctor & Gamble's New Model for Innovation," *Harvard Business Review,* March (2006), pp. 59–60.

Figure 6-3   Scope of Activity

Narrow	vs.	Wide
Single, geographic market	vs.	Multi-country
Single function	vs.	Complete value chain
Single industry/customer group	vs.	Multi-industry
Modest investment	vs.	Large scale
Existing business	vs.	New business
Limited term	vs.	Forever

Following the growing prominence and regulation pertaining to corporate governance in the domain of publicly traded firms, issues of governance have begun to attract increased attention within the realm of joint ventures.[8] Governance processes are particularly important in alliances characterized by a high level of integration. Consultants at McKinsey have recommended that parent companies should strive to focus their active participation on the joint venture or alliance's board to three areas that are directly related to the new entity's financial performance and the protection of shareholder interests—capital allocation, risk management, and performance management.[9] Additionally, they recommend that parents restrict their involvement in operational processes because the failure to do so can impinge upon the joint venture or alliance's ability to remain competitive and responsive to changing market forces. Ultimately, an alliance's governance structure must include clear rules pertaining to decision making among the entity's partners and its general manager.[10]

Managing Knowledge Flows: Integrating the Interface

Irrespective of the specific objectives of any alliance, the very process of collaboration creates flows of information across the boundaries of the participating companies and creates the potential for learning from each other. Managing these knowledge flows involves two kinds of tasks for the participating companies. First, they must ensure full exploitation of the created learning potential. Second, they must prevent the outflow of any information or knowledge that they do not wish to share with their alliance partners.

In terms of the first point, the key problem is that the individuals managing the interface may not be the best users of such knowledge. To maximize its learning from a partnership, a company must integrate its interface managers effectively into the rest of its organization. The gatekeepers must have knowledge of and access to the different individuals and management groups within the company that are likely to benefit most from the diverse kinds of information that flow through an alliance boundary. Managers familiar with the difficulties of managing information flows within the company's

---

[8]Jeffrey J. Reuer et al. "Building Corporate Governance to International Joint Ventures," *Global Strategy Journal,* 1 (2011), pp. 54–66.

[9]James Bamford, David Ernst, and David G. Fubini, "Launching a World-Class Joint Venture," *Harvard Business Review,* 82 (2004), pp. 91–100.

[10]Paul W. Beamish, *Joint Venturing* (Charlotte, North Carolina: Information Age Publishing, 2008).

boundaries will readily realize that such cross-boundary learning is unlikely to occur unless specific mechanisms are in place to make it happen.

The selection of appropriate interface managers is perhaps the single most important factor for facilitating such learning. Interface managers should have at least three key attributes: They must be well versed in the company's internal organizational process; they must have the personal credibility and status necessary to access key managers in different parts of the organization; and they must have a sufficiently broad understanding of the company's business and strategies to be able to recognize useful information and knowledge that might cross their path.

Merely placing the right managers at the interface is not sufficient to ensure effective learning, however. Supportive administrative processes also must be developed to facilitate the systematic transfer of information and to monitor the effectiveness of those transfers. Such support is often achieved most effectively through simple systems and mechanisms, such as task forces or periodic review meetings.

While exploiting the alliance's learning potential, however, each company must also manage the interface to prevent unintended flows of information to its partner. It is a delicate balancing task for the gatekeepers to ensure the free flow of information across the organizational boundaries while effectively regulating the flow of people and data to ensure that sensitive or proprietary knowledge is appropriately protected.

Providing Strategic Direction: The Governance Structure

The key to providing leadership and direction, ensuring strategic control, and resolving interorganizational conflicts is an effective governance structure. Unlike acquisitions, alliances are often premised on the equality of both partners, but an obsession to protect such equality can prevent companies from creating an effective governance structure for the partnership. Committees consisting of an equal number of participants from both companies and operating under strict norms of equality are often incapable of providing clear directions or forcing conflict resolution at lower levels. Indeed, many otherwise well conceived alliances have floundered because of their dependence on such committees for their leadership and control.

To find their way around such problems, partners must negotiate on the basis of *integrative* rather than *distributive* equality. With such an agreement, each committee is structured with clear, single-handed leadership, but each company takes the responsibility for different tasks. However, such delicately balanced arrangements can work only if the partners can agree on specific individuals, delegate the overall responsibility for the alliance to these individuals, and protect their ability to work in the best interests of the alliance itself rather than those of the parents.

Concluding Comments

Perspectives on strategic alliances have oscillated between the extremes of euphoria and disillusionment. Finally, however, there seems to be some recognition that though such partnerships may not represent perfect solutions, they are often the best solution available to a particular company at a particular point in time.

Easy—But Sometimes Not the Best Solution

Perhaps the biggest danger for many companies is to pretend that the "quick and easy" option of a strategic alliance is also the best or only option available. Cooperative arrangements are perhaps too tempting in catch-up situations in which the partnership might provide a façade of recovery that masks serious problems.

Yet although going it alone may well be the most desirable option for a specific objective or task in the long term, almost no company can afford to meet all its objectives in this way. When complete independence and self-sufficiency are not possible because of resource scarcity, lack of expertise and time—or any other such constraint—strategic alliances often become the most realistic option.

Alliances Need Not Be Permanent

Another important but commonly misunderstood factor is that the dissolution of a partnership is not synonymous with failure. Many companies appear to have suffered because of their unwillingness or inability to terminate partnership arrangements when changing circumstances made those arrangements inappropriate or because they failed to discuss upfront with their partner whether the alliance should have a sunset clause. All organizations create internal pressures for their own perpetuation, and an alliance is no exception to this enduring reality. One important task for senior managers of the participating companies is to ask periodically why the alliance should not be terminated and then continue with the arrangement only if they find compelling reasons to do so.

Flexibility Is Key

The original agreement for a partnership typically is based on limited information and unrealistic expectations. Experience gained from the actual process of working together provides the opportunity for fine-tuning and often finding better ways to achieve higher levels of joint value creation. In such circumstances, the flexibility to adapt the goals, scope, and management of the alliance to changing conditions is essential. In addition, changing environmental conditions may make original intentions and plans obsolete. Effective partnering requires the ability to monitor such changes and allow the partnership to evolve in response.

An Internal Knowledge Network: Basis for Learning

Finally, learning is one of the main benefits that a company can derive from a partnership, whether or not it represents one of the formal goals. For such learning to occur, however, a company must be receptive to the knowledge and skills available from the partner and have an organization able to diffuse and leverage such learning. In the absence of an internal knowledge network, information obtained from the partner cannot be transferred and applied, regardless of its potential value. Thus, building and managing an integrated network organization, as described in Chapter 4, is an essential prerequisite not only for effective internal processes, but also for effective management across organizational boundaries.

> ## Chapter 6 Readings
>
> - In Reading 6-1, Beamish discusses "The Design and Management of International Joint Ventures." This is typically the alliance form that requires the greatest level of interaction, cooperation, and investment. This reading focuses on two primary issues: the reasons why companies create international joint ventures and the requirements for international joint venture success.
> - In Reading 6-2, "How to Manage Alliances Better Than One at a Time," Wassmer, Dussauge, and Planellas focus on how companies can employ a more strategic approach to configuring effective alliance portfolios. The authors advocate a two-stage alliance assessment process (which includes both Individual Alliance Analysis and Alliance Portfolio Analysis) that can be used when considering any new alliance opportunity. They contend that when a company adds a new alliance to its portfolio, the firm tends to focus on how much value the alliance will create as a stand-alone transaction, while ignoring the fact that the composition of its entire alliance portfolio is an important determinant of the value that will emerge from the new alliance relationship.

Case 6-1   Sharp Corporation: Beyond Japan[1]

Derek Lehmberg

Mikio Katayama was the president of Sharp Corporation, a company that in the last 10 years had become recognized as a top-notch competitor in electronics products, leaving behind its image as a second-rate player. Sharp could brag about its leading positions in the Japanese cell phone handset and TV set markets as well as its worldwide reputation as a leader in liquid crystal display (LCD) technology. Despite these successes, however, the outlook for Sharp was far from optimistic. In the spring of 2009, Sharp reported its first loss since 1956, the year its shares began trading on the Tokyo Stock Exchange. At the subsequent annual shareholders' meeting, Katayama apologized for "causing great anxiety and trouble to shareholders," and also announced that the firm's dividend would be cut.[2] With slowing sales due to the deepest worldwide recession since the 1930s, Sharp's competitors were also facing hard times. However, Sharp's problems went beyond the current downturn. Katayama felt Sharp's fundamental way of doing business needed to be reconsidered.[3]

Richard Ivey School of Business
The University of Western Ontario

▌ [1]This case has been written on the basis of published sources only. Consequently, the interpretation and perspectives presented in this case are not necessarily those of Sharp Corporation or any of its employees.
▌ [2]"Sharp—Akajide Katayama-shachora Chinsha," *The Mainichi Newspaper,* Tokyo, June 24, 2009.
▌ [3]H. Sagimori, "Sharp Ishin: Saraba Kameyama Model," *Nikkei Business,* July 6, 2009, pp. 18–21.

Sharp Corporation

Sharp Corporation was an electronics company with headquarters in Osaka, Japan. Its business consisted of electronic products and electronic components (see **Exhibit 1**). Electronic products were grouped into three categories: audio-visual and communication equipment, health and environment equipment, and information equipment. Electronic components included LCDs, solar cells, and other electronic devices. Many of these components relied on Sharp's expertise in opto-electronics.

Sharp's technology strategy focused on synergies between electronic components and the end products Sharp made. End consumer products provided component sales as well as opportunities for Sharp to improve its component-related technologies. Sharp also looked for new market needs that it could meet using its component capabilities. It strove to develop and manufacture "Only-one" products: those that combined Sharp's knowledge and capabilities in ways other firms could not imitate. This approach had been at the heart of Sharp's impressive history of developing unique, groundbreaking products (see **Exhibit 2**).

Sharp was active in international markets, but had chosen to manufacture its electronic components exclusively in Japan. Often, these components employed cutting-edge technology and required capital-intensive plants to manufacture. Sharp's overseas plants, on the other hand, typically focused on the final assembly of products for local consumption. The Japanese domestic plants had become centres of high-value-added knowledge, whereas the overseas plants had not.

Exhibit 1   Sharp's Product Groupings

	Product Grouping	Major Products
Consumer/Information Products	Audio-Visual and Communication Equipment	LCD televisions, projectors, DVD recorders & players, Blu-ray Disc recorders & players, cell phones
	Health and Environment Equipment	Refrigerators, microwave ovens, small cooking appliances, air conditioners, electric heaters, air purifiers, dehumidifiers, humidifiers, washing machines, vacuum cleaners, LED lights
	Information Equipment	Personal computers, LCD computer monitors, electronic dictionaries, calculators, telephones, POS systems & cash registers, digital MFPs (multifunction printers), facsimiles
Electronic Components/ Devices	LCDs	LCD modules (Types: TFT-LCD, Duty, System)
	Solar Cells	Thin-film solar cells, crystalline solar cells
	Other	CCD/CMOS image sensors, LSIs for LCDs, microprocessors, flash and combination memory chips, laser diodes, LEDs, optical pickups, optical sensors, components for optical communications, broadcasting and tuning components, power supplies

Source: Company website.

Exhibit 2   Sharp Timeline

Year	Event
1925	Produces first Japanese-made radio set.
1953	First to mass produce TV sets in Japan. The technology is licensed from RCA.
1964	Produces world's first all-transistor-diode calculator.
1970	Licenses LCD technology from RCA, begins LCD development.
1973	Begins selling world's first LCD calculator, LC Mate EL805.
1974	Orient begins selling LCD watches with displays supplied by Sharp.
1986	Sharp's "Shoin" Japanese word processor with STN-LCD display becomes a hit product.
1987	Begins mass production of 3" color TFT LCD TVs.
1989	Releases video camera with LCD viewfinder.
1989	Uses LCD in car navigation application.
1991	Begins selling the world's first wall-hanging LCD TV. It has an 8.6" display and is priced at 500,000 yen.
1992	Begins selling LCD "View Cam" video camera with 3" TFT-LCD display.
1993	Introduces Zaurus LCD-based personal digital assistant (PDA).
1995	Introduces "Window" LCD TV in 10.4" and 8.4" sizes.
1995	Introduces Mebius line of laptop computers with Sharp-made LCDs.
1995	Introduces 43" rear projection TV using LCD microdisplays.
1998	Declares it will replace its entire TV lineup with LCD TVs by 2005.
1998	Announces world's first full lineup of flat panel TVs.
2001	Introduces AQUOS brand LCD TV line in 13, 15 and 20 inch sizes.
2002	Announces two 37" LCD TV models.
2004	Begins selling 45" full high definition LCD TV.
2004	Begins production on the world's first generation 6 LCD line at the Kameyama plant. This is the world's first LCD line dedicated to TV production.
2005	Teleases its final three CRT TV models for the Japanese market.
2005	Begins construction of Kameyama Number 2 LCD plant, which will be the world's first generation 8 plant. Plant to come on line in October, 2006; total investment is 150 billion yen.
2007	Announces it will build the world's first generation 10 LCD plant in Sakai, Japan. Sharp's investment will be approximately 380 billion yen. Production is planned to start in 2010.
2007	Announces world's largest LCD TV (108") at Consumer Electronics Show.

Source: Compiled from flat panel display industry serial publications including series from Nikkei BP (1991–2008), Sangyo Times (1990, 1992–2008), and Fuji Chimera (1998–2007).

Mikio Katayama

Mikio Katayama joined Sharp in 1981 after graduating from Tokyo University with a degree in engineering. He had followed an unusual career path at Sharp. Early in his career Katayama worked on solar panels, but he later moved into Sharp's LCD business. Katayama was promoted to the position of corporate director in 2003, and made corporate senior executive director in 2006, becoming responsible for both large LCDs and LCD TVs. Still in his 40s, Katayama was much younger than Sharp's other senior managers. In April 2007, Katayama became president of Sharp and the previous president, Katsuhiko Machida, was appointed chairman.[4]

Katayama had an unusual combination of abilities. Although he had an engineering background, his ability to develop and communicate a broad strategic vision made him stand out. Facing challenges on a number of fronts simultaneously, Sharp needed the kind of unconventional leadership Katayama could provide.

LCDs

Over the years, the name "Sharp" had become associated with leading LCD technology. The company first took notice of the technology after one of its engineers saw a TV clip showing an RCA LCD prototype in 1968. Sharp licensed the technology in 1970.[5] RCA's presentation of LCD technology had focused on its promise as a flat screen TV display. However, RCA had later concluded that the technological barriers LCD faced were too high and had ceased LCD development. Sharp had treated LCD very differently; LCD could be useful for many other applications besides TV. Calculators and watches were applications where even basic LCDs provided clear advantages to other display technologies.

Sharp had continued to develop LCD technology actively for many years. Although early LCD had many limitations, many of these were overcome as the technology developed. In the late 1980s, thin film transistor LCDs (TFT-LCDs) were developed, making possible bright, high-contrast displays. However, these were difficult and expensive to produce, limiting adoption to applications where the low energy usage and flat design of the LCD were absolute requirements. Sharp identified display applications where the

displays were attractive despite their high cost and small size, such as navigation systems and laptop computers.

Sharp was not alone in its pursuit of LCD technology. A number of other electronics firms, LCD fabrication equipment manufacturers, and input suppliers also invested heavily in LCD R&D. Much of the technological progress made in LCD technology during the 1990s was due to exchanging and integrating knowledge from these different kinds of firms. In particular, LCD production yields—the amount of usable displays producible from a certain amount of inputs—increased dramatically, resulting in lower production costs per display produced.

There was a downside to cooperation within the industry. By the time production technology reached its fifth generation, it had been improved to the point that firms with little LCD experience could buy a new plant and get it to function reasonably well with limited outside help. Improved production equipment, increased mobility of LCD engineering talent and technology transfer agreements had facilitated the development of LCD technology by firms in South Korea and Taiwan. Once these new competitors learned to operate, the incumbent Japanese LCD firms found it increasingly difficult to compete.

Although the industry's cooperative approach had facilitated the development of LCD production and cost performance, Sharp became concerned that too much of its proprietary knowledge was being learned by the outside world, decreasing its competitive lead. To protect its major investments in LCD and retain its cost advantage, Sharp decided to operate much more secretly. Beginning with the first of what would become two plants in Kameyama (Mie Prefecture, Japan), Sharp pursued a "black-box" approach to its manufacturing operations.[6] Outsiders were not allowed to see the inside of Sharp's LCD plants. Even key partners including suppliers and equipment producers were not admitted beyond the loading dock. Sharp believed this focus on secrecy

---

[4]Mikio Katayama interview with Nikkei Business, "Kukyo koso Seicho Vision," *Nikkei Business,* July 6, 2009, pp. 22–24.

[5]T. Numagami, *Ekisho Display no Gijutsu Kakushinshi,* Hakuto Shobo Publishing, Tokyo, 1999.

[6]"04 Nihon Keizai/3 Chusho-Hiseizogyo no Katusriki," *The Mainichi Newspaper,* Tokyo, July 21, 2004.

had helped it maintain its lead in proprietary technologies that otherwise might have been lost.[7]

Improvement of Other LCD Attributes

LCD had faced other performance issues in addition to production yield issues and high costs. Early LCDs looked blotchy when viewed from the side, could not display deep black, and had blurry output of moving images. These were not major concerns for some applications such as laptops, although they were major problems for video and TV applications.

Major LCD producers were concerned about these image quality issues and invested in R&D to rectify them. While Sharp had a respectable record in these areas, it was hardly the only firm that could claim this. Over time, many of these issues with LCDs were resolved to the point that typical consumers could not identify problems with LCDs produced by any of the major firms.

The Liquid Crystal Display Panel Industry

Sharp competed with a number of large-scale LCD producers. These firms were primarily located in South Korea and Taiwan, although China was interested in becoming a player in LCD production. Up until this point, Chinese LCD capabilities had been limited to simple LCD types and outdated-generation production facilities, but things appeared likely to change.

Some major LCD producers such as Sharp had large internal demand for their output, but others primarily sold LCD modules on the open market or to strategic partner companies. Although some displays were customized for specific applications, commonly used display sizes with standard resolutions were traded as commodities. Notebook computer displays, which were very profitable in the early 1990s, became an example of such a commoditized LCD product.

LCD production facilities were categorized by the generation of glass substrate they used (see **Exhibit 3**). With each introduction of new-generation production equipment, the size of the glass substrate used grew. Production using larger substrates was more cost-effective, although investment requirements were large. Due to the large scale of cutting-edge plants, each time one came on line it had a noticeable impact on market prices for LCD panels.

The LCD panel market was characterized by large price swings. These swings increased the volatility of LCD producers' earnings. This pattern of boom and bust had become known as "the crystal cycle." High levels of commoditization and rapid improvement in production efficiencies had also been behind the long-term trend towards lower LCD panel prices.

The Television Set Business

Although Sharp had been the first Japanese firm to produce a television set, it had never been a major player in the cathode ray tube-based (CRT) TV set business. Lacking its own CRT production capability, Sharp TVs had been made using tubes produced by its competitors. Sharp had considered itself to be at a major disadvantage in TVs for this reason.

As Sharp's LCD technology improved, the company began making LCD TV sets. Early models carried exorbitant price tags despite having very small screens. In 1995, Sharp introduced two LCD TVs with 8.4-inch and 10.4-inch diagonal screens. The 10.4-inch model carried a suggested retail price of 150,000 yen (approximately US$1,600 at the time).[8] Although the prices had fallen significantly compared with prior models, they were still quite expensive, and screen sizes remained small for TV set applications. Despite these drawbacks, the models sold more rapidly than Sharp had expected. The following year, Sharp added a larger 13-inch model and increased production of LCD TVs.[9]

Sharp's TV business had an important year in 1998. Sharp's president at the time, Katsuhiko Machida, announced the company's intent to make

---

[7]Sharp Corporation Annual Report 2006.

[8]*Flat Panel Display 1996*, Nikkei BP, Tokyo, 1996.
[9]*Ekisho Maker Keikaku Soran 1996*, Sangyo Times, Tokyo, 1995.

Exhibit 3 Substrate Size by Generation and Year of Production Start

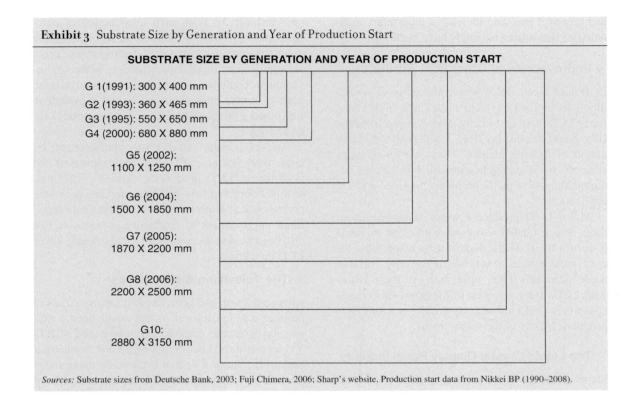

SUBSTRATE SIZE BY GENERATION AND YEAR OF PRODUCTION START

G 1(1991): 300 X 400 mm

G2 (1993): 360 X 465 mm

G3 (1995): 550 X 650 mm

G4 (2000): 680 X 880 mm

G5 (2002):
1100 X 1250 mm

G6 (2004):
1500 X 1850 mm

G7 (2005):
1870 X 2200 mm

G8 (2006):
2200 X 2500 mm

G10:
2880 X 3150 mm

Sources: Substrate sizes from Deutsche Bank, 2003; Fuji Chimera, 2006; Sharp's website. Production start data from Nikkei BP (1990–2008).

its entire TV lineup LCD-based by 2005. Inside the industry, this statement became known as "The Machida Declaration."[10] Considering the high price and limited screen size of LCDs at the time, this was a bold statement. CRT TVs provided much bigger screen sizes for a fraction of the cost, and had better image quality. Plasma TVs were also beginning to enter the market.

In 2001, Sharp introduced its Aquos line of LCD TV sets. These TVs featured an elegant industrial design in addition to the latest display technology. Sharp's advertising of the new line featured Sayuri Yoshinaga, a Japanese actress with whom many Japanese housewives strongly identified. This appeal to housewives was a new tactic in the Japanese TV set market. Considering the size of the

purchase, targeting the Japanese housewife—who generally managed the family finances—was viewed as smart.

The Aquos line caused a major sensation, dramatically improving Sharp's position in the TV set market. Sharp followed up with a stream of new models and continued brand development. While several other firms including Hitachi and Pioneer also benefited from early entry into flat panel televisions, their success was not long-lived. Sharp stood out as the only firm to maintain its newly attained market share over the long term.

Sharp had differentiated its TVs in the market through good product design, well-conceived advertising, and high-quality displays. As the quality of LCDs produced industry-wide had improved, advantages due to display quality had become smaller and smaller. In 2008, the Japanese news weekly Nikkei Business published an article

10"Sharp Braun-kan TV Zenpaihe 7-nengo madeni subete Ekishoka," *Sankei Shimbun,* Tokyo, August 19, 1998.

comparing a Sony LCD TV with a no-name brand LCD TV one-quarter its price. Although engineers extolled Sony's elegant design when the two products were disassembled, an image quality specialist was quoted as saying consumers would not be able to discern quality differences by comparing video on the two sets.[11]

Japanese consumer electronics maker Pioneer had differentiated its TV set offering based on high-quality imaging and display. Image quality experts applauded Pioneer's TV sets and the plasma displays used in them.[12] However, Pioneer's high-end pricing strategy had not worked well for the firm. Customers balked at paying thousands of dollars more for Pioneer TVs compared with competing models in the same size class. While its competitors realized lower costs through scale advantages and production experience, Pioneer fell far behind in cost effectiveness. Citing losses, the firm exited display production in 2008 and in early 2009 announced it would exit the TV business altogether.[13]

Pioneer's failure reaffirmed the limitations on differentiation in the TV business. Sharp could price a set in line with top brand names such as Sony and Panasonic, but it would have a difficult time convincing consumers that it was worth more unless the features of the set—not just the image quality—were greatly improved. Consumers clearly valued the display size; larger was generally better, all else being equal. Differentiation on size was possible because some of Sharp's competitors lacked the capability to produce large sets economically. However, there would be limitations to making ever-larger sets. There were limits to the size consumers could use practically, and once this size was reached it would only be a matter of time until competitors caught up to Sharp.

Other technologies that could bring about different dimensions of differentiation were in the works

at Sharp and its competitors. These included such features as dynamic light-emitting diode (LED) backlighting that could increase image contrast and decrease energy usage, edge backlighting using LEDs that could dramatically reduce the thickness of the set, enhanced color capability made possible by using more color filters in the LCDs, and displays capable of displaying 3D images. Sharp had also developed process technology to be implemented at the new Sakai plant that would both increase productivity and result in brighter displays.[14] While each was interesting, which, if any, of these technologies would lead to meaningful or lasting differentiation was not known.

Sharp's Business Model

Sharp had followed a formula of making large investments in production capability in Japan and exporting key devices such as LCDs. End products were assembled in Japan and overseas. Sharp's sales revenues by product type and location may be found in **Exhibit 4.**

Although the operating model wasn't new, Sharp's previous president, Katsuhiko Machida, had reemphasized the importance of keeping most manufacturing in Japan. According to Machida, Sharp was to develop and produce products that could only be made in Japan, products that only Sharp could design and produce.[15] This was especially the case with LCD. Although Sharp assembled some LCD TVs overseas, the highly capital- and knowledge-intensive process of producing LCD panels was performed exclusively in Japan. Panels used in Sharp's overseas TV assembly plants were either produced in Japan and shipped overseas or were procured from competing LCD producers overseas.

The "make in Japan, sell overseas" model had worked reasonably well for Sharp until recently. It had a number of advantages. Sharp's most important plants were relatively close to each other

[11]"Ekisho Terebi ha Daredemo Tsukureru," *Nikkei Business,* Tokyo, May 18, 2009.

[12]"Saishin Terebi Gijutsu," FPD International 2008 Forum Session G-21, Yokohama, Japan.

[13]"Usugata Terebi Jigyo Pioneer Tettai," *Sankei Shimbun,* Tokyo, February 8, 2009.

[14]Sharp Annual Report 2010.

[15]A. Miyamoto, *Sharp Dokoso no Himitsu: Naze Only One Shohin wo Dashitsuzukerunoka, Jitsugyo no Nihon sha,* Tokyo, 2007.

Exhibit 4   Sales Revenues by Product Segment, Financial Year 2009 (in millions of yen)

	International	Japan	Total
AV and Communications Equipment	495,341	872,259	1,367,600
Health and Environmental Equipment	97,842	127,448	225,290
Information Equipment	173,386	132,691	306,077
LCDs	514,338	59,516	573,854
Solar Cells	118,576	38,519	157,095
Other Electronic Devices	145,483	71,828	217,311

Source: Company website.

Exhibit 5   Sharp's LCD Facilities by Generation

Plant Name	LCD Generation	Production Start	Production End
Tenri NF-1	1	1991	1999
Tenri NF-3	2	1994	2001 (partial)
Mie #1	3	1995	
Mie #2	4	2001	2009 (partial)
Mie #3	4	2003	
Kameyama #1	6	2004	
Kameyama #2	8	2006	
Sakai	10	2010 (Planned)	

Source: Compiled by author based upon data from Nikkei BP (1990–2008) and Sankei Shimbun (2008).

(see **Exhibit 5**). The proximity kept a lid on travel costs, made it easier for people in different facilities to meet, and facilitated resource sharing. Keeping most production in Japan also made it easier for Sharp to maintain strong control over its plants and protect its proprietary technology.

Furthermore, Sharp's primary focus had been on the Japanese domestic market, and therefore maintaining its main production base in Japan had been practical. Recently, however, Sharp was becoming more international. Over the period of 2000 to 2009, the ratio of foreign sales to total revenues for Sharp grew from 34 per cent to 54 per cent.[16] Although Sharp was less international than its competitor Sony (for which international sales represented

76 per cent of total revenue in 2009), this growth put it on par with rival Panasonic in terms of proportion of international sales. As Sharp's international sales grew, the strain put on its business model became more apparent.

Currency risk was a major drawback to Sharp's operating model as the firm increased overseas sales. Sharp was spending Japanese yen to produce products that were shipped abroad and sold in local currencies. When the yen strengthened, the value of overseas revenues decreased in yen terms. This had recently happened (see **Exhibit 6**) and the impact on Sharp's bottom line was not inconsequential. The operating performance comparison (see **Exhibit 7**) breaks down the causes of decline in Sharp's operating income for the quarter ending December 31, 2008, with comparison to the same

[16]Sharp Annual Reports 2004 and 2009.

Exhibit 6 Japanese Yen to U.S. Dollar Exchange Rate (2006–2008)

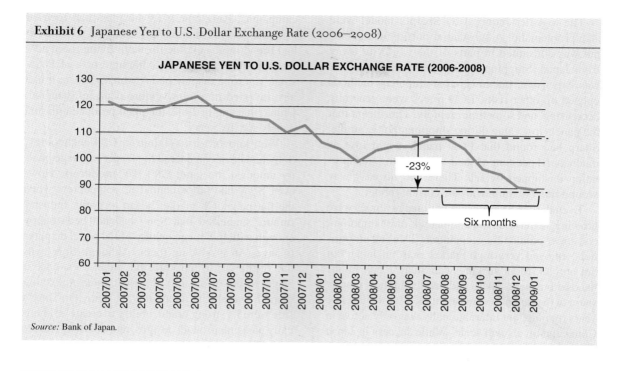

Source: Bank of Japan.

Exhibit 7   Sharp Operating Performance Comparison

	Units: billions of Japanese yen
Operating Income for Quarter Ending 12/07	51.9
Price Declines	−175.5
Forex Fluctuations	−19.5
Cost Reductions	127.3
Operating Income for Quarter Ending 12/08	−15.8

Source: Sharp quarterly report, March 31, 2008.

quarter in 2007. Sharp was not the only Japanese firm to be hurt by currency swings recently. Sony had also started losing money around the same time as Sharp.[17]

Extremely high infrastructure costs and high taxes were further disadvantages of producing in Japan. Corporate taxes in Japan were on average nearly double the level they were in Korea. A popular Japanese business magazine compared tax rates for Sharp and Samsung in 2008 and found that Samsung's tax rate was less than one-third of Sharp's.[18] Transportation and utility costs were also very high in Japan. Sharp was competing with firms in Taiwan and Korea that did not face these same disadvantages.

[17]"Denkigyokai Sokuzure Endaka Hanbaifushin ga Chokugeki Sony, Toshiba, Akaji no Mitoshi," *Yomiuri Shimbun*, Tokyo, January 14, 2009.

[18]"Nihon deha tatakaenai," *Nikkei Business*, October 11, 2010, p. 37.

The logistics required by Sharp's model were also problematic. A substantial portion of the output was consumed in parts of the world far away from Japan. Shipping LCD panels overseas by air was expensive, but lower-cost shipment methods opened up other risks. LCD prices were generally decreasing, and sometimes rapidly. This meant that the panels lost value during shipping. For example, Sharp had found that LCD panels could lose as much as 10 per cent of their value during transportation if shipped by sea. There was no easy way around this dilemma with the current model.

Even though Sharp's international revenues were growing, several of the company's most important consumer product lines, including TVs and air purifiers, enjoyed very high market share in Japan but not abroad. Most striking was Sharp's cell phone handset business. Sharp had had the highest market share in the Japanese handset market for the last five years running, but internationally was only active in China and on a small scale. While success in Japan did not necessarily translate into success overseas, Sharp's performance there suggested there were many opportunities for it to grow in international markets. Becoming closer to these markets might help Sharp better understand and penetrate them.

Sharp's operating model had not historically emphasized cooperation with other firms, but this was changing. Cooperative agreements, including joint ventures, were increasingly common. Sharp's new Sakai facility involved numerous partners including co-located suppliers such as glass and filter companies as well as firms using the output from the plant. Whether to cooperate and with whom were important questions Sharp's operating model did not answer.

Sharp's TV Set Competitors

In the days of CRT TV, Sharp was a third-tier competitor in TV sets. Now, however, Sharp was in league with the leading firms in Japan: Panasonic and Sony. Panasonic was an efficient manufacturer that had a goal of maintaining a large presence in the global market. In Japan, Panasonic was also known for implementing impressive marketing campaigns. Panasonic's TV business had focused primarily on plasma display technology, which it had found more suitable for large living room TV-sized displays than LCD. Although most of Panasonic's plasma display plants were in Japan, it had also invested in a joint venture plant in Shanghai, China. Starting in 2002, the plant produced plasma panels and TV sets.[19]

Well known for its Trinitron CRT technology, Sony had been considered the leader in image quality amongst the large CRT TV producers. However, Sony had fallen behind its competitors when the flat panel TV market began to grow. Industry rumors suggested that Sony had not been happy enough with the image quality of flat panel displays to invest in producing them. Although Sony was one of the last to introduce flat panel TVs, once it began to put effort into developing and marketing them, it was able to regain market share. On Sony's side were its strong brand, ability to create aesthetically pleasing product designs, and deep experience with TV set image quality. Sony did not have its own LCD or plasma display panel plant, and relied on other LCD producers for panel supply. In 2004, Sony invested in an LCD-producing joint venture with Samsung Electronics to obtain stable panel supply. The JV was located on a Samsung campus in South Korea. Recently, Sony agreed to enter a similar production JV with Sharp. In terms of final TV set assembly, Sony was moving towards increased outsourcing to contract manufacturers.

Outside of Japan, Sharp was a smaller player. In North America, Sharp's competitors ranged from the highly integrated global players, such as Samsung Electronics, to local and regional players, such as Vizio, that outsourced all production to firms largely from the personal computer supply chain.

Demand for TV Sets

Overseas, demand for flat panel TVs in high-income countries was forecast to fall. The current dismal economic conditions would dampen demand in the

---

[19]"Ekisho PDP EL Maker Keikaku Soran 2009 Nendoban," *Sangyo Times*, 2009.

Exhibit 8   Sharp Corporation Financial Summary

Financial Year (ending 3/31)	Units: millions of Japanese Yen				
	2009	2008	2007	2006	2005
Net Sales	2,847,227	3,417,736	3,127,771	2,797,109	2,359,859
Domestic	1,302,261	1,590,747	1,526,938	1,397,081	1,329,711
Overseas	1,544,966	1,826,989	1,600,833	1,400,028	1,210,148
Operating Income (Loss)	(55,481)	183,692	186,531	163,710	151,020
Net Income (Loss)	**(125,815)**	**101,922**	**101,717**	**88,671**	**76,845**
Capital Investment	260,337	344,262	314,301	238,839	243,388
R&D Expenditures	195,525	196,186	189,852	154,362	148,128
Return on Equity	−11.1%	8.4%	8.9%	8.4%	7.9%

Source: Company annual reports.

short run. An economic recovery would not necessarily increase demand in higher-income countries, because customers had already replaced their CRT TVs with flat panel TVs. In these areas, the number of replacement sales was on the decline.

In order to grow, Katayama felt it was imperative to capture a large number of middle- and lower-income customers overseas, particularly in emerging economies.[20] The Chinese market was especially important. Sharp's pursuit of the Chinese market had gained attention in the business press recently. To appeal to Chinese customers, Sharp had begun producing TVs developed especially to meet the needs of rural Chinese households. Amongst other modifications, the sets used particularly tough electrical cords to protect them from being chewed through by mice. Until recently, the Chinese market for flat panel TVs had primarily consisted of well-off families in coastal areas, but Sharp expected demand to expand rapidly in regional cities and rural areas.[21]

Sharp was not alone in pursuing these new customers. Sony and Panasonic, amongst others, were also actively competing in these emerging markets. Given the needs of these new customers and the strength of its competitors, Sharp could not win on

just product design or quality. Getting and maintaining low costs—far below their current levels—was an absolute requirement.

Sharp's Outlook

Sharp's current financial results were not looking good. Although times were tough now, Sharp had been doing well until quite recently (see **Exhibit 8**). During the first quarter of 2007, Sharp reported record profits. At the time, Sharp's investment in cutting-edge LCD production facilities had given it an advantage over its competitors. Whereas the average sale price of LCD TVs had fallen by 20 per cent industry-wide, Sharp had been able to increase its average sale price seven per cent by offering larger and larger sets. While increasing its average sales price, Sharp had also maintained a 50 per cent share of the Japanese TV market.

The construction of Sharp's Sakai plant was proceeding as planned. That was good news. More efficient than competitors' existing plants, and also capable of producing improved panels using Sharp's Four Primary Color Technology, Sakai would give Sharp some breathing room once finished. However, this lead would not last forever.

At the same time, the size of the Sakai project and the stage it was at reduced Mikio Katayama's room to maneuver. Perhaps the project could be completed more quickly than originally planned,

[20]H. Sagimori, "Sharp Ishin: Saraba Kameyama Model," *Nikkei Business,* July 6, 2009, pp. 18–21.
[21]Nikkan Kogyo Shimbun, "Keiei hitokoto / Sharp Hamano Toshishige fuku-shacho 'chugoku senryoku ha bantan," August 27, 2009.

but it simply was not feasible to dramatically change course on it now.

With its ability to produce large LCDs efficiently, the Sakai plant allowed Sharp to continue its strategy of maintaining profits by increasing the sizes of TV sets it offered. However, TV screens had already grown quite large. There was a limit to the size of TV sets consumers would be likely to buy. At some point, sooner or later, Sharp would reach that size.

The large production volume of the plant, while a source of its cost effectiveness, also raised another issue: Sharp could not use all of the panels it could make.[22] It would need to sell panels to its competitors. While Sharp had sold TV panels in the past, the volume would be much greater than before. To address the situation, Sony and Sharp had agreed to enter into a joint venture that would supply Sony with Sharp-made panels from the Sakai plant. Sony would gain reliable access to top-quality panels while Sharp reduced some of the investment risk in the plant.

Sharp was also aggressively investing in solar collector technology and production and the company believed the market for solar power would soon take off. Sharp's history with solar cells went back around fifty years, however, it had yet to develop into a major source of revenues. In fiscal year 2009, solar contributed to six per cent of Sharp's total revenues, the majority of which was from sales outside of Japan. In addition to producing LCDs, the new Sakai plant would also produce thin-film solar collectors.

Charting a New Direction for Sharp

With Sharp's recent losses, there was an increased sense of urgency. Investors and employees would want to see how the firm was going to rectify the situation. The fact that many other firms were experiencing difficulties due to the general economic situation was not comforting. From Katamaya's point of view, Sharp's losses were emblematic of a business model that no longer fit with the firm's strategy or the environment.[23]

Sharp was struggling with a change in its identity. No longer an "also ran," Sharp now found itself a major player in several technologies and product markets. Did that mean that Sharp needed to reconsider its priorities? The capabilities that had helped Sharp become a major player might not be those it would need to be successful in this new role over the longer term.

In a recent press interview, Katayama emphasized how Sharp needed to change its operating model to one where it produced in major markets. He suggested that Sharp's new model should put focus on developing and applying specialized knowledge and put less emphasis on large investments in physical plants. While discussing the direction of change, Katayama did not discuss actual plans. Given the scale and nature of the changes he envisioned, adjustments were likely to occur over a series of steps taking place over several years.

Sharp was exploring several options as next steps. If Sharp planned to produce in major overseas markets, it needed to identify where and how. Recently, Sharp was in contact with China's largest producer of cathode ray tubes, a firm called IRICO. IRICO was interested in purchasing the sixth-generation equipment at Sharp's Kameyama Number One plant and installing it in a new facility to be built in Nanjing, China. Sharp had an existing TV assembly plant in Nanjing that could be supplied with these panels.[24]

Sharp was also in discussions with CEC Panda, another Chinese company. CEC's plans were more ambitious. Like IRICO, CEC was also interested in purchasing the Kameyama sixth-generation production equipment, however, CEC and Sharp were also discussing a joint venture to build and operate an eighth-generation line. Like with IRICO, these facilities were to be located in Nanjing.[25] As part of this discussion, Sharp was considering building an LCD technology centre in China.

---

[22]*FPD 2008 Sangyo Doko Hen,* Nikkei BP, Tokyo, 2008, p. 45.
[23]Mikio Katayama interview with Nikkei Business, "Kukyo koso Seicho Vision," *Nikkei Business,* July 6, 2009, pp. 22-24.

[24]"Sharp, ekisho seizou sochi no baikyaku-de chuugoku saiko shudan to kosho," *Nikkan Kogyo Shimbun,* July 2, 2009.
[25]"Sharp, dai 6 sedai ekisho sochi-wo chugoku CEC Panda ni baikyaku," *Nikkan Kogyo Shimbun,* September 1, 2009.

Reliable, Sharp-related LCD production in China could give the company an edge in the growing Chinese TV set market. The larger the facilities' capacity, the greater this edge was likely to be. Sharp's Korean competitors LG and Samsung also heard the siren song from China's markets and were in the midst of considering options for building LCD production capabilities there for this same reason.

At the same time, moving Sharp's prized LCD technology abroad was risky, and it was considered controversial inside the company and in the Japanese business community. China's reputation

for problems related to intellectual property increased the concerns. After having spent great time and expense developing, maintaining, and protecting its proprietary technology, such a move would signal a major change in Sharp's direction and strategy. Once Sharp had moved operations and knowledge to China, it could not easily change its mind.

The China options, if implemented, would only be a start in the new direction. How early steps in the new direction worked out would have a profound impact on the path Sharp took thereafter. Katayama continued to contemplate how to become a major player beyond Japan.

Case 6-2   Nora-Sakari: A Proposed JV in Malaysia (Revised)

R. Azimah Ainuddin and Paul Beamish

On Monday, July 15, 2003 Zainal Hashim, vice-chairman of Nora Holdings Sdn Bhd[1] (Nora), arrived at his office about an hour earlier than usual.

R. Azimah Ainuddin prepared this case under the supervision of Professor Paul Beamish solely to provide material for class discussion. The authors do not intend to illustrate either effective or ineffective handling of a managerial situation. The authors may have disguised certain names and other identifying information to protect confidentiality.

[1]Sdn Bhd is an abbreviation for Sendirian Berhad, which means private limited company in Malaysia.

As he looked out the window at the city spreading below, he thought about the Friday evening reception which he had hosted at his home in Kuala Lumpur (KL), Malaysia, for a team of negotiators from Sakari Oy[2] (Sakari) of Finland. Nora was a leading supplier of telecommunications (telecom) equipment in Malaysia while Sakari, a Finnish conglomerate, was a leader in the manufacture of cellular phone sets and switching systems. The seven-member team from Sakari was in KL to negotiate with Nora the formation of a joint-venture (JV) between the two telecom companies.

This was the final negotiation which would determine whether a JV agreement would materialize. The negotiation had ended late Friday afternoon, having lasted for five consecutive days. The JV Company, if established, would be set up in Malaysia to manufacture and commission digital switching exchanges to meet the needs of the telecom industry in Malaysia and in neighbouring

[2]Oy is an abbreviation for Osakeyhtiot, which means private limited company in Finland.

countries, particularly Indonesia and Thailand. While Nora would benefit from the JV in terms of technology transfer, the venture would pave the way for Sakari to acquire knowledge and gain access to the markets of South-east Asia.

The Nora management was impressed by the Finnish capability in using high technology to enable Finland, a small country of only five million people, to have a fast-growing economy. Most successful Finnish companies were in the high-tech industries. It would be an invaluable opportunity for Nora to learn from the Finnish experience and emulate their success for Malaysia.

The opportunity emerged two and half years earlier when Peter Mattsson, president of Sakari's Asian regional office in Singapore, approached Zainal[3] to explore the possibility of forming a cooperative venture between Nora and Sakari. Mattsson said:

> While growth in the mobile telecommunications network is expected to be about 40 per cent a year in Asia in the next five years, growth in fixed networks would not be as fast, but the projects are much larger. A typical mobile network project amounts to a maximum of €50 million, but fixed network projects can be estimated in hundreds of millions. In Malaysia and Thailand, such latter projects are currently approaching contract stage. Thus it is imperative that Sakari establish its presence in this region to capture a share in the fixed network market.

The large potential for telecom facilities was also evidenced in the low telephone penetration rates for most South-east Asian countries. For example, in 1999, telephone penetration rates (measured by the number of telephone lines per 100 people) for Indonesia, Thailand, Malaysia and the Philippines ranged from three to 20 lines per 100 people compared to the rates in developed countries such as Canada, Finland, Germany, United States and Sweden where the rates exceeded 55 telephone lines per 100 people.

The Telecom Industry in Malaysia

Telekom Malaysia Bhd (TMB), the national telecom company, was given the authority by the Malaysian government to develop the country's telecom infrastructure. With a paid-up capital of RM2.4 billion,[4] it was also given the mandate to provide telecom services that were on par with those available in developed countries. TMB announced that it would be investing in the digitalization of its networks to pave the way for offering services based on the ISDN (integrated services digitalized network) standard, and investing in international fibre optic cable networks to meet the needs of increased telecom traffic between Malaysia and the rest of the world. TMB would also facilitate the installation of more cellular telephone networks in view of the increased demand for the use of mobile phones among the business community in KL and in major towns.

As the nation's largest telecom company, TMB's operations were regulated through a 20-year licence issued by the Ministry of Energy, Telecommunications and Posts. In line with the government's Vision 2020 program which targeted Malaysia to become a developed nation by the year 2020, there was a strong need for the upgrading of the telecom infrastructure in the rural areas. TMB estimated that it would spend more than RM1 billion each year on the installation of fixed networks, of which 25 per cent would be allocated for the expansion of rural telecom. The objective was to increase the telephone penetration rate to over 50 per cent by the year 2005.

Although TMB had become a large national telecom company, it lacked the expertise and technology to undertake massive infrastructure projects. In most cases, the local telecom companies would be invited to submit their bids for a particular contract. It was also common for these local companies to form partnerships with large multinational corporations (MNCs), mainly for technological support. For example, Pernas-NEC,

---

[3]The first name is used because the Malay name does not carry a family name. The first and/or middle names belong to the individual and the last name is his/her father's name.

[4]RM is Ringgit Malaysia, the Malaysian currency. As at December 31, 2002, US$1 = RM3.80.

a JV company between Pernas Holdings and NEC, was one of the companies that had been successful in securing large telecom contracts from the Malaysian authorities.

Nora's Search for a JV Partner

In October 2002, TMB called for tenders to bid on a five-year project worth RM2 billion for installing digital switching exchanges in various parts of the country. The project also involved replacing analog circuit switches with digital switches. Digital switches enhanced transmission capabilities of telephone lines, increasing capacity to approximately two million bits per second compared to the 9,600 bits per second on analog circuits.

Nora was interested in securing a share of the RM2 billion contract from TMB and more importantly, in acquiring the knowledge in switching technology from its partnership with a telecom MNC. During the initial stages, when Nora first began to consider potential partners in the bid for this contract, telecom MNCs such as Siemens, Alcatel, and Fujitsu seemed appropriate candidates. Nora had previously entered into a five-year technical assistance agreement with Siemens to manufacture telephone handsets.

Nora also had the experience of a long-term working relationship with Japanese partners which would prove valuable should a JV be formed with Fujitsu. Alcatel was another potential partner, but the main concern at Nora was that the technical standards used in the French technology were not compatible with the British standards already adopted in Malaysia. NEC and Ericsson were not considered, as they were already involved with other local competitors and were the current suppliers of digital switching exchanges to TMB. Their five-year contracts were due to expire soon.

Subsequent to Zainal's meeting with Mattsson, he decided to consider Sakari as a serious potential partner. He was briefed about Sakari's SK33, a digital switching system that was based on an open architecture, which enabled the use of standard components, standard software development tools, and standard software languages. Unlike the

switching exchanges developed by NEC and Ericsson which required the purchase of components developed by the parent companies, the SK33 used components that were freely available in the open market. The system was also modular, and its software could be upgraded to provide new services and could interface easily with new equipment in the network. This was the most attractive feature of the SK33 as it would lead to the development of new switching systems.

Mattsson had also convinced Zainal and other Nora managers that although Sakari was a relatively small player in fixed networks, these networks were easily adaptable, and could cater to large exchanges in the urban areas as well as small ones for rural needs. Apparently Sakari's smaller size, compared to that of some of the other MNCs, was an added strength because Sakari was prepared to work out customized products according to Nora's needs. Large telecom companies were alleged to be less willing to provide custom-made products. Instead, they tended to offer standard products that, in some aspects, were not consistent with the needs of the customer.

Prior to the July meeting, at least 20 meetings had been held either in KL or in Helsinki to establish relationships between the two companies. It was estimated that each side had invested not less than RM3 million in promoting the relationship. Mattsson and Ilkka Junttila, Sakari's representative in KL, were the key people in bringing the two companies together. (See **Exhibits 1** and **2** for brief background information on Malaysia and Finland respectively.)

Nora Holdings Sdn Bhd

Nora was one of the leading companies in the telecom industry in Malaysia. It was established in 1975 with a paid-up capital of RM2 million. Last year, the company recorded a turnover of RM320 million. Nora Holdings consisted of 30 subsidiaries, including two public-listed companies: Multiphone Bhd, and Nora Telecommunications Bhd. Nora had 3,081 employees, of which 513 were categorized as managerial (including 244 engineers) and 2,568 as non-managerial (including 269 engineers and technicians).

Exhibit 1 Malaysia: Background Information

Malaysia is centrally located in South-east Asia. It consists of Peninsular Malaysia, bordered by Thailand in the north and Singapore in the south, and the states of Sabah and Sarawak on the island of Borneo. Malaysia has a total land area of about 330,000 square kilometres, of which 80 per cent is covered with tropical rainforest. Malaysia has an equatorial climate with high humidity and high daily temperatures of about 26 degrees Celsius throughout the year.

In 2000, Malaysia's population was 22 million, of which approximately nine million made up the country's labour force. The population is relatively young, with 42 per cent between the ages of 15 and 39 and only seven per cent above the age of 55. A Malaysian family has an average of four children and extended families are common. Kuala Lumpur, the capital city of Malaysia, has approximately 1.5 million inhabitants.

The population is multiracial; the largest ethnic group is the Bumiputeras (the Malays and other indigenous groups such as the Ibans in Sarawak and Kadazans in Sabah), followed by the Chinese and Indians. Bahasa Malaysia is the national language but English is widely used in business circles. Other major languages spoken included various Chinese dialects and Tamil.

Islam is the official religion but other religions (mainly Christianity, Buddhism and Hinduism) are widely practised. Official holidays are allocated for the celebration of Eid, Christmas, Chinese New Year and Deepavali. All Malays are Muslims, followers of the Islamic faith.

During the period of British rule, secularism was introduced to the country, which led to the separation of the Islamic religion from daily life. In the late 1970s and 1980s, realizing the negative impact of secularism on the life of the Muslims, several groups of devout Muslims undertook efforts to reverse the process, emphasizing a dynamic and progressive approach to Islam. As a result, changes were introduced to meet the daily needs of Muslims. Islamic banking and insurance facilities were introduced and prayer rooms were provided in government offices, private companies, factories, and even in shopping complexes.

Malaysia is a parliamentary democracy under a constitutional monarchy. The Yang DiPertuan Agung (the king) is the supreme head, and appoints the head of the ruling political party to be the prime minister. In 2000 the Barisan Nasional, a coalition of several political parties representing various ethnic groups, was the ruling political party in Malaysia. Its predominance had contributed not only to the political stability and economic progress of the country in the last two decades, but also to the fast recovery from the 1997 Asian economic crisis.

The recession of the mid 1980s led to structural changes in the Malaysian economy which had been too dependent on primary commodities (rubber, tin, palm oil and timber) and had a very narrow export base. To promote the establishment of export-oriented industries, the government directed resources to the manufacturing sector, introduced generous incentives and relaxed foreign equity restrictions. In the meantime, heavy investments were made to modernize the country's infrastructure. These moves led to rapid economic growth in the late 1980s and early 1990s. The growth had been mostly driven by exports, particularly of electronics.

The Malaysian economy was hard hit by the 1997 Asian economic crisis. However, Malaysia was the fastest country to recover from the crisis after declining IMF assistance. It achieved this by pegging its currency to the USD, restricting outflow of money from the country, banning illegal overseas derivative trading of Malaysian securities and setting up asset management companies to facilitate the orderly recovery of bad loans. The real GDP growth rate in 1999 and 2000 were 5.4 per cent and 8.6 per cent, respectively (Table 1).

Malaysia was heavily affected by the global economic downturn and the slump in the IT sector in 2001 and 2002 due to its export-based economy. GDP in 2001 grew only 0.4 per cent due to an 11 per cent decrease in exports. A US $1.9 billion fiscal stimulus package helped the country ward off the worst of the recession and the GDP growth rate rebounded to 4.2 per cent in 2002 (Table 1). A relatively small foreign debt and adequate foreign exchange reserves make a crisis similar to the 1997 one unlikely. Nevertheless, the economy remains vulnerable to a more protracted slowdown in the U.S. and Japan, top export destinations and key sources of foreign investment.

(Continued)

Exhibit 1   *(Continued)*

Table 1   Malaysian Economic Performance 1999 to 2002

Economic Indicator	1999	2000	2001	2002
GDP per capita (US$)	3,596	3,680	3,678	3,814
Real GDP growth rate	5.4%	8.6%	0.4%	4.2%
Consumer price inflation	2.8%	1.6%	1.4%	1.8%
Unemployment rate	3.0%	3.0%	3.7%	3.5%

Source: IMD. Various years. "The World Competitiveness Report."

In 2002, the manufacturing sector was the leading contributor to the economy, accounting for about 30 percent of gross national product (GDP). Malaysia's major trading partners are United States, Singapore, Japan, China, Taiwan, Hong Kong and Korea.

Sources: Ernst & Young International. 1993. "Doing Business in Malaysia." Other online sources.

Exhibit 2   Finland: Background Information

Finland is situated in the north-east of Europe, sharing borders with Sweden, Norway and the former Soviet Union. About 65 per cent of its area of 338,000 square kilometres is covered with forest, about 15 per cent lakes and about 10 per cent arable land. Finland has a temperate climate with four distinct seasons. In Helsinki, the capital city, July is the warmest month with average mid-day temperature of 21 degrees Celsius and January is the coldest month with average mid-day temperature of –3 degrees Celsius.

Finland is one of the most sparsely populated countries in Europe with a 2002 population of 5.2 million, 60 per cent of whom lived in the urban areas. Helsinki had a population of about 560,000 in 2002. Finland has a well-educated work force of about 2.3 million. About half of the work force are engaged in providing services, 30 per cent in manufacturing and construction, and eight per cent in agricultural production. The small size of the population has led to scarce and expensive labour. Thus Finland had to compete by exploiting its lead in high-tech industries.

Finland's official languages are Finnish and Swedish, although only six per cent of the population speaks Swedish. English is the most widely spoken foreign language. About 87 per cent of the Finns are Lutherans and about one per cent Finnish Orthodox. Finland has been an independent republic since 1917, having previously been ruled by Sweden and Russia. A President is elected to a six-year term, and a 200-member, single-chamber parliament is elected every four years.

In 1991, the country experienced a bad recession triggered by a sudden drop in exports due to the collapse of the Soviet Union. During 1991–1993, the total output suffered a 10 per cent contraction and unemployment rate reached almost 20 per cent. Finnish Markka experienced a steep devaluation in 1991–1992, which gave Finland cost competitiveness in international market.

With this cost competitiveness and the recovery of Western export markets the Finnish economy underwent a rapid revival in 1993, followed by a period of healthy growth. Since the mid 1990s the Finnish growth has mainly been bolstered by intense growth in telecommunications equipment manufacturing. The Finnish economy peaked in the year 2000 with a real GDP growth rate of 5.6 per cent (Table 2).

(Continued)

Exhibit 2   *(Continued)*

Table 2   Finnish Economic Performance 1999 to 2002

Economic Indicator	1999	2000	2001	2002
GDP per capita (US$)	24,430	23,430	23,295	25,303
Real GDP growth rate	3.7%	5.6%	0.4%	1.6%
Consumer price inflation	1.2%	3.3%	2.6%	1.6%
Unemployment	10.3%	9.6%	9.1%	9.1%

Source: IMD. Various years. "The World Competitiveness Report."

Finland was one of the 11 countries that joined the Economic and Monetary Union (EMU) on January 1, 1999. Finland has been experiencing a rapidly increasing integration with Western Europe. Membership in the EMU provide the Finnish economy with an array of benefits, such as lower and stable interest rates, elimination of foreign currency risk within the Euro area, reduction of transaction costs of business and travel, and so forth. This provided Finland with a credibility that it lacked before accession and the Finnish economy has become more predictable. This will have a long-term positive effect on many facets of the economy.

Finland's economic structure is based on private ownership and free enterprise. However, the production of alcoholic beverages and spirits is retained as a government monopoly. Finland's major trading partners are Sweden, Germany, the former Soviet Union and United Kingdom.

Finland's standard of living is among the highest in the world. The Finns have small families with one or two children per family. They have comfortable homes in the cities and one in every three families has countryside cottages near a lake where they retreat on weekends. Taxes are high, the social security system is efficient and poverty is virtually non-existent.

Until recently, the stable trading relationship with the former Soviet Union and other Scandinavian countries led to few interactions between the Finns and people in other parts of the world. The Finns are described as rather reserved, obstinate, and serious people. A Finn commented, "We do not engage easily in small talk with strangers. Furthermore, we have a strong love for nature and we have the tendency to be silent as we observe our surroundings. Unfortunately, others tend to view such behaviour as cold and serious." Visitors to Finland are often impressed by the efficient public transport system, the clean and beautiful city of Helsinki with orderly road networks, scenic parks and lakefronts, museums, cathedrals, and churches.

Sources: Ernst & Young International. 1993. "Doing Business in Finland." Other online sources.

Since the inception of the company, Nora had secured two cable-laying projects. For the latter project worth RM500 million, Nora formed a JV with two Japanese companies, Sumitomo Electric Industries Ltd (held 10 per cent equity share) and Marubeni Corporation (held five per cent equity share). Japanese partners were chosen in view of the availability of a financial package that came together with the technological assistance needed by Nora. Nora also acquired a 63 per cent stake in a local cable-laying company, Selangor Cables Sdn Bhd.

Nora had become a household name in Malaysia as a telephone manufacturer. It started in 1980 when the company obtained a contract to supply telephone sets to the government-owned Telecom authority, TMB, which would distribute the sets to telephone subscribers on a rental basis. The contract, estimated at RM130 million, lasted for 15 years. In 1985 Nora secured licenses from Siemens and Nortel to manufacture telephone handsets and had subsequently developed Nora's own telephone sets—the N300S (single line), N300M (micro-computer controlled), and N300V (hands-free, voice-activated) models.

Upon expiry of the 15-year contract as a supplier of telephone sets to the TMB, Nora suffered a major setback when it lost a RM32 million contract to supply 600,000 N300S single line telephones. The contract was instead given to a Taiwanese manufacturer, Formula Electronics, which quoted a lower price of RM37 per handset compared to Nora's RM54. Subsequently, Nora was motivated to move towards the high end feature phone domestic market. The company sold about 3,000 sets of feature phones per month, capturing the high-end segment of the Malaysian market.

Nora had ventured into the export market with its feature phones, but industry observers predicted that Nora still had a long way to go as an exporter. The foreign markets were very competitive and many manufacturers already had well-established brands.

Nora's start-up in the payphone business had turned out to be one of the company's most profitable lines of business. Other than the cable-laying contract secured in 1980, Nora had a 15-year contract to install, operate and maintain payphones in the cities and major towns in Malaysia. In 1997, Nora started to manufacture card payphones under a license from GEC Plessey Telecommunications (GPT) of the United Kingdom. The agreement had also permitted Nora to sell the products to the neighbouring countries in South-east Asia as well as to eight other markets approved by GPT. While the payphone revenues were estimated to be as high as RM60 million a year, a long-term and stable income stream for Nora, profit margins were only about 10 per cent because of the high investment and maintenance costs.

The Management When Nora was established, Osman Jaafar, founder and chairman of Nora Holdings, managed the company with his wife, Nora Asyikin Yusof, and seven employees. Osman was known as a conservative businessman who did not like to dabble in acquisitions and mergers to make quick capital gains. He was formerly an electrical engineer who was trained in the United Kingdom

and had held several senior positions at the national Telecom Department in Malaysia.

Osman subsequently recruited Zainal Hashim for the position of deputy managing director at Nora. Zainal held a master's degree in microwave communications from a British university and had experience as a production engineer at Pernas-NEC Sdn Bhd, a manufacturer of transmission equipment. Zainal was later promoted to the position of managing director and six years later, the vice-chairman.

Industry analysts observed that Nora's success was attributed to the complementary roles, trust, and mutual understanding between Osman and Zainal. While Osman "likes to fight for new business opportunities," Zainal preferred a low profile and concentrated on managing Nora's operations. Industry observers also speculated that Osman, a former civil servant and an entrepreneur, was close to Malaysian politicians, notably the Prime Minister, while Zainal had been a close friend of the Finance Minister. Zainal disagreed with allegations that Nora had succeeded due to its close relationships with Malaysian politicians. However, he acknowledged that such perceptions in the industry had been beneficial to the company.

Osman and Zainal had an obsession for high-tech and made the development of research and development (R&D) skills and resources a priority in the company. About one per cent of Nora's earnings was reinvested into R&D activities. Although this amount was considered small by international standards, Nora planned to increase it gradually to five to six per cent over the next two to three years. Zainal said:

> We believe in making improvements in small steps, similar to the Japanese *kaizen* principle. Over time, each small improvement could lead to a major creation. To be able to make improvements, we must learn from others. Thus we would borrow a technology from others, but eventually, we must be able to develop our own to sustain our competitiveness in the industry. As a matter of fact, Sakari's SK33 system was developed based on a technology it obtained from Alcatel.

To further enhance R&D activities at Nora, Nora Research Sdn Bhd (NRSB), a wholly-owned subsidiary, was formed, and its R&D department was absorbed into this new company. NRSB operated as an independent research company undertaking R&D activities for Nora as well as private clients in related fields. The company facilitated R&D activities with other companies as well as government organizations, research institutions, and universities. NRSB, with its staff of 40 technicians/engineers, would charge a fixed fee for basic research and a royalty for its products sold by clients.

Zainal was also active in instilling and promoting Islamic values among the Malay employees at Nora. He explained:

> Islam is a way of life and there is no such thing as Islamic management. The Islamic values, which must be reflected in the daily life of Muslims, would influence their behaviours as employers and employees. Our Malay managers, however, were often influenced by their western counterparts, who tend to stress knowledge and mental capability and often forget the effectiveness of the softer side of management which emphasizes relationships, sincerity and consistency. I believe that one must always be sincere to be able to develop good working relationships.

Sakari Oy

Sakari was established in 1865 as a pulp and paper mill located about 200 kilometres northwest of Helsinki, the capital city of Finland. In the 1960s, Sakari started to expand into the rubber and cable industries when it merged with the Finnish Rubber Works and Finnish Cable Works. However, in 1975, the company recovered when Aatos Olkkola took over as Sakari's president. He led Sakari into competitive businesses such as computers, consumer electronics, and cellular phones via a series of acquisitions, mergers and alliances. Companies involved in the acquisitions included: the consumer electronics division of Standard Elektrik Lorenz AG; the data systems division of L.M. Ericsson; Vantala, a Finnish manufacturer of colour televisions; and Luxury, a Swedish state-owned electronics and computer concern.

In 1979, a JV between Sakari and Vantala, Sakari-Vantala, was set up to develop and manufacture mobile telephones. Sakari-Vantala had captured about 14 per cent of the world's market share for mobile phones and held a 20 per cent market share in Europe for its mobile phone handsets. Outside Europe, a 50-50 JV was formed with Tandy Corporation which, to date, had made significant sales in the United States, Malaysia and Thailand.

Sakari first edged into the telecom market by selling switching systems licensed from France's Alcatel and by developing the software and systems to suit the needs of small Finnish phone companies. Sakari had avoided head-on competition with Siemens and Ericsson by not trying to enter the market for large telephone networks. Instead, Sakari had concentrated on developing dedicated telecom networks for large private users such as utility and railway companies. In Finland, Sakari held 40 per cent of the market for digital exchanges. Other competitors included Ericsson (34 per cent), Siemens (25 per cent), and Alcatel (one per cent).

Sakari was also a niche player in the global switching market. Its SK33 switches had sold well in countries such as Sri Lanka, United Arab Emirates, China and the Soviet Union. A derivative of the SK33 main exchange switch called the SK33XT was subsequently developed to be used in base stations for cellular networks and personal paging systems.

Sakari attributed its emphasis on R&D as its key success factor in the telecom industry. Strong in-house R&D in core competence areas enabled the company to develop technology platforms such as its SK33 system that were reliable, flexible, widely compatible and economical. About 17 per cent of its annual sales revenue was invested into R&D and product development units in Finland, United Kingdom and France. Sakari's current strategy was to emphasize global operations in production and R&D. It planned to set up R&D centres in leading markets, including South-east Asia.

Despite having nearly $15 billion in telecom equipment sales, Sakari was still a small company by international standards. There were six larger competitors headquartered respectively in the United States (2), Sweden, France, Canada and Germany. Sakari lacked a strong marketing capability and had to rely on JVs such as the one with Tandy Corporation to enter the world market, particularly the United States. In its efforts to develop market position quickly, Sakari had to accept lower margins for its products, and often the Sakari name was not revealed on the product. In recent years, Sakari decided to emerge from its hiding place as a manufacturer's manufacturer and began marketing under the Sakari name.

In 1989 Mikko Koskinen took over as president of Sakari. Koskinen announced that telecommunications, computers, and consumer electronics would be maintained as Sakari's core business, and that he would continue Olkkola's efforts in expanding the company overseas. He believed that every European company needed global horizons to be able to meet global competition for future survival. To do so, he envisaged the setting up of alliances of varying duration, each designed for specific purposes. He said, "Sakari has become an interesting partner with which to cooperate on an equal footing in the areas of R&D, manufacturing and marketing."

The recession in Finland which began in 1990 led Sakari's group sales to decline substantially from FIM22 billion[5] in 1990 to FIM15 billion in 1991. The losses were attributed to two main factors: weak demand for Sakari's consumer electronic products, and trade with the Soviet Union which had come to almost a complete standstill. Consequently Sakari began divesting its less profitable companies within the basic industries (metal, rubber, and paper), as well as leaving the troubled European computer market with the sale of its computer subsidiary, Sakari Macro. The company's new strategy was to focus on three main areas: telecom systems and mobile phones in a

global framework, consumer electronic products in Europe, and deliveries of cables and related technology. The company's divestment strategy led to a reduction of Sakari's employees from about 41,000 in 1989 to 29,000 in 1991. This series of major strategic moves was accompanied by major leadership succession. In June 1992, Koskinen retired as Sakari's President and was replaced by Visa Ketonen, formerly the President of Sakari Mobile Phones. Ketonen appointed Ossi Kuusisto as Sakari's vice-president.

After Ketonen took over control, the Finnish economy went through a rapid revival in 1993, followed by a new period of intense growth. Since the mid 1990s the Finnish growth had been bolstered by intense growth in telecommunications equipment manufacturing as a result of an exploding global telecommunications market. Sakari capitalized on this opportunity and played a major role in the Finnish telecommunications equipment manufacturing sector.

In 2001, Sakari was Finland's largest publicly-traded industrial company and derived the majority of its total sales from exports and overseas operations. Traditionally, the company's export sales were confined to other Scandinavian countries, Western Europe and the former Soviet Union. However, in recent years, the company had succeeded in globalizing and diversifying its operations to make the most of its high-tech capabilities. As a result, Sakari emerged as a more influential player in international markets and had gained international brand recognition. One of Sakari's strategies was to form JVs to enter new foreign markets.

The Nora-Sakari Negotiation

Nora and Sakari had discussed the potential of forming a JV company in Malaysia for more than two years. Nora engineers were sent to Helsinki to assess the SK33 technology in terms of its compatibility with the Malaysian requirements, while Sakari managers travelled to KL mainly to assess both Nora's capability in manufacturing switching exchanges and the feasibility of gaining access to the Malaysian market.

[5]FIM is Finnish Markka, the Finnish currency until January 1, 1999. Markka coins and notes were not withdrawn from circulation until January 1, 2002, when Finland fully converted to the Euro. As at December 31, 2000, US$1 = FIM6.31, and €1 = FIM5.95.

In January 2003, Nora submitted its bid for TMB's RM2 billion contract to supply digital switching exchanges supporting four million telephone lines. Assuming the Nora-Sakari JV would materialize, Nora based its bid on supplying Sakari's digital switching technology. Nora competed with seven other companies short listed by TMB, all offering their partners' technology—Alcatel, Lucent, Fujitsu, Siemens, Ericsson, NEC, and Samsung. In early May, TMB announced five successful companies in the bid. They were companies using technology from Alcatel, Fujitsu, Ericsson, NEC, and Sakari. Each company was awarded one-fifth share of the RM2 billion contract and would be responsible for delivering 800,000 telephone lines over a period of five years. Industry observers were critical of TMB's decision to select Sakari and Alcatel. Sakari was perceived to be the least capable of supplying the necessary lines to meet TMB's requirements, as it was alleged to be a small company with little international exposure. Alcatel was criticized for having the potential of supplying an obsolete technology.

The May 21 Meeting   Following the successful bid and ignoring the criticisms against Sakari, Nora and Sakari held a major meeting in Helsinki on May 21 to finalize the formation of the JV. Zainal led Nora's five-member negotiation team which comprised Nora's general manager for corporate planning division, an accountant, two engineers, and Marina Mohamed, a lawyer. One of the engineers was Salleh Lindstrom who was of Swedish origin, a Muslim and had worked for Nora for almost 10 years.

Sakari's eight-member team was led by Kuusisto, Sakari's vice-president. His team comprised Junttila, Hussein Ghazi, Aziz Majid, three engineers, and Julia Ruola (a lawyer). Ghazi was Sakari's senior manager who was of Egyptian origin and also a Muslim who had worked for Sakari for more than 20 years while Aziz, a Malay, had been Sakari's manager for more than 12 years.

The meeting went on for several days. The main issue raised at the meeting was Nora's capability in penetrating the South-east Asian market. Other issues included Sakari's concerns over the efficiency of Malaysian workers in the JV in manufacturing the product, maintaining product quality and ensuring prompt deliveries.

Commenting on the series of negotiations with Sakari, Zainal said that this was the most difficult negotiation he had ever experienced. Zainal was Nora's most experienced negotiator and had single-handedly represented Nora in several major negotiations for the past 10 years. In the negotiation with Sakari, Zainal admitted making the mistake of approaching the negotiation applying the approach he often used when negotiating with his counterparts from companies based in North America or the United Kingdom. He said:

> Negotiators from the United States tend to be very open and often state their positions early and definitively. They are highly verbal and usually prepare well-planned presentations. They also often engage in small talk and 'joke around' with us at the end of a negotiation. In contrast, the Sakari negotiators tend to be very serious, reserved and 'cold.' They are also relatively less verbal and do not convey much through their facial expressions. As a result, it was difficult for us to determine whether they are really interested in the deal or not.

Zainal said that the negotiation on May 21 turned out to be particularly difficult when Sakari became interested in bidding a recently-announced tender for a major telecom contract in the United Kingdom. Internal politics within Sakari led to the formation of two opposing "camps." One "camp" held a strong belief that there would be very high growth in the Asia-Pacific region and that the JV company in Malaysia was seen as a hub to enter these markets. Although the Malaysian government had liberalized its equity ownership restrictions and allowed the formation of wholly-owned subsidiaries, JVs were still an efficient way to enter the Malaysian market for a company that lacked local knowledge. This group was represented mostly by Sakari's managers positioned in Asia and engineers who had made several trips to Malaysia, which usually included visits to Nora's facilities. They also had the support of Sakari's vice-president, Kuusisto, who was involved in most of the meetings with Nora, particularly when Zainal was present. Kuusisto had also made efforts to be present at meetings held in KL. This group also argued that Nora had already obtained the contract in Malaysia whereas the chance of getting the U.K. contract was quite low in view of the intense competition prevailing in that market.

The "camp" not in favour of the Nora-Sakari JV believed that Sakari should focus its resources on entering the United Kingdom, which could be used as a hub to penetrate the European Union (EU) market. There was also the belief that Europe was closer to home, making management easier, and that problems arising from cultural differences would be minimized. This group was also particularly concerned that Nora had the potential of copying Sakari's technology and eventually becoming a strong regional competitor. Also, because the U.K. market was relatively "familiar" and Sakari has local knowledge, Sakari could set up a wholly-owned subsidiary instead of a JV company and consequently, avoid JV-related problems such as joint control, joint profits, and leakage of technology.

Zainal felt that the lack of full support from Sakari's management led to a difficult negotiation when new misgivings arose concerning Nora's capability to deliver its part of the deal. It was apparent that the group in favour of the Nora-Sakari JV was under pressure to further justify its proposal and provide counterarguments against the U.K. proposal. A Sakari manager explained, "We are tempted to pursue both proposals since each has its own strengths, but our current resources are very limited. Thus a choice has to made, and soon."

The July 8 Meeting   Another meeting to negotiate the JV agreement was scheduled for July 8. Sakari's eight-member team arrived in KL on Sunday afternoon of July 7, and was met at the airport by the key Nora managers involved in the negotiation. Kuusisto did not accompany the Sakari team at this meeting.

The negotiation started early Monday morning at Nora's headquarters and continued for the next five days, with each day's meeting ending late in the evening. Members of the Nora team were the same members who had attended the May 21 meeting in Finland, except Zainal, who did not participate. The Sakari team was also represented by the same members in attendance at the previous meeting plus a new member, Solail Pekkarinen, Sakari's senior accountant. Unfortunately, on the third day of the negotiation, the Nora team requested that Sakari ask Pekkarinen to leave the negotiation. He was perceived as extremely arrogant and insensitive to the local culture, which tended to value modesty and diplomacy. Pekkarinen left for Helsinki the following morning.

Although Zainal had decided not to participate actively in the negotiations, he followed the process closely and was briefed by his negotiators regularly. Some of the issues which they complained were difficult to resolve had often led to heated arguments between the two negotiating teams. These included:

1. Equity Ownership   In previous meetings both companies agreed to form the JV company with a paid-up capital of RM5 million. However, they disagreed on the equity share proposed by each side. Sakari proposed an equity split in the JV company of 49 per cent for Sakari and 51 per cent for Nora. Nora, on the other hand, proposed a 30 per cent Sakari and 70 per cent Nora split. Nora's proposal was based on the common practice in Malaysia as a result of historical foreign equity regulations set by the Malaysian government that allowed a maximum of 30 per cent foreign equity ownership unless the company would export a certain percentage of its products. Though these regulations were liberalized by the Malaysian government effective from July, 1998 and new regulations had replaced the old ones, the 30–70 foreign—Malaysian ownership divide was still commonly observed.

Equity ownership became a major issue as it was associated with control over the JV company. Sakari was concerned about its ability to control the accessibility of its technology to Nora and about decisions concerning the activities of the JV as a whole. The lack of control was perceived by Sakari as an obstacle to protecting its interests. Nora also had similar concerns about its ability to exert control over the JV because it was intended as a key part of Nora's long-term strategy to develop its own digital switching exchanges and related high-tech products.

2. Technology Transfer Sakari proposed to provide the JV company with the basic structure of the digital switch. The JV company would assemble the switching exchanges at the JV plant and subsequently install the exchanges in designated locations identified by TMB. By offering Nora only the basic structure of the switch, the core of Sakari's switching technology would still be well-protected.

On the other hand, Nora proposed that the basic structure of the switch be developed at the JV company in order to access the root of the switching technology. Based on Sakari's proposal, Nora felt that only the technical aspects in assembling and installing the exchanges would be obtained. This was perceived as another "screw-driver" form of technology transfer while the core of the technology associated with making the switches would still be unknown.

3. Royalty Payment   Closely related to the issue of technology transfer was the payment of a royalty for the technology used in building the switches. Sakari proposed a royalty payment of five per cent of the JV gross sales while Nora proposed a payment of two per cent of net sales. (Net sales were overall sales minus returns, allowances for damaged or missing goods, plus any discounts.)

Nora considered the royalty rate of five per cent too high because it would affect Nora's financial situation as a whole. Financial simulations prepared by Nora's managers indicated that Nora's return on investment would be less than the desired 10 per cent if royalty rates exceeded three per cent of net sales. This was because Nora had already agreed to

make large additional investments in support of the JV. Nora would invest in a building which would be rented to the JV company to accommodate an office and the switching plant. Nora would also invest in another plant which would supply the JV with surface mounted devices (SMD), one of the major components needed to build the switching exchanges.

An added argument raised by the Nora negotiators in support of a two per cent royalty was that Sakari would receive side benefits from the JV's access to Japanese technology used in the manufacture of the SMD components. Apparently the Japanese technology was more advanced than Sakari's present technology.

4. Expatriates' Salaries and Perks To allay Sakari's concerns over Nora's level of efficiency, Nora suggested that Sakari provide the necessary training for the JV technical employees. Subsequently, Sakari had agreed to provide eight engineering experts for the JV company on two types of contracts, short-term and long-term. Experts employed on a short-term basis would be paid a daily rate of US$1260 plus travel/accommodation. The permanent experts would be paid a monthly salary of US$20,000. Three permanent experts would be attached to the JV company once it was established and the number would gradually be reduced to only one, after two years. Five experts would be available on a short-term basis to provide specific training needs for durations of not more than three months each year.

The Nora negotiation team was appalled at the exorbitant amount proposed by the Sakari negotiators. They were surprised that the Sakari team had not surveyed the industry rates, as the Japanese and other western negotiators would normally have done. Apparently Sakari had not taken into consideration the relatively low cost of living in Malaysia compared to Finland. In 2000, though the average monthly rent for a comfortable, unfurnished three-bedroom apartment was about the same (660 US$) in Helsinki and Kuala Lumpur, the cost of living was considerably lower in KL. The cost of living index (New York = 100) of basket of goods in major cities, excluding housing, for Malaysia was only 83.75, compared to 109.84 for Finland.[6]

In response to Sakari's proposal, Nora negotiators adopted an unusual "take-it or leave-it" stance. They deemed the following proposal reasonable in view of the comparisons made with other JVs which Nora had entered into with other foreign parties:

Permanent experts' monthly salary ranges to be paid by the JV company were as follows:

1. Senior expert (seven to 10 years experience) RM24,300–RM27,900
2. Expert (four to six years experience) RM22,500–RM25,200
3. Junior expert (two to three years experience) RM20,700–RM23,400
4. Any Malaysian income taxes payable would be added to the salaries.
5. A car for personal use.
6. Annual paid vacation of five weeks.
7. Return flight tickets to home country once a year for the whole family of married persons and twice a year for singles according to Sakari's general scheme.
8. Any expenses incurred during official travelling.

Temporary experts are persons invited by the JV company for various technical assistance tasks and would not be granted residence status. They would be paid the following fees:

1. Senior expert RM1,350 per working day
2. Expert RM1,170 per working day
3. The JV company would not reimburse the following:
   - Flight tickets between Finland (or any other country) and Malaysia.
   - Hotel or any other form of accommodation.
   - Local transportation.

[6]IMD & World Economic Forum. 2001. The World Competitiveness Report.

In defense of their proposed rates, Sakari's negotiators argued that the rates presented by Nora were too low. Sakari suggested that Nora's negotiators take into consideration the fact that Sakari would have to subsidize the difference between the experts' present salaries and the amount paid by the JV company. A large difference would require that large amounts of subsidy payments be made to the affected employees.

5. Arbitration   Another major issue discussed in the negotiation was related to arbitration. While both parties agreed to an arbitration process in the event of future disputes, they disagreed on the location for dispute resolution. Because Nora would be the majority stakeholder in the JV company, Nora insisted that any arbitration should take place in KL. Sakari, however, insisted on Helsinki, following the norm commonly practised by the company.

At the end of the five-day negotiation, many issues could not be resolved. While Nora could agree on certain matters after consulting Zainal, the Sakari team, representing a large private company, had to refer contentious items to the company board before it could make any decision that went beyond the limits authorized by the board.

The Decision

Zainal sat down at his desk, read through the minutes of the negotiation thoroughly, and was disappointed that an agreement had not yet been reached. He was concerned about the commitment Nora had made to TMB when Nora was awarded the switching contract. Nora would be expected to fulfill the contract soon but had yet to find a partner to provide the switching technology. It was foreseeable that companies such as Siemens, Samsung and Lucent, which had failed in the bid, could still be potential partners. However, Zainal had also not rejected the possibility of a reconciliation with Sakari. He could start by contacting Kuusisto in Helsinki. But should he?

Case 6-3   Eli Lilly in India: Rethinking the Joint Venture Strategy

Nikhil Celly, Charles Dhanaraj, and Paul Beamish

In August 2001, Dr. Lorenzo Tallarigo, president of Intercontinental Operations, Eli Lilly and Company (Lilly), a leading pharmaceutical firm based in the United States, was getting ready for a meeting in New York, with D. S. Brar, chairman and chief executive officer (CEO) of Ranbaxy Laboratories Limited (Ranbaxy), India. Lilly and Ranbaxy had started a joint venture (JV) in India, Eli Lilly-Ranbaxy Private Limited (ELR) that was incorporated in March 1993. The JV had steadily grown to a full-fledged organization employing more than 500 people in 2001. However, in recent months Lilly was re-evaluating the directions for the JV, with Ranbaxy signaling an intention to sell its stake. Tallarigo was scheduled to meet with Brar to decide on the next steps.

The Global Pharmaceutical Industry in the 1990s

The pharmaceutical industry had come about through both forward integration from the manufacture of organic chemicals and a backward

Richard Ivey School of Business
The University of Western Ontario

Nikhil Celly prepared this case under the supervision of Professors Charles Dhanaraj and Paul W. Beamish solely to provide material for class discussion. The authors do not intend to illustrate either effective or ineffective handling of a managerial situation. The authors may have disguised certain names and other identifying information to protect confidentiality.

integration from druggist-supply houses. The industry's rapid growth was aided by increasing worldwide incomes and a universal demand for better health care; however, most of the world market for pharmaceuticals was concentrated in North America, Europe and Japan. Typically, the largest four firms claimed 20 per cent of sales, the top 20 firms 50 per cent to 60 per cent and the 50 largest companies accounted for 65 per cent to 75 per cent of sales (see **Exhibit 1**). Drug discovery was an expensive process, with leading firms spending more than 20 per cent of their sales on research and development (R&D). Developing a drug, from discovery to launch in a major market, took 10 to 12 years and typically cost US$500 million to US$800 million (in 1992). Bulk production of active ingredients was the norm, along with the ability to decentralize manufacturing and packaging to adapt to particular market needs. Marketing was usually equally targeted to physicians and the paying customers. Increasingly, government agencies, such as Medicare, and health management organizations (HMOs) in the United States were gaining influence in the buying processes. In most countries, all activities related to drug research and manufacturing were strictly controlled by government agencies, such as the Food and Drug Administration (FDA) in the United States, the Committee on Proprietary Medicinal Products (CPMP) in Europe, and the Ministry of Health and Welfare (MHW) in Japan.

Patents were the essential means by which a firm protected its proprietary knowledge. The safety provided by the patents allowed firms to price their products appropriately in order to accumulate funds for future research. The basic reason to patent a new drug was to guarantee the exclusive legal right to profit from its innovation for a certain number of

Exhibit 1   World Pharmaceutical Suppliers 1992 and 2001 (US$ millions)

Company	Origin	1992 Sales*	Company	Origin	2001 Sales**
Glaxo	US	8,704	Pfizer	USA	25,500
Merck	UK	8,214	GlaxoSmithKline	UK	24,800
Bristol-Myers Squibb	US	6,313	Merck & Co	USA	21,350
Hoechst	GER	6,042	AstraZeneca	UK	16,480
Ciba-Geigy	SWI	5,192	Bristol-Myers Squibb	USA	15,600
SmithKline Beecham	US	5,100	Aventis	FRA	15,350
Roche	SWI	4,897	Johnson & Johnson	USA	14,900
Sandoz	SWI	4,886	Novartis	SWI	14,500
Bayer	GER	4,670	Pharmacia Corp	USA	11,970
American Home	US	4,589	Eli Lilly	USA	11,540
Pfizer	US	4,558	Wyeth	USA	11,710
Eli Lilly	US	4,537	Roche	SWI	8,530
Johnson & Johnson	US	4,340	Schering-Plough	USA	8,360
Rhone Poulenc Rorer	US	4,096	Abbot Laboratories	USA	8,170
Abbot	US	4,025	Takeda	JAP	7,770
			Sanofi-Synthélabo	FRA	5,700
			Boehringer Ingelheim	GER	5,600
			Bayer	GER	5,040
			Schering AG	GER	3,900
			Akzo Nobel	NTH	3,550

*Market Share Reporter, 1993.
**Pharmaceutical Executive, May 2002.

years, typically 20 years for a product patent. There was usually a time lag of about eight to 10 years from the time the patent was obtained and the time of regulatory approval to first launch in the United States or Europe. Time lags for emerging markets and in Japan were longer. The "product patent" covered the chemical substance itself, while a "process patent" covered the method of processing or manufacture. Both patents guaranteed the inventor a 20-year monopoly on the innovation, but the process patent offered much less protection, since it was fairly easy to modify a chemical process. It was also very difficult to legally prove that a process patent had been created to manufacture a product identical to that of a competitor. Most countries relied solely on process patents until the mid-1950s, although many countries had since recognized the product patent in law. While companies used the

global market to amortize the huge investments required to produce a new drug, they were hesitant to invest in countries where the intellectual property regime was weak.

As health-care costs soared in the 1990s, the pharmaceutical industry in developed countries began coming under increased scrutiny. Although patent protection was strong in developed countries, there were various types of price controls. Prices for the same drugs varied between the United States and Canada by a factor of 1.2 to 2.5.[1] Parallel trade or trade by independent firms

[1]Estimates of industry average wholesale price levels in Europe (with Spanish levels indexed at 100 in 1989) were: Spain 100; Portugal 107; France 113; Italy 118; Belgium 131; United Kingdom 201; The Netherlands 229; West Germany 251. Source: T. Malnight, Globalization of an Ethnocentric Firm: An Evolutionary Perspective, *Strategic Management Journal*, 1995, Vol. 16 p.128.

taking advantage of such differentials represented a serious threat to pharmaceutical suppliers, especially in Europe. Also, the rise of generics, unbranded drugs of comparable efficacy in treating the disease but available at a fraction of the cost of the branded drugs, were challenging the pricing power of the pharmaceutical companies. Manufacturers of generic drugs had no expense for drug research and development of new compounds and only had limited budgets for popularizing the compound with the medical community. The generic companies made their money by copying what other pharmaceutical companies discovered, developed and created a market for. Health management organizations (HMOs) were growing and consolidating their drug purchases. In the United States, the administration under President Clinton, which took office in 1992, investigated the possibility of a comprehensive health plan, which, among other things, would have allowed an increased use of generics and laid down some form of regulatory pressure on pharmaceutical profits.

The Indian Pharmaceutical Industry in the 1990s

Developing countries, such as India, although large by population, were characterized by low per capita gross domestic product (GDP). Typically, healthcare expenditures accounted for a very small share of GDP, and health insurance was not commonly available. The 1990 figures for per capita annual expenditure on drugs in India were estimated at US$3, compared to US$412 in Japan, US$222 in Germany and US$191 in the United Kingdom.[2] Governments and large corporations extended health coverage, including prescription drug coverage, to their workers.

In the years before and following India's independence in 1947, the country had no indigenous capability to produce pharmaceuticals, and was dependent on imports. The Patent and Designs Act of 1911, an extension of the British colonial rule,

enforced adherence to the international patent law, and gave rise to a number of multinational firms' subsidiaries in India, that wanted to import drugs from their respective countries of origin. Post-independence, the first public sector drug company, Hindustan Antibiotics Limited (HAL), was established in 1954, with the help of the World Health Organization, and Indian Drugs and Pharmaceutical Limited (IDPL) was established in 1961 with the help of the then Soviet Union.

The 1970s saw several changes that would dramatically change the intellectual property regime and give rise to the emergence of local manufacturing companies. Two such key changes were the passage of the Patents Act 1970 (effective April 1972) and the Drug Price Control Order (DPCO). The Patents Act in essence abolished the product patents for all pharmaceutical and agricultural products, and permitted process patents for five to seven years. The DPCO instituted price controls, by which a government body stipulated prices for all drugs. Subsequently, this list was revised in 1987 to 142 drugs (which accounted for 72 per cent of the turnover of the industry). Indian drug prices were estimated to be five per cent to 20 per cent of the U.S. prices and among the lowest in the world.[3] The DPCO also limited profits pharmaceutical companies could earn to approximately six per cent of sales turnover. Also, the post-manufacturing expenses were limited to 100 per cent of the production costs. At the World Health Assembly in 1982 Indira Gandhi, then Prime Minister of India, aptly captured the national sentiment on the issue in an often-quoted statement:

> The idea of a better-ordered world is one in which medical discoveries will be free of patents and there will be no profiteering from life and death.

With the institution of both the DPCO and the 1970 Patent Act, drugs became available more cheaply, and local firms were encouraged to make

[2]Organization of Pharmaceutical Producers of India Report.

[3]According to a study from Yale University, Ranitidine (300 tabs/10 pack) was priced at Rs18.53, whereas the U.S. price was 57 times more, and Ciprofloxacin (500 mg/4 pack) was at Rs28.40 in India, whereas the U.S. price was about 15 times more.

copies of drugs by developing their own processes, leading to bulk drug production. The profitability was sharply reduced for multinational companies, many of which began opting out of the Indian market due to the disadvantages they faced from the local competition. Market share of multinational companies dropped from 80 per cent in 1970 to 35 per cent in the mid-1990s as those companies exited the market due to the lack of patent protection in India.

In November 1984, there were changes in the government leadership following Gandhi's assassination. The dawn of the 1990s saw India initiating economic reform and embracing globalization. Under the leadership of Dr. Manmohan Singh, then finance minister, the government began the process of liberalization and moving the economy away from import substitution to an export-driven economy. Foreign direct investment was encouraged by increasing the maximum limit of foreign ownership to 51 per cent (from 40 per cent) in the drugs and pharmaceutical industry (see **Exhibit 2**). It was in this environment that Eli Lilly was considering getting involved.

Eli Lilly and Company

Colonel Eli Lilly founded Eli Lilly and Company in 1876. The company would become one of the largest pharmaceutical companies in the United States from the early 1940s until 1985 but it began with just $1,400 and four employees, including Lilly's 14-year-old son. This was accomplished with a company philosophy grounded in a commitment to scientific and managerial excellence. Over the years, Eli Lilly discovered, developed, manufactured and sold a broad line of human

Exhibit 2   India Economy at a Glance

	1992	1994	1996	1998	2000
Gross domestic product (GDP) at current market prices in US$	244	323	386	414	481
Consumer price index (June 1982 = 100) in local currency, period average	77.4	90.7	108.9	132.2	149.3
Recorded official unemployment as a percentage of total labor force	9.7	9.3	9.1	9.2	9.2
Stock of foreign reserves plus gold (national valuation), end-period	8,665	23,054	23,784	29,833	48,200
Foreign direct investment inflow (in US$ millions)[1]	252	974	2,525	2,633	2,319
Total exports	19,563	25,075	33,055	33,052	43,085
Total imports	23,580	26,846	37,376	42,318	49,907

Year	Population*
1991	846
2001	1,027

[1] United Nations Commission on Trade and Development
[2] 1991, 2001 Census of India
*In millions.
Source: The Economist Intelligence Unit.

health and agricultural products. Research and development was crucial to Lilly's long-term success.

Before 1950, most OUS (a company term for "Outside the United States") activities were export focused. Beginning in the 1950s, Lilly undertook systematic expansion of its OUS activities, setting up several affiliates overseas. In the mid-1980s, under the leadership of then chairman, Dick Wood, Lilly began a significant move toward global markets. A separate division within the company, Eli Lilly International Corporation, with responsibility for worldwide marketing of all its products, took an active role in expanding the OUS operations. By 1992, Lilly's products were manufactured and distributed through 25 countries and sold in more than 130 countries. The company had emerged as a world leader in oral and injectable antibiotics and in supplying insulin and related diabetic care products. In 1992, Lilly International was headed by Sidney Taurel, an MBA from Columbia University, with work experience in South America and Europe, and Gerhard Mayr, an MBA from Stanford, with extensive experience in Europe. Mayr wanted to expand Lilly's operations in Asia, where several countries including India were opening up their markets for foreign investment. Lilly also saw opportunities to use the world for clinical testing, which would enable it to move forward faster, as well as shape opinion with leaders in the medical field around the world; something that would help in Lilly's marketing stage.

Ranbaxy Laboratories

Ranbaxy began in the 1960s as a family business, but with a visionary management grew rapidly to emerge as the leading domestic pharmaceutical firm in India. Under the leadership of Dr. Parvinder Singh, who held a doctoral degree from the University of Michigan, the firm evolved into a serious research-oriented firm. Singh, who joined Ranbaxy to assist his father in 1967, rose to become the joint managing director in 1977, managing director in 1982, and vice-chairman and managing director in

1987. Singh's visionary management, along with the operational leadership provided by Brar, who joined the firm in 1977, was instrumental in turning the family business into a global corporation. In the early 1990s, when almost the entire domestic pharmaceutical industry was opposing a tough patent regime, Ranbaxy was accepting it as given. Singh's argument was unique within the industry in India:

> The global marketplace calls for a single set of rules; you cannot have one for the Indian market and the other for the export market. Tomorrow's global battles will be won by product leaders, not operationally excellent companies. Tomorrow's leaders must be visionaries, whether they belong to the family or not. Our mission at Ranbaxy is to become a research based international pharmaceutical company.[4]

By the early 1990s, Ranbaxy grew to become India's largest manufacturer of bulk drugs[5] and generic drugs, with a domestic market share of 15 per cent (see **Exhibit 3**).

One of Ranbaxy's core competencies was its chemical synthesis capability, but the company had begun to outsource some bulk drugs in limited quantities. The company produced pharmaceuticals in four locations in India. The company's capital costs were typically 50 per cent to 75 per cent lower than those of comparable U.S. plants and were meant to serve foreign markets in addition to the Indian market. Foreign markets, especially those in more developed countries, often had stricter quality control requirements, and such a difference meant that the manufacturing practices required to compete in those markets appeared to be costlier from the perspective of less developed markets. Higher prices in other countries provided the impetus for Ranbaxy to pursue international markets; the company had a presence in 47 markets outside India, mainly through exports handled through an international division. Ranbaxy's R&D efforts began at the end of the 1970s; in 1979, the company still had only 12 scientists. As Ranbaxy

[4] Quoted in *Times of India,* June 9, 1999.

[5] A bulk drug is an intermediate product that goes into manufacturing of pharmaceutical products.

Exhibit 3   Top 20 Pharmaceutical Companies in India by Sales 1996 to 2000 (Rs billions)

Company	1996*	Company	2000
Glaxo-Wellcome	4.97	Ranbaxy	20.00
Cipla	2.98	Cipla	12.00
Ranbaxy	2.67	Dr. Reddy's Labs	11.30
Hoechts-Roussel	2.60	Glaxo (India)	7.90
Knoll Pharmaceutical	1.76	Lupin Labs	7.80
Pfizer	1.73	Aurobindo Pharma	7.60
Alembic	1.68	Novartis	7.20
Torrent Pharma	1.60	Wockhardt Ltd.	6.80
Lupin Labs	1.56	Sun Pharma	6.70
Zydus-Cadila	1.51	Cadilla Healthcare	5.80
Ambalal Sarabhai	1.38	Nicholas Piramal	5.70
Smithkline Beecham	1.20	Aventis Pharma	5.30
Aristo Pharma	1.17	Alembic Ltd.	4.80
Parke Davis	1.15	Morepen Labs	4.70
Cadila Pharma	1.12	Torrent Pharma	4.40
E. Merck	1.11	IPCA Labs	4.20
Wockhardt	1.08	Knoll Pharma	3.70
John Wyeth	1.04	Orchid Chemicals	3.60
Alkem Laboratories	1.04	E Merck	3.50
Hindustan Ciba Geigy	1.03	Pfizer	3.40

*1996 figures are from ORG, Bombay as reported in Lanjouw, J.O., www.oiprc.ox.ac.uk/EJWP0799.html, NBER working paper No. 6366.
Source: "Report on Pharmaceutical Sector in India," *Scope Magazine,* September 2001, p.14.

entered the international market in the 1980s, R&D was responsible for registering its products in foreign markets, most of which was directed to process R&D; R&D expenditures ranged from two per cent to five per cent of the annual sales with future targets of seven per cent to eight per cent.

The Lilly Ranbaxy JV

Ranbaxy approached Lilly in 1992 to investigate the possibility of supplying certain active ingredients or sourcing of intermediate products to Lilly in order to provide low-cost sources of intermediate pharmaceutical ingredients. Lilly had had earlier relationships with manufacturers in India to produce human or animal insulin and then export the products to the Soviet Union using the Russia/India trade route, but those had never developed into on-the-ground relationships within the Indian

market. Ranbaxy was the second largest exporter of all products in India and the second largest pharmaceutical company in India after Glaxo (a subsidiary of the U.K.-based firm).

Rajiv Gulati, at that time a general manager of business development and marketing controller at Ranbaxy, who was instrumental in developing the strategy for Ranbaxy, recalled:

In the 1980s, many multinational pharmaceutical companies had a presence in India. Lilly did not. As a result of both the sourcing of intermediate products as well as the fact that Lilly was one of the only players not yet in India, we felt that we could use Ranbaxy's knowledge of the market to get our feet on the ground in India. Ranbaxy would supply certain products to the joint venture from its own portfolio that were currently being manufactured in India and then formulate and finish some of Lilly's products locally. The joint venture would buy the active ingredients and Lilly would have Ranbaxy finish the package and allow the joint venture to sell and distribute those products.

The first meeting was held at Lilly's corporate center in Indianapolis in late 1990. Present were Ranbaxy's senior executives, Dr. Singh, vice-chairman, and D.S. Brar, chief operating officer (COO), and Lilly's senior executives including Gene Step and Richard Wood, the CEO of Lilly. Rickey Pate, a corporate attorney at Eli Lilly who was present at the meeting, recalled:

> It was a very smooth meeting. We had a lot in common. We both believed in high ethical standards, in technology and innovation, as well as in the future of patented products in India. Ranbaxy executives emphasized their desire to be a responsible corporate citizen and expressed their concerns for their employees. It was quite obvious Ranbaxy would be a compatible partner in India.

Lilly decided to form the joint venture in India to focus on marketing of Lilly's drugs there, and a formal JV agreement was signed in November 1992. The newly created JV was to have an authorized capital of Rs200 million (equivalent of US$7.1 million), and an initial subscribed equity capital of Rs84 million (US$3 million), with equal contribution from Lilly and Ranbaxy, leading to an equity ownership of 50 per cent each. The board of directors for the JV would comprise six directors, three from each company. A management committee was also created comprising two directors, one from each company, and Lilly retained the right to appoint the CEO who would be responsible for the day-to-day operations. The agreement also provided for transfer of shares, in the event any one of the partners desired to dispose some or its entire share in the company.

In the mid-1990s, Lilly was investigating the possibility of extending its operations to include generics. Following the launch of the Indian JV, Lilly and Ranbaxy, entered into two other agreements related to generics, one in India to focus on manufacturing generics, and the other in the United States to focus on the marketing of generics.

However, within less than a year, Lilly made a strategic decision not to enter the generics market and the two parties agreed to terminate the JV agreements related to the generics. Mayr recalled:

> At that time we were looking at the Indian market although we did not have any particular time frame for entry. We particularly liked Ranbaxy, as we saw an alignment of the broad values. Dr. Singh had a clear vision of leading Ranbaxy to become an innovation driven company. And we liked what we saw in them. Of course, for a time we were looking at the generic business and wondering if this was something we should be engaged in. Other companies had separate division for generics and we were evaluating such an idea. However, we had a pilot program in Holland and that taught us what it took to be competitive in generics and decided that business wasn't for us, and so we decided to get out of generics.

The Start-up   By March 1993, Andrew Mascarenhas, an American citizen of Indian origin, who at the time was the general manager for Lilly's Caribbean basin, based in San Juan, Puerto Rico, was selected to become the managing director of the joint venture. Rajiv Gulati, who at the time spearheaded the business development and marketing efforts at Ranbaxy, was chosen as the director of marketing and sales at the JV. Mascarenhas recalled:

> Lilly saw the joint venture as an investment the company needed to make. At the time India was a country of 800 million people: 200 million to 300 million of them were considered to be within the country's middle class that represented the future of India. The concept of globalization was just taking hold at Lilly. India, along with China and Russia were seen as markets where Lilly needed to build a greater presence. Some resistance was met due to the recognition that a lot of Lilly's products were already being sold by Indian manufacturers due to the lack of patent protection and intellectual property rights so the question was what products should we put in there that could be competitive. The products that were already being manufactured had sufficient capacity; so it was an issue of trying to leverage the markets in which those products were sold into.

Lilly was a name that most physicians in India did not recognize despite its leadership position in the

United States, it did not have any recognition in India. Ranbaxy was the leader within India. When I was informed that the name of the joint venture was to be Lilly Ranbaxy, first thing I did was to make sure that the name of the joint venture was Eli Lilly Ranbaxy and not just Lilly Ranbaxy. The reason for this was based on my earlier experience in India, where "good quality" rightly or wrongly, was associated with foreign imported goods. Eli Lilly Ranbaxy sounded foreign enough!

Early on, Mascarenhas and Gulati worked on getting the venture up and running with office space and an employee base. Mascarenhas recalled:

> I got a small space within Ranbaxy's set-up. We had two tables, one for Rajiv and the other for me. We had to start from that infrastructure and move towards building up the organization from scratch. Rajiv was great to work with and we both were able to see eye-to-eye on most issues. Dr. Singh was a strong supporter and the whole of Ranbaxy senior management tried to assist us whenever we asked for help.

The duo immediately hired a financial analyst, and the team grew from there. Early on, they hired a medical director, a sales manager and a human resources manager. The initial team was a good one, but there was enormous pressure and the group worked seven days a week. Ranbaxy's help was used for getting government approvals, licenses, distribution and supplies. Recalled Gulati:

> We used Ranbaxy's name for everything. We were new and it was very difficult for us. We used their distribution network as we did not have one and Lilly did not want to invest heavily in setting up a distribution network. We paid Ranbaxy for the service. Ranbaxy was very helpful.

By the end of 1993, the venture moved to an independent place, began launching products and employed more than 200 people. Within another year, Mascarenhas had hired a significant sales force and had recruited medical doctors and financial people for the regulatory group with assistance from Lilly's Geneva office. Mascarenhas recalled:

> Our recruiting theme was 'Opportunity of a Lifetime' i.e., joining a new company, and to be part of its very

foundation. Many who joined us, especially at senior level, were experienced executives. By entering this new and untested company, they were really taking a huge risk with their careers and the lives of their families.

However, the employee turnover in the Indian pharmaceutical industry was very high. Sandeep Gupta, director of marketing recalled:

> Our biggest problem was our high turnover rate. A sales job in the pharmaceutical industry was not the most sought-after position. Any university graduate could be employed. The pharmaceutical industry in India is very unionized. Ranbaxy's HR practices were designed to work with unionized employees. From the very beginning, we did not want our recruits to join unions. Instead, we chose to show recruits that they had a career in ELR. When they joined us as sales graduates they did not just remain at that level. We took a conscious decision to promote from within the company. The venture began investing in training and used Lilly's training programs. The programs were customized for Indian conditions, but retained Lilly's values (see **Exhibit 4**).

Within a year, the venture team began gaining the trust and respect of doctors, due to the strong values adhered to by Lilly. Mascarenhas described how the venture fought the Indian stigma:

> Lilly has a code of ethical conduct called the Red Book, and the company did not want to go down the path where it might be associated with unethical behavior. But Lilly felt Ranbaxy knew how to do things the right way and that they respected their employees, which was a very important attribute. So following Lilly's Red Book values, the group told doctors the truth; both the positive and negative aspects of their drugs. If a salesperson didn't know the answer to something, they didn't lie or make up something; they told the doctor they didn't know. No bribes were given or taken, and it was found that honesty and integrity could actually be a competitive advantage. Sales people were trained to offer product information to doctors. The group gradually became distinguished by this "strange" behavior.

Exhibit 4   Values at Eli Lilly Ranbaxy Limited

People
"The people who make up this company are its most valuable assets"

- Respect for the individual
  - Courtesy and politeness at all times
  - Sensitivity to other people's views
  - Respect for ALL people regardless of caste, religion, sex or age
- Careers NOT jobs
  - Emphasis on individual's growth, personal and professional
  - Broaden experience via cross-functional moves

"The first responsibility of our supervisors is **to build men, then medicines.**"

Attitude
"There is very little difference between people. But that difference makes a BIG difference. The little difference is attitude. The BIG difference is... Whether it is POSITIVE or NEGATIVE"
"Are we part of the PROBLEM or part of the SOLUTION?"

Team
"None of us is as smart as all of us."

Integrity

- Integrity outside the company
  a. "We should not do anything or be expected to take any action that we would be ashamed to explain to our family or close friends"
  b. "The red-faced test"
  c. "Integrity can be our biggest competitive advantage"
- Integrity inside the company
  - With one another: openness, honesty

Excellence

- Serving our customers

"In whatever we do, we must ask ourselves: how does this serve my customer better?"

- Continuous improvement

"Nothing is being done today that cannot be done better tomorrow"

- Become the Industry Standard

"In whatever we do, we will do it so well that we become the Industry Standard"

Recalled Sudhanshu Kamat, controller of finance at ELR:

Lilly from the start treated us as its employees, like all its other affiliates worldwide. We followed the same systems and processes that any Lilly affiliate would worldwide.

Much of the success of the joint venture is attributed to the strong and cohesive working relationship of Mascarenhas and Gulati. Mascarenhas recalled:

We both wanted the venture to be successful. We both had our identities to the JV, and there was no Ranbaxy versus Lilly politics. From the very start when we had our office at Ranbaxy premises, I was invited to dine with their senior management. Even after moving to our own office, I continued the practice of having lunch at Ranbaxy HQ on a weekly basis. I think it helped a lot to be accessible at all times and to build on the personal relationship.

The two companies had very different business focuses. Ranbaxy was a company driven by the generics business. Lilly, on the other hand, was driven by innovation and discovery.

Mascarenhas focused his effort on communicating Eli Lilly's values to the new joint venture:

> I spent a lot of time communicating Lilly's values to newly hired employees. In the early days, I interviewed our senior applicants personally. I was present in the two-day training sessions that we offered for the new employees, where I shared the values of the company. That was a critical task for me to make sure that the right foundations were laid down for growth.

The first products that came out of the joint venture were human insulin from Lilly and several Ranbaxy products; but the team faced constant challenges in dealing with government regulations on the one hand and financing the affiliate on the other. There were also cash flow constraints.

The ministry of health provided limitations on Lilly's pricing, and even with the margin the Indian government allowed, most of it went to the wholesalers and the pharmacies, pursuant to formulas in the Indian ministry of health. Once those were factored out of the gross margin, achieving profitability was a real challenge, as some of the biggest obstacles faced were duties imposed by the Indian government on imports and other regulatory issues. Considering the weak intellectual property rights regime, Lilly did not want to launch some of its products, such as its top-seller, Prozac.[6] Gulati recalled:

> We focused only on those therapeutic areas where Lilly had a niche. We did not adopt a localization strategy such as the ones adopted by Pfizer and Glaxo[7]

[6]Used as an antidepressant medication.
[7]An industry study by McKinsey found that Glaxo sold 50 per cent of its volume, received three per cent of revenues and one per cent of profit in India.

that manufactured locally and sold at local prices. India is a high-volume, low price, low profit market, but it was a conscious decision by us to operate the way we did. We wanted to be in the global price band. So, we did not launch several patented products because generics were selling at 1/60th the price.

Product and marketing strategies had to be adopted to suit the market conditions. ELR's strategy evolved over the years to focus on two groups of products: one was off-patent drugs, where Lilly could add substantial value (e.g. Ceclor), and two, patented drugs, where there existed a significant barrier to entry (e.g. Reopro and Gemzar). ELR marketed Ceclor, a Ranbaxy manufactured product, but attempted to add significant value by providing medical information to the physicians and other unique marketing activities. By the end of 1996, the venture had reached the break-even and was becoming profitable.

The Mid-Term Organizational Changes   Mascarenhas was promoted in 1996 to managing director of Eli Lilly Italy, and Chris Shaw, a British national, who was then managing the operations in Taiwan, was assigned to the JV as the new managing director. Also, Gulati, who was formally a Ranbaxy employee, decided to join Eli Lilly as its employee, and was assigned to Lilly's corporate office in Indianapolis in the Business Development—Infectious Diseases therapeutic division. Chris Shaw recalled:

> When I went to India as a British national, I was not sure what sort of reception I would get, knowing its history. But my family and I were received very warmly. I found a dynamic team with a strong sense of values.

Shaw focused on building systems and processes to bring stability to the fast-growing organization; his own expertise in operations made a significant contribution during this phase. He hired a senior level manager and created a team to develop standard operating procedures (SOPs) for ensuring smooth operations. The product line also expanded. The JV continued to maintain a 50–50 distribution of products from Lilly and Ranbaxy, although there was no stipulation to maintain such a ratio. The clinical organization in India was received top-ratings in internal audits by Lilly, making it suitable for a wider range of clinical trials. Shaw also streamlined the sales and marketing activities around therapeutic areas to emphasize and enrich the knowledge capabilities of the company's sales force. Seeing the rapid change in the environment in India, ELR, with the support of Mayr, hired the management-consulting firm, McKinsey, to recommend growth options in India. ELR continued its steady performance with an annualized growth rate of about eight per cent during the late 1990s.

In 1999, Chris Shaw was assigned to Eli Lilly's Polish subsidiary, and Gulati returned to the ELR as its managing director, following his three-year tenure at Lilly's U.S. operations. Recalled Gulati:

> When I joined as MD in 1999, we were growing at eight per cent and had not added any new employees. I hired 150 people over the next two years and went about putting systems and processes in place. When we started in 1993 and during Andrew's time, we were like a grocery shop. Now we needed to be a company. We had to be a large durable organization and prepare

ourselves to go from sales of US$10 million to sales of US$100 million.

ELR created a medical and regulatory unit, which handled the product approval processes with government. Das, the chief financial officer (CFO), commented:

> We worked together with the government on the regulatory part. Actually, we did not take shelter under the Ranbaxy name but built a strong regulatory (medical and corporate affairs) foundation.

By early 2001, the venture was recording an excellent growth rate (see **Exhibit 5**), surpassing the average growth rate in the Indian pharmaceutical industry. ELR had already become the 46th largest pharmaceutical company in India out of 10,000 companies. Several of the multinational subsidiaries, which were started at the same time as ELR, had either closed down or were in serious trouble. Das summarized the achievements:

> The JV did add some prestige to Ranbaxy's efforts as a global player as the Lilly name had enormous credibility while Lilly gained the toehold in India. In 10 years we did not have any cannibalization of each other's employees, quite a rare event if you compare with the other JVs. This helped us build a unique culture in India.

Exhibit 5   ELI Lilly-Ranbaxy India Financials 1998 to 2001 (Rs'000s)

	1998-1999	1999-2000	2000-2001
Sales	559,766	632,188	876,266
Marketing Expenses	37,302	61,366	96,854
Other Expenses	157,907	180,364	254,822
Profit after Tax	5,898	12,301	11,999
Current Assets	272,635	353,077	466,738
Current Liabilities	239,664	297,140	471,635
Total Assets	303,254	386,832	516,241
No. of Employees	358	419	460
Exchange Rate (Rupees/US$)	42.6	43.5	46.8

Note: Financial year runs from April 1 to March 31.
Source: Company Reports.

The New World, 2001

The pharmaceutical industry continued to grow through the 1990s. In 2001, worldwide retail sales were expected to increase 10 per cent to about US$350 billion. The United States was expected to remain the largest and fastest growing country among the world's major drug markets over the next three years. There was a consolidation trend in the industry with ongoing mergers and acquisitions reshaping the industry. In 1990, the world's top 10 players accounted for just 28 per cent of the market, while in 2000, the number had risen to 45 per cent and continued to grow. There was also a trend among leading global pharmaceutical companies to get back to basics and concentrate on core high-margined prescription preparations and divest non-core businesses. In addition, the partnerships between pharmaceutical and biotechnology companies were growing rapidly. There were a number of challenges, such as escalating R&D costs, lengthening development and approval times for new products, growing competition from generics and follow-on products, and rising cost-containment pressures, particularly with the growing clout of managed care organizations.

By 1995, Lilly had moved up to become the 12th leading pharmaceutical supplier in the world, sixth in the U.S. market, 17th in Europe and 77th in Japan. Much of Lilly's sales success through the mid-1990s came from its antidepressant drug, Prozac. But with the wonder drug due to go off patent in 2001, Lilly was aggressively working on a number of high-potential products. By the beginning of 2001, Lilly was doing business in 151 countries, with its international sales playing a significant role in the company's success (see **Exhibits 6** and **7**). Dr. Lorenzo Tallarigo recalled:

> When I started as the president of the intercontinental operations, I realized that the world was very different in the 2000s from the world of 1990s. Particularly there were phenomenal changes in the markets in India and China. While I firmly believed that the partnership we had with Ranbaxy was really an excellent one, the fact that we were facing such a different market in the 21st century was reason enough to carefully evaluate our strategies in these markets.

Exhibit 6   Lilly Financials 1992 to 2000 (US$ millions)

	1992	1994	1996	1998	2000
Net sales	4,963	5,711	6,998	9,236	10,862
Foreign sales	2,207	2,710	3,587	3,401	3,858
Research and development expenses	731	839	1,190	1,739	2,019
Income from continuing operations before taxes and extraordinary items	1,194	1,699	2,131	2,665	3,859
Net income	709	1,286	1,524	2,097	3,058
Dividends per share*	1.128	1.260	0.694	0.830	1.060
Current assets	3,006	3,962	3,891	5,407	7,943
Current liabilities	2,399	5,670	4,222	4,607	4,961
Property and equipment	4,072	4,412	4,307	4,096	4,177
Total assets	8,673	14,507	14,307	12,596	14,691
Long-term debt	582	2,126	2,517	2,186	2,634
Shareholder equity	4,892	5,356	6,100	4,430	6,047
Number of employees*	24,500	24,900	27,400	29,800	35,700

*Actual value
Source: Company files.

Exhibit 7 Product Segment Information Lilly and Ranbaxy 1996 and 2000

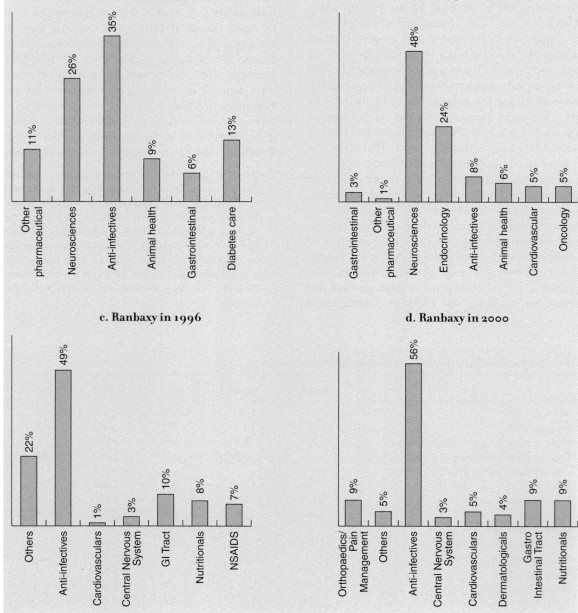

a. Eli Lilly in 1996

Other pharmaceutical	11%
Neurosciences	26%
Anti-infectives	35%
Animal health	9%
Gastrointestinal	6%
Diabetes care	13%

b. Eli Lilly in 2000

Gastrointestinal	3%
Other pharmaceutical	1%
Neurosciences	48%
Endocrinology	24%
Anti-infectives	8%
Animal health	6%
Cardiovascular	5%
Oncology	5%

c. Ranbaxy in 1996

Others	22%
Anti-infectives	49%
Cardiovasculars	1%
Central Nervous System	3%
GI Tract	10%
Nutritionals	8%
NSAIDS	7%

d. Ranbaxy in 2000

Orthopaedics/Pain Management	9%
Others	5%
Anti-infectives	56%
Central Nervous System	3%
Cardiovasculars	5%
Dermatologicals	4%
Gastro Intestinal Tract	9%
Nutritionals	9%

Ranbaxy, too, had witnessed changes through the 1990s. Dr. Singh became the new CEO in 1993 and formulated a new mission for the company: to become a research-based international pharmaceutical company with $1 billion in sales by 2003. This vision saw Ranbaxy developing new drugs through basic research, earmarking 20 per cent of the R&D budget for such work. In addition to its joint venture with Lilly, Ranbaxy made three other manufacturing/marketing investments in developed markets: a joint venture with Genpharm in Canada ($1.1 million), and the acquisitions of Ohm Labs in the United States ($13.5 million) and Rima Pharmaceuticals ($8 million) in Ireland. With these deals, Ranbaxy had manufacturing facilities around the globe. While China and Russia were expected to remain key foreign markets, Ranbaxy was looking at the United States and the United Kingdom as its core international markets for the future. In 1999, Dr. Singh handed over the reins of the company to Brar, and later the same year, Ranbaxy lost this visionary leader due to an untimely death. Brar continued Singh's vision to keep Ranbaxy in a leadership position. However, the vast network of international sales that Ranbaxy had developed created a large financial burden, depressing the company's 2000 results, and was expected to significantly affect its cash flow in 2001 (see **Exhibit 8**). Vinay Kaul, vice-chairman of Ranbaxy in 2001 and chairman of the board of ELR since 2000, noted:

> We have come a long way from where we started. Our role in the present JV is very limited. We had a smooth relationship and we have been of significant help to Lilly to establish a foothold in the market here in India. Also, we have opened up a number of opportunities for them to expand their network. However, we have also grown, and we are a global company with presence in a number of international markets including the United States. We had to really think if this JV is central to our operations, given that we have closed down the other two JV agreements that we had with Lilly on the generics manufacturing. It is common knowledge that whether we continue as a JV or not, we have created a substantial value for Lilly.

There were also significant changes in the Indian business environment. India signed the General Agreement on Tariffs and Trade (GATT) in April 1994 and became a World Trade Organization (WTO) member in 1995. As per the WTO, from the year 2005, India would grant product patent

Exhibit 8 Ranbaxy Financials 1992 to 2000 (Rs millions)

	1992–93	1994–95	1996–97	*1998	2000
Sales	4,607	7,122	11,482	10,641	17,459
Foreign sales	1,408	3,019	5,224	4,414	8,112
Profit before tax	358	1,304	1,869	1,240	1,945
Profit after tax	353	1,104	1,604	1,170	1,824
Equity dividend	66.50	199.80	379.10	560.10	869.20
Earnings per share (Rs)	16.21	25.59	32.47	13.46	15.74
Net current assets	1,737	5,790	9,335	8,321	8,258
Share capital	217.90	430.50	494.00	1,159.00	1,159.00
Reserves and surplus	1,028	6,000	11,056	12,849	16,448
Book value per share (Rs)	57.16	149.08	233.70	120.90	136.60
No. of employees	4,575	4,703	6,131	5,469	5,784
Exchange rate (US$1 = Rs)	29.00	31.40	35.90	42.60	46.80

*The financial year for Ranbaxy changed from April 1 to March 31 to calendar year in 1998. Also, the company issued a 1:2 bonus issue (see the changes in share capital and book value per share). The 1998 figures are based on nine months April to December 1998.
Source: Company files.

recognition to all new chemical entities (NCEs), i.e., bulk drugs developed from then onward. Also, the Indian government had made the decision to allow 100 per cent foreign direct investment into the drugs and pharmaceutical industry in 2001.[8] The Indian pharmaceutical market had grown at an average of 15 per cent through the 1990s, but the trends indicated a slowdown in growth, partly due to intense price competition, a shift toward chronic therapies and the entry of large players into the generic market. India was seeing its own internal consolidation of major companies that were trying to bring in synergies through economies of scale. The industry would see more mergers and alliances. And with India's entry into the WTO and its agreement to begin patent protection in 2004-2005, competition on existing and new products was expected to intensify. Government guidelines were expected to include rationalization of price controls and the encouragement of more research and development. Recalled Gulati:

> The change of institutional environment brought a great promise for Lilly. India was emerging into a market that had patent protection and with tremendous potential for adding value in the clinical trials, an important component in the pharmaceutical industry. In Ranbaxy, we had a partner with whom we could work very well, and one which greatly respected Lilly. However, there were considerable signals from both sides, which were forcing us to evaluate the strategy.

Dr. Vinod Mattoo, medical director of ELR commented:

> We have been able to achieve penetration in key therapeutic areas of diabetes and oncology. We have created a high caliber, and non-unionized sales force with world-class sales processes. We have medical infrastructure and expertise to run clinical trials to international standards. We have been able to provide clinical trial data to support global registrations, and an organization in place to maximize returns post-2005.

[8]In order to regulate the parallel activities of a foreign company, which had an ongoing joint venture in India, the regulations stipulated that the foreign partner must get a "No objection letter" from its Indian partner, before setting up a wholly owned subsidiary.

Evaluating Strategic Options

Considering these several developments, Tallarigo suggested a joint task force comprising senior executives from both companies:

> Soon after assuming this role, I visited India in early 2000, and had the pleasure of meeting Dr. Brar and the senior executives. It was clear to me that both Brar and I were in agreement that we needed to think carefully how we approached the future. It was there that I suggested that we create a joint task force to come up with some options that would help us make a final decision.

A task force was set up with two senior executives from Lilly's Asia-Pacific regional office (based in Singapore) and two senior executives from Ranbaxy. The task force did not include senior executives of the ELR so as to not distract the running of the day-to-day operations. Suman Das, the chief financial officer of ELR, was assigned to support the task force with the needed financial data. The task force developed several scenarios and presented different options for the board to consider.

There were rumors within the industry that Ranbaxy expected to divest the JV, and invest the cash in its growing portfolio of generics manufacturing business in international markets. There were also several other Indian companies that offered to buy Ranbaxy's stake in the JV. With India recognizing patent protection in 2005, several Indian pharmaceutical companies were keen to align with multinationals to ensure a pipeline of drugs. Although there were no formal offers from Ranbaxy, the company was expected to price its stakes as high as US$70 million. One of the industry observers in India commented:

> I think it is fair for Ranbaxy to expect a reasonable return for its investment in the JV, not only the initial capital, but also so much of its intangibles in the JV. Ranbaxy's stock has grown significantly. Given the critical losses that Ranbaxy has had in some of its investments abroad, the revenue from this sale may be a significant boost for Ranbaxy's cash flow this year.

Gerhard Mayr, who in 2001, was the executive vice-president and was responsible for Lilly's demand realization around the world, continued to emphasize the emerging markets in India, China and Eastern Europe. Mayr commented on Ranbaxy:

> India is an important market for us and especially after patent protection in 2005. Ranbaxy was a wonderful partner and our relationship with them was outstanding. The other two joint ventures we initiated with them in the generics did not make sense to us once we decided to get out of the generics business. We see India as a good market for Lilly. If a partner is what it takes to succeed, we should go with a partner. If it does not, we should have the flexibility to reconsider.

Tallarigo hoped that Brar would be able to provide a clear direction as to the venture's future. As he prepared for the meeting, he knew the decision was not an easy one, although he felt confident that the JV was in good shape. While the new regulations allowed Lilly to operate as a wholly-owned subsidiary in India, the partnership has been a very positive element in its strategy. Ranbaxy provided manufacturing and logistics support to the JV, and breaking up the partnership would require a significant amount of renegotiations. Also, it was not clear what the financial implications of such a move would be. Although Ranbaxy seemed to favor a sell-out, Tallarigo thought the price expectations might be beyond what Lilly was ready to accept. This meeting with Brar should provide clarity on all these issues.

Reading 6-1   The Design and Management of International Joint Ventures[1]

Paul W. Beamish

An international joint venture is a company that is owned by two or more firms of different nationality. International joint ventures may be formed from a starting (or greenfield) basis or may be the result of several established companies deciding to merge existing divisions. However they are formed, the purpose of most international joint ventures is to allow partners to pool resources and coordinate their efforts to achieve results that neither could obtain acting alone.

A broad range of strategic alliances exists. They vary widely in terms of the level of interaction and type. Most of the comments in this reading focus on equity joint venture—the alliance form usually requiring the greatest level of interaction, cooperation, and investment. While the discussion which follows usually considers a two-party joint venture,

it is worth noting that many joint ventures have three or more partners.

Joint ventures have moved from being a way to enter foreign markets of peripheral interest to become a part of the mainstream of corporate activity. Virtually all MNEs are using international joint ventures, many as a key element of their corporate strategies. For example, General Motors long-standing joint venture partnership in China with Shanghai Automotive Industry Corp. (2011 JV sales of $30 billion and profits of $3.2 billion) has expanded to include operations in Latin America and India. Similarly, General Motors has facilitated its decade-long foray into the Russian automotive marketplace through the continuing growth of its joint venture partnership with the Russian firm, AvtoVAZ. Even firms that have traditionally operated independently around the world are increasingly turning to joint ventures.

[1]For more detail, see Paul W. Beamish, *Joint Venturing*, (Charlotte, North Carolina: Information Age Publishing, 2008).

The popularity and use of international joint ventures and cooperative alliances has remained strong. The rate of joint venture use does not change much from year to year. In general, joint ventures are the mode of choice 25–35 percent of the time by U.S. multinationals and in about 40 percent of foreign subsidiaries formed by Japanese multinationals.

The popularity of alliances has continued despite their reputation for being difficult to manage. Failures exist and are usually widely publicized. For example, the 2007 joint venture announced between Tiffany & Co. and Swatch Group S.A., which was intended to grow into a decades-long partnership, devolved into a legal battle in which Swatch sued Tiffany for lost profits (estimated at $4.2 billion) and Tiffany filed a $590 million counterclaim. Also, after Lucent's joint venture in wireless handsets with Philips Electronics ended, Lucent took a $100 million charge at the time on selling its consumer phone equipment business. Similarly, HealthMatics, a joint venture between Glaxo Smith Kline and Physician Computer Network Inc., shut down after losing more than $50 million.

While early surveys suggested that as many as half the companies with international joint ventures were dissatisfied with their ventures' performance, there is reason to believe that some of the earlier concern can now be ameliorated. This is primarily because there is far greater alliance experience and insight to draw from. There is now widespread appreciation that joint ventures are not necessarily transitional organization forms, shorter-lived, or less profitable. For many organizations they are the mode of choice.

There now also exists an Association of Strategic Alliance Professionals (ASAP). It was created to support the professional development of alliance managers and executives to advance the state-of-the-art of alliance formation and management and to provide a forum for sharing alliance best practices, resources and opportunities to help companies improve their alliance management capabilities.

Why do managers keep creating new joint ventures? The reasons are presented in the remainder of this reading, as are some guidelines for international joint venture success.

Why Companies Create International Joint Ventures

International joint ventures can be used to achieve one of four basic purposes. As shown in **Exhibit 1,** these are: to strengthen the firm's existing business, to take the firm's existing products into new

Exhibit 1   Motives for International Joint Venture Formation

		Existing Products	New Products
New Markets		To take existing products to foreign markets	To diversify into a new business
Existing Markets		To strengthen the existing business	To bring foreign products to local markets

markets, to obtain new products that can be sold in the firm's existing markets, and to diversify into a new business.

Companies using joint ventures for each of these purposes will have different concerns and will be looking for partners with different characteristics. Firms wanting to strengthen their existing business, for example, will most likely be looking for partners among their current competitors, while those wanting to enter new geographic markets will be looking for overseas firms in related businesses with good local market knowledge. Although often treated as a single category of business activity, international joint ventures are remarkably diverse, as the following descriptions indicate.

Strengthening the Existing Business   International joint ventures are used in a variety of ways by firms wishing to strengthen or protect their existing businesses. Among the most important are joint ventures formed to achieve economies of scale, joint ventures that allow the firm to acquire needed technology and know-how, and ventures that reduce the financial risk of major projects. Joint ventures formed for the latter two reasons may have the added benefit of eliminating a potential competitor from a particular product or market area.

Achieving Economies of Scale   Firms often use joint ventures to attempt to match the economies of scale achieved by their larger competitors. Joint ventures have been used to give their parents economies of scale in raw material and component supply, in research and development, and in marketing and distribution. Joint ventures have also been used as a vehicle for carrying out divisional mergers, which yield economies across the full spectrum of business activity.

Very small, entrepreneurial firms are more likely to participate in a network than an equity joint venture in order to strengthen their business through economies of scale. Small firms may form a network to reduce the costs, and increase the potential, of foreign market entry, or to meet some other focused objective. Most of these networks

tend to have a relatively low ease of entry and exit and a loose structure and require a limited investment (primarily time, as they might be self-financing through fees). International equity joint ventures by very small firms are unusual because such firms must typically overcome some combination of liabilities of size, newness, foreignness, and relational orientation (often the small firms were initially successful because of their single-minded, do-it-themselves orientation).

Raw Material and Component Supply   In many industries the smaller firms create joint ventures to obtain raw materials or jointly manufacture components. Automakers, for instance, may develop a jointly owned engine plant to supply certain low-volume engines to each company. Producing engines for the parents provides economies of scale, with each company receiving engines at a lower cost than it could obtain if it were to produce them itself.

The managers involved in such ventures are quick to point out that these financial savings do not come without a cost. Design changes in jointly produced engines, for example, tend to be slow because all partners have to agree on them. In fact, one joint venture that produced computer printers fell seriously behind the state of the art in printer design because the parents could not agree on the features they wanted in the jointly designed printer. Because all of the venture's output was sold to the parents, the joint venture personnel had no direct contact with end customers and could not resolve the dispute.

Transfer pricing is another issue that arises in joint ventures that supply their parents. A low transfer price on products shipped from the venture to the parents, for instance, means that whichever parent buys the most product obtains the most benefit. Many higher-volume-taking parents claim that this is fair, as it is their volume that plays an important role in making the joint venture viable. On the other hand, some parents argue for a higher transfer price, which means that the economic benefits are captured in the venture and will flow, most likely via dividends, to the parents in proportion to their share holdings in the venture. As the share holdings generally reflect the original asset contributions to the venture and not the volumes taken out every year, this means that different parents will do well under this arrangement. Clearly, the potential for transfer price disputes is significant.

Research and Development   Shared research and development efforts are increasingly common. The rationale for such programs is that participating firms can save both time and money by collaborating and may, by combining the efforts of the participating companies' scientists, come up with results that would otherwise have been impossible.

The choice facing firms wishing to carry out collaborative research is whether to simply coordinate their efforts and share costs or to actually set up a jointly owned company. Hundreds of multi-company research programs are not joint ventures. Typically, scientists from the participating companies agree on the research objectives and the most likely avenues of exploration to achieve those objectives. If there are, say, four promising ways to attack a particular problem, each of four participating companies would be assigned one route and told to pursue it. Meetings would be held, perhaps quarterly, to share results and approaches taken and when (hopefully) one route proved to be successful, all firms would be fully informed on the new techniques and technology.

The alternative way to carry out collaborative research is to establish a jointly owned company and to provide it with staff, budget, and a physical location. Yet even here, problems may occur. In the United States, the president of a joint research company established by a dozen U.S. computer firms discovered that the participating companies were not sending their best people to the new company. He ended up hiring more than 200 of the firm's 330 scientists from the outside.

A sensitive issue for firms engaging in collaborative research, whether through joint ventures or not, is how far the collaboration should extend. Because the partners are usually competitors, the often expressed ideal is that the joint effort will focus only on "precompetitive" basic research and not,

for example, on product development work. This is often a difficult line to draw.

Marketing and Distribution   Many international joint ventures involve shared research, development, and production but stop short of joint marketing. The vehicles which came out of the NUMMI joint venture between Toyota and General Motors in California, which ceased operations in 2010, were clearly branded as GM or Toyota products and were sold competitively through each parent's distribution network. More recently, General Motors and South Korea's LG Corp. announced a joint venture to develop electric and hybrid vehicles by combining General Motors strength as an automaker with LG's leadership in electronics and lithium-ion battery technologies. Under the terms of the joint venture, LG is authorized to market any technologies that it co-develops with General Motors to other companies. Antitrust plays a role in the decision to keep marketing activities separate, but so does the partners' intrinsic desire to maintain separate brand identities and increase their own market share. These cooperating firms have not forgotten that they are competitors.

There are, nevertheless, some ventures formed for the express purpose of achieving economies in marketing and distribution. Here, each firm is hoping for wider market coverage at a lower cost. The trade-off is a loss of direct control over the sales force, potentially slower decision making, and a possible loss of direct contact with the customer.

Somewhat similar in intent are cooperative marketing agreements, which are not joint ventures but agreements by two firms with related product lines to sell one another's products. Here companies end up with a more complete line to sell, without the managerial complications of a joint venture. Sometimes the cooperative marketing agreement can in fact entail joint branding.

Divisional Mergers   Multinational companies with subsidiaries that they have concluded are too small to be economic have sometimes chosen to create a joint venture by combining their "too small" operations with those of a competitor. Fiat and Peugeot, for example, merged their automobile operations in Argentina, where both companies were doing poorly. The new joint venture started life with a market share of 35 percent and a chance for greatly improved economies in design, production, and marketing. Faced with similar pressures, Ford and Volkswagen did the same thing in Brazil, creating a jointly owned company called Auto Latina.

A divisional merger can also allow a firm a graceful exit from a business in which it is no longer interested. Honeywell gave up trying to continue alone in the computer industry when it folded its business into a venture with Machines Bull of France and NEC of Japan. Honeywell held a 40 percent stake in the resulting joint venture.

Acquiring Technology in the Core Business
Firms that have wanted to acquire technology in their core business area have traditionally done so through license agreements or by developing the technology themselves. Increasingly, however, companies are turning to joint ventures for this purpose, because developing technology in-house is seen as taking too long, and license agreements, while giving the firm access to patent rights and engineers' ideas, may not provide much in the way of shop floor know-how. The power of a joint venture is that a firm may be able to have its employees working shoulder to shoulder with those of its partner, trying to solve the same problems. For example, the General Motors joint venture with Toyota provided an opportunity for GM to obtain a source of low-cost small cars and to watch firsthand how Toyota managers, who were in operational control of the venture, were able to produce high-quality automobiles at low cost. Some observers even concluded that the opportunity for General Motors to learn new production techniques was potentially more valuable—if absorbed—than the supply of cars coming from the venture. More recently, General Motors' joint venture arrangement with LG Corp. has been designed to position General Motors to co-develop battery-powered vehicles more quickly than its competitors, as auto manufacturers

race to develop vehicles that will comply with new fuel economy regulations in the United States.

Reducing Financial Risk   Some projects are too big or too risky for firms to tackle alone. This is why oil companies use joint ventures to split the costs of searching for new oil fields, and why the aircraft industry is increasingly using joint ventures and "risk-sharing subcontractors" to put up some of the funds required to develop new aircraft and engines. When General Motors announced its joint venture to develop battery-powered vehicles with LG Corp., General Motors' Vice Chairman, Steve Girsky, was quoted as saying, "We don't know how big this market is going to be. This is a way to go at it in an efficient way that doesn't risk the company."

Do such joint ventures make sense? For the oil companies the answer is a clear yes. In these ventures, one partner takes a lead role and manages the venture on a day-to-day basis. Management complexity, a major potential drawback of joint ventures, is kept to a minimum. If the venture finds oil, transfer prices are not a problem—the rewards of the venture are easy to divide between the partners. In situations like this, forming a joint venture is an efficient and sensible way of sharing risk.

It is not as obvious that some other industry ventures are a good idea, at least not for industry leaders. Their partners are not entering these ventures simply in the hopes of earning an attractive return on their investment. They are gearing up to produce, sooner or later, their own product. Why would a company be willing to train potential competitors? For many firms, it is the realization that their partner is going to hook up with someone anyway, so better to have a portion of a smaller future pie than none at all, even if it means you may be eventually competing against yourself. This is consistent with the old adage: keep your friends close, and your enemies (here competitors) even closer.

Taking Products to Foreign Markets   Firms with domestic products that they believe will be successful in foreign markets face a choice. They can produce the product at home and export it, license the technology to local firms around the world, establish wholly owned subsidiaries in foreign countries, or form joint ventures with local partners. Many firms conclude that exporting is unlikely to lead to significant market penetration, building wholly owned subsidiaries is too slow and requires too many resources, and licensing does not offer an adequate financial return. The result is that an international joint venture, while seldom seen as an ideal choice, is often the most attractive compromise.

Moving into foreign markets entails a degree of risk, and most firms that decide to form a joint venture with a local firm are doing so to reduce the risk associated with their new market entry. Very often, they look for a partner that deals with a related product line and, thus, has a good feel for the local market. As a further risk-reducing measure, the joint venture may begin life as simply a sales and marketing operation, until the product begins to sell well and volumes rise. Then a "screwdriver" assembly plant may be set up to assemble components shipped from the foreign parent. Eventually, the venture may modify or redesign the product to better suit the local market and may establish complete local manufacturing, sourcing raw material and components locally. The objective is to withhold major investment until the market uncertainty is reduced.

Following Customers to Foreign Markets   Another way to reduce the risk of a foreign market entry is to follow firms that are already customers at home. Thus, many Japanese automobile suppliers have followed Honda, Toyota, and Nissan as they set up new plants in North America and Europe. Very often these suppliers, uncertain of their ability to operate in a foreign environment, decide to form a joint venture with a local partner. There are, for example, a great many automobile supplier joint ventures in the United States originally formed between Japanese and American auto suppliers to supply the Japanese "transplant" automobile manufacturers. For the Americans, such ventures provide a way to learn Japanese manufacturing techniques

and to tap into a growing market. Additionally, some joint ventures are established to satisfy legal requirements in order to permit a firm to follow its customers abroad. The Chinese air transport industry is regulated by laws that limit foreign ownership. NetJets, a Berkshire Hathaway subsidiary that specializes in private jet management, indicated that demand from existing customers in the United States and Europe, in addition to demand from prospective Chinese customers, motivated its entry into a joint venture with a consortium of Chinese investors to provide private aircraft management services within China to both corporate and individual clients.

Investing in "Markets of the Future"   Some joint ventures are established by firms taking an early position in what they see as emerging markets. These areas offer very large untapped markets, as well as a possible source of low-cost raw materials and labor. The major problems faced by Western firms in penetrating such markets are their unfamiliarity with the local culture, establishing Western attitudes toward quality, and, in some areas, repatriating earnings in hard currency. The solution (sometimes imposed by local government) has often been the creation of joint ventures with local partners who "know the ropes" and can deal with the local bureaucracy.

Bringing Foreign Products to Local Markets For every firm that uses an international joint venture to take its product to a foreign market, a local company sees the joint venture as an attractive way to bring foreign products to its existing market. It is, of course, this complementarity of interest that makes the joint venture possible. For example, Starbucks planned entry into India has been structured as a 50/50 joint venture agreement with Tata Global Beverages. While India has been traditionally regarded as a tea-drinking nation, consuming more than 800,000 metric tons of tea in 2010, both Starbucks and its Indian joint venture partner are optimistic that the country's more modest but increasing consumption of coffee (approximately 100,000 metric tons in 2010) will position the joint venture to succeed in developing the coffee chain's retail presence in India.

Local partners enter joint ventures to get better utilization of existing plants or distribution channels, to protect themselves against threatening new technology, or simply as an impetus for new growth. Typically, the financial rewards that the local partner receives from a venture are different from those accruing to the foreign partner. For example:

- Many foreign partners make a profit shipping finished products and components to their joint ventures. These profits are particularly attractive because they are in hard currency, which may not be true of the venture's profits, and because the foreign partner captures 100 percent of them, not just a share.
- Many foreign partners receive a technology fee, which is a fixed percentage of the sales volume of the joint venture. The local partner may or may not receive a management fee of like amount.
- Foreign partners typically pay a withholding tax on dividends remitted to them from the venture. Local firms do not.

As a result of these differences, the local partner is often far more concerned with the venture's bottom line earnings and dividend payout than the foreign partner. This means the foreign partner is likely to be happier to keep the venture as simply a marketing or assembly operation, as previously described, than to develop it to the point where it buys less imported material.

Although this logic is understandable, such thinking is shortsighted. The best example of the benefits that can come back to a parent from a powerful joint venture is Fuji Xerox, a venture begun in Japan in 1962 between Xerox and Fuji Photo. This is among the best known American–Japanese joint ventures in Japan.

For the first 10 years of its life, Fuji Xerox was strictly a marketing organization. It did its best to sell Xerox copiers in the Japanese market, even though the U.S. company had done nothing to adapt the machine to the Japanese market. For example,

to reach the print button on one model, Japanese secretaries had to stand on a box. After 10 years of operation, Fuji Xerox began to manufacture its own machines, and by 1975 it was redesigning U.S. equipment for the Japanese market. Soon thereafter, with the encouragement of Fuji Photo, and in spite of the resistance of Xerox engineers in the United States, the firm began to design its own copier equipment. Its goal was to design and build a copier in half the time and at half the cost of previous machines. When this was accomplished, the firm set its sights on winning the Deming award, a highly coveted Japanese prize for excellence in total quality control. Fuji Xerox won the award in 1980.

It was also in 1980 that Xerox, reeling under the impact of intense competition from Japanese copier companies, finally began to pay attention to the lessons that it could learn from Fuji Xerox. Adopting the Japanese joint venture's manufacturing techniques and quality programs, the parent company fought its way back to health in the mid-1980s. By 1991, Xerox International Partners was established as a joint venture between Fuji Xerox and Xerox Corporation to sell low-end printers in North America and Europe. In 1998, exports to the United States grew substantially with digital color copiers and COE printer engines. In 2000, Xerox Corporation transferred its China/Hong Kong Operations to Fuji Xerox and Fuji Photo raised its stake in the venture to 75 percent in 2001. By 2011, Fuji Xerox Co. Ltd. employed almost 43,000 people, had about $13.5 billion in revenues, was responsible for the design and manufacture of many digital color copiers and printers for Xerox worldwide, and was an active partner in research and development. Both the lessons learned from Fuji Xerox and the contributions they have made to Xerox have inevitably helped Xerox prosper as an independent company.

Using Joint Ventures for Diversification   As the previous examples illustrate, many joint ventures take products that one parent knows well into a market that the other knows well. However, some break new ground and move one or both parents into products and markets that are new to them.

Arrangements to acquire the skills necessary to compete in a new business is a long-term proposition, but one that some firms are willing to undertake. Given the fact that most acquisitions of unrelated businesses do not succeed, and that trying to enter a new business without help is extremely difficult, choosing partners who will help you learn the business may not be a bad strategy if you are already familiar with the partner. However, to enter a new market, with a new product, and a new partner—even when the probability of success for each is 80 percent—leaves one with an overall probability of success of (.8 .8 .8) about 50 percent!

Joint ventures can also be viewed as vehicles for learning. Here the modes of learning go beyond knowledge transfer (i.e., existing know-how) to include transformation and harvesting. In practice, most IJV partners engage in the transfer of existing knowledge, but stop short of knowledge transformation or harvesting. Although many multinational enterprises have very large numbers of international equity joint ventures and alliances, only a small percentage dedicate resources explicitly to learning about the alliance process. Few organizations go to the trouble of inventorying/cataloguing the corporate experience with joint ventures, let alone how the accumulated knowledge might be transferred within or between divisions. This oversight will be increasingly costly for firms, especially as some of the bilateral alliances become part of multilateral networks.

Requirements for International Joint Venture Success

The checklist in **Exhibit 2** presents many of the items that a manager should consider when establishing an international joint venture. Each of these is discussed in the following sections.

Testing the Strategic Logic   The decision to enter a joint venture should not be taken lightly. As mentioned earlier, joint ventures require a great deal of management attention, and, in spite of the care and attention they receive, many prove unsatisfactory to their parents.

Exhibit 2   Joint Venture Checklist

1. Test the strategic logic.
   - Do you really need a partner? For how long? Does your partner?
   - How big is the payoff for both parties? How likely is success?
   - Is a joint venture the best option?
   - Do congruent performance measures exist?
2. Partnership and fit.
   - Does the partner share your objectives for the venture?
   - Does the partner have the necessary skills and resources? Will you get access to them?
   - Will you be compatible?
   - Can you arrange an "engagement period"?
   - Is there a comfort versus competence trade-off?
3. Shape and design.
   - Define the venture's scope of activity and its strategic freedom vis-à-vis its parents.
   - Lay out each parent's duties and payoffs to create a win-win situation. Ensure that there are comparable contributions over time.
   - Establish the managerial role of each partner.
4. Doing the deal.
   - How much paperwork is enough? Trust versus legal considerations?
   - Agree on an endgame.
5. Making the venture work.
   - Give the venture continuing top management attention.
   - Manage cultural differences.
   - Watch out for inequities.
   - Be flexible.

Firms considering entering a joint venture should satisfy themselves that there is not a simpler way, such as a nonequity alliance, to get what they need. They should also carefully consider the time period for which they are likely to need help. Some joint ventures have been labeled "permanent solutions to temporary problems" by firms that entered a venture to get help on some aspect of their business; then, when they no longer needed the help, they were still stuck with the joint venture.

The same tough questions a firm may ask itself before forming a joint venture need to be asked of its partner(s). How long will the partner(s) need it? Is the added potential payoff high enough to each partner to compensate for the increased coordination/communications costs which go with the formation of a joint venture?

A major issue in the discussion of strategic logic is to determine whether congruent measures of performance exist. As **Exhibit 3** suggests, in many joint ventures, incongruity exists. In this example the foreign partner was looking for a joint venture that would generate 20 percent return on sales in a 1–2 year period and require a limited amount of senior management time. The local partner in turn was seeking a JV that would be quickly profitable and be able to justify some high-paying salaried positions (for the local partner and several family members/friends). While each partner's

performance objectives seem defensible, this venture would need to resolve several major problem areas in order to succeed. First, each partner did not make explicit all their primary performance objectives. Implicit measures (those below the dotted line in **Exhibit 3**), are a source of latent disagreement/misunderstanding. Second, the explicit versus implicit measures of each partner were internally inconsistent. The foreign partner wanted high profitability while using little senior management time and old technology. The local partner wanted quick profits but high-paying local salaries.

Congruity is not just an inter-partner issue. From an intra-partner perspective, it is also essential that the internal managers speak and act from a common platform.

Partnership and Fit Joint ventures are sometimes formed to satisfy complementary needs. But when one partner acquires (learns) another's capabilities, the joint venture becomes unstable. The acquisition of a partner's capabilities means that the partner is no longer needed. If capabilities are only

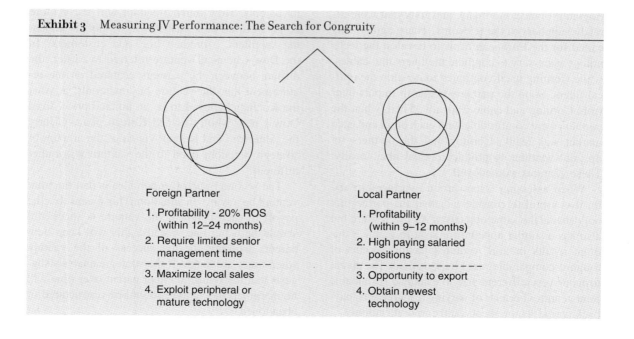

Exhibit 3   Measuring JV Performance: The Search for Congruity

Foreign Partner

1. Profitability - 20% ROS
   (within 12–24 months)
2. Require limited senior
   management time
   - - - - - - - - - - - - - - - -
3. Maximize local sales
4. Exploit peripheral or
   mature technology

Local Partner

1. Profitability
   (within 9–12 months)
2. High paying salaried
   positions
   - - - - - - - - - - - - - - - -
3. Opportunity to export
4. Obtain newest
   technology

accessed, the joint venture is more stable. It is not easy, before a venture begins, to determine many of the things a manager would most like to know about a potential partner, like the true extent of its capabilities, what its objectives are in forming the venture, and whether it will be easy to work with. A hasty answer to such questions may lead a firm into a bad relationship or cause it to pass up a good opportunity.

For these reasons, it is often best if companies begin a relationship in a small way, with a simple agreement that is important but not a matter of life and death to either parent. As confidence between the firms grows, the scope of the business activities can broaden.

A good example is provided by Corning Glass, which in 1970 made a major breakthrough in the development of optical fibers that could be used for telecommunication applications, replacing traditional copper wire or coaxial cable. The most likely customers of this fiber outside the United States were the European national telecoms, which were well known to be very nationalistic purchasers. To gain access to these customers, Corning set up development agreements with companies in England, France, Germany, and Italy that were already suppliers to the telecoms. These agreements called for the European firms to develop the technology necessary to combine the fibers into cables, while Corning itself continued to develop the optical fibers. Soon the partners began to import fiber from Corning and cable it locally. Then, when the partners were comfortable with each other and each market was ready, Corning and the partners set up joint ventures to produce optical fiber locally. These ventures worked well.

When assessing issues around partnership and fit, it is useful to consider whether the partner not only shares the same objectives for the venture but also has a similar appetite for risk. In practice this often results in joint ventures having parents of roughly comparable size. It is difficult for parent firms of very different size to establish sustainable joint ventures because of varying resource sets, payback period requirements, and corporate cultures.

Corporate culture similarity—or compatibility—can be a make-or-break issue in many joint ventures. It is not enough to find a partner with the necessary skills; you need to be able to get access to them and to be compatible. Managers are constantly told that they should choose a joint venture partner they trust. As these examples suggest, however, trust between partners is something that can only be developed over time as a result of shared experiences. You can't start with trust.

Shape and Design   In the excitement of setting up a new operation in a foreign country, or getting access to technology provided by an overseas partner, it is important not to lose sight of the basic strategic requirements that must be met if a joint venture is to be successful. The questions that must be addressed are the same when any new business is proposed: Is the market attractive? How strong is the competition? How will the new company compete? Will it have the required resources? And so on.

In addition to these concerns, three others are particularly relevant to joint venture design. One is the question of strategic freedom, which has to do with the relationship between the venture and its parents. How much freedom will the venture be given to do as it wishes with respect to choosing suppliers, a product line, and customers? In the Dow Chemical venture referred to earlier, the dispute between the partners centered on the requirement that the venture buy materials, at what the Koreans believed to be an inflated price, from Dow's new wholly owned Korean plant. Clearly the American and Korean vision of the amount of strategic freedom open to the venture was rather different.

The second issue of importance is that the joint venture be a win-win situation. This means that the payoff to each parent if the venture is successful should be a big one, because this will keep both parents working for the success of the venture when times are tough. If the strategic analysis suggests that the return to either parent over time will be marginal, the venture should be restructured or abandoned.

Finally, it is critical to decide on the management roles that each parent company will play. The venture will be easier to manage if one parent plays a dominant role and has a lot of influence over both the strategic and the day-to-day operations of the venture, or if one parent plays a lead role in the dayto-day operation of the joint venture. More difficult to manage are shared management ventures, in which both parents have a significant input into both strategic decisions and the everyday operations of the venture. A middle ground is split management decision making, where each partner has primary influence over those functional areas where it is most qualified. This is the most common and arguably most effective form.

In some ventures, the partners place too much emphasis on competing with each other about which one will have management control. They lose sight of the fact that the intent of the joint venture is to capture complementary benefits from two partners that will allow the venture (not one of the partners) to compete in the market better than would have been possible by going it alone.

The objective of most joint ventures is superior performance. Thus the fact that dominant-parent ventures are easier to manage than shared-management ventures does not mean they are the appropriate type of venture to establish. Dominant-parent ventures are most likely to be effective when one partner has the knowledge and skill to make the venture a success and the other party is contributing simply money, a trademark, or perhaps a one-time transfer of technology. Such a venture, however, begs the question "What are the unique continuing contributions of the partner?" Shared-management ventures are necessary when the venture needs active consultation between members of each parent company, as when deciding how to modify a product supplied by one parent for the local market that is well known by the other, or to modify a production process designed by one parent to be suitable for a workforce and working conditions well known by the other.

A joint venture is headed for trouble when a parent tries to take a larger role in its management than makes sense. An American company with a joint venture in Japan, for instance, insisted that one of its people be the executive vice president of the venture. This was not reasonable, because the manager had nothing to bring to the management of the venture. He simply served as a constant reminder to the Japanese that the American partner did not trust them. The Americans were pushing for a shared-management venture when it was more logical to allow the Japanese, who certainly had all the necessary skills, to be the dominant or at least the leading firm. The major American contribution to the venture was to allow it to use its world-famous trademarks and brand names.

A second example, also in Japan, involved a French firm. This company was bringing complex technology to the venture that needed to be modified for the Japanese market. It was clear that the French firm required a significant say in the management of the venture. On the other hand, the French had no knowledge of the Japanese market and, thus, the Japanese also needed a significant role in the venture. The logical solution would have been a shared-management venture and equal influence in decisions made at the board level. Unfortunately, both companies wanted to play a dominant role, and the venture collapsed in a decision-making stalemate.

Finally, every joint venture must resolve how much of the JV will be owned by each of the partners. Some firms equate ownership with control, assuming more is always better. Such an assumption would be incorrect. Research has shown that once a foreign firm has about a 40 percent equity stake, there is little difference in the survivability of that subsidiary than if they had had, for example, an 80 percent stake (see **Exhibit 4**).

Doing the Deal   Experienced managers argue that it is the relationship between the partners that is of key importance in a joint venture, not the legal agreement that binds them together. Nevertheless, most are careful to ensure that they have a good agreement in place—one that they understand and are comfortable with.

Most of the principal elements of a joint venture agreement are straightforward. One item that

Exhibit 4   Effect of Foreign Equity Holding on Subsidiary Mortality Risk

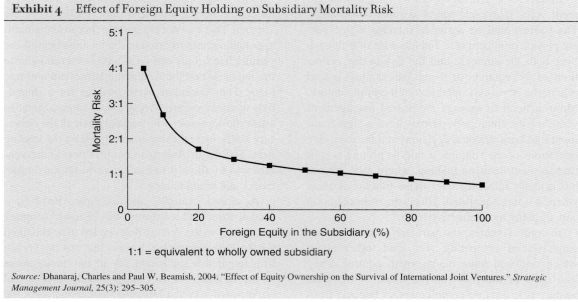

1:1 = equivalent to wholly owned subsidiary

Source: Dhanaraj, Charles and Paul W. Beamish. 2004. "Effect of Equity Ownership on the Survival of International Joint Ventures." *Strategic Management Journal,* 25(3): 295–305.

often goes un-discussed is the termination of the venture.

Although some managers balk at discussing termination during the getting-acquainted period, it is important to work out a method of terminating the venture in the event of a serious disagreement, and to do this at a time when heads are cool and goodwill abounds. The usual technique is to use a shotgun clause, which allows either party to name a price at which it will buy the other's shares in the venture. However, once this provision is activated and the first company has named a price, the second firm has the option of selling at this price or buying the first company's shares at the same price. This ensures that only fair offers are made, at least as long as both parents are large enough to be capable of buying each other out.

Making the Venture Work   Joint ventures need close and continuing attention, particularly in their early months. In addition to establishing a healthy working relationship between the parents and the venture general manager, and appropriate metrics, managers should be on the lookout for the impact that cultural differences may be having on the venture and for the emergence of unforeseen inequities.

International joint ventures, like any type of international activity, require that managers of different national cultures work together. This requires the selection of capable people in key roles. Unless managers have been sensitized to the characteristics of the culture that they are dealing with, this can lead to misunderstandings and serious problems. Many Western managers, for instance, are frustrated by the slow, consensus-oriented decision-making style of the Japanese. Equally, the Japanese find American individualistic decision making to be surprising, as the decisions are made so quickly, but the implementation is often so slow. Firms that are sophisticated in the use of international joint ventures are well aware of such problems and have taken action to minimize them. Ford, for example, has put more than 1,500 managers through courses to improve their ability to work with Japanese and Korean managers.

It is important to remember that cultural differences do not just arise from differences in nationality. For example:

- Small firms working with large partners are often surprised and dismayed by the fact that it can take months, rather than days, to get approval of a new project. In some cases the cultural differences appear to be greater between small and large firms of the same nationality than, say, between multinationals of different nationality, particularly if the multinationals are in the same industry.
- Firms working with two partners from the same country have been surprised to find how different the companies are in cultural habits. A Japanese automobile firm headquartered in rural Japan may be a very different company from one run from Tokyo.
- Cultural differences between managers working in different functional areas may be greater than those between managers in the same function in different firms. European engineers, for example, discovered when discussing a potential joint venture with an American partner that they had more in common with the American engineers than with the marketing people in their own company.

A very common joint venture problem is that the objectives of the parents, which coincided when the venture was formed, diverge over time. This divergence can be brought on by changes in the marketplace. For example, when the 50/50 joint venture between Sony and Ericsson was formed in 2001, both firms sought to improve their position in the growing high-end mobile handset market. Ten years later, with Apple dominating the premium end of the mobile handset market, Ericsson began to shift its focus to the supply of mobile and wireless networks, while Sony chose to focus its efforts on content delivery to personal computing devices such as tablets, PCs and mobile phones. Consequently, Sony acquired Ericsson's share of the joint venture, in order to facilitate Sony's efforts to capture greater market share in content delivery. Such divergences can also be brought on by changes in the fortunes of the partners. This was the case in the breakup of the General Motors–Daewoo joint venture in Korea. Relations between the partners were already strained due to GM's unwillingness to put further equity into the venture, in spite of a debt to equity ratio of more than 8 to 1, when, faced with rapidly declining market share, the Korean parent decided that the venture should go for growth and maximize market share. In contrast General Motors, itself in a poor financial position at the time, insisted that the emphasis be on current profitability. When Daewoo, without telling General Motors, introduced a concessionary financing program for the joint venture's customers, the relationship was damaged, never to recover.

A final note concerns the unintended inequities that may arise during the life of a venture. Due to an unforeseen circumstance, one parent may be winning from the venture while the other is losing. A venture established in the late 1990s between Indonesian and American parents, for instance, was buying components from the American parent at prices based in dollars. As the rupiah declined in value, the Indonesian partner could afford fewer components in each shipment. The advice of many experienced venture managers is that, in such a situation, a change in the original agreement should be made, so the hardship is shared between the parents. That was done in this case, and the venture is surviving, although it is not as profitable as originally anticipated.

In reviewing any checklist of the things to be considered when forming a joint venture, it is important to recognize that such a list will vary somewhat depending on where the international joint venture is established. The characteristics of joint ventures will vary according to whether they are established in developed versus emerging markets.

Most of the descriptions of the characteristics considered are self-explanatory. Yet, more fine-grained analyses are always possible. For

Exhibit 5   The True Joint Venture versus the Pseudo Joint Venture

	The True Alliance	The Pseudo Alliance
Planned level of parent input and involvement	Continuing	One-time
Distribution of risks/rewards	Roughly even	Uneven
Parent attitude toward the JV	A unique organization with unique needs	One more subsidiary
The formal JV agreement	Flexible guidelines	Frequently referenced rulebook
Performance objectives	Clearly specified and congruent	Partially overlapping/ambiguous

example, the discussion in this reading has generally assumed a traditional equity joint venture, one focused between two firms from two different countries. Yet other types of equity joint ventures exist, including those between firms from two different countries that set up in a third country (i.e., trinational), those formed between subsidiaries of the same MNE (i.e., intrafirm) and those formed with companies of the same nationality but located in a different country (i.e., cross-national domestic joint ventures). Further, many joint ventures have more than two partners. Interestingly, the traditional JVs (at least those formed by Japanese MNEs) tend to simultaneously be more profitable and to have a higher termination rate than the alternative structures available.

Summary

International joint ventures are an increasingly important part of the strategy of many firms. They are, however, sometime difficult to design and manage well, in part because some organizations do not treat them as "true" "joint" ventures (see **Exhibit 5**). The fact that some ventures are performing below their management's expectations should not be an excuse for firms to avoid such ventures. In many industries, the winners are going to be the companies that most quickly learn to manage international ventures effectively. The losers will be the managers who throw up their hands and say that joint ventures are too difficult, so we had better go it alone.

In the future, will we see more or fewer international joint ventures? Certainly the reduction in investment regulations in many countries, coupled with increased international experience by many firms, suggests there may be fewer joint ventures. Yet other countervailing pressures exist. With shortening product life cycles, it is increasingly difficult to go it alone. And with the increase in the number of MNEs from emerging markets, both the supply and demand of potential partners will likely escalate.

Reading 6-2 How to Manage Alliances Better Than One at a Time

By Ulrich Wassmer, Pierre Dussauge, and Marcel Planellas

Companies are remarkably myopic when they go about forming strategic partnerships. Systematizing the analysis process should produce more gain and less pain.

The French Food Giant Groupe Danone, long a leader in the Chinese market for beverages and

Ulrich Wassmer is a professor of management at Concordia University's John Molson School of Business in Montreal, Canada. **Pierre Dussauge** is a professor of strategic management at the HEC School of Management in Jouy-en-Josas, France. **Marcel Planellas** is a professor of business policy at the ESADE Business School in Barcelona, Spain.

Reprint 51305.

food products, has recently seen its position in this enormous market deteriorate drastically. The reason: Danone's strategic partnership with Hangzhou Wahaha Group Co. Ltd. is breaking up. Wahaha became the dominant player in the Chinese bottled water and other nonalcoholic beverage market through its 1996 alliance with Danone. But by 2007, Wahaha was blaming Danone for setting up competing joint ventures with other local companies, such as Robust, Aquarius, Mengniu Dairy and Bright Dairy & Food, while Danone was suing Wahaha for using the brand outside the scope of their joint ventures. Wahaha retaliated by dragging several Danone officials to court for conflict of interest because of their simultaneous membership

PARTNERING

By failing to analyze the consequences of partnering with McDonnell Douglas, CASA, a Spanish aerospace and defense company, ultimately damaged its long-standing prior partnership

on the boards of the Wahaha-Danone joint venture and other competing joint ventures Danone had in China. As a result, the relationship further deteriorated, and over 30 lawsuits were eventually filed on three different continents. By the end of 2009, a settlement was reached in which Danone pulled out of the alliance, which had accounted for a dominant share of the French company's sales in China of almost US$3 billion—about 10% of its total worldwide sales.

The Leading Question   How can companies form strategic alliances that create value on a stand-alone basis and at the alliance portfolio level?

Findings

- Use an alliance business case framework that takes into account the costs and benefits on both levels.
- Empower an individual or a department to oversee alliance formation decisions.
- Implement an integrated and codified decision process.

Danone's bungled approach to the formation of corporate alliances probably resulted in the destruction of several billion dollars' worth of market capitalization. Our study of how companies make decisions on the formation of alliances shows that this sort of dysfunctional behavior is all too common. Most companies now maintain an alliance portfolio comprising multiple simultaneous alliances with different partners.[1] In the global air transportation industry, for example, most airlines maintain broad portfolios of code-sharing alliances with other carriers, which allow them to significantly extend their route networks by offering services to their partners' destinations. In 1994, the average number of alliances per airline company

was only four. By 2008, however, the picture had changed dramatically: The average alliance portfolio size across the industry had increased to 12, with some airlines engaging simultaneously in as many as 30 or 40 alliances.[2] Despite this proliferation of corporate collaborations, research reveals a troublesome pattern. When a company adds a new alliance to its portfolio, it tends to focus on how much value the alliance will create as a stand-alone transaction but ignore the fact that the composition of its entire alliance portfolio is an important determinant of the value that will come from a new alliance. In other words, an alliance opportunity that promises to create value from a stand-alone perspective may not necessarily be value-creating from an alliance portfolio perspective. The formation of the new alliance may even be an overall value-destroying move.

By studying the global air transportation industry, we found concrete evidence of this proposition. (See "About the Research.") Formations of alliances that create synergies with other alliances in an existing alliance portfolio have a more positive effect on companies' stock prices than alliances with little or no synergy-creating potential. We also found that the stock market penalizes companies that enter into alliances that create conflict in the form of market overlap with existing alliance partners. Structural incentives at many companies often encourage a process that results in actions that may benefit one business unit while hurting the corporate whole.

Observation of this phenomenon raises three questions. Why do companies behave so thoughtlessly when forming alliances? What are the impediments to a more strategic approach to configuring effective alliance portfolios? And, finally, what's the way out—that is, what systems and processes should organizations adopt that will enable them to optimize the value of their alliance portfolios?

Understanding the counterproductive incentives that skew alliance formation allows us to propose a new decision-making process that we believe will

---

[1]See, for example, S. Parise and A. Casher, "Alliance Portfolios: Designing and Managing Your Network of Business-Partner Relationships," *Academy of Management Executive* 17, no. 4 (2003): 25–39; W.H. Hoffmann, "Strategies for Managing a Portfolio of Alliances," *Strategic Management Journal* 28, no. 8 (2007): 827–856; and U. Wassmer, "Alliance Portfolios: A Review and Research Agenda," *Journal of Management* 36, no. 1 (2010): 141–171.

[2]"Airline Business Alliance Survey," *Airline Business*, 1994–2008.

About the Research

We conducted two types of research. First, we conducted qualitative research and interviewed executives involved in alliance decisions in globally operating companies from industries in which alliance portfolios are an important strategic device and an essential part of business strategy. More specifically, we interviewed executives from the global air transportation sector (American Airlines, Air Canada, Air France, Delta Air Lines, Deutsche Lufthansa and others), packaged goods (Danone), aerospace and defense (EADS, SAFRAN), financial services (Banco Santander, Banco Bilbao Vizcaya Argentaria) and telecommunications (Telefónica de España, Ningbo Bird).

Second, we conducted quantitative research on companies in the global air transportation industry to better understand how alliance portfolios affect the value the companies derive from individual alliance formations. We examined 24 publicly traded, internationally operating airlines from 19 countries and their alliance portfolios as well as 259 formations of code-sharing alliances of these companies over a five-year period. We applied event study methodology and tracked the abnormal stock market returns following the announcements of the code-sharing alliances. To examine how the alliance portfolios of these 24 companies contribute to the explanation of the abnormal stock market return following individual alliance formations, we operationalized various alliance portfolio level measures and applied multivariate statistical techniques to analyze the impact on company value.

encourage companies to shift from the currently prevalent ad hoc approach to a smarter approach. In particular, companies should manage their alliances not as stand-alone arrangements but much more strategically, paying far more attention to how their various partnerships interact with one another.

Pitfalls of Alliance Portfolio Expansion

Alliance portfolios often result from a "sedimentary" accumulation process. That is, companies engage in multiple alliances over time, and all these partnerships accumulate haphazardly. Most alliances—even far-reaching partnerships that profoundly affect companies' overall performance—are initiated on an operational level as ad hoc responses to local business issues. In contrast, broad alliances promoted at the corporate level rarely translate into any actual business development.

As a result, one part of an organization, such as a business unit, will enter into partnerships that serve its own parochial interests, often without realizing or without regard for the impact on other parts of the organization or the company as a whole. It is not surprising that alliance formation decisions are often local matters and that coordination across units in the organization tends to be limited. Because business problems, and thus alliance formation opportunities, often are located in different units within an organization, problem owners are rarely the same individual. The issues associated with creating an alliance tend to affect different managers, who may interact with one another rarely, if ever. From an alliance portfolio perspective, such bottom-up alliance formation decision making is especially problematic when decision makers focus exclusively on criteria relevant to their local business problems and ignore how the new alliance fits into the company's alliance portfolio. Companies implement patchwork solutions that address problems for parts of a company but may actually create new troubles for other parts. The net result is often a failure to create value for the company overall—or, worse, a destruction of value overall.

Explanations for such silo thinking are manifold. Business-unit managers tend to have clear performance targets that are intrinsically linked to the success of their own units; this naturally leads to the prioritization of local needs over broader corporate needs. Academic research has also shown that managers frequently behave opportunistically and use alliance formations as ways to improve their own freedom of action.[3] Indeed, because alliance management is shared with a partner and because interpersonal relationships are often crucial in this process, it is difficult for corporate-level management to interfere. As a result, business-unit managers find themselves with a great deal of autonomy in alliance affairs.

Consider, for example, the decision of Construcciones Aeronauticas SA or CASA, a Spanish aerospace and defense company, to partner with McDonnell Douglas Corp. in the 1980s. This move originated at the plant level: CASA had idle manufacturing capacity that needed to be utilized. By becoming a partner in McDonnell Douglas's MD-80 commercial airliner project, CASA was able to create activity for one of its factories in Seville, Spain. The alliance with McDonnell Douglas thus solved a local business problem (unused manufacturing capacity). From an alliance portfolio perspective, however, the move was problematic. Since 1971, CASA had been collaborating with Airbus—a McDonnell Douglas rival and the manufacturer of the A319 aircraft, a direct competitor of the MD-80. As a result of its partnership with McDonnell Douglas, CASA's standing with Airbus suffered and it was not able to increase its share in new Airbus projects as it had hoped. Because the Seville plant was not involved in the Airbus collaboration, its managers lacked the perspective to fully understand and evaluate the consequences that would follow from teaming up with McDonnell Douglas.

Nor is that the only instance of a new alliance formation that appeared to be value-creating when viewed as a stand-alone transaction but turned out to be value-destroying from an alliance portfolio perspective. In the 1990s, the Spanish telecommunications company Telefónica de España maintained a key alliance with Unisource NV, a consortium that included telecommunications providers Koninklijke

KPN N.V. of the Netherlands; Stockholm, Sweden-based Telia; Swiss Telecom; and AT&T World Partners. In the late 1990s, one of Telefónica's business units, Telefónica Internacional or TISA, engaged in an alliance with Concert, a venture between British Telecom and MCI, in order to promote business in Latin America. While TISA managers focused on the value that Concert could add to Telefónica, they ignored the alliance's value-destroying effect from the portfolio-level perspective. Shortly after the TISA-Concert alliance was formed, Unisource partners raised concerns that Concert was becoming AT&T World Partners' main competitor and asked Telefónica to leave the Unisource alliance. As part of its exit, Telefónica paid more than 14 billion pesetas to Unisource (about US$94 million).

Making Alliances Fit

How can companies create alliances that not only are valuable at the local business-unit level but also work together to comprise a coherent alliance portfolio—a portfolio that is worth more than the sum of its parts? One part of the answer lies in having a corporate-level department that coordinates all alliance-related activity across a company's multiple units.[4] Such a department—what we call an alliance function—is crucial in ensuring the overall effectiveness of the alliance portfolio. Even though ideas for alliances have to come from low down in the organization, there must be an overall alliance portfolio compatibility check in order to ensure that value is created not only on the local, and thus individual, alliance level but also on the alliance portfolio level.

A dedicated alliance function should keep track of the alliance portfolio as it evolves over time and manage the balance between local problem solving and overall alliance portfolio effectiveness. The reality, however, is that such functions are often

[3]J.J. Reuer and R. Ragozzino, "Agency Hazards and Alliance Portfolios," *Strategic Management Journal* 27, no. 1 (2006): 27–43.

[4]P. Kale, J.H. Dyer and H. Singh, "Alliance Capability, Stock Market Response and Long-Term Alliance Success: The Role of the Alliance Function," *Strategic Management Journal* 23, no. 8 (2002): 747–767; and P. Kale, J.H. Dyer and H. Singh, "Value Creation and Success in Strategic Alliances: Alliancing Skills and the Role of Alliance Structure and Systems," *European Management Journal* 19, no. 5 (2001): 463–471.

performed by one of many internal corporate consulting units. Such units are run as cost centers, and their managers typically have little power over operational decision makers. Conflict between such a central function and the business unit that initiates particular alliances is often unavoidable due to diverging performance measures and interests. Although a dedicated alliance function is measured against overall alliance portfolio effectiveness and how well it enforces the company's overall alliance policy, individual alliances often tie into business-unit performance metrics for which the alliance initiator is responsible. The buck essentially stops at the business unit, not at the corporate staff level where the portfolio is coordinated.

Based on our research, we put forward a framework that will help managers to systematically make alliance formation decisions by considering interests both on the local and the alliance portfolio levels. The following three elements can help managers address this challenge: (1) an alliance business case framework that takes into account costs and benefits on the individual level as well as the alliance portfolio level of analysis, (2) an integrated and codified decision process involving managers on the business as well as the corporate levels, and (3) clearly defined roles and responsibilities for all actors involved in decision making.

Holistic Cost-Benefit Analysis

By engaging in strategic alliances, companies incur both costs and benefits.[5] Rationally behaving companies will enter into an alliance only when it creates value—that is, when its expected benefits exceed its

Between 1994 and 2008, the average number of alliances in the airline industry jumped from four to 12.

costs.[6] The construction of a business case for each alliance formation is therefore essential.[7]

Typically, alliance business cases tend to take into account only those benefits and costs that occur for a particular alliance, in isolation from existing ones. But such a myopic cost-benefit evaluation can be misleading. An alliance viewed on a stand-alone basis may appear to create value—but when the benefits and costs on the alliance portfolio level of analysis are taken into account, the picture can be quite different. To construct a robust business case, therefore, companies need to identify and quantify a broad range of benefits and costs both at the level of the individual alliance and at the portfolio level.

Costs and Benefits: Individual Alliance   Viewed on a stand-alone basis, alliances can help companies do four things:

- **Achieve economies of scale by pooling similar assets, knowledge or skills.** For example, Volkswagen AG and Renault S.A. teamed up to jointly develop and produce automatic gearboxes because the market for automatic cars in Europe

[5]P.J. Buckley and M. Casson, "A Theory of Cooperation in International Business," in "Cooperative Strategies in International Business," ed. F.J. Contractor and P. Lorange (Lexington, Massachusetts: Lexington Books, 1988): 31–53; A. Madhok and S.B. Tallman, "Resources, Transactions and Rents: Managing Value Through Inter-firm Collaborative Relationships," *Organization Science* 9, no. 3 (1998): 326–339; S.H. Park and D. Zhou, "Firm Heterogeneity and Competitive Dynamics in Alliance Formation," *Academy of Management Review* 30, no. 3 (2005): 531–554; and S. White and S.S. Lui, "Distinguishing Costs of Cooperation and Control in Alliances," *Strategic Management Journal* 26, no. 10 (2005): 913–932.

[6]Buckley and Casson, "Theory of Cooperation"; J. Koh and N. Venkatraman, "Joint Venture Formations and Stock Market Reactions: An Assessment in the Information Technology Sector," *Academy of Management Journal* 34, no. 4 (1991): 869–892; and Madhok and Tallman, "Resources, Transactions and Rents."

[7]J.H. Dyer, P. Kale and H. Singh, "How to Make Strategic Alliances Work," *MIT Sloan Management Review* 42, no. 4 (summer 2001): 37–43.

is small and neither company had large enough volume to achieve efficient production volumes.

- **Obtain access to a partner's complementary assets, knowledge and skills.** For example, Volkswagen teamed up with Shanghai Automotive Industry Corp. to create Shanghai VW, which leveraged VW's products and technology into China, where SAIC had local knowledge and access to manufacturing and distribution assets.
- **Obtain access to new skills.** Similarly, General Motors Co. and Toyota Motor Corp. formed the NUMMI alliance so that GM could learn about Toyota's lean manufacturing process and Toyota could take a cue from GM on how to deal with U.S. labor unions.
- **Reduce competition in the market and increase market power.** Rather than competing individually, DaimlerChrysler Aerospace AG (DASA), British Aerospace, CASA and Aerospatiale Matra formed the Airbus alliance, offering a jointly developed and manufactured product. The companies thus benefited from a less crowded playing field within the European market for commercial aircraft.

Still working from this stand-alone perspective, we can see that alliances also create costs for their partners. Most apparent are start-up costs, along with ongoing coordination costs. More subtle are the costs that stem from unexpected leakage, where one partner in the alliance acts opportunistically and appropriates skills or knowledge from the other. There are numerous examples of alliances in which one partner appropriates skills and knowledge from the other partner in an opportunistic fashion. Such poaching has afflicted even the seemingly genteel business of flower breeding. Meilland International, headquartered in France and one of the world's leading developers of rose hybrids, found that one of its former Chinese licensees was growing and marketing several of its patented varieties on a very large scale without paying any royalties.[8]

But it is not sufficient to focus only on the costs and benefits at the level of individual alliances: The alliance business case needs to be pushed further, to its impact at the level of a company's entire alliance portfolio.

Costs and Benefits: Alliance Portfolio   The benefits that a new alliance can create on the alliance portfolio level mainly stem from ways in which the new alliance and the existing ones can enhance each other. Two types of synergy are:

- **Sharing or recombining know-how.** Assets, knowledge and skills contributed or developed by a new alliance may be used in another, ongoing alliance. A new alliance may help a company develop a technology that may be of use in an existing alliance. Similarly, assets and knowledge contributed or developed by a new alliance may be combined with those associated with an existing alliance to create a new service or product. For example, California-based on-demand service provider Salesforce.com inc. has a portfolio of alliances that allows the company to combine physical and intellectual assets from various alliance partners to offer a more comprehensive service to its customers. Salesforce.com teamed up with Google Inc. to offer a joint product called Salesforce for Google Apps, a business productivity application that allows "business professionals to communicate, collaborate and work together in real time over the Web."[9] In order to offer its customers more computing power and allow them to host public Web sites and company intranets over its Force.com platform, Salesforce.com also engaged in an alliance with Amazon.com Inc. The online retailer, which maintains a vast network of servers, makes excess server capacity available to Saleforce.com. Thus, Salesforce.com is able to leverage both alliances and offer a broader and more comprehensive service to its customers.

[8] P. Dussauge, "Alliances, Joint-Ventures and Chinese Multinationals," in "Chinese Multinationals," ed. J.P. Larçon (Hackensack, New Jersey: World Scientific Publishing Company, 2008).

[9] "Salesforce.com and Google Introduce Salesforce for Google Apps: First Cloud Computing Suite for Business Productivity," April 14, 2008, www.google.com.

- **Reinforcing existing coalitions.** The airline industry provides a good example of this type of synergy. As a consequence of merging with Air France, KLM joined the Skyteam alliance that had previously been formed by Air France and Delta Air Lines Inc., while retaining its own long-standing relationship with Northwest Airlines Corp. Northwest eventually decided to follow its long-time partner KLM into Skyteam, rather than partner with other airlines, which strengthened the existing coalition. (Some years after this move, Northwest merged with Delta.)

The costs on the alliance portfolio level that a new alliance can create mainly stem from conflict resolution in existing alliances. These costs are related to re-establishing trust and good will with an existing alliance partner and can arise when a new alliance interferes with the relationship between a company and its existing partners. Such a disturbance may occur when the new alliance represents a competitive threat toward the existing partner—perhaps through imitating the other partner's technology or offering similar products or services.

When a newly formed alliance overlaps in product or market scope with an existing partner's business operations, the focal company may not only incur increased conflict resolution costs but in the worst case may also have to bear the consequences associated with dissolving the pre-existing alliance. An existing partner may decide to terminate an alliance altogether as a reaction to the formation of a new alliance and the resulting conflict. Such termination can result in the loss of valuable resources and particular revenue streams and therefore create a cost, as in the unhappy story of Danone and Wahaha.

Other examples can be found in the airline industry. British Airways Plc's decision to engage in an alliance with American Airlines Inc. directly led to the termination by US Airways Group Inc. of its existing code-share and frequent flyer partnership with British Airways. USAir likely felt threatened by the new links that BA was forging with American. Although BA called USAir's move "disappointing and puzzling,"[10] USAir may have suspected that BA would systematically favor its relationship with American, a larger and more powerful airline. BA might, for example, direct most of its flights toward American's hub cities or optimize its connections with American at USAir's expense. Another example is Singapore Airlines Limited, which entered into a multipartner alliance with Delta and Swissair involving equity swaps. Later, however, Singapore Airlines entered into a code-sharing and joint marketing agreement with Deutsche Lufthansa AG, leading to the termination of its alliance with Delta and Swissair.

The second source of tension between new partnerships and existing ones becomes salient when the focal company incurs costs associated with redundancy and value cannibalization as a result of a new alliance. Overlap in scope between a new alliance and an existing one can diminish either's benefits. It's true that redundancy is sometimes created deliberately to pursue various simultaneous options and thus spread risks, especially in research and development alliances to develop competing technologies. Nevertheless, companies that pursue such a strategy will incur redundancy costs because they will have to staff more people on the alliances than they would if they only had one alliance.

Toward Smarter Alliance Formation

Sound alliance formation decisions require an integrated decision process that involves actors on the business level as well as the corporate level in order to ensure a systematic assessment of the proposed alliance as well as the alliance portfolio level benefits and costs. The first phase of such a decision process should take an individual alliance perspective and the second phase an alliance portfolio perspective. Companies should assess alliance opportunities according to a rigorous set of criteria. (See "Alliance Assessment Decision Process.") By systematizing what is at present done on a mostly ad hoc basis, companies should be better able to ascertain that the partnership they are contemplating will do more good than harm.

[10]K. Schwartz, "USAir Ends Code Share with British Airways," *The Associated Press*, Oct. 24, 1996.

Alliance Assessment Decision Process

Any new alliance opportunity needs to be examined in two phases: first with regard to the alliance's impact on the individual business unit directly involved in the alliance, and then with regard to its impact on the company's overall alliance portfolio. If costs exceed benefits at the single alliance level, the proposed alliance should be rejected unless there are other strategic reasons for pursuing it. If the single alliance benefits exceed the costs, then the next step is to assess the impact from an alliance portfolio perspective. If the alliance portfolio level benefits exceed the costs, the formation for the alliance decision should be a "go." If, however, costs exceed benefits at the alliance portfolio level, then the company needs to do one further piece of analysis: comparing the value that the alliance is able to *create* on the single alliance level with the value that the alliance might *destroy* on the alliance portfolio level. Only if the expected value created exceeds expected value destroyed should the new alliance get the nod.

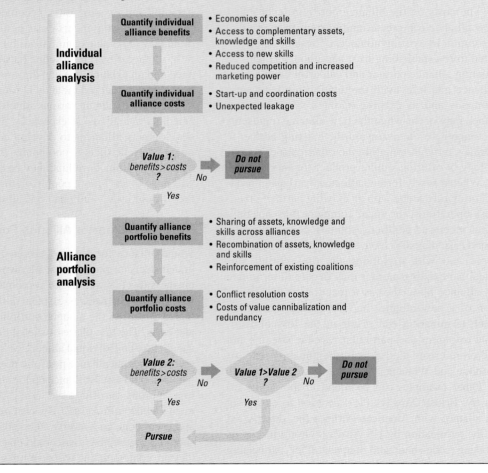

ALLIANCE DECISIONS: WHO'S RESPONSIBLE FOR WHAT?

Wise alliance formation decisions benefit from an integrated decision process. Many companies use a graphical representation of decision modeling that identifies each actor according to the following rubric, known by the initials of the key terms as RACI:

- Who is **R**esponsible? Which individuals have to perform the task?

- Who is **A**ccountable? Which individuals have the ultimate ownership of the task, and whose heads will roll if the task is not performed?

- Who needs to be **C**onsulted for input during this process step?

- Who should be kept **I**nformed and up to date during this process step?

Note especially the strong role played by the Manager of Alliance Function. This is an individual or department high in the central corporate hierarchy that is charged with the coordination of a company's alliance portfolio.

ALLIANCE DECISION PROCESS RACI DIAGRAM

	ALLIANCE SPONSOR	MANAGER OF ALLIANCE FUNCTION	MANAGERS OF OTHER ALLIANCES	MANAGERS OF OTHER BUSINESS UNITS	EXECUTIVE COMMITTEE
Identify alliance level benefits costs	AR	C			
Conduct alliance level cost-benefit evaluation	AR	C			
Identify alliance portfolio level benefits and costs	C	AR	C	C	
Conduct alliance portfolio level cost-benefit evaluation	I	AR	I	I	
Compare alliance level and alliance portfolio level costs and benefits	R	AR			
Raise awareness of benefits and conflict between alliances	I	AR	I	I	
Take final decision	I	I	I	I	AR

Alliance Sponsor: Owns the business problem that requires the alliance

Manager of the Central Alliance Function: Is responsible for the overall effectiveness of the company's alliance portfolio

Managers of Other Alliances: Are responsible for the other ongoing alliances in either the same business or a different business

Managers of Other Business Units: Have no vested interest in the alliance to be formed

Executive Committee: Is the ultimate "decision maker" that decides on the go-ahead of the alliance

The other critical step that companies should take to make sense of their alliance formation is to clarify exactly who in the organization plays what role in the process. Alliance formation decision making in companies with alliance portfolios is a complex undertaking that requires the involvement of a broad range of actors on both the business-unit and corporate levels.

To ensure effective alliance formation decision making, the exact roles and responsibilities of each individual player or committee in the process needs to be formalized, codified and communicated throughout the organization. One commonly used method of business process analysis, RACI analysis, tags the various actors in an organization as having one or more critical roles. Based on our research, we have developed a RACI diagram that precisely defines the various actors in the alliance formation process and assigns to each actor one or more RACI tags. (See "Alliance Decisions: Who's Responsible for What?")

A clearly defined decision process and explicitly codified roles and responsibilities could have helped companies such as Telefónica to see the bigger picture and avoid falling into the trap of forming alliances that appear to be value-creating deals from the business-unit perspective but create negative intra-alliance portfolio dynamics that destroy value overall. More specifically, it would have forced Telefónica's TISA unit to flush out the benefits as well as downsides of the new partnership and forced it to involve other parts of the organization in the decision. Through clear roles and responsibilities, the corporate alliance function could have put the potential outcomes in the context of the company's overall strategy.

Conclusion

There is no doubt that alliance portfolios have become a popular and important strategic device for companies seeking both to exploit opportunities and to neutralize threats. But surprisingly, many decisions pertaining to the formation of alliances are made on an operational level, without much regard for the impact on the company's overall alliance portfolio. By following a rigorous process that includes an integrated alliance business case and clear roles and responsibilities in decision making, companies can ensure that their alliance portfolios do not grow in a haphazard fashion and that their alliances are worth more as a whole than as the sum of their individual parts.

As noted by corporate management scholar D.A. Levinthal, "in complex decision problems, the discovery of the optimum is an extremely difficult task."[11] Such decisions are even more difficult if they span multiple organizational units within a company or if outside parties are involved. Alliance formation—which by definition entails bringing together multiple business units and inevitably requires interaction with independent partner companies—thus presents numerous possibilities for mismanagement. In fact, viewed in that light, alliance formation emerges as one of the most fraught and perilous moves an organization can make.

The tools described above are essentially a set of mechanisms that help companies address three common issues with alliance formation decisions from an alliance portfolio perspective: breaking down silo thinking, overcoming information asymmetries and balancing local and global needs across the organization. By sitting down around one table, decision makers from different units can better understand each others' perspectives, realize how a new alliance they are considering might be detrimental elsewhere in the organization and bargain with one another to arrive at a mutually acceptable solution. Also, by putting the responsibility for alliances in a central position, this approach will increase the status, influence and power that function has. As a result, companies will find it easier to arrive at decisions in which overall corporate objectives prevail over local, business-unit interests. Finally, working out the business case for an alliance will force all parties involved in the process to quantify, or at least estimate, the benefits and the downsides of the partnership being considered and allow for a somewhat more objective evaluation of the various implications of forming that particular alliance, both on the level of each individually affected business unit and on the overall corporate level.

Acknowledgments

The authors thank Silviya Svejenova for her helpful comments on earlier versions of this article. Pierre Dussauge acknowledges support from the HEC Accor-Air France-SNCF Chair on Service Management.

[11]D.A. Levinthal, "Organizational Adaptation and Environmental Selection: Interrelated Processes of Change," Organization Science 2, no. 1 (1991): 140–145.

Implementing the Strategy:
Building Multidimensional Capabilities

Just as the world's new transnational strategic imperatives put demands on the existing organizational capabilities of multinational enterprises (MNEs), so have evolving transnational organization models defined new managerial tasks for those operating within them. In this chapter, we examine the changing roles and responsibilities of three typical management groups that find themselves together at the decision-making table in today's transnational organizations: the global business manager, the worldwide functional manager, and the national subsidiary manager. Although different organizations may define the key roles differently (bringing global account managers or regional executives to the table, for example), the major challenge facing all MNEs is to allocate their many complex strategic tasks and organizational roles among key management groups, then give each of those groups the appropriate legitimacy and influence within the organization's ongoing decision-making process. After reviewing the new roles and responsibilities of these key executives, the chapter concludes with a look at the role of top management in integrating diverse interests and perspectives and engaging them in a common direction.

The 21st-century MNE is markedly different from its ancestors. It has been transformed by an environment in which multiple, often-conflicting forces accelerate simultaneously. The globalization of markets, the acceleration of product and technology life cycles, the assertion of national governments' demands, and above all, the intensification of global competition have created an environment of complexity, diversity, and change for most of today's MNEs.

As we have seen, the ability of a company to compete on the basis of a single dominant competitive advantage has morphed into a need to develop multiple strategic assets: global-scale efficiency and competitiveness, national responsiveness and flexibility, and worldwide innovation and learning capabilities. In turn, these new strategic demands have put pressure on existing organization structures and management processes. Traditional hierarchical structures, with their emphasis on either/or choices, have evolved toward organizational forms we have described as transnational, characterized by integrated networks of assets and resources, multidimensional management perspectives and capabilities, and flexible coordinative processes.

The managerial implications of all these changes are enormous. To succeed in today's international operating environment, transnational managers must be able to sense and interpret complex and dynamic environmental changes; they must be able to develop and integrate multiple strategic capabilities; and they must be able to build and manage complicated yet manageable new organizations required to deliver coordinated action on a worldwide basis. Unless those in key management positions are highly skilled and knowledgeable, their companies simply cannot respond well to the major new challenges that they face.

Yet surprisingly little attention has been devoted to the study of the implications of all these changes on the roles and responsibilities of those who manage today's MNEs. Academics, consultants, and even managers themselves focus an enormous amount of time and energy on analyzing the various international environmental forces, on refining the concepts of global strategy, and on understanding the characteristics of effective transnational organizations. But without effective managers in place, sophisticated strategies and organizations can and do fail. In simple terms, the great risk for most MNEs today is that they are often trying to implement third-generation strategies through second-generation organizations with first-generation managers.

In this chapter, we examine the management roles and responsibilities implied by the new challenges facing MNEs—those that take the manager beyond the first-generation assumptions. Rather than generalizing about tasks that differ considerably for those in different parts and different levels of the organization, we focus on the roles and responsibilities of three specific groups in the transnational company: the global business manager, the worldwide functional manager, and the country subsidiary manager. (Recall that in Chapter 4, we suggested that variations often occur in the nature of transnational structures. So bear in mind that other key executives—global account managers, for example—may also have a seat at the table.) To close the chapter, we review the role of top management in integrating these often-competing perspectives and capabilities.

Global Business Management

The challenge of developing global efficiency and competitiveness requires that management capture the various scale and scope economies available to the MNE, as well as capitalize on the potential competitive advantages inherent in its worldwide market positioning. These requirements demand a management with the acumen to see opportunities and risks across national boundaries and functional specialties, and the skill to coordinate and integrate activities across these barriers to capture the potential benefits. This is the fundamental task of the global business manager.

In implementing this important responsibility, the global business manager will be involved in a variety of diverse activities, whose balance varies considerably depending on the nature of the business and the company's administrative heritage. Nonetheless, there are three core roles and responsibilities that almost always fall to this key manager: he or she will be a global strategist, an architect of worldwide asset and resource configuration, and a coordinator and controller of cross-border transfers.

Global Business Strategist

Because competitive interaction increasingly takes place on a global chessboard, only a manager with a worldwide perspective and responsibility can assess the strategic position and capability of a given business. Therefore, companies must configure their information, planning, and control systems so that they can be consolidated into consistent, integrated global business reports. This does not imply that the global business manager alone has the perspective and capability to formulate strategic priorities, or that he or she should undertake that vital task unilaterally. Depending on the nature of the business, there will almost certainly be some need to incorporate the perspectives of geographic and functional managers who represent strategic interests that may run counter to the business manager's drive to maximize global efficiency. Equally important, the business strategy that is developed must fit within the broader corporate strategy which should provide a clear vision of what the company wants to be and explicit values pertaining to how it will accomplish its mission.

In the final analysis, however, the responsibility to reconcile different views falls to the global business manager, who will need to prepare an integrated strategy of how the company will compete in his or her particular business. In many companies, the manager's ability to do this is compromised because the company has created the position simply by anointing otherwise unprepared domestic product division managers with the title of "global business manager." Overseas subsidiary managers often feel that these managers are not only insensitive to nondomestic perspectives and interests, but also biased toward the domestic organization in making key strategic decisions such as product development and capacity plans. In many cases, their concerns are justified.

The ideal career path for a global business strategist would probably involve some experience as a country manager. The challenges facing the manager of a major national subsidiary are inevitably multidimensional and can serve as good training ground for future overall business strategists. And in the true transnational company, the global business manager need not necessarily be located in the home country; in fact, in many cases, great benefits can accrue to relocating several such management groups abroad.

Even well-established MNEs with a tradition of close control of their worldwide business strategy are changing. The head of IBM's $6 billion telecommunications business moved her division headquarters to London. She explained that the rationale was not only to move the command center closer to the booming European market for computer networking, but also "[to] give us a different perspective on all our markets." And when General Electric (GE) acquired Amersham, the British-based life sciences and diagnostics leader, it relocated its health care business headquarters to the United Kingdom to better leverage the technology, management talent, and entrepreneurial culture that came with this key acquisition.

Architect of Asset and Resource Configuration

Closely tied to the challenge of shaping an integrated business strategy is the global business manager's responsibility for overseeing the worldwide distribution of key assets and resources. Again, we do not mean to imply that he or she can make such decisions unilaterally. The input of interested geographic and functional managers must be weighed. It is the global business manager, however, who is normally best placed to initiate and lead the debate on where to locate key plants or develop vital resources, perhaps through a global strategy committee or a "world board" with membership drawn from key geographic and functional management groups.

In deciding such issues, the business manager can never assume a zero base. Indeed, these decisions must be rooted in the company's administrative heritage. In classic multinational companies like Philips, Unilever, ICI, and Nestlé, many of the key assets and resources that permitted them to expand internationally are deeply embedded in national companies operating as part of their decentralized federation structures. Any business manager trying to shape such companies' future configurations must build on rather than ignore or destroy the important benefits that such assets and resources represent. That does not mean that the existing configuration should become a constraint, but any reconfiguration involving closures or layoffs must be handled with social sensitivity and political dexterity to respond to the inevitable resistance from local stakeholders.

Recognizing that the task does not start from a zero base, the business manager's challenge is typically is to shape the future configuration by leveraging existing resources and capabilities and linking them to resemble the transnational's integrated network form. When GE Medical Systems (GEMS) reconfigured its global structure, it did so by scaling up operations in the most efficient production centers and making them global sources. This led to the designation of plants in Budapest, Shanghai, and Mexico City being designated "Centers of Excellence," while operations in Paris, Tokyo, and Milwaukee were scaled back to become specialized assembly operations. The same process redefined the roles of its research and development centers, making GEMS a classic model of a distributed yet integrated transnational structure.

Cross-Border Coordinator

The third key role played by most global business managers is that of a cross-border coordinator. Although less overtly strategic than the other two responsibilities, it is nonetheless a vital operating function because it involves deciding on sourcing patterns and managing cross-border transfer processes.

The task of coordinating flows of materials, components, and finished products becomes extremely complex as companies build transnational structures and capabilities. Rather than producing and shipping all products from a fully integrated central plant (the centralized hub model) or allowing local subsidiaries to develop self-sufficient capabilities (the decentralized federation model), transnational companies specialize their operations on a worldwide or perhaps regional basis, building on the most capable national operations and capitalizing on locations of strategic importance.

But the resulting integrated network of specialized operations is highly interdependent, as illustrated by the previously described structure that GEMS created to link its high-labor component plants in Eastern Europe and China with its highly skilled subassembly operations in Germany and Singapore, which in turn supply specialized finished-product plants in the United States, the United Kingdom, France, and Japan. The task is further complicated by the fact that it involves both corporate-owned and outsourced supply. The issues requiring resolution of issues range from allocating responsibilities for serving end users to controlling the quality of the product to managing the flow of design and production knowledge to subcontractors. And all of this must occur while trying to minimize the likelihood of technology loss if outsourcing is used.

The coordination mechanisms available to the global business manager vary from direct central control over quantities shipped and prices charged to the establishment of rules that essentially create an internal market mechanism to coordinate cross-border activities. The former means of control is more likely for products of high strategic importance (e.g., Pfizer's central coordination of quantities and pricing of the active ingredients of Viagra, or Coca-Cola's tight corporate control of the supply of Coke syrup worldwide).

As products become more commodity-like, however, global product managers recognize that internal transfers should reflect the competitive conditions set by the external environment. This recognition has led many to develop internal quasi-markets as the principal means of coordination. For example, in the consumer electronics giant Panasonic, once the parent company develops prototypes of the following year's models of consumer electronics products (ranging from video cameras to plasma TVs), global product managers offer them internally to buyers at merchandise meetings that are, in effect, huge internal trade fairs. At these meetings, national sales and marketing directors from the company's sales companies around the world enter into direct discussions with the global product managers, negotiating modifications in product design, price, and delivery schedule to meet their local market needs.

Worldwide Functional Management

Worldwide functional managers are the individuals with the specialist responsibility for activities like R&D, manufacturing, and marketing, as well as those responsible for support activities, such as the chief financial officer and the chief information officer. Their job, broadly speaking, is to provide support to line managers, particularly by diffusing innovations and transferring knowledge on a worldwide basis. This vital task is built on knowledge that is highly specialized by function—technological capability, marketing expertise, manufacturing know-how, and so on—and to do it effectively requires that functional managers evolve from the secondary roles that they may have played in the past and take a seat at the table, assuming active roles as transnational managers.

The tasks facing functional managers vary widely by specific function (e.g., in a biotech company, technology transfer may be more intensive than the transfer of marketing expertise) or by business (companies in transnational industries such as telecommunications usually demand more functional linkages and transfers than do those in multinational industries such as retailing). Nonetheless, we highlight three basic roles and responsibilities that most worldwide functional managers should play: worldwide scanner of specialized information and intelligence, cross-pollinator of "best practices," and champion of transnational innovation.

Worldwide Intelligence Scanner

Most innovations start with a stimulus that drives the company to respond to a perceived opportunity or threat. It may be a revolutionary technological breakthrough, an emerging consumer trend, a new competitive challenge, or a pending government regulation; and it may occur anywhere in the world. A typical example of this type of stimulus occurred with the rapid emergence of a commercial market for alternative energy in Europe soon after 2001. Strong public support backed by widespread government incentives and legislative requirements resulted in explosive growth in the demand for both wind- and solar-powered generators. By 2011, these two alternative-energy power sources accounted for 68 percent of new electric generation capacity installed in the European Union (E.U.) that year, and by 2020, 34 percent of Europe's electric demand was expected to come from renewable sources.

Those power-generation companies and equipment manufacturers that had good sensory mechanisms in Europe at the turn of the century recognized the significance of these developments early. This leading-edge information allowed them to track the development and make appropriate adjustments to their consumer communications, technological capabilities, and product line configuration. As these political forces and market demands spread worldwide over the following years, those companies that had not been monitoring the European development as an advance warning system found themselves trying to respond not only to the growing political and consumer pressures but also to more responsive competitors that had several years' head start in developing alternative energy technologies, products, and strategies.

But global awareness alone is insufficient. Historically, even when strategically important information was sensed in the foreign subsidiaries of classic multinational or global companies, it was rarely transmitted to those who could act on it or when it did get through was often ignored. The communication problem was due primarily to the fact that the intelligence was usually of a specialist nature, not always well understood by the geographic- or business-focused generalists who controlled the line organization. Capturing and transmitting such information across national boundaries required the establishment of functional specialist information channels to link local technologists, marketers, and production experts with others who understood their needs and shared their perspective.

In transnational companies, functional managers are often linked most effectively through informal networks that are nurtured and maintained through frequent meetings, visits, and transfers. Through such linkages, these managers develop the contacts and relationships that enable them to transmit information rapidly around the globe. The functional managers at the corporate level become the linchpins in this worldwide intelligence scanning effort and play a vital role as facilitators of communication and repositories of specialist information.

Fillippo Passorini, the corporate CIO of Procter & Gamble (P&G), has built a close relationship with all the company's global business managers by supporting the implementation of a digital strategy. The process aggregates consumer feedback collected from tweets, blogs, e-mails, and call center records worldwide, analyzing it to create a real-time digital dashboard that displays current information on consumer perceptions. By analyzing a massive amount of data from around the world, the CIO and his staff have also been able to provide global business executives and local subsidiary managers with a sales forecasting tool that has allowed the company to redeploy 5,000 staff who had been engaged in demand planning, replacing their spreadsheets with computer models that provide more accurate and timely aggregated demand forecasts.

Cross-Pollinator of "Best Practices"

Overseas subsidiaries can be more than sources of strategic intelligence, however. In a truly transnational company, they can also be the source of capabilities, expertise, and innovation that can be transferred to other parts of the organization. Caterpillar's leading-edge flexible manufacturing first emerged in its French and Belgian plants, for example, and much of P&G's liquid detergent technology was developed in its European Technology Center. In both cases, this expertise was transferred to other countries with important strategic impact.

Such an ability to transfer new ideas and developments requires a considerable amount of management time and attention to break down the not-invented-here (NIH) syndrome that often thrives in international business. In this process, those with worldwide functional responsibilities are ideally placed to play a central cross-pollination role. Not only do they have the specialist knowledge required to identify and evaluate leading-edge practices, they also tend to have a well-developed informal communications network developed with others in their functional area.

Through informal contacts, formal reviews, and frequent travel, corporate functional managers can often identify where the best practices are being developed and implemented. They are also in a position to arrange cross-unit visits and transfers, host conferences, form task forces, or take other initiatives that will expose others to the new ideas. For example, when the manufacturing of GE's highly successful, Europe-developed 2.5-megawatt (MW) wind turbines was starting up in Florida, in preparation for the 2010 launch of this product in the United States, it was a global manufacturing technology group in GE's power-generation business that linked the technical expertise developed in established plants in Germany and Spain to the new manufacturing site in Florida.

Champion of Transnational Innovation

The two previously identified roles ideally position the functional manager to play a key role in developing what we called transnational innovations. As described in Chapter 5, these are different from the predominantly local activity that dominated the innovation process in multinational companies or the centrally driven innovation in international and global companies. The simplest form of transnational innovation is what we call *locally leveraged.* By scanning their companies' worldwide operations, corporate functional managers can identify local innovations that have applications elsewhere. In Unilever, for example, product and marketing innovation for many of its global brands originated in national subsidiaries. Snuggle fabric softener was born in Unilever's German company, Timotei herbal shampoo originated in its Scandinavian operations, and Impulse body spray was first introduced by its South African unit. Recognizing the potential that these local innovations had for the wider company, the parent company's marketing and technical groups created the impetus to spread them to other subsidiaries.

The second type of transnational innovation, which we call *globally linked,* requires functional managers to play a more sophisticated role. This type of innovation fully exploits the company's access to worldwide information and expertise by linking and leveraging intelligence sources with internal centers of excellence, wherever they may be located. For example, the revolutionary design of GE's 2.5-MW wind turbine generator drew on jet engine turbine expertise developed in GE's transportation group in the United States, carbon composite materials technology from its corporate R&D facility, blade design developed in its engineering center in Warsaw, Poland, and software to locate the wind towers and feed power into the grid that was written in its Indian

R&D facility. That kind of sophisticated coordination can be identified, conceived, and executed only by functional technical experts with perspectives and responsibilities that reach across countries and across businesses.

Geographic Subsidiary Management

In many MNEs, a successful tour as a country subsidiary manager is often considered the acid test of general management potential. Indeed, it is often a necessary qualification on the résumé of any candidate for a top management position. Not only does it provide frontline exposure to the realities of today's international business environment, but it also puts the individual in a position where he or she must deal with enormous strategic complexity from an organizational position that is severely constrained. Indeed, as more MNEs move toward structures dominated by global business units and global customers, the role of "country manager" is, if anything, becoming more difficult. In such situations, the manager of the country is often held accountable for results but has only limited formal authority over the people and assets within his or her jurisdiction.

We have described the strategic challenge facing the MNE as one that requires resolving the conflicting demands for global efficiency, multinational responsiveness, and worldwide learning. The country manager is located at the nexus of this strategic tension—defending the company's market positions against global competitors, satisfying the demands of the host government, responding to the unique needs of local customers, serving as the "face" of the entire organization at the national level, and leveraging its local resources and capabilities to strengthen the company's competitive position worldwide.

There are many vital tasks that the country manager must play. In this section, we identify three that capture the complexity of the task and highlight its important linkage role: acting as a bicultural interpreter, becoming the chief advocate and defender of national needs, and executing the vital frontline responsibility of implementing the company's strategy.

Bicultural Interpreter

All country managers realize they must become the local expert who understands the needs of the local market, the strategy of competitors, and the demands of the host government. But his or her responsibilities are also much broader. Because managers at headquarters do not understand the environmental and cultural differences in the MNE's diverse foreign markets, the country manager must be able to analyze the information gathered, interpret its implications, and even predict the range of feasible outcomes. This role suggests an ability not only to act as an efficient sensor of the national environment, but also to become a cultural interpreter able to communicate the importance of that information to those whose perceptions may be obscured by ethnocentric biases.

In 1980, when Loy Weston, the general manager of KFC's Japanese subsidiary, suggested that the chain's classic "bucket of chicken" was too large for Japanese appetites, his request to introduce a new line of chicken pieces in a small serving size was rejected by corporate headquarters. It was a proposal that violated a strategy of rolling out KFC's successful U.S. menu as it expanded around the world. Only after McDonald's introduced its wildly successful Chicken McNuggets did the company recognize that the failure to learn in Japan had left a gap for its giant competitor to move in on KFC's previously impregnable chicken franchise.

There is another aspect to the country manager's role as an information broker that is sometimes ignored. Not only must the individual have a sensitivity to and understanding of the national culture, he or she must also be comfortable in the corporate culture at the MNE. Again, this liaison-style bicultural role implies much more than being an information conduit, communicating the corporation's goals, strategies, and values to a group of employees located thousands of miles from the parent company. The country subsidiary manager must also interpret those broad goals and strategies so that they become meaningful objectives and priorities at the local level of operation and apply those corporate values and organizational processes in a way that respects local cultural norms. And communicating in the opposite direction, they must also be able to present their ideas and proposals to corporate headquarters in a way that is sensitive to the company's overall strategy and values.

So although the KFC corporate executives had to accept much of the blame for missing the chicken nugget opportunity, country manager Weston also bore partial responsibility. In a location far removed from headquarters, Weston had established himself as a rebel willing to ignore the standard systems and challenge corporate directives. By distancing himself from corporate policies and procedures and openly resisting headquarters attempts to control him, he effectively undermined his credibility as a bicultural interpreter.

National Defender and Advocate

As important as the communication role is, it is not sufficient for the country manager to act solely as an intelligent mailbox. Information and analysis conveyed to corporate headquarters must be not only well understood but also acted upon, particularly in MNEs where strong business managers are arguing for a more integrated global approach and corporate functional managers are focusing on cross-border linkages. The country manager's role is to counterbalance these centralizing tendencies and ensure that the needs and opportunities that exist in the local environment are understood and incorporated into the decision-making process.

As the national organization evolves from its early independence to a more mature interdependent role as part of an integrated worldwide network, the country manager's drive for national self-sufficiency and personal autonomy (such as Loy Weston's dominant motivation in KFC) must be replaced by a less parochial perspective and a more corporate-oriented identity. This shift does not imply, however, that he or she should stop presenting the local perspective to headquarters management or stop defending national interests. Indeed, the company's ability to become a true transnational depends on having strong advocates of the need to differentiate its operations locally and be responsive to national demands and pressures.

Two distinct but related tasks are implied by this important role. The first requires that the country manager ensure that the overall corporate strategies, policies, and processes are appropriate from the national organization's perspective. If the interests of local constituencies are violated or the subsidiary's position might be compromised by the global strategy, it is the country manager's responsibility to become the defender of national needs and perspectives.

In addition to defending national differentiation and responsiveness, the country manager must become an advocate for his or her national organization's role in the corporation's worldwide integrated system, of which it is a part. As MNEs develop a more transnational strategy, national organizations compete not only for corporate resources but also for roles in the global operations. To ensure that each unit's full potential is realized, country managers must be able to identify and represent their particular national organization's key assets and capabilities, as well as the ways in which they can contribute to the MNE as a whole.

It is the country manager's job to mentor local employees and support those individuals in their fight for corporate resources and recognition. In doing so, they build local capability that can be a major corporate asset. As the former head of the Scottish subsidiary of a U.S. computer company observed, "It is my *obligation* to seek out new investment. No one else is going to stand up for these workers at head office. They are doing a great job, and I owe it to them to build up this operation. I get very angry with some of my counterparts in other parts of the company who just toe the party line. They have followed their orders to the letter, but when I visit their plants, I see unfulfilled potential everywhere."

Frontline Implementer of Corporate Strategy

Although the implementation of corporate strategy may seem the most obvious of tasks for the manager of a frontline operating unit, it is by no means the easiest. The first challenge stems from the multiplicity and diversity of constituents whose demands and pressures compete for the country manager's attention. Being a subsidiary company of some distant MNE seems to bestow a special status on many national organizations and subject them to a different and a more intense type of pressure than that put on other local companies. Governments may be suspicious of their motives, unions may distrust their national commitment, and customers may misunderstand their way of operating. Compounding the problem, corporate management often appears to the subsidiary general manager to underestimate the significance of these demands and pressures.

In addition, the country manager's implementation task is complicated by the corporate expectation that he or she take the broad corporate goals and strategies and translate them into specific actions that are responsive to the needs of the national environment. As we have seen, these global strategies are usually complex and finely balanced, reflecting multiple conflicting demands. Having been developed through subtle internal negotiation, they often leave the country manager with very little room to maneuver.

Pressured from without and constrained from within, the country manager needs a keen administrative sense to plot the negotiating range in which he or she can operate. The action decided on must be sensitive enough to respect the limits of the diverse local constituencies, pragmatic enough to achieve the expected corporate outcome, and creative enough to balance the diverse internal and external demands and constraints.

As if this were not enough, the task is made even more difficult by the fact that the country manager does not act solely as the implementer of corporate strategy. As we discussed previously, it is important that he or she also plays a key role in its formulation.

Thus, the strategy that the country manager is required to implement often will reflect some decisions against which he or she lobbied hard. Once the final decision is taken, however, the country manager must be able to convince his or her national organization to implement it with commitment and enthusiasm.

When Australian winemaker BRL Hardy wanted to introduce an entry-level wine brand worldwide, the company's U.K. subsidiary general manager, Christopher Carson, developed a detailed marketing strategy for a proposed brand he called Kelly's Revenge, which he believed would fit well in a market niche for a fun, relaxed product. When his proposal was rejected in favor of an Australian-originated idea for an environmentally conscious brand called Banrock Station, Carson was disappointed but put his organization's full efforts behind the new global rollout. Banrock Station subsequently became the top-selling wine brand in the United Kingdom.

Top-Level Corporate Management

Nowhere are the challenges facing management more extreme than at the top of an organization that is evolving toward becoming a transnational corporation. Not only do these senior executives have to integrate and provide direction for the diverse management groups that we have described, but in doing so, they also first have to break with many of the norms and traditions that defined their role in the past.

Historically, as increasingly complex hierarchical structures forced top management farther and farther from the frontlines of their businesses, its role became bureaucratized in a rising sea of systems and staff reports. As layers of management slowed decision making and the corporate headquarters role of coordination and support evolved to one of control and interference, top management's attention was distracted from the external demands of customers and competitive pressures and began to focus internally on an increasingly bureaucratic process.

The transnational organization of today cannot afford to operate this way. Like executives at all levels of the organization, top management must add value, which means liberating rather than constraining the organization below them. For those at the top of a transnational, this means more than just creating a diverse set of business, functional, and geographic management groups and assigning them specific roles and responsibilities. It also means maintaining the organizational legitimacy of each group, balancing and integrating their often-divergent influences in the ongoing management process, and maintaining a unifying sense of purpose and direction in the face of often-conflicting needs and priorities.

This constant balancing and integrating role is perhaps the most vital aspect of a top-level executive's job. It is reflected in the constant tension that these managers feel between ensuring long-term viability and achieving short-term results, or between providing a clear overall corporate direction and leaving sufficient room for experimentation. This tension is reflected in the three core top management tasks that we highlight here. The first, which focuses on the key role of providing long-term direction and purpose, is in some ways counterbalanced by the second, which highlights the need to achieve current results by leveraging performance. The third key task of ensuring continual renewal again focuses on long-term needs, but at the same time, it may require the organization to challenge its current directions and priorities.

Providing Direction and Purpose

In an organization built around the need for multidimensional strategic capabilities and competing management perspectives, diversity and internal tension can create an energizing free market of competing ideas and generate an enormous amount of individual and group motivation. But there is always the risk that these same powerful centrifugal forces could pull the company apart. So creating a common vision of the future and a shared set of values that govern managers' more parochial objectives becomes a vital task. In doing so, top management can, in effect, create a corporate lightning rod that captures this otherwise diffuse energy and channels it toward driving a single company engine.

We have identified three characteristics of an energizing strategic vision that distinguishes it from a catchy but ineffective public relations slogan. First, the vision must be clear—and here, simplicity, relevance, and continuous reinforcement are the key. NEC's integration of computers and communications—its C&C philosophy—is a good example of how clarity can make a vision more powerful and effective. Top management in NEC has applied the C&C concept so completely and effectively that management uses it not only to describe the company's enduring vision, but also to define its distinctive source of competitive advantage over large companies like IBM and AT&T, and to identify its major strategic and organizational priorities. Throughout the company, the many rich interpretations of C&C are understood and believed.

Second, continuity of a vision can provide direction and purpose. Despite shifts in leadership and continual adjustments in short-term business priorities, top management must remain committed to the company's core set of strategic objectives and organizational values. Without such continuity, the unifying vision takes on the transitory characteristics of the annual budget or quarterly targets—and engenders about as much organizational enthusiasm. Since first being articulated in 1977, NEC's concept of C&C has remained at the core of the company's strategy and is now embodied into its well-articulated underlying corporate philosophy.

Third, in communicating the vision and strategic direction, it is critical to establish consistency across organizational units—in other words, to ensure that the vision is shared by all. The cost of inconsistency can be horrendous. At a minimum, it can result in confusion and inefficiency; at worst, it can lead individuals and organizational units to pursue agendas that are mutually debilitating.

Leveraging Corporate Performance

Although aligning the company's resources, capabilities, and commitments to achieve common long-term objectives is vital, top management must also achieve results in the short term to remain viable among competitors and credible with stakeholders. Top management's key role in this task is to provide the controls, support, and coordination to leverage resources and capabilities to their highest level of performance.

In doing so, the leaders of transnational companies must abandon old notions of control that often saw their role primarily as monitoring and responding to below-budget financial results. Today's most effective top managers rely much more on control mechanisms that are personal and proactive. In discussions with each management group, they ensure that its particular responsibilities are understood in relation to the overall goal and that strategic and operational priorities are clearly identified and agreed upon. They set demanding standards and use frequent informal visits to discuss operations and identify new problems or opportunities quickly.

When such problems or opportunities are identified, the old model of top-down interference must be replaced by one driven by corporate-level support. Having created an organization staffed by experts and specialists, the most successful top managers resist the temptation to send in the headquarters "experts" to take charge at the first sign of difficulty. Far more effective is an approach of delegating clear responsibilities, backing them with rewards that align those responsibilities with corporate goals, then supporting each management group with resources, specialized expertise, and other forms of support available from the top levels of the company.

As top management tries to leverage the overall performance of the corporation, perhaps the most challenging task that it faces is to coordinate the activities of an organization deliberately designed around diverse perspectives and responsibilities. As we described in Chapter 4, there are three basic cross-organizational flows that must be managed carefully—goods, resources, and information—and each demands a different means of coordination. Goods flows can normally be routinized and managed through formal systems and procedures, a process that we describe as *for malization*. Decisions involving the allocation of scarce resources—capital allocation and key personnel assignments, for example—are usually ones in which top management wants to be involved directly and personally, a process we call *centralization*. And flows of information and knowledge are most effectively generated and diffused through the management of personal contacts in a process we describe as *socialization*.

These three flows are the lifeblood of any company, and any organization's ability to make them more efficient and effective depends on top management's ability to develop a rich portfolio of coordinative processes. By balancing the formalization, centralization, and socialization processes, they can fully exploit the company's assets and resources and greatly leverage its performance.

Ensuring Continual Renewal

Despite their enormous value, either of these first two top management roles, if pursued to the extreme, can result in a company's long-term demise. A fixation on an outmoded mission can be just as dangerous as a preoccupation with short-term performance because both of these tasks can focus management only on maintaining a company's ongoing positive current performance. The risk is that successful strategies can become elevated to the status of unquestioned wisdom and effective organizational processes become institutionalized as embedded routines. As strategies and processes ossify, management loses its flexibility, and eventually the organization sees its role as protecting its heritage.

It is top management's role to prevent this ossification from occurring, and there are several important ways it can ensure that the organization continues to renew itself rather than just reinventing its past. First, by constantly orienting the organization to its customers and benchmarking it against its best competitors, top management can ensure an external orientation. For example, when Jin Zhiguo became the president of China's massive Tsingtao Brewery Co. Ltd., he felt that the company had become too self-satisfied and inwardly focused. He saw his first priority as implementing internal reforms that would have management focus on the company's significant external competitive challenges. As he noted, "Tsingtao Brewery has been an arrogant company. We must have an open mind and learn from other companies. Only a strong learning ability will lead to powerful innovations."

An equally important top management role is the need to question, challenge, and change things constantly in a way that forces adaptation and learning. By creating a "dynamic imbalance" among those with different objectives, top management can prevent a myopic strategic posture from developing. Clearly, this delicate process requires a great deal of top management time if it is not to degenerate into anarchy or corporate politics. But it's a talent that the late Steve Jobs exhibited when he regained the leadership position of Apple in 1997. Through his ability to question, to push, and above all to challenge his organization, he turned a loss-making company with a shrinking market share into a market-sensitive, technology-driven global dynamo.

Third, top management can ensure renewal by defining the corporate mission and values so that they provide some strategic stretch and maneuverability while simultaneously legitimizing innovative new initiatives. More than this, those at the top levels must monitor closely the process of dynamic imbalance that they create and strongly support some of the more entrepreneurial experimentation or imaginative challenges to the status quo that emerge from the deliberately created instability. The champion of such long term adaptation has to be Nokia, a company that started its life as a forestry-based paper mill company. In the post–World War II era, it diversified into electric cable production, which in turn led it to become a TV set manufacturer. It was only in the 1990s that it finally evolved into a mobile phone company, the transformation that led to decades of global success.

Concluding Comments

In this chapter, we shifted the level of analysis down from the MNE as an organization to the individual manager. Rather than think in terms of the changing nature of the business environment or the conflicting strategic imperatives facing the MNE, we examined the new roles of three groups of managers—those responsible for a global business (e.g. a product SBU or division), a worldwide function (e.g., finance, marketing, or technology), and a geographic territory (e.g. a country or region). We also looked at the new role of top-level corporate management in integrating and providing direction for these three groups.

These new roles and responsibilities are hard to put in place because they require managers to rethink many of their traditional assumptions about the nature of their work. This is ultimately the biggest challenge facing the transnational organization—to create a generation of managers that have the requisite skills and the sense of perspective needed to operate in a multibusiness, multifunctional, multinational system.

Chapter 7 Readings

- In Reading 7-1, "Managing Executive Attention in the Global Company," Birkinshaw, Bouquet, and Ambos describe how executives can prioritize their time to ensure that they are focusing on the countries and subsidiaries that need the most attention. The authors describe two key strategies that a subsidiary can use to attract parent company attention: by using its "weight" as a player in an important market, and by exerting its "voice" and working through company channels.
- In Reading 7-2, "Tap Your Subsidiaries for Global Reach," Bartlett and Ghoshal introduce a simple conceptualization of the important roles for national subsidiaries in overall MNE success. In balancing the strategic importance of the local environment with the competence of the local organization, the authors define four very different roles for managers of country subsidiaries: strategic leader, contributor, implementer, and black hole.
- In Reading 7-3, "The Collaboration Imperative," Lash emphasizes the need for leaders who are able to achieve results even where they do not have direct control or authority over resources. The article describes the competencies required by these collaborative managers, who must be able to lead diverse groups across functional disciplines, regions, and cultures.

All these readings emphasize the multidimensional capabilities that must be built for effective strategy implementation in the transnational organization.

Case 7-1   Levendary Café: The China Challenge

Christopher A. Bartlett and Arar Han

Levendary Café was spun out from private equity ownership in January 2011, and the following month, Mia Foster was named as its new CEO. The departing CEO, Howard Leventhal, was the beloved founder of the popular chain of 3,500 cafés.

HBS Professor Christopher A. Bartlett and writer Arar Han prepared this case solely as a basis for class discussion and not as an endorsement, a source of primary data, or an illustration of effective or ineffective management. This case, though based on real events, is fictionalized, and any resemblance to actual persons or entities is coincidental. There are some references to actual companies in the narration.

He had grown a small Denver soup, salad, and sandwich restaurant into a $10 billion business, but after 32 years was moving on to new interests.

This was Foster's first job as CEO. Previously, the 47-year-old had been president of the U.S. business of a large American fast food company for seven years. She had started her career at a major global accounting firm, leaving to earn an MBA from Wharton. Upon graduation, she had become a consultant at McKinsey before taking a job in product management at P&G, where she worked her way up the ranks. Foster was known for her frank communication style and strong execution.

In spite of the promise held by the Levendary brand and Foster's strong track record, Wall Street was cautious about the stock. While the company's fundamentals were strong, and its performance generally in line with management forecasts, its shares traded at a discount to comparable restaurant stocks. There were two reasons for this. First, analysts were concerned that Levendary's domestic business was nearly tapped out. Second, given Foster's lack of previous international management experience, they were skeptical of her ability to build a multi-national brand.

Foster felt challenged by Wall Street's skepticism and wanted to address it head-on. In particular, she knew that Levendary's recent entry into the fast-growing China market would be closely watched. So she was concerned by reports that recently opened China locations incorporated some dramatic departures from Levendary's U.S. concept, particularly in store design and menu selection. She was also frustrated by the apparent unwillingness of Louis Chen, Leventhal's hand-picked president of Levendary China, to conform to the company's planning and reporting processes. To address these concerns, Foster decided she needed to visit the Chinese operations.

On May 25, 2011, Foster stepped out of the limo that Chen had arranged to pick her up at the Shanghai Pudong airport. Heading in to her first in-person meeting with Chen, she knew there were big decisions to be made. Indeed, they would determine the future of Levendary China.

The Multi-Unit Restaurant Business

In 2010, the U.S. restaurant and contract food-service industry was a $600 billion industry with 960,000 locations.[1] Multi-unit restaurant concepts represented approximately 30% of the industry by units, with independent operators as the balance. The restaurant and food service industry was highly fragmented, and even industry giant McDonald's generated just 2% of total revenues.

Multi-unit concepts were generally categorized into three industry segments:

- **Specialty Establishments** like Starbucks, Dunkin' Donuts, and Baskin-Robbins primarily served snacks and beverages under $5.

- **Quick Service Restaurants,** or so-called "fast food" concepts like McDonald's, Taco Bell, and Wendy's, provided counter or drive-through service with average tickets between $4 and $10.
- **Casual Dining** included brands like Olive Garden, Applebee's, and Outback, and offered table service for dinner entrees priced between $8 and $20. Within this group, fine dining concepts like Ruth's Chris and Capital Grille featured entrées into the $40 range.

While some concepts had bridged these categories for years (e.g., Friendly's offered casual dining coupled with a strong takeaway ice cream business), more recently several concepts had clustered around an emerging category often called "Quick Casual." For example, Panda Express was a quick service format of Chinese casual dining, while Chipotle offered a quick casual Mexican-American dining experience. Like other quick casual restaurants, Levendary promised more wholesome choices than its quick service cousins and a more informal self-serve dining experience than its casual dining relatives. Quick casual restaurants typically had average checks in the $8 to $12 range.

Restaurant Cost Structure   Restaurants had relatively simple cost structures which one industry expert defined as follows:[2]

- **Occupancy:** These costs included real estate rental, common area maintenance, and energy and waste disposal. In the United States, they hovered around 10% of revenues.
- **Labor:** Even at minimum wage, labor was typically the largest cost element. High turnover in the industry required restaurant companies to continually source and train new employees and to manage employee attrition. Labor typically represented 25% to 35% of total revenues.
- **Food:** Food costs accounted for 28% to 32%. This expense was influenced by not only the cost of the ingredients purchased, but also the amount of waste.

[1]"Freedonia Focus on Restaurants," *Freedonia Group.* February 2011.

[2]http://www.bakertilly.com/userfiles/BT_Retail_ RestaurantBench marks_web_small.pdf

- **Supply:** About 1% to 4% of revenues typically went to paper products at quick service restaurants or to linen and uniform cleaning at higher-end casual dining restaurants.

In a best case scenario, a restaurant might make up to 35% gross margin, but 20% to 25% was more typical. Franchised restaurants also paid a royalty, adding a 3% to 6% cost line, and a marketing fee which added a further 2% to 10% in costs. Depending on the size of the franchise organization, overhead might account for another 5% to 15% of cost.

Restaurants typically operated on razor-thin margins, with profitability a direct function of their ability to generate high traffic, execute consistently, and control costs. Traffic, in turn, was a function of the brand's appeal, marketing effectiveness, real estate location, and store experience.

Levendary Café: The Foundations

In the quick casual restaurant segment, Levendary Café was distinguished by two elements: wholesome soups, salads, and sandwiches using high-quality ingredients, and a commitment to service in a comfortable, friendly environment. Its corporate chefs were highly trained artisans from the Culinary Institute of America and other top cooking schools who took pride in creating everyday versions of gourmet fare. Customers raved, "Eating at Levendary makes me feel rich."

Levendary was also distinguished by its willingness to take risks, especially those that helped evolve its concept over time. It was an entrepreneurial characteristic traced to founder Howard Leventhal. The most recent risky change occurred five years before Foster became CEO, when the company decided to use only organic grains in its breads and hormone-free naturally raised meats in its sandwiches. To management's delight, customers willingly paid the premium price, resulting in increased revenues and margins and a simultaneous boost in customer trust in the brand.

The Organizational Foundation: Blending Concepts and Operations A complex organization supported Levendary's primarily U.S. business. The Denver headquarters housed the following activities (see **Exhibit 1** for a basic organizational chart):

- **Concept:** For 23 years, Howard Leventhal had relied on Chief Concept Officer (CCO) Lucian Leclerc to keep Levendary a top U.S. restaurant concept. Leclerc managed both the food development group and the marketing team that together determined what Levendary represented to the customer. With Leclerc's uncanny ability to sense nascent food trends and Leventhal's willingness to take calculated risks, the pair had kept the company at the forefront of changing tastes. Their shared commitment to healthful, wholesome eating was embedded in the company's culture and reflected in its well-known advertising slogan "Tasty Fresh Goodness" or TFG as insiders referred to it.

- **Marketing:** The Marketing group reported to the CCO. Its creative team worked with outside advertising agencies to convey the TFG concept through advertising copy and images. The logo, store decor, and media images used a palette of earth tones to communicate natural, wholesome goodness. The distribution team ensured that banners, table tents, window decals, and menu boards were properly placed in all 3,500 company and franchised stores, appropriately modified for differences in store size and layout. Preparing menus and menu boards was complicated by variations in menu items to respond to local market preferences and by pricing differences to meet local competition. But the comfortable, welcoming, and homey "look and feel" of stores always remained consistent.

- **Food:** A fully scaled test kitchen and food science laboratory also reported to the CCO, taking the items developed by the CCO's executive chefs and making the adaptations necessary to supply their components with quality and consistency to each of Levendary' 3,500 cafés. The food team was also responsible for conducting quality checks in the field.

- **Operations:** Led by Chief Operating Officer (COO) Nick White, who had 30 years of

Exhibit 1   Levendary Organizational Chart

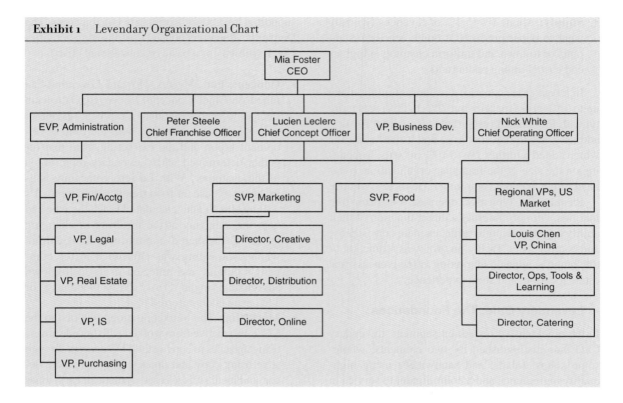

operating experience in U.S. franchised restaurant companies, this group managed the day-to-day restaurant business. Store managers at the 1,200 company-owned cafés reported to district managers, who in turn reported in to area directors, then market vice presidents. This structure allowed tight control of store level expenses and close monitoring of operations against the company's detailed and strict operating standards, policies, and practices. It also relayed any recommendations for modifications to the menu or variations in the store "look and feel" to the Concept group for consideration and approval.

The Operations group was also responsible for Operating Tools and Learning (OTL). As retail employees were often high school-aged or minimally educated, OTL set operating standards and provided materials to enhance employees' learning. Acting as a bridge between the Concept team and the stores, OTL also developed the training materials and processes to break down food preparation into steps that ensured quality local delivery of the chefs' gourmet creations. In general, OTL functioned as both an internal school and a standards enforcer.

• **Franchise:** About two-thirds of Levendary's 3,500 stores were franchised. Headed by Chief Franchise Officer Peter Steele, the franchise team recruited new franchisees, supported existing franchisees, and enforced brand and operating standards in franchised stores.

• **Business Development:** Staffed by former strategy consultants, this department sourced new revenue opportunities such as Levendary branded grocery items like coffee, cold cuts, and soups. This group also led research for the company's nascent international expansion and was responsible for an experimental licensing deal in Dubai. Launched in 2009, this opportunistic venture was run by a Saudi Arabian restaurant company owned by an old friend of Leventhal's. Aside from China, Dubai was Levendary's only international operation.

- **Administrative Staff Groups:** Real estate, finance and accounting, legal, purchasing, and information systems all reported to an Executive Vice President (EVP) of Administration.

Headquarters staff totaled approximately 300 in all. There was no separate international division.

The Strategic Base: Serving the U.S. Market

Levendary was built on a culture that emphasized "delighting the customer." As founder, Howard Leventhal was fond of telling store staff, "Forget today's profit. Have a positive impact on customers' lives. Make them want to come back. That's how we'll win in the long run." Day-to-day, this philosophy translated into a personalized approach that would accommodate customer requests such as removing sprouts from a sandwich or serving a soup extra hot. Such service appealed to Levendary's customer base of white-collar professionals and upper-middle-class women. "Heavy user" customers in these groups visited Levendary five or six times a week.

But this approach taxed Levendary's store-level operations. The two key store operating metrics of speed of service and order accuracy were driven by standardization, and personalization threatened both. In response to store operators who questioned his relentless drive to provide personal service, Leventhal would simply point to the company's impressive results. (See **Exhibit 2.**)

Leventhal's philosophy of delighting the customer also translated into local menu adaptions. With stores in urban, suburban, and rural environments across all 50 states, Levendary believed there was no such thing as "the American consumer." While McDonald's created one menu for its entire system, Levendary was more flexible. It offered fewer soup items and more drink options in the South, allowed one or two regional specialties to be added to its core menu, and listed its menu items in order of local popularity. While appreciated by customers, the menu variations represented a challenge for the Food, Operations, and Marketing teams.

Exhibit 2   Levendary Income Statement (2010)

	Year Ending December 31, 2010
Revenues	
Sales	9,248,134
Royalties	603,365
Ingredient & paper good sales to franchisees	945,924
Total	10,797,423
Costs and Expenses	
Food & Paper	2,623,712
Labor	2,933,980
Occupancy	706,790
Total	6,264,482
Food and paper good inventory	776,902
Depreciation and amortization	480,711
G&A	710,458
Marketing	1,239,413
Pre-opening expenses	29,974
Total costs and expenses	3,237,458
Operating profit	1,295,483
Interest expense	4,725
Other expense	29,624
Income before tax	1,261,134
Income tax	480,571
Net income	**780,563**

To keep the brand fresh in the eyes of the customer, the company was also committed to evolving menu choices, typically by featuring in-trend healthy ingredients like pomegranates or quinoa. The Concept team rolled out a suite of new products five times a year, often with minor variants adapted to the South's appetite for fattier, sweeter formulations, or the Northeast's love of turkey and cheddar cheese. Each new release was accompanied by a marketing program and new menu boards.

In truth, the new items boosted the company's image more than its sales. Systemwide sales were driven by a small number of core items. For 80% of locations, those included such Levendary classics as its turkey and avocado sandwich with cranberry dressing, its award-winning cheese soup, and its chicken Caesar salad. For the other 20% of outlets, the core sales drivers could be as diverse as espresso beverages, Howard's Famous Cookies, or a local seasonal special.

Expanding Abroad: China Dreams

In 2008, the company's domestic growth was slowing. Its geographic expansion strategy (jokingly referred to within the company as "follow the mommies," later adapted to "follow the yuppies") had plateaued. Recognizing that its concept did not translate well into small towns, particularly in the Midwest and South, the board of directors began discussions about overseas expansion. At the board's urging, management instructed its strategy team to research opportunities in China, a market that had attracted a great deal of attention among U.S. restaurant companies.

Opportunities in China With a population of 1.4 billion people and annual GDP growth of 14.5% over the past decade, China was ripe for investment. Two additional trends attracted U.S. restaurants: China's urban population rose from 36.2% of the total in 2000 to 46.6% in 2009, and a strong middle class emerged whose per capita income surged from RMB 6,282 to RMB 17,175. (In 2010, RMB 1 = USD 0.15.)

An affluent middle class, a large increase of women in the workforce, and a growing lifestyle trend to eat out all supported growth in the Chinese food services industry, which increased from RMB 1.106 trillion in 2004 to RMB 1.996 trillion five years later. Independent full-service restaurants still dominated the industry (there were 2,723,000 nationally), but the highly competitive quick service sector was growing the fastest, from RMB 254 billion in 2004 to RMB 471 billion in 2009.

While foreign fast food companies attracted the most attention, restaurants serving Asian food, primarily Chinese, took the biggest share of the quick service segment. These mostly independent restaurants appealed to locals' preference for rice-based

dishes and low prices. However, due to low margins, wide variation in regional food tastes, and most of all, the difficulty independents had experienced in standardizing operations, there were few successful local chains.

The most successful foreign fast food chain was KFC, which had more than 3,000 restaurants in 450 Chinese cities. In 2010, KFC opened on average one new store every day. Through its Chinese joint venture partners and local management, it had learned to adapt. It added a few items such as congee rice porridge and even altered the famous seasoning on its core fried chicken offering.

McDonald's entered China in 1992, five years after KFC, and by 2010 operated 1,100 restaurants in 110 cities. Its restaurants retained a consistent worldwide look and feel, and a menu featuring its Big Mac, McNuggets, and french fries. While its core menu was the same, localized specials such as the China Mac with black pepper sauce, pork burgers, and red bean ice cream had been added. Despite the fact that a plate of six pork buns cost 25 cents at a Chinese street stall, McDonald still charged $2.50 for its large fries, appealing to Chinese youth's willingness to indulge in foreign fare.

Pizza Hut's China strategy was notable for its departure from its U.S. original. Its 560 outlets were positioned as high-end casual dining restaurants, and its menu extended well beyond pizza to include scallop croquettes and escargot. Wine was served, reservations were accepted, and a 45-minute wait for a table was not uncommon. Young affluent Chinese went to Pizza Hut to impress their dates.

Despite these successes, many other American restaurants had struggled in China. When Applebee's replanted itself in Shanghai, the concept fizzled. So too did California Pizza Kitchen, forcing the founders to personally intervene to relaunch the effort. Many attributed Pretzel Time's failure in China to its white tile décor that reminded people of a bathroom.

More recently, Chinese chains had begun to learn from foreign competition and began to focus on standardization and tight control of raw materials, food preparation, and in-store service. After overtaking McDonald's as Hong Kong's leading chain, Dar Jia Le ("*Big Happy House*") took its tightly controlled operations to China. Other successful Asian chains in China included U.S.-listed Country Style Cooking (2009 Chinese sales of $495 million) serving Sichuan food, Hong Kong-based Little Sheep ($235 million) featuring Mongolian hot pot, and Japan's Ajisen ($256 million) ramen shops.

Leaping into China   After reviewing the research, Levendary's board and top management decided to enter China. The decision was hastened by the appearance of Louis Chen as a viable candidate to lead the effort. Chen heard about Levendary's interest in China through a Stanford MBA classmate who had become a partner at the private equity firm that had owned the company prior to its 2011 IPO. Chen gradually earned the confidence of CEO Leventhal and other key stakeholders. In time, Leventhal dropped his original idea of a joint venture with an established Chinese operator, and entrusted Levendary China to Chen, whose energy and entrepreneurial spirit reminded him of an earlier version of himself.

Chen's formal contract provided a two-year term starting in September 2009 with an option for annual renewal, but his relationship with the company was best described as a handshake agreement. While Chen formally reported to Leventhal, the CEO managed him with a very light touch. He asked Chen to establish a strong market position as a base for franchising outlets throughout China, but apart from a requirement to "do right by the concept," gave him broad latitude to execute.

To prepare for his assignment, Chen became a rotational intern in each of the major departments in Levendary's Denver headquarters as well as in a handful of stores. Over six weeks, his mandate was to pick up as much as he could and replicate it in China. The Denver team invited him to tap into their resources and expertise, interpreting and adapting them for use in the local Chinese stores. Before his departure for China, the board asked Chen about his plans. He was confident:

> It won't be easy but others have succeeded and we can too. I believe we have a good chance of building

a credible foundation of stores and breaking even within a year. We just have to be flexible. For example, Chinese eat few dairy products, so we should downplay our cheese soup. But a new generation now gives milk to its children, so tastes are evolving. And most people aren't familiar with turkey, but they love chicken, so we'll adapt the menu, just as we do in the States. It may take time, but I believe Levendary will connect with Chinese youth, and that's the future.

In spite of the monumental work ahead, the board was convinced that Chen was the right choice. The 34-year-old was bilingual in English and Mandarin Chinese, and his decade-long experience as a retail property developer gave him intimate familiarity with neighborhoods in Shanghai and Beijing—a valuable asset given the powerful impact of store location on profitability. Chen also had a network of contacts to help speed up the process of permitting, incorporating, and staffing stores. Finally, he was passionate about good food, and had long wanted to work in the restaurant industry.

Chen opened his first location in the expatriate-heavy Pudong region of Shanghai in January 2010, just three months after returning to China in his new role. Occupying the corner ground floor location of a new high-rise office building, the first restaurant was both prominent and luxurious. It was an instant hit among white-collar employees of the global financial firms housed above it. Taking a page from Pizza Hut's China playbook, Chen positioned the new location as casual dining with table service and higher prices than local fast food concepts. But with the real estate markets in Beijing and Shanghai heating up, and KFC and McDonald's snapping up sites, Chen wanted to move fast. His local knowledge and connections helped him lock in prime locations at good prices, and within a year, his initial location had grown into a chain of 23 restaurants.

Expansion in China: Key Decisions

During her interview process, Foster heard much about the great hopes for Levendary China. However, she had not had the opportunity to meet Chen or to closely examine the China business. When she became CEO in February 2011, the new CEO was surprised to find that the Chinese subsidiary submitted all management and financial reports to Denver in its own format. The finance group then "massaged" them to apply U.S. Generally Accepted Accounting Principles (GAAP) and adapt them to Levendary's internal monthly reporting format. Foster felt strongly that this would not be a sustainable practice as the China operations grew into a larger portion of total revenue.

The First Meeting: Raising the Questions   In considering her options for bringing the China reporting in line with the U.S., Foster favored hiring an international financial analyst for the Denver finance team, and thought Levendary's auditor should also manage the China audit. Both steps were expensive but seemed necessary for a publicly traded company that intended to stake its future on growth in the China market. During a video conference that Foster set up to meet Chen in her first week at Levendary, she shared these thoughts with him. He bristled at her suggestions, claiming that both changes would not only incur unnecessary costs but would also greatly inconvenience his local operations.

Chen's resistance struck Foster as either naïve or antagonistic, and she responded firmly: "You're going to have to make a change, Louis. We have to protect the integrity of our reporting structure." "Fine," Chen shot back. "But to operate here, we have to be compliant with local tax laws or we'll get shut down. If you need those changes, you're going to have to spend the money to set it up right." Saying she would follow up, Foster left the virtual meeting with a nagging feeling that developing a productive relationship with Chen was not going to be easy.

The next day, Foster added the China operations as an agenda item in the weekly executive meeting she held with her direct reports in Denver. The EVP of Administration agreed that using non-GAAP numbers from China in the financial reports was a risk, and that formalizing the reporting process was a necessary change. As the discussion broadened, COO Nick White, the person to whom Chen had reported since Leventhal's departure, spoke up:

> I talk to Louis every week or two. I'm floored by how quickly he got a couple dozen stores up and running. It's an amazing achievement. But the reality is that no senior executive has visited China since Howard officiated at the opening ceremony for the Pudong store a year ago. I'm sure a lot has changed since then, but I haven't been able to get Louis to give me much. Howard gave Louis a lot of freedom to establish the Chinese operations, and frankly, it shows. Louis is a great asset but I confess managing him has been a frustrating exercise.

By the end of the meeting, the executive team had agreed it was time to obtain more information about the China operations. Chief Franchise Officer Peter Steele agreed to conduct a comprehensive review of the 23 Levendary Cafés in that market. White said he would advise Chen of Steele's plans, emphasizing that this was a routine process regularly undertaken in all franchised and licensed cafés in the U.S. market, and that Steele had recently completed such a review in Dubai.

Steele spent 10 days in China, and at a weekly executive meeting in late March, presented his findings. He provided detailed descriptions of the 23 China locations, all in or around Beijing and Shanghai. Chen had taken many liberties with the look and feel of the cafés. While the first location in Pudong largely conformed to Levendary's design standards and menu selection, other locations held surprising and sometimes alarming changes. For example, the second location, located in Shanghai's historic Yu Garden area, was a take-away counter with no seating. The third location, on Beijing's embassy row, was similar to the first store in both design and offering, but the fourth, at the north entrance to Beijing's Forbidden City, not only had no salads on its menu, it replaced Levendary's classic wooden framed upholstered chairs with a plastic framed alternative from a local furniture supplier. By the opening of the 23rd location in a Korean expatriate-heavy suburb of Shanghai, all but one sandwich item had been removed from the menu, and replaced by a variety of local dumplings.

Immediately after the meeting, an irate Lucian Leclerc appeared in Foster's office. She was not surprised, given his visible agitation during Steele's presentation. "Plastic chairs and dumplings! This is a pure disaster," he exploded. "What's going on in China could destroy everything I've worked for over the past 23 years. Our customers travel a lot, and in one visit to just one of those places, our carefully nurtured concept and image will be ruined. Mia, you need to stop Louis now."

After letting him vent, Foster reassured Leclerc that she would give the issue her full attention. She turned to examine a chart comparing several Levendary locations in the United States and China (**Exhibit 3**). Inwardly, she knew that resolving this issue would be a big test for her.

Meeting Two: Confronting the Issues   In early April, Foster sent Chen a copy of Steele's findings in advance of a second video conference to which she also invited White. Foster opened the discussion by explaining that China was critical to Levendary's growth, so she wanted to be involved in discussions about its plans. She explained how concerned she and White had been about Steele's report. Chen's response sounded angry:

I don't think you guys appreciate the difficulty of managing a business in this environment. We've worked like crazy this past year and half. And in a tough market with minimum support from Denver, we've built a business that works in China. But now that we've opened 23 locations in just over a year and are about to turn a profit, you want me to change everything? Why would you do that?

Levendary as it exists in the U.S. simply will not work in China. Have you seen Denny's in Japan? It's wildly successful but it serves *tonkatsu* [a Japanese breaded and fried pork cutlet] and *ramen*. They understand that nobody wants pancakes and BLTs in Tokyo. People want the food they know but with cool American branding.

The only places where we can do what Levendary does in the U.S. are Pudong and Beijing's embassy row. Those locations are up and running using the American model. Everywhere else, we have to adapt our store design and menu. Otherwise, we won't be profitable. I think our performance speaks for itself (**Exhibit 4**).

Exhibit 3   Comparison of Two Levendary U.S. and Two Levendary China Locations

	Metro U.S./NYC	Suburban U.S./Denver area	Metro China/ Beijing Embassy	Metro–suburb China/Shanghai Koreatown
Annualized 2010 sales (USD)	$10,320,000	$2,126,000	$806,000	$288,000
Square footage	2,500	4,000	1,500	500
Seats	84	120	80	0 (counter only)
Staff (full-time equivalent)	24	26	20	13
Average traffic (guests per day)	3,210	560	260	430
Average check (USD)	$15	$12	$10	$2
Top 5 menu items	Turkey sand	Denver Melt sand.	Chicken soup	Chicken dumpling
	Cheese soup	Cheese soup	Chicken sand.	Pork dumpling
	Salmon salad	Turkey sand.	Roast beef sand.	Chicken sand.
	Chicken sand	Caesar salad	BBQ chicken sand.	BBQ chicken sand.
	Caesar salad	Howard's cookie	Thai veggie soup	Pu-erh tea
Outdoor seating?		X		
Personalized service?	X	X	X (simplified table service)	
Free WiFi?	X	X	X	

Exhibit 4   Levendary China Income
Statement (2010)

	Year Ending October 31, 2010
Sales (US$)	$ 3,261,598
Costs and Expenses	
Food & Paper	1,663,415
Labor	382,720
Occupancy	782,784
Total	2,828,919
Depreciation and amortization	6,523
G&A	163,080
Marketing	65,232
Pre-opening expenses	391,392
Total costs and expenses	3,455,145
Operating profit	−193,547
Interest expense	0
Other expense	5,925
Income before tax	−199,472
Income tax	−55,852
Net income	**−143,620**

Having reviewed the research, Foster was keenly aware of the difficulties of localizing a chain restaurant concept in a foreign market and the major tradeoffs entailed. She was aware that the Japanese company operating Denny's Japan had great success by radically changing its entire menu while keeping the stores' look and feel. But she also knew that the McDonald's approach was much more standardized worldwide. A McDonald's in Shanghai varied from one in New York City only in local marketing practices and some limited menu deletions and insertions. Indeed, Foster had been amazed to learn that McDonald's had even imported bricks to new markets it entered in Eastern Europe so that its restaurants would be as consistent as possible to its U.S. standards.

These were two opposite approaches, and Foster was not sure either model was appropriate for Levendary. She had yet to be convinced by Chen's assertion that growth in China required that the stores and menus be as different as they had become, and responded carefully:

> Louis, I think Peter's report gives us a good starting point to think about that issue going forward. You've provided us a great platform for our future growth in China. Now it's time for us to think through how we want to do that. The home office will probably need to step up and do more to support you. We'll also have to ensure the Levendary brand is positioned for growth, and that will require some consistency across borders. Nick and I will both commit to working with you to support your efforts. But we first need to fully understand your strategic plan for growth in China.

A more conciliatory-sounding Chen responded:

> Mia, you speak from a place of ideas, best practices, and compliance. But I'm here in the trenches running 23 restaurants that I've built one by one by reading market needs and sensing opportunities. I'm proud of Levendary's presence here. When you send in headquarters analysts and start telling me things need to change, I don't think you have a good sense of what it took to get us to where we are.
>
> You asked me about my strategic plan. Well I don't have one. And frankly, if I'd had one, I don't think we would have grown so quickly because we wouldn't have been as nimble or responded as flexibly to market needs. I'm willing to work with you to make some changes. But understand that I was given free rein for 18 months. If you start putting in new controls and tying local operations to the home office, I can't be held responsible if growth slows. If you make changes, we'll need to be very clear about what I'm responsible for, and what can I expect from Denver.

Foster found herself annoyed at what she sensed to be Chen's continued resistance and negative attitude. But there was no time for that now. Thoughts racing, she thanked Chen for his candor and expressed a desire to visit China to see in person what he had built, and also to finally meet him face-to-face. Chen welcomed her planned visit and offered his sympathy for the pressure she must be feeling from Wall Street. "Mia, I love what I'm doing, and I hope we can work things out. I really want to stay on when my contract expires in a few months," he said.

After ending the video conference, Foster reviewed the exchange with White. The conversation had raised some big issues that needed to be resolved: What strategy should Levendary adopt to drive its expansion in China? Who should have responsibility to make and implement those decisions? And what changes, if any, should be made in the roles, responsibilities, and relationships that linked China's management team to the home office? Acknowledging the importance of these issues, White agreed it was vital for Foster to get closer to the China business. A visit was set for May.

Meeting Three: Deciding the Future

On May 25, as her plane landed at Shanghai's Pudong International Airport, Foster felt a mix of excitement and concern. She was thrilled to finally visit this market that held such great potential for the Levendary brand and for her new role as CEO. But she was also grappling with some nagging doubts about whether Chen was right person for the job.

An old mentor had once told Foster that there were three types of managers in a new business's evolution to greater scale: the go-getter, the local baron, and the professional manager. All three types could be entrepreneurial in spirit, but not all were equally well suited for the various stages of a business's growth. Chen was clearly a go-getter who had evolved to become a local baron. The question in Foster's mind was whether he could transition to become a professional manager.

Two hours later, Mia Foster got out of the limousine that Louis Chen had arranged to pick her up at the airport. As she strode toward the entrance of Levendary's Shanghai office, she felt confident and prepared. Foster was ready for this conversation.

Case 7-2   Clayton Industries: Peter Arnell, Country Manager for Italy

Christopher A. Bartlett and Benjamin H. Barlow

In late September 2009, Peter Arnell, country manager of Clayton SpA, the Italian subsidiary of U.S.-based Clayton Industries, faced some daunting challenges as the global recession took its toll.

▍ HBS Professor Christopher A. Bartlett and writer Benjamin H. Barlow prepared this case solely as a basis for class discussion and not as an endorsement, a source of primary data, or an illustration of effective or ineffective management. The authors thank Sisto Merolla (HBS MBA 2002) of Merloni Termosanitari Spa of Fabriano, Italy, for his helpful contributions to the development of this case. This case, though based on real events, is fictionalized, and any resemblance to actual persons or entities is coincidental. There are occasional references to actual companies in the narration.

Sales were down 19%, and after decades of solid returns, Clayton SpA was in its third year of losses, now accumulating at more than $1 million a month.

Arnell's attention was sharpened by the imminent visit of Dan Briggs, Clayton's recently appointed CEO, and Simonne Buis, Arnell's direct boss and President of Clayton Europe. Both expected him to turn around Clayton SpA and position it for future growth. And although he had only been in Italy for just over two months, Arnell knew that Briggs and Buis would want to know exactly what action he intended to take.

The Parent Company: Clayton Industries

Founded in Milwaukee in 1938, Clayton Industries Inc. had built a successful business around window-mounted room air conditioners which it sold for residential and light-commercial applications. In the early 1980s, management perceived two important growth opportunities—one in the North American commercial sector, and the other in residential and commercial markets in Europe—and took steps to exploit both.

As it expanded abroad, Clayton established its position in Europe by acquiring four companies:

- Corliss, a U.K.-based manufacturer of home heating, ventilation, and air conditioning (HVAC) systems.
- Fontaire, a Brussels-based manufacturer of fans and ventilating equipment.
- Control del Clima, a Barcelona-based manufacturer of climate control products for industrial and commercial applications.
- AeroPuro, a Brescia, Italy-based manufacturer of compression chillers for large commercial, public, and institutional installations. (Chillers are the units at the core of most industrial air conditioners.)

To manage international expansion, Clayton restructured its organization in 1988. All operations in the United States and Canada were placed under Clayton North America, while the European acquisitions reported to a newly created Clayton Europe. Each of these entities was headed by a regional company president. (See **Exhibit 1** for the organizational chart.)

Clayton Europe

In 1989, Clayton Europe adopted the Brussels offices formerly occupied by Fontaire as its headquarters. Recognizing the need for strong management in each country where it had a presence, the new president of Clayton Europe appointed four country managers. They were given responsibility for sales of the full line of Clayton products in their home country and their allocated export markets in Europe.

Early progress was slow. While the European market for air conditioning began to grow in the 1990s, it was from a low base. Even in 1998, air-conditioning was in only 7% of homes in Italy, and 11% in Spain, compared with U.S. penetration of 71%. Many Europeans saw air conditioning as an expensive American luxury that harmed the environment.

Clayton's slow market penetration also reflected Europeans' different needs and national brand preferences. For example, Clayton's window units (assembled in Belgium from components shipped from the United States) did not sell as well as familiar local brands that Europeans seemed to prefer. And its central AC units also struggled in Europe where few buildings had duct work required for such systems. But a couple of Asian producers had been able to gain penetration in Europe, largely on the basis of price.

As a result of Europeans' strong national brand preferences, the Corliss-sourced HVAC systems and the Fontaire line of fans both sold much better in their home markets than elsewhere in Europe. But no product represented this geographic concentration more strongly than the chiller line built in Italy. A decade after it had been offered to all Clayton's European companies, sales outside Italy accounted for only 12% of the total.

In 2001, Simonne Buis, previously the hard-driving head of the Belgian company, was named president of Clayton Europe. Determined to create a more integrated European organization, her first priority was to increase the operational efficiency of Clayton's diverse portfolio of inherited plants. She set tough targets that required them to slash costs, build scale, or both. Then, to encourage Europe-wide penetration of the entire product line, she informed country managers that in addition to their national sales responsibility, they would now be held responsible for Europe-wide profitability of products produced in their plants. She encouraged them to emerge from their country subsidiary silos and collaborate. The simple geographic-based structure was evolving toward a product-overlaid matrix.

Over the next seven years, Europe became a major growth engine for Clayton, increasing its share of the company's global revenue from 33% in 2000 to 45% by 2009. During this period, Belgium/France overtook Italy as Clayton Europe's lead market, its 38% of 2009 revenues ahead of Italy's 30%. Spain accounted for 20%, and the U.K. for 12%.

But the European growth engine stalled when the global recession of 2008–09 hit. (**Exhibit 2** summarizes Clayton's financial statements.) It was a crisis

Exhibit 1 Clayton Industries: Organization of Operations, August 2009

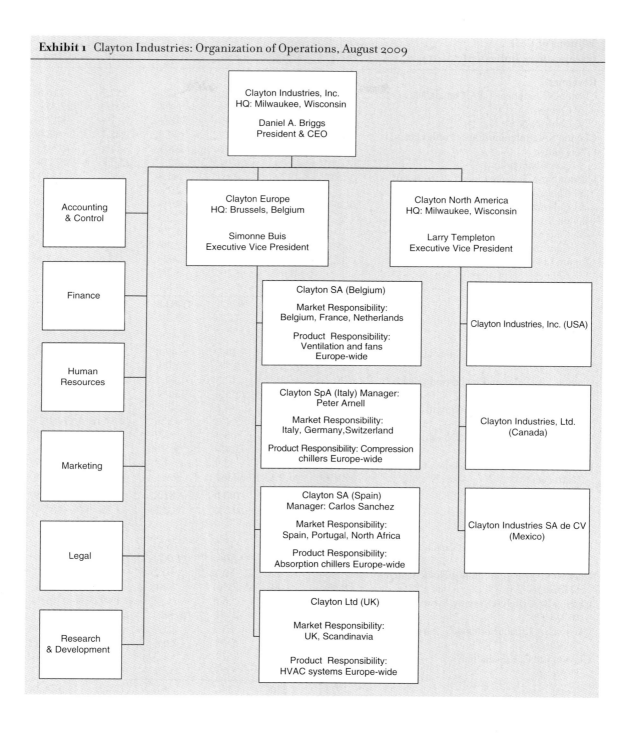

Exhibit 2 Clayton Industries: Income Statement—Summary, 2004–2009

Millions of USD (except where indicated)	2004	2005	2006	2007	2008	1H09
Revenues						
Clayton N. America (USA/Canada/Mexico)	565.7	577.1	590.0	598.1	557.7	216.6
% Change		*2.0%*	*2.2%*	*1.4%*	*(6.8%)*	*(22.3%)*
% Contribution	*63.2%*	*61.8%*	*60.7%*	*59.6%*	*58.0%*	*54.7%*
Clayton SA (Belgium/France/Netherlands)	107.5	118.6	129.7	142.3	148.7	68.0
% Change		*10.3%*	*9.3%*	*9.8%*	*4.4%*	*(8.5%)*
% Contribution	*12.0%*	*12.7%*	*13.3%*	*14.2%*	*15.5%*	*17.2%*
Clayton SpA (Italy/Germany/Switzerland)	125.0	132.5	138.0	141.8	134.3	54.1
% Change		*6.0%*	*4.2%*	*2.7%*	*(5.3%)*	*(19.4%)*
% Contribution	*14.0%*	*14.2%*	*14.2%*	*14.1%*	*14.0%*	*13.7%*
Clayton SA (Spain/Portugal/N. Africa)	58.1	62.9	68.1	72.3	72.2	36.0
% Change		*8.1%*	*8.4%*	*6.2%*	*(0.1%)*	*(0.3%)*
% Contribution	*6.5%*	*6.7%*	*7.0%*	*7.2%*	*7.5%*	*9.1%*
Clayton Ltd (UK/Scandinavia)	39.3	42.8	45.9	48.3	48.6	21.6
% Change		*8.9%*	*7.2%*	*5.2%*	*0.6%*	*(11.1%)*
% Contribution	*4.4%*	*4.6%*	*4.7%*	*4.8%*	*5.1%*	*5.5%*
Total	**895.7**	**933.8**	**971.7**	**1,002.8**	**961.4**	**396.3**
% Change		*4.3%*	*4.1%*	*3.2%*	*(4.1%)*	*(17.6%)*
EBITDA						
Clayton N. America (USA/Canada/Mexico)	70.7	69.2	53.1	47.8	27.9	6.5
% Margin	*12.5%*	*12.0%*	*9.0%*	*8.0%*	*5.0%*	*3.0%*
Clayton SA (Belgium/France/Netherlands)	20.2	21.3	17.5	17.1	11.1	3.1
% Margin	*18.8%*	*18.0%*	*13.5%*	*12.0%*	*7.5%*	*4.5%*
Clayton SpA (Italy/Germany/Switzerland)	25.1	24.5	18.1	5.2	(12.8)	(7.6)
% Margin	*20.1%*	*18.5%*	*13.1%*	*3.7%*	*(9.5%)*	*(14.1%)*
Clayton SA (Spain/Portugal/N. Africa)	10.0	10.4	8.4	6.9	6.6	3.2
% Margin	*17.2%*	*16.5%*	*12.4%*	*9.5%*	*9.1%*	*8.9%*
Clayton Ltd (UK/Scandinavia)	7.0	7.3	5.9	4.8	2.9	0.7
% Margin	*17.9%*	*17.2%*	*12.9%*	*9.9%*	*6.0%*	*3.4%*
Total	**133.0**	**132.8**	**103.0**	**81.8**	**35.8**	**5.9**
% Margin	*14.8%*	*14.2%*	*10.6%*	*8.2%*	*3.7%*	*1.5%*
Net income (loss)						
Clayton N. America (USA/Canada/Mexico)	31.1	28.9	11.8	(6.0)	(22.3)	(17.3)
% Margin	*5.5%*	*5.0%*	*2.0%*	*(1.0%)*	*(4.0%)*	*(8.0%)*
Clayton SA (Belgium/France/Netherlands)	8.9	9.5	10.1	10.2	5.9	0.7
% Margin	*8.3%*	*8.0%*	*7.8%*	*7.2%*	*4.0%*	*1.0%*
Clayton SpA (Italy/Germany/Switzerland)	10.8	10.5	6.0	(1.1)	(11.9)	(6.7)
% Margin	*8.7%*	*7.9%*	*4.4%*	*(0.8%)*	*(8.8%)*	*(12.3%)*
Clayton SA (Spain/Portugal/N. Africa)	4.1	4.1	3.7	1.9	0.2	0.0
% Margin	*7.1%*	*6.5%*	*5.4%*	*2.6%*	*0.3%*	*0.1%*
Clayton Ltd (UK/Scandinavia)	2.9	2.9	2.6	1.3	(0.3)	(0.9)
% Margin	*7.4%*	*6.8%*	*5.6%*	*2.7%*	*(0.5%)*	*(4.2%)*
Total	**57.9**	**55.8**	**34.2**	**6.4**	**(28.3)**	**(24.2)**
% Margin	*6.5%*	*6.0%*	*3.5%*	*0.6%*	*(2.9)%*	*(6.1)%*

Source: http://www.usatoday.com/, January 2008, accessed on May 29, 2011.

that triggered strategic adjustments and management changes in both the U.S. and European operations.

Crisis Response in the United States and Europe

As the economic crisis deepened in 2009, the Clayton Industries board convinced its 63-year-old, long-time CEO to step aside in favor of Dan Briggs, a 16-year company veteran who, along with Buis, had been groomed as a potential CEO successor. Briggs was a no-nonsense manager who was previously EVP of Clayton North America.

On assuming his new role in March 2009, Briggs quickly established two priorities. Facing a cash crisis, he underlined the urgency of reducing capital use and bringing costs under control. But he also emphasized that "great opportunities always reside inside crisis," and urged managers to use the downturn to rationalize the company's portfolio and focus on products that could position it for post-recession profitable growth.

As he discussed these priorities with Buis, Briggs told her that he saw Europe as a continued source of growth. But he questioned whether the company should continue its attempts to penetrate the commercial air conditioning sector. In Briggs's view, it was a business in which only the top three or four competitors in any market could make money, and he was skeptical that Clayton could get there from its current situation.

Buis argued that several record-breaking hot European summers were changing consumer attitudes and that the market was on the cusp of embracing air-conditioning. She felt that the company should be positioning for a post-recession expansion. Recognizing Buis's successes in Europe, Briggs asked her to prepare a growth plan to review with him.

To translate Briggs's corporate priorities into European actions, Buis met with her country managers and told them she wanted all country operations to achieve a 10/10/10 plan to cut both receivables and inventories by 10 days, and reduce headcount by 10%. She also announced the "Top Four in Four" initiative, and asked each manager to prepare plans showing how the product for which he had

Europe-wide responsibility would be in the top four in European market share within four years.

Problems at Clayton SpA

While these new targets would be difficult for all of Clayton's European companies, in Italy they would be a real challenge. Lagging other countries in revenue growth since 2004, Clayton SpA actually recorded a 5.3% sales decline in 2008, followed by a 19.4% drop in the first half of 2009. As a result, receivables and inventories were both above 120 days sales. In addition, headcount reduction faced tough local laws and a tense union relationship. In short, achieving the 10/10/10 plan would be very difficult.

The "Top Four in Four" requirement would also be a challenge for the Italian unit's Europe-wide responsibility for chillers. While this line accounted for 55% of 2009 Italian revenues, it generated only 12% of sales for the rest of Europe. (See **Exhibits 3** and **4** for industry sales and projections). Of the seven companies in the European chiller market, Clayton was in a distant fifth place with a 7% overall market share.

As performance declined, Paolo Lazzaro, president of Clayton SpA since 1998, claimed that the problems were due to the commodity cycle, and suggested that Clayton should "weather the storm." Frustrated by this attitude, Buis terminated Lazzaro in June 2009. As she began thinking about who could take over, her mind turned to Peter Arnell.

Peter Arnell   Peter Arnell was the 42-year-old head of the British subsidiary, Clayton Ltd. Raised in a working-class family on the outskirts of London, Arnell served seven years in the Royal Marines where he rose to the rank of Captain before attending business school in London. A brief stint in management consulting left him missing the sense of impact he had experienced in the Royal Marines. So in 1998 he joined Clayton's Birmingham office in a sales and marketing job that he thought would let him test himself again on the front lines.

An avid weekend footballer, Arnell was a born competitor, quick with both a handshake and a smile. He drove himself hard and expected the same from

Exhibit 3   Clayton Industries: Balance Sheet—Summary, 2004–2009

Millions of USD	2004	2005	2006	2007	2008	1H09
Current assets	**$ 277.0**	**$ 291.6**	**$ 303.8**	**$ 308.8**	**$ 284.2**	**$ 254.4**
Clayton SpA	$ 9.0	$ 54.1	$ 58.7	$ 62.6	$ 61.6	$ 59.6
Other Europe	$ 60.6	$ 66.5	$ 71.7	$ 75.2	$ 72.5	$ 71.5
North America	$ 167.4	$ 171.0	$ 173.5	$ 171.0	$ 150.1	$ 123.3
Facilities	**$ 417.6**	**$ 400.4**	**$ 385.5**	**$ 371.1**	**$ 354.4**	**$ 336.6**
Clayton SpA	$ 50.4	$ 54.6	$ 48.9	$ 44.7	$ 40.7	$ 38.0
Other Europe	$ 139.4	$ 129.4	$ 124.9	$ 118.7	$ 112.6	$ 109.6
North America	$ 227.9	$ 216.4	$ 211.6	$ 207.8	$ 201.1	$ 189.1
Other assets	**$ 88.0**	**$ 118.7**	**$ 124.1**	**$ 141.3**	**$ 125.2**	**$ 140.2**
Clayton SpA	$ 12.3	$ 16.8	$ 17.6	$ 20.0	$ 17.5	$ 19.1
Other Europe	$ 20.1	$ 28.5	$ 31.1	$ 37.0	$ 35.1	$ 44.4
North America	$ 55.6	$ 73.4	$ 75.4	$ 84.3	$ 72.6	$ 76.6
Total assets	**$ 782.7**	**$ 810.7**	**$ 813.4**	**$ 821.2**	**$ 763.8**	**$ 731.2**
Clayton SpA	$ 111.6	$ 125.5	$ 125.2	$ 127.2	$ 119.7	$ 116.7
Other Europe	$ 220.2	$ 224.4	$ 227.7	$ 230.9	$ 220.2	$ 225.5
North America	$ 450.9	$ 460.8	$ 460.5	$ 463.1	$ 423.8	$ 389.0
Current liabilities	**$ 204.3**	**$ 224.3**	**$ 238.6**	**$ 255.3**	**$ 251.7**	**$ 255.4**
Clayton SpA	$ 28.5	$ 32.9	$ 36.7	$ 41.2	$ 42.7	$ 45.5
Other Europe	$ 46.7	$ 51.3	$ 54.6	$ 58.4	$ 57.6	$ 58.4
North America	$ 129.0	$ 140.1	$ 147.3	$ 155.6	$ 151.4	$ 151.5
Long-term debt	**$ 310.5**	**$ 340.9**	**$ 362.6**	**$ 388.0**	**$ 382.5**	**$ 388.2**
Clayton SpA	$ 43.3	$ 50.0	$ 55.8	$ 62.7	$ 64.9	$ 69.1
Other Europe	$ 71.1	$ 81.9	$ 91.5	$ 102.8	$ 106.4	$ 113.4
North America	$ 196.1	$ 209.0	$ 215.3	$ 222.5	$ 211.3	$ 205.7
Stockholders' equity	**$ 267.9**	**$ 245.5**	**$ 212.3**	**$ 177.9**	**$ 129.6**	**$ 87.6**
Clayton SpA	$ 37.4	$ 32.2	$ 23.1	$ 12.2	$ (0.9)	$ (14.8)
Other Europe	$ 61.3	$ 61.5	$ 57.9	$ 54.1	$ 50.1	$ 59.9
North America	$ 169.2	$ 151.8	$ 131.3	$ 111.6	$ 80.4	$ 42.5
Total liabilities and equity	**$ 782.7**	**$ 810.7**	**$ 813.4**	**$ 821.2**	**$ 763.8**	**$ 731.2**
Clayton SpA	$ 109.2	$ 115.0	$ 115.6	$ 116.1	$ 106.7	$ 99.8
Other Europe	$ 179.1	$ 194.7	$ 204.0	$ 215.3	$ 214.1	$ 231.7
North America	$ 494.4	$ 501.0	$ 493.9	$ 489.8	$ 443.0	$ 399.6

others. While very outgoing, he expressed opinions bluntly and had alienated a few colleagues during his time at Clayton. Quickly promoted to marketing manager, Arnell had expanded Clayton's distribution network from four distributors in central England to 14 throughout the U.K. and Ireland, positioning Clayton's product line to capitalize on the U.K. real estate boom. In 2002, when the head of Clayton Ltd. retired, Buis promoted Arnell to fill the role.

Within weeks, Arnell took the tough decision of closing the old Corliss boiler plant—a move that was in line with the cost cutting program that Buis

Exhibit 4   Industry Sales of Air Treatment Products (including Chillers) 2003–2008

Millions of USD (except where indicated)	2003	2004	2005	2006	2007	2008
Units ('000)						
United States	61,263.4	64,104.4	67,137.1	70,380.4	71,142.0	71,410.2
% Change		*4.6%*	*4.7%*	*4.8%*	*1.1%*	*0.4%*
Europe	15,315.9	16,667.1	18,127.0	19,706.5	20,986.9	22,137.2
% Change		*8.8%*	*8.8%*	*8.7%*	*6.5%*	*5.5%*
Italy	2,718.9	2,832.2	2,940.5	3,074.6	3,273.6	3,482.5
% Change		*4.2%*	*3.8%*	*4.6%*	*6.5%*	*6.4%*
Millions of USD—current prices						
United States	5,794.7	6,012.4	6,386.9	6,862.9	6,886.9	6,921.7
% Change		*3.8%*	*6.2%*	*7.5%*	*0.3%*	*0.5%*
Europe[a]	1,997.4	2,386.8	2,519.8	2,683.3	3,502.2	4,274.1
% Change		*19.5%*	*5.6%*	*6.5%*	*30.5%*	*22.0%*
Italy[a]	755.7	861.0	887.8	934.5	1,149.3	1,336.4
% Change		*13.9%*	*3.1%*	*5.3%*	*23.0%*	*16.3%*
Millions of USD—constant prices						
United States	5,794.7	5,855.6	6,016.2	6,262.6	6,107.3	5,959.4
% Change		*1.1%*	*2.7%*	*4.1%*	*(2.5%)*	*(2.4%)*
Europe[a]	1,945.4	2,335.5	2,499.8	2,691.4	3,540.2	NA
% Change		*20.0%*	*7.0%*	*7.7%*	*31.5%*	
Italy[a]	736.1	820.5	829.7	855.3	1,030.2	NA
% Change		*11.5%*	*1.1%*	*3.1%*	*20.5%*	

[a]*Converted annually at following exchange rates:*
EUR/US$	0.8854	0.8051	0.8045	0.7970	0.7308	0.6834

Source: Euromonitor International and casewriter estimates.

had initiated a few months earlier. After enduring months of labor pressure and personal threats over the closure, he set about revitalizing the UK business by replacing the lost revenue. He solicited support from product managers of other Clayton lines to help them understand the UK market.

Buis was impressed by Arnell's military discipline and propensity for bold action and felt he could be the change agent Italy needed. She was also aware that years of summers spent in Italy with his maternal grandparents had given him a good command of Italian. When she asked him to consider taking on Clayton SpA, Arnell saw it as a career advancing opportunity to turn around a larger

operation that was key to Clayton's European strategy.

A New Subsidiary Manager Arrives   Arnell arrived in Brescia alone on July 20, 2009, having asked his wife and two children to follow in October so he could focus his energies on work. Buis met him and took him around the offices, personally introducing him to Brescia's 10 senior managers. At a group lunch, she told them that the future of Clayton SpA was in their hands. Reflecting her commitment to empowering country managers and encouraging them to take initiative, she said she would "get out of their way," and returned to Brussels.

That afternoon, Arnell called a management meeting to share his early assessment of Brescia's grave situation and to ask for their support. Emphasizing that this was a time for immediate action, he requested all of them to postpone vacation plans until further notice. August being the Italian vacation month, three managers expressed misgivings—the plant manager, the QC manager, and the company controller. Arnell asked them to meet with him individually before the end of the day. In those meetings, after each manager reiterated an unwillingness to change plans, Arnell dismissed them on the spot.

The following day, after a meeting with his HR director to identify strong successors, he announced internal replacements for all three positions. He then met individually with his top team, asking each to help him use his first 60 days to understand the situation and develop a strategy for the company. He then scheduled follow-up meetings with each of them to share their perspectives on the operations, and also to review their individual work plans for the next 60 days.

But events at Clayton SpA did not wait for Arnell to complete his 60-day analysis. On his second day, he arrived at work to find four union officials from Federazione dei Lavoratori della Manifatture (FILM) outside his office with a local TV news crew. These officials suggested he was a hatchet man sent to close the Brescia plant and implement a mass layoff. Arnell assured them he had no such directive, that his mind was open, and that all options were on the table. He told them he would keep them informed, and promised to meet with union representatives the following week.

On August 4, Arnell met seven FILM representatives to show them how much money the operations were losing. He explained that in the current economic environment, Clayton's U.S. parent could not subsidize these losses. (It was a presentation he had made earlier that day to Brescia's Mayor who expressed concern about a plant closure and had arrived for his appointment with press photographers in tow.) After hours of acrimonious discussion, FILM agreed to recommend shortened shifts to its Brescia members. But Arnell knew that the concessions were far less than the company needed to break even.

The following week, Arnell made an appointment to meet with Clayton's bank to renegotiate terms on the company's credit line. As a gesture of goodwill, and because he thought it would help his case, he invited a politically connected union representative to accompany him and his finance manager. The three men secured the bank's agreement to postpone large payments due over the coming quarter. Arnell knew that while these few changes would not return the plant to profitability, they might buy the company some time as he completed his assessment of the situation.

Assessing Clayton SpA's Situation   Over the next few weeks, in meetings with his management team, Arnell learned a great deal about the company's current situation as well as the history that brought it there. He learned that despite being given Europe-wide responsibility for compression chiller sales, Lazzaro had continued to focus on building political relationships to support large projects in Italy. As a result, chillers accounted for 55% of Italy's revenues, and its strong position in the public and institutional segments ensured its "top three" competitive position at home. However, it lagged among commercial customers who increasingly favored Asian products that promised lower life-cycle costs through more efficient design.

He also learned that Clayton's other product lines were struggling in Italy. Its central air-conditioning system fit poorly with Italian buildings, many of which lacked the duct work an integrated system required. In room air conditioners and ventilators, the market was split between low-priced foreign imports and familiar Italian brands. Offering neither low-price nor name familiarity, the Clayton and Fontaire brands struggled in Italy's residential climate-control market. And by focusing resources on the chiller line, the company had failed to develop a broader marketing capability needed to sell these other products.

On the production side, Arnell discovered that the unionized work force (which had tried to block Clayton's 1985 acquisition of AeroPuro) still enjoyed very generous benefits. For many years, the plant's high cost position was masked by political relationships that gave it an inside track on government contracts. It was because of these relationships that Lazzaro refused to consider permanent layoffs which were permitted in Italy only for "good cause" in firms with more than 15 employees. He even rejected using the Cassa Ingrazione Guardagni (CIG), a temporary layoff provision that exempted workers coming to work in exchange for a significant pay cut, with costs shared between the companies and the state.

This vulnerable cost position had put Brescia under threat in 2004 when Buis announced the second phase of her plant efficiency drive. Focusing on efficient sourcing, she had insisted that all plants become cost-effective European-scale operations. An early focus of the program was to decide whether Brescia or Barcelona should become Clayton's European source of commercial air conditioning chillers.

In conversations with Carlos Sanchez who headed the Spanish company, Arnell learned that after much political maneuvering, Lazzaro had convinced Buis to make Brescia the European source. Barcelona was smaller and older than the Italian plant, and was able to build only 300 to 1000 kW units compared to the 500 to 2000 kW units Brescia could make. So despite Barcelona's 20% lower labor costs and its more flexible work force, Buis felt that only the Italian operation had the capacity to meet European demand. She committed $18 million to upgrade and expand its operation, which eventually employed 203 people. But Sanchez told Arnell that he felt Brescia's staffing levels were still 20% to 30% too high.

Nonetheless, as Sanchez explained, with the support of labor, he had kept the Barcelona plant open by licensing technology to manufacture specialized absorption chillers suitable for Spain's growing thermal industry.[1] Sanchez was proud that with growing exports, this line contributed $35 million to his company's revenues in 2008, and with a 10% EBITDA, was already far more profitable than compression chillers had ever been.

---

[1] While compression chillers such as those made in Brescia rely on electricity, absorption chillers are driven by heat, often from waste hot water, and are increasingly solar-powered.

Arnell also wanted to understand why Brescia's chiller penetration outside Italy was poor. Its 7% European market share (well below the 21% Italy boasted) made Clayton a distant number five behind competitors with shares of 36%, 23%, 16%, and 12% respectively. He spoke with country manager colleagues in other major European markets as well as several major customers who told him that the product was too expensive and also behind competitors in innovative features such as variable speed technology. Furthermore, the Clayton chillers lagged the operating efficiencies of market-leading units by 15%.

Customers in some markets—particularly Scandinavia and Germany—told Arnell of a trend toward "district energy systems" which produced steam, hot water, or chilled water at a central plant and then piped it to buildings in the district for space heating, hot water, and air conditioning. Such systems favored absorption technology over the compression chillers Brescia produced. While compression chillers still had 85% of the market, environmentalists emphasized that absorption chillers were less carbon-intensive and used water instead of the ozone-depleting refrigerants that compression systems required.

Finally, Arnell's financial director reviewed current results showing that the company was currently losing more than $1 million a month. He felt the losses were primarily due to a 27% increase in steel prices in the past two years—a cost that could not be recouped due to foreign competitors' aggressive pricing. And rather than recognizing the problem, FILM, wielding great influence during a time of high unemployment, had increased its demands.

Decision Options

In early September, to help his senior team develop their plans, Arnell organized two internal conferences to expose them to outside input. At a manufacturing conference, production, engineering, and QC managers from Brescia described their situation and tested their emerging ideas with respected counterparts from the Spanish, Belgian, and UK plants. And in the marketing conference, the sales, marketing, and product development managers

Exhibit 5   Forecast Sales of Air Treatment Products (including Chillers), 2009–2013

Millions of USD (except where indicated)	2009	2010	2011	2012	2013
Units ('000)					
United States	72,391.6	73,911.5	75,532.5	77,253.8	79,130.0
% Change	*1.4%*	*2.1%*	*2.2%*	*2.3%*	*2.4%*
Europe	22,441.4	23,651.7	24,925.7	26,266.3	27,695.5
% Change		*5.4%*	*5.4%*	*5.4%*	*5.4%*
Italy	3,692.2	3,910.4	4,128.6	4,347.9	NA
% Change	*6.0%*	*5.9%*	*5.6%*	*5.3%*	
Millions of USD—current prices					
United States	7,013.6	7,139.2	7,287.8	7,462.0	7,632.0
% Change	*1.3%*	*1.8%*	*2.1%*	*2.4%*	*2.3%*
Europe	4,249.4	4,687.6	5,106.9	5,486.5	NA
% Change		*10.3%*	*8.9%*	*7.4%*	
Italy[a]	1,328.1	1,414.9	1,493.2	1,558.7	NA
% Change	*(0.6%)*	*6.5%*	*5.5%*	*4.4%*	
[a]Converted annually at following exchange rates:					
EUR/US$	0.7389	0.7389	0.7389	0.7389	0.7389

Source: Euromonitor International and casewriter estimates.

Exhibit 6   Brescia Plant Economics

Millions of USD (except where indicated)	2004	2005	2006	2007	2008	1H09
Units	348.0	372.0	382.0	386.0	375.0	155.0
Revenue Italy	67.1	73.2	76.7	79.0	76.0	29.9
Contribution to Clayton SpA	*53.7%*	*55.3%*	*55.6%*	*55.7%*	*56.6%*	*55.2%*
Other	10.9	11.3	11.1	11.3	11.5	4.1
Total	75.2	82.4	86.7	89.6	86.7	34.0
Operating Expense						
Direct materials	19.7	23.7	29.2	37.5	50.1	18.5
Labor	16.1	16.6	16.9	15.3	15.7	7.2
Overhead—Fixed	29.0	31.3	32.2	34.9	33.6	15.7
Total	64.8	71.5	78.3	87.6	99.4	41.3
EBITDA	10.4	10.9	8.4	2.0	(12.8)	(7.3)
EBITDA Margin	*13.8%*	*13.2%*	*9.7%*	*2.3%*	*(14.7%)*	*(21.5%)*
Capital Expenditures	10.8	11.2	2.3	2.8	3.0	0.8
Capex Margin	*14.4%*	*13.6%*	*2.7%*	*3.1%*	*3.5%*	*2.3%*
Headcount	190	196	204	208	204	203
[a]Converted annually at following exchange rates:						
EUR/US$	**0.8051**	**0.8045**	**0.7970**	**0.7308**	**0.6834**	**0.7389**

exchanged views with colleagues invited from other Clayton country organizations.

Not surprisingly, the Italian managers' presentations focused on restoring Brescia's profitability and ensuring its long-term viability. Their emerging plan involved programs to boost plant efficiency, product development initiatives to revitalize the compression chiller line, and a sales and marketing plan to expand market share outside Italy. Early cost estimates of those plans were about $5 million, with most of that investment in the first 12 months.

Meanwhile, Arnell had been in ongoing discussions with Sanchez who had raised an alternative option. He explained to Arnell that he had approached Buis several times to fund a major new plant in Spain, but she had told him she was not convinced that absorption chillers would ever be more than a niche market. She had also told him that she had placed her investment bet on Brescia, and wanted to give Italy a chance to prove itself.

"But the absorption chiller is the market of the future, and we have the license for a first-class technology," Sanchez said. "We still can't produce large-scale chillers in Barcelona, and we're site-constrained to grow the plant. Why don't you phase out your compression chiller line and convert capacity to absorption chillers to meet the growing market? Together, we could make Clayton a dominant force in this segment."

It was an intriguing idea, but one that would involve significant costs in layoffs and restructuring, even with the gradual phased changeover process. Arnell estimated the investment would be about $15 million over five years, with most costs starting in the phase-out and re-structuring stages two to three years out.

A third option was proposed by Arnell's finance director who felt that it was too early to make major strategic commitments in an economy that was still unstable. He was skeptical of the government's July draft budget which projected a 2009 contraction of 4.8% in the Italian economy, before a rebound to 0.7% growth in 2010. He argued for a tight focus on efficiency measures to restore profitability while studying the various strategic options for at least another six months or until things became clearer.

In considering these alternatives, Arnell knew that while he did not have all the answers, what he did know was that Briggs and Buis were booked at the Hotel Ambasciatori for two nights the following week. They would expect to hear his analysis, his vision for a healthy Clayton SpA, his plans for a turnaround, and the results he expected to achieve.

Case 7-3   Silvio Napoli at Schindler India (A)

Perry L. Fagan, Michael Y. Yoshino, and Christopher A. Bartlett

"Monsieur Napoli, si vous vous plantez ici vous êtes fini! Mais si vous réussissez, vous aurez une très bonne carrière." (Translation: "Mr. Napoli, if you fall on your face here you are finished! But if you succeed, you will have a very nice career.") The words echoed off the walls of Silvio Napoli's empty living room and disappeared down the darkened hallway like startled ghosts. The parquet was

Senior Research Associate Perry L. Fagan and Professor Michael Y. Yoshino prepared the original version of this case, "Silvio Napoli at Schindler India (A)," HBS No. 302-053 (Boston: Harvard Business School Publishing, 2002). This version was prepared by Professor Christopher A. Bartlett. HBS cases are developed solely as the basis for class discussion. Cases are not intended to serve as endorsements, sources of primary data, or illustrations of effective or ineffective management.

still wet from the five inches of water that had flooded the first floor of the Napoli home in suburban New Delhi several days before, during one of the sewer system's periodic backups. Standing in the empty room were Napoli and Luc Bonnard, vice chairman, board of directors of Schindler Holdings Ltd., the respected Swiss-based manufacturer of elevators and escalators. It was November 1998, and Bonnard was visiting New Delhi for the first time to review progress on the start-up of the company's Indian subsidiary, which Napoli had been dispatched to run eight months earlier. Things were not going according to plan.

Napoli, a 33-year-old Italian former semiprofessional rugby player, had arrived in March with his pregnant wife and two young children and had quickly set about creating an entirely new organization from scratch. Since March, he had established offices in New Delhi and Mumbai, hired five Indian top managers, and begun to implement the aggressive business plan he had written the previous year while head of corporate planning in Switzerland. The plan called for a $10 million investment and hinged on selling "core, standardized products," with no allowance for customization. To keep costs down and avoid India's high import tariffs, the plan also proposed that all manufacturing and logistics activities be outsourced to local suppliers.

Shortly before Bonnard's visit, however, Napoli was confronted with three challenges to his plan. First, he learned that for the second time in two months, his Indian managers had submitted an order for a nonstandard product—calling for a glass rear wall in one of the supposedly standard elevators. At the same time, his business plan had come under intense cost pressures, first from a large increase in customs duties on imported elevator components, then from an unanticipated rise in transfer prices for the "low-cost" components and materials imported from Schindler's European factories. Finally, as Napoli began accelerating his strategy of developing local sources for elevator components, he found that his requests for parts lists, design specifications, and engineering support were not forthcoming from Schindler's European plants.

As the implementation of his business plan stalled, Napoli wondered what he should do. Eight months in India and he still had not installed a single elevator, while his plan showed first-year sales of 50 units. And now Bonnard was visiting. Should he seek his help, propose a revised plan, or try to sort out the challenges himself? These were the thoughts running through Napoli's head as the vice chairman asked him, "So, how are things going so far, Mr. Napoli?"

Schindler's India Explorations

Schindler had a long and rather disjointed history with the Indian market. Although its first elevator in India was installed in 1925, the company did not have a local market presence until it appointed a local distributor in the late 1950s. Almost 40 years later, Schindler decided it was time to take an even bolder step and enter the market through its own wholly owned subsidiary.

The Growing Commitment   Established in 1874 in Switzerland by Robert Schindler, the company began manufacturing elevators in 1889. Almost a century later, the 37-year-old Alfred N. Schindler became the fourth generation of the family to lead the company, in 1987. Over the next decade, he sought to transform the company's culture from that of an engineering-based manufacturing company to one of a customer-oriented service company.

By 1998, Schindler had worldwide revenues of 6.6 billion Swiss francs (US$4 billion) and was widely perceived as a technology leader in elevators. It was also the number one producer of escalators in the world. The company employed over 38,000 people in 97 subsidiaries but did not yet have its own operations in India, a market Alfred Schindler felt had great potential.

Although the first Schindler elevator in India was installed in 1925, it was not until 1958 that the company entered into a long-term distribution agreement with ECE, an Indian company. In 1985, Schindler terminated that agreement and entered into a technical collaboration with Mumbai-based Bharat Bijlee Ltd. (BBL) to manufacture, market, and sell its elevators. After acquiring a 12% equity stake in BBL, Schindler supported the local company as it became the number two player in the Indian elevator market, with a 10%–15% share a decade later.

On assuming the role of chairman in 1995, Alfred Schindler decided to take a six-month "sabbatical" during which he wanted to step back and review the long-term strategy of Schindler. As part of that process, he undertook to travel through several markets—China, Japan, and several other Far Eastern markets—that he felt were important to the company's growth. He spent several weeks in India, traveling over 3,000 kilometers in a small Ford rental car. "After his trip Mr. Schindler saw India as a second China," said a manager in Switzerland. "He saw huge growth potential. And once he targets something, he's like a hawk."

With the objective of raising its involvement, Schindler proposed to BBL that a separate joint venture be created solely for the elevator business, with Schindler taking management control. But negotiations proved difficult and eventually collapsed. In late 1996, collaboration with BBL ended, and Schindler began considering options to establish its own operation in India.

Silvio Napoli's Role   Meanwhile, after graduating from the MBA program at Harvard Business School, Silvio Napoli had joined Schindler in September 1994. He accepted a position at the company's headquarters in Ebikon, Switzerland, reporting directly to the CEO as head of corporate planning.

With its 120 years of history, Schindler was a formal Swiss company where the hierarchy was clear, politeness important, and first names rarely used. Napoli's office was on the top floor of the seven-story headquarters building, a floor reserved for the three members of the company's executive committee and the legal counsel. (For profiles of top management, see **Exhibit 1.**) "As soon as I arrived, I was aware that people were very responsive to my requests," said Napoli. "Just by my physical location, I generated fearful respect, and I realized I would have to manage my situation very carefully." A 20-year Schindler veteran recalled his reaction

to Napoli's arrival: "He was the assistant to Mr. Schindler, so I knew I'd better be nice to him."

As head of corporate planning, Napoli was responsible for coordinating the annual strategic review process and undertaking external benchmarking and competitor analysis. But his most visible role was as staff to the corporate executive committee, the Verwaltungsrat Ausschuss (VRA)—which was composed of Alfred Schindler, Luc Bonnard, and Alfred Spöerri, the chief financial officer. As the only nonmember to attend VRA meetings, Napoli was responsible for taking meeting minutes and for following up on action items and special projects defined by the VRA.

The Swatch Project   In 1995, Napoli took on the Swatch Project, a major assignment that grew out of a concern by VRA members that margins on new-product sales were eroding as each competitor strove to expand its installed base of elevators. Since such sales were a vital source of profitable long-term maintenance and service contracts, the project's goal was to develop a standardized elevator at a dramatically lower cost than the existing broad line of more customized products. It was an assignment that involved the young newcomer in sensitive discussions with Schindler's plants in Switzerland, France, and Spain to discuss design, determine costs, and explore sourcing alternatives. Napoli described the process and outcome of the Swatch Project:

> As you might imagine, I was viewed with some suspicion and concern. Here was this young MBA talking about getting costs down or outsourcing core tasks that the plants felt they owned... In the end, we developed the S001, a standard elevator that would not be customized, incorporated processes never before seen in the group, and used many parts sourced from outside suppliers. All of this was unthinkable in the past. We redesigned the entire supply chain and in doing so, halved the industry's standard 20- to 30-week cycle time.

The Indian Entry Project   Meanwhile, as negotiations with BBL broke down in India, the VRA engaged Boston Consulting Group to identify and evaluate

Exhibit 1	Schindler Top Management Profiles		
Name:	**Alfred N. Schindler**	**Luc Bonnard**	**Alfred Spöerri**
Position:	Chairman and Chief Executive Officer	Vice Chairman of the Board and Member of the Executive Committee	Member of the Board of Directors Member of the Executive Committee
Date of Birth:	March 21, 1949	October 8, 1946	August 22, 1938
Education:	*1976–1978:* MBA, Wharton, USA *1974–1976:* Certified Public Accountant School, Bern *1969–1974:* University of Basel–Law School (lic. jur.), Abschluss:lic.iur.	*1971:* Diploma in Electrical Engineering at ETH (Technical University), Zurich	
Experience:	*Since 1995:* Chairman of the Board and Chief Executive Officer *1985–1995:* Chairman of the Corporate Executive (CEO) *1984–1985:* Member of Corporate Management *1982–1984:* Head of Corporate Planning *1978–1979:* Deputy Head of Corporate Planning	*1996:* Vice Chairman *1991–1996:* Member of the Executive Committee *1986–1990:* COO Elevators and Escalators, Member Corporate Executive Committee *1985–1986:* Member, Executive Committee *1983–1985:* Group Management Member, North Europe *1973:* Management, Schindler, in France	*1991–1998:* Member, Executive Committee *1997–1998:* Chief Financial Officer *1979–1988:* Corporate Controller—Treasurer *1975–1979:* COO of Mexico *1971–1974:* Area Controller, Latin America *1968–1974:* Financial Officer of Mexico *1968:* Joined Schindler Group

Source: Schindler India.

alternative local partners with whom Schindler might build its business in India. As the company's point man on the project, Napoli worked with the consultants to narrow the list of 34 potential partners to eight candidates for review by the VRA. As the team pursued the final choices, however, it concluded that there was no ideal partner. But it learned that it was now legally feasible to start up a 100% wholly owned company in India. The VRA then asked Napoli and the head of Schindler's mergers and acquisitions department to explore that option.

Napoli contacted experts in India who helped him expand his understanding of the situation. Through discussions with market experts and studies by local consultants, Napoli spent nine months developing a detailed analysis of the market size, legal environment, and competitive situation in the Indian elevator market. He integrated this into a business plan for Schindler's market entry and submitted it to the VRA. The plan was approved in October. Soon after, Napoli was offered the job of creating the Indian subsidiary. Napoli recalled his reaction:

> I realized that the future manager of the new company would be key to the success of the business plan I had been working on. I was conscious that my early involvement in the project made me a candidate, so when the offer came, I was not surprised. Deep down, I knew I could do it. More surprising was the reaction

of my headquarters' colleagues, who thought I was crazy to take such a high-risk career move that involved dragging my family to a developing country.

Bonnard explained the choice of Napoli:

There are two possible profiles in a country like India. The first is a young guy who knows the company, people, and products; the second is someone who is 55 years old with grown kids looking for a new challenge... Mr. Napoli knew lots of people. He was open to go new ways. We needed someone who could handle different cultures, who was young and flexible. We needed to trust the person we sent, and we trusted him 100%. And we needed a generalist, not a pure specialist. We needed someone who had courage. Finally, I believe that the people who make the business plan should have to realize it. Of course, we also needed to have someone who was willing to go.

In November Napoli and his wife Fabienne, a French-German dual national, made their first trip to India. "We went on a 'look and see' visit, starting in Mumbai," Napoli recounted. "When we arrived in Delhi my wife looked around and said she would be more comfortable living here. After reaching an agreement on the relocation package back in Switzerland, I accepted the job."

Over the next several months, Napoli made three more trips to India to lay the groundwork for the move. In one key move, he engaged the executive search firm Egon Zehnder to identify candidates for his top management team. Although he had to await government approval to start the new company, when he moved to India, he wanted to have key managers in place.

Forming Schindler India

As vice president for South Asia, Napoli was responsible for India and a few nearby export markets in Schindler's elevators and escalators division (see **Exhibit 2**). In March, Napoli relocated to India and began the task of building the company that would implement his business plan.

New Culture, New Challenges   On his first day in the Delhi office, Napoli got stuck in one of BBL's elevators. As he recalled, it proved to be an omen of things to come:

On our first morning in Delhi, six hours after the family had landed, my two-year-old daughter opened her forehead falling in the hotel room. The deep wound required hospitalization and stitching under total anesthesia. Two weeks later, my wife Fabienne got infectious food poisoning, which required one-week hospitalization, even threatening a miscarriage. The day she came back from hospital, my three-year-old son fell in the hotel bathroom and broke his front tooth. Rushing to an emergency dentist in a hotel car, I really wondered, for the only time in my life, whether I could stand this much longer.

Although Napoli and his family were in New Delhi, where he had opened a marketing and service office, he spent most of a typical week at the company's headquarters in Mumbai. "The first two months were really a hard-fought battle between family relocation and company start-up," he recalled. "Weeks were consumed shuttling between Delhi and Mumbai, hunting for office space, filing government registrations, and completing legal paperwork. On the family front, I had to get them started in a totally different system: housing, schools, doctors, grocery shopping. . . all things which are totally different in India."

In the process, Napoli found he had to adapt his management approach. "For example," he recalled, "all types of characters started to approach me offering their services. They had heard that I was representing a Swiss firm about to invest in India. I soon learned to be careful in deciding who I could trust."

Recruiting the Team   Over the previous couple of months, Egon Zehnder had identified several promising candidates who became the pool from which Napoli recruited for his top positions in the new company. Mehar Karan ("M.K.") Singh, 42, was tapped for the role of managing director, a position that reported to Napoli but was viewed as a stepping stone to heading the subsidiary. (For profiles of key Indian managers, see **Exhibit 3**). "At some point in your career you will report to someone younger than yourself," said Singh. "I decided

Exhibit 2 Schindler Organization Chart, Elevator and Escalator Division

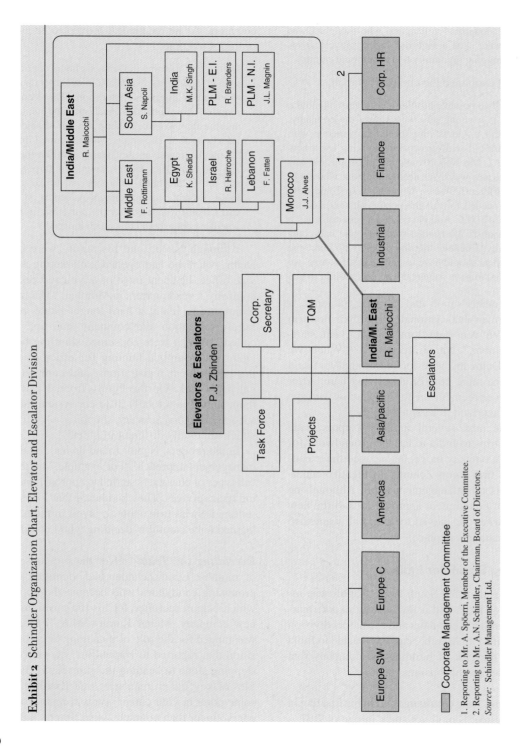

Corporate Management Committee

1. Reporting to Mr. A. Spöerri, Member of the Executive Committee.
2. Reporting to Mr. A.N. Schindler, Chairman, Board of Directors.
Source: Schindler Management Ltd.

Exhibit 3 Schindler India: Key Managers' Profiles

Name:	Silvio Napoli	Mehar Karan (M.K.) Singh	T.A.K. Matthews	Ronnie Dante	Jujudhan Jena
Position:	Vice President, Schindler South Asia	Managing Director	Vice President—Field Operations	General Manager—Engineering	Chief Financial Officer
Date of Birth:	August 23, 1965	April 12, 1955	March 12, 1964	November 3, 1959	March 3, 1967
Education:	*1992–1994:* MBA, Harvard University Graduate School of Business Administration, Boston, Massachusetts *1984–1989:* Graduate degree in Materials Science Engineering, Swiss Federal Institute of Technology (EPFL), Lausanne, Switzerland; Lausanne University rugby captain (1987) *1983–1984:* Ranked among top 20% foreign students admitted to EPFL, one-year compulsory selection program, Swiss Federal Institute of Technology (EPFL), Cours de Mathematiques Special, Lausanne, Switzerland	*1977:* B.E.—Mechanical Engineering; ranked top of his class in Indian Institute of Technology, Delhi, India *1979:* MBA, Indian Institute of Management, Ahmedabad, India (Awarded President of India's Gold Medal)	*1986:* B.Sc.—Civil Engineering, University of Dar-E-Salaam, Tanzania *1989:* MBA, Birla Institute of Technology, Ranchi, India	*1977:* HSC, D.G. Ruparel College, Mumbai, India	*1990:* Chartered Accountant, Institute of Chartered Accountancy, India

Experience:

Since 1998: Vice President, South Asia, Schindler Management Ltd.	*Since 1998:* Managing Director, Schindler India Pvt. Ltd., Mumbai, India	*Since 1998:* Vice President—Field Operations, Schindler India Pvt. Ltd., Mumbai	*Since 1998:* General Manager—Engineering, Schindler India Pvt. Ltd., Mumbai	*Since 1998:* Chief Financial Officer, Schindler India Pvt. Ltd., Mumbai
1994–1997: Vice President, Head of Corporate Planning, Schindler, Switzerland	*1979–1998:* Head of Projects and Development Group, Taj Group of Hotels, India (setting up hotels in India and abroad; joint ventures with state governments, local authorities, and international investors, including the Singapore Airlines, Gulf Co-operation Council Institutional investors. Responsible for financial restructuring of the international operations after the Gulf War, culminating with the successful 1995 GDR offering).	*1998:* Modernization Manager, Otis Elevator Company, Mumbai	*1995–1998:* National Field Engineering Manager, Otis Elevator, Mumbai	*1997–1998:* Financial Controller, Kellogg India Ltd., Mumbai
1991–1992: Technical Market Development Specialist, Dow Europe, Rheinmuenster, Germany		*1989–1998:* Otis Elevator Company, New Delhi	*1991–1995:* National Field Auditor, Otis Elevator, Mumbai	*1996–1997:* Group Manager, Procter & Gamble India Ltd., Mumbai
1989–1991: Technical Service & Development Engineer, Dow Deutschland, Rheinmuenster, Germany		• Service & Service Sales Manager	*1989–1991:* Supervisor, Otis Elevator	*1995–1996:* Treasury Manager, Procter & Gamble India Ltd.
1989–1992: French Semi-Pro Rugby League (Strasbourg)		• Construction Manager	*1984–1989:* Commissioning of New Products, Otis Elevator, Singapore, Malaysia, and Mumbai	*1990–1995:* Financial Analyst, Procter & Gamble India Ltd.
		• Assistant Construction Manager	*1982–1984:* Commissioning Engineer, Otis Elevator Company, Gujarat	
		• Management Trainee	*1977–1982:* Apprentice, Otis Elevator Company, Maharashtra	
		1986–1987: Civil Engineer, Construction Companies, Tanzania		

Source: Schindler India.

that Schindler was an exciting opportunity to test this scenario."

Napoli explained the choice of Singh: "Having led construction projects for some of India's largest hotels, M.K. had firsthand experience in building an organization from scratch. But most of all, he had been on our customers' side. He would know how to make a difference in service." In addition, being 10 years older and having grown up in India, Singh brought valuable experience and a different perspective. He was also more sensitive to organizational power and relationships, as Napoli soon recognized:

> The first question M.K. asked me after joining the company was, "Who are your friends inside the company? Who doesn't like you?" I never thought about it this way. And I said to him: "Listen, you will have to develop a sense of that yourself. As far as I know, probably people are a little bit cautious of me because they know I used to work for the big bosses at headquarters. But we will have to wait and see."

To head field operations (sales, installation, and maintenance) Napoli hired T.A.K. Matthews, 35, who had worked for nine years at Otis India. Matthews recalled: "I had been approached before by elevator people, but after hearing a bit about Schindler's plans, I realized that you don't have a chance to get involved with a start-up every day." For Napoli, Matthews brought the business expertise he needed: "With M.K. and I as generalists, I absolutely needed someone with in-depth elevator experience to complement our management team. T.A.K. came across as a dynamic and ambitious hands-on manager waiting for the chance to exploit his potential."

Next, Napoli hired Ronnie Dante, 39, as his general manager for engineering. Dante had 24 years of experience at Otis. "Even with T.A.K., we missed a real hard-core elevator engineer capable of standing his ground in front of his European counterparts," said Napoli. "Such people are the authentic depositories of an unpublished science, and they are really very hard to find. Honestly, nobody in the group expected us to find and recruit someone like Ronnie. He is truly one of the best."

Hired to head the company's human resources department, Pankaj Sinha, 32, recalled his interview: "Mr. Napoli and Mr. Singh interviewed me together. There was a clarity in terms of what they were thinking that was very impressive." Napoli offered his assessment of Sinha: "Mr. Schindler had convinced me that the company really needed a front-line HR manager who was capable of developing a first-class organization. But I certainly did not want a traditional Indian ivory tower personnel director. Pankaj convinced us to hire him through his sheer commitment to care about our employees."

Finally, he recruited Jujudhan Jena, 33, as his chief financial officer. (See **Exhibit 4** for an organization chart.) Napoli explained his approach to hiring: "You try to see whether the character of the person is compatible with yours, whether you have a common set of values, which in our case range from high ethical standards, integrity, assiduousness to work, and drive. Mostly we were looking for people with the right attitude and energy, not just for elevator people."

Developing the Relationships   As soon as the senior managers were on board, Napoli began working to develop them into an effective team. He recalled the early meetings with his new hires:

> Because some of them were still finishing up their previous jobs, the first Schindler India staff meetings were held at night, in the Delhi Hotel lounge. I'll never forget working together on our first elevator project offer, late after holding a series of interviews for the first employees who would report to the top team. But most of those "undercover" sessions were dedicated to educating the new team about their new company and building consensus around our business plan... The team was really forged through days of late work, fueled by the common motivation to see our project succeed.

In the team-forming process, the different management styles and personal characteristics of Schindler India's new leaders became clear. Even before he was assigned to India, Napoli was recognized as a "strong-headed and single-minded manager," as one manager at Swiss headquarters

Exhibit 4   Schindler India Organization Chart

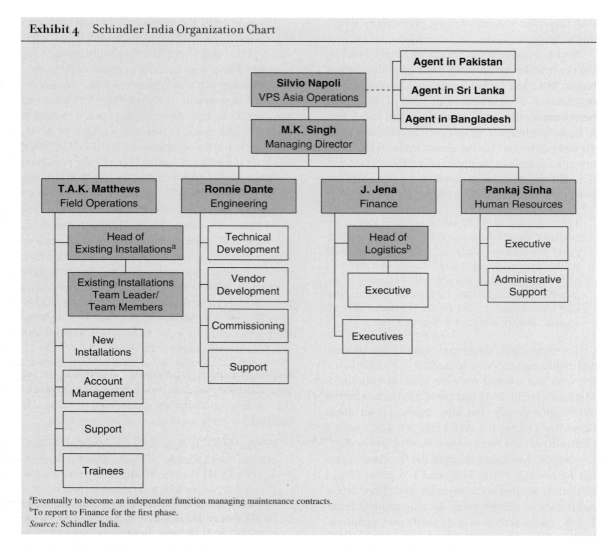

[a]Eventually to become an independent function managing maintenance contracts.
[b]To report to Finance for the first phase.
Source: Schindler India.

described him. "There couldn't have been a better environment to send Silvio than India," said another Swiss colleague. "He wants everything done yesterday. And in India, things don't get done yesterday."

Napoli acknowledged the personal challenge. "To survive in India you have to be half monk and half warrior," he said. "I was certainly more inclined to the warrior side, and when I left Switzerland, Mr. Bonnard told me, 'You will have to work on your monk part.'"

Napoli's Indian staff and colleagues described him as "driving very hard," "impulsive," "impatient," and at times "over-communicative." "Mr. Napoli gets angry when deadlines are not met," added a member of his New Delhi staff. "He's a pretty hard taskmaster." The HR director, Sinha, was more circumspect: "Silvio has a lot of energy. When he focuses on an issue he manages to get everybody else's focus in that direction."

Descriptions of Napoli contrasted sharply with those of Singh, whom one manager saw as "friendly and easygoing." Another described him as "much more patient, but he can also be tough." Jena, the finance director, reflected on his first encounter with the two company leaders: "During the interview Silvio came across banging on the table, but I don't think that concerned me. Still, I remember wondering during the interview how two guys as different as M.K. and Silvio would fit together in a start-up." Matthews, the field operations manager, added another perspective:

It's true that if you look at Silvio, M.K., and me we are all very different. At first we had sessions where the discussion would get pulled in every direction, but I think in the end, it did bring about a balance. . . I would put it this way. Silvio came to India from Switzerland. But things here are very different: You can't set your watch by the Indian trains. M.K. came from the hotel industry where even if you say "no," it's always made to sound like "yes."

"Silvio was the driver and clearly was the boss," said another Indian executive. "M.K. was great in helping Silvio understand the Indian environment. Having worked in the hotel industry he had a very good network. He had been on the customer side. But he had to learn the elevator business."

Out of this interaction emerged a company culture that employees described as "informal," "open," "responsive," and "proactive." It was also a lean, efficient organization. For example, furniture and office space were rented, and there were only two secretaries in the company—one for the Delhi office and one for Mumbai. "People must do their own administrative work or they won't survive," said Singh.

The India Business Plan

As soon as his team was in place, Napoli worked to gain their commitment to his business plan. At its core were two basic elements: the need to sell a focused line of standard products, and the ability to outsource key manufacturing and logistics functions. This plan had been built on an analysis of the Indian market and competitive environment that Napoli also communicated to his team (see **Exhibits 5** and **6** for data from the plan).

The Indian Elevator Market   Economic liberalization in India in the early 1990s had revived the construction industry, and along with it, the fortunes of the elevator industry. Roughly 50% of demand was for low-tech manual elevators, typically fitted with unsafe manual doors (see **Exhibit 5**). But a ban on collapsible gate elevators had been approved by the Indian Standards Institute, and, at the urging of the Indian government, individual states were making the ban legally enforceable. This low end of the market was characterized by intense competition among local companies, but was expected to make this market segment more interesting to major international players when the ban was fully implemented.

The middle segment of low- and mid-rise buildings was promising due to India's rapid urbanization which had led to a shortage of space in Mumbai and fast-growing cities such as Bangalore, Pune, and Madras. Concurrently, traditional builders were becoming more sophisticated and professionalized, leading to an emphasis on better services and facilities and on higher quality, safer, and more technologically advanced elevators.

At the top end of the market, there was small but growing demand for top-quality, high-rise office facilities, particularly from multinational companies. Tourism was also expanding, greatly aiding the domestic hotel industry, a major buyer of top-line elevators. The average value per top end elevator was five to six times that of low end installations.

At the end of 1997, the installed base of elevators in India was 40,000, with an estimated 5,600 units sold during the year. Although this installed base was small compared with those of China (140,000 units) and Japan (400,000 units), India's growth potential was significant. The rapidly expanding residential segment accounted for 70% of the Indian market, followed by the commercial segment (office buildings and shopping centers) with a 20% share. The balance was accounted for by hotels (4%) and others (6%). Total revenues for the industry were US$125 million, including service income. For the first half of the decade, the market grew at a compound annual rate of 17%

Exhibit 5   Indian Elevator Market, Structure, and Product Segmentation

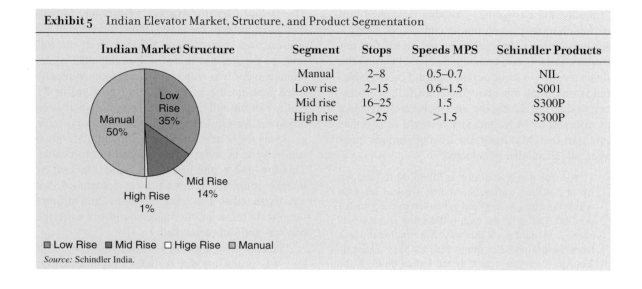

Segment	Stops	Speeds MPS	Schindler Products
Manual	2–8	0.5–0.7	NIL
Low rise	2–15	0.6–1.5	S001
Mid rise	16–25	1.5	S300P
High rise	>25	>1.5	S300P

Source: Schindler India.

in units and 27% by value, but due to a slump in the real estate market, the unit growth forecast for 1998 was just 5%. It was expected to rise to 8%–12% in subsequent years. Together, Mumbai and New Delhi represented 60% of the total Indian elevator market.

In India, most sales were of single-speed elevators (65%), followed by two-speed (20%), variable frequency (13%), and hydraulic (2%). Sales of single-speed elevators dominated the residential market, while variable frequency was most commonly used in higher-end commercial applications. Although the Indian market was biased toward the simplest products, it was expected to shift gradually toward two-speed or higher technology in the future.

Competition   Napoli's business plan also documented that four major players accounted for more than three-quarters of the Indian market value: Otis (50%), BBL (8.6%), Finland's Kone (8.8%), and ECE (8.4%). Mitsubishi had recently begun importing premium elevators for hotels and commercial developments, and Hyundai Elevators had entered into a joint venture to manufacture high-end elevators in India. At this stage, however, they

accounted for only 1% of sales. With the exception of Mitsubishi, all multinational players relied on local manufacturing for the majority of their components. The remaining 23% of the market—mostly the price-sensitive low end—was controlled by 25 regional players characterized by a lack of technical expertise and limited access to funds.

Otis India had an installed base of 26,000 elevators, 16,000 of which were under maintenance contracts. It manufactured its own components, spare parts, and fixtures at an aging plant in Mumbai and a new state-of-the art manufacturing plant near Bangalore. The company staffed 70 service centers, including a national service center in Mumbai, and held an estimated 85% of the high-end hotels and commercial segment. ("You couldn't name any building over 15 floors that did not have an Otis elevator," said ex-Otis employee Matthews. "Otis, Otis, Otis. Any special equipment, it goes Otis. Any fast elevator goes Otis.") Otis was reportedly one of the most profitable industrial companies in India, and its 3,500 employees had an average tenure of 20 years.

The Indian market was highly price sensitive, and most analysts agreed that elevators were becoming commodity products and that price pressures would increase. However, surveys indicated that service was also important in the buying decision, as were the financial terms (**Exhibit 6**).

The elevator life cycle had seven distinct phases: engineering, production, installation, service, repair, modernization, and replacement. Over the 30-year life cycle of an elevator, the first three stages accounted for about one-third of the labor content but only 20% of the profits. In contrast, the latter four accounted for two-thirds of labor content but 80% of profits. As a result, annual maintenance contracts covering routine maintenance and breakdown service were vital. (High-margin spare parts were billed separately.) Service response time varied across segments. Most five-star hotels with multiple installations had a technician on call or on-site; for important commercial buildings and hospitals, the response time was usually within two hours, but many residential and some commercial customers reported an average response time of between six and eight hours.

The Standard Product Strategy   Napoli felt that Schindler could not compete just by matching what others did. It had to find its own unique source of advantage. His analysis of the Indian environment coupled with his work on the Swatch Project led

Exhibit 6   Market Research on Indian Elevator Market, 1996

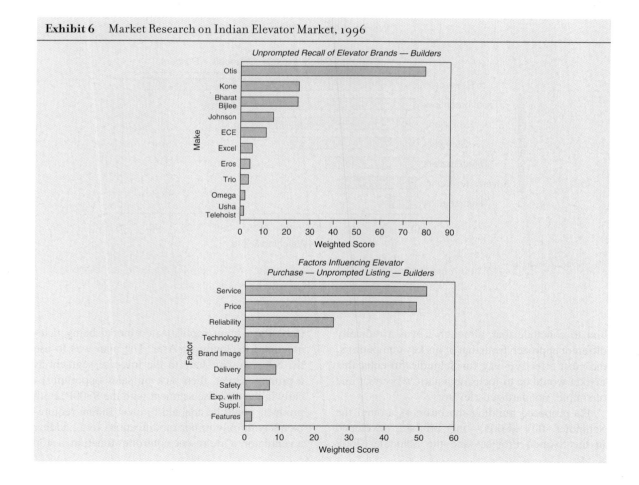

Exhibit 6   Market Research on Indian Elevator Market, 1996

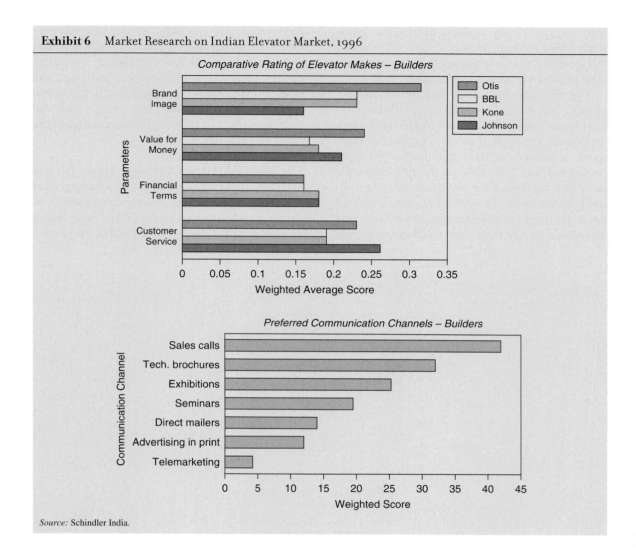

Source: Schindler India.

him to conclude that, although it was a radically different approach from that of his key competitors, the most effective way for Schindler to enter this market would be to focus on a narrow product line of simple, standardized elevators.

He proposed building the business around the Schindler 001 (S001)—the product developed in the Swatch Project—and the Schindler 300P

(S300P), a more sophisticated model being manufactured in Southeast Asia. The plan was to use the S001 to win share in the low-rise segment as a primary target, then pick up sales opportunistically in the mid-rise segment with the S300P. Both products could be adapted to meet Indian requirements with only minor modifications (e.g., adding a ventilator, a fire rescue controller function, a stop button, and different guide rails). Equally important, as long as the company stuck to the principle of no customization, both products could be priced appropriately for the local market. The plan called for Schindler India to sell 50 units in the first year and to win a 20% share of the target segments in five years. It also projected Schindler India would break even after four years and eventually would generate double-digit margins.

After communicating this strategy to his Indian management team, Napoli was pleased when they came back with an innovative approach to selling the standard line. If the product was standardized, they argued, the sales and service should be differentiated. Singh's experience with hotel construction led him to conclude that projects were more effectively managed when one individual was responsible for designing, planning, contracting, and implementing. Yet, as Matthews knew, the traditional sales structure in the elevator industry had different specialists dedicated to sales, technical, and installation, each of whom handed the project off to the next person. Together, these managers proposed to Napoli that Schindler organize around an account-management concept designed to give the customer a single "hassle-free" point of contact.

The Outsourcing Strategy   India's high import duties had forced most foreign elevator companies to manufacture locally. But again, Napoli chose a different approach. To keep overheads low, his business plan proposed a radical sourcing concept for the S001 that was expected to account for 75% of sales: Schindler India would have no in-house manufacturing, no centralized assembly, and no logistics infrastructure. Instead, the production of most components for the dominant S001 model would be outsourced to approved local suppliers. (The S300P would be wholly imported from Southeast Asia.) Only safety-related components (the safety gear and speed governor, together representing 10% of the value), would be imported from Schindler plants in Europe. In

addition, the entire logistics function would be handled by to an internationally reputed logistics service provider. And some basic installation work—part of the on-site assembly of the drive, controller, car, doors, rails, and counterweight—would also be outsourced. However, maintenance contracts resulting from new sales would stay with Schindler.

Inspired by the local automotive industry—Mercedes outsourced most components of its Indian vehicles—Napoli believed he could set up a local manufacturing network that would preserve Schindler's quality reputation. To ensure this, localization of each component would follow the same "product-creation process" criteria used by Schindler worldwide. Furthermore, before the first pre-series batch could be released, it would face an additional hurdle of testing and approval by experts from Schindler's European factories and competence centers.

From Analysis to Action: Implementing the Plan

By June, Napoli's management team members had settled into their roles, and the newly hired sales force was in the field. Almost immediately, however, the young expatriate leader began to experience questions, challenges, and impediments to his carefully prepared business plan.

Business Challenges   From the outset, several of Napoli's new management team had questioned him on the feasibility of his plan. In particular, those from the elevator industry wondered how the company would survive selling only standard elevators. They also worried about the outsourcing strategy, since no other company in the industry worked this way. "Some of the doubts were expressed as questions," said Napoli. "Many more were unspoken. My guess is they thought, 'We'll soon convince this crazy guy from Europe that we have to do something a bit less unusual.'"

In August, Napoli traveled to Italy to be with his wife when she gave birth to their third child. On one of his daily telephone calls to key managers in India, he discovered that the company had accepted an order for an expensive custom glass pod elevator that was to be imported from Europe. "I was at first just surprised, and then pretty angry, since it clearly was a violation of the strategy we had all agreed on," said Napoli. "The project was committed, and it was too late to stop it. But I had a long talk with M.K. and followed it up with an e-mail reminding him and the others of our strategy."

After his return to India, Napoli was delighted when he heard that the company was ready to accept another order for four S001 elevators for a government building in Mumbai. But in later conversations with a field salesman he discovered that there was a good possibility that each of the elevators would be specified with a glass wall. Although the managers insisted that this was really a minor modification to the standard S001 product, Napoli believed that, especially for a new team, installing it would be much more difficult than they expected.

The next challenge to his plan came when price estimates for the proposal was received to Schindler's plants in Europe. (Sources had not yet been qualified for local production.) Napoli was shocked when he saw the transfer prices on the basic S001 elevators at 30% above the costs he had used to prepare his original plans. "When I called to complain, they told me that my calculations had been correct six months ago, but costs had increased, and a new transfer costing system had also been introduced," recalled Napoli.

The impact of the transfer price increase was made worse by the new budget the Indian government had passed during the summer. It included increased import duties on specific "noncore goods" including elevators, whose rates increased from 22% to 56%. Napoli recalled the impact:

> This was devastating to our planned break-even objectives. The first thing I did was to accelerate our plans to outsource the S001 to local suppliers as soon as possible. We immediately started working with the European plants to get design details and production specifications. Unfortunately, the plants were not quick to respond, and we were becoming frustrated at our inability to get their assistance in setting up alternative local sources.

Reflections of a Middle Manager   As darkness enveloped the neighborhood surrounding his townhouse, Napoli sat in his living room reflecting on his job. Outside, the night was filled with the sounds of barking dogs and the piercing whistles of the estate's security patrol. "Each family here has its own security guard," he explained. "But because guards fall asleep at their posts, our neighborhood association hired a man who patrols the neighborhood blowing his whistle at each guard post and waiting for a whistle in response. But now the whistling has gotten so bad that some families have begun paying this man not to whistle in front of their houses. Incredible, isn't it?"

Thinking back on his eight months in his new job, Napoli described the multiple demands. On one hand, he had to resolve the challenges he faced in India. On the other, he had to maintain contact with the European organization to ensure he received the support he needed. And on top of both these demands was an additional expectation that the company's top management had of this venture. Napoli explained:

> When we were discussing the business plan with Mr. Schindler, he said, "India will be our Formula One racing track." In the auto industry, 90% of all innovations are developed for and tested on Formula One cars and then reproduced on a much larger scale and adapted for the mass market. We are testing things in India—in isolation and on a fast track—that probably could not be done anywhere else in the company. The expectation is that what we prove can be adapted to the rest of the group.

While the viability of the Formula One concept was still unclear, Alfred Schindler commented on Napoli's experience:

> This job requires high energy and courage. It's a battlefield experience. This is the old economy, where you have to get involved in the nitty-gritty. We don't

pay the big salaries or give stock options. We offer the pain, surprises, and challenges of implementation. The emotions start when you have to build what you have written. Mr. Napoli is feeling what it means to be in a hostile environment where nothing works as it should.

Napoli reflected, "You know the expression, 'It's lonely at the top?' Well, I'm not at the top, but I feel lonely in the middle... Somehow I have to swim my way through this ocean. Meanwhile, we have yet to install a single elevator and have no maintenance portfolio." At this point, Napoli's reflections were interrupted by the question of visiting vice chairman Luc Bonnard, "So, how are things going so far, Mr. Napoli?"

Case 7-4 Managing a Global Team: Greg James at Sun Microsystems, Inc. (A)

Tsedal Neeley and Thomas J. Delong

Greg James, a global manager at Sun Microsystems, Inc. (Sun), slumped on the edge of his bed in the company's corporate flat in Paris. He struggled to even move after only three hours of sleep.

James had embarked on this unexpected trip from Sun's Santa Clara, California, headquarters six days earlier. With only a few hours' notice, he had set out to meet with his entire 45-member customer implementation team spread across India, France, the United Arab Emirates (UAE), and the United States (US). He had already met with his team members in the US, India, and the UAE. France was his final

⬛ Professors Tsedal Neeley and Thomas J. DeLong prepared this case with the assistance of Research Associates Alison Comings and Patricia Hernandez. Certain details have been disguised. HBS cases are developed solely as the basis for class discussion. Cases are not intended to serve as endorsements, sources of primary data, or illustrations of effective or ineffective management.

stop before heading home. For the second time, the team had failed to respond promptly to a customer system outage as required by a service contract agreement. James had begun this trip assuming he would find a swift resolution to the rapidly escalating customer situation that had motivated it. Unfortunately, that had not been the case.

James knew that if he could just make it to the gym, exercise would invigorate him and clear his head: "Five more minutes and then I'll go." Twenty minutes later, still in his room, he grabbed his laptop and launched his e-mail.

⬛ Re: HS Holdings

James scanned his inbox, reliving the events that had plunged him into this predicament. Six days earlier, he had received a string of e-mails, forwarded to him by his team. Rahul Ashok, service manager for the Mumbai team, was in touch with Praveen Devilal (one of Ashok's team members in Mumbai) and Nick Elliott and Robert Chan in Santa Clara to trace the source of the breakdown:

To: Greg James (Global Manager, Santa Clara)
Fw: FYI in re: HS Holdings
Date: Mon, 26 May 2008 06:58:40 PST
From: Robert Chan (Sales Account Manager, Santa Clara Team): *V. Urgent*
To: Rahul Ashok (Customer Service Manager, Mumbai Team)

Rahul,

We have a major problem with HS Holdings. Their server went down on Sunday at 23:30 PST, and TIC [Technology Integration Company], their tech support group, called us for help. The issue was at a critical level because their entire system was down for two hours. This was a disaster for their online banking business. They're now struggling to respond to their customers who are furious.

They have a 24 × 7 Sun software premium—a $300K service—annual contract, but NOBODY engaged them. They're outraged. They've escalated the matter to Sun's higher management and are threatening a lawsuit because we violated their service contract. We need to find out what happened and respond to their complaints immediately. I've also left you a voicemail and a txt message about this.

Help!

Robert

Date: Mon, 26 May 2008 19:51:44 IST
From: Rahul Ashok (Customer Service Manager, Mumbai Team): *V. Urgent*
To: Nick Elliott (Application Support Engineer, Santa Clara Team); Chan, Robert
Re: HS Holdings

Nick,

Re: HS Holdings, we have paged the US team three times and left numerous voicemails for the past several hours. We haven't been able to get a hold of the customer either. Pls investigate why the US didn't provide any assistance on Sunday. They should be on call to handle critical issues. We need to revert to the customer and our senior management with an explanation ASAP. Customer threatening lawsuit.

Rahul

Date: Mon, 26 May 2008 11:30:24 PST
From: Nick Elliott (Application Support Engineer, Santa Clara Team): *V. Urgent*
To: Rahul Ashok (Customer Service Manager, Mumbai Team); Chan, Robert
Re: HS Holdings

I checked the system and it shows that HS Holdings' situation was logged in 12 hours ago in the wrong queue for resolution. We did not receive any pages about their system outage because it was in the wrong queue! (It looks like it was the queue that is used to hold issues pending support service account number verifications. The question is who programmed this queuing error? Jamal in Dubai? Praveen in Mumbai?)

Nick

Date: Tues, 27 May 2008 11:36:16 IST
From: Rahul Ashok (Customer Service Manager, Mumbai Team)
To: Praveen Devilal (Support Engineer, Mumbai Team); Elliott, Nick; Chan, Robert
Re: HS Holdings

Praveen, no page was received by the US support team. I am trying to understand where the ball was dropped. I understand that US and Mumbai folks have exchanged messages.

Robert, the engineers have restarted the server. But we need to talk to the customer for confirmation that related networks are not affected. We're all on the conference bridge, but the customer has not called in. We left a couple of voicemails at his ext. (45890) to join the conference call. We need him on the line . . .

Thanks,

Rahul

At the end of the team members' messages was Spurlock's.

Date: Tues, 27 May 2008 08:33:12 PST
From: Stephen Spurlock (Global Vice President, Santa Clara): *V. Urgent*
To: Greg James (Global Manager, Santa Clara)
Re: HS Holdings: Lawsuit?!?

Greg,

Just got a call from HS Holdings' attorneys. They said that their server went down for two hours. Cost them thousands in lost revenue. They are asking us to pay for that loss … and they want the $300K service contract money returned to them. Said it was the second time this has happened. I talked to Rahul, and he alluded to problems with your team … Did you know about this? What the hell is going on?

SS

Before James left the office, he asked his team in India to address the technical failure at HS Holdings. He then booked a ticket to India, the UAE, and France to investigate and resolve the issues.

James's Journey

Though the HS Holdings' system was up and running, the face-to-face meetings with his team had uncovered deeper, more complex, interpersonal issues. James decided to seek counsel from another vice president (VP), Pam Lawry. He picked up his cell phone and sent her a text message: "Can u video chat? I really need 2 talk to u." A few moments later, his cell phone buzzed. He quickly read her response, "B on in 30 mins."

James tried to gather his thoughts. When he joined Sun, one manager had described him as "one of the best hires that I have ever had work for me." When Sun launched the Open Work program that allowed people to work from anywhere, anytime, and anyplace, James had felt as if he were part of the most cutting-edge company in the world. Yet, here he was struggling with his distributed team.

His ruminations were interrupted when Lawry's video call screen popped up. "Hi, Pam."

"What's going on? Where are you?" Lawry asked with urgency in her voice.

"I'm in Paris." James quickly explained his conversation with Spurlock and the HS Holdings incident. "I spoke with Nick Elliott, who's the primary contact for the account. He worked closely with HS Holdings and TIC, their system integration contractor, to customize our software products for their online banking system (see **Exhibit 1**). I wanted to know why Nick wasn't the first to respond. Nick was mad and explained that no one called him. Even though his cell phone was off, all the engineers have his home number for emergencies. He didn't learn about the problem until the next day. I also spoke with Robert Chan who said that he didn't know about the problem until he checked his e-mail on Monday morning. Both Robert and Nick think that Mumbai dropped the

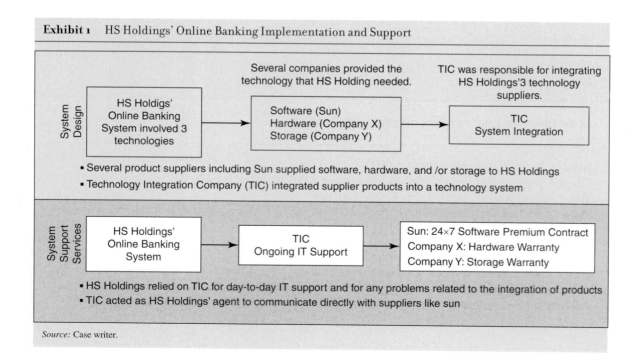

Exhibit 1   HS Holdings' Online Banking Implementation and Support

System Design

HS Holdigs' Online Banking System involved 3 technologies → Software (Sun) Hardware (Company X) Storage (Company Y) → TIC System Integration

Several companies provided the technology that HS Holding needed.

TIC was responsible for integrating HS Holdings'3 technology suppliers.

- Several product suppliers including Sun supplied software, hardware, and /or storage to HS Holdings
- Technology Integration Company (TIC) integrated supplier products into a technology system

System Support Services

HS Holdings' Online Banking System → TIC Ongoing IT Support → Sun: 24×7 Software Premium Contract Company X: Hardware Warranty Company Y: Storage Warranty

- HS Holdings relied on TIC for day-to-day IT support and for any problems related to the integration of products
- TIC acted as HS Holdings' agent to communicate directly with suppliers like sun

Source: Case writer.

ball. They should have gotten in touch with Nick or resolved the outage themselves."

"So did Mumbai drop the ball? Why didn't they call Nick?" Lawry asked.

"When I was in Mumbai, I talked to Rahul Ashok about it. He said that as soon as Praveen Devilal got the call, he paged the on-call, after-hours US manager three times. In his rush to reach the on-call manager, Praveen used the weekday contact protocol instead of the weekend protocol. He forgot that it was still the weekend in California."

"Do you need to make your protocol procedures more error proof?" Lawry asked.

"Well, it's not just a protocol problem," James said. He thought about the long and revealing conversation he had had with Devilal. "I asked Praveen why he hadn't tracked down Nick directly. He said that in the past he'd felt insulted by Nick. It appears Nick was overheard saying that the Indian team wasn't competent."

"Really?" Lawry asked.

"Yes, the issues are more complex than I realized," James responded. "So instead of calling Nick's home number, Praveen tried to fix the problem with the help of his colleagues in India. He tried numerous times to access the information about the client, but it wasn't in their support queue where all the client requests for help are stored. To make matters worse, the phone number that we had for HS Holdings was disconnected. Praveen and Rahul insisted that the HS Holdings crisis was caused by a queue that was poorly programmed and did not notify the appropriate people in time. And Rahul's team had nothing to do with that queue. Jamal, an engineer in Dubai, programmed it."

James continued:

"There had been some miscommunication between the US, India, and the UAE about what the queue should do. The US wanted to streamline the way that missing account numbers were assigned to projects. They asked Rahul to get someone on his team to program it, but it ended up being done in Dubai. Jamal said his assignment was to create a queue for accounts with missing contract numbers. So the queue he created sends an e-mail to Robert in Santa Clara to fill in the missing contract number. According to Jamal, this queue was not supposed to be used for emergency requests. The Mumbai team is responsible for

programming anything that has to do with customer emergencies."

"Why didn't anyone check the queue before it went live?" Lawry said.

"Ahmed Nazr, the manager for the Dubai team, had a second programmer check Jamal's work, and he didn't find any problems with it. But they were both working from the wrong instructions. The queue should've been connected to the support queue that everyone checks regularly, and it should have also sent an automatic page to the managers on call," said James.

"Greg, your team members are all acting like they're on separate teams... But, I still don't get the wrong client phone number part in all of this?" Lawry asked.

"Seems like our contact person at HS Holdings moved departments a few months ago; Nick should have updated the contact number on file, but he figured that anyone who needed to get in touch with them would go through him."

"What a mess! How was Elisabeth Fournier's role in this? Paris is the Customer Advocate for European accounts, right?" Lawry asked.

"I spoke with Elisabeth, and she did receive a call from HS Holdings manager, Michael Thoene, an hour after their server crashed. As you can imagine, Michael was very upset. Elisabeth immediately called Nick and me, but neither of us answered. She then contacted Praveen, who returned Michael's call, but by then Michael was out of the office. Elisabeth had been dealing with angry HS Holdings managers all week, and she was upset that no one in the US had answered her calls on Monday. She said that the Santa Clara team was always the hardest to reach and the slowest to respond."

James and Lawry spoke for some time before ending the call.

"Build consensus," James repeated to himself, "everyone fully engaged," "keep it simple," "manage disparate voices." Lawry's parting phrases ran like a ticker tape through his mind. James was feeling the heat from all corners of the world and from every corner of the organization.

Greg James

Greg James's early career had been promising. He had earned a bachelor of science in computer engineering from Stanford University, where he was regarded as a star engineer among the technical elites. His computer science professor described James as possessing "an uncanny knack" for solving complex technical problems. He had been sought by preeminent Silicon Valley technology companies, including Sun, which he chose after extensive research. James opined:

> Sun was perfect for me because it represented a combination of opportunities that I felt I just couldn't find anywhere else. I had the chance to help define the cutting edge of technological innovation. At the same time, Sun had the stability of a fairly established technology company where I could grow and develop professionally. It felt like it was the best of both worlds.

Within four years, he had risen through development projects to managing a team and budget in the Data Protection and Recovery Department. His team had consistently generated work that received rave reviews from customers. One customer sent James an e-mail praising his team for its "outstanding customer service from the beginning to the conclusion of the installation." Five years after joining Sun, he was one of 50 managers to receive the coveted Sun Outstanding Manager award.

In the pursuit of a growing global presence for Sun, Lawry, the Global Markets VP, had tapped James for a high-profile global team management position geared at implementing the firm's latest enterprise-wide solutions for large *Fortune* 100 companies. This position required a team to implement and maintain systems across several countries. If a multinational organization had 20 sites in Europe, Asia, and the Middle East, it was up to James's global team to seamlessly execute a plan to safeguard the data for that customer at those 20 sites. The Sun team had usually been contacted after the customer's own IT group could not resolve the problem.

▌ Sun Microsystems, Inc.

Sun Microsystems, Inc., provided companies with complete information technology (IT) solutions that included hardware, software, storage, and services. Espousing the notion that core innovations

should not be proprietary, Sun had made its technologies open source. The company's philosophy was that innovation was sparked when people were free to assemble, participate, and create. This, in turn, enabled market expansion, which had boded well for developers, consumers, and Sun.

Sun had originated in a student project at Stanford University. In 1982, Vinod Khosla, Scott McNealy, and Andy Bechtolsheim founded Sun Microsystems, deriving its name from the Stanford University Network (SUN). A year later, Sun signed a $40 million agreement with Computervision, a computer-aided design and manufacturing company. The company continued developing innovative network technology, as well as personal computers and supercomputers. Sun's ownership of some of the leading products in network computing, namely the Solaris operating system, the UltraSPARC processor, and the Java technology platform had given it an advantage over its peers. As a "systems" company, Sun controlled all of these elements directly, as opposed to leveraging and integrating the parts from other companies (e.g., suppliers of middleware, chips, etc.). In addition, Sun's strategy for forming strategic alliances, even with competitors like Microsoft, had paid off. By 2007, Sun had reached $14 billion in revenues with approximately 35,000 employees in 47 countries.

Competitive Industry Sun was in a fast-paced industry that was characterized by high product turnover. Companies not able to keep ahead of the technology curve quickly fell by the wayside. Consequently, industry members had to invest heavily in research and development to succeed in an environment that was rapidly changing in size and capacity. The last few years had been particularly difficult, as profit margins were squeezed from both sides. High input prices were raising the cost of production, and competitors were involved in an intense price war. Loss of revenue had forced companies to look for other ways to slash costs, resulting in outsourcing to Asia, Eastern Europe, and Latin America.

Global Talent   One of Sun's competitive strategies had been to form global teams. By spreading out across the globe, Sun was able to be closer to its customers, have access to a larger pool of talent, and provide service to its customers at any hour of the day.

When Sun was developing or implementing a new product, it had chosen employees to support the product based on talent or leadership rather than on location. If Sun wanted to create a new product, it might find the professionals best suited to lead and conduct the project from diverse countries. Lawry described some of the benefits of having global teams:

> Our customers have offices in Asia, Europe, and throughout North and South America. If we are to understand and respond to their needs, we need to have people on the ground in each of these areas. How are we going to get the best people if we try to run three work shifts in Santa Clara? You are not going to get an engineer with 15 years' experience to agree to work the graveyard shift, and even if he did, there would be errors and he'd quit after not seeing his family for a few months. Our policy is to follow the sun—teams come online as the sun rises in their region and take over projects from areas where the sun is setting.

These global teams ranged in size and composition, but the majority of them had been structured so that each manager had 11 direct reports. This was in response to Sun's code, called the "Rule of 11," that established a norm that each manager should have direct supervision over approximately 11 employees.

Open Work   At Sun, diverse employees had to work together across multiple time zones and function within their workplace locations. In addition, employees had expressed a need for more flexible work schedules and a better structure for balancing professional and private choices. In response, in 1995, Sun's top management had begun to brainstorm about possible alternatives to its workplace arrangement and had designed and launched an alternative work environment.

The Open Work program combined technologies, tools, and support processes that enabled employees to work from anywhere, anytime, using any technology.[1] According to the findings of one of Sun's studies, roughly 35% of all employees did not use their assigned buildings on a typical workday. By implementing Open Work, Sun reduced its real estate holdings by more than 15% (2.6 million square feet), resulting in savings of nearly a half-billion dollars over the course of 10 years. In 2008, nearly 60% of Sun's employees had participated in the program.

According to Seema Iyer, the Open Work program manager, employees had a choice of flexible work arrangements. When new hires joined Sun, they decided, along with their managers, whether their work was suitable for an Open Work arrangement. The Open Work program consisted of three components. The first was a suite of enabling technologies referred to as "mobility with security," in which people moved between work sites and had consistent mobile access to personal computer sessions. The second involved access to workplaces on a day-to-day basis in spaces that included the Sun campus, a drop-in office, a hotelling site, or a client site. Third, employees worked from home, and, when an alternative space was needed, they used Sun workspaces. Organizational policies like monthly allowances that included Internet, telephone, and hardware for mobile employees and training to work in this environment were in place to support this program.

Iyer noted:

> With Open Work, we've dramatically reduced our operating costs, and we pride ourselves for developing an eco-responsible system in line with our "green approach to business."[2] Our employee satisfaction has risen and productivity remains strong. While satisfaction with the program is high, it still has a number of critics who believe that face-to-face interaction is key to innovation.

---

[1] This and other case details were taken from interviews with the following Sun managers: Seema Iyer, Wajid Jalaldin, Robert Latham, Chris James, Will Rahim, and William Franklin.

[2] Sun estimates that the average Open Worker emits 1.25 fewer metric tons of CO_2 per year compared to a typical employee assigned to a particular location. It is also estimated that each Open Worker avoids 135 gallons of annual fuel consumption (Sun & University of Colorado, 2008).

Exhibit 2   Sample Open Work Suitability Survey Questions

Work Preferences & Characteristics: Please check (√) the description that best captures you and your work situation.

[ ] I am good at planning and organizing my work so that it can be done effectively from any location.

[ ] When I am away from the office environment, I find it difficult to motivate myself to set my own goals and accomplish them.

[ ] I have the self-discipline necessary to work productively in an unstructured work setting like my home.

[ ] The office environment is not an important source of social contact for me.

[ ] I would miss people or feel isolated working by myself at home.

[ ] My coworkers accept and respect those who do not to come into the office every day (i.e., work from home, etc.).

[ ] The ability to work anytime, anywhere is very important to me.

[ ] I need flexibility in my workplace choices as a way of balancing my work/nonwork needs.

[ ] I prefer the stability of using the same office space on a routine basis, rather than choosing where I work each day to suit my work needs.

[ ] I often travel to customer, partner, vendor, or other non-Sun locations as part of my work.

[ ] My work has discrete time lines and milestones that can be quantified, measured, and monitored.

[ ] I always make sure my manager, coworkers, and/or customers know how to quickly find or reach me, no matter where I am working.

[ ] Information sharing and knowledge exchange occur informally, through direct person-to-person contacts on the job.

[ ] Much of my dealings with coworkers and customers involve communicating electronically using phone, e-mail, or other online technologies.

[ ] Most of the in-person interaction I have with others at work is impromptu, informal, and spontaneous.

Source: Company.

Sun had set up a suitability assessment for employees who wanted to participate in Open Work. Managers filled out a category assessment survey that polled work patterns, activities, resources, work style, and background (see **Exhibit 2**). Sun examined factors such as the amount of work time spent at different locations, whether the employee worked alone or with others, the need for communication, and whether communication was electronic or in person. The data-collection process also looked at the amount of interaction with other team members and internal or external customers, how frequently he or she worked from home, and whether the employee was a self-starter.

Sun had established organizational systems, such as training for managers and employees working in global teams, resources for home-based employees, and workshops on Open Work. James's team had completed these training programs and used many of the resources.

James's Team

Recruitment   Twelve months earlier, James had recruited his 45-person team composed of 7 members in France, 16 in India, 11 in the UAE, and 11 in the US to serve Sun's enterprise customers in Asia and Europe (see **Exhibit 3**). James had been pleased with the ease by which the global team came together:

Exhibit 3 Organization Chart for Greg James's Team

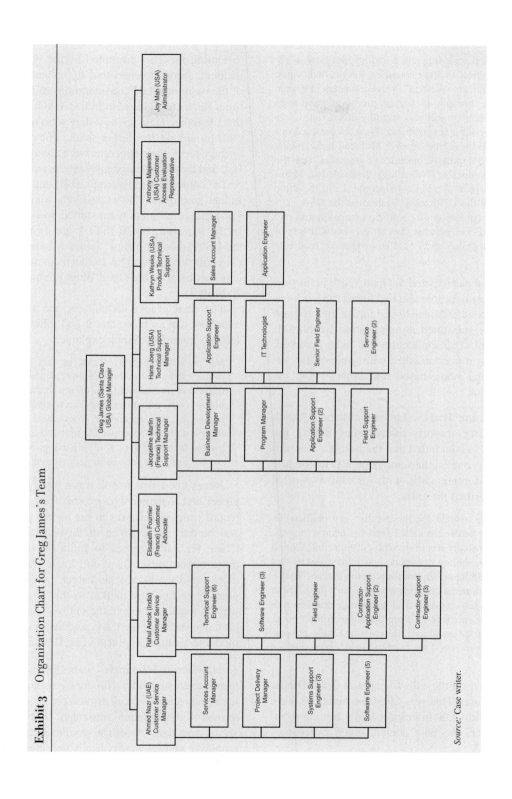

Source: Case writer.

When I first took this job, I had no idea how to recruit new hires in other countries, but the team came together quickly. We had several engineers in France who were brought in for an unrelated short-term project. Their project was winding down, and I was able to recruit a few of them. Then, I contacted our local human resources team in Mumbai, India, which sent me 75 impressive résumés of graduates from the Indian Institutes of Technology. I traveled to Mumbai for a week and hired 16 people. I did the same thing with the UAE team. I inherited the USA guys from an acquisition of a start-up company, and that worked out well because they already had a history of working together and could be productive relatively quickly.

James had participated in Open Work in his previous management role and had found the work environment beneficial. He hoped to use the program again, so he submitted an application for himself and his team. The application had been accepted, and his team was established with some of the employees being home-based and others using the flexible option.

Time Zone and Work   James had kept in touch with his direct reports many times during the week. He also concluded that the best way for him to keep everyone on the same page was to conduct weekly conference calls with his entire team of 45. He described the calls:

I keep the agenda for these calls very predictable. The night before the call, I send the team a "topics' list" that usually has to do with customer installation schedules, service contracts, and related issues that we must address. We run through the list, and I push for commitments on next steps for every item. These calls can get very technical and drawn out. My role is to make sure that we keep the big picture in mind. And because I understand the meeting time is not perfect for everyone, I try hard to always start and end on time.

James had set the calls to begin at 08:00 Pacific Standard Time. This was 20:30 in India, 19:00 in the UAE, and 17:00 in France. James felt the meeting time was the best choice, given everyone's constraints.

During the visit prompted by the HS Holdings incident, James learned that he had missed some of the more nuanced considerations of the meeting time. His technical lead in India, Ashok, told James that the Indian team felt as if they were second-class citizens among the larger team. They had fewer agenda items, their concerns were always reviewed last, and they felt consistently interrupted. By being on the conference calls from 20:30 until 22:00, the Indian employees had excessively long days. Beyond that, the Indian team started work very early in the morning (06:30 IST) to get briefed before the US team went offline. James wondered if these concerns were behind his Indian team members' recent feedback on the Open Work environment (see **Exhibit 4**).

The final crucial irritant for the Indian team members was so basic that it had initially escaped James's attention. Ashok explained:

My guys are unhappy about the fact that they are often left to do customer maintenance work. They think their focus should be on initial customer technology customization and innovation. The other teams get the interesting work. But the moment there's a problem, we are the first ones dispatched to put out technical fires. If we are that good, how come we are not good enough to get the creative work?

James knew that Ashok was a highly skilled engineer and manager who got his team working in record time. Ashok was in his eighth year at Sun, and he had spent seven of those years in Santa Clara. He had returned to India because he saw more opportunities there and knew that he could more rapidly advance his career, given the burgeoning technology market in that region. Ashok was on track to manage the entire Asia-Pacific region that included the UAE, and he served as a role model to younger engineers like Devilal.

Compensation Mismatch   James felt each country's team was frustrated for a different reason. The French team had recently voiced displeasure about what they termed "compensation mismatch" between themselves and their American counterparts. Although employee salaries were typically kept confidential, an

Exhibit 4   Surveys of Satisfaction with Open Work for Greg James's Team

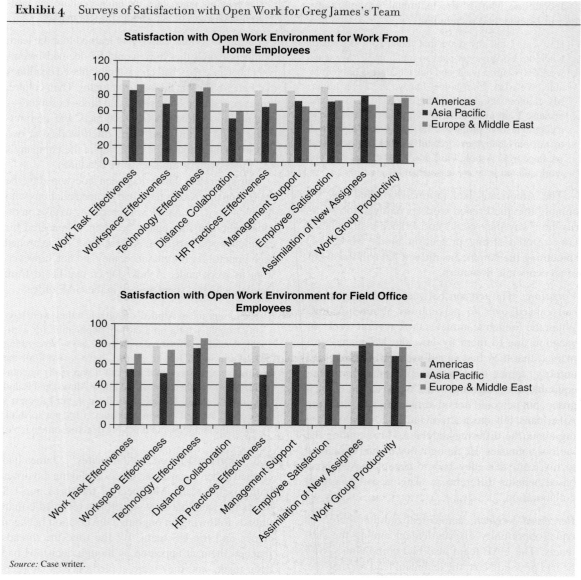

Source: Case writer.

American team member had inadvertently disclosed his higher salary to his French teammate.

James recalled:

> There was an immediate firestorm within the team. The French members did not understand why they were making 30% less than their American coworkers, even though they were trained at the top technical institutions in their country. I tried to explain to them that their salaries were consistent with their local market.

Jacqueline Martin, the technical support manager in France, had responded:

> How can I tell my team that their work is valued, when the US guys get paid so much more? My team works 50 hours a week and our schedule is unpredictable. We work from home, but we are never home. My children say that they don't spend time with me because I am always on my laptop or on the phone trying to resolve problems. Just two weeks ago, I had to miss my daughter's recital when I got an urgent message from Ashok. I just don't understand why our work and our time are less valuable.

The Americans had rationalized their pay by opining that the French workers enjoyed job security in a way they could not: France's strict labor laws offered strong protection to its workforce, something the Americans did not have in the event of an economic downturn.

Vacation   The tension between these two teams had carried over to perceptions about time off. When the French teammates took several weeks of vacation due to them by law, the US team complained that they had ended up carrying their load unfairly. James tried to make the situation more equitable by assigning more work to the French group, but he could not advertise that fact. Still, the Americans felt unsatisfied. James could do nothing about the differing regulatory laws among the various countries. He thought that he had explained to his team that they had to accept the country-based benefits differences: "This is part of global collaboration."

Perceived Neglect   James realized that there was equal-opportunity disgruntlement among the subteams. The UAE team also had complaints. After he had pressed Nazr, the technical lead for that site, he learned that the team felt they did not have sufficient face-to-face contact with James, and they were nervous about becoming a subgroup to the India office, which would have placed them even further away from James.

Nazr went on to explain:

> The team feels disconnected not just from you, but from the company as a whole. In fact, we all worry that our performance evaluations will suffer because

you may not understand the unique culture and business challenges of our Middle Eastern market.

For the first time, James had learned that the team members feared that they would be deemed incompetent because they had consistently missed deadlines that James had set in the last few months. Their culture, however, required extensive—and time-consuming—relationship building before contracts and commitments could be finalized. They often worked at two paces—at their country's pace, and at the company's faster pace with its time-sensitive deadlines.

During his trip, James had been sideswiped by the realization that Nazr's team had strained relations with Ashok's team. As Ashok was preparing to take on responsibility for the region, he often volunteered his experience and expertise. At first, the UAE team had been grateful for his guidance; they did not, however, want to work under Ashok. James had heard from Devlal, who had spent a week in the UAE office:

> Rahul sent me to Ahmed's team when they were having trouble setting up a custom application for a client. I really sympathize with those guys—everything takes so much longer, so they have to work all the time to make our deadlines. But it was really uncomfortable to be there, because I know Ahmed and Rahul don't get along. No one talks about it, but I think it's because Ahmed is from Pakistan. I try not to think about those things, but it is a big deal for some people.

U.S. Subteam Viewed as "Favorites"   James had cringed when he was accused of playing favorites with his US team. Members of the three non-US teams had said that they sometimes received e-mail threads following an ongoing conversation between James and the US team. By the time the threads reached them, it appeared as though decisions had been made, and they were copied only as an afterthought. James realized that he had spent more time with the US team: "We do have more of the water-cooler conversations, but I do not understand how that makes me a bad guy. I overheard one of my guys say, 'With Greg, the rich get richer and the poor get poorer.' I really felt the sting of that comment."

All this passed through James's mind as he ended the video conference with Lawry. He noted the cold comfort of her words:

Global markets are pressuring us to span operations across multiple time zones. There is no going back. You need to figure out how to build consensus. You're not going to be able to get that developer from China and India and Prague all in the same room, and a lot of issues quite frankly are time sensitive. You have to make sure that everyone is fully engaged because you are managing systems for our most important clients.

Moving Forward

James knew that Sun was under tremendous pressure from its competitors and could not risk losing customers. He considered himself lucky to have survived the HS Holdings disaster by averting a lawsuit, but he knew that if he did not find a solution to his team's troubles, his meticulous career planning might fall off course.

James recalled sitting in his boss's office, soon after he had received Spurlock's terse e-mail. He had never seen him that angry. Being on the receiving end of such criticism for the first time was shocking to James. His heart raced as he remembered Spurlock's stern warning: "Fix it. Fix it now. Greg, I want you to tell me your short- and long-term plan to make certain that this never, ever happens again. Something in your process is broken!"

The lack of face-to-face interaction with his teams in France, the UAE, and India was a problem, and he wondered whether he should increase face time by traveling to every site on the first and third weeks of the month or do the opposite and reduce face-to-face interaction with everyone, including the US team. James also considered conducting multiple all-team meetings throughout the week to increase communication across cultural and national boundaries. He questioned whether his problems were with the larger structure of his team. He also had doubts about whether his customer demands were even suited to the number of team members and the Open Work environment. He wondered, most of all, if he had mismanaged the team. What could he do differently moving forward?

Reading 7-1   Managing Executive Attention in the Global Company

Julian Birkinshaw, Cyril Bouquet, and Tina C. Ambos

How can executives prioritize their time to ensure that they are focusing on the countries and subsidiaries that need the most attention?

Many companies today are truly global in reach. Shell Oil has operations in more than 140 countries, Coca-Cola sells its products in more than 200 countries, and Nestlé boasts that it has factories or operations in almost every country in the world. For the executives running these companies, the challenge of keeping abreast of events in markets around the world is mind boggling. Interestingly, the biggest problem is not a lack of information: Executives are deluged with monthly reports and market analyses for every country in which they operate. The problem is having the time and energy to process the information. Indeed, executive attention is a scarce resource, one that needs to be carefully managed.[1]

▌ **Julian Birkinshaw** is professor of strategic and international management at London Business School and a senior fellow of the Advanced Institute of Management Research. Cyril Bouquet is an assistant professor of strategic management at the Schulich School of Business, York University in Toronto. Tina C. Ambos is a lecturer at the University of Edinburgh and an assistant professor of economics and business administration at Vienna University. Comment on this article or contact the authors through smrfeedback@mit.edu.

▌[1]Several studies have examined the challenges of managing executive attention. See T.H. Davenport and J.C. Beck, "The Attention Economy: Understanding the New Currency of Business" (Boston: Harvard Business School Press, 2001); C. Bouquet, "Building Global Mindsets: An Attention-Based Perspective" (New York: Palgrave Macmillan, 2005); W. Ocasio, "Towards an Attention-Based View of the Firm," *Strategic Management Journal* 18, special issue (Dec. 4, 1998): 187–206; and M.T. Hansen and M.R. Haas, "Competing For Attention in Knowledge Markets: Electronic Document Dissemination in a Management Consulting Company," *Administrative Science Quarterly* 46, no. 1 (March 2001): 1–28.

How should executives prioritize their time to ensure that it is focused on the countries and subsidiaries that need their attention? Which markets should they emphasize, and which can they allow to fall off their radar screen? We have researched executive attention in global companies for the past five years, interviewing 50 executives at 30 corporations. (See "About the Research," p. 40.) Despite the best of intentions and irrespective of the exhortation that companies should "think global, act local," the evidence shows clearly that corporate executives end up prioritizing a handful of markets at the expense of the others. One reason for selective attention is ethnocentric thinking—the tendency to assume that the home market is most important. Of course, no executive would state this directly, but the evidence of a home-country bias is widespread and undisputed.[2]

Another factor is the so-called "herd mentality," which causes companies to focus on markets that competitors have identified. It is human nature to go "where the action is," and as a result some countries (most recently, China and India) attract a disproportionate amount of executive attention.

Both of these approaches are entirely defensible: They help channel resources to the most important areas of activity, and they seem relatively safe. But they can also be very wrong. Because executive attention is so limited, focusing on the home market or on a hot market will always come at the expense of other opportunities. The resulting mismatch between what's possible and what's needed can be quite damaging: Too much attention can disempower or suffocate subsidiary managers. As one executive noted, managers can become so preoccupied with representing their operations to executives that they don't have enough time to manage the business.

Too little attention can lead to even bigger problems, because it can result in missed opportunities and decisions by talented employees to leave. Consider, for example, the case of Dun & Bradstreet Corp.'s Australian subsidiary, which was ignored by the U.S. head office for years in the belief that

Australia was not a "strategic" market. Frustrated by the lack of attention, the subsidiary's CEO persuaded the parent company to sell the business to a local private equity company in 2001; within three years, it had doubled in size and increased earnings tenfold. As a subsidiary company, its access to investment capital had been hamstrung by how corporate executives viewed Australia; as a standalone company, it could invest in whichever opportunities offered a promising investment return.

In this article, we examine the nature of executive attention and identify mechanisms by which subsidiary companies draw attention from the top executives of their organizations. Although attention can be harmful as well as helpful, we focus on the positive aspects. In particular, we see executive attention as consisting of three important elements: support, in terms of how headquarters executives interact with and help subsidiary managers achieve their goals; visibility, in terms of the public statements headquarters executives make about how the subsidiary is doing; and relative standing, in terms of the subsidiary's perceived status vis-à-vis other subsidiaries in the organization.

Conceptualized in this way, we address two important questions: How can a subsidiary attract more attention? And what can headquarters executives do to make sure that the right subsidiaries receive the attention they deserve?

Allocating Attention Across the Corporate Portfolio

How do headquarters executives decide which markets to focus on? While ethnocentric bias and herdlike behavior influence executive attention in profound ways, most global companies have nonetheless established reasonably sophisticated mechanisms for directing attention to the markets that need it most. These mechanisms include choices about lines of reporting, which meetings to attend and which individuals to put in positions of influence. Such mechanisms don't just channel executive attention to particular markets or issues. They also provide an important signal within the company about which markets matter most.

---

[2]See A.M. Rugman and A. Verbeke, "Subsidiary-Specific Advantages in Multinational Enterprises," *Strategic Management Journal* 22, no. 3 (January 2001): 237–250.

About the Research

Our research study was organized into two parts. In the first part, we conducted about 50 interviews with executives in corporate headquarters and subsidiaries of 30 global companies. The interviews were conducted in Australia, Canada, the United Kingdom, France, Sweden, Switzerland and the United States. We asked headquarters executives about the systems they used for managing attention in their companies and how they allocated their attention among competing claims from subsidiaries. We also asked subsidiary company executives to discuss strategies they used for gaining the attention of executives at the parent companies. In the second part of the study, we developed a questionnaire to ask managers about the "weight" and the "voice" of the subsidiaries, and the amount of attention the subsidiaries actually received. We received completed questionnaires from 283 subsidiary managers in four countries (Australia, Canada, the United Kingdom, and the United States). We also collected secondary data on the same subsidiary companies: how often they were mentioned in the annual report of their parent company, and market share and sales volume in the local country.

Subsidiary Weight and Attention   Our baseline hypothesis was that attention decisions would be based partially on the structural positions that subsidiary units occupy within the corporate system—their "weight." To test this hypothesis, we undertook a series of regression analyses, which showed that attention correlates with such factors as (1) the size of the subsidiary (measured in terms of total sales, employees and number of officers in the top management team); (2) the strategic importance of the local market (whether conceptualized in terms of sales figures or flows of foreign direct investment); and (3) the strength

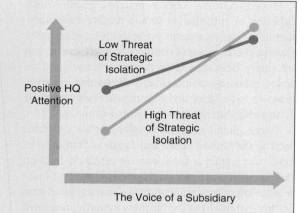

of the subsidiary's operations (an index capturing the extent to which the subsidiary occupies a highly valued role in the global organization).

Subsidiary Voice and Attention   Our second hypothesis was that subsidiaries also had a "voice" of their own that they could use to attract attention. To test this idea, we asked questions about a range of subsidiary-level activities, out of which we created two indexes (one for initiative taking, the other for profile building). Both factors were found to positively correlate with the level of attention granted to the subsidiary, indicating support for our second hypothesis.

Strategic Isolation and Attention   The third hypothesis was that the relationship between subsidiary voice and headquarters attention would be moderated by two specific aspects of the subsidiary's historical situation, which have often contributed to the subsidiary's strategic isolation: geographic distance and a competence anchored in the downstream part of the value chain. Using a series of regression analyses, we found support for this hypothesis. The more subsidiaries are at risk of strategic isolation, the greater the importance of voice in shaping levels of executive attention.

Top executives obtain insights about which countries or subsidiaries should receive their attention in two ways: externally, in the form of industry reports, the media and competitor intelligence; and internally, from standard reporting processes and the active lobbying of individuals. From this information, we have identified four distinct markets. (See "Attracting Attention in the Global Company.")

Large global companies often regard countries such as the United States and Japan as "major markets" that attract a high level of attention through both internal and external channels. China and India receive lots of media attention and thus are often seen as "honey pots," but the business opportunities there may not live up to the buzz. In many companies, Canada and Australia receive attention based on relationships; we characterize such markets as "squeaky wheels" because they represent established operations whose achievements are well known to headquarters executives, even if the markets themselves don't justify the emphasis. We call the last group the "forgotten markets" because they have difficulty getting onto the corporate radar screen. Note that our framework says nothing about whether the subsidiary is performing well or badly, only the level of management attention the subsidiary receives. Some squeaky wheels are troubled operations that need to be turned around; others might be rising stars; and some of the forgotten markets, like Dun & Bradstreet (Australia) Pty. Ltd., may actually be hidden gems.

Attracting Attention in the Global Company

Subsidiary units can be categorized on two dimensions: the amount of attention they gain through external or top-down channels, and the amount of attention they gain through internal or bottom-up channels. Where the subsidiary is located will define the appropriate strategy for gaining additional attention.

Our framework suggests that a subsidiary can use two very different strategies to attract the attention of executives at the parent company: It can count on its weight as a player in an important market, and it can exert its voice by working through channels within the company. Some subsidiaries focus on one or the other, while others pursue both approaches in parallel. We will explain how these two approaches work.

Attracting Attention With "Weight"

In global organizations, subsidiaries that play pivotal roles in the success of the overall business have no trouble getting attention. China, for example, is a critical market for ABB Ltd., the Switzerland-based engineering group: In 2006, ABB's Chinese subsidiaries contributed $2.9 billion in revenues—approximately 12% of ABB's global business. The previous year, it captured capital funds and investments of $80 million out of $454 million for the whole corporate portfolio. Like other multinational corporations, ABB has high hopes for the Chinese market in the years ahead. But as China prepares for elections in 2008, there is considerable uncertainty about how best to maintain a positive climate for investment. ABB executives spend several hours a week on conference calls with their Chinese counterparts to identify and mobilize the necessary corporate resources and to ensure that the company's executives in Zurich are up to speed on major developments in the region. Ulrich Spiesshofer, ABB's head of corporate development, recently noted that "questions related to the activities of our Chinese business get top management preoccupied on a daily basis."[3]

A subsidiary's weight is not simply a function of its size. In many cases, it also reflects the impact it has on the company's global network. Subsidiaries occupying highly valued roles—for example, as centers of competence or as technological hubs— have significant weight as well. Pratt & Whitney Canada Corp., for example, is recognized for its expertise in the small aircraft turbine market. Because of its highly skilled labor force and advanced technologies, many sister subsidiaries look to it for technological advice and support.

Attracting Attention With "Voice"

How does a subsidiary that lacks weight capture the attention of top management? Our research found that subsidiaries without weight often seek other

[3]U. Spiesshofer, "Managing the Balance: A Global Player's Perspective On Institutional Change" (keynote address at the 26th Annual Conference of the Strategic Management Society, Vienna, Austria, Oct. 30, 2006).

ways to gain visibility in a global company. Many managers rely on two types of proactive efforts: initiative taking and profile building.

Initiative Taking   This approach involves strategically selecting projects or ventures to grow the subsidiary, perhaps by developing new products, penetrating new markets or simply generating new ideas.[4] Such actions can influence the attention of the parent company in very direct ways. For example, when Fred Kindle, the CEO of ABB, visited the managers of the company's Czech subsidiary, he learned that managers there had found an innovative way of networking the company's administrative computers at night (when they were not used) to leverage their built-in processing capacity. This enabled the company to run complex research and development algorithms more quickly and, in turn, gave the Czech subsidiary valuable recognition and corporate support.

Initiative taking can also draw attention from headquarters in ways that are less direct. Individuals behind successful initiatives, for example, can build reputations that open doors to opportunities. For instance, Sara Lee Corp.'s Australian subsidiary became known within the company for its leadership on diversity issues, thus making Angela Laing, the diversity champion, a rising star. She soon became vice president of human resources for the company's worldwide household and body care division, and several others from Sara Lee Australia moved into senior positions elsewhere in the corporation. Nestlé Canada Inc., which developed a new line selling custom batches of frozen foods to food service operators, has leveraged this innovation into increased attention overall. (See "Defining a Value-Added Role for Nestlé Canada.")

Profile Building   Subsidiary managers use a variety of mechanisms to improve their image, credibility and reputation within the global company. If initiative taking occurs in the local context, profile building focuses on the things managers do within the broader corporate network. We found that successful profile builders focused on three types of activities.

They build a stellar track record.   The managers of profile building subsidiaries delivered results above the expectations of the parent company for a number of years. As Mark Masterson, vice president of health care product maker Abbott Laboratories' Pacific, Asia and Africa operations, observed, "Getting attention is about establishing credibility, and it doesn't happen within a short period of time. People need time to evaluate how you run a business. If you demonstrate predictability and results over time, you start to gain more confidence to put more challenging options to the company."[5]

They support corporate objectives.   To the extent that managers pursued their own local priorities, they did not downplay corporate concerns in the least. This may be common sense to seasoned executives, but it can also call for some careful juggling as subsidiary managers attempt to balance local initiatives with commitments to the corporate cause. Many of the subsidiary managers we spoke to described how they "push back" on some corporate requests and how they explain problems to their immediate bosses. "You are stupid if you don't keep some things up your sleeve," one manager explained. "You have to manage expectations, which involves not telling the whole story until you are ready. So I act as a buffer."

They work as internal brokers.   Successful subsidiary managers spend a lot of time building relationships within and beyond their corporate network. Some of this work is to build awareness—letting other parts of the company know what the unit does, how well it does it and what it might be able to contribute in the future. It can also be targeted toward specific projects and take the form of pre-selling ideas and lobbying with key power brokers in the corporate hierarchy. For example, one manager talked about the preselling process: getting

---

[4]See J.M. Birkinshaw and N. Fry, "Subsidiary Initiative to Develop New Markets," *Sloan Management Review* 39, no. 3 (spring 1998): 51–61.

[5]Interestingly, a poor track record is also conducive to getting attention, but not the type of attention that subsidiary managers feel is most conducive to creating the right set of conditions for the subsidiary to develop in the future. 3M Co., for instance, recently reacted to the disappointing results of its Canadian subsidiary by almost completely replacing the local management structure. Four out of five VPs were let go; the Canadian CEO who completed our survey was moved to a lesser position in the United States; and a substantial number of middle-level managers ended up being replaced.

all interested parties involved early and "oiling the wheels" so that when the formal proposal is presented it encounters no resistance. Another manager noted the importance of timing: "If you tell the story too early, you risk getting shot down or building up unreasonable expectations; if you tell it too late and they get mad, you will struggle to get support." It is important to recognize the level of planning required for a successful campaign to build support for new investment and new initiatives.

The Threat of Strategic Isolation

In addition to the strategic approaches subsidiaries used for attracting attention, we found two particular contexts where initiative taking and profile building were especially important: when subsidiaries were located far away from corporate headquarters and when the subsidiary's activities were focused solely on the local market. This finding is not entirely surprising: Remote operations are especially likely to fall off the radar screen of headquarters executives. But for subsidiary managers, it is reassuring to know that there are ways to overcome the "tyranny of distance."

We found that profile building was the more effective approach to capturing attention, either on its own or in combination with initiative taking. One of the dangers of subsidiary managers pursuing initiatives on their own is that unless they have already built a track record with the parent company, the initiatives can be seen as empire building. The initiatives may also compete with the entrepreneurial activities of subsidiaries in other parts of the world for headquarters' attention. Subsidiary managers often seek to mitigate these concerns by approaching initiatives cautiously: focusing on ideas and projects that will add value to the rest of the global company or collaborating with peers in other countries. For example, the CEO of Oracle Corp. Australia Pty. Ltd. Sponsored the design of an integrated approach to education, which he believed had the potential to revolutionize methods of learning within the K-12 school system. But pursuing this initiative required substantial funds and did not fit into the existing corporate research and development priorities. By lining up support from his overseas colleagues, the Australian CEO was able to build a critical mass and attract notice from the head office.

Defining a Value-Added Role for Nestlé Canada

In the years following the North American Free Trade Agreement, Nestlé Canada, like many Canadian subsidiaries, found it increasingly difficult to add value to the company's low-growth lines of business. The reality was that most Canadian markets could be tapped more efficiently from the United States. Nestlé Canada's best hope was to define a distinctive role within the global company. Management came up with the idea of a new line of products: custom batches of restaurant-quality frozen food for food service operators, who would then market to hospitals, hotels and airlines. If successful, it would provide a new revenue stream while positioning Nestlé Canada to test market other new products.

Nestlé Canada has turned into a major success story. In 2006, it employed 3,600 people in 16 facilities across the country, with sales of $2.3 billion, mostly from direct exports to 70 countries worldwide. "Canada has highly sophisticated consumers, and yet [it has] a population base that allows us to experiment without breaking the bank," said Frank Cella, former president and chief executive of Nestlé Canada, who went on to become a senior executive with the corporate parent.[i] "We made a case for allowing us to be an experimental lab, and that has given us a uniqueness that we would not have otherwise. We add value by innovation, by trying new ideas and getting them to market faster. We are so innovative that the worldwide group is sending people [to Canada] to learn about how we do it."

[i] See Business Council on National Issues, "Going For Gold: Winning Corporate Strategies and Their Impact on Canada," working paper released at the CEO Summit 2000, Toronto, April 5, 2000.

Subsidiary managers often argue that their ability to influence their own destiny is undermined by their lack of decision-making power. However, we found that a subsidiary's degree of decision-making autonomy has no meaningful effect on the level of executive attention it receives. Indeed, in many instances subsidiary managers used their limited degrees of freedom to great effect. For example, Yum! Restaurants International's KFC division in Australia has built a reputation as a leading innovator in its global business. One of its most notable breakthroughs involved its drive-through business. For a variety of reasons (some of which had to do with technical problems relating to the drive-through speaker box), customers at many stores had been reluctant to use the drive-through window. With a modest investment, however, Yum Australia redesigned the entire drive-through experience: It expanded the order window, redesigned the menu board and trained employees to assist customers with their menu choices. The result was a dramatic increase in drive-through sales and customer satisfaction and enhanced visibility for Yum Australia within the corporate system, reinforcing its position as a leading global innovator.

Refocusing Executive Attention

What lessons can corporate headquarters executives draw from our research? What sorts of changes should they make to get the most out of their portfolio of subsidiary companies? Our findings suggest four broad approaches.

Create channels for attention. Attention is channeled through a number of formal and informal mechanisms, many of which are designed explicitly to direct executive attention to the biggest or weightiest issues. But if executives want to find ways to amplify the voice of their subsidiaries around the world, they need to give creative thought to the meetings, events and forums they participate in. Some examples of what we observed include:

- Holding performance reviews in the country or region being evaluated. One Australian

subsidiary manager had been meeting his European boss in Bangkok as a way to share the travel time. But once he was able to persuade his boss to travel to Sydney, he noticed a dramatic—and positive—change in his boss's attitude toward the subsidiary.
- Locating board meetings overseas. Companies have found that this often leads to dramatic changes in outlook, providing board members with opportunities to talk directly with distant customers and examine production operations firsthand. Melbourne- and London-based global mining company Rio Tinto, for example, took its entire board to China for a week in 2005. London-based engineering consultancy Arup Group Ltd. holds every other board meeting in an overseas location such as Poland or Brazil.
- Cultivating interpersonal ties. The attention headquarters executives pay to subsidiaries typically stems from past interactions and how well executives know the local people. Accordingly, many companies host forums for the purpose of cultivating ties among different players in the organization. For example, ABB brings its country managers together at least twice a year both to socialize and to share important local insights. In addition, staff from subsidiaries around the world meet with headquarters staff regularly through their involvement in cross-country teams.
- Assigning mentorship responsibilities. At Procter & Gamble Co., country managers are formally linked to a corporate executive, who is expected to keep his antennae out and play a championing role in helping the subsidiary gain access to corporate resources. Ultimately, however, it is up to the subsidiary staff to inform mentors of interesting local developments and to build the case for what they can contribute to the company as a whole.
- Recognizing that regional support for subsidiaries can cut both ways. Regional headquarters can help subsidiaries attract attention, but they can also act as a harmful buffer. IBM Corp., for example, re-evaluated the role of its European headquarters recently, and ended up replacing its Paris headquarters with two new focused

headquarters serving North/East Europe and South/West Europe, respectively.

Seek out the hidden gems and give them a platform   It is worth paying special attention to subsidiary companies that deliver surprisingly good results in relation to their overall stature. Over and above delivering stellar numbers financially, they may also be sources of new insights or practices. Finding these subsidiaries is partly a matter of opening up the attention channels. But it also may require some extra analysis. Which subsidiaries are attracting more interest internally than their market position might warrant? And which are responsible for the biggest annual jumps in sales and profits?

Groupe Danone, the French food products company, does a good job of giving a platform to its hidden gems. Following a major initiative aimed at increasing the company's top-line growth, Danone recently identified the leading countries in the world for certain activities and designated them as the corporate "champions" that others could learn from. Frucor Beverages Group Ltd., Danone's New Zealand subsidiary, became a center for innovation, and executives from elsewhere in the company have been encouraged to spend time in New Zealand to understand how it has been able to deliver revenue growth of 7% to 10% over the past 10 years in a flat market. Similarly, Indonesia was recognized for its expertise in "affordability."

Measure returns on executive attention   A slightly different challenge is how to assess the value of investments in attention, particularly as they relate to big emerging markets: In essence, this involves understanding how to leverage attention into capability. General Electric Co.'s experience in this area provides useful insights. Like executives of most global companies, GE executives pay huge amounts of attention to growth opportunities in China, India, Russia and markets in the Middle East and Latin America. But they are highly disciplined about how they go about it so that the investment opportunities aren't wasted. Their motto is: "Go big and continuously look back." Indeed, they don't get involved unless they

can help the company win mega project proposals in the region—for example, airport expansion programs in China or major water-power programs in India. Less significant opportunities are left for local talent to ponder. Perhaps more importantly, they continually evaluate whether these investments are delivering against their performance expectations, and this analysis becomes a significant input into subsequent investment decisions.[6]

Give subsidiaries a chance to contribute   Good subsidiary managers are looking for ways to contribute to the company as a whole over and above achieving good results in their own business. One of the roles of headquarters managers is to define the needs. For example, executives at several Australian subsidiaries spoke about how their parent wanted them to develop management talent for the rest of the company. Many were reluctant to give up their most promising managers to careers in Europe or North America. But Roger Eaton, the CEO of Yum Australia, decided to make exporting talent a cornerstone of his strategy. Each year he recommended three senior managers for key assignments outside Australia; as these individuals have excelled in their new assignments, the reputation of the Australian operation has grown. "You can't avoid the Aussies in YUM globally," notes Eaton. "If you look at the top 200 executives in the company, you'd find over 20 Australians!"

MANAGING ATTENTION IN A GLOBAL COMPANY often boils down to specific and apparently small actions: holding a board meeting in a remote city, initiating a forum to discuss emerging market opportunities or asking a division head to groom executives for overseas assignments. However, in an environment where high-level attention is in such short supply, small actions can have enormous consequences. They can furnish opportunities for subsidiaries to showcase their initiatives or gain access to expansion capital. They can trigger

---

[6]J. Immelt (untitled presentation at Electrical Products Group conference, Long Boat Keys, Florida, May 24, 2006).

important shifts in the parent company's overall growth trajectory.

We are accustomed to thinking of subsidiaries as having fairly fixed roles.[7] But actually, the roles can be fairly fluid, changing to reflect evolving opportunities and new competencies the subsidiary can contribute. Executive attention can facilitate these internal shifts. Attention may not be the

[7]See C.A. Bartlett and S. Ghoshal, "Tap Your Subsidiaries For Global Reach," *Harvard Business Review* 64, no. 6 (November 1986): 87-94.

ultimate objective, but it is a necessary ingredient for any subsidiary that seeks to play a more pivotal role in the global company.

Acknowledgments

The authors wish to thank the Advanced Institute of Management Research, the Social Sciences and Humanities Research Council of Canada, York University's Institute for Social Research and CEO Forum Group (Australia) for their support.

Reading 7-2   Tap Your Subsidiaries for Global Reach

by Christopher A. Bartlett and Sumantra Ghoshal

In 1972, EMI developed the CAT scanner. This technological breakthrough seemed to be the innovation that the U.K.-based company had long sought in order to relieve its heavy dependence on the cyclical music and entertainment business and to strengthen itself in international markets. The medical community hailed the product, and within four years EMI had established a medical electronics business that was generating 20% of the company's worldwide earnings. The scanner enjoyed a dominant market position, a fine reputation, and a strong technological leadership situation.

Nevertheless, by mid-1979 EMI had started losing money in this business, and the company's deteriorating performance eventually forced it to

Christopher A. Bartlett teaches management of international business at the Harvard Business School, where he is an associate professor. Before joining HBS he was a consultant for McKinsey & Company and general manager of the French subsidiary of Baxter Travenol Laboratories.

Sumantra Ghoshal is an assistant professor of business policy at the European Institute of Business Administration (INSEAD) in Fontainebleau, France. Before turning to teaching, he held line and staff positions with the Indian Oil Corporation Ltd. and directed domestic and foreign marketing for a large private commercial organization in India.

accept a takeover bid from Thorn Electric. Thorn immediately divested the ailing medical electronics business. Ironically, the takeover was announced the same month that Godfrey Hounsfield, the EMI scientist who developed the CAT scanner, was awarded a Nobel Prize for the invention.

How could such a fairy-tale success story turn so quickly into a nightmare? There were many contributing causes, but at the center were a structure and management process that impeded the company's ability to capitalize on its technological assets and its worldwide market position.

The concentration of EMI's technical, financial, and managerial resources in the United Kingdom made it unresponsive to the varied and changing needs of international markets. As worldwide demand built up, delivery lead times for the scanner stretched out more than 12 months. Despite the protests of EMI's U.S. managers that these delays were opening opportunities for competitive entry, headquarters continued to fill orders on the basis of when they were received rather than on how strategically important they were. Corporate management would not allow local sourcing or duplicate manufacturing of the components that were the bottlenecks causing delays.

The centralization of decision making in London also impaired the company's ability to guide strategy to meet the needs of the market. For example, medical practitioners in the United States, the key market for CAT scanners, considered reduction of scan time to be an important objective, while EMI's central research laboratory, influenced by feedback from the domestic market, concentrated on improving image resolution. When General Electric eventually brought out a competitive product with a shorter scan time, customers deserted EMI.

In the final analysis, it was EMI's limited organizational capability that prevented it from capitalizing on its large resource base and its strong global competitive position. The company lacked:

The ability to sense changes in market needs and industry structure occurring away from home.

The resources to analyze data and develop strategic responses to competitive challenges that were emerging worldwide.

The managerial initiative, motivation, and capability in its overseas operations to respond imaginatively to diverse and fast-changing operating environments.

While the demise of its scanner business represents an extreme example, the problems EMI faced are common. With all the current attention being given to global strategy, companies risk underestimating the organizational challenge of managing their global operations. Indeed, the top management in almost every one of the MNCs we have studied has had an excellent idea of what it needed to do to become more globally competitive; it was less clear on how to organize to achieve its global strategic objectives.

United Nations Model & HQ Syndrome

Our study covered nine core companies in three industries and a dozen secondary companies from a more diverse industrial spectrum. They were selected from three areas of origin—the United States, Europe, and Japan. Despite this diversity, most of these companies had developed their international operations around two common assumptions on how to organize. We dubbed these well-ingrained beliefs the "U.N. model assumption" and the "headquarters hierarchy syndrome."

Although there are wide differences in importance of operations in major markets like Germany, Japan, or the United States, compared with subsidiaries in Argentina, Malaysia, or Nigeria, for example, most multinationals treat their foreign subsidiaries in a remarkably uniform manner. One executive we talked to termed this approach "the U.N. model of multinational management." Thus it is common to see managers express subsidiary roles and responsibilities in the same general terms, apply their planning control systems uniformly systemwide, involve country managers to a like degree in planning, and evaluate them against standardized criteria. The uniform systems and procedures tend to paper over any differences in the informal treatment of subsidiaries.

When national units are operationally self-sufficient and strategically independent, uniform treatment may allow each to develop a plan for dealing with its local environment. As a company reaches for the benefits of global integration, however, there is little need for uniformity and symmetry among units. Yet the growing complexity of the corporate management task heightens the appeal of a simple system.

The second common assumption we observed, the headquarters hierarchy syndrome, grows out of and is reinforced by the U.N. model assumption. The symmetrical organization approach encourages management to envision two roles for the organization, one for headquarters and another for the national subsidiaries. As companies moved to build a consistent global strategy, we saw a strong tendency for headquarters managers to try to coordinate key decisions and control global resources and have the subsidiaries act as implementers and adapters of the global strategy in their localities.

As strategy implementation proceeded, we observed country managers struggling to retain their freedom, flexibility, and effectiveness, while their counterparts at the center worked to maintain their control and legitimacy as administrators of the global strategy. It's not surprising that relationships between the center and the periphery often became strained and even adversarial.

The combined effect of these two assumptions is to severely limit the organizational capability of a company's international operations in three important ways. First, the doctrine of symmetrical treatment results in an overcompensation for the needs of smaller or less crucial markets and a simultaneous under-responsiveness to the needs of strategically important countries. Moreover, by relegating the national subsidiaries to the role of local implementers and adapters of global directives, the head office risks grossly underutilizing the company's worldwide assets and organizational capabilities. And finally, ever-expanding control by headquarters deprives the country managers of outlets for their skills and creative energy. Naturally, they come to feel demotivated and even disenfranchised.

Dispersed Responsibility

The limitations of the symmetrical, hierarchical mode of operation have become increasingly clear to MNC executives, and in many of the companies we surveyed we found managers experimenting with alternative ways of managing their worldwide operations. And as we reviewed these various approaches, we saw a new pattern emerging that suggested a significantly different model of global organization based on some important new assumptions and beliefs. We saw companies experimenting with ways of selectively varying the roles and responsibilities of their national organizations to reflect explicitly the differences in external environments and internal capabilities. We also saw them modifying central administrative systems to legitimize the differences they encountered.

Such is the case with Procter & Gamble's European operations. More than a decade ago, P&G's European subsidiaries were free to adapt the parent company's technology, products, and marketing approaches to their local situation as they saw fit—while being held responsible, of course, for sales and earnings in their respective countries. Many of these subsidiaries had become large and powerful.

By the mid-1970s, economic and competitive pressures were squeezing P&G's European profitability. The head office in Cincinnati decided that the loose organizational arrangement inhibited product development, curtailed the company's ability to capture Europewide scale economies, and afforded poor protection against competitors' attempts to pick off product lines country by country.

So the company launched what became known as the Pampers experiment—an approach firmly grounded in the classic U.N. and HQ assumptions. It created a position at European headquarters in Brussels to develop a Pampers strategy for the whole continent. By giving this manager responsibility for the Europewide product and marketing strategy, management hoped to be able to eliminate the diversity in brand strategy by coordinating activities across subsidiary boundaries. Within 12 months, the Pampers experiment had failed. It not only ignored local knowledge and underutilized subsidiary strengths but also demotivated the country managers to the point that they felt no responsibility for sales performance of the brand in their areas.

Obviously, a different approach was called for. Instead of assuming that the best solutions were to be found in headquarters, top management decided to find a way to exploit the expertise of the national units. For most products, P&G had one or two European subsidiaries that had been more creative, committed, and successful than the others. By extending the responsibilities and influence of these organizations, top management reasoned, the company could make the success infectious. All that was needed was a means for promoting intersubsidiary cooperation that could offset the problems caused by the company's dispersed and independent operations. For P&G the key was the creation of "Eurobrand" teams.

For each important brand the company formed a management team that carried the responsibility for development and coordination of marketing strategy for Europe. Each Eurobrand team was headed not by a manager from headquarters but by the general manager and the appropriate brand group from the "lead" subsidiary—a unit selected for its success and creativity with the brand. Supporting them were brand managers from other subsidiaries, functional managers from headquarters, and anyone else involved in strategy for the particular product. Team meetings became forums for the lead-country group to pass on ideas, propose action, and hammer out agreements.

The first Eurobrand team had charge of a new liquid detergent called Vizir. The brand group in the lead country, West Germany, had undertaken product and market testing, settled on the package design and advertising theme, and developed the marketing strategy. The Eurobrand team ratified all these elements, then launched Vizir in six new markets within a year. This was the first time the company had ever introduced a new product in that many markets in so brief a span. It was also the first time the company had got agreement in several subsidiaries on a single product formulation, a uniform advertising theme, a standard packaging line, and a sole manufacturing source. Thereafter, Eurobrand teams proliferated; P&G's way of organizing and directing subsidiary operations had changed fundamentally.

On reflection, company managers feel that there were two main reasons why Eurobrand teams succeeded where the Pampers experiment had failed. First, they captured the knowledge, the expertise, and most important, the commitment of managers closest to the market. Equally significant was the fact that relationships among managers on Euro-brand teams were built on interdependence rather than on independence, as in the old organization, or on dependence, as with the Pampers experiment. Different subsidiaries had the lead role for different brands, and the need for reciprocal cooperation was obvious to everyone.

Other companies have made similar discoveries about new ways to manage their international operations—at NEC and Philips, at L.M. Ericsson and Matsushita, at ITT and Unilever, we observed executives challenging the assumptions behind the traditional head office—subsidiary relationship. The various terms they used—lead-country concept, key-market subsidiary, global-market mandate, center of excellence—all suggested a new model based on a recognition that their organizational task was

Exhibit Roles for national subsidiaries

focused on a single problem: the need to resolve imbalances between market demands and constraints on the one hand and uneven subsidiary capabilities on the other. Top officers understand that the option of a zero-based organization is not open to an established multinational organization. But they seem to have hit on an approach that works.

Black Holes, Etc.   The actions these companies have taken suggest an organizational model of differentiated rather than homogeneous subsidiary roles and of dispersed rather than concentrated responsibilities. As we analyzed the nature of the emerging subsidiary roles and responsibilities, we were able to see a pattern in their distribution and identify the criteria used to assign them. The **Exhibit** represents a somewhat oversimplified conceptualization of the criteria and roles, but it is true enough for discussion purposes.

The strategic importance of a specific country unit is strongly influenced by the significance of its national environment to the company's global strategy. A large market is obviously important, and so is a competitor's home market or a market that is particularly sophisticated or technologically advanced. The organizational competence of a particular subsidiary can, of course, be in technology, production, marketing, or any other area.

Strategic Leader   This role can be played by a highly competent national subsidiary located in a strategically important market. In this role, the subsidiary serves as a partner of headquarters in developing and implementing strategy. It must not only be a sensor for detecting signals of change but also a help in analyzing the threats and opportunities and developing appropriate responses.

The part played by the U.K. subsidiary of Philips in building the company's strong leadership position in the teletext-TV business provides an illustration. In the early 1970s, the BBC and ITV (an independent British TV company) simultaneously launched projects to adapt existing transmission capacity to permit broadcast of text and simple diagrams. But teletext, as it was called, required a TV receiver that would accept and decode the modified transmissions. For TV set manufacturers, the market opportunity required a big investment in R&D and production facilities, but commercial possibilities of teletext were highly uncertain, and most producers decided against making the investment. They spurned teletext as a typical British toy—fancy and not very useful. Who would pay a heavy premium just to read text on a TV screen?

Philips' U.K. subsidiary, however, was convinced that the product had a future and decided to pursue its own plans. Its top officers persuaded Philips' component manufacturing unit to design and produce the integrated-circuit chip for receiving teletext and commissioned their Croydon plant to build the teletext decoder.

In the face of poor market acceptance (the company sold only 1,000 teletext sets in its first year), the U.K. subsidiary did not give up. It lent support to the British government's efforts to promote teletext and make it widely available. Meanwhile, management kept up pressure on the Croydon factory to find ways of reducing costs and improving reception quality—which it did.

In late 1979, teletext took off, and by 1982 half a million sets were being sold annually in the United Kingdom. Today almost three million teletext sets are in use in Britain, and the concept is spreading abroad. Philips has built up a dominant position in markets that have accepted the service. Corporate management has given the U.K. subsidiary formal responsibility to continue to exercise leadership in the development, manufacture, and marketing of teletext on a companywide basis. The Croydon plant is recognized as Philips' center of competence and international sourcing plant for teletext-TV sets.

Contributor   Filling this role is a subsidiary operating in a small or strategically unimportant market but having a distinctive capability. A fine example is the Australian subsidiary of L.M. Ericsson, which played a crucial part in developing its successful AXE digital telecommunications switch. The down-under group gave impetus to the conversion of the system from its initial analog design to the digital form. Later its engineers helped construct several key components of the system.

This subsidiary had built up its superior technological capability when the Australian telephone authority became one of the first in the world to call for bids on electronic telephone switching equipment. The government in Canberra, however, had insisted on a strong local technical capability as a condition for access to the market. Moreover, heading this unit of the Swedish company was a willful, independent, and entrepreneurial country manager who strengthened the R&D team, even without full support from headquarters.

These various factors resulted in the local subsidiary having a technological capability and an R&D resource base that was much larger than subsidiaries in other markets of similar size or importance. Left to their own devices, management worried that such internal competencies would focus on local tasks and priorities that were unnecessary or even detrimental to the overall global strategy. But if the company inhibited the development activities of the local units, it risked losing these special skills. Under the circumstances, management saw the need to coopt this valuable subsidiary expertise and channel it toward projects of corporate importance.

Implementer   In the third situation, a national organization in a less strategically important market has just enough competence to maintain its local operation. The market potential is limited, and the corporate resource commitment reflects it. Most national units of most companies are given this role. They might include subsidiaries in the developing countries, in Canada, and in the smaller European countries. Without access to critical information, and having to control scarce resources, these national organizations lack the potential to become contributors to the company's strategic planning. They are deliverers of the company's value added; they have the important task of generating the funds that keep the company going and underwrite its expansion.

The implementers' efficiency is as important as the creativity of the strategic leaders or contributors—and perhaps more so, for it is this group that provides the strategic leverage that affords MNCs their competitive advantage. The implementers produce the opportunity to capture economies of scale and scope that are crucial to most companies' global strategies.

In Procter & Gamble's European introduction of Vizir, the French company played an important contributing role by undertaking a second market test and later modifying the advertising approach. In the other launches during the first year, Austria, Spain, Holland, and Belgium were implementers; they took the defined strategy and made it work in their markets. Resisting any temptation to push for change in the formula, alteration of the package, or adjustment of the advertising theme, these national subsidiaries enabled P&G to extract profitable efficiencies.

The black hole   Philips in Japan, Ericsson in the United States, and Matsushita in Germany are black holes. In each of these important markets, strong local presence is essential for maintaining the company's global position. And in each case, the local company hardly makes a dent.

The black hole is not an acceptable strategic position. Unlike the other roles we have described, the objective is not to manage it but to manage one's way out of it. But building a significant local presence in a national environment that is large, sophisticated, and competitive is extremely difficult, expensive, and time consuming.

One common tack has been to create a sensory outpost in the black hole environment so as to exploit the learning potential, even if the local business potential is beyond reach. Many American and European companies have set up small establishments in Japan to monitor technologies, market trends, and competitors. Feedback to headquarters, so the thinking goes, will allow further analysis of the global implications of local developments and will at least help prevent erosion of the company's position in other markets. But this strategy has often been less fruitful than the company had hoped. Look at the case of Philips in Japan.

Although Philips had two manufacturing joint ventures with Matsushita, not until 1956 did it enter Japan by establishing a marketing organization. When Japan was emerging as a significant force in the consumer electronics market in the late 1960s, the company decided it had to get further into that market. After years of unsuccessfully trying to penetrate the captive distribution channels of the principal Japanese manufacturers, headquarters settled for a Japan "window" that would keep it informed of technical developments there. But results were disappointing. The reason, according to a senior manager of Philips in Japan, is that to sense effectively, eyes and ears are not enough. One must get "inside the bloodstream of the business," he said, with constant and direct access to distribution channels, component suppliers, and equipment manufacturers.

Detecting a new development after it has occurred is useless, for there is no time to play catch-up. One needs to know of developments as they emerge, and for that one must be a player, not a spectator. Moreover, being confined to window status, the local company is prevented from playing a strategic role. It is condemned to a permanent existence as a black hole.

So Philips is trying to get into the bloodstream of the Japanese market, moving away from the window concept and into the struggle for market share. The local organization now sees its task as winning market share rather than just monitoring local developments. But it is being very selective and focusing on areas where it has advantages over strong local competition. The Japanese unit started with coffee makers and electric shavers. Philips' acquisition of Marantz, a hi-fi equipment producer, gives it a bid to expand on its strategic base and build the internal capabilities that will enable the Japanese subsidiary to climb out of the black hole.

Another way to manage one's way out of the black hole is to develop a strategic alliance. Such coalitions can involve different levels of cooperation. Ericsson's joint venture with Honeywell in the United States and AT&T's with Philips in Europe are examples of attempts to fill up a black hole by obtaining resources and competence from a strong local organization in exchange for capabilities available elsewhere.

Shaping, Building, Directing

Corporate management faces three big challenges in guiding the dispersion of responsibilities and differentiating subsidiaries' tasks. The first is in setting the strategic direction for the company by identifying its mission and its business objectives. The second is in building the differentiated organization, not only by designing the diverse roles and distributing the assignments but also by giving the managers responsible for filling them the legitimacy and power to do so. The final challenge is in directing the process to ensure that the several roles are coordinated and that the distributed responsibilities are controlled.

Setting the course   Any company (or any organization, for that matter) needs a strong, unifying sense of direction. But that need is particularly strong in an organization in which tasks are differentiated and responsibilities dispersed. Without it, the decentralized management process will quickly degenerate into strategic anarchy. A visitor to any NEC establishment in the world will see everywhere the company motto "C&C," which stands for computers and communications. This simple pairing of words is much more than a definition of NEC's product markets; top managers have made it the touchstone of a common global strategy. They emphasize it to focus the attention of employees on the key strategy of linking two technologies. And they employ it to help managers think how NEC can compete with larger

companies like IBM and AT&T, which are perceived as vulnerable insofar as they lack a balance in the two technologies and markets.

Top management at NEC headquarters in Tokyo strives to inculcate its worldwide organization with an understanding of the C&C strategy and philosophy. It is this strong, shared understanding that permits greater differentiation of managerial processes and the decentralization of tasks.

But in addition to their role of developing and communicating a vision of the corporate mission, the top officers at headquarters also retain overall responsibility for the company's specific business strategies. While not abandoning this role at the heart of the company's strategic process, executives of many multinational companies are co-opting other parts of the organization (and particularly its diverse national organizations) into important business strategy roles, as we have already described. When it gives up its lead role, however, headquarters management always tracks that delegated responsibility.

Building differentiation   In determining which units should be given the lead, contributor, or follower roles, management must consider the motivational as well as the strategic impact of its decisions. If unfulfilled, the promise offered by the new organization model can be as demotivating as the symmetrical hierarchy, in which all foreign subsidiaries are assigned permanent secondary roles. For most national units, an organization in which lead and contributor roles are concentrated in a few favorite children represents little advance from old situations in which the parent dominated the decision making. In any units continually obliged to implement strategies developed elsewhere, skills atrophy, entrepreneurship dies, and any innovative spark that existed when it enjoyed more independence now sputters.

By dealing out lead or contributing roles to the smaller or less developed units, even if only for one or two strategically less important products, the headquarters group will give them a huge incentive. Although Philips N.V. had many other subsidiaries closer to large markets or with better access to corporate know-how and expertise, headquarters awarded the Taiwan unit the lead role in the small-screen monitor business. This vote of confidence gave the Taiwanese terrific motivation to do well and made them feel like a full contributing partner in the company's worldwide strategy.

But allocating roles isn't enough; the head office has to empower the units to exercise their voices in the organization by ensuring that those with lead positions particularly have access to and influence in the corporate decision-making process. This is not a trivial task, especially if strategic initiative and decision-making powers have long been concentrated at headquarters.

NEC discovered this truth about a decade ago when it was trying to transform itself into a global enterprise. Because NTT, the Japanese telephone authority, was dragging its feet in converting its exchanges to the new digital switching technology, NEC was forced to diverge from its custom of designing equipment mainly for its big domestic customer. The NEAC 61 digital switch was the first outgrowth of the policy shift; it was aimed primarily at the huge, newly deregulated U.S. telephone market.

Managers and engineers in Japan developed the product; the American subsidiary had little input. Although the hardware drew praise from customers, the switch had severe software deficiencies that hampered its penetration of the U.S. market.

Recognizing the need to change its administrative setup, top management committed publicly to becoming "a genuine world enterprise" rather than a Japanese company operating abroad. To permit the U.S. subsidiary a greater voice, headquarters helped it build a local software development capability. This plus the unit's growing knowledge about the Bell operating companies—NEC's target customers—gave the American managers legitimacy and power in Japan.

NEC's next-generation digital switch, the NEAC 61E, evolved quite differently. Exercising their new influence at headquarters, U.S. subsidiary managers took the lead in establishing its features and specifications and played a big part in the design.

Another path to empowerment takes the form of dislodging the decision-making process from the home office. Ericsson combats the headquarters hierarchy syndrome by appointing product and functional managers from headquarters to subsidiary boards. The give-and-take in board meetings is helpful for both subsidiary and parent. Matsushita holds an annual review of each major worldwide function (like manufacturing and human resource management) in the offices of a national subsidiary it considers to be a leading exponent of the particular function. In addition to the symbolic value for employees of the units, the siting obliges officials from Tokyo headquarters to consider issues that the front lines are experiencing and gives local managers the home-court advantage in seeking a voice in decision making.

Often the most effective means of giving strategy access and influence to national units is to create entirely new channels and forums. This approach permits roles, responsibilities, and relationships to be defined and developed with far less constraint than through modification of existing communication patterns or through shifting of responsibility boundaries. Procter & Gamble's Eurobrand teams are a case in point.

Directing the process   When the roles of operating units are differentiated and responsibility is more dispersed, corporate management must be prepared to deemphasize its direct control over the strategic content but develop an ability to manage the dispersed strategic process. Furthermore, headquarters must adopt a flexible administrative stance that allows it to differentiate the way it manages one subsidiary to the next and from business to business within a single unit, depending on the particular role it plays in each business.

In units with lead roles, headquarters plays an important role in ensuring that the business strategies developed fit the company's overall goals and priorities. But control in the classic sense is often quite loose. Corporate management's chief function is to support those with strategy leadership responsibility by giving them the resources and the freedom needed for the innovative and entrepreneurial role they have been asked to play.

With a unit placed in a contributor role, the head-office task is to redirect local resources to programs outside the unit's control. In so doing, it has to counter the natural hierarchy of loyalties that in most national organizations puts local interests above global ones. In such a situation, headquarters must be careful not to discourage the local managers and technicians so much that they stop contributing or leave in frustration. This has happened to many U.S. companies that have tried to manage their Canadian subsidiaries in a contributor role. Ericsson has solved the problem in its Australian subsidiary by attaching half the R&D team to headquarters, which farms out to these engineers projects that are part of the company's global development program.

The head office maintains tighter control over a subsidiary in an implementer role. Because such a group represents the company's opportunity to capture the benefits of scale and learning from which it gets and sustains its competitive advantage, headquarters stresses economy and efficiency in selling the products. Communication of strategies developed elsewhere and control of routine tasks can be carried out through systems, allowing headquarters to manage these units more efficiently than most others.

As for the black hole unit, the task for top executives is to develop its resources and capabilities to make it more responsive to its environment. Managers of these units depend heavily on headquarters for help and support, creating an urgent need for intensive training and transfer of skills and resources.

Firing the Spark Plugs

Multinational companies often build cumbersome and expensive infrastructures designed to control their widespread operations and to coordinate the diverse and often conflicting demands they make. As the coordination and control task expands, the typical headquarters organization becomes larger and more powerful, while the national subsidiaries are increasingly regarded as pipelines for centrally developed products and strategy.

But an international company enjoys a big advantage over a national one: it is exposed to a wider and more diverse range of environmental stimuli. The broader range of customer preferences, the wider spectrum of competitive behavior, the more serious array of government demands, and the more diverse sources of technological information represent potential triggers of innovation and thus a rich source of learning for the company. To capitalize on this advantage requires an organization that is sensitive to the environment and responsive in absorbing the information it gathers.

So national companies must not be regarded as just pipelines but recognized as sources of information and expertise that can build competitive advantage. The best way to exploit this resource is not through centralized direction and control but through a cooperative effort and co-option of dispersed capabilities. In such a relationship, the entrepreneurial spark plugs in the national units can flourish.

Reading 7-3   The Collaboration Imperative

By Rick Lash

For various reasons, the management challenges ahead will require the skills of a collaborative leader. Many leaders, however, lack the required skills to collaborate meaningfully.

Rick Lash is the National Practice leader, Leadership and Talent, the Hay Group. This is his third article for Ivey Business Journal. His most recent, Change From the Inside, was published in the November-December, 2008 edition.

Readers will learn what those skills are and how they can develop them in this article

Organizations face an increasingly complex and unpredictable competitive landscape, and one that is filled with new, aggressive competitors. A few years ago, for example, who would have predicted that electronics manufacturer Samsung would offer stiff competition to GE in the appliance and lighting marketplaces?

In the years ahead volatility and uncertainty will tyrannize markets, and companies will need leaders who are highly adaptive, continuous learners, able to lead diverse groups across functional disciplines, regions and cultures. They will also need to accomplish the difficult feat of driving results even where they do not have formal direct control or authority over resources. Achieving more growth through greater innovation, searching for new business opportunities across customer segments and leveraging best business practices to improve operational efficiency are all tasks that demand that leaders know how to work across organizational boundaries. Whether it's across national boundaries or across teams, leaders will need to collaborate. This article will focus on the skills that leaders will need to develop if they are to collaborate successfully in the years ahead.

Getting to the Root of Collaboration Challenges

The vast majority of participants in Hay Group's recent global Best Companies for Leadership survey indicated that their organizations have become flatter and more matrixed. Individuals may be assigned to work on different project teams and report to multiple managers. The advantages can be huge—new innovations, increased sharing of information and better capacity to solve complex problems. And yet the more matrixed organizations become the greater the challenges in making lines of authority and accountability clear. Decisions can take longer and the costs for bringing people together can add to a company's bottom line. In addition, the skills required for effective collaboration are not the same as knowing how to work effectively in a functional team. These same companies also reported that their people had trouble understanding how to relate to each other and in a more collaborative way, as their new organizational structures required.

These survey results are not surprising, given that another Hay Group study of over 300 organizations covering almost 4,500 leaders found that executives still need the most development in competencies such as influence, inspirational leadership, coaching, mentoring and emotional self-awareness—the competencies that are critical for collaboration. Leadership skills and capabilities have not kept pace with the rapid evolution of flatter, more matrixed organizational structures.

Why has the development of collaborative leadership skills lagged the evolution of organizational structures? Organizations usually get the kind of behaviour they reward, and they have historically rewarded achievement-oriented leaders who drive short-term results. As a result, companies have ended up with leaders who excel at the achievement orientation, teamwork and organizational awareness competencies that are associated with strong functional leadership.

The problem is that companies face a mismatch: They have developed a strong base of operational leaders who perform well when they have direct control over a specific set of resources that they can deploy to achieve accountable results. Unfortunately, the matrixed, global structure that is becoming the norm for many organizations requires leaders who can *subordinate* their agenda, *yield* power and *give up* resources for the greater good. These concepts are foreign to many leaders who attempt to lead collaborative efforts by applying their usual functional skill-set—and that predictably lead to poor results. Even leaders who possess some of the necessary competencies find themselves working at cross-purposes with an organizational structure and rewards system that discourages collaboration.

Collaborating in the Matrix

Despite popular belief, collaboration is not the same as teamwork. Traditional functional leaders in hierarchical organizations may excel at "teamwork" in the sense of motivating their business unit or division toward collective action and consensus around a common goal.

But matrixed organizations are different. Matrixed companies group employees by both function *and* product. Matrixed organizations typically have moved away from hierarchy toward a much flatter structure in which employees operate with less direct supervision from functional leaders. Leaders in the matrixed organization need to know how to promote collaboration across business units and functional areas, and to coordinate and motivate employees, over whom they may have no direct authority, to achieve a goal whose value may not be immediately apparent to all team members.

In a matrixed world, good collaboration can lead to the rapid launch of next-generation, market-changing products. Bad collaboration can end up wasting time and money on a slow, tortuous path toward a "me-too" flop. In his seminal book *Collaboration,* UC Berkeley professor Morten Hansen illustrates the value of collaboration by tracing the success of Apple's iPod music player versus the belated launch of a similar product by Sony. Hansen notes that it took Apple just eight months starting from scratch to collaborate across its organization and find a way to create the iPod. Sony, on the other hand, spent three years engaged in internal infighting before launching a competing MP3 player that had little success.

Apple did not win because it had better technology. In fact, Apple actually sourced its iPod battery from Sony! The success of the iPod can be attributed more to Apple's ability to manage rapid innovation through excellent internal and external collaborative networks. At Sony, where the culture encouraged internal competition over collaboration, a digital music player did not make as much sense from a P&L standpoint for any individual business unit. As a result, the project did not move forward, even though it held the potential to deliver large P&L benefits for the entire organization.

It turns out that collaborative leaders are able to see past their own P&L calculations to recognize and pursue initiatives that have the potential to add value for the entire corporation. But companies should not expect such collaborative behaviour to materialize spontaneously. As mentioned earlier, organizations tend to exhibit the kind of behaviour that they reward. It is difficult to generate much enthusiasm for collaboration initiatives if managers are only rewarded based on their own P&L. Best-in-class organizations have recognized this problem and begun looking for ways to measure the global

P&L impact of collaborative projects and reward leaders accordingly, **even if those projects result in lower P&L for the manager's own business unit.**

Building a Collaborative Culture

Senior executives have both the responsibility and the power to encourage and foster a culture of collaboration. Consider the impact that collaboration had on Procter & Gamble (P&G). In early 2000, P&G was in disarray. The company's share price had fallen by nearly 50 percent, wiping out $85 billion in market capital. Despite spending heavily on research & development (R&D), productivity had plateaued and the company's innovation success rate (the percentage of new products that reached financial objectives) was stuck around an unsatisfactory 35 percent.

The company's new CEO, A.G. Lafley, recognized that collaboration would be key to helping P&G recover its value and improve its innovation performance. He proclaimed that he was determined to make P&G known as the company that "collaborates, inside and out, better than any other company in the world." Lafley and his team conducted an analysis showing that most of P&G's most profitable innovations came either from internal collaboration across business units or from external collaboration with outside researchers. Determined to encourage both kinds of collaboration, Lafley established 20 cross-functional "communities of practice" within P&G and declared that 50 percent of P&G's products, ideas and technologies would be developed by external sources.

These collaboration initiatives paid off handsomely. By 2008, P&G had improved its R&D productivity by nearly 60 percent, more than doubled its innovation success rate, and lowered its cost of innovation. From 2000 to 2008, R&D investment as a percentage of sales fell from 4.8 percent to 3.4 percent.[1]

---

[1] For more details on how P&G created a collaborative culture and the benefits it reaped from that culture, see "Connect and Develop: Inside Procter & Gamble's New Model for Innovation," *Harvard Business Review,* Vol. 84, No. 3, March 2006.

Key Collaborative Competencies

Leadership and organizational structure matter in building a collaborative culture, but organizations still need the right people with the right skills to lead collaboration initiatives toward the desired outcomes. Hay Group research findings on matrixed organizations show that the best collaborative leaders have a strong understanding of both the organization and its people. They distinguish themselves on six key capabilities:

1. **Enterprise perspective**—they have a comprehensive understanding of the company's overall business strategy and how the joint work they are leading aligns with that strategy. They use this understanding to resolve any conflicts that may arise.
2. **Cross-functional perspective**—they understand the needs, metrics, incentives and deliverables of different functions and business units. They can align these competing priorities within the operating model.
3. **Customer perspective**—they not only understand the customers' interests and needs, they also know how to keep the team focused on making the decisions that enhance the overall customer experience.
4. **Self-management**—they exhibit self-control when challenged. They have patience when dealing with colleagues who may have trouble understanding the shared purpose of the collaboration initiative. They do not take disagreements personally.
5. **Listen with respect**—they listen objectively and respectfully to multiple opinions. They empathize with colleagues whose position, situation or perspective may differ from their own. They start with the assumption that collaborators are capable and will do their best.
6. **Matrix influencing**—they excel at communicating with different stakeholders and influencing them to support collaborative projects.

Cultivating Collaborative Leaders

How can organizations identify candidates that will succeed in matrixed leadership positions that require strong collaborative skills? Hay Group's Role-Profile Matrix shows that the best collaborative leaders excel at interpersonal understanding, relationship building and commitment to the enterprise. This makes sense because collaborative leaders have to be able to *understand* the motives and fears of potential collaborative partners throughout the organization. Collaborative leaders have to be able to *build* relationships that will enable them to persuade their partners to join in a collaborative effort that may entail short-term risks or costs for certain partners. And collaborative leaders need to be *committed* to enterprise-wide goals since collaborative projects are typically bigger than any one department or business unit.

Given the need for collaborative leaders in matrixed organizations, companies should plan to start trying to develop collaborative behaviours as early as possible in a junior executive's career. Giving young executives a variety of experiences and ensuring that they have exposure to managing diverse groups can help them to develop a collaborative skill set. Companies like P&G and GE plan 5–10 years into the future when considering the development of their leadership corps. If they see that a certain junior executive has growth potential, they consider which experiences will give the executive the opportunity to develop the broad collaborative leadership capabilities that will be essential in the future. IBM pairs promising young talent with the best possible bosses so that the next generation of leaders will be able to see what strong collaborative leadership looks like in action.

That is not to say that training can mold any leadership candidate into a capable collaborative leader. Broadly speaking, leaders are motivated by a combination of three needs: achievement, affiliation and power. Every collaborative leader has these motives, though in different proportions. Hay Group's research has shown that the most effective collaborative matrixed leaders tend to have flat profiles that show a relatively equal distribution of the 3 motives.

This makes sense. Matrixed leadership roles are complex precisely because they demand so many different skills. Leaders who are motivated primarily by personal achievement will often become frustrated by the time it takes to align agendas or the need to rely on collaborators to get things done. Conversely, leaders who enjoy the harmony of building relationships for their own sake will be more likely to enjoy and thrive in a collaborative leadership position with a heavy relationship-building component.

Collaborating More, Collaborating Better

Collaboration is not a universal solution. As mentioned earlier, collaboration has costs—direct investment costs and opportunity costs associated with the time spent pursuing collaborative initiatives. Companies should assess and qualify collaboration opportunities just as they qualify sales leads to decide whether a particular collaboration effort makes sense. In most cases, organizations should only pursue those collaboration initiatives where the potential benefits clearly exceed the potential costs.

But if choosing collaboration opportunities wisely depends on calculating costs and benefits (as Hansen emphasizes in his perspective), then one way to enlarge the universe of attractive collaboration initiatives is to lower the costs of collaborating across the board. That was part of the approach taken by Cisco Systems when the company decided to prioritize internal collaboration to meet its customers' demand for integrated solutions. Cisco drove down the direct costs of collaboration by leveraging wikis (websites built and edited by communities of users) and pioneering telepresence technologies (enhanced videoconferencing) that enabled affordable long-distance collaboration among employees around the world, thereby reducing the hard costs and opportunity costs of collaboration. By innovating on collaboration technologies and cultivating collaborative behaviour and management practices, Cisco saved $691 million and increased productivity by 4.9 percent in fiscal year 2008.[2]

Reducing the costs of collaboration improves the chance that a collaboration initiative will have

[2]McBrearty, Rachael, Brian Suckow and Joel Barbier, "The Economics of Collaboration at Cisco," Cisco Point of View document, 2009. http://www.cisco.com/web/about/ac79/docs/pov/Economics_Collaboration_POV_FINAL_041009.pdf

a positive ROI. However, companies can improve their odds even further by following five guidelines for successful collaboration:

1. **Be clear about the destination**—define the goalposts and communicate those definitions to collaboration partners. Know when to start the collaboration and when the collaboration has achieved maximum benefits and can be dissolved. Hay Group research has shown that nearly 70 percent of best-practice collaboration initiatives are based from the start on a clear purpose, whereas only 40 percent of less successful matrixed collaboration teams had that clear purpose from the beginning.
2. **Develop mutual understanding**—collaborative success depends on trust, and trust depends on good communication. Collaborative leaders must not only be clear about their own goals, they must also understand and respect their collaborative partners' goals in order to find ways to bring these diverse goals into alignment. Achieving this alignment is a requisite for motivating all collaboration partners to achieve the best possible results. According to Hay Group research, more than 60 percent of best-practice collaboration initiatives get early buy-in on shared goals from collaboration partners. The same can be said for less than 10 percent of the less successful collaboration teams.
3. **Know when to lead and when to follow**—it sounds paradoxical, but the best collaborative leaders are those who are comfortable occasionally letting their partners take a leadership role. At certain times, partners may be the only ones with the resources necessary to push a project forward. Partners who play leadership roles are also more likely to feel a sense of ownership in the project, which can increase their motivation and performance. Nearly 70 percent of best-practice collaborators clarify roles from the start in order to find out which collaboration partners excel in certain areas or have the best customer insights. Again, less than 10 percent of less successful collaborators take the time to clarify roles in this way early on.

4. **Set schedules and stick to them**—many collaborative efforts are undertaken to accelerate innovation in fast-moving markets. Sticking to a realistic timetable avoids conflicts and prevents disappointment. Collaborative tools such as the wikis and telepresence technologies discussed above, or information-sharing forums like SharePoint, can help speed up the process and keep everyone on schedule.

5. **Encourage information sharing**—for functional leaders used to managing and controlling their own resources, collaborative leadership roles can be challenging and even a little mystifying. Experienced mentors who have already led profitable collaboration projects can help teach new collaborative leaders what it takes to succeed. Once they know the ropes, collaborative leaders can pass along their knowledge by guiding others, codifying their knowledge in wikis or other information sharing forums, and establishing guidelines to encourage useful collaborative activity.

Done hastily or sloppily, collaboration can be a time-consuming exercise. Done right, collaboration can unleash latent creativity and help companies spur innovation and growth while fulfilling unmet customer needs.

Sidebar #1—Collaboration Is a Goal, Not a Journey

Despite the importance of *useful* collaboration, collaboration should not be set on a pedestal and worshiped for its own sake. As organizations strive to foster collaboration by training leaders, revamping rewards programs and making structural changes, they should remember that not all collaboration is good collaboration.

As UC Berkeley professor Morten Hansen has eloquently articulated, collaboration frequently requires a significant and sustained investment of time, money and other resources. Beyond the direct costs of collaboration, there are opportunity costs associated with not spending time on initiatives that are particular to one's own group or division.

Organizations can sort good collaboration from the frivolous by making sure that all collaboration initiatives have a clearly defined purpose. Collaboration should not be seen as a valuable trait or an end in itself, but rather should only be used as a solution to a compelling business problem that requires people from different functional areas to work together and cooperate to innovate, improve operations or drive sales. Thus Procter & Gamble used collaboration to good effect when it brought together innovators from multiple divisions including polymers, oral health and adhesives to create Crest White Strips, a market-changing product.

How can you spot poor collaboration initiatives before they cause damage? Symptoms of bad collaboration include lots of meetings with no clear agenda, time-consuming attempts to reach full consensus on all business decisions and relationships that are prioritized over results. Sorting worthwhile and worthless collaboration initiatives and figuring out which ones to encourage and which ones to shut down may be one of the most important capabilities for organizations to cultivate.

Sidebar #2—Collaboration Assessment Tool

As organizations consider candidates for collaborative leadership roles, they should ask the following six questions:

1. Can this leader achieve results by influencing rather than directing?
2. Can this leader share ownership, even if it means sharing credit and rewards?
3. Can this leader delegate and let others deliver results?
4. Has this leader demonstrated the ability to motivate groups of diverse individuals who may not share her viewpoints or perspectives?
5. Has this leader demonstrated the ability to make and implement decisions collaboratively?
6. Can this leader get results even when he has no direct control over people or resources?

The Future of the Transnational:
An Evolving Global Role

Following several decades in which powerful forces of globalization unleashed a period of growth that drove the overseas development and expansion of many multinational enterprises (MNEs), questions are now being raised about what responsibilities come with the power that these large global companies have accumulated. In this final chapter, we address this question by examining the role of the MNE in the global political economy of the early twenty-first century.

This period of growth in the global economy has also advanced the progress of most large nation-states in which MNEs operated, as their economic and social infrastructure benefited from the value created through booming cross-border trade and investment. However, another group of countries has remained largely in the backwash of the powerful development forces of globalization. While the richest nations argued that the rising tide of globalization would lift all boats, to those in the poorest countries, it appeared to be lifting mainly the luxury yachts. And despite half a century of effort, the government-sponsored aid programs designed to narrow the growing gap between rich and poor nations have exhibited surprisingly little positive impact. With a third of the world's population subsisting on less than $2 a day, many have begun to feel that the MNEs that benefited so greatly from global economic expansion now have a responsibility to help deal with the unequal distribution of their benefits.

After discussing this evolving situation, this chapter will describe four different postures that MNEs have adopted in recent decades, ranging from the exploitative and the transactional to the responsive and the transformational. Although these are presented as descriptive generalizations rather than definitive normative categories, in today's global environment, there is a strong push to have companies move away from the exploitive end of the spectrum toward the responsive and even transformative end. These expectations are set out in documents ranging from the U.N. Global Compact to the voluntary industry norms and standards that have been established to provide guidance to the way the MNEs might think about their responsibilities abroad as they expand their operations into the 21st century.

For most transnational companies, the dawning of the new millennium offered exciting prospects of continued growth and prosperity. Yet, in the poorest nations on Earth, the reputation of large MNEs from the world's most developed countries was shaky at best, and in some quarters, it was in complete tatters. Indeed, a series of widely publicized events in the closing years of the twentieth century led many to ask what additional constraints and controls needed to be placed on their largely unregulated activities:

- In Indonesia, Nike employed children in unhealthy work environments, paying them $1.80 a day to make athletic shoes being sold for a $150 a pair to affluent Western buyers.
- In Europe, Coca-Cola refused to take responsibility when consumers of soft drinks produced at its Belgian plant reported getting sick, then finally acknowledging the problem only after 100 people had been hospitalized and five countries had banned the sale of its products.
- In India, a regional government was trying to cancel a contract with Enron for the construction of the Dabhol power station and the supply of power, citing the company's "fraud and misrepresentation" during the original negotiations.
- In South Africa, 39 Western pharmaceutical companies sued the government and President Nelson Mandela to prevent the importation of cheap generic versions of patented AIDS drugs to treat the country's 4.5 million HIV-positive patients.

Each of these situations involved complex, multifaceted issues to which intelligent managers presumably believed that they were responding in a logical, justifiable manner—conforming to local labor laws and practices at Nike, conducting quality tests and communicating the data at Coke, enforcing legal contract provisions at Enron, and protecting intellectual property rights by the drug companies. Yet in the court of public opinion, their rational, abstract, or legalistic arguments were swamped by an overarching view of Western multinational companies operating out of greed, arrogance, and self-interest. They were seen as hammers driving home a widening wedge between the "haves" and the "have nots."

The Growing Discontent

Partly as a result of this growing distrust of MNEs, a popular groundswell against globalization began to gather strength in the early years of the 21st century. Prior to this movement, globalization had been widely viewed as a powerful engine of economic development, spreading the benefits of free market capitalism around the world. Yet the increasingly apparent reality was that far fewer developing countries had seen the benefits of this much-discussed tidal wave of trade and investment. Indeed, to some who lived in these countries, the growing gap between the rich and the poor offered clear evidence that "globalization" was just the latest term for their continued exploitation by the developed world through the agency of MNEs.

As a result, delegates from a number of developing nations agreed to block what they saw as unfair rules being imposed by richer nations at the World Trade Organization (WTO) meeting in Seattle in 1999. Supported by a large number of demonstrators, this conference represented the first high-profile protest against the increasing globalization of the world's economy, which many in the West believed was as beneficial as it was inevitable. The prime targets of the protests were the trade ministers from the world's richest countries and the multinational corporations that the demonstrators saw as the main drivers and beneficiaries of globalization. It became a watershed moment that forced many MNEs to review their past practices and their future priorities.

The Seattle protests received even more public attention when police began using pepper spray and tear gas against demonstrators, mobilizing a great deal of public sympathy and support for their cause. In subsequent years, as the protesters continued their actions, their arguments were being buttressed by powerful allies, including the Nobel laureate Joseph Stiglitz, a former chairman of the Council of Economic Advisors and chief economist at the World Bank. In his book *Globalization and Its Discontents,* Stiglitz suggests that previous actions of the WTO, the International Monetary Fund (IMF), and the World Bank had often damaged developing countries' economies more than they had helped them.[1] He pointed out that although the First World preached the benefits of free trade, it still protected and subsidized agricultural products, textiles, and apparel—precisely the goods exported by Third World countries. And rather than seeing MNEs as creating value in developing countries, Stiglitz suggested that their effect was often to crowd out local enterprise, and then use their monopoly power to raise prices.

But the developing world's arguments were most dramatically confirmed by the World Bank's ongoing annual reports on the number of people worldwide living below the poverty threshold.[2] The data confirmed modest progress in reducing the number of people living on less than $2 a day (in constant purchasing price parity) from 2.59 billion in 1981 to 2.47 billion in 2008. Yet despite the impressive growth of countries like India and China during that time, after almost three decades of globalization-driven growth, the World Bank's data showed that more than a third of the world's 7 billion people were still living in extreme poverty.

The Challenge Facing MNEs

Given the extent of global poverty and the lack of clear significant progress in reducing it, a growing view began to emerge that it was time to radically rethink an approach that relied so heavily on government-funded aid programs. William Easterly, a former research economist at the World Bank, pointed out that after developed countries had provided $2.3 trillion of aid to developing countries over the past five decades, it is clear that the West's model of development has failed.[3] He argued that a large portion of foreign aid takes a paternalistic view in defining both the problems and the solutions and providing for neither accountability nor feedback. As a result, for example, $5 billion of internationally funded aid has been spent over the past 30 years on a publicly owned steel mill in Nigeria that has yet to produce any steel.

In contrast, the outstanding success stories in India and China have been achieved by unleashing the power of their market economies rather than through massive aid programs. In what the World Bank has called "the greatest poverty reduction program in human history," hundreds of millions of people in China have moved out of poverty since the late 1970s. In large part, this amazing transformation has been due to the

---

[1]Joseph E. Stiglitz, *Globalization and Its Discontents* (New York: WW Norton & Company, 2002).
[2]World Bank, *Poverty Reduction and the World Bank* (Washington, D.C.: World Bank, 1999); World Bank, *Attacking Poverty* (New York: Oxford University Press, 2001).
[3]William Easterly, *White Man's Burden* (New York: Penguin Press, 2006).

investment of $870 billion by 300,000 approved foreign enterprises in the 30 years following the announcement of China's open-door policy in 1979. Included in that total are 490 of the world's top 500 companies, who not only see China providing them access to low-cost labor and a huge fast-growing market, but also as a technology source in which they have established 1,160 R&D centers. In addition to helping China, their investments are now having a significant economic impact on these firms, which sent almost $300 billion in profits out of China in the period from 1990 to 2007. Such a win-win consequence is due to one undeniable reality: The faster the poor gain wealth, the faster they become customers.

In light of this impressive record, the eyes of many in the international community began to turn toward the MNEs to provide at least a part of the solution to the intractable problems that many developing countries faced. But this has required more than just a public relations exercise extolling the benefits of free trade and openness to foreign investment. It has meant understanding what role MNEs might play in dealing with some of the underlying causes of the widespread discontent in the developing world. In financial power alone, the World Bank estimated that the flows of foreign direct investment into developing countries in 2010 was about $416 billion, more than four times the amount of foreign aid and development funding flowing into that same group of countries.

For the MNEs, the immediate challenge has been to decide how to respond to the growing public resistance to the globalization forces that drove their growth and expansion during the previous half-century. Their longer-term challenge is to determine whether they are willing to step up and take a leadership role in dealing with the problems that are the underlying causes of the anti-globalization movement.

Responding to Developing World Needs: Four MNE Postures

To understand how MNEs have faced such issues in the past and how they might in the future, we will describe four somewhat archetypical responses along a spectrum of possible action, ranging from an approach we label "exploitive" to one we describe as "transformative." Our observations suggest that most MNEs have moved away from the former model; many believe that it is in their long-term interest to shift toward the latter.

The Exploitive MNE: Taking Advantage of Disadvantage

As we saw in Chapter 1, because one of the strongest and most enduring motivations for a company to internationalize is its desire to access low-cost factors of production, the ability to locate cheap labor has long encouraged many MNEs to enter emerging markets. To anyone operating in these environments, it soon became clear that not only were the wages significantly below those in developed countries, but so were the health and safety standards, the working conditions, and even the human rights of the workers. The question facing MNE management was how to respond to that situation.

For a subset of the companies that we describe as "exploitive MNEs," the lower the labor rate, the longer the workweek, the fewer the restrictions on working conditions, and the less regulation on workers' rights, the better. The companies that we place in this category believe that cross-country differences in wages, working conditions, legal requirements, and living standards all represent unfettered opportunities for them to capture competitive advantage.

Such an attitude received its strongest support in the 1970s in the writings of University of Chicago economist Milton Friedman. Guided by the view that companies had a responsibility to maximize profits and that shareholders were their only legitimate stakeholder, he argued that "[those who believe that] business has a 'social conscience' and takes seriously its responsibilities for providing employment, eliminating discrimination, avoiding pollution . . . are preaching pure and unadulterated socialism."[4] Such bold, clear absolutes from a Nobel laureate in economics provided the exploitive MNEs all the cover they needed to embrace their oppressive stance, and during the 1960s and 1970s, many did. Surprisingly, a few still operate this way today.

One of the most commonly held negative images of MNEs relates to the use of "sweatshops"—workplaces characterized by some combination of hot, crowded, poorly ventilated, poorly lit, and unsafe environments—in which the labor force, often including children, works long hours for less than a "living wage." Unfortunately, these are not just examples of extreme situations from an era long past. In 2006, *The New York Times* reported that a large number of workers from Bangladesh each paid $1,000 to $3,000 to agents in return for the promise of work in Jordanian factories producing garments for Target and Wal-Mart. After they arrived at their new place of work, their passports were confiscated to ensure that they did not quit. Not only were they paid less than promised (and far less than the country's minimum wage), they were forced to work 20-hour days and were hit by supervisors if they complained.[5]

Most MNEs have tried to avoid criticism around the sweatshop issue by outsourcing manufacturing to arm's-length suppliers. But as Nike, Wal-Mart, and many other high-profile companies found, such tactics are no longer effective in insulating the MNE from responsibility. Stories such as the one in *The New York Times* have resulted in widespread consumer outrage and public demands that MNEs take responsibility for the suppliers with whom they contract to make their products. In recent years, major companies, including Apple, Nike, and Wal-Mart, have all yielded to the pressure of consumer boycotts and public criticism to step up monitoring of their suppliers.

Yet despite the risks, when the pressure from governments, nongovernmental organizations (NGOs), and supranational agencies becomes too great, MNEs committed to an exploitive approach will simply close down and move their factory to another city, state, or country. These companies understand that many countries are actively working to develop employment, increase their tax base, and capture spin-off benefits from new investment, and they do not hesitate to play countries against one another. A classic example was provided by several companies making soccer balls in Pakistan. When publicity about the widespread use of child labor forced them to change their practices, many simply provided the employees materials that could be stitched by the children in their

[4]Milton Friedman. "The Social Responsibility of Business Is to Increase its Profits," *The New York Times Magazine,* September 13, 1970.

[5]Steven Greenhouse and Michael Barbaro, "An Ugly Side of Free Trade: Sweatshops in Jordan," *The New York Times,* May 3, 2006.

homes. Others simply responded to government incentives to relocate to Bangladesh, where the use of child labor continued.

In countries where corruption and bribery are common, this push for concessions and subsidies from local government officials and regulators has led some exploitive MNEs to engage in illegal activities. Justifying their actions with an attitude of "when in Rome . . . ," some firms have been willing to engage in such practices in the name of maximizing profits. In a couple of notorious examples from the 1970s, United Brands was charged with bribing the president of Honduras to help maintain a banana monopoly, and the U.S. conglomerate ITT was accused of conspiring to work with the Central Intelligence Agency (CIA) to overthrow the democratically elected government of Chile.[6] In response, the U.S. Congress passed the Foreign Corrupt Practices Act (FCPA) in 1977. Yet corrupt payments have continued, as confirmed by the fact that between 2007 and 2011, the U.S. government collected almost $4 billion in FCPA fines, the most recent high-profile case being Wal-Mart's cover-up of millions of dollars in bribes in Mexico to obtain permits to allow store development.

Global exploitation can move well beyond an ethics-free pursuit of low-cost labor and subsidized investment. It has led some companies to seek market expansion regardless of the likely resulting economic, social, or cultural damage. One classic example unfolded in the mid-1970s, when Nestlé and other infant formula manufacturers became concerned that birth rates in most industrialized countries were flattening and declining. Shifting their attention to what seemed like huge opportunities in these emerging-country markets, they began a major marketing push in those countries. Their tactics involved employing sales promoters dressed as nurses to hand out samples and providing hospitals with discharge kits of bottles and baby milk powder.

Subsequent reports of increases in infant mortality and malnourishment soon had many concerned that the practice was having major negative health consequences. It was discovered that mothers saw infant formula as "modern and Western," and the practice of breastfeeding declined. But because they could not afford to use the formula at the recommended level, they diluted it. Not only was the baby not receiving necessary nutrients, but the water being used to mix the formula often was unsanitary, leading to diarrhea, dehydration, and malnutrition. Worse still, the baby was not receiving all the immunities normally transferred from the mother via breastfeeding, again making the child less resistant to sickness.

In the ensuing public outrage, consumers worldwide boycotted Nestlé products. Even today, more than three decades later, that boycott continues, supported by NGOs such as Save the Children, CARE, and World Vision, protesting what they believe to be continued unethical practices promoting infant formula in Laos, Bangladesh, and other developing countries.

Beyond the direct way that it affects the lives of its employees and customers, the MNE also has an impact on the local communities in which it operates. In its single-minded focus on maximizing profit, however, an exploitive MNE accepts no responsibility for the social or environmental consequences of its actions.

---

[6]Anthony Sampson, *The Sovereign State of ITT* (New York: Stein and Day, 1973).

One of the most severe industrial tragedies in history involved a massive gas leak from a Union Carbide facility in Bhopal, India, in 1984, an accident that resulted in 18,000 deaths and 50,000 permanent disabilities. The company was fined $470 million, and criminal proceedings were initiated against its key executives. The case was finally resolved in Indian courts in 2010, but it was immediately appealed by the government, which felt that a sentence of two years in prison for seven Indian company executives was too lenient.[7]

Subsequent decades have been punctuated by similar disasters for which MNEs have been held responsible. Some, such as BP's 2010 Deep Horizon oil rig explosion in the Gulf of Mexico, have been highly publicized. Others, such as the ongoing series of spills in the Niger Delta—at least 50 times the impact of the 1989 Exxon *Valdez* oil spill, according to the World Wildlife Fund (WWF)—go largely unreported. Shell and Exxon claim that most have been the result of oil pipeline thieves and militant activists.

Because MNEs are able to operate outside the legal framework of any single government, some believe that they need to be better regulated and controlled. However, most supranational organizations and agencies (e.g., ILO, UNCTAD, and UNESCO) have been relatively ineffective in providing such oversight. As a result, many global NGOs have begun to assume the role of monitors and controllers of exploitive MNEs. As Nestlé, Nike, and Shell learned firsthand, these NGOs could exercise their power effectively through their ability to organize protests, boycotts, or political action, targeting the MNE's customers, stock owners, or regulators.

Not surprisingly, exploitive MNEs soon developed adversarial attitudes toward NGOs, and that relationship was reciprocated. Consider the example of the multinational tobacco companies that had been targeting developing country markets for decades as regulatory pressure and consumer education shrank their markets in the West. During the early 1990s, when the former Soviet Union split into several independent countries, the laws previously in place banning tobacco advertising, forbidding smoking in many public places, and requiring health warnings on cigarette packages were no longer binding in the newly created states. According to researchers, "post-transition, the tobacco companies exploited confusion over the legality of this Soviet legislation by advertising heavily to establish their brands."[8] Subsequent surveys indicated that in a part of the world where tobacco was already responsible for twice the number of deaths among men as in the West, there has been a significant increase in youth smoking.

The response from public health researchers and antismoking NGOs was loud and sustained. They lobbied various newly established governments to reestablish antismoking controls and worked actively to publicize the negative implications of MNE activities in the region. The tobacco companies countered by emphasizing the job creation and increased taxes available to local governments from the investments they have made.

The adversarial relationship between the groups continues. In 2011, when British American Tobacco (BAT) threatened to sue the Namibian government over its plan to require warning statements and photos on cigarette packages, NGOs from 50 countries

---

[7]See www.bhopal.com and www.responsiblecare.org.

[8]A. B. Gilmore and M. McKee, "Tobacco and Transition: An Overview of Industry Investment, Impact, and Influence in the Former Soviet Union," *Tobacco Control* 13 (2004), pp. 136–42.

banded together to communicate their support of the government's actions and their willingness to help it defend against what they described as BAT's "bullying."

Overall, the picture of the exploitive MNE is not a pretty one. It is an organization that is willing to collude with political elites, violate environmental norms, ignore the welfare of consumers and employees, and expose emerging market communities to potential harm. Fortunately, it seems to be a species in decline.

The Transactional MNE: Doing Deals, Respecting Laws

Although the examples cited in the previous section indicate that some companies still exhibit at least some elements of the exploitive MNE, there are few companies today that are still driven only by the objective of maximizing profit in the sole service of the shareholder. In the pure form articulated and advocated by economist Milton Friedman, this philosophy opposed corporations making any charitable donations or acting in response to any social issue. Today, most publicly owned corporations demonstrate at least a little charitable generosity and show at least some sensitivity toward their communities. And because of widespread public rejection of extreme profit maximization behavior, the minimum expectation of MNE behavior today tends to be based on what we describe as a "transactional attitude."

The difference between the transactional MNE and the exploitive one is that the former adopts an approach that is both legally compliant and non-oppressive in its emerging market dealings. Yet despite adopting a relationship with its environment that is almost exclusively commercial, the transactional MNE, unlike its exploitive counterpart, does not pursue the bottom line at all costs. Indeed, many companies that once were insensitive to the serious problems that their aggressive or indifferent attitudes created have evolved from their exploitive approach to adopt a more responsible transactional posture.

The transactional MNE's relationship with its emerging market customers avoids the egregious missteps highlighted in the Nestlé experience. This implies having the sensitivity to recognize that products originally developed for consumers with very different needs or markets with very different characteristics should not be promoted where they are socially, culturally, or economically inappropriate. Beyond this understanding, these companies are often willing to make minor product or service adaptations to meet local needs or preferences, but only if such a change is likely to expand market share, increase profits, or meet some other commercial need.

For example, global fast-food giants such as McDonald's and KFC are often willing to make minor changes to their product offering or service approach on a country-by-country basis, but they seldom stray very far from their standard menus. And although they are generally regarded as law-abiding, taxpaying corporate citizens in the countries in which they operate, they have also been accused of cultural insensitivity or worse. Particularly in the area of public health, many government agencies have expressed concern about the increasing health risks for people in developing countries who are being persuaded to change their eating habits from the high-fiber, natural foods of their local diets to the high-fat, refined foods that dominate fast-food menus.

With regard to employee relations, because the transactional MNE respects local labor laws and International Labor Organization (ILO) guidelines, it usually relates to its employees in a much less brutal or oppressive way than the exploitive company. For example, the transactional MNE would not be willing to have its own employees, or those of its subcontractors, work in the sweatshop-like conditions that we described in the previous section. Yet, though they conform to labor laws and workplace regulations, these companies still would be likely to maintain pressure on employees and suppliers to capture the value of the lower-cost labor that attracted their original investment.

In one widely publicized recent example, Apple was forced to move some way along this learning curve in the face of growing reports of harsh working conditions in its suppliers' plants. For many years, Apple had sidestepped pressure from NGOs about labor practices employed in the manufacture of its products, arguing that it was the subcontractors, not Apple, that employed the workers. Finally, in response to pressure, it began publishing audits of factories where its products were sourced in 2007. But in May 2010, press reports that the ninth suicide of the year had occurred at a Foxconn factory in southern China producing Apple products sparked public outrage. In response, Foxconn put up safety nets to prevent suicide jumps from dormitories, improved factory conditions, and raised wages. But a year later, a watchdog group reported that Foxconn was forcing employees to work up to 100 hours a week without proper compensation.

To ensure greater compliance and transparency, Apple subsequently joined the Fair Labor Association (the first high-tech company to do so), and invited that nonprofit group to conduct inspections of its suppliers' factories. In its 2012 annual report on conditions in its suppliers' factories, Apple released the names of 156 companies that supplied it with parts and their compliance with its standards. Following the report and discussions with Apple, Foxconn raised the wages of workers by 25 percent and promised its employees that they would no longer have to work beyond the 49-hour workweek limit set by Chinese law.

In its attitude toward local communities and the broader society, the transactional MNE does not exhibit the same level of indifference and irresponsibility that characterizes the exploitive MNE. One lesson that transactional-oriented MNEs appear to have learned from the experiences of Nestlé in Africa, Union Carbide in Bhopal, and tobacco companies in the former Soviet Union is that it usually makes economic sense to obey both the letter and the spirit of local and international laws and regulations.

Evidence of this shift began appearing in the years following the signing of the North American Free Trade Agreement (NAFTA). Many had predicted that Mexico would become a pollution haven for MNEs with dirty chemical, metals, or paper plants hoping to take advantage of that country's low environmental standards or lax enforcement. Yet more than a decade later, careful research has concluded that "no discernible migration of dirty industry has occurred."[9] The fact that there has been no such large-scale migration to Mexico of companies fleeing tightening U.S. regulations tends to suggest that most MNEs have established a law-abiding, non-exploitive attitude toward emerging markets.

At a minimum, the transactional-oriented MNE takes the equivalent of a Hippocratic oath to communities. (The ancient Greek physician Hippocrates is credited with the

[9]Gustavo Alanis-Ortega, "Is Global Environmental Governance Working?" *The Environmental Forum,* May/June 2006, p. 23.

expression "First, do no harm," which forms part of the oath taken by physicians.) Such an attitude applied to MNEs increases the likelihood that the worst potential corporate abuses will be avoided, but that does not mean that transactional MNEs will be fully trusted or that their actions will not be carefully monitored by regulators or NGOs. And in recent years, it has often been the global NGOs that have taken the more active role in pushing MNEs to take more responsibility for their social, economic, and environmental impact.

Take the case of Nike. Despite the major concessions that the company made to the NGOs' demands in the late 1990s—for example, to increase its working minimum age for footwear manufacture from 14 to 16, and eventually to 18—it was clear that NGOs would remain interested in the company's practices simply because Nike is a highly profitable, highly visible industry leader, dealing with 700 factories that collectively employ over half a million people, mostly in emerging markets. But Nike's relationship with the many NGOs with which it sparred in the mid-1990s has slowly changed. Although some remnants of the activist-driven boycotts and protests remain, the heat has been greatly reduced. As the company moved to comply with more of their demands, the NGOs' role evolved from active adversary to vigilant watchdog.

Although not always enthusiastically embracing each other, this relationship between NGOs and transactional companies is based less on confrontation and accusation and more on monitoring and challenging. And while the NGOs might agree that "doing no harm" is certainly a positive characteristic, they also challenge companies to consider whether that is a sufficient role for the multinational enterprise of the 21st century.

The Responsive MNE: Making a Difference

In the past, a large number—perhaps a majority—of MNEs might have exhibited behavior that was significantly or even predominantly exploitive or transactional, as we have described those behaviors. In recent years, however, management's concept of a sustainable strategy has migrated from a passing acknowledgment of the need to develop a responsible corporate environmental policy to a recognition that companies must articulate a philosophy that reflects their long-term viability as participants in and contributors to the broader social and economic environment. This perspective requires managers to take a broader view of their constituencies and their roles and responsibilities in the societies in which they operate.

A 2006 McKinsey study supports the notion that executives around the world are becoming more aware of their larger responsibilities and increasingly convinced that they have a broader role to play. The McKinsey survey of 4,238 executives from 116 countries found that only 16 percent of respondents saw their responsibility as being to focus on the maximization of shareholder returns, whereas 84 percent expressed the opinion that high returns to shareholders must be balanced with contributions to a broader good.[10]

The responsive MNE, as we have dubbed it, reflects this view and undertakes to be more than just a law-abiding entity: it makes a conscious commitment to be a contributing corporate citizen in all the environments in which it operates. In contrast to its exploitive

---

[10]"McKinsey Global Survey of Business Executives: Business and Society," *McKinsey Quarterly,* January 2006, available at http://www.mckinseyquarterly.com/article_page.aspx?ar=1741&L2=39&L3=29.

and transactional counterparts, the responsive MNC is more sensitive to the different needs of the stakeholders in developing countries and manifests this behavior more proactively in the way in which it deals with its customers, employees, and the community at large.

In his book *The Fortune at the Bottom of the Pyramid,* C. K. Prahalad argues that MNEs have a responsibility to contribute to development in the poorest nations of the world. In his words, "Big corporations should solve big problems." But he also made the case that in doing so, they can avail themselves of a huge opportunity to access a largely untapped market of 4 billion people. By investing in developing markets, creating jobs, generating wealth, and catering to underserved consumers, Prahalad argued that MNEs have an opportunity to bring into the marketplace millions of consumers from the two-thirds of the global population that earns less than $2,000 per year.[11]

Some companies have understood this opportunity for decades, none more so than Hindustan Lever. As Unilever's operating company in India for more than a century, this company has long understood that the key to developing scale and driving growth in that densely populated country is to expand its target market well beyond the middle- and upper-class consumers that are the typical focus of most MNEs in India. For many decades, Hindustan Lever has aimed at expanding its operations to serve the rural poor by adapting the company's products and technologies to their very different needs and economic means. For example, it developed a way to incorporate Unilever's advanced detergent technology into simple, laundry bars, thereby providing superior washing capabilities in the cold-water, hand-washing methods that characterize India's widespread practice of doing laundry in the local stream or village washhouse. The company also adapted to local economic realities and social structures by selling through small rural shops and a network of 50,000 *shakti* women who make a living on sales commissions earned by selling products from their homes in remote villages.

Even in sophisticated product markets such as medical diagnostic equipment, there is the opportunity for MNEs to adopt a more responsive approach that can bring advanced technology to developing countries. For example, GE Healthcare invested $60 million in its Indian R&D center to develop a range of diagnostic products adapted to the simpler needs and more cost-constrained budgets of developing country health care systems. Although the economy model of its computed tomography (CT) scanner sells for about 40 percent less than the price of the advanced models in the United States, the potential for such a product in less developed markets is huge. The company is currently adapting its latest positron emission tomography (PET)—CT scanners that provide improved diagnosis for cancer, heart disease, and brain disorders—and it plans to have a system costing 30 percent to 40 percent less than current models by 2014.

To meet the needs of this large, previously unserved market, GE has gone beyond the adaptation of its current line to create a business it calls its Gold Seal Program. Through this program, the company acquires used x-ray machines and CT scanners, refurbishes them to their original specifications, and then resells them to developing-country markets. Although these may not be the latest models with the most up-to-date technological features, they are in high demand, and GE's initiative has earned it a

[11]C. K. Prahalad, *The Fortune at the Bottom of the Pyramid* (Upper Saddle River, NJ: Wharton School Publishing/Pearson, 2005).

30 percent share of a $1 billion global market for refurbished diagnostic equipment. Better still, the market is growing at 15 percent per year.

But the responsive MNE accepts a role beyond that of a commercial participant in developing countries' economies, no matter how flexible and responsive. These companies also feel the responsibility to be good corporate citizens that have a positive impact on those whose lives they touch. For example, Starbucks has accepted the responsibility to help its farmer suppliers obtain higher prices for their coffee while simultaneously enhancing local environmental and labor practices. In 2004, it collaborated with Conservation International to create its Coffee and Farmer Equity (CAFE) practices, which proposed key points of a new agreement between Starbucks and the farmers. In return for compliance with labor and environmental standards independently set and monitored by Conservation International, farmers who meet CAFE standards would be offered "preferred supplier" status, including long-term contracts and a price premium. In 2011, 86 percent of Starbucks' coffee supply—367 million pounds worth $875 million— came from farms that followed its CAFE guidelines.

Many of the actions of these and other responsive MNEs reflect the aspirational standards of behavior contained in the voluntary Global Compact, signed by more than 8,600 companies from 130 countries in the years since its introduction in 1999 at the World Economic Forum in Davos by Kofi Annan, then Secretary General of the United Nations (U.N.).[12] (See Exhibit 8-1 for a summary of the key principles of the Global Compact.) Although it is a voluntary, self-regulated set of aspirational norms rather than a legislated and enforceable code, the Global Compact seems to represent a way

---

Exhibit 8-1   The Global Compact's ten principles

Human Rights
1. Businesses should support and respect the protection of internationally proclaimed human rights; and
2. make sure that they are not complicit in human rights abuses.

Labour Standards
3. Businesses should uphold the freedom of association and the effective recognition of the right to collective bargaining;
4. the elimination of all forms of forced and compulsory labor;
5. the effective abolition of child labor; and
6. the elimination of discrimination in respect of employment and occupation.

Environment
7. Businesses should support a precautionary approach to environmental challenges;
8. undertake initiatives to promote greater environmental responsibility; and
9. encourage the development and diffusion of environmentally friendly technologies

Anti-Corruption
10. Businesses should work against all forms of corruption, including extortion and bribery.

Source: www.unglobalcompact.org/AboutTheGC/TheTenPrinciples/index.html

---

[12]More recently, the Global Compact has helped establish the Principles for Responsible Management Education (PRME). Its mission is to "inspire and champion responsible management education, research, and thought leadership globally."

forward that can encourage MNEs to embrace a more responsive and constructive role in the developing world.

The Transformative MNE: Leading Broad Change

In recent years, there has been a growing number of examples of private sector organizations not only being sensitive and responsive to the problems and needs of the developing world, but also taking the lead in broad-scale efforts to deal with their root causes. Because of the cost and commitment required to take such action, it is hardly surprising that the boldest and most visible of such initiatives have been those taken by private individuals and/or their foundations. Highly visible current era global philanthropists like Bill Gates and George Soros have created foundations that have committed billions of dollars to attacking some of the biggest problems of health, education, and welfare among the world's neediest populations.

Several large companies have also stepped up to the challenge. Despite the huge commitment required, these pioneering transformative MNEs are leading major initiatives to help deal with problems facing the developing world. Beyond being good corporate citizens, they have concluded that they can and should take a larger role in the less advantaged countries in which they operate by bringing their resources to bear on the massive problems that the populations and governments of these countries face.

Most transformative MNEs evolve to this high level of commitment from the more modest business-linked activities that characterized those companies we described as responsive MNEs. For example, Heineken responded to the AIDS epidemic in Africa in the 1990s when it created a prevention and education program for its 6,000 African employees. In 2001, the company expanded the program to offer free antiretroviral drugs to all infected employees, later extending the benefit to cover all of their family members. In subsequent years, Heineken continued expanding its clinics which by 2007 provided care to 30,000 HIV-positive patients. The subsequent formation of the Heineken Africa Foundation allow it to extend its programs to a variety of prevention, treatment, and research programs in eight sub-Saharan African countries.

Another company whose recent commitments have vaulted it into the transformational MNC category is Unilever. Its Sustainable Living Plan provides a commitment that by the year 2020, the company will improve the health and well-being of 1 billion people worldwide, will cut the environmental impact of its products by 50 percent, and will source 100 percent of its agricultural products from sustainable producers. The bold plan is broken into more than 60 social, economic, and environmental targets, each of which is monitored and reported on annually. Early progress has been impressive. In 2011, the first year of reporting, a sampling of reports on the 60 metrics showed that the company had reached 100 million people with its hand washing and oral care programs and 35 million with the safe drinking water project; it had increased its percentage of sustainably sourced raw materials from 14 percent to 24 percent; and it had engaged with 500,000 small farmers and 75,000 small-scale distributors worldwide to bring them into the program. Paul Polman, Unilever's CEO, explained that he simply believed that this is the way responsible companies should act: "I'm not interested whether the plan brings competitive advantage ... It's the only way to do business in the long term."

Because they often deal with long-term problems or challenge deeply embedded practices, such transformational programs can be difficult to implement, particularly when social and economic environments are governed by very different cultural norms and legal frameworks. As a result, it often requires a long process of learning, adaptation, and above all, commitment to achieving results. One of the most sustained examples of transformational change has been Merck's commitment to eradicate river blindness, a disease that exists almost entirely in the developing world. When the pharmaceutical giant developed a drug to prevent river blindness in 1987, it recognized that few of the more than 18 million sufferers of this debilitating disease or the 100 million who were at risk could afford the treatment. So the company decided to make the drug freely available for as long as it was needed to anyone suffering from or at risk of becoming exposed. Over the past 25 years, in partnership with numerous U.N. and governmental agencies, NGOs, and local communities, the program has delivered Mectizan tablets without charge to treat more than 700 million patients in Africa and South America. It currently reaches 100 million people annually and prevents an estimated 40,000 cases of blindness each year.

As the preceding examples have shown, in implementing these activities, MNEs often find themselves working in partnership with NGOs or supragovernment agencies that can provide expertise in social program delivery that the companies typically lack. In doing so, they develop very different relationships with these groups than the adversarial or defensive exchanges that characterize exploitive or transactional MNEs' experiences with such organizations. It is a partnership leverages the resources and capabilities of both groups and may well prove to be the engine that can drive the changes that have been so elusive in attempts to accelerate economic and social development in the world's poorest nations. If so, it will create a future role for the MNE that will make it an even more important and respected player on the world stage.

Concluding Comments

Over time, there has been an evolution in the roles, responsibilities, and expectations of MNEs operating in host countries around the world. In his seminal books *Sovereignty at Bay* and *Storm over the Multinationals,* both published in the 1970s, Harvard Professor Ray Vernon expressed concerns about the "economic hegemony and economic dependence" that often characterized the relationship between MNEs and host-country governments in the developing world in that era.[13] And various corrupt or exploitive acts by those companies during this time period created what Vernon described as a sense of "tension and anxiety on the part of many nation-states."

As the anecdotes that open this chapter illustrate, MNEs are still susceptible to charges of insensitivity and irresponsibility. But in the three decades since Vernon's research was published, the concern that MNEs were holding "sovereignty at bay" has gradually subsided. And although there has been little success in creating the effective supranational agencies that once were thought vital to reining in the unfettered power of the MNE, the rise of numerous, highly effective global NGOs has filled the role of

---

[13]Raymond Vernon, *Sovereignty at Bay* (New York: Basic Books, 1971); Raymond Vernon, *Storm Over the Multinationals: The Real Issues* (Cambridge, MA: Harvard University Press, 1977).

the active "watchdog." As the several examples cited in this chapter show, NGOs have become very effective at using their clout with consumers, shareholders, and other company stakeholders as a way to bring about change.

But the biggest change has occurred in the evolving attitudes of companies toward their sense of corporate social responsibility and their commitment to a strategy of sustainability. Although a few firms have remained stuck in an exploitive mode, most have adopted, at a minimum, a transactional approach. And with the growing influence of public, government, and NGO demands, and increasingly rising shareholder expectations, the trend is clearly moving toward responsive and even transformative models.

The social needs in emerging markets are great, and MNEs and their managers are feeling both pressure and encouragement to respond. In addition to transforming the lives of those at the "bottom of the pyramid," their commitment of resources to such activities may very well represent one of the most important investments that the MNE will ever make.

Chapter 8 Readings

- In Reading 8-1, "A Global Leader's Guide to Managing Business Conduct," Paine, Deshpandé, and Margolis use the results of a large-scale survey to challenge multinational corporations to reconsider their current internal standards of business behavior. Their findings suggest that there is surprising agreement on what those standards should be, as well as a consensus that companies are falling short of their basic responsibilities in the international environment. They provide guidance on the development and monitoring of an appropriate set of standards.

- In Reading 8-2, "Serving the World's Poor, Profitably," Prahalad and Hammond detail how multinationals can build businesses aimed at the bottom of the economic pyramid in order to build competitive advantage. They argue that such investments in the world's poorest markets can result in both tangible business benefits and major contributions to poverty reduction.

The roles and responsibilities of the MNE continue to evolve, as these readings suggest. MNEs have much to contribute.

MNE/Stakeholder Relationships in Emerging Markets: A Typology

	Stakeholders					
	Economic			Societal	Political/Regulatory	
MNE Responses and Attitudes	Shareholders	Customers	Employees/Suppliers	Local Communities	Government and Supranational Agencies/Regulators (e.g., U.N. Agencies)	NGOs
Exploitive *Views differences in wages, working conditions and living standards as exploitable opportunities.*	Adopts classic Milton Friedman view: Its only legitimate role is to maximize returns to shareholders.	Sells existing products and services, even if they have negative social or economic impact.	Exploits existing local wages, working conditions, and suppliers, driving them lower if possible.	Accepts no community responsibility for its social or environmental impact.	Seeks concessions and subsidies, using bargaining power to play national investment boards against each other. If bribery and corruption exist, engages in local practices to win benefits.	An adversary: NGOs actively work to force the MNE to change its behavior through protests, boycotts, political activism, etc.
Transactional *Engages in law-abiding, nonexploitive, commercial interactions.*	Focus on shareholder returns, but believes a pure Friedman approach is inconsistent with the long-term interests of its shareholders.	Treats it as any another market. Makes product adaptations if they are economically viable and can increase market share.	Complies with local labor laws and workplace regulations. Uses cost-efficient local sources, pressuring them on price.	Adopts a Hippocratic Oath approach toward communities: (i.e., "First, do no harm").	Obeys local laws and regulations but uses country differences to gain competitive advantage.	A watchdog: NGO monitors the MNE's actions, urging or pushing it to do more.

Stakeholders

	Economic		Societal		Political/Regulatory	
	Shareholders	**Customers**	**Employees/ Suppliers**	**Local Communities**	**Government and Supranational Agencies/ Regulators (e.g., U.N. Agencies)**	**NGOs**
Responsive *Acts in a way that is sensitive and responsive to the needs of all its immediate stakeholders.*	Feels a responsibility to be a "good corporate citizen" in the environments in which it operates.	Invests in potentially significant product or service developments and/or adaptations to meet local needs.	Committed to caring for its employees and developing their skills. Actively engages local sources, using its buyer power to improve working conditions for employees.	Aims to affect positively those whose lives it touches in communities in which it operates.	Sets its standard of behavior above minimum local legal requirements. Conforms to higher international standards (e.g., set by ILO or UNESCO).	An observer: NGO may be neutral or partially engaged with MNE. Limited mutual trust.
Transformative *Commits to leading initiatives to bring life-enhancing changes to the broader society.*	Persuades investors of the need for companies to be part of the solution by bringing their resources to bear on the root causes of problems.	Believes that by helping move people out of poverty, it will create stability and goodwill and help grow the world's customer base. Develops products or services specifically to meet local needs.	Committed to upgrading the lives of its employees, inside and outside the workplace. Brings work standard–compliant local suppliers into global supply chain networks.	Leads in developing the quality of life in the broad community (e.g., upgrading health, education).	Actively raises local standards (e.g., transferring developed world workplace health and safety standards.) Supports change agenda of international agencies (e.g., WHO, UNESCO).	A partner: NGO works with and supports the MNE working toward the same objectives.

641

Case 8-1   Barrick Gold Corporation—Tanzania[1]

Aloysius Newenham-Kahindi and Paul W. Beamish

By March 2009, Canadian mining company Barrick Gold Corporation (Barrick) had only been operating in the Lake Victoria Zone in Tanzania for a decade. In the same year, Barrick had adopted a new name for its business in Tanzania, African Barrick Gold plc (ABG), which was also listed on the London Stock Exchange. The company was widely considered to be one of the more "responsive" global corporations in the mining industry.[2] Its extensive mining activities in the region employed thousands of local people, and Barrick was engaged in social development projects in various Tanzanian communities.[3] By October 2010, the company operated four main gold mining sites in the country.[4]

Despite Barrick's efforts to support social development initiatives in the Lake Victoria Zone over the past decade, discontent and resistance at one of its mining sites in North Mara still remained. This

IVEY

Richard Ivey School of Business
The University of Western Ontario

▌ [1]This case has been written on the basis of published sources only. Consequently, the interpretation and perspectives presented in this case are not necessarily those of Barrick Gold Corporation or any of its employees.
▌ [2]www.barrick.com/CorporateResponsibility/BeyondBorders/default.aspx, accessed March 24, 2009.
▌ [3]www.barrick.com/News/PressReleases/PressReleaseDetails/2010/Barrick-Named-to-Dow-Jones-Sustainability-World-Index-for-Third-Consecutive-Year/default.aspx, accessed September 27, 2010.
▌ [4]www.tanzaniagold.com/barrick.html, accessed October 1, 2010.

area posed challenges. A key question was why the tension and violence had not stopped in certain mining sites in the North Mara mining area, and whether there was much more Barrick could reasonably be expected to do to resolve the problem.

Background on Tanzania

Tanzania was a developing country located in East Africa, with a total land size of 945,087 square kilometres. It had one of the highest levels of unemployment and poverty in Sub-Saharan Africa. Its economy was heavily dependent on agriculture, which accounted for half of the gross domestic product (GDP), provided 85 per cent of the country's exports and employed 90 per cent of the work force. Topography and climatic conditions, however, limited cultivated crops to only four per cent of the land area. Industry was mainly limited to processing agricultural products and light consumer goods.

Like most developing nations, Tanzania had a very weak national institutional and legal system. It also had a very high rate of corruption.[5] The country needed support from foreign direct investment (FDI) and transnational corporations (TNCs) in order to promote businesses, employment, and other opportunities for its citizens. Tanzania wanted its institutions to be more transparent and accountable, and to regulate the activities of FDI and TNCs in addressing the country's social and ecological issues. Both local and international not-for-profit organizations (NFOs), however, had continued to create a significant impact with respect to promoting responsive behaviour in corporate governance practices, positively influencing all involved stakeholders and other social actors to address social issues.

Following independence in 1961, Tanzania opted for a socialist command economic and institutional system, with socialist policies ("*Ujamaa*" in Swahili) being implemented in 1967. The emphasis of these

▌ [5]*See data on Tanzania at* www.transparency.org.

policies was to promote co-operative institutions and collective villages with the aim of building an egalitarian society, eliminating ethnic and gender barriers, and creating a common language of Swahili for all. Within the practice of Ujamaa, the country had managed to unite its ethnic groups under a common language, with the result that the central government had created strong post-colonial nationalistic ideologies, unity, ethnic harmony and peace among its people. Compared to many post-colonial Sub-Saharan African countries that went through civil and ethnic strife and conflicts after independence in the 1960s and 1970s, Tanzania under Ujamaa appeared to be a successful model.

Towards the end of the 1980s, however, Tanzania began to experience significant economic stagnation and social problems. To combat these issues, in the early 1990s the government sought to privatize its economy and reform its institutions in order to attract foreign investment. The introduction of the famous post-Ujamaa Investment Act of 1997 was intended to encourage free market and trade liberalization in the country. Investment in various private sectors such as mining, tourism, fishing, banking and agriculture under foreign-owned TNCs served to bolster the country's reforms by creating employment opportunities for the local economy.

As the country continued to privatize and reform its national institutional and legal systems, many foreign companies sought to invest in its economy. The Tanzania Investment Centre (TIC) was created in the early 2000s as a tool for identifying possible investment opportunities and aiding potential investors in navigating any procedural barriers that might exist during the process of investment in the country.[6] The liberalization of the banking industry in 2002, for example, saw the former Ujamaa Cooperative and Rural Development Bank replaced by the Commercial Rural Development Bank (CRDB) and the National Microfinance Bank (NMB), which promoted community investments across the country. In February 2009, the Tanzania Private Sector Foundation (TPSF) was created with the aim of strengthening the entrepreneurial culture among its

citizens by providing communities and individuals across the country with entrepreneurial business ideas and grants. In June 2009, the government started an ambitious national resolution under the so-called "Kilimo Kwanza" policies (meaning "Agriculture First" in Swahili) to boost the standard of living among the *eighty per cent* of citizens who relied on agriculture for their livelihood.[7] It was based on Green Revolution principles aimed at boosting Tanzania's agriculture into the modern and commercial sector, and mobilizing for-profit organizations (FPOs) such as local private businesses and foreign-owned TNCs in the country to increase their investment engagement with the agriculture sector, both at the macro and micro levels (i.e. along with local communities).

In order to ensure that there was sufficient security and peace for private and foreign-owned investors (i.e. TNCs), in 2005 the government introduced a new entity called "Tanzania Security Industry Association." The association was based on local, professional private security firms and groups whose main tasks were to safeguard business firms' activities rather than letting the firms rely on local police forces. The largest and best-known local security firm was "Moku Security Services Limited," based in Dar Es Salaam, which had over 13,000 employees across the country. Other security groups with over 400 employees were "Ultimate Security Company," "Dragon Security," "Tele-security Company Limited," and "Group Four Security Company." Private security employees were mainly retired army and police officers; young people who had lost their previous jobs following the collapse of the Ujamaa policies that provided "jobs for everyone and for life"; and individuals who sought better remuneration in the security sector than in the government public sector. However, due to increased demand for better security across businesses, many foreign-owned TNCs sought the services of security firms from abroad, mainly from South Africa's professional security firms such as the South African Intruder Detection

[6]www.tic.co.tz, accessed April 1, 2009.

[7]www.actanzania.org/index.php?option=com_content&task=view&id=121&Itemid=39, accessed February 12, 2010.

Service Association (SAIDS). Some security personnel had combat experience, which helped them handle sophisticated forms of crime and intrusion.

The Tanzanian economy continued to grow and create job opportunities, training and innovative development prospects for its people. Earlier, the country had introduced new mining legislation such as the Mining Act of 1998 and the Mining Regulation Act of 1999 in order to harmonize investment relations between FDI and local interests. However, in April 2010 the government passed another new mining Act, following consultations with civil society groups such as the Foundation for Civil Society Tanzania (FCST), companies and other stakeholders. The legislation of a new mining Act imposed a new form of royalties that required all TNCs and local companies to be listed in the country and gave the state a stake in future projects.[8]

The country possessed vast amounts of natural resources like gold, diamond, copper, platinum, natural gas, and zinc deposits that remained underdeveloped. It was one of the more peaceful countries in Sub-Saharan Africa. In order to attract and protect the interests of FDI and TNCs and, of course, its own people, Tanzania had attempted to harmonize its investment practices and labour legislation. In order to create responsible institutional policies, in February 2010 the National Assembly of Tanzania enlisted a group of local environmental and toxicity experts to investigate environmental and toxic effects on the people and livestock in the North Mara gold mine in Tarime District, Mara Region, by the Tigithe River.[9]

For a number of reasons, Tanzania was a willing host nation for FDI. The country needed the input of TNCs in order to create employment and prosperity. In return, Tanzania could provide TNCs with low-cost labour and a readily available labour force. Low labour costs were an opportunity to support a host nation's development policy in attracting FDI and ultimately in creating a knowledge-based society in the midst of the globalization challenges that were faced by so many developing countries.

Furthermore, Tanzania continued to create a local business environment in conjunction with various TNCs' global business interests in order to generate sustainable development policies and practices. It also engaged in market development initiatives that represented innovative learning opportunities and entrepreneurship ventures for its citizens.

Lake Victoria Background

Tanzania's Lake Victoria was surrounded by the three East African countries of Kenya, Tanzania and Uganda. The lake itself was named after the former Queen of England, Queen Victoria, and stood as the world's largest tropical lake and the second-largest freshwater lake after Lake Superior in North America. Covering a total of 69,000 square kilometres, the lake was as large as the Republic of Ireland and lay in the Rift Valley of East Africa, a 3,500-mile system of deep cracks in the earth's crust, running from the Red Sea south to Mozambique. Lake Victoria was the source of the Nile River, which passed through the Sudan and Egypt and finally reached the Mediterranean Sea.

Lake Victoria Zone in Tanzania   The Lake Victoria Zone consisted of the three regions of Mwanza, Mara (formerly called Musoma) and Kagera (formerly called Bukoba), and was one of the most densely populated regions in Africa. Population growth around Lake Victoria was significantly higher than in the rest of Sub-Saharan Africa. During the last five decades, population growth within a 100-kilometre buffer zone around the lake had outpaced the continental average, which had led to growing dependency and pressure on the lake's resources.

Prior to the mining extraction boom in the early 1990s and following the collapse of Ujamaa, most people living in this region were mainly engaged in rudimentary forms of fishing, agricultural farming and keeping cattle, as well as other forms of co-operative activities that had been engineered by the country's former Ujamaa policies. Irrigation was limited to a small scale and often used rudimentary technologies to support both individual

[8]www.mining-journal.com/finance/new-tanzanian-mining-act, accessed September 27, 2010.
[9]www.dailynews.co.tz, accessed February 10, 2010.

and co-operative farming activities. Noted for its temperate climate, the area had a mean temperature of between 26 and 30 degrees Celsius in the hot season and 15 and 18 degrees Celsius in the cooler months. The area was rich with tropical vegetation and fruits such as bananas, mangoes, corn, pineapple and many others. The lake was essential to more than 15 million people, providing potable water, hydroelectric power, and inland water transport, as well as support for tourism and wildlife.

The area remained one of the most fertile for farming activities and continued to attract immigrants from other regions of the country, as well as from Tanzania's neighbors in the war-torn populations of Burundi, Rwanda and the Democratic Republic of Congo. The presence of hundreds of TNCs engaged in various activities in the area was the main "draw" for these immigrants, who came seeking employment and new sources of livelihood.

The resulting population increase in the Lake Victoria Zone created several problems with respect to the lake and the environment. According to a report by World Watch Institute in Washington, D.C., the once clear, life-abounding lake had become murky, smelly and choked with algae. It had been reported that:

> The ecological health of Lake Victoria has been affected profoundly as a result of a rapidly growing population, clearance of natural vegetation along the shores, a booming fish-export industry, the disappearance of several fish species native to the lake, prolific growth of algae, and dumping of untreated effluent by several industries. Much of the damage is vast and irreversible. Traditional lifestyles of lakeshore communities have been disrupted and are crumbling.[10]

As a result of the overuse of natural resources in the area, the traditional lifestyles of the lakeshore communities were significantly disrupted, a situation that prompted both social and ecological concerns for the area and its residents.

The fishing industry was badly affected in the region following the introduction of Nile perch (Lates Niloticus) and Nile tilapia (Oreochromis Niloticus)

into the lake. For example, in the 1980s a survey of the lake revealed an abrupt and unexpected increase in numbers among the Nile perch, constituting 80 per cent of all fish in the lake. In spite of working harder, local fishermen caught fewer fish since the populations of smaller fish, which traditionally had been the fishermen's primary source of livelihood, became decimated. In addition, the big oily Nile perch, generally referred to as "Mbuta," swam too far out in the open waters for the little local fishing boats and was too big to be caught in the locals' unsophisticated nets.

In response to an increased international demand for the Nile perch, commercial fishing fleets owned by foreign firms displaced local fishermen and many women in lakeside communities who worked as fish processors. The processing of fish, traditionally performed by women, was gradually taken over by large filleting plants. The women resorted to processing fish waste, commonly referred to as *mgongo-wazi,* or "bare-back" in Swahili. The waste, comprised of fish heads, backbones and tails, was sun-dried and then deep-fried and sold to local people who were drawn to its low price and nutritional value. Many fishermen were forced to look for alternative sources of livelihood, mainly seeking employment in extractive mining corporations and other industries as manual labourers.

The water hyacinth posed another threat to the health of Lake Victoria. With the deceptive appearance of a lush, green carpet, the hyacinth was in fact a merciless, free-floating weed, reproducing rapidly and covering any uncovered territory. First noticed in 1989, the weed spread rapidly and covered areas in all three surrounding countries. It formed a dense mat, blocking the sunlight from reaching the organisms below, depleting the already-low concentrations of oxygen and trapping fishing boats and nets of all sizes. The hyacinth was also an ideal habitat for poisonous snakes and disease-carrying snails that caused bilharzias. The government, in partnership with other international agencies, had tried desperately to control the weed. Its most promising approach involved harvesting the hyacinth and using it either for compost or for biogas production.

The health implications associated with the declining state of the lake were extensive. Dumping

[10]www.cichlid-forum.com/articles/lake_victoria_sick.php, accessed April 1, 2009.

untreated sewage in the lake and nearby rivers exposed people to waterborne diseases, such as typhoid, cholera and diarrhea, and chronic forms of malaria. The Lake Victoria Zone was known to have the most dangerous types of malaria in the world. As fish prices soared, protein malnutrition became a significant threat for communities living in the zone. Lack of regular income also meant that many people in the area could not afford to be treated for waterborne typhoid, yellow fever, and various forms of tropical worms such as tapeworms and hookworms.

Mining in Tanzania   Gold mining activities around the Lake Victoria Zone in Tanzania started during the German colonial period in 1894, when Tanzania was called Tanganyika. The First and Second World Wars accelerated the demand for gold production in the region and, following the introduction of Ujamaa in 1967, mining became a state-directed activity. By nationalizing the industry, the government hoped to capture more benefits from mining through the creation of local employment, direct spending on social services for mining communities, and higher budget revenues from having a direct stake in the business. However, despite these high hopes, the mining sector failed to stimulate the industrialization of the country's economy. During Ujamaa, the production of gold declined significantly due to limited government funding and limited technological know-how within the industry. Mining activities that were performed illegally by small-scale operators contributed to several environmental and social problems.[11]

The collapse of Ujamaa in 1990s, however, resulted in new opportunities for the country to attract mining companies from Canada, the United Kingdom, Australia and South Africa, all of whom were interested in gold exploration and development activities. Following successful exploration mining activities that began in 1995, Barrick invested in Tanzania in 1999 at the Lake Victoria Zone. It acquired gold reserves in the Bulyanhulu mine, located in northwest Tanzania, East Africa, approximately 55 kilometres south of Lake Victoria and approximately 150 kilometres from the city of Mwanza; Buzwagi near Kahama District; Tulawaka in Biharamulo, Kagera Region; and later at the North Mara gold mine in the northwestern part of Tanzania in Tarime District of Mara Region, approximately 100 kilometres east of Lake Victoria and 20 kilometres south of the Kenyan border.

According to the Tanzanian Mineral Authority and Tanzania Chamber of Minerals and Energy (TCME), since 2000 production of gold had been growing, making the Lake Victoria Zone one of the most attractive areas for employment opportunities as well as for business opportunities in other industries. Tanzania was Africa's third-largest producer of gold, after Ghana and South Africa.[12] Tanzania was also richly endowed with other minerals, including cobalt, copper, nickel, platinum group metals, and silver, as well as diamonds and a variety of gemstones. The energy sector was dominated by natural gas. Commercial quantities of oil had yet to be discovered. In 2008, TCME reported that a total of US$2 billion in the past decade had been injected into the Tanzanian economy by mining TNCs, and in total mining TNCs had paid the government over US$255 million in taxes within the same period.[13]

In 2002, Tanzania joined the African Union's development blueprint, an endeavour that was governed by the New Economic Partnership for African Development (NEPAD), to oversee an African Mining Partnership (AMP) with global mining corporations. The goal of this partnership was to promote sustainable development and best-practice guidelines for African governments as a way to ensure that their mining laws protected ecological and community welfare while maximizing remittances from the mining TNCs to the government budgets in a transparent and accountable way.

The country did, however, develop competitive tax packages and incentives to attract TNCs to

[11]www.douglaslakeminerals.com/mining.html, accessed February 26, 2009.

[12]www.mineweb.co.za/mineweb/view/mineweb/en/page67?oid=39782&sn=Detail, accessed May 1, 2009.

[13]Ibid.

Exhibit 1   Three Types of Engagement Behaviors

Dimension	Transactional	Transitional	Transformational
Corporate Stance	"Giving Back" Community Investment	"Building Bridges" Community Involvement	"Changing Society" Community Integration
Communication	One-Way	Two-Way	Two-Way
# of Community Partners	Many	Many	Few
Nature of Trust	Limited	Evolutionary	Relational
Frequency of Interaction	Occasional	Repeated	Frequent
Learning	Transferred from Firm	Transferred to Firm	Jointly Generated
Control over Process	Firm	Firm	Shared
Benefit & Outcomes	Distinct	Distinct	Joint

Source: F. Bowen, A. Newenham-Kahindi and H. Irene, "Engaging the Community: A Synthesis of Academic and Practitioner Knowledge on Best Practices in Community Engagement," *Canadian Research Network for Business Sustainability, Knowledge Project Series, Ivey School of Business,* 1:1, 2008, pp. 1–34.

invest in high-risk and complex exploration areas such as the Lake Victoria Zone. The government did not devise a practical and engaging strategy to utilize mining resources and revenues paid by TNCs to support the local communities that were situated around mining sites and who had lost their livelihood, homes, health, natural resources and recreation with little or no compensation.[14] Also, the government did not come up with a concrete strategy to deal with the chronic sewage and environmental issues in the area.

Like any TNC engaged in extractive mining activities in a developing country such as Tanzania with so many social problems and legal and institutional weaknesses, Barrick had faced conflicting pressures with regard to the way it engaged in locally based community social partnership (see **Exhibit 1**). Such partnerships were meant to address the social problems of unemployment, poverty, diseases and environmental concerns in a sustainable way. Barrick strictly followed Western legal and property approvals to legitimize its mining activities in the country. It also continued to face challenges with respect to its efforts to strike

a balance between its global strategies and those of the local subsidiary operations in Tanzania. Mineral wealth continued to fuel and prolong violent behaviour by local communities mainly in North Mara, thus failing to diversify economic growth and contribute to the development of communities in the Lake Victoria Zone. Corruption and weak institutional capabilities to enact or enforce the democratic, transparent and agreed-upon rules and laws that governed the operation and taxation of mining activities were a source of ongoing problems.[15] Also, some local communities did not see the potential benefits of large corporations in their communities.

Barrick Gold Corp in Tanzania

As a gold producer on the world stage, Barrick used advanced exploration technological systems for its mining development projects.[16] The company owned one of the world's largest gold mineral reserves and a large land position across its subsidiary mining extraction activities. These were located across the five continents of North America, South America, Africa, Australia and Asia. As one of the largest Canadian mining companies, Barrick shares were traded on the Toronto and New York

[14]"The Challenge of Mineral Wealth in Tanzania: using resource endowments to foster sustainable development," International Council on Mining & Metals, 2006.
[15]www.revenuewatch.org/our-work/countries/tanzania.php, accessed May 1, 2009.

[16]www.tanzaniagold.com/barrick.html, accessed, May 1, 2009.

stock exchanges and on other major global stock index centres in London, as well as on the Swiss Stock Exchanges and the Euronext-Paris. It was a shareholder-driven firm. Barrick invested in Tanzania in 1999, following the completion of exploration activities that had started in 1995. The company's initial mining activities were limited to Bulyanhulu in Kahama Dictrict until 2004, when it expanded to other areas surrounding the Lake Victoria Zone.

Socialization was part of the corporate culture used to manage human resources (HRM)[17] in Tanzania. Each mining site had a training department. Barrick recruited university graduates who worked on administrative activities in corporate offices, and assigned manual labourers to mining sites to work along with expatriates and locals who had experience in mining activities. Also, the company was involved in developing the so-called Integrated Mining Technical Training (IMTT) program, a joint project with the Tanzania Chamber of Minerals and Energy and the Tanzanian government. The goal was to offer locals the skills they needed to participate in the country's burgeoning mining sector and to reduce the industry's reliance on foreign-trained expatriates.[18] Barrick used its Global Succession Planning Program (GSPP) that provided expatriates with a chance to increase their knowledge and expertise by transferring them into assignments at other Barrick sites in Tanzania, and sites in other countries where the company operated.[19] The major role of GSPP was to instill the corporate culture through the training of employees regarding various mining technology skills, and to run the company's daily practices in accordance with the corporate business interests of the company.

Mission, Vision and Values   Given the questionable reputation of some global mining corporations with respect to sustainable development projects in developing societies, Barrick's core vision and values were to continue finding, acquiring, developing and producing quality reserves in a safe, profitable and socially responsible manner. Barrick claimed to promote long-term benefits to the communities in which it operated and to foster a culture of excellence and collaboration with its employees, governments and local stakeholders.

The company followed global corporate social responsibility standards as part of its larger global business strategies, using the vocabularies of business ethics, human rights and development. Among these strategies, the company placed significant emphasis on its social relationships with local communities and the right to operate in their land.[20]

Building Social Development Initiatives   Barrick was committed to making a positive difference in the communities where it operated. The company focused on responsible behaviour as its duty, as well as creating opportunities to generate greater value for its shareholders, while at the same time fostering sustainable development in the communities and countries where it operated. As a global TNC, Barrick strove to earn the trust of its employees, of the communities where its subsidiary operations were based, of the host nations' governments, and of any other persons or parties with whom the company was engaged in the sustainable development of mineral resources.[21]

In 2008, the corporation established a locally based mining institution in Moshi, Kilimanjaro Region. The aim of the institute was to provide training skills and opportunities for Barrick's mining sites and other mining TNCs in the country.[22] Local individuals involved in the training program included fresh university graduates in engineering and geology, and dedicated individuals from local communities where Barrick operated. Such an initiative supported Barrick's sense of corporate responsibility towards these two groups of people

[17]www.barrick.com/CorporateResponsibility/Employees/Attracting Retaining/default.aspx, accessed April 24, 2009.

[18]www.barrick.com/Theme/Barrick/files/docs_csr/BeyondBorder 2008July.pdf#page=4, accessed September 27, 2010.

[19]www.barrick.com/CorporateResponsibility/Employees/Attracting Retaining/default.aspx, accessed September 27, 2010.

[20]www.barrick.com/CorporateResponsibility/OurCommitment/default .aspx, accessed September 27, 2010.

[21]www.barrick.com/CorporateResponsibility/default.aspx, accessed March 25, 2009.

[22]www.ippmedia.com/ipp/guardian/2008/04/11/112164.html, accessed February 13, 2009.

by providing tangible benefits to their communities in the form of employment opportunities and co-operative relationships.

Yet among community leaders and NFOs, there was clear discontent regarding the various foreign companies:

> "The government has not addressed the role of foreign companies in our communities. Some communities have been compensated by the government to clear land for the mining company, but some did not receive any money. Most communities would tell you what was given to them by the government, which is very little. They cannot build a house and send children to school and so on. They feel their livelihood is gone forever."

> "The mining corporation does not compensate people nor does it explain why it is operating in our communities. Of course, these companies have official binding contracts and the right to operate in our communities from the government. Local communities are in despair . . . the government is nowhere to be seen! The people are angry with the government and the mining company."

> "People are not happy with the government. They are aware of the extent of corruption among the government officials in the region and districts, but they cannot confront the government the way they are now confronting the mining company. They think that the company might be more sympathetic to them than the government would be with respect to offering them jobs and other opportunities."

> "The company has initiated several development projects in our communities [North Mara] in education, health and infrastructure. But we do not have jobs to access these better equipped services (education and health) nor essential means to support us to build community enterprises where we could apply our local skills in many activities. Though the company is doing very good projects here, we are still unhappy with the company. Our problems are long-term; they need serious engagement with us."

> "The company discharges water to the land, which is causing lots of environmental problems on our farms such as land erosion and polluting of the rivers. We have more mosquitoes, snakes and snails at the moment than any time in our lives because of stagnant water caused by the company's water discharge. The exploration and explosive activities conducted at

night on mining sites have caused shockwaves, panic and sleepless nights among neighborhood villages, making big cracks on community farms and land."

Two community leaders (representing local stakeholders' interests) commented:

> "The other night we were all suddenly shaken by the mining blast tremor. Initially, we thought it was the so-called earthquake ("Tetemeko la Ardhi" in Swahili). What is on all the people's minds here in Bulyanhulu is, 'When will all this end?'"

> "We need a mutual partnership with foreign companies investing in our communities. There are so many potential benefits we can get from the company with respect to jobs and skill development; also, the company can learn a lot from us when it comes to negotiation strategies with our communities. If the company responds positively to our concerns, we will strive to protect its business interests here and it will operate in harmony in our communities. But the government needs to sit with local communities and tell them why the government has allowed the company to come to practice mining in their land and tell us what potential benefit it will bring in our communities. For the time being, the company is left to itself to address these issues with the local communities."

Amid this climate of discontent among the native Tanzanians, Barrick's mining operations were subject to some hostilities from local stakeholders. In response, the company put into place several CSR initiatives that were aimed at developing sustainable benefits within the communities and around its business operations in the core mining sites of Tulawaka, Bulyanhulu and Buzigwa. Two NFO officials in Mwanza cut to the nature of the problem:

> "The company initially attempted to collaborate with local communities and the local government to address the social and ecological issues during its initial stage of entry into the country. But it was not easy to find serious stakeholders right away. Because of the nature of the local institutions, it was also not easy to have things done quickly due to the degree of bureaucracy and the culture of corruption."

> "The recent protests in North Mara from local communities can be resolved only if the government, company and other social awareness groups sit together to address this situation. Shooting protestors, closing the mining site

and sending employees home without pay won't solve the problem in the long run. And the company's legal insistence of its right to operate in the communities isn't enough to convince these angry communities."

"The company is not wrong at all . . . it has followed all legal procedures and has the right to be here [in the Lake Victoria Zone], but for local communities, legal papers are NOTHING. The company finds people very unpredictable. The answer is so simple: it is all about deep understanding, integration, and building a trusting relationship."

"Mining companies are granted too many tax contracts and subsidies in order to create jobs. During this process, it is very possible for companies to avoid paying taxes that would actually benefit poor countries. There are often 'secret contracts' with corrupt government officials. The lack of institutional capacity is also a major problem; the people have not been made to see how these companies can benefit our poor societies. That's why there is still so much poverty, and that's why communities around the mining sites are angry and desperate."

Several local communities felt they were isolated when it came to the social issues that concerned them, e.g., land issues, compensation, employment, and how the presence of the company in their communities would benefit them generally. According to community leaders, few projects were initiated by the company within the various neighbourhood communities, and the ones that were enacted showed a lack of any significant sense of local ownership and influence; they did not possess the diverse forms of institutional infrastructure that fostered accountability values in communities and in the management of the company itself. As a consequence, local communities lost interest in pursuing most of the developmental projects that Barrick had initiated.

Following community tensions with Barrick between 2007 and 2009, a different strategy was developed. Implementing a locally based interaction model that promoted mutual partnership with communities seemed like the best strategic legitimacy approach. In early 2009, Barrick encountered discontent from the local communities, as well as from the local media, activists groups and lobby groups, who felt that the company had not done enough to promote sustainable and inclusive development in the communities where it operated. Barrick's new mining site at North Mara was featured several times in the media.[23] Two local NFOs commented on the dispute:

> "The government needs to educate its people as to what benefits TNCs would bring to its citizens; the mining company is extracting our natural resources, causing environmental degradation and pollution, and displacing people, all with a lack of accountability, and is not doing enough for the host communities to create prosperity, jobs, local innovation and entrepreneurship initiatives."

> "The source of discontent is from local communities and small-scale miners who feel neglected by the government. We strongly feel that their livelihoods have been destroyed with little or no compensation. They also feel that the government and local authorities have been giving foreign investors much attention at the expense of local people. Corruption and lack of accountability on the government side is the source of all these problems. The company is caught in the middle!"

Creating a Corporate Responsive Agenda
Barrick developed a responsive initiative to deal with the company's challenges in its international business activities abroad, including Tanzania. It established a community department in all four mining areas to oversee development initiatives. It also adopted standardized global CSR strategies as part of its larger international and localization business strategies, stating that "as a global corporation, we endorse the definition of Corporate Social Responsibility as proposed by the World Bank—Corporate Social Responsibility is the commitment of business to contribute to sustainable economic development—working with employees, their families, the local community and society at large to improve the quality of life, in ways that are both good for business and good for development."[24]

---

[23]Several protests by local communities against Barrick's mining activities in Tanzania had been reported. See www.protestbarrick.net/article.php?list=type&type=12, accessed February 17, 2009.

[24]www.barrick.com/CorporateResponsibility/Ethics/PoliciesStandards/default.aspx, accessed February 17, 2009.

1. **Education in partnership with local communities**

   Through its newly established community department, Barrick had made a concerted attempt to identify self-employment opportunities to the communities around the Bulyanhulu gold mine. In partnership with local governments, NFOs and communities, the company had used educated locals to promote a broad array of social entrepreneurship skills in a variety of areas such as finance, accounting and marketing (see **Exhibit 2**).

   The communities surrounding the mine needed a great deal of support in terms of education in order to be able to exploit the area's potential. By 2008, Barrick had committed to working closely with eight villages before expanding to another eight villages along the Bulyanhulu-Kahama road in Bulyanhulu. Seven of the eight villages were in the Bugarama ward and one was in the Mwingilo ward, but all were located in the Bulyanhulu mining area.

2. **Community-based entrepreneurship**

   In collaboration with local community authorities, Barrick went on to assist several community groups that already possessed local skills and entrepreneurship initiatives and which had local resources to generate business activities. Other community development projects had also been started and were engineered under the same procedure of governance (**Exhibit 3**).

3. **Health**

   Barrick committed itself to upgrading the Sungusungu Health Centre into what became called the Nyamongo Hospital in the Bulyanhulu area under the so-called phase I. Organized by the Evangelical Lutheran Church in the area, several NFOs had entered into an agreement with the local District Office and the Village Councils to provide health care that was affordable to the many local residents to treat diseases such as malaria, waterborne diseases, typhoid, yellow fever and other epidemiology problems. The community trust committed $30,000 towards beds and fittings and for a general upgrade to the hospital. Barrick's overall objective was to make health services available to many disadvantaged communities, and to attempt to curb the number of deaths that occurred

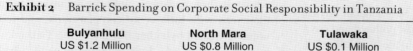

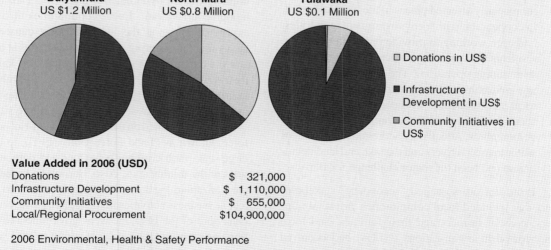

Exhibit 2   Barrick Spending on Corporate Social Responsibility in Tanzania

Bulyanhulu
US $1.2 Million

North Mara
US $0.8 Million

Tulawaka
US $0.1 Million

☐ Donations in US$

■ Infrastructure Development in US$

▨ Community Initiatives in US$

Value Added in 2006 (USD)

Donations	$ 321,000
Infrastructure Development	$ 1,110,000
Community Initiatives	$ 655,000
Local/Regional Procurement	$104,900,000

2006 Environmental, Health & Safety Performance

Note: Total amount of money in U.S. dollars spent on health & safety training and emergency response training in 2006.
Source: www.barrick.com/Theme/Barrick/files/docs_ehss/2007%20Africa%20Regional%20Rpt.pdf, accessed April 30, 2009.

Exhibit 3   Total Amount of Money Spent on Community Development Projects, 2006

Community	2006	2005	2004	2003
Donations in US$				
Bulyanhulu	20,193	14,000	410,000	485,000
North Mara	294,220	50,000	0	0
Tulawaka	6,778	7,662	5,894	n/a
Infrastructure Development in US$				
Bulyanhulu	631,222	3,570,000	4,374,000	572,000
North Mara	389,384	360,000	350,000	100,000
Tulawaka	89,020	43,697	6,250	n/a
Community Initiatives in US$				
Bulyanhulu	519,793	609,000	0	0
North Mara	135,015	0	not measured	
Tulawaka	304	0	0	n/a
Regional Purchases of Goods & Services in US$				
Bulyanhulu	65,600,000		not measured	
North Mara	37,700,000		not measured	
Tulawaka	1,600,000		not measured	

Source: www.barrick.com/Theme/Barrick/files/docs_ehss/2007%20Africa%20Regional%20Rpt.pdf, accessed April 30, 2009.

among pregnant women when they travelled from the poor communities to the district hospital.

4. **Environment**

The Lake Victoria Zone was one of the most densely populated areas in Sub-Saharan Africa, but it was also one of the most polluted and environmentally affected places in the world. Barrick, in cooperation with local government authorities, had been working to provide opportunities to the residents of the mining areas to orient themselves with mining operations. The company was creating environmental awareness in order to create local "ambassadors" who could then go out and speak positively about the mining sites to other communities. Adequately addressing the issues of water toxins on rivers and the lake and land degradation had been the major challenge for Barrick.

Protests from so-called "secondary" stakeholders that included local communities, artisanal miners, peasant farmers and their families, and local not-for-profit organizations (NFOs) had occurred to address specific social, environmental, and land heritage and resettlement issues. All these stakeholders had widely varying claims, interests and rights. In addition, subgroups and individuals with multiple and changing roles and interests existed. They included manual mining workers who felt they had been unfairly dismissed from their jobs with little or no compensation, and felt unjustly treated by either Barrick or the Tanzanian labour court system. Local communities also had expressed anger at the level of noise caused by heavy machines during mining explorations at night and the extent of the company's impact on land in their neighborhoods. There were also individuals, mainly unemployed youths, who were engaged in intrusion, vandalism and theft at the mining sites.

Barrick had relied on the Tanzanian anti-riot police force, known as "Field Force Unit" (FFU), to quell large-scale mob criminal behaviour and demonstrations at the mining sites. Also, Barrick had relied on the Tanzanian legal system and government to protect its business activities in the region. However, the behaviour of the FFU, the weak government institutional system, and the loyalty of administrative workers to Barrick had increased anger, frustration, and resentment among communities, small-scale artisan miners and NFOs. The FFU had been regarded by local communities as brutal and uncompromising during confrontations. Responses by the FFU had even led to death,[25] long-term imprisonment of community campaigners' leaders, intimidation and harassment.[26] The government had been viewed as lacking vision and leadership to reap the benefits of the mining activities in the region and had been criticized for failing to protect the interests of its citizens.

Conclusion

By 2010, a variety of corporate social responsibility (CSR) initiatives were established based on ABG's commitment to building a sustainable relationship with local communities. The overall aim was to ensure that the company would build mutual respect,

active partnerships, and a long-term commitment with its secondary stakeholders who tended to have disparate goals, demands and opinions. Mutual respect, it was argued, was important if such relationships were to be lasting, beneficial and dynamic. In addition, the company had used its social development department in each of the mining sites to develop practical guidelines in order to facilitate the implementation of its organizational values and mission, including building long-term relationships of mutual benefit between the operations and their host communities, and to avoid costly disputes and hostilities with local stakeholders.[27] Although significant progress and successful collaborations had evolved across local communities at its mining sites, African Barrick Gold still faced serious, unique problems and increased pressure to manage conflicts and reconcile stakeholders' demands in places such as North Mara.

[25]A recent incident at a Barrick mining site in the Mara region had led the Tanzanian FFU to kill an intruder (see www.protestbarrick.net/article.php?list=type&type=12, accessed April 17, 2009).

[26]For the behaviour of Tanzania's FFU in quelling demonstrations, see www.protestbarrick.net/article.php?id=369, accessed April 17, 2009.

[27]Further CSR programs are available at www.barrick.com/CorporateResponsibility/default.aspx, accessed February 24, 2009.

Case 8-2   IKEA's Global Sourcing Challenge: Indian Rugs and Child Labor (A)

Christopher A. Bartlett, Vincent Dessain, and Anders Sjöman

In May 1995, Marianne Barner faced a tough decision. After just two years with IKEA, the world's largest furniture retailer, and less than a year into her job

Professor Christopher A. Bartlett, Executive Director of the HBS Europe Research Center Vincent Dessain, and Research Associate Anders Sjöman prepared this case. HBS cases are developed solely as the basis for class discussion. Certain details have been disguised. Cases are not intended to serve as endorsements, sources of primary data, or illustrations of effective or ineffective management.

as business area manager for carpets, she was faced with the decision of cutting off one of the company's major suppliers of Indian rugs. While such a move would disrupt supply and affect sales, she found the reasons to do so quite compelling. A German TV station had just broadcast an investigative report naming the supplier as one that used child labor in the production of rugs made for IKEA. What frustrated Barner was that, like all other IKEA suppliers, this large, well-regarded company had recently signed an addendum to its supply contract explicitly forbidding the use of child labor on pain of termination.

Even more difficult than this short-term decision was the long-term action Barner knew IKEA must take on this issue. On one hand, she was being urged to sign up to an industry-wide response to growing concerns about the use of child labor in the Indian carpet industry. A recently formed partnership of manufacturers, importers, retailers, and Indian non-governmental organizations (NGOs) was proposing to issue and monitor the use of "Rugmark," a label to be put on carpets certifying that they were made without child labor. Simultaneously, Barner had been conversing with people at the Swedish Save the Children organization who were urging IKEA to ensure that its response to the situation was "in the best interest of the child"—whatever that might imply. Finally, there were some who wondered if IKEA should not just leave this hornet's nest. Indian rugs accounted for a tiny part of IKEA's turnover, and to these observers, the time, cost, and reputation risk posed by continuing this product line seemed not worth the profit potential.

The Birth and Maturing of a Global Company[1]

To understand IKEA's operations, one had to understand the philosophy and beliefs of its 70-year-old founder, Ingvar Kamprad. Despite stepping down as CEO in 1986, almost a decade later, Kamprad retained the title of honorary chairman and was still very involved in the company's activities. Yet perhaps even more powerful than his ongoing presence were his strongly held values and beliefs, which long ago had been deeply embedded in IKEA's culture.

Kamprad was 17 years old when he started the mail-order company he called IKEA, a name that combined his initials with those of his family farm, Elmtaryd, and parish, Agunnaryd, located in the forests of southern Sweden. Working out of the family kitchen, he sold goods such as fountain pens, cigarette lighters, and binders he purchased from low-priced sources and then advertised in a newsletter to local shopkeepers. When Kamprad matched his competitors by adding furniture to his

newsletter in 1948, the immediate success of the new line led him to give up the small items.

In 1951, to reduce product returns, he opened a display store in nearby Älmhult village to allow customers to inspect products before buying. It was an immediate success, with customers traveling seven hours from the capital Stockholm by train to visit. Based on the store's success, IKEA stopped accepting mail orders. Later Kamprad reflected, "The basis of the modern IKEA concept was created [at this time] and in principle it still applies. First and foremost, we use a catalog to tempt people to visit an exhibition, which today is our store... Then, catalog in hand, customers can see simple interiors for themselves, touch the furniture they want to buy and then write out an order."[2]

As Kamprad developed and refined his furniture retailing business model he became increasingly frustrated with the way a tightly knit cartel of furniture manufacturers controlled the Swedish industry to keep prices high. He began to view the situation not just as a business opportunity but also as an unacceptable social problem that he wanted to correct. Foreshadowing a vision for IKEA that would later be articulated as "creating a better life for the many people," he wrote: "A disproportionately large part of all resources is used to satisfy a small part of the population... IKEA's aim is to change this situation. We shall offer a wide range of home furnishing items of good design and function at prices so low that the majority of people can afford to buy them... We have great ambitions."[3]

The small newsletter soon expanded into a full catalog. The 1953 issue introduced what would become another key IKEA feature: self-assembled furniture. Instead of buying complete pieces of furniture, customers bought them in flat packages and put them together themselves at home. Soon, the "knockdown" concept was fully systemized, saving transport and storage costs. In typical fashion,

[1]This section draws on company histories detailed in Bertil Torekull, "Leading by Design—The IKEA Story" (New York: Harper Business, 1998), and on the IKEA website, available at http://www.ikea.com/ms/en_GB/about_ikea/splash.html, accessed October 5, 2005.

[2]Ingvar Kamprad, as quoted in Torekull, "Leading by Design—The IKEA Story," p. 25.
[3]Quoted in Christopher A. Bartlett and Ashish Nanda, "Ingvar Kamprad and IKEA," HBS No. 390-132 (Boston: Harvard Business School Publishing, 1990).

Kamprad turned the savings into still lower prices for his customers, gaining an even larger following among young postwar householders looking for well-designed but inexpensive furniture. Between 1953 and 1955, the company's sales doubled from SEK 3 million to SEK 6 million.[4]

Managing Suppliers: Developing Sourcing Principles   As its sales took off in the late 1950s, IKEA's radically new concepts began to encounter stiff opposition from Sweden's large furniture retailers. So threatened were they that when IKEA began exhibiting at trade fairs, they colluded to stop the company from taking orders at the fairs and eventually even from showing its prices. The cartel also pressured manufacturers not to sell to IKEA, and the few that continued to do so often made their deliveries at night in unmarked vans.

Unable to meet demand with such constrained local supply, Kamprad was forced to look abroad for new sources. In 1961, he contracted with several furniture factories in Poland, a country still in the Communist eastern bloc. To assure quality output and reliable delivery, IKEA brought its know-how, taught its processes, and even provided machinery to the new suppliers, revitalizing Poland's furniture industry as it did so. Poland soon became IKEA's largest source and, to Kamprad's delight, at much lower costs—once again allowing him to reduce his prices.

Following its success in Poland, IKEA adopted a general procurement principle that it should not own its means of production but should seek to develop close ties by supporting its suppliers in a long-term relationship.[a] Beyond supply contracts and technology transfer, the relationship led IKEA to make loans to its suppliers at reasonable rates, repayable through future shipments. "Our objective is to develop long-term business partners," explained a senior purchasing manager. "We commit to doing all we can to keep them competitive—as long as they remain equally committed to us. We are in this for the long run."

Although the relationship between IKEA and its suppliers was often described as one of mutual dependency, suppliers also knew that they had to remain competitive to keep their contract. From the outset they understood that if a more cost-effective alternative appeared, IKEA would try to help them respond, but if they could not do so, it would move production.

In its constant quest to lower prices, the company developed an unusual way of identifying new sources. As a veteran IKEA manager explained: "We do not buy products from our suppliers. We buy unused production capacity." It was a philosophy that often led its purchasing managers to seek out seasonal manufacturers with spare off-season capacity. There were many classic examples of how IKEA matched products to supplier capabilities: they had sail makers make seat cushions, window factories produce table frames, and ski manufacturers build chairs in their off-season. The manager added, "We've always worried more about finding the right management at our suppliers than finding high-tech facilities. We will always help good management to develop their capacity."

Growing Retail: Expanding Abroad   Building on the success of his first store, Kamprad self-financed a store in Stockholm in 1965. Recognizing a growing use of automobiles in Sweden, he bucked the practice of having a downtown showroom and opted for a suburban location with ample parking space. When customers drove home with their furniture in flat packed boxes, they assumed two of the costliest parts of traditional furniture retailing—home delivery and assembly.

In 1963, even before the Stockholm store had opened, IKEA had expanded into Oslo, Norway. A decade later, Switzerland became its first non-Scandinavian market, and in 1974 IKEA entered Germany, which soon became its largest market.

---

[4]Ibid.

[a]This policy was modified after a number of East European suppliers broke their contracts with IKEA after the fall of the Berlin Wall opened new markets for them. IKEA's subsequent supply chain problems and loss of substantial investments led management to develop an internal production company, Swedwood, to ensure delivery stability. However, it was decided that only a limited amount of IKEA's purchases (perhaps 10%) should be sourced from Swedwood.

Exhibit 1   IKEA Stores, Fiscal Year Ending
August 1994

a. Historical Store Growth

	1954	1964	1974	1984	1994
Number of Stores	0	2	9	52	114

b. Country's First Store

First Store (with city)		
Year	**Country**	**City**
1958	Sweden	Älmhult
1963	Norway	Oslo
1969	Denmark	Copenhagen
1973	Switzerland	Zürich
1974	Germany	Munich
1975	Australia	Artamon
1976	Canada	Vancouver
1977	Austria	Vienna
1978	Netherlands	Rotterdam
1978	Singapore	Singapore
1980	Spain	Gran Canaria
1981	Iceland	Reykjavik
1981	France	Paris
1983	Saudi Arabia	Jeddah
1984	Belgium	Brussels
1984	Kuwait	Kuwait City
1985	United States	Philadelphia
1987	United Kingdom	Manchester
1988	Hong Kong	Hong Kong
1989	Italy	Milan
1990	Hungary	Budapest
1991	Poland	Platan
1991	Czech Republic	Prague
1991	United Arab Emirates	Dubai
1992	Slovakia	Bratislava
1994	Taiwan	Taipei

Source: IKEA website, http://franchisor.ikea.com/txtfacts.html, accessed October 15, 2004.

(See **Exhibit 1** for IKEA's worldwide expansion.) At each new store the same simple Scandinavian-design products were backed up with a catalog and offbeat advertising, presenting the company as "those impossible Swedes with strange ideas." And reflecting the company's conservative values, each new entry was financed by previous successes.[b]

During this expansion, the IKEA concept evolved and became increasingly formalized. (**Exhibit 2** summarizes important events in IKEA's corporate history.) It still built large, suburban stores with knockdown furniture in flat packages the customers brought home to assemble themselves. But as the concept was refined, the company required that each store follow a predetermined design, set up to maximize customers' exposure to the product range. The concept mandated, for instance, that the living room interiors should follow immediately after the entrance. IKEA also serviced customers with features such as a playroom for children, a low-priced restaurant, and a "Sweden Shop" for groceries that had made IKEA Sweden's leading food exporter. At the same time, the range gradually expanded beyond furniture to include a full line of home furnishing products such as textiles, kitchen utensils, flooring, rugs and carpets, lamps, and plants.

The Emerging Culture and Values[5]   As Kamprad's evolving business philosophy was formalized into the IKEA vision statement, "To create a better everyday life for the many people," it became the foundation of the company's strategy of selling affordable, good-quality furniture to mass-market consumers around the world. The cultural norms and values that developed to support the strategy's implementation were also, in many ways, an extension of Kamprad's personal beliefs and style. "The true IKEA spirit," he remarked, "is founded on our enthusiasm, our constant will to renew, on our cost-consciousness, on our willingness to assume responsibility and to help, on our humbleness before the task, and on the simplicity of our behavior." As well as a summary of his aspiration for the company's behavioral norms, it was also a good statement of Kamprad's own personal management style.

---

[b]By 2005, company lore had it that IKEA had only taken one bank loan in its corporate history—which it had paid back as soon as the cash flow allowed.

[5]Ibid.

Exhibit 2   IKEA History: Selected Events

Year	Event
1943	IKEA is founded. Ingvar Kamprad constructs the company name from his initials (**I**ngvar **K**amprad), his home farm (**E**lmtaryd), and its parish (**A**gunnaryd).
1945	The first IKEA ad appears in press, advertising mail-order products.
1948	Furniture is introduced into the IKEA product range. Products are still only advertised through ads.
1951	The first IKEA catalogue is distributed.
1955	IKEA starts to design its own furniture.
1956	Self-assembly furniture in flat packs is introduced.
1958	The first IKEA store opens in Älmhult, Sweden.
1961	Contract with Polish sources, IKEA's first non-Scandinavian suppliers. First delivery is 20,000 chairs.
1963	The first IKEA store outside Sweden opens in Norway.
1965	IKEA opens in Stockholm, introducing the self-serve concept to furniture retailing.
1965	IKEA stores add a section called the "The Cook Shop," offering quality utensils at low prices.
1973	The first IKEA store outside Scandinavia opens in Spreitenbach, Switzerland.
1974	A plastic chair developed at a supplier that usually makes buckets.
1978	The BILLY bookcase is introduced to the range, becoming an instant top seller.
1980	One of IKEA's best-sellers, the KLIPPAN sofa with removable, washable covers, is introduced.
1980	Introduction of LACK coffee table, made from a strong, light material by an interior door factory.
1985	The first IKEA Group store opens in the U.S.
1985	MOMENT sofa with frame built by a supermarket trolley factory is introduced. Wins a design prize.
1991	IKEA establishes its own industrial group, Swedwood

Source: Adapted from IKEA Facts and Figures, 2003 and 2004 editions and IKEA internal documents.

Over the years a very distinct organizational culture and management style emerged in IKEA reflecting these values. For example, the company operated very informally as evidenced by the open-plan office landscape, where even the CEO did not have a separate office, and the familiar and personal way all employees addressed one another. But that informality often masked an intensity that derived from the organization's high self-imposed standards. As one senior executive explained, "Because there is no security available behind status or closed doors, this environment actually puts pressure on people to perform."

The IKEA management process also stressed simplicity and attention to detail. "Complicated rules paralyze!" said Kamprad. The company organized "anti-bureaucrat week" every year, requiring all managers to spend time working in a store to reestablish contact with the front line and the consumer. The work pace was such that executives joked that IKEA believed in "management by running around."

Cost consciousness was another strong part of the management culture. "Waste of resources," said Kamprad, "is a mortal sin at IKEA. Expensive solutions are often signs of mediocrity, and an idea without a price tag is never acceptable." Although cost consciousness extended into all aspects of the operation, travel and entertainment expenses were particularly sensitive. "We do not set any price on time," remarked an executive, recalling that he had once phoned Kamprad to get approval to fly first class. He explained that economy class was full and that he had an urgent appointment to keep. "There is no first class in IKEA," Kamprad had replied. "Perhaps you should go by car." The executive completed the 350-mile trip by taxi.

The search for creative solutions was also highly prized with IKEA. Kamprad had written, "Only while sleeping one makes no mistakes. The fear of making mistakes is the root of bureaucracy and the enemy of all evolution." Though planning for the future was encouraged, overanalysis was not. "Exaggerated planning can be fatal," Kamprad advised his executives. "Let simplicity and common sense characterize your planning."

Exhibit 3   "A Furniture Dealer's Testament"—A Summarized Overview

In 1976, Ingvar Kamprad listed nine aspects of IKEA that he believed formed the basis of the IKEA culture together with the vision statement "To create a better everyday life for the many people." These aspects are given to all new employees through a pamphlet titled "A Furniture Dealer's Testament." The following table summarizes the major points:

Cornerstone	Summarize Description
1. The Product Range—Our Identity	IKEA sells well-designed, functional home furnishing products at prices so low that as many people as possible can afford them.
2. The IKEA Spirit—A Strong and Living Reality	IKEA is about enthusiasm, renewal, thrift, responsibility, humbleness toward the task and simplicity.
3. Profit Gives Us Resources	IKEA will achieve profit (which Kamprad describes as a "wonderful word") through the lowest prices, good quality, economical development of products, improved purchasing processes and cost savings.
4. Reaching Good Results with Small Means	"Waste is a deadly sin."
5. Simplicity is a Virtue	Complex regulations and exaggerated planning paralyze. IKEA people stay simple in style and habits as well as in their organizational approach.
6. Doing it a Different Way	IKEA is run from a small village in the woods. IKEA asks shirt factories to make seat cushions and window factories to make table frames. IKEA discounts its umbrellas when it rains. IKEA does things differently.
7. Concentration—Important to Our Success	"We can never do everything everywhere, all at the same time." At IKEA, you choose the most important thing to do and finish that before starting a new project.
8. Taking Responsibility—A Privilege	"The fear of making mistakes is the root of bureaucracy." Everyone has the right to make mistakes; in fact, everyone has obligation to make mistakes.
9. Most Things Still Remain to be Done. A Glorious Future!	IKEA is only at the beginning of what it might become. 200 stores is nothing. "We are still a small company at heart."

Source: Adapted by casewriters from IKEA's "A Furniture Dealer's Testament"; Bertil Torekull, "Leading by Design: The IKEA Story" (New York: Harper Business, 1998, p. 112); and interviews.

In 1976, Kamprad felt the need to commit to paper the values that had developed in IKEA during the previous decades. His thesis, *Testament of a Furniture Dealer,* became an important means for spreading the IKEA philosophy, particularly during its period of rapid international expansion. (Extracts of the *Testament* are given in **Exhibit 3.**) Specially trained "IKEA ambassadors" were assigned to key positions in all units to spread the company's philosophy and values by educating their subordinates and by acting as role models.

In 1986, when Kamprad stepped down, Anders Moberg, a company veteran who had once been Kamprad's personal assistant, took over as president and CEO. But Kamprad remained intimately involved as chairman, and his influence extended well beyond the ongoing daily operations: he was the self-appointed guardian of IKEA's deeply embedded culture and values.

Waking up to Environmental and Social Issues

By the mid-1990s, IKEA was the world's largest specialized furniture retailer. Sales for the IKEA Group for the financial year ending August 1994 totaled SEK 35 billion (about $4.5 billion). In the previous year, more than 116 million people had visited one of the 98 IKEA stores in 17 countries, most of them drawn there by the company's product catalog, which was printed yearly in 72 million copies in 34 languages. The privately held company did not report profit levels, but one estimate put its net margin at 8.4% in 1994, yielding a net profit of SEK 2.9 billion (about $375 million).[6]

After decades of seeking new sources, in the mid-1990s IKEA worked with almost 2,300 suppliers in 70 countries, sourcing a range of around 11,200 products. Its relationship with its suppliers was dominated by commercial issues, and its 24 trading service offices in 19 countries primarily monitored production, tested new product ideas, negotiated prices, and checked quality. (See **Exhibit 4** for selected IKEA figures in 1994.) That

Exhibit 4   IKEA in Figures, 1993/1994
(fiscal year ending August 31, 1994)

a. Sales

Country/Region	SEK Billion	Percentage
Germany	10.4	29.70%
Sweden	3.9	11.20%
Austria, France, Italy, Switzerland	7.7	21.90%
Belgium, Netherlands, United Kingdom, Norway	7.3	20.80%
North America (U.S.A and Canada)	4.9	13.90%
Czech Republic, Hungary, Poland, Slovakia	0.5	1.50%
Australia	0.4	1.00%
	35.0	

b. Purchasing

Country/Region	Percentage
Nordic Countries	33.4%
East and Central Europe	14.3%
Rest of Europe	29.6%
Rest of the World	22.7%

Source: IKEA Facts and Figures, 1994.

[6]Estimation in Bo Pettersson, "Han släpper aldrig taget," *Veckans Affärer*, March 1, 2004, pp. 30–48.

relationship began to change during the 1980s, however, when environmental problems emerged with some of its products. And it was even more severely challenged in the mid-1990s when accusations of IKEA suppliers using child labor surfaced.

The Environmental Wake-Up: Formaldehyde
In the early 1980s, Danish authorities passed regulations to define limits for formaldehyde emissions permissible in building products. The chemical compound was used as binding glue in materials such as plywood and particleboard and often seeped out as gas. At concentrations above 0.1 mg/kg in air, it could cause watery eyes, headaches, a burning sensation in the throat, and difficulty breathing. With IKEA's profile as a leading local furniture retailer using particleboard in many of its products, it became a prime target for regulators wanting to publicize the new standards. So when tests showed that some IKEA products emitted more formaldehyde than was allowed by legislation, the case was widely publicized and the company was fined. More significantly—and the real lesson for IKEA—was that due to the publicity, its sales dropped 20% in Denmark.

In response to this situation, the company quickly established stringent requirements regarding formaldehyde emissions but soon found that suppliers were failing to meet its standards. The problem was that most of its suppliers bought from sub-suppliers, who in turn bought the binding materials from glue manufacturers. Eventually, IKEA decided it would have to work directly with the glue-producing chemical companies and, with the collaboration of companies such as ICI and BASF, soon found ways to reduce the formaldehyde off-gassing in its products.[7]

A decade later, however, the formaldehyde problem returned. In 1992, an investigative team from a large German newspaper and TV company found that IKEA's best-selling bookcase series, Billy, had emissions higher than German legislation allowed.

[7]Based on case study by The Natural Step, "Organizational Case Summary: IKEA," available at http://www.naturalstep.org/learn/docs/cs/case_ikea.pdf, accessed October 5, 2005.

This time, however, the source of the problem was not the glue but the lacquer on the bookshelves. In the wake of headlines describing "deadly poisoned bookshelves," IKEA immediately stopped both the production and sales of Billy bookcases worldwide and corrected the problem before resuming distribution. Not counting the cost of lost sales and production or the damage to goodwill, the Billy incident was estimated to have cost IKEA $6 million to $7 million.[8]

These events prompted IKEA to address broader environmental concerns more directly. Since wood was the principal material in about half of all IKEA products, forestry became a natural starting point. Following discussions with both Greenpeace and World Wide Fund for Nature (WWF, formerly World Wildlife Fund) and using standards set by the Forest Stewardship Council, IKEA established a forestry policy stating that IKEA would not accept any timber, veneer, plywood, or layer-glued wood from intact natural forests or from forests with a high conservation value. This meant that IKEA had to be willing to take on the task of tracing all wood used in IKEA products back to its source.[9] To monitor compliance, the company appointed forest managers to carry out random checks of wood suppliers and run projects on responsible forestry around the world.

In addition to forestry, IKEA identified four other areas where environmental criteria were to be applied to its business operations: adapting the product range; working with suppliers; transport and distribution; and ensuring environmentally conscious stores. For instance, in 1992, the company began using chlorine-free recycled paper in its catalogs; it redesigned the best-selling OGLA chair—originally manufactured from beech—so it could be made using waste material from yogurt cup production; and it redefined its packaging principles to eliminate any use of PVC. The company also maintained its partnership with WWF, resulting

in numerous projects on global conservation, and funded a global forest watch program to map intact natural forests worldwide. In addition, it engaged in an ongoing dialogue with Greenpeace on forestry.[10]

The Social Wake-Up: Child Labor   In 1994, as IKEA was still working to resolve the formaldehyde problems, a Swedish television documentary showed children in Pakistan working at weaving looms. Among the several Swedish companies mentioned in the film as importers of carpets from Pakistan, IKEA was the only high-profile name on the list. Just two months into her job as business area manager for carpets, Marianne Barner recalled the shockwaves that the TV program sent through the company:

> The use of child labor was not a high-profile public issue at the time. In fact, the U.N. Convention on the Rights of the Child had only been published in December 1989. So, media attention like this TV program had an important role to play in raising awareness on a topic not well known and understood—including at IKEA... We were caught completely unaware. It was not something we had been paying attention to. For example, I had spent a couple of months in India learning about trading but got no exposure to child labor. Our buyers met suppliers in their city offices and rarely got out to where production took place... Our immediate response to the program was to apologize for our ignorance and acknowledge that we were not in full control of this problem. But we also committed to do something about it.

As part of its response, IKEA sent a legal team to Geneva to seek input and advice from the International Labor Organization (ILO) on how to deal with the problem. They learned that Convention 138, adopted by the ILO in 1973 and ratified by 120 countries, committed ratifying countries to working for the abolition of labor by children under 15 or the age of compulsory schooling in that country. India, Pakistan, and Nepal were not signatories to the convention.[11] Following these discussions with the

---

[8]Ibid.

[9]"IKEA—Social and Environmental Responsibility Report 2004," p. 33, available at http://www.ikea-group.ikea.com/corporate/PDF/IKEA_SaER.pdf, accessed October 5, 2005.

[10]Ibid., pp. 19–20.

[11]Ratification statistics available on ILO website, page titled "Convention No. C138 was ratified by 142 countries," available at http://www.ilo.org/ilolex/cgi-lex/ratifce.pl?C138, accessed December 4, 2005.

ILO, IKEA added a clause to all supply contracts—a "black-and-white" clause, as Barner put it—stating simply that if the supplier employed children under legal working age, the contract would be cancelled.

To take the load off field trading managers and to provide some independence to the monitoring process, the company appointed a third-party agent to monitor child labor practices at its suppliers in India and Pakistan. Because this type of external monitoring was very unusual, IKEA had some difficulty locating a reputable and competent company to perform the task. Finally, they appointed a well-known Scandinavian company with extensive experience in providing external monitoring of companies' quality assurance programs and gave them the mandate not only to investigate complaints but also to undertake random audits of child labor practices at suppliers' factories.

Early Lessons: A Deeply Embedded Problem
With India being the biggest purchasing source for carpets and rugs, Barner contacted Swedish Save the Children, UNICEF, and the ILO to expand her understanding and to get advice about the issue of child labor, especially in South Asia. She soon found that hard data was often elusive. While estimates of child labor in India varied from the government's 1991 census figure of 11.3 million children under 15 working[12] to Human Rights Watch's estimate of between 60 million and 115 million child laborers,[13] it was clear that a very large number of Indian children as young as five years old worked in agriculture, mining, quarrying, and manufacturing, as well as acting as household servants, street vendors, or beggars. Of this total, an estimated 200,000 were employed in the carpet industry, working on looms in large factories, for small subcontractors, and in homes where whole families worked on looms to earn extra income.[14]

Children could be bonded—essentially placed in servitude—in order to pay off debts incurred by their parents, typically in the range of 1,000 to 10,000 rupees ($30 to $300). But due to the astronomical interest rates and the very low wages offered to children, it could take years to pay off such loans. Indeed, some indentured child laborers eventually passed on the debt to their own children. The Indian government stated that it was committed to the abolition of bonded labor, which had been illegal since the Children (Pledging of Labour) Act passed under British rule in 1933. The practice continued to be widespread, however, and to reinforce the earlier law, the government passed the Bonded Labour System (Abolition) Act in 1976.[15]

But the government took a less absolute stand on unbonded child labor, which it characterized as "a socioeconomic phenomenon arising out of poverty and the lack of development." The Child Labour (Prohibition and Regulation) Act of 1986 prohibited the use of child labor (applying to those under 14) in certain defined "hazardous industries" and regulated children's hours and working conditions in others. But the government felt that the majority of child labor involved "children working alongside and under the supervision of their parents" in agriculture, cottage industries, and service roles. Indeed, the law specifically permitted children to work in craft industries "in order not to outlaw the passage of specialized handicraft skills from generation to generation."[16] Critics charged that even with these laws on the books, exploitive child labor—including bonded labor—was widespread because laws were poorly enforced and prosecution rarely severe.[17]

Action Required: New Issues, New Options

In the fall of 1994, after managing the initial response to the crisis, Barner and her direct manager traveled to India, Nepal, and Pakistan to learn

[12]Indian Government Policy Statements, "Child Labor and India," available at http://www.indianembassy.org/policy/Child_Labor/childlabor_2000.htm, accessed October 1, 2005.

[13]Human Rights Watch figures, available at http://www.hrw.org/reports/1996/India3.htm, accessed October 1, 2005.

[14]Country Reports in Human Rights, U.S. State Department, February 2000, available at http://www.state.gov/g/drl/rls/hrrpt/2000/, accessed October 1, 2005.

[15]Indian Government Policy Statements, "Child Labor and India," available at http://www.indianembassy.org/policy/Child_Labor/childlabor_2000.htm, accessed October 1, 2005.

[16]Ibid.

[17]Human Rights Watch data, available at http://www.hrw.org/reports/1996/India3.htm, accessed October 1, 2005.

more. Barner recalled the trip: "We felt the need to educate ourselves, so we met with our suppliers. But we also met with unions, politicians, activists, NGOs, U.N. organizations, and carpet export organizations. We even went out on unannounced carpet factory raids with local NGOs; we saw child labor, and we were thrown out of some places."

On the trip, Barner also learned of the formation of the Rugmark Foundation, a recently initiated industry response to the child labor problem in the Indian carpet industry. Triggered by a consumer awareness program started by human rights organizations, consumer activists, and trade unions in Germany in the early 1990s, the Indo-German Export Promotion Council had joined up with key Indian carpet manufacturers and exporters and some Indian NGOs to develop a label certifying that the hand-knotted carpets to which it was attached were made without the use of child labor. To implement this idea, the Rugmark Foundation was organized to supervise the use of the label. It expected to begin exporting rugs carrying a unique identifying number in early 1995. As a major purchaser of Indian rugs, IKEA was invited to sign up with Rugmark as a way of dealing with the ongoing potential for child labor problems on products sourced from India.

On her return to Sweden, Barner again met frequently with the Swedish Save the Children's expert on child labor. "The people there had a very forward-looking view on the issue and taught us a lot," said Barner. "Above all, they emphasized the need to ensure you always do what is in the best interests of the child." This was the principle set at the heart of the U.N. Convention on the Rights of the Child (1989), a document with which Barner was now quite familiar. (See **Exhibit 5** for Article 32 from the U.N. Convention on the Rights of the Child.)

The more Barner learned, the more complex the situation became. As a business area manager with full profit-and-loss responsibility for carpets, she knew she had to protect not only her business but also the IKEA brand and image. Yet she viewed her responsibility as broader than this: She felt the company should do something that would make a difference in the lives of the children she had seen. It was a view that was not universally held within IKEA, where many were concerned that a very proactive stand could put the business at a significant cost disadvantage to its competitors.

A New Crisis   Then, in the spring of 1995, a year after IKEA began to address this issue, a well-known German documentary maker notified the company that a film he had made was about to be broadcast on German television showing children working at looms at Rangan Exports, one of IKEA's major suppliers. While refusing to let the company preview the video, the filmmaker produced still shots taken directly from the video. The producer then invited IKEA to send someone to take part in a live discussion during the airing of the

---

Exhibit 5   The U.N. Convention on the Rights of the Child: Article 32

1. States Parties recognize the right of the child to be protected from economic exploitation and from performing any work that is likely to be hazardous or to interfere with the child's education, or to be harmful to the child's health or physical, mental, spiritual, moral, or social development.
2. States Parties shall take legislative, administrative, social, and educational measures to ensure the implementation of the present article. To this end, and having regard to the relevant provisions of other international instruments, States Parties shall in particular:

   a. Provide for a minimum age for admission to employment
   b. Provide for appropriate regulation of hours and conditions of employment
   c. Provide for appropriate or other sanctions to ensure the effective enforcement of the present article.

Source: Excerpt from "Convention on the Rights of the Child," from the website of the Office of the United Nations High Commissioner for Human Rights, available at http://www.unhchr.ch/html/menu3/b/k2crc.htm, accessed October 2005.

program. Said Barner, "Compared to the Swedish program, which documented the use of child labor in Pakistan as a serious report about an important issue without targeting any single company, it was immediately clear that this German-produced program planned to take a confrontational and aggressive approach aimed directly at IKEA and one of its suppliers."

For Barner, the first question was whether to recommend that IKEA participate in the program or decline the invitation. Beyond the immediate public relations issue, she also had to decide how to deal with Rangan Exports' apparent violation of the contractual commitment it had made not to use child labor. And finally, this crisis raised the issue of whether the overall approach IKEA had been taking to the issue of child labor was appropriate. Should the company continue to try to deal with the issue through its own relationships with its suppliers? Should it step back and allow Rugmark to monitor the use of child labor on its behalf? Or should it recognize that the problem was too deeply embedded in the culture of these countries for it to have any real impact and simply withdraw?

Case 8-3   Genzyme's CSR Dilemma: How to Play Its HAND

Christopher A. Bartlett, Tarun Khanna, and Prithwiraj Choudhury

On a cold but sunny day in January 2009, as sunlight reflected through the adjustable mirror panels of Genzyme's landmark "green" headquarters, Jim Geraghty was reflecting on discussions in a just-concluded phone call. Geraghty, senior vice president at Genzyme, had been instrumental in creating the Humanitarian Assistance for Neglected Diseases (HAND) program. Launched in April 2006, HAND was a cornerstone of Genzyme's corporate social responsibility (CSR) initiatives, and its steering committee had just completed a conference call meeting to decide its future priorities.

▌Professors Christopher A. Bartlett and Tarun Khanna and Doctoral Candidate Prithwiraj Choudhury prepared this case. HBS cases are developed solely as the basis for class discussion. Cases are not intended to serve as endorsements, sources of primary data, or illustrations of effective or ineffective management.

Two special invitees on the call—Sandeep Sahney, managing director of Genzyme India, and Rogerio Vivaldi, senior vice president and head of the Latin American operations—had been asked to provide information to help the committee decide which HAND initiative to support going forward. Sahney was championing the malaria research project with the Indian partner ICGEB, while Vivaldi was making a strong case for extending the Brazilian research program on Chagas disease with local partner Fiocruz. There were other options on the table, including the idea of starting a HAND tuberculosis project.

When Sahney and Vivaldi left the call, Geraghty focused the committee members on the recommendations they would take to Henri Termeer, Genzyme CEO. Which research initiative would have maximum impact? What was the right future model for partnering? And what were the funding and resource needs for scaling up the program?

Laying the Corporate Foundation Stones[a]

From modest beginnings in 1981 as a supplier of enzymes, fine chemicals, and reagents to research labs and pharmaceutical companies, Genzyme had

grown to become a leader in biotechnology with revenues of almost $4 billion in 2007 (see **Exhibit 1** for key financial indicators and **Exhibit 2** for stock price movement). It had done so by identifying its patients' needs, targeting a focused technology capability, and developing a set of values that clearly defined its role as a corporation within society.

[a]This section is adapted from Christopher A. Bartlett and Andrew McLean, "Genzyme's Gaucher Initiative: Global Risk and Responsibility," HBS No. 303-048 (Boston: Harvard Business School Publishing, 2002).

Exhibit 1   Key Financial Indicators at Genzyme

(Dollars in thousands, except for share data)	2003	2004	2005	2006	2007	2008
Revenues	1,574,817	2,201,145	2,734,842	3,187,013	3,813,519	4,605,039
Gross margin	1,143,123	1,599,997	2,082,030	2,433,856	2,856,774	3,414,436
Operating income (loss)	174,012	252,913	600,862	(190,509)	653,865	581,479
Net income (loss)	94,283	86,527	441,489	(16,797)	480,193	421,081
Earnings per share (diluted)	$0.42	$0.37	$1.65	$(0.06)	$1.74	$1.50
Cash and investments	1,227,460	1,079,454	1,089,102	1,285,604	1,460,394	973,691
Working capital	930,951	1,009,231	1,114,976	1,338,062	1,137,904	1,601,852
Total assets	5,004,528	6,069,421	6,878,865	7,191,188	8,314,375	8,671,276
Long-term obligations	1,676,091	1,064,867	1,178,975	879,038	217,511	451,000
Stockholder's equity	2,936,412	4,380,156	5,149,867	5,660,711	6,612,937	7,305,993

Source: Genzyme website, http://www.genzyme.com/corp/investors/2008_annualreport.pdf, accessed on 08/12/2009.

Exhibit 2   Genzyme's Stock Price Movement Benchmarked Against Pharmaceutical Index (2003–2008)

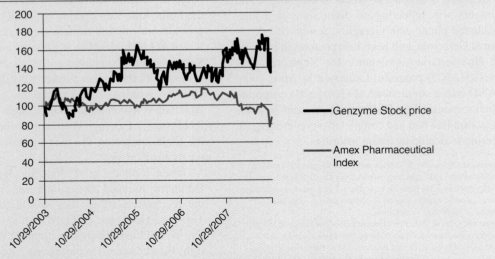

Source: Genzyme stock price data from Thomson Datastream, accessed on March 31, 2009; Amex pharmaceutical index data, http://www.amex.com/othProd/prodInf/OpPiChartDet.jsp?monthVal=12&Product_Symbol=DRG, accessed on March 31, 2009.

From its earliest days, Genzyme had focused on orphaned diseases (those with too small a population of sufferers to attract drug development attention), a strategy reflected in its portfolio of drugs (see **Exhibit 3** for its major products and **Exhibit 4** for a portfolio of products for orphan and neglected diseases).

Nurturing an Early Breakthrough   Two years after creating the company, founder Henry Blair recognized that he needed help in managing his fast-growing start-up. In 1983, he hired Henri Termeer, a 36-year-old division president at medical products giant Baxter International, bringing him in as Genzyme's president. Recognizing the

Exhibit 3   Genzyme's Product Portfolio

Major Current products ranked by sales*

Product Name	Disease/Condition	Is the Medication for an "Orphan Disease"?	Revenue in 2007
Cerezyme®	Gaucher disease	Yes	$1.13 billion
Renagel®	End-stage renal disease	No	$603 million
Fabrazyme®	Fabry disease	Yes	$424 million
Synvisc®	Osteoarthritis of the knee	No	$242 million

*List incomplete

Products in the Pipeline

Product Name	Disease/Condition
Mozobil™ (plerixafor)	Stem cell transplant
Alemtuzumab (Campath®)	Multiple sclerosis
Clolar® (clofarabine)	Adult acute myeloid leukemia
Mipomersen	High-risk hypercholesterolemia

Revenue Breakdown by Product Area

2000 REVENUES $752M*

2007 REVENUES $3,814M

Source: Genzyme company documents.

Exhibit 4   Genzyme's Existing Product Portfolio for Orphan or Neglected Diseases

Neglected/Orphan Disease	Treatment	First Approved	Patients on Therapy as of January 1, 2008	Approx. Annual Treatment Cost Per Patient ($)	Percentage of Patients Who Get Free Treatment
Type 1 Gaucher disease	Cerezyme	1991 (first-generation product Ceredase)	5,200	$200,000	10% (through Project Hope)
Fabry disease	Fabrazyme	2001	2,200	$200,000	10%
MPS I	Aldurazyme (with BioMarin Pharmaceutical)	2003	600	$200,000	10%
Pompe disease	Myozyme	2006	900	$300,000	10%

Note: As the last column of this table indicates, Genzyme sells most of these products commercially. The HAND program is completely separate to these initiatives.
Source: Interviews with Genzyme executives.

importance of R&D to build a diversified pipeline of products, Termeer initiated a series of weekend technology strategy discussions involving top management, MIT and Harvard faculty, key investors, and a few outside advisers.

One potential opportunity that caught Termeer's eye was an ongoing trial being conducted by Dr. Roscoe Brady of the National Institutes of Health (NIH). Brady was conducting research on Gaucher (pronounced GO-shay) disease, and Genzyme had received a contract to supply an enzyme called GCR. Gaucher is an extremely rare and deadly condition caused by the body's inability to manufacture the GCR enzyme. It affected fewer than six of every one million people, of whom only a quarter were thought to be ill enough to require treatment.

Early trials of Brady's treatment were disappointing. Only one of seven patients in the trial showed any response to the therapy, but the intriguing fact was that in this particular case, the symptoms were dramatically reversed. Most within Genzyme were pessimistic about the therapy. In addition to questions about the therapy's efficacy, there were two other major concerns—whether it was safe (the enzyme was extracted from human placentas and there

were risks of HIV and hepatitis C transmission), and whether the investment would earn a significant return.

But Termeer wasn't ready to give up. After learning that the one patient in dramatic recovery was a four-year-old boy from the Washington, D.C., area, he visited the boy's family regularly over the next few months and was impressed with the treatment's effectiveness. Eventually, despite the many concerns being expressed, Termeer decided to proceed with the development.

In 1985, soon after Termeer was appointed CEO and had taken the company public, Genzyme made an orphan drug application for the Ceredase enzyme under the Orphan Drug Act.[b] The company estimated that *if* further trials were successful and *if* the orphan drug status was awarded, it could serve around 2,000 patients worldwide, with projected annual sales of $100 million. Finally, in 1991, the U.S. Food and Drug Administration approved Ceredase for marketing in the United States.

[b]Under the Orphan Drug Act of January 1983, companies doing research on rare diseases affecting fewer than 200,000 people in the United States were awarded tax breaks and marketing exclusivity on that drug for seven years postapproval.

Weathering Political and Regulatory Pressures
Ceredase was launched into a difficult political environment for pharmaceutical and biotech companies. President Clinton's emphasis on health-care reform turned the spotlight on high-priced therapies, and with Gaucher medication costing $50,000 to $100,000 a year per patient, Genzyme came under scrutiny. Termeer's response was to go to Washington and meet with members of Congress and the regulatory authorities. As he recalled later, "I invited them to visit our operations and offered to open our books so they could see what it cost to develop and produce the product. Our approach was to be completely open and transparent. We were proud of what we had done and had nothing to hide."

After showing his visitors the facilities and giving the Congressional Office of Technology Assessment (OTA) open access to Genzyme's books, Termeer explained the company's philosophy: "Since the beginning, I have told this organization that our first responsibility is to treat patients with the disease, not to maximize financial returns." With this objective, even before Ceredase was approved, Genzyme created the Ceredase Assistance Program (CAP) to provide free medication to the patients in most need. After a detailed examination, in October 1992, the OTA concluded that while the Orphan Drug Act protection did reduce risks, Genzyme had invested significantly in R&D and production facilities and the company's pretax margin on the drug was within industry norms.

Building a Global Organization   As the Ceredase trials continued, Genzyme began building a new $180 million manufacturing facility. With such a small population of Gaucher sufferers, Termeer realized the company needed to expand into global markets in order to generate volume for the plant. As Genzyme expanded abroad, the CEO insisted that the marketing focus be on the core corporate value of "putting patients first."

Assembling a go-to-market team for an extremely expensive therapy for a rare and seldom diagnosed disease was a daunting task. Salespeople would have to educate doctors, pharmacies, and hospitals about the disease in a variety of different health-care environments. Management quickly concluded that the key was to recruit "passionate practical dreamers" as they called them. Termeer tapped his Baxter alumni network to hire senior people to lead Genzyme's entry into Europe, the Middle East, Asia, Canada, and Latin America into the new millennium.

Paralleling its domestic commitment to provide treatment to all Gaucher sufferers, in 1998 the company launched a global version of CAP called the Gaucher Initiative with the objective of delivering treatment to those in less developed countries. To help deliver treatment to these countries, Genzyme teamed up with Project HOPE (Health Opportunities for People Everywhere) as its global nongovernmental organization (NGO) partner, deciding to focus first on untreated sufferers in Egypt and China.

In implementing the Gaucher Initiative, the embedded corporate value of putting patients first was translated into a "two-price policy" for the drug—full price, or free for patients who could not afford it. An independent six-member medical review board was created to review and approve economically challenged patients. Project HOPE would handle the drug's delivery to developing countries, while Genzyme agreed to provide free drugs, pay for the program manager and the secretariat, and provide training, travel, and office peripherals for local treatment centers. In 1998, the Gaucher Initiative took on 60 patients worldwide. Three years later, this number was 140.

Shaping a New Industry Image   While Genzyme was developing the Gaucher Initiative, Termeer was becoming increasingly concerned about the failure of the pharmaceutical industry to create sustainable goodwill with NGOs, government agencies, and the public at large, especially in emerging markets. He was astounded in 1999, when 28 big pharmaceutical companies sued the South African government and President Mandela personally for passing a law allowing the import of affordable generic versions of patented AIDS drugs to treat millions of sufferers for the first time. While the companies argued that the law treated them unfairly, NGOs and AIDS activists argued that commercial interests could not override the human rights of people who were simply trying to stay alive."[1]

Termeer was determined to take a radically different approach at Genzyme. Given the company's patient-focused culture and its sense of corporate social responsibility, he saw an opportunity to seize the initiative by responding to requests from governments in developing countries to invest locally in helping them respond to neglected diseases—diseases that were not attracting drug development attention despite the large number of sufferers. The company was accustomed to working with government health-care agencies worldwide to achieve its goal of obtaining treatment for rare orphan diseases like Gaucher. Now he felt it might be able to leverage those relationships and offer help in finding solutions for more common neglected diseases.

Beyond Orphan Diseases to Neglected Diseases

In the spring of 2005, as Termeer began testing this idea with his staff, Peter Wirth, Genzyme's corporate counsel, suggested that he talk to his wife Dyann Wirth, chair of the Department of Immunology and Infectious Diseases at the Harvard School of Public Health. It was the first step in an exploration of neglected diseases where Genzyme's capabilities could be brought to bear.

Malaria   In her conversation with Termeer, Dyann Wirth described the work she was doing on malaria in collaboration with the Broad Institute, a joint venture of the Massachusetts Institute of Technology (MIT), Harvard, and the Whitehead Institute. Following that discussion, Termeer asked Geraghty to schedule a follow-up meeting with Wirth and Eric Lander, MIT professor and director of the Broad Institute. At that meeting, Termeer and Geraghty learned that an estimated 500 million people were affected by malaria, a number that was expected to increase to 1 billion by 2025.

[1]March 5, 2001, press article,"South Africa battles for cheap AIDS drugs," http://www.thepost.ohiou.edu/archives3/mar01/030501/brief4.html, accessed August 15, 2009.

They also learned that while malaria caused more than 1 million deaths every year, only 0.3% of global health R&D was spent on its drug research. Geraghty explained the potential for Genzyme to contribute: "We had complementary skills to academics like Wirth and Lander who were experts in basic research focused on drug discovery. Genzyme had skills in translating projects from the research stage to a clinical case. Between us, we could make a real contribution."

Chagas Disease/Sleeping Sickness   Another candidate for the emerging idea of developing cures for neglected diseases was brought to light by conversations Geraghty had with a Brazilian researcher he had met at a malaria conference. They had discussed a parasitic illness called Chagas disease, or American trypanosomiasis. That conversation triggered a recollection. In March 2004, Genzyme had bought Ilex Oncology Inc., a biotechnology company focused on the treatment of bladder cancer, solid tumors, and other forms of cancer. But as part of its oncology repertoire, Ilex had on its shelves a drug called eflornithine, which had been shown to have an unexpected yet positive effect on African trypanosomiasis, or sleeping sickness.

Sleeping sickness is a parasitic disease in people and animals that is transmitted by the tsetse fly. It is especially prevalent in Sub-Saharan Africa and affects around 50,000 to 70,000 people a year. After it was nearly eradicated in the twentieth century, relaxation in control methods led to a resurgence. Although treatments existed, they were highly toxic, and resistance was spreading fast. Early research indicated that eflornithine was very effective in treating Stage II sleeping sickness, with the only problem being that its requirement for intravenous treatment four times per day was too difficult to be practical in remote sections of Africa.

Chagas disease, named after the Brazilian physician Carlos Chagas who first described it in 1909, is caused by a related parasite and is widespread in Latin America. A disease without a vaccine, it is transmitted to humans and other mammals mostly by blood-sucking assassin bugs.

Tuberculosis   A third major neglected disease candidate presented itself in 2006 in discussions that followed an approach from the Global Alliance for TB Drug Development, a New York–based nonprofit dedicated to the discovery and development of faster-acting and more affordable tuberculosis (TB) treatments. Through that contact, Geraghty began to learn about TB, and felt Genzyme might be able to help.

A widespread and highly infectious disease, TB has a footprint across large parts of Africa, China, South Asia, and elsewhere and is responsible for among the highest deaths of all neglected diseases (see **Exhibit 5** for a comparison of neglected

Exhibit 5   Comparison of Key Neglected Diseases

	Malaria	Chagas	Sleeping Sickness	Tuberculosis
Region affected	In the equatorial areas of the Americas, Asia, and Africa. However, 85%–90% of malaria fatalities occur in Sub-Saharan Africa	Mexico, Central and South America	36 countries in Sub-Saharan Africa	Throughout the developing world; 22 "high-burden" countries include India, Pakistan, China, Indonesia, Nigeria, and Bangladesh
Total people affected every year	250 million cases every year	16–18 million	~500,000	~25 million
Total number of people for whom the disease poses a threat	3.3 billion	100 million	60 million	>4 billion
Number of deaths every year	1 million	50,000	>40,000	1.5–2 million
Spread	Caused by protozoan parasites spread by female Anopheles mosquitoes. Two strains: *falciparum* (Africa, India, elsewhere) and *vivax* (mostly in India)	Transmission is mainly through triatomine bugs, which hide during the day, but emerge at night to bite and infect sleeping victims	Infected tsetse fly injects metacyclic trypomastigotes parasite into the skin tissue while biting the mammalian host.	Spread through the air, when people who have the disease cough, sneeze, or spit.

Source: Data collected from interviews with Genzyme executives and from the following websites:
http://www.who.int/mediacentre/factsheets/fs094/ en/index.html, accessed on March 31, 2009.
http://www.who.int/features/factfiles/malaria/en/index.html, accessed on August 12, 2009.
http://www.who.int/ neglected_diseases/diseases/chagas/en/index.html, accessed on March 31, 2009.
http://www.who.int/ mediacentre/factsheets/fs259/en/, accessed on March 31, 2009.
http://www.sleepingsickness.org/Background.html, accessed on August 15, 2009.

diseases). It infects one-third of the world's population and is spread when those with the disease cough or spit, causing new infections at the rate of one per second. Although most of these cases are latent, about 1 in 10 became full-blown TB. If left untreated, the disease will kill more than half its victims. In 2004, there were almost 15 million active chronic cases of TB, 9 million new cases, and 1.6 million deaths in the year, almost all in developing countries.

Despite these disturbing statistics, TB was still being treated by a combination of four drugs developed in the 1960s. Pharmaceutical companies had done little R&D in recent decades due to the disease's concentration in developing countries, which could not afford expensive health care. Drugs were available to less than half of the most infectious cases, and even when they were provided, treatment took six months. The need for constant drug administration and monitoring was beyond the capability of most developing countries, so treatment was often abandoned before it was completed. This had fueled the rise of XDR-TB, a new and highly drug-resistant form of the disease.

▮ Opening a Helping HAND: Forming the Program

With these exploratory discussions in motion, Termeer decided to outline his vision for how Genzyme could contribute to the plight of those suffering from such widespread, neglected diseases. The opening of Genzyme's U.K. R&D center in September 2005 provided him with an opportunity. In his speech dedicating the center, he said: "In the new millennium the challenge will be to find dramatic new ways to serve people suffering from neglected diseases around the world, especially the billions ignored by traditional pharma companies in emerging markets."

Caren Arnstein, vice president of corporate communications at Genzyme, recalled listening to the speech: "Henri's speech caught us all a bit by surprise. He was way ahead of us. But what he said was not only uplifting and inspirational; it also showed his deep personal commitment to act. It was as if he was trying to raise the game for all of us. That's how the HAND initiative was born."

Setting Goals and Guidelines   After many internal conversations, in February 2006, Termeer formed a steering committee of Geraghty; Arnstein; Ted Sybertz, senior vice president of scientific affairs; and Jeff Klinger, vice president of infectious diseases. In April, the committee formally launched the Humanitarian Assistance for Neglected Diseases (HAND) program. Termeer articulated the thinking behind the program's creation: "Genzyme's customers are mostly government agencies that buy expensive medication for rare diseases like Gaucher. In the long term, these organizations are not comfortable engaging on the basis of cold commerce alone, and neither are we. The HAND initiative is Genzyme's way of giving back."

Technically, any entry on the World Health Organization (WHO) list of Neglected Tropical Diseases could qualify for the HAND program. However, the steering committee proposed some simple criteria to guide its choices going ahead (see **Exhibit 6** for minutes from a committee meeting). Projects had to be related to an "important unmet medical need" where Genzyme had "technological capability," "credible partners," and the "ability to afford the next phase of development, ideally with long-term funding."

Geraghty explained the rationale behind the company's strong preference for engaging others in partnerships: "Even if we increased our own investment by two- or threefold to $6 million to $10 million, we would have very little incremental impact. We not only need to leverage our own capabilities, we want to influence others and become an industry role model." He also explained that HAND's objectives were explicitly "beyond narrow commercial interests" and emphasized that Genzyme "would not seek profit from these programs." Indeed, the company committed to make available all intellectual property generated from the HAND program so that partners and governments around the world could benefit.

Building Capability   HAND was going to require significant resources, and the challenge for Genzyme was to provide it with the technology

Exhibit 6   HAND Steering Committee Meeting Minutes, February 2006 (selected text)

Mission of HAND Program

Neglected diseases such as malaria are enormous public health problems in many areas, killing more than a million people each year, mostly children. There is an urgent need to discover new and effective drugs. Industry has a unique contribution to make by applying drug discovery and preclinical development capabilities to create new solutions. In partnership with others, Genzyme seeks to be a catalyst in advancing the development of novel therapies for neglected diseases.

Objectives

- Partner with others in conducting work that can advance the development of novel therapies for important neglected diseases
- Create a vehicle for Genzyme's global health initiative that has a structure and process for screening, selecting and accounting for scientific projects
- Establish a process for making IP available for use in the field

Project Selection Criteria

- Important unmet medical need, ideally recognized as public health priority
- Medically effective product profile, ideally very inexpensive
- Evidence-based scientific rationale, ideally with a well-defined pathway and development plan
- Ability to make a significant impact for patients, ideally using unique capabilities
- Credible academic and medical partners, ideally with a well-organized framework
- Ability to afford the next phase of development, ideally with long-term funding

Source: Interviews with Genzyme executives.

access it needed without compromising the commercial activities that would fund and support the program. (**Exhibit 7** describes Genzyme's R&D operations.)

Like the Gaucher Initiative, HAND created a lot of excitement among employees. Many at the Waltham, Massachusetts, R&D center that housed its projects wanted to contribute, and for the first year or so, researchers mostly worked on the program in their free time. A couple of the first to participate described the excitement: "A lot of people wanted to be on this program, given its social impact. We were just lucky to be among the first employees assigned to projects."

As the exploration of various neglected diseases and potential partnerships expanded, Genzyme found it had to commit more resources to the program. As Klinger described it, "HAND started to transform itself from being a hip-pocket organization to being

more formal, almost a shadow organization." From the employees' perspective, this created issues of being recognized for working on HAND. One project member quipped, "I work on a HAND project, but I also report to my regular cost-center manager. It's like working 150%. At the end of the day, I am not even sure my manager knows what my contribution to the HAND program has been."

Furthermore, as key researchers' time and energy were diverted to the HAND program, there was push-back from cost-center managers and project managers. Jim Burns, who managed resources in Waltham, often had to play the role of referee. "The HAND program is the right thing to do and we can add real value in areas like formulation," he said. "But there is a fine balance and we must not overcommit ourselves." Klinger agreed: "Everyone is after scarce technical resources like DMPK (Drug Metabolism and Pharmacokinetics)

Exhibit 7   R&D, Employee, and CSR Indicators at Genzyme

Indicator	Value in Year 2008
Total number of employees	11,000
Total number of R&D employees[a]	~900
R&D employees at the Waltham center (that housed the HAND projects)	205
Total R&D budget	$750 million
R&D budget for drugs and biomaterials devices division[b]	~$80 million
Average fully loaded cost of 1 R&D FTE	~$300,000
Global product donations (for year 2007)	$110 million
U.S. cash donations (for year 2007)	$14 million

[a]The R&D organization at Genzyme has the following locations: (1) Drug and biomaterials R&D focused on small molecules and biomaterial devices (based in Waltham MA); (2) Therapeutic proteins division focused on cell and gene therapies (based in Framingham MA); (3) Molecular antibiotics division based in Cambridge U.K. and two smaller centers in Oklahoma and San Antonio. The Waltham center had around 205 scientists and engineers. Framingham had around 600 R&D employees, while Cambridge U.K., Oklahoma and San Antonio had around 50, 12 and 12 R&D employees respectively
[b]Most of the remaining R&D budget at Genzyme is allocated to the Therapeutic Proteins division
Source: Data on total employees, total R&D budget from http://www.genzyme.com/corp/structure/fastfacts.asp, accessed on August 12, 2009. Data on number of R&D employees in Waltham, R&D budget for drugs and biomaterials, cost of FTE, and other data, from interviews with Genzyme executives.

and medicinal chemistry[c]—commercial project managers as well the HAND program partners. So the question is not just how many resources HAND needs, but what kinds of resources."

HAND in Hand: Engaging Partners

Along with engaging its own internal resources in HAND, Genzyme also began exploring various partnerships that seemed to offer the potential for collaborative research in each of the identified neglected disease areas. It was a slow, iterative process that gradually identified a portfolio of potential long-term research collaborators.

The DNDi Experience   In 2006, early in its search for partners, Genzyme initiated discussions with the Drugs for Neglected Diseases initiative. DNDi was a global organization formed in 2003 when five public-sector institutions joined forces with leading NGO Doctors Without Borders and the Special

[c]Medicinal chemistry is at the intersection of pharmacology and chemistry and involves testing, synthesizing, and developing chemical entities suitable for therapeutic use.

Programme for Research and Training in Tropical Diseases (TDR) sponsored by the United Nations Development Programme (UNDP), the World Bank, and the World Health Organization (WHO).

Given DNDi's expertise in neglected diseases and its worldwide presence, it appeared to be an ideal partner with which to develop and test novel compounds to treat sleeping sickness. In discussions about this possibility, DNDi seemed glad to involve Genzyme, and even proposed bringing additional partners like the Swiss Tropical Institute into the project to do some testing.

However, DNDi was in the midst of a transition, and the new team took a different view of how development should proceed. DNDi was also sponsoring research on other promising sleeping-sickness drug candidates. Soon, the two organizations started moving in different directions on the project.

The relationship remained cordial, and Genzyme continued to use DNDi facilities to test compounds. But while the possibility of future collaboration remained open, by 2008 the two organizations no longer funded projects jointly. For Genzyme, it was an early lesson in how difficult it could be to pursue an objective on a project where partners had different interests.

The Broad/Harvard/MMV Negotiations   Meanwhile, the malaria work with Broad and Harvard was moving ahead. The Broad Institute would contribute in the area of medicinal chemistry and cheminformatics,[d] the Harvard School of Public Health had expertise in molecular genetics and clinical investigation, and Genzyme would screen its chemical libraries of millions of compounds to check whether any of the compounds were effective in treating the disease targets.

But in this partnership also, differences cropped up—this time over funding. In an initial budget meeting, the partners estimated annual funding needs of about $1.6 million in the first year of the project, increasing to around $6.6 million in year three. Initially, the Broad Institute explored the possibility that Genzyme act as the sponsor for the work at the Broad. After making it clear that they were not in a position to finance the entire program, Genzyme's representatives offered to help raise the money.

The search for both funding and additional capabilities led to the Medicines for Malaria Venture (MMV), a Geneva-based nonprofit organization that focused on the public-private partnership model involving academics, NGOs, and pharma companies like Novartis and GlaxoSmithKline (GSK). With $263 million in funding (much of it from the Gates Foundation), MMV was looking for new partners, and the Broad-Genzyme-Harvard partnership looked very attractive, given the credibility of the partners and their complementary skills. Soon, Genzyme and its partners received funding of $4 million from MMV and began work on five projects focused on malaria.

Looking back, Geraghty saw the early tension with Broad as a blessing in disguise. "It was a pleasant surprise to learn that we also could get funding," he said. "It freed us to contribute our people and technology to the program, without the constraint of funding it 100% ourselves."

The Fiocruz Relationship   In 2006, soon after the HAND program was announced, Latin American general manager Rogerio Vivaldi opened discussions with the Oswald Cruz Institute or Fiocruz, a Brazilian public science organization that was part of the Ministry of Health. It conducted research, produced vaccines, and was involved in public health education. Fiocruz had previously approached Vivaldi with a request for the technology to produce Cerezyme (a later version of Ceredase) in Brazil. Vivaldi had responded by saying that perhaps the two organizations could create more value by working together on neglected diseases like Chagas.

To explore this possibility, Vivaldi proposed sending Fiocruz scientists to Genzyme's Waltham R&D center to learn how to take new therapies through the drug development process. From Genzyme's point of view, while the visit provided a way to get to know this potential partner, it was not without its challenges. "Our most valuable resource is the time and energy of our scientists and those who manage them," said Geraghty. "Clearly a partnership with an organization like Fiocruz makes more of a demand on that resource than a local partnership, but our scientists also learn from it."

The TB Alliance Discussions   As Geraghty continued his discussions with the Global Alliance for TB Drug Development (or the TB Alliance, as it was known), he learned that it was a product development partnership that operated like a virtual biotechnology firm. It had significant financial support from the Gates and Rockefeller foundations as well as several governments worldwide, and used those funds to outsource the development of potential drugs to pharmaceutical companies like Bayer and GSK. However, unlike traditional product development in those companies, the clear objective of these projects was to create treatments that were both affordable and accessible to the developing world.

As an initial project, the TB Alliance proposed funding a specific research program in which Genzyme would take responsibility for screening some existing targets by allocating scientists with DMPK and medicinal chemistry skills to the project.

Geraghty indicated that these were scarce resources at Genzyme, but that he would take the proposal to the company for consideration.

Extending the HAND: Exploring New Opportunities

After almost three years, HAND's activities were beginning to coalesce around the malaria and Chagas projects. But as Geraghty and the HAND steering committee began talking about the program's future, they wondered if they had identified the most appropriate neglected diseases, were engaged in the most effective partnerships, and were applying the most appropriate resources to the program. With a review in process, advocates and champions for each of the options quickly arose.

The Chagas Project: A Champion in Brazil   As soon as the HAND program was announced, Vivaldi had seen an opportunity to link this initiative to the growth of Genzyme's operations in Brazil. Vivaldi was a doctor who had treated Brazil's first Gaucher patient in 1991. After Genzyme opened an office in São Paolo in 1997, Vivaldi had painstakingly built up the operations and had elevated Genzyme Brazil into the top tier of pharmaceutical companies in the country, with 100 employees on its rolls.

While Genzyme Brazil was in a start-up mode, José Serra, São Paulo's mayor, was positioning himself as a presidential candidate in 2002. National health-care reform was a priority for Serra, widely credited with boosting the generics industry in Brazil and creating ANVISA (Agência Nacional de Vigilância Sanitária), the Brazilian food and drug regulatory agency. In this context, Vivaldi succeeded in getting Cerezyme on the list of exceptional drugs for rare diseases, thereby ensuring direct reimbursement from the federal government. In 2008, $100 million of the $108 million in revenues that Genzyme had in Brazil came from federal reimbursements. "Brazil has created a template for emerging markets in Latin America, South Asia, and Eastern Europe," said Geraghty. "We were able to convince governments in countries like Chile and Venezuela to follow the example of Brazil and create programs that supported the treatment of Gaucher."

Still, retaining Cerezyme's place on the coveted list wasn't easy. "There were health-care officials who claimed that they could eradicate tuberculosis in Brazil with the money being a directed into Gaucher," Vivaldi explained. "What really helped us was our commitment to treating poor patients under the Gaucher Initiative and our direct communication with the government." But the list for "exceptional drugs" was coming up for a revision in 2011, and more than 100 drugs had staked their claim to be included, including 5 from Genzyme. To Vivaldi, the HAND project represented an important means of raising Genzyme's profile ahead of that decision.

Following Geraghty's meeting with a leading Fiocruz scientist, Vivaldi began exploring with his Brazilian partner how the two organizations might work together in other disease areas like malaria and tuberculosis. Within Genzyme, he became an extremely strong and passionate advocate for such extended partnership activity.

On the January 2009 HAND conference call, Vivaldi was very upbeat about the Chagas initiative, which he emphasized would be a true giveback to Brazil. He also reminded them that several Brazilian Health Ministry officials had involvement with Fiocruz, and that continued success in the project would enhance Genzyme's credibility with federal health authorities, a particularly important objective, given that the list of federally approved drugs would soon be updated.

The Malaria Initiative: Lobbying in India   On the other side of the world, Sandeep Sahney, managing director of Genzyme India, was equally excited about HAND. Genzyme had entered India in 2002 when it launched Synvisc, a biotech product indicated for the treatment of osteoarthritis of the knee. In 2007, the company hired Sahney, a local industry veteran, to build the organization.

Genzyme was still in a start-up mode in India, compared to its position in Brazil. Even though the government had no program to reimburse Gaucher patients, Genzyme hoped to generate sales of $30 million to $50 million within five years. But without government reimbursement, most of this growth would have to come from sales of treatments for cancer, osteoarthritis, and renal disease to private-practice doctors and for-profit hospitals.

But Sahney also believed that Genzyme had another great untapped opportunity in India—to access world-class R&D resources in government and private labs. He felt that the HAND program provided the ideal platform to bring together resources and ideas across various local labs and tap into that knowledge. Supported by Geraghty and Sybertz, Sahney spent much of 2007 and 2008 in discussions with several Indian public science organizations, like the Council for Scientific and Industrial Research. "The Indian scientific community has great talent, but its people work in silos," Sahney said." Genzyme could help break some of the walls."

Given malaria's widespread occurrence in India, Sahney saw HAND providing an opportunity to begin discussions with ICGEB, a Delhi-based organization working on developing a new vaccine for the disease. "ICGEB is funded by the United Nations and the Indian government, and has great skills in vaccines," Sahney reported. "It has been working on malaria vaccines for 15 years and has deep knowledge of local issues, like how the disease is spread here."

ICGEB also had new expertise to contribute to the project. Most human malaria is caused by two distinct species—*Plasmodium falciparum* and *Plasmodium vivax*. Though most of the existing malaria research (including the Broad-Harvard initiative) was focused on the former, in India 65% of the disease cases were attributed to the latter. This lesser-researched species appeared to have caused more virulent disease in recent years, and ICGEB had demonstrated novel ideas for targets and certain plant-based treatment strategies effective for both *vivax* and *falciparum*.

Genzyme decided to explore this potential partnership, and it was agreed that ICGEB, like Fiocruz, would get rights to all the intellectual property (IP) that came out of the program in the field of neglected diseases. But early communication problems with the new Indian collaborators underscored how challenging cross-border partnerships could be. Klinger recalled, "On an early video conference call, I was bringing the discussion to a close by listing the seven initiatives that seemed to interest

people. But when I asked for suggestions about how to prioritize them, someone on the Indian side said, 'It's very inefficient to prioritize. Why not do all of them at the same time?' At that point, it was clear that our approaches might be different."

Meanwhile, Genzyme had committed to a partnership with Advinus, an Indian research company with great skills in chemistry, DMPK, and crystallography. But the deal with Advinus was fundamentally different from that with ICGEB: the partner would be paid on an hourly basis for specific assignments, and its services would be used on an "as needed basis" by multiple HAND program teams, including the Broad and Harvard malaria research team.

With time, the ICGEB relationship had overcome some of the initial cultural barriers, and on the conference call, Sahney was passionate about the need to support this emerging partnership. He explained that malaria, especially the *vivax* strain, was a real unsolved problem in India, and ICGEB had shown great promise by coming up with concrete ideas on molecules that could be tested. He firmly believed that success in this project would position Genzyme as an "Indian" R&D player and build its reputation with the local medical and research communities. Sahney also suggested that the Indian malaria template could be used in other countries like Brazil and in parts of Africa.

The TB Option: A Voice in the Center   Meanwhile, at Genzyme's Cambridge, Massachusetts, headquarters, Geraghty wanted to keep questioning the assumptions and challenging the priorities that shaped HAND's future direction. In that role, one of the issues he had kept alive was the question about whether Genzyme could devote resources and capabilities to helping develop treatments for TB.

A year after Geraghty's initial contact with the TB Alliance in 2006, the CEO with whom he had been having discussions resigned and the relationship stalled. In 2008, at a Gates Foundation meeting, he struck up a conversation with the new CEO, and promptly invited him to visit Genzyme. "We sat down with scientists from both organizations to discuss collaborative possibilities," said Geraghty. "We all learned a lot, but had difficulty finding a way to get started. Beyond our normal worry about being stretched too thin, some of our people expressed concerns that we did not know much about TB. But as I pointed out, we didn't know much about malaria either until the HAND program started."

About this time, Geraghty was also contacted by scientists working on TB at the Harvard School of Public Health (led by outgoing dean Barry Bloom, a world authority on TB) and at the Broad Institute. The scientists had developed novel assays and had identified unique targets for TB drugs using sophisticated genomic analyses and felt that Genzyme could help move them forward, as in the case of malaria. Geraghty offered assistance on project management, but the relationship did not develop. Still, it was a potential resource that might be engaged in the future.

One question the HAND steering committee faced was deciding which neglected diseases offered the most effective use of its scarce resources going forward. By this criterion, TB demanded attention because it was such a massive global health-care problem. In comparison, the number of people affected by Chagas was relatively small and its impact was focused on Central and South America (see **Exhibit 5**).While malaria was more widespread and had higher morbidity and mortality rates, it had recently attracted significant funding and technological resources, particularly due to its priority status within the Gates Foundation. One outcome of this was that in early 2009, Bill Gates announced a potential breakthrough vaccine that could be ready by 2014.[2] Given the large number of global players and the significant resources aimed at malaria's cure, some industry observers had begun questioning whether it could still be classified as a "neglected disease."

In contrast, despite the fact that TB was a worldwide problem with among the highest mortality rates, it received much less global attention. In that context, Geraghty wondered whether Genzyme should restart discussions with the TB Alliance, the Harvard School of Public Health, and the Broad Institute. "I remain a champion for HAND to consider TB because I think

it is good if we keep questioning how we are using our scarce resources," he said. And a project with partners based in New York and Boston could be a lot easier to manage than one linked into Brazil or India.

On One HAND: Weighing the Options

After presenting their cases, the two invited guests dropped off the conference call, leaving the steering committee members to review some of the other opportunities and risk factors they would have to take into account in making their recommendations about HAND's future direction and priorities.

END of U.S. Government Inaction   On the positive side, Genzyme and its partners had received good news from Washington, where the U.S. Senate had recently adopted the Elimination of Neglected Diseases Act (END) amendment to the Food and Drug Administration Reauthorization Bill. The END Act would award a "treatment priority review voucher" to any company that brought to market a treatment for a neglected disease.

The voucher, which could be used for any new drug coming up for review, would ensure that an FDA priority review could be completed in about 6 months compared to 18 months under a regular review. The 12 months saved could be worth up to $300 million to a pharma or biotech company—perhaps more for a blockbuster drug. Senator Sam Brownback commented: "We are blessed to live in a nation in which diseases like malaria and cholera are not serious threats, but must not forget that one-sixth of the world's population faces death and suffering from easily treatable diseases... Private companies have the potential to be major players in the fight against neglected diseases."[3]

The IP Risk: The Novartis Experience   Of greater concern to the HAND steering committee were developments involving an ongoing patent dispute between Novartis and the Indian government. After Indian regulatory authorities refused to grant Novartis a patent on its cancer drug Glivec, Novartis

[2]Gates Foundation, annual letter, p. 15, http://www.gatesfoundation .org/annual-letter/Documents/2009-bill-gates-annual-letter.pdf, accessed August 15, 2009.

[3]News release,"Brownback Applauds Adoption of Neglected Diseases Amendment" September 21, 2007, http://brownback.senate.gov/public/ press/record.cfm?id=283848, accessed August 15, 2009.

had taken legal action challenging India's 2005 law, which allowed patents to be refused for drug modifications that could not prove significant increases in the original drug's efficacy. The company contended that this was in violation of WTO rules relating to trade-related intellectual property rights.[4]

The appeal created headlines, causing several NGOs to strongly criticize Novartis's actions. For example, a spokesman for Doctors Without Borders, an organization that relied on India as a source of 84% of its generic AIDS drugs, said, "People the world over who rely on India as a source of their medicines may be affected if Novartis gets its way."[5] After pointing out that 99% of patients treated with Glivec in India received it free from Novartis, a company spokesman said, "Our actions in India do not hinder the supply of medicines to poor countries given the international safeguards now in place. We are seeking clarity about India's laws ... We believe that limiting patents only to new chemical entities does not recognize genuine innovation. Medical progress happens through steps in innovation, also called incremental innovation."[6]

Through its contact with Novartis at MMV, Genzyme had become increasingly aware of the company's commitment to finding cures for neglected diseases. In addition to its involvement in nine MMV projects, it had created its own nonprofit Institute for Tropical Diseases in collaboration with the Singapore Economic Development Board. But, apparently, these commitments to developing countries' needs had not carried much weight with the Indian government.

As corporate counsel, Peter Wirth was concerned about these developments. Previously a respected partner at a Boston law firm, Wirth was known to ask difficult but insightful questions within Genzyme. "While most of us would be looking at the bright side, Peter would be thinking of the potential risks and pulling us back to reality," said Geraghty. Taking that

role, Wirth challenged the HAND committee to think about what implications the Novartis case held for Genzyme—its relationships with India, its intellectual property positions, and even its altruistic motives.

The question led Geraghty to reflect on a recent Gates Foundation discussion about how to stimulate more corporate research involvement in neglected diseases. The two major impediments cited by most companies were the difficulty of making money in neglected diseases and the fear of losing control of their intellectual property. Rightly or wrongly, they believed some developing countries did not have the same respect for IP as most developed countries did.

The Management Challenge: Managing Partnerships and Expectations Wirth also articulated concerns about "setting the right expectations" with Genzyme's various partners, especially those in developing countries where each party's future hopes and expectations were not always made clear. He recalled that during the Gaucher Initiative, its government and NGO partners had expressed strong concerns when Genzyme eventually applied for partial reimbursement for supplying Cerezyme to patients in Egypt when the local health-care system could eventually afford it. This had led to tensions and disputes that Wirth did not want to repeat.

In his opinion, Genzyme would have to clearly define upfront where it could help and where it could not. However, with the barriers of language, culture, and distance, Wirth saw lots of opportunity for miscommunication. "It will be imperative for us to etch a strong impression in the minds of partners, governments, and the public at large of our constraints and limitations," he said.

Geraghty too was concerned about the increasing network of complex partnerships. Although the initial start-up challenges with DNDi and Broad had taught him important lessons, over the last couple of years, HAND had added many more partners to its projects. The sleeping sickness team now included Pace University in New York, the Swiss Tropical Institute, and most recently, Fiocruz in Brazil. In addition to Broad and Harvard, the malaria initiative now involved ICGEB and Advinus, with

[4]http://www.medicalnewstoday.com/articles/61932.php, accessed August 15, 2009.

[5]http://doctorswithoutborders.org/press/release.cfm?id=1870, accessed August 15, 2009.

[6] Novartis release, http://www.novartis.com/downloads/about-novartis/Novartis_position-Glivec_Gleevec_patent_case_india.pdf, accessed August 15, 2009.

Fiocruz showing interest. "It takes a lot to manage all these relationships," said Geraghty. "Maintaining the managerial bandwidth to deal with this level of complexity is very challenging."

The Resource Decision: Allocating Funds and Capabilities   HAND had moved far beyond the part-time volunteer staffing of its early days, and by 2009, there were around 10 employees in Waltham working virtually full-time on its projects. With the fully loaded cost of an employee at around $300,000, this was an annual investment of around $3 million. In addition, Klinger's title was now vice president of infectious diseases and neglected diseases, with

---

Exhibit 8   Malaria–Scientific Strategy and Skills of Partners

Recent scientific breakthroughs

- Sequencing of multiple strains of *P. falciparum* has provided information on available targets and their diversity.
- High-density genetic mapping (HapMap) has enabled detailed mapping of genes responsible for disease severity and drug resistance.
- New drug-discovery efforts focused on Protease inhibitors.

	Novel Target Discovery	Compound Screening	Lead Selection & Optimization	Preclinical Development	Clinical Trials & Approvals
Genzyme	Support role	Lead role: make libraries comprising millions of compounds available for screening to find 'hits' with target	Lead role: design and synthesize hundreds of analogues of 'hits' to improve property of 'hits'	Lead role: confirm potency and safety of drug using animal and lab tests	Support role
Broad & Harvard	Lead role: lead biology research in identifying potential intervention points (targets) for the disease	Lead role: contribute library of 120,000 compounds to screen compounds to screen for anti-plasmodial activity using Kan reactors	Lead role: share medicinal chemistry effort with Genzyme	Lead role: share cheminformatics effort with Genzyme	Support role
MMV	Support role	Support role	Support role	Support role	Lead role: organize testing and animal models
ICGEB	Lead role: target ideas for vivax and falciparum	Support role	Support role	Support role on cheminformatics	Possible support role

Source: Interviews with Genzyme executives.

the latter designation reflecting the amount of time and attention he was now giving to HAND.

Watching this growing activity, Wirth questioned whether Genzyme could sustainably invest the financial and human resources to manage multiple programs and partners. He urged the committee to balance global medical need with the best fit of technology and partner (**Exhibits 5, 8,** and **9** provide data). He also worried that pursuing too

many initiatives would lead to less oversight and therefore greater risk.

• • •

With all this advice ringing in his ears, Geraghty knew that the time for analysis was over. Now was the time for decisions. Termeer would be expecting the HAND steering committee to provide some clear proposals about which projects to undertake, which partners to engage, and what resources to allocate to them.

Exhibit 9   Chagas–Scientific Strategy and Skills of Partners

Recent scientific breakthroughs

- Two focus areas: (1) Identifying novel biological targets within the parasite that causes Chagas disease; (2) Test effectiveness of using monoclonal antibodies to neutralize a protein that contributes to heart damage in Chagas disease.
- New drug discovery efforts focused on Megazol Analogs.

	Novel Target Discovery	Compound Screening	Lead Selection & Optimization	Preclinical Development	Clinical Trials & Approvals
Genzyme	Support role	Lead role: make libraries comprising million of compounds available for screening to find 'hits' with target. Also test compounds that have been effective in sleeping sickness parasite	Lead role: design and synthesize hundreds of analogues of 'hits' to improve property of 'hits'	Lead role: confirm potency and safety of drug using animal and lab tests	Support role
Fiocruz	Lead role: scientists at Fiocruz have developed metabolic maps of the Trypanosoma cruzi parasite that causes the disease; these maps will be used to explore specific metabolic pathways that may serve as targets for potential drugs	Support role	Support role	Support role	Support role

Source: Interviews with Genzyme executives.

Reading 8-1   A Global Leader's Guide to Managing Business Conduct

by Lynn S. Paine, Rohit Deshpandé, and Joshua D. Margolis

Managers working outside their home environments often find that their companies' norms are inconsistent with practices followed by other businesses in the area. In response, many follow the time-honored advice given in the fourth century by the bishop of Milan to Augustine of Hippo: When in Rome, do as the Romans do.

But that's a perilous approach. Consider the outrage in the United States when the media reported that BP oil rigs in the Gulf of Mexico lacked safeguards required on similar machinery in Norway and Brazil—even though the failed equipment in the Gulf met U.S. legal requirements. Or the worldwide outcry over working conditions at Foxconn in China after some employees committed suicide, although the company's factories were arguably no worse than thousands of others nearby. Or consider the hot water that Siemens, Lucent, and DaimlerChrysler landed in after paying bribes and making various types of side payments that were common in the countries where the companies were operating.

These and other incidents show that conformance with local law and practice does not guarantee stakeholder or public approval of a corporation's behavior. But does that mean companies should automatically default to their home-country practices?

Our research suggests that the answer is no. In surveys of more than 6,200 employees from the top ranks to the front lines of four leading multinationals based in the U.S., Europe, and Japan, we found a strong consensus on basic standards of conduct that companies should follow worldwide. Our findings indicate, further, that meeting those standards

will require new approaches to managing business conduct. The compliance and ethics programs of most companies today fall short of addressing multinationals' basic responsibilities—such as developing their people or delivering high-quality products—let alone such vexing issues as how to stay competitive in markets where rivals follow different rules. Instead of intensifying their focus on compliance, companies must bring to the management of business conduct the same performance tools and concepts that they use to manage quality, innovation, and financial results. Leaders need an approach that is guided by global standards, informed by systematic data, grounded in the business context, and focused on positive goals.

This need is particularly acute right now. Despite the widespread adoption of ethics programs by companies around the world in recent decades, failures of corporate responsibility are all too frequent and public trust in business remains distressingly low. At the same time, expectations continue to rise. The UK created a new antibribery law that took effect July 1, 2011, and broadens the range of companies—both domestic and foreign—that can be prosecuted in the UK for bribery or for failure to prevent bribery by an associated person or entity, regardless of where the offending act took place.

In this article, we offer guidelines for navigating the increasingly rugged ethical terrain that multinationals face every day.

Identify Your Conduct Gaps

Government officials and members of the public aren't the only ones calling for better business conduct. Employees, too, see a need for improvement in corporate behavior. Surveys we conducted in 2006 and 2007 at some of the world's leading global

Lynn S. Paine is a John G. McLean Professor of Business Administration,
Rohit Deshpandé is the Sebastian S. Kresge Professor of Marketing, and
Joshua D. Margolis is the James Dinan and Elizabeth Miller Professor of Business Administration at Harvard Business School.

corporations reveal that while there is a strong consensus on the standards that should be met, many employees feel that their companies don't fully live up to those standards. (See the exhibit "The Conduct Gap.")

The Conduct Gap

Surveys we conducted at leading multinational corporations show that employees tend to agree on what companies should do, but many believe their employers don't fully live up to those standards; we also found greater consensus among employees on what companies should do as compared with what their own companies actually do.

The surveys, whose findings have been supported by a companion study of global executives that has 880 respondents to date, show that employees from every level in those organizations strongly support adherence to the 62 standards in the Global Business Standards Codex, which we developed some years ago on the basis of leading codes of corporate conduct. These standards, described in our 2005 HBR article "Up to Code," cover all of a company's responsibilities, from respecting employees' dignity to refraining from bribery to creating innovative products and technologies.

Despite wide differences in cultural origins and business environments, the employees, when asked

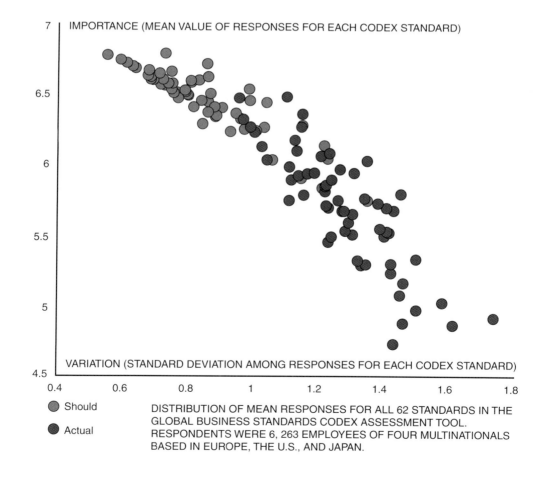

IMPORTANCE (MEAN VALUE OF RESPONSES FOR EACH CODEX STANDARD)

VARIATION (STANDARD DEVIATION AMONG RESPONSES FOR EACH CODEX STANDARD)

● Should
● Actual

DISTRIBUTION OF MEAN RESPONSES FOR ALL 62 STANDARDS IN THE GLOBAL BUSINESS STANDARDS CODEX ASSESSMENT TOOL. RESPONDENTS WERE 6, 263 EMPLOYEES OF FOUR MULTINATIONALS BASED IN EUROPE, THE U.S., AND JAPAN.

the extent to which they thought companies should adhere to each of the standards, responded with an average value of 6.44 on a scale of 1 to 7. Even on items that we thought would be controversial—such as respecting dignity and human rights—we found strong support. These surveys bolster our earlier research, in which we hypothesized an emerging consensus on widely accepted standards of conduct for global companies, and they belie the assumption that relativism should guide cross-border business practices.

But the gap between "should" and "do" was troubling: The average score on adherence to the standards was just 5.68 on the same seven-point scale. Moreover, we found a greater range of responses on the actuals than on the shoulds, which means employee perceptions of what their companies do are more varied than their perceptions of what the companies should do. Although every company will have a different profile of gaps between its conduct and what employees feel that conduct should be, we observed three patterns that we suspect are widespread.

The altitude effect. Those at the top of the corporate hierarchy generally have a more positive view of their companies' conduct. For the bulk of the standards, respondents who identified themselves as corporate or division-level executives reported smaller gaps between "should" and "do" than those who identified themselves as middle management, junior management, or non-management employees. The altitude effect was most pronounced for employee-related issues, but it was also strongly in evidence for basic standards of business integrity such as fair dealing and promise keeping and for basic standards of human welfare such as protecting health and safety. Whether the rosier view from the top indicates that executives are better informed or that they are merely out of touch, the discrepancy between their assessments and those offered by other employees is cause for some concern. At the very least, it indicates that executives need to rely on more than their own views to assess their companies' ethical performance.

Basics matter. We found that gaps for standards of business integrity were among the widest.

Although environmental issues emerged, somewhat predictably, with wide gaps, we also found larger-than-average gaps for fair dealing, promise keeping, and conflict-of-interest disclosure. These findings are a reminder that business leaders must remain vigilant about basic business integrity even as they strive to meet emerging standards of corporate citizenship concerning the environment, human rights, and supplier practices.

Employees are an early-alert system. Gaps relating to fair compensation, responsiveness to employees' concerns, communication with employees, and developing employees' skills topped the list. In the next tier, not far below, were gaps relating to free association, employee dignity, equal employment opportunity, and employment dislocations. Employees may well be most sensitive to practices that affect them, but that shouldn't provide much solace to executives. A large body of research has consistently shown that employees who feel mistreated exact a cost from the company, and many companies espouse the importance of treating employees the way they want employees to treat customers. The sizable gaps we found on employee standards may be an early warning of brewing trouble.

Develop Data-Driven Tools

With governments, the public, and employees expressing a desire to see better corporate behavior, how can companies take measurable steps to improve their conduct?

While many executives say that their companies adhere to the highest ethical standards, very few have data to assess the stringency of those standards or even a way to determine what standards their companies actually follow. Instead they typically point with pride to the company's written code, the excellent people the company hires, or how some particular misdeed was handled.

Such unsubstantiated claims would be unacceptable in any other aspect of business. An executive who claimed that his company's sales were among the best in the industry but whose only evidence was the company's written sales plan, its great salespeople, or last week's big sale would quickly be shown the door and perhaps even sued for fraud or negligence. The lack of data and rigor in assessing and managing business conduct is tolerated because many assume that ethics and conduct are "soft" topics not amenable to measurement or evaluation.

To be sure, many companies do track the use of their hotlines and collect data on alleged code-of-conduct violations. And some companies do survey employees on their perceptions of company values or adherence to espoused standards. What is largely lacking, however, is a systematic approach to assessing company performance on the standards of conduct that are expected of leading companies today.

To address this problem and help leaders more accurately gauge their companies' ethical performance, we developed an assessment tool based on the Global Business Standards Codex to survey the four global companies. Compared with more-common assessment tools, this one has several important features. First, it is based on objective rather than subjective standards (those that the company has chosen) that we have found to be widely accepted by diverse business, government, and multisector groups. Second, it generates data from throughout the company—up and down the hierarchy and across multiple units—and covers multiple dimensions of performance. Third, it focuses not just on negative standards and the prevalence of misconduct but on positive standards and the company's performance against affirmative benchmarks.

The codex assessment tool allows business leaders to construct an organization-wide picture of the company's ethical strengths, weaknesses, and performance. Admittedly, it captures perceptions and beliefs rather than actual behavior, and perceptions can be mistaken. (An independent third-party assessment would be useful additional input.) But perceptions from a broad and diverse group of employees are a useful first approximation of actual conduct—and perceptions are crucial in and of themselves, because they drive attitudes and opinions within the company. They are also useful for helping managers take three necessary steps: identifying issues that need further inquiry, pinpointing

potential risks to the company and its reputation, and finding areas of strength and opportunities for learning.

The Global Business Standards Project

In response to a lack of clear, comprehensive guidelines for the conduct of global companies, we set out in 2004 to create a business-ethics index that companies could use to benchmark their behavior over time.

As a first step, we systematically analyzed a select group of codes of corporate conduct. Distilling precepts from 23 sources, including 14 of the world's largest companies and institutions—among them the United Nations, the OECD, the Global Reporting Initiative, and the Caux Round Table—we created the Global Business Standards Codex, a compilation of widely endorsed standards.

We then conducted multilanguage field surveys to determine the extent to which businesspeople around the world believe that companies should—and do—adhere to these standards. Two data sets emerged from this work, which drew on respondents from some 23 countries and regions: findings from 880 executives in Harvard Business School's Advanced Management Program (2006 to the present), and survey results from more than 6,200 employees of four leading global companies (2006 and 2007).

Go Beyond Compliance-as-Usual

Over the past two decades, many executives have appointed chief compliance officers and established programs to foster adherence to their companies' codes of conduct. A typical compliance program comprises best-practice elements—from a defined set of conduct standards and policies to an implementation and oversight structure that goes all the way up to the board of directors, often via the board's audit committee or a compliance committee. Companies that follow such programs communicate their standards to employees, appoint ombudspeople, set up anonymous hotlines, and install monitoring and auditing processes to ferret out code violations and risks. They are quick to respond to violations by going after the causes and the offenders.

These programs are predicated on a well-functioning legal system, and their approach to influencing behavior relies heavily on the lawyer's tool kit of rules and penalties. Violations are presumed to originate with individuals acting against otherwise prevailing norms, so the idea is to detect and deter breaches by fostering transparency and strengthening disincentives. The apparatus is focused on activities inside the organization and is largely indifferent to the economic and societal context in which the organization operates. Moreover, it is much the same whatever the business and whatever the content of the code.

But this approach seems markedly out of step with other areas of business practice. Our research suggests the need for richer tools and a more contextual approach to improving ethical performance. When we delved more deeply into the gaps between "should" and "do," we found that aspects of the broader context in which respondents were working related to the size of the gaps they reported. In particular, we found that employees in the emerging markets of China, India, Brazil, and Southeast Asia reported larger gaps than those in the United States, the UK, Western Europe, and Japan. More generally, those in low-income countries reported larger gaps than those in middle- and high-income ones. The discrepancy between emerging and developed markets was in evidence across a wide range of areas—from competitive practices and employee development to community relations and anticorruption efforts. In only one area—providing customers with accurate information about products and services—did developed-market respondents report significantly larger gaps than emerging-market respondents.

Gaps associated with broad contextual factors such as the economic and legal environments are difficult to address with a compliance program focused on detecting and deterring individual violators. For such factors, low adherence to the codex standards may have more to do with the environment in which people are working than with deficiencies in the character or motivation of particular individuals, so replacing one set of employees with another is unlikely to make much of a difference.

What's needed is a multifaceted response that takes account of how legal or economic differences shape behavior and support (or discourage) adherence to the standards in question.

Consider the large gaps for workplace health and safety that we found in some regions. As many companies have learned, an effective program for improving workplace safety may include investment in equipment and infrastructure, redesign of facilities, changes in work processes, education and training of employees, and modification of performance measures. Engagement with external parties—to establish standards, improve enforcement practices, and focus public attention on safety—may also be required. None of these elements is included in the typical compliance tool kit.

Similarly, efforts to combat bribery in an environment where corruption is widespread must be multifaceted. Instructing employees to "just say no" and punishing violators may work, but it carries a risk to the business and may drive corruption further underground. A more promising approach recognizes that the best protection against corruption is a superior product that adds value for the customer and is not readily available elsewhere. Excellent sales and marketing skills are also important, because without them sales personnel are much more dependent on supplying personal favors, gifts, and entertainment. As in the case of workplace safety, changes in internal processes may be required—for example, approvals for certain marketing expenses—and it may be essential to engage with external parties such as standard setters, regulatory officials, and anticorruption groups.

The usual compliance tool kit is useful for reinforcing certain standards in certain operating environments, but as these examples show, business leaders will need a much more extensive set of tools to improve performance in many of the gap areas identified by our research. It is not enough to establish codes of conduct, oversight structures, reporting processes, and disciplinary systems. Managers also need to examine core aspects of the business and the operating environment and craft a performance-improvement plan that is tailored to those specifics using the full range of management tools at their disposal—from product, process, and plant design to employee training, development, and motivation; marketing strategy; external relations; and community engagement. Leaders must change the context within which people are working. To do so, they will need to go well beyond the activities performed by the typical compliance and ethics function.

Revise Your Mental Model

Many executives who are serious about business conduct view the challenge with the legalistic mentality that informs most compliance programs. This mentality is characterized by binary categories—ethical versus unethical, compliant versus noncompliant, legal versus illegal—that leave little room for degrees of performance or gradual improvement. It focuses on standards requiring or prohibiting actions that can be readily specified in advance, such as rules against bribery, insider trading, or collusion among competitors. Executives in this camp sometimes pride themselves on having zero tolerance for unethical behavior or for insisting that ethics are nonnegotiable; compliance must be immediate, and it must be complete.

Although compliance thinking and zero tolerance have their place, our research underscores the need for business leaders to see a profile of corporate conduct that is broad, dynamic, and affirmative.

By broad, we mean including not just "Thou shalt not . . ." but also the standards that have traditionally been called "imperfect duties." Unlike legalistic standards that require specific acts or omissions, imperfect duties allow for a significant degree of freedom in how they may be satisfied. Consider, for example, the codex standards on respecting employee dignity and on fair treatment of minority shareholders. The actions required to meet those standards cannot be easily stated in generic, auditable terms. A full third of the codex standards are of this indefinite type. (One-third are definite, and one-third are of a mixed character.) We found that in general, gaps are larger for indefinite than for definite standards. Indeed, among the largest gaps revealed in our multinational

surveys, about half were associated with standards that are indefinite or mixed in nature—for example, providing employees with fair compensation, protecting the environment, helping employees develop skills and knowledge, and, among emerging-market respondents, cooperating with others to eliminate bribery and corruption. A company stuck in a compliance mind-set may be patrolling violations effectively while missing out on crucial opportunities to upgrade its performance in these ethical areas.

By dynamic, we mean capturing how performance shifts over time. As macroeconomic and industry conditions change, the pressures and opportunities that shape individual and company conduct also change. Periodic assessments of how the company is performing on the codex standards are crucial for spotting emerging risks and opportunities.

By affirmative, we mean treating ethics as goals to strive for rather than just lapses to avoid. Business leaders will need to think in terms of continuous improvement as they seek to create the conditions and institutions necessary to support adherence to the whole range of codex standards across differing operating contexts.

A broad, dynamic, and affirmative approach to managing business conduct represents a new way of looking at corporate ethics. For companies to foster this new way, a corporate-conduct dashboard may prove essential. Using data gathered with the codex assessment tool, managers can provide a snapshot of the company's performance on key indicators to make conduct issues across the organization visible to business leaders. The data can be aggregated in various ways. For instance, they can be organized to show the extent to which employees support the "should" consensus or how employees rate the company's performance on ethical principles or responsibilities to stakeholders.

The dashboard can also convey the largest gaps as seen by employees across the company and within different business units, regions, functions, and hierarchical levels. Depending on how the data are analyzed, it can allow for more-granular comparisons of gaps for particular standards—or topic areas—across various geographies and business units. For instance, results for the cluster of standards relating to the environment can be aggregated, and an indicator for environmental issues in different regions can be included in the dashboard.

A codex dashboard is only the beginning of a conversation. To understand what accounts for the findings that it captures, managers and directors will need to look beneath the surface and to interpret the indicators with care and judgment in light of other facts and data. Still, a codex dashboard can help executives shift from what they sense to what systematic data reveal and from a compliance-oriented review of hotline usage, investigations, and disciplinary actions to a more holistic examination of the company's overall performance on critical standards. Instead of debating whether a spike in reported cases is good (because it shows that employees are not afraid to use the reporting system) or bad (because misconduct is, in fact, escalating), business heads and board members can focus on where the threats and opportunities may lie and how the company can achieve its conduct goals.

With an enriched tool kit and new ways of thinking, business leaders can, we hope, improve their companies' ability to perform to the standards increasingly expected of multinationals the world over. We think that doing so is crucial for maintaining the public's trust in business and the free-market system.

Reading 8-2   Serving the World's Poor, Profitably

by C.K. Prahalad and Allen Hammond

Consider this bleak vision of the world 15 years from now: The global economy recovers from its current stagnation but growth remains anemic. Deflation continues to threaten, the gap between rich and poor keeps widening, and incidents of economic chaos, governmental collapse, and civil war plague developing regions. Terrorism remains a constant threat, diverting significant public and private resources to security concerns. Opposition to the global market system intensifies. Multinational companies find it difficult to expand, and many become risk averse, slowing investment and pulling back from emerging markets.

Now consider this much brighter scenario: Driven by private investment and widespread entrepreneurial activity, the economies of developing regions grow vigorously, creating jobs and wealth and bringing hundreds of millions of new consumers into the global marketplace every year. China, India, Brazil, and, gradually, South Africa become new engines of global economic growth, promoting prosperity around the world. The resulting decrease in poverty produces a range of social benefits, helping to stabilize many developing regions and reduce civil and cross-border conflicts. The threat of terrorism and war recedes. Multinational companies expand rapidly in an era of intense innovation and competition.

Both of these scenarios are possible. Which one comes to pass will be determined primarily by one factor: the willingness of big, multinational companies to enter and invest in the world's poorest markets. By stimulating commerce and development at the bottom of the economic pyramid, MNCs could radically improve the lives of billions of people and help bring into being a more stable, less dangerous world. Achieving this goal does not require multinationals to spearhead global social development initiatives for charitable purposes. They need only

C.K. Prahalad is the Harvey C. Fruehauf Professor of Business Administration at the University of Michigan Business School in Ann Arbor and the chairman of Praja, a software company in San Diego. Allen Hammond is the CIO, senior scientist, and director of the Digital Dividend project at the World Resources Institute in Washington, DC.

act in their own self-interest, for there are enormous business benefits to be gained by entering developing markets. In fact, many innovative companies—entrepreneurial outfits and large, established enterprises alike—are already serving the world's poor in ways that generate strong revenues, lead to greater operating efficiencies, and uncover new sources of innovation. For these companies—and those that follow their lead—building businesses aimed at the bottom of the pyramid promises to provide important competitive advantages as the twenty-first century unfolds.

Big companies are not going to solve the economic ills of developing countries by themselves, of course. It will also take targeted financial aid from the developed world and improvements in the governance of the developing nations themselves. But it's clear to us that prosperity can come to the poorest regions only through the direct and sustained involvement of multinational companies. And it's equally clear that the multinationals can enhance their own prosperity in the process.

Untapped Potential

Everyone knows that the world's poor are distressingly plentiful. Fully 65% of the world's population earns less than $2,000 each per year—that's 4 billion people. But despite the vastness of this market, it remains largely untapped by multinational companies. The reluctance to invest is easy to understand. Companies assume that people with such low incomes have little to spend on goods and services and that what they do spend goes to basic needs like food and shelter. They also assume that various barriers to commerce—corruption, illiteracy, inadequate infrastructure, currency fluctuations, bureaucratic red tape—make it impossible to do business profitably in these regions.

But such assumptions reflect a narrow and largely outdated view of the developing world. The fact is, many multinationals already successfully do business in developing countries (although most currently focus on selling to the small upper-middle-class segments of these markets), and their experience shows that the barriers to commerce—although

real—are much lower than is typically thought. Moreover, several positive trends in developing countries—from political reform, to a growing openness to investment, to the development of low-cost wireless communication networks—are reducing the barriers further while also providing businesses with greater access to even the poorest city slums and rural areas. Indeed, once the misperceptions are wiped away, the enormous economic potential that lies at the bottom of the pyramid becomes clear.

Take the assumption that the poor have no money. It sounds obvious on the surface, but it's wrong. While individual incomes may be low, the aggregate buying power of poor communities is actually quite large. The average per capita income of villagers in rural Bangladesh, for instance, is less than $200 per year, but as a group they are avid consumers of telecommunications services. Grameen Telecom's village phones, which are owned by a single entrepreneur but used by the entire community, generate an average revenue of roughly $90 a month—and as much as $1,000 a month in some large villages. Customers of these village phones, who pay cash for each use, spend an average of 7% of their income on phone services—a far higher percentage than consumers in traditional markets do.

It's also incorrect to assume that the poor are too concerned with fulfilling their basic needs to "waste" money on nonessential goods. In fact, the poor often do buy "luxury" items. In the Mumbai shantytown of Dharavi, for example, 85% of households own a television set, 75% own a pressure cooker and a mixer, 56% own a gas stove, and 21% have telephones. That's because buying a house in Mumbai, for most people at the bottom of the pyramid, is not a realistic option. Neither is getting access to running water. They accept that reality, and rather than saving for a rainy day, they spend their income on things they can get now that improve the quality of their lives.

Another big misperception about developing markets is that the goods sold there are incredibly cheap and, hence, there's no room for a new competitor to come in and turn a profit. In reality, consumers at the bottom of the pyramid pay much higher prices for most things than middle-class consumers do, which means that there's a real opportunity for companies, particularly big corporations with economies of scale and efficient supply chains, to capture market share by offering higher quality goods at lower prices while maintaining attractive margins. In fact, throughout the developing world, urban slum dwellers pay, for instance, between four and 100 times as much for drinking water as middle- and upper-class families. Food also costs 20% to 30% more in the poorest communities since there is no access to bulk discount stores. On the service side of the economy, local moneylenders charge interest of 10% to 15% *per day,* with annual rates running as high as 2,000%. Even the lucky small-scale entrepreneurs who get loans from nonprofit microfinance institutions pay between 40% and 70% interest per year—rates that are illegal in most developed countries. (For a closer look at how the prices of goods compare in rich and poor areas, see the exhibit "The High-Cost Economy of the Poor.")

It can also be surprisingly cheap to market and deliver products and services to the world's poor. That's because many of them live in cities that are densely populated today and will be even more so in the years to come. Figures from the UN and the World Resources Institute indicate that by 2015, in Africa,

225 cities will each have populations of more than 1 million; in Latin America, another 225; and in Asia, 903. The population of at least 27 cities will reach or exceed 8 million. Collectively, the 1,300 largest cities will account for some 1.5 billion to 2 billion people, roughly half of whom will be bottom-of-the-pyramid (BOP) consumers now served primarily by informal economies. Companies that operate in these areas will have access to millions of potential new customers, who together have billions of dollars to spend. The poor in Rio de Janeiro, for instance, have a total purchasing power of $1.2 billion ($600 per person). Shantytowns in Johannesburg or Mumbai are no different.

The slums of these cities already have distinct ecosystems, with retail shops, small businesses, schools, clinics, and moneylenders. Although there are few reliable estimates of the value of commercial transactions in slums, business activity appears to be thriving. Dharavi—covering an area of just 435 acres—boasts scores of businesses ranging from leather, textiles, plastic recycling, and surgical sutures to gold jewelry, illicit liquor, detergents, and groceries. The scale of the businesses varies from one-person operations to bigger, well-recognized producers of brand-name products. Dharavi generates an estimated $450 million in manufacturing

The High-Cost Economy of the Poor

When we compare the costs of essentials in Dharavi, a shantytown of more than 1 million people in the heart of Mumbai, India, with those of Warden Road, an upper-class community in a nice Mumbai suburb, a disturbing picture emerges. Clearly, costs could be dramatically reduced if the poor could benefit from the scope, scale, and supply-chain efficiencies of large enterprises, as their middle-class counterparts do. This pattern is common around the world, even in developed countries. For instance, a similar, if less exaggerated, disparity exists between the inner-city poor and the suburban rich in the United States.

Cost	Dharavi	Warden Road	Poverty premium
Credit (annual interest)	600%–1,000%	12%–18%	53X
municipal-grade water (per cubic meter)	$1.12	$0.03	37X
phone call (per minute)	$0.04–$0.05	$0.025	1.8X
diarrhea medication	$20	$2	10X
rice (per kilogram)	$0.28	$0.24	1.2X

revenues, or about $1 million per acre of land. Established shantytowns in São Paulo, Rio, and Mexico City are equally productive. The seeds of a vibrant commercial sector have been sown.

While the rural poor are naturally harder to reach than the urban poor, they also represent a large untapped opportunity for companies. Indeed, 60% of India's GDP is generated in rural areas. The critical barrier to doing business in rural regions is distribution access, not a lack of buying power. But new information technology and communications infrastructures—especially wireless—promise to become an inexpensive way to establish marketing and distribution channels in these communities.

Conventional wisdom says that people in BOP markets cannot use such advanced technologies, but that's just another misconception. Poor rural women in Bangladesh have had no difficulty using GSM cell phones, despite never before using phones of any type. In Kenya, teenagers from slums are being successfully trained as Web page designers. Poor farmers in El Salvador use telecenters to negotiate the sale of their crops over the Internet. And women in Indian coastal villages have in less than a week learned to use PCs to interpret real-time satellite images showing concentrations of schools of fish in the Arabian Sea so they can direct their husbands to the best fishing areas. Clearly, poor communities are ready to adopt new technologies that improve their economic opportunities or their quality of life. The lesson for multinationals: Don't hesitate to deploy advanced technologies at the bottom of the pyramid while, or even before, deploying them in advanced countries.

A final misperception concerns the highly charged issue of exploitation of the poor by MNCs. The informal economies that now serve poor communities are full of inefficiencies and exploitive intermediaries. So if a microfinance institution charges 50% annual interest when the alternative is either 1,000% interest or no loan at all, is that exploiting or helping the poor? If a large financial company such as Citigroup were to use its scale to offer microloans at 20%, is that exploiting or helping the poor? The issue is not just cost but also

quality—quality in the range and fairness of financial services, quality of food, quality of water. We argue that when MNCs provide basic goods and services that reduce costs to the poor and help improve their standard of living—while generating an acceptable return on investment—the results benefit everyone.

The Business Case

The business opportunities at the bottom of the pyramid have not gone unnoticed. Over the last five years, we have seen nongovernmental organizations (NGOs), entrepreneurial start-ups, and a handful of forward-thinking multinationals conduct vigorous commercial experiments in poor communities. Their experience is a proof of concept: Businesses can gain three important advantages by serving the poor—a new source of revenue growth, greater efficiency, and access to innovation. Let's look at examples of each.

Top-Line Growth   Growth is an important challenge for every company, but today it is especially critical for very large companies, many of which appear to have nearly saturated their existing markets. That's why BOP markets represent such an opportunity for MNCs: They are fundamentally new sources of growth. And because these markets are in the earliest stages of economic development, growth can be extremely rapid.

Latent demand for low-priced, high-quality goods is enormous. Consider the reaction when Hindustan Lever, the Indian subsidiary of Unilever, recently introduced what was for it a new product category—candy—aimed at the bottom of the pyramid. A high-quality confection made with real sugar and fruit, the candy sells for only about a penny a serving. At such a price, it may seem like a marginal business opportunity, but in just six months it became the fastest-growing category in the company's portfolio. Not only is it profitable, but the company estimates it has the potential to generate revenues of $200 million per year in India and comparable markets in five years. Hindustan Lever has had similar successes in India with low-priced detergent and iodized salt. Beyond generating new sales, the company is establishing its business and its brand in a vast new market.

There is equally strong demand for affordable services. TARAhaat, a start-up focused on rural India, has introduced a range of computer-enabled education services ranging from basic IT training to English proficiency to vocational skills. The products are expected to be the largest single revenue generator for the company and its franchisees over the next several years.[1] Credit and financial services are also in high demand among the poor. Citibank's ATM-based banking experiment in India, called Suvidha, for instance, which requires a minimum deposit of just $25, enlisted 150,000 customers in one year in the city of Bangalore alone.

Small-business services are also popular in BOP markets. Centers run in Uganda by the Women's Information Resource Electronic Service (WIRES) provide female entrepreneurs with information on markets and prices, as well as credit and trade support services, packaged in simple, ready-to-use formats in local languages. The centers are planning to offer other small-business services such as printing, faxing, and copying, along with access to accounting, spreadsheet, and other software. In Bolivia, a start-up has partnered with the Bolivian Association of Ecological Producers Organizations to offer business information and communications services to more than 25,000 small producers of ecoagricultural products.

It's true that some services simply cannot be offered at a low-enough cost to be profitable, at least not with traditional technologies or business models. Most mobile telecommunications providers, for example, cannot yet profitably operate their networks at affordable prices in the developing world. One answer is to find alternative technology. A microfinance organization in Bolivia named PRODEM, for example, uses multilingual smart-card ATMs to substantially reduce its marginal cost per customer. Smart cards store

[1]Andrew Lawlor, Caitlin Peterson, and Vivek Sandell, "Catalyzing Rural Development: TARAhaat.com" (World Resources Institute, July 2001).

a customer's personal details, account numbers, transaction records, and a fingerprint, allowing cash dispensers to operate without permanent network connections—which is key in remote areas. What's more, the machines offer voice commands in Spanish and several local dialects and are equipped with touch screens so that PRODEM's customer base can be extended to illiterate and semiliterate people.

Another answer is to aggregate demand, making the community—not the individual—the network customer. Gyandoot, a start-up in the Dhar district of central India, where 60% of the population falls below the poverty level, illustrates the benefits of a shared access model. The company has a network of 39 Internet-enabled kiosks that provide local entrepreneurs with Internet and telecommunications access, as well as with governmental, educational, and other services. Each kiosk serves 25 to 30 surrounding villages; the entire network reaches more than 600 villages and over half a million people.

Networks like these can be useful channels for marketing and distributing many kinds of low-cost products and services. Aptech's Computer Education division, for example, has built its own network of 1,000 learning centers in India to market and distribute Vidya, a computer-training course specially designed for BOP consumers and available in seven Indian languages. Pioneer Hi-Bred, a DuPont company, uses Internet kiosks in Latin America to deliver agricultural information and to interact with customers. Farmers can report different crop diseases or weather conditions, receive advice over the wire, and order seeds, fertilizers, and pesticides. This network strategy increases both sales and customer loyalty.

Reduced Costs   No less important than top-line growth are cost-saving opportunities. Outsourcing operations to low-cost labor markets has, of course, long been a popular way to contain costs, and it has led to the increasing prominence of China in manufacturing and India in software. Now, thanks to the rapid expansion of high-speed digital networks, companies are realizing even greater savings by

The World Pyramid

Most companies target consumers at the upper tiers of the economic pyramid, completely overlooking the business potential at its base. But though they may each be earning the equivalent of less than $2,000 a year, the people at the bottom of the pyramid make up a colossal market 4 billion strong—the vast majority of the world's population.

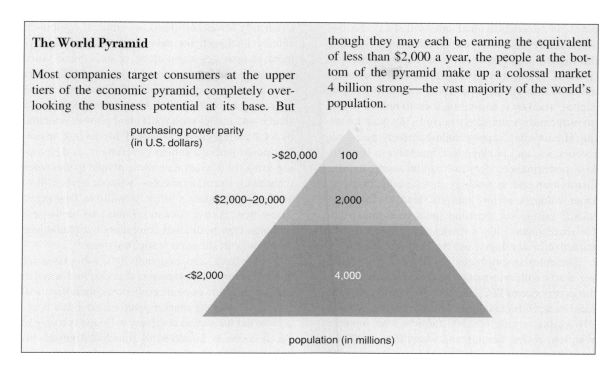

purchasing power parity
(in U.S. dollars)

>$20,000   100

$2,000–20,000   2,000

<$2,000   4,000

population (in millions)

locating such labor-intensive service functions as call centers, marketing services, and back-office transaction processing in developing areas. For example, the nearly 20 companies that use OrphanIT.com's affiliate-marketing services, provided via its telecenters in India and the Philippines, pay one-tenth the going rate for similar services in the United States or Australia. Venture capitalist Vinod Khosla describes the remote-services opportunity this way: "I suspect that by 2010, we will be talking about [remote services] as the fastest-growing part of the world economy, with many trillions of dollars of new markets created." Besides keeping costs down, outsourcing jobs to BOP markets can enhance growth, since job creation ultimately increases local consumers' purchasing power.

But tapping into cheap labor pools is not the only way MNCs can enhance their efficiency by operating in developing regions. The competitive necessity of maintaining a low cost structure in these areas can push companies to discover creative ways to configure their products, finances, and supply chains to enhance productivity. And these discoveries can often be incorporated back into their existing operations in developed markets.

For instance, companies targeting the BOP market are finding that the shared access model, which disaggregates access from ownership, not only widens their customer base but increases asset productivity as well. Poor people, rather than buying their own computers, Internet connections, cell phones, refrigerators, and even cars, can use such equipment on a pay-per-use basis. Typically, the providers of such services get considerably more revenue per dollar of investment in the underlying assets. One shared Internet line, for example, can serve as many as 50 people, generating more revenue per day than if it were dedicated to a single customer at a flat fee. Shared access creates the opportunity to gain far greater returns from all sorts of infrastructure investments.

In terms of finances, to operate successfully in BOP markets, managers must also rethink their business metrics—specifically, the traditional focus on high gross margins. In developing markets, the profit margin on individual units will always be low. What really counts is capital efficiency—getting the highest possible returns on capital employed (ROCE). Hindustan Lever, for instance, operates a $2.6 billion business portfolio with zero working capital. The key is constant efforts to reduce capital investments by extensively outsourcing manufacturing, streamlining supply chains, actively managing receivables, and paying close attention to distributors' performance. Very low capital needs, focused distribution and technology investments, and very large volumes at low margins lead to very high ROCE businesses, creating great economic value for shareholders. It's a model that can be equally attractive in developed and developing markets.

Streamlining supply chains often involves replacing assets with information. Consider, for example, the experience of ITC, one of India's largest companies. Its agribusiness division has deployed a total of 970 kiosks serving 600,000 farmers who supply it with soy, coffee, shrimp, and wheat from 5,000 villages spread across India. This kiosk program, called e-Choupal, helps increase the farmers' productivity by disseminating the latest information on weather and best practices in farming, and by supporting other services like soil and water testing, thus facilitating the supply of quality inputs to both the farmers and ITC. The kiosks also serve as an e-procurement system, helping farmers earn higher prices by minimizing transaction costs involved in marketing farm produce. The head of ITC's agribusiness reports that the company's procurement costs have fallen since e-Choupal was implemented. And that's despite paying higher prices to its farmers: The program has enabled the company to eliminate multiple transportation, bagging, and handling steps—from farm to local market, from market to broker, from broker to processor—that did not add value in the chain.

Innovation BOP markets are hotbeds of commercial and technological experimentation. The Swedish wireless company Ericsson, for instance, has developed a small cellular telephone system, called a MiniGSM, that local operators in BOP markets can use to offer cell phone service to a small area at

a radically lower cost than conventional equipment entails. Packaged for easy shipment and deployment, it provides stand-alone or networked voice and data communications for up to 5,000 users within a 35-kilometer radius. Capital costs to the operator can be as low as $4 per user, assuming a shared-use model with individual phones operated by local entrepreneurs. The MIT Media Lab, in collaboration with the Indian government, is developing low-cost devices that allow people to use voice commands to communicate—without keyboards— with various Internet sites in multiple languages. These new access devices promise to be far less complex than traditional computers but would perform many of the same basic functions.[2]

As we have seen, connectivity is a big issue for BOP consumers. Companies that can find ways to dramatically lower connection costs, therefore, will have a very strong market position. And that is exactly what the Indian company n-Logue is trying to do. It connects hundreds of franchised village kiosks containing both a computer and a phone with centralized nodes that are, in turn, connected to the national phone network and the Internet. Each node, also a franchise, can serve between 30,000 and 50,000 customers, providing phone, e-mail, Internet services, and relevant local information at affordable prices to villagers in rural India. Capital costs for the n-Logue system are now about $400 per wireless "line" and are projected to decline to $100—at least ten times lower than conventional telecom costs. On a per-customer basis, the cost may amount to as little as $1.[3] This appears to be a powerful model for ending rural isolation and linking untapped rural markets to the global economy.

New wireless technologies are likely to spur further business model innovations and lower costs even more. Ultrawideband, for example, is

[2]Michael Best and Colin M. Maclay, "Community Internet Access in Rural Areas: Solving the Economic Sustainability Puzzle," *The Global Information Technology Report 2001–2002: Readiness for the Networked World*, ed., Geoffrey Kirkman (Oxford University Press, 2002), available on-line at http://www.cid.harvard.edu/cr/gitrr_030202.html.
[3]Joy Howard, Erik Simanis, and Charis Simms, "Sustainable Deployment for Rural Connectivity: The n-Logue Model" (World Resources Institute, July 2001).

currently licensed in the United States only for limited, very low-power applications, in part because it spreads a signal across already-crowded portions of the broadcast spectrum. In many developing countries, however, the spectrum is less congested. In fact, the U.S.-based Dandin Group is already building an ultrawideband communications system for the Kingdom of Tonga, whose population of about 100,000 is spread over dozens of islands, making it a test bed for a next-generation technology that could transform the economics of Internet access.

E-commerce systems that run over the phone or the Internet are enormously important in BOP markets because they eliminate the need for layers of intermediaries. Consider how the U.S. start-up Voxiva has changed the way information is shared and business is transacted in Peru. The company partners with Telefónica, the dominant local carrier, to offer automated business applications over the phone. The inexpensive services include voice mail, data entry, and order placement; customers can check account balances, monitor delivery status, and access prerecorded information directories. According to the Boston Consulting Group, the Peruvian Ministry of Health uses Voxiva to disseminate information, take pharmaceutical orders, and link health care workers spread across 6,000 offices and clinics. Microfinance institutions use Voxiva to process loan applications and communicate with borrowers. Voxiva offers Web-based services, too, but far more of its potential customers in Latin America have access to a phone.

E-commerce companies are not the only ones turning the limitations of BOP markets to strategic advantage. A lack of dependable electric power stimulated the UK-based start-up Freeplay Group to introduce hand-cranked radios in South Africa that subsequently became popular with hikers in the United States. Similar breakthroughs are being pioneered in the use of solar-powered devices such as battery chargers and water pumps. In China, where pesticide costs have often limited the use of modern agricultural techniques, there are now 13,000 small farmers—more than in the rest of the world combined—growing cotton that has been genetically engineered to be pest resistant.

Strategies for Serving BOP Markets

Certainly, succeeding in BOP markets requires multinationals to think creatively. The biggest change, though, has to come in the attitudes and practices of executives. Unless CEOs and other business leaders confront their own preconceptions, companies are unlikely to master the challenges of BOP markets. The traditional workforce is so rigidly conditioned to operate in higher-margin markets that, without formal training, it is unlikely to see the vast potential of the BOP market. The most pressing need, then, is education. Perhaps MNCs should create the equivalent of the Peace Corps: Having young managers spend a couple of formative years in BOP markets would open their eyes to the promise and the realities of doing business there.

To date, few multinationals have developed a cadre of people who are comfortable with these markets. Hindustan Lever is one of the exceptions. The company expects executive recruits to spend at least eight weeks in the villages of India to get a gut-level experience of Indian BOP markets. The new executives must become involved in some community project—building a road, cleaning up a water catchment area, teaching in a school, improving a health clinic. The goal is to engage with the local population. To buttress this effort, Hindustan Lever is initiating a massive program for managers at all levels—from the CEO down—to reconnect with their poorest customers. They'll talk with the poor in both rural and urban areas, visit the shops these customers frequent, and ask them about their experience with the company's products and those of its competitors.

In addition to expanding managers' understanding of BOP markets, companies will need to make structural changes. To capitalize on the innovation potential of these markets, for example, they might set up R&D units in developing countries that are specifically focused on local opportunities. When Hewlett-Packard launched its e-Inclusion division, which concentrates on rural markets, it established a branch of its famed

HP Labs in India charged with developing products and services explicitly for this market. Hindustan Lever maintains a significant R&D effort in India, as well.

Companies might also create venture groups and internal investment funds aimed at seeding entrepreneurial efforts in BOP markets. Such investments reap direct benefits in terms of business experience and market development. They can also play an indirect but vital role in growing the overall BOP market in sectors that will ultimately benefit the multinational. At least one major U.S. corporation is planning to launch such a fund, and the G8's Digital Opportunity Task Force is proposing a similar one focused on digital ventures.

MNCs should also consider creating a business development task force aimed at these markets. Assembling a diverse group of people from across the corporation and empowering it to function as a skunk works team that ignores conventional dogma will likely lead to greater innovation. Companies that have tried this approach have been surprised by the amount of interest such a task force generates. Many employees want to work on projects that have the potential to make a real difference in improving the lives of the poor. When Hewlett-Packard announced its e-Inclusion division, for example, it was overwhelmed by far more volunteers than it could accommodate.

Making internal changes is important, but so is reaching out to external partners. Joining with businesses that are already established in these markets can be an effective entry strategy, since these companies will naturally understand the market dynamics better. In addition to limiting the risks for each player, partnerships also maximize the existing infrastructure—both physical and social. MNCs seeking partners should look beyond businesses to NGOs and community groups. They are key sources of knowledge about customers' behavior, and they often experiment the most with new services and new delivery models. In fact, of the social enterprises experimenting with creative uses of digital technology that the Digital Dividend

Project Clearinghouse tracked, nearly 80% are NGOs. In Namibia, for instance, an organization called SchoolNet is providing low-cost, alternative technology solutions—such as solar power and wireless approaches—to schools and community-based groups throughout the country. SchoolNet is currently linking as many as 35 new schools every month.

Entrepreneurs also will be critical partners. According to an analysis by McKinsey & Company, the rapid growth of cable TV in India—there are 50 million connections a decade after introduction—is largely due to small entrepreneurs. These individuals have been building the last mile of the network, typically by putting a satellite dish on their own houses and laying cable to connect their neighbors. A note of caution, however. Entrepreneurs in BOP markets lack access to the advice, technical help, seed funding, and business support services available in the industrial world. So MNCs may need to take on mentoring roles or partner with local business development organizations that can help entrepreneurs create investment and partnering opportunities.

It's worth noting that, contrary to popular opinion, women play a significant role in the economic development of these regions. MNCs, therefore, should pay particular attention to women entrepreneurs. Women are also likely to play the most critical role in product acceptance not only because of their childcare and household management activities but also because of the social capital that they have built up in their communities. Listening to and educating such customers is essential for success.

Regardless of the opportunities, many companies will consider the bottom of the pyramid to be too risky. We've shown how partnerships can limit risk; another option is to enter into consortia. Imagine sharing the costs of building a rural network with the communications company that would operate it, a consumer goods company seeking channels to expand its sales, and a bank that is financing the construction and wants to make loans to and collect deposits from rural customers.

Sharing Intelligence

What creative new approaches to serving the bottom-of-the-pyramid markets have digital technologies made possible? Which sectors or countries show the most economic activity or the fastest growth? What new business models show promise? What kinds of partnerships—for funding, distribution, public relations—have been most successful?

The Digital Dividend Project Clearinghouse (digitaldividend.org) helps answer those types of questions. The Web site tracks the activities of organizations that use digital tools to provide connectivity and deliver services to underserved populations in developing countries. Currently, it contains information on 700 active projects around the world. Maintained under the auspices of the nonprofit World Resources Institute, the site lets participants in different projects share experiences and swap knowledge with one another. Moreover, the site provides data for trend analyses and other specialized studies that facilitate market analyses, local partnerships, and rapid, low-cost learning.

Investing where powerful synergies exist will also mitigate risk. The Global Digital Opportunity Initiative, a partnership of the Markle Foundation and the UN Development Programme, will help a small number of countries implement a strategy to harness the power of information and communications technologies to increase development. The countries will be chosen in part based on their interest and their willingness to make supportive regulatory and market reforms. To concentrate resources and create reinforcing effects, the initiative will encourage international aid agencies and global companies to assist with implementation.

All of the strategies we've outlined here will be of little use, however, unless the external barriers we've touched on—poor infrastructure, inadequate connectivity, corrupt intermediaries, and the like—are removed. Here's where technology holds the most promise. Information and communications technologies can grant access to otherwise isolated communities, provide marketing and distribution channels, bypass intermediaries, drive down transaction costs, and help aggregate demand and buying power. Smart cards and other emerging technologies are inexpensive ways to give poor customers a secure identity, a transaction or credit history, and even a virtual address—prerequisites for interacting with the formal economy. That's why high-tech companies aren't the only ones that should be interested in closing the global digital divide; encouraging the spread of low-cost digital networks at the bottom of the pyramid is a priority for virtually all companies that want to enter and engage with these markets. Improved connectivity is an important catalyst for more effective markets, which are critical to boosting income levels and accelerating economic growth.

Moreover, global companies stand to gain from the effects of network expansion in these markets. According to Metcalfe's Law, the usefulness of a network equals the square of the number of users. By the same logic, the value and vigor of the economic activity that will be generated when hundreds of thousands of previously isolated rural communities can buy and sell from one another and from urban markets will increase dramatically—to the benefit of all participants.

• • •

Since BOP markets require significant rethinking of managerial practices, it is legitimate for managers to ask: Is it worth the effort?

We think the answer is yes. For one thing, big corporations should solve big problems—and what is a more pressing concern than alleviating the poverty that 4 billion people are currently mired in? It is hard to argue that the wealth of technology and talent within leading multinationals is better allocated to producing incremental variations of existing products than to addressing the real needs—and real opportunities—at the bottom of the pyramid. Moreover, through competition, multinationals are likely to bring to BOP markets a level of accountability for performance and resources that neither international development agencies nor national governments have demonstrated during the last 50 years. Participation by MNCs could set a new standard, as well as a new market-driven paradigm, for addressing poverty.

But ethical concerns aside, we've shown that the potential for expanding the bottom of the market is just too great to ignore. Big companies need to focus on big market opportunities if they want to generate real growth. It is simply good business strategy to be involved in large, untapped markets that offer new customers, cost-saving opportunities, and access to radical innovation. The business opportunities at the bottom of the pyramid are real, and they are open to any MNC willing to engage and learn.

Index

('f' indicates a figure; 'n' indicates a note; 't' indicates a table)